CREDITS

'85-'86 Edition

MAGPIE PRESS
NEW JERSEY

CREDITS

By Debbie Brenner & Gary Hill

'85-'86 Edition

VOLUME III
BY INDIVIDUAL

Software design by Reliant Systems, Inc., New York.

Production Consultants: Kyla Kanz & K. Hamilton Pucci.

Published by Magpie Press, 16 Main Avenue, Wallington, New Jersey 07057.

Printed in the United States of America

ISSN 088406456

ISBN 0-935469-00-1 **(complete set)**
ISBN 0-935469-01-X **(Volume I)**
ISBN 0-935469-02-8 **(Volume II)**
ISBN 0-935469-03-6 **(Volume III)**

10 9 8 7 6 5 4 3 2 1

CREDITS is presented in 3 Volumes. Volume I is listed by Film Title; Volume II is cross referenced by Production Category; and Volume III is cross referenced by Individual Names.

In Volumes II & III some CREDITS are followed by an asterisk (*). This denotes that this particular CREDIT was shared by two or more individuals (whose names can be found in Volume I).

A

HARRIOTTE AARON
SCRIPT SUPERVISOR
'83 PRIVATE SCHOOL

PAUL AARON
DIRECTOR
'79 FORCE OF ONE, A
'83 DEADLY FORCE

SIDNEY AARON
SCREENPLAY
'80 ALTERED STATES

SONNY ABAGNALE
MISCELLANEOUS
'84 ONCE UPON A TIME IN AMERICA

PAUL ABASCAL
HAIR
'83 OSTERMAN WEEKEND, THE*
'84 THIEF OF HEARTS

SYLVIA ABASCAL
HAIR
'80 URBAN COWBOY*
'83 HEART LIKE A WHEEL
'84 STAR TREK III:
THE SEARCH FOR SPOCK

RASHID ABBASI
UNIT MANAGER
'82 GANDHI*
'84 PASSAGE TO INDIA, A
LOCATIONS
'83 OCTOPUSSY*

JUDY ABBOTT
CASTING
'79 EUROPEANS, THE

KATHY "STYLE K" ABBOTT
MISCELLANEOUS
'84 BREAKIN 2 ELECTRIC BOOGALOO

L.B. ABBOTT
MISCELLANEOUS
'79 1941
'80 WHEN TIME RAN OUT
'83 WRONG IS RIGHT

MAGGIE ABBOTT
ASSOCIATE PRODUCER
'79 NIGHTWING*

NICK ABDO
ASSOCIATE PRODUCER
'82 YOUNG DOCTORS IN LOVE*
'84 FLAMINGO KID, THE
2ND UNIT DIRECTOR
'84 FLAMINGO KID, THE

PAULA ABDUL
CHOREOGRAPHER
'83 PRIVATE SCHOOL

MALEK ABDUL-MANSOUR
MISCELLANEOUS
'80 INSIDE MOVES

NASSER ABDULLA
LOCATIONS
'84 RAZOR'S EDGE, THE*

CAROLYN ABE
ASSISTANT EDITOR
'80 ISLAND, THE
'84 CRACKERS*

MASATO ABE
HAIR
'82 CHALLENGE, THE

MIKE ABE
1ST ASST. DIRECTOR
'82 CHALLENGE, THE*

FRED ABELES
CINEMATOGRAPHER
'81 WOLFEN*

SHELLY ABEND
ASSOCIATE PRODUCER
'80 WHY WOULD I LIE?*

LYNN ABER
SCRIPT SUPERVISOR
'80 BIG RED ONE, THE
'80 FINAL COUNTDOWN, THE

JIM ABRAHAMS
DIRECTOR
'80 AIRPLANE*
'84 TOP SECRET!*
SCREENPLAY
'80 AIRPLANE*
'84 TOP SECRET!*
EXECUTIVE PRODUCER
'84 TOP SECRET!*

JON ABRAHAMS
EXECUTIVE PRODUCER
'80 AIRPLANE*

MORT ABRAHAMS
EXEC IN CHARGE PROD
'80 HOPSCOTCH
'82 CHOSEN, THE

CHRISTER ABRAHAMSEN
ASSOCIATE PRODUCER
'81 MONTENEGRO*

BARRY ABRAMS
CINEMATOGRAPHER
'80 FRIDAY THE 13TH
'82 STRANGER IS WATCHING, A

BOB ABRAMS
PUBLICIST
'81 BLOOD BEACH
'82 LIAR'S MOON

LARRY ABRAMS
EXECUTIVE PRODUCER
'84 C.H.U.D.

MORRIS ABRAMS
EXEC IN CHARGE PROD
'84 STONE BOY, THE

PHILIP ABRAMSON
MISCELLANEOUS
'83 JAWS 3-D

SHIRLEY ABRAMSON
CASTING
'84 NOT FOR PUBLICATION*

EDWARD ABROMS
EDITOR
'83 BLUE THUNDER*
'83 OSTERMAN WEEKEND, THE*

STEVE ABRUMS
MAKEUP
'79 AMITYVILLE HORROR, THE
'81 BUDDY, BUDDY*
'81 CHU CHU AND THE PHILLY FLASH
'82 SIX WEEKS*
'82 THAT CHAMPIONSHIP SEASON
'83 SCARFACE*

DEL ACEVEDO
MAKEUP
'78 DEER HUNTER, THE*
'79 HARDCORE
'79 JERK, THE
'79 WINTER KILLS
'80 CHANGELING, THE*
'80 FORMULA, THE
'83 SPACEHUNTER: ADVENTURES IN THE FORBIDDEN ZONE
'84 FIRESTARTER*

JEAN ACHACHE
1ST ASST. DIRECTOR
'84 CHEECH AND CHONG'S THE CORSICAN BROTHERS*

JIM ACHESON
COSTUMES
'81 TIME BANDITS*
'83 MONTY PYTHON'S THE MEANING OF LIFE

WERNER ACHMANN
ART DIRECTOR
'80 AMERICAN SUCCESS COMPANY,THE

ANDREW ACKERMAN
2ND ASST. DIRECTOR
'81 BLOOD BEACH
'81 DEAD AND BURIED*

JACK ACKERMAN
PROPS
'80 USED CARS
'83 RISKY BUSINESS
'83 BRAINSTORM

JOHN ACKERMAN
PROPS
'84 GHOSTBUSTERS*

CHRIS ACKLAND
ASSISTANT EDITOR
'79 CLASS OF MISS MACMICHAEL,THE

BRIAN ACKLAND-SNOW
ART DIRECTOR
'79 DRACULA
'82 DARK CRYSTAL, THE*
'83 SUPERMAN III*
'84 LASSITER*
'84 SCANDALOUS*

RITA ACKLAND-SNOW
ASSISTANT EDITOR
'84 SUPERGIRL*

TERRY ACKLAND-SNOW
ART DIRECTOR
'81 GREAT MUPPET CAPER, THE*
'82 DARK CRYSTAL, THE*
'83 SUPERMAN III*
'84 SUPERGIRL

CAL ACORD
SPECIAL EFFECTS
'81 BLOW OUT
'84 PLACES IN THE HEART

MARGARET ADACHI
ASSISTANT EDITOR
'79 NORMA RAE*
'80 HERO AT LARGE*
'80 WHOLLY MOSES!*
'81 BACK ROADS*
'82 I OUGHT TO BE IN PICTURES*
'83 TRADING PLACES*

DWIGHT ADAIR
MISCELLANEOUS
'81 HARD COUNTRY

SANDRA ADAIR
ASSISTANT EDITOR
'82 JEKYLL AND HYDE TOGETHER AGAIN

SANDRA ADAIR
CASTING
'80 HOLLYWOOD KNIGHTS, THE*

KEN ADAM
ASSOCIATE PRODUCER
'81 PENNIES FROM HEAVEN
PRODUCTION DESIGNER
'79 MOONRAKER
MISCELLANEOUS
'81 PENNIES FROM HEAVEN

WILLIAM ADAMS III
2ND ASST. DIRECTOR
'80 MANIAC*

JOHN ADAMS
ASSISTANT EDITOR
'80 BATTLE BEYOND THE STARS*
'81 GALAXY OF TERROR*

JULIE ADAMS
MISCELLANEOUS
'84 RIVER, THE

KEN ADAMS
KEY GRIP
'79 OVER THE EDGE*
'80 GONG SHOW MOVIE, THE

MARILYN MCMAHON ADAMS
ASSISTANT EDITOR
'84 STREETS OF FIRE*

MYRON ADAMS
LOCATIONS
'81 MODERN PROBLEMS*
'82 AUTHOR, AUTHOR

PHIL ADAMS
STUNT COORDINATOR
'79 C.H.O.M.P.S.
'79 FAST COMPANY*
'83 MR. MOM*

RON ADAMS
MISCELLANEOUS
'81 BUDDY, BUDDY

SUSIE ADAMS
MAKEUP
'84 GIVE MY REGARDS TO BROAD STREET

TERRY ADAMS
PROPS
'82 ENDANGERED SPECIES*

TONY ADAMS
PRODUCER
'79 10*
'81 S.O.B.*
'82 VICTOR/VICTORIA*
'83 CURSE OF THE PINK PANTHER*
'83 MAN WHO LOVED WOMEN, THE*
'83 TRAIL OF THE PINK PANTHER*
'84 MICKI AND MAUDE

CHUCK ADAMSON
MISCELLANEOUS
'81 THIEF
'84 BEVERLY HILLS COP
'84 THIEF OF HEARTS

KEITH ADDIS
EXECUTIVE PRODUCER
'83 BREATHLESS

JOHN ADDISON
MUSIC
'83 STRANGE INVADERS

RICHARD ADEE
PROPS
'80 WILLIE & PHIL
'81 EYEWITNESS
'82 AMITYVILLE II: THE POSSESSION*
'83 EXPOSED*
'83 TOUGH ENOUGH
'84 FLAMINGO KID, THE
SPECIAL EFFECTS
'80 OH! HEAVENLY DOG*

WALLY ADEE
PROPS
'82 AMITYVILLE II: THE POSSESSION*

HERB ADELMAN
2ND ASST. DIRECTOR
'80 SERIAL
'80 WHOLLY MOSES!
'81 KING OF THE MOUNTAIN
'81 PATERNITY
'83 INDEPENDENCE DAY*

GARY ADELSON
PRODUCER
'84 LAST STARFIGHTER, THE*

ALAN ADLER
PRODUCER
'82 MAKING LOVE*
'83 METALSTORM: THE DESTRUCTION OF JARED-SYN*
SCREENPLAY
'82 PARASITE*
'83 METALSTORM: THE DESTRUCTION OF JARED-SYN

GALE ADLER
STILLS
'80 GALAXINA
'81 TAKE THIS JOB AND SHOVE IT
'83 CUJO*
'83 PRIVATE SCHOOL*
'83 JOYSTICKS
'84 BREAKIN 2 ELECTRIC BOOGALOO*

GIL ADLER
PRODUCER
'80 HOME MOVIES*

LOU ADLER
EXECUTIVE PRODUCER
'81 SHOCK TREATMENT*

RICHARD AELLEN
SCRIPT SUPERVISOR
'83 SWEET SIXTEEN

WERNER AELLEN
PRODUCER
'82 BY DESIGN*

MINDY AFFRIME
PRODUCER
'80 TELL ME A RIDDLE*

BEN-AMI AGMON
LOCATIONS
'81 HALLOWEEN II
'82 HALLOWEEN III: SEASON OF THE WITCH

LINDA LOU AGNELLI
PROPS
'82 BEASTMASTER, THE*
'83 PRIVATE SCHOOL

GUS AGOSTI
1ST ASST. DIRECTOR
'79 PLAYERS*

MARISA AGOSTINI
SCRIPT SUPERVISOR
'83 1990: THE BRONX WARRIORS

RITA AGOSTINI
UNIT MANAGER
'83 1990: THE BRONX WARRIORS*

CLAUDE AGOSTINO
CINEMATOGRAPHER
'81 SUNDAY LOVERS*
'82 QUEST FOR FIRE

MARTIN AGUILAR
KEY GRIP
'83 MAUSOLEUM

SEGUNDO AGUINALDO JR.
PROPS
'83 BLIND RAGE

JULIE BILSON AHLBERG
PROD. COORDINATOR
'84 DREAMSCAPE

MAC AHLBERG
CINEMATOGRAPHER
'81 HELL NIGHT
'82 SEDUCTION, THE
'82 PARASITE
'83 CHAINED HEAT
'83 METALSTORM: THE DESTRUCTION OF JARED-SYN
'83 MY TUTOR

PAUL AHRENS
PROPS
'84 NIGHT OF THE COMET

LAURIE AIELLO
MAKEUP
'80 MOTHER'S DAY

STUART AIKENS
CASTING
'79 BLACK STALLION, THE*
'79 LOST AND FOUND*
'84 MRS. SOFFEL*

EDDIE AIONA
PROPS
'79 ELECTRIC HORSEMAN, THE
'79 HARDCORE
'80 ANY WHICH WAY YOU CAN
'80 CARNY
'80 ORDINARY PEOPLE
'81 ABSENCE OF MALICE
'82 FIREFOX
'82 HONKYTONK MAN
'83 SUDDEN IMPACT
'84 CITY HEAT
'84 TIGHTROPE

SEDAT AKDEMIR
ASSOCIATE PRODUCER
'83 YOR*

RANDLE AKERSON
ASSISTANT EDITOR
'83 ECHOES*

BOB AKESTER
2ND ASST. DIRECTOR
'82 OUT OF THE BLUE

DAVID ALAJKO
SOUND
'81 TUCK EVERLASTING

JOSE MARIA ALARCON
ART DIRECTOR
'84 CONAN THE DESTROYER*

TONY ALATIS
PRODUCTION MANAGER
'80 FOR THE LOVE OF BENJI*
1ST ASST. DIRECTOR
'80 FOR THE LOVE OF BENJI

DICK ALBAIN
SPECIAL EFFECTS
'79 REAL LIFE
'79 MOUNTAIN FAMILY ROBINSON
'81 TAKE THIS JOB AND SHOVE IT
'82 SHOOT THE MOON
'82 FORCED VENGEANCE
'82 ZAPPED!*

DICK ALBAIN JR.
SPECIAL EFFECTS
'80 FOG, THE

ARTHUR ALBERT
CINEMATOGRAPHER
'84 NIGHT OF THE COMET

ROSS ALBERT
EDITOR
'83 SUBURBIA
ASSOCIATE EDITOR
'81 DEAD AND BURIED
'84 2010*
ASSISTANT EDITOR
'79 ROCKY II*
'80 GONG SHOW MOVIE, THE*

TED ALBERT
PUBLICIST
'80 HEAVEN'S GATE
'81 FORT APACHE, THE BRONX
'82 STRANGER IS WATCHING, A
'83 EXPOSED*
'84 MISUNDERSTOOD
UNIT PUBLICIST
'81 WHOSE LIFE IS IT ANYWAY?

ARLENE ALBERTSON
PROD. OFFICE COORD.
'79 LAST EMBRACE
'80 DEFIANCE
'80 FAME
PROD. COORDINATOR
'81 FORT APACHE, THE BRONX

ERIC ALBERTSON

EDITOR
'80 FIRST DEADLY SIN
MISCELLANEOUS
'80 UNION CITY

PETER ALBIEZ

SPECIAL EFFECTS
'79 CONCORDE-AIRPORT '79, THE*
'82 CANNERY ROW*

RENE ALBOUIZE

PROPS
'80 FIENDISH PLOT OF DR. FU MANCHU, THE

MIKE ALBRECHTSON

SPECIAL EFFECTS
'79 MURDER BY DECREE
'80 DEATH SHIP

MARISA ALCARAZ

PROD. COORDINATOR
'79 AMERICATHON
'79 APOCALYPSE NOW*

PAMELA ALCH

SCRIPT SUPERVISOR
'80 HOLLYWOOD KNIGHTS, THE
'81 BODY HEAT
'83 BIG CHILL, THE

JOHN ALCOTT

CINEMATOGRAPHER
'80 SHINING, THE
'80 TERROR TRAIN
'81 FORT APACHE, THE BRONX
'82 BEASTMASTER, THE
'82 VICE SQUAD
'83 UNDER FIRE
'84 GREYSTOKE: THE LEGEND OF TARZAN, LORD OF THE APES

ALAN ALDA

DIRECTOR
'81 FOUR SEASONS, THE
SCREENPLAY
'79 SEDUCTION OF JOE TYNAN, THE
'81 FOUR SEASONS, THE

RICHARD ALDERETE

ASSISTANT EDITOR
'83 FLASHDANCE*
'84 KARATE KID, THE*

JANE ALDERMAN

CASTING
'83 BAD BOYS*

THEONI ALDREDGE

COSTUMES
'79 ROSE, THE
'79 CHAMP, THE
'80 CAN'T STOP THE MUSIC*
'80 CHANGE OF SEASONS, A*
'80 FIRST DEADLY SIN*
'80 LOVING COUPLES*
'80 MIDDLE AGE CRAZY*
'81 RICH AND FAMOUS
'82 ANNIE
'82 MONSIGNOR
'84 GHOSTBUSTERS

ADELL ALDRICH

SCRIPT SUPERVISOR
'84 MASS APPEAL

ADELL ALDRICH

2ND UNIT DIRECTOR
'81 ...ALL THE MARBLES

ELIZABETH ALDRICH

CHOREOGRAPHER
'79 EUROPEANS, THE*
'80 QUARTET

HANK ALDRICH

ART DIRECTOR
'79 NATURAL ENEMIES

ROBERT ALDRICH

DIRECTOR
'79 FRISCO KID, THE
'81 ...ALL THE MARBLES

WILLIAM ALDRICH

PRODUCER
'81 ...ALL THE MARBLES

JACK ALDWORTH

1ST ASST. DIRECTOR
'79 LOVE AND BULLETS
'80 SEEMS LIKE OLD TIMES

ARLENE ALEN

ART DIRECTOR
'81 SATURDAY THE 14TH

JOHN ALESE

MAKEUP
'79 GOING IN STYLE*

BILL ALEXANDER

ART DIRECTOR
'80 LADY VANISHES, THE*

DICK ALEXANDER

LOCATIONS
'80 USED CARS

DORIS ALEXANDER

MAKEUP
'79 BUDDY HOLLY STORY, THE*

JIM ALEXANDER

SOUND
'79 CONCORDE-AIRPORT '79, THE
'80 COAL MINER'S DAUGHTER
'81 BUSTIN' LOOSE
'81 GHOST STORY
'81 HEARTBEEPS
'82 STAR TREK II THE WRATH OF KHAN
'83 NIGHTMARES
'83 PSYCHO II
'83 TERMS OF ENDEARMENT
'84 SIXTEEN CANDLES

LARRY ALEXANDER

PROPS
'83 SAVANNAH SMILES

LEE ALEXANDER

SOUND
'79 FAST BREAK
'79 GREAT SANTINI, THE
'80 LOVING COUPLES
'83 TESTAMENT
'84 BODY ROCK

URSULA ALEXANDER

UNIT PROD. MANAGER
'79 GREAT BANK HOAX, THE

APRIL ALEXANDRE

HAIR
'84 CHOOSE ME*

MILLIE ALEXICH

MISCELLANEOUS
'83 OUTSIDERS, THE

CHARLIE ALFANO

MISCELLANEOUS
'81 NIGHTHAWKS

LUIGI ALFANO

1ST ASST. DIRECTOR
'79 ESCAPE FROM ALCATRAZ
'80 HOLLYWOOD KNIGHTS, THE

WALTER ALFORD

PUBLICIST
'79 GREAT TRAIN ROBBERY, THE
'80 OUTSIDER, THE

GLORIA ALGEO

HAIR
'79 PROMISE, THE

JANEY ALHANTI

MISCELLANEOUS
'83 BREATHLESS

HOSSAM ALI
UNIT MANAGER
'81 SPHINX*

SHAWKI ABU ALI
PROD. COORDINATOR
'81 GALLIPOLI

GUY ALIME
MISCELLANEOUS
'83 NEVER SAY NEVER AGAIN

PATRICE ALINO
CHOREOGRAPHER
'84 WEEKEND PASS

TED ALLAN
SCREENPLAY
'84 LOVE STREAMS*

TED ALLAN
SOUND
'83 BLIND RAGE*

TOR ALLAN
MISCELLANEOUS
'84 SHEENA

ERIC ALLARD
SPECIAL EFFECTS
'83 BRAINSTORM*

NICK ALLDER
SPECIAL EFFECTS
'79 ALIEN
'81 SEA WOLVES, THE*
'81 NIGHTHAWKS*
'82 SENDER, THE
'83 FINAL OPTION, THE
'83 KEEP, THE
SP. EFFECTS SUPERV.
'82 CONAN THE BARBARIAN
'84 TOP SECRET!
MISCELLANEOUS
'80 EMPIRE STRIKES BACK, THE

ANGELA ALLEN
SCRIPT SUPERVISOR
'79 AVALANCHE EXPRESS*
'80 ROUGH CUT
'80 FFOLKES
'81 SEA WOLVES, THE
'81 EYE OF THE NEEDLE*
'83 ENIGMA
'83 YELLOWBEARD*
'84 SCANDALOUS

BARBARA ALLEN
PROD. COORDINATOR
'81 DOGS OF WAR, THE
'83 YENTL
'84 KILLING FIELDS, THE*

CANDACE ALLEN
2ND ASST. DIRECTOR
'80 FORMULA, THE*
'82 HANKY PANKY*
'84 HARD TO HOLD

CHARLES ALLEN
LOCATIONS
'81 BEAST WITHIN, THE
'82 SIX PACK

CHRIS ALLEN
SCREENPLAY
'80 IN GOD WE TRUST*

DAVID ALLEN
MISCELLANEOUS
'81 CAVEMAN
'82 Q: QUETZALCOATL

DEBRA ALLEN
CHOREOGRAPHER
'79 FISH THAT SAVED PITTSBURGH,THE

DEDE ALLEN
EXECUTIVE PRODUCER
'81 REDS*
EDITOR
'81 REDS*
'84 HARRY & SON
'84 MIKE'S MURDER*

DICK ALLEN
MISCELLANEOUS
'83 HUNGER, THE

IRWIN ALLEN
PRODUCER
'79 BEYOND THE POSEIDON ADVENTURE
'80 WHEN TIME RAN OUT
DIRECTOR
'79 BEYOND THE POSEIDON ADVENTURE

JAMES ALLEN
ART DIRECTOR
'84 STREETS OF FIRE

JANIS ALLEN
SCREENPLAY
'79 MEATBALLS*

JAY PRESSON ALLEN
PRODUCER
'80 JUST TELL ME WHAT YOU WANT*
SCREENPLAY
'80 JUST TELL ME WHAT YOU WANT
'81 PRINCE OF THE CITY*
'82 DEATHTRAP
EXECUTIVE PRODUCER
'80 IT'S MY TURN
'81 PRINCE OF THE CITY
'82 DEATHTRAP

LEWIS ALLEN
PRODUCER
'83 NEVER CRY WOLF*

MARK ALLEN
1ST ASST. DIRECTOR
'82 LAST AMERICAN VIRGIN, THE

MICHAEL ALLEN
MISCELLANEOUS
'83 REUBEN, REUBEN

PATRICE ALLEN
PROD. COORDINATOR
'82 GREY FOX, THE
'82 OUT OF THE BLUE
'83 NEVER CRY WOLF*
'84 ICEMAN

RICHARD ALLEN
2ND ASST. DIRECTOR
'80 MOTEL HELL

STANFORD ALLEN
EDITOR
'79 ROCKY II*
'80 HOLLYWOOD KNIGHTS, THE*
'83 MORTUARY
ASSISTANT EDITOR
'81 NIGHTHAWKS

SUSAN ALLEN
PROD. SECRETARY
'80 BRONCO BILLY

SYLVIA ALLEN
MISCELLANEOUS
'83 ANGEL OF H.E.A.T.

THOMAS ALLEN
PROPS
'83 BABY IT'S YOU
'84 RECKLESS
'84 BOSTONIANS, THE

WOODY ALLEN
DIRECTOR
'79 MANHATTAN
'80 STARDUST MEMORIES
'82 MIDSUMMER NIGHT'S SEX COMEDY, A
'83 ZELIG
'84 BROADWAY DANNY ROSE
SCREENPLAY
'79 MANHATTAN*
'80 STARDUST MEMORIES
'82 MIDSUMMER NIGHT'S SEX COMEDY, A
'83 ZELIG
'84 BROADWAY DANNY ROSE

JOHN ALLENBY
PROPS
'82 FIVE DAYS ONE SUMMER

DAN ALLINGHAM
ASSOCIATE PRODUCER
'83 REUBEN, REUBEN*
PRODUCTION MANAGER
'83 TWILIGHT ZONE, THE MOVIE*
1ST ASST. DIRECTOR
'79 ROLLER BOOGIE
'80 BALTIMORE BULLET, THE
'83 REUBEN, REUBEN

KAY ALLISON
MISCELLANEOUS
'84 BEAR, THE

SANDY ALLISON
CASTING
'84 RIDDLE OF THE SANDS

PETER ALLWORK
MISCELLANEOUS
'83 HIGH ROAD TO CHINA
'83 NEVER SAY NEVER AGAIN

ERIC ALLWRIGHT
MAKEUP
'80 HOPSCOTCH*
'80 MIRROR CRACK'D, THE*
'80 NOTHING PERSONAL*
'81 FOR YOUR EYES ONLY*
'84 PASSAGE TO INDIA, A*

WILLIAM ALLYN
PRODUCER
'81 RICH AND FAMOUS

NESTOR ALMENDROS
CINEMATOGRAPHER
'79 KRAMER VS. KRAMER
'80 BLUE LAGOON
'82 SOPHIE'S CHOICE
'82 STILL OF THE NIGHT
'84 PLACES IN THE HEART

JOHN ALONZO
CINEMATOGRAPHER
'79 NORMA RAE
'80 TOM HORN
'81 BACK ROADS
'81 ZORRO, THE GAY BLADE
'83 SCARFACE
'83 BLUE THUNDER
'83 CROSS CREEK
'84 RUNAWAY
MISCELLANEOUS
'80 CLOSE ENCOUNTERS OF THE THIRD KIND SPECIAL EDITION

RICHARD ALONZO
MISCELLANEOUS
'81 NESTING, THE

BUD ALPER
SOUND
'79 BREAKING AWAY
'80 WHY WOULD I LIE?
'82 SIX PACK
'82 BLADERUNNER
'82 DEAD MEN DON'T WEAR PLAID
'82 LOVE AND MONEY
'83 MAN WITH TWO BRAINS, THE
'83 TWO OF A KIND
'84 MARVIN AND TIGE

JOHN ALPER
LOCATIONS
'79 RICH KIDS

VICKIE ALPER
PROD. COORDINATOR
'82 BLADERUNNER

SUSAN ALSCHULER
PUBLICIST
'80 FOXES
'81 CHU CHU AND THE PHILLY FLASH
'81 EYE FOR AN EYE, AN
'83 ROMANTIC COMEDY
UNIT PUBLICIST
'82 SECOND THOUGHTS

ALLEN ALSOBROOK
PRODUCTION MANAGER
'84 REPO MAN
UNIT PROD. MANAGER
'82 SWORD AND THE SORCERER, THE

JANE ALSOBROOK
PUBLICIST
'82 CREEPSHOW

EMMETT ALSTON
2ND UNIT DIRECTOR
'81 ENTER THE NINJA

HOWARD ALSTON
EXEC IN CHARGE PROD
'82 SOPHIE'S CHOICE
'84 WHERE THE BOYS ARE
'84 EVIL THAT MEN DO, THE
MISCELLANEOUS
'80 BORDERLINE
'81 HARD COUNTRY
'82 BARBAROSA

DAWNE ALSTROM
PROD. COORDINATOR
'81 VICTORY*
PROD. SECRETARY
'83 BLACK STALLION RETURNS, THE*

GREG ALT
ASSOCIATE PRODUCER
'81 ZORRO, THE GAY BLADE*

JOSEPH ALTADONNA
ART DIRECTOR
'80 BIG BRAWL, THE
'80 MOTEL HELL

ELIO ALTAMURA
PROPS
'82 TEMPEST*

PHYLLIS ALTENHAUS-SMITH
ASSISTANT EDITOR
'79 WARRIORS, THE*

ERIC ALTER
SCREENPLAY
'84 HARDBODIES*

UDO ALTER
LOCATIONS
'84 MOSCOW ON THE HUDSON*

KAREN ALTMAN
PROD. COORDINATOR
'81 UNDER THE RAINBOW*
'83 OSTERMAN WEEKEND, THE*
'83 MAN WHO WASN'T THERE, THE
'84 FRIDAY THE 13TH PART IV THE FINAL CHAPTER

KATE ALTMAN
ART DIRECTOR
'84 PARIS, TEXAS

ROBERT ALTMAN
PRODUCER
'79 QUINTET
'79 PERFECT COUPLE, A
'79 REMEMBER MY NAME
'80 HEALTH
'83 STREAMERS*
DIRECTOR
'79 QUINTET
'79 PERFECT COUPLE, A
'80 HEALTH
'80 POPEYE
'82 COME BACK TO THE 5 & 10, JIMMY DEAN, JIMMY DEAN
'83 STREAMERS
SCREENPLAY
'79 QUINTET*
'79 PERFECT COUPLE, A*
'80 HEALTH*
EXECUTIVE PRODUCER
'79 RICH KIDS

STEPHEN ALTMAN
ART DIRECTOR
'83 STREAMERS
PROPS
'79 QUINTET
'79 PERFECT COUPLE, A
'80 HEALTH
'80 POPEYE
'82 COME BACK TO THE 5 & 10, JIMMY DEAN, JIMMY DEAN
'82 ENDANGERED SPECIES*

PETER ALTOBELLI
MAKEUP
'82 BEST LITTLE WHOREHOUSE IN TEXAS, THE*
'84 STARMAN

JOE ALVES
DIRECTOR
'83 JAWS 3-D
PRODUCTION DESIGNER
'80 CLOSE ENCOUNTERS OF THE THIRD KIND SPECIAL EDITION
'81 ESCAPE FROM NEW YORK
2ND UNIT DIRECTOR
'84 STARMAN

STEVE ALVES
ASSISTANT EDITOR
'80 EYES OF A STRANGER*

MOHAMED HOSSAM EL DIN ALY
LOCATIONS
'80 AWAKENING, THE*

TARAK BEN AMAR
EXECUTIVE PRODUCER
'79 MONTY PYTHON'S LIFE OF BRIAN*

CHLOE AMATEAU
2ND ASST. DIRECTOR
'84 LOVELESS, THE

CHLOE AMATEAU
MISCELLANEOUS
'79 FEDORA

CHLOE AMATEAU
LOCATIONS
'81 STRANGE BEHAVIOR

ROD AMATEAU
2ND UNIT DIRECTOR
'83 OSTERMAN WEEKEND, THE

BARBARA AMATO
SCRIPT SUPERVISOR
'79 JUST YOU AND ME KID

JUN AMAZAN
1ST ASST. DIRECTOR
'81 ENTER THE NINJA
'84 PURPLE HEARTS

KIM AMBLER
SCREENPLAY
'80 HOME MOVIES*

STAN AMBORN
SPECIAL EFFECTS
'81 STRIPES

DAVID AMBROSE
SCREENPLAY
'79 FIFTH MUSKETEER, THE
'80 FINAL COUNTDOWN, THE*

GEORGE AMERICAN HORSE
MISCELLANEOUS
'79 FRISCO KID, THE

PRESTON AMES
PRODUCTION DESIGNER
'79 BEYOND THE POSEIDON ADVENTURE
'80 LAST FLIGHT OF NOAH'S ARK, THE
'80 OH GOD! BOOK II
'81 PURSUIT OF D.B. COOPER, THE

JOHN ALAN AMICARELLA
ASSISTANT EDITOR
'83 STAYING ALIVE*

GIANFRANCO AMICUCCI
EDITOR
'83 1990: THE BRONX WARRIORS

ROBERTO AMICUCCI
ASSISTANT EDITOR
'83 1990: THE BRONX WARRIORS*

JEAN PIERRE AMIEL
CHOREOGRAPHER
'82 DARK CRYSTAL, THE

MARTIN AMIS
SCREENPLAY
'80 SATURN 3

TARAK BEN AMMAR
PRODUCER
'84 MISUNDERSTOOD

JOHN AMPLAS
CASTING
'79 DAWN OF THE DEAD

FRANCO AMURRI
1ST ASST. DIRECTOR
'82 TEMPEST*

ANDY ANDERSON
2ND ASST. DIRECTOR
'81 CONTINENTAL DIVIDE*
'81 HAND, THE
'82 ENDANGERED SPECIES*
'82 ESCAPE ARTIST, THE*

BARBARA ANDERSON
COSTUMES
'82 CREEPSHOW

BERNADINE ANDERSON
MAKEUP
'79 CHINA SYNDROME, THE*
'79 ELECTRIC HORSEMAN, THE*
'80 NINE TO FIVE*
'81 ROLLOVER*
'83 BUDDY SYSTEM, THE*
'84 SOLDIER'S STORY, A

BOB ANDERSON
UNIT PROD. MANAGER
'80 HOLLYWOOD KNIGHTS, THE

CARL ANDERSON
ART DIRECTOR
'79 VILLAIN, THE
PRODUCTION DESIGNER
'81 ...ALL THE MARBLES

CLETUS ANDERSON
PRODUCTION DESIGNER
'81 KNIGHTRIDERS
'82 CREEPSHOW
COSTUMES
'81 KNIGHTRIDERS
MISCELLANEOUS
'82 CREEPSHOW

DAVID ANDERSON
ASSOCIATE PRODUCER
'82 PIRATE MOVIE, THE
PRODUCTION MANAGER
'80 FLASH GORDON*
'81 STRANGE BEHAVIOR
1ST ASST. DIRECTOR
'79 FIFTH MUSKETEER, THE*
'81 CATTLE ANNIE AND LITTLE BRITCHES
'84 LOVELESS, THE
MISCELLANEOUS
'78 DEER HUNTER, THE

GLENN ANDERSON
SOUND
'79 ICE CASTLES*
'80 STIR CRAZY
'80 MOUNTAIN MEN, THE
'80 OCTAGON, THE
'81 SOUTHERN COMFORT*
'82 48 HOURS
'82 ZAPPED!*

HESPER ANDERSON
SCREENPLAY
'80 TOUCHED BY LOVE

HOWARD ANDERSON II
MISCELLANEOUS
'79 AVALANCHE EXPRESS

IRA ANDERSON
SPECIAL EFFECTS
'79 BREAKING AWAY

IRA ANDERSON JR.
SPECIAL EFFECTS
'81 MODERN PROBLEMS

JOHN ANDERSON
COSTUME SUPERVISOR
'80 RAISE THE TITANIC

JOHN ANDERSON
MISCELLANEOUS
'83 SILKWOOD

JON ANDERSON
1ST ASST. DIRECTOR
'80 BRUBAKER
'80 COMPETITION, THE
'82 AMATEUR, THE

LANCE ANDERSON
MAKEUP
'84 RED DAWN*
MISCELLANEOUS
'82 PARASITE
'84 LAST STARFIGHTER, THE

LAURIE ANDERSON
MISCELLANEOUS
'83 MAN WITH TWO BRAINS, THE

LINDSAY ANDERSON
DIRECTOR
'83 BRITANNIA HOSPITAL

LORNA ANDERSON
ASSISTANT EDITOR
'84 TERMINATOR, THE*

MARK ANDERSON
LOCATIONS
'84 REPO MAN

MAX ANDERSON
2ND UNIT DIRECTOR
'84 ICE PIRATES, THE
'84 PHILADELPHIA EXPERIMENT, THE
MISCELLANEOUS
'82 ZAPPED!
'84 CHILDREN OF THE CORN
'84 ICE PIRATES, THE
'84 PHILADELPHIA EXPERIMENT, THE

MICHAEL ANDERSON
EDITOR
'79 LOVE AND BULLETS*
'81 SPHINX*
'82 YES, GIORGIO

MICHAEL ANDERSON
STILLS
'82 SAFARI 3000

NICK ANDERSON
UNIT PROD. MANAGER
'79 BOULEVARD NIGHTS

PETER ANDERSON
PROD. COORDINATOR
'79 BUCK ROGERS

RICH ANDERSON
LOCATIONS
'80 HUMAN FACTOR, THE
'82 QUEST FOR FIRE

WILLIAM ANDERSON
EDITOR
'81 GALLIPOLI
'83 TENDER MERCIES
'83 YEAR OF LIVING DANGEROUSLY,THE

WILLIAM ANDERSON
MUSIC
'79 PENITENTIARY*

ROBERT ANDRE
ART DIRECTOR
'79 FEDORA

FRANCOISE ANDREJKA
MAKEUP
'79 LITTLE ROMANCE, A*

ROBERT ANDRES
KEY GRIP
'82 FIGHTING BACK*

STEPHEN ANDREW
1ST ASST. DIRECTOR
'80 MANIAC

ANDY ANDREWS
PROPS
'79 DRACULA
'79 MURDER BY DECREE
'80 FLASH GORDON
'81 FINAL CONFLICT, THE

CHRISTOPHER ANDREWS
EDITOR
'81 MS. 45

JAN ANDREWS
HAIR
'80 AWAKENING, THE*

JOSH ANDREWS
1ST ASST. DIRECTOR
'84 PREPPIES

LEA ANDREWS
PROD. COORDINATOR
'80 JAZZ SINGER, THE
PROD. SECRETARY
'80 UP THE ACADEMY
'82 STAR TREK II
THE WRATH OF KHAN

MARY ANDREWS
ASSISTANT EDITOR
'80 GONG SHOW MOVIE, THE*
'84 RACING WITH THE MOON

RUFUS ANDREWS
UNIT MANAGER
'81 PRIEST OF LOVE
2ND ASST. DIRECTOR
'84 CHAMPIONS*
LOCATIONS
'82 MOONLIGHTING

STEVE ANDREWS
2ND ASST. DIRECTOR
'81 GALLIPOLI
'81 EARTHLING, THE

ROSANNE ANDREWS-BAXTER
PROD. COORDINATOR
'82 ROAD WARRIOR, THE

GUI ANDRISANO
CHOREOGRAPHER
'84 POPE OF GREENWICH VILLAGE,THE

JEFF ANGELL
MAKEUP
'79 ROSE, THE
'80 DIVINE MADNESS*
'82 HAMMETT*
'82 JINXED*
'82 ONE FROM THE HEART*
'83 TABLE FOR FIVE
'84 CRACKERS*

CONRAD ANGONE
PRODUCTION DESIGNER
'82 BEASTMASTER, THE

NEIL ANGWIN
ART DIRECTOR
'79 MY BRILLIANT CAREER

EDWARD ANHALT
SCREENPLAY
'79 ESCAPE TO ATHENA*

HAGIT ANIN
ASSISTANT EDITOR
'82 PARADISE*

KEN ANNAKIN
DIRECTOR
'79 FIFTH MUSKETEER, THE
'80 CHEAPER TO KEEP HER
'82 PIRATE MOVIE, THE

JEAN-JACQUE ANNAUD
DIRECTOR
'82 QUEST FOR FIRE

BRIGITTA ANSARY
MAKEUP
'84 NEVERENDING STORY, THE*

VICTOR ANSELMO
MISCELLANEOUS
'82 BEASTMASTER, THE

MIKKI ANSIN
STILLS
'84 BOSTONIANS, THE*

DIANNE ANTHONY
COSTUMES
'81 HARD COUNTRY

RICHARD ANTHONY
SCREENPLAY
'83 ECHOES

SAL ANTHONY
MISCELLANEOUS
'84 POPE OF GREENWICH VILLAGE,THE

TONY ANTHONY
PRODUCER
'81 COMIN' AT YA!

PETE ANTICO
MISCELLANEOUS
'83 TOUGH ENOUGH

CLEO MARY ANTON
SCRIPT SUPERVISOR
'81 FORCE FIVE

FRANCO ANTONELLI
COSTUMES
'83 HIGH ROAD TO CHINA*

LOU ANTONIO
EXECUTIVE PRODUCER
'84 MICKI AND MAUDE*

JOY ANZAROUTH
PROD. OFFICE COORD.
'81 ZORRO, THE GAY BLADE
PROD. COORDINATOR
'83 WAR GAMES
'84 IRRECONCILABLE DIFFERENCES

ALBERTO ANZELLOTTI
KEY GRIP
'83 HANNA K*

MAURO ANZELLOTTI
KEY GRIP
'82 FIGHTING BACK*

APACHE
KEY GRIP
'84 CONAN THE DESTROYER

IRENE APARICIO
HAIR
'82 SIX PACK
'83 SPRING BREAK

CHARLES APERIA
EXECUTIVE PRODUCER
'82 BRAINWAVES*

ALLAN APONE
2ND UNIT DIRECTOR
'83 METALSTORM: THE DESTRUCTION OF JARED-SYN
MISCELLANEOUS
'83 METALSTORM: THE DESTRUCTION OF JARED-SYN
'83 GOLDEN SEAL, THE

MICHAEL APPEL
ASSOCIATE PRODUCER
'84 FLASHPOINT*

JEFF APPLE
PRODUCER
'82 ZAPPED!
EXECUTIVE PRODUCER
'84 WHERE THE BOYS ARE*

MAX APPLE
SCREENPLAY
'81 SMOKEY BITES THE DUST

LAWRENCE APPLEBAUM
EXECUTIVE PRODUCER
'82 PENITENTIARY II*

DAVID APPLEBY
STILLS
'79 MONTY PYTHON'S LIFE OF BRIAN
'80 FFOLKES
'81 REDS
'82 PINK FLOYD: THE WALL
'82 VICTOR/VICTORIA
'83 CURSE OF THE PINK PANTHER
'83 MONTY PYTHON'S THE MEANING OF LIFE
'83 TRAIL OF THE PINK PANTHER
'84 KILLING FIELDS, THE

GEORGE APPLEBY
EDITOR
'79 SILENT PARTNER, THE
'80 NOTHING PERSONAL

DAVID APPLETON
1ST ASST. DIRECTOR
'84 BOSTONIANS, THE

MICHAEL APTED
DIRECTOR
'79 AGATHA
'80 COAL MINER'S DAUGHTER
'81 CONTINENTAL DIVIDE
'83 GORKY PARK
'84 FIRSTBORN
'84 KIPPERBANG

RENE ARAM
MISCELLANEOUS
'83 HOUSE ON SORORITY ROW

JORGE ARANETA
CO-PRODUCER
'81 SEA WOLVES, THE

PAUL ARATOW
PRODUCER
'84 SHEENA

BEN ARBEID
EXECUTIVE PRODUCER
'83 ENIGMA

GERRY ARBEID
PRODUCTION MANAGER
'80 TRIBUTE*
1ST ASST. DIRECTOR
'80 KIDNAPPING OF THE PRESIDENT, THE

RENATE ARBES
CASTING
'79 AVALANCHE EXPRESS
'79 BLOODLINE
'80 AMERICAN SUCCESS COMPANY, THE*
'80 FORMULA, THE*
'82 FIREFOX*

ROY ARBOGAST
SPECIAL EFFECTS
'81 ESCAPE FROM NEW YORK
'82 THING, THE
SP. EFFECTS SUPERV.
'81 CAVEMAN
'83 RETURN OF THE JEDI
'83 CHRISTINE
'84 STARMAN
MISCELLANEOUS
'80 CLOSE ENCOUNTERS OF THE THIRD KIND SPECIAL EDITION
'83 JAWS 3-D

JENNY ARBOUR
HAIR
'80 PROM NIGHT
'83 DEAD ZONE, THE
'84 JUST THE WAY YOU ARE*

FRANCO ARCALLO
SCREENPLAY
'84 ONCE UPON A TIME IN AMERICA*

ALEX ARCHAMBAULT
HAIR
'80 FIENDISH PLOT OF DR. FU MANCHU, THE*
'81 CONDORMAN

MONIQUE ARCHAMBAULT
MAKEUP
'79 MOONRAKER*

ERNEST ARCHER
ART DIRECTOR
'83 PIRATES OF PENZANCE, THE*

RON ARCHER
COSTUMES
'82 DEATHWISH II

SIMON ARCHER
KEY GRIP
'83 DRAUGHTSMAN CONTRACT, THE

VERN ARCHER
SPECIAL EFFECTS
'79 DREAMER

PRUDENCE ARDNT
ASSISTANT EDITOR
'83 LIANNA*

GIOVANNI ARDUINI
CASTING
'83 BLACK STALLION RETURNS, THE*
1ST ASST. DIRECTOR
'83 BLACK STALLION RETURNS, THE*

FRANCISCO ARDURA
MISCELLANEOUS
'82 CONAN THE BARBARIAN

PACO ARDURO
MISCELLANEOUS
'81 REDS

JULIE ARENAL
CHOREOGRAPHER
'81 FOUR FRIENDS

BRAD ARENSMAN
EDITOR
'82 PARASITE
'83 METALSTORM: THE DESTRUCTION OF JARED-SYN

DARIO ARGENTO
MUSIC
'79 DAWN OF THE DEAD*

ALAN ARKIN
EXECUTIVE PRODUCER
'79 IN-LAWS, THE

LOUIS ARKOFF
EXECUTIVE PRODUCER
'84 UP THE CREEK

SAMUEL ARKOFF
EXECUTIVE PRODUCER
'79 AMITYVILLE HORROR, THE
'79 C.H.O.M.P.S.
'80 HOW TO BEAT THE HIGH COST OF LIVING
EXEC IN CHARGE PROD
'84 UP THE CREEK

ALLAN ARKUSH
DIRECTOR
'79 ROCK 'N ROLL HIGH SCHOOL
'81 HEARTBEEPS
'83 GET CRAZY

PAT ARLEDGE
LOCATIONS
'80 URBAN COWBOY*

ALICE ARLEN
SCREENPLAY
'83 SILKWOOD*

LESLIE ARLISS
SCREENPLAY
'83 WICKED LADY, THE*

MARY ARMANTROUT
SCRIPT SUPERVISOR
'84 EL NORTE*

KAY ARMATAGE
LOCATIONS
'79 MEATBALLS

CARMEN ARMENDAREZ
LOCATIONS
'79 SUNBURN

JAMES ARMFIELD
STILLS
'79 PRIZE FIGHTER, THE
'83 SPRING BREAK*
'83 NIGHT IN HEAVEN, A

ANDY ARMSTRONG
1ST ASST. DIRECTOR
'83 DRESSER, THE
'84 ANOTHER COUNTRY
2ND ASST. DIRECTOR
'79 HANOVER STREET*
'80 ROUGH CUT*
'81 RAGTIME*
'83 KRULL*

DEL ARMSTRONG
MAKEUP
'79 NIGHTWING
'79 IN-LAWS, THE*
'80 MOUNTAIN MEN, THE*
'80 TOM HORN
'81 CAVEMAN
'82 SILENT RAGE
'82 MAKING LOVE*
'84 LONELY GUY, THE*
'84 TEACHERS*

DOUG ARMSTRONG
KEY GRIP
'81 NESTING, THE
'83 ECHOES

GILLIAN ARMSTRONG
DIRECTOR
'79 MY BRILLIANT CAREER
'82 STARSTRUCK
'84 MRS. SOFFEL

KAY ARMSTRONG
SOUND
'80 GILDA LIVE*

MICHAEL ARMSTRONG
SCREENPLAY
'82 HOUSE OF THE LONG SHADOWS

STUART ARMSTRONG
ASSISTANT EDITOR
'80 ROUGH CUT*

SU ARMSTRONG
PRODUCTION MANAGER
'81 GALLIPOLI*
'81 EARTHLING, THE*

VIC ARMSTRONG
STUNT COORDINATOR
'79 UNIDENTIFIED FLYING ODDBALL
'79 ESCAPE TO ATHENA
'80 WATCHER IN THE WOODS, THE
'81 SUPERMAN II*
'83 KRULL
'83 NEVER SAY NEVER AGAIN
'84 CONAN THE DESTROYER*
'84 INDIANA JONES AND THE TEMPLE OF DOOM*

WILLIAM ARMSTRONG
MISCELLANEOUS
'79 BREAKING AWAY

LEO ARNAUD
MISCELLANEOUS
'80 COMPETITION, THE

DAVID ARNDT
KEY GRIP
'80 RETURN OF THE SECAUCUS SEVEN, THE

GORDON ARNELL
PUBLICIST
'79 BUTCH AND SUNDANCE: THE EARLY YEARS
'79 DRACULA
'80 FLASH GORDON*
'80 MIRROR CRACK'D, THE
'81 RAGTIME
'82 EVIL UNDER THE SUN
'84 SUPERGIRL*

M. JAMES ARNETT
2ND UNIT DIRECTOR
'79 WINTER KILLS
'81 GAS
'81 TAPS
'82 ANNIE
'83 D.C. CAB*
'83 DOCTOR DETROIT
STUNT COORDINATOR
'79 NIGHTWING
'80 FOXES
'80 NINE TO FIVE
'80 STEEL
'80 WHEN TIME RAN OUT
'81 GAS
'81 TAPS
'82 SHOOT THE MOON
'82 ANNIE*
'82 GREASE 2
'83 DOCTOR DETROIT
'84 ADVENTURES OF BUCKAROO BANZAI ACROSS THE 8TH DIMENSION, THE
'84 BIRDY
'84 2010
'84 IMPULSE
'84 DREAMSCAPE

ALAN ARNOLD
PUBLICIST
'80 EMPIRE STRIKES BACK, THE
'82 FIVE DAYS ONE SUMMER
'83 BETRAYAL
'84 GIVE MY REGARDS TO BROAD STREET

JEFF ARNOLD
LOCATIONS
'80 FOXES

MELBOURNE ARNOLD
SPECIAL EFFECTS
'81 BUSTIN' LOOSE
'83 PSYCHO II

MONROE ARNOLD
MISCELLANEOUS
'79 BELL JAR, THE

NEWTON ARNOLD
1ST ASST. DIRECTOR
'79 CONCORDE-AIRPORT '79, THE
'79 JERK, THE
'80 CHEECH AND CHONG'S NEXT MOVIE
'82 SIX PACK
'82 BLADERUNNER*
'82 DEAD MEN DON'T WEAR PLAID
'83 D.C. CAB
'83 TABLE FOR FIVE
'83 WAR GAMES
'84 SIXTEEN CANDLES

PAMELA ARNOLD
ASSISTANT EDITOR
'83 ZELIG*

PIA ARNOLD
ASSOCIATE PRODUCER
'80 AMERICAN SUCCESS COMPANY, THE
MISCELLANEOUS
'80 OH! HEAVENLY DOG

SUSAN ARNOLD
CASTING
'81 HOWLING, THE*
'82 SOUP FOR ONE*
'83 INDEPENDENCE DAY*
'83 NATIONAL LAMPOON'S VACATION*
'84 GREMLINS
'84 REVENGE OF THE NERDS*
'84 TOP SECRET!*

WILMA ARNOLD
SCRIPT SUPERVISOR
'79 PENITENTIARY

DAVID ARNTZEN
2ND ASST. DIRECTOR
'82 GREASE 2*

DONN ARON
ASSISTANT EDITOR
'84 POPE OF GREENWICH VILLAGE,

RICARDO ARONOVICH
CINEMATOGRAPHER
'80 OUTSIDER, THE
'82 MISSING
'83 HANNA K

BRAD ARONSON
PRODUCTION MANAGER
'83 YELLOWBEARD*
UNIT PROD. MANAGER
'81 INCHON
MISCELLANEOUS
'81 HIGH RISK

BUD ARONSON
LOCATIONS
'82 BARBAROSA
'82 DEATHWISH II*

LYNETTE ARONSON
SCRIPT SUPERVISOR
'81 HIGH RISK

ITZHAK BEN AROYA
KEY GRIP
'82 SAFARI 3000

FERNANDO ARRIBAS
CINEMATOGRAPHER
'81 COMIN' AT YA!

LUCIANA ARRIGHI
PRODUCTION DESIGNER
'79 MY BRILLIANT CAREER
'83 PRIVATES ON PARADE
'84 MRS. SOFFEL
COSTUMES
'82 STARSTRUCK*
'83 PRIVATES ON PARADE

RICHARD ARRINGTON
MAKEUP
'82 BUTTERFLY
'82 LAST AMERICAN VIRGIN, THE
'83 SAVANNAH SMILES*
'84 PURPLE RAIN*
HAIR
'83 SAVANNAH SMILES*

COLIN ARTHUR
MAKEUP
'79 CLASS OF MISS MACMICHAEL, THE
'81 CATTLE ANNIE AND LITTLE BRITCHES*
MISCELLANEOUS
'81 CLASH OF THE TITANS
'84 NEVERENDING STORY, THE

DONALD ARTHUR
MISCELLANEOUS
'81 MONTENEGRO

DUANE ARTHUR
KEY GRIP
'80 HE KNOWS YOU'RE ALONE

VICTORIA ARTHUR
UNIT PUBLICIST
'80 CARNY
'80 HOW TO BEAT THE HIGH COST OF LIVING*

TONY ARTIEDA
MAKEUP
'82 DON'T CRY, IT'S ONLY THUNDER*

STUART ARTINGSTALL
HAIR
'82 DARK CRYSTAL, THE
MISCELLANEOUS
'82 DARK CRYSTAL, THE

LINDA ARTUSO
MISCELLANEOUS
'79 WANDERERS, THE

MARY GAIL ARTZ
CASTING
'81 HALLOWEEN II
'83 BAD BOYS*

MARLENE ARVAN
2ND ASST. DIRECTOR
'82 COME BACK TO THE 5 & 10, JIMMY DEAN, JIMMY DEAN
LOCATIONS
'82 I'M DANCING AS FAST AS I CAN

PAULA SQUIRES ASAFF
SCRIPT SUPERVISOR
'84 NOT FOR PUBLICATION

MEL ASCH
PUBLICIST
'81 MODERN PROBLEMS

KENNY ASCHER
MUSIC
'79 MUPPET MOVIE, THE*

HAL ASHBY
DIRECTOR
'79 BEING THERE
'82 LOOKIN' TO GET OUT
'83 LET'S SPEND THE NIGHT TOGETHER

MARIE ASHBY
PROD. SECRETARY
'79 GAME OF DEATH

ANN ASHCRAFT
PROD. OFFICE COORD.
'82 ANNIE*
'82 BEST FRIENDS

LANI ASHER
PROPS
'83 SMITHEREENS*

MARIE ASHTON
CASTING
'82 DON'T CRY, IT'S ONLY THUNDER

ROY ASHTON
MAKEUP
'79 UNIDENTIFIED FLYING ODDBALL*

ANDREA ASIMOV
ASSOCIATE PRODUCER
'83 TESTAMENT

ISAAC ASIMOV
MISCELLANEOUS
'79 STAR TREK-THE MOTION PICTURE

PETER ASKIN
SCREENPLAY
'83 SMITHEREENS*

DIANE ASNES
ASSISTANT EDITOR
'82 COME BACK TO THE 5 & 10, JIMMY DEAN, JIMMY DEAN*

DALE ASPIN
STUNT COORDINATOR
'82 STARSTRUCK
MISCELLANEOUS
'82 ROAD WARRIOR, THE

MAX ASPIN
STUNT COORDINATOR
'82 ROAD WARRIOR, THE

TAMARA ASSEYEV
PRODUCER
'79 NORMA RAE*

OVIDIO ASSONITIS
EXECUTIVE PRODUCER
'83 PIRANHA II: THE SPAWNING

JARVIS ASTAIRE
PRODUCER
'79 AGATHA*

GUY ASTIER
MAKEUP
'81 RICHARD PRYOR: LIVE ON THE SUNSET STRIP

PETER ASTON
MISCELLANEOUS
'83 BRITANNIA HOSPITAL

MARIANNA ASTROM-DEFINA
MAKEUP
'84 HOT DOG...THE MOVIE*

NADER ATASSI
EXECUTIVE PRODUCER
'82 BEASTMASTER, THE*

STEVE ATHA
MAKEUP
'79 HEARTLAND
'83 EDDIE AND THE CRUISERS
HAIR
'79 HEARTLAND
'83 EDDIE AND THE CRUISERS

BHANU ATHAIYA
COSTUMES
'82 GANDHI*

KEN ATHERFOLD
KEY GRIP
'84 LASSITER

MEHIZ ATHMANE
LOCATIONS
'83 BLACK STALLION RETURNS, THE*

DARRYL ATHONS
COSTUME SUPERVISOR
'82 BARBAROSA

DAVID ATKINS
CHOREOGRAPHER
'82 STARSTRUCK
'82 PIRATE MOVIE, THE

ADRIENNE ATKINSON
ART DIRECTOR
'83 LOCAL HERO*
PRODUCTION DESIGNER
'84 COMFORT AND JOY

BETTY ATKINSON
PROD. OFFICE COORD.
'82 CHILLY SCENES OF WINTER
PROD. COORDINATOR
'79 ROSE, THE
'79 DREAMER

MARTIN ATKINSON
ART DIRECTOR
'81 FINAL CONFLICT, THE

NANCY ATLAS
ASSISTANT EDITOR
'80 UNION CITY*

RICHARD ATTENBOROUGH
PRODUCER
'82 GANDHI
DIRECTOR
'82 GANDHI

WENDY ATTERBURY
SCRIPT SUPERVISOR
'80 THOSE LIPS, THOSE EYES
'81 POSTMAN ALWAYS RINGS TWICE, THE
'82 SOME KIND OF HERO
'82 CANNERY ROW

DAN ATTIAS
2ND ASST. DIRECTOR
'81 PURSUIT OF D.B. COOPER, THE*
'82 E.T. THE EXTRA-TERRESTRIAL
'82 HAMMETT*
'82 ONE FROM THE HEART*
'83 TWILIGHT ZONE, THE MOVIE*

GRAHAM ATTWOOD
STILLS
'79 MURDER BY DECREE
'80 AWAKENING, THE*
'81 SEA WOLVES, THE
'81 CHARIOTS OF FIRE
'82 FIVE DAYS ONE SUMMER*
'83 BETRAYAL
'83 FINAL OPTION, THE*
'83 KEEP, THE
'83 LOCAL HERO*

HUGH ATTWOOLL
ASSOCIATE PRODUCER
'79 UNIDENTIFIED FLYING ODDBALL
'80 WATCHER IN THE WOODS, THE
'81 CONDORMAN

COLLEEN ATWOOD
COSTUMES
'84 FIRSTBORN

JOE AUBEL
ART DIRECTOR
'81 DEAD AND BURIED*

RALPH AUBERT
PROPS
'79 WHEN YOU COMIN' BACK, RED RYDER?
MISCELLANEOUS
'79 AVALANCHE EXPRESS

PATRICK AUBREE
1ST ASST. DIRECTOR
'81 SUNDAY LOVERS*

GREG AUER
SPECIAL EFFECTS
'79 PROMISE, THE

RANDY AUERBACH
MISCELLANEOUS
'80 ELEPHANT MAN, THE

HY AUERBACK
DIRECTOR
'84 WHERE THE BOYS ARE

ANNE AULENTA-SPIRA
MAKEUP
'83 CHAINED HEAT*
'84 HARDBODIES
HAIR
'83 CHAINED HEAT*
'84 HARDBODIES

JOSEPH AULISI
COSTUMES
'80 LITTLE DARLINGS
'81 NIGHT THE LIGHTS WENT OUT IN GEORGIA, THE
'82 STRANGER IS WATCHING, A
'83 BUDDY SYSTEM, THE
'83 EASY MONEY
'83 MAN WOMAN AND CHILD*
'84 POPE OF GREENWICH VILLAGE, THE

JAMES AUPPERLE
MISCELLANEOUS
'84 DREAMSCAPE

GIUSEPPE AURIEMMA
PRODUCTION MANAGER
'83 LONELY LADY, THE

ROBERT ALAN AURTHUR
PRODUCER
'79 ALL THAT JAZZ
SCREENPLAY
'79 ALL THAT JAZZ*

BUD AUSTIN
EXECUTIVE PRODUCER
'84 JOHNNY DANGEROUSLY*

GEOFFREY AUSTIN
LOCATIONS
'84 CHAMPIONS*
'84 SCANDALOUS*

JEAN AUSTIN
HAIR
'81 PURSUIT OF D.B. COOPER, THE*

LEO AUSTIN
PRODUCTION DESIGNER
'84 BOSTONIANS, THE

MARY ANN AUSTIN
CASTING
'84 PLACES IN THE HEART*

MICHAEL AUSTIN
SCREENPLAY
'79 SHOUT, THE*
'82 FIVE DAYS ONE SUMMER
'84 GREYSTOKE: THE LEGEND OF TARZAN, LORD OF THE APES*
ASSOCIATE PRODUCER
'79 SHOUT, THE

STEPHANIE AUSTIN
PROD. COORDINATOR
'79 FAST BREAK

TERESA AUSTIN
MAKEUP
'80 GALAXINA
HAIR
'80 GALAXINA

ARAM AVAKIAN
EDITOR
'80 HONEYSUCKLE ROSE*

HOWARD AVEDIS
PRODUCER
'83 MORTUARY*
DIRECTOR
'83 MORTUARY
SCREENPLAY
'83 MORTUARY*

KIMBERLY AVERY
PROD. COORDINATOR
'83 REVENGE OF THE NINJA*

JEAN-PIERRE AVICE
PRODUCTION MANAGER
'83 NEVER SAY NEVER AGAIN*
'84 CHEECH AND CHONG'S THE CORSICAN BROTHERS

JOHN AVILDSEN
DIRECTOR
'80 FORMULA, THE
'81 NEIGHBORS
'83 NIGHT IN HEAVEN, A
'84 KARATE KID, THE
EDITOR
'80 FORMULA, THE*
'83 NIGHT IN HEAVEN, A
'84 KARATE KID, THE*
MISCELLANEOUS
'81 NEIGHBORS

TOM AVILDSEN
DIRECTOR
'82 THINGS ARE TOUGH ALL OVER
EDITOR
'84 CHEECH AND CHONG'S THE CORSICAN BROTHERS
ASSISTANT EDITOR
'80 CHEECH AND CHONG'S NEXT MOVIE*
'81 CHEECH AND CHONG'S NICE DREAMS*

ALFONSO AVINCOLA
STILLS
'81 BEYOND THE REEF
'82 FIGHTING BACK

JON AVNET
PRODUCER
'80 COAST TO COAST*
'83 RISKY BUSINESS*
EXECUTIVE PRODUCER
'83 DEAL OF THE CENTURY*

ROBERT AVRECH
SCREENPLAY
'84 BODY DOUBLE*

FRANCES AVRUT-BAUER
ASSOCIATE PRODUCER
'79 BUDDY HOLLY STORY, THE
'81 UNDER THE RAINBOW

NEWTON AVRUTIS
SOUND
'79 FIREPOWER*

DAVID AXELROD
SCREENPLAY
'81 CHARLIE CHAN AND THE CURSE OF THE DRAGON QUEEN*
ASSOCIATE PRODUCER
'80 HEARTBEAT

GEORGE AXELROD
SCREENPLAY
'80 LADY VANISHES, THE

KIRK AXTELL
ART DIRECTOR
'80 RAGING BULL*

YVONNE AXWORTHY

SCRIPT SUPERVISOR
'79 BLOODLINE*
'81 INCHON
'81 DOGS OF WAR, THE
'82 CONAN THE BARBARIAN
'84 DUNE

WILLIAM AYDELOTT

PRODUCER
'80 RETURN OF
THE SECAUCUS SEVEN, THE*

JANE AYER

PUBLICIST
'83 TIMERIDER

M.C. AYERS

PROPS
'80 HOPSCOTCH*
'81 S.O.B.
'81 BUDDY, BUDDY
'83 MAN WHO LOVED WOMEN, THE
'84 MICKI AND MAUDE

DAN AYKROYD

SCREENPLAY
'80 BLUES BROTHERS*
'84 GHOSTBUSTERS*

DENYS AYLING

MISCELLANEOUS
'79 ALIEN

BRUCE AYRES

STILLS
'82 BRAINWAVES*

GERALD AYRES

PRODUCER
'80 FOXES*
SCREENPLAY
'80 FOXES
'81 RICH AND FAMOUS

JORGE AZCARATE

ASSISTANT EDITOR
'84 ROMANCING THE STONE*

FAROUK ABDEL AZIZ

KEY GRIP
'81 GALLIPOLI*

IRVING AZOFF

PRODUCER
'80 URBAN COWBOY*
'82 FAST TIMES AT RIDGEMONT HIGH*

THO. AZZARI

ART DIRECTOR
'84 CANNONBALL RUN II

B

ANDY BABBISH
SOUND
'81 PRIVATE LESSONS

DAVID BACA
COSTUMES
'84 BREAKIN 2 ELECTRIC BOOGALOO*

DOROTHY BACA
COSTUMES
'84 BREAKIN 2 ELECTRIC BOOGALOO*

ABDELKRIM BACCAR
LOCATIONS
'81 RAIDERS OF THE LOST ARK*

STEVEN BACH
PRODUCER
'79 BUTCH AND SUNDANCE: THE EARLY YEARS*

BURT BACHARACH
MUSIC
'81 ARTHUR
'82 NIGHT SHIFT

LAWRENCE BACHMANN
PRODUCER
'81 WHOSE LIFE IS IT ANYWAY?

BARBARA BACK
PROD. OFFICE COORD.
'82 CONAN THE BARBARIAN

NELIA BACMEISTER
2ND ASST. DIRECTOR
'80 MANIAC*

WILLIAM BADALATO
PRODUCTION MANAGER
'79 LOVE AT FIRST BITE
'81 NIGHTHAWKS*
'82 YOUNG DOCTORS IN LOVE
'83 MAN WITH TWO BRAINS, THE
UNIT PROD. MANAGER
'81 RICH AND FAMOUS*
'81 CONTINENTAL DIVIDE*
UNIT MANAGER
'82 CAT PEOPLE*

LAUREN BADAMI
ASSISTANT EDITOR
'83 GET CRAZY*

RANDALL BADGER
LOCATIONS
'80 STARDUST MEMORIES*
'82 STRANGER IS WATCHING, A

JOHN BADHAM
DIRECTOR
'79 DRACULA
'81 WHOSE LIFE IS IT ANYWAY?
'83 BLUE THUNDER
'83 WAR GAMES

ANAUR BADIN
PRODUCTION MANAGER
'83 BEYOND THE LIMIT*
MISCELLANEOUS
'80 HERBIE GOES BANANAS
'84 DUNE
'84 CONAN THE DESTROYER

HANANIA BAER
CINEMATOGRAPHER
'83 ECHOES
'84 BREAKIN 2 ELECTRIC BOOGALOO
MISCELLANEOUS
'80 ALLIGATOR

JOHN BAER
MUSIC
'84 WEEKEND PASS

JERRY BAERWITZ
UNIT PROD. MANAGER
'81 RICHARD PRYOR: LIVE ON THE SUNSET STRIP
'82 TEX
'82 TOY, THE

TED BAFALOUKOS
MISCELLANEOUS
'84 NATURAL, THE

BRUCE BAGGOT
ASSISTANT EDITOR
'80 SEEMS LIKE OLD TIMES
'83 STRANGE BREW*

KING BAGGOT
CINEMATOGRAPHER
'80 CHEECH AND CHONG'S NEXT MOVIE
'81 HAND, THE
'82 SOME KIND OF HERO
'82 SECOND THOUGHTS
'83 DOCTOR DETROIT
'84 LAST STARFIGHTER, THE
'84 REVENGE OF THE NERDS
'84 OH GOD, YOU DEVIL
MISCELLANEOUS
'79 FISH THAT SAVED PITTSBURGH, THE

BRUCE BAHRENBURG
PUBLICIST
'82 BARBAROSA
'82 JINXED
'84 RACING WITH THE MOON
'84 TEACHERS
UNIT PUBLICIST
'79 NORTH DALLAS FORTY
'81 NIGHTHAWKS
'82 AUTHOR, AUTHOR
'83 LOVESICK
'83 TO BE OR NOT TO BE
'84 RIVER, THE
'84 ONCE UPON A TIME IN AMERICA

BILL BAILES
SPECIAL EFFECTS
'82 I, THE JURY*

HILLARY BAILEY
CASTING
'82 FIRST TIME, THE*

JOHN BAILEY
CINEMATOGRAPHER
'79 AMERICAN GIGOLO
'79 BOULEVARD NIGHTS
'80 ORDINARY PEOPLE
'81 CONTINENTAL DIVIDE
'81 HONKY TONK FREEWAY
'82 CAT PEOPLE
'82 THAT CHAMPIONSHIP SEASON
'83 BIG CHILL, THE
'83 WITHOUT A TRACE
'84 POPE OF GREENWICH VILLAGE, THE
'84 RACING WITH THE MOON
MISCELLANEOUS
'79 WINTER KILLS

JOHN BAILEY
SCREENPLAY
'84 RIDDLE OF THE SANDS*

ROBERT BAILEY
SCREENPLAY
'83 YOR*

SALLI BAILEY
HAIR
'80 CHANGELING, THE*
'82 BY DESIGN
'82 FIRST BLOOD
'82 OUT OF THE BLUE

GARY BAIM
SCREENPLAY
'79 ICE CASTLES*

KEITH BAIN
MISCELLANEOUS
'79 MY BRILLIANT CAREER

JOHN BAIRD
MISCELLANEOUS
'79 MY BRILLIANT CAREER
'82 PIRATE MOVIE, THE

STUART BAIRD
EDITOR
'81 OUTLAND
'82 FIVE DAYS ONE SUMMER
'83 BEYOND THE LIMIT

STUART BAIRD
ASSOCIATE PRODUCER
'80 ALTERED STATES

BUDDY BAKER
MUSIC
'79 APPLE DUMPLING GANG RIDES AGAIN, THE
'81 DEVIL AND MAX DEVLIN, THE

CLEO BAKER
MISCELLANEOUS
'79 CONCORDE-AIRPORT '79, THE

DAVID BAKER
MISCELLANEOUS
'79 MAN, A WOMAN AND A BANK, A

DIANE BAKER
PROD. SECRETARY
'84 MASS APPEAL

DON BAKER
MISCELLANEOUS
'83 BRAINSTORM

G. THOMAS BAKER
EXEC IN CHARGE PROD
'83 EDDIE AND THE CRUISERS

GRAHAM BAKER
DIRECTOR
'81 FINAL CONFLICT, THE
'84 IMPULSE

HERBERT BAKER
SCREENPLAY
'80 JAZZ SINGER, THE

IAN BAKER
CINEMATOGRAPHER
'82 BARBAROSA
'84 ICEMAN

KAREN BAKER
ASSISTANT EDITOR
'83 ENIGMA*

KEN BAKER
1ST ASST. DIRECTOR
'79 STEVIE

LEONARD BAKER
ASSOCIATE PRODUCER
'79 TOURIST TRAP

MARK BAKER
LOCATIONS
'81 FRIDAY THE 13TH PART TWO

MARTIN BAKER
LOCATIONS
'81 GREAT MUPPET CAPER, THE
MISCELLANEOUS
'79 MUPPET MOVIE, THE

MICHAEL CONWAY BAKER
MUSIC
'82 GREY FOX, THE

RICK BAKER
MISCELLANEOUS
'81 AMERICAN WEREWOLF IN LONDON, AN
'81 FUNHOUSE, THE
'81 INCREDIBLE SHRINKING WOMAN, THE
'83 VIDEODROME
'84 GREYSTOKE: THE LEGEND OF TARZAN, LORD OF THE APES
'84 GREYSTOKE: THE LEGEND OF TARZAN, LORD OF THE APES
'84 STARMAN

ROY BAKER
ASSISTANT EDITOR
'83 MONTY PYTHON'S THE MEANING OF LIFE*

SHERRY BAKER
PROD. SECRETARY
'79 GREAT BANK HOAX, THE

STEVE BAKER
KEY GRIP
'84 ONCE UPON A TIME IN AMERICA*

EDLE BAKKE
SCRIPT SUPERVISOR
'79 BEING THERE
'80 COAST TO COAST
'82 TRON
'83 SOMETHING WICKED THIS WAY COMES

ROBERTO BAKKER
PRODUCTION MANAGER
'84 BLAME IT ON RIO*

ASSMA EL BAKRY
MISCELLANEOUS
'80 AWAKENING, THE

FRANCISCO BALANGUE
ART DIRECTOR
'84 PURPLE HEARTS

BALAZS
MAKEUP
'83 SAVANNAH SMILES*
HAIR
'83 SAVANNAH SMILES*

CHARLES BALAZS
MAKEUP
'82 BOOGENS, THE
HAIR
'80 BATTLE BEYOND THE STARS

KAROLY BALAZS
MAKEUP
'80 HANGAR 18
HAIR
'80 PRIVATE EYES, THE

PETER BALDDOCK
ASSISTANT EDITOR
'84 KIPPERBANG*

VERENA BALDEO
PROD. SECRETARY
'83 BLACK STALLION RETURNS, THE*

FERDINANDO BALDI
DIRECTOR
'81 COMIN' AT YA!

SAM BALDONI
1ST ASST. DIRECTOR
'83 FRIGHTMARE
2ND UNIT DIRECTOR
'83 FRIGHTMARE

BOB BALDWIN
CINEMATOGRAPHER
'80 EXTERMINATOR, THE
'84 EXTERMINATOR II*

SIDNEY BALDWIN
STILLS
'79 BEING THERE
'79 MUPPET MOVIE, THE*
'79 PROMISES IN THE DARK
'79 REMEMBER MY NAME
'80 STIR CRAZY
'80 BLACK MARBLE, THE
'82 ENDANGERED SPECIES*
'82 THINGS ARE TOUGH ALL OVER
'83 SCARFACE
'84 STARMAN*
'84 WOMAN IN RED, THE

CYNTHIA BALES
COSTUMES
'83 UNDER FIRE

SILVANO BALICAS
KEY GRIP
'84 PURPLE HEARTS

DAVID BALL
PRODUCTION MANAGER
'81 CATTLE ANNIE AND LITTLE BRITCHES
'83 YELLOWBEARD*
MISCELLANEOUS
'83 ENIGMA

DEREK BALL
SOUND
'79 EUROPEANS, THE
'79 ESCAPE TO ATHENA
'79 GREAT TRAIN ROBBERY, THE
'80 SATURN 3
'80 HOPSCOTCH*
'81 FOR YOUR EYES ONLY
'82 FIVE DAYS ONE SUMMER
'83 OCTOPUSSY
'84 KIPPERBANG
'84 SUPERGIRL

EARL POOLE BALL
MISCELLANEOUS
'81 THEY ALL LAUGHED

GEORGE BALL
PROPS
'79 HANOVER STREET
'80 SATURN 3
'81 GREAT MUPPET CAPER, THE
'81 REDS
'82 DARK CRYSTAL, THE
'82 MISSIONARY, THE
'83 KEEP, THE
'84 RAZOR'S EDGE, THE

PHIL BALL
2ND ASST. DIRECTOR
'83 MAUSOLEUM

BONNIE BALLARD
PROPS
'82 FRIDAY THE 13TH PART THREE IN 3D

CARROLL BALLARD
DIRECTOR
'79 BLACK STALLION, THE
'83 NEVER CRY WOLF

TERRY BALLARD
PROPS
'83 MAN WHO WASN'T THERE, THE
'84 MEATBALLS PART II
MISCELLANEOUS
'82 FRIDAY THE 13TH PART THREE IN 3D
'84 FRIDAY THE 13TH PART IV THE FINAL CHAPTER

FRANCO BALLATI
UNIT MANAGER
'79 BLACK STALLION, THE

BILL BALLES
SPECIAL EFFECTS
'81 PURSUIT OF D.B. COOPER, THE*
'83 MR. MOM

MICHAEL BALLHAUS
CINEMATOGRAPHER
'83 BABY IT'S YOU
'84 RECKLESS

HUMBERT BALSAIN
ASSOCIATE PRODUCER
'80 QUARTET*

ALAN BALSAM
EDITOR
'81 DEAD AND BURIED
'83 TO BE OR NOT TO BE
'84 REVENGE OF THE NERDS
ASSISTANT EDITOR
'80 FATSO

FRANK BALSAMO
SOUND
'83 RETURN OF THE ALIENS: THE DEADLY SPAWN
MISCELLANEOUS
'83 RETURN OF THE ALIENS: THE DEADLY SPAWN

MICHAEL BALSON
EDITOR
'82 ROAD WARRIOR, THE*

BOB BANAS
CHOREOGRAPHER
'83 HEART LIKE A WHEEL

PEPINO BANCHELLI
MAKEUP
'82 TEMPEST*

ANNE BANCROFT
DIRECTOR
'80 FATSO
SCREENPLAY
'80 FATSO

ALBERT BAND
EXECUTIVE PRODUCER
'83 METALSTORM: THE DESTRUCTION OF JARED-SYN*

CHARLES BAND
PRODUCER
'82 PARASITE
'83 METALSTORM: THE DESTRUCTION OF JARED-SYN*
DIRECTOR
'82 PARASITE
'83 METALSTORM: THE DESTRUCTION OF JARED-SYN
EXECUTIVE PRODUCER
'79 TOURIST TRAP

RICHARD BAND
MUSIC
'82 PARASITE
'83 HOUSE ON SORORITY ROW
'83 METALSTORM: THE DESTRUCTION OF JARED-SYN
'84 MUTANT

LES BANDA
2ND ASST. DIRECTOR
'84 BROADWAY DANNY ROSE*

MARTIN BANDEER
MUSIC SUPERVISOR
'84 BEAR, THE*

SYLVETTE BANDROT
SCRIPT SUPERVISOR
'82 MISSING

MOHINI BANERJI
MISCELLANEOUS
'84 PASSAGE TO INDIA, A

BEATRICE BANFI
CASTING
'83 HANNA K*

ANTHONY BANKS
MUSIC
'79 SHOUT, THE*
'83 WICKED LADY, THE

GORDON BANKS
MISCELLANEOUS
'82 PENITENTIARY II

GILDA BARACCHI
SCRIPT SUPERVISOR
'79 PICNIC AT HANGING ROCK

NINI BARAGLI
EDITOR
'84 ONCE UPON A TIME IN AMERICA

LORENZO BARALDI
ART DIRECTOR
'81 SUNDAY LOVERS

JACK BARAN
1ST ASST. DIRECTOR
'79 AMERICATHON
'83 BREATHLESS

CATHY BARANCIK
MISCELLANEOUS
'84 FALLING IN LOVE

PAUL BARATTA
ASSOCIATE PRODUCER
'81 TAKE THIS JOB AND SHOVE IT*

LILLIAN BARB
HAIR
'81 HONKY TONK FREEWAY*
'83 WRONG IS RIGHT
'84 RACING WITH THE MOON

FRANCOIS BARBEAU
COSTUMES
'81 ATLANTIC CITY

OSCAR BARBER
MISCELLANEOUS
'79 HOT STUFF

JOSEPH BARBERA
PRODUCER
'79 C.H.O.M.P.S.
SCREENPLAY
'79 C.H.O.M.P.S.*

LARRY BARBIER
STILLS
'80 IN GOD WE TRUST
'80 JAZZ SINGER, THE
'80 XANADU
'81 UNDER THE RAINBOW
'82 NIGHT SHIFT
'82 SECOND THOUGHTS
'83 STAR CHAMBER
'83 TWO OF A KIND
'84 UNFAITHFULLY YOURS
'84 AMERICAN DREAMER

GATO BARBIERI
MUSIC
'79 FIREPOWER
'84 STRANGERS KISS

BRUCE PAUL BARBOUR
STUNT COORDINATOR
'84 CHILDREN OF THE CORN

CLEMENT BARCLAY
EDITOR
'84 PREPPIES

DEBRA BARD
ASSISTANT EDITOR
'84 COTTON CLUB, THE*

HERBERT BARD
MISCELLANEOUS
'83 ANGELO, MY LOVE

SARAH BARDO
COSTUMES
'81 SATURDAY THE 14TH
'83 LOVE LETTERS

FRANK BARE
STUNT COORDINATOR
'84 SILENT NIGHT, DEADLY NIGHT

ED BARGER
MISCELLANEOUS
'80 FADE TO BLACK

FRANK BARHYDT
SCREENPLAY
'79 QUINTET*
'80 HEALTH*

ROBERT BARICH
PRODUCER
'83 MAUSOLEUM*
SCREENPLAY
'83 MAUSOLEUM*
CINEMATOGRAPHER
'83 MAUSOLEUM

LENNIE BARIN
COSTUMES
'81 HELL NIGHT

KEITH BARISH
PRODUCER
'82 SOPHIE'S CHOICE*
EXECUTIVE PRODUCER
'81 ENDLESS LOVE
'84 MISUNDERSTOOD*

KEVAN BARKER
1ST ASST. DIRECTOR
'83 HEAT AND DUST
LOCATIONS
'84 GIVE MY REGARDS
TO BROAD STREET*

MARCO BARLA
PUBLICIST
'83 SUDDEN IMPACT
UNIT PUBLICIST
'82 FIREFOX
'82 HONKYTONK MAN
'84 TIGHTROPE

MICHAEL BARLOWE
ASSOCIATE PRODUCER
'81 POSTMAN ALWAYS
RINGS TWICE, THE

IRA RICHARD BARMAK
PRODUCER
'84 SILENT NIGHT, DEADLY NIGHT

BETTY BARNARD
PRODUCTION MANAGER
'79 TIM

STEVE BARNCARD
MISCELLANEOUS
'81 GALAXY OF TERROR

MICHAEL BARNES
CASTING
'81 GREAT MUPPET CAPER, THE

ROSS BARNES
MISCELLANEOUS
'82 FIRST TIME, THE

MASTER SGT. JIM BARNET
MISCELLANEOUS
'80 PRIVATE BENJAMIN

JOHN BARNETT
PRODUCER
'81 STRANGE BEHAVIOR*

KEN BARNETT
SCREENPLAY
'83 DEADLY FORCE*

PETER BARNETT
LOCATIONS
'83 ANGEL OF H.E.A.T.

STEVE BARNETT
1ST ASST. DIRECTOR
'79 BELL JAR, THE
'79 SUNBURN
'80 IN GOD WE TRUST
'80 WHY WOULD I LIE?
'81 WOLFEN*
'82 HANKY PANKY
'84 HARD TO HOLD

ALAN BARNETTE
ASSOCIATE PRODUCER
'83 NIGHTMARES

VICTORIA BARNEY
PROD. OFFICE COORD.
'83 PORKY'S II THE NEXT DAY
PROD. COORDINATOR
'80 HEALTH
MISCELLANEOUS
'79 QUINTET

FRED BARON
LOCATIONS
'82 CAT PEOPLE*
'82 YOUNG DOCTORS IN LOVE*
'83 MAN WITH TWO BRAINS, THE
'84 IRRECONCILABLE DIFFERENCES*

NORMAN BARON
ART DIRECTOR
'79 FAST BREAK
'79 FORCE OF ONE, A
'80 HERO AT LARGE*
PRODUCTION DESIGNER
'83 LONE WOLF MCQUADE

SUZANNE BARON
EDITOR
'81 ATLANTIC CITY
'81 MY DINNER WITH ANDRE
'84 CRACKERS

ENZO BARONE
EXECUTIVE PRODUCER
'79 KILLER FISH*

CHRIS BARR
PROPS
'84 ANGEL

MATTHEW BARR
SCREENPLAY
'81 DEADLY BLESSING*
ASSOCIATE PRODUCER
'81 DEADLY BLESSING*

RICHARD BARR
CASTING
'82 BORDER, THE

SUE BARRADELL
MAKEUP
'81 FRENCH LIEUTENANT'S WOMAN,THE

EUGENE "GENO" BARRAGY
KEY GRIP
'80 SMALL CIRCLE OF FRIENDS, A

JONTY BARRAUD
PRODUCTION MANAGER
'84 BOUNTY, THE*
2ND ASST. DIRECTOR
'83 MERRY CHRISTMAS, MR. LAWRENCE

ROBERT BARRERE
EDITOR
'79 OVER THE EDGE
ASSOCIATE EDITOR
'81 THEY ALL LAUGHED

STAN BARRET
2ND UNIT DIRECTOR
'84 HARRY & SON

ALAN BARRETT
COSTUMES
'80 NIJINSKY

ALISON BARRETT
CASTING
'81 GALLIPOLI
'83 YEAR OF LIVING DANGEROUSLY, THE*
'84 PHAR LAP

CLIVE BARRETT
ASSISTANT EDITOR
'80 FFOLKES*
'82 PINK FLOYD: THE WALL*
'84 ANOTHER COUNTRY
'84 BIRDY*

LEW BARRETT
STILLS
'82 STRANGER IS WATCHING, A
'82 HANKY PANKY

STAN BARRETT
STUNT COORDINATOR
'79 WHEN A STRANGER CALLS

TERRY BARRETT
PROPS
'84 RIDDLE OF THE SANDS

GEORGE BARRIE
EXECUTIVE PRODUCER
'79 CLASS OF MISS MACMICHAEL, THE

CHUCK BARRIS
DIRECTOR
'80 GONG SHOW MOVIE, THE
SCREENPLAY
'80 GONG SHOW MOVIE, THE*

DAVID BARRON
2ND ASST. DIRECTOR
'84 KILLING FIELDS, THE*
LOCATIONS
'81 FRENCH LIEUTENANT'S WOMAN,THE

EDDIE BARRON
HAIR
'79 NORTH AVENUE IRREGULARS, THE
'80 LAST FLIGHT OF NOAH'S ARK, THE

FRANK BARRON
PUBLICIST
'82 SWORD AND THE SORCERER, THE

FRED BARRON
SCREENPLAY
'79 SOMETHING SHORT OF PARADISE

SIMON BARRON
2ND ASST. DIRECTOR
'83 JOYSTICKS

STEVE BARRON
DIRECTOR
'84 ELECTRIC DREAMS

ZELDA BARRON
ASSOCIATE PRODUCER
'80 COAL MINER'S DAUGHTER
'81 CONTINENTAL DIVIDE*
SCRIPT SUPERVISOR
'79 AGATHA
'79 YANKS
'81 REDS*
'83 YENTL
MISCELLANEOUS
'81 REDS

B.H. BARRY
MISCELLANEOUS
'83 PIRATES OF PENZANCE, THE

JACK BARRY
EXECUTIVE PRODUCER
'81 PRIVATE LESSONS*
1ST ASST. DIRECTOR
'80 MOTEL HELL

JEFF BARRY
MUSIC
'80 IDOLMAKER, THE

JOHN BARRY
MUSIC
'79 BLACK HOLE, THE
'79 HANOVER STREET
'79 MOONRAKER
'79 STARCRASH
'79 GAME OF DEATH
'80 RAISE THE TITANIC
'80 SOMEWHERE IN TIME
'80 INSIDE MOVES
'80 TOUCHED BY LOVE
'81 BODY HEAT
'81 LEGEND OF THE LONE RANGER, THE
'82 FRANCES
'82 HAMMETT
'83 HIGH ROAD TO CHINA
'83 OCTOPUSSY
'83 GOLDEN SEAL, THE*
'84 COTTON CLUB, THE
'84 MIKE'S MURDER*
'84 UNTIL SEPTEMBER

JOHN BARRY
PRODUCTION DESIGNER
'81 SUPERMAN II*

JOHN BARRY
2ND UNIT DIRECTOR
'80 EMPIRE STRIKES BACK, THE*

JULIAN BARRY
SCREENPLAY
'84 RIVER, THE*

LISA BARSAMIAN
EXECUTIVE PRODUCER
'81 FRIDAY THE 13TH PART TWO*
'82 FRIDAY THE 13TH PART THREE IN 3D
'84 FRIDAY THE 13TH PART IV THE FINAL CHAPTER*
'84 MEATBALLS PART II
PRODUCTION MANAGER
'81 FRIDAY THE 13TH PART TWO

ROBERT BARSAMIAN
EXECUTIVE PRODUCER
'84 FRIDAY THE 13TH PART IV THE FINAL CHAPTER*

AARON BARSKY
1ST ASST. DIRECTOR
'84 ALPHABET CITY
2ND ASST. DIRECTOR
'82 AMITYVILLE II: THE POSSESSION*

PETER BART
EXECUTIVE PRODUCER
'84 REVENGE OF THE NERDS*

PAUL BARTEL
DIRECTOR
'82 EATING RAOUL
'84 NOT FOR PUBLICATION
SCREENPLAY
'82 EATING RAOUL*
'84 NOT FOR PUBLICATION*

F. DIETER BARTELS
ART DIRECTOR
'79 BLOODLINE*

JANET BARTELS
ASSISTANT EDITOR
'82 YOUNG DOCTORS IN LOVE*

BOB BARTH
2ND ASST. DIRECTOR
'79 WARRIORS, THE*
'80 RAGING BULL*
'80 SIMON

CARL BARTH
2ND UNIT DIRECTOR
'83 NATIONAL LAMPOON'S VACATION

BEAU BARTHEL
ASSISTANT EDITOR
'79 MOUNTAIN FAMILY ROBINSON*
'81 BEAST WITHIN, THE*
'84 RIVER, THE*

ANDRZEJ BARTKOWIAK
CINEMATOGRAPHER
'81 PRINCE OF THE CITY
'82 DEATHTRAP
'82 VERDICT, THE
'83 DANIEL
'83 TERMS OF ENDEARMENT
'84 GARBO TALKS

DENNIS BARTLETT
MISCELLANEOUS
'84 SUPERGIRL

SCOTT BARTLETT
MISCELLANEOUS
'80 ALTERED STATES

BILL BARTMAN
MISCELLANEOUS
'80 CAN'T STOP THE MUSIC

FRANCESCA BARTOCCINI
PROPS
'80 BATTLE BEYOND THE STARS*
'81 GALAXY OF TERROR

BELA BARTOK
MUSIC
'80 SHINING, THE

FIDELIO DELIA BARTOLOMEO
HAIR
'82 COME BACK TO THE 5 & 10, JIMMY DEAN, JIMMY DEAN

SEAN BARTON
EDITOR
'81 EYE OF THE NEEDLE

BILL BARVIN
2ND ASST. DIRECTOR
'81 STUDENT BODIES

HAL BARWOOD
PRODUCER
'81 DRAGONSLAYER
SCREENPLAY
'81 DRAGONSLAYER*

CONNIE BARZAGHI
SCRIPT SUPERVISOR
'84 BREAKIN 2 ELECTRIC BOOGALOO

TINO BARZIE
EXECUTIVE PRODUCER
'82 BUTTERFLY
ASSOCIATE PRODUCER
'83 LONELY LADY, THE

TONI BASIL
CHOREOGRAPHER
'79 ROSE, THE
'80 DIVINE MADNESS

PIERLUIGI BASILE
ART DIRECTOR
'80 NIJINSKY*
'81 INCHON*
'82 CONAN THE BARBARIAN*
PRODUCTION DESIGNER
'82 AMITYVILLE II: THE POSSESSION
'84 CONAN THE DESTROYER

MARIO BASILI
LOCATIONS
'83 HANNA K*

PAMELA BASKER
CASTING
'80 CHEECH AND CHONG'S NEXT MOVIE*
'80 FADE TO BLACK*
'81 BUDDY, BUDDY*
'81 CHEECH AND CHONG'S NICE DREAMS*
'81 CHU CHU AND THE PHILLY FLASH*
'81 FUNHOUSE, THE*
'82 THINGS ARE TOUGH ALL OVER*
'83 MAN WHO WASN'T THERE, THE*
'84 BREAKIN 2 ELECTRIC BOOGALOO*
'84 POLICE ACADEMY*
'84 FRIDAY THE 13TH PART IV THE FINAL CHAPTER*
'84 MEATBALLS PART II*

RICHARD BASKIN
MUSIC SUPERVISOR
'80 HONEYSUCKLE ROSE

SONNY BASKIN
ASSOCIATE EDITOR
'84 NO SMALL AFFAIR
ASSISTANT EDITOR
'83 EDDIE AND THE CRUISERS*

BERNARD BASLEY
2ND ASST. DIRECTOR
'83 RICHARD PRYOR: HERE AND NOW

BOBBY BASS
STUNT COORDINATOR
'80 SERIAL
'81 SHARKEY'S MACHINE
'81 CANNONBALL RUN, THE
'81 INCREDIBLE SHRINKING WOMAN, THE
'82 MEGAFORCE

LINDA BASS
COSTUMES
'82 SEDUCTION, THE
'84 DREAMSCAPE

CRAIG BASSETT
ASSISTANT EDITOR
'83 DEAL OF THE CENTURY*
'84 KARATE KID, THE*

STEVEN BASSIN
MISCELLANEOUS
'81 PRIVATE LESSONS

LAWRENCE BASSOFF
DIRECTOR
'84 WEEKEND PASS
SCREENPLAY
'84 WEEKEND PASS

BILL BATCHELOR
PUBLICIST
'80 HUMAN FACTOR, THE*

MICHAEL BATEMAN
ASSISTANT EDITOR
'80 FFOLKES*
'81 FINAL CONFLICT, THE*
'82 SENDER, THE*

CATHY BATES
ASSISTANT EDITOR
'80 PRIVATE EYES, THE*

LEWIS BATES JR.
ASSISTANT EDITOR
'83 RICHARD PRYOR: HERE AND NOW

SANDY BATES
COSTUME SUPERVISOR
'82 BUTTERFLY
'83 SAVANNAH SMILES

FRED BATKA
CINEMATOGRAPHER
'80 LITTLE DARLINGS
MISCELLANEOUS
'81 NIGHT THE LIGHTS WENT OUT IN GEORGIA, THE

WILLIAM BATLINER
CASTING
'79 CONCORDE-AIRPORT '79, THE*
'80 RESURRECTION*
'80 LITTLE MISS MARKER*
'80 NUDE BOMB, THE*
'81 HEARTBEEPS*

BERNARD BATS
SOUND
'80 ISLAND, THE*
'80 QUARTET
'80 OUTSIDER, THE

BERT BATT
1ST ASST. DIRECTOR
'81 SEA WOLVES, THE
'83 HIGH ROAD TO CHINA*
'83 NATE & HAYES
'84 CHAMPIONS*

FRANK BATT
KEY GRIP
'83 YENTL
'84 ELECTRIC DREAMS

FATHER JOSEPH BATTAGLIA
MISCELLANEOUS
'84 MASS APPEAL

BRAD BATTERSBY
STILLS
'80 HOME MOVIES

SIMON BATTERSBY
ASSISTANT EDITOR
'81 AMERICAN WEREWOLF IN LONDON, AN

GREGG BATTES
MISCELLANEOUS
'82 TRON

LLOYD BATTISTA
SCREENPLAY
'81 COMIN' AT YA!*

WALTER BATTISTELLI
SPECIAL EFFECTS
'83 1990: THE BRONX WARRIORS*

LAWRENCE BATTLE
MISCELLANEOUS
'83 HERCULES

BEN BATZDORF
KEY GRIP
'80 BATTLE BEYOND THE STARS

RON BATZDORFF
STILLS
'79 ONION FIELD, THE
'81 MODERN PROBLEMS
'82 HALLOWEEN III: SEASON OF THE WITCH
'83 PSYCHO II
'84 REVENGE OF THE NERDS
'84 SPLASH*

SYLVETTE BAUDROT
SCRIPT SUPERVISOR
'80 TESS
'83 HANNA K*
'84 JUST THE WAY YOU ARE*

FRED BAUER
PRODUCER
'79 BUDDY HOLLY STORY, THE
'81 UNDER THE RAINBOW

MARY BAUER
ASSISTANT EDITOR
'79 HEARTLAND
'80 WHOLLY MOSES!*
'81 WOLFEN

MICHAEL BAUGH
PRODUCTION DESIGNER
'81 RICHARD PRYOR: LIVE ON THE SUNSET STRIP
'84 WHERE THE BOYS ARE

DAVID BAUGHN
PRODUCER
'81 GRADUATION DAY*

CAROL BAUM
EXECUTIVE PRODUCER
'84 RECKLESS

FRED BAUM
CO-PRODUCER
'84 UP THE CREEK

THOMAS BAUM
SCREENPLAY
'80 CARNY
'82 SENDER, THE

ALAN BAUMGARTEN
ASSISTANT EDITOR
'84 OVER THE BROOKLYN BRIDGE*

CRAIG BAUMGARTEN
EXECUTIVE PRODUCER
'84 MISUNDERSTOOD*

KARL BAUMGARTNER
SPECIAL EFFECTS
'82 FIREFOX*
'84 LITTLE DRUMMER GIRL, THE

FRANK BAUR
ASSOCIATE PRODUCER
'79 NORTH DALLAS FORTY
PRODUCTION MANAGER
'80 CHANGE OF SEASONS, A
UNIT PROD. MANAGER
'79 DREAMER
'79 NORTH DALLAS FORTY
MISCELLANEOUS
'79 METEOR

JACK BAUR
CASTING
'79 BEYOND THE POSEIDON ADVENTURE
'80 WHEN TIME RAN OUT
'81 INCHON

CRAIG BAXLEY
2ND UNIT DIRECTOR
'81 REDS
STUNT COORDINATOR
'79 WARRIORS, THE
'80 LONG RIDERS, THE
'80 WHOLLY MOSES!
'81 TAKE THIS JOB AND SHOVE IT
'82 SEDUCTION, THE

GARY BAXLEY
STUNT COORDINATOR
'83 EDDIE MACON'S RUN

PAUL BAXLEY
2ND UNIT DIRECTOR
'79 SUNBURN
'81 DEATH HUNT*
STUNT COORDINATOR
'79 SUNBURN
'80 IN GOD WE TRUST

LES BAXTER
MUSIC
'81 BEAST WITHIN, THE

FRANK BAYER
CASTING
'82 ZOOT SUIT*

LUSTER BAYLESS
COSTUMES
'79 VILLAIN, THE*

TROU BAYLESS
KEY GRIP
'81 STRANGE BEHAVIOR

JEREMY BAYLIS
ASSISTANT EDITOR
'84 OXFORD BLUES*

ROBERT BAYLIS
ASSOCIATE PRODUCER
'81 DEATH HUNT
PRODUCTION MANAGER
'79 MEATBALLS

RAYMOND BAYLISS
MISCELLANEOUS
'80 CHANGELING, THE

JIM BEACH
CO-PRODUCER
'84 HOTEL NEW HAMPSHIRE, THE

RUTH BEACH
ASSISTANT EDITOR
'82 ROAD WARRIOR, THE*

BILL BEAIRD
KEY GRIP
'79 FRISCO KID, THE

JOHN BEAIRD
SCREENPLAY
'81 MY BLOODY VALENTINE

JOHN BEAL
MUSIC
'81 FUNHOUSE, THE

PETER BEALE
EXECUTIVE PRODUCER
'82 FIVE DAYS ONE SUMMER

BILL BEAM
KEY GRIP
'80 MOUNTAIN MEN, THE
'80 OCTAGON, THE

HENRY BEAN
SCREENPLAY
'83 RUNNING BRAVE*

PATRICIA BEAN
COSTUME SUPERVISOR
'82 THINGS ARE TOUGH ALL OVER

ROBERT BEAN
MISCELLANEOUS
'84 NATURAL, THE

LYNETTE BEAR
MISCELLANEOUS
'84 AGAINST ALL ODDS

TED BEAR
MISCELLANEOUS
'84 AGAINST ALL ODDS

FRANK BEASCOECHEA
CINEMATOGRAPHER
'79 BUCK ROGERS

BILL BEASLEY
1ST ASST. DIRECTOR
'80 CAN'T STOP THE MUSIC
'81 HALLOWEEN II
'81 ONLY WHEN I LAUGH
'82 MY FAVORITE YEAR
'82 PERSONAL BEST*
'83 STAR CHAMBER
'83 STAYING ALIVE
'84 JOHNNY DANGEROUSLY
'84 RACING WITH THE MOON
'84 2010
2ND ASST. DIRECTOR
'79 AMERICAN GIGOLO
'79 BREAKING AWAY

ERIC BEASON
ASSISTANT EDITOR
'80 FIRST DEADLY SIN*

ALEX BEATON
EXECUTIVE PRODUCER
'83 NIGHTMARES*

ANNE BEATTS
SCREENPLAY
'80 GILDA LIVE*

WARREN BEATTY
PRODUCER
'81 REDS
DIRECTOR
'81 REDS
SCREENPLAY
'81 REDS*

JOSEPH BEAUBIEN
EXECUTIVE PRODUCER
'81 ATLANTIC CITY*

JAMES BEAUCHAMP
SPECIAL EFFECTS
'83 FOOTLOOSE
MISCELLANEOUS
'84 THIS IS SPINAL TAP

WAYNE BEAUCHAMP
SPECIAL EFFECTS
'80 BORDERLINE
'81 BACK ROADS

KEN BEAUCHANE
SOUND
'81 GALAXY OF TERROR

MICHAEL BEAUDETTE
PRODUCTION MANAGER
'83 SMITHEREENS

CRAIG BEAUDINE
2ND ASST. DIRECTOR
'79 SCAVENGER HUNT*
'84 COUNTRY

WILLIAM BEAUDINE JR.
PRODUCTION MANAGER
'84 COUNTRY
MISCELLANEOUS
'84 COUNTRY

SKIP BEAUDINE
1ST ASST. DIRECTOR
'80 FIRST FAMILY

NICHOLAS BEAUMAN
EDITOR
'79 MY BRILLIANT CAREER
'82 STARSTRUCK
'84 MRS. SOFFEL

JENNY BEAVAN
COSTUMES
'84 BOSTONIANS, THE*

JACKIE BEAVERS
CASTING
'83 TERMS OF ENDEARMENT*

ARTHUR BEAVIS
SPECIAL EFFECTS
'83 YELLOWBEARD*

DAVE BEAVIS
SPECIAL EFFECTS
'84 LASSITER

GEORGE BEAVIS
KEY GRIP
'81 DRAGONSLAYER*

ALEXANDER BECK
EXECUTIVE PRODUCER
'80 MOTHER'S DAY

MAURIE BECK
ASSISTANT EDITOR
'80 THOSE LIPS, THOSE EYES
'82 HALLOWEEN III:
SEASON OF THE WITCH

STANLEY BECK
EXECUTIVE PRODUCER
'83 MAN WOMAN AND CHILD
CO-PRODUCER
'82 DEATH VALLEY*

CLAUDIA BECKER
CASTING
'83 BEYOND THE LIMIT*
'84 ROMANCING THE STONE*
'84 EVIL THAT MEN DO, THE*

FRAWLEY BECKER
LOCATIONS
'83 FOOTLOOSE

HAROLD BECKER

DIRECTOR
'79 ONION FIELD, THE
'80 BLACK MARBLE, THE
'81 TAPS

LOUIS BECKER

2ND ASST. DIRECTOR
'83 HANNA K*

MARTIN BECKER

SPECIAL EFFECTS
'82 FRIDAY THE 13TH PART THREE IN 3D
SP. EFFECTS SUPERV.
'83 MAN WHO WASN'T THERE, THE
'84 FRIDAY THE 13TH PART IV THE FINAL CHAPTER
'84 MEATBALLS PART II

MICHAEL BECKER

SOUND
'80 KIDS ARE ALL RIGHT, THE*

ROBERT BECKER

1ST ASST. DIRECTOR
'82 VICE SQUAD

SUSAN BECKER

COSTUMES
'80 BLACK MARBLE, THE
'81 KING OF THE MOUNTAIN

BARRY BECKERMAN

PRODUCER
'84 RED DAWN*

SIDNEY BECKERMAN

PRODUCER
'79 BLOODLINE*
'80 SERIAL
'82 STRANGER IS WATCHING, A
EXECUTIVE PRODUCER
'81 BLOOD BEACH
'84 ADVENTURES OF BUCKAROO BANZAI ACROSS THE 8TH DIMENSION, THE
'84 RED DAWN

RAYMOND BECKET

2ND ASST. DIRECTOR
'79 ALIEN*
'80 OH! HEAVENLY DOG

BARRY BECKETT

LOCATIONS
'81 FRENCH LIEUTENANT'S WOMAN, THE*

DAVID BECKETT

HAIR
'79 IN PRAISE OF OLDER WOMEN

RAY BECKETT

SOUND
'83 HEAT AND DUST
'84 BOSTONIANS, THE

CLAIRE BECKHAM

PROD. COORDINATOR
'79 HEARTLAND

RON BECKMAN

PRODUCER
'82 CHALLENGE, THE*

SUSAN BECTON

PROD. COORDINATOR
'83 SOMETHING WICKED THIS WAY COMES*

IVOR BEDDOES

MISCELLANEOUS
'81 SUPERMAN II

RICHARD BEDFORD

EDITOR
'81 SHOCK TREATMENT

BARRY BEDIG

PROPS
'79 ONION FIELD, THE
'80 CRUISING*
'80 INSIDE MOVES
'81 ENTITY, THE
'81 LOOKER
'81 GOING APE!
'82 SIX WEEKS
'83 DEAL OF THE CENTURY
'83 MAN WOMAN AND CHILD
'83 TWO OF A KIND
'84 NATURAL, THE

DAVID BEECROFT

HAIR
'80 HAPPY BIRTHDAY, GEMINI
'82 IF YOU COULD SEE WHAT I HEAR

WALLY BEENE

PUBLICIST
'80 INSIDE MOVES
'81 FIRST MONDAY IN OCTOBER
'81 HAND, THE
UNIT PUBLICIST
'79 WHEN YOU COMIN' BACK, RED RYDER?
'79 OLD BOYFRIENDS

BEBORAH IMOGEN BEER

STILLS
'83 LONELY LADY, THE*

JEFFREY BEER

LOCATIONS
'82 I, THE JURY

JERE BEERY

MISCELLANEOUS
'84 MAKING THE GRADE

DAVID BEESLEY

EDITOR
'83 CURSE OF THE PINK PANTHER*
ASSISTANT EDITOR
'83 TRAIL OF THE PINK PANTHER*

MATT BEESLEY

ASSISTANT EDITOR
'79 DOUBLE MCGUFFIN, THE*
'80 FOR THE LOVE OF BENJI*

MATT EARL BEESLEY

2ND ASST. DIRECTOR
'84 CITY HEAT*

PAUL BEESON

CINEMATOGRAPHER
'79 UNIDENTIFIED FLYING ODDBALL
'79 STARCRASH*
MISCELLANEOUS
'83 NEVER SAY NEVER AGAIN

SAMUEL BEETLEY

EDITOR
'79 FIVE DAYS FROM HOME
'82 SAFARI 3000

FRANK BEETSON

PRODUCTION MANAGER
'81 ON THE RIGHT TRACK
UNIT PROD. MANAGER
'80 STUNT MAN, THE
1ST ASST. DIRECTOR
'80 STUNT MAN, THE
'82 DEATH VALLEY*
'84 LOVE STREAMS*

DAVID BEGELMAN

EXECUTIVE PRODUCER
'80 WHOLLY MOSES!

RICHARD BEGGS

SOUND
'82 ONE FROM THE HEART
MISCELLANEOUS
'83 RUMBLEFISH
'83 OUTSIDERS, THE

JEFF BEGUN

PRODUCER
'84 HARDBODIES*
CO-PRODUCER
'81 SATURDAY THE 14TH

JIM BEHNKE

2ND ASST. DIRECTOR
'84 RED DAWN*

JACK BEHR

SCREENPLAY
'84 BIRDY*

DON BEHRNS
PRODUCER
'82 LIAR'S MOON
EXEC IN CHARGE PROD
'84 BODY ROCK
PRODUCTION MANAGER
'79 ROLLER BOOGIE
'80 FOG, THE

JERRY BEIGEL
PUBLICIST
'84 MIKE'S MURDER

PATTY BEIGEL
MAKEUP
'83 METALSTORM: THE DESTRUCTION OF JARED-SYN*

HANS BEIMLER
2ND ASST. DIRECTOR
'82 NIGHT SHIFT

LUIS BEKRIS
PRODUCTION MANAGER
'81 ZORRO, THE GAY BLADE*

HARRY BELAFONTE
PRODUCER
'84 BEAT STREET*

RICHARD BELDING
EDITOR
'81 TAKE THIS JOB AND SHOVE IT

GRAHAM BELIN
PRODUCER
'80 UNION CITY

ALAN BELKIN
PRODUCER
'79 FORCE OF ONE, A
EXECUTIVE PRODUCER
'80 OCTAGON, THE*
'81 CHARLIE CHAN AND THE CURSE OF THE DRAGON QUEEN*

ANN HUNTER BELL
CASTING
'79 RAVAGERS
'79 CIRCLE OF IRON
'79 JAGUAR LIVES*
'79 ROLLER BOOGIE*
'80 SCHIZOID

HAL BELL
1ST ASST. DIRECTOR
'81 HARDLY WORKING
2ND ASST. DIRECTOR
'81 PENNIES FROM HEAVEN*

JEFF BELL
ASSISTANT EDITOR
'83 MAN WHO WASN'T THERE, THE

JOHN BELL
UNIT MANAGER
'81 LAST CHASE, THE
LOCATIONS
'80 NOTHING PERSONAL

ROLAND BELL
STILLS
'84 JOY OF SEX, THE

THOM BELL
MUSIC
'79 FISH THAT SAVED PITTSBURGH, THE

WAYNE BELL
MUSIC
'84 LAST NIGHT AT THE ALAMO*

JOCELYNE BELLEMARE
MAKEUP
'81 HAPPY BIRTHDAY TO ME

HERCULES BELLEVILLE
2ND UNIT DIRECTOR
'80 TESS

DAVINA BELLING
PRODUCER
'83 BRITANNIA HOSPITAL*
'84 COMFORT AND JOY*

FRANCO BELLOMO
STILLS
'83 BLACK STALLION RETURNS, THE

ADRIANA BELLONE
ART DIRECTOR
'83 LONELY LADY, THE*

GABRIELLA BELLONI
MISCELLANEOUS
'82 NATIONAL LAMPOON'S CLASS REUNION
'83 MAN WITH TWO BRAINS, THE

HERCULES BELLVILLE
CO-PRODUCER
'84 STRANGERS KISS

VERA BELMONT
CO-PRODUCER
'82 QUEST FOR FIRE*

HENRI BELOLO
PRODUCER
'80 CAN'T STOP THE MUSIC*

VALERIE BELSKY
PRODUCER
'83 ECHOES*

JERRY BELSON
DIRECTOR
'82 JEKYLL AND HYDE TOGETHER AGAIN
SCREENPLAY
'80 SMOKEY AND THE BANDIT II*
'82 JEKYLL AND HYDE TOGETHER AGAIN*
EXECUTIVE PRODUCER
'81 STUDENT BODIES*

JORDAN BELSON
MISCELLANEOUS
'83 RIGHT STUFF, THE

WILLIAM BELT
PROPS
'83 EDDIE MACON'S RUN*

JON BELYEU
SPECIAL EFFECTS
'82 HALLOWEEN III: SEASON OF THE WITCH
'82 OUT OF THE BLUE
'83 DEAD ZONE, THE

HANS ANTHONY BEMLER
2ND ASST. DIRECTOR
'84 SPLASH*

YORAM BEN-AMI
PRODUCER
'83 LONE WOLF MCQUADE*
EXECUTIVE PRODUCER
'84 SHEENA
UNIT PROD. MANAGER
'82 SWAMP THING*
1ST ASST. DIRECTOR
'81 EYE FOR AN EYE, AN

ELI BEN-ARI
STILLS
'79 CIRCLE OF IRON

TAMI BEN-HORIN
STILLS
'83 REVENGE OF THE NINJA*

JOSEE BENABENT
PUBLICIST
'80 TESS

PASQUINO BENASSATI
SPECIAL EFFECTS
'83 1990: THE BRONX WARRIORS*

DENNIS BENATAR
2ND ASST. DIRECTOR
'84 ONCE UPON A TIME IN AMERICA*

PETER BENCHLEY
SCREENPLAY
'80 ISLAND, THE

PHOEBE BENDIGER
SOUND
'83 LIQUID SKY*

BARBARA BENEDEK
SCREENPLAY
'83 BIG CHILL, THE*

MAX BENEDICT
EDITOR
'79 CLASS OF MISS MACMICHAEL, THE

BILL BENENSON
PRODUCER
'79 BOULEVARD NIGHTS

GLENN BENEST
SCREENPLAY
'81 DEADLY BLESSING*
ASSOCIATE PRODUCER
'81 DEADLY BLESSING*

ANTONIO BENETTI
STILLS
'83 1990: THE BRONX WARRIORS

PAUL BENGSTON
CASTING
'84 ICE PIRATES, THE

LOUIS BENIOFF
ASSISTANT EDITOR
'83 RIGHT STUFF, THE*

JANIS BENJAMIN
PROD. COORDINATOR
'80 LOVING COUPLES
'82 SUMMER LOVERS
'84 SONGWRITER

JEFFREY BENJAMIN
ASSOCIATE PRODUCER
'81 KING OF THE MOUNTAIN

RICHARD BENJAMIN
DIRECTOR
'82 MY FAVORITE YEAR
'84 CITY HEAT
'84 RACING WITH THE MOON

TOM BENKO
EDITOR
'80 HEALTH*
MISCELLANEOUS
'82 BEASTMASTER, THE

HARRY BENN
PRODUCER
'84 RAZOR'S EDGE, THE*
ASSOCIATE PRODUCER
'79 HANOVER STREET*
'80 AWAKENING, THE
'82 VENOM

RICHARD BENNER
DIRECTOR
'80 HAPPY BIRTHDAY, GEMINI
SCREENPLAY
'80 HAPPY BIRTHDAY, GEMINI

ELISABETH BENNETT
LOCATIONS
'84 SONGWRITER

HARVE BENNETT
PRODUCER
'84 STAR TREK III: THE SEARCH FOR SPOCK
SCREENPLAY
'84 STAR TREK III: THE SEARCH FOR SPOCK
EXECUTIVE PRODUCER
'82 STAR TREK II THE WRATH OF KHAN

JACK BENNETT
ART DIRECTOR
'80 FOR THE LOVE OF BENJI
PROPS
'79 DOUBLE MCGUFFIN, THE
SPECIAL EFFECTS
'79 DOUBLE MCGUFFIN, THE
'81 DEADLY BLESSING
'82 SILENT RAGE
'82 SPLIT IMAGE

JOHN BENNETT
PRODUCER
'79 MAN, A WOMAN AND A BANK, A*
'82 FORCED VENGEANCE

KIMBERLEY BENNETT
ASSISTANT EDITOR
'84 EVIL THAT MEN DO, THE

LEROY BENNETT
MISCELLANEOUS
'84 PURPLE RAIN

MICHAEL BENNETT
PRODUCTION MANAGER
'80 BATTLE BEYOND THE STARS
'81 BODY AND SOUL
'81 FEAR NO EVIL

PETER BENNETT
UNIT MANAGER
'81 FOR YOUR EYES ONLY*
LOCATIONS
'80 WATCHER IN THE WOODS, THE*
'81 FOR YOUR EYES ONLY*
'81 DOGS OF WAR, THE*
'83 OCTOPUSSY*
'84 INDIANA JONES AND THE TEMPLE OF DOOM*

PHILLIP BENNETT
ART DIRECTOR
'80 ORDINARY PEOPLE*

RICHARD RODNEY BENNETT
MUSIC
'79 YANKS

YUDI BENNETT
1ST ASST. DIRECTOR
'81 FOUR SEASONS, THE
'81 NEIGHBORS
'82 AUTHOR, AUTHOR
'82 CHOSEN, THE
2ND ASST. DIRECTOR
'79 SEDUCTION OF JOE TYNAN, THE
'79 KRAMER VS. KRAMER
'80 STARDUST MEMORIES
'80 WILLIE & PHIL

PETER BENOIT
PUBLICIST
'79 GOLDENGIRL
'80 HOLLYWOOD KNIGHTS, THE
'84 IMPULSE

SUZANNE BENOIT
MAKEUP
'82 QUEST FOR FIRE*
'84 JUST THE WAY YOU ARE*

STEPH BENSEMAN
LOCATIONS
'80 DIE LAUGHING
'80 FOOLIN AROUND
'81 CHU CHU AND THE PHILLY FLASH
'84 THIEF OF HEARTS*

ANNETTE BENSON
CASTING
'83 VALLEY GIRL
'84 NIGHTMARE ON ELM STREET, A
'84 NIGHT OF THE COMET
'84 JOY OF SEX, THE

DALE BENSON
LOCATIONS
'79 ROCKY II
'80 RAGING BULL*
'81 TRUE CONFESSIONS
'82 ROCKY III

JONATHAN BENSON
1ST ASST. DIRECTOR
'79 AGATHA
'79 MONTY PYTHON'S LIFE OF BRIAN
'81 CHARIOTS OF FIRE
'83 LOCAL HERO

KEVIN BENSON
MUSIC SUPERVISOR
'84 HARDBODIES*

PETER BENSON
MISCELLANEOUS
'80 TERROR TRAIN

RAY BENSON
MUSIC
'82 LIAR'S MOON

ROBBY BENSON
PRODUCER
'80 DIE LAUGHING*
SCREENPLAY
'80 DIE LAUGHING*
MUSIC
'80 DIE LAUGHING*

DAN BENTLEY
PROPS
'80 UP THE ACADEMY

LON BENTLEY
MAKEUP
'79 FAST BREAK
'79 GREAT SANTINI, THE
'80 CHANGE OF SEASONS, A*
'80 MOUNTAIN MEN, THE*
'80 WHY WOULD I LIE?
'83 HIGH ROAD TO CHINA*
'84 LASSITER*
'84 RUNAWAY*

BI BENTON
PROD. COORDINATOR
'82 DARK CRYSTAL, THE

ROBERT BENTON
DIRECTOR
'79 KRAMER VS. KRAMER
'82 STILL OF THE NIGHT
'84 PLACES IN THE HEART
SCREENPLAY
'79 KRAMER VS. KRAMER
'82 STILL OF THE NIGHT
'84 PLACES IN THE HEART

LEONARDO BENVENUTI
SCREENPLAY
'84 ONCE UPON A TIME IN AMERICA*

SIMON BENZAKEIN
PROD. COORDINATOR
'83 TRENCHCOAT

CHRISTINE BERARDO
ASSOCIATE PRODUCER
'83 BLACK STALLION RETURNS, THE

ROBERT BERBERIAN
UNIT MANAGER
'83 CAN SHE BAKE A CHERRY PIE?

STEVE BERENS
MISCELLANEOUS
'84 UP THE CREEK

BRUCE BERESFORD
DIRECTOR
'83 TENDER MERCIES

JEAN BEREZIUK
SCRIPT SUPERVISOR
'83 GOLDEN SEAL, THE
'84 NEVERENDING STORY, THE

JON BERG
MISCELLANEOUS
'80 EMPIRE STRIKES BACK, THE

STEVE BERG
MISCELLANEOUS
'79 HEARTLAND

TONY BERG
MUSIC SUPERVISOR
'80 DIVINE MADNESS*

WAYNER BERG
MISCELLANEOUS
'80 STUNT MAN, THE

JOHN BERGER
PROPS
'80 CHANGELING, THE
'81 DEATH HUNT
'81 TICKET TO HEAVEN
'82 AMATEUR, THE
'84 POLICE ACADEMY

PETER BERGER
EDITOR
'79 PROMISE, THE
'80 LAST MARRIED COUPLE IN AMERICA, THE
'80 OH GOD! BOOK II
'81 FIRST MONDAY IN OCTOBER
'81 MOMMIE DEAREST
'82 MONSIGNOR

RENATE BERGER
PROD. SECRETARY
'84 NEVERENDING STORY, THE*

RICHARD BERGER
ART DIRECTOR
'79 ROCKY II
'79 SCAVENGER HUNT

LEE BERGLUND
PROPS
'83 LOSIN' IT
'84 PHILADELPHIA EXPERIMENT, THE

ANDREW BERGMAN
DIRECTOR
'81 SO FINE
SCREENPLAY
'79 IN-LAWS, THE
'81 SO FINE
'84 OH GOD, YOU DEVIL

FRANKIE BERGMAN
HAIR
'79 VILLAIN, THE*
'81 ESCAPE FROM NEW YORK
'81 HALLOWEEN II
'82 HALLOWEEN III: SEASON OF THE WITCH
'83 CHRISTINE

PETER BERGQUIST
1ST ASST. DIRECTOR
'83 BUDDY SYSTEM, THE
2ND ASST. DIRECTOR
'79 BUTCH AND SUNDANCE: THE EARLY YEARS*
'79 DREAMER
'79 FRISCO KID, THE
'79 REMEMBER MY NAME*

ERIC BERGREN
SCREENPLAY
'80 ELEPHANT MAN, THE*
'82 FRANCES*

ELEANOR BERGSTEIN
SCREENPLAY
'80 IT'S MY TURN

BARRY BERGTHORSON
1ST ASST. DIRECTOR
'80 MIDDLE AGE CRAZY

IRENE BERKMAN
PROD. OFFICE COORD.
'80 CAN'T STOP THE MUSIC

JEFFREY BERLATSKY
ASSOCIATE PRODUCER
'81 HARDLY WORKING*

ALFREDO BERLINCHON
2ND ASST. DIRECTOR
'84 BOLERO

LESTER BERMAN
PRODUCER
'79 SOMETHING SHORT OF PARADISE*
ASSOCIATE PRODUCER
'79 GREAT BANK HOAX, THE
'79 SCALPEL*
PRODUCTION MANAGER
'82 DON'T CRY, IT'S ONLY THUNDER
'83 TIMERIDER

AGNES BERMEJO
PROD. SECRETARY
'84 CHEECH AND CHONG'S THE CORSICAN BROTHERS*

BURT BERNAM
2ND ASST. DIRECTOR
'84 UP THE CREEK*

ALAN BERNARD
SOUND
'83 CHRISTMAS STORY, A
'83 PORKY'S II THE NEXT DAY

DUSTIN BERNARD
2ND ASST. DIRECTOR
'83 SPRING BREAK
'83 MR. MOM

JUDD BERNARD

PRODUCER
'79 CLASS OF MISS MACMICHAEL, THE
'81 ENTER THE NINJA*
SCREENPLAY
'79 CLASS OF MISS MACMICHAEL, THE

BARRY BERNARDI

ASSOCIATE PRODUCER
'81 ESCAPE FROM NEW YORK
'81 HALLOWEEN II
'82 HALLOWEEN III: SEASON OF THE WITCH
'83 CHRISTINE
CO-PRODUCER
'84 STARMAN
PROD. COORDINATOR
'79 ROLLER BOOGIE
'80 FOG, THE
LOCATIONS
'81 ESCAPE FROM NEW YORK
'82 LIAR'S MOON

CLIFF BERNAY

PROPS
'82 PARTNERS

SUSAN BERNAY

2ND ASST. DIRECTOR
'82 AIRPLANE II: THE SEQUEL*

GEORGE BERNDT

EDITOR
'80 GALAXINA*
'84 MEATBALLS PART II
SP. EFFECTS SUPERV.
'80 GALAXINA
MISCELLANEOUS
'83 MY TUTOR

BRIAN BERNER

HAIR
'84 CHOOSE ME*

FRED BERNER

EXEC IN CHARGE PROD
'81 STUDENT BODIES
PRODUCTION MANAGER
'83 ECHOES
1ST ASST. DIRECTOR
'81 NESTING, THE
MISCELLANEOUS
'83 EASY MONEY

HARVEY BERNHARD

PRODUCER
'81 BEAST WITHIN, THE*
'81 FINAL CONFLICT, THE

STEVEN BERNHARDT

PRODUCER
'81 FUNHOUSE, THE*
CO-PRODUCER
'82 TEMPEST*

ALAIN BERNHEIM

PRODUCER
'84 RACING WITH THE MOON*
EXECUTIVE PRODUCER
'81 BUDDY, BUDDY
'82 YES, GIORGIO*

HARMON BERNS

CO-PRODUCER
'82 NATIONAL LAMPOON'S CLASS REUNION*

NORMAN BERNS

1ST ASST. DIRECTOR
'79 SCALPEL
'81 MY DINNER WITH ANDRE

ARMYAN BERNSTEIN

DIRECTOR
'84 WINDY CITY
SCREENPLAY
'82 ONE FROM THE HEART*
'84 WINDY CITY
CO-PRODUCER
'82 ONE FROM THE HEART

CHARLES BERNSTEIN

MUSIC
'79 LOVE AT FIRST BITE
'80 COAST TO COAST
'80 FOOLIN AROUND
'81 ENTITY, THE
'83 CUJO
'83 INDEPENDENCE DAY
'84 NIGHTMARE ON ELM STREET, A

ELMER BERNSTEIN

MUSIC
'79 GREAT SANTINI, THE
'79 MEATBALLS
'80 SATURN 3
'80 AIRPLANE
'81 STRIPES
'81 AMERICAN WEREWOLF IN LONDON, AN
'81 HONKY TONK FREEWAY*
'81 GOING APE!
'82 AIRPLANE II: THE SEQUEL*
'82 CHOSEN, THE
'82 FIVE DAYS ONE SUMMER
'83 SPACEHUNTER: ADVENTURES IN THE FORBIDDEN ZONE
'83 CLASS
'83 TRADING PLACES
'84 BOLERO*
'84 GHOSTBUSTERS
MUSIC SUPERVISOR
'84 BOLERO
MISCELLANEOUS
'80 BLUES BROTHERS

JACK BERNSTEIN

EXECUTIVE PRODUCER
'79 NORTH DALLAS FORTY
'81 BEAST WITHIN, THE
ASSOCIATE PRODUCER
'79 BUTCH AND SUNDANCE: THE EARLY YEARS
'82 SIX PACK
'84 UNFAITHFULLY YOURS
PRODUCTION MANAGER
'81 BEAST WITHIN, THE
UNIT PROD. MANAGER
'82 SIX PACK
'84 UNFAITHFULLY YOURS

JAY BERNSTEIN

EXECUTIVE PRODUCER
'79 SUNBURN*
'80 NOTHING PERSONAL*

JONATHAN BERNSTEIN

PRODUCER
'83 TESTAMENT*
EXECUTIVE PRODUCER
'82 CHOSEN, THE
ASSOCIATE PRODUCER
'80 HOPSCOTCH*
PRODUCTION MANAGER
'80 HOPSCOTCH

NAN BERNSTEIN

LOCATIONS
'83 ANGELO, MY LOVE

PETER BERNSTEIN

MUSIC
'82 SILENT RAGE*
'82 NATIONAL LAMPOON'S CLASS REUNION*
'84 BOLERO*
'84 HOT DOG...THE MOVIE

RICHARD BERNSTEIN

ASSISTANT EDITOR
'81 THIEF*

WALTER BERNSTEIN

DIRECTOR
'80 LITTLE MISS MARKER
SCREENPLAY
'79 YANKS*
'80 LITTLE MISS MARKER

BOBBY BEROSINI

MISCELLANEOUS
'81 GOING APE!

CLAUDE BERRI

PRODUCER
'80 TESS

GINA BERRIAULT

SCREENPLAY
'84 STONE BOY, THE

JULIE BERRIAULT
PUBLICIST
'84 STONE BOY, THE

JEAN-PIERRE BERROYER
HAIR
'79 LITTLE ROMANCE, A
'80 QUARTET
'83 HUNGER, THE*
'84 UNTIL SEPTEMBER

DON BERRY
MISCELLANEOUS
'79 DAWN OF THE DEAD

WAYNE BERRY
1ST ASST. DIRECTOR
'83 YEAR OF LIVING DANGEROUSLY, THE*

ADRIANA BERSELLI
COSTUMES
'79 KILLER FISH*

TIVADAR BERTALAN
ART DIRECTOR
'80 NIJINSKY*

SANH BERTI
MUSIC
'81 CATTLE ANNIE AND LITTLE BRITCHES*

JOHN BERTUCCI
EDITOR
'83 BALLAD OF GREGORIO CORTEZ, THE*

JOSEPH BERUH
EXECUTIVE PRODUCER
'80 HE KNOWS YOU'RE ALONE*

RAY BERWICK
MISCELLANEOUS
'84 GREMLINS
'84 UP THE CREEK

JAMES BESHEARS
PRODUCER
'82 HOME WORK
DIRECTOR
'82 HOME WORK

JAMES BESHEARS
EDITOR
'83 HERCULES

PETER BESTON
EDITOR
'84 GIVE MY REGARDS TO BROAD STREET

JONATHAN BETUEL
SCREENPLAY
'84 LAST STARFIGHTER, THE

HORTENSE BEVERIDGE
EDITOR
'80 HAPPY BIRTHDAY, GEMINI*
ASSISTANT EDITOR
'79 NATURAL ENEMIES

KENT BEYDA
EDITOR
'81 SATURDAY THE 14TH*
'83 GET CRAZY*
'84 THIS IS SPINAL TAP*
ASSISTANT EDITOR
'79 ROCK 'N ROLL HIGH SCHOOL*
'80 HUMANOIDS FROM THE DEEP
'81 HOWLING, THE

ED BEYER
CO-PRODUCER
'83 HOUSE ON SORORITY ROW

EDWARD BEYER
EDITOR
'79 RICH KIDS
'79 ALAMBRISTA!
'80 ONE-TRICK PONY*

JERRY BHANA
HAIR
'80 AMERICAN SUCCESS COMPANY, THE

ATUL BHASIN
UNIT MANAGER
'84 RAZOR'S EDGE, THE

EDWARD BIANCHI
DIRECTOR
'81 FAN, THE
2ND UNIT DIRECTOR
'80 TIMES SQUARE*

RICHARD BIANCHI
ART DIRECTOR
'79 VOICES

TONY BIANCHI
MISCELLANEOUS
'83 HIGH ROAD TO CHINA

FRANK BIANCO
HAIR
'79 STARTING OVER
'79 WARRIORS, THE
'80 SIMON
'80 TRIBUTE*
'81 ROLLOVER*
'81 TAPS
'81 WOLFEN
'82 SOPHIE'S CHOICE
'83 TRADING PLACES
'83 I AM THE CHEESE

JOHN BIBTRUNK
STUNT COORDINATOR
'80 GALAXINA

FABIENNE BICHET
CASTING
'83 EXPOSED*

JERRY BICK
EXECUTIVE PRODUCER
'84 AGAINST ALL ODDS

STEVEN BICKEL
ASSOCIATE PRODUCER
'80 SOMEWHERE IN TIME

DAVE BICKERS
STUNT COORDINATOR
'83 OCTOPUSSY*
MISCELLANEOUS
'81 AMERICAN WEREWOLF IN LONDON, AN

MARY ANN BIDDLE
ART DIRECTOR
'83 ALL THE RIGHT MOVES

TERRY BIDDLECOMBE
MISCELLANEOUS
'84 CHAMPIONS

CHARLES BIEDERMANN
MAKEUP
'84 BEST DEFENSE*

NICKY BIEDERMANN
HAIR
'84 BEST DEFENSE*

STANLEY BIELECKI
PUBLICIST
'81 FINAL CONFLICT, THE*

SANDRA BIELER
PROD. COORDINATOR
'82 DEATH VALLEY

EDWARD BIERY
EDITOR
'80 WHEN TIME RAN OUT*

JURGEN BIESKE
UNIT MANAGER
'84 NEVERENDING STORY, THE

KATHRYN BIGELOW
DIRECTOR
'84 LOVELESS, THE*
SCREENPLAY
'84 LOVELESS, THE*
SCRIPT SUPERVISOR
'80 UNION CITY

BRUCE BIGG
PROPS
'83 HUNGER, THE*

CAROLINE BIGGERSTAFF
EDITOR
'84 SOLDIER'S STORY, A*

KATHRYN BIHR
MAKEUP
'83 JAWS 3-D

LEON BIJOU
CINEMATOGRAPHER
'80 FOXES

DOUGLAS BILGE
MISCELLANEOUS
'81 THEY ALL LAUGHED

BRIAN BILGORRI
LOCATIONS
'80 HOPSCOTCH*

DAVID BILL
ASSOCIATE PRODUCER
'84 KIPPERBANG

TONY BILL
PRODUCER
'79 GOING IN STYLE*
DIRECTOR
'80 MY BODYGUARD
'82 SIX WEEKS
EXECUTIVE PRODUCER
'79 BOULEVARD NIGHTS

MARION BILLINGS
PUBLICIST
'79 KRAMER VS. KRAMER
'80 RAGING BULL
'81 TAPS*
'83 KING OF COMEDY, THE

WILLIAM BILOWIT
PRODUCTION DESIGNER
'84 C.H.U.D.

BRUCE BILSON
DIRECTOR
'79 NORTH AVENUE IRREGULARS, THE

GREGG BILSON
PROPS
'83 WAR GAMES

JULIE BILSON
PROD. COORDINATOR
'82 SEDUCTION, THE

JOHN BINDER
SCREENPLAY
'80 HONEYSUCKLE ROSE*
'82 ENDANGERED SPECIES*

MAURICE BINDER
MISCELLANEOUS
'80 FINAL COUNTDOWN, THE
'84 OXFORD BLUES

MACK BING
PRODUCER
'81 HARD COUNTRY*
ASSOCIATE PRODUCER
'80 WHERE THE BUFFALO ROAM
PRODUCTION MANAGER
'81 HARD COUNTRY
'82 BORDER, THE*
UNIT PROD. MANAGER
'80 WHERE THE BUFFALO ROAM
1ST ASST. DIRECTOR
'81 BUSTIN' LOOSE*
'84 WHERE THE BOYS ARE

HOWARD BINGHAM
STILLS
'79 ELECTRIC HORSEMAN, THE

LESLIE BINNS
ART DIRECTOR
'83 MAN FROM SNOWY RIVER, THE

MATTHEW BINNS
UNIT MANAGER
'84 OXFORD BLUES
2ND ASST. DIRECTOR
'81 CHARIOTS OF FIRE*
'83 LOCAL HERO*
LOCATIONS
'84 OXFORD BLUES

RUSSELL BINTLIFF
MISCELLANEOUS
'81 NIGHTHAWKS

CLAUDE BINYON JR.
PRODUCTION MANAGER
'78 DEER HUNTER, THE
UNIT PROD. MANAGER
'79 RAVAGERS
'79 JUST YOU AND ME KID
'82 THINGS ARE TOUGH ALL OVER*

PATRICIA BIRCH
DIRECTOR
'82 GREASE 2
CHOREOGRAPHER
'80 GILDA LIVE
'82 ZOOT SUIT
'82 GREASE 2

WILLIAM BIRCH
MISCELLANEOUS
'81 ...ALL THE MARBLES

ROY BIRCHLEY
ASSISTANT EDITOR
'80 SATURN 3
'80 MIRROR CRACK'D, THE
'82 EVIL UNDER THE SUN

LARRY BIRD
PROPS
'79 ESCAPE FROM ALCATRAZ
'80 RAISE THE TITANIC*
'80 SMALL CIRCLE OF FRIENDS, A
'81 WHOSE LIFE IS IT ANYWAY?
'82 DINER*
'83 BLUE THUNDER
'84 STARMAN

MICHAEL BIRD
PROPS
'79 RUNNING*
'81 FOUR FRIENDS
'82 I, THE JURY
SPECIAL EFFECTS
'80 OH! HEAVENLY DOG*

NANCY BIRD, R.N.
MISCELLANEOUS
'79 ALL THAT JAZZ

JOY BIRDSONG
2ND ASST. DIRECTOR
'84 BROTHER FROM ANOTHER PLANET, THE

LYNNE BIRDT
PROD. COORDINATOR
'81 BODY HEAT
'81 HALLOWEEN II
'81 KING OF THE MOUNTAIN

ANDREW BIRKIN
SCREENPLAY
'81 FINAL CONFLICT, THE
ASSOCIATE PRODUCER
'81 FINAL CONFLICT, THE*

BRUCE BIRMELIN
STILLS
'80 DEFIANCE*
'80 WHOLLY MOSES!
'81 MODERN ROMANCE
'82 STAR TREK II THE WRATH OF KHAN
'84 ICE PIRATES, THE
'84 ROMANCING THE STONE*
'84 OH GOD, YOU DEVIL

FATHER THOMAS BIRMINGHAM
MISCELLANEOUS
'82 AMITYVILLE II: THE POSSESSION

HARVEY BIRNBAUM
CINEMATOGRAPHER
'83 RETURN OF THE ALIENS: THE DEADLY SPAWN

RICHARD BIRNBAUM
SOUND
'81 EYE FOR AN EYE, AN
'84 OH GOD, YOU DEVIL

ROBERT BIRNBAUM
1ST ASST. DIRECTOR
'81 REDS*

STUART BIRNBAUM
SCREENPLAY
'83 SMOKEY AND THE BANDIT III*

HARRIET BIRNHOLZ
PROD. OFFICE COORD.
'82 PORKY'S

DON BIRNKRANT
CINEMATOGRAPHER
'84 TANK

JOSEPH BIROC
CINEMATOGRAPHER
'79 BEYOND THE POSEIDON ADVENTURE
'80 AIRPLANE
'81 ...ALL THE MARBLES
'82 AIRPLANE II: THE SEQUEL
'82 HAMMETT

LARRY BISCHOF
SCREENPLAY
'79 DREAMER*

LARRY BISCHOFF
1ST ASST. DIRECTOR
'83 AMERICANA

BRUCE BISENZ
SOUND
'79 NORMA RAE
'79 10
'80 FINAL COUNTDOWN, THE
'81 CHARLIE CHAN AND THE CURSE OF THE DRAGON QUEEN
'82 PERSONAL BEST
'83 SOMETHING WICKED THIS WAY COMES
'83 BREATHLESS
'84 PURPLE RAIN

CHARLES BISHOP
ART DIRECTOR
'79 MOONRAKER*
'81 GREAT MUPPET CAPER, THE*
'82 SENDER, THE*
MISCELLANEOUS
'82 DARK CRYSTAL, THE

DENNIS BISHOP
LOCATIONS
'83 LOCAL HERO*
MISCELLANEOUS
'84 NOT FOR PUBLICATION

SHELTON BISHOP III
PRODUCTION DESIGNER
'84 FRIDAY THE 13TH PART IV THE FINAL CHAPTER

MEL BISHOP
1ST ASST. DIRECTOR
'84 MUTANT

PHIL BISHOP
MISCELLANEOUS
'84 MEATBALLS PART II

TONY BISHOP
PRODUCER
'84 MEATBALLS PART II*
ASSOCIATE PRODUCER
'83 MAN WHO WASN'T THERE, THE
CO-PRODUCER
'82 FRIDAY THE 13TH PART THREE IN 3D
'84 FRIDAY THE 13TH PART IV THE FINAL CHAPTER
PRODUCTION MANAGER
'81 KING OF THE MOUNTAIN
'83 MAN WHO WASN'T THERE, THE
'84 FRIDAY THE 13TH PART IV THE FINAL CHAPTER
1ST ASST. DIRECTOR
'79 OLD BOYFRIENDS
'84 FRIDAY THE 13TH PART IV THE FINAL CHAPTER
2ND UNIT DIRECTOR
'84 MEATBALLS PART II
MISCELLANEOUS
'83 MAN WHO WASN'T THERE, THE

JAMES BISSELL
ART DIRECTOR
'84 LAST STARFIGHTER, THE
PRODUCTION DESIGNER
'82 E.T. THE EXTRA-TERRESTRIAL

JOHN BISSELL
PRODUCTION DESIGNER
'83 TWILIGHT ZONE, THE MOVIE

MARC BITTIAN
STILLS
'82 FIRST TIME, THE

GAIL BIXBY
COSTUMES
'80 ROADIE*

BRUCE BIXLER
STILLS
'79 MR. MIKE'S MONDO VIDEO

PETER BIZIOU
CINEMATOGRAPHER
'79 MONTY PYTHON'S LIFE OF BRIAN
'81 TIME BANDITS
'82 PINK FLOYD: THE WALL
'84 ANOTHER COUNTRY

BIRGITTA BJERKE
COSTUMES
'84 PARIS, TEXAS
MISCELLANEOUS
'82 SECOND THOUGHTS

B.J. BJORKMAN
SCRIPT SUPERVISOR
'81 FAN, THE
'82 WORLD ACCORDING TO GARP, THE
'83 LOVESICK

IAN BLACK
MISCELLANEOUS
'83 FINAL OPTION, THE

JEAN BLACK
MAKEUP
'84 NOT FOR PUBLICATION*
HAIR
'84 NOT FOR PUBLICATION*

JOHN BLACK
KEY GRIP
'81 WHOSE LIFE IS IT ANYWAY?
'82 SIX PACK
'83 LET'S SPEND THE NIGHT TOGETHER*

NOEL BLACK
DIRECTOR
'79 MAN, A WOMAN AND A BANK, A
'83 PRIVATE SCHOOL

PHILIP BLACK
2ND ASST. DIRECTOR
'79 STEVIE

TREVOR BLACK
SOUND
'82 BUTTERFLY*
UNIT PROD. MANAGER
'84 EL NORTE*

RICHARD BLACKBURN
SCREENPLAY
'82 EATING RAOUL*
ASSOCIATE PRODUCER
'82 EATING RAOUL

BARRY BLACKMORE
1ST ASST. DIRECTOR
'81 EXCALIBUR
2ND ASST. DIRECTOR
'80 OUTSIDER, THE*

CHARLES BLACKWELL
SOUND
'81 DOZENS, THE

CHRIS BLACKWELL
EXECUTIVE PRODUCER
'84 CHOOSE ME*

GREG BLACKWELL
PRODUCER
'81 TAKE THIS JOB AND SHOVE IT

DENNIS BLAIR
SCREENPLAY
'83 EASY MONEY*

DONNA BLAIR
ASSISTANT EDITOR
'79 MOUNTAIN FAMILY ROBINSON*

FRANK BLAIR
ART DIRECTOR
'84 MARVIN AND TIGE*

RICHARD BLAIR
MAKEUP
'82 JINXED*
'83 BUDDY SYSTEM, THE*
'83 MAN WOMAN AND CHILD
'84 MASS APPEAL

ROBERT BLAIR
KEY GRIP
'82 BARBAROSA

BILL BLAKE
EXECUTIVE PRODUCER
'81 NIGHT THE LIGHTS WENT OUT IN GEORGIA, THE*
CO-PRODUCER
'84 RHINESTONE*

CAROL BLAKE
EXECUTIVE PRODUCER
'81 NIGHT THE LIGHTS WENT OUT IN GEORGIA, THE*

GRACE BLAKE
ASSOCIATE PRODUCER
'83 STAR 80
PROD. OFFICE COORD.
'79 ALL THAT JAZZ
'81 EYEWITNESS
'82 STILL OF THE NIGHT
'82 TEMPEST
PROD. COORDINATOR
'80 WILLIE & PHIL
MISCELLANEOUS
'84 COTTON CLUB, THE

HARRY BLAKE
MAKEUP
'80 XANADU*

HOWARD BLAKE
MUSIC
'80 FLASH GORDON*
'83 AMITYVILLE 3D
'83 LORDS OF DISCIPLINE, THE
'84 RIDDLE OF THE SANDS
MISCELLANEOUS
'80 CHANGELING, THE

MICHAEL BLAKE
MAKEUP
'81 BUSTIN' LOOSE*

WALTER BLAKE
ASSOCIATE PRODUCER
'81 ...ALL THE MARBLES*

YVONNE BLAKE
COSTUMES
'79 ESCAPE TO ATHENA
'81 SUPERMAN II*
'84 FINDERS KEEPERS

MICHAEL BLAKEMORE
DIRECTOR
'83 PRIVATES ON PARADE

CAROL BLALACK
PROD. COORDINATOR
'81 HARD COUNTRY

ROBERT BLALACK
MISCELLANEOUS
'81 HEARTBEEPS
'81 WOLFEN
'82 CAT PEOPLE
'82 ZAPPED!
'82 ESCAPE ARTIST, THE
'83 GET CRAZY

ALICE BLANCHARD
2ND ASST. DIRECTOR
'80 JAZZ SINGER, THE*

SUE BLANE
COSTUMES
'81 SHOCK TREATMENT
'83 DRAUGHTSMAN CONTRACT, THE

ERICA BLANGSTED
ASSISTANT EDITOR
'84 MARVIN AND TIGE*

BETSY BLANKETT
EDITOR
'79 PENITENTIARY
'84 EL NORTE

FREDRIC BLANKFEIN
PRODUCTION MANAGER
'84 BROADWAY DANNY ROSE
1ST ASST. DIRECTOR
'79 MANHATTAN
'80 STARDUST MEMORIES
'82 MIDSUMMER NIGHT'S SEX COMEDY, A
'83 TWO OF A KIND
'83 ZELIG*
2ND ASST. DIRECTOR
'80 HIDE IN PLAIN SIGHT*

RICHARD BLANSHARD
STILLS
'84 GIVE MY REGARDS TO BROAD STREET*

JOEL BLASBERG
ASSOCIATE PRODUCER
'80 FOXES*

MARA BLASETTI
PRODUCTION MANAGER
'81 FOR YOUR EYES ONLY*
'82 TEMPEST*

RAFE BLASI
PUBLICIST
'82 48 HOURS
'84 STREETS OF FIRE

ALEXIS BLASINI
COSTUMES
'81 NESTING, THE

DANIEL BLATT
PRODUCER
'80 AMERICAN SUCCESS COMPANY, THE*
'83 CUJO*
'83 INDEPENDENCE DAY*
EXECUTIVE PRODUCER
'81 HOWLING, THE*

JERRY BLATT
SCREENPLAY
'80 DIVINE MADNESS*

WILLIAM PETER BLATTY
PRODUCER
'80 TWINKLE TWINKLE "KILLER" KANE
DIRECTOR
'80 TWINKLE TWINKLE "KILLER" KANE
SCREENPLAY
'80 TWINKLE TWINKLE "KILLER" KANE

FRED BLAU
MAKEUP
'84 JOY OF SEX, THE*

FRED BLAU JR.
MAKEUP
'79 APOCALYPSE NOW*
'80 SMALL CIRCLE OF FRIENDS, A*
'81 TATTOO*
'82 MAKING LOVE*

WILLIAM WARREN BLAYLOCK
PRODUCER
'84 GRANDVIEW, U.S.A.*

BOBBY BLECKMAN
MISCELLANEOUS
'84 FRIDAY THE 13TH PART IV THE FINAL CHAPTER

JOSH BLEIBTREU
SOUND
'84 STONE BOY, THE*

BERT BLESSING
<u>SCREENPLAY</u>
'82 JINXED*

DAVID BLEWITT
<u>EDITOR</u>
'79 BUDDY HOLLY STORY, THE
'80 COMPETITION, THE
'80 IN GOD WE TRUST
'80 STEEL
'81 UNDER THE RAINBOW
'83 SMOKEY AND THE BANDIT III*
'83 D.C. CAB
'84 GHOSTBUSTERS*

JOHN BLEZARD
<u>ART DIRECTOR</u>
'83 WICKED LADY, THE
<u>PRODUCTION DESIGNER</u>
'79 FIREPOWER*
'80 NIJINSKY

WILLIAM BLINN
<u>SCREENPLAY</u>
'84 PURPLE RAIN*

DAVID BLITSTEIN
<u>SPECIAL EFFECTS</u>
'84 ADVENTURES OF BUCKAROO BANZAI ACROSS THE 8TH DIMENSION,THE*

ANDY BLOCH
<u>MISCELLANEOUS</u>
'80 JAZZ SINGER, THE

CHARLES BLOCH
<u>EXECUTIVE PRODUCER</u>
'80 FOG, THE

CHERYL BLOCH
<u>ASSISTANT EDITOR</u>
'83 TESTAMENT
'84 ADVENTURES OF BUCKAROO BANZAI ACROSS THE 8TH DIMENSION, THE*

IVAN BLOCH
<u>PRODUCER</u>
'84 STONE BOY, THE*

BECKY BLOCK
<u>ART DIRECTOR</u>
'84 NOT FOR PUBLICATION*

BRUCE BLOCK
<u>2ND UNIT DIRECTOR</u>
'84 BACHELOR PARTY
<u>MISCELLANEOUS</u>
'84 IRRECONCILABLE DIFFERENCES
'84 BACHELOR PARTY

LARRY BLOCK
<u>SCREENPLAY</u>
'81 FUNHOUSE, THE

DAVID BLOCKER
<u>PRODUCER</u>
'84 CHOOSE ME*

MICHAEL BLOECHER
<u>ASSOCIATE EDITOR</u>
'84 TERMINATOR, THE
<u>ASSISTANT EDITOR</u>
'84 MUTANT*

ELIZABETH BLOMME
<u>PUBLICIST</u>
'80 PROM NIGHT
'82 GREY FOX, THE

HENRI BLONDEAU
<u>SOUND</u>
'79 IN PRAISE OF OLDER WOMEN
'80 DEATH SHIP

KATHRYN BLONDELL
<u>HAIR</u>
'79 CHAPTER TWO
'79 ICE CASTLES
'79 PROMISES IN THE DARK
'79 WINTER KILLS
'80 SEEMS LIKE OLD TIMES
'80 HERO AT LARGE
'80 PRIVATE BENJAMIN*
'81 MOMMIE DEAREST*
'81 ONLY WHEN I LAUGH
'82 BEST FRIENDS*
'82 DEAD MEN DON'T WEAR PLAID
'82 HAMMETT*
'83 CLASS*
'83 MAN WITH TWO BRAINS, THE
'84 PROTOCOL*
'84 ROMANCING THE STONE
'84 SWING SHIFT*

ERIC BLOOM
<u>SCREENPLAY</u>
'80 EYES OF A STRANGER*

JEFFREY BLOOM
<u>DIRECTOR</u>
'81 BLOOD BEACH
<u>SCREENPLAY</u>
'81 BLOOD BEACH
'83 NIGHTMARES*

JIM BLOOM
<u>ASSOCIATE PRODUCER</u>
'80 EMPIRE STRIKES BACK, THE*
<u>CO-PRODUCER</u>
'83 RETURN OF THE JEDI*
<u>2ND ASST. DIRECTOR</u>
'80 CLOSE ENCOUNTERS OF THE THIRD KIND SPECIAL EDITION

JOHN BLOOM
<u>EDITOR</u>
'79 DRACULA
'81 FRENCH LIEUTENANT'S WOMAN, THE
'82 GANDHI
'83 BETRAYAL
'83 UNDER FIRE*

LES BLOOM
<u>PROPS</u>
'79 SEDUCTION OF JOE TYNAN, THE
'79 MANHATTAN
'83 LOVESICK

GEORGE BLOOMFIELD
<u>DIRECTOR</u>
'80 NOTHING PERSONAL

JOHN BLOOMFIELD
<u>COSTUMES</u>
'80 FIENDISH PLOT OF DR. FU MANCHU, THE
'81 EYE OF THE NEEDLE
'82 CONAN THE BARBARIAN
'83 WICKED LADY, THE
'84 BOUNTY, THE
'84 CONAN THE DESTROYER

LISA BLOOMFIELD
<u>STILLS</u>
'83 INDEPENDENCE DAY*

JOHN BLOSS
<u>PRODUCTION MANAGER</u>
'79 APPLE DUMPLING GANG RIDES AGAIN, THE
'79 BLACK HOLE, THE
'79 NORTH AVENUE IRREGULARS, THE
'80 HERBIE GOES BANANAS
'80 LAST FLIGHT OF NOAH'S ARK,THE
'80 MIDNIGHT MADNESS
'81 AMY
'81 CONDORMAN*
'81 DEVIL AND MAX DEVLIN, THE

JIM BLOUNT
<u>SPECIAL EFFECTS</u>
'79 TIME AFTER TIME*

LORI BLOUSTEIN
<u>ASSISTANT EDITOR</u>
'80 GLORIA
'82 AMITYVILLE II: THE POSSESSION*

CRYSTAL BLUE
<u>MISCELLANEOUS</u>
'82 PENITENTIARY II

BUET BLUESTEIN
<u>1ST ASST. DIRECTOR</u>
'80 SOMEWHERE IN TIME

SUSAN BLUESTEIN
<u>CASTING</u>
'83 PRIVATE SCHOOL*

ARTHUR BLUM
<u>KEY GRIP</u>
'84 RECKLESS*

DEBBIE BLUM
<u>PRODUCTION MANAGER</u>
'80 KIDS ARE ALL RIGHT, THE

HARRY BLUM
EXECUTIVE PRODUCER
'79 MAGICIAN OF LUBLIN, THE

JACK BLUM
CASTING
'79 MEATBALLS*

JOANIE BLUM
SCRIPT SUPERVISOR
'80 RESURRECTION
'80 CARNY
'80 HEARTBEAT
'81 CUTTER'S WAY
'82 HAMMETT*
'82 ONE FROM THE HEART
'83 FLASHDANCE
'83 TABLE FOR FIVE*
'83 UNCOMMON VALOR

LEN BLUM
SCREENPLAY
'79 MEATBALLS*
'81 STRIPES*
'83 SPACEHUNTER: ADVENTURES IN THE FORBIDDEN ZONE*

JUDITH BLUME
ASSISTANT EDITOR
'82 WORLD ACCORDING TO GARP, THE*

ANDY BLUMENTHAL
EDITOR
'84 HARDBODIES
ASSISTANT EDITOR
'80 STUNT MAN, THE*
'80 MY BODYGUARD*
'81 ZORRO, THE GAY BLADE*
'82 SIX WEEKS

HERMAN BLUMENTHAL
PRODUCTION DESIGNER
'79 CHAMP, THE
'80 BALTIMORE BULLET, THE
'80 FORMULA, THE
'81 ZORRO, THE GAY BLADE

CHRIS BLUNDEN
ASSISTANT EDITOR
'84 CHAMPIONS
'84 ELECTRIC DREAMS*

MARYCE BLYMER
HAIR
'80 LITTLE DARLINGS

SUGAR BLYMER
HAIR
'83 ALL THE RIGHT MOVES*

GINGER BLYMYER
HAIR
'84 SONGWRITER

EUGENE BLYTHE
CASTING
'82 ZOOT SUIT*

JEFFREY BOAM
SCREENPLAY
'83 DEAD ZONE, THE

JOHN BOARD
ASSOCIATE PRODUCER
'82 GREY FOX, THE
1ST ASST. DIRECTOR
'79 BROOD, THE
'81 ATLANTIC CITY
'82 GREY FOX, THE
'83 DEAD ZONE, THE
'83 VIDEODROME

TIM BOARD
ASSISTANT EDITOR
'80 LITTLE DARLINGS
'80 NINE TO FIVE
'81 ZORRO, THE GAY BLADE*
'82 GREASE 2*
'83 NATIONAL LAMPOON'S VACATION
'84 RHINESTONE*

JOHN LANGE BOARDMAN
MAKEUP
'83 I AM THE CHEESE

ROBYN BOARDMAN
MISCELLANEOUS
'83 I AM THE CHEESE

ILONA BOBAK
HAIR
'83 RISKY BUSINESS

RON BOCHAR
ASSISTANT EDITOR
'82 CREEPSHOW

LARRY BOCK
EDITOR
'79 ROCK 'N ROLL HIGH SCHOOL*
'80 ALLIGATOR*
'81 SMOKEY BITES THE DUST
'81 GALAXY OF TERROR*
'83 JOYSTICKS

MITCHELL BOCK
2ND ASST. DIRECTOR
'79 SCAVENGER HUNT*
'80 FATSO
'80 HOW TO BEAT THE HIGH COST OF LIVING
'81 HISTORY OF THE WORLD PART I
'82 DEAD MEN DON'T WEAR PLAID

RICHARD CHRISTOPHER BOCK
EDITOR
'83 MAUSOLEUM
ASSISTANT EDITOR
'81 ENTER THE NINJA*

GAVIN BOCQUET
MISCELLANEOUS
'80 SATURN 3

MICHAEL BODDICKER
MUSIC
'83 GET CRAZY
'84 ADVENTURES OF BUCKAROO BANZAI ACROSS THE 8TH DIMENSION, THE

RALF BODE
CINEMATOGRAPHER
'79 RICH KIDS
'80 COAL MINER'S DAUGHTER
'80 DRESSED TO KILL
'81 RAGGEDY MAN
'82 LITTLE SEX, A
'83 GORKY PARK
'84 FIRSTBORN

DAVID BODEN
KEY GRIP
'84 HARDBODIES

KRISTINA BODEN
ASSISTANT EDITOR
'83 BABY IT'S YOU*
'84 BODY DOUBLE

RENEE BODNER
SCRIPT SUPERVISOR
'80 FAME
'80 IT'S MY TURN*
'80 JUST TELL ME WHAT YOU WANT
'82 CHOSEN, THE
'82 HANKY PANKY
'82 I, THE JURY
'82 TOOTSIE
'83 TRADING PLACES

TED BOEHLER
MISCELLANEOUS
'80 HUMANOIDS FROM THE DEEP

DAVE BOEHLKE
MISCELLANEOUS
'81 CONTINENTAL DIVIDE

TODD BOEKELHEIDE
MUSIC SUPERVISOR
'84 MRS. SOFFEL

TODD BOEKELHEIDE
ASSOCIATE EDITOR
'79 BLACK STALLION, THE*

MENNO BOEREMA
ASSISTANT EDITOR
'83 CHEECH AND CHONG'S STILL SMOKIN'*

JEAN BOFFETY
CINEMATOGRAPHER
'79 QUINTET
'82 BY DESIGN

PAUL BOGART
DIRECTOR
'84 OH GOD, YOU DEVIL

PETER BOGART
UNIT PROD. MANAGER
'80 BLUE LAGOON
1ST ASST. DIRECTOR
'79 AMERICAN GIGOLO
'79 MAN, A WOMAN AND A BANK, A
'80 BLUE LAGOON
'80 DEFIANCE
'81 CAVEMAN
'81 THIEF*
'83 TESTAMENT*
'83 TOUGH ENOUGH
'84 BEVERLY HILLS COP
'84 OH GOD, YOU DEVIL

PETER BOGDANOVICH
DIRECTOR
'79 SAINT JACK
'81 THEY ALL LAUGHED
SCREENPLAY
'79 SAINT JACK*
'81 THEY ALL LAUGHED

WILLY BOGNER
MISCELLANEOUS
'81 FOR YOUR EYES ONLY

BARBARA BOGUSKI
ASSISTANT EDITOR
'83 SWEET SIXTEEN

JACK BOHRER
UNIT PROD. MANAGER
'81 HONKY TONK FREEWAY*

ROBERT BOHUS
STILLS
'83 RETURN OF THE ALIENS: THE DEADLY SPAWN
SCRIPT SUPERVISOR
'83 RETURN OF THE ALIENS: THE DEADLY SPAWN

TED BOHUS
PRODUCER
'83 RETURN OF THE ALIENS: THE DEADLY SPAWN

MARIE-THERESE BOICHE
PROD. OFFICE COORD.
'84 GREYSTOKE: THE LEGEND OF TARZAN, LORD OF THE APES

JOHN BOISSEAU
KEY GRIP
'80 EYES OF A STRANGER

DOMINIQUE BOISVERT
EDITOR
'80 HOG WILD

PETER BOITA
EDITOR
'79 UNIDENTIFIED FLYING ODDBALL

YOUSAF BOKHARI
1ST ASST. DIRECTOR
'84 BOLERO

ALEX BOLADO JR.
UNIT MANAGER
'83 BLIND RAGE

JOSEPH BOLESTA
KEY GRIP
'80 MOTHER'S DAY

MARTIN BOLGER
SOUND
'79 WHEN A STRANGER CALLS
'79 FORCE OF ONE, A*
'80 PRIVATE BENJAMIN
'80 UP THE ACADEMY
'83 NATIONAL LAMPOON'S VACATION

CLAUDE BOLLING
MUSIC
'80 AWAKENING, THE
'80 WILLIE & PHIL

PATRICIA BOLOMET
COSTUMES
'82 SWAMP THING*

LEE BOLON
LOCATIONS
'81 EYE OF THE NEEDLE*

CHARLES BOLT
SCREENPLAY
'84 NO SMALL AFFAIR*

ROBERT BOLT
SCREENPLAY
'84 BOUNTY, THE

GREGORY BOLTON
ART DIRECTOR
'83 WITHOUT A TRACE
'84 COTTON CLUB, THE*

MICHAEL BOLTON
ART DIRECTOR
'82 MOTHER LODE*
'83 STAR 80*
'84 RUNAWAY

JOHN BOLZ
SOUND
'80 DRESSED TO KILL
'80 FIRST DEADLY SIN
'83 HUNGER, THE*
'84 FIRSTBORN

TIMOTHY BOND
SCREENPLAY
'81 HAPPY BIRTHDAY TO ME*

PETER BONERZ
DIRECTOR
'81 NOBODY'S PERFEKT

TOM BONGALIS
MISCELLANEOUS
'82 GREY FOX, THE

ANDREW BONIME
PRODUCER
'84 C.H.U.D.

ANDY BONIN M.D.
MISCELLANEOUS
'81 HALLOWEEN II

BOB BONNEY
SCREENPLAY
'81 NIGHT THE LIGHTS WENT OUT IN GEORGIA, THE

GLAUDE BONNIERE
PRODUCTION DESIGNER
'82 PARADISE

FRANCOISE BONNOT
EDITOR
'82 MISSING
'83 HANNA K

STEVE BONO
PRODUCTION MANAGER
'81 NIGHT THE LIGHTS WENT OUT IN GEORGIA, THE

ALBERT BONOMI
KEY GRIP
'79 LITTLE ROMANCE, A

TERESA BOOK
ASSISTANT EDITOR
'83 BLACK STALLION RETURNS, THE
'84 AMADEUS*

COLIN BOOKER
MAKEUP
'80 FADE TO BLACK
HAIR
'80 FADE TO BLACK

JOHN BOORMAN
PRODUCER
'81 EXCALIBUR
DIRECTOR
'81 EXCALIBUR
SCREENPLAY
'81 EXCALIBUR*

H. GORDON BOOS
<u>1ST ASST. DIRECTOR</u>
'84 NIGHT OF THE COMET
<u>2ND ASST. DIRECTOR</u>
'83 VALLEY GIRL

GENE BOOTH
<u>PROPS</u>
'82 FORCED VENGEANCE*

JAMES BOOTH
<u>SCREENPLAY</u>
'79 SUNBURN*

MARGARET BOOTH
<u>ASSOCIATE PRODUCER</u>
'79 CHAPTER TWO
'80 SEEMS LIKE OLD TIMES
'82 TOY, THE
<u>EDITOR</u>
'79 CHAPTER TWO*
'82 ANNIE*
<u>MISCELLANEOUS</u>
'80 SEEMS LIKE OLD TIMES

TOM BOOTH
<u>HAIR</u>
'80 HOG WILD
'83 SPACEHUNTER: ADVENTURES IN THE FORBIDDEN ZONE
'83 VIDEODROME*

VALERIE BOOTH
<u>SCRIPT SUPERVISOR</u>
'81 EYE OF THE NEEDLE*
'83 BRITANNIA HOSPITAL

MILAN BOR
<u>SOUND</u>
'84 NEVERENDING STORY, THE*

PAUL BORCHARDT
<u>KEY GRIP</u>
'80 THOSE LIPS, THOSE EYES
'82 LOOKIN' TO GET OUT
'82 CHILLY SCENES OF WINTER

RICK BORCHARDT
<u>KEY GRIP</u>
'79 VILLAIN, THE
'83 INDEPENDENCE DAY
'83 TWILIGHT ZONE, THE MOVIE*
'84 RHINESTONE
'84 SIXTEEN CANDLES

DONALD BORCHERS
<u>PRODUCER</u>
'84 ANGEL*
'84 CHILDREN OF THE CORN*
<u>ASSOCIATE PRODUCER</u>
'81 FEAR NO EVIL*
'82 BEASTMASTER, THE
<u>CO-PRODUCER</u>
'84 CRIMES OF PASSION
<u>2ND ASST. DIRECTOR</u>
'81 EYE FOR AN EYE, AN*

MARSHALL BORDEN
<u>EDITOR</u>
'81 WOLFEN*

WILLIAM BORDEN
<u>ASSOCIATE PRODUCER</u>
'84 AGAINST ALL ODDS
<u>LOCATIONS</u>
'81 STRIPES*
'81 HISTORY OF THE WORLD PART I
'83 NATIONAL LAMPOON'S VACATION*

PATRICK BORDIER
<u>LOCATIONS</u>
'80 TESS*

ROBERT BORDIGA
<u>PRODUCTION MANAGER</u>
'84 C.H.U.D.
<u>UNIT PROD. MANAGER</u>
'82 SWAMP THING*
<u>MISCELLANEOUS</u>
'84 C.H.U.D.

RITA BORDONARO
<u>HAIR</u>
'80 PRIVATE BENJAMIN*

GEORG BORGEL
<u>1ST ASST. DIRECTOR</u>
'84 NEVERENDING STORY, THE*

JOHNNY BORGESE
<u>SPECIAL EFFECTS</u>
'82 ZOOT SUIT
'83 STING II, THE

GABE BORGO
<u>HAIR</u>
'79 NATURAL ENEMIES
'80 SMOKEY AND THE BANDIT II*
'81 SHARKEY'S MACHINE*
'81 CANNONBALL RUN, THE
'82 BEST FRIENDS*
'83 STROKER ACE*
'84 TANK*

ROBERT BORIS
<u>DIRECTOR</u>
'84 OXFORD BLUES
<u>SCREENPLAY</u>
'82 SOME KIND OF HERO*
'83 DOCTOR DETROIT*
'84 OXFORD BLUES
<u>ASSOCIATE PRODUCER</u>
'82 SOME KIND OF HERO

RENE BORISEWITZ
<u>SOUND</u>
'79 PLAYERS
'82 VENOM*
'84 RAZOR'S EDGE, THE
'84 RIDDLE OF THE SANDS

MORITZ BORMAN
<u>PRODUCER</u>
'84 UNDER THE VOLCANO*

CHARLES BORNSTEIN
<u>EDITOR</u>
'80 FOG, THE*
'84 ANGEL*
<u>ASSISTANT EDITOR</u>
'80 CLOSE ENCOUNTERS OF THE THIRD KIND SPECIAL EDITION*
'82 YOUNG DOCTORS IN LOVE*

KEN BORNSTEIN
<u>ASSISTANT EDITOR</u>
'83 REVENGE OF THE NINJA*
'84 BREAKIN 2 ELECTRIC BOOGALOO

PETER BOROWSKY
<u>MISCELLANEOUS</u>
'81 SCANNERS
'83 OF UNKNOWN ORIGIN

PHILLIP BORSOS
<u>DIRECTOR</u>
'82 GREY FOX, THE
<u>CO-PRODUCER</u>
'82 GREY FOX, THE*

ORIN BORSTEN
<u>UNIT PUBLICIST</u>
'81 ZORRO, THE GAY BLADE
'82 PORKY'S

RADU BORUSESCU
<u>ART DIRECTOR</u>
'81 MONTENEGRO

PAOLO BORZELLI
<u>HAIR</u>
'83 HIGH ROAD TO CHINA

SIMON BOSANQUET
<u>PRODUCTION MANAGER</u>
'84 ANOTHER COUNTRY
'84 GREYSTOKE: THE LEGEND OF TARZAN, LORD OF THE APES
<u>LOCATIONS</u>
'81 CHARIOTS OF FIRE*

VALLEY VIA BOSCHO
<u>LOCATIONS</u>
'81 BACK ROADS

TINA BOSSIDY
<u>COSTUMES</u>
'80 HOME MOVIES

DEREK BOTELL
<u>MISCELLANEOUS</u>
'80 FLASH GORDON

PERRY BOTKIN

MUSIC
'81 TARZAN, THE APE MAN
'84 SILENT NIGHT, DEADLY NIGHT

ROB BOTTIN

ASSOCIATE PRODUCER
'81 HOWLING, THE
MISCELLANEOUS
'79 ROCK 'N ROLL HIGH SCHOOL
'80 HUMANOIDS FROM THE DEEP
'81 HOWLING, THE
'82 THING, THE
'83 TWILIGHT ZONE, THE MOVIE

CLAUDINE BOUCHE

ASSISTANT EDITOR
'79 LITTLE ROMANCE, A*

PASCALE BOUCHE

ASSISTANT EDITOR
'83 HANNA K*

FRANCE BOUDREAU

SCRIPT SUPERVISOR
'80 HOG WILD
'81 SCANNERS
'81 GAS
'83 OF UNKNOWN ORIGIN

MYCHELE BOUDRIAS

PRODUCTION MANAGER
'84 HOTEL NEW HAMPSHIRE, THE

JOREEN BOUILLET

STILLS
'80 ROADIE*
'80 CARNY*
'81 NIGHT THE LIGHTS WENT OUT IN GEORGIA, THE
'83 PORKY'S II THE NEXT DAY

YAACOV BOUKMAN

KEY GRIP
'83 HANNA K*

SARA BOULDER

ASSISTANT EDITOR
'80 HOME MOVIES*

LUCY BOULTING

CASTING
'83 DRAUGHTSMAN CONTRACT, THE
'84 TOP SECRET!*
MISCELLANEOUS
'84 ANOTHER COUNTRY

ADRIENNE BOURBEAU

1ST ASST. DIRECTOR
'79 MR. MIKE'S MONDO VIDEO*
2ND ASST. DIRECTOR
'81 FUNHOUSE, THE
'81 HARDLY WORKING*

MICHAEL BOURCHIER

2ND ASST. DIRECTOR
'84 PHAR LAP

YVON BOURGEOIS

MISCELLANEOUS
'79 MAN, A WOMAN AND A BANK, A

FERGUS BOURKE

STILLS
'79 GREAT TRAIN ROBBERY, THE*

MEL BOURNE

PRODUCTION DESIGNER
'79 MANHATTAN
'80 STARDUST MEMORIES
'80 WINDOWS
'81 THIEF
'82 STILL OF THE NIGHT
'82 MIDSUMMER NIGHT'S SEX COMEDY, A
'83 ZELIG
'84 BROADWAY DANNY ROSE
'84 NATURAL, THE*

TIMOTHY MARSHALL BOURNE

LOCATIONS
'82 MIDSUMMER NIGHT'S SEX COMEDY, A*
'83 ZELIG
'84 BROADWAY DANNY ROSE
'84 FALLING IN LOVE

ULLA BOURNE

SCRIPT SUPERVISOR
'79 MUPPET MOVIE, THE
'80 SOMEWHERE IN TIME

JEAN BOURRET

PROPS
'80 HOG WILD
'81 SCANNERS
'81 GAS

TRACY BOUSMAN

ART DIRECTOR
'79 NORMA RAE
'82 YOUNG DOCTORS IN LOVE
'84 PROTOCOL

GABRIEL BOUSTANY

EXECUTIVE PRODUCER
'81 ATLANTIC CITY*

ALAN BOUSTEAD

MISCELLANEOUS
'84 AMADEUS

GIUSU BOVINO

HAIR
'80 FLASH GORDON*

DAVID BOWDEN

ART DIRECTOR
'84 PHAR LAP

LIBBY BOWDEN

2ND ASST. DIRECTOR
'79 BROOD, THE
'80 HAPPY BIRTHDAY, GEMINI
'83 VIDEODROME*

BARBARA BOWEN

PROD. SECRETARY
'83 JOYSTICKS

CHANTAL BOWEN

ASSISTANT EDITOR
'81 MY BLOODY VALENTINE

DEIRDRE BOWEN

CASTING
'83 RUNNING BRAVE*
'83 DEAD ZONE, THE*
'83 OF UNKNOWN ORIGIN*

HOLLY BOWER

STILLS
'79 KRAMER VS. KRAMER
'80 DRESSED TO KILL
'80 FAME*
'81 FOUR SEASONS, THE
'83 EASY MONEY
'83 WITHOUT A TRACE

MARTIN BOWER

MISCELLANEOUS
'79 ALIEN

ELAINE BOWERBANK

HAIR
'79 MAN, A WOMAN AND A BANK, A
'79 GREAT TRAIN ROBBERY, THE
'80 ROUGH CUT*
'81 SPHINX*
'84 PASSAGE TO INDIA, A*

DOUG BOWERMAN

MISCELLANEOUS
'83 METALSTORM: THE DESTRUCTION OF JARED-SYN

GEORGE BOWERS

DIRECTOR
'81 BODY AND SOUL
'83 MY TUTOR
EDITOR
'80 GALAXINA*
'84 ADVENTURES OF BUCKAROO BANZAI ACROSS THE 8TH DIMENSION, THE*

IRENE BOWERS

ASSISTANT EDITOR
'83 MY TUTOR

MARGE BOWERS

COSTUMES
'83 RUMBLEFISH
'83 OUTSIDERS, THE

PHIL BOWLES
<u>1ST ASST. DIRECTOR</u>
'79 BUCK ROGERS*
'81 GHOST STORY*

WILLIAM BOWLING
<u>LOCATIONS</u>
'81 MODERN PROBLEMS*
'83 DEAL OF THE CENTURY*
'84 BEVERLY HILLS COP*

BETTY BOX
<u>MUSIC</u>
'80 FOR THE LOVE OF BENJI*

EUEL BOX
<u>MUSIC</u>
'79 DOUBLE MCGUFFIN, THE
'80 FOR THE LOVE OF BENJI*
'80 OH! HEAVENLY DOG

JOHN BOX
<u>PRODUCTION DESIGNER</u>
'83 KEEP, THE
'84 PASSAGE TO INDIA, A

TIM BOXELL
<u>MISCELLANEOUS</u>
'84 ELECTRIC DREAMS
'84 C.H.U.D.

JOHN BOXER
<u>COSTUMES</u>
'79 STARTING OVER
'79 VOICES
'80 RAGING BULL*
'81 FORT APACHE, THE BRONX
'81 NEIGHBORS
'81 WOLFEN
'82 FIGHTING BACK
'83 REUBEN, REUBEN

NAT BOXER
<u>SOUND</u>
'79 RUNNING*
'79 BLACK STALLION, THE*
'79 WANDERERS, THE
'80 MY BODYGUARD*
'81 EYEWITNESS
'81 FOUR FRIENDS*
'82 STILL OF THE NIGHT
'83 BLACK STALLION RETURNS, THE
'83 I AM THE CHEESE

MICHAEL BOYADJIEW
<u>1ST ASST. DIRECTOR</u>
'84 NEVERENDING STORY, THE*

CHRISTINE BOYAR
<u>COSTUMES</u>
'82 SWORD AND THE SORCERER, THE

LES BOYCE
<u>SCRIPT SUPERVISOR</u>
'82 JINXED

DON BOYD
<u>PRODUCER</u>
'81 HONKY TONK FREEWAY*

JACK BOYD
<u>MISCELLANEOUS</u>
'81 CONDORMAN

ROBERT BOYD
<u>ASSISTANT EDITOR</u>
'81 SCANNERS*

RUSSELL BOYD
<u>CINEMATOGRAPHER</u>
'79 PICNIC AT HANGING ROCK
'81 GALLIPOLI
'82 STARSTRUCK
'83 TENDER MERCIES
'83 YEAR OF
LIVING DANGEROUSLY, THE
'84 PHAR LAP
'84 SOLDIER'S STORY, A
'84 MRS. SOFFEL

SUSAN BOYD
<u>HAIR</u>
'84 ICEMAN

ERIC BOYD-PERKINS
<u>EDITOR</u>
'82 MOTHER LODE
<u>ASSISTANT EDITOR</u>
'81 FOR YOUR EYES ONLY

MANON BOUGER BOYER
<u>MISCELLANEOUS</u>
'82 PARADISE

ROBERT BOYETT
<u>PRODUCER</u>
'82 BEST LITTLE WHOREHOUSE
IN TEXAS, THE*

ALAN BOYLE
<u>MAKEUP</u>
'83 BRITANNIA HOSPITAL*
'83 DRESSER, THE
'83 GORKY PARK*
'83 KRULL

MARC BOYLE
<u>STUNT COORDINATOR</u>
'81 FINAL CONFLICT, THE
'83 WICKED LADY, THE
'84 LASSITER
'84 FINDERS KEEPERS

MIKE BOYLE
<u>MISCELLANEOUS</u>
'82 BARBAROSA

PETER BOYLE
<u>EDITOR</u>
'84 RAZOR'S EDGE, THE
<u>ASSISTANT EDITOR</u>
'79 FIFTH MUSKETEER, THE

ROBERT BOYLE
<u>PRODUCTION DESIGNER</u>
'79 WINTER KILLS
'80 PRIVATE BENJAMIN
'82 BEST LITTLE WHOREHOUSE
IN TEXAS, THE
'82 LOOKIN' TO GET OUT
'83 STAYING ALIVE
'83 TABLE FOR FIVE
'84 NO SMALL AFFAIR
'84 RHINESTONE

PETER BOYSEY
<u>MISCELLANEOUS</u>
'79 ALIEN

STEVE BOYUM
<u>STUNT COORDINATOR</u>
'82 BEASTMASTER, THE
<u>MISCELLANEOUS</u>
'80 MOUNTAIN MEN, THE

RON BOZMAN
<u>PRODUCTION MANAGER</u>
'80 MIDDLE AGE CRAZY*
<u>UNIT PROD. MANAGER</u>
'82 SPLIT IMAGE*
<u>UNIT MANAGER</u>
'83 ECHOES
<u>1ST ASST. DIRECTOR</u>
'83 SMOKEY AND THE BANDIT III
'84 MRS. SOFFEL*
<u>LOCATIONS</u>
'79 PROMISE, THE
<u>2ND UNIT DIRECTOR</u>
'84 MRS. SOFFEL*

JOHN BRABOURNE
<u>PRODUCER</u>
'80 MIRROR CRACK'D, THE*
'82 EVIL UNDER THE SUN*
'84 PASSAGE TO INDIA, A*

GERARD BRACH
<u>SCREENPLAY</u>
'80 TESS*
'82 QUEST FOR FIRE

BIFF BRACHT
<u>ASSISTANT EDITOR</u>
'80 GALAXINA

FRANK BRACHT
<u>EDITOR</u>
'79 SOMETHING SHORT OF PARADISE

JOHN BRACKEN
<u>ASSISTANT EDITOR</u>
'84 ADVENTURES OF BUCKAROO BANZAI
ACROSS THE 8TH DIMENSION, THE*

RICHARD BRACKEN
<u>EDITOR</u>
'81 DEADLY BLESSING
'82 SWAMP THING

LEIGH BRACKETT
SCREENPLAY
'80 EMPIRE STRIKES BACK, THE*

JACOB BRACKMAN
PRODUCER
'80 TIMES SQUARE*
SCREENPLAY
'80 TIMES SQUARE

DAVID BRACKNELL
1ST ASST. DIRECTOR
'82 QUEST FOR FIRE*
'84 INDIANA JONES AND THE TEMPLE OF DOOM*

PAUL BRADBURN
PROPS
'83 BEYOND THE LIMIT

RAY BRADBURY
SCREENPLAY
'83 SOMETHING WICKED THIS WAY COMES

MAC BRADDEN
2ND ASST. DIRECTOR
'81 GAS
'83 RUNNING BRAVE

HUB BRADEN
ART DIRECTOR
'84 MIKE'S MURDER

WILLIAM BRADEN
2ND ASST. DIRECTOR
'82 DEATH VALLEY*
MISCELLANEOUS
'82 SEDUCTION, THE

DEBRA "EBONY" BRADFORD
COSTUMES
'79 PENITENTIARY*

KAREN BRADLEY
MAKEUP
'83 RIGHT STUFF, THE*

OWEN BRADLEY
MUSIC SUPERVISOR
'80 COAL MINER'S DAUGHTER

PAT BRADLEY
SCREENPLAY
'81 UNDER THE RAINBOW*

PAUL BRADLEY
ASSOCIATE PRODUCER
'84 BOSTONIANS, THE*

MICHAEL BRADSELL
EDITOR
'82 I'M DANCING AS FAST AS I CAN
'82 VENOM
'83 LOCAL HERO
'84 SCANDALOUS
2ND UNIT DIRECTOR
'82 VENOM

JOAN BRADSHAW
PRODUCTION MANAGER
'81 FAN, THE
UNIT PROD. MANAGER
'79 GOING IN STYLE
'82 YES, GIORGIO
'83 WRONG IS RIGHT*

BERNADETTE BRADY
COSTUMES
'84 HARDBODIES

BOB BRADY
CASTING
'83 LIQUID SKY

BOB BRADY
MISCELLANEOUS
'84 BEAT STREET

DAVID BRADY
EXECUTIVE PRODUCER
'82 GREY FOX, THE

JERRY BRADY
EDITOR
'80 BALTIMORE BULLET, THE

CHARLES BRAIVE
1ST ASST. DIRECTOR
'79 IN PRAISE OF OLDER WOMEN
'80 DEATH SHIP
'81 HAPPY BIRTHDAY TO ME
2ND ASST. DIRECTOR
'79 QUINTET
2ND UNIT DIRECTOR
'81 HAPPY BIRTHDAY TO ME

ROBERT BRALVER
2ND UNIT DIRECTOR
'82 SENDER, THE
STUNT COORDINATOR
'79 JAGUAR LIVES

MALCOLM BRALY
SCREENPLAY
'79 ON THE YARD

MARTIN BRAM
EDITOR
'81 WOLFEN*

BILL BRAME
EDITOR
'79 BEYOND THE POSEIDON ADVENTURE

RICHARD BRAMS
ASSOCIATE PRODUCER
'81 THIEF

JOHN BRANAGAN
MISCELLANEOUS
'83 SUBURBIA

ANTHONY BRAND
1ST ASST. DIRECTOR
'84 PURPLE RAIN*

THOMAS BRANDAU
SOUND
'83 LIANNA*

CLIFTON BRANDON
PRODUCTION MANAGER
'79 FIREPOWER*
'83 WICKED LADY, THE

JANICE BRANDOW
HAIR
'81 HARD COUNTRY
'82 CAT PEOPLE
'82 FAST TIMES AT RIDGEMONT HIGH
'83 SCARFACE*
'83 BUDDY SYSTEM, THE*

EVE BRANDSTEIN
CASTING
'80 BIG BRAWL, THE*
'84 CHAMPIONS*
'84 THIS IS SPINAL TAP

BYRON "BUZZ" BRANDT
EDITOR
'79 PRISONER OF ZENDA, THE
'80 IT'S MY TURN*
'83 SMOKEY AND THE BANDIT III*

CARYL BRANDT
PRODUCTION MANAGER
'79 FAST COMPANY

JERROLD BRANDT
MISCELLANEOUS
'82 I, THE JURY

JERROLD BRANDT JR.
PRODUCER
'79 BELL JAR, THE*
EXEC IN CHARGE PROD
'82 I, THE JURY
'83 TOUGH ENOUGH

RAYMOND BRANDT
PRODUCTION DESIGNER
'81 INCREDIBLE SHRINKING WOMAN, THE

RICHARD BRANDT
PROPS
'79 RICH KIDS

TONY BRANDT
1ST ASST. DIRECTOR
'80 NIJINSKY*
'82 YES, GIORGIO*

HOWARD BRANDY
PUBLICIST
'82 THINGS ARE TOUGH ALL OVER
'83 GORKY PARK
'84 POPE OF GREENWICH VILLAGE,THE*
UNIT PUBLICIST
'83 NIGHT IN HEAVEN, A*

RICHARD BRANSON
EXECUTIVE PRODUCER
'84 ELECTRIC DREAMS

JOHN BRASCIA
PRODUCER
'80 BALTIMORE BULLET, THE
SCREENPLAY
'80 BALTIMORE BULLET, THE*

FRANCINE BRASSEUR
MISCELLANEOUS
'81 HAPPY BIRTHDAY TO ME

MONIQUE BRASSEUR
PROD. SECRETARY
'80 DEATH SHIP

ARNOLD BRAUN
SOUND
'83 AMERICANA*

SHONY ALEX BRAUN
MISCELLANEOUS
'80 BLACK MARBLE, THE

TONY BRAUN
MISCELLANEOUS
'81 SEA WOLVES, THE

ZEV BRAUN
PRODUCER
'80 FIENDISH PLOT
OF DR. FU MANCHU, THE*

ANDREW BRAUNSBERG
PRODUCER
'79 BEING THERE
'84 ALPHABET CITY
EXECUTIVE PRODUCER
'81 POSTMAN ALWAYS
RINGS TWICE, THE
'82 LOOKIN' TO GET OUT

GEORGE BRAUNSTEIN
PRODUCER
'80 FADE TO BLACK*

RICHARD BRAUSE
SOUND
'84 ALPHABET CITY

CHARLES BRAVERMAN
2ND UNIT DIRECTOR
'80 CAN'T STOP THE MUSIC

RAMON BRAVO
MISCELLANEOUS
'79 SUNBURN
'81 BEYOND THE REEF

ALAN BRAWER
MISCELLANEOUS
'81 BURNING, THE

TINA BRAWNER
ASSOCIATE PRODUCER
'84 LAST NIGHT AT THE ALAMO
PRODUCTION MANAGER
'84 LAST NIGHT AT THE ALAMO

PETER BRAY
UNIT MANAGER
'82 QUEST FOR FIRE

PHIL BRAY
STILLS
'84 AMADEUS*

PETER BRAYHAM
STUNT COORDINATOR
'81 TIME BANDITS*
'82 PINK FLOYD: THE WALL
'84 RAZOR'S EDGE, THE
'84 SCANDALOUS

ANN BREBNER
MISCELLANEOUS
'80 DIE LAUGHING

KENNETH BRECHER
CO-PRODUCER
'82 ZOOT SUIT*

DEREK BRECHIN
ASSISTANT EDITOR
'80 JAZZ SINGER, THE*
'80 LOVING COUPLES*
'81 ENTITY, THE*
'83 TRENCHCOAT

STEPHEN BRECHT
MISCELLANEOUS
'80 GALAXINA

CHARLES BREEN
ART DIRECTOR
'80 BATTLE BEYOND THE STARS*

KATHY BREEN
PROD. COORDINATOR
'84 TERMINATOR, THE

PHILIP BREEN
EXECUTIVE PRODUCER
'84 NATURAL, THE*

KEN BREESE
MISCELLANEOUS
'83 DRAUGHTSMAN CONTRACT, THE

LAURENT BREGEAT
1ST ASST. DIRECTOR
'84 RAZOR'S EDGE, THE*

MARTIN BREGMAN
PRODUCER
'79 SEDUCTION OF JOE TYNAN, THE
'80 SIMON
'81 FOUR SEASONS, THE
'82 VENOM
'83 SCARFACE

CARLA BREITNER
2ND ASST. DIRECTOR
'79 GOLDENGIRL*

ROBERT BREMSON
EXECUTIVE PRODUCER
'79 FIVE DAYS FROM HOME
'80 ALLIGATOR
'82 SWORD AND THE SORCERER, THE
ASSOCIATE PRODUCER
'79 OVER THE EDGE*

ALLISON BRENNAN
PUBLICIST
'83 AMERICANA

JIM BRENNAN
PRODUCTION MANAGER
'82 EVIL UNDER THE SUN
'84 PASSAGE TO INDIA, A*
LOCATIONS
'79 DRACULA*
'80 ROUGH CUT
'83 YENTL*

KEVIN BRENNAN
MISCELLANEOUS
'83 MAN WITH TWO BRAINS, THE

RICHARD BRENNAN
PRODUCER
'82 STARSTRUCK*

ALBERT BRENNER
PRODUCTION DESIGNER
'80 DIVINE MADNESS
'80 HERO AT LARGE
'81 LEGEND OF
THE LONE RANGER, THE
'81 ONLY WHEN I LAUGH
'82 I OUGHT TO BE IN PICTURES
'83 MAX DUGAN RETURNS
'83 TWO OF A KIND
'84 2010
'84 UNFAITHFULLY YOURS

DEBBIE BRENNER
PROD. OFFICE COORD.
'82 SWAMP THING*

FAYE BRENNER
SCRIPT SUPERVISOR
'84 LAST STARFIGHTER, THE

GORDON BRENNER
EDITOR
'79 APPLE DUMPLING GANG RIDES AGAIN, THE
'79 NORTH AVENUE IRREGULARS, THE
'80 HERBIE GOES BANANAS
'80 LAST FLIGHT OF NOAH'S ARK, THE
'81 CONDORMAN
'82 NIGHT CROSSING

JULES BRENNER
CINEMATOGRAPHER
'79 WHEN YOU COMIN' BACK, RED RYDER?

MARTIN BRESIN
SPECIAL EFFECTS
'83 BRAINSTORM*
MISCELLANEOUS
'83 RUMBLEFISH
'83 OUTSIDERS, THE

HERBERT BRESLIN
EXECUTIVE PRODUCER
'82 YES, GIORGIO*

MARTIN BREST
DIRECTOR
'79 GOING IN STYLE
'84 BEVERLY HILLS COP
SCREENPLAY
'79 GOING IN STYLE

DAVID BRETHERTON
EDITOR
'79 WINTER KILLS
'79 GREAT TRAIN ROBBERY, THE
'80 FORMULA, THE*
'82 BEST LITTLE WHOREHOUSE IN TEXAS, THE*
'82 CANNERY ROW
'83 MAN WOMAN AND CHILD

ELAYNE BRETHERTON
ASSISTANT EDITOR
'80 CHANGE OF SEASONS, A
'82 BEST FRIENDS

MELLISSA BRETHERTON
ASSISTANT EDITOR
'80 HEAVEN'S GATE*
'84 LONELY GUY, THE
'84 THIEF OF HEARTS

DENISE BRETON
PUBLICIST
'84 UNTIL SEPTEMBER*

ERIC BREVIG
MISCELLANEOUS
'83 MAN WHO WASN'T THERE, THE

ART BREWER
SPECIAL EFFECTS
'80 BLUES BROTHERS*
'80 CARNY*

COLIN BREWER
EXECUTIVE PRODUCER
'83 KEEP, THE
ASSOCIATE PRODUCER
'79 ESCAPE TO ATHENA

NEIL BREWER
ASSISTANT EDITOR
'82 BEST LITTLE WHOREHOUSE IN TEXAS, THE*

JERRY BRICK
PRODUCER
'84 SWING SHIFT

MAGDALEN BRICK
2ND ASST. DIRECTOR
'81 BURNING, THE

RICHARD BRICK
PRODUCTION MANAGER
'83 SILKWOOD
'84 PLACES IN THE HEART
LOCATIONS
'81 RAGTIME*

GREG BRICKMAN
STUNT COORDINATOR
'80 HANGAR 18*

MARK BRICKMAN
MISCELLANEOUS
'84 STREETS OF FIRE

MARSHALL BRICKMAN
DIRECTOR
'80 SIMON
'83 LOVESICK
SCREENPLAY
'79 MANHATTAN*
'80 SIMON
'83 LOVESICK

PAUL BRICKMAN
DIRECTOR
'83 RISKY BUSINESS
SCREENPLAY
'83 RISKY BUSINESS
'83 DEAL OF THE CENTURY
EXECUTIVE PRODUCER
'83 DEAL OF THE CENTURY*

JEFF BRICMONT
1ST ASST. DIRECTOR
'79 GREAT BANK HOAX, THE

WENDY BRICMONT
EDITOR
'80 ON THE NICKEL
ASSOCIATE EDITOR
'83 ALL THE RIGHT MOVES
ASSISTANT EDITOR
'79 GREAT BANK HOAX, THE

LESLIE BRICUSSE
SCREENPLAY
'81 SUNDAY LOVERS*

JOAN BRIDGE
COSTUMES
'79 HANOVER STREET

JAMES BRIDGES
DIRECTOR
'79 CHINA SYNDROME, THE
'80 URBAN COWBOY
'84 MIKE'S MURDER
SCREENPLAY
'79 CHINA SYNDROME, THE*
'80 URBAN COWBOY*
'84 MIKE'S MURDER

RICHARD BRIDGES
EXECUTIVE PRODUCER
'79 GREAT BANK HOAX, THE*

SUSAN GESTON BRIDGES
MISCELLANEOUS
'80 AMERICAN SUCCESS COMPANY, THE

ERIC BRIEMAN
1ST ASST. DIRECTOR
'84 HARDBODIES

HANK BRIERE
KEY GRIP
'80 HONEYSUCKLE ROSE

ELISA LIVIA BRIGANTI
SCREENPLAY
'83 1990: THE BRONX WARRIORS*

JACK BRIGGS
LOCATIONS
'82 SWAMP THING

JOHN BRIGHT
COSTUMES
'84 BOSTONIANS, THE*

RICHARD BRIGHT
EXECUTIVE PRODUCER
'80 TRIBUTE

JOHN BRIGLEB
MISCELLANEOUS
'82 COME BACK TO THE 5 & 10, JIMMY DEAN, JIMMY DEAN

JOHN BRILEY
SCREENPLAY
'82 GANDHI
'83 ENIGMA

BERNIE BRILLSTEIN
EXECUTIVE PRODUCER
'80 BLUES BROTHERS
'80 UP THE ACADEMY
'81 CONTINENTAL DIVIDE*
'81 NEIGHBORS*
'83 DOCTOR DETROIT
'84 GHOSTBUSTERS

DOUGLAS BRINDLEY
CASTING
'81 BEAST WITHIN, THE*

BOB BRING
EDITOR
'81 FORCE FIVE
MISCELLANEOUS
'82 ZAPPED!

CONNIE BRINK
SPECIAL EFFECTS
'80 GLORIA*
'80 NIGHT OF THE JUGGLER*
'81 ENDLESS LOVE
'81 FORT APACHE, THE BRONX
'81 WOLFEN*
'82 SOUP FOR ONE
'82 STRANGER IS WATCHING, A
'82 I, THE JURY*
'83 AMITYVILLE 3D*
'84 COTTON CLUB, THE

JOHN BRINSON
KEY GRIP
'82 MOTHER LODE
'83 SPACEHUNTER: ADVENTURES IN THE FORBIDDEN ZONE
'84 RUNAWAY

DANIEL BRISSEAU
SOUND
'79 MOONRAKER
'80 FIENDISH PLOT OF DR. FU MANCHU, THE
'81 SUNDAY LOVERS*
'82 MISSING*
'83 EDUCATING RITA*
'83 EXPOSED*
'84 JUST THE WAY YOU ARE
'84 UNTIL SEPTEMBER

CAROL BRISTOW
MISCELLANEOUS
'82 SAFARI 3000

OSSIE BRISTOW
MISCELLANEOUS
'82 SAFARI 3000

VIVIAN BRISTOW
MISCELLANEOUS
'82 SAFARI 3000

MICHAEL BRITTON
2ND ASST. DIRECTOR
'80 ORDINARY PEOPLE

SHOTGUN BRITTON
MAKEUP
'80 BLUES BROTHERS

MIKE BRIXEY
MISCELLANEOUS
'84 FINAL TERROR, THE

ALBERT BROCCOLI
PRODUCER
'79 MOONRAKER
'81 FOR YOUR EYES ONLY
'83 OCTOPUSSY

TONY BROCCOLI
2ND ASST. DIRECTOR
'81 FOR YOUR EYES ONLY*
'83 OCTOPUSSY*

DON BROCHU
ASSISTANT EDITOR
'82 THINGS ARE TOUGH ALL OVER*
'82 TOOTSIE*
'83 SPACEHUNTER: ADVENTURES IN THE FORBIDDEN ZONE*
'84 AGAINST ALL ODDS*

BILL BROCIOUS
KEY GRIP
'82 LOVE AND MONEY

CHRIS BROCK
2ND ASST. DIRECTOR
'83 LORDS OF DISCIPLINE, THE
'84 LASSITER
'84 SHEENA*

MEINER BROCK
HAIR
'82 VENOM

TRICIA BROCK
ASSOCIATE PRODUCER
'79 MR. MIKE'S MONDO VIDEO

JIM BROCKETT
MISCELLANEOUS
'82 SWORD AND THE SORCERER, THE

DAVID BROCKHURST
PRODUCTION DESIGNER
'81 PRIEST OF LOVE*

SUSAN BROCKMAN
PUBLICIST
'80 JUST TELL ME WHAT YOU WANT

ANN BRODIE
MAKEUP
'80 SATURN 3*
'81 LAST CHASE, THE*
'84 SUPERGIRL

BILL BRODIE
PRODUCTION DESIGNER
'82 GREY FOX, THE

JAN BRODIN
SOUND
'80 FADE TO BLACK
'80 GALAXINA
'81 HELL NIGHT
'82 SEDUCTION, THE

JACK BRODSKY
CO-PRODUCER
'84 ROMANCING THE STONE*

BRUCE BRODY
MISCELLANEOUS
'82 DINER

MARCEL BROEKMAN
ASSOCIATE PRODUCER
'81 NIGHT THE LIGHTS WENT OUT IN GEORGIA, THE*

KAREN BROMLEY
PRODUCTION DESIGNER
'80 MIDDLE AGE CRAZY

HENRY BRONCHTEIN
1ST ASST. DIRECTOR
'83 EDDIE AND THE CRUISERS
2ND ASST. DIRECTOR
'81 ENDLESS LOVE
'81 THEY ALL LAUGHED
'82 CHOSEN, THE
'82 I, THE JURY
'83 EASY MONEY
'83 ECHOES
'84 COTTON CLUB, THE*

EDGAR BRONFMAN JR.
PRODUCER
'82 BORDER, THE

TOM BRONSON
COSTUMES
'80 TWINKLE TWINKLE "KILLER" KANE
'81 VICTORY
'82 ROCKY III
'82 FIRST BLOOD
'83 STAYING ALIVE*
'83 TWO OF A KIND
'84 BEVERLY HILLS COP
'84 RHINESTONE*
COSTUME SUPERVISOR
'81 SOUTHERN COMFORT

FRANCESCO BRONZI
ART DIRECTOR
'79 KILLER FISH

LOMA LEE BROOKBANK
PROPS
'80 FADE TO BLACK
'81 HELL NIGHT
'82 EATING RAOUL

KEN BROOKE
MAKEUP
'79 SILENT PARTNER, THE
'79 LOST AND FOUND*
'80 CHANGELING, THE*
'80 TRIBUTE*
'82 AMATEUR, THE
'82 IF YOU COULD SEE WHAT I HEAR
'83 STRANGE INVADERS*
'83 CHRISTMAS STORY, A
'84 POLICE ACADEMY

LEONARD BROOKE
MISCELLANEOUS
'81 THEY ALL LAUGHED

ART BROOKER
KEY GRIP
'79 GREAT SANTINI, THE
'79 WHEN YOU COMIN' BACK, RED RYDER?

TOMMY BROOKER
MISCELLANEOUS
'84 BEAR, THE

ADAM BROOKS
SCRIPT SUPERVISOR
'83 BABY IT'S YOU
'83 LIANNA
'84 RECKLESS

ALBERT BROOKS
DIRECTOR
'79 REAL LIFE
'81 MODERN ROMANCE
SCREENPLAY
'79 REAL LIFE*
'81 MODERN ROMANCE*

BOB BROOKS
ASSISTANT EDITOR
'80 HOME MOVIES*

BOB BROOKS
DIRECTOR
'81 TATTOO

DICK BROOKS
PUBLICIST
'81 PRIVATE LESSONS
'82 SEDUCTION, THE
'83 CHAINED HEAT
UNIT PUBLICIST
'82 LOVE AND MONEY*

DONALD BROOKS
COSTUMES
'79 BELL JAR, THE

JAMES BROOKS
PRODUCER
'79 STARTING OVER*
'83 TERMS OF ENDEARMENT
DIRECTOR
'83 TERMS OF ENDEARMENT
SCREENPLAY
'79 STARTING OVER
'83 TERMS OF ENDEARMENT

JOSEPH BROOKS
PRODUCER
'83 EDDIE AND THE CRUISERS*

MEL BROOKS
PRODUCER
'81 HISTORY OF THE WORLD PART I
'83 TO BE OR NOT TO BE
DIRECTOR
'81 HISTORY OF THE WORLD PART I
SCREENPLAY
'81 HISTORY OF THE WORLD PART I

RICHARD BROOKS
PRODUCER
'83 WRONG IS RIGHT
DIRECTOR
'83 WRONG IS RIGHT
SCREENPLAY
'83 WRONG IS RIGHT

RICHARD BROOKS
CINEMATOGRAPHER
'79 NATURAL ENEMIES

ROLAND BROOKS
ART DIRECTOR
'83 I AM THE CHEESE

JUNE BROOM
PUBLICIST
'80 FLASH GORDON*
'84 SUPERGIRL*

BRIAN BROSNAN
LOCATIONS
'83 TERMS OF ENDEARMENT*
'84 BEST DEFENSE*

STANLEY BROSSETTE
PUBLICIST
'79 ROCKY II
'80 SMALL CIRCLE OF FRIENDS, A
'81 SHARKEY'S MACHINE
'81 INCREDIBLE SHRINKING WOMAN, THE
'81 PATERNITY
'82 BEST FRIENDS
'82 BEST LITTLE WHOREHOUSE IN TEXAS, THE
'83 STROKER ACE
UNIT PUBLICIST
'80 SMOKEY AND THE BANDIT II
'81 CANNONBALL RUN, THE*
'84 BEVERLY HILLS COP
'84 CITY HEAT
'84 CANNONBALL RUN II

FREDERIC BROST
UNIT PROD. MANAGER
'80 RESURRECTION

J.C. BROTHERHOOD
KEY GRIP
'82 FIRST TIME, THE

PEGI BROTMAN
ASSOCIATE PRODUCER
'84 PHILADELPHIA EXPERIMENT, THE
CASTING
'81 ESCAPE FROM NEW YORK
MISCELLANEOUS
'80 FOG, THE

DON BROUGH
2ND ASST. DIRECTOR
'80 KIDNAPPING OF THE PRESIDENT, THE*
'80 TRIBUTE
'82 PORKY'S
'83 CHRISTMAS STORY, A
PROD. COORDINATOR
'83 PORKY'S II THE NEXT DAY

PETER BROUGHAN
PROD. OFFICE COORD.
'83 DRAUGHTSMAN CONTRACT, THE

BRUCE BROUGHTON
MUSIC
'84 ICE PIRATES, THE

CHARLOTTE BROUSSARD
PROD. SECRETARY
'79 ICE CASTLES

JOYCE BROUSSARD
ASSISTANT EDITOR
'79 ICE CASTLES*

BARBARA BROWN
ASSISTANT EDITOR
'84 HOTEL NEW HAMPSHIRE, THE*

CHANTAL BROWN
ASSISTANT EDITOR
'83 OF UNKNOWN ORIGIN*

COURTNEY BROWN
STUNT COORDINATOR
'79 HOT STUFF
'83 JAWS 3-D

DAVID BROWN
PRODUCER
'80 ISLAND, THE*
'81 NEIGHBORS*
'82 VERDICT, THE*

DAVID BROWN
PRODUCTION MANAGER
'84 COMFORT AND JOY
2ND ASST. DIRECTOR
'84 KILLING FIELDS, THE*
LOCATIONS
'83 LOCAL HERO*

DAVID GAVIN BROWN
ART DIRECTOR
'79 PHANTASM

DEBORAH BROWN
CASTING
'81 DRAGONSLAYER*
'81 MOMMIE DEAREST*
'81 NIGHT THE LIGHTS WENT OUT IN GEORGIA, THE*
'82 I, THE JURY
'83 REUBEN, REUBEN*

EMMETT BROWN
KEY GRIP
'81 ENTITY, THE
'82 ESCAPE ARTIST, THE
'82 DEATH VALLEY
'83 RUMBLEFISH
'83 OUTSIDERS, THE
'84 BODY DOUBLE

ERMAN BROWN
HAIR
'81 BEYOND THE REEF

G. MAC BROWN
PRODUCTION MANAGER
'82 AMITYVILLE II: THE POSSESSION
UNIT PROD. MANAGER
'83 AMITYVILLE 3D
'83 I AM THE CHEESE

GARRETT BROWN
MISCELLANEOUS
'79 ROCKY II
'80 SHINING, THE
'80 CAN'T STOP THE MUSIC
'80 XANADU
'81 TAPS
'81 UNDER THE RAINBOW
'81 WOLFEN
'82 DEATHTRAP
'82 LITTLE SEX, A
'83 RETURN OF THE JEDI
'83 BABY IT'S YOU
'83 KING OF COMEDY, THE
'83 LET'S SPEND THE NIGHT TOGETHER
'83 NIGHT IN HEAVEN, A
'83 TWILIGHT ZONE, THE MOVIE
'83 YENTL
'84 GIVE MY REGARDS TO BROAD STREET
'84 INDIANA JONES AND THE TEMPLE OF DOOM

GEORGE BROWN
ART DIRECTOR
'84 PREPPIES

GEORGE MICHAEL BROWN
MISCELLANEOUS
'82 FRIDAY THE 13TH PART THREE IN 3D

GINA BROWN
ASSISTANT EDITOR
'80 DEFIANCE
'82 CHOSEN, THE

GORDON BROWN
ASSISTANT EDITOR
'83 BRITANNIA HOSPITAL*

GREG BROWN
ASSISTANT EDITOR
'82 ZAPPED!*

HILYARD BROWN
ART DIRECTOR
'80 COAST TO COAST
'82 SIX WEEKS

HOWARD BROWN
PRODUCER
'80 CHEECH AND CHONG'S NEXT MOVIE
'81 CHEECH AND CHONG'S NICE DREAMS
'82 THINGS ARE TOUGH ALL OVER

JAMES BROWN
HAIR
'79 BROOD, THE
'80 TRIBUTE*
'81 LAST CHASE, THE*
'81 TICKET TO HEAVEN
'83 RUNNING BRAVE
'83 CHRISTMAS STORY, A
'84 POLICE ACADEMY

JAMIE BROWN
MAKEUP
'82 MOTHER LODE*
'83 GOLDEN SEAL, THE

JEANNIE JEFFRIES BROWN
MAKEUP
'81 KNIGHTRIDERS

JOANNA BROWN
PROD. SECRETARY
'83 OCTOPUSSY*

JOPHERY BROWN
STUNT COORDINATOR
'79 AMERICAN GIGOLO
'83 SCARFACE

LEAH BROWN
PROD. COORDINATOR
'82 PERSONAL BEST*

LEIGH BROWN
SCREENPLAY
'83 CHRISTMAS STORY, A*

LINDA BROWN
MAKEUP
'79 MAN, A WOMAN AND A BANK, A*
'80 CHANGELING, THE*

MICHAEL BROWN
EDITOR
'83 NIGHTMARES*

O. NICHOLAS BROWN
EDITOR
'83 HEART LIKE A WHEEL

R. ANTHONY BROWN
2ND ASST. DIRECTOR
'81 PURSUIT OF D.B. COOPER, THE*
'83 WRONG IS RIGHT*

RAY BROWN
KEY GRIP
'80 BLUE LAGOON
'82 STARSTRUCK
'83 YEAR OF LIVING DANGEROUSLY, THE
'84 PHAR LAP

RICK BROWN
UNIT MANAGER
'82 CREEPSHOW*

RICK BROWN
PROPS
'84 HOT DOG...THE MOVIE

ROBERT BROWN
EDITOR
'80 BRUBAKER
'81 BEAST WITHIN, THE*
'84 POLICE ACADEMY*
'84 POPE OF GREENWICH VILLAGE,THE

ROBERT BROWN
MISCELLANEOUS
'81 FEAR NO EVIL

ROBERT BROWN JR.
EDITOR
'79 AMITYVILLE HORROR, THE

ROBERT LATHAM BROWN
PRODUCTION MANAGER
'82 THING, THE
'84 ICEMAN*
'84 INDIANA JONES AND THE TEMPLE OF DOOM*
UNIT PROD. MANAGER
'79 CONCORDE-AIRPORT '79, THE
'80 NUDE BOMB, THE
'81 ALL NIGHT LONG*
'81 BUSTIN' LOOSE*
'81 GHOST STORY*
'84 BEST DEFENSE*
UNIT MANAGER
'80 BLUES BROTHERS*

ROBIN BROWN

MISCELLANEOUS
'84 PASSAGE TO INDIA, A

ROSS BROWN

1ST ASST. DIRECTOR
'83 TO BE OR NOT TO BE
2ND ASST. DIRECTOR
'80 PRIVATE BENJAMIN
'82 CANNERY ROW
'82 JEKYLL AND HYDE TOGETHER AGAIN
'83 STING II, THE*
'83 NATIONAL LAMPOON'S VACATION

ROSS BROWN

CASTING
'79 WINTER KILLS*
'81 PENNIES FROM HEAVEN*

SAM BROWN

SCREENPLAY
'84 CITY HEAT*

SAMAI BROWN

PROD. COORDINATOR
'79 LOVE AT FIRST BITE

STEVE BROWN

EXECUTIVE PRODUCER
'82 SECOND THOUGHTS

THOMAS BROWN

MISCELLANEOUS
'82 ONE FROM THE HEART

TONY BROWN

1ST ASST. DIRECTOR
'82 HONKYTONK MAN
'84 JOY OF SEX, THE*

VICTOR BROWN

CHOREOGRAPHER
'84 MAKING THE GRADE

WENDY STERNE BROWN

SCRIPT SUPERVISOR
'82 FRANCES

ROBIN BROWNE

MISCELLANEOUS
'83 KEEP, THE

RICOU BROWNING

2ND UNIT DIRECTOR
'79 HOT STUFF
'80 CADDYSHACK
'81 NOBODY'S PERFEKT
MISCELLANEOUS
'80 RAISE THE TITANIC
'83 NEVER SAY NEVER AGAIN

ROD BROWNING

SCREENPLAY
'80 OH! HEAVENLY DOG*

JOHN BROWNJOHN

SCREENPLAY
'80 TESS*

DAVID BROWNLOW

SOUND
'83 VALLEY GIRL
'84 HARDBODIES

MICHAEL BROWNSTONE

LOCATIONS
'82 AMATEUR, THE*
'83 STRANGE INVADERS*
'84 POLICE ACADEMY

JAMES BRUBAKER

EXECUTIVE PRODUCER
'83 RIGHT STUFF, THE
ASSOCIATE PRODUCER
'81 TRUE CONFESSIONS
'84 RHINESTONE*
PRODUCTION MANAGER
'80 RAGING BULL
'81 TRUE CONFESSIONS
'82 ROCKY III
'83 RIGHT STUFF, THE
UNIT PROD. MANAGER
'83 STAYING ALIVE*
'84 RHINESTONE
MISCELLANEOUS
'83 STAYING ALIVE

TONY BRUBAKER

STUNT COORDINATOR
'79 BUCK ROGERS*

BENJAMIN BRUCE

LOCATIONS
'80 FINAL COUNTDOWN, THE*

JAMES BRUCE

ASSISTANT EDITOR
'81 MY DINNER WITH ANDRE*
PROD. COORDINATOR
'81 MY DINNER WITH ANDRE

JERRY BRUCKHEIMER

PRODUCER
'79 AMERICAN GIGOLO
'80 DEFIANCE*
'81 THIEF*
'82 YOUNG DOCTORS IN LOVE
'83 FLASHDANCE*
'84 BEVERLY HILLS COP*
'84 THIEF OF HEARTS*
EXECUTIVE PRODUCER
'82 CAT PEOPLE

PIETER JAN BRUGGE

EXEC IN CHARGE PROD
'84 BREAKIN 2 ELECTRIC BOOGALOO
PRODUCTION MANAGER
'84 MAKING THE GRADE

TOM BRUMBERGER

SPECIAL EFFECTS
'80 EXTERMINATOR, THE

RICHARD BRUMMER

EDITOR
'80 SCHIZOID*
'82 BRAINWAVES

JAMES BRUNER

SCREENPLAY
'81 EYE FOR AN EYE, AN*
ASSOCIATE PRODUCER
'81 EYE FOR AN EYE, AN*

VITO BRUNETTI

SOUND
'83 SMITHEREENS*

ROBERT BRUNNER

MUSIC
'79 NORTH AVENUE IRREGULARS, THE
'81 AMY

DOMINICK BRUNO

PROPS
'81 DEAD AND BURIED
'84 JOY OF SEX, THE

RICHARD BRUNO

COSTUMES
'79 ICE CASTLES
'79 PLAYERS
'79 WHEN A STRANGER CALLS
'80 RAGING BULL*
'81 STRIPES
'83 GORKY PARK
'83 KING OF COMEDY, THE
'84 FALLING IN LOVE

FRANK BRUTON

PROPS
'80 EMPIRE STRIKES BACK, THE
'81 RAIDERS OF THE LOST ARK*

JERRY BRUTSCHE

STUNT COORDINATOR
'80 HOLLYWOOD KNIGHTS, THE
'82 ANNIE*
'84 BODY DOUBLE

MARY BRUYERE

SCRIPT SUPERVISOR
'83 REVENGE OF THE NINJA

REV. ROSALYN BRUYERE

MISCELLANEOUS
'80 RESURRECTION

CLYDE BRYAN

MISCELLANEOUS
'79 ROCK 'N ROLL HIGH SCHOOL

LESLIE BRYAN
KEY GRIP
'79 LEGACY, THE
'81 CAVEMAN

CELIA BRYANT
COSTUMES
'82 I, THE JURY

CHARLSIE BRYANT
SCRIPT SUPERVISOR
'80 CLOSE ENCOUNTERS OF THE THIRD KIND SPECIAL EDITION

CHRIS BRYANT
SCREENPLAY
'80 AWAKENING, THE*

ALAN BRYCE
SPECIAL EFFECTS
'81 FRENCH LIEUTENANT'S WOMAN, THE*

HOPE BRYCE
COSTUMES
'80 HUMAN FACTOR, THE

IAN BRYCE
2ND ASST. DIRECTOR
'84 ELECTRIC DREAMS*
'84 INDIANA JONES AND THE TEMPLE OF DOOM*

BILL BRYDEN
SCREENPLAY
'80 LONG RIDERS, THE*

PASQUALE BUBA
EDITOR
'81 KNIGHTRIDERS*
'82 CREEPSHOW*
1ST ASST. DIRECTOR
'81 KNIGHTRIDERS

TONY BUBA
SOUND
'79 DAWN OF THE DEAD
ASSISTANT EDITOR
'81 KNIGHTRIDERS*

KEVIN BUBRISKI
STILLS
'83 BALLAD OF GREGORIO CORTEZ, THE

DIANE BUCCI
ASSISTANT EDITOR
'84 PREPPIES*

NICOLA BUCCI
PROPS
'79 BLACK STALLION, THE*

TERENCE BUCHINSKY
2ND ASST. DIRECTOR
'80 WHY WOULD I LIE?*
'83 10 TO MIDNIGHT
'84 EVIL THAT MEN DO, THE*

HARRY BUCHMAN
MAKEUP
'79 FISH THAT SAVED PITTSBURGH, THE*

IRVING BUCHMAN
MAKEUP
'79 ON THE YARD
'79 VOICES
'80 MY BODYGUARD*
'80 WINDOWS
'80 NIGHT OF THE JUGGLER
'81 GHOST STORY*
'82 DINER
'82 YES, GIORGIO*
'83 ALL THE RIGHT MOVES
'83 EXPOSED*
'83 WITHOUT A TRACE*
'84 FLAMINGO KID, THE*

FERN BUCHNER
MAKEUP
'79 ALL THAT JAZZ
'79 MANHATTAN
'80 STARDUST MEMORIES
'81 ARTHUR
'81 NIGHTHAWKS
'81 REDS*
'82 SOUP FOR ONE
'82 MIDSUMMER NIGHT'S SEX COMEDY, A
'83 LOVESICK
'83 ZELIG
'84 BROADWAY DANNY ROSE
'84 FIRSTBORN

ROMAN BUCHOK
2ND ASST. DIRECTOR
'84 JUST THE WAY YOU ARE*

DON BUCHSBAUM
PRODUCTION MANAGER
'80 HOG WILD
'81 SCANNERS
'83 RUNNING BRAVE

HAROLD BUCK
ASSOCIATE PRODUCER
'81 SEA WOLVES, THE

JANE BUCK
SCRIPT SUPERVISOR
'79 EUROPEANS, THE
'80 QUARTET
'81 CHARIOTS OF FIRE
'83 HEAT AND DUST

MARY BUCK
CASTING
'82 STAR TREK II THE WRATH OF KHAN

NORMAN BUCK
KEY GRIP
'79 BELL JAR, THE
'81 ARTHUR
'82 SOUP FOR ONE
'83 EASY MONEY
'83 EXPOSED
'83 KING OF COMEDY, THE
'84 GHOSTBUSTERS*
'84 FIRSTBORN

RONALD BUCK
PRODUCER
'84 HARRY & SON*
SCREENPLAY
'84 HARRY & SON*

STEPHEN BUCK
2ND ASST. DIRECTOR
'82 ANDROID
'84 MAKING THE GRADE

MARK BUCKALEW
KEY GRIP
'84 EL NORTE*

KEN BUCKLE
MISCELLANEOUS
'79 FIFTH MUSKETEER, THE

BETTY BUCKLEY
PROD. OFFICE COORD.
'83 TENDER MERCIES
PROD. COORDINATOR
'81 DEADLY BLESSING
'83 TOUGH ENOUGH

NORMAN BUCKLEY
ASSISTANT EDITOR
'84 PLACES IN THE HEART*

MICHAEL BUCUR
ART DIRECTOR
'81 TUCK EVERLASTING

ZORAN BUDAK
1ST ASST. DIRECTOR
'83 HIGH ROAD TO CHINA*

J. TRACY BUDD
PROPS
'82 PORKY'S
'83 CHRISTMAS STORY, A
'83 PORKY'S II THE NEXT DAY
'84 MRS. SOFFEL

ROY BUDD
MUSIC
'81 SEA WOLVES, THE

AVERY BUDDY
SCREENPLAY
'81 ON THE RIGHT TRACK*
CO-PRODUCER
'81 ON THE RIGHT TRACK*

JOS BUDIE
2ND ASST. DIRECTOR
'83 CHEECH AND CHONG'S STILL SMOKIN'

DANIEL BUDIN
ART DIRECTOR
'84 CHEECH AND CHONG'S THE CORSICAN BROTHERS

PATRICIA BUDZ
HAIR
'79 BUCK ROGERS

JOHN BUECHLER
MISCELLANEOUS
'82 ANDROID
'83 MAUSOLEUM

JACK BUEHLER
COSTUMES
'79 ROCK 'N ROLL HIGH SCHOOL
'79 ROLLER BOOGIE
'81 HOWLING, THE
'83 CUJO
'83 TIMERIDER

FRANK BUENO
2ND ASST. DIRECTOR
'79 VILLAIN, THE*
'80 SMOKEY AND THE BANDIT II*
'81 CANNONBALL RUN, THE
'82 MEGAFORCE*
'82 TOY, THE*

NORTON BUFFALO
MUSIC
'83 EDDIE MACON'S RUN

ELAINE BUFFINGTON
MAKEUP
'84 MARVIN AND TIGE*
HAIR
'84 MARVIN AND TIGE*

JEFF BUHAI
SCREENPLAY
'84 REVENGE OF THE NERDS*

YACOV BUKMAN
KEY GRIP
'82 PARADISE

BILL BUKOWSKI
MISCELLANEOUS
'81 COMIN' AT YA!
'83 MAN WHO WASN'T THERE, THE

ENZO BULGARELLI
PRODUCTION DESIGNER
'83 LONELY LADY, THE

DONKO BULJAN
MISCELLANEOUS
'83 HIGH ROAD TO CHINA

FRANCO BULLATI
UNIT MANAGER
'83 BLACK STALLION RETURNS, THE*

HENRY BUMSTEAD
PRODUCTION DESIGNER
'79 CONCORDE-AIRPORT '79, THE
'79 LITTLE ROMANCE, A
'80 SMOKEY AND THE BANDIT II
'82 WORLD ACCORDING TO GARP, THE
'84 HARRY & SON
'84 LITTLE DRUMMER GIRL, THE

PATTY BUNCH
MAKEUP
'83 JOYSTICKS

JOHN BUNKER
SPECIAL EFFECTS
'81 TIME BANDITS

DAVID BUNNETT
MISCELLANEOUS
'81 DRAGONSLAYER

MARK BUNTZMAN
PRODUCER
'80 EXTERMINATOR, THE
'84 EXTERMINATOR II*
DIRECTOR
'84 EXTERMINATOR II
SCREENPLAY
'84 EXTERMINATOR II*

JOYCE BUNUEL
SCREENPLAY
'81 TATTOO

LYNDA BURBANK
ART DIRECTOR
'84 REPO MAN*

CURTIS BURCH
SCREENPLAY
'83 JOYSTICKS*
ASSOCIATE PRODUCER
'80 WITHOUT WARNING*
'83 JOYSTICKS*
EDITOR
'80 WITHOUT WARNING
CASTING
'83 JOYSTICKS

JACKIE BURCH
CASTING
'83 D.C. CAB*
'84 CLOAK AND DAGGER*
'84 SIXTEEN CANDLES

WILLIAM BURCH
MISCELLANEOUS
'82 THINGS ARE TOUGH ALL OVER

JEFFREY BURCHELL
PROPS
'84 CHOOSE ME

PATRICIA BURCK
HAIR
'80 IN GOD WE TRUST
'80 MOTEL HELL

FRANCOIS BUREAU
LOCATIONS
'84 CHEECH AND CHONG'S THE CORSICAN BROTHERS

BARBARA BURGDORF
COSTUMES
'80 OCTAGON, THE

CORKY BURGER
EXEC IN CHARGE PROD
'81 BURNING, THE

AL BURGESS
PRODUCTION MANAGER
'79 GREAT TRAIN ROBBERY, THE
MISCELLANEOUS
'80 NIJINSKY

ANTHONY BURGESS
MISCELLANEOUS
'82 QUEST FOR FIRE

BRIAN BURGESS
MISCELLANEOUS
'81 FINAL CONFLICT, THE

ERIC BURGESS
MISCELLANEOUS
'79 MOONRAKER

HOVEY BURGESS
CHOREOGRAPHER
'80 POPEYE*

RITA BURGESS
ASSISTANT EDITOR
'80 FLASH GORDON*

GEOFFREY BURGON
MUSIC
'79 MONTY PYTHON'S LIFE OF BRIAN
'81 DOGS OF WAR, THE

CHRIS BURKE
ART DIRECTOR
'80 DEATH SHIP*
'82 PINK FLOYD: THE WALL*

JOHN BURKE

SPECIAL EFFECTS
'82 ENDANGERED SPECIES*

JOHN BURKE SR.

SPECIAL EFFECTS
'81 S.O.B.

MARTYN BURKE

PRODUCER
'81 LAST CHASE, THE*
DIRECTOR
'81 LAST CHASE, THE
SCREENPLAY
'81 LAST CHASE, THE*
'84 TOP SECRET!*

MICHELE BURKE

MAKEUP
'80 TERROR TRAIN*
'82 QUEST FOR FIRE*

MILDRED BURKE

MISCELLANEOUS
'81 ...ALL THE MARBLES

ROBERT BURKE

ASSOCIATE PRODUCER
'79 NATURAL ENEMIES*

SHARON BURKE

ASSISTANT EDITOR
'84 IMPULSE*

JEFF BURKHART

SCREENPLAY
'84 WHERE THE BOYS ARE*

ELLIS BURMAN

MISCELLANEOUS
'79 PROPHECY

GLENN BURMAN

ASSISTANT EDITOR
'82 QUEST FOR FIRE

TOM BURMAN

MISCELLANEOUS
'79 PROPHECY
'80 HEAVEN'S GATE
'81 BEAST WITHIN, THE
'81 HAND, THE
'81 MY BLOODY VALENTINE
'82 CAT PEOPLE
'82 HALLOWEEN III: SEASON OF THE WITCH
'82 MOTHER LODE
'83 SPACEHUNTER: ADVENTURES IN THE FORBIDDEN ZONE
'84 BODY DOUBLE

MARK BURNER

MISCELLANEOUS
'83 BALLAD OF GREGORIO CORTEZ, THE

JOHN BURNETT

EDITOR
'79 ...AND JUSTICE FOR ALL
'80 CAN'T STOP THE MUSIC
'81 RICH AND FAMOUS
'81 DEATH HUNT*
'82 GREASE 2
'84 IRRECONCILABLE DIFFERENCES
MISCELLANEOUS
'83 STAYING ALIVE

FRED BURNHAM

SOUND
'83 LIANNA*
STILLS
'80 RETURN OF THE SECAUCUS SEVEN, THE
'83 LIANNA

ALLAN BURNS

SCREENPLAY
'79 BUTCH AND SUNDANCE: THE EARLY YEARS
'79 LITTLE ROMANCE, A
'84 JUST THE WAY YOU ARE

BARBARA BURNS

PROD. COORDINATOR
'80 GILDA LIVE

BRIAN BURNS

MISCELLANEOUS
'81 GALLIPOLI

FRANCIS BURNS

SCREENPLAY
'80 ROUGH CUT

JACK BURNS

SCREENPLAY
'79 MUPPET MOVIE, THE*

MARK BURNS

ASSISTANT EDITOR
'83 WITHOUT A TRACE

MILLY BURNS

ART DIRECTOR
'79 YANKS
PRODUCTION DESIGNER
'81 TIME BANDITS

PATRICK BURNS

2ND ASST. DIRECTOR
'83 LET'S SPEND THE NIGHT TOGETHER*

RALPH BURNS

MUSIC
'82 MY FAVORITE YEAR
'83 STAR 80
'83 KISS ME GOODBYE
'83 NATIONAL LAMPOON'S VACATION
MUSIC SUPERVISOR
'80 URBAN COWBOY
MISCELLANEOUS
'79 ALL THAT JAZZ
'82 ANNIE

ROBERT BURNS

ART DIRECTOR
'79 TOURIST TRAP
'81 HOWLING, THE
'83 MAUSOLEUM

STAN BURNS

SCREENPLAY
'81 CHARLIE CHAN AND THE CURSE OF THE DRAGON QUEEN*

TOMMY BURNS

2ND ASST. DIRECTOR
'84 BREAKIN 2 ELECTRIC BOOGALOO*

PETER BURRELL

PRODUCER
'82 ZOOT SUIT
ASSOCIATE PRODUCER
'80 SMOKEY AND THE BANDIT II
UNIT PROD. MANAGER
'80 SMOKEY AND THE BANDIT II
MISCELLANEOUS
'80 NUDE BOMB, THE

WALTER BURRELL

PUBLICIST
'79 BUDDY HOLLY STORY, THE

TIMOTHY BURRILL

PRODUCER
'84 SUPERGIRL
EXECUTIVE PRODUCER
'83 ANOTHER TIME, ANOTHER PLACE
CO-PRODUCER
'80 TESS
'83 PIRATES OF PENZANCE, THE

GEOFF BURROWES

PRODUCER
'83 MAN FROM SNOWY RIVER, THE

JAMES BURROWS

DIRECTOR
'82 PARTNERS

JOHN BURROWS

ASSOCIATE PRODUCER
'84 NIGHTMARE ON ELM STREET, A
PRODUCTION MANAGER
'84 NIGHTMARE ON ELM STREET, A

ROSEMARY BURROWS

COSTUME SUPERVISOR
'79 ARABIAN ADVENTURE
'80 HOPSCOTCH

ALLEN BURRY

PUBLICIST
- '81 GREAT MUPPET CAPER, THE
- '82 SHOOT THE MOON*
- '82 MOONLIGHTING
- '82 PINK FLOYD: THE WALL
- '83 SUPERMAN III*
- '83 YENTL

UNIT PUBLICIST
- '84 ANOTHER COUNTRY
- '84 ELECTRIC DREAMS

TOM BURSTALL

1ST ASST. DIRECTOR
- '81 ROAD GAMES

JESSICA BURSTEIN

STILLS
- '80 GLORIA*

CHRIS BURT

PRODUCTION MANAGER
- '81 FRENCH LIEUTENANT'S WOMAN, THE

CHRISTINE BURT

LOCATIONS
- '80 HOG WILD
- '81 SCANNERS

BILLY BURTON

STUNT COORDINATOR
- '79 PROPHECY*
- '81 EYEWITNESS

MISCELLANEOUS
- '79 GAME OF DEATH

SEAN BURTON

EDITOR
- '83 RETURN OF THE JEDI*
- '84 UNTIL SEPTEMBER

2ND UNIT DIRECTOR
- '84 UNTIL SEPTEMBER

WILLIE BURTON

SOUND
- '79 BUDDY HOLLY STORY, THE
- '80 ALTERED STATES
- '80 INSIDE MOVES
- '80 URBAN COWBOY
- '81 DEVIL AND MAX DEVLIN, THE
- '81 ENTITY, THE
- '81 UNDER THE RAINBOW
- '82 SIX WEEKS
- '83 DEAL OF THE CENTURY
- '83 INDEPENDENCE DAY
- '83 WAR GAMES
- '84 ALL OF ME
- '84 HARD TO HOLD
- '84 MIKE'S MURDER

BEN BURTT

MISCELLANEOUS
- '82 DARK CRYSTAL, THE
- '82 E.T. THE EXTRA-TERRESTRIAL
- '84 INDIANA JONES AND THE TEMPLE OF DOOM

STEPHEN BURUM

CINEMATOGRAPHER
- '81 ENTITY, THE
- '82 ESCAPE ARTIST, THE
- '82 DEATH VALLEY
- '83 RUMBLEFISH
- '83 SOMETHING WICKED THIS WAY COMES
- '83 OUTSIDERS, THE
- '83 UNCOMMON VALOR
- '84 BODY DOUBLE

MISCELLANEOUS
- '79 APOCALYPSE NOW
- '79 BLACK STALLION, THE

LOUIS BURWELL

MAKEUP
- '83 DRAUGHTSMAN CONTRACT, THE

TERRY BUSBY

ASSISTANT EDITOR
- '80 FAME*
- '81 DOGS OF WAR, THE*

DICK BUSH

CINEMATOGRAPHER
- '79 LEGACY, THE*
- '79 YANKS
- '80 ONE-TRICK PONY
- '81 FAN, THE
- '82 VICTOR/VICTORIA
- '83 CURSE OF THE PINK PANTHER
- '83 TRAIL OF THE PINK PANTHER
- '84 CRIMES OF PASSION
- '84 PHILADELPHIA EXPERIMENT, THE

GIANNINA BUSH

MAKEUP
- '79 FRISCO KID, THE*

JOHN BUSH

LOCATIONS
- '79 TIME AFTER TIME
- '80 THOSE LIPS, THOSE EYES*
- '81 HONKY TONK FREEWAY*

JOHN BUSH

STILLS
- '83 CUJO*

JOHN ROSS BUSH

1ST ASST. DIRECTOR
- '81 HELL NIGHT
- '82 SWORD AND THE SORCERER, THE

LOCATIONS
- '84 NO SMALL AFFAIR

RAYMOND BUSH

EDITOR
- '83 RICHARD PRYOR: HERE AND NOW

CATHARINE BUSHNELL

STILLS
- '79 LAST EMBRACE*
- '79 VOICES
- '80 FAME*
- '82 DINER
- '82 YES, GIORGIO*
- '83 HUNGER, THE*

SCOTT BUSHNELL

PRODUCER
- '82 COME BACK TO THE 5 & 10, JIMMY DEAN, JIMMY DEAN

ASSOCIATE PRODUCER
- '79 PERFECT COUPLE, A*
- '79 REMEMBER MY NAME*
- '80 HEALTH*
- '80 POPEYE
- '83 STREAMERS

COSTUMES
- '79 QUINTET
- '80 POPEYE
- '82 COME BACK TO THE 5 & 10, JIMMY DEAN, JIMMY DEAN
- '83 STREAMERS

WILLIAM BUSHNELL

ASSOCIATE PRODUCER
- '80 ON THE NICKEL

PRODUCTION MANAGER
- '80 ON THE NICKEL

MARK BUSSAN

MAKEUP
- '79 IN-LAWS, THE*

MISCELLANEOUS
- '82 JEKYLL AND HYDE TOGETHER AGAIN

ALFREDO BUSTOS

MISCELLANEOUS
- '84 EL NORTE

LOU BUTERA

MISCELLANEOUS
- '80 BALTIMORE BULLET, THE
- '84 RACING WITH THE MOON

MARLENE BUTLAND

PROD. SECRETARY
- '80 SHINING, THE*

AARON BUTLER

CASTING
- '81 GRADUATION DAY

AARON BUTLER

MISCELLANEOUS
- '83 CHAINED HEAT

BILL BUTLER
CINEMATOGRAPHER
'79 ROCKY II
'79 ICE CASTLES
'80 CAN'T STOP THE MUSIC
'80 IT'S MY TURN
'81 STRIPES
'81 NIGHT THE LIGHTS WENT OUT IN GEORGIA, THE
'82 ROCKY III
'83 STING II, THE

BILL BUTLER
EDITOR
'79 LOST AND FOUND
'80 HOW TO BEAT THE HIGH COST OF LIVING
'81 ON THE RIGHT TRACK
'82 LITTLE SEX, A
'84 UP THE CREEK

DAVID BUTLER
MISCELLANEOUS
'82 MEGAFORCE
'84 BIRDY

DICK BUTLER
STUNT COORDINATOR
'80 DIE LAUGHING
'80 UP THE ACADEMY

GAE BUTLER
HAIR
'80 WHY WOULD I LIE?

JOHN BUTLER
SOUND
'81 KNIGHTRIDERS

MICHAEL BUTLER
CINEMATOGRAPHER
'80 SMALL CIRCLE OF FRIENDS, A
'80 SMOKEY AND THE BANDIT II
'81 CANNONBALL RUN, THE
'82 MEGAFORCE

MICHAEL BUTLER
PRODUCER
'79 HAIR*

MICHAEL BUTLER
SCREENPLAY
'84 FLASHPOINT*

MIKE BUTLER
COSTUMES
'81 UNDER THE RAINBOW

PETER BUTLER
1ST ASST. DIRECTOR
'80 KIDS ARE ALL RIGHT, THE*

ROBERT BUTLER
DIRECTOR
'80 NIGHT OF THE JUGGLER
'84 UP THE CREEK

STEVE BUTLER
ASSISTANT EDITOR
'80 HOW TO BEAT THE HIGH COST OF LIVING
'81 ON THE RIGHT TRACK
'82 LITTLE SEX, A*
'84 UP THE CREEK

LIZ BUTTERFIELD
PRODUCTION MANAGER
'79 RUNNING*
'79 SILENT PARTNER, THE*
'80 MIDDLE AGE CRAZY*

ED BUTTERWORTH
MAKEUP
'78 DEER HUNTER, THE*
'80 AIRPLANE
'80 DIVINE MADNESS*
'80 LAST MARRIED COUPLE IN AMERICA, THE*
'81 CANNONBALL RUN, THE*
'81 MAN WHO SAW TOMORROW, THE*
'82 BARBAROSA*
'83 BRAINSTORM*

ROY BUTTON
2ND ASST. DIRECTOR
'80 EMPIRE STRIKES BACK, THE*
'81 RAIDERS OF THE LOST ARK*
'83 RETURN OF THE JEDI*
'83 NEVER SAY NEVER AGAIN*
'84 INDIANA JONES AND THE TEMPLE OF DOOM*

JAN BYCZYCKI
MISCELLANEOUS
'82 SOPHIE'S CHOICE

GLENN BYDWELL
PRODUCTION DESIGNER
'80 TERROR TRAIN

MINDY BYER
ASSISTANT EDITOR
'82 CHILLY SCENES OF WINTER

ARMELDA BYRD
MAKEUP
'83 BIG SCORE, THE
HAIR
'83 BIG SCORE, THE

JOSEPH BYRD
MUSIC
'80 HEALTH

RODNEY BYRD
SPECIAL EFFECTS
'84 SWING SHIFT*

BOBBY BYRNE
CINEMATOGRAPHER
'79 VILLAIN, THE
'80 THOSE LIPS, THOSE EYES
'81 PATERNITY
'82 THINGS ARE TOUGH ALL OVER
'82 CHILLY SCENES OF WINTER
'84 SIXTEEN CANDLES
MISCELLANEOUS
'80 DIVINE MADNESS
'80 INSIDE MOVES
'81 LEGEND OF THE LONE RANGER,THE
'82 BEST LITTLE WHOREHOUSE IN TEXAS, THE
'83 BREATHLESS

DOROTHY BYRNE
HAIR
'79 VILLAIN, THE*
'83 UNCOMMON VALOR*
'84 WOMAN IN RED, THE*

MARGARET BYRNE
PRODUCTION MANAGER
'81 MAN WHO SAW TOMORROW, THE*

SEAMUS BYRNE
PRODUCTION MANAGER
'80 OUTSIDER, THE

JOHN BYRUM
DIRECTOR
'80 HEARTBEAT
'84 RAZOR'S EDGE, THE
SCREENPLAY
'80 HEARTBEAT
'81 SPHINX
'84 RAZOR'S EDGE, THE*
'84 SCANDALOUS*

C

JAMES CAAN
DIRECTOR
'80 HIDE IN PLAIN SIGHT

RONNIE CAAN
PRODUCER
'81 THIEF*

LUCIANA CABARGA
PROD. COORDINATOR
'84 UNDER THE VOLCANO*

RUFINO CABRALES
ASSISTANT EDITOR
'83 BLIND RAGE

JOHN CABRERA
CINEMATOGRAPHER
'79 JAGUAR LIVES

JOSE LUIS CABRERA
MAKEUP
'81 SPHINX*

JOHN CACAVAS
MUSIC
'80 HANGAR 18
'83 MORTUARY

SANDRA CADE
CASTING
'82 SPLIT IMAGE*

PATRICK CADELL
1ST ASST. DIRECTOR
'84 PASSAGE TO INDIA, A*
2ND ASST. DIRECTOR
'81 RAIDERS OF THE LOST ARK*

RICHARD CADGER
ASSISTANT EDITOR
'80 TRIBUTE
'82 PORKY'S
'83 CHRISTMAS STORY, A*
'83 PORKY'S II THE NEXT DAY
'84 RHINESTONE*

ROGER CADIEUX
KEY GRIP
'82 BY DESIGN

DAVID CADWALLADER
KEY GRIP
'79 HANOVER STREET
'79 PRISONER OF ZENDA, THE*
'81 OUTLAND

FITCH CADY
UNIT PROD. MANAGER
'82 THING, THE
UNIT MANAGER
'83 NEVER CRY WOLF
'83 GOLDEN SEAL, THE
'84 ICEMAN
LOCATIONS
'82 BY DESIGN

JOHN CAFFERTY
MUSIC
'83 EDDIE AND THE CRUISERS

RICHARD CAFFEY
PRODUCER
'79 BUCK ROGERS

JOHN CAGLIONE
MISCELLANEOUS
'82 QUEST FOR FIRE
'83 AMITYVILLE 3D
'83 ZELIG
'84 BIRDY

JOHN CAGLIONE JR.
MISCELLANEOUS
'82 AMITYVILLE II:THE POSSESSION
'84 COTTON CLUB, THE
'84 C.H.U.D.

ROBIN CAGNEY
MISCELLANEOUS
'83 NATE & HAYES

DON CAHILL
MISCELLANEOUS
'81 THIEF

KATHY CURTIS CAHILL
ART DIRECTOR
'80 SCHIZOID
PROPS
'79 ROLLER BOOGIE
'80 GALAXINA
'80 SCHIZOID

PATRICIA CAHILL
PROD. SECRETARY
'83 OF UNKNOWN ORIGIN

DANIEL TODD CAHN
ASSISTANT EDITOR
'79 ICE CASTLES*
'79 1941
'80 OH GOD! BOOK II
'81 ...ALL THE MARBLES*

DANN CAHN
EDITOR
'80 OCTAGON, THE
'83 TOUGH ENOUGH

DIANNE CAHOON
COSTUME SUPERVISOR
'81 PURSUIT OF D.B. COOPER, THE*

CHRISTOPHER CAIN
DIRECTOR
'84 STONE BOY, THE

MAURICE CAIN
ART DIRECTOR
'81 SEA WOLVES, THE
'83 FINAL OPTION, THE
PRODUCTION DESIGNER
'83 NATE & HAYES

ROGER CAIN
ART DIRECTOR
'84 INDIANA JONES AND THE TEMPLE OF DOOM*

SYD CAIN
PRODUCTION DESIGNER
'81 SEA WOLVES, THE
'83 FINAL OPTION, THE

ALLISON CAINE
MISCELLANEOUS
'80 CARNY

JOSEPH CALA
SCREENPLAY
'84 ANGEL*

PAUL CALABRIA
MISCELLANEOUS
'83 SUDDEN IMPACT
'84 CITY HEAT
'84 TIGHTROPE

BEN CALDWELL
STILLS
'79 PENITENTIARY

HELEN CALDWELL
SCRIPT SUPERVISOR
'84 LOVE STREAMS
'84 PARIS, TEXAS

STEVEN CALDWELL
MISCELLANEOUS
'82 ANDROID

SUSAN CALDWELL
HAIR
'84 PURPLE RAIN*

CHARLES CALELLO
MUSIC
'83 LONELY LADY, THE

RICHARD CALKINS
MISCELLANEOUS
'82 E.T. THE EXTRA-TERRESTRIAL
'82 POLTERGEIST
'84 RACING WITH THE MOON

COLLEEN CALLAGHAN
HAIR
'79 SEDUCTION OF JOE TYNAN, THE
'80 CARNY*
'80 MY BODYGUARD
'82 STRANGER IS WATCHING, A
'82 AUTHOR, AUTHOR
'82 DEATHTRAP
'83 WITHOUT A TRACE

DUKE CALLAGHAN
CINEMATOGRAPHER
'82 CONAN THE BARBARIAN

VINCE CALLAGHAN
MAKEUP
'80 GLORIA
'81 FOUR FRIENDS
'82 LITTLE SEX, A
'83 WITHOUT A TRACE*
MISCELLANEOUS
'83 AMITYVILLE 3D

ED CALLAHAN
PROPS
'83 SWEET SIXTEEN

GENE CALLAHAN
PRODUCTION DESIGNER
'79 CHAPTER TWO
'80 SEEMS LIKE OLD TIMES
'80 LAST MARRIED COUPLE IN AMERICA, THE
'81 WHOSE LIFE IS IT ANYWAY?
'82 GREASE 2
'83 SURVIVORS, THE
'84 PLACES IN THE HEART

VICKI CALLAHAN
MISCELLANEOUS
'82 LOVE CHILD

JERRY CALLAWAY
MISCELLANEOUS
'83 LONE WOLF MCQUADE

BARRY CALLIER
LOCATIONS
'83 HEART LIKE A WHEEL*

CHRISTOPHER CALLIS
CINEMATOGRAPHER
'84 TOP SECRET!

DAVID CALLOWAY
MISCELLANEOUS
'84 HARDBODIES

BRUCE CALNAN
CO-PRODUCER
'80 HAPPY BIRTHDAY, GEMINI

ADAMS CALVERT
SPECIAL EFFECTS
'80 CARNY*
'80 MOTEL HELL
'81 FORCE FIVE
'82 FIGHTING BACK

JOHN CALVERT
MISCELLANEOUS
'79 APOCALYPSE NOW

JOSE CALVO
ASSISTANT EDITOR
'80 GUYANA: CULT OF THE DAMNED

ROBERTO CAMACHO
SOUND
'81 HIGH RISK
'84 EVIL THAT MEN DO, THE

RAUL CAMARENA
SPECIAL EFFECTS
'80 GUYANA: CULT OF THE DAMNED

JACQUELINE CAMBAS
EDITOR
'82 ZOOT SUIT
'84 CITY HEAT
'84 RACING WITH THE MOON
ASSISTANT EDITOR
'79 HARDCORE

DONN CAMBERN
EDITOR
'79 TIME AFTER TIME
'80 SMOKEY AND THE BANDIT II*
'80 WILLIE & PHIL
'81 CANNONBALL RUN, THE*
'81 PATERNITY
'82 TEMPEST
'84 ROMANCING THE STONE*
2ND UNIT DIRECTOR
'82 TEMPEST

ALLAN CAMERON
ART DIRECTOR
'81 FRENCH LIEUTENANT'S WOMAN, THE*
PRODUCTION DESIGNER
'83 BEYOND THE LIMIT

ANNE CAMERON
SCREENPLAY
'81 TICKET TO HEAVEN*

DENZEL CAMERON
MISCELLANEOUS
'83 LONE WOLF MCQUADE
'83 MAN FROM SNOWY RIVER, THE
'84 BACHELOR PARTY

JAMES CAMERON
DIRECTOR
'83 PIRANHA II: THE SPAWNING
'84 TERMINATOR, THE
SCREENPLAY
'84 TERMINATOR, THE*
ART DIRECTOR
'80 BATTLE BEYOND THE STARS*
PRODUCTION DESIGNER
'81 GALAXY OF TERROR*
2ND UNIT DIRECTOR
'81 GALAXY OF TERROR

JOAN CAMERON
ASSISTANT EDITOR
'79 ALL THAT JAZZ*

JOHN CAMERON
MUSIC
'79 LOST AND FOUND
'79 SUNBURN
'80 MIRROR CRACK'D, THE

RUTH CAMERON
MISCELLANEOUS
'80 AMERICAN SUCCESS COMPANY, THE

TRICIA CAMERON
HAIR
'83 GORKY PARK

JAMES CAMOMILE
SPECIAL EFFECTS
'80 HEAVEN'S GATE*
'81 TAPS*
'82 NATIONAL LAMPOON'S CLASS REUNION*

JOE CAMP
PRODUCER
'79 DOUBLE MCGUFFIN, THE
'80 OH! HEAVENLY DOG
DIRECTOR
'79 DOUBLE MCGUFFIN, THE
'80 FOR THE LOVE OF BENJI
'80 OH! HEAVENLY DOG
SCREENPLAY
'79 DOUBLE MCGUFFIN, THE
'80 FOR THE LOVE OF BENJI
'80 OH! HEAVENLY DOG*
EXECUTIVE PRODUCER
'80 FOR THE LOVE OF BENJI

CARLO CAMPANA
KEY GRIP
'80 PROM NIGHT
'82 QUEST FOR FIRE
'83 SCREWBALLS

ALISON CAMPBELL
PROD. SECRETARY
'84 COMFORT AND JOY

BRUCE CAMPBELL
EXECUTIVE PRODUCER
'83 EVIL DEAD, THE*

CHRIS CAMPBELL
ART DIRECTOR
'84 PHILADELPHIA EXPERIMENT, THE

DAVID CAMPBELL
MUSIC
'83 ALL THE RIGHT MOVES

MALCOLM CAMPBELL
EDITOR
'81 AMERICAN WEREWOLF IN LONDON, AN
'83 TRADING PLACES
'83 TWILIGHT ZONE, THE MOVIE*
ASSISTANT EDITOR
'80 BLUES BROTHERS*

MIKE CAMPBELL
EDITOR
'80 DEATH SHIP

SALLY CAMPBELL
PROPS
'82 STARSTRUCK*
MISCELLANEOUS
'79 MY BRILLIANT CAREER

STEWART CAMPBELL
ART DIRECTOR
'80 URBAN COWBOY
'81 TRUE CONFESSIONS
'83 RIGHT STUFF, THE*
'84 BIRDY*
PRODUCTION DESIGNER
'83 INDEPENDENCE DAY
MISCELLANEOUS
'84 PHILADELPHIA EXPERIMENT, THE

TOM CAMPBELL
MISCELLANEOUS
'81 GALAXY OF TERROR

SAM CAMPOREALE
ASSISTANT EDITOR
'83 ANGELO, MY LOVE

FILIPPO CAMPUS
LOCATIONS
'83 HANNA K*

DANIEL CANDIB
ASSISTANT EDITOR
'82 SHOOT THE MOON*
'84 BIRDY*

RICHARD CANDIB
ASSISTANT EDITOR
'82 SHOOT THE MOON*
'83 KING OF COMEDY, THE
'84 BIRDY*

TARA CANDOLI
MAKEUP
'82 BEASTMASTER, THE

VIOLET CANE
COSTUME SUPERVISOR
'83 UNCOMMON VALOR*

JOHN CANEMAKER
MISCELLANEOUS
'82 WORLD ACCORDING TO GARP, THE

SERENA CANEVARI
SCRIPT SUPERVISOR
'83 BLACK STALLION RETURNS, THE

WILLIAM CANFIELD
SPECIAL EFFECTS
'79 STARTING OVER

BERT CANN
STILLS
'80 NIJINSKY
'81 SPHINX

MARY ELLEN CANNIFF
2ND ASST. DIRECTOR
'80 BORDERLINE
'83 LET'S SPEND THE NIGHT TOGETHER*

JAY CANNISTRACI
MAKEUP
'82 AUTHOR, AUTHOR
'82 I, THE JURY
'82 TEMPEST*
'83 BAD BOYS

BRUCE CANNON
ASSISTANT EDITOR
'83 BIG CHILL, THE*

GREG CANNON
MISCELLANEOUS
'80 WITHOUT WARNING

POPPY CANNON
COSTUMES
'84 EVIL THAT MEN DO, THE
COSTUME SUPERVISOR
'83 10 TO MIDNIGHT

REUBEN CANNON
CASTING
'81 ...ALL THE MARBLES
'81 DEATH HUNT
'82 SECOND THOUGHTS
'84 SOLDIER'S STORY, A

TERRI CANNON
HAIR
'80 SMOKEY AND THE BANDIT II*
'81 ABSENCE OF MALICE
'81 BACK ROADS
'82 THINGS ARE TOUGH ALL OVER
'83 KISS ME GOODBYE

VINCE CANNON
ASSOCIATE PRODUCER
'80 COAST TO COAST

LARRY CANO
EXECUTIVE PRODUCER
'83 SILKWOOD*

MILENA CANONERO
COSTUMES
'80 SHINING, THE
'81 CHARIOTS OF FIRE
'83 HUNGER, THE
'84 COTTON CLUB, THE
'84 GIVE MY REGARDS TO BROAD STREET

LARRY CANSLER
MUSIC
'83 SMOKEY AND THE BANDIT III
MISCELLANEOUS
'84 SONGWRITER

GENE CANTAMESSA
SOUND
'79 1941
'79 PROPHECY
'80 BORDERLINE
'80 CLOSE ENCOUNTERS OF THE THIRD KIND SPECIAL EDITION
'80 COAST TO COAST
'80 HIDE IN PLAIN SIGHT
'81 STRIPES
'81 HISTORY OF THE WORLD PART I*
'82 ANNIE
'82 E.T. THE EXTRA-TERRESTRIAL
'82 THAT CHAMPIONSHIP SEASON
'82 TOY, THE
'83 BIG CHILL, THE
'83 TO BE OR NOT TO BE
'83 WRONG IS RIGHT
'84 GHOSTBUSTERS
'84 STAR TREK III: THE SEARCH FOR SPOCK
'84 2010

STEVE CANTAMESSA
SOUND
'81 HISTORY OF THE WORLD PART I*

STANLEY CANTER
PRODUCER
'84 GREYSTOKE: THE LEGEND OF TARZAN, LORD OF THE APES*

MARK CANTON
PRODUCER
'80 DIE LAUGHING*
EXEC IN CHARGE PROD
'80 CADDYSHACK

NEIL CANTON

PRODUCER
'84 ADVENTURES OF BUCKAROO BANZAI ACROSS THE 8TH DIMENSION,THE*
ASSOCIATE PRODUCER
'81 BLOOD BEACH

JOE CANUTT

2ND UNIT DIRECTOR
'80 MOUNTAIN MEN, THE
'82 MOTHER LODE
'83 GOLDEN SEAL, THE

DON CAPEL

KEY GRIP
'79 BLACK HOLE, THE
'81 GOING APE!

MARGOT CAPELIER

CASTING
'79 LITTLE ROMANCE, A*
'79 MOONRAKER*
'80 FIENDISH PLOT OF DR. FU MANCHU, THE*
'82 FIVE DAYS ONE SUMMER*
'83 HANNA K*

JOHN CAPER JR.

MUSIC
'83 JOYSTICKS

GWEN CAPETANOS

COSTUMES
'79 MUPPET MOVIE, THE

LEON CAPETANOS

SCREENPLAY
'82 TEMPEST*
'84 MOSCOW ON THE HUDSON*

ELLIOT CAPLAN

1ST ASST. DIRECTOR
'83 SMITHEREENS*

HARRY CAPLAN

UNIT PROD. MANAGER
'79 AVALANCHE EXPRESS

PHIL CAPLAN

ASSOCIATE EDITOR
'83 AMERICANA*

RONALD CAPLAN

COSTUME SUPERVISOR
'84 CLOAK AND DAGGER

RAY CAPLE

MISCELLANEOUS
'79 ALIEN
'79 CIRCLE OF IRON
'81 CHARIOTS OF FIRE

CLIFFORD CAPONE

COSTUMES
'80 WINDOWS
'83 AMITYVILLE 3D
'83 TOUGH ENOUGH

DIXIE CAPP

PROD. COORDINATOR
'80 TOM HORN
'81 DEAD AND BURIED

LOU CAPPETO

KEY GRIP
'80 WILLIE & PHIL
'81 TATTOO
'82 HANKY PANKY
'84 SPLASH*

AL CAPPS

MUSIC
'83 STROKER ACE
'84 CANNONBALL RUN II
MISCELLANEOUS
'81 CANNONBALL RUN, THE

DENNIS CAPPS

2ND ASST. DIRECTOR
'80 HEARTBEAT
'80 HEAVEN'S GATE*
'84 WOMAN IN RED, THE

JOANNA CAPPUCCILLI

ASSOCIATE EDITOR
'84 2010*
ASSISTANT EDITOR
'81 MODERN PROBLEMS
'83 STAR CHAMBER
'83 TWO OF A KIND*

FRANK CAPRA III

1ST ASST. DIRECTOR
'82 ZAPPED!

FRANK CAPRA JR.

PRODUCER
'80 BLACK MARBLE, THE
'81 EYE FOR AN EYE, AN
'84 FIRESTARTER
EXECUTIVE PRODUCER
'82 SEDUCTION, THE*
'82 VICE SQUAD*

GIANCARLO CAPUANO

PROPS
'79 BLACK STALLION, THE*

GAIL CAR

CASTING
'79 FAST COMPANY

JIM CARABATSOS

SCREENPLAY
'81 BEYOND THE REEF*

STEVEN CARABATSOS

SCREENPLAY
'80 LAST FLIGHT OF NOAH'S ARK, THE*

JOSEPH CARACCIOLO

UNIT PROD. MANAGER
'82 VERDICT, THE
'83 NIGHT IN HEAVEN, A
'84 POPE OF GREENWICH VILLAGE,THE
UNIT MANAGER
'82 DEATHTRAP
PROPS
'79 HAIR
'79 WANDERERS, THE
'80 FAME
'80 JUST TELL ME WHAT YOU WANT
'81 PRINCE OF THE CITY
'82 AUTHOR, AUTHOR*

JOSEPH CARACCIOLO JR.

PROPS
'81 RAGTIME*
'82 VERDICT, THE
'83 SURVIVORS, THE
'84 GHOSTBUSTERS*
'84 GARBO TALKS

GIANNI CARAMANICO

STILLS
'83 PIRANHA II: THE SPAWNING

GILBERTO CARBONARO

SPECIAL EFFECTS
'83 PIRANHA II: THE SPAWNING*

RINO CARBONI

MAKEUP
'83 LONELY LADY, THE*

LAMAR CARD

EXECUTIVE PRODUCER
'80 TERROR TRAIN

RON CARDARELLI

KEY GRIP
'80 WHOLLY MOSES!
'81 UNDER THE RAINBOW
'82 GREASE 2

ENZO CARDELLA

HAIR
'84 ONCE UPON A TIME IN AMERICA*

CATHERINE CARDIFF

CHOREOGRAPHER
'81 STRANGE BEHAVIOR

JACK CARDIFF

CINEMATOGRAPHER
'79 AVALANCHE EXPRESS
'79 FIFTH MUSKETEER, THE
'79 MAN, A WOMAN AND A BANK, A
'80 AWAKENING, THE
'81 GHOST STORY
'81 DOGS OF WAR, THE
'83 WICKED LADY, THE
'84 SCANDALOUS
'84 CONAN THE DESTROYER

RENE CARDONA JR.

PRODUCER
'80 GUYANA: CULT OF THE DAMNED
DIRECTOR
'80 GUYANA: CULT OF THE DAMNED
SCREENPLAY
'80 GUYANA: CULT OF THE DAMNED*

JOHN "BUD" CARDOS

DIRECTOR
'84 MUTANT

JOANN CARELLI

PRODUCER
'80 HEAVEN'S GATE
ASSOCIATE PRODUCER
'78 DEER HUNTER, THE*
MISCELLANEOUS
'78 DEER HUNTER, THE

FRANK CARERE

SPECIAL EFFECTS
'83 VIDEODROME

ELAINE CAREW

MAKEUP
'79 MONTY PYTHON'S LIFE OF BRIAN*
'81 TIME BANDITS*
'82 STARSTRUCK
'83 PRIVATES ON PARADE*
HAIR
'79 MONTY PYTHON'S LIFE OF BRIAN*
'81 TIME BANDITS*

TOPPER CAREW

PRODUCER
'83 D.C. CAB

NICK CAREY

SPECIAL EFFECTS
'80 RESURRECTION

EDWARD CARFAGNO

PRODUCTION DESIGNER
'79 TIME AFTER TIME
'79 METEOR
'80 LITTLE MISS MARKER
'82 HONKYTONK MAN
'83 STING II, THE
'83 SUDDEN IMPACT
'83 WRONG IS RIGHT
'84 ALL OF ME
'84 CITY HEAT
'84 TIGHTROPE

GARY CARFAGNO

ASSISTANT EDITOR
'82 ZAPPED!*

VIVIANNE MANOELLE CARLEY

ASSISTANT EDITOR
'84 STONE BOY, THE

CLAUDE CARLIEZ

STUNT COORDINATOR
'80 FIENDISH PLOT OF DR. FU MANCHU, THE

CLANCY CARLILE

SCREENPLAY
'82 HONKYTONK MAN

TOM CARLILE

PUBLICIST
'79 BLOODLINE

ED CARLIN

PRODUCER
'80 BATTLE BEYOND THE STARS

LEWIS JOHN CARLINO

DIRECTOR
'79 GREAT SANTINI, THE
'83 CLASS
SCREENPLAY
'79 GREAT SANTINI, THE
'80 RESURRECTION

MARTA CARLISKI

PUBLICIST
'80 QUARTET

ANNE CARLISLE

SCREENPLAY
'83 LIQUID SKY*

WENDY CARLOS

MUSIC
'82 TRON

LARRY CARLTON

MUSIC
'84 AGAINST ALL ODDS*

PAMELA CARLTON

SCRIPT SUPERVISOR
'79 DRACULA
'81 DEATH HUNT
'82 FIVE DAYS ONE SUMMER
'83 SUPERMAN III
'84 SUPERGIRL*
'84 FINDERS KEEPERS

ROGER CARLTON

1ST ASST. DIRECTOR
'83 ANGEL OF H.E.A.T.*
2ND ASST. DIRECTOR
'82 DEATHWISH II

DON CARMODY

PRODUCER
'82 PORKY'S*
'83 SPACEHUNTER: ADVENTURES IN THE FORBIDDEN ZONE*
'83 PORKY'S II THE NEXT DAY*
MISCELLANEOUS
'80 TERROR TRAIN

JAKI CARMODY

ASSISTANT EDITOR
'81 HAPPY BIRTHDAY TO ME*

STEVAN CARNER

CINEMATOGRAPHER
'79 BUDDY HOLLY STORY, THE

PAUL CARNIE

1ST ASST. DIRECTOR
'82 HOUSE OF THE LONG SHADOWS*

JOHN CARNOCHAN

ASSISTANT EDITOR
'80 STUNT MAN, THE*
'82 SILENT RAGE*

TRISH CAROSELLI

ASSOCIATE PRODUCER
'84 MICKI AND MAUDE

A.J. CAROTHERS

SCREENPLAY
'80 HERO AT LARGE

JILL CARPENTER

MAKEUP
'80 MIRROR CRACK'D, THE*
'80 WATCHER IN THE WOODS, THE*
'82 EVIL UNDER THE SUN
'83 PIRATES OF PENZANCE, THE
'84 PASSAGE TO INDIA, A*

JOAN CARPENTER

HAIR
'79 YANKS
'79 STEVIE
'81 EYE OF THE NEEDLE*
'81 GREAT MUPPET CAPER, THE
'81 REDS*
'83 BETRAYAL*
'83 PRIVATES ON PARADE
'84 TOP SECRET!*

JOHN CARPENTER
PRODUCER
'81 HALLOWEEN II*
'82 HALLOWEEN III:
SEASON OF THE WITCH*
DIRECTOR
'80 FOG, THE
'81 ESCAPE FROM NEW YORK
'82 THING, THE
'83 CHRISTINE
'84 STARMAN
SCREENPLAY
'80 FOG, THE*
'81 ESCAPE FROM NEW YORK*
'81 HALLOWEEN II*
EXECUTIVE PRODUCER
'84 PHILADELPHIA EXPERIMENT, THE
MUSIC
'80 FOG, THE
'81 ESCAPE FROM NEW YORK*
'81 HALLOWEEN II*
'82 HALLOWEEN III:
SEASON OF THE WITCH*
'83 CHRISTINE*

SCOTT CARPENTER
MISCELLANEOUS
'83 NEVER SAY NEVER AGAIN

STEVE CARPENTER
PROPS
'83 SUBURBIA

DON CARPENTIER
ART DIRECTOR
'84 BOSTONIANS, THE*
PROPS
'79 EUROPEANS, THE

PETER CARPENTIER
1ST ASST. DIRECTOR
'83 CHEECH AND CHONG'S
STILL SMOKIN'

ADRIAN CARR
EDITOR
'83 MAN FROM SNOWY RIVER, THE

ALLAN CARR
PRODUCER
'80 CAN'T STOP THE MUSIC*
'82 GREASE 2*
'84 CLOAK AND DAGGER
'84 WHERE THE BOYS ARE
SCREENPLAY
'80 CAN'T STOP THE MUSIC*

DENNIS CARR
SOUND
'81 FEAR NO EVIL

J. PARKER CARR
PROD. COORDINATOR
'83 METALSTORM: THE DESTRUCTION
OF JARED-SYN

JOHN CARR
ASSISTANT EDITOR
'82 BEST LITTLE
WHOREHOUSE IN TEXAS, THE*
'83 TWO OF A KIND*

PATRICIA CARR
PRODUCTION MANAGER
'84 INDIANA JONES
AND THE TEMPLE OF DOOM*

RICHARD CARR
SCREENPLAY
'83 AMERICANA

RON CARR
LOCATIONS
'80 STIR CRAZY
'82 ZAPPED!

TERRY CARR
EXECUTIVE PRODUCER
'80 COAST TO COAST
ASSOCIATE PRODUCER
'82 YES, GIORGIO
PRODUCTION MANAGER
'83 GET CRAZY
UNIT PROD. MANAGER
'80 COAST TO COAST
'81 ON GOLDEN POND*
'84 RIVER, THE
MISCELLANEOUS
'81 ON GOLDEN POND

WARREN CARR
2ND ASST. DIRECTOR
'84 ICEMAN
LOCATIONS
'83 SPACEHUNTER: ADVENTURES
IN THE FORBIDDEN ZONE

BRUCE CARRADINE
STILLS
'83 AMERICANA*

DAVID CARRADINE
PRODUCER
'83 AMERICANA
DIRECTOR
'83 AMERICANA
EDITOR
'83 AMERICANA*

JAVIER CARRASCO
2ND ASST. DIRECTOR
'79 CUBA*

AL CARRAZA
MISCELLANEOUS
'80 HOLLYWOOD KNIGHTS, THE

JAVIER CARRENO
2ND ASST. DIRECTOR
'83 UNDER FIRE*
'84 ROMANCING THE STONE
'84 EVIL THAT MEN DO, THE*

CHRIS CARRERAS
1ST ASST. DIRECTOR
'83 ENIGMA*
2ND ASST. DIRECTOR
'79 GREAT TRAIN ROBBERY, THE*
'80 HOPSCOTCH*
'80 ISLAND, THE*
'83 HIGH ROAD TO CHINA

MICHAEL CARRERAS
EXECUTIVE PRODUCER
'80 LADY VANISHES, THE*

FERNANDO CARRERE
PRODUCTION DESIGNER
'80 FINAL COUNTDOWN, THE
'80 FOOLIN AROUND

LLOYD CARRICK
SOUND
'82 ROAD WARRIOR, THE

ROBERT CARRINGTON
SCREENPLAY
'82 VENOM

FRANCIS CARRISOSA
MISCELLANEOUS
'83 METALSTORM: THE DESTRUCTION
OF JARED-SYN

BENJI CARROLL
MISCELLANEOUS
'81 TICKET TO HEAVEN

BILL CARROLL
1ST ASST. DIRECTOR
'84 ICE PIRATES, THE

GORDON CARROLL
PRODUCER
'79 ALIEN*
'83 BLUE THUNDER

J. LARRY CARROLL
PRODUCER
'79 TOURIST TRAP
SCREENPLAY
'79 TOURIST TRAP*
MISCELLANEOUS
'82 PARASITE

JOHN CARROLL
ART DIRECTOR
'79 TIM

LYNNE CARROW
CASTING
'82 BY DESIGN*
'83 STAR 80*
MISCELLANEOUS
'84 MRS. SOFFEL

WILLIAM CARRUTH
EDITOR
'79 SAINT JACK
'80 CADDYSHACK
'81 THEY ALL LAUGHED*
'84 STRANGERS KISS

ALAN CARRUTHERS
STILLS
'80 TERROR TRAIN

L.M. KIT CARSON
SCREENPLAY
'83 BREATHLESS*

SARAH CARSON
PROD. OFFICE COORD.
'81 ENDLESS LOVE
'84 GARBO TALKS
PROD. COORDINATOR
'83 EDDIE AND THE CRUISERS

BILL CARTER
ASSISTANT EDITOR
'80 PROM NIGHT*

JAMES CARTER
CINEMATOGRAPHER
'80 HOME MOVIES
'83 SWEET SIXTEEN
MISCELLANEOUS
'82 SWORD AND THE SORCERER, THE

JOHN CARTER
SOUND
'80 LITTLE MISS MARKER

JOHN CARTER
EDITOR
'80 FORMULA, THE*

JOHN CARTER
SP. EFFECTS SUPERV.
'82 SWORD AND THE SORCERER, THE

MARIE CARTER
MAKEUP
'80 MOTEL HELL
'82 PENITENTIARY II

MAURICE CARTER
PRODUCTION DESIGNER
'79 GREAT TRAIN ROBBERY, THE
'80 FFOLKES

META CARTER
SCRIPT SUPERVISOR
'80 MOTHER'S DAY

PAMELA CARTER
PROD. OFFICE COORD.
'82 EATING RAOUL

PETER CARTER
LOCATIONS
'83 FINAL OPTION, THE
'84 CHAMPIONS*
'84 SCANDALOUS*

RANDY CARTER
1ST ASST. DIRECTOR
'84 LOVE STREAMS*
2ND ASST. DIRECTOR
'79 NORTH AVENUE IRREGULARS, THE
'80 BLUES BROTHERS*

RANDY CARTER
CASTING
'79 APOCALYPSE NOW*

RICHARD CARTER
ART DIRECTOR
'84 ADVENTURES OF BUCKAROO BANZAI ACROSS THE 8TH DIMENSION, THE*

MAGGIE CARTIER
CASTING
'80 ELEPHANT MAN, THE
'81 RAGTIME*
'83 HUNGER, THE*
'83 NEVER SAY NEVER AGAIN*
'84 AMADEUS*
'84 DUNE*
'84 SHEENA*
MISCELLANEOUS
'81 HISTORY OF THE WORLD PART I

WILLIAM CARTLIDGE
ASSOCIATE PRODUCER
'79 MOONRAKER

ALAN CARTWRIGHT
MISCELLANEOUS
'80 BRONCO BILLY

BOB CARTWRIGHT
ART DIRECTOR
'79 BLOODLINE*
'79 HANOVER STREET*
'80 ELEPHANT MAN, THE
MISCELLANEOUS
'81 HISTORY OF THE WORLD PART I

JOHN CARTWRIGHT
ART DIRECTOR
'81 FIRST MONDAY IN OCTOBER
'82 OFFICER AND A GENTLEMAN, AN
'83 KISS ME GOODBYE

CELSO AL CARUNUNGAN
MISCELLANEOUS
'83 YEAR OF LIVING DANGEROUSLY, THE

FRED CARUSO
PRODUCER
'79 WINTER KILLS
EXECUTIVE PRODUCER
'81 BLOW OUT
EXEC IN CHARGE PROD
'82 FIGHTING BACK
'84 ONCE UPON A TIME IN AMERICA
ASSOCIATE PRODUCER
'79 WANDERERS, THE
'80 DRESSED TO KILL
'80 FIRST DEADLY SIN
PRODUCTION MANAGER
'80 DRESSED TO KILL
'81 BLOW OUT
UNIT PROD. MANAGER
'79 WANDERERS, THE
'80 FIRST DEADLY SIN
'82 FIGHTING BACK

JOSIE CARUSO
COSTUMES
'79 DAWN OF THE DEAD
MISCELLANEOUS
'80 MOTHER'S DAY

LUIGI CARUSO
HAIR
'81 KNIGHTRIDERS*

VERNE CARUSO
HAIR
'80 RAGING BULL*
'80 DEFIANCE*
'80 GLORIA
'80 HEAVEN'S GATE*
'81 THEY ALL LAUGHED*
'84 WHERE THE BOYS ARE

KATHRYN CARVER
MISCELLANEOUS
'81 NIGHT THE LIGHTS WENT OUT IN GEORGIA, THE

RICHARD CARVER
HAIR
'79 PRIZE FIGHTER, THE*

ROSS CARVER
HAIR
'84 ANOTHER COUNTRY

STEVE CARVER
PRODUCER
'83 LONE WOLF MCQUADE*
DIRECTOR
'80 STEEL
'81 EYE FOR AN EYE, AN
'83 LONE WOLF MCQUADE

LINDA CARWIN
EXEC IN CHARGE PROD
'81 ZORRO, THE GAY BLADE

CHRIS CASADY
MISCELLANEOUS
'81 FEAR NO EVIL

GEORGES CASATI
MISCELLANEOUS
'79 LOVE AND BULLETS

CARLO CASCIOLI
PROPS
'83 LONELY LADY, THE*

ENNIO CASCIOLI
HAIR
'83 LONELY LADY, THE*

TOM CASE
MAKEUP
'79 CHAPTER TWO
'79 PROMISES IN THE DARK*
'80 SEEMS LIKE OLD TIMES
'80 BALTIMORE BULLET, THE
'80 PRIVATE BENJAMIN*
'81 ONLY WHEN I LAUGH
'82 BEST FRIENDS*
'82 DEAD MEN DON'T WEAR PLAID*
'83 MAN WITH TWO BRAINS, THE*
'84 KARATE KID, THE
'84 PROTOCOL*
'84 ROMANCING THE STONE
'84 SWING SHIFT*

JACK CASEY
PUBLICIST
'80 FINAL COUNTDOWN, THE
'80 HONEYSUCKLE ROSE
UNIT PUBLICIST
'80 HIDE IN PLAIN SIGHT

JIM CASEY
MISCELLANEOUS
'83 MAN WHO LOVED WOMEN, THE

KEVIN CASEY
ASSISTANT EDITOR
'80 CHEAPER TO KEEP HER*

PATRICIA CASEY
ASSOCIATE PRODUCER
'79 CLASS OF MISS MACMICHAEL,THE

DON CASH
MAKEUP
'81 ABSENCE OF MALICE*

MARY CASILLO
MISCELLANEOUS
'81 BURNING, THE

ALAN CASO
MISCELLANEOUS
'82 SWORD AND THE SORCERER, THE

DAVID CASS
2ND UNIT DIRECTOR
'83 SMOKEY AND THE BANDIT III
'83 SAVANNAH SMILES
STUNT COORDINATOR
'81 ALL NIGHT LONG
'83 SMOKEY AND THE BANDIT III
'83 SAVANNAH SMILES

JOHN CASSAVETES
PRODUCER
'80 GLORIA
DIRECTOR
'80 GLORIA
'84 LOVE STREAMS
SCREENPLAY
'80 GLORIA
'84 LOVE STREAMS*

PATRICK CASSAVETTI
LOCATIONS
'81 TIME BANDITS

LOUISE CASSELMAN
2ND ASST. DIRECTOR
'80 MIDDLE AGE CRAZY*

BILL CASSIDY
2ND UNIT DIRECTOR
'81 NIGHTHAWKS

JOHN CASSIDY
KEY GRIP
'84 PREPPIES

TINA CASSIDY
HAIR
'80 FOG, THE

WILLIAM CASSIDY
PRODUCTION DESIGNER
'80 CARNY
'82 ROCKY III
'83 RISKY BUSINESS
'83 NIGHT IN HEAVEN, A
'84 KARATE KID, THE

ALAN CASSIE
ART DIRECTOR
'80 WATCHER IN THE WOODS, THE
'81 DRAGONSLAYER
'82 EVIL UNDER THE SUN
'83 LORDS OF DISCIPLINE, THE
'83 PIRATES OF PENZANCE, THE*

DENISE CASSOTTI
PROD. SECRETARY
'84 UNTIL SEPTEMBER

FABRIZIO CASTELLANI
1ST ASST. DIRECTOR
'84 ONCE UPON A TIME IN AMERICA

ENZO CASTELLARI
DIRECTOR
'83 1990: THE BRONX WARRIORS
SCREENPLAY
'83 1990: THE BRONX WARRIORS*

DEBORAH CASTLE
ASSOCIATE PRODUCER
'80 FOOLIN AROUND

GENE CASTLE
CHOREOGRAPHER
'83 KISS ME GOODBYE

MICHAEL CASTLE
EXEC IN CHARGE PROD
'80 GALAXINA
CO-PRODUCER
'83 MY TUTOR
'84 WEEKEND PASS

NICK CASTLE
DIRECTOR
'84 LAST STARFIGHTER, THE
SCREENPLAY
'81 ESCAPE FROM NEW YORK*

MONICA CASTRO
PROPS
'84 BLAME IT ON RIO*

OSCAR CASTRO-NEVES
MISCELLANEOUS
'84 BLAME IT ON RIO

MARIE CASTRO-VASQUEZ
ASSISTANT EDITOR
'82 MISSING

MARGOT CATALAA
SCRIPT SUPERVISOR
'80 OUTSIDER, THE

ROSALYN CATANIA
PROD. COORDINATOR
'79 C.H.O.M.P.S.
'79 FORCE OF ONE, A
'80 FATSO
PROD. SECRETARY
'83 TWILIGHT ZONE, THE MOVIE*

BILL CATCHING
STUNT COORDINATOR
'79 RUNNER STUMBLES, THE
'81 HIGH RISK

GILBERT CATES
PRODUCER
'80 OH GOD! BOOK II
DIRECTOR
'79 PROMISE, THE
'80 LAST MARRIED COUPLE IN AMERICA, THE
'80 OH GOD! BOOK II
EXECUTIVE PRODUCER
'80 LAST MARRIED COUPLE IN AMERICA, THE*

JANE CATES
MISCELLANEOUS
'80 LAST MARRIED COUPLE IN AMERICA, THE

JOSEPH CATES
EXECUTIVE PRODUCER
'80 LAST MARRIED COUPLE IN AMERICA, THE*

DELIO CATINI
SPECIAL EFFECTS
'83 BLACK STALLION RETURNS, THE*

HAZEL CATMILL
HAIR
'79 ROSE, THE
'81 WHOSE LIFE IS IT ANYWAY?*

MIMMO CATTARINICH
STILLS
'82 TEMPEST*

BERNADETTE CAULFIELD
PROD. COORDINATOR
'81 BODY AND SOUL
'81 FEAR NO EVIL

DON CAULFIELD
KEY GRIP
'80 TERROR TRAIN

MICHAEL CAULFIELD
MISCELLANEOUS
'79 MY BRILLIANT CAREER

WILLIAM CAULFIELD
PROPS
'82 HANKY PANKY

TOMMY CAUSEY
SOUND
'81 ESCAPE FROM NEW YORK
'81 HALLOWEEN II
'82 HALLOWEEN III: SEASON OF THE WITCH
'82 THING, THE
'83 CHRISTINE
'83 GET CRAZY
'83 TWILIGHT ZONE, THE MOVIE*
'84 CLOAK AND DAGGER
'84 STARMAN

GREER CAVAGNARO
STILLS
'78 DEER HUNTER, THE*
'79 WHEN YOU COMIN' BACK, RED RYDER?

PAUL CAVAGNERO
ASSISTANT EDITOR
'79 GAME OF DEATH*
'80 KIDS ARE ALL RIGHT, THE*
'81 NEIGHBORS*

CESAR CAVALCANTI
LOCATIONS
'84 BLAME IT ON RIO

JOE CAVALIER
ASSOCIATE PRODUCER
'79 C.H.O.M.P.S.
'81 CARBON COPY
'82 JINXED*
PRODUCTION MANAGER
'79 C.H.O.M.P.S.
'82 JINXED

KIKU CAVALIER
PROD. COORDINATOR
'82 JINXED

ROBERT CAVALLO
PRODUCER
'84 PURPLE RAIN*

LARRY CAVANAUGH
SPECIAL EFFECTS
'79 ...AND JUSTICE FOR ALL
'80 SMALL CIRCLE OF FRIENDS, A*
'80 LONG RIDERS, THE*
'81 SOUTHERN COMFORT
'82 BEST FRIENDS
'82 ESCAPE ARTIST, THE
'83 BIG CHILL, THE
SP. EFFECTS SUPERV.
'81 HALLOWEEN II
'84 PHILADELPHIA EXPERIMENT, THE

KEITH CAVELE
MISCELLANEOUS
'81 BURNING, THE

CLINTON CAVERS
ART DIRECTOR
'82 PINK FLOYD: THE WALL*
'82 QUEST FOR FIRE
'83 HUNGER, THE
'84 ANOTHER COUNTRY

CLINTON CAVERS
LOCATIONS
'79 AGATHA*

CLINTON CAVERS
MISCELLANEOUS
'79 ALIEN

GERRY CAVIGAN
2ND ASST. DIRECTOR
'80 ELEPHANT MAN, THE

BRUCE CAWARDINE
SOUND
'81 TICKET TO HEAVEN*

BOB CAWLEY
PROD. COORDINATOR
'82 BUTTERFLY

JEAN-JACQUES CAZIOT
ART DIRECTOR
'80 QUARTET

SHARON CECCATI
MISCELLANEOUS
'81 KNIGHTRIDERS

IOLE CECCHINI
HAIR
'83 LONELY LADY, THE*

TONY CECERE
2ND ASST. DIRECTOR
'82 SWAMP THING

ELAYNE CEDER
ASSOCIATE PRODUCER
'84 MARVIN AND TIGE
ART DIRECTOR
'82 FIREFOX*
'83 GET CRAZY
PRODUCTION DESIGNER
'79 WHEN A STRANGER CALLS

CELIA
COSTUMES
'81 BODY AND SOUL

FERNANDO CELIS
STUNT COORDINATOR
'84 ICE PIRATES, THE
'84 PHILADELPHIA EXPERIMENT, THE

AL CERILLO
MISCELLANEOUS
'82 Q: QUETZALCOATL

BEDRICH CERMAK
PROPS
'84 AMADEUS*

KAREL CERNY
ART DIRECTOR
'84 AMADEUS*

JACQUES CEROID
ASSISTANT EDITOR
'84 BOUNTY, THE*

MARCO CEROVAC
COSTUME SUPERVISOR
'83 HIGH ROAD TO CHINA

DON CERRONE
KEY GRIP
'82 Q: QUETZALCOATL
'84 NOT FOR PUBLICATION*

RICHARD CERRONE
MISCELLANEOUS
'84 NATURAL, THE

EUGENE CERVENY
MISCELLANEOUS
'82 NIGHT CROSSING

GARY CERVENY
MISCELLANEOUS
'82 NIGHT CROSSING

JAROSLAV CESAL
PROPS
'84 AMADEUS*

GUSMANO CESARETTI
MISCELLANEOUS
'81 THIEF

HABIB CHAARI
LOCATIONS
'81 RAIDERS OF THE LOST ARK*

THIERRY CHABERT
1ST ASST. DIRECTOR
'80 TESS

BETTE CHADWICK
CASTING
'82 BY DESIGN*
MISCELLANEOUS
'83 RUNNING BRAVE

JILL CHADWICK
ASSOCIATE PRODUCER
'83 CLASS*

WARREN CHADWICK
ASSOCIATE EDITOR
'82 SEDUCTION, THE
ASSISTANT EDITOR
'81 HELL NIGHT*
'83 CHAINED HEAT

RICHARD CHAFFEE
SCRIPT SUPERVISOR
'80 ON THE NICKEL

ROB CHAFFEE
PROPS
'82 PENITENTIARY II

DON CHAFFEY
DIRECTOR
'79 C.H.O.M.P.S.

CHRISTOPHER CHALLIS
CINEMATOGRAPHER
'80 MIRROR CRACK'D, THE
'82 EVIL UNDER THE SUN
'84 RIDDLE OF THE SANDS

DRUMMOND CHALLIS
PRODUCER
'84 RIDDLE OF THE SANDS
MISCELLANEOUS
'81 BURNING, THE

CATHY CHAMBERLAIN
MUSIC
'80 HAPPY BIRTHDAY, GEMINI*

CREW CHAMBERLAIN
SOUND
'84 STREETS OF FIRE*

JACQUES CHAMBERLAND
PROPS
'83 OF UNKNOWN ORIGIN
'84 HOTEL NEW HAMPSHIRE, THE

JOHN CHAMBERS
MAKEUP
'82 NATIONAL LAMPOON'S CLASS REUNION
MISCELLANEOUS
'81 HALLOWEEN II

ROBIN CHAMBERS
ASSISTANT EDITOR
'80 SCHIZOID*
'81 BODY AND SOUL

ALAIN CHAMMAS
PRODUCER
'83 BUDDY SYSTEM, THE

ANDREE CHAMPAGNE
CASTING
'82 QUEST FOR FIRE*

MONIQUE CHAMPAGNE
SCRIPT SUPERVISOR
'79 QUINTET
'81 HAPPY BIRTHDAY TO ME
'82 BY DESIGN
'82 PARADISE

FERN CHAMPION
CASTING
'80 CHEECH AND CHONG'S NEXT MOVIE*
'80 FADE TO BLACK*
'81 BUDDY, BUDDY*
'81 CHEECH AND CHONG'S NICE DREAMS*
'81 CHU CHU AND THE PHILLY FLASH*
'81 FUNHOUSE, THE*
'82 THINGS ARE TOUGH ALL OVER*
'83 MAN WHO WASN'T THERE, THE*
'84 BREAKIN 2 ELECTRIC BOOGALOO*
'84 POLICE ACADEMY*
'84 FRIDAY THE 13TH PART IV THE FINAL CHAPTER*
'84 MEATBALLS PART II*

GILL CHAMPION
CO-PRODUCER
'81 FORT APACHE, THE BRONX*

GREGG CHAMPION
ASSOCIATE PRODUCER
'83 BLUE THUNDER

MARC CHAMPION
CINEMATOGRAPHER
'82 OUT OF THE BLUE

MARGE CHAMPION
CHOREOGRAPHER
'81 WHOSE LIFE IS IT ANYWAY?

AMOS CHAN
STILLS
'80 UNION CITY

DAVID CHAN
PRODUCTION MANAGER
'79 GAME OF DEATH

GEORGE CHAN
PRODUCTION DESIGNER
'82 FORCED VENGEANCE

MADALENA CHAN
LOCATIONS
'79 GAME OF DEATH*

PATTY CHAN
1ST ASST. DIRECTOR
'84 INDIANA JONES AND THE TEMPLE OF DOOM*

BODIE CHANDLER
MUSIC SUPERVISOR
'82 LOVE AND MONEY

JULIE CHANDLER
LOCATIONS
'80 BLUES BROTHERS*
'81 THIEF*

MICHAEL CHANDLER
EDITOR
'83 NEVER CRY WOLF*
'84 AMADEUS*

ESTELLE CHANGAS
PROD. OFFICE COORD.
'82 ONE FROM THE HEART

SIMON CHANNING-WILLIAMS
1ST ASST. DIRECTOR
'84 GREYSTOKE: THE LEGEND OF TARZAN, LORD OF THE APES*

DOUG CHAPIN
PRODUCER
'79 WHEN A STRANGER CALLS*
'84 AMERICAN DREAMER

KAY CHAPIN
SCRIPT SUPERVISOR
'79 GOING IN STYLE
'79 MANHATTAN
'80 STARDUST MEMORIES
'80 WINDOWS
'81 SO FINE*
'81 ARTHUR
'82 MIDSUMMER NIGHT'S SEX COMEDY, A
'82 VERDICT, THE
'83 ZELIG
'84 BROADWAY DANNY ROSE
'84 POPE OF GREENWICH VILLAGE,

BETTY CHAPLIN
SCRIPT SUPERVISOR
'79 AVALANCHE EXPRESS*
'80 PRIVATE BENJAMIN
'82 MAKING LOVE
'83 ROMANTIC COMEDY
'84 LONELY GUY, THE
'84 WOMAN IN RED, THE

BILL CHAPMAN
PROD. OFFICE COORD.
'81 TAPS

DAVID CHAPMAN
ART DIRECTOR
'79 SEDUCTION OF JOE TYNAN, THE
'81 WOLFEN
'84 COTTON CLUB, THE*
PRODUCTION DESIGNER
'81 FOUR FRIENDS

DIANNE FINN CHAPMAN
COSTUMES
'79 GREAT BANK HOAX, THE

FRED CHAPMAN
PROPS
'83 STING II, THE

GRAHAM CHAPMAN
SCREENPLAY
'79 MONTY PYTHON'S LIFE OF BRIAN*
'82 MONTY PYTHON LIVE AT THE HOLLYWOOD BOWL*
'83 MONTY PYTHON'S THE MEANING OF LIFE*
'83 YELLOWBEARD*

JOAN CHAPMAN
EDITOR
'82 FIRST BLOOD
ASSISTANT EDITOR
'84 REPO MAN*
'84 RED DAWN*

LEIGH CHAPMAN
SCREENPLAY
'79 BOARDWALK*
'80 OCTAGON, THE
'80 STEEL

LESLIE CHAPMAN
LOCATIONS
'81 KNIGHTRIDERS

MATTHEW CHAPMAN
DIRECTOR
'84 STRANGERS KISS
SCREENPLAY
'84 STRANGERS KISS*

MICHAEL CHAPMAN
DIRECTOR
'83 ALL THE RIGHT MOVES
CINEMATOGRAPHER
'79 HARDCORE
'79 WANDERERS, THE
'80 RAGING BULL
'82 DEAD MEN DON'T WEAR PLAID
'82 PERSONAL BEST
'83 MAN WITH TWO BRAINS, THE

PRISCILLA CHAPMAN
SCREENPLAY
'81 FAN, THE*

TERRY CHAPMAN
KEY GRIP
'84 BOLERO

MORRIS CHAPNICK
UNIT PROD. MANAGER
'83 REUBEN, REUBEN
2ND ASST. DIRECTOR
'82 BLADERUNNER*

FRANCOISE CHAPUIS
MAKEUP
'84 JUST THE WAY YOU ARE*

ESTA CHARKHAM
CASTING
'79 CLASS OF MISS MACMICHAEL,THE
'81 CHARIOTS OF FIRE
'83 FINAL OPTION, THE
'83 LORDS OF DISCIPLINE, THE*
'84 SUPERGIRL*
'84 UNTIL SEPTEMBER*

COLIN CHARLES
SOUND
'80 FOR THE LOVE OF BENJI
'80 OH! HEAVENLY DOG
'81 VICTORY
'83 CHEECH AND CHONG'S STILL SMOKIN'
'84 CHEECH AND CHONG'S THE CORSICAN BROTHERS
'84 INDIANA JONES AND THE TEMPLE OF DOOM*
'84 UNDER THE VOLCANO

DAVID CHARLES
ART DIRECTOR
'79 MEATBALLS

SANDY CHARLES
ASSOCIATE PRODUCER
'83 SWEET SIXTEEN

JIM CHARLESTON
2ND ASST. DIRECTOR
'81 HELL NIGHT

VALERIE CHARLTON
MISCELLANEOUS
'83 MONTY PYTHON'S THE MEANING OF LIFE

ROY CHARMAN
SOUND
'79 CUBA
'81 RAIDERS OF THE LOST ARK
'81 SUPERMAN II
'81 FINAL CONFLICT, THE
'82 MONSIGNOR
'82 VICTOR/VICTORIA
'83 SUPERMAN III
'83 CURSE OF THE PINK PANTHER
'83 TRAIL OF THE PINK PANTHER
'84 ELECTRIC DREAMS

MARMIE CHARNDOFF
PROPS
'80 PROM NIGHT

EUDIE CHARNES
PROD. OFFICE COORD.
'81 STRIPES
PROD. SECRETARY
'80 OH GOD! BOOK II

ROBERT CHARTOFF
PRODUCER
'79 ROCKY II*
'80 RAGING BULL*
'81 TRUE CONFESSIONS*
'82 ROCKY III*
'83 RIGHT STUFF, THE*

ANNE CHARVEIN
EDITOR
'83 EXPOSED*

BRANDON CHASE
PRODUCER
'80 ALLIGATOR
'82 SWORD AND THE SORCERER, THE*

KEN CHASE
MAKEUP
'80 STUNT MAN, THE
'81 SHARKEY'S MACHINE*
'81 ESCAPE FROM NEW YORK
'81 LOOKER
'81 GOING APE!
'82 THING, THE
'82 TOY, THE*
'83 STAR 80
'83 STING II, THE*
'83 SMOKEY AND THE BANDIT III*
'84 IRRECONCILABLE DIFFERENCES

MARIANNE CHASE
PRODUCER
'82 SWORD AND THE SORCERER, THE*
EXEC IN CHARGE PROD
'80 ALLIGATOR

MARYDITH CHASE
COSTUME SUPERVISOR
'83 MORTUARY
LOCATIONS
'79 DOUBLE MCGUFFIN, THE

GARY CHASON
CASTING
'81 STUDENT BODIES

JAY CHATTAWAY
MUSIC
'80 MANIAC
'83 BIG SCORE, THE

ROSEANN CHATTERTON
PROD. COORDINATOR
'82 BARBAROSA*

BARRY CHATTINGTON
MISCELLANEOUS
'84 SCANDALOUS

ELEANOR CHAUDHURI
PROD. SECRETARY
'83 OCTOPUSSY*
'84 PASSAGE TO INDIA, A

PAUL CHAVEZ
2ND ASST. DIRECTOR
'80 RAISE THE TITANIC*
'80 FADE TO BLACK
'81 GOING APE!*

SUSAN CHAVEZ
PUBLICIST
'81 BEAST WITHIN, THE

NORA CHAVOOSHIAN
PRODUCTION DESIGNER
'84 BROTHER FROM
ANOTHER PLANET, THE

ROBERT CHECCHI
PRODUCTION DESIGNER
'82 DON'T CRY,IT'S ONLY THUNDER

DOUGLAS CHEEK
DIRECTOR
'84 C.H.U.D.

STEPHEN CHEIKES
MISCELLANEOUS
'82 BRAINWAVES

DOMINIQUE CHEMINAL
CASTING
'82 QUEST FOR FIRE*

SHERRY CHEN
CASTING
'82 FORCED VENGEANCE*

ZVI CHEN
LOCATIONS
'84 BEST DEFENSE*

ELLEN CHENOWETH
CASTING
'81 SHOCK TREATMENT*
'82 DINER
'82 MY FAVORITE YEAR*
'82 QUEST FOR FIRE*
'83 STRANGE INVADERS*
'83 LORDS OF DISCIPLINE, THE*
'83 TERMS OF ENDEARMENT*
'84 NATURAL, THE

MOHAMED ALI CHERIF
MISCELLANEOUS
'84 MISUNDERSTOOD

BARRY CHERIN
UNIT PUBLICIST
'82 ZAPPED!

JEFFREY CHERNOV
EXEC IN CHARGE PROD
'82 HALLOWEEN III:
SEASON OF THE WITCH
ASSOCIATE PRODUCER
'83 DEAD ZONE, THE
PRODUCTION MANAGER
'81 HALLOWEEN II
UNIT PROD. MANAGER
'82 HALLOWEEN III:
SEASON OF THE WITCH
1ST ASST. DIRECTOR
'84 PHILADELPHIA EXPERIMENT,THE*
2ND ASST. DIRECTOR
'81 BODY HEAT
'81 CUTTER'S WAY
'81 ESCAPE FROM NEW YORK
'82 THING, THE
'84 STARMAN
LOCATIONS
'79 FAST BREAK
MISCELLANEOUS
'84 CHILDREN OF THE CORN

PETER CHESNEY
SPECIAL EFFECTS
'83 OSTERMAN WEEKEND, THE

GIRAUD CHESTER
EXECUTIVE PRODUCER
'82 COME BACK TO THE 5 & 10,
JIMMY DEAN, JIMMY DEAN

PAUL CHEUNG
STILLS
'82 FORCED VENGEANCE*

BRUCE CHEVILLAT
UNIT PROD. MANAGER
'84 CHOOSE ME
1ST ASST. DIRECTOR
'84 CHOOSE ME

RICHARD CHEW
EDITOR
'79 WHEN YOU COMIN' BACK,
RED RYDER?
'82 MY FAVORITE YEAR
'83 RISKY BUSINESS

MICHAEL CHEYKO
1ST ASST. DIRECTOR
'79 MOONRAKER
'80 ISLAND, THE
'83 EDUCATING RITA
'83 ENIGMA*
'83 EXPOSED*
'83 TRAIL OF THE PINK PANTHER*
'84 UNTIL SEPTEMBER

AGNES CHIA
CASTING
'79 SAINT JACK*

JEANNINE CHIALVO
ASSISTANT EDITOR
'81 GALLIPOLI*
'83 YEAR OF
LIVING DANGEROUSLY, THE*

FRANCESCO CHIANESE
ART DIRECTOR
'84 AMADEUS*

MARC CHIASSON
SOUND
'81 TICKET TO HEAVEN*

DEBBIE CHIATE
ASSISTANT EDITOR
'79 PENITENTIARY
'80 BATTLE BEYOND THE STARS*
'82 FAST TIMES AT RIDGEMONT HIGH*
'84 JOHNNY DANGEROUSLY

JEAN CLAUDE CHICOT
HAIR
'83 ENIGMA

LIZ MI CHIE
HAIR
'81 GALLIPOLI*

MARTIN CHIELENS
ASSISTANT EDITOR
'80 RAISE THE TITANIC
'84 STAR TREK III:
THE SEARCH FOR SPOCK*

YVAN CHIFFRE
STUNT COORDINATOR
'84 CHEECH AND CHONG'S THE
CORSICAN BROTHERS
MISCELLANEOUS
'84 CHEECH AND CHONG'S THE
CORSICAN BROTHERS

PAUL CHIHARA
MUSIC
'81 PRINCE OF THE CITY
'83 SURVIVORS, THE
'84 CRACKERS
'84 IMPULSE

JOHN CHILBERG II
ART DIRECTOR
'84 STAR TREK III: THE SEARCH FOR SPOCK

CATHERINE CHILDERS
HAIR
'83 RIGHT STUFF, THE*

COLIN CHILVERS
SPECIAL EFFECTS
'80 SATURN 3
SP. EFFECTS SUPERV.
'81 SUPERMAN II
'81 CONDORMAN
MISCELLANEOUS
'83 SUPERMAN III

BRIAN CHIN
MISCELLANEOUS
'81 ESCAPE FROM NEW YORK
'81 GALAXY OF TERROR
'81 GALAXY OF TERROR

MICHAEL CHINICH
CASTING
'80 BLUES BROTHERS
'80 COAL MINER'S DAUGHTER
'80 MELVIN AND HOWARD
'80 WHERE THE BUFFALO ROAM
'81 RAGGEDY MAN*
'81 AMERICAN WEREWOLF IN LONDON, AN*
'81 CONTINENTAL DIVIDE*
'83 STROKER ACE

BERTNA CHIO
HAIR
'83 YELLOWBEARD

JIMMY CHIPPERFIELD
MISCELLANEOUS
'84 GREYSTOKE: THE LEGEND OF TARZAN, LORD OF THE APES

JOHN CHISHOLM
PROPS
'83 DRESSER, THE

DIANE CHITTELL
PROD. COORDINATOR
'84 KILLING FIELDS, THE*

TIM CHITWOOD
STUNT COORDINATOR
'81 NOBODY'S PERFEKT

BENNETT CHOATE
COSTUMES
'82 SWAMP THING*

ARTHUR CHOBANIAN
ASSOCIATE PRODUCER
'79 ROCKY II

CHRISTINE CHOLVIN
ASSISTANT EDITOR
'84 THIS IS SPINAL TAP

MARVIN CHOMSKY
DIRECTOR
'84 TANK

SHELBY CHONG
ASSOCIATE PRODUCER
'82 THINGS ARE TOUGH ALL OVER*

THOMAS CHONG
DIRECTOR
'80 CHEECH AND CHONG'S NEXT MOVIE
'81 CHEECH AND CHONG'S NICE DREAMS
'83 CHEECH AND CHONG'S STILL SMOKIN'
'84 CHEECH AND CHONG'S THE CORSICAN BROTHERS
SCREENPLAY
'80 CHEECH AND CHONG'S NEXT MOVIE*
'81 CHEECH AND CHONG'S NICE DREAMS*
'82 THINGS ARE TOUGH ALL OVER*
'83 CHEECH AND CHONG'S STILL SMOKIN'*
'84 CHEECH AND CHONG'S THE CORSICAN BROTHERS*

LEON CHOOLUCK
PRODUCTION MANAGER
'79 AMERICATHON
'79 APOCALYPSE NOW*
UNIT MANAGER
'80 LOVING COUPLES

JAMES CHORY
2ND ASST. DIRECTOR
'81 ATLANTIC CITY*
'83 ZELIG*
'84 BROADWAY DANNY ROSE*
'84 FALLING IN LOVE

TERRY CHOSTNER
STILLS
'83 RETURN OF THE JEDI

LESTER CHOTT
SPECIAL EFFECTS
'80 LITTLE MISS MARKER

JAMES CHOW
ART DIRECTOR
'82 MOTHER LODE*
PROPS
'79 MAN, A WOMAN AND A BANK, A
'83 GOLDEN SEAL, THE
'84 RUNAWAY

RAYMOND CHOW
PRODUCER
'79 GAME OF DEATH
EXECUTIVE PRODUCER
'80 BIG BRAWL, THE
'81 CANNONBALL RUN, THE
'81 DEATH HUNT*
'82 MEGAFORCE
'83 HIGH ROAD TO CHINA
'84 LASSITER*
'84 CANNONBALL RUN II*

CHRIS CHRISAFIS
EXECUTIVE PRODUCER
'81 SEA WOLVES, THE
'83 FINAL OPTION, THE

FRED CHRISS
PROPS
'82 ZAPPED!*

BRYANT CHRIST
LOCATIONS
'79 PROMISES IN THE DARK

TAWNY CHRIST
ASSISTANT EDITOR
'80 COAST TO COAST*

SAM CHRISTENSEN
CASTING
'79 CHAMP, THE*
'79 FORCE OF ONE, A*
'80 DEFIANCE*
'80 HERO AT LARGE*
'80 IN GOD WE TRUST*
'81 CLASH OF THE TITANS*

H.R. CHRISTIAN
SCREENPLAY
'81 KING OF THE MOUNTAIN

ROGER CHRISTIAN
DIRECTOR
'82 SENDER, THE
ART DIRECTOR
'79 ALIEN*
'79 MONTY PYTHON'S LIFE OF BRIAN

ED CHRISTIANO
SOUND
'82 BRAINWAVES*

BILL CHRISTIANS
COSTUMES
'81 SO FINE*

ROBERT CHRISTIANSEN
PRODUCER
'80 HIDE IN PLAIN SIGHT*

ROBERT CHRISTIDES
ART DIRECTOR
'79 BLOODLINE*

BOB CHRISTIE
PUBLICIST
'83 MERRY CHRISTMAS, MR. LAWRENCE*

CHRISTODOULOS
MISCELLANEOUS
'79 ESCAPE TO ATHENA

MALCOLM CHRISTOPHER
PRODUCTION MANAGER
'81 RAGTIME*
'83 NEVER SAY NEVER AGAIN*
MISCELLANEOUS
'80 RAISE THE TITANIC

BERTHA CHU
HAIR
'81 CATTLE ANNIE AND LITTLE BRITCHES*

CALDECOT CHUBB
LOCATIONS
'83 LOVE LETTERS

FRED CHULACK
EDITOR
'79 DREAMER*
'80 TOUCHED BY LOVE
'81 PRIVATE LESSONS
'83 PRIVATE SCHOOL

JEFFREY CHUMAS
MISCELLANEOUS
'84 HOT DOG...THE MOVIE

LAI FUN CHUNG
CHOREOGRAPHER
'83 UNCOMMON VALOR
MISCELLANEOUS
'82 SPLIT IMAGE

LAU CHI CHUNG
LOCATIONS
'79 GAME OF DEATH*

RICHARD CHURCH
SOUND
'81 ...ALL THE MARBLES
'84 SPLASH

TERRY CHURCHER
PRODUCTION MANAGER
'79 MOONRAKER*
'80 OH! HEAVENLY DOG*
'84 SUPERGIRL*

PAT CHURCHILL
PRODUCTION MANAGER
'81 RAGTIME*
'83 LOCAL HERO*
PROD. OFFICE COORD.
'79 ALAMBRISTA!*

TED CHURCHILL
CINEMATOGRAPHER
'80 GILDA LIVE*
MISCELLANEOUS
'81 TAPS
'82 PORKY'S
'83 RISKY BUSINESS
'83 BAD BOYS
'83 KING OF COMEDY, THE
'83 NIGHT IN HEAVEN, A
'83 MAN WHO WASN'T THERE, THE
'84 BIRDY
'84 FALLING IN LOVE
'84 PURPLE RAIN

LISA CHURGIN
ASSISTANT EDITOR
'79 WARRIORS, THE*
'81 SOUTHERN COMFORT*

SUZANNE CIANI
MUSIC
'81 INCREDIBLE SHRINKING WOMAN, THE

ANDREW CIANNELLA
MAKEUP
'79 BELL JAR, THE
'82 STRANGER IS WATCHING, A

MATT CIMBER
PRODUCER
'82 BUTTERFLY
DIRECTOR
'82 BUTTERFLY
SCREENPLAY
'82 BUTTERFLY*

MICHAEL CIMINO
PRODUCER
'78 DEER HUNTER, THE*
DIRECTOR
'78 DEER HUNTER, THE
'80 HEAVEN'S GATE
SCREENPLAY
'80 HEAVEN'S GATE

FRANCESCO CINIERI
CASTING
'82 MONSIGNOR*
'82 YES, GIORGIO*

DELIA CIRCELLO
PROD. OFFICE COORD.
'84 SOLDIER'S STORY, A

CRISTINA CIRNE
PROPS
'84 BLAME IT ON RIO*

MARIO CISNEROS
1ST ASST. DIRECTOR
'80 OCTAGON, THE*
'81 ZORRO, THE GAY BLADE*
'83 YELLOWBEARD*
2ND ASST. DIRECTOR
'79 SUNBURN
'81 CAVEMAN

RICHARD CIUPKA
CINEMATOGRAPHER
'81 ATLANTIC CITY

ELAINA CIZEK
HAIR
'82 DEATH VALLEY

BARBARA CLAMAN
CASTING
'79 BOARDWALK*
'80 CHANGELING, THE*
'80 TIMES SQUARE
'81 ENTITY, THE
'81 HAND, THE
'81 MODERN ROMANCE*
'82 SUMMER LOVERS*
'82 LIAR'S MOON*
'84 PURPLE HEARTS

DOUGLAS CLAPP
UNIT PROD. MANAGER
'81 FEAR NO EVIL

NIKKI CLAPP
SCRIPT SUPERVISOR
'79 HURRICANE
'80 FOR THE LOVE OF BENJI
'80 OH! HEAVENLY DOG
'83 HIGH ROAD TO CHINA
'84 CHAMPIONS*
'84 ELECTRIC DREAMS

JAMES STEVEN CLARIDGE
MISCELLANEOUS
'84 SPLASH

ALBERT CLARK
STILLS
'81 RAIDERS OF THE LOST ARK

B.D. CLARK
DIRECTOR
'81 GALAXY OF TERROR
SCREENPLAY
'81 GALAXY OF TERROR*

BOB CLARK
PRODUCER
'79 MURDER BY DECREE*
'82 PORKY'S*
'83 CHRISTMAS STORY, A*
'83 PORKY'S II THE NEXT DAY*
DIRECTOR
'79 MURDER BY DECREE
'80 TRIBUTE
'82 PORKY'S
'83 CHRISTMAS STORY, A
'83 PORKY'S II THE NEXT DAY
'84 RHINESTONE
SCREENPLAY
'82 PORKY'S
'83 CHRISTMAS STORY, A*
'83 PORKY'S II THE NEXT DAY*

BRIAN CLARK
SCREENPLAY
'81 WHOSE LIFE IS IT ANYWAY?*

CURTIS CLARK
CINEMATOGRAPHER
'83 DRAUGHTSMAN CONTRACT, THE

FRANK CLARK
DIRECTOR
'81 BEYOND THE REEF
2ND UNIT DIRECTOR
'79 HURRICANE

GREYDON CLARK
PRODUCER
'80 WITHOUT WARNING
'83 JOYSTICKS
DIRECTOR
'80 WITHOUT WARNING
'83 JOYSTICKS

HILARY CLARK
PUBLICIST
'84 SWING SHIFT
UNIT PUBLICIST
'83 TWILIGHT ZONE, THE MOVIE*

HOPE CLARK
MISCELLANEOUS
'81 BODY AND SOUL

JANIS CLARK
HAIR
'82 NIGHT SHIFT
'83 STROKER ACE*

JIM CLARK
EDITOR
'79 AGATHA
'79 YANKS
'81 HONKY TONK FREEWAY
'83 PRIVATES ON PARADE
'84 KILLING FIELDS, THE
2ND UNIT DIRECTOR
'81 HONKY TONK FREEWAY

JIM CLARK
LOCATIONS
'83 OUTSIDERS, THE

JOHN CLARK
PRODUCER
'83 HOUSE ON SORORITY ROW*

KATHIE CLARK
MISCELLANEOUS
'83 METALSTORM: THE DESTRUCTION OF JARED-SYN

LAURENCE CLARK
ASSISTANT EDITOR
'81 HONKY TONK FREEWAY*

MICHAEL CLARK
ASSISTANT EDITOR
'79 SILENT PARTNER, THE

PAUL CLARK
SOUND
'80 BLUE LAGOON
'81 STRANGE BEHAVIOR
'81 ROAD GAMES
'82 PIRATE MOVIE, THE

ROBIN CLARK
PRODUCTION MANAGER
'80 RAISE THE TITANIC*
UNIT PROD. MANAGER
'82 SPLIT IMAGE*

STEVE CLARK
KEY GRIP
'79 BUCK ROGERS

BUD CLARKE
ASSISTANT EDITOR
'79 VILLAIN, THE

BUDDY CLARKE
PUBLICIST
'81 HARDLY WORKING

NOBBY CLARKE
SPECIAL EFFECTS
'81 FRENCH LIEUTENANT'S WOMAN, THE*

LAURIE CLARKSON
SOUND
'79 HURRICANE

LISA CLARKSON
CASTING
'82 TEX*

ANTHONY CLAVET
MAKEUP
'83 MERRY CHRISTMAS, MR. LAWRENCE*
MISCELLANEOUS
'83 HUNGER, THE

ANTONY CLAVET
MISCELLANEOUS
'84 COTTON CLUB, THE

DOUG CLAYBOURNE
PRODUCER
'82 ESCAPE ARTIST, THE*
'83 RUMBLEFISH*
'83 BLACK STALLION RETURNS,THE*
1ST ASST. DIRECTOR
'79 BLACK STALLION, THE
'83 BLACK STALLION RETURNS,THE*

NANCY CLAYCOMB
PROD. SECRETARY
'80 WHEN TIME RAN OUT

JACK CLAYTON
DIRECTOR
'83 SOMETHING WICKED THIS WAY COMES

PATRICK CLAYTON
1ST ASST. DIRECTOR
'80 HOPSCOTCH*
'82 ROAD WARRIOR, THE*
'84 LASSITER
'84 SHEENA
MISCELLANEOUS
'82 ROAD WARRIOR, THE
'83 KEEP, THE

JOHN CLEESE
SCREENPLAY
'79 MONTY PYTHON'S LIFE OF BRIAN*
'82 MONTY PYTHON LIVE AT THE HOLLYWOOD BOWL*
'83 MONTY PYTHON'S THE MEANING OF LIFE*

TERRENCE CLEGG
EXECUTIVE PRODUCER
'83 HUNGER, THE
EXEC IN CHARGE PROD
'80 ELEPHANT MAN, THE
'82 GANDHI
PRODUCTION MANAGER
'80 SATURN 3

HARRY CLEIN
PUBLICIST
'79 STARTING OVER
'80 JAZZ SINGER, THE*

BRIAN CLEMENS
SCREENPLAY
'80 WATCHER IN THE WOODS, THE*

DICK CLEMENT
SCREENPLAY
'79 PRISONER OF ZENDA, THE*

JACQUES CLEMENTE
MAKEUP
'80 AMERICAN SUCCESS COMPANY,THE*

JUAN CLEMENTE
LOCATIONS
'82 CONAN THE BARBARIAN
'84 DUNE
'84 CONAN THE DESTROYER

CANDACE CLEMENTS
COSTUMES
'80 MANIAC
COSTUME SUPERVISOR
'84 OVER THE BROOKLYN BRIDGE
MAKEUP
'80 MANIAC

JACK CLEMENTS
UNIT PROD. MANAGER
'84 JOY OF SEX, THE

GABRIELLE CLERY
PROD. SECRETARY
'81 TICKET TO HEAVEN

CARL CLIFFORD
PRODUCTION MANAGER
'84 OVER THE BROOKLYN BRIDGE
1ST ASST. DIRECTOR
'81 BURNING, THE
'83 ANGELO, MY LOVE*
2ND ASST. DIRECTOR
'82 CREEPSHOW

GRAEME CLIFFORD
DIRECTOR
'82 FRANCES
EDITOR
'81 POSTMAN ALWAYS RINGS TWICE, THE

JEFFREY CLIFFORD
SPECIAL EFFECTS
'80 BIG RED ONE, THE*
'82 ROAD WARRIOR, THE

MICHAEL CLIFFORD
SPECIAL EFFECTS
'82 AMATEUR, THE*

EDWARD CLINTON
SCREENPLAY
'81 HONKY TONK FREEWAY

GEORGE CLINTON
MUSIC
'83 CHEECH AND CHONG'S STILL SMOKIN'
MISCELLANEOUS
'82 VICE SQUAD

JACK CLINTON
2ND ASST. DIRECTOR
'80 JAZZ SINGER, THE*

ZILLA CLINTON
PRODUCTION MANAGER
'79 DAWN OF THE DEAD
'81 KNIGHTRIDERS

RICH CLISE
SPECIAL EFFECTS
'83 MAN FROM SNOWY RIVER, THE

GHISLAIN CLOQUET
CINEMATOGRAPHER
'80 TESS*
'81 FOUR FRIENDS

LEON CLORE
PRODUCER
'81 FRENCH LIEUTENANT'S WOMAN, THE

MURRAY CLOSE
STILLS
'82 DARK CRYSTAL, THE
'82 MOONLIGHTING
'84 BOUNTY, THE
'84 GREYSTOKE: THE LEGEND OF TARZAN, LORD OF THE APES

CLOUDIA
MISCELLANEOUS
'83 OSTERMAN WEEKEND, THE

ROBERT CLOUSE
DIRECTOR
'79 GAME OF DEATH
'80 BIG BRAWL, THE
'81 FORCE FIVE
SCREENPLAY
'80 BIG BRAWL, THE
'81 FORCE FIVE

ALAN CLUER
ASSOCIATE PRODUCER
'79 GOLDENGIRL

VIOLETTA COATA
PROD. SECRETARY
'83 BLACK STALLION RETURNS, THE*

ANNE COATES
EDITOR
'79 LEGACY, THE
'80 ELEPHANT MAN, THE
'81 RAGTIME*
'83 PIRATES OF PENZANCE, THE
'84 GREYSTOKE: THE LEGEND OF TARZAN, LORD OF THE APES

BRYAN COATES
LOCATIONS
'81 RAIDERS OF THE LOST ARK*
'81 CLASH OF THE TITANS
'81 FINAL CONFLICT, THE*
'83 KEEP, THE*

LEWIS COATES
DIRECTOR
'79 STARCRASH
'83 HERCULES
SCREENPLAY
'79 STARCRASH*
'83 HERCULES

DAVID COATSWORTH
PRODUCTION MANAGER
'84 KILLING FIELDS, THE*
2ND ASST. DIRECTOR
'80 MIDDLE AGE CRAZY*
'81 LAST CHASE, THE*
LOCATIONS
'79 BROOD, THE
'83 DEAD ZONE, THE
'83 VIDEODROME
'84 JUST THE WAY YOU ARE*

RON COBB
PRODUCTION DESIGNER
'82 CONAN THE BARBARIAN
'84 LAST STARFIGHTER, THE
MISCELLANEOUS
'79 ALIEN

ROBERT COBERT
MUSIC
'79 SCALPEL

JAMES COBLENTZ
EDITOR
'80 FOXES
'80 IT'S MY TURN*
'83 CHEECH AND CHONG'S STILL SMOKIN'*
MISCELLANEOUS
'80 WHOLLY MOSES!

WALTER COBLENZ
PRODUCER
'79 ONION FIELD, THE
'81 LEGEND OF THE LONE RANGER, THE
'83 STRANGE INVADERS

DICK COBOS
MAKEUP
'80 STIR CRAZY
'84 WOMAN IN RED, THE*

ARTHUR COBURN
EDITOR
'83 BALLAD OF GREGORIO CORTEZ, THE*
'84 BEVERLY HILLS COP*

BOB COBURN
STILLS
'80 MOTEL HELL

FRANK COCCARO
ART DIRECTOR
'83 ANGEL OF H.E.A.T.
PROPS
'83 ANGEL OF H.E.A.T.

ROBERT COCCO
LOCATIONS
'83 TABLE FOR FIVE*

ROBERTO COCCO
PRODUCTION MANAGER
'81 INCHON*

THOMAS COCHEO
PROPS
'82 LOVE CHILD
'83 BLUE SKIES AGAIN
'84 HARRY & SON
'84 WHERE THE BOYS ARE

COCO
CHOREOGRAPHER
'79 HURRICANE

STACEY CODIKOW
STILLS
'81 GRADUATION DAY

CARYL CODON
HAIR
'79 BUDDY HOLLY STORY, THE*

DEBRA COE
MISCELLANEOUS
'84 ICEMAN

JIM COE
STILLS
'79 RAVAGERS
'80 CLOSE ENCOUNTERS OF THE THIRD KIND SPECIAL EDITION*
'80 FINAL COUNTDOWN, THE
'80 HONEYSUCKLE ROSE
'80 MY BODYGUARD
'80 STEEL
'81 BACK ROADS
'81 ESCAPE FROM NEW YORK*
'82 SILENT RAGE

JOEL COEN
ASSISTANT EDITOR
'81 FEAR NO EVIL
'83 EVIL DEAD, THE

MADELEINE COFANO
HAIR
'79 FIFTH MUSKETEER, THE*

JOE COFFEY
MISCELLANEOUS
'82 STILL OF THE NIGHT

ADOLFO COFINO
ART DIRECTOR
'79 JAGUAR LIVES

RONNIE COGAN
HAIR
'84 KILLING FIELDS, THE

RONALD COGSWELL
SOUND
'79 LOVE AT FIRST BITE
'79 ON THE YARD
'80 USED CARS
'83 STING II, THE

ALBERT COHEN
MISCELLANEOUS
'81 SATURDAY THE 14TH

ANDREW COHEN
ASSISTANT EDITOR
'82 YES, GIORGIO

BARNEY COHEN
SCREENPLAY
'84 FRIDAY THE 13TH PART IV THE FINAL CHAPTER

BETTY COHEN
ASSISTANT EDITOR
'81 INCREDIBLE SHRINKING WOMAN, THE*

DON COHEN
SOUND
'80 HOG WILD
'81 SCANNERS
'83 OF UNKNOWN ORIGIN

EDWARD COHEN
EXECUTIVE PRODUCER
'79 BUDDY HOLLY STORY, THE
'81 UNDER THE RAINBOW

GEORGE BERNARD COHEN
MISCELLANEOUS
'83 ECHOES

HOWARD COHEN
DIRECTOR
'81 SATURDAY THE 14TH
SCREENPLAY
'81 SATURDAY THE 14TH

JOEL COHEN
ASSOCIATE PRODUCER
'83 STRANGE INVADERS*

JONATHAN COHEN
ASSISTANT EDITOR
'79 BREAKING AWAY*

LARRY COHEN
PRODUCER
'82 Q: QUETZALCOATL
DIRECTOR
'82 Q: QUETZALCOATL
SCREENPLAY
'80 AMERICAN SUCCESS COMPANY,THE*
'82 I, THE JURY
'82 Q: QUETZALCOATL

LAURIE COHEN
SCRIPT SUPERVISOR
'80 GALAXINA
'82 SEDUCTION, THE

LAWRENCE COHEN
SCREENPLAY
'81 GHOST STORY

MARLA COHEN
LOCATIONS
'80 BLUES BROTHERS*

MARTIN COHEN
PRODUCER
'80 HUMANOIDS FROM THE DEEP
ASSISTANT EDITOR
'84 BEST DEFENSE*
'84 FALLING IN LOVE*
'84 MEATBALLS PART II

MICHELLE COHEN
PUBLICIST
'80 URBAN COWBOY

NORMAN COHEN
UNIT PROD. MANAGER
'81 FUNHOUSE, THE
1ST ASST. DIRECTOR
'81 FUNHOUSE, THE

RANDY COHEN
SPECIAL EFFECTS
'79 MR. MIKE'S MONDO VIDEO*

ROB COHEN
DIRECTOR
'80 SMALL CIRCLE OF FRIENDS, A
'84 SCANDALOUS
SCREENPLAY
'84 SCANDALOUS*
EXECUTIVE PRODUCER
'84 RAZOR'S EDGE, THE

ROBERT COHEN
UNIT PROD. MANAGER
'84 MEATBALLS PART II
1ST ASST. DIRECTOR
'81 CHEECH AND CHONG'S NICE DREAMS
'81 KING OF THE MOUNTAIN
'82 SILENT RAGE
'82 NATIONAL LAMPOON'S CLASS REUNION
'83 NATIONAL LAMPOON'S VACATION
'83 MAN WHO WASN'T THERE, THE
'84 MEATBALLS PART II
2ND ASST. DIRECTOR
'79 LOVE AT FIRST BITE
'79 PROPHECY*
'79 FORCE OF ONE, A*
'80 WHEN TIME RAN OUT*

RONALD COHEN
PRODUCER
'79 RUNNING*
'80 MIDDLE AGE CRAZY*
EXECUTIVE PRODUCER
'81 TICKET TO HEAVEN

SHERRY COHEN
PROD. COORDINATOR
'79 FAST COMPANY

SHURA COHEN
COSTUMES
'79 LEGACY, THE

STEVEN COHEN
ASSISTANT EDITOR
'79 RUNNER STUMBLES, THE
'80 OCTAGON, THE*

STUART COHEN
CO-PRODUCER
'82 THING, THE

MICHAEL COHL
EXECUTIVE PRODUCER
'81 BURNING, THE*

ELIE COHN
1ST ASST. DIRECTOR
'81 BLOOD BEACH
'81 VICTORY
'82 MISSING
'83 TWILIGHT ZONE, THE MOVIE*
2ND ASST. DIRECTOR
'79 ROCKY II
'80 RAGING BULL*

LAURIE COHN
SCRIPT SUPERVISOR
'79 ROLLER BOOGIE*
'80 ALLIGATOR
'82 FIGHTING BACK
'82 LIAR'S MOON

BARUCH COHON
MISCELLANEOUS
'79 FRISCO KID, THE

BILL COKER
UNIT PROD. MANAGER
'83 STROKER ACE*
'84 CANNONBALL RUN II
1ST ASST. DIRECTOR
'81 CANNONBALL RUN, THE
'82 MEGAFORCE
2ND ASST. DIRECTOR
'80 SMOKEY AND THE BANDIT II*

HARLEY COKLISS
2ND UNIT DIRECTOR
'80 EMPIRE STRIKES BACK, THE*

DANNY COLANGELO
PROPS
'84 INDIANA JONES
AND THE TEMPLE OF DOOM*

ALDO COLANZI
PROPS
'84 MISUNDERSTOOD

ALDO COLANZI
KEY GRIP
'84 SHEENA

RENAUD COLAS
PROPS
'83 EXPOSED*

RONALD COLBY
PRODUCER
'82 HAMMETT*
UNIT PROD. MANAGER
'82 HAMMETT*
'83 OUTSIDERS, THE
1ST ASST. DIRECTOR
'82 HAMMETT*
'83 DEADLY FORCE
LOCATIONS
'79 HAIR*

TERRY COLBY
MISCELLANEOUS
'79 DOUBLE MCGUFFIN, THE

BILL COLE
STUNT COORDINATOR
'82 IF YOU COULD SEE WHAT I HEAR*

DOUG COLE
PROD. OFFICE COORD.
'82 COME BACK TO THE 5 & 10,
JIMMY DEAN, JIMMY DEAN
PROD. COORDINATOR
'83 STREAMERS

GARY COLE
PROPS
'84 BREAKIN 2 ELECTRIC BOOGALOO

HERMAN COLE
MISCELLANEOUS
'79 PENITENTIARY
'82 PENITENTIARY II

HOWARD COLE
PROPS
'82 DON'T CRY, IT'S ONLY THUNDER
'83 MAUSOLEUM

JOHN COLE
PROPS
'83 MONTY PYTHON'S
THE MEANING OF LIFE*

STAN COLE
EDITOR
'79 MURDER BY DECREE
'82 PORKY'S
'83 CHRISTMAS STORY, A
'83 PORKY'S II THE NEXT DAY
'84 RHINESTONE*

ALBERT COLEMAN
ASSISTANT EDITOR
'83 TERMS OF ENDEARMENT*

CHARLES COLEMAN
ASSISTANT EDITOR
'81 HARDLY WORKING*
'81 ZORRO, THE GAY BLADE*

CLIFFORD COLEMAN
1ST ASST. DIRECTOR
'80 IDOLMAKER, THE
'80 TOM HORN
'81 BUSTIN' LOOSE*
'82 ROCKY III
'83 GET CRAZY
'84 KARATE KID, THE

CY COLEMAN
MUSIC
'84 GARBO TALKS

DONALD COLEMAN
MISCELLANEOUS
'83 METALSTORM: THE DESTRUCTION
OF JARED-SYN

JERRY COLEMAN
MISCELLANEOUS
'83 BLUE SKIES AGAIN

STAN COLEMAN
EXECUTIVE PRODUCER
'84 CHEECH AND CHONG'S THE
CORSICAN BROTHERS*

THOMAS COLEMAN
EXECUTIVE PRODUCER
'83 VALLEY GIRL*
'84 NIGHT OF THE COMET*
'84 ALPHABET CITY*

CHRIS COLES
PRODUCTION MANAGER
'83 SUPERMAN III*
MISCELLANEOUS
'80 JAZZ SINGER, THE

JOHN DAVID COLES
ASSISTANT EDITOR
'84 COTTON CLUB, THE*

ROBERT COLESBERRY
ASSOCIATE PRODUCER
'81 TATTOO
'83 BABY IT'S YOU
'83 KING OF COMEDY, THE
'84 FALLING IN LOVE
'84 NATURAL, THE
'84 RECKLESS
PRODUCTION MANAGER
'81 TATTOO*
'83 BABY IT'S YOU
'83 KING OF COMEDY, THE
UNIT PROD. MANAGER
'84 FALLING IN LOVE
'84 NATURAL, THE
'84 RECKLESS
1ST ASST. DIRECTOR
'79 BOARDWALK
'80 FAME
'80 WINDOWS
MISCELLANEOUS
'79 BOARDWALK

PAT COLL
LOCATIONS
'81 HARDLY WORKING

BILL COLLARD
2ND ASST. DIRECTOR
'83 FRIGHTMARE

YANOU COLLART
PUBLICIST
'84 CHEECH AND CHONG'S THE CORSICAN BROTHERS

TONINO DELLI COLLI
CINEMATOGRAPHER
'81 SUNDAY LOVERS*
'83 TRENCHCOAT
'84 ONCE UPON A TIME IN AMERICA

CYRIL COLLICK
SOUND
'79 CIRCLE OF IRON
'80 BIG RED ONE, THE

ALAN COLLINS
EDITOR
'79 BROOD, THE

BARRY COLLINS
CHOREOGRAPHER
'80 FIENDISH PLOT OF DR. FU MANCHU, THE

CLAY COLLINS
ASSISTANT EDITOR
'81 ZORRO, THE GAY BLADE*

JOE COLLINS
KEY GRIP
'79 MUPPET MOVIE, THE
'79 FORCE OF ONE, A
'80 SOMEWHERE IN TIME
'81 CONTINENTAL DIVIDE
'81 MODERN ROMANCE

KENNETH COLLINS
2ND ASST. DIRECTOR
'80 AIRPLANE
'80 CHEAPER TO KEEP HER*
'82 ONE FROM THE HEART*
'83 CROSS CREEK
'83 GET CRAZY*

NORMA COLLINS
HAIR
'81 TARZAN, THE APE MAN

ROBERT COLLINS
MISCELLANEOUS
'81 KING OF THE MOUNTAIN

RUSSELL COLLINS
ART DIRECTOR
'81 STRANGE BEHAVIOR

TOM COLLINS
STILLS
'80 OUTSIDER, THE
'83 EDUCATING RITA

PETER COLLINSON
DIRECTOR
'81 EARTHLING, THE

JACK COLLIS
ART DIRECTOR
'79 NORTH AVENUE IRREGULARS,THE*
PRODUCTION DESIGNER
'79 JERK, THE
'80 LONG RIDERS, THE
'81 FOUR SEASONS, THE
'81 PATERNITY
'82 NIGHT SHIFT
'82 TEX
'83 NATIONAL LAMPOON'S VACATION
'84 IMPULSE
'84 SPLASH

TERRY COLLIS
PRODUCTION MANAGER
'82 FRIDAY THE 13TH PART THREE IN 3D

MICHEL COLOMBIER
MUSIC
'80 STEEL
'84 AGAINST ALL ODDS*
'84 PURPLE RAIN

HARRY COLOMBY
SCREENPLAY
'84 JOHNNY DANGEROUSLY*
EXECUTIVE PRODUCER
'84 JOHNNY DANGEROUSLY*
CO-PRODUCER
'83 MR. MOM

KERRY COLONNA
MISCELLANEOUS
'83 DEAL OF THE CENTURY

MARY COLQUHOUN
CASTING
'82 SOUP FOR ONE*
'84 BEAT STREET*

CHRIS COLUMBUS
SCREENPLAY
'84 GREMLINS
'84 RECKLESS

CHUCK COLWELL
MISCELLANEOUS
'80 GALAXINA
'84 TERMINATOR, THE

K.C. COLWELL
2ND ASST. DIRECTOR
'82 ZAPPED!*
'84 IRRECONCILABLE DIFFERENCES
'84 IMPULSE

GARY COMBS
STUNT COORDINATOR
'79 VILLAIN, THE
'80 HUNTER, THE
'80 TOM HORN
'81 HISTORY OF THE WORLD PART I
'81 PURSUIT OF D.B. COOPER, THE
'82 BLADERUNNER
'82 HANKY PANKY
'82 NIGHT SHIFT
'83 STROKER ACE
'83 UNDER FIRE

GILBERT COMBS
STUNT COORDINATOR
'83 STAR 80
'83 ANGEL OF H.E.A.T.

BILL COMFORD
ASSOCIATE PRODUCER
'82 BOOGENS, THE*

JOHN COMFORT
ASSOCIATE PRODUCER
'82 SENDER, THE*
'83 BRITANNIA HOSPITAL
PRODUCTION MANAGER
'81 EYE OF THE NEEDLE
LOCATIONS
'79 MOONRAKER*
MISCELLANEOUS
'81 SHOCK TREATMENT
'84 RAZOR'S EDGE, THE

C. COMISKY
SPECIAL EFFECTS
'80 BATTLE BEYOND THE STARS*
MISCELLANEOUS
'80 BATTLE BEYOND THE STARS

JO COMPTON
PROD. COORDINATOR
'82 DEAD MEN DON'T WEAR PLAID

RICHARD COMPTON
DIRECTOR
'79 RAVAGERS

SAMUEL COMSTOCK
MISCELLANEOUS
'81 DRAGONSLAYER
'82 STAR TREK II THE WRATH OF KHAN
'82 E.T. THE EXTRA-TERRESTRIAL

FRANCOIS COMTET
PRODUCTION DESIGNER
'83 ENIGMA

GUY COMTOIS
ART DIRECTOR
'80 TERROR TRAIN
PRODUCTION DESIGNER
'82 QUEST FOR FIRE*
'83 CUJO
'84 BODY ROCK

BILL CONDON
SCREENPLAY
'81 STRANGE BEHAVIOR*
'83 STRANGE INVADERS*
ASSOCIATE PRODUCER
'81 STRANGE BEHAVIOR

CHRIS CONDON
MISCELLANEOUS
'82 PARASITE
'83 JAWS 3-D
'83 METALSTORM: THE DESTRUCTION OF JARED-SYN

LAUREY CONDON
ASSISTANT EDITOR
'79 TIME AFTER TIME*

CANDIDA CONERY
HAIR
'80 XANADU*
'81 RICH AND FAMOUS*
'82 ANNIE*
'83 MAN WOMAN AND CHILD
'84 ICE PIRATES, THE*

RUTH CONFORTE
CASTING
'80 OH! HEAVENLY DOG*

HELEN CONKLIN
MISCELLANEOUS
'80 ANY WHICH WAY YOU CAN

KATHLEEN CONKLIN
PROD. COORDINATOR
'83 SWEET SIXTEEN

JOSEPH CONLAN
MUSIC
'83 CHAINED HEAT

DAN CONLEY
PROPS
'83 STRANGE INVADERS*

RENIE CONLEY
COSTUMES
'81 BODY HEAT

TOM CONLEY
KEY GRIP
'84 MEATBALLS PART II

KEVIN CONLIN
ART DIRECTOR
'84 BACHELOR PARTY*

MIKE CONNELL
ASSISTANT EDITOR
'82 MOONLIGHTING

COLETTE CONNER
PUBLICIST
'84 PREPPIES

MICHAEL CONNER
ASSISTANT EDITOR
'79 STEVIE

CRIN CONNOLLY
PROD. COORDINATOR
'80 HIDE IN PLAIN SIGHT

DON CONNOLY
SOUND
'79 PICNIC AT HANGING ROCK
'79 MY BRILLIANT CAREER
'81 GALLIPOLI
'81 EARTHLING, THE

FRANK CONNOR
STILLS
'79 HURRICANE
'80 ELEPHANT MAN, THE
'80 DEATH SHIP
'81 FRENCH LIEUTENANT'S WOMAN, THE
'83 BRITANNIA HOSPITAL
'83 GORKY PARK
'83 OCTOPUSSY*
'84 PASSAGE TO INDIA, A

KEVIN CONNOR
DIRECTOR
'79 ARABIAN ADVENTURE
'80 MOTEL HELL

SEAN-MICHAEL CONNOR
ASSISTANT EDITOR
'79 REMEMBER MY NAME*

TOM CONNORS III
1ST ASST. DIRECTOR
'82 TEX

TOM CONNORS
1ST ASST. DIRECTOR
'80 STEEL
'83 STROKER ACE
'84 CANNONBALL RUN II

JACK CONRAD
PRODUCER
'81 HOWLING, THE*

RANDALL CONRAD
PRODUCER
'81 DOZENS, THE*
DIRECTOR
'81 DOZENS, THE*
SCREENPLAY
'81 DOZENS, THE*
EDITOR
'81 DOZENS, THE*

SCOTT CONRAD
EDITOR
'80 CHEECH AND CHONG'S NEXT MOVIE
'80 HOLLYWOOD KNIGHTS, THE*
'81 CHEECH AND CHONG'S NICE DREAMS
'83 SPACEHUNTER: ADVENTURES IN THE FORBIDDEN ZONE

BILL CONSENTINO
2ND ASST. DIRECTOR
'79 PERFECT COUPLE, A
'79 REMEMBER MY NAME*
'82 BARBAROSA

MARIE CONSIGLIO
PRODUCTION MANAGER
'81 SATURDAY THE 14TH

DAVID CONSTABLE
ART DIRECTOR
'79 METEOR

JOE CONSTANTINO
PRODUCTION MANAGER
'84 PURPLE HEARTS

JEAN PATRICK CONSTATINI
UNIT MANAGER
'79 LITTLE ROMANCE, A*
1ST ASST. DIRECTOR
'79 FEDORA*

D. CONSTANTINE CONTE
PRODUCER
'82 FIGHTING BACK
'84 HARD TO HOLD
EXECUTIVE PRODUCER
'82 CONAN THE BARBARIAN*
'82 48 HOURS

MARK CONTE
EDITOR
'83 UNDER FIRE*

MARK CONTER
ASSISTANT EDITOR
'81 ON GOLDEN POND

BILL CONTI
MUSIC
'79 ROCKY II
'79 SEDUCTION OF JOE TYNAN, THE
'79 DREAMER
'79 MAN, A WOMAN AND A BANK, A
'79 FIVE DAYS FROM HOME
'80 FORMULA, THE
'80 GLORIA
'80 PRIVATE BENJAMIN
'81 FOR YOUR EYES ONLY
'81 NEIGHBORS
'81 VICTORY
'82 ROCKY III
'82 SPLIT IMAGE
'82 I, THE JURY
'82 THAT CHAMPIONSHIP SEASON
'83 RIGHT STUFF, THE
'83 BAD BOYS
'84 KARATE KID, THE
'84 UNFAITHFULLY YOURS
'84 BEAR, THE
'84 MASS APPEAL

JAMES CONTNER
CINEMATOGRAPHER
'80 CRUISING
'80 GILDA LIVE*
'80 TIMES SQUARE
'81 SO FINE
'81 NIGHTHAWKS
'83 EDDIE MACON'S RUN
'83 JAWS 3-D
'83 TOUGH ENOUGH
'84 FLAMINGO KID, THE
'84 WHERE THE BOYS ARE

ARMANDO CONTRERAS
KEY GRIP
'81 TARZAN, THE APE MAN
'84 MICKI AND MAUDE

BILL CONWAY
MISCELLANEOUS
'82 ANDROID

JAMES CONWAY
DIRECTOR
'80 HANGAR 18
'82 BOOGENS, THE

MARC CONWAY
MISCELLANEOUS
'81 MY BLOODY VALENTINE
'83 STRANGE BREW

RICHARD CONWAY
MISCELLANEOUS
'80 FLASH GORDON
'84 INDIANA JONES AND THE TEMPLE OF DOOM

TIM CONWAY
SCREENPLAY
'79 PRIZE FIGHTER, THE*
'80 PRIVATE EYES, THE*

CRAIG CONWELL
ASSISTANT EDITOR
'84 AMERICAN DREAMER*

RY COODER
MUSIC
'80 LONG RIDERS, THE
'81 SOUTHERN COMFORT
'82 BORDER, THE
'84 STREETS OF FIRE
'84 PARIS, TEXAS

BRIAN COOK
1ST ASST. DIRECTOR
'80 SHINING, THE
'80 FFOLKES
'80 FLASH GORDON
'80 HEAVEN'S GATE*
'80 KIDS ARE ALL RIGHT, THE*

DEBBIE COOK
PROD. COORDINATOR
'83 SCREWBALLS

JAN COOK
HAIR
'81 DEAD AND BURIED

LISA COOK
PROD. COORDINATOR
'83 CHAINED HEAT

NORMAN COOK
PRODUCTION MANAGER
'79 BEYOND THE POSEIDON ADVENTURE
'81 TAPS*

PETER COOK
SCREENPLAY
'83 YELLOWBEARD*

RANDY COOK
MISCELLANEOUS
'82 Q: QUETZALCOATL

SKIP COOK
KEY GRIP
'81 TAKE THIS JOB AND SHOVE IT
'82 SEDUCTION, THE

T.S. COOK
SCREENPLAY
'79 CHINA SYNDROME, THE*

TOMMY COOK
ASSOCIATE PRODUCER
'79 PLAYERS

VIRGINIA COOK
PROD. COORDINATOR
'79 WHEN A STRANGER CALLS
'80 BLACK MARBLE, THE
'81 PURSUIT OF D.B. COOPER, THE*
'84 HARD TO HOLD

MALCOLM COOKE
EDITOR
'79 FIFTH MUSKETEER, THE
'80 FLASH GORDON
'84 SUPERGIRL

ANTHONY COOKSON
2ND ASST. DIRECTOR
'83 NEVER CRY WOLF*

MARTHA COOLIDGE
DIRECTOR
'83 VALLEY GIRL
'84 JOY OF SEX, THE

MICHAEL COONEY
2ND ASST. DIRECTOR
'81 TAPS*

RAY COONEY
EXECUTIVE PRODUCER
'81 WHOSE LIFE IS IT ANYWAY?*

TIM COONEY
SOUND
'83 BLUE THUNDER*
'83 SWEET SIXTEEN

DENYS COOP
CINEMATOGRAPHER
'82 VENOM*
MISCELLANEOUS
'81 SUPERMAN II

JACK COOPER
SCREENPLAY
'83 GOIN' ALL THE WAY*

KARIN COOPER
SCRIPT SUPERVISOR
'83 10 TO MIDNIGHT

LOU COOPER
SPECIAL EFFECTS
'84 MASS APPEAL

MARTIN COOPER
ASSOCIATE PRODUCER
'81 GALLIPOLI*

RALPH COOPER
MISCELLANEOUS
'84 COTTON CLUB, THE

ROBERT COOPER
PRODUCER
'79 RUNNING*
'80 MIDDLE AGE CRAZY*

SAUL COOPER
UNIT PUBLICIST
'84 EVIL THAT MEN DO, THE

TED COOPER
PROPS
'79 C.H.O.M.P.S.

JACK COOPERMAN
MISCELLANEOUS
'80 ALLIGATOR
'82 OFFICER AND A GENTLEMAN, AN
'83 BLUE THUNDER
'83 GOLDEN SEAL, THE

CLIVE COOTE
STILLS
'81 TIME BANDITS
'82 VENOM
'83 BEYOND THE LIMIT
'83 PRIVATES ON PARADE
MISCELLANEOUS
'84 ANOTHER COUNTRY

LISSA COOTE
PROPS
'82 STARSTRUCK*
'83 NATE & HAYES

GEORGE COPANAS
EDITOR
'83 GOIN' ALL THE WAY*

CARL COPELAND
ART DIRECTOR
'79 HEARTLAND
'83 BALLAD OF GREGORIO CORTEZ, THE

STEWART COPELAND
MUSIC
'83 RUMBLEFISH

CARON COPLAN
COSTUMES
'80 FRIDAY THE 13TH

YVONNE COPPARD
MAKEUP
'79 ARABIAN ADVENTURE*
'83 ANOTHER TIME, ANOTHER PLACE
'84 COMFORT AND JOY

DAVID COPPERFIELD
MISCELLANEOUS
'80 TERROR TRAIN

DAVID COPPING
ART DIRECTOR
'79 PICNIC AT HANGING ROCK
'81 EARTHLING, THE*

ROBIN COPPING
CINEMATOGRAPHER
'82 PIRATE MOVIE, THE

CARMINE COPPOLA
MUSIC
'79 APOCALYPSE NOW*
'79 BLACK STALLION, THE
'83 OUTSIDERS, THE

FRANCIS COPPOLA
PRODUCER
'79 APOCALYPSE NOW
DIRECTOR
'79 APOCALYPSE NOW
'82 ONE FROM THE HEART
'83 RUMBLEFISH
'83 OUTSIDERS, THE
'84 COTTON CLUB, THE
SCREENPLAY
'79 APOCALYPSE NOW*
'82 ONE FROM THE HEART*
'83 RUMBLEFISH*
'84 COTTON CLUB, THE*
EXECUTIVE PRODUCER
'79 BLACK STALLION, THE
'82 HAMMETT
'82 ESCAPE ARTIST, THE*
'83 RUMBLEFISH
'83 BLACK STALLION RETURNS, THE
MUSIC
'79 APOCALYPSE NOW*

GIAN-CARLO COPPOLA
ASSOCIATE PRODUCER
'83 RUMBLEFISH*
'83 OUTSIDERS, THE
2ND UNIT DIRECTOR
'84 COTTON CLUB, THE

ROMAN COPPOLA
ASSOCIATE PRODUCER
'83 RUMBLEFISH*

JOHN COQUILLON
CINEMATOGRAPHER
'80 CHANGELING, THE
'82 AMATEUR, THE
'83 OSTERMAN WEEKEND, THE

JAMES CORBETT
2ND ASST. DIRECTOR
'84 SCANDALOUS*

RAY CORBETT
1ST ASST. DIRECTOR
'82 PINK FLOYD: THE WALL
'83 CURSE OF THE PINK PANTHER
'83 MONTY PYTHON'S THE MEANING OF LIFE
'83 TRAIL OF THE PINK PANTHER*
'83 KEEP, THE*
'84 GREYSTOKE: THE LEGEND OF TARZAN, LORD OF THE APES*
'84 RAZOR'S EDGE, THE*

BILL CORCORAN
1ST ASST. DIRECTOR
'81 TICKET TO HEAVEN
LOCATIONS
'79 BLACK STALLION, THE*

KEVIN CORCORAN
ASSOCIATE PRODUCER
'79 NORTH AVENUE IRREGULARS, THE
CO-PRODUCER
'80 HERBIE GOES BANANAS*

FOSTER CORDER
STILLS
'82 PENITENTIARY II

KEITH CORDER
ASSISTANT EDITOR
'84 OXFORD BLUES*

BILL "BEAST" CORDERO
MISCELLANEOUS
'84 BEAT STREET

LAURENCIO CORDERO
SPECIAL EFFECTS
'79 SUNBURN*
'81 CATTLE ANNIE AND LITTLE BRITCHES*
'81 HIGH RISK
'82 MISSING*
'83 UNDER FIRE*
'84 ROMANCING THE STONE*
'84 EVIL THAT MEN DO, THE

RALPH CORDERO
MISCELLANEOUS
'84 BROTHER FROM ANOTHER PLANET, THE

JOHN CORIGLIANO
MUSIC
'80 ALTERED STATES

CHRIS CORMACK
STILLS
'79 EUROPEANS, THE
'83 HEAT AND DUST

CIS CORMAN
CASTING
'78 DEER HUNTER, THE
'79 VOICES
'80 RAGING BULL
'80 HEAVEN'S GATE*
'81 NIGHTHAWKS
'81 WOLFEN
'82 AUTHOR, AUTHOR
'83 KING OF COMEDY, THE
'83 YENTL
'84 ONCE UPON A TIME IN AMERICA*

GENE CORMAN
PRODUCER
'80 BIG RED ONE, THE
EXECUTIVE PRODUCER
'82 IF YOU COULD SEE WHAT I HEAR*
MISCELLANEOUS
'82 PARADISE

JULIE CORMAN
PRODUCER
'81 SATURDAY THE 14TH

RICHARD CORMAN
STILLS
'84 OVER THE BROOKLYN BRIDGE*

ROGER CORMAN
PRODUCER
'79 SAINT JACK
'81 SMOKEY BITES THE DUST
'81 GALAXY OF TERROR
'83 LOVE LETTERS
EXECUTIVE PRODUCER
'79 ROCK 'N ROLL HIGH SCHOOL
'80 BATTLE BEYOND THE STARS

TODD CORMAN
1ST ASST. DIRECTOR
'82 SWAMP THING
2ND ASST. DIRECTOR
'80 BIG RED ONE, THE
'83 LONE WOLF MCQUADE

PETER CORNBERG
PRODUCTION MANAGER
'83 TESTAMENT
UNIT PROD. MANAGER
'80 BIG RED ONE, THE
1ST ASST. DIRECTOR
'82 BLADERUNNER*

PAUL CORNELL
MISCELLANEOUS
'83 RETURN OF THE ALIENS: THE DEADLY SPAWN

STUART CORNFELD
PRODUCER
'80 FATSO
EXECUTIVE PRODUCER
'80 ELEPHANT MAN, THE
ASSOCIATE PRODUCER
'81 HISTORY OF THE WORLD PART I*

BILL CORNFOLD
ASSOCIATE PRODUCER
'80 HANGAR 18

BRIAN CORNFORD
PROPS
'82 BOOGENS, THE

SOPHIE CORNU
ASSISTANT EDITOR
'79 SAINT JACK*

JACK CORNWELL
ART DIRECTOR
'80 DEFIANCE

RANDY CORONATO
MAKEUP
'84 ONCE UPON A TIME IN AMERICA*
HAIR
'84 ONCE UPON A TIME IN AMERICA*

EUGENE CORR
MISCELLANEOUS
'83 NEVER CRY WOLF

PHILLIP CORR
UNIT MANAGER
'84 PHAR LAP
LOCATIONS
'82 PIRATE MOVIE, THE*

ANGELO CORRAO
ASSISTANT EDITOR
'83 SILKWOOD*

CHARLES CORRELL
CINEMATOGRAPHER
'79 FAST BREAK
'80 IN GOD WE TRUST
'81 CHEECH AND CHONG'S NICE DREAMS
'84 STAR TREK III: THE SEARCH FOR SPOCK
'84 JOY OF SEX, THE
MISCELLANEOUS
'80 DIE LAUGHING

MARIA TERESA CORRIDONI
HAIR
'80 POPEYE
'82 MONSIGNOR
'84 ONCE UPON A TIME IN AMERICA*

ANTONIO CORRIDORI
SPECIAL EFFECTS
'83 PIRANHA II: THE SPAWNING*
'83 1990: THE BRONX WARRIORS*

JOEY CORSARO
HAIR
'84 JUST THE WAY YOU ARE*

MICHAEL CORSENTINO
HAIR
'79 CHAMP, THE*

JOHN CORSO
ART DIRECTOR
'81 BUSTIN' LOOSE*
PRODUCTION DESIGNER
'80 COAL MINER'S DAUGHTER
'80 XANADU
'81 HEARTBEEPS
'83 PSYCHO II
'84 SIXTEEN CANDLES

JOHN CORSO
MISCELLANEOUS
'84 BEAT STREET

CARLOS CORTES
PROPS
'83 YELLOWBEARD*

ROBERT CORTES
PRODUCER
'84 CRACKERS*
'84 RIVER, THE*

STANLEY CORTEZ
MISCELLANEOUS
'80 WHEN TIME RAN OUT

BRUNO CORTINI
2ND ASST. DIRECTOR
'79 LITTLE ROMANCE, A*

ANTHONY CORTINO
HAIR
'81 FOUR FRIENDS
'82 LITTLE SEX, A
'83 EXPOSED*
'84 FLAMINGO KID, THE*
'84 BEAT STREET

JUDITH CORY
HAIR
'79 BOULEVARD NIGHTS
'81 LOOKER*
'82 NATIONAL LAMPOON'S CLASS REUNION*
'84 LONELY GUY, THE
'84 PROTOCOL*
'84 CANNONBALL RUN II

PHIL CORY
SPECIAL EFFECTS
'79 RUNNER STUMBLES, THE
'79 BOULEVARD NIGHTS
'79 BUTCH AND SUNDANCE: THE EARLY YEARS
'79 ONION FIELD, THE
'79 SCAVENGER HUNT*
'80 HUNTER, THE
'80 TOM HORN
'81 SHARKEY'S MACHINE
'81 HISTORY OF THE WORLD PART I
'81 UNDER THE RAINBOW
'82 ANNIE
'82 THINGS ARE TOUGH ALL OVER*
'83 STROKER ACE
'84 PROTOCOL
'84 CANNONBALL RUN II

D.A. COSCARELLI
PRODUCER
'79 PHANTASM

DON COSCARELLI
DIRECTOR
'79 PHANTASM
'82 BEASTMASTER, THE
SCREENPLAY
'79 PHANTASM
'82 BEASTMASTER, THE*
CINEMATOGRAPHER
'79 PHANTASM
EDITOR
'79 PHANTASM

JOE COSCIA
MAKEUP
'82 CHOSEN, THE*
HAIR
'79 KRAMER VS. KRAMER
'81 ENDLESS LOVE
'81 FORT APACHE, THE BRONX
'81 NEIGHBORS
'82 CHOSEN, THE*
'82 HANKY PANKY
'82 TOOTSIE*
'83 EASY MONEY
'83 NIGHT IN HEAVEN, A
'84 POPE OF GREENWICH VILLAGE, THE

BILL COSENTINO
2ND ASST. DIRECTOR
'81 ENTITY, THE

PATRICK COSGROVE
2ND ASST. DIRECTOR
'83 BRAINSTORM
'84 CRACKERS*

RICHARD COSGROVE
MISCELLANEOUS
'83 DEAD ZONE, THE

MARIE COSINDAS
STILLS
'84 BOSTONIANS, THE*

VLADIMIR COSMA
MUSIC
'84 JUST THE WAY YOU ARE

GEORGE COSMATOS
DIRECTOR
'79 ESCAPE TO ATHENA
'83 OF UNKNOWN ORIGIN

TONY COSTA
MISCELLANEOUS
'84 NO SMALL AFFAIR

COSTA-GAVRAS
PRODUCER
'83 HANNA K
DIRECTOR
'82 MISSING
'83 HANNA K
SCREENPLAY
'82 MISSING*
'83 HANNA K*

CELIA COSTAS
LOCATIONS
'81 ROLLOVER
'82 SOPHIE'S CHOICE

GEORGE COSTELLO
ART DIRECTOR
'82 SWORD AND THE SORCERER, THE
'82 LIAR'S MOON*
'84 TERMINATOR, THE
PRODUCTION DESIGNER
'84 BEAR, THE

PAUL COSTELLO
MISCELLANEOUS
'83 YOR

HAZEL COTE
COSTUMES
'81 TIME BANDITS*

DEE COTHERN
CASTING
'82 TOY, THE*

LANNY COTLER
SCREENPLAY
'81 EARTHLING, THE

MARIO COTONE
MISCELLANEOUS
'84 ONCE UPON A TIME IN AMERICA

JAMES COTTEN
MISCELLANEOUS
'81 ENTITY, THE

PETER COTTEN
1ST ASST. DIRECTOR
'82 MOONLIGHTING

AL COTTER
SPECIAL EFFECTS
'80 PROM NIGHT

JOHN COTTER
DIRECTOR
'79 MOUNTAIN FAMILY ROBINSON

CARLO COTTI
1ST ASST. DIRECTOR
'83 TRENCHCOAT*

GRAHAM COTTLE
1ST ASST. DIRECTOR
'80 NIJINSKY*
MISCELLANEOUS
'84 PROTOCOL

PETER COTTON
2ND ASST. DIRECTOR
'84 CHAMPIONS*
LOCATIONS
'84 SHEENA*

EDITH COTTRELL
CASTING
'80 BIG RED ONE, THE*

PIERRE COTTRELL
MISCELLANEOUS
'79 SAINT JACK

BILL COUCH
STUNT COORDINATOR
'79 FAST BREAK
'79 LAST EMBRACE*
'80 FINAL COUNTDOWN, THE
'81 DEAD AND BURIED
'82 STAR TREK II THE WRATH OF KHAN
'82 VICE SQUAD*
'83 STRANGE BREW
'83 BRAINSTORM
'83 TWILIGHT ZONE, THE MOVIE*

CHUCK COUCH
STUNT COORDINATOR
'82 DEATHWISH II*

LIONEL COUCH
ART DIRECTOR
'80 AWAKENING, THE*

SAVIN COUELLE
1ST ASST. DIRECTOR
'79 BLOODLINE*

JACK COUFFER
PRODUCER
'83 NEVER CRY WOLF*
2ND UNIT DIRECTOR
'84 SHEENA

CARI COUGHLIN
ASSISTANT EDITOR
'83 STING II, THE
'83 ALL THE RIGHT MOVES
'84 FLASHPOINT*

ANNE COUK
ASSISTANT EDITOR
'83 ECHOES*

CAPT. P.C.G COULTER, USMC
MISCELLANEOUS
'79 GREAT SANTINI, THE

ALEXANDER COURAGE
MISCELLANEOUS
'82 YES, GIORGIO

JEROME COURTLAND

PRODUCER
'81 AMY
'81 DEVIL AND MAX DEVLIN, THE

STEVE COURTLEY

SPECIAL EFFECTS
'81 GALLIPOLI*

DON COURTNEY

SPECIAL EFFECTS
'79 MORE AMERICAN GRAFFITTI

JUDY COURTNEY

MISCELLANEOUS
'84 RECKLESS

MARY COURTNEY-EDWARDS

PROD. SECRETARY
'83 DOCTOR DETROIT

GEOFF COUSINS

MISCELLANEOUS
'84 GIVE MY REGARDS TO BROAD STREET

JEAN-FRANCOIS COUSSON

SPECIAL EFFECTS
'83 HANNA K*

THIERRY COUTURIER

EDITOR
'84 EXTERMINATOR II*
ASSOCIATE EDITOR
'81 ENTER THE NINJA
'82 BUTTERFLY
ASSISTANT EDITOR
'80 SCHIZOID*

JANE COVNER

PUBLICIST
'80 BATTLE BEYOND THE STARS
'81 SATURDAY THE 14TH
'81 GALAXY OF TERROR
UNIT PUBLICIST
'84 THIS IS SPINAL TAP

PAUL COWAN

ASSOCIATE PRODUCER
'83 ANOTHER TIME, ANOTHER PLACE

THEO COWAN

PUBLICIST
'81 SEA WOLVES, THE*

ADGAR COWANS

STILLS
'79 RUNNING*
'80 SIMON
'80 GLORIA*
'81 ROLLOVER
'81 FAN, THE*
'81 ON GOLDEN POND
'84 COTTON CLUB, THE

BRIAN COWDEN

MISCELLANEOUS
'84 PLACES IN THE HEART

JACK COWDEN

SCRIPT SUPERVISOR
'79 HOT STUFF
'81 NOBODY'S PERFEKT
'82 LOVE CHILD
'83 SPRING BREAK
'83 SMOKEY AND THE BANDIT III
'84 HARRY & SON

STANLEY COWELL

MISCELLANEOUS
'81 RAGTIME

RICK COWITT

PROPS
'83 D.C. CAB

ALBERT COWLARD

KEY GRIP
'81 DRAGONSLAYER*

ALEX COX

DIRECTOR
'84 REPO MAN
SCREENPLAY
'84 REPO MAN

BETSY COX

COSTUMES
'79 BREAKING AWAY
'80 SEEMS LIKE OLD TIMES
'80 PRIVATE BENJAMIN
'81 LOOKER
'82 BEST FRIENDS
'82 ENDANGERED SPECIES
'82 YES, GIORGIO*
'83 DOCTOR DETROIT
'84 LONELY GUY, THE
'84 RUNAWAY
'84 WINDY CITY

JOEL COX

EDITOR
'80 BRONCO BILLY*
'82 HONKYTONK MAN*
'82 DEATH VALLEY
'83 SUDDEN IMPACT
'84 TIGHTROPE

MONTY COX

STUNT COORDINATOR
'79 MOUNTAIN FAMILY ROBINSON

MONTY COX

MISCELLANEOUS
'84 IMPULSE

VINCENT COX

MISCELLANEOUS
'82 SAFARI 3000

KIMBERLEY COY

PUBLICIST
'79 APPLE DUMPLING GANG RIDES AGAIN, THE*
'80 JAZZ SINGER, THE*
'81 DEAD AND BURIED
UNIT PUBLICIST
'81 HEARTBEEPS

BOB COYLE

STILLS
'83 BAD BOYS*

GIANNI COZZO

1ST ASST. DIRECTOR
'81 SO FINE*
'81 INCHON
'82 MONSIGNOR
2ND ASST. DIRECTOR
'79 BLOODLINE*

JAMES CRABE

CINEMATOGRAPHER
'79 CHINA SYNDROME, THE
'79 PLAYERS
'80 BALTIMORE BULLET, THE
'80 FORMULA, THE
'80 HOW TO BEAT THE HIGH COST OF LIVING
'82 NIGHT SHIFT
'84 KARATE KID, THE

DEREK CRACKNELL

1ST ASST. DIRECTOR
'79 ESCAPE TO ATHENA
'80 OH! HEAVENLY DOG
'80 MIRROR CRACK'D, THE
'82 EVIL UNDER THE SUN
'83 KRULL
'84 SCANDALOUS
'84 SUPERGIRL
2ND UNIT DIRECTOR
'83 KRULL
MISCELLANEOUS
'79 BLOODLINE

CHUCK CRAFTS

MAKEUP
'79 BEYOND THE POSEIDON ADVENTURE*
'80 WHEN TIME RAN OUT*
'81 INCHON*
'83 PSYCHO II*

DAVID CRAIG

MISCELLANEOUS
'83 CHRISTMAS STORY, A

GEORGE CRAIG

ASSOCIATE EDITOR
'81 TATTOO

LOUIS CRAIG

SPECIAL EFFECTS
'83 OF UNKNOWN ORIGIN*
'84 HOTEL NEW HAMPSHIRE, THE*

STUART CRAIG
PRODUCTION DESIGNER
'80 SATURN 3
'80 ELEPHANT MAN, THE
'82 GANDHI
'84 GREYSTOKE: THE LEGEND OF TARZAN, LORD OF THE APES
MISCELLANEOUS
'81 HISTORY OF THE WORLD PART I

VALERIE CRAIG
PROD. COORDINATOR
'84 OXFORD BLUES

FRED CRAMER
SPECIAL EFFECTS
'78 DEER HUNTER, THE
'79 RAVAGERS
'79 10
'81 BEAST WITHIN, THE
'81 INCHON*
'81 TAPS*
SP. EFFECTS SUPERV.
'84 KILLING FIELDS, THE

GERRY CRAMPTON
STUNT COORDINATOR
'82 GANDHI
'83 LORDS OF DISCIPLINE, THE

ROGET CRANDALL
PROPS
'83 CUJO

JIM CRANSTON
PRODUCTION MANAGER
'84 AGAINST ALL ODDS*
MISCELLANEOUS
'79 SUNBURN

JOE CRANZANO
MAKEUP
'80 DRESSED TO KILL*
'80 WILLIE & PHIL*
'81 BLOW OUT*
'82 DEATHTRAP*
'82 FIRST TIME, THE*
'82 HANKY PANKY*
'82 VERDICT, THE*
'83 DANIEL
'84 GARBO TALKS
'84 MOSCOW ON THE HUDSON*

GARTH CRAVEN
EDITOR
'82 I, THE JURY
'83 EDUCATING RITA
2ND UNIT DIRECTOR
'80 CARNY

JENNY CRAVEN
ASSOCIATE PRODUCER
'82 HOUSE OF THE LONG SHADOWS
PUBLICIST
'80 FFOLKES
UNIT PUBLICIST
'79 MAGICIAN OF LUBLIN, THE*

RICHARD CRAVEN
LOCATIONS
'81 HONKY TONK FREEWAY*

WES CRAVEN
DIRECTOR
'81 DEADLY BLESSING
'82 SWAMP THING
'84 NIGHTMARE ON ELM STREET, A
SCREENPLAY
'81 DEADLY BLESSING*
'82 SWAMP THING
'84 NIGHTMARE ON ELM STREET, A

ARIONNA CRAWFORD
MISCELLANEOUS
'83 MAN WHO LOVED WOMEN, THE

GLEN CRAWFORD
UNIT PUBLICIST
'81 ROAD GAMES

JAMES CRAWFORD
ASSOCIATE PRODUCER
'81 CHARIOTS OF FIRE

LEE CRAWFORD
HAIR
'79 FRISCO KID, THE
'80 WHOLLY MOSES!*
'80 WHEN TIME RAN OUT*
'82 ANNIE*

LORETTA CRAWFORD
MISCELLANEOUS
'83 MAN FROM SNOWY RIVER, THE

PATRICK CRAWFORD
EDITOR
'80 PRIVATE EYES, THE

ROBERT CRAWFORD
PRODUCER
'79 LITTLE ROMANCE, A*
'82 WORLD ACCORDING TO GARP,THE*
'84 LITTLE DRUMMER GIRL, THE

SHIRLEY CRAWFORD
HAIR
'81 ZORRO, THE GAY BLADE*
'82 YOUNG DOCTORS IN LOVE*

WAYNE CRAWFORD
PRODUCER
'83 VALLEY GIRL*
'84 NIGHT OF THE COMET*
SCREENPLAY
'83 VALLEY GIRL*

EVERETT CREACH
STUNT COORDINATOR
'79 PROPHECY*
'79 TIME AFTER TIME
'80 CHEAPER TO KEEP HER
'80 DEFIANCE*
'82 SIX PACK
'83 BREATHLESS
'84 BEST DEFENSE

WILLIAM CREBER
PRODUCTION DESIGNER
'80 ANY WHICH WAY YOU CAN
'80 HOPSCOTCH
'82 SIX PACK
'82 YES, GIORGIO

EUGENE CREDEDIO
KEY GRIP
'80 MY BODYGUARD*

ROGER CREED
STUNT COORDINATOR
'79 AMITYVILLE HORROR, THE
'79 METEOR
'81 HOWLING, THE
'84 TANK

YVON CREEN
UNIT MANAGER
'83 HANNA K

KEVIN CREMIN
1ST ASST. DIRECTOR
'83 NIGHTMARES
2ND ASST. DIRECTOR
'80 FIRST FAMILY

VINCENT CRESCIMAN
ART DIRECTOR
'84 RED DAWN

PILAR CRESPI
MISCELLANEOUS
'84 SCANDALOUS

ANA CRIADO
HAIR
'79 FIFTH MUSKETEER, THE*

CHRISTOBAL CRIADO
MAKEUP
'84 BOLERO

MIK CRIBBEN
UNIT MANAGER
'83 RETURN OF THE ALIENS: THE DEADLY SPAWN

DON CRICHTON
CHOREOGRAPHER
'81 CHU CHU AND THE PHILLY FLASH

MICHAEL CRICHTON
DIRECTOR
'79 GREAT TRAIN ROBBERY, THE
'81 LOOKER
'84 RUNAWAY
SCREENPLAY
'79 GREAT TRAIN ROBBERY, THE
'81 LOOKER
'84 RUNAWAY

TONY CRIDLIN
KEY GRIP
'80 HEAVEN'S GATE*
'83 BRITANNIA HOSPITAL
'83 TRAIL OF THE PINK PANTHER

NICK CRIMI
MAKEUP
'80 DEFIANCE*

IVO CRISTANTE
ART DIRECTOR
'84 WEEKEND PASS
PRODUCTION DESIGNER
'83 PRIVATE SCHOOL
PROPS
'81 SATURDAY THE 14TH
'81 HOWLING, THE
'81 TAKE THIS JOB AND SHOVE IT

MICHAEL CRISTOFER
SCREENPLAY
'84 FALLING IN LOVE

CORRADO CRISTOFORI
HAIR
'83 LONELY LADY, THE*

DIANNE CRITTENDEN
CASTING
'79 GOING IN STYLE*
'79 IN-LAWS, THE
'79 MAIN EVENT, THE*
'79 TIME AFTER TIME
'80 HEARTBEAT
'80 HONEYSUCKLE ROSE*
'82 BARBAROSA*
'83 BLUE THUNDER
'84 BEST DEFENSE
'84 WINDY CITY
'84 TEACHERS

ANTHONY SANTA CROCE
SOUND
'79 ROLLER BOOGIE
'82 BEASTMASTER, THE
'82 EATING RAOUL
'84 BEAR, THE

GERARD CROCE
PRODUCTION MANAGER
'81 SUNDAY LOVERS*
MISCELLANEOUS
'84 JUST THE WAY YOU ARE

DICK CROCKETT
STUNT COORDINATOR
'79 10

CAROL CROFT
MISCELLANEOUS
'80 CARNY

SYLVIA CROFT
MAKEUP
'79 GREAT TRAIN ROBBERY, THE*

ROBERT CRONE
MISCELLANEOUS
'82 AMATEUR, THE

DAVID CRONENBERG
DIRECTOR
'79 BROOD, THE
'79 FAST COMPANY
'81 SCANNERS
'83 DEAD ZONE, THE
'83 VIDEODROME
SCREENPLAY
'79 BROOD, THE
'79 FAST COMPANY*
'81 SCANNERS
'83 VIDEODROME

JORDAN CRONENWETH
CINEMATOGRAPHER
'80 ALTERED STATES
'81 CUTTER'S WAY
'82 BEST FRIENDS
'82 BLADERUNNER

CHIP CRONKITE
ASSISTANT EDITOR
'81 NEIGHBORS*
'83 NIGHT IN HEAVEN, A

CHRIS CRONYN
UNIT PROD. MANAGER
'84 COTTON CLUB, THE*
LOCATIONS
'80 RAGING BULL*
'81 HONKY TONK FREEWAY*

PAUL CROSFIELD
EXECUTIVE PRODUCER
'80 HUMAN FACTOR, THE

GERARD CROSNER
PRODUCTION MANAGER
'83 HANNA K

BEVERLEY CROSS
SCREENPLAY
'81 CLASH OF THE TITANS

DICK CROSS
SPECIAL EFFECTS
'82 THINGS ARE TOUGH ALL OVER*
'84 TANK*

WALLACE CROWDER
STUNT COORDINATOR
'83 LOSIN' IT

CAMERON CROWE
SCREENPLAY
'82 FAST TIMES AT RIDGEMONT HIGH

CHRISTOPHER CROWE
PRODUCER
'83 NIGHTMARES
SCREENPLAY
'83 NIGHTMARES*

PATRICK CROWLEY
1ST ASST. DIRECTOR
'83 LOSIN' IT
'83 UNDER FIRE*
'84 NATURAL, THE*

DEBRA CROWNINGSHIELD
MISCELLANEOUS
'83 JAWS 3-D

JOHN CROWTHER
SCREENPLAY
'84 EVIL THAT MEN DO, THE*
CASTING
'83 10 TO MIDNIGHT

DAVID CROZIER
SOUND
'83 FINAL OPTION, THE

AURELIO CRUGNOLA
ART DIRECTOR
'79 BLACK STALLION, THE*
'83 BLACK STALLION RETURNS, THE
PRODUCTION DESIGNER
'79 STARCRASH
SPECIAL EFFECTS
'79 BLACK STALLION, THE

ART CRUICKSHANK
SPECIAL EFFECTS
'79 APPLE DUMPLING GANG RIDES AGAIN, THE*
'79 NORTH AVENUE IRREGULARS, THE*
'80 HERBIE GOES BANANAS
'80 LAST FLIGHT OF NOAH'S ARK,THE*
'81 DEVIL AND MAX DEVLIN, THE*
MISCELLANEOUS
'79 BLACK HOLE, THE
'80 WATCHER IN THE WOODS, THE
'81 CONDORMAN

SALLY CRUIKSHANK
MISCELLANEOUS
'83 TWILIGHT ZONE, THE MOVIE

BILL CRUSE
MISCELLANEOUS
'82 BEASTMASTER, THE

WILLIAM CRUSE
MISCELLANEOUS
'79 AMITYVILLE HORROR, THE
'81 ENTITY, THE

ARNOLD CRUST
EDITOR
'79 FIREPOWER
'82 DEATHWISH II*
'83 WICKED LADY, THE

EDILBERTO CRUZ
ASSISTANT EDITOR
'83 REUBEN, REUBEN*

HONORIO CRUZ
PROPS
'84 BOLERO

JAVIER RUVALCABA CRUZ
CINEMATOGRAPHER
'84 EVIL THAT MEN DO, THE

GABRIELLA CSORBA
MAKEUP
'82 ZOOT SUIT*

CLIFF CUDNEY
STUNT COORDINATOR
'80 EXTERMINATOR, THE
'81 SO FINE
'81 FRIDAY THE 13TH PART TWO
'81 NESTING, THE*

JOSEPH CUERVO
MAKEUP
'79 RICH KIDS
'80 FAME
'81 RAGTIME*
'81 FAN, THE*
'82 AMITYVILLE II: THE POSSESSION
HAIR
'80 FAME

GEORGE CUKOR
DIRECTOR
'81 RICH AND FAMOUS

VICTOR CULINA
PROPS
'84 TANK

CINDY JAMES CULLEN
MISCELLANEOUS
'84 AGAINST ALL ODDS
'84 LONELY GUY, THE

CLINT CULLEN
MISCELLANEOUS
'81 HONKY TONK FREEWAY

JOHN CULLEN
KEY GRIP
'79 MOUNTAIN FAMILY ROBINSON

CLIFF CULLEY
MISCELLANEOUS
'79 ARABIAN ADVENTURE
'79 UNIDENTIFIED FLYING ODDBALL
'81 CLASH OF THE TITANS

MIKE CULLING
MISCELLANEOUS
'81 RAIDERS OF THE LOST ARK
'84 INDIANA JONES AND THE TEMPLE OF DOOM

PETER CULVERWELL
ASSISTANT EDITOR
'83 ENIGMA*

PATRICK CUMMINGS
COSTUMES
'82 DEATH VALLEY

JACK CUMMINS
ASSOCIATE PRODUCER
'79 BOARDWALK
'83 CHAINED HEAT*
1ST ASST. DIRECTOR
'81 HOWLING, THE
'84 NOT FOR PUBLICATION*
2ND UNIT DIRECTOR
'81 HOWLING, THE*

JACQUELINE CUMMINS
COSTUMES
'81 FEAR NO EVIL

DEAN CUNDEY
CINEMATOGRAPHER
'79 ROCK 'N ROLL HIGH SCHOOL
'79 ROLLER BOOGIE
'80 FOG, THE
'80 WITHOUT WARNING
'80 GALAXINA
'81 ESCAPE FROM NEW YORK
'81 HALLOWEEN II
'82 HALLOWEEN III: SEASON OF THE WITCH
'82 THING, THE
'83 D.C. CAB
'83 PSYCHO II
'84 ROMANCING THE STONE

JESSIE CUNETA
LOCATIONS
'83 YEAR OF LIVING DANGEROUSLY, THE
'84 PURPLE HEARTS

ANTHON CUNHA
STILLS
'80 ALLIGATOR
'82 PARASITE

ELBY CUNIBERTI
MISCELLANEOUS
'81 ON THE RIGHT TRACK

ANTHONY CUNNINGHAM
LOCATIONS
'82 HAMMETT*
'82 ESCAPE ARTIST, THE*

CAROLYN CUNNINGHAM
PROD. COORDINATOR
'83 YEAR OF LIVING DANGEROUSLY, THE*
PROD. SECRETARY
'81 GALLIPOLI

GARRY CUNNINGHAM
ART DIRECTOR
'79 RAVAGERS

GARY CUNNINGHAM
SOUND
'81 FOUR SEASONS, THE
'81 MAN WHO SAW TOMORROW, THE*

GLENN CUNNINGHAM
ASSISTANT EDITOR
'80 HONEYSUCKLE ROSE*
'81 FOUR FRIENDS*
'82 WORLD ACCORDING TO GARP, THE*
'84 MISUNDERSTOOD

JACK CUNNINGHAM
UNIT PROD. MANAGER
'79 BUCK ROGERS*

SEAN CUNNINGHAM
PRODUCER
'80 FRIDAY THE 13TH
'83 SPRING BREAK
DIRECTOR
'80 FRIDAY THE 13TH
'82 STRANGER IS WATCHING, A
'83 SPRING BREAK

SUSAN CUNNINGHAM
EDITOR
'81 FRIDAY THE 13TH PART TWO
'82 STRANGER IS WATCHING, A
'83 SPRING BREAK

VIRGINIA CUNNINGHAM
MISCELLANEOUS
'84 SHEENA

BILL CURBISHLEY
PRODUCER
'80 KIDS ARE ALL RIGHT, THE*

RON CURFMAN
SOUND
'81 STUDENT BODIES
'82 CHILLY SCENES OF WINTER

JOHN CURRAN

1ST ASST. DIRECTOR
'80 GALAXINA
LOCATIONS
'82 NATIONAL LAMPOON'S CLASS REUNION

LAUREN CURRIER

SCREENPLAY
'83 CUJO*

JOHN CURRIN

ASSISTANT EDITOR
'80 WHOLLY MOSES!*
'81 RICHARD PRYOR: LIVE ON THE SUNSET STRIP*
'82 VICE SQUAD
'83 DEADLY FORCE*

GREG CURRY

SOUND
'84 STRANGER THAN PARADISE*

J. YVONNE CURRY

MAKEUP
'81 EYE FOR AN EYE, AN
'81 PRIVATE LESSONS*
'83 RIGHT STUFF, THE*

HOYT CURTIN

MUSIC
'79 C.H.O.M.P.S.

THERESA CURTIN

ASSOCIATE PRODUCER
'83 KEEP, THE*

VALERIE CURTIN

SCREENPLAY
'79 ...AND JUSTICE FOR ALL*
'80 INSIDE MOVES*
'82 BEST FRIENDS*
'84 UNFAITHFULLY YOURS*

BRUCE COHN CURTIS

PRODUCER
'79 ROLLER BOOGIE
'81 HELL NIGHT*
'82 SEDUCTION, THE*
'84 DREAMSCAPE

DOUGLAS CURTIS

PRODUCER
'84 PHILADELPHIA EXPERIMENT, THE*

GREG CURTIS

SPECIAL EFFECTS
'84 IMPULSE*

JOHN CURTIS

MISCELLANEOUS
'80 BORDERLINE

TOM CURTIS

EXECUTIVE PRODUCER
'84 DREAMSCAPE*
ASSOCIATE PRODUCER
'82 SEDUCTION, THE

TONY CURTIS

ART DIRECTOR
'82 VENOM
'83 KRULL*

ALAN CURTISS

2ND ASST. DIRECTOR
'80 COAST TO COAST*
'81 MOMMIE DEAREST*
'83 ROMANTIC COMEDY
'83 MAX DUGAN RETURNS
'84 CLOAK AND DAGGER
'84 LONELY GUY, THE
'84 2010
LOCATIONS
'80 HEAVEN'S GATE*
'82 I OUGHT TO BE IN PICTURES

KATHERINE ANN CURTISS

PROD. COORDINATOR
'84 2010

INDRID CUSIEL

SOUND
'80 HAPPY BIRTHDAY, GEMINI

JOSEPH CUSUMANO

MISCELLANEOUS
'84 COTTON CLUB, THE

BERNIE CUTLER

ART DIRECTOR
'80 SMOKEY AND THE BANDIT II
'81 PENNIES FROM HEAVEN*
'83 D.C. CAB

YVETTE CUTRARA

PROD. SECRETARY
'82 BY DESIGN*

MARY CYBULSKI

PROD. OFFICE COORD.
'84 BROTHER FROM ANOTHER PLANET, THE

RAY CYMOSZINSKI

SOUND
'80 MY BODYGUARD*
'81 FOUR FRIENDS*
'83 CLASS
'83 BIG SCORE, THE

D

JOE D'AGOSTA
CASTING
'84 JUST THE WAY YOU ARE
MISCELLANEOUS
'84 RED DAWN

CESARE D'AMICO
ASSISTANT EDITOR
'81 VICTORY*
'82 MONSIGNOR*

GINETTE D'AMICO
CASTING
'83 OF UNKNOWN ORIGIN*

JOANNE D'ANTONIO
EDITOR
'81 SATURDAY THE 14TH*

KAREN SCOURBY D'ARC
ASSISTANT EDITOR
'80 HOME MOVIES*
PROPS
'80 HOME MOVIES

SUSAN D'ARCY
PUBLICIST
'84 GREYSTOKE: THE LEGEND OF TARZAN, LORD OF THE APES
UNIT PUBLICIST
'83 LOCAL HERO
'84 INDIANA JONES AND THE TEMPLE OF DOOM

TOM D'ARCY
MAKEUP
'84 BROTHER FROM ANOTHER PLANET, THE
HAIR
'84 BROTHER FROM ANOTHER PLANET, THE

JANE D'ARISTA
MISCELLANEOUS
'81 ROLLOVER

RENE D'AURIAC
PRODUCTION DESIGNER
'80 GLORIA

D'DEE
CHOREOGRAPHER
'82 FIVE DAYS ONE SUMMER

LOUIS D'ESPOSITO
2ND ASST. DIRECTOR
'84 COTTON CLUB, THE*
'84 FIRSTBORN

ROBERTO D'ETTORRE
CINEMATOGRAPHER
'79 STARCRASH*

CATHERINE D'HOUR
ASSISTANT EDITOR
'84 CHEECH AND CHONG'S THE CORSICAN BROTHERS*

DAVID DAGLEY
STILLS
'84 GIVE MY REGARDS TO BROAD STREET*

ETIENNE DAHENE
2ND ASST. DIRECTOR
'84 JUST THE WAY YOU ARE*

BOB DAHLIN
1ST ASST. DIRECTOR
'80 POPEYE*
2ND ASST. DIRECTOR
'79 ...AND JUSTICE FOR ALL
'79 BUTCH AND SUNDANCE: THE EARLY YEARS*
'80 HEALTH
'80 HUNTER, THE

GARY DAIGLER
1ST ASST. DIRECTOR
'79 NIGHTWING
'79 MAIN EVENT, THE*
'80 ALTERED STATES
'80 NINE TO FIVE
'81 BUDDY, BUDDY
'81 ON GOLDEN POND
'82 YES, GIORGIO*
'82 GREASE 2
'83 DOCTOR DETROIT
'84 ADVENTURES OF BUCKAROO BANZAI ACROSS THE 8TH DIMENSION, THE
'84 GHOSTBUSTERS*
'84 RECKLESS

PAUL DAL PORTO
PROPS
'83 RIGHT STUFF, THE*

GROVER DALE
CHOREOGRAPHER
'81 SO FINE

SHAWN DALE
COSTUMES
'83 LOCAL HERO*

BARBARA DALEY
MISCELLANEOUS
'84 GIVE MY REGARDS TO BROAD STREET

HARRY DALEY
ASSOCIATE PRODUCER
'79 NATURAL ENEMIES*

ROBERT DALEY
EXECUTIVE PRODUCER
'79 ESCAPE FROM ALCATRAZ
'80 ANY WHICH WAY YOU CAN
'80 BRONCO BILLY

MALCOLM DALGLISH
MUSIC
'81 TUCK EVERLASTING*

CHRISTINE DALL
PRODUCER
'81 DOZENS, THE*
DIRECTOR
'81 DOZENS, THE*
SCREENPLAY
'81 DOZENS, THE*
EDITOR
'81 DOZENS, THE*

ANITA DALLAS
PROPS
'84 NOT FOR PUBLICATION*

BURT DALTON
SPECIAL EFFECTS
'80 XANADU*

KEN DALTON
PRODUCER
'84 HARDBODIES*

KIM DALTON
2ND ASST. DIRECTOR
'79 PICNIC AT HANGING ROCK

PHYLLIS DALTON
COSTUMES
'79 UNIDENTIFIED FLYING ODDBALL
'80 AWAKENING, THE
'80 MIRROR CRACK'D, THE

RICHARD DALTON
ASSOCIATE PRODUCER
'83 BEYOND THE LIMIT

JACK DALTON SR.
SOUND
'79 HOT STUFF
'81 FUNHOUSE, THE
'81 HARDLY WORKING

SUE DALTON
SPECIAL EFFECTS
'81 MS. 45*

ROBERT DALVA
DIRECTOR
'83 BLACK STALLION RETURNS, THE
EDITOR
'79 BLACK STALLION, THE

BILL DALY
SOUND
'79 GREAT BANK HOAX, THE
'80 EXTERMINATOR, THE
'82 DON'T CRY, IT'S ONLY THUNDER
'83 TIMERIDER

GLENIS DALY
HAIR
'83 MERRY CHRISTMAS, MR.LAWRENCE

JERRY DALY
2ND ASST. DIRECTOR
'84 TOP SECRET!*

JOHN DALY
PRODUCER
'79 SUNBURN*
SCREENPLAY
'79 SUNBURN*
EXECUTIVE PRODUCER
'81 STRANGE BEHAVIOR*
'81 CATTLE ANNIE AND LITTLE BRITCHES*
'81 HIGH RISK
'81 GOING APE!
'83 DEADLY FORCE
'83 YELLOWBEARD
'84 TERMINATOR, THE*

DENNIS DALZELL
CINEMATOGRAPHER
'81 BUSTIN' LOOSE
'81 HARD COUNTRY

DAMIANO DAMIANI
DIRECTOR
'82 AMITYVILLE II: THE POSSESSION

MARK DAMIEN
STUNT COORDINATOR
'79 FAST COMPANY*

MARK DAMON
EXECUTIVE PRODUCER
'84 NEVERENDING STORY, THE*

MEL DAMSKI
DIRECTOR
'83 YELLOWBEARD

BARBARA DANA
SCREENPLAY
'81 CHU CHU AND THE PHILLY FLASH

BILL DANA
SCREENPLAY
'80 NUDE BOMB, THE*

RONNY DANA
ASSISTANT EDITOR
'84 LOVE STREAMS*

BILL DANCE
MISCELLANEOUS
'84 MASS APPEAL

STEPHEN DANE
ART DIRECTOR
'84 ADVENTURES OF BUCKAROO BANZAI ACROSS THE 8TH DIMENSION, THE*

HOWARD DANELOWITZ
MISCELLANEOUS
'80 HOME MOVIES

MERCEDES DANEVIC
ASSISTANT EDITOR
'79 RICH KIDS*

NENA DANEVIC
EDITOR
'84 AMADEUS*
ASSISTANT EDITOR
'80 ONE-TRICK PONY*
'81 RAGTIME

MARY DANGERFIELD
MISCELLANEOUS
'84 IMPULSE

RODNEY DANGERFIELD
SCREENPLAY
'83 EASY MONEY*

DANNY DANIEL
SOUND
'79 GAME OF DEATH
'82 NIGHT CROSSING

FRANCIS DANIEL
SOUND
'79 BOARDWALK

MALISSA DANIEL
COSTUMES
'80 GALAXINA

GRACIELA DANIELE
CHOREOGRAPHER
'83 PIRATES OF PENZANCE, THE

ALICE DANIELS
MISCELLANEOUS
'82 TOY, THE

DANNY DANIELS
CHOREOGRAPHER
'81 PENNIES FROM HEAVEN
'83 ZELIG
'84 INDIANA JONES AND THE TEMPLE OF DOOM

DONNE DANIELS
KEY GRIP
'84 NIGHT OF THE COMET

PENNY DANIELS
SCRIPT SUPERVISOR
'80 SATURN 3

STAN DANIELS
SCREENPLAY
'84 LONELY GUY, THE*

JOE DANTE
DIRECTOR
'81 HOWLING, THE
'83 TWILIGHT ZONE, THE MOVIE*
'84 GREMLINS
EDITOR
'81 HOWLING, THE*

CHRIS DANTON
2ND ASST. DIRECTOR
'81 LAST CHASE, THE*

RICHARD CHRISTIAN DANUS
SCREENPLAY
'80 XANADU*

MARTIN DANZIG
PRODUCTION MANAGER
'79 MANHATTAN
'81 THEY ALL LAUGHED
UNIT MANAGER
'79 CHAPTER TWO
LOCATIONS
'79 HAIR*
'80 HERO AT LARGE

SUSAN DANZIG
UNIT MANAGER
'84 LOVELESS, THE
PROD. OFFICE COORD.
'79 WANDERERS, THE
'80 STARDUST MEMORIES
PROD. COORDINATOR
'82 STRANGER IS WATCHING, A

JEAN-LOUIS DAOUST
KEY GRIP
'79 QUINTET
'81 HAPPY BIRTHDAY TO ME

NORMA JEAN DARDEN
MISCELLANEOUS
'84 COTTON CLUB, THE

JENNIFER DARIEN
SCRIPT SUPERVISOR
'82 PENITENTIARY II*

MASON DARING
MUSIC
'80 RETURN OF THE SECAUCUS SEVEN, THE
'83 LIANNA
'84 BROTHER FROM ANOTHER PLANET, THE

GREG DARK
2ND ASST. DIRECTOR
'83 NEVER SAY NEVER AGAIN*

JOHN DARK
PRODUCER
'79 ARABIAN ADVENTURE

DICK DARLING
EDITOR
'79 C.H.O.M.P.S.*

LARRY DARR
MAKEUP
'81 PURSUIT OF D.B. COOPER, THE*

GAUTAM DAS
ASSOCIATE PRODUCER
'84 BACHELOR PARTY

DAVID DASHER
SCREENPLAY
'83 SMOKEY AND THE BANDIT III*

DAVID DASHEV
PRODUCER
'79 FISH THAT SAVED PITTSBURGH, THE*

RAUL DASILVA
MISCELLANEOUS
'81 FEAR NO EVIL

MARK DASSAS
PRODUCTION MANAGER
'83 STRANGE BREW
LOCATIONS
'84 MRS. SOFFEL*

NICK DAUBENY
2ND ASST. DIRECTOR
'82 SENDER, THE
'82 MOONLIGHTING
'82 VENOM
'84 CHAMPIONS*

PASCALE DAUMAN
ASSOCIATE PRODUCER
'84 PARIS, TEXAS

ROBERTO FORGES DAVANZATI
MISCELLANEOUS
'83 PIRANHA II: THE SPAWNING

BOBBY DAVENPORT
MISCELLANEOUS
'79 VILLAIN, THE
'81 LEGEND OF THE LONE RANGER,THE
'82 BEST LITTLE WHOREHOUSE IN TEXAS, THE
'84 COUNTRY

LARRY DAVENPORT
ASSISTANT EDITOR
'82 NIGHT SHIFT*

MICHAEL DAVES
1ST ASST. DIRECTOR
'79 TIME AFTER TIME
'80 COAST TO COAST
'80 LITTLE DARLINGS
'80 MY BODYGUARD
'81 MOMMIE DEAREST
'82 SIX WEEKS
'83 BLUE SKIES AGAIN
'84 DREAMSCAPE*

BERT DAVEY
ART DIRECTOR
'79 GREAT TRAIN ROBBERY, THE
'80 FFOLKES
'81 EYE OF THE NEEDLE*
'81 DOGS OF WAR, THE*
'83 SUPERMAN III*

ALLEN DAVIAU
CINEMATOGRAPHER
'82 E.T. THE EXTRA-TERRESTRIAL
'83 TWILIGHT ZONE, THE MOVIE*

GOLDA DAVID
ASSOCIATE PRODUCER
'81 BACK ROADS

HERMAN DAVID
MISCELLANEOUS
'79 ONION FIELD, THE

PIERRE DAVID
EXECUTIVE PRODUCER
'79 BROOD, THE*
'80 HOG WILD*
'81 SCANNERS*
'81 GAS*
'83 VIDEODROME*
'83 OF UNKNOWN ORIGIN

PIERRE DAVID
HAIR
'80 DEATH SHIP
'84 HOTEL NEW HAMPSHIRE, THE*

SAUL DAVID
EXECUTIVE PRODUCER
'79 RAVAGERS

ANDREAS DAVIDESCU
CINEMATOGRAPHER
'84 FINAL TERROR, THE

KENNETH DAVIDOW
ASSISTANT EDITOR
'79 DAWN OF THE DEAD

ARLENE DAVIDSON
SCREENPLAY
'83 EDDIE AND THE CRUISERS*
ASSOCIATE PRODUCER
'83 EDDIE AND THE CRUISERS

BOAZ DAVIDSON
DIRECTOR
'82 LAST AMERICAN VIRGIN, THE
SCREENPLAY
'82 LAST AMERICAN VIRGIN, THE

BRURIA DAVIDSON
EDITOR
'82 LAST AMERICAN VIRGIN, THE

CAROL DAVIDSON
MAKEUP
'80 NOTHING PERSONAL*

DENNIS DAVIDSON
PUBLICIST
'79 SHOUT, THE

GORDON DAVIDSON
EXECUTIVE PRODUCER
'82 ZOOT SUIT

MARTIN DAVIDSON
DIRECTOR
'80 HERO AT LARGE
'83 EDDIE AND THE CRUISERS
SCREENPLAY
'83 EDDIE AND THE CRUISERS*

SANDRA DAVIDSON
COSTUMES
'80 COAST TO COAST
'80 HERO AT LARGE
'83 EDDIE AND THE CRUISERS

WILLIAM DAVIDSON
PRODUCTION MANAGER
'80 DEFIANCE*
'81 HONKY TONK FREEWAY

CARMEL DAVIES
ASSISTANT EDITOR
'81 SOUTHERN COMFORT*
'82 48 HOURS*
'84 STREETS OF FIRE*

ERIC DAVIES
LOCATIONS
'83 SUBURBIA

FREEMAN DAVIES
EDITOR
'80 WHEN TIME RAN OUT*
'81 SOUTHERN COMFORT
'82 48 HOURS*
'83 BRAINSTORM*
'84 STREETS OF FIRE*
MISCELLANEOUS
'79 MAIN EVENT, THE

JACK DAVIES
SCREENPLAY
'80 FFOLKES

PAUL DAVIES
EDITOR
'81 PRIEST OF LOVE

PETER DAVIES
EDITOR
'83 OCTOPUSSY*
ASSISTANT EDITOR
'79 ESCAPE TO ATHENA
'81 SEA WOLVES, THE

RICHARD DAVIES
LOCATIONS
'83 OSTERMAN WEEKEND, THE*

T. HUW DAVIES
LOCATIONS
'84 UNFAITHFULLY YOURS

TOM DAVIES
2ND ASST. DIRECTOR
'83 BLUE THUNDER*
'84 BIRDY
'84 NATURAL, THE*

NELSON DAVILA
ASSISTANT EDITOR
'84 PREPPIES*

ANDREW DAVIS
DIRECTOR
'84 FINAL TERROR, THE
SCREENPLAY
'84 BEAT STREET*

ANDY DAVIS
CINEMATOGRAPHER
'79 OVER THE EDGE
'84 ANGEL

B.J. DAVIS
STUNT COORDINATOR
'83 CHAINED HEAT
'83 DEADLY FORCE
'84 HARDBODIES

BART DAVIS
SCREENPLAY
'84 IMPULSE*

BATTLE DAVIS
ASSISTANT EDITOR
'81 ...ALL THE MARBLES*

BILL DAVIS
SCREENPLAY
'84 MASS APPEAL

BILLY DAVIS
MISCELLANEOUS
'80 HOLLYWOOD KNIGHTS, THE

CARL DAVIS
MUSIC
'81 FRENCH LIEUTENANT'S WOMAN, THE
'84 CHAMPIONS

CHARLES DAVIS
ART DIRECTOR
'81 BUSTIN' LOOSE*

CHRISTINE DAVIS
MISCELLANEOUS
'80 GALAXINA

DAVID DAVIS
MISCELLANEOUS
'83 TERMS OF ENDEARMENT

DEBRA SHARON DAVIS
SPECIAL EFFECTS
'80 COMPETITION, THE

DESMOND DAVIS
DIRECTOR
'81 CLASH OF THE TITANS

FREEMAN DAVIS
ASSISTANT EDITOR
'80 LONG RIDERS, THE

GARY DAVIS
STUNT COORDINATOR
'81 KNIGHTRIDERS
'84 AGAINST ALL ODDS

GERRY DAVIS
SCREENPLAY
'80 FINAL COUNTDOWN, THE*

IVAN DAVIS
SCREENPLAY
'83 HUNGER, THE*

JOHN DAVIS
PRODUCTION MANAGER
'79 MURDER BY DECREE
'83 NEVER SAY NEVER AGAIN*
MISCELLANEOUS
'84 INDIANA JONES AND THE TEMPLE OF DOOM

MARK DAVIS
MUSIC
'80 CHEECH AND CHONG'S NEXT MOVIE
'81 BUSTIN' LOOSE

MAXINE DAVIS
PROD. COORDINATOR
'84 PURPLE RAIN

NOEL DAVIS
CASTING
'79 YANKS*
'81 REDS*
'83 DRESSER, THE
'83 KEEP, THE*
'83 PRIVATES ON PARADE

PAMELA DAVIS
SCRIPT SUPERVISOR
'81 SUPERMAN II*
'81 DRAGONSLAYER
'83 BETRAYAL
'83 PRIVATES ON PARADE
'84 TOP SECRET!

PETER DAVIS
PRODUCER
'80 STEEL*
'83 OSTERMAN WEEKEND, THE*

PHILIP DAVIS
SOUND
'84 LAST NIGHT AT THE ALAMO

RICHARD DAVIS
EXEC IN CHARGE PROD
'82 PIRATE MOVIE, THE
'84 PHAR LAP
LOCATIONS
'84 KARATE KID, THE

RICHARD DAVIS
1ST ASST. DIRECTOR
'82 FRIDAY THE 13TH PART THREE IN 3D

RICHARD DAVIS JR.
LOCATIONS
'84 AGAINST ALL ODDS

SANDRA DAVIS
ASSISTANT EDITOR
'82 MEGAFORCE*
'84 CITY HEAT

T. BATTLE DAVIS
EDITOR
'80 TWINKLE TWINKLE "KILLER" KANE*

TOM DAVIS
LOCATIONS
'83 REVENGE OF THE NINJA

CARILINE DAVIS-DYER
SCRIPT SUPERVISOR
'80 ALTERED STATES
'80 FOXES
'84 RED DAWN

JON DAVISON
PRODUCER
'80 AIRPLANE
'84 TOP SECRET!*
ASSOCIATE PRODUCER
'83 TWILIGHT ZONE, THE MOVIE*
2ND UNIT DIRECTOR
'79 ROCK 'N ROLL HIGH SCHOOL*
'81 HOWLING, THE*

RUTH DAVISON
LOCATIONS
'80 WATCHER IN THE WOODS, THE*
'81 DRAGONSLAYER

ANATOLY DAVYDOV
MISCELLANEOUS
'83 GORKY PARK

RUSSELL DAWE
MISCELLANEOUS
'84 CLOAK AND DAGGER

TONY DAWE
SOUND
'81 DRAGONSLAYER
'82 SENDER, THE
'83 RETURN OF THE JEDI*

BIFF DAWES
SOUND
'81 RICHARD PRYOR: LIVE ON THE SUNSET STRIP*

JIM DAWES
KEY GRIP
'81 FRENCH LIEUTENANT'S WOMAN, THE

SANDRA DAWES
MISCELLANEOUS
'81 GHOST STORY

RICHARD DAWKING
ART DIRECTOR
'83 MONTY PYTHON'S THE MEANING OF LIFE
'84 ELECTRIC DREAMS

ANITA DAWN
CASTING
'80 SMOKEY AND THE BANDIT II
'81 ALL NIGHT LONG
'81 BUSTIN' LOOSE*
'81 HEARTBEEPS*
'81 INCREDIBLE SHRINKING WOMAN, THE
'82 THING, THE
'82 ZOOT SUIT*
'83 NIGHTMARES

BOB DAWN
MAKEUP
'79 CHAMP, THE*
'79 NORTH DALLAS FORTY*
'80 RAISE THE TITANIC*
'82 CHALLENGE, THE*
'82 LOOKIN' TO GET OUT
'83 CHRISTINE

JEFFERSON DAWN
MAKEUP
'84 TERMINATOR, THE

WES DAWN
MAKEUP
'79 BOULEVARD NIGHTS*
'80 URBAN COWBOY*
'82 YOUNG DOCTORS IN LOVE*
'83 HEART LIKE A WHEEL
'84 STAR TREK III: THE SEARCH FOR SPOCK*
'84 RED DAWN*

ANTHONY DAWSON
DIRECTOR
'79 KILLER FISH
'83 YOR
SCREENPLAY
'83 YOR*

BOB DAWSON
SPECIAL EFFECTS
'79 PROPHECY
'80 DEFIANCE
'81 REDS*
'82 AIRPLANE II: THE SEQUEL
SP. EFFECTS SUPERV.
'82 STAR TREK II THE WRATH OF KHAN
'84 STAR TREK III: THE SEARCH FOR SPOCK

DEREK DAWSON
EXECUTIVE PRODUCER
'81 CATTLE ANNIE AND LITTLE BRITCHES*

DICK DAWSON
MAKEUP
'79 PRISONER OF ZENDA, THE*

DOUGIE DAWSON
STILLS
'84 OXFORD BLUES

ELEANOR DAWSON
MISCELLANEOUS
'78 DEER HUNTER, THE

PETER DAWSON
SPECIAL EFFECTS
'80 BIG RED ONE, THE*
'83 NATE & HAYES
MISCELLANEOUS
'81 RAIDERS OF THE LOST ARK

THOMAS DAWSON
COSTUMES
'84 SOLDIER'S STORY, A

BRYAN DAY
SOUND
'79 BROOD, THE
'79 FAST COMPANY
'80 PROM NIGHT
'81 LAST CHASE, THE
'83 DEAD ZONE, THE
'83 VIDEODROME

ERNEST DAY
CINEMATOGRAPHER
'81 SPHINX
'84 PASSAGE TO INDIA, A

ERNIE DAY
2ND UNIT DIRECTOR
'79 MOONRAKER*

FRANCISCO DAY
UNIT PROD. MANAGER
'80 WHY WOULD I LIE?*

JENNY DAY
PROD. COORDINATOR
'81 EARTHLING, THE

JOE DAY
SPECIAL EFFECTS
'79 HURRICANE*
'80 FINAL COUNTDOWN, THE*
'81 HONKY TONK FREEWAY
'81 LOOKER
'82 MOTHER LODE*
'83 DEAL OF THE CENTURY*

JONATHAN DAY
ASSISTANT EDITOR
'79 BREAKING AWAY*

LISA DAY
EDITOR
'83 LET'S SPEND THE NIGHT TOGETHER*
ASSISTANT EDITOR
'80 XANADU
'81 CONTINENTAL DIVIDE

SHARON DAY
COSTUMES
'81 CHEECH AND CHONG'S NICE DREAMS

WENDY DAY
PUBLICIST
'81 GALLIPOLI

LISA DE ALVA
PROPS
'84 MAKING THE GRADE

FABRIZIO DE AMGELIS
PRODUCER
'83 1990: THE BRONX WARRIORS

GUIDO DE ANGELIS
MUSIC
'79 KILLER FISH*

MAURIZIO DE ANGELIS
MUSIC
'79 KILLER FISH*

REMO DE ANGELIS
STUNT COORDINATOR
'81 INCHON*

DICK DE BENEDICTIS
MUSIC
'81 EARTHLING, THE

MARK DE ERNSTED
KEY GRIP
'81 MY BLOODY VALENTINE

HUBERT DE LA BOUILLERIE
ASSISTANT EDITOR
'82 SOUP FOR ONE*

FERRY ANDRE DE LA FORTE
STILLS
'83 CHEECH AND CHONG'S STILL SMOKIN'

JEAN- DE LA QUERANTONNAIS
MISCELLANEOUS
'80 QUARTET

SILVIE DE LA RIVIERE
PUBLICIST
'80 UNION CITY

NELSON DE LACRUZ
PROD. COORDINATOR
'83 BLIND RAGE*

GIANCARLO DE LEONARDIS
HAIR
'79 BLOODLINE*
'81 INCHON*

BRIAN DE MELLIER
SOUND
'83 GOIN' ALL THE WAY*

PATRICIA DE OLIVEIRA
PROD. OFFICE COORD.
'82 SHOOT THE MOON

UL DE RICO
MISCELLANEOUS
'84 NEVERENDING STORY, THE

EVERETT DE ROCHE
SCREENPLAY
'81 ROAD GAMES

PASQUALINO DE SANTIS
CINEMATOGRAPHER
'84 SHEENA

IRENE DE'ATLEY
HAIR
'82 BEST LITTLE WHOREHOUSE IN TEXAS, THE*
'83 NIGHTMARES

KAREN DEA
CASTING
'79 GOING IN STYLE*

VINCE DEADRICK
STUNT COORDINATOR
'84 ROMANCING THE STONE*

ROGER DEAKINS
CINEMATOGRAPHER
'83 ANOTHER TIME, ANOTHER PLACE

DARWIN DEAN
MISCELLANEOUS
'84 MRS. SOFFEL

FRED DEAN
MISCELLANEOUS
'81 EYE FOR AN EYE, AN
'83 LONE WOLF MCQUADE

JOEL DEAN
EXECUTIVE PRODUCER
'82 SUMMER LOVERS

RICHARD DEAN
MAKEUP
'80 UNION CITY

RICHARD DEAN
SPECIAL EFFECTS
'82 VENOM*

SAMANTHA DEAN
PUBLICIST
'79 ALL THAT JAZZ*

WILLIAM DEAR
DIRECTOR
'83 TIMERIDER
SCREENPLAY
'83 TIMERIDER*

WILLIAM DEAR
MISCELLANEOUS
'79 HARDCORE

ROBERT DEARBERG
EDITOR
'82 HOUSE OF THE LONG SHADOWS

SPLINTERS DEASON
SCRIPT SUPERVISOR
'84 RIDDLE OF THE SANDS

JERRY DEATS
KEY GRIP
'79 ON THE YARD
'81 INCREDIBLE SHRINKING WOMAN, THE

RICHARD DEATS
KEY GRIP
'79 SEDUCTION OF JOE TYNAN, THE*
'80 HEAVEN'S GATE*
'81 BLOW OUT
'82 JINXED
'83 TABLE FOR FIVE
'84 NO SMALL AFFAIR
'84 RIVER, THE

STEVE DEAVER
MISCELLANEOUS
'82 MONTY PYTHON LIVE AT THE HOLLYWOOD BOWL

MICHEL DEBATS
LOCATIONS
'84 JUST THE WAY YOU ARE*

PHILLIP DEBBS
MAKEUP
'82 BRAINWAVES*

ALEX DEBENEDETTI
CO-PRODUCER
'82 FIGHTING BACK*

PIERO DEBERNARDO
SCREENPLAY
'84 ONCE UPON A TIME IN AMERICA*

AUSTIN DEBESCHE
CINEMATOGRAPHER
'80 RETURN OF THE SECAUCUS SEVEN, THE
'83 LIANNA

RON DEBLASIO
MISCELLANEOUS
'79 ROSE, THE

JAN DEBONT
CINEMATOGRAPHER
'81 PRIVATE LESSONS
'82 I'M DANCING AS FAST AS I CAN
'83 ALL THE RIGHT MOVES
'83 CUJO

HENRI DECAE
CINEMATOGRAPHER
'80 ISLAND, THE
'83 EXPOSED

L. SPRAGUE DECAMP
MISCELLANEOUS
'82 CONAN THE BARBARIAN
'84 CONAN THE DESTROYER

DAVE DECARLO
ART DIRECTOR
'82 BUTTERFLY

TOM DECILLO
CINEMATOGRAPHER
'84 STRANGER THAN PARADISE

ALEX DECKER
LOCATIONS
'82 VERDICT, THE*
'84 BOSTONIANS, THE

LYNN DECKER
HAIR
'80 BIG BRAWL, THE
'81 DEADLY BLESSING
'82 SPLIT IMAGE*
'83 TENDER MERCIES

ROBERT DECKER
LOCATIONS
'83 WAR GAMES*
'84 BEVERLY HILLS COP*

JOHN DECUIR
PRODUCTION DESIGNER
'79 LOVE AND BULLETS
'80 RAISE THE TITANIC
'82 DEAD MEN DON'T WEAR PLAID
'82 MONSIGNOR
'84 GHOSTBUSTERS

JOHN DECUIR JR.
ART DIRECTOR
'80 RAISE THE TITANIC
'84 GHOSTBUSTERS*

ANGEL DEDIEGO
MAKEUP
'79 JAGUAR LIVES

MELISSA DEDMAN
STUNT COORDINATOR
'83 LIQUID SKY*

MICHAEL DEELEY
PRODUCER
'78 DEER HUNTER, THE*
'82 BLADERUNNER

MARC DEERNSTED
KEY GRIP
'83 OF UNKNOWN ORIGIN

JIM DEETH
MISCELLANEOUS
'84 STARMAN

WALT DEFARIA
PRODUCER
'82 DON'T CRY, IT'S ONLY THUNDER
2ND ASST. DIRECTOR
'82 DON'T CRY, IT'S ONLY THUNDER

FRANK DEFELITTA
SCREENPLAY
'81 ENTITY, THE

BARBARA DEFINA
ASSOCIATE PRODUCER
'83 SPRING BREAK
UNIT PROD. MANAGER
'83 SPRING BREAK
UNIT MANAGER
'81 PRINCE OF THE CITY
2ND ASST. DIRECTOR
'80 GILDA LIVE
PROD. COORDINATOR
'80 HAPPY BIRTHDAY, GEMINI

DON DEFINA
ART DIRECTOR
'84 HOT DOG...THE MOVIE

DAVID DEGEUS
ASSISTANT EDITOR
'83 REUBEN, REUBEN*
'83 SPACEHUNTER: ADVENTURES IN THE FORBIDDEN ZONE*

JACKSON DEGOVIA
ART DIRECTOR
'79 BUTCH AND SUNDANCE: THE EARLY YEARS
PRODUCTION DESIGNER
'79 BOULEVARD NIGHTS
'80 IT'S MY TURN
'80 MY BODYGUARD
'83 SPACEHUNTER: ADVENTURES IN THE FORBIDDEN ZONE
'84 RED DAWN

ALEXANDER DEGRUNWALD
PRODUCTION MANAGER
'80 FLASH GORDON*
'82 GANDHI*
LOCATIONS
'79 LEGACY, THE
MISCELLANEOUS
'81 HISTORY OF THE WORLD PART I
'83 NEVER SAY NEVER AGAIN
'83 PIRATES OF PENZANCE, THE

RICARDO DEGUZMAN
2ND ASST. DIRECTOR
'84 PURPLE HEARTS

CARTER DEHAVEN
PRODUCER
'81 CARBON COPY*
'83 YELLOWBEARD
EXECUTIVE PRODUCER
'84 SCANDALOUS

MARK DEITCH
MISCELLANEOUS
'83 LOSIN' IT

JORDAN DEITCHER
CASTING
'80 OH! HEAVENLY DOG*

LISA DEJAGER
PROD. COORDINATOR
'82 FIRST TIME, THE

STEVEN DEJARNATT
SCREENPLAY
'83 STRANGE BREW*

RENALDO DEJUAN
MISCELLANEOUS
'83 ECHOES

HISAYUKI DEKURA
PRODUCTION MANAGER
'81 TATTOO*

GIANCARLO DEL BROCCO
MAKEUP
'80 POPEYE
'83 HIGH ROAD TO CHINA*

LYNN DEL KAIL
HAIR
'79 GREAT SANTINI, THE
'80 MOUNTAIN MEN, THE
'80 TOM HORN
'81 CAVEMAN
'82 NATIONAL LAMPOON'S CLASS REUNION*
'84 RIVER, THE
'84 TEACHERS

DONNA DEL PIZZO
MISCELLANEOUS
'83 JOYSTICKS

EMILIO RUIZ DEL RIO
MISCELLANEOUS
'84 CONAN THE DESTROYER

DANNY DEL ROSARIO
SOUND
'83 BLIND RAGE*

GUY DEL RUSSO
MAKEUP
'80 CARNY*

MARIE DEL RUSSO
MAKEUP
'82 LOVE CHILD

THOMAS DEL RUTH
CINEMATOGRAPHER
'80 MOTEL HELL
'82 DEATHWISH II*
'83 GET CRAZY
'84 IMPULSE

ROBERT DEL VALLE
UNIT MANAGER
'79 PHANTASM

ROSINE DELAMARE
COSTUMES
'79 LITTLE ROMANCE, A

FRANCOIS DELAMOTHE
ART DIRECTOR
'79 LITTLE ROMANCE, A
'84 JUST THE WAY YOU ARE

BARRY DELANEY
COSTUME SUPERVISOR
'82 SECOND THOUGHTS*

ANNA DELANZO
SOUND
'82 FIRST TIME, THE
'83 CHAINED HEAT

HUGUES DELAUGARDIERE
1ST ASST. DIRECTOR
'80 QUARTET
2ND ASST. DIRECTOR
'80 TESS*

DINO DELAURENTIIS
PRODUCER
'79 HURRICANE
'80 FLASH GORDON
'81 RAGTIME
EXECUTIVE PRODUCER
'83 DEAD ZONE, THE

RAFFAELLA DELAURENTIIS
PRODUCER
'81 BEYOND THE REEF
'82 CONAN THE BARBARIAN*
'84 DUNE
'84 CONAN THE DESTROYER

ROBERT DELAURENTIS
PRODUCER
'82 LITTLE SEX, A*
SCREENPLAY
'82 LITTLE SEX, A

LOOLEE DELEON
PROD. COORDINATOR
'79 APOCALYPSE NOW*

GEORGES DELERUE
MUSIC
'79 LITTLE ROMANCE, A
'81 RICH AND FAMOUS
'81 TRUE CONFESSIONS
'82 LITTLE SEX, A
'82 PARTNERS
'82 ESCAPE ARTIST, THE
'83 BLACK STALLION RETURNS, THE
'83 EXPOSED
'83 MAN WOMAN AND CHILD
'83 SILKWOOD

RAYMOND DELEUW
EDITOR
'81 DEVIL AND MAX DEVLIN, THE

ROBERTA DELGADI
MISCELLANEOUS
'82 ZOOT SUIT

TOM DELGENIO
SPECIAL EFFECTS
'80 COAL MINER'S DAUGHTER*

JOE DELIA
MUSIC
'81 MS. 45

ALFRED DELIAGRE JR.
ASSOCIATE PRODUCER
'82 DEATHTRAP

WANDA DELL
PRODUCER
'80 PRIVATE EYES, THE*
'84 MARVIN AND TIGE
SCREENPLAY
'84 MARVIN AND TIGE*
CO-PRODUCER
'79 PRIZE FIGHTER, THE
CASTING
'84 MARVIN AND TIGE*

ALDO DELL'ACQUA
STUNT COORDINATOR
'83 YOR*

DEBORAH DELL'AMICO
2ND ASST. DIRECTOR
'81 BUDDY, BUDDY*
'82 YES, GIORGIO*
'83 DOCTOR DETROIT

MEL DELLAR
ASSOCIATE PRODUCER
'79 FRISCO KID, THE
'80 SERIAL
'82 AIRPLANE II: THE SEQUEL
PRODUCTION MANAGER
'80 SERIAL
UNIT PROD. MANAGER
'81 PATERNITY*
'82 SOME KIND OF HERO
'82 AIRPLANE II: THE SEQUEL
'83 UNCOMMON VALOR
1ST ASST. DIRECTOR
'79 FRISCO KID, THE
MISCELLANEOUS
'81 BLOOD BEACH

JACQUE DELONGEVILLE
2ND ASST. DIRECTOR
'83 LONELY LADY, THE*

GAYE DELORNE
MUSIC
'82 THINGS ARE TOUGH ALL OVER

MARISA DELPINO
ASSISTANT EDITOR
'79 JAGUAR LIVES

JOSEE DELUCA
MAKEUP
'83 EXPOSED*

NEAL DELUCA
ART DIRECTOR
'83 ECHOES

RUDY DELUCA
SCREENPLAY
'81 CAVEMAN*

TERESA DELUCA
ASSISTANT EDITOR
'83 OF UNKNOWN ORIGIN*

MILTON DELUGG
MUSIC
'80 GONG SHOW MOVIE, THE

DOM DELUISE
DIRECTOR
'79 HOT STUFF

TONY DELUMEN
UNIT MANAGER
'81 ENTER THE NINJA

CARLO DEMARCHIS
MISCELLANEOUS
'82 CONAN THE BARBARIAN

FRANK DEMARCO
SPECIAL EFFECTS
'79 ROCK 'N ROLL HIGH SCHOOL*
'82 BEASTMASTER, THE*
'83 LONE WOLF MCQUADE*
'84 TERMINATOR, THE*
MISCELLANEOUS
'80 BATTLE BEYOND THE STARS

FABRIZIO DEMARTINO
UNIT MANAGER
'83 1990: THE BRONX WARRIORS*

FRANCESCO DEMASI
MUSIC
'83 LONE WOLF MCQUADE

GASTONI DEMATTIA
LOCATIONS
'79 LITTLE ROMANCE, A*

DANI DEMBROSKY
MISCELLANEOUS
'80 CARNY

JILL DEMBY
ASSISTANT EDITOR
'83 TRADING PLACES*
'83 TWILIGHT ZONE, THE MOVIE*

FRANCOISE DEMENIL
ASSOCIATE PRODUCER
'80 STIR CRAZY

ATHENA DEMETRIOS
MAKEUP
'83 MAUSOLEUM*

ALAN DEMKOWICZ
HAIR
'84 FLAMINGO KID, THE*

EVELYN PURCELL DEMME
2ND UNIT DIRECTOR
'79 LAST EMBRACE

JONATHAN DEMME
DIRECTOR
'79 LAST EMBRACE
'80 MELVIN AND HOWARD
'84 SWING SHIFT

ROBERT DEMORA
COSTUMES
'79 WANDERERS, THE
'79 WINTER KILLS
'80 AMERICAN SUCCESS COMPANY,THE*
'80 CRUISING
'80 DIVINE MADNESS
'81 NIGHTHAWKS*
'82 SOUP FOR ONE
'82 JINXED
'82 GREASE 2
'83 RISKY BUSINESS

PIERRE DEMORO
DIRECTOR
'83 SAVANNAH SMILES

GARY DEMOS
MISCELLANEOUS
'84 LAST STARFIGHTER, THE

DIONE DEMSKY
HAIR
'80 CHANGE OF SEASONS, A*

EDWARD DENAULT
PRODUCER
'84 LAST STARFIGHTER, THE*

RICHARD DENAULT
2ND ASST. DIRECTOR
'84 LAST STARFIGHTER, THE

MIKE DENECKE
SOUND
'84 LOVE STREAMS*

"PETE" DENENBERG
ASSISTANT EDITOR
'79 FAST BREAK

VICTOR DENICOLA
HAIR
'84 OVER THE BROOKLYN BRIDGE

CLAIRE DENIS
1ST ASST. DIRECTOR
'83 HANNA K
'84 PARIS, TEXAS

SUSAN DENISON
COSTUMES
'83 SPRING BREAK*

JIM DENNETT
PRODUCTION MANAGER
'84 FINAL TERROR, THE

SARA DENNING
COSTUMES
'83 SPRING BREAK*

CHARLES DENNIS
SCREENPLAY
'84 FINDERS KEEPERS*

SALLY DENNISON
CASTING
'79 CHINA SYNDROME, THE
'79 MEATBALLS*
'79 1941
'80 TOM HORN
'80 USED CARS
'81 ENDLESS LOVE*
'82 GREASE 2
'83 HEART LIKE A WHEEL
'84 FLASHPOINT*

REG DENT
MISCELLANEOUS
'79 DRACULA

EUMIR DEODATO
MUSIC
'79 ONION FIELD, THE

STEFANI DEOUL
PROD. COORDINATOR
'84 BREAKIN 2 ELECTRIC BOOGALOO

CAROL DEPACE
ASSISTANT EDITOR
'83 AMERICANA*

BRIAN DEPALMA
PRODUCER
'80 HOME MOVIES*
'84 BODY DOUBLE
DIRECTOR
'80 DRESSED TO KILL
'80 HOME MOVIES
'81 BLOW OUT
'83 SCARFACE
'84 BODY DOUBLE
SCREENPLAY
'80 DRESSED TO KILL
'81 BLOW OUT
'84 BODY DOUBLE*
MISCELLANEOUS
'82 FIRST TIME, THE

ALAIN DEPARDIEU
UNIT MANAGER
'80 QUARTET
'80 TESS

LESLEY DEPETTITT
CASTING
'79 LEGACY, THE
'79 PRISONER OF ZENDA, THE
'82 QUEST FOR FIRE*

PAT DEPEW
SCRIPT SUPERVISOR
'81 THEY ALL LAUGHED

THEDA DERAMUS
COSTUMES
'84 REPO MAN

BO DEREK
PRODUCER
'81 TARZAN, THE APE MAN
'84 BOLERO

JOHN DEREK
DIRECTOR
'81 TARZAN, THE APE MAN
'84 BOLERO
SCREENPLAY
'84 BOLERO
CINEMATOGRAPHER
'81 TARZAN, THE APE MAN
'84 BOLERO

PAUL DEROLF
CHOREOGRAPHER
'79 1941*

GIANNETTO DEROSSI
SPECIAL EFFECTS
'83 PIRANHA II: THE SPAWNING*
MISCELLANEOUS
'83 PIRANHA II: THE SPAWNING
'83 PIRANHA II: THE SPAWNING
'84 DUNE
'84 CONAN THE DESTROYER

MASSIMO DEROSSI
MAKEUP
'79 HURRICANE
'80 FLASH GORDON*

MIRELLA DEROSSI
HAIR
'84 DUNE
'84 CONAN THE DESTROYER

GENE DERVELLE
2ND ASST. DIRECTOR
'79 FISH THAT SAVED PITTSBURGH, THE*

MICHEL DERVELLE
MAKEUP
'79 BLOODLINE*

REGAS DES PLAS
ART DIRECTOR
'84 UNTIL SEPTEMBER

PASQUALINO DESANTIS
CINEMATOGRAPHER
'84 MISUNDERSTOOD

SUSIE DESANTO
COSTUMES
'83 JOYSTICKS*

WILLIE DESANTOS
MISCELLANEOUS
'83 BLIND RAGE

MONIQUE DESART
HAIR
'80 OH GOD! BOOK II*

JOSIANE DESCHAMP
MAKEUP
'82 QUEST FOR FIRE*

CALEB DESCHANEL
DIRECTOR
'82 ESCAPE ARTIST, THE
CINEMATOGRAPHER
'79 BEING THERE
'79 BLACK STALLION, THE
'79 MORE AMERICAN GRAFFITTI
'83 RIGHT STUFF, THE
'83 LET'S SPEND THE NIGHT TOGETHER*
'84 NATURAL, THE
MISCELLANEOUS
'79 APOCALYPSE NOW

GERRY DESCHENES
PROPS
'79 MEATBALLS

PAUL DESENNEVILLE
MUSIC
'84 IRRECONCILABLE DIFFERENCES*

WILLIAM DESETA
ART DIRECTOR
'79 SOMETHING SHORT OF PARADISE
PRODUCTION DESIGNER
'79 SCALPEL

GIORGIO DESIDERI
ART DIRECTOR
'81 CLASH OF THE TITANS*
COSTUMES
'83 LONELY LADY, THE

DAVID DESILVA
PRODUCER
'80 FAME*

RITA DESILVA
PROD. SECRETARY
'84 INDIANA JONES AND THE TEMPLE OF DOOM*

WILLIE DESILVA
PRODUCTION MANAGER
'84 INDIANA JONES AND THE TEMPLE OF DOOM*

TOM DESIMONE
DIRECTOR
'81 HELL NIGHT

PHIL DESJARDINS
LOCATIONS
'79 RUNNING*

DICK DESMOND
SCREENPLAY
'81 ENTER THE NINJA

FRANK DESMOND
PROPS
'83 ECHOES*

PHILLIPPE DESMOULINS
LOCATIONS
'80 TESS*
'84 JUST THE WAY YOU ARE*

JOHN DESORMEAUX
UNIT MANAGER
'81 MY BLOODY VALENTINE
LOCATIONS
'81 MY BLOODY VALENTINE

BETTY DESOUCHES
CASTING
'84 RAZOR'S EDGE, THE*

STEVEN DESOUZA
SCREENPLAY
'82 48 HOURS*

NICOS DESPOTIDES
SOUND
'82 SUMMER LOVERS

KATIA DESPOTIDOU
MAKEUP
'82 SUMMER LOVERS*

MICHEL DESROIS
SOUND
'79 LITTLE ROMANCE, A

MARK DESROSCHERS
LOCATIONS
'82 OUT OF THE BLUE

ED DESSISSO
LOCATIONS
'84 COTTON CLUB, THE*

LORENZO DESTEFANO
ASSOCIATE EDITOR
'84 DREAMSCAPE
ASSISTANT EDITOR
'82 THAT CHAMPIONSHIP SEASON
'83 LOSIN' IT

BOB DESTOCKI
MUSIC SUPERVISOR
'82 FAST TIMES AT RIDGEMONT HIGH

ROBERT DESTOLFE
STILLS
'81 FUNHOUSE, THE
'82 LOVE CHILD
'83 SMOKEY AND THE BANDIT III
'83 BLUE SKIES AGAIN

MARJORIE DEUTSCH
ASSISTANT EDITOR
'79 ON THE YARD
'80 LOVING COUPLES*

STEPHEN DEUTSCH
PRODUCER
'80 SOMEWHERE IN TIME
'83 ALL THE RIGHT MOVES

MARY JO DEVENNY
SOUND
'83 FRIGHTMARE

SPENCER DEVERILL
ART DIRECTOR
'79 FISH THAT SAVED PITTSBURGH, THE
'80 HEAVEN'S GATE*
'80 JAZZ SINGER, THE
'83 TWO OF A KIND

LINDA DEVETTA
MAKEUP
'83 BRITANNIA HOSPITAL*

GIORGIO DEVINCENZO
ASSISTANT EDITOR
'83 LONELY LADY, THE*

JAMES DEVIS
CINEMATOGRAPHER
'81 DEATH HUNT
'81 TAKE THIS JOB AND SHOVE IT
MISCELLANEOUS
'81 FOR YOUR EYES ONLY

JIMMY DEVIS
2ND UNIT DIRECTOR
'84 PROTOCOL

C. TAD DEVLIN
2ND ASST. DIRECTOR
'80 HIDE IN PLAIN SIGHT*
'81 ON THE RIGHT TRACK
'82 DEATH VALLEY*

DON DEVLIN
PRODUCER
'80 MY BODYGUARD

FRANK DEVOL
MUSIC
'79 FRISCO KID, THE
'80 HERBIE GOES BANANAS
'81 ...ALL THE MARBLES

CHRISTOPHER DEVORE
SCREENPLAY
'80 ELEPHANT MAN, THE*
'82 FRANCES*

GARY DEVORE
SCREENPLAY
'81 BACK ROADS
'81 DOGS OF WAR, THE*

BARRY DEVORZON
MUSIC
'79 WARRIORS, THE
'80 TWINKLE TWINKLE "KILLER" KANE
'81 LOOKER
'81 TATTOO
'82 JEKYLL AND HYDE TOGETHER AGAIN

ROBERT DEVRIES
2ND ASST. DIRECTOR
'84 CHILDREN OF THE CORN

STEPHANIE MILLS DEVRIES
PROD. SECRETARY
'81 FEAR NO EVIL

KAREN DEW
MISCELLANEOUS
'83 NATIONAL LAMPOON'S VACATION
'84 CITY HEAT

LARRY DEWAAY
PRODUCER
'81 DOGS OF WAR, THE
'84 ELECTRIC DREAMS*
EXECUTIVE PRODUCER
'83 YENTL
PRODUCTION MANAGER
'79 ...AND JUSTICE FOR ALL

H. DAN DEWEY
LOCATIONS
'83 ALL THE RIGHT MOVES

JAN DEWITT
2ND ASST. DIRECTOR
'81 GHOST STORY*
'83 STROKER ACE*
'84 CANNONBALL RUN II*

JACK DEWOLF
PRODUCTION DESIGNER
'80 WITHOUT WARNING

GERRY DEY
SCREENPLAY
'79 BLACK HOLE, THE*

CAROLE DEYONG
MISCELLANEOUS
'83 MONTY PYTHON'S THE MEANING OF LIFE

ALICIA DHANIFU
CO-PRODUCER
'79 PENITENTIARY*

EMMA DI VITTORIO
MAKEUP
'82 AIRPLANE II: THE SEQUEL

AUGUSTO DIAMANTI
KEY GRIP
'84 ONCE UPON A TIME IN AMERICA*

I.A.L. DIAMOND
SCREENPLAY
'79 FEDORA*
'81 BUDDY, BUDDY*
ASSOCIATE PRODUCER
'79 FEDORA

KATHERINE DIAMOND
MISCELLANEOUS
'79 VOICES

MONTY DIAMOND
UNIT PROD. MANAGER
'84 NOT FOR PUBLICATION
UNIT MANAGER
'81 TATTOO
'84 MRS. SOFFEL*
LOCATIONS
'80 SIMON

NEIL DIAMOND
MUSIC
'80 JAZZ SINGER, THE

PETER DIAMOND
STUNT COORDINATOR
'79 LEGACY, THE
'80 EMPIRE STRIKES BACK, THE
'83 NATE & HAYES
MISCELLANEOUS
'79 FIFTH MUSKETEER, THE

KEN DIAZ
MAKEUP
'82 ZOOT SUIT*

REHEIM "ZODIAC" DIAZ
MISCELLANEOUS
'84 BREAKIN 2 ELECTRIC BOOGALOO

JOE DIBELLA
MAKEUP
'80 CHEAPER TO KEEP HER

CRAIG DIBONA
MISCELLANEOUS
'80 TRIBUTE
'82 PORKY'S
'84 SPLASH

RICHARD DIBONA
EXECUTIVE PRODUCER
'82 Q: QUETZALCOATL*

THOMAS DICILLO
CINEMATOGRAPHER
'81 PERMANENT VACATION

ROGER DICKEN
MISCELLANEOUS
'79 ALIEN
'83 HUNGER, THE

ROB DICKENSON
MISCELLANEOUS
'83 NEVER SAY NEVER AGAIN

BRETT DICKER
PUBLICIST
'79 APOCALYPSE NOW

ERNEST DICKERSON
CINEMATOGRAPHER
'84 BROTHER FROM ANOTHER PLANET, THE

BOB DICKINSON
MISCELLANEOUS
'80 IDOLMAKER, THE

DIDI DICKSON
MISCELLANEOUS
'83 MERRY CHRISTMAS, MR. LAWRENCE

PHILIP DICKSON
ASSISTANT EDITOR
'82 ROAD WARRIOR, THE*

JOAN DIDION
SCREENPLAY
'81 TRUE CONFESSIONS*

DEBBIE DIERENZO
PROD. COORDINATOR
'84 UP THE CREEK

BOBBIE DIES
ASSISTANT EDITOR
'79 HURRICANE

BILL DIETZ
PROPS
'79 ROCKY II
'79 CONCORDE-AIRPORT '79, THE
'80 IDOLMAKER, THE
'81 INCREDIBLE SHRINKING WOMAN, THE*
'82 ROCKY III
'84 COUNTRY

HEDY DIETZ
STILLS
'80 WITHOUT WARNING

ROBERT DIETZ
SOUND
'80 WITHOUT WARNING

JOE DIGAETANO
SPECIAL EFFECTS
'83 WAR GAMES

ADRIAN DIGHTAM
MISCELLANEOUS
'84 BREAKIN 2 ELECTRIC BOOGALOO

FRANCO DIGIACOMO
CINEMATOGRAPHER
'82 AMITYVILLE II: THE POSSESSION
'82 FIGHTING BACK

LOUIS DIGIAMO
CASTING
'80 CRUISING
'80 FIRST DEADLY SIN
'82 MONSIGNOR*
MISCELLANEOUS
'80 TIMES SQUARE
'81 NIGHTHAWKS
'83 EASY MONEY

CAROL ANN DIGIUSEPPE
ASSISTANT EDITOR
'81 HISTORY OF THE WORLD PART I*
'83 STROKER ACE*
'84 CANNONBALL RUN II*

RANDY DIGRAZIO
CHOREOGRAPHER
'84 HARDBODIES

ROBERT DIJOUX
PRODUCTION MANAGER
'80 PRIVATE EYES, THE
UNIT PROD. MANAGER
'79 PRIZE FIGHTER, THE

VERA DIKA
ASSISTANT EDITOR
'80 HE KNOWS YOU'RE ALONE
SCRIPT SUPERVISOR
'80 HE KNOWS YOU'RE ALONE

RICHARD DILELLO
SCREENPLAY
'83 BAD BOYS

MARIO DILEO
CINEMATOGRAPHER
'83 NIGHTMARES*

DOUGLAS DILGE
PRODUCER
'84 STRANGERS KISS
MUSIC
'81 THEY ALL LAUGHED

LESLIE DILLEY
ART DIRECTOR
'79 ALIEN*
'80 EMPIRE STRIKES BACK, THE*
'81 RAIDERS OF THE LOST ARK
'81 AMERICAN WEREWOLF IN LONDON, AN
'83 NEVER SAY NEVER AGAIN

CHRIS DILLINGER
ASSOCIATE PRODUCER
'80 HUMAN FACTOR, THE*

JAMES DILLON
2ND ASST. DIRECTOR
'82 FAST TIMES AT RIDGEMONT HIGH*

ROBERT DILLON
SCREENPLAY
'84 RIVER, THE*

EDWARD DILORENZO
SCREENPLAY
'80 IDOLMAKER, THE

NINO DIMARCO
EDITOR
'83 CHAINED HEAT

TONY DIMARCO
EDITOR
'81 HELL NIGHT
'82 SEDUCTION, THE

ROBERT DIMILIA
CO-PRODUCER
'80 HE KNOWS YOU'RE ALONE*
UNIT PROD. MANAGER
'80 HE KNOWS YOU'RE ALONE

DIMITRI DIMITRIADIS
PRODUCTION MANAGER
'80 RAISE THE TITANIC*
LOCATIONS
'83 TABLE FOR FIVE*

OLGA DIMITROV
COSTUMES
'79 IN PRAISE OF OLDER WOMEN
'81 DEATH HUNT
'83 DEAD ZONE, THE

SAUL DINNERSTEIN
MISCELLANEOUS
'83 LIQUID SKY

MARTIN DINNES D.V.M.
MISCELLANEOUS
'83 GOLDEN SEAL, THE

DENISE DINOVA
MISCELLANEOUS
'83 VIDEODROME

RICHARD DIOGUARDI
MISCELLANEOUS
'78 DEER HUNTER, THE

DEBRA DION
CASTING
'83 METALSTORM: THE DESTRUCTION OF JARED-SYN*
PROD. COORDINATOR
'82 PARASITE

DENNIS DION
SPECIAL EFFECTS
'81 ...ALL THE MARBLES
'81 TAPS*
'82 SECOND THOUGHTS
'83 OUTSIDERS, THE
SP. EFFECTS SUPERV.
'83 RUMBLEFISH
'84 SOLDIER'S STORY, A

MICHELE DION
MAKEUP
'79 IN PRAISE OF OLDER WOMEN
'83 OF UNKNOWN ORIGIN*

CARLO DIPALMA
CINEMATOGRAPHER
'83 BLACK STALLION RETURNS, THE

JAMES DIPASQUALE
MUSIC
'79 FAST BREAK*

MICHAEL DIPASQUALE
UNIT PUBLICIST
'84 BREAKIN 2 ELECTRIC BOOGALOO
'84 MAKING THE GRADE

GERALD DIPEGO
SCREENPLAY
'81 SHARKEY'S MACHINE

JOHN DIRLAM
MISCELLANEOUS
'83 FRIGHTMARE

MARIO DISALVIO
MAKEUP
'80 FLASH GORDON*

TOM DISCHERT
KEY GRIP
'84 BOSTONIANS, THE

FRANK DISESSO
MISCELLANEOUS
'83 MAUSOLEUM

MOE DISESSO
MISCELLANEOUS
'82 ANNIE

JOE DISHNER
LOCATIONS
'84 NOT FOR PUBLICATION*

EILEEN DISS
PRODUCTION DESIGNER
'83 BETRAYAL

ANN DITCHBURN
CHOREOGRAPHER
'82 SIX WEEKS

BRUCE DITCHFIELD
STILLS
'84 CHEECH AND CHONG'S THE CORSICAN BROTHERS

DAVID DITTMAR
MAKEUP
'82 HONKYTONK MAN
'84 OH GOD, YOU DEVIL

MIKE DITZ
STILLS
'83 EVIL DEAD, THE

WILLIAM DIVER
ASSISTANT EDITOR
'79 SHOUT, THE*

JOANNE DIVITO
CHOREOGRAPHER
'83 EDDIE AND THE CRUISERS

BARBARA DIXON
ASSISTANT EDITOR
'84 RUNAWAY*

CURTIS DIXON
SPECIAL EFFECTS
'82 YOUNG DOCTORS IN LOVE*

HUMPHREY DIXON
EDITOR
'79 EUROPEANS, THE
'80 QUARTET
'83 HEAT AND DUST

JOHN DIXON
SCREENPLAY
'83 MAN FROM SNOWY RIVER, THE
2ND UNIT DIRECTOR
'83 MAN FROM SNOWY RIVER, THE

PAUL DIXON
ASSISTANT EDITOR
'81 CUTTER'S WAY*

PEGGY DIXON
CHOREOGRAPHER
'81 DRAGONSLAYER

TRAVIS DIXON
HAIR
'80 WILLIE & PHIL*

ANDRE DJAOUI
EXECUTIVE PRODUCER
'81 BURNING, THE*

DEBRA DJENDEM
ART DIRECTOR
'83 STRANGE BREW*

MICHAEL DMTRYK
2ND UNIT DIRECTOR
'80 HERBIE GOES BANANAS

BILL DOANE
SP. EFFECTS SUPERV.
'81 HAPPY BIRTHDAY TO ME*

BENNIE DOBBINS
STUNT COORDINATOR
'79 GREAT SANTINI, THE
'79 LOVE AND BULLETS*
'80 CHANGE OF SEASONS, A
'81 SOUTHERN COMFORT
'82 48 HOURS
'84 STREETS OF FIRE

MIKE DOBIE
ASSISTANT EDITOR
'82 PERSONAL BEST*

NEAL DOBROFSKY
PRODUCER
'80 BRONCO BILLY*

RICHARD DOBSON
1ST ASST. DIRECTOR
'80 KIDS ARE ALL RIGHT, THE*

KATHRYN DOBY
CHOREOGRAPHER
'81 ...ALL THE MARBLES

RUDY DOCHTERMANN
SCREENPLAY
'80 FIENDISH PLOT OF DR. FU MANCHU, THE*

SAM DOCKREY
SPECIAL EFFECTS
'79 CHAPTER TWO

GEORGE DOCKSTADER
MISCELLANEOUS
'80 ANY WHICH WAY YOU CAN

E.L. DOCTOROW
SCREENPLAY
'83 DANIEL
EXECUTIVE PRODUCER
'83 DANIEL*

GARY DODD
KEY GRIP
'79 NORMA RAE
'80 HOLLYWOOD KNIGHTS, THE
'80 NINE TO FIVE
'81 SHARKEY'S MACHINE
'81 PATERNITY
'82 BEST LITTLE WHOREHOUSE IN TEXAS, THE
'83 WAR GAMES
'84 IRRECONCILABLE DIFFERENCES

PATRICK DODD
EDITOR
'81 GAS

JOHN DODDS
2ND ASST. DIRECTOR
'84 GIVE MY REGARDS TO BROAD STREET

GEORGE DODGE
MISCELLANEOUS
'80 BATTLE BEYOND THE STARS

JOHN DODS
ASSOCIATE PRODUCER
'83 RETURN OF THE ALIENS: THE DEADLY SPAWN
SPECIAL EFFECTS
'83 RETURN OF THE ALIENS: THE DEADLY SPAWN

ANGELA DODSON
COSTUMES
'84 UNDER THE VOLCANO

MARY DODSON
ART DIRECTOR
'81 THIEF*

CRAIG DOERGE
MUSIC
'79 RICH KIDS

ROBERT DOHERTY
2ND ASST. DIRECTOR
'80 CHEECH AND CHONG'S NEXT MOVIE
'80 COAST TO COAST*
'80 LITTLE DARLINGS
'81 MOMMIE DEAREST*
'82 SIX WEEKS
'82 I'M DANCING AS FAST AS I CAN*
'82 PERSONAL BEST*
'83 BLUE SKIES AGAIN*
'83 WAR GAMES
'84 DREAMSCAPE*

EVERLYN DOHRING
MAKEUP
'82 NIGHT CROSSING*
HAIR
'79 FEDORA*
'82 NIGHT CROSSING*

CHUCK DOLAN
SPECIAL EFFECTS
'84 GRANDVIEW, U.S.A.*

DENNIS DOLAN
EDITOR
'81 WOLFEN*
'82 THINGS ARE TOUGH ALL OVER
'83 CLASS*
'84 REPO MAN
ASSISTANT EDITOR
'79 BOULEVARD NIGHTS
'80 CARNY

JUDY DOLAN
COSTUMES
'80 OUTSIDER, THE

IGNAZIO DOLCE
1ST ASST. DIRECTOR
'83 YOR

KLAUS DOLDINGER
MUSIC
'84 NEVERENDING STORY, THE*

PETER DOLMAN
LOCATIONS
'81 FRENCH LIEUTENANT'S WOMAN, THE*

SUE DOLPH
MAKEUP
'80 ALLIGATOR
'80 BATTLE BEYOND THE STARS
'81 GALAXY OF TERROR
'82 ANDROID
'82 ZAPPED!
'83 PRIVATE SCHOOL*
HAIR
'80 ALLIGATOR

ROLLY SANTO DOMINGO
SPECIAL EFFECTS
'83 BLIND RAGE

CESAR DOMINGUEZ
MISCELLANEOUS
'84 PURPLE HEARTS

DANNY DOMINGUEZ
SPECIAL EFFECTS
'82 DON'T CRY, IT'S ONLY THUNDER
'83 YEAR OF LIVING DANGEROUSLY, THE
'84 PURPLE HEARTS

EFREN DOMINGUEZ
PRODUCTION MANAGER
'83 BLIND RAGE

H. FRANK DOMINGUEZ
EXECUTIVE PRODUCER
'83 BALLAD OF GREGORIO CORTEZ, THE*

PINO DONAGGIO
MUSIC
'79 TOURIST TRAP
'80 DRESSED TO KILL
'80 HOME MOVIES
'81 BLOW OUT
'81 FAN, THE
'81 HOWLING, THE
'82 TEX
'83 HERCULES
'84 BODY DOUBLE
'84 OVER THE BROOKLYN BRIDGE

LYNN DONAHUE
MAKEUP
'81 FOUR SEASONS, THE*

TERRY DONAHUE
MISCELLANEOUS
'83 RICHARD PRYOR: HERE AND NOW

ROGER DONALDSON
DIRECTOR
'84 BOUNTY, THE

ANDREW DONALLY
PRODUCER
'81 PRIEST OF LOVE*

DANILO DONATI
PRODUCTION DESIGNER
'79 HURRICANE
'80 FLASH GORDON
COSTUMES
'79 HURRICANE
'80 FLASH GORDON

STANLEY DONEN
PRODUCER
'80 SATURN 3
'84 BLAME IT ON RIO
DIRECTOR
'80 SATURN 3
'84 BLAME IT ON RIO

DONFELD
COSTUMES
'79 CHINA SYNDROME, THE
'81 INCHON
'83 BRAINSTORM
'83 CLASS

JOHN DONNALLY
KEY GRIP
'80 DIVINE MADNESS

KEVIN DONNELLY
PRODUCTION MANAGER
'84 UP THE CREEK
MISCELLANEOUS
'80 NUDE BOMB, THE

TERRY DONNELLY

EXECUTIVE PRODUCER
'84 WHERE THE BOYS ARE*
ASSOCIATE PRODUCER
'80 WILLIE & PHIL
'81 ALL NIGHT LONG*
UNIT PROD. MANAGER
'79 DOUBLE MCGUFFIN, THE
'82 AUTHOR, AUTHOR
'84 WHERE THE BOYS ARE
1ST ASST. DIRECTOR
'79 DOUBLE MCGUFFIN, THE
'80 WILLIE & PHIL
'81 ALL NIGHT LONG
'83 DEAL OF THE CENTURY
'83 WITHOUT A TRACE
'84 REVENGE OF THE NERDS

THOMAS MICHAEL DONNELLY

SCREENPLAY
'80 DEFIANCE
ASSOCIATE PRODUCER
'80 DEFIANCE

CLIVE DONNER

DIRECTOR
'80 NUDE BOMB, THE
'81 CHARLIE CHAN AND THE CURSE OF THE DRAGON QUEEN

RICHARD DONNER

DIRECTOR
'80 INSIDE MOVES
'82 TOY, THE
EXECUTIVE PRODUCER
'81 FINAL CONFLICT, THE

EDDY DONNO

1ST ASST. DIRECTOR
'84 LOVE STREAMS*
STUNT COORDINATOR
'79 NORTH AVENUE IRREGULARS, THE
'84 LOVE STREAMS

MARY AGNES DONOGHUE

SCREENPLAY
'83 BUDDY SYSTEM, THE

QUINN DONOGHUE

PUBLICIST
'79 CIRCLE OF IRON
'79 CUBA
'83 SUPERMAN III*
'84 FINDERS KEEPERS

QUINN DONOGHUE

ASSOCIATE PRODUCER
'79 JAGUAR LIVES

ARLENE DONOVAN

PRODUCER
'82 STILL OF THE NIGHT
'84 PLACES IN THE HEART

BRIAN DONOVAN

PROPS
'84 COMFORT AND JOY

MARTIN DONOVAN

SCREENPLAY
'80 LOVING COUPLES

AL DOOLEY

MISCELLANEOUS
'81 SMOKEY BITES THE DUST

PAUL DOOLEY

SCREENPLAY
'80 HEALTH*

SIMON DOONAN

MISCELLANEOUS
'84 BEVERLY HILLS COP

CLAUDE DORAL

LOCATIONS
'79 SAINT JACK

LINDSAY DORAN

EXEC IN CHARGE PROD
'84 THIS IS SPINAL TAP

GARY DORF

LOCATIONS
'81 CHEECH AND CHONG'S NICE DREAMS

STEVE DORFF

MISCELLANEOUS
'80 ANY WHICH WAY YOU CAN

JACQUES DORFMANN

CO-PRODUCER
'82 QUEST FOR FIRE*

BARBARA DORIO

PROD. COORDINATOR
'82 LOVE AND MONEY

JEAN-PIERRE DORLEAC

COSTUMES
'79 BUCK ROGERS
'80 SOMEWHERE IN TIME
'80 BLUE LAGOON
'82 NATIONAL LAMPOON'S CLASS REUNION

JAN DORMAN

HAIR
'80 HUMAN FACTOR, THE

TERI DORMAN

ASSISTANT EDITOR
'81 SOUTHERN COMFORT*

NORMAN DORME

ART DIRECTOR
'80 SATURN 3
'81 FRENCH LIEUTENANT'S WOMAN, THE*
'82 GANDHI*
'83 KRULL*
'84 GREYSTOKE: THE LEGEND OF TARZAN, LORD OF THE APES*

DODY DORN

ASSISTANT EDITOR
'81 HIGH RISK
'82 ENDANGERED SPECIES

JOEL DORN

MUSIC SUPERVISOR
'83 BABY IT'S YOU

MIKE DORNFELD

MISCELLANEOUS
'84 RUNAWAY

WALTON DORNISCH

ASSISTANT EDITOR
'84 WINDY CITY*

WILLIAM DORNISCH

EDITOR
'82 STAR TREK II THE WRATH OF KHAN

ROBERT DORSEY

KEY GRIP
'83 HOUSE ON SORORITY ROW

ROSEMARY DORSEY

SCRIPT SUPERVISOR
'80 LITTLE DARLINGS
'83 TERMS OF ENDEARMENT*

JUDITH DORSMAN

COSTUMES
'79 PICNIC AT HANGING ROCK
'81 EARTHLING, THE

ATTILA DORY

STILLS
'81 ATLANTIC CITY
'84 HOTEL NEW HAMPSHIRE, THE

SUDY DOSTAL

PROD. COORDINATOR
'80 OCTAGON, THE

JO DOSTER

CASTING
'79 GREAT SANTINI, THE*
'80 ROADIE
'81 CONTINENTAL DIVIDE*

BENJAMIN DOUBLAS

MAKEUP
'79 AMERICATHON

ROBERT DOUDELL
PRODUCTION MANAGER
'83 CHRISTINE

ROBIN DOUET
PRODUCTION MANAGER
'79 UNIDENTIFIED FLYING ODDBALL
'83 LOCAL HERO*
MISCELLANEOUS
'84 KILLING FIELDS, THE

MARION DOUGHERTY
CASTING
'79 LITTLE ROMANCE, A*
'80 URBAN COWBOY*
'81 HONKY TONK FREEWAY*
'81 REDS*
'82 FIREFOX*
'82 HONKYTONK MAN
'82 WORLD ACCORDING TO GARP, THE
'83 SUDDEN IMPACT
'83 MAN WITH TWO BRAINS, THE*
'84 KILLING FIELDS, THE*
'84 SWING SHIFT
'84 LITTLE DRUMMER GIRL, THE

MICHAEL DOUGHERTY
MISCELLANEOUS
'80 BLACK MARBLE, THE

TIM DOUGHTEN
KEY GRIP
'81 SATURDAY THE 14TH
'82 LIAR'S MOON*

ANDRE DOUGLAS
MUSIC
'79 PENITENTIARY*

JOEL DOUGLAS
CO-PRODUCER
'84 ROMANCING THE STONE*
1ST ASST. DIRECTOR
'84 ROMANCING THE STONE*

MICHAEL DOUGLAS
PRODUCER
'79 CHINA SYNDROME, THE
'84 ROMANCING THE STONE
EXECUTIVE PRODUCER
'84 STARMAN

PETER VINCENT DOUGLAS
PRODUCER
'80 FINAL COUNTDOWN, THE
'83 SOMETHING WICKED
THIS WAY COMES

CHRIS DOUGLAS-MORRIS
ASSISTANT EDITOR
'81 FINAL CONFLICT, THE*

MAX DOUY
ART DIRECTOR
'79 MOONRAKER*

SERGE DOUY
ART DIRECTOR
'80 PRIVATE BENJAMIN*

DICK DOVA
KEY GRIP
'80 DIE LAUGHING

KATHY DOVER
COSTUMES
'82 EATING RAOUL

WILLIAM DOW
STILLS
'81 FORCE FIVE

KEVIN DOWD
SOUND
'81 PERMANENT VACATION

NED DOWD
2ND ASST. DIRECTOR
'83 STREAMERS

JON DOWDING
ART DIRECTOR
'80 BLUE LAGOON
PRODUCTION DESIGNER
'81 ROAD GAMES

PETER DOWKER
MISCELLANEOUS
'81 SCANNERS
'83 OF UNKNOWN ORIGIN

TOM DOWNER
MISCELLANEOUS
'79 PICNIC AT HANGING ROCK

JOHN DOWNES
2ND ASST. DIRECTOR
'81 DRAGONSLAYER*
LOCATIONS
'80 FFOLKES
'81 DOGS OF WAR, THE*

CHERYL DOWNEY
1ST ASST. DIRECTOR
'81 FOUR FRIENDS
2ND ASST. DIRECTOR
'79 ICE CASTLES*

ROBERT DOWNEY
DIRECTOR
'80 UP THE ACADEMY
SCREENPLAY
'80 GONG SHOW MOVIE, THE*

ROY DOWNEY
SPECIAL EFFECTS
'80 HOPSCOTCH*
'81 KING OF THE MOUNTAIN
'82 DEATH VALLEY
'83 MAN WHO LOVED WOMEN, THE
'84 MICKI AND MAUDE

HUNT DOWNS
PUBLICIST
'79 GREAT SANTINI, THE
'81 SPHINX

PETER DOWNSBOROUGH
SOUND
'81 SUBWAY RIDERS

BRIAN DOYLE
PUBLICIST
'81 SEA WOLVES, THE*
'83 EDUCATING RITA
'84 TOP SECRET!
UNIT PUBLICIST
'79 ALIEN
'84 RIDDLE OF THE SANDS

JIM DOYLE
SPECIAL EFFECTS
'84 NIGHTMARE ON ELM STREET, A
MISCELLANEOUS
'82 SWORD AND THE SORCERER, THE
'84 NIGHTMARE ON ELM STREET, A
'84 BREAKIN 2 ELECTRIC BOOGALOO

JULIAN DOYLE
EDITOR
'79 MONTY PYTHON'S LIFE OF BRIAN
'81 TIME BANDITS
'82 MONTY PYTHON LIVE AT
THE HOLLYWOOD BOWL*
'83 MONTY PYTHON'S
THE MEANING OF LIFE

MARGARITA DOYLE
ASSISTANT EDITOR
'83 MONTY PYTHON'S
THE MEANING OF LIFE*

MICHAEL DOYLE
SPECIAL EFFECTS
'81 EXCALIBUR*

BRIAN DOYLE-MURRAY
SCREENPLAY
'80 CADDYSHACK*

GARTH DRABINSKY
PRODUCER
'80 CHANGELING, THE*
'80 TRIBUTE*
'82 AMATEUR, THE*
EXECUTIVE PRODUCER
'79 SILENT PARTNER, THE
'83 LOSIN' IT*

NATALIE DRACHE
SCRIPT SUPERVISOR
'79 SILENT PARTNER, THE
'83 BUDDY SYSTEM, THE

BERT DRAGIN
PRODUCER
'83 SUBURBIA

STAN DRAGOTI
DIRECTOR
'79 LOVE AT FIRST BITE
'83 MR. MOM

VICTOR DRAI
PRODUCER
'84 WOMAN IN RED, THE

DICK DRAKE
MISCELLANEOUS
'81 HONKY TONK FREEWAY

LEONARD DRAKE
HAIR
'80 COMPETITION, THE*
'81 WHOSE LIFE IS IT ANYWAY?*
'83 STING II, THE*
'83 BUDDY SYSTEM, THE*
'83 MR. MOM
'83 TRENCHCOAT
'84 SOLDIER'S STORY, A

MILLER DRAKE
2ND UNIT DIRECTOR
'80 ALLIGATOR*

SIMON DRAKE
MISCELLANEOUS
'84 SCANDALOUS

T.Y. DRAKE
SCREENPLAY
'80 TERROR TRAIN

JAY DRANCH
ASSISTANT EDITOR
'79 RICH KIDS*
'79 ALAMBRISTA!

PAUL DRANE
PRODUCER
'81 MAN WHO SAW TOMORROW, THE*

EMILY DRAPER
COSTUMES
'84 MAKING THE GRADE

BARI DREIBAND
MAKEUP
'79 BUCK ROGERS*
'82 BORDER, THE
'84 ADVENTURES OF BUCKAROO BANZAI ACROSS THE 8TH DIMENSION,THE
MISCELLANEOUS
'84 BODY DOUBLE

BARRY DRESNER
ASSISTANT EDITOR
'81 GRADUATION DAY
'83 MORTUARY

HAL DRESNER
SCREENPLAY
'81 ZORRO, THE GAY BLADE

DAVID DREYFUSS
2ND ASST. DIRECTOR
'84 PLACES IN THE HEART
2ND UNIT DIRECTOR
'83 SCARFACE

GEORGE DREYFUSS
MUSIC
'83 TENDER MERCIES

CHARLOTTE DRIEMAN
PROD. COORDINATOR
'81 CHEECH AND CHONG'S NICE DREAMS
'83 ALL THE RIGHT MOVES

JOHN DRIMMER
SCREENPLAY
'84 ICEMAN*

SARA DRIVER
PRODUCER
'84 STRANGER THAN PARADISE
PRODUCTION MANAGER
'81 PERMANENT VACATION
'84 STRANGER THAN PARADISE
1ST ASST. DIRECTOR
'81 PERMANENT VACATION

EDWARD DROHAN
PROPS
'83 HUNGER, THE*
SPECIAL EFFECTS
'79 WARRIORS, THE
'80 SIMON
'81 NEIGHBORS*
'82 HANKY PANKY*
'84 LOVELESS, THE*
SP. EFFECTS SUPERV.
'81 RAGTIME*

BUDGE DRURY
CASTING
'79 MOONRAKER*

WESTON DRURY JR.
CASTING
'83 EDUCATING RITA*

GEORDIE DRYDEN
KEY GRIP
'79 PICNIC AT HANGING ROCK

DAVID DRYER
MISCELLANEOUS
'82 BLADERUNNER
'83 NEVER SAY NEVER AGAIN

ANNA DRYHURST
MAKEUP
'80 OUTSIDER, THE
'81 EXCALIBUR*

MICHAEL DRYHURST
ASSOCIATE PRODUCER
'81 EXCALIBUR
'83 NEVER SAY NEVER AGAIN
1ST ASST. DIRECTOR
'79 LEGACY, THE
'80 LADY VANISHES, THE
MISCELLANEOUS
'83 SUPERMAN III

JOSE DUARTE
ART DIRECTOR
'81 FUNHOUSE, THE

DAVID DUBAY
ASSOCIATE PRODUCER
'82 BRAINWAVES

RANI DUBE
CO-PRODUCER
'82 GANDHI

ARTHUR DUBS
PRODUCER
'79 MOUNTAIN FAMILY ROBINSON
SCREENPLAY
'79 MOUNTAIN FAMILY ROBINSON

JEAN-LOUIS DUCARME
SOUND
'83 ENIGMA
'83 TRENCHCOAT*

SUSAN DUDECK
ASSISTANT EDITOR
'82 PARASITE

STANLEY DUDELSON
EXECUTIVE PRODUCER
'84 NIGHTMARE ON ELM STREET, A*

LEON DUDEVOIR
1ST ASST. DIRECTOR
'80 HANGAR 18
'82 BOOGENS, THE

NICK DUDMAN
MAKEUP
'83 BEYOND THE LIMIT*

DON DUFFIELD
KEY GRIP
'80 JAZZ SINGER, THE
'81 CHEECH AND CHONG'S NICE DREAMS
'84 SOLDIER'S STORY, A

DON DUFFIELD JR.
KEY GRIP
'84 TANK

FARRELL DUFFY
ASSISTANT EDITOR
'81 BURNING, THE
'83 EDDIE MACON'S RUN

WILLIAM DUFFY
ASSOCIATE PRODUCER
'81 LAST CHASE, THE

VALERIE DUGALE
PUBLICIST
'81 TICKET TO HEAVEN

DAN DUGAN
1ST ASST. DIRECTOR
'84 WEEKEND PASS

MICHAEL DUGAN
DIRECTOR
'83 MAUSOLEUM

FRANCOIS DUHAMEL
STILLS
'84 LOVE STREAMS*
'84 UNDER THE VOLCANO

DARYL DUKE
DIRECTOR
'79 SILENT PARTNER, THE

SUSAN DUKOW
PROD. COORDINATOR
'82 THAT CHAMPIONSHIP SEASON
'83 SPACEHUNTER: ADVENTURES IN THE FORBIDDEN ZONE*
PROD. SECRETARY
'80 ISLAND, THE

AYANNA DULANEY
ASSOCIATE PRODUCER
'82 PENITENTIARY II*

JIM DULTZ
ART DIRECTOR
'81 TAKE THIS JOB AND SHOVE IT
'82 LAST AMERICAN VIRGIN, THE
PROPS
'80 BATTLE BEYOND THE STARS*

JOHN DUMAS
EDITOR
'79 BUCK ROGERS

NADINE DUMAS
HAIR
'83 EXPOSED*

DON CARLOS DUNAWAY
SCREENPLAY
'83 CUJO*
'84 IMPULSE*

TED DUNCAN
STUNT COORDINATOR
'82 SWAMP THING
'83 TIMERIDER*
'84 EXTERMINATOR II

NORA DUNFEE
MISCELLANEOUS
'84 MRS. SOFFEL

DUWAYNE DUNHAM
EDITOR
'83 RETURN OF THE JEDI*
ASSISTANT EDITOR
'79 MORE AMERICAN GRAFFITTI*

BOB DUNN
MISCELLANEOUS
'83 OF UNKNOWN ORIGIN
'84 BACHELOR PARTY

JIM DUNN
KEY GRIP
'80 BIG RED ONE, THE

MICHAEL DUNN
PROPS
'79 GREAT SANTINI, THE
'80 ROADIE*
'80 SERIAL
'81 SHARKEY'S MACHINE
'81 KING OF THE MOUNTAIN
'81 PATERNITY

NAN DUNN
MAKEUP
'81 MAN WHO SAW TOMORROW, THE*

NATHANIEL DUNN
ASSOCIATE PRODUCER
'84 MUTANT
PRODUCTION MANAGER
'84 MUTANT

NATHANIEL DUNN
KEY GRIP
'83 OSTERMAN WEEKEND, THE

STEPHEN DUNN
2ND ASST. DIRECTOR
'82 CAT PEOPLE
'82 YOUNG DOCTORS IN LOVE
'83 BIG CHILL, THE*
'83 MAN WITH TWO BRAINS, THE
'84 THIEF OF HEARTS

GRIFFIN DUNNE
PRODUCER
'82 CHILLY SCENES OF WINTER*
'83 BABY IT'S YOU*

JOE DUNNE
STUNT COORDINATOR
'81 S.O.B.
'83 CURSE OF THE PINK PANTHER
'83 FLASHDANCE
'83 MAN WHO LOVED WOMEN, THE
'83 MAN WITH TWO BRAINS, THE
'83 TRAIL OF THE PINK PANTHER
'84 MICKI AND MAUDE
'84 BACHELOR PARTY

JOHN GREGORY DUNNE
SCREENPLAY
'81 TRUE CONFESSIONS*

BARBARA DUNNING
ASSISTANT EDITOR
'79 CHAPTER TWO
'81 KING OF THE MOUNTAIN*
'81 ZORRO, THE GAY BLADE*
'84 2010*

JOHN DUNNING
PRODUCER
'81 HAPPY BIRTHDAY TO ME*
'81 MY BLOODY VALENTINE*
'83 SPACEHUNTER: ADVENTURES IN THE FORBIDDEN ZONE*
EXECUTIVE PRODUCER
'79 MEATBALLS*

BARBARA DUNPHY
ART DIRECTOR
'83 RUNNING BRAVE
'83 DEAD ZONE, THE

MAURICE DUNSTER
ASSOCIATE PRODUCER
'79 MAN, A WOMAN AND A BANK, A

MONICA DUPASQUIER
PROD. SECRETARY
'81 HIGH RISK*

FRANCOISE DUPERE
KEY GRIP
'81 SCANNERS
'81 GAS

PENNIE DUPONT
CASTING
'82 TOY, THE*
'84 KARATE KID, THE*

RENE DUPONT
PRODUCER
'79 MURDER BY DECREE*
'83 CHRISTMAS STORY, A*

JOHN DUPREZ
MUSIC
'84 OXFORD BLUES

STEPHAN DUPUIS
MISCELLANEOUS
'81 SCANNERS
'82 QUEST FOR FIRE
'83 OF UNKNOWN ORIGIN

CHUCHO DURAN
SPECIAL EFFECTS
'84 UNDER THE VOLCANO

JESUS DURAN
SPECIAL EFFECTS
'79 SUNBURN*
'81 CATTLE ANNIE AND LITTLE BRITCHES*
'82 MISSING*
'83 UNDER FIRE*

DUKE DURFEE
ART DIRECTOR
'84 FLAMINGO KID, THE

JAMES KELLY DURGIN
SCRIPT SUPERVISOR
'83 AMERICANA

EXA DURHAM
PROD. COORDINATOR
'84 BACHELOR PARTY

MARCEL DURHAM
ASSISTANT EDITOR
'81 GREAT MUPPET CAPER, THE

GILLES DURIEUX
UNIT PUBLICIST
'79 MOONRAKER*

PIERRE DURY
STILLS
'81 GAS*

DANIEL DUSEK
LOCATIONS
'82 SILENT RAGE

PHIL DUSENBERRY
SCREENPLAY
'84 NATURAL, THE*

MICHAEL DUTHIE
EDITOR
'81 ENTER THE NINJA*
'83 REVENGE OF THE NINJA*
'84 MUTANT

JOHN DUTTON
SCRIPT SUPERVISOR
'79 WHEN YOU COMIN' BACK, RED RYDER?

SYD DUTTON
MISCELLANEOUS
'79 BUCK ROGERS
'83 PSYCHO II

LAURENCE DUVAL
SCRIPT SUPERVISOR
'82 QUEST FOR FIRE*

ROBERT DUVALL
DIRECTOR
'83 ANGELO, MY LOVE
SCREENPLAY
'83 ANGELO, MY LOVE
CO-PRODUCER
'83 TENDER MERCIES*

CLAUDE DUVERNOY
ASSISTANT EDITOR
'80 SCHIZOID*

RUSS DVONCH
SCREENPLAY
'79 ROCK 'N ROLL HIGH SCHOOL*

SUE DWIGGINS
PROD. COORDINATOR
'82 E.T. THE EXTRA-TERRESTRIAL

OTTO BORIS DWORAK
PRODUCTION MANAGER
'82 AMATEUR, THE*

RICH DWYER
ASSISTANT EDITOR
'81 KNIGHTRIDERS*

DORIS DYCK
EDITOR
'82 OUT OF THE BLUE

LYNDA DYE
PROPS
'81 STRANGE BEHAVIOR

MARY DYE
COSTUMES
'79 APPLE DUMPLING GANG RIDES AGAIN, THE*

JAMES ROBERT DYER
UNIT PROD. MANAGER
'82 VICE SQUAD

JIM DYER
1ST ASST. DIRECTOR
'83 MR. MOM

LEE DYER
MISCELLANEOUS
'82 TRON
'83 SOMETHING WICKED THIS WAY COMES

LOU DYER
PUBLICIST
'81 INCHON
UNIT PUBLICIST
'82 CHALLENGE, THE

NORMAN DYHRENFURTH
2ND UNIT DIRECTOR
'82 FIVE DAYS ONE SUMMER
MISCELLANEOUS
'82 FIVE DAYS ONE SUMMER

JOHN DYKSTRA
SPECIAL EFFECTS
'79 AVALANCHE EXPRESS*
MISCELLANEOUS
'79 STAR TREK-THE MOTION PICTURE
'80 CADDYSHACK

CAROL DYSINGER
1ST ASST. DIRECTOR
'83 LIANNA

TOM DZURISON
MISCELLANEOUS
'80 MY BODYGUARD

E

PAUL EADS
ART DIRECTOR
'81 SO FINE
'81 FAN, THE
'82 TEMPEST*
'83 JAWS 3-D*

NANCY EAGLES
SCRIPT SUPERVISOR
'79 BROOD, THE

DAVID EAMES
SCREENPLAY
'82 BY DESIGN*

DAVID EARL
MUSIC
'84 KIPPERBANG

DAVID EARL
2ND ASST. DIRECTOR
'79 BLACK STALLION, THE*

CAPTAIN JOHN EARLY
MISCELLANEOUS
'84 RED DAWN

ROBERT EASTMAN
1ST ASST. DIRECTOR
'80 EYES OF A STRANGER

SPENCER EASTMAN
SCREENPLAY
'80 HIDE IN PLAIN SIGHT

BILL EASTON
MISCELLANEOUS
'83 RUNNING BRAVE

SCOTT EASTON
1ST ASST. DIRECTOR
'81 LOOKER
'82 DINER*
'84 BLAME IT ON RIO*
2ND ASST. DIRECTOR
'79 NIGHTWING
'79 ONION FIELD, THE
'79 PLAYERS
'80 RAISE THE TITANIC*
'80 BRUBAKER
'80 CHANGE OF SEASONS, A*
'81 GOING APE!*
'82 CHILLY SCENES OF WINTER

LORI EASTSIDE
CHOREOGRAPHER
'84 ALPHABET CITY

CLINT EASTWOOD
PRODUCER
'82 FIREFOX
'82 HONKYTONK MAN
'83 SUDDEN IMPACT
'84 TIGHTROPE*
DIRECTOR
'80 BRONCO BILLY
'82 FIREFOX
'82 HONKYTONK MAN
'83 SUDDEN IMPACT

LAURENCE EASTWOOD
PRODUCTION DESIGNER
'84 PHAR LAP

BRIAN EATWELL
PRODUCTION DESIGNER
'79 BUTCH AND SUNDANCE: THE EARLY YEARS
'79 ONION FIELD, THE
'83 EXPOSED
'84 AMERICAN DREAMER

BOB EBER
SOUND
'84 THIS IS SPINAL TAP

THOM EBERHARDT
DIRECTOR
'84 NIGHT OF THE COMET
SCREENPLAY
'84 NIGHT OF THE COMET

JACK EBERHART
PROPS
'84 PLACES IN THE HEART

ROBERT EBERLEIN
MISCELLANEOUS
'82 ONE FROM THE HEART

ROBERT EBINGER
CINEMATOGRAPHER
'81 STUDENT BODIES

AL EBNER
PUBLICIST
'80 CHANGELING, THE*
'80 CLOSE ENCOUNTERS OF THE THIRD KIND SPECIAL EDITION*
'80 ISLAND, THE
'81 ALL NIGHT LONG
'83 HIGH ROAD TO CHINA
'83 TOUGH ENOUGH
'84 GRANDVIEW, U.S.A.
UNIT PUBLICIST
'82 MEGAFORCE
'84 PHILADELPHIA EXPERIMENT, THE

JOHN ECKERT
CO-PRODUCER
'79 RUNNING
'80 MIDDLE AGE CRAZY
PRODUCTION MANAGER
'83 DEAD ZONE, THE

MICHAEL ECONOMOU
ASSOCIATE PRODUCER
'81 FOUR SEASONS, THE
EDITOR
'81 FOUR SEASONS, THE

HAMID EDDEUCH
PRODUCTION MANAGER
'84 PROTOCOL*

SCOTT EDDO
MAKEUP
'80 GONG SHOW MOVIE, THE

ROBERT EDELEN
EXECUTIVE PRODUCER
'79 PENITENTIARY*

DANA EDELMAN
SCREENPLAY
'80 HOME MOVIES*
LOCATIONS
'80 HOME MOVIES

RICK EDELSTEIN
MISCELLANEOUS
'83 YENTL

WAYNE EDGAR
SPECIAL EFFECTS
'82 HONKYTONK MAN

DUANE EDGE
MISCELLANEOUS
'83 RUNNING BRAVE

JED EDGE
MISCELLANEOUS
'81 RAIDERS OF THE LOST ARK

NORM EDGE
MISCELLANEOUS
'83 RUNNING BRAVE

STEVE EDGE
MISCELLANEOUS
'81 RAIDERS OF THE LOST ARK

ANNE EDGEWORTH
PROPS
'84 BROTHER FROM
ANOTHER PLANET, THE

MICHAEL EDGLEY
EXECUTIVE PRODUCER
'83 MAN FROM SNOWY RIVER, THE*

RICHARD EDLUND
MISCELLANEOUS
'79 CHINA SYNDROME, THE
'80 EMPIRE STRIKES BACK, THE
'81 RAIDERS OF THE LOST ARK
'82 POLTERGEIST
'83 RETURN OF THE JEDI
'84 GHOSTBUSTERS
'84 2010

BOB EDMISTON
CASTING
'79 BUCK ROGERS
'80 EMPIRE STRIKES BACK, THE*

PAUL EDMONDS
ASSISTANT EDITOR
'81 SHOCK TREATMENT

ANN EDWARDS
SCRIPT SUPERVISOR
'79 LOST AND FOUND
'83 WICKED LADY, THE
'83 KEEP, THE
'84 LASSITER

BEN EDWARDS
PRODUCTION DESIGNER
'81 FORT APACHE, THE BRONX
'82 HANKY PANKY

BERNARD EDWARDS
MUSIC
'82 SOUP FOR ONE*

BLAKE EDWARDS
PRODUCER
'79 10*
'81 S.O.B.*
'82 VICTOR/VICTORIA*
'83 CURSE OF THE PINK PANTHER*
'83 MAN WHO LOVED WOMEN, THE*
'83 TRAIL OF THE PINK PANTHER*
DIRECTOR
'79 10
'81 S.O.B.
'82 VICTOR/VICTORIA
'83 CURSE OF THE PINK PANTHER
'83 MAN WHO LOVED WOMEN, THE
'83 TRAIL OF THE PINK PANTHER
'84 MICKI AND MAUDE
SCREENPLAY
'79 10
'81 S.O.B.
'82 VICTOR/VICTORIA
'83 CURSE OF THE PINK PANTHER*
'83 MAN WHO LOVED WOMEN, THE*
'83 TRAIL OF THE PINK PANTHER*

BUCK EDWARDS
1ST ASST. DIRECTOR
'84 BEAR, THE
2ND ASST. DIRECTOR
'80 COMPETITION, THE*
LOCATIONS
'79 MUPPET MOVIE, THE

ERIC EDWARDS
CINEMATOGRAPHER
'84 LAST NIGHT AT THE ALAMO*
STILLS
'84 LAST NIGHT AT THE ALAMO*

GEOFFREY EDWARDS
SCREENPLAY
'83 CURSE OF THE PINK PANTHER*
'83 MAN WHO LOVED WOMEN, THE*
'83 TRAIL OF THE PINK PANTHER*
ASSISTANT EDITOR
'79 10*
'81 S.O.B.*

JOAN EDWARDS
ASSOCIATE PRODUCER
'83 TWO OF A KIND*

KATE EDWARDS
ASSOCIATE PRODUCER
'83 TWO OF A KIND*

MERVYN EDWARDS
UNIT PROD. MANAGER
'84 STONE BOY, THE

PATRICIA EDWARDS
COSTUMES
'79 10
'80 STIR CRAZY
'80 CHANGE OF SEASONS, A*
'81 TARZAN, THE APE MAN
'83 CURSE OF THE PINK PANTHER
'83 TRAIL OF THE PINK PANTHER

R. BEN EFRAIM
PRODUCER
'81 PRIVATE LESSONS
'83 PRIVATE SCHOOL*

EDWARD EGAN
PUBLICIST
'82 STAR TREK II
THE WRATH OF KHAN

DENNIS EGER
MISCELLANEOUS
'82 Q: QUETZALCOATL

ANTON EGERER
KEY GRIP
'84 NEVERENDING STORY, THE

MARK EGERTON
1ST ASST. DIRECTOR
'79 PICNIC AT HANGING ROCK
'79 MY BRILLIANT CAREER
'81 GALLIPOLI
'81 EARTHLING, THE
'83 YEAR OF
LIVING DANGEROUSLY, THE*
'84 MRS. SOFFEL*

MARK EGGENWEILER
ASSISTANT EDITOR
'80 JAZZ SINGER, THE*
'80 ON THE NICKEL
'81 ENTITY, THE*
'83 AMITYVILLE 3D
'84 CONAN THE DESTROYER

ROBERT EGGENWEILER
ASSOCIATE PRODUCER
'79 REMEMBER MY NAME*
'79 PERFECT COUPLE, A*
UNIT PROD. MANAGER
'80 HEALTH
LOCATIONS
'80 POPEYE
'81 ENTITY, THE
'82 SIX WEEKS*
'83 WAR GAMES*

WILLY EGGER
MISCELLANEOUS
'79 AVALANCHE EXPRESS
'79 FEDORA
'79 MAGICIAN OF LUBLIN, THE
'80 FORMULA, THE

JOHN EGGETT
MISCELLANEOUS
'81 FEAR NO EVIL

RICHARD EGLSEDER
PROPS
'84 NEVERENDING STORY, THE*

CORKY EHLERS
EDITOR
'83 JAWS 3-D*

LAURIE EICHENGREEN
2ND ASST. DIRECTOR
'79 WANDERERS, THE

EILEEN EICHENSTEIN
PROD. OFFICE COORD.
'80 GLORIA
'80 WINDOWS
'81 FAN, THE
'81 FOUR FRIENDS
'82 VERDICT, THE
'83 WRONG IS RIGHT
'84 BEAT STREET*
PROD. COORDINATOR
'82 I, THE JURY*

BERND EICHINGER
PRODUCER
'84 NEVERENDING STORY, THE*

KAREN EIFERT
COSTUME SUPERVISOR
'80 TIMES SQUARE

PAMELA EILERSON
2ND ASST. DIRECTOR
'81 CHARLIE CHAN AND THE CURSE OF THE DRAGON QUEEN*
'82 AIRPLANE II: THE SEQUEL*
'82 OFFICER AND A GENTLEMAN, AN
'83 TO BE OR NOT TO BE
'83 UNCOMMON VALOR*
'84 SONGWRITER

MARY EILTS
2ND ASST. DIRECTOR
'82 GREY FOX, THE

REBECCA EINFELD
ASSISTANT EDITOR
'82 BARBAROSA*

RICHARD EINHORN
MUSIC
'80 EYES OF A STRANGER

DANIEL EISENBERG
2ND ASST. DIRECTOR
'84 HARDBODIES

JOAN EISENBERG
PUBLICIST
'79 MORE AMERICAN GRAFFITTI
'80 BORDERLINE
'81 ONLY WHEN I LAUGH
'82 FAST TIMES AT RIDGEMONT HIGH
'83 SCARFACE
'84 CLOAK AND DAGGER
UNIT PUBLICIST
'80 SEEMS LIKE OLD TIMES
'80 PRIVATE BENJAMIN
'80 WHERE THE BUFFALO ROAM
'83 EDDIE MACON'S RUN
'83 PSYCHO II

ROBERT EISENSTEIN
EXECUTIVE PRODUCER
'81 EXCALIBUR*

SUSAN EKINS
PROD. SECRETARY
'84 CANNONBALL RUN II

GREG ELAM
STUNT COORDINATOR
'82 ENDANGERED SPECIES*

KEVIN ELDERS
MISCELLANEOUS
'84 PURPLE HEARTS

ZOLTAN ELEK
MAKEUP
'81 DEAD AND BURIED*
'81 ENTITY, THE
'81 HEARTBEEPS*

MARTIN ELFAND
PRODUCER
'80 IT'S MY TURN
'82 OFFICER AND A GENTLEMAN, AN

DAVID ELFICK
PRODUCER
'82 STARSTRUCK*

PETER ELFORD
LOCATIONS
'81 FINAL CONFLICT, THE*
'84 KIPPERBANG
'84 RAZOR'S EDGE, THE*

BURTON ELIAS
ASSOCIATE PRODUCER
'83 UNCOMMON VALOR*
UNIT PUBLICIST
'82 FIRST BLOOD

CAROLYN ELIAS
MAKEUP
'81 REDS*
HAIR
'79 RUNNER STUMBLES, THE
'80 TOUCHED BY LOVE*
'82 SECOND THOUGHTS*

JONATHAN ELIAS
MUSIC
'84 CHILDREN OF THE CORN

LOUIE ELIAS
STUNT COORDINATOR
'79 APPLE DUMPLING GANG RIDES AGAIN, THE
MISCELLANEOUS
'84 BEAR, THE

MICHAEL ELIAS
SCREENPLAY
'79 FRISCO KID, THE*
'79 JERK, THE*
'80 SERIAL*
'82 YOUNG DOCTORS IN LOVE*

WILLIAM ELIAS
EDITOR
'84 JOY OF SEX, THE*

JOYCE ELIASON
SCREENPLAY
'80 TELL ME A RIDDLE*

NICHOLAS ELIOPOULAS
EDITOR
'82 BEST LITTLE WHOREHOUSE IN TEXAS, THE*

DREW ELISIUS
MISCELLANEOUS
'84 SIXTEEN CANDLES

BOB ELKINS
LOCATIONS
'80 HONEYSUCKLE ROSE

BUD ELKINS
STUNT COORDINATOR
'82 JEKYLL AND HYDE TOGETHER AGAIN

SUSAN ELKINS
LOCATIONS
'84 PARIS, TEXAS*

COCO ELLACOTT
CHOREOGRAPHER
'81 BEYOND THE REEF

HARRISON ELLENSHAW
ASSOCIATE PRODUCER
'82 TRON
MISCELLANEOUS
'79 BLACK HOLE, THE
'80 EMPIRE STRIKES BACK, THE
'82 TRON
'83 SOMETHING WICKED THIS WAY COMES

PETER ELLENSHAW
PRODUCTION DESIGNER
'79 BLACK HOLE, THE
MISCELLANEOUS
'79 BLACK HOLE, THE

DUKE ELLINGTON
MUSIC
'80 ROUGH CUT

TOM ELLINGWOOD
MAKEUP
'79 STARTING OVER*
'79 BEYOND THE POSEIDON ADVENTURE*
'79 DREAMER*
'79 NORMA RAE*
'80 ROUGH CUT*
'80 SMOKEY AND THE BANDIT II*
'80 LITTLE DARLINGS
'81 SHARKEY'S MACHINE*
'81 CANNONBALL RUN, THE*
'81 PATERNITY*
'82 BEST FRIENDS*
'82 BEST LITTLE WHOREHOUSE IN TEXAS, THE*
'83 STROKER ACE*
'83 MAN WHO LOVED WOMEN, THE*
'84 CITY HEAT*
'84 CANNONBALL RUN II

ILOE ELLIOT
HAIR
'80 TOUCHED BY LOVE*

JIM ELLIOT
MISCELLANEOUS
'84 UP THE CREEK

PETER ELLIOT
MISCELLANEOUS
'84 GREYSTOKE: THE LEGEND OF TARZAN, LORD OF THE APES

DELORES ELLIOTT
ASSISTANT EDITOR
'81 TATTOO

JACK ELLIOTT
MUSIC
'79 JERK, THE
'79 JUST YOU AND ME KID

JAMES ELLIOTT
MISCELLANEOUS
'82 PENITENTIARY II

JOHN ELLIOTT
MAKEUP
'80 HUNTER, THE
'81 PURSUIT OF D.B. COOPER, THE*
'83 TWILIGHT ZONE, THE MOVIE*

JOHN ELLIOTT
SPECIAL EFFECTS
'84 BEST DEFENSE*
'84 JOY OF SEX, THE

JOHN ELLIOTT JR.
MAKEUP
'82 JEKYLL AND HYDE TOGETHER AGAIN
'83 INDEPENDENCE DAY
'83 TO BE OR NOT TO BE

LANG ELLIOTT
PRODUCER
'79 PRIZE FIGHTER, THE
'80 PRIVATE EYES, THE*
DIRECTOR
'80 PRIVATE EYES, THE
CASTING
'79 PRIZE FIGHTER, THE
'80 PRIVATE EYES, THE

M.J. ELLIOTT
STILLS
'82 ANDROID
'83 CHAINED HEAT
'84 CHILDREN OF THE CORN
'84 NOT FOR PUBLICATION
'84 DREAMSCAPE*
'84 PHILADELPHIA EXPERIMENT, THE*

MARIANNA ELLIOTT
COSTUMES
'81 WHOSE LIFE IS IT ANYWAY?
'83 BLUE THUNDER

PAUL ELLIOTT
MISCELLANEOUS
'81 STUDENT BODIES

WILLIAM ELLIOTT
MISCELLANEOUS
'83 PIRATES OF PENZANCE, THE

DAVID ELLIS
STUNT COORDINATOR
'80 CARNY
'81 BACK ROADS
'81 KING OF THE MOUNTAIN
'82 AIRPLANE II: THE SEQUEL
'82 SECOND THOUGHTS
'83 GORKY PARK
MISCELLANEOUS
'79 GAME OF DEATH

DON ELLIS
MUSIC
'79 NATURAL ENEMIES

DULANIE ELLIS
SCRIPT SUPERVISOR
'83 LOSIN' IT
'84 STONE BOY, THE

JAMIE ELLIS
SCRIPT SUPERVISOR
'84 PREPPIES

JOSEPH ELLIS
PRODUCTION MANAGER
'79 OVER THE EDGE
'81 FORCE FIVE
'84 MARVIN AND TIGE

KIM ELLIS
MISCELLANEOUS
'82 ZAPPED!

MICHAEL ELLIS
EDITOR
'83 BRITANNIA HOSPITAL
'83 LORDS OF DISCIPLINE, THE
'84 COMFORT AND JOY

PAM ELLIS
PROD. COORDINATOR
'81 FORCE FIVE
'84 MARVIN AND TIGE

SARAH ELLIS
ASSISTANT EDITOR
'84 BOUNTY, THE*

CARRIE ELLISON
ASSISTANT EDITOR
'82 HAMMETT*

CHARLES ELLISON
ASSISTANT EDITOR
'79 MAN, A WOMAN AND A BANK, A

CHUCK ELLISON
ASSISTANT EDITOR
'81 DEADLY BLESSING
'82 YOUNG DOCTORS IN LOVE*

GARY ELMENDORF
SPECIAL EFFECTS
'80 FINAL COUNTDOWN, THE*
'81 TAPS*
'83 BUDDY SYSTEM, THE
'84 RACING WITH THE MOON
'84 RHINESTONE

PAT ELMENDORF
SPECIAL EFFECTS
'80 FINAL COUNTDOWN, THE*

FREDERICK ELMES
CINEMATOGRAPHER
'83 VALLEY GIRL
MISCELLANEOUS
'84 RED DAWN

RAFAEL ELORTEGUI
1ST ASST. DIRECTOR
'80 CHEAPER TO KEEP HER
2ND ASST. DIRECTOR
'79 REAL LIFE
'79 BOULEVARD NIGHTS
'79 FAST BREAK*
'80 IT'S MY TURN*
'81 ABSENCE OF MALICE
'81 CHARLIE CHAN AND THE CURSE OF THE DRAGON QUEEN*
'84 HARRY & SON

STEPHEN ELSBREE
HAIR
'83 BLUE THUNDER

JOHN ELSENBACH
MISCELLANEOUS
'79 LOVE AT FIRST BITE

JOSEF ELSHER
SPECIAL EFFECTS
'80 TERROR TRAIN

BILL ELVIN
2ND ASST. DIRECTOR
'80 BLACK MARBLE, THE*
'81 TAPS*
'81 TRUE CONFESSIONS*
'83 SURVIVORS, THE*
'83 BAD BOYS*
'84 AGAINST ALL ODDS
'84 AMERICAN DREAMER*

CASSIAN ELWES
PRODUCER
'84 OXFORD BLUES*

SHANNON ELY
HAIR
'82 FRIDAY THE 13TH PART THREE IN 3D
'84 HOT DOG...THE MOVIE

DAVE EMANN
CASTING
'82 FRIDAY THE 13TH PART THREE IN 3D*

FRANCOISE EMBRY
MAKEUP
'83 ENIGMA*

KATY EMDE
ASSOCIATE PRODUCER
'81 INCREDIBLE SHRINKING WOMAN, THE*
1ST ASST. DIRECTOR
'81 INCREDIBLE SHRINKING WOMAN, THE
'81 WHOSE LIFE IS IT ANYWAY?
'82 E.T. THE EXTRA-TERRESTRIAL
'84 CLOAK AND DAGGER
2ND ASST. DIRECTOR
'79 CONCORDE-AIRPORT '79, THE
'80 COAL MINER'S DAUGHTER

KEITH EMERSON
MUSIC
'81 NIGHTHAWKS

LAVAR EMERT
PROPS
'80 COAST TO COAST

PRUDENCE EMERY
PUBLICIST
'83 STRANGE BREW
'83 STRANGE INVADERS
'83 DEAD ZONE, THE
'84 HOTEL NEW HAMPSHIRE, THE
UNIT PUBLICIST
'79 RUNNING
'80 MIDDLE AGE CRAZY

ALBERTO EMIDI
KEY GRIP
'80 POPEYE*

PETE EMMET
PUBLICIST
'82 SIX WEEKS
'84 KARATE KID, THE
UNIT PUBLICIST
'80 CHANGE OF SEASONS, A
'82 ANNIE
'82 TOY, THE
'84 JOHNNY DANGEROUSLY
'84 REVENGE OF THE NERDS

ROBERT ENDERS
PRODUCER
'79 STEVIE
DIRECTOR
'79 STEVIE

ESTELLE ENDLER
EXECUTIVE PRODUCER
'83 EASY MONEY

MICHAEL ENDLER
SCREENPLAY
'83 EASY MONEY*

KENNY ENDOSO
STUNT COORDINATOR
'84 JOY OF SEX, THE

JACK ENGEL
MAKEUP
'83 TRADING PLACES

DAVID ENGELBACH
SCREENPLAY
'82 DEATHWISH II

MORT ENGELBERG
PRODUCER
'79 VILLAIN, THE
'79 HOT STUFF
'80 HUNTER, THE
'81 NOBODY'S PERFEKT
'83 SMOKEY AND THE BANDIT III

PAUL ENGELEN
MAKEUP
'79 MOONRAKER*
'80 FFOLKES
'81 RAGTIME*
'81 REDS*
'82 PINK FLOYD: THE WALL*
'82 VICTOR/VICTORIA*
'83 SUPERMAN III*
'83 CURSE OF THE PINK PANTHER*
'83 TRAIL OF THE PINK PANTHER*
'84 BOUNTY, THE
'84 GREYSTOKE: THE LEGEND OF TARZAN, LORD OF THE APES
'84 LITTLE DRUMMER GIRL, THE*

GITA ENGELHART
PROD. COORDINATOR
'84 BLAME IT ON RIO

LEONARD ENGELMAN
MAKEUP
'79 SUNBURN
'80 SATURN 3*
'80 IN GOD WE TRUST
'80 JAZZ SINGER, THE*
'81 WHOSE LIFE IS IT ANYWAY?
'82 CAT PEOPLE
'82 SECOND THOUGHTS
'84 BEVERLY HILLS COP*
'84 GHOSTBUSTERS*

ROBERT ENGELMAN
2ND ASST. DIRECTOR
'82 THAT CHAMPIONSHIP SEASON
'83 STING II, THE*
'83 FOOTLOOSE*
'84 TEACHERS

ROSHANI ENGINEER-WISKES
SCRIPT SUPERVISOR
'79 PRIZE FIGHTER, THE
'81 EYE FOR AN EYE, AN

BRYAN ENGLAND
CINEMATOGRAPHER
'84 WEEKEND PASS

IRA ENGLANDER
PRODUCER
'83 RUNNING BRAVE

JACK ENGLISH
LOCATIONS
'79 APOCALYPSE NOW
'79 AVALANCHE EXPRESS
'80 BLACK MARBLE, THE
'81 EYE FOR AN EYE, AN
'81 CARBON COPY
'82 DEATHWISH II*

TERRY ENGLISH
MISCELLANEOUS
'81 EXCALIBUR

RORY ENKE
LOCATIONS
'84 BIRDY

BRIAN ENO
MISCELLANEOUS
'84 DUNE

DON ENRIGHT
PRODUCER
'83 PRIVATE SCHOOL*
EXECUTIVE PRODUCER
'81 PRIVATE LESSONS*

ANDROS EPAMINONDAS
PRODUCER
'84 GIVE MY REGARDS TO BROAD STREET

NORA EPHRON
SCREENPLAY
'83 SILKWOOD*

JEANNIE EPPER
STUNT COORDINATOR
'84 FINAL TERROR, THE

TONY EPPER
STUNT COORDINATOR
'81 CATTLE ANNIE AND LITTLE BRITCHES

MICKEY EPPS
SCREENPLAY
'83 JOYSTICKS*

JULIUS EPSTEIN
SCREENPLAY
'83 REUBEN, REUBEN
CO-PRODUCER
'83 REUBEN, REUBEN

MARCELO EPSTEIN
DIRECTOR
'84 BODY ROCK

NORMAN EPSTEIN
EXECUTIVE PRODUCER
'79 REAL LIFE*

PHILIP EPSTEIN
ASSOCIATE PRODUCER
'83 REUBEN, REUBEN*

S. KAREN EPSTEIN
STILLS
'84 SPLASH*

SAMUEL EPSTEIN
2ND ASST. DIRECTOR
'83 YELLOWBEARD*

RENE ERAM
CASTING
'83 HOUSE ON SORORITY ROW*
2ND UNIT DIRECTOR
'83 HOUSE ON SORORITY ROW

MICKY ERBE
MUSIC
'81 TICKET TO HEAVEN*

NICOLETTA ERCOLE
COSTUMES
'83 PIRANHA II: THE SPAWNING

EDDY ERFMANN
MAKEUP
'84 NEVERENDING STORY, THE*
'84 LITTLE DRUMMER GIRL, THE*

LEON ERICKSEN
ART DIRECTOR
'82 HAMMETT*
'84 ICEMAN*
PRODUCTION DESIGNER
'79 QUINTET
MISCELLANEOUS
'82 BARBAROSA

C.O. ERICKSON
PRODUCER
'81 ZORRO, THE GAY BLADE*
EXECUTIVE PRODUCER
'80 POPEYE
'80 URBAN COWBOY
'82 FAST TIMES AT RIDGEMONT HIGH
'84 CLOAK AND DAGGER
EXEC IN CHARGE PROD
'82 BLADERUNNER
PRODUCTION MANAGER
'80 URBAN COWBOY
UNIT PROD. MANAGER
'79 PLAYERS
'82 FAST TIMES AT RIDGEMONT HIGH
'84 CLOAK AND DAGGER
'84 LONELY GUY, THE*
MISCELLANEOUS
'79 PLAYERS
'84 LONELY GUY, THE

KAY ERICKSON
ASSISTANT EDITOR
'84 GRANDVIEW, U.S.A.

PAULA ERICKSON
PROD. COORDINATOR
'83 REVENGE OF THE NINJA*
'84 OVER THE BROOKLYN BRIDGE*
MISCELLANEOUS
'84 BREAKIN 2 ELECTRIC BOOGALOO

PAULA ERICKSON
MUSIC SUPERVISOR
'82 LAST AMERICAN VIRGIN, THE

ROSS ERICKSON
KEY GRIP
'79 MY BRILLIANT CAREER
'79 TIM
'81 GALLIPOLI*

KERSTIN ERIKSDOTTER
SCRIPT SUPERVISOR
'81 MONTENEGRO

DAN ERIKSON
1ST ASST. DIRECTOR
'82 STRANGER IS WATCHING, A*

MICHAEL ERLER
ART DIRECTOR
'80 ALLIGATOR
'80 HUMANOIDS FROM THE DEEP

MARTIN ERLICHMAN
PRODUCER
'83 BREATHLESS

FRANK ERNST
UNIT PROD. MANAGER
'84 GREYSTOKE: THE LEGEND OF TARZAN, LORD OF THE APES
1ST ASST. DIRECTOR
'81 DEATH HUNT
LOCATIONS
'78 DEER HUNTER, THE*
'79 MOONRAKER*
'81 INCHON*

JOHN ESCOBAR
STUNT COORDINATOR
'79 BOULEVARD NIGHTS

PEDRO ESCOBEDO
MISCELLANEOUS
'84 UNDER THE VOLCANO

VINCENTE ESCRIVIA JR.
PRODUCTION MANAGER
'79 JAGUAR LIVES
'81 REDS*
'82 CONAN THE BARBARIAN
'83 CURSE OF THE PINK PANTHER*

VINCENTE ESCRIVIA
PRODUCTION MANAGER
'83 KRULL*
MISCELLANEOUS
'84 DUNE

FERNANDO PEREZ ESCURA
SPECIAL EFFECTS
'79 LOVE AND BULLETS*

JACI ESHEL
MISCELLANEOUS
'84 BEST DEFENSE

STEVEN ESHELMAN
PRODUCTION MANAGER
'83 MY TUTOR
1ST ASST. DIRECTOR
'83 MY TUTOR

MARCEL ESKENATY
STILLS
'83 FRIGHTMARE*

PETER ESMONDE
ASSISTANT EDITOR
'84 BEAT STREET*

MOCTESUMA ESPARZA
PRODUCER
'83 BALLAD OF GREGORIO CORTEZ, THE*

PHILLIP ESPARZA
ASSOCIATE PRODUCER
'82 ZOOT SUIT

RICHARD ESPINOZA
2ND ASST. DIRECTOR
'82 STAR TREK II THE WRATH OF KHAN
'82 BORDER, THE
'82 VICE SQUAD
'83 YELLOWBEARD*
'84 UP THE CREEK*

ANTHONY ESPOSITO
HAIR
'82 SWORD AND THE SORCERER, THE
'83 ALL THE RIGHT MOVES*

WILLIAM ESSARY
ASSISTANT EDITOR
'82 BEST LITTLE WHOREHOUSE IN TEXAS, THE*
'83 REUBEN, REUBEN*
'83 BAD BOYS
'84 TEACHERS

ENRIQUE ESTEVEZ
ART DIRECTOR
'84 EVIL THAT MEN DO, THE

CATHY ESTOCIN
MAKEUP
'82 BRAINWAVES*

MARTHA ESTRELLA
MISCELLANEOUS
'84 CRACKERS

TOMMY ESTRIDGE
PROPS
'82 SWAMP THING
'82 LIAR'S MOON
'84 LOVE STREAMS
'84 THIS IS SPINAL TAP
'84 BEAR, THE
'84 TERMINATOR, THE

ROBERT ESTRIN
EDITOR
'83 BREATHLESS

JOHN ESTY
MUSIC
'79 ROLLER BOOGIE

JOE ESZTERHAS
SCREENPLAY
'83 FLASHDANCE*

KIRSTEEN ETHERINGTON
CHOREOGRAPHER
'83 VIDEODROME

CHANTAL ETHIER
MAKEUP
'83 OF UNKNOWN ORIGIN*

ERICA EULANND
MAKEUP
'80 SCHIZOID

WILLIAM EUSTACE
2ND ASST. DIRECTOR
'79 FAST BREAK*
'79 GOING IN STYLE
'80 DRESSED TO KILL
'81 FAN, THE
'83 EXPOSED*
'83 HUNGER, THE*
'84 GHOSTBUSTERS*

RICH EUSTIS
SCREENPLAY
'80 SERIAL*
'82 YOUNG DOCTORS IN LOVE*

ANDY EVANS
SPECIAL EFFECTS
'80 XANADU*
'83 YELLOWBEARD*

BRUCE EVANS
SCREENPLAY
'79 MAN, A WOMAN AND A BANK, A*
'84 STARMAN*

CERI EVANS
SCRIPT SUPERVISOR
'80 AWAKENING, THE
'80 ELEPHANT MAN, THE
'81 FINAL CONFLICT, THE
'82 VENOM
'83 HUNGER, THE
'84 INDIANA JONES AND THE TEMPLE OF DOOM*

CHARLES EVANS
EXECUTIVE PRODUCER
'82 TOOTSIE

DAVID EVANS
MAKEUP
'79 MEATBALLS

JOHN EVANS
SPECIAL EFFECTS
'79 MOONRAKER
SP. EFFECTS SUPERV.
'84 SUPERGIRL
MISCELLANEOUS
'83 OCTOPUSSY

ROBERT EVANS
PRODUCER
'79 PLAYERS
'80 POPEYE
'80 URBAN COWBOY*
'84 COTTON CLUB, THE

ROY EVANS
MISCELLANEOUS
'81 CHARIOTS OF FIRE

SHIRLEY EVANS
UNIT PUBLICIST
'83 SWEET SIXTEEN*

D.S. EVERETT
DIRECTOR
'83 RUNNING BRAVE

GORDON EVERETT
SOUND
'79 BLOODLINE
'80 AMERICAN SUCCESS COMPANY, THE

WILLIAM EVERETT M.D.
MISCELLANEOUS
'81 WHOSE LIFE IS IT ANYWAY?

HELEN EVERINGHAM
PROD. SECRETARY
'79 MY BRILLIANT CAREER

JULIA EVERSHADE
ASSISTANT EDITOR
'80 WITHOUT WARNING

DEBORAH EVERTON
COSTUME SUPERVISOR
'84 TERMINATOR, THE

MICHAEL EVJE
SOUND
'79 PROMISE, THE
'80 RAGING BULL*
'80 CADDYSHACK*
'80 FOOLIN AROUND
'84 ADVENTURES OF BUCKAROO BANZAI ACROSS THE 8TH DIMENSION, THE
'84 CHAMPIONS*
'84 RHINESTONE

SAM EWALT
KEY GRIP
'81 FRIDAY THE 13TH PART TWO

CAROLINA EWERT

COSTUMES
'80 HOW TO BEAT
THE HIGH COST OF LIVING

BUD EWING

SPECIAL EFFECTS
'79 BUCK ROGERS*

MARTY EWING

2ND ASST. DIRECTOR
'81 CONTINENTAL DIVIDE*
'82 SOME KIND OF HERO
'82 FAST TIMES AT RIDGEMONT HIGH*
'83 FLASHDANCE
'83 TERMS OF ENDEARMENT
'84 ALL OF ME
'84 MIKE'S MURDER

CLIVE EXTON

SCREENPLAY
'80 AWAKENING, THE*

JEAN-PIERRE EYCHENNE

MAKEUP
'83 HANNA K*

JOHN EYLER

2ND ASST. DIRECTOR
'80 JAZZ SINGER, THE*
'81 DEADLY BLESSING

PENNY EYLES

SCRIPT SUPERVISOR
'81 TIME BANDITS
'83 BEYOND THE LIMIT
'83 MONTY PYTHON'S
THE MEANING OF LIFE
'84 KILLING FIELDS, THE

DAVID EYRE

SCREENPLAY
'81 CATTLE ANNIE
AND LITTLE BRITCHES*
'81 WOLFEN*

F

PAOLO FABBRI
LOCATIONS
'82 MONSIGNOR
'83 KRULL*
'84 AMADEUS*

CHRIS FABIASCHI
2ND ASST. DIRECTOR
'81 FEAR NO EVIL*

ALLEN FACEMIRE
MISCELLANEOUS
'81 UNDER THE RAINBOW

MICHELL FACTOR
2ND ASST. DIRECTOR
'82 EATING RAOUL*

JACK FAGGARD
SPECIAL EFFECTS
'79 BUCK ROGERS*
'80 SOMEWHERE IN TIME

ZYAD FAHOUM
2ND ASST. DIRECTOR
'83 HANNA K*

JONATHAN FAIRBANKS
MISCELLANEOUS
'82 LOVE CHILD

FERDINAND FAIRFAX
DIRECTOR
'83 NATE & HAYES

JOHN FALABELLA
COSTUMES
'81 NIGHTHAWKS*

LOUIS FALCO
CHOREOGRAPHER
'80 FAME

DALE FALCONER
EXECUTIVE PRODUCER
'82 IF YOU COULD SEE WHAT I HEAR*

MORT FALLICK
EDITOR
'79 LOVE AT FIRST BITE*

RAUL FALOMIR
SPECIAL EFFECTS
'83 YELLOWBEARD*

HAROLD FALTERMEYER
MUSIC
'84 BEVERLY HILLS COP
'84 THIEF OF HEARTS

STEFANIA FALZETTI
ASSISTANT EDITOR
'83 1990: THE BRONX WARRIORS*

JAMAA FANAKA
PRODUCER
'79 PENITENTIARY
'82 PENITENTIARY II
DIRECTOR
'79 PENITENTIARY
'82 PENITENTIARY II
SCREENPLAY
'79 PENITENTIARY
'82 PENITENTIARY II

HAMPTON FANCHER
SCREENPLAY
'82 BLADERUNNER*
EXECUTIVE PRODUCER
'82 BLADERUNNER*

STEPHEN FANFARA
EDITOR
'80 HAPPY BIRTHDAY, GEMINI*
ASSISTANT EDITOR
'82 AMATEUR, THE*

MARGARET FANNIN
PROD. COORDINATOR
'84 THIS IS SPINAL TAP

EDWARD FANTL
ASSISTANT EDITOR
'81 FOUR SEASONS, THE*
'82 I, THE JURY*

FREDERICO FARFAN
SPECIAL EFFECTS
'83 BEYOND THE LIMIT

STEVEN FARGNOLI
PRODUCER
'84 PURPLE RAIN*

JAMES FARGO
DIRECTOR
'82 FORCED VENGEANCE

ANNIE FARGUE
ASSOCIATE PRODUCER
'81 VICTORY

ERNEST FARINO
MISCELLANEOUS
'81 SATURDAY THE 14TH
'81 GALAXY OF TERROR

JAMES FARIS
MISCELLANEOUS
'81 TAPS

BILL FARLEY
HAIR
'80 WILLIE & PHIL*
'80 NIGHT OF THE JUGGLER
'81 EYEWITNESS
'82 I, THE JURY
'82 TEMPEST
'83 HUNGER, THE*

CLAIR FARLEY
EXECUTIVE PRODUCER
'83 JOYSTICKS*

TIM FARLEY
STILLS
'83 TIMERIDER

DIAMOND FARNSWORTH
STUNT COORDINATOR
'84 RHINESTONE

GLENN FARR
EDITOR
'80 DIVINE MADNESS
'80 FATSO
'83 RIGHT STUFF, THE*
'84 RUNAWAY

TREVOR FARRANT
SCREENPLAY
'82 PIRATE MOVIE, THE

JOHN FARRAR
MUSIC
'80 XANADU*

BERNARD FARREL
PRODUCTION MANAGER
'80 FIENDISH PLOT OF DR. FU MANCHU, THE
1ST ASST. DIRECTOR
'84 MISUNDERSTOOD
2ND ASST. DIRECTOR
'80 OUTSIDER, THE*
2ND UNIT DIRECTOR
'79 BLOODLINE
MISCELLANEOUS
'79 BLOODLINE

DANIEL FARRELL
ASSOCIATE PRODUCER
'84 STONE BOY, THE*

DAVID FARRELL
STILLS
'79 SHOUT, THE
'81 EYE OF THE NEEDLE
'82 MISSIONARY, THE
'83 WICKED LADY, THE
'84 SHEENA

NEIL FARRELL
ASSISTANT EDITOR
'83 TRAIL OF THE PINK PANTHER*

PEGGY FARRELL
COSTUMES
'79 NATURAL ENEMIES
'80 GLORIA*
'80 NIGHT OF THE JUGGLER

FLOYD FARRINGTON
PROPS
'81 INCREDIBLE SHRINKING WOMAN, THE*

TRACY FARRINGTON
PROPS
'84 LAST STARFIGHTER, THE
'84 OH GOD, YOU DEVIL

GRAHAM FARROW
ASSISTANT EDITOR
'83 HIGH ROAD TO CHINA

JOHN GLEN FARROW
LOCATIONS
'82 MAKING LOVE*

MIKE FASH
CINEMATOGRAPHER
'83 BETRAYAL
'83 BRITANNIA HOSPITAL

TONY FASO
COSTUMES
'79 OLD BOYFRIENDS*

AMY FATES
ASSISTANT EDITOR
'81 CATTLE ANNIE AND LITTLE BRITCHES*

LAURA FATTORE
LOCATIONS
'83 BLACK STALLION RETURNS, THE*

LISA FAUERSHAM
ASSOCIATE PRODUCER
'84 RUNAWAY

STEPHANO FAVA
MAKEUP
'84 SHEENA

ROBERT FAWCETT
ASSISTANT EDITOR
'80 FOOLIN AROUND*
'83 PRIVATE SCHOOL*

DAVID FAY
KEY GRIP
'81 PURSUIT OF D.B. COOPER, THE*

PAT FAY
LOCATIONS
'84 FIRESTARTER
MISCELLANEOUS
'83 HEART LIKE A WHEEL

SYLVIA FAY
MISCELLANEOUS
'80 RAGING BULL
'81 TATTOO
'82 TOOTSIE
'83 ECHOES
'83 WITHOUT A TRACE

WILLIAM FAY
UNIT MANAGER
'84 NIGHT OF THE COMET
LOCATIONS
'83 DEADLY FORCE

DODI FAYED
EXECUTIVE PRODUCER
'81 CHARIOTS OF FIRE

WILLIAM FAYMAN
EXECUTIVE PRODUCER
'81 STRANGE BEHAVIOR*

FAZ FAZAKAS
MISCELLANEOUS
'81 GREAT MUPPET CAPER, THE

ELEANOR FAZAN
CHOREOGRAPHER
'79 YANKS
'80 HEAVEN'S GATE
'84 LASSITER

TOM FEARS
MISCELLANEOUS
'79 NORTH DALLAS FORTY

DAVID FECHTOR
ASSISTANT EDITOR
'84 WEEKEND PASS

ALEX FEDACK
SCRIPT SUPERVISOR
'79 GREAT BANK HOAX, THE*

ANDREW FEDERMAN
ASSISTANT EDITOR
'82 DEATHTRAP
'82 VERDICT, THE

JAMES FEE
PRODUCTION MANAGER
'84 AMADEUS*

MICHAEL FEFFER
PROPS
'82 VICE SQUAD

RUDI FEHR
EDITOR
'82 ONE FROM THE HEART*

HENRY FEHREN
MISCELLANEOUS
'81 TRUE CONFESSIONS

JULES FEIFFER
SCREENPLAY
'80 POPEYE

FRANCIS FEIGHAN
PUBLICIST
'79 AMERICATHON

GERALD FEIL
CINEMATOGRAPHER
'80 HE KNOWS YOU'RE ALONE
'82 FRIDAY THE 13TH PART THREE IN 3D
'83 LET'S SPEND THE NIGHT TOGETHER*

IRVING FEIN
PRODUCER
'79 JUST YOU AND ME KID*
EXECUTIVE PRODUCER
'84 OH GOD, YOU DEVIL

AL FEINBERG
SPECIAL EFFECTS
'79 MR. MIKE'S MONDO VIDEO*

JANE FEINBERG

<u>CASTING</u>
'79 AMITYVILLE HORROR, THE*
'79 ...AND JUSTICE FOR ALL*
'79 BREAKING AWAY*
'79 BUTCH AND SUNDANCE: THE EARLY YEARS*
'79 DREAMER*
'79 ICE CASTLES*
'79 NORMA RAE*
'79 SUNBURN*
'80 RAISE THE TITANIC*
'80 SMALL CIRCLE OF FRIENDS, A*
'80 FATSO*
'80 HOW TO BEAT THE HIGH COST OF LIVING*
'80 INSIDE MOVES*
'80 LAST MARRIED COUPLE IN AMERICA, THE*
'80 LITTLE DARLINGS*
'80 LONG RIDERS, THE*
'81 RAIDERS OF THE LOST ARK*
'81 RICH AND FAMOUS*
'81 SPHINX*
'81 GHOST STORY*
'81 HISTORY OF THE WORLD PART I*
'81 LEGEND OF THE LONE RANGER, THE*
'81 NIGHT THE LIGHTS WENT OUT IN GEORGIA, THE*
'81 ZORRO, THE GAY BLADE*
'81 DOGS OF WAR, THE*
'81 CARBON COPY*
'82 SIX PACK*
'82 SIX WEEKS*
'82 AMATEUR, THE*
'82 BEST FRIENDS*
'82 BLADERUNNER*
'82 ENDANGERED SPECIES*
'82 E.T. THE EXTRA-TERRESTRIAL*
'82 MEGAFORCE*
'82 MONSIGNOR*
'82 PARTNERS*
'82 POLTERGEIST*
'82 PORKY'S*
'83 RUNNING BRAVE*
'83 LOSIN' IT*
'83 SUPERMAN III*
'83 ALL THE RIGHT MOVES*
'83 BLUE SKIES AGAIN*
'83 BUDDY SYSTEM, THE*
'83 CHRISTMAS STORY, A*
'83 FOOTLOOSE*
'83 KISS ME GOODBYE*
'83 MAN WHO LOVED WOMEN, THE*
'83 NEVER SAY NEVER AGAIN*
'83 PORKY'S II THE NEXT DAY*
'83 TIMERIDER*
'83 TWILIGHT ZONE, THE MOVIE*
'83 TWO OF A KIND*
'83 WITHOUT A TRACE*
'83 SAVANNAH SMILES*
'84 JOHNNY DANGEROUSLY*
'84 RUNAWAY*
'84 SHEENA*
'84 WOMAN IN RED, THE*
'84 INDIANA JONES AND THE TEMPLE OF DOOM*
'84 FINDERS KEEPERS*
'84 CANNONBALL RUN II*

NINA FEINBERG

<u>EDITOR</u>
'80 SIMON
'83 LOVESICK

JULIE FEINER

<u>ASSISTANT EDITOR</u>
'84 DREAMSCAPE

BARRY FEINSTEIN

<u>STILLS</u>
'84 BEAR, THE

JOAN FEINSTEIN

<u>1ST ASST. DIRECTOR</u>
'81 ROLLOVER*
'84 MARVIN AND TIGE
<u>2ND ASST. DIRECTOR</u>
'79 MANHATTAN
'79 VOICES
'80 RAGING BULL*
'81 FOUR SEASONS, THE

BUZZ FEITSHANS

<u>PRODUCER</u>
'79 HARDCORE
'79 1941
'82 CONAN THE BARBARIAN*
'82 FIRST BLOOD
'83 UNCOMMON VALOR*
'84 RED DAWN*

STEVE FEKE

<u>PRODUCER</u>
'79 WHEN A STRANGER CALLS*
<u>SCREENPLAY</u>
'79 WHEN A STRANGER CALLS*

RICHARD FELBER

<u>STILLS</u>
'83 EDDIE AND THE CRUISERS

CRAIG FELBURG

<u>SOUND</u>
'79 MOUNTAIN FAMILY ROBINSON
'80 FOG, THE
'82 BUTTERFLY*
'83 10 TO MIDNIGHT
'84 ANGEL
'84 CRIMES OF PASSION

RICHARD FELD

<u>LOCATIONS</u>
'83 RISKY BUSINESS

STEVEN FELDER

<u>UNIT PROD. MANAGER</u>
'81 FOUR FRIENDS*
<u>1ST ASST. DIRECTOR</u>
'81 WOLFEN*
<u>2ND ASST. DIRECTOR</u>
'79 LAST EMBRACE
'81 TATTOO
'82 HANKY PANKY*

CHARLES FELDMAN

<u>MISCELLANEOUS</u>
'83 TENDER MERCIES

EDWARD FELDMAN

<u>PRODUCER</u>
'80 LAST MARRIED COUPLE IN AMERICA, THE*
'82 SENDER, THE
'84 HOT DOG...THE MOVIE
<u>EXECUTIVE PRODUCER</u>
'82 SIX PACK*

LAURETTA FELDMAN

<u>ASSOCIATE PRODUCER</u>
'80 IN GOD WE TRUST

MARTY FELDMAN

<u>DIRECTOR</u>
'80 IN GOD WE TRUST
<u>SCREENPLAY</u>
'80 IN GOD WE TRUST*

PHIL FELDMAN

<u>PRODUCER</u>
'82 TOY, THE
<u>EXECUTIVE PRODUCER</u>
'83 BLUE THUNDER*

RANDOLPH FELDMAN

<u>SCREENPLAY</u>
'81 HELL NIGHT

ROBERT FELDMAN

<u>KEY GRIP</u>
'80 MANIAC
'81 FEAR NO EVIL
'84 REPO MAN

SHARI FELDMAN

<u>COSTUMES</u>
'82 SENDER, THE*
'84 HOT DOG...THE MOVIE

TOM FELDMAN

<u>KEY GRIP</u>
'84 STRANGERS KISS

TRACY FELDMAN

<u>ASSISTANT EDITOR</u>
'84 BACHELOR PARTY

CLAIRE FELICEN

<u>SCRIPT SUPERVISOR</u>
'84 PURPLE HEARTS

JON FELTHEIMER

<u>EXECUTIVE PRODUCER</u>
'84 BODY ROCK*

DOLLY FENDEL

<u>ASSISTANT EDITOR</u>
'80 STUNT MAN, THE*
'80 BLUE LAGOON

LILLY FENICHEL
COSTUMES
'79 CIRCLE OF IRON

SUZANNE FENN
ASSISTANT EDITOR
'79 WINTER KILLS*

ELSA FENNELL
COSTUMES
'81 SEA WOLVES, THE

LORRAINE FENNELL
PROD. COORDINATOR
'83 ENIGMA
'83 YELLOWBEARD

JOHN FENNER
ART DIRECTOR
'81 FOR YOUR EYES ONLY
'83 OCTOPUSSY
'84 TOP SECRET!*

CAROL FENSTER
LOCATIONS
'80 EYES OF A STRANGER*

KAY FENTON
SCRIPT SUPERVISOR
'79 ALIEN
'80 WATCHER IN THE WOODS, THE
'81 FRENCH LIEUTENANT'S WOMAN, THE
'82 VICTOR/VICTORIA

MIKE FENTON
CASTING
'79 AMITYVILLE HORROR, THE*
'79 ...AND JUSTICE FOR ALL*
'79 BREAKING AWAY*
'79 BUTCH AND SUNDANCE: THE EARLY YEARS*
'79 DREAMER*
'79 ICE CASTLES*
'79 NORMA RAE*
'79 SUNBURN*
'80 RAISE THE TITANIC*
'80 SMALL CIRCLE OF FRIENDS, A*
'80 FATSO*
'80 HOW TO BEAT THE HIGH COST OF LIVING*
'80 INSIDE MOVES*
'80 LAST MARRIED COUPLE IN AMERICA, THE*
'80 LITTLE DARLINGS*
'80 LONG RIDERS, THE*
'81 RAIDERS OF THE LOST ARK*
'81 RICH AND FAMOUS*
'81 SPHINX*
'81 GHOST STORY*
'81 HISTORY OF THE WORLD PART I*
'81 LEGEND OF THE LONE RANGER, THE*
'81 NIGHT THE LIGHTS WENT OUT IN GEORGIA, THE*
'81 ZORRO, THE GAY BLADE*
'81 DOGS OF WAR, THE*
'81 CARBON COPY*
'82 SIX PACK*
'82 SIX WEEKS*
'82 AMATEUR, THE*
'82 BEST FRIENDS*
'82 BLADERUNNER*
'82 ENDANGERED SPECIES*
'82 E.T. THE EXTRA-TERRESTRIAL*
'82 MEGAFORCE*
'82 MONSIGNOR*
'82 PARTNERS*
'82 POLTERGEIST*
'82 PORKY'S*
'83 RUNNING BRAVE*
'83 LOSIN' IT*
'83 SUPERMAN III*
'83 ALL THE RIGHT MOVES*
'83 BLUE SKIES AGAIN*
'83 BUDDY SYSTEM, THE*
'83 CHRISTMAS STORY, A*
'83 FOOTLOOSE*
'83 KISS ME GOODBYE*
'83 MAN WHO LOVED WOMEN, THE*
'83 NEVER SAY NEVER AGAIN*
'83 PORKY'S II THE NEXT DAY*
'83 TIMERIDER*
'83 TWILIGHT ZONE, THE MOVIE*
'83 TWO OF A KIND*
'83 WITHOUT A TRACE*
'83 SAVANNAH SMILES*
'84 JOHNNY DANGEROUSLY*
'84 RUNAWAY*
'84 SHEENA*
'84 WOMAN IN RED, THE*
'84 INDIANA JONES AND THE TEMPLE OF DOOM*
'84 FINDERS KEEPERS*
'84 CANNONBALL RUN II*

ROBERT FENTON
EXECUTIVE PRODUCER
'82 HOME WORK

ROBERT FENTRESS
PRODUCER
'81 DEAD AND BURIED*

JEANNE FERBER
PRODUCTION MANAGER
'82 HOUSE OF THE LONG SHADOWS

ALLYN FERGUSON
MUSIC
'79 AVALANCHE EXPRESS

CAROLYN FERGUSON
HAIR
'79 BUTCH AND SUNDANCE: THE EARLY YEARS
'80 COMPETITION, THE*
'80 HONEYSUCKLE ROSE*

MARY JANE FERGUSON
SCRIPT SUPERVISOR
'82 STAR TREK II THE WRATH OF KHAN

JOAO FERNANDES
CINEMATOGRAPHER
'81 NESTING, THE
'83 BIG SCORE, THE
'84 FRIDAY THE 13TH PART IV THE FINAL CHAPTER

ANTONIO FERNANDEZ
KEY GRIP
'82 CONAN THE BARBARIAN*

BENJAMIN FERNANDEZ
ART DIRECTOR
'82 CONAN THE BARBARIAN*
'84 DUNE

JULIAN FERNANDEZ
KEY GRIP
'82 CONAN THE BARBARIAN*

ROBERTO FERNANDEZ
HAIR
'80 CHANGELING, THE*

WALDO FERNANDEZ
MISCELLANEOUS
'80 CAN'T STOP THE MUSIC

DEAN RAPHAEL FERRANDINI
STUNT COORDINATOR
'82 NATIONAL LAMPOON'S CLASS REUNION
'84 INDIANA JONES AND THE TEMPLE OF DOOM*

ABEL FERRARA
DIRECTOR
'81 MS. 45

ANTHONY FERRARA
MISCELLANEOUS
'84 NATURAL, THE

FRANKIE FERRARA
STUNT COORDINATOR
'82 TEMPEST*

BRAN FERREN
MISCELLANEOUS
'80 ALTERED STATES
'82 DEATHTRAP
'82 TEMPEST
'84 PLACES IN THE HEART

ALEJANDRO FERRER
LOCATIONS
'83 BEYOND THE LIMIT

SEAN FERRER
ASSOCIATE PRODUCER
'84 STRANGERS KISS

ROBERT FERRETTI
EDITOR
'82 ZAPPED!
ASSOCIATE EDITOR
'81 FORCE FIVE

ALICE FERRIER
PROD. COORDINATOR
'79 SILENT PARTNER, THE
'84 MRS. SOFFEL*

RALPH FERRIN
1ST ASST. DIRECTOR
'80 ON THE NICKEL

FRANCO FERRINI
SCREENPLAY
'84 ONCE UPON A TIME IN AMERICA*

CAROLINE FERRIOL
EDITOR
'80 STUNT MAN, THE*

BETH FERRIS
PRODUCER
'79 HEARTLAND*
SCREENPLAY
'79 HEARTLAND

HUGGY-BEAR FERRIS
MISCELLANEOUS
'81 TATTOO

ANTHONY FERRO
CHOREOGRAPHER
'81 SHARKEY'S MACHINE

APRIL FERRY
COSTUME SUPERVISOR
'83 BIG CHILL, THE
'84 MIKE'S MURDER

CHRISTIAN FERRY
ASSOCIATE PRODUCER
'84 SHEENA*

EMILY FERRY
PROPS
'80 RAGING BULL*
'81 ON GOLDEN POND
'84 AGAINST ALL ODDS

STEVE FERRY
PROPS
'83 LONE WOLF MCQUADE

JOHN FETHERS
MISCELLANEOUS
'82 PIRATE MOVIE, THE

PETER FETTERMAN
PRODUCER
'82 YES, GIORGIO

GARY FETTIS
PROPS
'80 MELVIN AND HOWARD*

TERI FETTIS
PROD. COORDINATOR
'82 HAMMETT
'83 RUMBLEFISH
'83 OUTSIDERS, THE

HOWARD FEUER
CASTING
'79 ALL THAT JAZZ*
'79 GOING IN STYLE*
'79 HAIR*
'79 ON THE YARD*
'79 YANKS*
'79 WARRIORS, THE*
'80 ALTERED STATES*
'80 CAN'T STOP THE MUSIC*
'80 DEFIANCE*
'80 FAME*
'80 THOSE LIPS, THOSE EYES*
'81 RICH AND FAMOUS*
'81 SO FINE*
'81 ARTHUR*
'81 EYEWITNESS*
'81 FOUR SEASONS, THE*
'81 TATTOO*
'82 ANNIE*
'82 LITTLE SEX, A*
'83 STAR 80*
'83 AMITYVILLE 3D*
'83 BAD BOYS*
'84 HOTEL NEW HAMPSHIRE, THE*
'84 PLACES IN THE HEART*

RICHARD FEURY
UNIT MANAGER
'82 CREEPSHOW*
1ST ASST. DIRECTOR
'82 FIRST TIME, THE
2ND ASST. DIRECTOR
'81 FRIDAY THE 13TH PART TWO
STILLS
'80 FRIDAY THE 13TH

PAUL FEYDER
1ST ASST. DIRECTOR
'80 FIENDISH PLOT OF DR. FU MANCHU, THE
2ND ASST. DIRECTOR
'81 CONDORMAN*

FELIX FIBICH
MISCELLANEOUS
'82 CHOSEN, THE

FREDDIE FICE
STUNT COORDINATOR
'81 HELL NIGHT

JUNE FICKS
HAIR
'83 ANGEL OF H.E.A.T.

LES FIDDESS
ASSISTANT EDITOR
'82 ROAD WARRIOR, THE*

SHELBY FIDDIS
ASSOCIATE PRODUCER
'81 CHEECH AND CHONG'S NICE DREAMS
'83 CHEECH AND CHONG'S STILL SMOKIN'*
'84 CHEECH AND CHONG'S THE CORSICAN BROTHERS*

HARRIET FIDLOW
ASSISTANT EDITOR
'81 EYEWITNESS

MARIE FIDUCCIA
PROD. COORDINATOR
'81 KNIGHTRIDERS

BRAD FIEDEL
MUSIC
'84 TERMINATOR, THE

ERICK FIEDLER
MAKEUP
'84 MUTANT*

MONT FIEGUTH
PROPS
'79 PICNIC AT HANGING ROCK
SPECIAL EFFECTS
'81 GALLIPOLI*

JEANIE FIELD
1ST ASST. DIRECTOR
'82 HOME WORK

ROBERT FIELD
EXECUTIVE PRODUCER
'83 LIQUID SKY

ROY FIELD
MISCELLANEOUS
'80 SATURN 3
'81 SUPERMAN II
'81 CLASH OF THE TITANS
'81 OUTLAND
'83 SUPERMAN III
'84 SUPERGIRL

TED FIELD
PRODUCER
'84 REVENGE OF THE NERDS*

VIRGINIA FIELD
ART DIRECTOR
'80 FRIDAY THE 13TH
'82 STRANGER IS WATCHING, A
'84 EXTERMINATOR II*
PRODUCTION DESIGNER
'81 FRIDAY THE 13TH PART TWO
'83 SPRING BREAK

JENE FIELDER
MAKEUP
'82 ONE FROM THE HEART*

JERRY FIELDING
MUSIC
'79 BEYOND
THE POSEIDON ADVENTURE

FREDDIE FIELDS
PRODUCER
'80 WHOLLY MOSES!
'81 VICTORY
EXECUTIVE PRODUCER
'79 AMERICAN GIGOLO

JAMES FIELDS
MISCELLANEOUS
'83 EXPOSED

KATHY FIELDS
STILLS
'79 C.H.O.M.P.S.*

R. FIELDS
ASSISTANT EDITOR
'82 POLTERGEIST

RICHARD FIELDS
ASSISTANT EDITOR
'80 SOMEWHERE IN TIME
'81 RAGGEDY MAN*

RICK FIELDS
ASSISTANT EDITOR
'79 WARRIORS, THE*

ROY FIELDS
MISCELLANEOUS
'82 DARK CRYSTAL, THE

ROBERT FIELDSTEEL
MISCELLANEOUS
'84 LOVE STREAMS

STEVE FIERBERG
CINEMATOGRAPHER
'82 FIRST TIME, THE

MARCEL FIEVE
HAIR
'83 LIQUID SKY

RANDY FIFE
STUNT COORDINATOR
'83 TENDER MERCIES
'84 NOT FOR PUBLICATION

CHRISTOPHER FIGG
1ST ASST. DIRECTOR
'84 PASSAGE TO INDIA, A*
2ND ASST. DIRECTOR
'83 DRESSER, THE
'84 ANOTHER COUNTRY*

SUSIE FIGGIS
CASTING
'81 DOGS OF WAR, THE*
'82 GANDHI
'83 HEAT AND DUST
'83 LOCAL HERO*
'84 COMFORT AND JOY
'84 ELECTRIC DREAMS*
'84 KILLING FIELDS, THE*

GABRIEL FIGUEROA
CINEMATOGRAPHER
'84 UNDER THE VOLCANO

LENNY FIKE
MISCELLANEOUS
'84 FINAL TERROR, THE

SONNY FILIPPINI
SCRIPT SUPERVISOR
'80 JAZZ SINGER, THE
'81 GHOST STORY

DENNIS FILL
COSTUME SUPERVISOR
'79 FRISCO KID, THE

JONATHAN FILLEY
2ND ASST. DIRECTOR
'84 BROADWAY DANNY ROSE*
LOCATIONS
'81 NEIGHBORS
'82 TOOTSIE*
'83 EASY MONEY

LENNART FILPPU
UNIT PUBLICIST
'81 FEAR NO EVIL

TOM FINAN
ASSISTANT EDITOR
'80 COAL MINER'S DAUGHTER
'81 HEARTBEEPS
'84 GREMLINS

CHARLES FINANCE
SP. EFFECTS SUPERV.
'84 DUNE
MISCELLANEOUS
'84 CONAN THE DESTROYER

LES FINCHER
LOCATIONS
'84 OVER THE BROOKLYN BRIDGE

NORBERT FINCK
LOCATIONS
'80 FORMULA, THE*

BILLY FINE
PRODUCER
'83 CHAINED HEAT
EXECUTIVE PRODUCER
'82 PENITENTIARY II*
MISCELLANEOUS
'83 SWEET SIXTEEN

BOBBY FINE
MISCELLANEOUS
'83 HOUSE ON SORORITY ROW

DEBORAH FINE
MISCELLANEOUS
'79 MORE AMERICAN GRAFFITTI
'84 INDIANA JONES
AND THE TEMPLE OF DOOM

DAVID FINFER
EDITOR
'79 REAL LIFE
'80 DEFIANCE
'81 MODERN ROMANCE

JOHN FINK II
EDITOR
'80 BORDERLINE

MARGARET FINK
PRODUCER
'79 MY BRILLIANT CAREER

MICHAEL FINK
MISCELLANEOUS
'83 WAR GAMES
'84 ADVENTURES OF BUCKAROO BANZAI ACROSS THE 8TH DIMENSION,THE

STUART FINK
PUBLICIST
'82 CAT PEOPLE
'82 YOUNG DOCTORS IN LOVE
'83 SILKWOOD

WAYNE FINKELMAN
COSTUMES
'82 PARTNERS
'84 PROTOCOL

CLAUDE FINKLE
ASSISTANT EDITOR
'82 ANDROID*

CLAUDIA FINKLE
ASSISTANT EDITOR
'83 GET CRAZY*
'84 BEST DEFENSE*
'84 BEVERLY HILLS COP*

KEN FINKLEMAN
DIRECTOR
'82 AIRPLANE II: THE SEQUEL
SCREENPLAY
'82 AIRPLANE II: THE SEQUEL
'82 GREASE 2

PENNEY FINKLEMAN
CO-PRODUCER
'83 TERMS OF ENDEARMENT*

WAYNE FINKLEMAN
COSTUME SUPERVISOR
'84 GRANDVIEW, U.S.A.

BRUCE FINLAYSON
COSTUMES
'81 STRANGE BEHAVIOR

TOM FINLAYSON
CASTING
'83 NATE & HAYES*

W. FRANKLIN FINLEY
SCREENPLAY
'82 FIRST TIME, THE*

KEVIN FINNEGAN
1ST ASST. DIRECTOR
'82 SENDER, THE*
2ND ASST. DIRECTOR
'83 MAN WHO LOVED WOMEN, THE*

PAT FINNEGAN
PROD. OFFICE COORD.
'81 NESTING, THE

MICHAEL FINNELL
PRODUCER
'79 ROCK 'N ROLL HIGH SCHOOL
'81 HOWLING, THE*
'84 GREMLINS
ASSOCIATE PRODUCER
'83 TWILIGHT ZONE, THE MOVIE*

GERALD PERRY FINNERMAN
CINEMATOGRAPHER
'83 NIGHTMARES*

DANIEL FINNERTY
ASSISTANT EDITOR
'84 STAR TREK III: THE SEARCH FOR SPOCK*

JIM FINNERTY
KEY GRIP
'79 SEDUCTION OF JOE TYNAN, THE*
'79 GOING IN STYLE
'80 JUST TELL ME WHAT YOU WANT
'80 ONE-TRICK PONY
'80 NIGHT OF THE JUGGLER
'81 FAN, THE
'82 AUTHOR, AUTHOR
'82 LITTLE SEX, A
'83 SURVIVORS, THE
'83 WITHOUT A TRACE
'84 LONELY GUY, THE*
'84 MOSCOW ON THE HUDSON*
'84 BEAT STREET

GENE FIORAMONTI
LOCATIONS
'79 BEYOND THE POSEIDON ADVENTURE
'80 PRIVATE BENJAMIN*
'80 WHEN TIME RAN OUT
'84 JOY OF SEX, THE

ROBERT FIORE
CINEMATOGRAPHER
'83 CAN SHE BAKE A CHERRY PIE?

TOM FIORELLO
PRODUCER
'81 FORT APACHE, THE BRONX*

TOM FIORELLO
MISCELLANEOUS
'79 SCAVENGER HUNT

CARLOS FIORES
PRODUCTION MANAGER
'80 OCTAGON, THE*

SAM FIRSTENBERG
DIRECTOR
'83 REVENGE OF THE NINJA
'84 BREAKIN 2 ELECTRIC BOOGALOO

MICHAEL FIRTH
MISCELLANEOUS
'79 MUPPET MOVIE, THE

D.G. FISCHER
SOUND
'80 CADDYSHACK*

INGRID FISCHER
CASTING
'80 TERROR TRAIN*

LEE FISCHER
ART DIRECTOR
'80 HOLLYWOOD KNIGHTS, THE
'82 LOVE AND MONEY
PRODUCTION DESIGNER
'82 VICE SQUAD

RICHARD FISCHOFF
ASSOCIATE PRODUCER
'79 KRAMER VS. KRAMER

JAY FISHBURN
MISCELLANEOUS
'80 LAST FLIGHT OF NOAH'S ARK, THE
'82 BARBAROSA

DAVID FISHER
DIRECTOR
'82 LIAR'S MOON
SCREENPLAY
'82 LIAR'S MOON

F.L. FISHER
PRODUCTION MANAGER
'83 CAN SHE BAKE A CHERRY PIE?

GEORGE FISHER
STUNT COORDINATOR
'81 FOUR SEASONS, THE
'84 OH GOD, YOU DEVIL

GERRY FISHER
CINEMATOGRAPHER
'79 FEDORA
'80 TWINKLE TWINKLE "KILLER" KANE
'81 VICTORY
'81 WOLFEN*
'83 LOVESICK
'83 YELLOWBEARD

JERRY FISHER
MISCELLANEOUS
'84 KARATE KID, THE

JOHN FISHER
PROPS
'79 RUNNING*
'79 BLACK STALLION, THE*
'80 HAPPY BIRTHDAY, GEMINI
'82 IF YOU COULD SEE WHAT I HEAR

LELAND "BUD" FISHER
SPECIAL EFFECTS
'82 AMATEUR, THE*

MARIANNE FISHER
2ND UNIT DIRECTOR
'84 HARDBODIES

MARY ANN FISHER
PRODUCER
'82 ANDROID
EXEC IN CHARGE PROD
'81 GALAXY OF TERROR
ASSOCIATE PRODUCER
'80 BATTLE BEYOND THE STARS

RENE FISHER
HAIR
'83 RICHARD PRYOR: HERE AND NOW

SARAH FISHER
ASSOCIATE PRODUCER
'82 LIAR'S MOON

STEPHEN FISHER
UNIT PROD. MANAGER
'81 MODERN ROMANCE*

TOM FISHER
SPECIAL EFFECTS
'79 FAST COMPANY
'79 QUINTET
'79 PERFECT COUPLE, A
'81 DEATH HUNT*
'81 LAST CHASE, THE
'82 FIRST BLOOD
'84 IMPULSE*
'84 RED DAWN*

JACK FISK
DIRECTOR
'81 RAGGEDY MAN
PRODUCTION DESIGNER
'80 HEARTBEAT

JEFFREY ALAN FISKIN
SCREENPLAY
'81 CUTTER'S WAY
'81 PURSUIT OF D.B. COOPER, THE
'84 CRACKERS

MAUREEN FITZGERALD
2ND ASST. DIRECTOR
'80 KIDNAPPING OF
THE PRESIDENT, THE*

MICHAEL FITZGERALD
EXECUTIVE PRODUCER
'84 UNDER THE VOLCANO

ROGER FITZGERALD
EDITOR
'80 SCHIZOID*

JAMES FITZPATRICK
2ND ASST. DIRECTOR
'83 DEADLY FORCE
LOCATIONS
'84 AMERICAN DREAMER

SARAH FITZSIMMONS
PROD. OFFICE COORD.
'84 PARIS, TEXAS*

JACK FITZSTEPHENS
EDITOR
'80 JUST TELL ME WHAT YOU WANT

JOHN FITZSTEPHENS
EDITOR
'81 PRINCE OF THE CITY
'82 DEATHTRAP
'82 FIGHTING BACK*

GIANNI FIUMI
PROPS
'84 ONCE UPON A TIME IN AMERICA

DOROTHY FIX
HAIR
'79 PRISONER OF ZENDA, THE*

KEN FIX
LOCATIONS
'83 LOSIN' IT

MARCOS FLAKSMAN
ART DIRECTOR
'84 BLAME IT ON RIO

NICKY FLAN
ASSOCIATE PRODUCER
'83 SCREWBALLS*

CANDY FLANAGAN
SPECIAL EFFECTS
'80 UP THE ACADEMY
'81 FOUR SEASONS, THE*
'81 HARDLY WORKING
'81 VICTORY
'83 GORKY PARK*

GARY FLANAGAN
LOCATIONS
'79 LOST AND FOUND*

WILLARD FLANAGIN
SPECIAL EFFECTS
'80 TWINKLE TWINKLE
"KILLER" KANE

RICHARD FLANZER
MISCELLANEOUS
'80 IDOLMAKER, THE

ERICA FLAUM
EDITOR
'84 FINAL TERROR, THE*
ASSISTANT EDITOR
'80 BIG RED ONE, THE
'82 BEST LITTLE WHOREHOUSE
IN TEXAS, THE*
'83 MAN WOMAN AND CHILD

SETH FLAUM
ASSISTANT EDITOR
'82 PERSONAL BEST*
'83 DEAL OF THE CENTURY*
'84 KARATE KID, THE*

JERRY FLECK
2ND ASST. DIRECTOR
'82 BOOGENS, THE

JOHN FLECKENSTEIN
MISCELLANEOUS
'82 DEATH VALLEY

LINDA FLEISCHER
MISCELLANEOUS
'84 ADVENTURES OF BUCKAROO BANZAI
ACROSS THE 8TH DIMENSION, THE

MARK FLEISCHER
ASSOCIATE PRODUCER
'83 TOUGH ENOUGH

RICHARD FLEISCHER
DIRECTOR
'80 JAZZ SINGER, THE
'83 AMITYVILLE 3D
'83 TOUGH ENOUGH
'84 CONAN THE DESTROYER

DARCY FLEMING
MISCELLANEOUS
'80 XANADU

JOHN FLEMING
KEY GRIP
'84 OXFORD BLUES

MIKE FLEMING
MISCELLANEOUS
'80 XANADU

STU FLEMING
ASSOCIATE PRODUCER
'79 VILLAIN, THE
UNIT PROD. MANAGER
'79 VILLAIN, THE
'80 LITTLE DARLINGS
'80 WHOLLY MOSES!
'83 BREATHLESS

CHARLOTTE FLEMMING
COSTUMES
'79 FEDORA

COLIN FLETCHER
2ND ASST. DIRECTOR
'82 STARSTRUCK*

RED FLETCHER
PROPS
'79 ON THE YARD

ROBERT FLETCHER
COSTUMES
'79 STAR TREK-THE MOTION PICTURE
'81 CAVEMAN
'82 STAR TREK II
THE WRATH OF KHAN
'84 LAST STARFIGHTER, THE
'84 STAR TREK III:
THE SEARCH FOR SPOCK

ROBERT FLETCHER
STILLS
'80 HIDE IN PLAIN SIGHT*
'81 NEIGHBORS*
'81 TATTOO
'84 BEAT STREET*

ANDRE FLEUREN
ASSISTANT EDITOR
'79 PICNIC AT HANGING ROCK

ROGER FLEYTOUX
PRODUCTION MANAGER
'84 UNTIL SEPTEMBER

SCOTT FLOREN
KEY GRIP
'82 SENDER, THE

SYLVIA FLORES
MAKEUP
'83 FRIGHTMARE
HAIR
'83 FRIGHTMARE

ROBERT FLORIO
EDITOR
'84 BEAR, THE

RICHARD FLOWER
2ND ASST. DIRECTOR
'84 MRS. SOFFEL*

VERKINA FLOWER
COSTUMES
'84 SILENT NIGHT, DEADLY NIGHT

A.D. FLOWERS
SPECIAL EFFECTS
'79 APOCALYPSE NOW*
'79 1941

PENNY FLOWERS
2ND ASST. DIRECTOR
'79 MUPPET MOVIE, THE

ALAN FLYNG
COSTUMES
'82 HOUSE OF THE LONG SHADOWS*

JOHN FLYNN
DIRECTOR
'80 DEFIANCE

VERONICA FLYNN
SCRIPT SUPERVISOR
'81 SATURDAY THE 14TH
'82 PARASITE
'83 VALLEY GIRL
'84 WEEKEND PASS

ALLAN FOENANDER
CASTING
'80 FFOLKES
'80 LADY VANISHES, THE*

ANDREW FOGELSON
EXECUTIVE PRODUCER
'83 BLUE THUNDER*
'83 WRONG IS RIGHT

LYLA FOGGIA
PUBLICIST
'83 CROSS CREEK
'83 MR. MOM
'83 WAR GAMES
UNIT PUBLICIST
'81 SOUTHERN COMFORT
'81 ENTITY, THE
'82 E.T. THE EXTRA-TERRESTRIAL
'84 SPLASH

MICHELINE FOISY
MAKEUP
'84 HOTEL NEW HAMPSHIRE, THE*

MIKHAIL FOKINE
CHOREOGRAPHER
'80 NIJINSKY*

SOL FOL
1ST ASST. DIRECTOR
'79 NATURAL ENEMIES

BRIAN FOLEY
CHOREOGRAPHER
'79 ICE CASTLES
MISCELLANEOUS
'81 FOR YOUR EYES ONLY

JAMES FOLEY
DIRECTOR
'84 RECKLESS

LT. COLONEL DENNIS FOLEY
MISCELLANEOUS
'80 PRIVATE BENJAMIN
'82 SOME KIND OF HERO

TRISH FOLEY
PROD. COORDINATOR
'83 MAN FROM SNOWY RIVER, THE
PROD. SECRETARY
'81 ROAD GAMES*

TOM FOLINO
MISCELLANEOUS
'80 LAST MARRIED COUPLE
IN AMERICA, THE
'80 OH GOD! BOOK II

LINDA FOLK
ASSISTANT EDITOR
'83 BALLAD OF
GREGORIO CORTEZ, THE

ROBERT FOLK
MUSIC
'84 POLICE ACADEMY
'84 PURPLE HEARTS

EDWINA FOLLOWS
1ST ASST. DIRECTOR
'83 STRANGE BREW*

GEORGE FOLSEY JR.
PRODUCER
'81 AMERICAN WEREWOLF
IN LONDON, AN
EXECUTIVE PRODUCER
'83 TRADING PLACES
ASSOCIATE PRODUCER
'80 BLUES BROTHERS*
'83 TWILIGHT ZONE, THE MOVIE*
EDITOR
'79 GREAT SANTINI, THE*
'80 BLUES BROTHERS
2ND UNIT DIRECTOR
'83 TRADING PLACES

PIERO FONDI
SOUND
'83 PIRANHA II: THE SPAWNING

LEO FONG
SCREENPLAY
'83 BLIND RAGE*

KATHLEEN FONMARTY
SCRIPT SUPERVISOR
'84 CHEECH AND CHONG'S THE
CORSICAN BROTHERS

GREGG FONSECA
PRODUCTION DESIGNER
'84 NIGHTMARE ON ELM STREET, A
'84 HARDBODIES

CAROLE FONTANA
PROD. COORDINATOR
'83 REUBEN, REUBEN

LINDSAY FONTANA
1ST ASST. DIRECTOR
'79 MR. MIKE'S MONDO VIDEO*

JACQUES FONTERAY
COSTUMES
'79 MOONRAKER

LLOYD FONVIELLE

SCREENPLAY
'83 LORDS OF DISCIPLINE, THE*

GEOFFREY FOOT

EDITOR
'79 SUNBURN
'80 WATCHER IN THE WOODS, THE

HORTON FOOTE

SCREENPLAY
'83 TENDER MERCIES
CO-PRODUCER
'83 TENDER MERCIES*

JIM FOOTE

LOCATIONS
'80 GLORIA*

BRYAN FORBES

DIRECTOR
'81 SUNDAY LOVERS*
SCREENPLAY
'80 HOPSCOTCH*

DAVID FORBES

EXECUTIVE PRODUCER
'83 BIG SCORE, THE*

DOUGLAS FORBES

LOCATIONS
'84 CHOOSE ME*

BERT FORD

PUBLICIST
'79 OVER THE EDGE
'80 DEFIANCE*

C. ROMANIA FORD

MAKEUP
'82 TOOTSIE*
'83 SURVIVORS, THE
'84 BEAT STREET

GRAHAM FORD

PRODUCTION MANAGER
'81 TIME BANDITS
'82 MISSIONARY, THE
'83 BEYOND THE LIMIT*
LOCATIONS
'80 ELEPHANT MAN, THE
'82 GANDHI*

JO FORD

ART DIRECTOR
'83 NATE & HAYES*

ROCHELLE FORD

HAIR
'83 MAN FROM SNOWY RIVER, THE

RUBY FORD

HAIR
'79 WHEN A STRANGER CALLS*
'80 OH GOD! BOOK II*
'82 MY FAVORITE YEAR*

JET FORE

UNIT PUBLICIST
'83 MAN WOMAN AND CHILD

RONN FORELLA

CHOREOGRAPHER
'81 STRIPES*

CARL FOREMAN

SCREENPLAY
'80 WHEN TIME RAN OUT*

ELAINE FOREMAN

ASSISTANT EDITOR
'80 KIDNAPPING OF
THE PRESIDENT, THE
'83 DEAD ZONE, THE*
'83 VIDEODROME*

JOHN FOREMAN

PRODUCER
'79 GREAT TRAIN ROBBERY, THE
'84 ICE PIRATES, THE

JON FOREMAN

PUBLICIST
'80 FADE TO BLACK

RICHARD FOREMAN

STILLS
'84 BREAKIN 2 ELECTRIC BOOGALOO*

RONALD KENT FOREMAN

ART DIRECTOR
'81 HIGH RISK
'82 ROCKY III
'84 ICE PIRATES, THE*

CARMINE FORESTA

LOCATIONS
'80 CRUISING

BETTINA FORG

2ND ASST. DIRECTOR
'82 NIGHT CROSSING*

MILOS FORMAN

DIRECTOR
'79 HAIR
'81 RAGTIME
'84 AMADEUS

MILTON FORMAN

MISCELLANEOUS
'84 COTTON CLUB, THE

MILTON FORMAN

MISCELLANEOUS
'79 HURRICANE

NANCY FORNER

ASSISTANT EDITOR
'81 DEAD AND BURIED
'83 TO BE OR NOT TO BE
'84 REVENGE OF THE NERDS

ARTHUR FORNEY

ASSISTANT EDITOR
'80 ALTERED STATES*
'82 FAST TIMES AT RIDGEMONT HIGH*
'84 RECKLESS

BOB FORREST

SCRIPT SUPERVISOR
'79 PRISONER OF ZENDA, THE
'80 COAL MINER'S DAUGHTER
'80 WHERE THE BUFFALO ROAM
'81 RAGGEDY MAN

CHRISTINE FORREST

1ST ASST. DIRECTOR
'79 DAWN OF THE DEAD

CLIFF FORREST

KEY GRIP
'79 DAWN OF THE DEAD*

DAVID CRAIG FORREST

MAKEUP
'79 GREAT BANK HOAX, THE
'79 SCALPEL
'82 COME BACK TO THE 5 & 10,
JIMMY DEAN, JIMMY DEAN
'84 OVER THE BROOKLYN BRIDGE
HAIR
'79 SCALPEL
'83 JAWS 3-D

JAMES FORREST

CINEMATOGRAPHER
'81 BODY AND SOUL

TERRY FORRESTAL

STUNT COORDINATOR
'84 KILLING FIELDS, THE

MARK FORSTATER

EXECUTIVE PRODUCER
'84 NOT FOR PUBLICATION

PAT FORSTER

COSTUMES
'79 TIM

BILL FORSYTH
DIRECTOR
'83 LOCAL HERO
'84 COMFORT AND JOY
SCREENPLAY
'83 LOCAL HERO
'84 COMFORT AND JOY

GAIL JOYCE FORTMULLER
2ND ASST. DIRECTOR
'84 PHILADELPHIA EXPERIMENT, THE

BRUCE FORTUNE
ASSISTANT EDITOR
'84 STAR TREK III: THE SEARCH FOR SPOCK*

BOB FOSSE
DIRECTOR
'79 ALL THAT JAZZ
'83 STAR 80
SCREENPLAY
'79 ALL THAT JAZZ*
'83 STAR 80
CHOREOGRAPHER
'79 ALL THAT JAZZ

WILLIAM FOSSER
ART DIRECTOR
'81 ON THE RIGHT TRACK

BART FOSTER
PRODUCTION MANAGER
'84 SILENT NIGHT, DEADLY NIGHT

DAVID FOSTER
PRODUCER
'79 LEGACY, THE
'81 CAVEMAN*
'82 THING, THE*
'84 MASS APPEAL*
DIRECTOR
'82 SECOND THOUGHTS

JACK FOSTER
EDITOR
'81 NESTING, THE

JAN FOSTER
SCRIPT SUPERVISOR
'83 ANGELO, MY LOVE

JOHN FOSTER
PRODUCTION MANAGER
'82 FIRST TIME, THE
STILLS
'81 FRIDAY THE 13TH PART TWO

KAREN FOSTER
ASSISTANT EDITOR
'81 GALLIPOLI*

NORMAN FOSTER
PRODUCTION MANAGER
'81 SEA WOLVES, THE*

PENELOPE FOSTER
1ST ASST. DIRECTOR
'81 ON THE RIGHT TRACK

STEVE FOSTER
CASTING
'83 FRIGHTMARE*

STEVE FOSTER
MISCELLANEOUS
'80 POPEYE

DIANE FOTI
LOCATIONS
'83 STRANGE INVADERS*

MICHAEL FOTTRELL
PRODUCTION MANAGER
'81 HELL NIGHT
'82 SEDUCTION, THE
LOCATIONS
'80 FADE TO BLACK
'81 TAKE THIS JOB AND SHOVE IT
'83 SCARFACE*

ED FOUNTAIN
MISCELLANEOUS
'82 CREEPSHOW

LILI FOURNIER
SCRIPT SUPERVISOR
'82 IF YOU COULD SEE WHAT I HEAR

VINCENT FOURNIER
PROPS
'81 MY DINNER WITH ANDRE

ROGER FOUTS PHD
MISCELLANEOUS
'84 GREYSTOKE: THE LEGEND OF TARZAN, LORD OF THE APES

CHIP FOWLER
PROD. OFFICE COORD.
'79 ROCKY II
'79 BUTCH AND SUNDANCE: THE EARLY YEARS
'81 ESCAPE FROM NEW YORK
'82 VICE SQUAD
'83 BLUE THUNDER
PROD. COORDINATOR
'80 BRUBAKER
'81 CAVEMAN*
'82 HALLOWEEN III: SEASON OF THE WITCH
'83 DEADLY FORCE*
'83 MAN WHO LOVED WOMEN, THE

GRAHAM FOWLER
1ST ASST. DIRECTOR
'81 PRIEST OF LOVE

GENE FOWLER JR.
EDITOR
'81 CAVEMAN

KIM FOWLER
ASSISTANT EDITOR
'81 CAVEMAN*

MARJORIE FOWLER
EDITOR
'80 IT'S MY TURN*

MAURICE FOWLER
ART DIRECTOR
'80 HEAVEN'S GATE*
'81 SUPERMAN II
'83 EDUCATING RITA
'83 HEAT AND DUST*

RICHARD FOWLER
2ND ASST. DIRECTOR
'82 IF YOU COULD SEE WHAT I HEAR

EDDIE FOWLIE
PROPS
'84 PASSAGE TO INDIA, A*
LOCATIONS
'84 PASSAGE TO INDIA, A

HENRY FOWNES
EXECUTIVE PRODUCER
'84 MUTANT*

BERYL FOX
PRODUCER
'82 BY DESIGN*

CELESTIA FOX
CASTING
'81 EYE OF THE NEEDLE
'82 PINK FLOYD: THE WALL*
'83 NATE & HAYES*
'84 ANOTHER COUNTRY
'84 OXFORD BLUES

CHARLES FOX
MUSIC
'80 LAST MARRIED COUPLE IN AMERICA, THE
'80 LITTLE DARLINGS
'80 NINE TO FIVE
'80 OH GOD! BOOK II
'80 WHY WOULD I LIE?
'82 SIX PACK
'82 LOVE CHILD
'82 ZAPPED!
'83 STRANGE BREW
'83 TRENCHCOAT

CHRISTINE FOX
2ND ASST. DIRECTOR
'79 EUROPEANS, THE

DOUG FOX
PROPS
'84 REPO MAN

FRED FOX
SCREENPLAY
'80 OH GOD! BOOK II*

FREDDIE FOX
MISCELLANEOUS
'82 EVIL UNDER THE SUN

J. RAE FOX
ART DIRECTOR
'84 REPO MAN*

JIM FOX
PROPS
'84 FLASHPOINT

JOHN FOX
2ND UNIT DIRECTOR
'81 BLOW OUT

ROBERT FOX
EXECUTIVE PRODUCER
'84 ANOTHER COUNTRY*

STEVE FOX
ASSISTANT EDITOR
'80 MY BODYGUARD*

WILLIAM FRAKER
DIRECTOR
'81 LEGEND OF THE LONE RANGER, THE
CINEMATOGRAPHER
'79 1941
'79 OLD BOYFRIENDS
'80 DIVINE MADNESS
'80 HOLLYWOOD KNIGHTS, THE
'81 SHARKEY'S MACHINE
'82 BEST LITTLE WHOREHOUSE IN TEXAS, THE
'83 WAR GAMES
'84 IRRECONCILABLE DIFFERENCES
'84 PROTOCOL
MISCELLANEOUS
'80 CLOSE ENCOUNTERS OF THE THIRD KIND SPECIAL EDITION

JOSEPH FRALEY
SCREENPLAY
'82 SILENT RAGE

HARRY FRAMPTON
MAKEUP
'79 PRISONER OF ZENDA, THE*
'82 VICTOR/VICTORIA*
'83 CURSE OF THE PINK PANTHER*
'83 TRAIL OF THE PINK PANTHER*

PETER FRAMPTON
MAKEUP
'81 RAGTIME*
'82 PINK FLOYD: THE WALL*
'82 VICTOR/VICTORIA*
'83 CURSE OF THE PINK PANTHER*
'83 TRAIL OF THE PINK PANTHER*
'84 OXFORD BLUES

PAOLO FRANCESCHI
HAIR
'81 SO FINE*

RENATA FRANCHESCHI
SCRIPT SUPERVISOR
'83 PIRANHA II: THE SPAWNING

CAPTAIN JEAN FRANCHI
MISCELLANEOUS
'79 CONCORDE-AIRPORT '79, THE

EDDIE FRANCIS
PROPS
'84 ELECTRIC DREAMS
'84 SUPERGIRL

FREDDIE FRANCIS
CINEMATOGRAPHER
'80 ELEPHANT MAN, THE
'81 FRENCH LIEUTENANT'S WOMAN, THE
'84 DUNE

KIRK FRANCIS
SOUND
'83 LOSIN' IT
'83 UNDER FIRE
'84 GRANDVIEW, U.S.A.
'84 DREAMSCAPE*

LINDA FRANCIS
CASTING
'80 FATSO*
'81 DEAD AND BURIED
'83 SPRING BREAK*
'83 STRANGE INVADERS*
'84 ANGEL*
'84 CHILDREN OF THE CORN
'84 PHILADELPHIA EXPERIMENT, THE*

MURRAY FRANCIS
UNIT MANAGER
'83 YEAR OF LIVING DANGEROUSLY, THE

PAMELA MANN FRANCIS
SCRIPT SUPERVISOR
'83 RETURN OF THE JEDI
'83 NEVER SAY NEVER AGAIN
'84 INDIANA JONES AND THE TEMPLE OF DOOM*

REA FRANCIS
PUBLICIST
'83 NATE & HAYES

SHARON FRANCIS
MAKEUP
'83 ANGEL OF H.E.A.T.
'84 MAKING THE GRADE
'84 REPO MAN
HAIR
'84 MAKING THE GRADE
'84 REPO MAN

RICKY FRANCISCO
STILLS
'84 PURPLE HEARTS

DAVID FRANCO
MUSIC SUPERVISOR
'83 OF UNKNOWN ORIGIN

JOHN FRANCO
SCRIPT SUPERVISOR
'79 ON THE YARD
'79 PROPHECY
'80 WHY WOULD I LIE?
'81 VICTORY
'83 STAR CHAMBER
'83 WRONG IS RIGHT
'84 HARD TO HOLD
'84 UNDER THE VOLCANO

LARRY FRANCO
PRODUCER
'81 ESCAPE FROM NEW YORK*
'84 STARMAN
ASSOCIATE PRODUCER
'82 THING, THE
CO-PRODUCER
'83 CHRISTINE
1ST ASST. DIRECTOR
'79 ROSE, THE
'80 FOG, THE
'81 CUTTER'S WAY
'81 ESCAPE FROM NEW YORK
'82 THING, THE
'83 CHRISTINE
'84 STARMAN
2ND ASST. DIRECTOR
'79 APOCALYPSE NOW

ROBERT FRANCO
PROPS
'84 C.H.U.D.

HARRIET FRANK JR.
SCREENPLAY
'79 NORMA RAE*

KIMBERLY FRANK
MISCELLANEOUS
'84 TANK

MELVIN FRANK
PRODUCER
'79 LOST AND FOUND
DIRECTOR
'79 LOST AND FOUND
SCREENPLAY
'79 LOST AND FOUND*

PETER FRANK
EDITOR
'82 VERDICT, THE
'83 DANIEL

DAVID FRANKE
ASSOCIATE PRODUCER
'81 MY DINNER WITH ANDRE*

JERRY FRANKEL
EXECUTIVE PRODUCER
'79 FAST BREAK
'80 CHEAPER TO KEEP HER

FRANNI FRANKEN
PROD. COORDINATOR
'79 MR. MIKE'S MONDO VIDEO

JOHN FRANKENHEIMER
DIRECTOR
'79 PROPHECY
'82 CHALLENGE, THE

BRIAN FRANKISH
PRODUCER
'82 VICE SQUAD
ASSOCIATE PRODUCER
'83 STRANGE BREW
1ST ASST. DIRECTOR
'81 DEAD AND BURIED
'83 SPRING BREAK
'83 STRANGE BREW*
'84 LAST STARFIGHTER, THE

TERRIE FRANKLE
ASSISTANT EDITOR
'82 SWORD AND THE SORCERER, THE

DANIEL FRANKLIN
UNIT PROD. MANAGER
'84 SIXTEEN CANDLES

MARLAYNA FRANKLIN
ASSISTANT EDITOR
'79 STARTING OVER*

RICHARD FRANKLIN
PRODUCER
'81 ROAD GAMES
DIRECTOR
'81 ROAD GAMES
'83 PSYCHO II
'84 CLOAK AND DAGGER
CO-PRODUCER
'80 BLUE LAGOON

WARREN FRANKLIN
MISCELLANEOUS
'84 INDIANA JONES AND THE TEMPLE OF DOOM

MIKE FRANKOVICH JR.
PRODUCTION MANAGER
'84 PURPLE RAIN

JERRY FRANKS
CASTING
'82 SWORD AND THE SORCERER, THE*

MICHAEL FRANZESE
EXECUTIVE PRODUCER
'83 MAUSOLEUM*

DENNIS FRASER
KEY GRIP
'81 AMERICAN WEREWOLF IN LONDON, AN

GEORGE MACDONALD FRASER
SCREENPLAY
'83 OCTOPUSSY*

IAN FRASER
MUSIC
'80 HOPSCOTCH
'81 FIRST MONDAY IN OCTOBER
'81 ZORRO, THE GAY BLADE

JILL FRASER
MUSIC
'82 PERSONAL BEST*

MARTY FRASER
LOCATIONS
'80 BLUES BROTHERS*

FRANCO FRATICELLI
EDITOR
'81 COMIN' AT YA!

KATTERLI FRAUENFELDER
2ND ASST. DIRECTOR
'81 CONTINENTAL DIVIDE*
'83 BAD BOYS*
'83 CLASS
'84 ADVENTURES OF BUCKAROO BANZAI ACROSS THE 8TH DIMENSION,THE
'84 GHOSTBUSTERS*
LOCATIONS
'81 ON THE RIGHT TRACK

BONY FRAULO
PROPS
'82 MONSIGNOR

JAMES FRAWLEY
DIRECTOR
'79 MUPPET MOVIE, THE

LOGAN FRAZEE
SPECIAL EFFECTS
'84 TANK*

TERRY FRAZEE
SPECIAL EFFECTS
'81 LEGEND OF THE LONE RANGER, THE
'82 BLADERUNNER

ROBERT FRAZEN
ASSISTANT EDITOR
'83 CROSS CREEK*
'84 RIVER, THE*

STANLEY FRAZEN
MISCELLANEOUS
'82 YOUNG DOCTORS IN LOVE

JIMMY FRAZIER
EDITOR
'82 MONTY PYTHON LIVE AT THE HOLLYWOOD BOWL*

JOHN FRAZIER
SPECIAL EFFECTS
'79 WHEN YOU COMIN' BACK, RED RYDER?
'80 ROADIE*
'80 AIRPLANE
SP. EFFECTS SUPERV.
'83 DOCTOR DETROIT
'84 FLASHPOINT

BILL FREDA
EDITOR
'80 FRIDAY THE 13TH

DAVE FREDERICK
ASSISTANT EDITOR
'81 NESTING, THE

LYNNE FREDERICK
MISCELLANEOUS
'80 FIENDISH PLOT OF DR. FU MANCHU, THE

WILLIAM FREDERICK
MISCELLANEOUS
'82 MEGAFORCE

ADAM FREDERICKS
ASSISTANT EDITOR
'84 OVER THE BROOKLYN BRIDGE*
'84 FRIDAY THE 13TH PART IV THE FINAL CHAPTER*

JIM FREDERICKS
PROPS
'81 THEY ALL LAUGHED*

GRAY FREDERICKSON
PRODUCER
'82 ONE FROM THE HEART*
'83 OUTSIDERS, THE*
CO-PRODUCER
'79 APOCALYPSE NOW*

MARC FREDERIX
ART DIRECTOR
'81 CONDORMAN

GRAHAM FREEBORN
MAKEUP
'79 SAINT JACK
'79 GAME OF DEATH
'80 EMPIRE STRIKES BACK, THE
'81 DRAGONSLAYER*
'83 KEEP, THE*
'84 LASSITER*

RAY FREEBORN
LOCATIONS
'81 AMERICAN WEREWOLF IN LONDON, AN
'83 HIGH ROAD TO CHINA
'84 LASSITER

STUART FREEBORN
MAKEUP
'81 SUPERMAN II
'81 GREAT MUPPET CAPER, THE
'83 SUPERMAN III*
'84 TOP SECRET!
MISCELLANEOUS
'80 EMPIRE STRIKES BACK, THE
'83 RETURN OF THE JEDI

DONNA FREED
PROD. COORDINATOR
'80 HOW TO BEAT THE HIGH COST OF LIVING

HERB FREED
PRODUCER
'81 GRADUATION DAY*
DIRECTOR
'81 GRADUATION DAY
SCREENPLAY
'81 GRADUATION DAY*

REUBEN FREED
ART DIRECTOR
'80 CHANGELING, THE
'80 PROM NIGHT
'80 TRIBUTE*
'82 BY DESIGN
PRODUCTION DESIGNER
'82 PORKY'S
'83 CHRISTMAS STORY, A
MISCELLANEOUS
'83 PORKY'S II THE NEXT DAY

JAMES FREEDMAN
MISCELLANEOUS
'83 TOUGH ENOUGH

JEFF FREEDMAN
UNIT PUBLICIST
'82 PERSONAL BEST

JERROLD FREEDMAN
DIRECTOR
'80 BORDERLINE
SCREENPLAY
'80 BORDERLINE*

JOEL FREEDMAN
EXECUTIVE PRODUCER
'83 BRAINSTORM

SARA FREELAND
ASSISTANT EDITOR
'80 HERO AT LARGE*

ANTHONY FREEMAN
MISCELLANEOUS
'81 EXCALIBUR

DAVID FREEMAN
SCREENPLAY
'82 BORDER, THE*

GEOFF FREEMAN
PUBLICIST
'81 FINAL CONFLICT, THE*
'82 VENOM
'82 VICTOR/VICTORIA
'83 CURSE OF THE PINK PANTHER*
'83 PIRATES OF PENZANCE, THE
'84 CHAMPIONS*

JACK FREEMAN
MAKEUP
'80 COMPETITION, THE*

JEANETTE FREEMAN
HAIR
'80 AWAKENING, THE*
'80 FIENDISH PLOT OF DR. FU MANCHU, THE*
'82 SENDER, THE
'84 SHEENA

JEFF FREEMAN
ASSISTANT EDITOR
'79 LOVE AT FIRST BITE*
'81 EYE FOR AN EYE, AN
'81 INCREDIBLE SHRINKING WOMAN, THE*
'82 NATIONAL LAMPOON'S CLASS REUNION*
'83 TERMS OF ENDEARMENT*
'83 SILKWOOD*

JILL FREEMAN
SCRIPT SUPERVISOR
'81 EARTHLING, THE

JOEL FREEMAN
PRODUCER
'79 LOVE AT FIRST BITE
'80 OCTAGON, THE

JOHN ALFRED FREEMAN
MAKEUP
'80 TOUCHED BY LOVE*

LOIS FREEMAN
ASSISTANT EDITOR
'79 HAIR

LYN FREEMAN
SCREENPLAY
'80 WITHOUT WARNING*
CO-PRODUCER
'80 WITHOUT WARNING*

ROBERT FREEMAN
DIRECTOR
'83 GOIN' ALL THE WAY
EDITOR
'83 GOIN' ALL THE WAY*

RUDY FREEMAN
ASSISTANT EDITOR
'80 CHEAPER TO KEEP HER*

TOM FREEMAN
PROPS
'83 HEAT AND DUST

DAWN FREER
SCRIPT SUPERVISOR
'83 REUBEN, REUBEN
'84 C.H.U.D.

JIM FREIBURGER
ART DIRECTOR
'83 10 TO MIDNIGHT

ANITA FREIDMAN
MAKEUP
'82 HOME WORK

CURTIS FREILICH
ASSISTANT EDITOR
'84 MARVIN AND TIGE*

JAMES FREITAG
2ND ASST. DIRECTOR
'80 ON THE NICKEL
'81 STRIPES*
'81 TAKE THIS JOB AND SHOVE IT
'82 SPLIT IMAGE
'83 DEAL OF THE CENTURY
'83 OUTSIDERS, THE
'84 REVENGE OF THE NERDS
'84 WHERE THE BOYS ARE*

MICHAEL FREMER
MISCELLANEOUS
'82 TRON

DON FRENCH
1ST ASST. DIRECTOR
'80 FORMULA, THE*
'82 FIREFOX*
'84 NEVERENDING STORY, THE*
'84 LITTLE DRUMMER GIRL, THE
2ND ASST. DIRECTOR
'79 AVALANCHE EXPRESS
'79 FEDORA
'82 NIGHT CROSSING*

ED FRENCH
MISCELLANEOUS
'83 SMITHEREENS
'84 EXTERMINATOR II
'84 ALPHABET CITY

CANTOR URI FRENKEL
MISCELLANEOUS
'80 JAZZ SINGER, THE

JOHN FRETZ
<u>1ST ASST. DIRECTOR</u>
'80 HOG WILD
'81 GAS
'83 OF UNKNOWN ORIGIN

BARBARA FREUDE
<u>PROPS</u>
'79 FEDORA*

HARRY FREUDE
<u>PROPS</u>
'79 FEDORA*

BUD FRIEDGEN JR.
<u>EDITOR</u>
'79 FISH THAT SAVED PITTSBURGH, THE*

TONY FRIEDKIN
<u>STILLS</u>
'83 METALSTORM: THE DESTRUCTION OF JARED-SYN
'83 MY TUTOR
'84 WEEKEND PASS

WILLIAM FRIEDKIN
<u>DIRECTOR</u>
'80 CRUISING
'83 DEAL OF THE CENTURY
<u>SCREENPLAY</u>
'80 CRUISING

ALAN FRIEDMAN
<u>MAKEUP</u>
'79 FISH THAT SAVED PITTSBURGH, THE*
'83 STROKER ACE*
<u>MISCELLANEOUS</u>
'80 TERROR TRAIN

BRUCE JAY FRIEDMAN
<u>SCREENPLAY</u>
'80 STIR CRAZY
'83 DOCTOR DETROIT*
'84 SPLASH*

DAVE FRIEDMAN
<u>STILLS</u>
'80 HUNTER, THE
'80 TOM HORN
'82 LOOKIN' TO GET OUT
'82 THAT CHAMPIONSHIP SEASON*
'84 UP THE CREEK

JEANNE FRIEDMAN
<u>STILLS</u>
'83 ANGELO, MY LOVE

JOSEPH FRIEDMAN
<u>CINEMATOGRAPHER</u>
'83 ANGELO, MY LOVE

KEN FRIEDMAN
<u>SCREENPLAY</u>
'83 HEART LIKE A WHEEL

LOUIS FRIEDMAN
<u>2ND ASST. DIRECTOR</u>
'84 INDIANA JONES AND THE TEMPLE OF DOOM*

NANCY FRIEDMAN
<u>PROD. COORDINATOR</u>
'81 SMOKEY BITES THE DUST

ROBERTA FRIEDMAN
<u>ASSOCIATE PRODUCER</u>
'84 ALPHABET CITY

STEPHEN FRIEDMAN
<u>PRODUCER</u>
'79 FAST BREAK
'80 HERO AT LARGE
'80 LITTLE DARLINGS
'81 EYE OF THE NEEDLE
'84 ALL OF ME

TULLY FRIEDMAN
<u>EXECUTIVE PRODUCER</u>
'79 PROMISE, THE

ANDY FRIENDLY
<u>PRODUCER</u>
'83 RICHARD PRYOR: HERE AND NOW*

LYNDA FRIENDLY
<u>PUBLICIST</u>
'80 CHANGELING, THE*
'82 AMATEUR, THE
<u>UNIT PUBLICIST</u>
'80 TRIBUTE

CHARLES FRIES
<u>PRODUCER</u>
'82 CAT PEOPLE

KIM FRIESE
<u>PRODUCTION MANAGER</u>
'84 LAST STARFIGHTER, THE
<u>1ST ASST. DIRECTOR</u>
'82 LOVE AND MONEY
<u>2ND ASST. DIRECTOR</u>
'79 HARDCORE

RAY FRIFT
<u>PRODUCTION MANAGER</u>
'80 RAISE THE TITANIC*

CAROL FRILEGH
<u>PUBLICIST</u>
'83 LOSIN' IT

ROBERT FRIPP
<u>MUSIC</u>
'81 SUBWAY RIDERS*

JULIA FRITTAION
<u>PUBLICIST</u>
'82 OUT OF THE BLUE

KEN FRITZ
<u>STUNT COORDINATOR</u>
'84 TERMINATOR, THE

TOM FRITZ
<u>2ND ASST. DIRECTOR</u>
'80 GLORIA
'80 IT'S MY TURN*

LOUISE FROGLEY
<u>COSTUMES</u>
'83 ANOTHER TIME, ANOTHER PLACE

CLAYTON FROHMAN
<u>SCREENPLAY</u>
'83 UNDER FIRE*

MEL FROHMAN
<u>SCREENPLAY</u>
'81 ...ALL THE MARBLES

LISA FROMER
<u>ASSISTANT EDITOR</u>
'82 HOME WORK*

DOMINIC FRONTIERE
<u>MUSIC</u>
'80 STUNT MAN, THE
'80 DEFIANCE
'81 MODERN PROBLEMS

GEORGE FROST
<u>MAKEUP</u>
'80 AWAKENING, THE
'81 FOR YOUR EYES ONLY*
'81 PRIEST OF LOVE
'82 FIVE DAYS ONE SUMMER
'83 BETRAYAL
'83 OCTOPUSSY
'84 RAZOR'S EDGE, THE

LEE FROST
<u>KEY GRIP</u>
'84 BREAKIN 2 ELECTRIC BOOGALOO

BRIAN FROUD
<u>MISCELLANEOUS</u>
'82 DARK CRYSTAL, THE
'82 DARK CRYSTAL, THE

LISA FRUCHTMAN
<u>EDITOR</u>
'79 APOCALYPSE NOW*
'80 HEAVEN'S GATE*
'83 RIGHT STUFF, THE*

DENNIS FRUIN

PROPS
'79 AGATHA
'81 FRENCH LIEUTENANT'S WOMAN, THE
'84 SCANDALOUS

RON FRY

PRODUCTION MANAGER
'82 VENOM

WILLIAM FRYE

PRODUCER
'80 RAISE THE TITANIC

LEO FUCHS

PRODUCER
'81 SUNDAY LOVERS
'84 JUST THE WAY YOU ARE

LARRY FUENTES

SPECIAL EFFECTS
'79 TIME AFTER TIME*
'80 STIR CRAZY
'84 NO SMALL AFFAIR

DENIS FUGERE

STILLS
'81 SCANNERS
'81 GAS*

RICHARD FUHRMAN

ART DIRECTOR
'80 WINDOWS

CHRISTIAN FUIN

2ND ASST. DIRECTOR
'80 FIENDISH PLOT OF DR. FU MANCHU, THE

TAK FUJIMOTO

CINEMATOGRAPHER
'79 LAST EMBRACE
'79 REMEMBER MY NAME
'80 BORDERLINE
'80 MELVIN AND HOWARD
'80 WHERE THE BUFFALO ROAM
'83 HEART LIKE A WHEEL
'84 SWING SHIFT

DOMINIC FULFORD

1ST ASST. DIRECTOR
'82 VENOM
'84 KIPPERBANG

JOSIE FULFORD

SCRIPT SUPERVISOR
'83 LORDS OF DISCIPLINE, THE

DINO FULGONI

MISCELLANEOUS
'79 ONION FIELD, THE

CHARLES FULLER

SCREENPLAY
'84 SOLDIER'S STORY, A

PARMER FULLER

MUSIC
'81 SATURDAY THE 14TH

SAMUEL FULLER

DIRECTOR
'80 BIG RED ONE, THE
SCREENPLAY
'80 BIG RED ONE, THE

CARL FULLERTON

MAKEUP
'81 EYEWITNESS
MISCELLANEOUS
'81 FRIDAY THE 13TH PART TWO
'81 WOLFEN
'82 I, THE JURY
'83 HUNGER, THE

JERRY FULTON

MISCELLANEOUS
'81 BEAST WITHIN, THE

FRANCO FUMAGALLIL

PRODUCTION DESIGNER
'80 OUTSIDER, THE

AINE "ONYA" FUREY

LOCATIONS
'80 PROM NIGHT

LEWIS FUREY

MUSIC
'84 AMERICAN DREAMER

SIDNEY FURIE

PRODUCER
'84 PURPLE HEARTS
DIRECTOR
'81 ENTITY, THE
'84 PURPLE HEARTS
SCREENPLAY
'84 PURPLE HEARTS*

RENEE FURST

PUBLICIST
'79 DAWN OF THE DEAD

RON FURY

EXEC IN CHARGE PROD
'79 SCAVENGER HUNT
ASSOCIATE PRODUCER
'81 BEAST WITHIN, THE
UNIT PROD. MANAGER
'79 SCAVENGER HUNT
1ST ASST. DIRECTOR
'80 FADE TO BLACK
'81 BEAST WITHIN, THE

LOU FUSARO

PRODUCTION MANAGER
'83 EASY MONEY*
UNIT MANAGER
'79 LAST EMBRACE
'80 TIMES SQUARE
2ND ASST. DIRECTOR
'80 WINDOWS
PROD. COORDINATOR
'79 VOICES

EVA FYER

PROD. OFFICE COORD.
'83 AMITYVILLE 3D
'83 ECHOES

DAVID FYSON

PROPS
'80 AWAKENING, THE*

G

PETER GABARINI
<u>MISCELLANEOUS</u>
'80 GLORIA

ENRIQUE GABRIEL
<u>2ND ASST. DIRECTOR</u>
'81 SPHINX*

PETER GABRIEL
<u>MUSIC</u>
'84 BIRDY

BERT GADSDEN
<u>PROPS</u>
'82 HOUSE OF THE LONG SHADOWS

BERNIE GAGLIANO
<u>MISCELLANEOUS</u>
'82 TRON

BERNARD GAGNE
<u>MISCELLANEOUS</u>
'83 GOIN' ALL THE WAY

HUGETTE GAGNE
<u>COSTUMES</u>
'81 HAPPY BIRTHDAY TO ME

ANDRE GAGNON
<u>MUSIC</u>
'79 RUNNING

AL GAIL
<u>ASSOCIATE PRODUCER</u>
'79 BEYOND THE POSEIDON ADVENTURE
'80 WHEN TIME RAN OUT*

DEBRA GAIL
<u>ASSISTANT EDITOR</u>
'79 BEYOND THE POSEIDON ADVENTURE*
'80 WHEN TIME RAN OUT*

LYNN GAILEY
<u>PROD. SECRETARY</u>
'82 STARSTRUCK

LEONARD GAINES
<u>EXECUTIVE PRODUCER</u>
'79 GOING IN STYLE

HERB GAINS
<u>1ST ASST. DIRECTOR</u>
'81 FAN, THE
<u>2ND ASST. DIRECTOR</u>
'79 STARTING OVER

LYN GALBRAITH
<u>LOCATIONS</u>
'83 NATE & HAYES

BOB GALE
<u>PRODUCER</u>
'80 USED CARS
<u>SCREENPLAY</u>
'79 1941*
'80 USED CARS*

CHARLES GALE
<u>ASSISTANT EDITOR</u>
'84 MAKING THE GRADE

TIMOTHY GALFAS
<u>CINEMATOGRAPHER</u>
'82 SUMMER LOVERS
'84 RHINESTONE

VICTOR GALIANT
<u>PRODUCTION MANAGER</u>
'83 HERCULES

STEVE GALICH
<u>SPECIAL EFFECTS</u>
'82 ENDANGERED SPECIES*

ELIZABETH GALLAGHER
<u>SCRIPT SUPERVISOR</u>
'82 FORCED VENGEANCE

JOHN GALLAGHER
<u>KEY GRIP</u>
'83 CAN SHE BAKE A CHERRY PIE?

LARRY GALLAGHER
<u>KEY GRIP</u>
'81 DOZENS, THE

TRICIA GALLAHER
<u>2ND ASST. DIRECTOR</u>
'80 MIDDLE AGE CRAZY*

TRISHA GALLAHER
<u>PROPS</u>
'84 FIRESTARTER*

SHERI GALLAWAY
<u>ASSISTANT EDITOR</u>
'84 SONGWRITER*

DICK GALLEGLY
<u>ASSOCIATE PRODUCER</u>
'81 LEGEND OF THE LONE RANGER, THE
<u>PRODUCTION MANAGER</u>
'81 GREAT MUPPET CAPER, THE
'81 LEGEND OF THE LONE RANGER, THE
<u>UNIT PROD. MANAGER</u>
'82 BARBAROSA

KARLENE GALLEGLY
<u>LOCATIONS</u>
'81 BUDDY, BUDDY*
'82 JINXED
'83 CHRISTINE

SUSAN GALLEGLY
<u>PROD. COORDINATOR</u>
'80 BIG BRAWL, THE

BOOTH GALLETT
<u>LOCATIONS</u>
'79 BUTCH AND SUNDANCE: THE EARLY YEARS*

JOYCE GALLIE
<u>CASTING</u>
'80 FIENDISH PLOT OF DR. FU MANCHU, THE*
'83 WICKED LADY, THE
'84 KIPPERBANG

SANDY GALLIN
<u>EXECUTIVE PRODUCER</u>
'84 RHINESTONE*

DENNIS GALLING
<u>ASSISTANT EDITOR</u>
'79 AMITYVILLE HORROR, THE
'82 SUMMER LOVERS*

ORLANDO GALLINI
<u>EDITOR</u>
'81 SUBWAY RIDERS*

ALBERTO GALLITTI
<u>EDITOR</u>
'81 SUNDAY LOVERS*

FRED GALLO
PRODUCER
'79 GOING IN STYLE*
'81 BODY HEAT
ASSOCIATE PRODUCER
'80 HIDE IN PLAIN SIGHT
UNIT PROD. MANAGER
'80 HIDE IN PLAIN SIGHT

GUY GALLO
SCREENPLAY
'84 UNDER THE VOLCANO

PHIL GALLO
MUSIC
'80 MOTHER'S DAY*

BARBARA GALLOWAY
HAIR
'83 REUBEN, REUBEN*

LIZ GALLOWAY
PROD. OFFICE COORD.
'83 MR. MOM

MARY GALLOWAY
LOCATIONS
'80 SMALL CIRCLE OF FRIENDS, A*
'80 LONG RIDERS, THE
'81 SOUTHERN COMFORT
'82 48 HOURS
'84 STREETS OF FIRE

NICK GALT
ASSISTANT EDITOR
'83 TRAIL OF THE PINK PANTHER*

DIANA GALVIN
PROD. COORDINATOR
'84 NIGHT OF THE COMET

JIMMY GAMBINA
MISCELLANEOUS
'79 CHAMP, THE

EMILY GAMBOA
PROD. OFFICE COORD.
'82 MISSING
PROD. COORDINATOR
'83 UNDER FIRE*

BRIAN GAMBY
PROPS
'82 MOONLIGHTING

PIERRE GAMET
SOUND
'83 HANNA K*

DENNIS GAMIELLO
KEY GRIP
'80 GLORIA
'82 STRANGER IS WATCHING, A
'82 AMITYVILLE II:THE POSSESSION
'82 YES, GIORGIO*
'83 TRADING PLACES

DOUGLAS GAMLEY
MUSIC
'83 ENIGMA*

BILL GAMMAGE
MISCELLANEOUS
'81 GALLIPOLI

ISABELLE GAMSOHN
HAIR
'84 JUST THE WAY YOU ARE*

MITCHELL GAMSON
ASSOCIATE PRODUCER
'82 PARTNERS
UNIT PROD. MANAGER
'82 PARTNERS

NORMAN GAN
ASSOCIATE PRODUCER
'80 IT'S MY TURN

CONSTANTINE GANAKES
MISCELLANEOUS
'80 MIDNIGHT MADNESS

PAUL GANAPOLER
PRODUCTION MANAGER
'79 BLOODLINE

PEDRO GANDOL
2ND ASST. DIRECTOR
'80 DEATH SHIP

BARBARA GANDOLFO
ASSISTANT EDITOR
'84 STREETS OF FIRE*

GLENDA GANIS
PRODUCTION DESIGNER
'79 BOARDWALK

BEN GANNNON
ASSOCIATE PRODUCER
'81 GALLIPOLI*

JOE GANNON
SCRIPT SUPERVISOR
'80 HONEYSUCKLE ROSE

DOUGLAS GANTON
SOUND
'80 KIDNAPPING OF
THE PRESIDENT, THE

JULIE GANTON
COSTUMES
'82 PARADISE*

ARMIN GANZ
ART DIRECTOR
'84 BIRDY*

JEFFREY GANZ
ASSOCIATE PRODUCER
'82 YOUNG DOCTORS IN LOVE*

LOWELL GANZ
SCREENPLAY
'82 NIGHT SHIFT*
'84 SPLASH*

MICHELINE GARANT
UNIT MANAGER
'81 ATLANTIC CITY*

ROBIN GARB
MUSIC SUPERVISOR
'83 STAYING ALIVE

DAVID GARBER
MISCELLANEOUS
'79 BUCK ROGERS

ELLISE GARBER
MAKEUP
'82 FIRST TIME, THE*
HAIR
'82 FIRST TIME, THE*

JOHN GARBER
MISCELLANEOUS
'81 WHOSE LIFE IS IT ANYWAY?
'83 BLUE THUNDER

ABYZAK GARCIA
PROD. SECRETARY
'84 EVIL THAT MEN DO, THE*

CARLOS GARCIA
PRODUCTION MANAGER
'79 SUNBURN

DARNELL GARCIA
PROD. COORDINATOR
'83 BLIND RAGE*

JOSE GARCIA
SOUND
'82 MISSING*

ROSA GARCIA
CASTING
'79 JAGUAR LIVES*

GEOFFREY GARDINER
ASSOCIATE PRODUCER
'79 TIM

RALPH GARDINER
MISCELLANEOUS
'83 MERRY CHRISTMAS, MR. LAWRENCE

ARTHUR GARDNER
PRODUCER
'82 SAFARI 3000*

DEREK GARDNER
2ND ASST. DIRECTOR
'82 BY DESIGN

JACK GARDNER
ASSISTANT EDITOR
'80 FAME*

PHYLLIS GARDNER
PUBLICIST
'79 IN-LAWS, THE
'79 LOVE AT FIRST BITE
'80 COAST TO COAST
UNIT PUBLICIST
'81 ...ALL THE MARBLES

ROBBIE GARDNER
HAIR
'83 DRAUGHTSMAN CONTRACT, THE*

ROSEMARY GARDNER
MAKEUP
'79 RUNNING*
'80 TRIBUTE*

EVA GARDOS
EDITOR
'83 VALLEY GIRL
MISCELLANEOUS
'84 JOY OF SEX, THE

CHRIS GARDYASZ
PROPS
'81 FRIDAY THE 13TH PART TWO*

BRIAN GARFIELD
SCREENPLAY
'80 HOPSCOTCH*
ASSOCIATE PRODUCER
'80 HOPSCOTCH*

DAVID GARFIELD
EDITOR
'80 HERO AT LARGE
'82 CHOSEN, THE
'83 STING II, THE
'83 ALL THE RIGHT MOVES
'84 FLASHPOINT
MISCELLANEOUS
'81 BEAST WITHIN, THE

PAOLO GARGANO
UNIT MANAGER
'83 1990: THE BRONX WARRIORS*

ARNOLD GARGIULO
MAKEUP
'83 RETURN OF THE ALIENS: THE DEADLY SPAWN
MISCELLANEOUS
'83 RETURN OF THE ALIENS: THE DEADLY SPAWN

JESUS GARGOLES
MISCELLANEOUS
'82 EVIL UNDER THE SUN

SAM GARITE
LOCATIONS
'83 ECHOES

TOM GARK
PROPS
'79 RAVAGERS
'79 AMERICATHON
'80 CHEAPER TO KEEP HER

ROBERT GARLAND
SCREENPLAY
'79 ELECTRIC HORSEMAN, THE

GLEN GARNER
MISCELLANEOUS
'83 CUJO

LEONARD GARNER JR.
2ND ASST. DIRECTOR
'80 BLUES BROTHERS*

GARREN
HAIR
'80 SATURN 3*

SNUFF GARRETT
MUSIC SUPERVISOR
'80 SMOKEY AND THE BANDIT II
'80 ANY WHICH WAY YOU CAN
'80 BRONCO BILLY
'81 CANNONBALL RUN, THE
'82 HONKYTONK MAN
'84 CANNONBALL RUN II

JOAQUIN GARRIDO
MISCELLANEOUS
'84 UNDER THE VOLCANO

KELLI GARRIS
PUBLICIST
'81 ESCAPE FROM NEW YORK

JOSEPH GARRITY
ART DIRECTOR
'84 MAKING THE GRADE
PRODUCTION DESIGNER
'84 BREAKIN 2 ELECTRIC BOOGALOO

ANDREW GARRONI
PRODUCER
'80 MANIAC*
UNIT PROD. MANAGER
'80 MANIAC

WILLIAM GARRONI
MISCELLANEOUS
'81 ROLLOVER

EDOUARD GARROUSTE
PROD. COORDINATOR
'80 PRIVATE BENJAMIN*

WILMA GARSCADDEN-GAHRET
SCRIPT SUPERVISOR
'80 IT'S MY TURN*
'81 ABSENCE OF MALICE
'81 BUSTIN' LOOSE*
'83 MAN WHO WASN'T THERE, THE
'84 BODY DOUBLE
'84 SOLDIER'S STORY, A

SAM GART
ASSISTANT EDITOR
'84 LOVE STREAMS*

CHARLES GARTH
CHOREOGRAPHER
'79 EUROPEANS, THE*

JAMES GARTLAND
KEY GRIP
'80 TIMES SQUARE
'81 FOUR FRIENDS
'83 TOUGH ENOUGH

NORMAN GARWOOD
ART DIRECTOR
'81 TIME BANDITS
'82 MISSIONARY, THE

CHUCK GASPAR
SPECIAL EFFECTS
'79 ESCAPE FROM ALCATRAZ
'80 ALTERED STATES
'80 ANY WHICH WAY YOU CAN*
'80 NINE TO FIVE*
'82 FIREFOX*
'83 SUDDEN IMPACT
'83 BLUE THUNDER
'83 DEAL OF THE CENTURY*
'83 WRONG IS RIGHT
SP. EFFECTS SUPERV.
'84 GHOSTBUSTERS

ALDO GASPARRI
SPECIAL EFFECTS
'83 BLACK STALLION RETURNS, THE*

ERNIE GASSER
MAKEUP
'79 UNIDENTIFIED FLYING ODDBALL*
'80 WATCHER IN THE WOODS, THE*

HELMUT GASSNER
ART DIRECTOR
'79 BLOODLINE*
'84 LITTLE DRUMMER GIRL, THE*

HELENA GASTAL
COSTUME SUPERVISOR
'84 BLAME IT ON RIO

DEAN GATES
MISCELLANEOUS
'80 EYES OF A STRANGER

JERRY GATLIN
STUNT COORDINATOR
'80 COAST TO COAST*
'81 LEGEND OF THE LONE RANGER, THE

KIM GATTI
PUBLICIST
'83 HERCULES

BOB GAUDIO
MISCELLANEOUS
'80 JAZZ SINGER, THE

JOHN GAUDIOSO
UNIT PROD. MANAGER
'80 CHEAPER TO KEEP HER
'80 IN GOD WE TRUST

JOHN GAUGHN
MISCELLANEOUS
'82 ESCAPE ARTIST, THE

LESLIE GAUL
SCRIPT SUPERVISOR
'83 HERCULES

GLEN GAUTHIER
SOUND
'81 TICKET TO HEAVEN*

GERRY GAVIGAN
2ND ASST. DIRECTOR
'79 GREAT TRAIN ROBBERY, THE*
'81 CLASH OF THE TITANS*
'81 DOGS OF WAR, THE*
2ND UNIT DIRECTOR
'79 DRACULA

JAMES GAVIN
2ND UNIT DIRECTOR
'80 LAST FLIGHT OF NOAH'S ARK, THE
'82 HANKY PANKY
'82 NIGHT CROSSING
'83 BLUE THUNDER*
MISCELLANEOUS
'82 FIREFOX
'84 DREAMSCAPE

ROB GAVIN
ASSISTANT EDITOR
'84 NEVERENDING STORY, THE

STEVE GAWLEY
MISCELLANEOUS
'82 STAR TREK II THE WRATH OF KHAN
'83 RETURN OF THE JEDI

MARCIA GAY
2ND ASST. DIRECTOR
'83 BETRAYAL

NORMAN GAY
EDITOR
'80 HONEYSUCKLE ROSE*

FRANKIE GAYE
MUSIC
'79 PENITENTIARY*

CHUCK GAYLORD
MISCELLANEOUS
'83 FOOTLOOSE

KERRY GAYNOR
MISCELLANEOUS
'81 ENTITY, THE

JOE GAYTON
SCREENPLAY
'83 UNCOMMON VALOR

DAVID GEARHARDT
MISCELLANEOUS
'84 MAKING THE GRADE

FRED GEBLER
SPECIAL EFFECTS
'80 LAST MARRIED COUPLE IN AMERICA, THE
'82 BEST LITTLE WHOREHOUSE IN TEXAS, THE

SIDNEY GECKER
SCRIPT SUPERVISOR
'79 WANDERERS, THE
'80 CRUISING
'80 GILDA LIVE*
'81 WOLFEN
'83 EXPOSED*

MAGGIE GEDDES
MISCELLANEOUS
'82 PIRATE MOVIE, THE

TIMOTHY GEE
EDITOR
'81 CLASH OF THE TITANS

DAVID GEFFEN
EXECUTIVE PRODUCER
'82 PERSONAL BEST

ARNOLD GEFSKY
ASSOCIATE PRODUCER
'84 UNDER THE VOLCANO*

GAIL GEIBEL
PROD. OFFICE COORD.
'79 WARRIORS, THE
'80 ONE-TRICK PONY
'81 REDS
'82 WORLD ACCORDING TO GARP, THE

RUDI GEIGLER
MISCELLANEOUS
'79 AVALANCHE EXPRESS

ZIGGY GEIKE
MISCELLANEOUS
'81 DEAD AND BURIED

ELLIOT GEISINGER
PRODUCER
'79 AMITYVILLE HORROR, THE*
'81 NIGHT THE LIGHTS WENT OUT IN GEORGIA, THE*

ROBERT MICHAEL GEISLER
EXECUTIVE PRODUCER
'83 STREAMERS*

DIETER GEISSLER
PRODUCER
'84 NEVERENDING STORY, THE*

SUSAN GELB
1ST ASST. DIRECTOR
'84 CHILDREN OF THE CORN

LARRY GELBART
SCREENPLAY
'81 NEIGHBORS
'82 TOOTSIE*
'84 BLAME IT ON RIO*
EXECUTIVE PRODUCER
'84 BLAME IT ON RIO

LIZ GELBER
ASSISTANT EDITOR
'83 HERCULES*

M.A. GELENG
PRODUCTION DESIGNER
'83 HERCULES

XAVIER GELIN
ASSOCIATE PRODUCER
'84 WOMAN IN RED, THE*

BRUCE GELLER
HAIR
'83 RIGHT STUFF, THE*

GIL GELLER
MISCELLANEOUS
'81 NEIGHBORS

ANDREW GELLIS
EXECUTIVE PRODUCER
'84 GRANDVIEW, U.S.A.*

HENRY GELLIS
EXECUTIVE PRODUCER
'83 FRIGHTMARE

JUDY GELLMAN
COSTUMES
'79 MEATBALLS

MICHAEL GEMMELL
MISCELLANEOUS
'79 LEGACY, THE

JOHN GEMPEL
ASSISTANT EDITOR
'80 OH! HEAVENLY DOG*

JEAN-FRANCOIS GENEIX
LOCATIONS
'84 RAZOR'S EDGE, THE*

HARVEY GENKINS
CINEMATOGRAPHER
'79 FIVE DAYS FROM HOME

SERGIO GENNARI
HAIR
'84 MISUNDERSTOOD

ROBBIE GENSLER
PROD. COORDINATOR
'82 SILENT RAGE

PETER GENT
SCREENPLAY
'79 NORTH DALLAS FORTY*

GIORGIO GENTILI
1ST ASST. DIRECTOR
'80 OUTSIDER, THE

MARIO GENTILINI
PROPS
'83 LONELY LADY, THE*

BILL GENTRY
ASSISTANT EDITOR
'84 NIGHT OF THE COMET

BOB GEORGE
KEY GRIP
'79 TOURIST TRAP

CHRISTINE GEORGE
HAIR
'82 DINER

GEORGE GEORGE
PRODUCER
'79 RICH KIDS*
'81 MY DINNER WITH ANDRE*

JON GEORGE
SCREENPLAY
'84 FINAL TERROR, THE*

KEN GEORGE
STILLS
'83 MERRY CHRISTMAS, MR. LAWRENCE*

LASZLO GEORGE
CINEMATOGRAPHER
'79 RUNNING
'80 NOTHING PERSONAL*
'84 BEAR, THE

ROGER GEORGE
SPECIAL EFFECTS
'79 ROCK 'N ROLL HIGH SCHOOL*
'80 DIE LAUGHING
'80 HUMANOIDS FROM THE DEEP
'80 STEEL
'81 EYE FOR AN EYE, AN
'81 HOWLING, THE
'82 BEASTMASTER, THE*
'83 LONE WOLF MCQUADE*
'84 ANGEL
'84 REPO MAN*
'84 TERMINATOR, THE*
MISCELLANEOUS
'80 BATTLE BEYOND THE STARS
'81 SATURDAY THE 14TH
'82 ANDROID
'82 PARASITE
'83 MAUSOLEUM
'83 MAUSOLEUM

ANNE GERARD
SCREENPLAY
'82 LOVE CHILD*

BRYSON PETER GERARD
MISCELLANEOUS
'79 BUCK ROGERS

JACK GEREGHTY
STILLS
'79 NIGHTWING
'82 CHILLY SCENES OF WINTER

ROBERTO GERHARD
1ST ASST. DIRECTOR
'84 EL NORTE*

PAT GERHARDT
MAKEUP
'84 STONE BOY, THE
HAIR
'84 STONE BOY, THE

GREG GERLICH
CASTING
'80 HOLLYWOOD KNIGHTS, THE*

GREGORY GERLICH
ASSISTANT EDITOR
'79 ROCKY II*
'82 ROCKY III*
'82 BARBAROSA*
'84 RHINESTONE*
'84 2010*

MICHAEL GERMAIN
MAKEUP
'79 RUNNER STUMBLES, THE
'80 LONG RIDERS, THE
'80 WHEN TIME RAN OUT*
'81 SOUTHERN COMFORT
'81 HALLOWEEN II
'82 48 HOURS*
'82 ESCAPE ARTIST, THE
'83 BIG CHILL, THE*
'83 WAR GAMES*
'84 STREETS OF FIRE

BRIGITTE GERMAINE
SCRIPT SUPERVISOR
'80 TERROR TRAIN

SUSAN GERMAINE
HAIR
'79 1941
'80 SERIAL
'80 NINE TO FIVE*
'82 ENDANGERED SPECIES
'82 MAKING LOVE
'82 PERSONAL BEST
'83 STAR 80
'84 CRACKERS
'84 IRRECONCILABLE DIFFERENCES

MICHELE GERMANO
PRODUCTION MANAGER
'83 YOR*

GARY GERO
MISCELLANEOUS
'80 FINAL COUNTDOWN, THE
'81 BLOOD BEACH
'81 HAND, THE
'84 BIRDY
'84 LAST STARFIGHTER, THE

CHAS GERRETSEN
STILLS
'79 APOCALYPSE NOW*

WILLIAM GERRITY
ASSOCIATE PRODUCER
'82 SOPHIE'S CHOICE
UNIT PROD. MANAGER
'79 STARTING OVER
'81 WOLFEN
'83 TRADING PLACES
UNIT MANAGER
'82 SOPHIE'S CHOICE*
2ND UNIT DIRECTOR
'81 NIGHT THE LIGHTS WENT OUT IN GEORGIA, THE

GEORGE GERSHWIN
MUSIC
'79 MANHATTAN

BERNARD GERSTEN
EXECUTIVE PRODUCER
'82 ONE FROM THE HEART

RALPH GERVAIS
SPECIAL EFFECTS
'80 IDOLMAKER, THE*

GUNTHER GERZSO
PRODUCTION DESIGNER
'84 UNDER THE VOLCANO

ROBERT GETCHELL
SCREENPLAY
'81 MOMMIE DEAREST*

PAUL GIACOBBE
LOCATIONS
'81 NESTING, THE
'84 PREPPIES

LAURETTE DEMORO GIAFFERI
ASSOCIATE PRODUCER
'83 SAVANNAH SMILES

JOAN GIAMMARCO
ASSISTANT EDITOR
'80 PROM NIGHT*

JOHN GIAMMARCO
ASSISTANT EDITOR
'81 LAST CHASE, THE*

SUSAN GIAMMUSSO
MAKEUP
'84 C.H.U.D.
HAIR
'84 C.H.U.D.

MARIA GIANANDREA
ASSISTANT EDITOR
'83 HERCULES*

ROBERTO GIANANDREA
ASSISTANT EDITOR
'83 HERCULES*

JOHN GIANNINI
STILLS
'81 LAST CHASE, THE

JOE GIANNONE
HAIR
'83 LOSIN' IT*
'84 PHILADELPHIA EXPERIMENT, THE

RON GIANNOTTO
EXECUTIVE PRODUCER
'83 RETURN OF THE ALIENS: THE DEADLY SPAWN*

MARILYN GIARDINO
SCRIPT SUPERVISOR
'80 BLUE LAGOON
'80 USED CARS
'81 CHEECH AND CHONG'S NICE DREAMS
'82 SUMMER LOVERS

TONY GIARRANTANO
KEY GRIP
'81 MS. 45

RODNEY GIBBONS
CINEMATOGRAPHER
'81 MY BLOODY VALENTINE

ALAN GIBBS
STUNT COORDINATOR
'82 BORDER, THE
'82 FIGHTING BACK*
'84 RIVER, THE
'84 CANNONBALL RUN II
MISCELLANEOUS
'79 AVALANCHE EXPRESS
'80 HANGAR 18

ANTONY GIBBS
EDITOR
'79 BUTCH AND SUNDANCE: THE EARLY YEARS
'81 RAGTIME*
'81 DOGS OF WAR, THE
'83 BAD BOYS
'84 DUNE

BARBARA GIBBS
PRODUCTION MANAGER
'81 ROAD GAMES*
'82 STARSTRUCK

GARY GIBBS
PRODUCER
'83 GOIN' ALL THE WAY*

GEORGE GIBBS
SPECIAL EFFECTS
'80 FLASH GORDON
'83 BRITANNIA HOSPITAL
'83 TRAIL OF THE PINK PANTHER
SP. EFFECTS SUPERV.
'79 ARABIAN ADVENTURE
'81 RAGTIME*
'81 EYE OF THE NEEDLE
'83 MONTY PYTHON'S THE MEANING OF LIFE
MISCELLANEOUS
'84 INDIANA JONES AND THE TEMPLE OF DOOM

JEREMY GIBBS
ASSISTANT EDITOR
'82 PINK FLOYD: THE WALL*

PAULA GIBBS
PRODUCTION MANAGER
'84 PHAR LAP

ALEX GIBNEY
ASSOCIATE EDITOR
'83 GOLDEN SEAL, THE

KATHRYN GIBNEY
SCRIPT SUPERVISOR
'81 FEAR NO EVIL

CARL GIBSON
KEY GRIP
'81 PENNIES FROM HEAVEN

DEREK GIBSON
PRODUCER
'79 JAGUAR LIVES
'80 DEATH SHIP*
EXECUTIVE PRODUCER
'84 TERMINATOR, THE*

J. KATHLEEN GIBSON
ASSISTANT EDITOR
'84 BEAT STREET*

MARCELLE GIBSON
PROD. COORDINATOR
'81 MY BLOODY VALENTINE*

SANDY GIBSON
MUSIC SUPERVISOR
'84 TEACHERS

NELSON GIDDING
SCREENPLAY
'79 BEYOND THE POSEIDON ADVENTURE

AL GIDDINGS
MISCELLANEOUS
'81 FOR YOUR EYES ONLY

JACK GIDDY
MISCELLANEOUS
'81 GALLIPOLI

RAYNOLD GIDEON
SCREENPLAY
'79 MAN, A WOMAN AND A BANK, A*
'84 STARMAN*

NANCY GIEBINK
UNIT PROD. MANAGER
'84 BIRDY
UNIT MANAGER
'82 SHOOT THE MOON

ZIGGY GIEKE
MISCELLANEOUS
'81 HEARTBEEPS

H.R. GIGER
MISCELLANEOUS
'79 ALIEN

GIUSEPPE GIGLIETTI
1ST ASST. DIRECTOR
'83 1990: THE BRONX WARRIORS*

CARLOS GIL
1ST ASST. DIRECTOR
'84 INDIANA JONES
AND THE TEMPLE OF DOOM*
2ND ASST. DIRECTOR
'83 NEVER SAY NEVER AGAIN*

GILBERT AND SULLIVAN
MISCELLANEOUS
'83 PIRATES OF PENZANCE, THE

BRUCE GILBERT
PRODUCER
'80 NINE TO FIVE
'81 ROLLOVER
'81 ON GOLDEN POND
EXECUTIVE PRODUCER
'79 CHINA SYNDROME, THE

DAVID GILBERT
SCREENPLAY
'84 BEAT STREET*

DONNA GILBERT
HAIR
'82 NATIONAL LAMPOON'S
CLASS REUNION*

JANE GILBERT
PRODUCTION MANAGER
'83 NATE & HAYES

KEN GILBERT
1ST ASST. DIRECTOR
'84 FLASHPOINT*

KENNETH GILBERT
SCRIPT SUPERVISOR
'84 GREMLINS

LEWIS GILBERT
PRODUCER
'83 EDUCATING RITA
DIRECTOR
'79 MOONRAKER
'83 EDUCATING RITA

MICKEY GILBERT
STUNT COORDINATOR
'79 FRISCO KID, THE*
'80 STIR CRAZY
'80 BRUBAKER
'80 LITTLE MISS MARKER
'81 ...ALL THE MARBLES
MISCELLANEOUS
'82 SWAMP THING

PAT GILBERT
ASSISTANT EDITOR
'83 ENIGMA*

STANLEY GILBERT
MISCELLANEOUS
'80 CADDYSHACK

SYDNEY GILBERT
COSTUMES
'80 STEEL*

TERRY GILBERT
CHOREOGRAPHER
'84 BOUNTY, THE

GILDA
HAIR
'79 FIFTH MUSKETEER, THE*

DAVID GILER
PRODUCER
'79 ALIEN*
'81 SOUTHERN COMFORT
SCREENPLAY
'81 SOUTHERN COMFORT*

AMANDA GILL
2ND ASST. DIRECTOR
'84 EL NORTE

GARY GILL
KEY GRIP
'84 BIRDY

JEAN GILL
MISCELLANEOUS
'84 EL NORTE

JIM GILL
MISCELLANEOUS
'84 LOVELESS, THE

JUDITH GILL
PROD. COORDINATOR
'80 IDOLMAKER, THE
'84 NO SMALL AFFAIR
'84 CANNONBALL RUN II

LINDA GILL
MAKEUP
'83 STRANGE BREW*

MARK GILL
ASSISTANT EDITOR
'83 BEYOND THE LIMIT*

STUART GILLARD
DIRECTOR
'82 PARADISE
SCREENPLAY
'82 IF YOU COULD SEE WHAT I HEAR
'82 PARADISE
CO-PRODUCER
'82 IF YOU COULD SEE WHAT I HEAR

MARTIN GILLEN
PRODUCTION MANAGER
'82 PORKY'S

JIM GILLESPIE
MAKEUP
'83 SWEET SIXTEEN
MISCELLANEOUS
'83 MORTUARY

PAULA GILLESPIE
HAIR
'80 ELEPHANT MAN, THE*
'82 GANDHI
'83 HUNGER, THE*
'83 WICKED LADY, THE*
'84 CHAMPIONS

RON GILLHAM
KEY GRIP
'79 SILENT PARTNER, THE
'79 BLACK STALLION, THE
'79 LOST AND FOUND
'80 TRIBUTE*
'82 AMATEUR, THE
'83 STRANGE INVADERS
'83 CHRISTMAS STORY, A
'84 POLICE ACADEMY
'84 MRS. SOFFEL

TERRY GILLIAM
PRODUCER
'81 TIME BANDITS
DIRECTOR
'81 TIME BANDITS
SCREENPLAY
'79 MONTY PYTHON'S LIFE OF BRIAN*
'81 TIME BANDITS*
'82 MONTY PYTHON LIVE AT
THE HOLLYWOOD BOWL*
'83 MONTY PYTHON'S
THE MEANING OF LIFE*
MISCELLANEOUS
'79 MONTY PYTHON'S LIFE OF BRIAN
'83 MONTY PYTHON'S
THE MEANING OF LIFE

LESLIE GILLIAT
MISCELLANEOUS
'81 PRIEST OF LOVE

THOMAS GILLIGAN
KEY GRIP
'84 AMADEUS

GARY GILLINGHAM
EXECUTIVE PRODUCER
'82 BRAINWAVES*

JOVON GILLOHM
ASSISTANT EDITOR
'82 PENITENTIARY II*
1ST ASST. DIRECTOR
'79 PENITENTIARY

NICHOLAS GILLOTT
PRODUCTION MANAGER
'79 FIREPOWER*
'80 LADY VANISHES, THE*

ANDREW GILMORE
SOUND
'81 HARD COUNTRY

DEAN GILMORE
SOUND
'80 RAISE THE TITANIC*

WILLIAM GILMORE
PRODUCER
'80 DEFIANCE*
'83 TOUGH ENOUGH
'84 AGAINST ALL ODDS*
EXECUTIVE PRODUCER
'81 DEADLY BLESSING

DAVID GILMOUR
MISCELLANEOUS
'82 PINK FLOYD: THE WALL

SANDRA GIMPEL
STUNT COORDINATOR
'79 TOURIST TRAP

BRYAN GINDOFF
PRODUCER
'83 LOSIN' IT*

ANTHONY GINNANE
PRODUCER
'81 STRANGE BEHAVIOR*

DONALD GINSBERG
ASSOCIATE EDITOR
'80 HAPPY BIRTHDAY, GEMINI

MICHAEL GINSBURG
STILLS
'79 STARTING OVER
'79 WARRIORS, THE
'80 DEFIANCE*
'81 FORT APACHE, THE BRONX
'81 WOLFEN
'83 ALL THE RIGHT MOVES*
'83 BIG CHILL, THE
'84 GHOSTBUSTERS*
'84 BEAT STREET*

ROCCO GIOFFRE
MISCELLANEOUS
'83 NATIONAL LAMPOON'S VACATION

DOMENIC GIORGIO
KEY GRIP
'82 SIX WEEKS

JAMES GIOVANNETTI JR.
2ND ASST. DIRECTOR
'84 SIXTEEN CANDLES
'84 WINDY CITY

CORRIDORI GIOVANNI
SPECIAL EFFECTS
'83 HANNA K*

GEORGE GIPE
SCREENPLAY
'82 DEAD MEN DON'T WEAR PLAID*
'83 MAN WITH TWO BRAINS, THE*

MARCIA GIRARD
SCRIPT SUPERVISOR
'80 CHEAPER TO KEEP HER
'81 RICHARD PRYOR: LIVE
ON THE SUNSET STRIP*

JEAN "MOEBIUS" GIRAUD
MISCELLANEOUS
'82 TRON

JIMMY GIRITLIAN
ASSISTANT EDITOR
'80 RESURRECTION

ROBERT GIROLAMI
UNIT PROD. MANAGER
'83 EDDIE AND THE CRUISERS
'84 LONELY GUY, THE*
1ST ASST. DIRECTOR
'79 BLOODLINE*
'81 ENDLESS LOVE
'81 NIGHTHAWKS
'81 THEY ALL LAUGHED
'83 EASY MONEY
'84 COTTON CLUB, THE
'84 FIRSTBORN

ROCCO GISMONDI
2ND ASST. DIRECTOR
'83 VIDEODROME*

MARIE-JOSE GISSAURT
SCRIPT SUPERVISOR
'83 EXPOSED*

ANTHONY GITTELSON
2ND ASST. DIRECTOR
'82 STILL OF THE NIGHT
'82 MIDSUMMER NIGHT'S
SEX COMEDY, A*
'83 STAR 80
'83 ZELIG*
'84 MRS. SOFFEL*
LOCATIONS
'79 SOMETHING SHORT OF PARADISE
'80 FINAL COUNTDOWN, THE*

HARRY GITTES
PRODUCER
'83 TIMERIDER

ROBERT GITTLER
SCREENPLAY
'79 BUDDY HOLLY STORY, THE

PETER GIULIANO
PRODUCTION MANAGER
'79 MR. MIKE'S MONDO VIDEO*
1ST ASST. DIRECTOR
'84 GHOSTBUSTERS*

ANNE GLANFIELD
LOCATIONS
'83 NEVER SAY NEVER AGAIN

BAYLIS GLASCOCK
ASSISTANT EDITOR
'82 TRON*

JOHN GLASCOCK
SOUND
'81 WHOSE LIFE IS IT ANYWAY?
'82 CHALLENGE, THE
'83 BLUE THUNDER*

KARIN GLASER
MAKEUP
'80 AMERICAN SUCCESS COMPANY, THE*
HAIR
'80 AMERICAN SUCCESS COMPANY, THE*

BETTY GLASGOW
HAIR
'79 SHOUT, THE
'80 FLASH GORDON*
'81 FINAL CONFLICT, THE
'84 KIPPERBANG
'84 TOP SECRET!*

SANDY GLASS
SCREENPLAY
'80 LAST FLIGHT
OF NOAH'S ARK, THE*

TOM GLASS

MISCELLANEOUS
'82 GREY FOX, THE
'83 DEAD ZONE, THE

BERT GLATSTEIN

ASSOCIATE EDITOR
'82 SWORD AND THE SORCERER, THE

WOLFGANG GLATTES

PRODUCER
'83 STAR 80*
ASSOCIATE PRODUCER
'79 ALL THAT JAZZ*
'82 STILL OF THE NIGHT*
UNIT MANAGER
'79 ALL THAT JAZZ
1ST ASST. DIRECTOR
'79 ALL THAT JAZZ
'82 STILL OF THE NIGHT
'83 STAR 80

DAVID GLAZER

PROPS
'82 SEDUCTION, THE
'83 DEADLY FORCE
'84 DREAMSCAPE

MITCHELL GLAZER

SCREENPLAY
'79 MR. MIKE'S MONDO VIDEO*

ED GLEASON

SOUND
'80 GILDA LIVE*

PHIL GLEASON

SOUND
'80 GILDA LIVE*

PIERRE WILLIAM GLEEN

CINEMATOGRAPHER
'79 LITTLE ROMANCE, A

JOHN GLEN

DIRECTOR
'81 FOR YOUR EYES ONLY
'83 OCTOPUSSY
EDITOR
'79 MOONRAKER
'81 SEA WOLVES, THE
2ND UNIT DIRECTOR
'79 MOONRAKER*

MATTHEW GLEN

ASSISTANT EDITOR
'83 FINAL OPTION, THE

FRANK GLENN

1ST ASST. DIRECTOR
'81 TAKE THIS JOB AND SHOVE IT

JAMES GLENNON

CINEMATOGRAPHER
'83 RETURN OF THE JEDI*
'84 UP THE CREEK
'84 EL NORTE

EARL GLICK

EXECUTIVE PRODUCER
'84 CHILDREN OF THE CORN*

MICHAEL GLICK

PRODUCER
'81 BUSTIN' LOOSE*
MISCELLANEOUS
'79 ROCKY II
'82 SUMMER LOVERS

JAMES GLICKENHAUS

DIRECTOR
'80 EXTERMINATOR, THE*

WENDY GLICKSTEIN

PROD. OFFICE COORD.
'79 GOING IN STYLE
'80 NIGHT OF THE JUGGLER
'81 ROLLOVER
'83 SURVIVORS, THE
PROD. COORDINATOR
'82 AMITYVILLE II:
THE POSSESSION*

CARY GLIEBERMAN

UNIT PROD. MANAGER
'84 CHAMPIONS
'84 THIS IS SPINAL TAP

TERRY GLINWOOD

EXECUTIVE PRODUCER
'83 MERRY CHRISTMAS,
MR. LAWRENCE*

BRYAN GLISERMAN

MISCELLANEOUS
'81 DEATH HUNT

JAMES GLOBUS

STILLS
'79 METEOR
'79 OLD BOYFRIENDS
'80 CHANGE OF SEASONS, A
'80 HEARTBEAT*
'81 FIRST MONDAY IN OCTOBER

RAM GLOBUS

STILLS
'83 HERCULES

YORAM GLOBUS

PRODUCER
'79 MAGICIAN OF LUBLIN, THE*
'80 SCHIZOID*
'81 BODY AND SOUL*
'81 ENTER THE NINJA*
'82 DEATHWISH II*
'82 LAST AMERICAN VIRGIN, THE*
'82 THAT CHAMPIONSHIP SEASON*
'82 HOUSE OF THE LONG SHADOWS*
'83 REVENGE OF THE NINJA*
'83 HERCULES*
'83 WICKED LADY, THE*
'84 BREAKIN 2 ELECTRIC BOOGALOO*
'84 LOVE STREAMS*
'84 OVER THE BROOKLYN BRIDGE*
EXECUTIVE PRODUCER
'83 10 TO MIDNIGHT*
'84 BOLERO*
'84 MAKING THE GRADE*
'84 EXTERMINATOR II*

DENNIS GLOUNER

MISCELLANEOUS
'79 PRISONER OF ZENDA, THE
'81 HEARTBEEPS
'83 PSYCHO II

RICHARD GLOUNER

CINEMATOGRAPHER
'80 GONG SHOW MOVIE, THE

GEOFF GLOVER

MISCELLANEOUS
'80 EMPIRE STRIKES BACK, THE

LEONHARD GMUR

PRODUCTION MANAGER
'80 AMERICAN SUCCESS COMPANY, THE
'82 FIVE DAYS ONE SUMMER*
'83 OCTOPUSSY*
UNIT PROD. MANAGER
'79 BLOODLINE*

MARSHA GNAIZDA

SCRIPT SUPERVISOR
'80 EYES OF A STRANGER

PAUL GOBEL

MAKEUP
'83 HUNGER, THE

RUSSELL GOBLE

PROPS
'80 FORMULA, THE
'81 TAPS
'82 BARBAROSA
'82 E.T. THE EXTRA-TERRESTRIAL
'83 SILKWOOD
'84 HARD TO HOLD
'84 NO SMALL AFFAIR

THE GOBLINS

MUSIC
'79 DAWN OF THE DEAD*

LES GOBRUEGGE

ART DIRECTOR
'79 MUPPET MOVIE, THE

GARY GOCH

ASSOCIATE PRODUCER
'82 PORKY'S
'83 CHRISTMAS STORY, A
'83 PORKY'S II THE NEXT DAY*

KEN GOCH

1ST ASST. DIRECTOR
'80 TRIBUTE*
'82 PORKY'S
'83 CHRISTMAS STORY, A
'83 PORKY'S II THE NEXT DAY

GODFREY GODAR

CINEMATOGRAPHER
'79 GAME OF DEATH
MISCELLANEOUS
'80 WATCHER IN THE WOODS, THE

JACQUES GODBOUT

SPECIAL EFFECTS
'83 OF UNKNOWN ORIGIN*
'84 HOTEL NEW HAMPSHIRE, THE*

GARY GODDARD

SCREENPLAY
'81 TARZAN, THE APE MAN*

IAN GODDARD

LOCATIONS
'82 PIRATE MOVIE, THE*

NICK GODDEN

1ST ASST. DIRECTOR
'82 HOUSE OF THE LONG SHADOWS*

SUSAN GODFREY

ASSISTANT EDITOR
'82 PENITENTIARY II*

TED GOETZ

ASSOCIATE PRODUCER
'80 BALTIMORE BULLET, THE

IVAN GOFF

SCREENPLAY
'81 LEGEND OF
THE LONE RANGER, THE*

JOHN GOFF

SCREENPLAY
'82 BUTTERFLY*

MENAHEM GOLAN

PRODUCER
'79 MAGICIAN OF LUBLIN, THE*
'80 SCHIZOID*
'81 BODY AND SOUL*
'82 DEATHWISH II*
'82 LAST AMERICAN VIRGIN, THE*
'82 THAT CHAMPIONSHIP SEASON*
'82 HOUSE OF THE LONG SHADOWS*
'83 REVENGE OF THE NINJA*
'83 HERCULES*
'83 WICKED LADY, THE*
'84 BREAKIN 2 ELECTRIC BOOGALOO*
'84 LOVE STREAMS*
'84 OVER THE BROOKLYN BRIDGE*
DIRECTOR
'79 MAGICIAN OF LUBLIN, THE
'81 ENTER THE NINJA
'84 OVER THE BROOKLYN BRIDGE
SCREENPLAY
'79 MAGICIAN OF LUBLIN, THE*
EXECUTIVE PRODUCER
'83 10 TO MIDNIGHT*
'84 BOLERO*
'84 MAKING THE GRADE*
'84 EXTERMINATOR II*

NAOMI GOLAN

COSTUME SUPERVISOR
'83 REVENGE OF THE NINJA

ALAN GOLAND

ASSOCIATE PRODUCER
'81 MAN WHO SAW TOMORROW, THE*

BARRY GOLD

ASSISTANT EDITOR
'80 NIGHT OF THE JUGGLER
'81 BUDDY, BUDDY
'81 CHU CHU AND THE PHILLY FLASH
'83 EXPOSED*

BERT GOLD

UNIT PROD. MANAGER
'81 DEADLY BLESSING
1ST ASST. DIRECTOR
'80 TOUCHED BY LOVE

ERNEST GOLD

MUSIC
'79 RUNNER STUMBLES, THE
'80 TOM HORN
'82 SAFARI 3000

MICHAEL SCOTT GOLDBAUM

SOUND
'79 HEARTLAND
'83 BALLAD OF
GREGORIO CORTEZ, THE

BETTY GOLDBERG

SCRIPT SUPERVISOR
'79 REAL LIFE
'84 BEVERLY HILLS COP
'84 THIEF OF HEARTS

DAN GOLDBERG

PRODUCER
'79 MEATBALLS
'81 STRIPES*
SCREENPLAY
'79 MEATBALLS*
'81 STRIPES*
'83 SPACEHUNTER: ADVENTURES
IN THE FORBIDDEN ZONE*

DANNY GOLDBERG

MUSIC SUPERVISOR
'84 BACHELOR PARTY*

JOYCE GOLDBERG

PROD. SECRETARY
'80 CLOSE ENCOUNTERS OF THE THIRD
KIND SPECIAL EDITION

LEONARD GOLDBERG

PRODUCER
'81 ALL NIGHT LONG*
EXECUTIVE PRODUCER
'79 WINTER KILLS*
'83 WAR GAMES

MARY GOLDBERG

CASTING
'79 ALIEN*
'79 PROMISE, THE*
'81 RAGTIME*
'82 SENDER, THE*
'82 CAT PEOPLE
'83 CLASS*
'83 HUNGER, THE*
'83 SILKWOOD
'84 AMADEUS*
'84 ICEMAN

TIKKI GOLDBERG

PRODUCTION MANAGER
'80 FADE TO BLACK

MARK GOLDBLATT

EDITOR
'80 HUMANOIDS FROM THE DEEP
'81 ENTER THE NINJA*
'81 HALLOWEEN II*
'81 HOWLING, THE*
'83 GET CRAZY*
'84 OVER THE BROOKLYN BRIDGE
'84 TERMINATOR, THE

PHILIP GOLDBLATT

MAKEUP
'83 KING OF COMEDY, THE

STEPHEN GOLDBLATT

CINEMATOGRAPHER
'81 OUTLAND
'83 HUNGER, THE
'84 COTTON CLUB, THE

DAVID GOLDEN
PRODUCTION MANAGER
'79 KRAMER VS. KRAMER
'81 ENDLESS LOVE
'81 FORT APACHE, THE BRONX
UNIT PROD. MANAGER
'80 FAME
'84 COTTON CLUB, THE*

JOANNE GOLDEN
UNIT MANAGER
'80 EYES OF A STRANGER

KAREN ROSE GOLDEN
SCRIPT SUPERVISOR
'84 MAKING THE GRADE

KEN GOLDEN
PRODUCTION MANAGER
'81 ATLANTIC CITY*
UNIT PROD. MANAGER
'81 HONKY TONK FREEWAY*

PAT GOLDEN
CASTING
'84 KILLING FIELDS, THE*
'84 BEAT STREET*

PETER GOLDEN
CASTING
'84 PURPLE RAIN*

BILLY GOLDENBERG
MUSIC
'79 SCAVENGER HUNT
'83 REUBEN, REUBEN

MARK GOLDENBERG
MUSIC
'82 SILENT RAGE*
'82 NATIONAL LAMPOON'S CLASS REUNION*

PHILLIP GOLDFARB
ASSOCIATE PRODUCER
'80 MY BODYGUARD
CO-PRODUCER
'83 ALL THE RIGHT MOVES
PRODUCTION MANAGER
'81 TAPS*
UNIT PROD. MANAGER
'79 ICE CASTLES
'80 MY BODYGUARD
'81 CHEECH AND CHONG'S NICE DREAMS
'83 ALL THE RIGHT MOVES

GAYLE GOLDIN
PROD. COORDINATOR
'83 PRIVATE SCHOOL

JERELYN GOLDING
ASSISTANT EDITOR
'79 ROCKY II*

PAUL GOLDING
SCREENPLAY
'84 BEAT STREET*

BO GOLDMAN
SCREENPLAY
'79 ROSE, THE*
'80 MELVIN AND HOWARD
'82 SHOOT THE MOON

CHARLENE GOLDMAN
MISCELLANEOUS
'84 CANNONBALL RUN II
'84 OH GOD, YOU DEVIL

DON GOLDMAN
PRODUCTION MANAGER
'79 BUDDY HOLLY STORY, THE
'79 WHEN YOU COMIN' BACK, RED RYDER?
'81 UNDER THE RAINBOW
'84 FIRESTARTER

ERWIN GOLDMAN
SCREENPLAY
'83 SWEET SIXTEEN

HAL GOLDMAN
SCREENPLAY
'80 OH GOD! BOOK II*

LOUIS GOLDMAN
STILLS
'79 WANDERERS, THE
'80 JUST TELL ME WHAT YOU WANT
'81 BLOW OUT
'81 PRINCE OF THE CITY
'82 DEATHTRAP
'82 VERDICT, THE
'84 MOSCOW ON THE HUDSON
'84 POPE OF GREENWICH VILLAGE, THE

LYNN GOLDMAN
LOCATIONS
'84 NATURAL, THE*

MIA GOLDMAN
EDITOR
'84 CHOOSE ME
ASSISTANT EDITOR
'81 BODY HEAT
'83 BIG CHILL, THE*

MICHAEL GOLDMAN
MISCELLANEOUS
'80 WHOLLY MOSES!

DAVID GOLDNER
MISCELLANEOUS
'80 IDOLMAKER, THE

BARRY GOLDSMITH
MISCELLANEOUS
'81 FOR YOUR EYES ONLY

GEORGE GOLDSMITH
SCREENPLAY
'84 CHILDREN OF THE CORN

GLADYS GOLDSMITH
SCRIPT SUPERVISOR
'79 LEGACY, THE

JERRY GOLDSMITH
MUSIC
'79 ALIEN
'79 PLAYERS
'79 STAR TREK-THE MOTION PICTURE
'79 GREAT TRAIN ROBBERY, THE
'81 RAGGEDY MAN
'81 FINAL CONFLICT, THE
'81 INCHON
'81 OUTLAND
'82 CHALLENGE, THE
'82 FIRST BLOOD
'82 POLTERGEIST
'82 NIGHT CROSSING
'83 PSYCHO II
'83 TWILIGHT ZONE, THE MOVIE
'83 UNDER FIRE
'84 LONELY GUY, THE
'84 GREMLINS
'84 RUNAWAY
'84 SUPERGIRL

JOEL GOLDSMITH
MUSIC
'83 MAN WITH TWO BRAINS, THE

PAUL GOLDSMITH
CINEMATOGRAPHER
'82 HOME WORK

ERIC GOLDSTEIN
KEY GRIP
'82 BRAINWAVES

JEFF GOLDSTEIN
ART DIRECTOR
'84 AMERICAN DREAMER

SARAH RACHEL GOLDSTEIN
PUBLICIST
'84 BACHELOR PARTY

WILLIAM GOLDSTEIN
MUSIC
'81 EYE FOR AN EYE, AN
'81 FORCE FIVE
'82 FORCED VENGEANCE
'84 UP THE CREEK

ROBERT GOLDSTON
EXECUTIVE PRODUCER
'79 BELL JAR, THE

JAMES GOLDSTONE
DIRECTOR
'80 WHEN TIME RAN OUT

JOHN GOLDSTONE
PRODUCER
'79 MONTY PYTHON'S LIFE OF BRIAN
'81 SHOCK TREATMENT
'83 MONTY PYTHON'S THE MEANING OF LIFE

ARTHUR GOLDWEIT
CHOREOGRAPHER
'81 STRIPES*

SAMUEL GOLDWYN JR.
PRODUCER
'83 GOLDEN SEAL, THE

JOANNA GOLLINS
LOCATIONS
'82 MISSIONARY, THE

RICHARD GOLOMB
STILLS
'82 CREEPSHOW*

SUSAN GOLOMB
STILLS
'82 CREEPSHOW*

UMIT GOLSOY
MISCELLANEOUS
'83 YOR

CARLOS GOMERI
MAKEUP
'80 EYES OF A STRANGER

AL GOMEZ
SCREENPLAY
'83 JOYSTICKS*

ESPERANZA GOMEZ
HAIR
'82 MISSING*
'83 UNDER FIRE
'84 EVIL THAT MEN DO, THE

MIGUEL ANGEL GOMEZ
PRODUCTION MANAGER
'80 GUYANA: CULT OF THE DAMNED

MIKE GOMEZ
MISCELLANEOUS
'82 BORDER, THE

SERGEI GONCHAROFF
MISCELLANEOUS
'80 BLACK MARBLE, THE

FERNANDO GARCIA GONZALES
MAKEUP
'84 UNDER THE VOLCANO*
HAIR
'84 UNDER THE VOLCANO*

CONRAD GONZALEZ
ASSISTANT EDITOR
'84 LAST STARFIGHTER, THE

FERNANDO GONZALEZ
ART DIRECTOR
'81 CLASH OF THE TITANS*

BRENDA GOOD
HAIR
'84 JOY OF SEX, THE

GLEN GOODCHILD
KEY GRIP
'80 HAPPY BIRTHDAY, GEMINI

FRED GOODICH
CINEMATOGRAPHER
'81 FEAR NO EVIL
MISCELLANEOUS
'81 BUSTIN' LOOSE

COURTNEY GOODIN
SOUND
'79 TOURIST TRAP
'84 FLASHPOINT

BOBBY GOODMAN
MISCELLANEOUS
'81 PENNIES FROM HEAVEN
'82 CANNERY ROW

DAVID GOODMAN
SCREENPLAY
'82 FIGHTING BACK*
'83 MAN WOMAN AND CHILD*

GEORGE GOODMAN
EXEC IN CHARGE PROD
'83 REUBEN, REUBEN

JOEL GOODMAN
EDITOR
'84 FRIDAY THE 13TH PART IV THE FINAL CHAPTER

JUDI GOODMAN
HAIR
'80 TIMES SQUARE
'81 FOUR SEASONS, THE
'83 TOUGH ENOUGH
'84 SPLASH*

LORRAINE GOODMAN
PROD. COORDINATOR
'84 BOSTONIANS, THE

MICHAEL GOODMAN
2ND ASST. DIRECTOR
'82 FIRST TIME, THE

MILES GOODMAN
MUSIC
'82 JINXED*
'83 MAN WHO WASN'T THERE, THE

RICHARD GOODMAN
SOUND
'79 PRIZE FIGHTER, THE
'80 ROADIE
'82 HAMMETT*
'83 OSTERMAN WEEKEND, THE
'84 IMPULSE

RONALD GOODMAN
MISCELLANEOUS
'81 SUPERMAN II
'83 SUPERMAN III

BILL GOODSON
CHOREOGRAPHER
'84 BREAKIN 2 ELECTRIC BOOGALOO

LYZANNE GOODSON
MAKEUP
'81 NESTING, THE

GEOFF GOODWIN
MISCELLANEOUS
'79 FAST COMPANY

HOPE GOODWIN
2ND ASST. DIRECTOR
'80 IDOLMAKER, THE
'81 BUSTIN' LOOSE*
'82 ROCKY III
'82 SIX PACK*
'83 GET CRAZY*
'84 CHOOSE ME
'84 KARATE KID, THE
'84 UNFAITHFULLY YOURS

R.W. GOODWIN
PRODUCER
'80 INSIDE MOVES*

RICHARD GOODWIN
PRODUCER
'80 MIRROR CRACK'D, THE*
'82 EVIL UNDER THE SUN*
'84 PASSAGE TO INDIA, A*

ROBIN GOODWIN
CINEMATOGRAPHER
'82 SWAMP THING

RON GOODWIN
MUSIC
'79 UNIDENTIFIED FLYING ODDBALL

KEN GORDAN
SCRIPT SUPERVISOR
'82 FIRST TIME, THE

WILLIAM GORDEAN
EDITOR
'80 SMOKEY AND THE BANDIT II*
'81 SHARKEY'S MACHINE
'81 CANNONBALL RUN, THE*
'83 STROKER ACE*
'84 CANNONBALL RUN II*

ALIXE GORDIN

CASTING
'79 SEDUCTION OF JOE TYNAN, THE
'80 LITTLE DARLINGS*
'80 NIGHT OF THE JUGGLER
'81 FAN, THE
'82 SOPHIE'S CHOICE
'83 SCARFACE

BARRY MARK GORDON

EDITOR
'83 SOMETHING WICKED THIS WAY COMES*
ASSISTANT EDITOR
'80 WHEN TIME RAN OUT*
'81 VICTORY*

BEATRICE GORDON

EXECUTIVE PRODUCER
'79 PENITENTIARY*

CELINE GORDON

PROD. COORDINATOR
'82 PENITENTIARY II
LOCATIONS
'79 PENITENTIARY*

DAN GORDON

SCREENPLAY
'84 TANK

EDWIN GORDON

SCREENPLAY
'82 CHOSEN, THE

ELKE GORDON

MAKEUP
'79 BOARDWALK

JOSEPH GORDON

LOCATIONS
'79 PENITENTIARY*

JUDY GORDON

ASSOCIATE PRODUCER
'84 LONELY GUY, THE

KEITH GORDON

SOUND
'82 COME BACK TO THE 5 & 10, JIMMY DEAN, JIMMY DEAN*

LAWRENCE GORDON

PRODUCER
'79 WARRIORS, THE
'80 XANADU
'81 PATERNITY*
'82 48 HOURS*
'82 JEKYLL AND HYDE TOGETHER AGAIN
'84 STREETS OF FIRE*

LYNETTE GORDON

PROD. SECRETARY
'81 STRANGE BEHAVIOR

MELINDA SUE GORDON

STILLS
'83 TESTAMENT

PATRICK GORDON

UNIT MANAGER
'83 ENIGMA

ROBERT GORDON

EDITOR
'80 BLUE LAGOON
'82 SUMMER LOVERS
'84 GRANDVIEW, U.S.A.

ROBERT GORDON

MISCELLANEOUS
'83 MAUSOLEUM

ROBERT GORDON SR.

EXECUTIVE PRODUCER
'79 PENITENTIARY*

SAM GORDON

PROPS
'79 AVALANCHE EXPRESS
'79 1941
'79 WINTER KILLS
'80 CLOSE ENCOUNTERS OF THE THIRD KIND SPECIAL EDITION
'80 COMPETITION, THE
'81 STRIPES
'82 ANNIE
'82 TOY, THE
'84 KARATE KID, THE

SHEP GORDON

EXECUTIVE PRODUCER
'84 CHOOSE ME*

STEVE GORDON

DIRECTOR
'81 ARTHUR
SCREENPLAY
'81 ARTHUR

SUZANNE GORDON

PUBLICIST
'79 STAR TREK- THE MOTION PICTURE*

CHRISTOPHER GORE

SCREENPLAY
'80 FAME

MICHAEL GORE

MUSIC
'80 FAME
'83 TERMS OF ENDEARMENT

KATHLEEN GORE-MISKO

COSTUME SUPERVISOR
'84 SONGWRITER*

GREG GORMAN

MISCELLANEOUS
'80 FADE TO BLACK

MICHAEL GORMAN

PROPS
'81 KNIGHTRIDERS

CATHERINE GORNE

COSTUMES
'84 CHEECH AND CHONG'S THE CORSICAN BROTHERS

ALLAN GORNICK JR.

MISCELLANEOUS
'82 PERSONAL BEST

MICHAEL GORNICK

CINEMATOGRAPHER
'79 DAWN OF THE DEAD
'81 KNIGHTRIDERS
'82 CREEPSHOW

MARJOE GORTNER

PRODUCER
'79 WHEN YOU COMIN' BACK, RED RYDER?

ADRIAN GORTON

ART DIRECTOR
'80 BALTIMORE BULLET, THE
'81 ZORRO, THE GAY BLADE

ASSHETON GORTON

PRODUCTION DESIGNER
'81 FRENCH LIEUTENANT'S WOMAN, THE

JOE GOSHAY

MISCELLANEOUS
'81 HONKY TONK FREEWAY

RAJA GOSNELL

EDITOR
'84 LONELY GUY, THE*
ASSISTANT EDITOR
'79 QUINTET*
'79 PERFECT COUPLE, A*
'79 REMEMBER MY NAME*
'80 HEALTH*
'82 AUTHOR, AUTHOR
'82 MAKING LOVE
'83 YELLOWBEARD

DANETTE GOSS

LOCATIONS
'83 TENDER MERCIES

JOE GOSS

SPECIAL EFFECTS
'79 CONCORDE-AIRPORT '79, THE*
'80 CHEECH AND CHONG'S NEXT MOVIE

KEN GOSS
KEY GRIP
'79 KRAMER VS. KRAMER
'81 ENDLESS LOVE
'81 FORT APACHE, THE BRONX
'82 TEMPEST*
'84 COTTON CLUB, THE

VICTOR GOSS
MISCELLANEOUS
'83 TABLE FOR FIVE

BOB GOSSOM
1ST ASST. DIRECTOR
'80 MIDNIGHT MADNESS

HOWARD GOTTFRIED
PRODUCER
'80 ALTERED STATES
EXECUTIVE PRODUCER
'84 BODY DOUBLE

JOE GOTTFRIED
EXECUTIVE PRODUCER
'84 HARD TO HOLD

CARL GOTTLIEB
DIRECTOR
'81 CAVEMAN
SCREENPLAY
'79 JERK, THE*
'81 CAVEMAN*
'83 DOCTOR DETROIT*
'83 JAWS 3-D*

KIM GOTTLIEB
STILLS
'80 FOG, THE
'81 ESCAPE FROM NEW YORK*
'81 HALLOWEEN II
'83 CHRISTINE

MORTON GOTTLIEB
PRODUCER
'83 ROMANTIC COMEDY*

PAUL GOTTLIEB
SCREENPLAY
'79 IN PRAISE OF OLDER WOMEN

JANUSZ GOTTWALD
COSTUMES
'80 UNION CITY*

LAURA GOTTWALD
COSTUMES
'80 UNION CITY*

HEYWOOD GOULD
SCREENPLAY
'81 FORT APACHE, THE BRONX

LEWIS GOULD
1ST ASST. DIRECTOR
'84 C.H.U.D.
2ND ASST. DIRECTOR
'80 FIRST DEADLY SIN
'81 BLOW OUT
'83 KING OF COMEDY, THE
'83 LOVESICK
LOCATIONS
'80 CAN'T STOP THE MUSIC*

NICHOLAS GOULD
PROPS
'82 FIRST TIME, THE
'82 Q: QUETZALCOATL

CHRISTINE GOULDING
COSTUMES
'80 PRIVATE EYES, THE
'84 MARVIN AND TIGE*

LUDMILLA GOULIAN
PRODUCTION MANAGER
'79 FEDORA*
'79 LITTLE ROMANCE, A

ROMAIN GOUPIL
2ND ASST. DIRECTOR
'80 TESS*

ANNE GOURSAND
EDITOR
'81 NIGHT THE LIGHTS WENT OUT IN GEORGIA, THE
'82 ONE FROM THE HEART*
'83 OUTSIDERS, THE
'84 AMERICAN DREAMER

JEFF GOURSON
EDITOR
'80 SOMEWHERE IN TIME
'81 INCREDIBLE SHRINKING WOMAN, THE*
'82 TRON
'84 MIKE'S MURDER*

RAMON GOW
HAIR
'80 RAISE THE TITANIC*
'80 ROUGH CUT*
'81 ON GOLDEN POND
'81 DOGS OF WAR, THE
'82 EVIL UNDER THE SUN
'82 MISSIONARY, THE
'83 PIRATES OF PENZANCE, THE

WONG GOW
PROPS
'79 GAME OF DEATH

KIP GOWANS
1ST ASST. DIRECTOR
'79 SHOUT, THE
'80 HUMAN FACTOR, THE

MIKE GOWANS
1ST ASST. DIRECTOR
'79 GAME OF DEATH

LIZ'BETH GOWER
PROD. COORDINATOR
'83 TIMERIDER

PATRICK GOWERS
MUSIC
'79 STEVIE

ALAN GRABELSKY
LOCATIONS
'83 GORKY PARK

HOWARD GRACE
1ST ASST. DIRECTOR
'81 AMY

SUZANNE GRACE
COSTUMES
'79 OLD BOYFRIENDS*
'80 TRIBUTE
'82 AMATEUR, THE

ED GRACZYK
SCREENPLAY
'82 COME BACK TO THE 5 & 10, JIMMY DEAN, JIMMY DEAN

HELMUT GRAEF
SPECIAL EFFECTS
'79 FIFTH MUSKETEER, THE*

GORDON GRAFF
SPECIAL EFFECTS
'82 LOVE AND MONEY

STEPHEN GRAFF
ART DIRECTOR
'82 BRAINWAVES

BATIA GRAFKA
PROPS
'84 OVER THE BROOKLYN BRIDGE*

ANGELO GRAHAM
ART DIRECTOR
'79 APOCALYPSE NOW
'82 HAMMETT*
'82 ONE FROM THE HEART
'82 ESCAPE ARTIST, THE*
PRODUCTION DESIGNER
'83 WAR GAMES
'84 BEVERLY HILLS COP
'84 NATURAL, THE*

CARL GRAHAM
ASSOCIATE EDITOR
'84 NIGHT OF THE COMET

DAVID GRAHAM
CASTING
'81 FIRST MONDAY IN OCTOBER
'84 PURPLE RAIN*

JANICE LEE GRAHAM
SCREENPLAY
'84 UNTIL SEPTEMBER

JERRY GRAHAM
PROPS
'79 ROSE, THE
'79 GOLDENGIRL
'80 SMOKEY AND THE BANDIT II
'81 CANNONBALL RUN, THE
'81 PURSUIT OF D.B. COOPER, THE

KATHLEEN GRAHAM
MAKEUP
'83 STRANGE BREW*

RITA GRAHAM
CHOREOGRAPHER
'82 NATIONAL LAMPOON'S CLASS REUNION

RONNY GRAHAM
SCREENPLAY
'83 TO BE OR NOT TO BE*
'84 FINDERS KEEPERS*

SARAH GRAHAME
SCRIPT SUPERVISOR
'80 PROM NIGHT
'81 LAST CHASE, THE
'81 TICKET TO HEAVEN
'83 SPACEHUNTER: ADVENTURES IN THE FORBIDDEN ZONE

MICHAEL GRAIS
SCREENPLAY
'81 DEATH HUNT*
'82 POLTERGEIST*

DICK GRAMAGLIA
SOUND
'79 BELL JAR, THE

JOSE RODRIGUEZ GRANADA
ART DIRECTOR
'81 CAVEMAN
'84 UNDER THE VOLCANO

DON GRANBERY
1ST ASST. DIRECTOR
'81 LAST CHASE, THE
'82 BY DESIGN
'82 MOTHER LODE

ROBERT GRAND
ASSOCIATE PRODUCER
'81 BODY HEAT
'83 NATIONAL LAMPOON'S VACATION
PRODUCTION MANAGER
'80 HEAVEN'S GATE*
'81 BODY HEAT
UNIT PROD. MANAGER
'83 NATIONAL LAMPOON'S VACATION

JERRY GRANDEY
1ST ASST. DIRECTOR
'79 FISH THAT SAVED PITTSBURGH, THE
'79 ICE CASTLES
'80 RAGING BULL*
'82 I'M DANCING AS FAST AS I CAN
'82 PERSONAL BEST*
'82 SECOND THOUGHTS
'83 RISKY BUSINESS
'83 ALL THE RIGHT MOVES
'83 CUJO
'84 BEST DEFENSE*

HORST GRANDT
PROPS
'79 ICE CASTLES
'79 MUPPET MOVIE, THE
'80 CHANGE OF SEASONS, A
'80 GONG SHOW MOVIE, THE
'81 ...ALL THE MARBLES
'82 AIRPLANE II: THE SEQUEL
'84 BODY DOUBLE
'84 ICEMAN*

MADELINE GRANETO
COSTUMES
'81 HEARTBEEPS*

DENYS GRANIER-DEFERRE
1ST ASST. DIRECTOR
'79 SAINT JACK
2ND ASST. DIRECTOR
'81 CONDORMAN*

BUDD GRANOFF
PRODUCER
'80 GONG SHOW MOVIE, THE

BARRA GRANT
SCREENPLAY
'84 MISUNDERSTOOD

LEE GRANT
DIRECTOR
'80 TELL ME A RIDDLE

PETER GRANT
PROPS
'84 GIVE MY REGARDS TO BROAD STREET*

ROBIN GRANTHAM
MAKEUP
'79 ARABIAN ADVENTURE*
'80 RAISE THE TITANIC*
'80 ROUGH CUT*
'81 AMERICAN WEREWOLF IN LONDON, AN*
'83 NEVER SAY NEVER AGAIN*
MISCELLANEOUS
'79 LEGACY, THE

DORIS GRAU
SCRIPT SUPERVISOR
'79 CHAMP, THE
'79 FRISCO KID, THE
'80 HUNTER, THE
'81 CAVEMAN
'81 PURSUIT OF D.B. COOPER, THE

FEDERICO GRAU
STILLS
'79 JAGUAR LIVES

ROBERT GRAVENOR
SOUND
'79 RICH KIDS
'79 BOULEVARD NIGHTS*
'79 QUINTET
'79 PERFECT COUPLE, A*
'79 REMEMBER MY NAME*
'80 HEALTH*
'80 POPEYE
'80 XANADU
'82 BARBAROSA
'83 ALL THE RIGHT MOVES
'83 HEART LIKE A WHEEL
'84 PHILADELPHIA EXPERIMENT, THE

GARY GRAVER
CINEMATOGRAPHER
'81 SMOKEY BITES THE DUST
'83 MORTUARY
2ND UNIT DIRECTOR
'82 HOME WORK
MISCELLANEOUS
'82 EATING RAOUL
'83 SWEET SIXTEEN

CAPT. WILLIAM GRAVES
MISCELLANEOUS
'80 RAISE THE TITANIC
'80 FINAL COUNTDOWN, THE
'82 OFFICER AND A GENTLEMAN, AN

ED GRAVES
MISCELLANEOUS
'79 AVALANCHE EXPRESS

RICHARD GRAVES
2ND ASST. DIRECTOR
'79 ESCAPE FROM ALCATRAZ*
'80 BRONCO BILLY*
'80 HEAVEN'S GATE*
'81 THIEF
'82 BEASTMASTER, THE
'83 SMOKEY AND THE BANDIT III
'83 TESTAMENT*
'83 TOUGH ENOUGH
'84 BEVERLY HILLS COP

BILL GRAY
UNIT PROD. MANAGER
'83 PSYCHO II

BOB GRAY
PRODUCTION MANAGER
'79 MAN, A WOMAN AND A BANK, A
LOCATIONS
'79 LOST AND FOUND*

FEDERICO GOMEZ GRAY
STILLS
'79 CUBA

JAMES GRAY
KEY GRIP
'80 IT'S MY TURN*

KAY GRAY
UNIT PUBLICIST
'81 SCANNERS

MIKE GRAY
SCREENPLAY
'79 CHINA SYNDROME, THE*

NICK GRAY
UNIT MANAGER
'83 RUNNING BRAVE

STEPHEN GRAY
CINEMATOGRAPHER
'83 SAVANNAH SMILES

TOM GRAY
PUBLICIST
'80 HEALTH
'83 RIGHT STUFF, THE
UNIT PUBLICIST
'79 HURRICANE
'79 VILLAIN, THE
'84 BIRDY
'84 RHINESTONE
'84 UNDER THE VOLCANO

WARREN GRAY
2ND ASST. DIRECTOR
'84 SOLDIER'S STORY, A

WILLIAM GRAY
SCREENPLAY
'80 CHANGELING, THE*
'80 PROM NIGHT
'81 EYE FOR AN EYE, AN*
'84 PHILADELPHIA EXPERIMENT,THE*

RICHARD GRAYDON
STUNT COORDINATOR
'79 LOVE AND BULLETS*
MISCELLANEOUS
'84 CHAMPIONS

JOHN GRAYSMARK
ART DIRECTOR
'79 ESCAPE TO ATHENA
'80 FLASH GORDON
'82 FIREFOX*
PRODUCTION DESIGNER
'81 RAGTIME
'83 LORDS OF DISCIPLINE, THE
'84 BOUNTY, THE

BRIAN GRAZER
PRODUCER
'82 NIGHT SHIFT
'84 SPLASH

STEVE GRAZIANI
ART DIRECTOR
'81 GALAXY OF TERROR*

WENDY GREAN
CO-PRODUCER
'82 PARADISE
UNIT MANAGER
'79 IN PRAISE OF OLDER WOMEN
LOCATIONS
'79 IN PRAISE OF OLDER WOMEN

WILLIAM GREAVES
EXECUTIVE PRODUCER
'81 BUSTIN' LOOSE

ANTHONY GRECO
PROPS
'81 LAST CHASE, THE

EDWARD GRECO
STUNT COORDINATOR
'83 HERCULES

MARIA GRECO
CASTING
'84 ALPHABET CITY*

ALAN GREEDY
SCRIPT SUPERVISOR
'79 RAVAGERS
'79 BEYOND THE POSEIDON ADVENTURE
'80 BLACK MARBLE, THE
'80 IDOLMAKER, THE
'80 WHEN TIME RAN OUT
'81 MODERN PROBLEMS
'82 SIX PACK
'83 INDEPENDENCE DAY
'83 NATIONAL LAMPOON'S VACATION

REBECCA GREELEY
PROD. SECRETARY
'84 DREAMSCAPE

ALAN GREEN
2ND ASST. DIRECTOR
'79 APPLE DUMPLING GANG RIDES AGAIN, THE

ALEX GREEN
STUNT COORDINATOR
'81 DEATH HUNT

BOB GREEN
STILLS
'79 ROCKY II*

BRUCE GREEN
ASSISTANT EDITOR
'81 RAIDERS OF THE LOST ARK*
'81 KING OF THE MOUNTAIN*
'83 TABLE FOR FIVE
'84 INDIANA JONES AND THE TEMPLE OF DOOM*

CAROL GREEN
2ND ASST. DIRECTOR
'83 KISS ME GOODBYE
'84 CRACKERS*
'84 GREMLINS
'84 JOHNNY DANGEROUSLY*

CAROL GREEN
PUBLICIST
'84 ICE PIRATES, THE
UNIT PUBLICIST
'82 GREASE 2

CLIFF GREEN
SCREENPLAY
'79 PICNIC AT HANGING ROCK

DOUGLAS GREEN
EXECUTIVE PRODUCER
'81 HEARTBEEPS
CO-PRODUCER
'81 GHOST STORY

DR. RICHARD GREEN
MISCELLANEOUS
'82 STAR TREK II THE WRATH OF KHAN
'84 STAR TREK III: THE SEARCH FOR SPOCK

FRANK GREEN
UNIT MANAGER
'80 FIENDISH PLOT OF DR. FU MANCHU, THE*

GERALD GREEN
PRODUCER
'79 SUNBURN*
'81 HIGH RISK*

GERALD GREEN
MISCELLANEOUS
'84 DUNE

HILTON GREEN
PRODUCER
'83 PSYCHO II
'84 SIXTEEN CANDLES

HUGH GREEN
HAIR
'83 BETRAYAL*

JACK GREEN
MISCELLANEOUS
'84 CITY HEAT

LEONARD GREEN
ASSISTANT EDITOR
'80 FAME*
'82 SHOOT THE MOON*
'82 PINK FLOYD: THE WALL*
'84 BIRDY*

MARGUERITE GREEN
PROD. COORDINATOR
'84 SUPERGIRL

MARY LOU GREEN
HAIR
'81 SUBWAY RIDERS

MICHAEL GREEN
2ND ASST. DIRECTOR
'79 YANKS
'81 HONKY TONK FREEWAY*
'81 REDS*
'82 FRANCES
'83 CUJO

MICHAEL GREEN
MISCELLANEOUS
'83 TOUGH ENOUGH

PATRICIA GREEN
MAKEUP
'84 MRS. SOFFEL

PAUL GREEN
EDITOR
'82 MISSIONARY, THE

STEVE GREEN
SCREENPLAY
'84 HARDBODIES*

WILLARD GREEN
MISCELLANEOUS
'79 PHANTASM

PETER GREENAWAY
DIRECTOR
'83 DRAUGHTSMAN CONTRACT, THE
SCREENPLAY
'83 DRAUGHTSMAN CONTRACT, THE

ADAM GREENBERG
CINEMATOGRAPHER
'80 BIG RED ONE, THE
'82 LAST AMERICAN VIRGIN, THE
'82 PARADISE
'82 SAFARI 3000
'83 10 TO MIDNIGHT
'84 OVER THE BROOKLYN BRIDGE
'84 TERMINATOR, THE

GERALD GREENBERG
EDITOR
'79 APOCALYPSE NOW*
'79 KRAMER VS. KRAMER
'80 DRESSED TO KILL
'80 HEAVEN'S GATE*
'82 STILL OF THE NIGHT
'83 SCARFACE*
'84 BODY DOUBLE*

HAROLD GREENBERG
PRODUCER
'80 TERROR TRAIN
'80 DEATH SHIP*
EXECUTIVE PRODUCER
'79 IN PRAISE OF OLDER WOMEN*
'82 PORKY'S*
'83 PORKY'S II THE NEXT DAY*

JEFF GREENBERG
CASTING
'84 ANGEL*

MARC GREENBERG
PRODUCTION MANAGER
'83 CURSE OF THE PINK PANTHER*
UNIT MANAGER
'81 FAN, THE
LOCATIONS
'79 LAST EMBRACE*

RICHARD GREENBERG
MISCELLANEOUS
'80 RESURRECTION

ROBERT GREENBERG
MISCELLANEOUS
'80 RESURRECTION

DAN GREENBURG
SCREENPLAY
'81 PRIVATE LESSONS
'83 PRIVATE SCHOOL*

STEPHEN GREENBURG
MISCELLANEOUS
'82 PORKY'S

CHRISTOPHER GREENBURY
EDITOR
'79 MUPPET MOVIE, THE
'80 WHERE THE BUFFALO ROAM
'82 SOME KIND OF HERO
'82 LIAR'S MOON
'83 SMOKEY AND THE BANDIT III*
'83 DOCTOR DETROIT

DANFORD GREENE
EDITOR
'79 VOICES
'82 PARTNERS
'83 BLUE SKIES AGAIN
MISCELLANEOUS
'79 ROCKY II
'80 HOLLYWOOD KNIGHTS, THE

DAVID GREENE
PRODUCER
'81 HARD COUNTRY*
DIRECTOR
'81 HARD COUNTRY

JUSTIS GREENE
PRODUCTION MANAGER
'84 ICEMAN*

MELADY GREENE
SCRIPT SUPERVISOR
'82 THAT CHAMPIONSHIP SEASON

MERRIL GREENE
COSTUMES
'82 ANDROID*

PAT GREENE
COSTUMES
'83 AMERICANA

RICHARD GREENE
MISCELLANEOUS
'81 CATTLE ANNIE AND LITTLE BRITCHES

ROGER GREENE
ASSISTANT EDITOR
'80 CHEECH AND CHONG'S NEXT MOVIE*
'82 THINGS ARE TOUGH ALL OVER*
'83 MAN WITH TWO BRAINS, THE
'84 ALL OF ME

ROMAINE GREENE
HAIR
'79 ALL THAT JAZZ
'79 MANHATTAN
'80 CAN'T STOP THE MUSIC*
'80 FINAL COUNTDOWN, THE
'81 ARTHUR
'81 NIGHTHAWKS
'82 SOUP FOR ONE
'82 MIDSUMMER NIGHT'S SEX COMEDY, A
'83 LOVESICK
'83 ZELIG
'84 BROADWAY DANNY ROSE

WENDY GREENE
EDITOR
'83 LOVE LETTERS

JOSH GREENFIELD
SCREENPLAY
'80 OH GOD! BOOK II*

RAYMOND GREENFIELD
1ST ASST. DIRECTOR
'82 SHOOT THE MOON
'83 BABY IT'S YOU
2ND ASST. DIRECTOR
'80 FAME

ROBERT GREENHUT
PRODUCER
'80 STARDUST MEMORIES
'81 ARTHUR
'82 MIDSUMMER NIGHT'S SEX COMEDY, A
'83 ZELIG
'84 BROADWAY DANNY ROSE
EXECUTIVE PRODUCER
'79 MANHATTAN
'83 KING OF COMEDY, THE
ASSOCIATE PRODUCER
'79 HAIR
UNIT MANAGER
'79 HAIR
1ST ASST. DIRECTOR
'81 ARTHUR

MICHAEL GREENLEAF
ASSISTANT EDITOR
'80 FLASH GORDON*

ADAM GREENMAN
LOCATIONS
'80 DEFIANCE*
'80 INSIDE MOVES

ADOR GREENMAN
LOCATIONS
'82 EATING RAOUL*

ALVIN GREENMAN
SCRIPT SUPERVISOR
'79 ICE CASTLES
'80 GONG SHOW MOVIE, THE
'80 OCTAGON, THE*
'81 CHARLIE CHAN AND THE CURSE OF THE DRAGON QUEEN
'81 DEAD AND BURIED
'84 KARATE KID, THE

HAROLD GREENSILL
MISCELLANEOUS
'79 MY BRILLIANT CAREER

DR. MORTON GREENSPOON
MISCELLANEOUS
'83 MAUSOLEUM

FRANCIE GREENSPOON
PROD. SECRETARY
'80 TRIBUTE

ROBERT GREENWALD
DIRECTOR
'80 XANADU

STEPHEN GREENWALD
PRODUCER
'82 AMITYVILLE II: THE POSSESSION*

DAVID GREENWALT
SCREENPLAY
'83 CLASS*
'84 AMERICAN DREAMER*
ASSOCIATE PRODUCER
'83 CLASS*

CHRISTOPHER GREENWOOD
EDITOR
'84 WOMAN IN RED, THE

JANE GREENWOOD
COSTUMES
'79 LAST EMBRACE
'80 CAN'T STOP THE MUSIC*
'81 ARTHUR
'81 FOUR SEASONS, THE

SYD GREENWOOD
PROPS
'79 NIGHTWING
'79 IN-LAWS, THE
'80 ALTERED STATES
'82 MAKING LOVE
'82 NATIONAL LAMPOON'S CLASS REUNION
'83 ROMANTIC COMEDY
'84 CLOAK AND DAGGER
'84 LONELY GUY, THE
'84 TEACHERS

DAN GREER
EDITOR
'79 MOUNTAIN FAMILY ROBINSON*

DONN GREER
ART DIRECTOR
'83 JOYSTICKS

ANDRE GREGORY
SCREENPLAY
'81 MY DINNER WITH ANDRE*

GILLIAN GREGORY
CHOREOGRAPHER
'81 SHOCK TREATMENT
'81 REDS*
'82 PINK FLOYD: THE WALL
'83 PRIVATES ON PARADE
'84 TOP SECRET!

GORDON GREGORY
ASSOCIATE PRODUCER
'83 METALSTORM: THE DESTRUCTION OF JARED-SYN

ROBIN GREGORY
SOUND
'79 DRACULA
'79 HANOVER STREET
'80 ELEPHANT MAN, THE
'81 CLASH OF THE TITANS
'81 OUTLAND
'81 PRIEST OF LOVE
'83 KEEP, THE
'84 BEST DEFENSE*

PAUL GREIMANN
PRODUCTION DESIGNER
'84 FLASHPOINT

ALAN GREISMAN
PRODUCER
'80 HEARTBEAT*
'81 MODERN PROBLEMS*
'84 WINDY CITY

ORA GREN
HAIR
'81 HEARTBEEPS

SERGE GRENIER
KEY GRIP
'80 OH! HEAVENLY DOG
'84 HOTEL NEW HAMPSHIRE, THE

JARED EDD GRENN
COSTUMES
'80 ROADIE*

GEORGE GRENVILLE
ASSOCIATE PRODUCER
'83 WRONG IS RIGHT
EDITOR
'80 BIG BRAWL, THE
'80 TOM HORN
'83 WRONG IS RIGHT
'84 PURPLE HEARTS*

LARRY GRENVILLE
ASSISTANT EDITOR
'80 BIG BRAWL, THE
'80 TOM HORN
'83 WRONG IS RIGHT
'84 PURPLE HEARTS*

GLORIA GRESHAM
COSTUMES
'80 URBAN COWBOY
'81 ZORRO, THE GAY BLADE
'82 AUTHOR, AUTHOR
'82 DINER
'82 ESCAPE ARTIST, THE
'83 FOOTLOOSE
'83 WITHOUT A TRACE
'84 BODY DOUBLE
'84 NATURAL, THE*

CLAUDE GRESSET
UNIT MANAGER
'84 LASSITER

BRAD GREY
MISCELLANEOUS
'81 BURNING, THE

ROBIN GREY
UNIT MANAGER
'81 BURNING, THE
'83 ANGELO, MY LOVE
PROD. COORDINATOR
'84 OVER THE BROOKLYN BRIDGE*

GREYFOX

EDITOR
'80 LOVING COUPLES*

BERNARD GRIBBLE

EDITOR
'80 MOTEL HELL
'84 TOP SECRET!

HARRY GRIER

LOCATIONS
'84 SPLASH*

PETER GRIES

1ST ASST. DIRECTOR
'80 LONG RIDERS, THE
'81 RAGGEDY MAN
2ND ASST. DIRECTOR
'79 WARRIORS, THE*
'80 DEFIANCE*

NEIL GRIEVE

ASSISTANT EDITOR
'83 CHRISTMAS STORY, A*

ROBERT GRIEVE

MISCELLANEOUS
'81 WOLFEN

GARY GRIFFEN

EDITOR
'81 BLOOD BEACH

BETTY ABBOTT GRIFFIN

SCRIPT SUPERVISOR
'79 CONCORDE-AIRPORT '79, THE
'80 LITTLE MISS MARKER
'80 XANADU
'81 ALL NIGHT LONG
'81 BUSTIN' LOOSE*
'82 JEKYLL AND HYDE TOGETHER AGAIN
'82 ZOOT SUIT
'82 GREASE 2
'83 STAR 80*
'83 DEAL OF THE CENTURY
'83 MAN WHO LOVED WOMEN, THE
'83 PSYCHO II
'84 CLOAK AND DAGGER
'84 MICKI AND MAUDE

CHRIS GRIFFIN

2ND ASST. DIRECTOR
'84 FLAMINGO KID, THE*
'84 SPLASH*

CHRIS GRIFFIN

PRODUCER
'84 KIPPERBANG

CLAIR GRIFFIN

COSTUMES
'81 MAN WHO SAW TOMORROW, THE*

FRANK GRIFFIN

MAKEUP
'80 URBAN COWBOY*
'81 PENNIES FROM HEAVEN
'81 THIEF
'82 FAST TIMES AT RIDGEMONT HIGH
'82 I OUGHT TO BE IN PICTURES*
'83 DEAL OF THE CENTURY
'83 NATIONAL LAMPOON'S VACATION
'83 TWO OF A KIND*
'84 PROTOCOL*
'84 REVENGE OF THE NERDS

FRANK GRIFFIN JR.

MAKEUP
'79 GOLDENGIRL
'80 HIDE IN PLAIN SIGHT

SHAY GRIFFIN

CASTING
'84 MUTANT*

CARY GRIFFITH

KEY GRIP
'79 C.H.O.M.P.S.
'79 HARDCORE
'79 MAIN EVENT, THE
'80 MOTEL HELL
'81 CUTTER'S WAY
'82 BEST FRIENDS
'82 BLADERUNNER
'82 DEAD MEN DON'T WEAR PLAID
'82 PERSONAL BEST
'83 MAN WITH TWO BRAINS, THE
'84 IMPULSE

CHARLES GRIFFITH

DIRECTOR
'81 SMOKEY BITES THE DUST

DOW GRIFFITH

LOCATIONS
'79 ...AND JUSTICE FOR ALL
'79 JERK, THE
'82 BEST FRIENDS*

EUGENE GRIFFITH

KEY GRIP
'79 BUDDY HOLLY STORY, THE
'79 GOLDENGIRL
'82 STAR TREK II THE WRATH OF KHAN

JILL GRIFFITH

LOCATIONS
'81 SMOKEY BITES THE DUST

WILLIAM GRIFFITH

MISCELLANEOUS
'80 NIJINSKY

MARK GRIFFITHS

DIRECTOR
'84 HARDBODIES
SCREENPLAY
'84 HARDBODIES*

RACHEL GRIFFITHS

SCRIPT SUPERVISOR
'83 TRENCHCOAT

TREVOR GRIFFITHS

SCREENPLAY
'81 REDS*

DEWEY GRIGG

SPECIAL EFFECTS
'82 JEKYLL AND HYDE TOGETHER AGAIN

GENE GRIGG

SPECIAL EFFECTS
'79 LOVE AND BULLETS*
'80 CHANGELING, THE
'80 MOUNTAIN MEN, THE
'80 OCTAGON, THE
'81 CHARLIE CHAN AND THE CURSE OF THE DRAGON QUEEN*
'81 PURSUIT OF D.B. COOPER, THE*
'82 AMATEUR, THE*
SP. EFFECTS SUPERV.
'83 HIGH ROAD TO CHINA
MISCELLANEOUS
'84 POLICE ACADEMY

MARIANNE GRIGG

MAKEUP
'79 EUROPEANS, THE*

WILLIAM GRIGG

SOUND
'83 GOIN' ALL THE WAY*

HERMAN GRIGSBY

PRODUCTION MANAGER
'81 GRADUATION DAY
'83 MORTUARY
1ST ASST. DIRECTOR
'83 MORTUARY

DAMION GRILL

HAIR
'80 IT'S MY TURN*

MICHAEL GRILLO

UNIT PROD. MANAGER
'84 THIEF OF HEARTS
1ST ASST. DIRECTOR
'79 BREAKING AWAY
'80 HEAVEN'S GATE*
'80 INSIDE MOVES
'81 BODY HEAT
'82 CAT PEOPLE
'82 YOUNG DOCTORS IN LOVE
'83 BIG CHILL, THE
'83 MAN WITH TWO BRAINS, THE
'84 IRRECONCILABLE DIFFERENCES
'84 THIEF OF HEARTS
'84 WOMAN IN RED, THE
2ND ASST. DIRECTOR
'78 DEER HUNTER, THE
2ND UNIT DIRECTOR
'80 INSIDE MOVES
MISCELLANEOUS
'84 WOMAN IN RED, THE

ADA GRIMALDI
ASSISTANT EDITOR
'83 PIRANHA II: THE SPAWNING

ROBERT GRIMALDI
HAIR
'79 RICH KIDS
'80 CRUISING
'80 DRESSED TO KILL*
'80 WINDOWS
'81 TATTOO*
'82 FIRST TIME, THE*
'82 VERDICT, THE
'82 WORLD ACCORDING TO GARP, THE
'83 DANIEL
'84 FLAMINGO KID, THE*
'84 GARBO TALKS

COLIN GRIMES
ART DIRECTOR
'79 LOVE AND BULLETS
'83 DRESSER, THE
'83 KRULL*

FRANK GRIMES
MISCELLANEOUS
'83 BRITANNIA HOSPITAL

STEPHEN GRIMES
PRODUCTION DESIGNER
'79 ELECTRIC HORSEMAN, THE
'80 URBAN COWBOY
'81 ON GOLDEN POND
'81 TRUE CONFESSIONS
'83 DRESSER, THE
'83 KRULL
'83 NEVER SAY NEVER AGAIN*
2ND UNIT DIRECTOR
'81 ON GOLDEN POND

DAVID GRIMSDALE
ASSISTANT EDITOR
'84 SCANDALOUS*

JOHN GRISSMER
PRODUCER
'79 SCALPEL*
DIRECTOR
'79 SCALPEL
SCREENPLAY
'79 SCALPEL

AL GRISWOLD
SPECIAL EFFECTS
'79 HAIR
'80 GLORIA*
'80 NIGHT OF THE JUGGLER*
'81 FOUR FRIENDS
'82 WORLD ACCORDING TO GARP, THE
'83 AMITYVILLE 3D*
'84 BEAT STREET

ANNA GRIZI
LOCATIONS
'79 LITTLE ROMANCE, A*

DANIEL GRODNICK
SCREENPLAY
'80 WITHOUT WARNING*
CO-PRODUCER
'80 WITHOUT WARNING*

KEES GROENEWEGEN
LOCATIONS
'84 RIDDLE OF THE SANDS*

OTTO GROKENBERGER
EXECUTIVE PRODUCER
'84 STRANGER THAN PARADISE

DAVID GROOVER
ASSISTANT EDITOR
'79 SCALPEL

DAVID GROPMAN
PRODUCTION DESIGNER
'82 COME BACK TO THE 5 & 10, JIMMY DEAN, JIMMY DEAN

ULU GROSBARD
DIRECTOR
'81 TRUE CONFESSIONS
'84 FALLING IN LOVE

ROSSIE GROSE
2ND ASST. DIRECTOR
'79 SILENT PARTNER, THE

BRADLEY GROSS
2ND ASST. DIRECTOR
'81 CHU CHU AND THE PHILLY FLASH

CHARLES GROSS
MUSIC
'79 HEARTLAND
'79 ON THE YARD
'84 COUNTRY

DANIEL GROSS
ASSISTANT EDITOR
'83 ANGEL OF H.E.A.T.

EDGAR GROSS
EXECUTIVE PRODUCER
'81 EXCALIBUR*

JOANNE GROSS
ASSOCIATE PRODUCER
'83 SMITHEREENS
CASTING
'83 SMITHEREENS

LARRY GROSS
SCREENPLAY
'82 48 HOURS*
'84 STREETS OF FIRE*

LARRY GROSS
MISCELLANEOUS
'82 SPLIT IMAGE

LEE GROSS
PUBLICIST
'79 ALL THAT JAZZ*

MICHAEL GROSS
ASSOCIATE PRODUCER
'84 GHOSTBUSTERS*

MICHAEL GROSS
SOUND
'79 PHANTASM

STUART GROSS
1ST ASST. DIRECTOR
'80 FOXES

JACK GROSSBERG
EXECUTIVE PRODUCER
'83 STRANGE BREW
EXEC IN CHARGE PROD
'83 BRAINSTORM
ASSOCIATE PRODUCER
'79 FAST BREAK
'82 STRANGER IS WATCHING, A
UNIT PROD. MANAGER
'79 FAST BREAK
'82 STRANGER IS WATCHING, A
'83 STRANGE BREW
'83 BRAINSTORM*

DAVID GROSSMAN
2ND ASST. DIRECTOR
'81 RICHARD PRYOR: LIVE ON THE SUNSET STRIP*

DOUG GROSSMAN
MISCELLANEOUS
'79 NORTH DALLAS FORTY

KAREN GROSSMAN
MISCELLANEOUS
'82 EATING RAOUL

MARNI GROSSMAN
STILLS
'82 IF YOU COULD SEE WHAT I HEAR*

TED GROSSMAN
STUNT COORDINATOR
'79 LAST EMBRACE*
'80 ISLAND, THE
'83 MR. MOM*

NIKKI ALLYN GROSSO
PROD. COORDINATOR
'84 ROMANCING THE STONE

SONNY GROSSO
MISCELLANEOUS
'80 CRUISING

UTAH GROUND
CHOREOGRAPHER
'84 NOT FOR PUBLICATION

JOHN GROVER

EDITOR
'81 FOR YOUR EYES ONLY
'83 FINAL OPTION, THE
'83 OCTOPUSSY*

PAT GROVER

HAIR
'81 EYE FOR AN EYE, AN
'82 SILENT RAGE
'83 RIGHT STUFF, THE*

RON GROVER

STILLS
'79 ESCAPE FROM ALCATRAZ
'80 SERIAL
'80 IDOLMAKER, THE
'82 FAST TIMES AT RIDGEMONT HIGH

JOHN GROVES

SCREENPLAY
'83 GOLDEN SEAL, THE

PIERRE GROZDANIC

LOCATIONS
'84 JUST THE WAY YOU ARE*

BENJAMIN GRUBERG

PRODUCTION MANAGER
'84 ALPHABET CITY
MISCELLANEOUS
'84 ALPHABET CITY

LAURA LEE GRUBICH

HAIR
'80 HIDE IN PLAIN SIGHT
'80 LOVING COUPLES*

JIM GRUEBEL

KEY GRIP
'83 EDDIE AND THE CRUISERS

TOM GRUENBERG

EXECUTIVE PRODUCER
'81 FRIDAY THE 13TH PART TWO*

CECILIA GRUESSING

CHOREOGRAPHER
'80 AMERICAN SUCCESS COMPANY,THE

TED GRUMBT

SPECIAL EFFECTS
'80 ROUGH CUT
'83 LORDS OF DISCIPLINE, THE

TOM GRUNKE

KEY GRIP
'82 COME BACK TO THE 5 & 10,
JIMMY DEAN, JIMMY DEAN

PIERRE GRUNSTEIN

EXECUTIVE PRODUCER
'80 TESS

DAVE GRUSIN

MUSIC
'79 ...AND JUSTICE FOR ALL
'79 CHAMP, THE
'79 ELECTRIC HORSEMAN, THE
'80 MY BODYGUARD
'81 ABSENCE OF MALICE
'81 ON GOLDEN POND
'82 AUTHOR, AUTHOR
'82 TOOTSIE
'84 FALLING IN LOVE
'84 POPE OF GREENWICH VILLAGE,THE
'84 RACING WITH THE MOON
'84 SCANDALOUS
'84 LITTLE DRUMMER GIRL, THE
MISCELLANEOUS
'81 REDS

LARRY GRUSIN

SCREENPLAY
'84 GARBO TALKS

MICHAEL GRUSKOFF

PRODUCER
'82 MY FAVORITE YEAR
'84 UNTIL SEPTEMBER
EXECUTIVE PRODUCER
'82 QUEST FOR FIRE

DORAIN GRUSMAN

CHOREOGRAPHER
'84 REVENGE OF THE NERDS

CHARLES GUANCI

PROPS
'83 SPRING BREAK
'83 NIGHT IN HEAVEN, A

JOHN GUARE

SCREENPLAY
'81 ATLANTIC CITY

PETER GUBER

PRODUCER
'82 SIX WEEKS*
EXECUTIVE PRODUCER
'81 AMERICAN WEREWOLF
IN LONDON, AN*
'82 MISSING*
'83 D.C. CAB*
'83 FLASHDANCE*

BARBARA GUEDEL

MAKEUP
'81 PURSUIT OF D.B. COOPER, THE*
'83 SCARFACE*
'83 STRANGE INVADERS*
'83 SUDDEN IMPACT
'84 BODY DOUBLE
'84 TIGHTROPE
MISCELLANEOUS
'79 ROLLER BOOGIE

ROBERT GUENETTE

PRODUCER
'81 MAN WHO SAW TOMORROW, THE*
DIRECTOR
'81 MAN WHO SAW TOMORROW, THE
SCREENPLAY
'81 MAN WHO SAW TOMORROW, THE*

ANN GUERIN

PUBLICIST
'79 BELL JAR, THE
'80 GLORIA
'80 LITTLE DARLINGS
'81 FOUR FRIENDS
'81 FOUR SEASONS, THE
'82 STILL OF THE NIGHT
'84 NATURAL, THE
UNIT PUBLICIST
'79 VOICES
'82 TOOTSIE

MAX GUERIN

HAIR
'79 BLOODLINE*
'83 HANNA K

PAUL-ANDRE GUERIN

COSTUMES
'83 OF UNKNOWN ORIGIN

LEO GUERRA

ASSISTANT EDITOR
'80 KIDS ARE ALL RIGHT, THE*

ROBERT GUERRA

ART DIRECTOR
'82 ANNIE

ROSA GUERRERO

MAKEUP
'81 CATTLE ANNIE
AND LITTLE BRITCHES*

CHRISTOPHER GUEST

SCREENPLAY
'84 THIS IS SPINAL TAP*
MUSIC
'84 THIS IS SPINAL TAP*

DON GUEST

PRODUCER
'82 HAMMETT*
'84 PARIS, TEXAS*
ASSOCIATE PRODUCER
'83 OSTERMAN WEEKEND, THE*
PRODUCTION MANAGER
'82 SECOND THOUGHTS
'83 OSTERMAN WEEKEND, THE

MICHAEL GUEST

ASSOCIATE PRODUCER
'82 MOONLIGHTING

WILLIAM GUEST
MISCELLANEOUS
'82 BEASTMASTER, THE

PIERRE GUFFROY
PRODUCTION DESIGNER
'80 TESS
'83 HANNA K

GUIDARINO GUIDI
CASTING
'83 TRENCHCOAT*

DON GUIDICE
ASSISTANT EDITOR
'79 PROMISES IN THE DARK
'82 LOVE CHILD
'84 HARD TO HOLD*

SYDNEY GUILAROFF
MISCELLANEOUS
'81 ...ALL THE MARBLES

MICHEL GUILLERM
2ND ASST. DIRECTOR
'84 JUST THE WAY YOU ARE*

JOHN GUILLERMAN
DIRECTOR
'84 SHEENA

KATE GUINZBURG
PROD. OFFICE COORD.
'83 EASY MONEY
'84 FIRSTBORN
'84 MOSCOW ON THE HUDSON
PROD. COORDINATOR
'84 GHOSTBUSTERS*

GREG GUIRARD
MISCELLANEOUS
'81 SOUTHERN COMFORT

TONY GULLIVER
STILLS
'80 LITTLE DARLINGS

BETTY GUMM
ASSOCIATE PRODUCER
'79 VOICES

JAN GUNDERSON
2ND ASST. DIRECTOR
'81 GRADUATION DAY

ROBERT GUNDLACH
ART DIRECTOR
'80 HERO AT LARGE*
'80 TRIBUTE*
'82 FIGHTING BACK
PRODUCTION DESIGNER
'79 FIREPOWER*
'82 I, THE JURY

GLORIA GUNN
ASSISTANT EDITOR
'79 MORE AMERICAN GRAFFITTI*
'79 TOURIST TRAP*
'82 HOME WORK*

JOHN GUNTER
COSTUMES
'79 STEVIE

RANDY GUNTER
PROPS
'83 10 TO MIDNIGHT

CHAT GUNTHER
SOUND
'84 LOVELESS, THE

LYNDA GURASICH
HAIR
'80 SMALL CIRCLE OF FRIENDS, A*
'80 DIVINE MADNESS*
'80 HOLLYWOOD KNIGHTS, THE
'81 SHARKEY'S MACHINE*
'81 LEGEND OF THE LONE RANGER, THE
'81 PATERNITY
'82 BEST FRIENDS*
'82 BEST LITTLE WHOREHOUSE IN TEXAS, THE*
'82 JINXED
'83 UNCOMMON VALOR*
'83 WAR GAMES
'84 MIKE'S MURDER
'84 NO SMALL AFFAIR

JOSEPH GURESKY
ASSISTANT EDITOR
'79 RAVAGERS
'79 ICE CASTLES*
'80 LITTLE MISS MARKER
'81 FORT APACHE, THE BRONX

DAVID GURFINKEL
CINEMATOGRAPHER
'79 MAGICIAN OF LUBLIN, THE
'81 ENTER THE NINJA
'83 REVENGE OF THE NINJA

PAUL GURIAN
PRODUCER
'81 CUTTER'S WAY

MIGUEL GURZA
MISCELLANEOUS
'84 ROMANCING THE STONE

KJELL GUSTAFFSSON
MISCELLANEOUS
'81 MONTENEGRO

THURE GUSTAFSON
ASSISTANT EDITOR
'79 WHEN YOU COMIN' BACK, RED RYDER?

BETH GUTCHEON
SCREENPLAY
'83 WITHOUT A TRACE

JUNE RACHEL GUTERMAN
LOCATIONS
'81 FOUR FRIENDS

BERT GUTHRIE
MISCELLANEOUS
'84 NOT FOR PUBLICATION

JAMES GUTHRIE
MISCELLANEOUS
'82 PINK FLOYD: THE WALL

LYNN GUTHRIE
ASSOCIATE PRODUCER
'79 AVALANCHE EXPRESS
PRODUCTION MANAGER
'81 S.O.B.
UNIT PROD. MANAGER
'81 BUDDY, BUDDY

GARY GUTIERREZ
MISCELLANEOUS
'83 RIGHT STUFF, THE

JAMES GUTMAN
PRODUCER
'79 SOMETHING SHORT OF PARADISE*

JOSEPH GUTOWSKI
ASSISTANT EDITOR
'84 BOSTONIANS, THE*

JONATHAN GUTTERES
KEY GRIP
'79 MORE AMERICAN GRAFFITTI
'82 SHOOT THE MOON
'83 RIGHT STUFF, THE

MARTIN GUTTERIDGE
SPECIAL EFFECTS
'79 HANOVER STREET
'82 PINK FLOYD: THE WALL*
'83 SUPERMAN III*
SP. EFFECTS SUPERV.
'84 RAZOR'S EDGE, THE

NORMAN GUY
KEY GRIP
'84 ONCE UPON A TIME IN AMERICA*

KATIE GUYMON
MISCELLANEOUS
'81 WHOSE LIFE IS IT ANYWAY?

CLAUDIO GUZMAN
ART DIRECTOR
'80 TOUCHED BY LOVE

PATO GUZMAN

CO-PRODUCER
'82 TEMPEST*
'84 MOSCOW ON THE HUDSON

PRODUCTION DESIGNER
'79 IN-LAWS, THE
'80 HIDE IN PLAIN SIGHT
'80 WILLIE & PHIL
'82 TEMPEST
'84 MOSCOW ON THE HUDSON

JOANNA GUZZETTA

LOCATIONS
'81 KING OF THE MOUNTAIN

ANNE GYORY

SCRIPT SUPERVISOR
'84 AMADEUS*

ANNE GYORY

LOCATIONS
'82 MIDSUMMER NIGHT'S SEX COMEDY, A*

H

CRAIG HAAGENSEN
MISCELLANEOUS
'83 I AM THE CHEESE

ROBERT HAAGENSEN
MISCELLANEOUS
'83 BRAINSTORM

CHARLES HAAS
SCREENPLAY
'79 OVER THE EDGE*
'82 TEX*

LEE HAAS
UNIT PROD. MANAGER
'83 STAYING ALIVE*

WENDI HAAS
PROD. OFFICE COORD.
'83 JAWS 3-D
PROD. COORDINATOR
'82 I'M DANCING AS FAST AS I CAN

TONY HABEEB
PUBLICIST
'79 BEYOND THE POSEIDON ADVENTURE
'80 WHEN TIME RAN OUT

DAVID HABER
ART DIRECTOR
'81 LEGEND OF THE LONE RANGER, THE
'81 ONLY WHEN I LAUGH
'83 MAX DUGAN RETURNS
'84 ICE PIRATES, THE*
PRODUCTION DESIGNER
'81 BEAST WITHIN, THE

SHELDON HABER
ART DIRECTOR
'80 RAGING BULL*

ABE HABERMAN
MAKEUP
'81 ALL NIGHT LONG*

SHAMA HABIBULLAH
PRODUCTION MANAGER
'82 GANDHI*
'84 PASSAGE TO INDIA, A*
PROD. COORDINATOR
'83 HEAT AND DUST
MISCELLANEOUS
'83 OCTOPUSSY

MICHAEL HACKER
1ST ASST. DIRECTOR
'83 VALLEY GIRL*

NANCY HACKERMAN
LOCATIONS
'82 DINER

JONATHAN HACKETT
KEY GRIP
'79 RUNNING*
'80 MIDDLE AGE CRAZY*
'82 PORKY'S

TAYLOR HACKFORD
PRODUCER
'84 AGAINST ALL ODDS*
DIRECTOR
'80 IDOLMAKER, THE
'82 OFFICER AND A GENTLEMAN, AN
'84 AGAINST ALL ODDS

DENNIS HACKIN
PRODUCER
'80 BRONCO BILLY*
SCREENPLAY
'80 BRONCO BILLY

ALFRED DER HACOPIAN
MISCELLANEOUS
'84 MEATBALLS PART II

JOHN HADDY
MISCELLANEOUS
'83 MAN FROM SNOWY RIVER, THE

PENNY HADFIELD
ART DIRECTOR
'81 MY BLOODY VALENTINE
COSTUMES
'80 TERROR TRAIN

VIRGINIA HADFIELD
HAIR
'79 AMERICATHON
'81 HAND, THE

MARIA HADJIMATTHEOU
PROD. COORDINATOR
'82 TEMPEST
PROD. SECRETARY
'80 FOR THE LOVE OF BENJI*

VIVIANE HADNAGY
MISCELLANEOUS
'84 CHEECH AND CHONG'S THE CORSICAN BROTHERS

RAZI HAEN
MISCELLANEOUS
'82 PARADISE

ZION HAEN
2ND ASST. DIRECTOR
'82 PARADISE

FRANCINE HAENDIGES
HAIR
'79 IN-LAWS, THE*

JOHN HAGGAR
ASSISTANT EDITOR
'79 BLOODLINE*
'82 STAR TREK II THE WRATH OF KHAN*
'82 DEAD MEN DON'T WEAR PLAID
'83 STAYING ALIVE*
'84 BEVERLY HILLS COP*
'84 STAR TREK III: THE SEARCH FOR SPOCK*

PIERS HAGGARD
DIRECTOR
'80 FIENDISH PLOT OF DR. FU MANCHU, THE
'82 VENOM

DAN HAGGARTY
STUNT COORDINATOR
'83 AMERICANA*
MISCELLANEOUS
'83 AMERICANA

CAPTAIN HAGGERTY
MISCELLANEOUS
'84 PREPPIES

NORD HAGGERTY
PRODUCTION DESIGNER
'84 ALPHABET CITY

ROSS HAHN
MISCELLANEOUS
'79 AVALANCHE EXPRESS

PETER HAHNE
MISCELLANEOUS
'79 MAGICIAN OF LUBLIN, THE

OLIVER HAILEY
SCREENPLAY
'79 JUST YOU AND ME KID*

VIKKI HAIMILIA
PROD. SECRETARY
'80 TOUCHED BY LOVE

JEFFREY HAINES
HAIR
'84 BOSTONIANS, THE*

MICHAEL HAINES
SOUND
'84 NOT FOR PUBLICATION*

RICHARD HAINES
ASSISTANT EDITOR
'80 MOTHER'S DAY*
'82 CANNERY ROW

JACQUES HAITKIN
CINEMATOGRAPHER
'79 PRIZE FIGHTER, THE
'80 PRIVATE EYES, THE
'81 GALAXY OF TERROR
'83 ANGEL OF H.E.A.T.
'84 NIGHTMARE ON ELM STREET, A
'84 MAKING THE GRADE
MISCELLANEOUS
'83 OSTERMAN WEEKEND, THE

ALEX HAJDU
ART DIRECTOR
'81 GALAXY OF TERROR*

LISA HALAS
2ND ASST. DIRECTOR
'79 JUST YOU AND ME KID

IRA HALBERSTADT
1ST ASST. DIRECTOR
'84 NOT FOR PUBLICATION*
2ND ASST. DIRECTOR
'82 EATING RAOUL*
'82 Q: QUETZALCOATL*
'83 BABY IT'S YOU

JOE HALE
MISCELLANEOUS
'79 BLACK HOLE, THE
'80 WATCHER IN THE WOODS, THE

SIANA LEE HALE
CHOREOGRAPHER
'79 ROCK 'N ROLL HIGH SCHOOL

JONATHAN HALES
SCREENPLAY
'80 MIRROR CRACK'D, THE*

MIKE HALEY
ASSOCIATE PRODUCER
'79 ON THE YARD
'81 SO FINE*
1ST ASST. DIRECTOR
'79 ON THE YARD
'80 SMALL CIRCLE OF FRIENDS, A
'80 GILDA LIVE
'80 GLORIA
'80 NIGHT OF THE JUGGLER*
'80 TRIBUTE*
'81 SO FINE*
'82 ESCAPE ARTIST, THE
'83 EDDIE MACON'S RUN

PHIL HALEY
PROPS
'80 NUDE BOMB, THE

MIROSLAC HALIK
MISCELLANEOUS
'84 AMADEUS

ELIZABETH HALKO
2ND ASST. DIRECTOR
'83 SPACEHUNTER: ADVENTURES IN THE FORBIDDEN ZONE*

ALLEN HALL
SPECIAL EFFECTS
'79 LOVE AT FIRST BITE
'80 IN GOD WE TRUST
'81 ZORRO, THE GAY BLADE
'82 NIGHT SHIFT
SP. EFFECTS SUPERV.
'80 POPEYE
'83 D.C. CAB
'83 MAN WITH TWO BRAINS, THE

CLEVE HALL
MISCELLANEOUS
'83 METALSTORM: THE DESTRUCTION OF JARED-SYN

JOHN HALL
MISCELLANEOUS
'81 KING OF THE MOUNTAIN

KAREN HALL
PROD. OFFICE COORD.
'83 SILKWOOD*

MARLIN HALL
KEY GRIP
'79 AMERICAN GIGOLO
'79 BOULEVARD NIGHTS
'80 CHEECH AND CHONG'S NEXT MOVIE
'80 DEFIANCE
'81 HAND, THE
'82 SECOND THOUGHTS
'83 DOCTOR DETROIT
'84 LAST STARFIGHTER, THE
'84 REVENGE OF THE NERDS
'84 OH GOD, YOU DEVIL

PARNELL HALL
SCREENPLAY
'84 C.H.U.D.

RAY HALL
KEY GRIP
'79 DRACULA

ROBERT HALL
MISCELLANEOUS
'82 BLADERUNNER
'83 BRAINSTORM

ROBIN HALL
COSTUMES
'83 MAN FROM SNOWY RIVER, THE

ROGER HALL
ART DIRECTOR
'81 CHARIOTS OF FIRE

SUSAN HALL
COSTUMES
'81 MY BLOODY VALENTINE

LISA HALLAS
2ND ASST. DIRECTOR
'80 SMALL CIRCLE OF FRIENDS, A

BERT HALLBERG
SOUND
'79 ESCAPE FROM ALCATRAZ
'80 ANY WHICH WAY YOU CAN
'80 BRONCO BILLY
'81 ABSENCE OF MALICE
'81 TAPS

E. DARRELL HALLENBECK
PRODUCTION MANAGER
'80 JAZZ SINGER, THE
UNIT PROD. MANAGER
'83 TRENCHCOAT

DANIEL HALLER
DIRECTOR
'79 BUCK ROGERS

LYNDA HALLER
PROD. OFFICE COORD.
'79 MEATBALLS*

MICHAEL HALLER
PRODUCTION DESIGNER
'79 BEING THERE

ISABEL HALLIBURTON
CASTING
'79 PROMISE, THE*

ISABEL HALLIBURTON
ASSOCIATE PRODUCER
'79 STARTING OVER*

BOB HALLIDAY
MISCELLANEOUS
'82 VENOM

DICK HALLIGAN
MUSIC
'79 FORCE OF ONE, A
'80 CHEAPER TO KEEP HER
'80 OCTAGON, THE

RICHARD HALLINAN
CASTING
'80 OUTSIDER, THE

JANE HALLORAN
CASTING
'80 HEAVEN'S GATE*
'80 UNION CITY

TODD HALLOWELL
ART DIRECTOR
'84 CLOAK AND DAGGER

LEE HALLS
MAKEUP
'83 CROSS CREEK

DAVID HALPERN JR.
DIRECTOR
'79 SOMETHING SHORT OF PARADISE

PHILLIP HALPIN
MISCELLANEOUS
'79 ONION FIELD, THE

PATRICK HALPINE
2ND ASST. DIRECTOR
'83 EXPOSED*

DAVID HALSEY
MISCELLANEOUS
'81 FOR YOUR EYES ONLY

KIM HALSEY
ASSISTANT EDITOR
'80 HOME MOVIES*

RICHARD HALSEY
EDITOR
'79 AMERICAN GIGOLO
'79 BOULEVARD NIGHTS
'80 TRIBUTE
'82 AMATEUR, THE
'82 THAT CHAMPIONSHIP SEASON
'83 LOSIN' IT
'84 MOSCOW ON THE HUDSON
'84 BODY ROCK
'84 DREAMSCAPE
2ND UNIT DIRECTOR
'82 AMATEUR, THE

JIM HALTY
STUNT COORDINATOR
'81 CAVEMAN*

RON HAMADY
PRODUCER
'80 FADE TO BLACK*

ADRIENNE HAMALIAN
SCRIPT SUPERVISOR
'83 ECHOES

GERRY HAMBLING
EDITOR
'80 FAME
'82 SHOOT THE MOON
'82 PINK FLOYD: THE WALL
'84 ANOTHER COUNTRY
'84 BIRDY

GERRY HAMBLING
ASSOCIATE PRODUCER
'80 FOXES*

ROBERT HAMBLING
ASSISTANT EDITOR
'82 PINK FLOYD: THE WALL*

DAVID HAMBURGER
ASSOCIATE PRODUCER
'81 CANNONBALL RUN, THE
'82 MEGAFORCE
UNIT PROD. MANAGER
'81 CANNONBALL RUN, THE
'82 MEGAFORCE
1ST ASST. DIRECTOR
'79 BEING THERE
'79 VILLAIN, THE
'80 SMOKEY AND THE BANDIT II

ROUSHADI HAMED
PROPS
'80 AWAKENING, THE*

ALAN HAMEL
EXECUTIVE PRODUCER
'80 NOTHING PERSONAL*

YONI HAMENAHEM
STILLS
'79 MAGICIAN OF LUBLIN, THE
'82 PARADISE

BRIAN HAMILL
ASSOCIATE PRODUCER
'83 EXPOSED
STILLS
'80 RAGING BULL*
'80 STARDUST MEMORIES
'80 WINDOWS
'81 ARTHUR
'82 LITTLE SEX, A
'82 MIDSUMMER NIGHT'S SEX COMEDY, A
'82 TOOTSIE
'83 AMITYVILLE 3D
'83 EXPOSED*
'83 ZELIG*
'84 BROADWAY DANNY ROSE
'84 FIRSTBORN
'84 NATURAL, THE*

BIG JOHN HAMILTON
LOCATIONS
'80 BIG BRAWL, THE

CHICO HAMILTON
MUSIC
'82 BY DESIGN

GEORGE HAMILTON
PRODUCER
'81 ZORRO, THE GAY BLADE*
EXECUTIVE PRODUCER
'79 LOVE AT FIRST BITE*

GEORGE HAMILTON
PROPS
'79 HURRICANE

GEORGINA HAMILTON
SCRIPT SUPERVISOR
'79 UNIDENTIFIED FLYING ODDBALL

GUY HAMILTON
DIRECTOR
'80 MIRROR CRACK'D, THE
'82 EVIL UNDER THE SUN

JAMES HAMILTON
STILLS
'81 KNIGHTRIDERS
'82 CREEPSHOW*

JANE HAMILTON
COSTUMES
'84 RIDDLE OF THE SANDS

JEFF HAMILTON
MAKEUP
'82 ANNIE*

JOHN HAMILTON
STILLS
'81 ENTITY, THE
'81 LEGEND OF THE LONE RANGER, THE

JUDD HAMILTON
EXECUTIVE PRODUCER
'80 MANIAC*

NANCY HAMILTON
PUBLICIST
'80 FIRST FAMILY
'80 UP THE ACADEMY
UNIT PUBLICIST
'82 LOVE AND MONEY*

POLLY HAMILTON
COSTUMES
'82 HOUSE OF THE LONG SHADOWS*

SANDY HAMILTON
ART DIRECTOR
'80 MOTHER'S DAY
PROPS
'80 HE KNOWS YOU'RE ALONE

TED HAMILTON
EXECUTIVE PRODUCER
'82 PIRATE MOVIE, THE

TERRIS HAMILTON
HAIR
'83 DEADLY FORCE

YANCE HAMLET
2ND ASST. DIRECTOR
'79 PENITENTIARY*

MARVIN HAMLISCH
MUSIC
'79 STARTING OVER
'79 CHAPTER TWO
'79 ICE CASTLES
'80 SEEMS LIKE OLD TIMES
'81 PENNIES FROM HEAVEN*
'82 SOPHIE'S CHOICE
'82 I OUGHT TO BE IN PICTURES
'83 ROMANTIC COMEDY
MISCELLANEOUS
'80 ORDINARY PEOPLE

MICHAEL HAMLYN
2ND ASST. DIRECTOR
'81 SPHINX*

SAM HAMM
SCREENPLAY
'83 NEVER CRY WOLF*

BRUCE HAMME
KEY GRIP
'82 BUTTERFLY
'83 CUJO
'83 SAVANNAH SMILES

THOMAS HAMMEL
ASSOCIATE PRODUCER
'82 ZAPPED!*
UNIT PROD. MANAGER
'82 BEASTMASTER, THE
'83 RUMBLEFISH

JAN HAMMER
MUSIC
'83 NIGHT IN HEAVEN, A

WYNN HAMMER
STILLS
'78 DEER HUNTER, THE*
'79 OVER THE EDGE
'80 OH GOD! BOOK II
'81 BLOOD BEACH
'81 KING OF THE MOUNTAIN
'82 MAKING LOVE
'83 HEART LIKE A WHEEL
'84 CLOAK AND DAGGER*

CHARLIE HAMMERSCHMIDT
MISCELLANEOUS
'84 BIRDY

VIC HAMMOND
KEY GRIP
'84 BLAME IT ON RIO

CHRISTOPHER HAMPTON
SCREENPLAY
'83 BEYOND THE LIMIT

JANICE HAMPTON
EDITOR
'79 ROCKY II*
'82 HAMMETT*

SANFORD HAMPTON
1ST ASST. DIRECTOR
'82 BUTTERFLY

TIM HAMPTON
ASSOCIATE PRODUCER
'79 MONTY PYTHON'S LIFE OF BRIAN

KEITH HAMSHERE
STILLS
'79 LOST AND FOUND
'80 SATURN 3
'81 SUPERMAN II
'81 CLASH OF THE TITANS
'81 FOR YOUR EYES ONLY
'83 SUPERMAN III
'83 KRULL
'84 INDIANA JONES
AND THE TEMPLE OF DOOM*

HERBIE HANCOCK
MUSIC
'84 SOLDIER'S STORY, A

MICHAEL HANCOCK
MAKEUP
'79 BUTCH AND SUNDANCE:
THE EARLY YEARS*
'80 ALTERED STATES
'81 TATTOO*

PETER HANCOCK
PROPS
'80 SHINING, THE
'81 RAIDERS OF THE LOST ARK*
'81 SPHINX
'83 RETURN OF THE JEDI
'83 NEVER SAY NEVER AGAIN

SCOTT HANCOCK
ASSOCIATE EDITOR
'84 GRANDVIEW, U.S.A.
ASSISTANT EDITOR
'79 PRIZE FIGHTER, THE
'80 PRIVATE EYES, THE*
'82 SUMMER LOVERS*
'84 MARVIN AND TIGE*

GALEN HANDEE
MISCELLANEOUS
'81 GALAXY OF TERROR

PETER HANDFORD
SOUND
'80 LADY VANISHES, THE
'84 FINDERS KEEPERS

CATHY HANDLEMAN
PROD. SECRETARY
'80 OUTSIDER, THE*

DAVID HANDMAN
ASSISTANT EDITOR
'83 STAYING ALIVE*
'83 FOOTLOOSE*

KEVIN HANEY
MISCELLANEOUS
'84 C.H.U.D.

BILL HANKINS
MISCELLANEOUS
'84 THIS IS SPINAL TAP

BILL HANKINS
PROPS
'80 BIG RED ONE, THE

BARBARA HANLEY
CASTING
'81 EYE FOR AN EYE, AN*
'82 SWAMP THING*
'82 ZAPPED!*

DANIEL HANLEY
EDITOR
'82 NIGHT SHIFT*
'84 SPLASH*

MARGARET HANLY
SCRIPT SUPERVISOR
'79 FAST COMPANY
'81 BLOOD BEACH

ROSS HANN
SPECIAL EFFECTS
'79 C.H.O.M.P.S.

BILLY HANNA
EXECUTIVE PRODUCER
'82 LIAR'S MOON*

R.L. "BOBBY" HANNAH
STUNT COORDINATOR
'80 KIDNAPPING OF THE PRESIDENT, THE
'82 AMATEUR, THE

RICHARD HANNAH
CINEMATOGRAPHER
'83 STAR CHAMBER

PETER HANNAN
CINEMATOGRAPHER
'82 MISSIONARY, THE
'83 MONTY PYTHON'S
THE MEANING OF LIFE
'84 RAZOR'S EDGE, THE

BRIAN HANNANT

SCREENPLAY
'82 ROAD WARRIOR, THE*
1ST ASST. DIRECTOR
'82 ROAD WARRIOR, THE*
2ND UNIT DIRECTOR
'82 ROAD WARRIOR, THE

WALTER HANNEMANN

EDITOR
'79 VILLAIN, THE
'80 NUDE BOMB, THE*
'81 CHARLIE CHAN AND THE CURSE OF THE DRAGON QUEEN*

BILL HANSARD

MISCELLANEOUS
'81 DEAD AND BURIED
'81 ROAD GAMES
'82 ANNIE
'83 BREATHLESS

CHARLES HANSEN

SOUND
'82 VICE SQUAD

KRISTINA HANSEN

LOCATIONS
'83 CLASS

NANCY HANSEN

SCRIPT SUPERVISOR
'79 BOULEVARD NIGHTS
'80 AIRPLANE
'81 HAND, THE

ROGER HANSEN

SPECIAL EFFECTS
'80 BLUES BROTHERS*
'82 CHALLENGE, THE
'84 NATURAL, THE
'84 POLICE ACADEMY*

ARTHUR HANSON

PROPS
'79 PRISONER OF ZENDA, THE*
'80 IN GOD WE TRUST

BERNARD HANSON

LOCATIONS
'83 LORDS OF DISCIPLINE, THE
'84 GREYSTOKE: THE LEGEND OF TARZAN, LORD OF THE APES*
MISCELLANEOUS
'79 LOST AND FOUND

CURTIS HANSON

DIRECTOR
'83 LOSIN' IT
SCREENPLAY
'79 SILENT PARTNER, THE
'83 NEVER CRY WOLF*
ASSOCIATE PRODUCER
'79 SILENT PARTNER, THE

DENNIS HANSON

MISCELLANEOUS
'83 10 TO MIDNIGHT

JOHN HANSON

ASSISTANT EDITOR
'81 BLOOD BEACH*

OTTA HANUS

2ND ASST. DIRECTOR
'82 AMATEUR, THE
'82 FIRST BLOOD
'83 DEAD ZONE, THE
LOCATIONS
'82 IF YOU COULD SEE WHAT I HEAR

NATASJA HANUSOVA

SCRIPT SUPERVISOR
'83 CHEECH AND CHONG'S STILL SMOKIN'

ALEX HAPSAS

1ST ASST. DIRECTOR
'79 STARTING OVER
'81 ROLLOVER*
'81 FORT APACHE, THE BRONX
'81 WOLFEN*
'82 SOPHIE'S CHOICE
'84 MOSCOW ON THE HUDSON*
2ND ASST. DIRECTOR
'79 FIREPOWER*

MASATO HARA

EXECUTIVE PRODUCER
'83 MERRY CHRISTMAS, MR. LAWRENCE*

JOE HARADA

STILLS
'80 STUNT MAN, THE*

TARAK HARBI

PRODUCTION MANAGER
'84 MISUNDERSTOOD*

ROBERT HARDERS

SCREENPLAY
'80 HOME MOVIES*

DAVID HARDIE

SPECIAL EFFECTS
'81 GALLIPOLI*

MACK HARDING

UNIT PROD. MANAGER
'81 CONTINENTAL DIVIDE*

MALCOLM HARDING

ASSOCIATE PRODUCER
'84 HARRY & SON

STEVE HARDING

2ND ASST. DIRECTOR
'79 ALIEN*
'83 NEVER SAY NEVER AGAIN*
'84 INDIANA JONES AND THE TEMPLE OF DOOM*

STEWART HARDING

ASSOCIATE PRODUCER
'83 SPACEHUNTER: ADVENTURES IN THE FORBIDDEN ZONE
MISCELLANEOUS
'81 HAPPY BIRTHDAY TO ME

CATHERINE HARDMAN

ASSISTANT EDITOR
'79 DOUBLE MCGUFFIN, THE*
'80 OH! HEAVENLY DOG*

CATHERINE HARDMAN

SCRIPT SUPERVISOR
'82 SPLIT IMAGE

GINETTE HARDY

PRODUCTION MANAGER
'81 HAPPY BIRTHDAY TO ME
'84 ONCE UPON A TIME IN AMERICA

THEO HARISCH

ART DIRECTOR
'79 FIFTH MUSKETEER, THE

EFREM HARKHAM

ASSOCIATE PRODUCER
'83 GORKY PARK*

URI HARKHAM

ASSOCIATE PRODUCER
'83 GORKY PARK*

JAN HARLAN

EXECUTIVE PRODUCER
'80 SHINING, THE

FRANZ HARLAND

ART DIRECTOR
'83 SMITHEREENS

ROB HARLAND

LOCATIONS
'83 BLUE THUNDER*

RUSS HARLING

2ND ASST. DIRECTOR
'83 D.C. CAB*
'83 TABLE FOR FIVE
'83 UNDER FIRE*

HUGH HARLOW

PRODUCTION MANAGER
'79 DRACULA
MISCELLANEOUS
'83 OCTOPUSSY

PAULINE HARLOW
SCRIPT SUPERVISOR
'80 KIDNAPPING OF THE PRESIDENT, THE

BOB HARMAN
MISCELLANEOUS
'81 SUPERMAN II
'84 BIRDY
'84 SUPERGIRL
'84 2010

J. BOYCE HARMAN
PRODUCTION MANAGER
'79 SOMETHING SHORT OF PARADISE
'80 EXTERMINATOR, THE

LEE HARMAN
MAKEUP
'79 CHAMP, THE*
'79 MAIN EVENT, THE
'80 HERO AT LARGE
'80 HONEYSUCKLE ROSE*
'80 IT'S MY TURN
'81 MOMMIE DEAREST*
'82 I'M DANCING AS FAST AS I CAN
'82 MONSIGNOR
'83 HANNA K*
'83 WICKED LADY, THE*

ALLAN HARMON
2ND ASST. DIRECTOR
'84 POLICE ACADEMY

MARGARET HARMON
PROD. OFFICE COORD.
'83 I AM THE CHEESE

ROBERT HARMON
STILLS
'79 ROLLER BOOGIE
'79 TOURIST TRAP
'80 FADE TO BLACK
'81 HELL NIGHT

PAULA HAROLD
CASTING
'84 REVENGE OF THE NERDS*

PETER HAROLD
UNIT PROD. MANAGER
'82 NATIONAL LAMPOON'S CLASS REUNION

DENNIS HARPER
KEY GRIP
'83 LORDS OF DISCIPLINE, THE
'84 STAR TREK III: THE SEARCH FOR SPOCK
'84 JOY OF SEX, THE

HENRY HARPER
SCREENPLAY
'79 SCAVENGER HUNT*

FRED HARPMAN
ART DIRECTOR
'81 RICH AND FAMOUS
PRODUCTION DESIGNER
'80 CHEECH AND CHONG'S NEXT MOVIE

MARK HARRAH
MISCELLANEOUS
'83 TERMS OF ENDEARMENT

MICHELE HARRAH
CASTING
'82 BARBAROSA*

MICHAEL HARRESCHOU
SCREENPLAY
'82 SAFARI 3000

JIM HARRICK
MISCELLANEOUS
'79 FAST BREAK

GRAHAM HARRINGTON
MISCELLANEOUS
'83 HIGH ROAD TO CHINA

ANDY HARRIS
ART DIRECTOR
'84 COMFORT AND JOY

BOBBY HARRIS
STUNT COORDINATOR
'79 CHINA SYNDROME, THE*

BOOZIE HARRIS
HAIR
'83 STREAMERS

BRIAN HARRIS
KEY GRIP
'83 MERRY CHRISTMAS, MR. LAWRENCE

BURTT HARRIS
PRODUCER
'81 PRINCE OF THE CITY
'82 DEATHTRAP
'83 DANIEL
'84 GARBO TALKS*
EXECUTIVE PRODUCER
'82 VERDICT, THE
ASSOCIATE PRODUCER
'80 CRUISING
'80 GILDA LIVE
'80 JUST TELL ME WHAT YOU WANT
PRODUCTION MANAGER
'80 CRUISING
'80 GILDA LIVE
1ST ASST. DIRECTOR
'80 JUST TELL ME WHAT YOU WANT
'82 DEATHTRAP
'82 VERDICT, THE
'83 DANIEL

CHERYL ANN HARRIS
MISCELLANEOUS
'83 CROSS CREEK

DAVID HARRIS
MISCELLANEOUS
'84 ELECTRIC DREAMS

DORIAN HARRIS
ASSISTANT EDITOR
'81 FOUR FRIENDS*
'82 HAMMETT*
'83 RUMBLEFISH
'83 BABY IT'S YOU*
'84 COTTON CLUB, THE*

EVANNA HARRIS
MISCELLANEOUS
'81 EARTHLING, THE
'84 PHAR LAP

HEATH HARRIS
MISCELLANEOUS
'81 GALLIPOLI
'81 ROAD GAMES
'81 EARTHLING, THE
'84 PHAR LAP

HELENE HARRIS
PROD. COORDINATOR
'82 BEASTMASTER, THE
'82 ZAPPED!
'83 BREATHLESS

JACK HARRIS
STILLS
'79 ...AND JUSTICE FOR ALL*
'79 JUST YOU AND ME KID
'82 HAMMETT*

JEFF HARRIS
SCREENPLAY
'84 JOHNNY DANGEROUSLY*

JONATHAN HARRIS
EXECUTIVE PRODUCER
'83 RETURN OF THE ALIENS: THE DEADLY SPAWN*

ROBERT HARRIS JR.
COSTUMES
'79 SCAVENGER HUNT
'81 GOING APE!

JULIE HARRIS
COSTUMES
'79 DRACULA
'79 LOST AND FOUND
'81 GREAT MUPPET CAPER, THE

KIRK HARRIS
SOUND
'80 FOXES

LEON HARRIS
ART DIRECTOR
'79 ON THE YARD
'79 STAR TREK-THE MOTION PICTURE*
'81 DEVIL AND MAX DEVLIN, THE*
'82 DINER
MISCELLANEOUS
'80 WATCHER IN THE WOODS, THE

LOWELL HARRIS
SOUND
'79 PRISONER OF ZENDA, THE*
'80 NUDE BOMB, THE

MARK HARRIS
SOUND
'80 HUMANOIDS FROM THE DEEP

MAURY HARRIS
SOUND
'79 AMITYVILLE HORROR, THE
'81 BODY HEAT
'82 MAKING LOVE
'83 EDDIE MACON'S RUN
'84 ICE PIRATES, THE*

PETER HARRIS
MISCELLANEOUS
'84 ANOTHER COUNTRY

RICHARD HARRIS
EDITOR
'80 ISLAND, THE
'82 TOY, THE*
'83 SURVIVORS, THE

ROB HARRIS
PUBLICIST
'84 GREMLINS
'84 FIRESTARTER
UNIT PUBLICIST
'84 BODY DOUBLE

ROBERT HARRIS
COSTUMES
'79 ON THE YARD

ROZ HARRIS
SCRIPT SUPERVISOR
'84 AMERICAN DREAMER

SUSAN HARRIS
EXECUTIVE PRODUCER
'83 RETURN OF THE ALIENS: THE DEADLY SPAWN*

TIMOTHY HARRIS
SCREENPLAY
'80 CHEAPER TO KEEP HER*
'83 TRADING PLACES*

WILLIAM HARRIS
PRODUCTION DESIGNER
'83 RICHARD PRYOR: HERE AND NOW*

EVANGELINE HARRISON
COSTUMES
'83 SUPERMAN III

GEORGE HARRISON
EXECUTIVE PRODUCER
'79 MONTY PYTHON'S LIFE OF BRIAN*
'81 TIME BANDITS*
'82 MISSIONARY, THE*
'82 MONTY PYTHON LIVE AT THE HOLLYWOOD BOWL*
'83 PRIVATES ON PARADE*

HARVEY HARRISON
CINEMATOGRAPHER
'81 BURNING, THE
'83 CHEECH AND CHONG'S STILL SMOKIN'
'84 CHEECH AND CHONG'S THE CORSICAN BROTHERS

JOHN HARRISON
MUSIC
'82 CREEPSHOW
1ST ASST. DIRECTOR
'82 CREEPSHOW

KEN HARRISON
MUSIC
'84 MEATBALLS PART II

PHILIP HARRISON
PRODUCTION DESIGNER
'79 HANOVER STREET
'81 OUTLAND
'83 NEVER SAY NEVER AGAIN*
'84 RAZOR'S EDGE, THE
MISCELLANEOUS
'83 BLUE THUNDER

TED HARRISON
KEY GRIP
'80 FORMULA, THE

MAXI HARRITER
ART DIRECTOR
'79 BLOODLINE*

RAY HARRYHAUSEN
PRODUCER
'81 CLASH OF THE TITANS*
MISCELLANEOUS
'81 CLASH OF THE TITANS

HAZEL HARSTE
ASSISTANT EDITOR
'80 HUMAN FACTOR, THE

CLYDE HART
KEY GRIP
'79 BEING THERE
'80 ORDINARY PEOPLE*
'81 RICHARD PRYOR: LIVE ON THE SUNSET STRIP*
'81 HONKY TONK FREEWAY
'82 CAT PEOPLE
'84 NATURAL, THE

JAMES HART
2ND ASST. DIRECTOR
'82 LIAR'S MOON

RICHARD HART
MISCELLANEOUS
'84 ROMANCING THE STONE

SCOTT HART
MISCELLANEOUS
'80 SEEMS LIKE OLD TIMES

MICHAEL HARTE
COSTUME SUPERVISOR
'80 UP THE ACADEMY

ROMAN HARTE
MISCELLANEOUS
'82 SOPHIE'S CHOICE

CLIVE HARTLEY
ASSISTANT EDITOR
'84 GIVE MY REGARDS TO BROAD STREET*

NEIL HARTLEY
PRODUCER
'84 HOTEL NEW HAMPSHIRE, THE
EXECUTIVE PRODUCER
'82 BORDER, THE

RICHARD HARTLEY
MUSIC
'80 LADY VANISHES, THE
'81 SHOCK TREATMENT*
'84 SHEENA

GENE HARTLINE
STUNT COORDINATOR
'80 MOTEL HELL
'81 SMOKEY BITES THE DUST*
'82 ANDROID
'83 TIMERIDER*

JOHN HARTMANN
CO-PRODUCER
'81 HARD COUNTRY

JOHN HARTWELL
SCREENPLAY
'81 FAN, THE*

LOIS KRAMER HARTWICK
UNIT PROD. MANAGER
'81 PATERNITY*
'81 DOGS OF WAR, THE
PROD. OFFICE COORD.
'79 HAIR
LOCATIONS
'79 AMERICAN GIGOLO
'80 STARDUST MEMORIES*
MISCELLANEOUS
'84 RACING WITH THE MOON

RAY HARTWICK

ASSOCIATE PRODUCER
'81 SO FINE*
'81 PRINCE OF THE CITY
PRODUCTION MANAGER
'79 RUNNING*
'80 JUST TELL ME WHAT YOU WANT
'81 PRINCE OF THE CITY
'83 SCARFACE
'84 BODY DOUBLE
UNIT PROD. MANAGER
'80 CAN'T STOP THE MUSIC*
'81 SO FINE
'82 ANNIE*
MISCELLANEOUS
'80 NIGHT OF THE JUGGLER

KOICHI HARUTA

KEY GRIP
'82 CHALLENGE, THE

ANTHONY HARVEY

DIRECTOR
'79 PLAYERS

BERYL HARVEY

PROD. OFFICE COORD.
'79 BLACK STALLION, THE*

CHARLOTTE HARVEY

HAIR
'80 CARNY*

GAIL HARVEY

STILLS
'84 MRS. SOFFEL*

JOAN HARVEY

PROPS
'81 FEAR NO EVIL

MARSHALL HARVEY

EDITOR
'82 SWORD AND THE SORCERER, THE
2ND UNIT DIRECTOR
'82 SWORD AND THE SORCERER, THE*

RICHARD HARVEY

MUSIC
'82 HOUSE OF THE LONG SHADOWS

RUPERT HARVEY

EXECUTIVE PRODUCER
'82 ANDROID*

BO HARWOOD

MUSIC
'81 HAPPY BIRTHDAY TO ME*
'84 LOVE STREAMS
SOUND
'80 TERROR TRAIN
'81 MY BLOODY VALENTINE
'84 LOVE STREAMS*

JOANNE HARWOOD

SCRIPT SUPERVISOR
'81 MY BLOODY VALENTINE
'82 QUEST FOR FIRE*

MARC HARWOOD

EDITOR
'83 RETURN OF THE ALIENS: THE DEADLY SPAWN

RONALD HARWOOD

SCREENPLAY
'83 DRESSER, THE

SHUNA HARWOOD

COSTUMES
'82 MISSIONARY, THE

RICHARD HASHIMOTO

ASSOCIATE PRODUCER
'83 WAR GAMES
'84 IRRECONCILABLE DIFFERENCES
PRODUCTION MANAGER
'80 CARNY
'80 HEARTBEAT
'84 IRRECONCILABLE DIFFERENCES
UNIT PROD. MANAGER
'80 NINE TO FIVE
'81 ON GOLDEN POND*
'83 WAR GAMES
1ST ASST. DIRECTOR
'79 HARDCORE
2ND ASST. DIRECTOR
'80 STEEL

JIMMIE HASKELL

MUSIC
'81 HARD COUNTRY

TERRY HASKELL

PROPS
'84 SILENT NIGHT, DEADLY NIGHT

SALAH HASSANEIN

EXECUTIVE PRODUCER
'81 KNIGHTRIDERS
'82 CREEPSHOW

WILLIAM HASSELL

1ST ASST. DIRECTOR
'80 HOPSCOTCH*
'83 EXPOSED*
'83 HUNGER, THE*
'83 TESTAMENT*

JOHN HATELEY

MISCELLANEOUS
'83 TIMERIDER

BOB HATHAWAY

SOUND
'83 TRENCHCOAT*
MISCELLANEOUS
'84 SPLASH

BRIAN HATHAWAY

MISCELLANEOUS
'84 KILLING FIELDS, THE

JOHN HATT

MISCELLANEOUS
'84 DUNE

DON HAUER

2ND ASST. DIRECTOR
'82 BLADERUNNER*
'83 REUBEN, REUBEN
'83 FOOTLOOSE*

WILLIAM HAUGSE

EDITOR
'81 CATTLE ANNIE AND LITTLE BRITCHES

GLORIA HAUSER

PROD. OFFICE COORD.
'80 TIMES SQUARE*

ROBERT HAUSER

CINEMATOGRAPHER
'79 FRISCO KID, THE

WINGS HAUSER

ASSOCIATE PRODUCER
'83 UNCOMMON VALOR*

MICHAEL HAUSMAN

PRODUCER
'79 RICH KIDS*
'79 ALAMBRISTA!*
'79 HEARTLAND*
'83 BALLAD OF GREGORIO CORTEZ, THE*
'83 SILKWOOD*
EXECUTIVE PRODUCER
'81 RAGTIME*
'84 AMADEUS*
'84 PLACES IN THE HEART
CO-PRODUCER
'80 ONE-TRICK PONY
1ST ASST. DIRECTOR
'79 RICH KIDS
'79 HAIR
'79 HEARTLAND
'80 ONE-TRICK PONY
'81 RAGTIME
'83 BALLAD OF GREGORIO CORTEZ, THE
'83 SILKWOOD
'84 AMADEUS

DANIEL HAUSMANN

CASTING
'80 HOG WILD
'81 SCANNERS

MISCHA HAUSSERMAN

MISCELLANEOUS
'80 WHY WOULD I LIE?
'83 10 TO MIDNIGHT

GENO HAVENS
CASTING
'79 JERK, THE*
'79 MORE AMERICAN GRAFFITTI*
'80 ALLIGATOR
'84 HARDBODIES

BRENDA HAVERSTOCK
2ND ASST. DIRECTOR
'82 SWORD AND THE SORCERER, THE

CLIFF HAWKINS
MISCELLANEOUS
'83 NATE & HAYES

DIANA HAWKINS
PUBLICIST
'82 GANDHI
'84 PASSAGE TO INDIA, A

JEREMIAH HAWKINS
LOCATIONS
'84 ALPHABET CITY

JIM HAWKINS
SOUND
'84 MUTANT

GOLDIE HAWN
EXECUTIVE PRODUCER
'80 PRIVATE BENJAMIN
'84 PROTOCOL

TED HAWORTH
PRODUCTION DESIGNER
'79 BLOODLINE
'79 WHEN YOU COMIN' BACK, RED RYDER?
'80 ROUGH CUT
'81 DEATH HUNT
'81 CARBON COPY
'82 JINXED

JOHN HAY
COSTUMES
'82 QUEST FOR FIRE*
MISCELLANEOUS
'80 HEALTH

PAT HAY
MAKEUP
'81 SHOCK TREATMENT
HAIR
'80 NIJINSKY*

RY HAY
MISCELLANEOUS
'79 ROLLER BOOGIE

JEFF HAYES
SOUND
'82 Q: QUETZALCOATL

JOHN HAYES
1ST ASST. DIRECTOR
'84 LAST NIGHT AT THE ALAMO

KERRY HAYES
STILLS
'83 ZELIG*
'84 BIRDY*

TERRY HAYES
SCREENPLAY
'82 ROAD WARRIOR, THE*

RODNEY HAYKIN
SOUND
'82 IF YOU COULD SEE WHAT I HEAR
'82 PORKY'S

BRIAN HAYLES
SCREENPLAY
'79 ARABIAN ADVENTURE

BRIAN HAYNES
LOCATIONS
'84 CLOAK AND DAGGER

JEFF HAYNES
MISCELLANEOUS
'81 WOLFEN

SHEILA HAYNES
MISCELLANEOUS
'84 TANK

MICHAEL HAYNIE
PRODUCTION MANAGER
'81 MAN WHO SAW TOMORROW, THE*

RON HAYS
MISCELLANEOUS
'79 STARCRASH

CHUCK HAYWARD
STUNT COORDINATOR
'79 FRISCO KID, THE*

WILLIAM HAYWARD
STILLS
'81 STRANGE BEHAVIOR*

CLAUDE HAZANAVICIUS
SOUND
'82 QUEST FOR FIRE

PHILIP HAZARD
MISCELLANEOUS
'81 SUBWAY RIDERS

RICHARD HAZARD
MUSIC
'81 ALL NIGHT LONG*
'82 AIRPLANE II: THE SEQUEL*

KAREN HAZZARD
CASTING
'79 RUNNING*
'79 SILENT PARTNER, THE
'80 PROM NIGHT*
'82 QUEST FOR FIRE*
'83 CHRISTMAS STORY, A*
MISCELLANEOUS
'80 HAPPY BIRTHDAY, GEMINI

EDITH HEAD
COSTUMES
'80 LAST MARRIED COUPLE IN AMERICA, THE*
'82 DEAD MEN DON'T WEAR PLAID

BARRY HEALEY
CO-PRODUCER
'82 GREY FOX, THE*

LES HEALEY
ASSISTANT EDITOR
'79 ALIEN
'80 AWAKENING, THE*
'81 CHARIOTS OF FIRE
'83 YENTL

TIM HEALEY
UNIT MANAGER
'84 BREAKIN 2 ELECTRIC BOOGALOO
LOCATIONS
'84 BREAKIN 2 ELECTRIC BOOGALOO

JANET HEALY
ASSOCIATE PRODUCER
'79 1941*

ANGELA HEARD
PROD. COORDINATOR
'83 RUNNING BRAVE

HOWARD HEARD
ASSISTANT EDITOR
'81 LEGEND OF THE LONE RANGER, THE*
'82 MY FAVORITE YEAR*
'83 RISKY BUSINESS
'84 POLICE ACADEMY

BERT HEARN
PROPS
'79 LOST AND FOUND
'80 ROUGH CUT
'81 RAGTIME*
'83 SUPERMAN III*
'84 BOUNTY, THE
'84 PASSAGE TO INDIA, A*

JAMES HEARN
EXECUTIVE PRODUCER
'84 BEAR, THE

ERWIN HEARNE
ASSOCIATE PRODUCER
'80 FOR THE LOVE OF BENJI*

RAY HEARNE
STILLS
'79 STEVIE

PHILIP HEARNSHAW
UNIT MANAGER
'81 GALLIPOLI
LOCATIONS
'81 GALLIPOLI

MARK HEBSON
ASSISTANT EDITOR
'82 PENITENTIARY II*

AMY HECKERLING
DIRECTOR
'82 FAST TIMES AT RIDGEMONT HIGH
'84 JOHNNY DANGEROUSLY

ROB HEDDEN
PUBLICIST
'82 ZOOT SUIT
'84 HARD TO HOLD

BOB HEDGES
PROPS
'79 SHOUT, THE*
'81 EXCALIBUR

CLIVE HEDGES
LOCATIONS
'84 ELECTRIC DREAMS*

ANDERS HEDIN
2ND ASST. DIRECTOR
'83 GORKY PARK*

TOM HEDLEY
SCREENPLAY
'82 FIGHTING BACK*
'83 FLASHDANCE*
'84 HARD TO HOLD
ASSOCIATE PRODUCER
'82 FIGHTING BACK

KEN HEELEY-RAY
ASSOCIATE PRODUCER
'83 PORKY'S II THE NEXT DAY*

JOHANNA HEER
PRODUCER
'81 SUBWAY RIDERS*
CINEMATOGRAPHER
'81 SUBWAY RIDERS
EDITOR
'81 SUBWAY RIDERS*

DAN HEFFNER
2ND ASST. DIRECTOR
'81 RICHARD PRYOR: LIVE ON THE SUNSET STRIP*
'82 PERSONAL BEST*
'83 BIG CHILL, THE*

RICHARD HEFFRON
DIRECTOR
'80 FOOLIN AROUND
'82 I, THE JURY

HUGH HEFNER
EXECUTIVE PRODUCER
'79 SAINT JACK*
'80 FIENDISH PLOT OF DR. FU MANCHU, THE

JOYCE HEFTEL
SCRIPT SUPERVISOR
'79 BUCK ROGERS*

GERHARD HEGELE
UNIT MANAGER
'84 MOSCOW ON THE HUDSON

ALAN HEIM
EDITOR
'79 ALL THAT JAZZ
'79 HAIR*
'81 SO FINE
'81 FAN, THE
'83 STAR 80

BETSY HEIMANN
COSTUMES
'83 HIGH ROAD TO CHINA*

BOB HEINLEIN
MISCELLANEOUS
'80 HUNTER, THE

JAY HEIT
MISCELLANEOUS
'79 PROMISES IN THE DARK

DONALD HEITZER
PRODUCTION MANAGER
'79 OLD BOYFRIENDS
'81 CAVEMAN*
'82 ONE FROM THE HEART*
1ST ASST. DIRECTOR
'80 CHANGE OF SEASONS, A*
'80 MELVIN AND HOWARD
'83 CROSS CREEK
'84 GRANDVIEW, U.S.A.
'84 JOY OF SEX, THE*

LEN HEKEL
STILLS
'80 FOXES
'81 ALL NIGHT LONG
'81 WHOSE LIFE IS IT ANYWAY?
'82 MY FAVORITE YEAR
'83 BRAINSTORM*
'84 JOHNNY DANGEROUSLY
'84 MICKI AND MAUDE
'84 RACING WITH THE MOON

WALTER HEKKING
ASSISTANT EDITOR
'82 TRON*

HARRIET HELBERG
CASTING
'80 JAZZ SINGER, THE
'84 UP THE CREEK*

SANDY HELBERG
MISCELLANEOUS
'84 UP THE CREEK

CHRIS HELCERMANAS-BENGE
STILLS
'82 GREY FOX, THE*
'82 MOTHER LODE*
'84 ICEMAN*
'84 MRS. SOFFEL*

RALPH HELFER
MISCELLANEOUS
'82 QUEST FOR FIRE

MARK HELFRICH
EDITOR
'83 REVENGE OF THE NINJA*
ASSISTANT EDITOR
'79 ROCK 'N ROLL HIGH SCHOOL*
'82 LAST AMERICAN VIRGIN, THE

J. ROY HELLAND
MAKEUP
'82 STILL OF THE NIGHT
'83 SILKWOOD
'84 FALLING IN LOVE*
HAIR
'82 STILL OF THE NIGHT
'83 SILKWOOD
'84 FALLING IN LOVE*

BUD HELLER
KEY GRIP
'80 TOM HORN
'81 BACK ROADS
'81 ZORRO, THE GAY BLADE
'83 SCARFACE
'83 BLUE THUNDER
'83 CROSS CREEK

GREGORY HELLER
SCREENPLAY
'84 ALPHABET CITY*

PAUL HELLER
PRODUCER
'79 PROMISE, THE*
'81 FIRST MONDAY IN OCTOBER*

RABBI MEYER HELLER
MISCELLANEOUS
'79 FRISCO KID, THE

ROSILYN HELLER
EXECUTIVE PRODUCER
'79 ICE CASTLES

JEROME HELLMAN
PRODUCER
'79 PROMISES IN THE DARK
DIRECTOR
'79 PROMISES IN THE DARK

JOY HELLMAN
PUBLICIST
'83 DRESSER, THE
'84 SHEENA

GEOFFREY HELMAN
ASSOCIATE PRODUCER
'81 FRENCH LIEUTENANT'S WOMAN, THE*
'83 KRULL

RICHARD HELMER
SPECIAL EFFECTS
'79 TOURIST TRAP
'80 ALLIGATOR
'81 CHU CHU AND THE PHILLY FLASH
'82 THAT CHAMPIONSHIP SEASON
MISCELLANEOUS
'80 AIRPLANE

PAUL HELMICK
PRODUCTION MANAGER
'82 CHILLY SCENES OF WINTER

EMAD HELMY
ART DIRECTOR
'83 STRANGE INVADERS

BRUCE HELPER
ASSISTANT EDITOR
'81 MAN WHO SAW TOMORROW, THE

SIR ROBERT HELPMANN
MISCELLANEOUS
'83 MAN FROM SNOWY RIVER, THE

ILONA HEMAN
MAKEUP
'83 NEVER SAY NEVER AGAIN*
HAIR
'83 NEVER SAY NEVER AGAIN*

CAROL HEMMING
HAIR
'83 HEAT AND DUST
'84 BOSTONIANS, THE*

LINDY HEMMING
COSTUME SUPERVISOR
'84 COMFORT AND JOY*

DAVID HEMMINGS
EXECUTIVE PRODUCER
'81 STRANGE BEHAVIOR*

HANNAH HEMPSTEAD
PRODUCER
'83 LOSIN' IT*
ASSOCIATE PRODUCER
'80 TRIBUTE
MISCELLANEOUS
'82 AMATEUR, THE

JIM HENDERLING
PRODUCTION MANAGER
'80 OCTAGON, THE*

ANNE HENDERSON
EDITOR
'80 TERROR TRAIN

BRUCE HENDERSON
SPECIAL EFFECTS
'81 GALLIPOLI*

CATHY HENDERSON
CASTING
'81 EYE FOR AN EYE, AN*
'81 TAKE THIS JOB AND SHOVE IT
'82 SWAMP THING*
'82 ZAPPED!*

CHARLEY HENDERSON
PUBLICIST
'79 PRIZE FIGHTER, THE
'80 PRIVATE EYES, THE

CLARK HENDERSON
ASSISTANT EDITOR
'81 GALAXY OF TERROR*

DALE HENDERSON
HAIR
'84 BLAME IT ON RIO

DUNCAN HENDERSON
1ST ASST. DIRECTOR
'84 RHINESTONE
2ND ASST. DIRECTOR
'81 HALLOWEEN II
'81 TRUE CONFESSIONS*
'82 MY FAVORITE YEAR
'83 STAR CHAMBER
'83 STAYING ALIVE*
'84 RACING WITH THE MOON

JAMES HENDERSON
PROPS
'84 STRANGERS KISS

SANDRA HENDERSON
HAIR
'80 SOMEWHERE IN TIME*

WILT HENDERSON
EDITOR
'84 ANGEL*

KEN HENDLER
MISCELLANEOUS
'84 NATURAL, THE

WILLIAM HENDRICKS
MISCELLANEOUS
'79 DREAMER

CALISTA HENDRICKSON
MISCELLANEOUS
'79 MUPPET MOVIE, THE
'81 GREAT MUPPET CAPER, THE

STEPHEN HENDRICKSON
PRODUCTION DESIGNER
'79 GOING IN STYLE
'81 ARTHUR
'82 LITTLE SEX, A
MISCELLANEOUS
'80 CAN'T STOP THE MUSIC

SHIRL HENDRYX
SCREENPLAY
'83 RUNNING BRAVE*

LUTZ HENGST
MISCELLANEOUS
'79 FEDORA

KIM HENKEL
PRODUCER
'84 LAST NIGHT AT THE ALAMO*
SCREENPLAY
'84 LAST NIGHT AT THE ALAMO
EDITOR
'84 LAST NIGHT AT THE ALAMO*

W. PAUL HENLEY
LOCATIONS
'82 MY FAVORITE YEAR*

DAN HENNAH
ART DIRECTOR
'83 NATE & HAYES*

JOHN HENNESSY
KEY GRIP
'79 WHEN A STRANGER CALLS
'81 KING OF THE MOUNTAIN

DALE HENNESY
PRODUCTION DESIGNER
'80 COMPETITION, THE
'80 ISLAND, THE
'80 WHOLLY MOSES!
'82 ANNIE

EDOUARD HENRIQUES
MAKEUP
'79 NORTH DALLAS FORTY*
'80 SERIAL*
'80 HEARTBEAT
'81 DEAD AND BURIED*
'83 UNDER FIRE*
'84 SIXTEEN CANDLES*
MISCELLANEOUS
'79 PROPHECY

EDOUARD HENRIQUES III
MAKEUP
'80 THOSE LIPS, THOSE EYES
'82 CANNERY ROW*
'82 48 HOURS*
'84 TEACHERS*

MAX HENRIQUEZ
MAKEUP
'79 HAIR
'79 LAST EMBRACE
'80 ONE-TRICK PONY
'81 RAGTIME*

BUCK HENRY
DIRECTOR
'80 FIRST FAMILY
SCREENPLAY
'80 FIRST FAMILY
'84 PROTOCOL

CHRIS HENRY
ART DIRECTOR
'81 GRADUATION DAY

DAVID LEE HENRY
SCREENPLAY
'84 EVIL THAT MEN DO, THE*

MIKE HENRY
LOCATIONS
'81 GHOST STORY

RICHARD HENRY
2ND ASST. DIRECTOR
'83 MAN WOMAN AND CHILD*

ANNE HENSHAW
MISCELLANEOUS
'82 MONTY PYTHON LIVE AT THE HOLLYWOOD BOWL

JERE HENSHAW
EXEC IN CHARGE PROD
'79 AMITYVILLE HORROR, THE
'79 METEOR
'80 DEFIANCE
'80 HOW TO BEAT THE HIGH COST OF LIVING
'81 DEADLY BLESSING
MISCELLANEOUS
'80 NOTHING PERSONAL

PAUL HENSLER
SCREENPLAY
'82 DON'T CRY, IT'S ONLY THUNDER
CO-PRODUCER
'82 DON'T CRY, IT'S ONLY THUNDER
MISCELLANEOUS
'79 MORE AMERICAN GRAFFITTI

DALE HENSON
LOCATIONS
'83 STAYING ALIVE

JIM HENSON
PRODUCER
'79 MUPPET MOVIE, THE
'82 DARK CRYSTAL, THE*
DIRECTOR
'81 GREAT MUPPET CAPER, THE
'82 DARK CRYSTAL, THE*

DAVID HENTSCHEL
MUSIC
'83 EDUCATING RITA

NICK HEPWORTH
ART DIRECTOR
'82 PIRATE MOVIE, THE
PROPS
'80 BLUE LAGOON

PETER HERALD
ASSOCIATE PRODUCER
'79 NIGHTWING*
'83 D.C. CAB
'83 DOCTOR DETROIT
CO-PRODUCER
'82 NATIONAL LAMPOON'S CLASS REUNION*
UNIT PROD. MANAGER
'79 NIGHTWING
'83 D.C. CAB
'83 DOCTOR DETROIT

LEN HERBERMAN
EXECUTIVE PRODUCER
'79 MURDER BY DECREE

JACQUES HERBERT
1ST ASST. DIRECTOR
'82 OUT OF THE BLUE

JAMES HERBERT
ASSOCIATE PRODUCER
'79 DREAMER
2ND ASST. DIRECTOR
'81 MODERN PROBLEMS
LOCATIONS
'80 OCTAGON, THE
'80 THOSE LIPS, THOSE EYES*
'82 LOOKIN' TO GET OUT
'82 MAKING LOVE*
'83 MAX DUGAN RETURNS
'84 BEVERLY HILLS COP*

JOCELYN HERBERT
PRODUCTION DESIGNER
'84 HOTEL NEW HAMPSHIRE, THE
COSTUMES
'84 HOTEL NEW HAMPSHIRE, THE

KATHY HERBERT
PROD. COORDINATOR
'83 BUDDY SYSTEM, THE

EARLE HERDAN
EDITOR
'83 RUNNING BRAVE*

STEVE HEREK
ASSISTANT EDITOR
'82 ANDROID*

JOYCE HERLIHY
ASSOCIATE PRODUCER
'83 MERRY CHRISTMAS, MR. LAWRENCE*
PRODUCTION MANAGER
'79 SHOUT, THE
'79 AGATHA
'79 EUROPEANS, THE
'81 AMERICAN WEREWOLF IN LONDON, AN
'81 CHARIOTS OF FIRE

BRUCE HERMAN
STILLS
'79 FAST BREAK
'79 MORE AMERICAN GRAFFITTI
'83 MAN WOMAN AND CHILD*

FRAN HERMAN
SCRIPT SUPERVISOR
'79 VOICES

ILONA HERMAN
MAKEUP
'82 FIRST BLOOD*
'82 GREY FOX, THE
'84 RUNAWAY*
'84 FINDERS KEEPERS

LESLIE HERMAN
PROD. SECRETARY
'80 EYES OF A STRANGER

MIKI HERMAN
UNIT PROD. MANAGER
'83 RETURN OF THE JEDI
PROD. COORDINATOR
'80 EMPIRE STRIKES BACK, THE

NORMAN HERMAN
EXECUTIVE PRODUCER
'80 IN GOD WE TRUST

DAVID HERMELIN
ASSOCIATE PRODUCER
'84 STONE BOY, THE*

JOHN HERNANDES
KEY GRIP
'84 FIRESTARTER

JEFFREY HERNANDEZ
UNIT MANAGER
'81 STUDENT BODIES

KING HERNANDEZ
SP. EFFECTS SUPERV.
'81 HAPPY BIRTHDAY TO ME*

ROBERT HERNANDEZ
ASSISTANT EDITOR
'82 48 HOURS*

WALTER SCOTT HERNDON
PRODUCTION DESIGNER
'79 NORMA RAE
'79 PROMISES IN THE DARK
'80 THOSE LIPS, THOSE EYES
'81 SHARKEY'S MACHINE
'81 BACK ROADS
'83 CROSS CREEK
'84 SOLDIER'S STORY, A

J. BARRY HERON
MISCELLANEOUS
'83 STRANGE BREW

CLAUDE HEROUX
PRODUCER
'79 BROOD, THE
'79 IN PRAISE OF OLDER WOMEN*
'80 HOG WILD
'81 SCANNERS
'81 GAS
'83 VIDEODROME
'83 OF UNKNOWN ORIGIN

DENIS HEROUX
PRODUCER
'81 ATLANTIC CITY
'82 QUEST FOR FIRE*

JUSTIN HEROUX
ASSOCIATE PRODUCER
'81 ATLANTIC CITY*
PRODUCTION MANAGER
'81 ATLANTIC CITY*

ROGER HEROUX
PRODUCTION MANAGER
'79 IN PRAISE OF OLDER WOMEN
'80 DEATH SHIP
'81 GAS
PROD. COORDINATOR
'83 VIDEODROME
MISCELLANEOUS
'83 OF UNKNOWN ORIGIN

CRAIG HERRING
ASSISTANT EDITOR
'84 2010*

PAM HERRING
EDITOR
'83 NATIONAL LAMPOON'S VACATION

PEMBROKE HERRING
EDITOR
'79 RUNNER STUMBLES, THE
'80 LITTLE DARLINGS
'80 NINE TO FIVE
'82 BEST LITTLE WHOREHOUSE IN TEXAS, THE*
'84 JOHNNY DANGEROUSLY
MISCELLANEOUS
'81 ZORRO, THE GAY BLADE

EUGENE HERRLY
KEY GRIP
'80 OUTSIDER, THE

GERRY HERROD
EXECUTIVE PRODUCER
'79 BOARDWALK

JIMMIE HERRON JR.
PROPS
'79 FORCE OF ONE, A

KATHI HERSCH
PROD. OFFICE COORD.
'84 C.H.U.D.

PHIL HERSEE
STILLS
'80 CHANGELING, THE
'82 GREY FOX, THE*
'82 OUT OF THE BLUE

DAVID HERSEY
MISCELLANEOUS
'80 NIJINSKY

JANE HERSHCOPF
1ST ASST. DIRECTOR
'80 EXTERMINATOR, THE

PAT HERSKOVIC
PRODUCER
'81 DEADLY BLESSING*

MILTON HERSON
EXECUTIVE PRODUCER
'83 SPRING BREAK*

MICHAEL HERTZBERG
PRODUCER
'84 JOHNNY DANGEROUSLY

MICHAEL HERZ
ASSOCIATE PRODUCER
'80 MOTHER'S DAY*

JOHN HERZFELD
DIRECTOR
'83 TWO OF A KIND
SCREENPLAY
'79 VOICES
'83 TWO OF A KIND

PAUL HESLIN
LOCATIONS
'81 HARD COUNTRY

FRED HESPER
MISCELLANEOUS
'79 GREAT SANTINI, THE

MELINDA HESS
ASSISTANT EDITOR
'84 ALPHABET CITY

SUE HESSEL
CASTING
'83 SURVIVORS, THE*

RUSS HESSEY
SPECIAL EFFECTS
'81 RAGGEDY MAN
'81 THIEF
'83 CROSS CREEK

CHARLTON HESTON
DIRECTOR
'82 MOTHER LODE

FRASER CLARKE HESTON
PRODUCER
'82 MOTHER LODE
SCREENPLAY
'80 MOUNTAIN MEN, THE
'82 MOTHER LODE

LYDIA CLARKE HESTON
STILLS
'82 MOTHER LODE*

MARILYN HESTON
PUBLICIST
'82 MOTHER LODE

LEROY HEUGLIN
MISCELLANEOUS
'81 STRIPES

YOSKI HEUSDORFF
MISCELLANEOUS
'82 PARADISE

VIC HEUTSCHY
PUBLICIST
'79 AVALANCHE EXPRESS
'79 MAIN EVENT, THE
'80 CADDYSHACK
'80 DIE LAUGHING
'81 CONTINENTAL DIVIDE
'81 TRUE CONFESSIONS
'82 MISSING
'82 MY FAVORITE YEAR
'83 STAR 80
'83 BRAINSTORM*
'83 D.C. CAB
'84 CRACKERS
'84 UNTIL SEPTEMBER*
UNIT PUBLICIST
'80 BIG RED ONE, THE
'84 HOT DOG...THE MOVIE
'84 NO SMALL AFFAIR

JERRY HEWITT
STUNT COORDINATOR
'81 NESTING, THE*
'84 PREPPIES

NORMAN HEYMAN
PRODUCER
'83 BEYOND THE LIMIT

PAULINE HEYS
MAKEUP
'83 LORDS OF DISCIPLINE, THE

LOUIS HEYWARD
EXEC IN CHARGE PROD
'79 C.H.O.M.P.S.

VICKI HIATT
ASSISTANT EDITOR
'80 FADE TO BLACK*
'83 DOCTOR DETROIT
'84 WOMAN IN RED, THE

EDDIE HICE
STUNT COORDINATOR
'80 CHEECH AND CHONG'S NEXT MOVIE
'82 BEST LITTLE WHOREHOUSE IN TEXAS, THE
'82 VICE SQUAD*
'84 REPO MAN

MICHAEL HICKEY
SCREENPLAY
'84 SILENT NIGHT, DEADLY NIGHT

IAN HICKINBOTHAM
COSTUMES
'82 SENDER, THE*
COSTUME SUPERVISOR
'83 BRITANNIA HOSPITAL
2ND ASST. DIRECTOR
'84 ELECTRIC DREAMS*

GAIL MORGAN HICKMAN
SCREENPLAY
'83 BIG SCORE, THE

NEILL HICKS
SCREENPLAY
'84 FINAL TERROR, THE*

BERNARD HIDES
ART DIRECTOR
'81 EARTHLING, THE*

RICHARD HIERNONYMUS
MUSIC
'83 GOIN' ALL THE WAY

BILLY HIGGINS
LOCATIONS
'83 BAD BOYS*
'84 SIXTEEN CANDLES
MISCELLANEOUS
'83 DOCTOR DETROIT

COLIN HIGGINS
DIRECTOR
'80 NINE TO FIVE
'82 BEST LITTLE WHOREHOUSE IN TEXAS, THE
SCREENPLAY
'80 NINE TO FIVE*
'82 BEST LITTLE WHOREHOUSE IN TEXAS, THE*

DENNIS HIGGINS
PUBLICIST
'82 LOVE CHILD

DOUGLAS HIGGINS
ART DIRECTOR
'80 KIDNAPPING OF THE PRESIDENT, THE
PRODUCTION DESIGNER
'82 MOTHER LODE
'83 GOLDEN SEAL, THE
'84 RUNAWAY

JEAN HIGGINS
EXEC IN CHARGE PROD
'80 OCTAGON, THE

JUNE HIGGINS
HAIR
'80 DEFIANCE*

MICHAEL HIGGINS
2ND ASST. DIRECTOR
'84 TOP SECRET!*
MISCELLANEOUS
'83 HIGH ROAD TO CHINA

ROY HIGGINS
MISCELLANEOUS
'84 PHAR LAP

VIRGINIA HIGGINS
CASTING
'83 SOMETHING WICKED THIS WAY COMES*

J. ALLEN HIGHFILL
COSTUMES
'80 HEAVEN'S GATE
'83 BREATHLESS

DAVE HIGHGATE
MISCELLANEOUS
'84 GIVE MY REGARDS TO BROAD STREET

PADDY HIGSON
ASSOCIATE PRODUCER
'84 COMFORT AND JOY

CHRIS HILBER
2ND UNIT DIRECTOR
'84 UP THE CREEK

FRANK HILDEBRAND
ASSOCIATE PRODUCER
'82 VICE SQUAD

RITA HILDEBRANDT
EXECUTIVE PRODUCER
'83 RETURN OF THE ALIENS: THE DEADLY SPAWN*

TIM HILDEBRANDT
EXECUTIVE PRODUCER
'83 RETURN OF THE ALIENS: THE DEADLY SPAWN*
MISCELLANEOUS
'83 RETURN OF THE ALIENS: THE DEADLY SPAWN

KIM HILDER
ART DIRECTOR
'82 STARSTRUCK

BOB HILDITCH
ART DIRECTOR
'81 EARTHLING, THE*

DAVID HILDYARD
SOUND
'79 FEDORA
'80 FFOLKES
'81 SEA WOLVES, THE
'82 SAFARI 3000
'83 PIRATES OF PENZANCE, THE
'83 YENTL
'84 CHAMPIONS*
'84 FIRESTARTER

MARIE HILDYARD
SCRIPT SUPERVISOR
'82 SAFARI 3000

CLAYTON HILL
2ND ASST. DIRECTOR
'81 KNIGHTRIDERS*
MISCELLANEOUS
'79 DAWN OF THE DEAD

DAVE HILL

STILLS
'81 STRANGE BEHAVIOR*

DEBRA HILL

PRODUCER
'80 FOG, THE
'81 ESCAPE FROM NEW YORK*
'81 HALLOWEEN II*
'82 HALLOWEEN III: SEASON OF THE WITCH*
'83 DEAD ZONE, THE
SCREENPLAY
'80 FOG, THE*
'81 HALLOWEEN II*

DENNIS HILL

EDITOR
'79 QUINTET
'80 HEALTH*
'82 LOVE AND MONEY

GEORGE HILL

KEY GRIP
'79 ROCKY II
'79 ICE CASTLES
'80 CAN'T STOP THE MUSIC
'80 IT'S MY TURN*
'81 STRIPES
'82 ROCKY III
'83 STING II, THE

GEORGE ROY HILL

PRODUCER
'82 WORLD ACCORDING TO GARP,THE*
DIRECTOR
'79 LITTLE ROMANCE, A
'82 WORLD ACCORDING TO GARP, THE
'84 LITTLE DRUMMER GIRL, THE

JOHN HILL

SCREENPLAY
'81 HEARTBEEPS
ASSOCIATE PRODUCER
'81 HEARTBEEPS

JOHN ANDREW HILL

ASSISTANT EDITOR
'84 LITTLE DRUMMER GIRL, THE*

LESLIE HILL

ASSOCIATE PRODUCER
'80 FIRST FAMILY*

MICHAEL HILL

EDITOR
'82 NIGHT SHIFT*
'84 SPLASH*

WALTER HILL

PRODUCER
'79 ALIEN*
DIRECTOR
'79 WARRIORS, THE
'80 LONG RIDERS, THE
'81 SOUTHERN COMFORT
'82 48 HOURS
'84 STREETS OF FIRE
SCREENPLAY
'79 WARRIORS, THE*
'81 SOUTHERN COMFORT*
'82 48 HOURS*
'84 STREETS OF FIRE*

WILLIAM HILL

PRODUCTION MANAGER
'79 PLAYERS

ARTHUR HILLER

PRODUCER
'79 IN-LAWS, THE*
'84 LONELY GUY, THE
DIRECTOR
'79 NIGHTWING
'79 IN-LAWS, THE
'82 AUTHOR, AUTHOR
'82 MAKING LOVE
'83 ROMANTIC COMEDY
'84 LONELY GUY, THE
'84 TEACHERS

MARGARET HILLIARD

PRODUCTION MANAGER
'84 BOUNTY, THE*
PROD. COORDINATOR
'83 MERRY CHRISTMAS, MR. LAWRENCE

MARY HILLMAN

MAKEUP
'81 CHARIOTS OF FIRE
'84 CHAMPIONS

VICKI HILLMAN

MISCELLANEOUS
'84 THIS IS SPINAL TAP

GEOFF HILLS

PRODUCTION MANAGER
'84 BOUNTY, THE*

JOAN HILLS

HAIR
'81 CHARIOTS OF FIRE

CAROL HILSON

PROD. COORDINATOR
'83 DEADLY FORCE*

JACK HILTON

ASSISTANT EDITOR
'82 MOTHER LODE
'82 OUT OF THE BLUE*
'84 RUNAWAY*
'84 HARDBODIES

TOM HILTON

STILLS
'84 COMFORT AND JOY

CAROL HIMES

1ST ASST. DIRECTOR
'79 BUDDY HOLLY STORY, THE

CELESTE HINES

ASSISTANT EDITOR
'82 COME BACK TO THE 5 & 10, JIMMY DEAN, JIMMY DEAN*

MAURICE HINES SR.

MISCELLANEOUS
'84 COTTON CLUB, THE

WILLIAM HINEY

ART DIRECTOR
'80 FIRST FAMILY
PRODUCTION DESIGNER
'80 LITTLE DARLINGS
'82 DEATHWISH II
'84 UP THE CREEK

RUDY HINKLE

MISCELLANEOUS
'83 REUBEN, REUBEN

SIMON HINKLY

1ST ASST. DIRECTOR
'81 TIME BANDITS
'83 BEYOND THE LIMIT

S.E. HINTON

SCREENPLAY
'83 RUMBLEFISH*
MISCELLANEOUS
'83 OUTSIDERS, THE

PAUL HIPP

CINEMATOGRAPHER
'80 HANGAR 18
'82 BOOGENS, THE

ROBERT HIPPARD

LOCATIONS
'82 VICE SQUAD

TOSHINORI HIRAYANAGI

2ND ASST. DIRECTOR
'82 CHALLENGE, THE*

BUZZ HIRSCH

EXECUTIVE PRODUCER
'83 SILKWOOD*

KATHARINA HIRSCH

MAKEUP
'83 VALLEY GIRL

PAUL HIRSCH
EDITOR
'80 EMPIRE STRIKES BACK, THE
'81 BLOW OUT
'82 CREEPSHOW*
'83 BLACK STALLION RETURNS, THE
'83 FOOTLOOSE
'84 PROTOCOL
MISCELLANEOUS
'80 HOME MOVIES

STEVE HIRSCH
STILLS
'80 MANIAC*

TINA HIRSCH
EDITOR
'79 MORE AMERICAN GRAFFITTI
'81 HEARTBEEPS
'83 TWILIGHT ZONE, THE MOVIE*
'84 GREMLINS
MISCELLANEOUS
'80 XANADU

ALEC HIRSCHFELD
CINEMATOGRAPHER
'83 LOVE LETTERS

GERALD HIRSCHFELD
CINEMATOGRAPHER
'79 AMERICATHON
'79 BELL JAR, THE
'80 WHY WOULD I LIE?
'81 NEIGHBORS
'81 SUNDAY LOVERS*
'82 MY FAVORITE YEAR
'83 TO BE OR NOT TO BE

NORMAN HIRSCHFIELD
EXECUTIVE PRODUCER
'80 NOTHING PERSONAL*

KURT HIRSCHLER
MISCELLANEOUS
'79 RUNNING

PHYLLIS GARDNER HIRSEN
UNIT PUBLICIST
'84 OH GOD, YOU DEVIL

JACK HIRSHBERG
PUBLICIST
'80 BRUBAKER
'80 ORDINARY PEOPLE
UNIT PUBLICIST
'79 ELECTRIC HORSEMAN, THE

JANET HIRSHENSON
CASTING
'82 HAMMETT*
'83 RUMBLEFISH
'83 DEAD ZONE, THE*
'83 OUTSIDERS, THE*
'84 BODY DOUBLE*
'84 COTTON CLUB, THE*
'84 HARD TO HOLD*
'84 GRANDVIEW, U.S.A.*
'84 RED DAWN*

MAUREEN HISCOX
COSTUME SUPERVISOR
'83 GOLDEN SEAL, THE

RONDI HISTROM-DAVIS
COSTUMES
'84 NOT FOR PUBLICATION

CLAUDE HITCHCOCK
SOUND
'79 STEVIE
'81 CAVEMAN
'81 EYE OF THE NEEDLE

DAVID HITCHCOCK
ASSISTANT EDITOR
'80 FLASH GORDON*
'84 SHEENA*

PAUL HITCHCOCK
ASSOCIATE PRODUCER
'82 FIREFOX

RON HITCHCOCK
MISCELLANEOUS
'80 JAZZ SINGER, THE

HALL HITZIG
2ND ASST. DIRECTOR
'81 CATTLE ANNIE
AND LITTLE BRITCHES*
'81 WOLFEN

RUPERT HITZIG
PRODUCER
'80 HAPPY BIRTHDAY, GEMINI
'81 CATTLE ANNIE
AND LITTLE BRITCHES*
'81 WOLFEN
'83 JAWS 3-D
2ND UNIT DIRECTOR
'81 WOLFEN
'83 JAWS 3-D

GEORGE HIVELY
EDITOR
'82 FRIDAY THE 13TH
PART THREE IN 3D
'84 BLAME IT ON RIO*

KIM HIX
MISCELLANEOUS
'83 SPACEHUNTER: ADVENTURES
IN THE FORBIDDEN ZONE

KEN HIXON
SCREENPLAY
'84 GRANDVIEW, U.S.A.

RUNE HJELM
PRODUCTION MANAGER
'81 MONTENEGRO

PETUR HLIDDAL
SOUND
'80 IDOLMAKER, THE
'80 WHERE THE BUFFALO ROAM
'81 CUTTER'S WAY
'81 MODERN PROBLEMS
'82 HOME WORK
'84 WINDY CITY

A. KITMAN HO
PRODUCER
'84 LOVELESS, THE*
PRODUCTION MANAGER
'79 HEARTLAND
'81 REDS*
'83 HUNGER, THE
UNIT MANAGER
'80 ONE-TRICK PONY
'82 MY FAVORITE YEAR*
LOCATIONS
'79 WARRIORS, THE*
'80 FIRST DEADLY SIN

REX HOBBS
PROPS
'83 BETRAYAL

RON HOBBS
ART DIRECTOR
'78 DEER HUNTER, THE*
'80 TOM HORN
'83 SMOKEY AND THE BANDIT III
PRODUCTION DESIGNER
'79 RAVAGERS
'79 JUST YOU AND ME KID
'80 HUNTER, THE
'82 PERSONAL BEST
'83 FOOTLOOSE
'84 COUNTRY

WILLIAM HOBBS
MISCELLANEOUS
'80 FLASH GORDON
'81 EXCALIBUR

MARY-ANN HOBEL
EXECUTIVE PRODUCER
'83 TENDER MERCIES

PHILLIP HOBEL
PRODUCER
'83 TENDER MERCIES

JOHN HOBLETT
MAKEUP
'83 GOIN' ALL THE WAY*

GENE HOBSON
MUSIC
'81 STUDENT BODIES

PETER HOCK
STUNT COORDINATOR
'82 Q: QUETZALCOATL

JOHN HOCKRIDGE
1ST ASST. DIRECTOR
'84 STAR TREK III: THE SEARCH FOR SPOCK

PAUL STERLING HODARA
STILLS
'80 BATTLE BEYOND THE STARS

BERNARD HODES
ASSOCIATE PRODUCER
'83 MORTUARY*

ROBERT HODES
SCRIPT SUPERVISOR
'80 SIMON
'83 KING OF COMEDY, THE*

STUART HODES
CHOREOGRAPHER
'79 VOICES

DEAN HODGES
SOUND
'79 FORCE OF ONE, A*
'84 ICE PIRATES, THE*
'84 KARATE KID, THE

MIKE HODGES
DIRECTOR
'80 FLASH GORDON

JOAN HODGINS
HAIR
'79 FAST COMPANY

TERRY HODGKINSON
LOCATIONS
'83 BETRAYAL

PAUL HODGSON
ASSISTANT EDITOR
'84 COMFORT AND JOY*

GILLY HODSON
PUBLICIST
'84 KILLING FIELDS, THE

DOV HOENIG
EDITOR
'79 MAGICIAN OF LUBLIN, THE
'81 THIEF
'82 YOUNG DOCTORS IN LOVE
'83 KEEP, THE
'84 BEAT STREET

MICHAEL HOENIG
MISCELLANEOUS
'81 GALAXY OF TERROR

THOMAS HOERBER
MAKEUP
'81 BEAST WITHIN, THE
'84 BEST DEFENSE*
'84 NATURAL, THE*

JOHN HOESLI
ART DIRECTOR
'81 EYE OF THE NEEDLE*

LARRY HOFF
SOUND
'83 REUBEN, REUBEN

PAUL HOFFERT
MUSIC
'82 PARADISE

ADRIAN HOFFMAN
HAIR
'79 SILENT PARTNER, THE

ALICE HOFFMAN
SCREENPLAY
'83 INDEPENDENCE DAY

BEVERLY HOFFMAN
MISCELLANEOUS
'82 E.T. THE EXTRA-TERRESTRIAL

BRUCE HOFFMAN
MISCELLANEOUS
'79 ROCKY II

INGRID HOFFMAN
COSTUMES
'79 MAGICIAN OF LUBLIN, THE

JOE HOFFMAN
ART DIRECTOR
'84 FRIDAY THE 13TH PART IV THE FINAL CHAPTER

MARLA HOFFMAN
PROD. COORDINATOR
'79 SCAVENGER HUNT*

VALERIE HOFFMAN
UNIT PUBLICIST
'84 NOT FOR PUBLICATION

RINA HOFMANIS
MAKEUP
'81 ENTER THE NINJA

JACK HOFSIS
DIRECTOR
'82 I'M DANCING AS FAST AS I CAN

JACK HOFSTRA
EDITOR
'80 STUNT MAN, THE*
'81 FUNHOUSE, THE
'82 BEST LITTLE WHOREHOUSE IN TEXAS, THE*
'83 TWO OF A KIND*

BARBARA HOGAN
SCRIPT SUPERVISOR
'79 WHEN A STRANGER CALLS
'81 BEAST WITHIN, THE
'82 BORDER, THE

TIM HOGAN
KEY GRIP
'79 MAN, A WOMAN AND A BANK, A
'82 FIRST BLOOD
'82 GREY FOX, THE
'83 GOLDEN SEAL, THE
'84 ICEMAN

LOIS HOHENFELS
MAKEUP
'81 ROAD GAMES
'82 PIRATE MOVIE, THE

R.J. HOHMAN
SPECIAL EFFECTS
'82 PIRATE MOVIE, THE
MISCELLANEOUS
'80 POPEYE

KIRK HOKANSON
LOCATIONS
'84 PURPLE RAIN

KAJ HOLBERG
PRODUCTION MANAGER
'81 REDS*

GERRY HOLBROOK
LOCATIONS
'82 Q: QUETZALCOATL

JOHN HOLBROOK
MISCELLANEOUS
'82 FIRST BLOOD

AARON HOLDEN
PROPS
'83 BAD BOYS
'83 BIG SCORE, THE

DAVID HOLDEN
EDITOR
'79 WARRIORS, THE
'80 LONG RIDERS, THE
'81 BUSTIN' LOOSE
'84 IMPULSE
2ND UNIT DIRECTOR
'81 BUSTIN' LOOSE

HILARY HOLDEN
CASTING
'79 BROOD, THE
'80 WHY WOULD I LIE?
'84 EVIL THAT MEN DO, THE*

LEE HOLDRIDGE
MUSIC
'82 BEASTMASTER, THE
'83 MR. MOM
'84 MICKI AND MAUDE
'84 SPLASH

MARY HOLDSWORTH
SCRIPT SUPERVISOR
'83 GORKY PARK
'84 KIPPERBANG

FRED HOLE
ART DIRECTOR
'83 RETURN OF THE JEDI*

WILLIAM HOLE
1ST ASST. DIRECTOR
'79 DREAMER

ADAM HOLENDER
CINEMATOGRAPHER
'79 SEDUCTION OF JOE TYNAN, THE
'79 PROMISES IN THE DARK
'80 SIMON
'80 IDOLMAKER, THE

FRANK HOLGATE
MISCELLANEOUS
'79 ...AND JUSTICE FOR ALL
'80 STUNT MAN, THE
'80 HUNTER, THE
'80 USED CARS
'82 HANKY PANKY
'83 BLUE THUNDER
'83 UNCOMMON VALOR
'84 IMPULSE

BISHOP HOLIDAY
MUSIC
'84 JOY OF SEX, THE*

GARY HOLIFF
STILLS
'80 HAPPY BIRTHDAY, GEMINI

BYRD HOLLAND
MAKEUP
'79 FISH THAT
SAVED PITTSBURGH, THE*

LAJA HOLLAND
ASSISTANT EDITOR
'83 CAN SHE BAKE A CHERRY PIE?*

ROB HOLLAND
MISCELLANEOUS
'80 MOTHER'S DAY
'83 HOUSE ON SORORITY ROW

SIMON HOLLAND
ART DIRECTOR
'79 SHOUT, THE
'79 AGATHA
'81 REDS
'84 GREYSTOKE: THE LEGEND OF
TARZAN, LORD OF THE APES*

TOM HOLLAND
SCREENPLAY
'81 BEAST WITHIN, THE
'83 PSYCHO II
'84 CLOAK AND DAGGER

MARY CAY HOLLANDER
PROD. COORDINATOR
'79 ELECTRIC HORSEMAN, THE
'80 ORDINARY PEOPLE
'82 THINGS ARE TOUGH ALL OVER
'83 WRONG IS RIGHT

TEDD HOLLIDAY
PRODUCTION MANAGER
'79 BLACK STALLION, THE*

LORINDA HOLLINGSHEAD
EDITOR
'83 LET'S SPEND
THE NIGHT TOGETHER*
ASSISTANT EDITOR
'83 TRADING PLACES*

C. ROBERT HOLLOWAY
LOCATIONS
'82 YOUNG DOCTORS IN LOVE*
'83 PRIVATE SCHOOL

FRED HOLLOWAY
PROPS
'84 MUTANT

RICHARD HOLLOWAY
MISCELLANEOUS
'79 MUPPET MOVIE, THE

NORMAN HOLLYN
ASSISTANT EDITOR
'80 FAME*

PETER HOLLYWOOD
EDITOR
'84 RIDDLE OF THE SANDS
ASSOCIATE EDITOR
'83 SUPERMAN III

CHRISTOPHER HOLMES
EDITOR
'79 SCAVENGER HUNT
'81 NIGHTHAWKS
MISCELLANEOUS
'79 ROCKY II
'83 STAYING ALIVE

GILBERT HOLMES
MISCELLANEOUS
'79 ICE CASTLES

JOHN HOLMES
EDITOR
'79 JUST YOU AND ME KID
ASSISTANT EDITOR
'80 POPEYE*

JOHN HOLMES
MISCELLANEOUS
'79 DRACULA

PRESTON HOLMES
2ND ASST. DIRECTOR
'82 HANKY PANKY*

R. DUDLEY "ACE" HOLMES
PROPS
'79 DREAMER
'79 NORMA RAE
'80 URBAN COWBOY
'81 BACK ROADS
'81 ZORRO, THE GAY BLADE
'82 FAST TIMES AT RIDGEMONT HIGH
'83 CROSS CREEK

ROBERT HOLMES
MISCELLANEOUS
'79 FAST COMPANY

RUPERT HOLMES
MUSIC
'84 NO SMALL AFFAIR

ERIC HOLST
PROPS
'82 LAST AMERICAN VIRGIN, THE

SVEN-GOSTA HOLST
UNIT MANAGER
'81 MONTENEGRO

JUDITH HOLSTRA
CASTING
'81 SOUTHERN COMFORT
'82 48 HOURS
'83 CUJO*
'83 LONE WOLF MCQUADE*
'84 STREETS OF FIRE*

DENIS HOLT
ASSOCIATE PRODUCER
'80 FFOLKES
PRODUCTION MANAGER
'83 YELLOWBEARD*

GEORGE HOLT
MISCELLANEOUS
'83 EVIL DEAD, THE

SARAH HOLT
ASSISTANT EDITOR
'83 LIANNA*

WILLY HOLT
PRODUCTION DESIGNER
'82 FIVE DAYS ONE SUMMER

ALLAN HOLTZMAN
EDITOR
'80 BATTLE BEYOND THE STARS*

ROGER HOLZBERG
PROPS
'82 SWORD AND THE SORCERER, THE
MISCELLANEOUS
'82 SWORD AND THE SORCERER, THE

ALLAN HOLZMAN
EXEC IN CHARGE PROD
'84 FINAL TERROR, THE

ALLAN HOLZMAN
2ND UNIT DIRECTOR
'81 SMOKEY BITES THE DUST

LEVIA HON
CASTING
'83 HANNA K*

RON HONE
MISCELLANEOUS
'84 NEVERENDING STORY, THE

MARTIN HONER
2ND ASST. DIRECTOR
'79 MAGICIAN OF LUBLIN, THE

HERB HONIS
PUBLICIST
'80 STIR CRAZY
UNIT PUBLICIST
'81 FORCE FIVE
'82 HANKY PANKY

PETER HONESS
EDITOR
'84 CHAMPIONS
'84 ELECTRIC DREAMS
ASSISTANT EDITOR
'81 DOGS OF WAR, THE*
'83 HUNGER, THE

RON HONSA
MISCELLANEOUS
'79 MR. MIKE'S MONDO VIDEO

EVE LIGHT HONTHANER
UNIT PROD. MANAGER
'84 HOT DOG...THE MOVIE

LARRY HOOBERRY
SOUND
'80 CHANGE OF SEASONS, A

DAVID HOOD
2ND ASST. DIRECTOR
'84 JUST THE WAY YOU ARE*

KEES'T HOOFT
ASSISTANT EDITOR
'84 PASSAGE TO INDIA, A*

MICHAEL HOOK
1ST ASST. DIRECTOR
'84 INDIANA JONES
AND THE TEMPLE OF DOOM*

BUDDY JOE HOOKER
2ND UNIT DIRECTOR
'81 KING OF THE MOUNTAIN
STUNT COORDINATOR
'80 CLOSE ENCOUNTERS OF THE THIRD
KIND SPECIAL EDITION
'80 DEFIANCE*
'80 HERBIE GOES BANANAS
'81 HAND, THE
'83 RIGHT STUFF, THE
'83 RUMBLEFISH
'83 BEYOND THE LIMIT
'83 OUTSIDERS, THE
MISCELLANEOUS
'79 GAME OF DEATH

LANCE HOOL
PRODUCER
'83 10 TO MIDNIGHT*
EXECUTIVE PRODUCER
'84 EVIL THAT MEN DO, THE

WILLIAM HOOL
MISCELLANEOUS
'83 10 TO MIDNIGHT

SPIKE ALLISON HOOPER
ASSISTANT EDITOR
'84 TERMINATOR, THE*

TOBE HOOPER
DIRECTOR
'81 FUNHOUSE, THE
'82 POLTERGEIST

ARTHUR HOPCRAFT
SCREENPLAY
'79 AGATHA*

KATHRYN RUTH HOPE
EDITOR
'81 STUDENT BODIES

ALAN HOPGOOD
SCREENPLAY
'81 MAN WHO SAW TOMORROW, THE*

ALAN HOPKINS
1ST ASST. DIRECTOR
'79 WANDERERS, THE
'80 CRUISING
'80 TIMES SQUARE
'81 PRINCE OF THE CITY
'81 REDS*
'82 WORLD ACCORDING TO GARP, THE
'83 STRANGE INVADERS*
'83 JAWS 3-D*
'83 NIGHT IN HEAVEN, A
'83 WRONG IS RIGHT*
'84 GARBO TALKS
'84 BEAT STREET*

JOHN HOPKINS
SCREENPLAY
'79 MURDER BY DECREE

SPEED HOPKINS
ART DIRECTOR
'82 MIDSUMMER NIGHT'S
SEX COMEDY, A
'83 ZELIG
'84 FALLING IN LOVE
'84 NATURAL, THE*

MATEEL HOPPE
ASSISTANT EDITOR
'84 CRACKERS*

MICHAEL HOPPE
MUSIC
'84 MISUNDERSTOOD

DENNIS HOPPER
DIRECTOR
'82 OUT OF THE BLUE

DARBY HOPPIN
HAIR
'79 BEYOND THE POSEIDON ADVENTURE*
'80 WHEN TIME RAN OUT*
'81 INCHON*

NANCY HOPTON
SCRIPT SUPERVISOR
'80 GILDA LIVE*
'80 GLORIA
'81 FOUR FRIENDS

JOHN HORA
CINEMATOGRAPHER
'81 HOWLING, THE
'82 LIAR'S MOON
'83 TWILIGHT ZONE, THE MOVIE*
'84 GREMLINS

PATRICK HORGAN
MISCELLANEOUS
'83 ZELIG

JACK HORGER
EDITOR
'79 FRISCO KID, THE*

GEORGE HORN
STILLS
'83 MORTUARY

KENNETH HORN
MISCELLANEOUS
'81 HELL NIGHT

JEFFREY HORNADAY
CHOREOGRAPHER
'83 D.C. CAB
'83 FLASHDANCE
'84 STREETS OF FIRE
'84 ROMANCING THE STONE

JOE HORNAK
MISCELLANEOUS
'81 WOLFEN

DAVID HORNE
UNIT MANAGER
'82 MONTY PYTHON LIVE AT THE HOLLYWOOD BOWL

CHRIS HORNER
ART DIRECTOR
'83 JAWS 3-D*

HARRY HORNER
PRODUCTION DESIGNER
'80 JAZZ SINGER, THE

JAMES HORNER
MUSIC
'80 BATTLE BEYOND THE STARS
'80 HUMANOIDS FROM THE DEEP
'81 DEADLY BLESSING
'81 HAND, THE
'81 PURSUIT OF D.B. COOPER, THE
'81 WOLFEN
'82 STAR TREK II THE WRATH OF KHAN
'82 48 HOURS
'83 SOMETHING WICKED THIS WAY COMES
'83 BRAINSTORM
'83 DRESSER, THE
'83 GORKY PARK
'83 KRULL
'83 TESTAMENT
'83 UNCOMMON VALOR
'84 STAR TREK III: THE SEARCH FOR SPOCK
'84 STONE BOY, THE

LINDA HORNER
ASSOCIATE PRODUCER
'83 STAYING ALIVE
'84 BEVERLY HILLS COP
'84 RHINESTONE*

JOSEPH HORNOK
MISCELLANEOUS
'79 C.H.O.M.P.S.
'84 DREAMSCAPE

MARTIN HORNSTEIN
ASSOCIATE PRODUCER
'82 I, THE JURY
'83 BAD BOYS
UNIT PROD. MANAGER
'82 I, THE JURY
'83 BAD BOYS

HOWIE HOROWITZ
2ND ASST. DIRECTOR
'82 LITTLE SEX, A*

ISRAEL HOROWITZ
SCREENPLAY
'82 AUTHOR, AUTHOR

DAVID HORTON
MISCELLANEOUS
'79 QUINTET

GAYLOR HORTON
MUSIC SUPERVISOR
'84 BODY ROCK

JOHN HORTON
MISCELLANEOUS
'81 FIRST MONDAY IN OCTOBER

MICHAEL HORTON
2ND UNIT DIRECTOR
'83 NATE & HAYES

LOUIS HORVATH
CINEMATOGRAPHER
'81 STRANGE BEHAVIOR
'83 STRANGE INVADERS

ROBERT HORVATICH
SPECIAL EFFECTS
'80 FOXES

ANDY HORVITCH
EDITOR
'82 ANDROID*

NICK HOSKER
ASSISTANT EDITOR
'81 EYE OF THE NEEDLE

JOE HOSKING
LOCATIONS
'82 YOUNG DOCTORS IN LOVE*

TRACY HOTCHNER
SCREENPLAY
'81 MOMMIE DEAREST*

JOHN HOUGH
DIRECTOR
'80 WATCHER IN THE WOODS, THE

BUCK HOUGHTON
PRODUCER
'82 ESCAPE ARTIST, THE*

SHELLEY HOUIS
PROD. OFFICE COORD.
'83 BABY IT'S YOU
'83 DANIEL
'83 KING OF COMEDY, THE
'84 NATURAL, THE

PETER HOULT
2ND ASST. DIRECTOR
'82 VICTOR/VICTORIA*

RICHARD HOULT
1ST ASST. DIRECTOR
'80 WATCHER IN THE WOODS, THE
'81 FRENCH LIEUTENANT'S WOMAN, THE
'82 VICTOR/VICTORIA

CHARLES HOUSE
MAKEUP
'81 STRIPES*
'81 BUSTIN' LOOSE*

JENNIFER HOUSTON
ASSISTANT EDITOR
'83 FRIGHTMARE*

JOHN HOUSTON
1ST ASST. DIRECTOR
'83 NEVER CRY WOLF*

ELLEN HOVDE
EDITOR
'80 GILDA LIVE*

ADRIAN HOWARD
ASSOCIATE PRODUCER
'80 DEATH SHIP

ANDY HOWARD
CO-PRODUCER
'82 SILENT RAGE
MISCELLANEOUS
'84 STONE BOY, THE

CATHERINE HOWARD
PROD. COORDINATOR
'82 MOTHER LODE

JEFF HOWARD
ART DIRECTOR
'80 PRIVATE BENJAMIN*

JOHN HOWARD
EDITOR
'79 NIGHTWING
'79 AMERICATHON
'80 WHY WOULD I LIE?
'81 HISTORY OF THE WORLD PART I
'83 ROMANTIC COMEDY

LINDA HOWARD
<u>ASSOCIATE PRODUCER</u>
'80 GONG SHOW MOVIE, THE
'83 RICHARD PRYOR: HERE AND NOW
<u>UNIT PROD. MANAGER</u>
'83 RICHARD PRYOR: HERE AND NOW
<u>1ST ASST. DIRECTOR</u>
'83 RICHARD PRYOR: HERE AND NOW

MEL HOWARD
<u>ASSOCIATE PRODUCER</u>
'82 CHOSEN, THE
'84 BEAT STREET
<u>1ST ASST. DIRECTOR</u>
'80 NIGHT OF THE JUGGLER*

RON HOWARD
<u>DIRECTOR</u>
'82 NIGHT SHIFT
'84 SPLASH

SANDY HOWARD
<u>PRODUCER</u>
'79 CIRCLE OF IRON*
'83 DEADLY FORCE
<u>SCREENPLAY</u>
'82 VICE SQUAD*
<u>EXECUTIVE PRODUCER</u>
'79 JAGUAR LIVES
'79 METEOR*
'80 DEATH SHIP
'82 VICE SQUAD*

TONI HOWARD
<u>CASTING</u>
'81 MODERN PROBLEMS*
'82 AIRPLANE II: THE SEQUEL*
'82 FIRST BLOOD*
'82 HANKY PANKY*
'82 MAKING LOVE*
'82 TOOTSIE*
'83 RIGHT STUFF, THE*
'83 BRAINSTORM*
'83 CLASS*
'83 MR. MOM*
'83 UNCOMMON VALOR*
'84 LONELY GUY, THE*
'84 HARRY & SON*
'84 SUPERGIRL*
'84 UNFAITHFULLY YOURS*

ALAN HOWARTH
<u>MUSIC</u>
'81 ESCAPE FROM NEW YORK*
'81 HALLOWEEN II*
'82 HALLOWEEN III:
SEASON OF THE WITCH*
'83 CHRISTINE*

DEREK HOWARTH
<u>MISCELLANEOUS</u>
'81 DRAGONSLAYER
'84 INDIANA JONES
AND THE TEMPLE OF DOOM

BONES HOWE
<u>MISCELLANEOUS</u>
'84 ADVENTURES OF BUCKAROO BANZAI
ACROSS THE 8TH DIMENSION,THE

DAVID HOWE
<u>ASSISTANT EDITOR</u>
'79 BUCK ROGERS*

JIM HOWE
<u>ASSISTANT EDITOR</u>
'82 VENOM*
'84 SCANDALOUS*

LARRY HOWE
<u>STUNT COORDINATOR</u>
'83 METALSTORM: THE DESTRUCTION
OF JARED-SYN*

MONICA HOWE
<u>MISCELLANEOUS</u>
'83 BRITANNIA HOSPITAL

CAMRON "BUD" HOWELL
<u>KEY GRIP</u>
'79 FISH THAT
SAVED PITTSBURGH, THE
'79 10
'81 FORCE FIVE

CHRIS HOWELL
<u>STUNT COORDINATOR</u>
'80 JAZZ SINGER, THE
'80 URBAN COWBOY
'80 NIGHT OF THE JUGGLER
'81 ENTITY, THE
'81 SMOKEY BITES THE DUST*
'83 AMITYVILLE 3D

ENID HOWELL
<u>MISCELLANEOUS</u>
'82 LOVE CHILD

SUZIE HOWIE
<u>PUBLICIST</u>
'84 PHAR LAP
<u>UNIT PUBLICIST</u>
'83 MAN FROM SNOWY RIVER, THE

PETER HOWITT
<u>ART DIRECTOR</u>
'81 CLASH OF THE TITANS*

ROBERT HOWLAND
<u>PROPS</u>
'82 ANDROID
'82 PARASITE
'83 LOVE LETTERS

RICHARD HOWORTH
<u>ASSOCIATE PRODUCER</u>
'81 MS. 45*
<u>ASSISTANT EDITOR</u>
'81 MS. 45
<u>PRODUCTION MANAGER</u>
'81 MS. 45*

MAYSIE HOY
<u>ASSISTANT EDITOR</u>
'79 REMEMBER MY NAME*

WILLIAM HOY
<u>ASSISTANT EDITOR</u>
'79 QUINTET*
'80 HEALTH*
'84 ICE PIRATES, THE

LESTER HOYLE
<u>SCRIPT SUPERVISOR</u>
'79 SUNBURN
'81 CATTLE ANNIE
AND LITTLE BRITCHES
'84 GRANDVIEW, U.S.A.

ROBERT HOYT
<u>SOUND</u>
'79 PRISONER OF ZENDA, THE*

VICTOR HSU
<u>1ST ASST. DIRECTOR</u>
'79 NORTH DALLAS FORTY
'82 LITTLE SEX, A
<u>2ND ASST. DIRECTOR</u>
'79 WHEN YOU COMIN'
BACK, RED RYDER?

AUGUSTIN HUARTE
<u>ART DIRECTOR</u>
'84 ROMANCING THE STONE

CHARLES HUBBARD
<u>2ND ASST. DIRECTOR</u>
'84 KILLING FIELDS, THE*

JANE HUBBARD
<u>PROD. OFFICE COORD.</u>
'80 HOME MOVIES

GILL HUBBS
<u>CINEMATOGRAPHER</u>
'81 FORCE FIVE

BRIAN HUBERMAN
<u>CINEMATOGRAPHER</u>
'84 LAST NIGHT AT THE ALAMO*

AXEL ANTON HUBERT
<u>ASSISTANT EDITOR</u>
'83 SOMETHING WICKED
THIS WAY COMES
'84 AMERICAN DREAMER*

JACQUES HUBERT
<u>2ND ASST. DIRECTOR</u>
'82 MOTHER LODE

RAY HUBLEY
<u>ASSISTANT EDITOR</u>
'84 FIRSTBORN*

JOHN HUCK
<u>SOUND</u>
'82 BRAINWAVES*
'83 SUBURBIA

BILL HUCR
MISCELLANEOUS
'80 EYES OF A STRANGER

ROBERT HUDDLESTON
UNIT PROD. MANAGER
'82 HAMMETT*

JOHN HUDECEK
KEY GRIP
'83 BIG SCORE, THE

WENDY HUDOLIN
COSTUMES
'83 RUNNING BRAVE

CLAUDE HUDSON
PRODUCTION MANAGER
'84 KILLING FIELDS, THE*
MISCELLANEOUS
'81 EYE OF THE NEEDLE

HUGH HUDSON
PRODUCER
'84 GREYSTOKE: THE LEGEND OF TARZAN, LORD OF THE APES*
DIRECTOR
'81 CHARIOTS OF FIRE
'84 GREYSTOKE: THE LEGEND OF TARZAN, LORD OF THE APES

KAREN HUDSON
COSTUMES
'80 MOTEL HELL*

WILLIAM HUDSON
PROPS
'79 SUNBURN
'80 BIG BRAWL, THE
'80 MOTEL HELL

KARL HUEGLIN
ART DIRECTOR
'83 WRONG IS RIGHT

ARMANDO HUERTA
2ND ASST. DIRECTOR
'81 ALL NIGHT LONG

TOM HUFF
STUNT COORDINATOR
'83 OSTERMAN WEEKEND, THE
'84 WOMAN IN RED, THE

PHYLLIS HUFFMAN
CASTING
'80 XANADU
'82 SOUP FOR ONE*
'83 INDEPENDENCE DAY*
'83 NATIONAL LAMPOON'S VACATION*
'84 TIGHTROPE

STEVEN HUFSTETER
MUSIC
'84 REPO MAN*

ED HUGETZ
EXECUTIVE PRODUCER
'84 LAST NIGHT AT THE ALAMO

JERE HUGGINS
ASSISTANT EDITOR
'80 CRUISING*

ADRIAN HUGHES
MISCELLANEOUS
'79 JAGUAR LIVES

BOB HUGHES
MISCELLANEOUS
'83 NATE & HAYES

CHARLES HUGHES
ART DIRECTOR
'83 MAN WHO WASN'T THERE, THE

COOPER HUGHES
MUSIC
'84 C.H.U.D.

DICK HUGHES
ART DIRECTOR
'81 FOUR FRIENDS

ERIC HUGHES
SCREENPLAY
'84 AGAINST ALL ODDS

JOHN HUGHES
DIRECTOR
'84 SIXTEEN CANDLES
SCREENPLAY
'82 NATIONAL LAMPOON'S CLASS REUNION
'83 MR. MOM
'83 NATE & HAYES*
'83 NATIONAL LAMPOON'S VACATION
'84 SIXTEEN CANDLES

JULIE HUGHES
CASTING
'80 FRIDAY THE 13TH*
'81 ENDLESS LOVE*
'82 STRANGER IS WATCHING, A*
'83 SPRING BREAK*
MISCELLANEOUS
'84 COTTON CLUB, THE

KATHLEEN HUGHES
PROPS
'80 FOG, THE
'80 HUMANOIDS FROM THE DEEP
'81 PRIVATE LESSONS
'82 I'M DANCING AS FAST AS I CAN

STEPHANIE HUGHES
MISCELLANEOUS
'83 FRIGHTMARE

TERRY HUGHES
PRODUCER
'82 MONTY PYTHON LIVE AT THE HOLLYWOOD BOWL
DIRECTOR
'82 MONTY PYTHON LIVE AT THE HOLLYWOOD BOWL*

WHITEY HUGHES
STUNT COORDINATOR
'82 DEATH VALLEY
'84 COUNTRY

MICHAEL HUGO
CINEMATOGRAPHER
'80 MOUNTAIN MEN, THE
'80 OCTAGON, THE

JAY HUMBROCK
ASSISTANT EDITOR
'81 PURSUIT OF D.B. COOPER, THE*

ALAN HUME
CINEMATOGRAPHER
'79 ARABIAN ADVENTURE
'79 LEGACY, THE*
'80 WATCHER IN THE WOODS, THE
'81 CAVEMAN
'81 EYE OF THE NEEDLE
'81 FOR YOUR EYES ONLY
'83 RETURN OF THE JEDI*
'83 OCTOPUSSY
'84 SUPERGIRL

JEREMY HUME
ASSISTANT EDITOR
'80 FLASH GORDON*
'80 TESS*
'81 FRENCH LIEUTENANT'S WOMAN, THE*
'83 BETRAYAL

BRIAN HUMPHREY
PROPS
'81 FOR YOUR EYES ONLY
'83 GORKY PARK
'83 MONTY PYTHON'S THE MEANING OF LIFE*
'84 FINDERS KEEPERS

DAVE HUMPHREYS
KEY GRIP
'83 RUNNING BRAVE

NED HUMPHREYS
EDITOR
'84 JOY OF SEX, THE*
ASSISTANT EDITOR
'80 CRUISING*

RICHARD HUMPHREYS
STUNT COORDINATOR
'84 DUNE

CRAIG HUNDLEY
MUSIC
'80 ROADIE
'80 ALLIGATOR
'80 SCHIZOID
'83 AMERICANA

MEG HUNNEWELL
UNIT PROD. MANAGER
'84 COTTON CLUB, THE*
LOCATIONS
'79 LAST EMBRACE*
'80 WINDOWS*

BOB HUNT
SCREENPLAY
'82 BOOGENS, THE*

COLIN HUNT
MISCELLANEOUS
'83 PRIVATES ON PARADE

DENNIS HUNT
STUNT COORDINATOR
'81 GALLIPOLI*

GEOLF HUNT
UNIT MANAGER
'83 MAN FROM SNOWY RIVER, THE

PAUL HUNT
ASSOCIATE EDITOR
'83 AMERICANA*

PETER HUNT
DIRECTOR
'81 DEATH HUNT

TERESA HUNT
MISCELLANEOUS
'83 OUTSIDERS, THE

ALBERTA HUNTER
MUSIC
'79 REMEMBER MY NAME

DENISE HUNTER
ASSISTANT EDITOR
'82 PIRATE MOVIE, THE

JEFF HUNTER
STILLS
'79 GREAT BANK HOAX, THE

JOHN HUNTER
SCREENPLAY
'82 GREY FOX, THE

MICHAEL HUNTER
PROPS
'80 OH! HEAVENLY DOG*
'83 DRAUGHTSMAN CONTRACT, THE*

TERRY HUNTER
PROD. COORDINATOR
'79 ROCK 'N ROLL HIGH SCHOOL

THOMAS HUNTER
SCREENPLAY
'80 FINAL COUNTDOWN, THE*

TIM HUNTER
DIRECTOR
'82 TEX
SCREENPLAY
'79 OVER THE EDGE*
'82 TEX*

EARL HUNTOON
PROPS
'81 CATTLE ANNIE
AND LITTLE BRITCHES

GALE ANN HURD
PRODUCER
'84 TERMINATOR, THE
SCREENPLAY
'84 TERMINATOR, THE*
CO-PRODUCER
'81 SMOKEY BITES THE DUST

IRA HURVITZ
2ND ASST. DIRECTOR
'83 SMITHEREENS

HARRY HURWITZ
DIRECTOR
'82 SAFARI 3000

HARRY HURWITZ
SCREENPLAY
'81 UNDER THE RAINBOW*

HARRY HURWITZ
EXECUTIVE PRODUCER
'83 BIG SCORE, THE*

MARK HURWITZ
LOCATIONS
'79 WINTER KILLS

CHUNKY HUSE
KEY GRIP
'79 AVALANCHE EXPRESS
'80 ISLAND, THE
'81 SPHINX
'81 FOR YOUR EYES ONLY

PERRY HUSMAN
2ND ASST. DIRECTOR
'84 SILENT NIGHT, DEADLY NIGHT

CRAIG HUSTON
1ST ASST. DIRECTOR
'79 RUNNER STUMBLES, THE
'80 RESURRECTION
'80 BIG BRAWL, THE
'80 FOOLIN AROUND
'80 THOSE LIPS, THOSE EYES
'82 SPLIT IMAGE
'82 FIRST BLOOD
'83 UNCOMMON VALOR

JOHN HUSTON
DIRECTOR
'81 VICTORY
'82 ANNIE
'84 UNDER THE VOLCANO

ETELVINA HUTCHINS
MISCELLANEOUS
'83 ECHOES

BRENDA HUTCHINSON
MUSIC
'83 LIQUID SKY*

BRUCE HUTCHINSON
MAKEUP
'82 NIGHT SHIFT

JOHN HUTCHINSON III, M.D.
MISCELLANEOUS
'79 ALL THAT JAZZ

JOIE HUTCHINSON
COSTUME SUPERVISOR
'81 FORCE FIVE

PETER HUTCHINSON
SPECIAL EFFECTS
'80 KIDNAPPING OF
THE PRESIDENT, THE
'81 EXCALIBUR*
'83 PRIVATES ON PARADE
'84 GREYSTOKE: THE LEGEND OF
TARZAN, LORD OF THE APES
SP. EFFECTS SUPERV.
'84 SHEENA

TIM HUTCHINSON
ART DIRECTOR
'81 EXCALIBUR
'82 VICTOR/VICTORIA*
'83 CURSE OF THE PINK PANTHER
'83 TRAIL OF THE PINK PANTHER*

JOSEPH HUTSHING
ASSISTANT EDITOR
'83 VALLEY GIRL

BRIAN HUTTON
DIRECTOR
'80 FIRST DEADLY SIN
'83 HIGH ROAD TO CHINA

CHRIS HUTTON
ASSISTANT EDITOR
'81 SCANNERS*

WILLARD HUYCK
DIRECTOR
'84 BEST DEFENSE
SCREENPLAY
'84 BEST DEFENSE*
'84 INDIANA JONES AND THE TEMPLE OF DOOM*

LUCIA HWONG
MISCELLANEOUS
'82 HAMMETT

PETER HYAMS
PRODUCER
'84 2010
DIRECTOR
'79 HANOVER STREET
'81 OUTLAND
'83 STAR CHAMBER
'84 2010
SCREENPLAY
'79 HANOVER STREET
'80 HUNTER, THE*
'81 OUTLAND
'83 STAR CHAMBER*
'84 2010
CINEMATOGRAPHER
'84 2010

JOHN HYDE
EXEC IN CHARGE PROD
'80 CHANGE OF SEASONS, A
'80 FINAL COUNTDOWN, THE
'81 DEAD AND BURIED

JOHN HYDE
PRODUCER
'79 RAVAGERS

JOHN HYDE
EXECUTIVE PRODUCER
'84 NEVERENDING STORY, THE*

VERNON HYDE
SPECIAL EFFECTS
'79 PRIZE FIGHTER, THE*
'84 LOVELESS, THE*
MISCELLANEOUS
'84 MUTANT

DICK HYMAN
MUSIC
'83 ZELIG
MUSIC SUPERVISOR
'84 BROADWAY DANNY ROSE

RICHARD HYMNS
ASSISTANT EDITOR
'82 SHOOT THE MOON*
'84 BIRDY*

PENELOPE HYNAM
SCRIPT SUPERVISOR
'79 RUNNING
'80 MIDDLE AGE CRAZY
'82 MOTHER LODE
'83 STRANGE BREW
'84 POLICE ACADEMY
'84 MRS. SOFFEL

DR. J. ALLEN HYNEK
MISCELLANEOUS
'80 CLOSE ENCOUNTERS OF THE THIRD KIND SPECIAL EDITION

JOEL HYNEK
MISCELLANEOUS
'80 XANADU

I

ED IACOBELLI
STUNT COORDINATOR
'79 SEDUCTION OF JOE TYNAN, THE

GEORGE "IACO" IACONELLI
PROPS
'84 CHEECH AND CHONG'S THE CORSICAN BROTHERS
SPECIAL EFFECTS
'83 ENIGMA
'83 TRENCHCOAT
'84 CHEECH AND CHONG'S THE CORSICAN BROTHERS

NILO IACOPONI
MAKEUP
'81 THEY ALL LAUGHED*

ARTHUR IBBETSON
CINEMATOGRAPHER
'79 PRISONER OF ZENDA, THE
'80 HOPSCOTCH
'80 NOTHING PERSONAL*
'84 BOUNTY, THE

PAUL IBBETSON
1ST ASST. DIRECTOR
'79 ALIEN

MOYA ICETON
SCRIPT SUPERVISOR
'79 MY BRILLIANT CAREER
'81 GALLIPOLI
'83 YEAR OF LIVING DANGEROUSLY, THE

ALOMA ICHINOSE
STILLS
'83 LOSIN' IT
'84 BACHELOR PARTY
'84 DREAMSCAPE*

ERIC IDLE
SCREENPLAY
'79 MONTY PYTHON'S LIFE OF BRIAN*
'82 MONTY PYTHON LIVE AT THE HOLLYWOOD BOWL*
'83 MONTY PYTHON'S THE MEANING OF LIFE*

RACHEL IGEL
ASSISTANT EDITOR
'80 CADDYSHACK
'81 ALL NIGHT LONG*
'83 BREATHLESS

CHRIS IKEDA
PROD. COORDINATOR
'81 BUDDY, BUDDY

SHIGEKAZU IKUNO
ART DIRECTOR
'81 INCHON*

PETER ILARDI
SOUND
'79 ALL THAT JAZZ*
'81 NEIGHBORS*
'82 HANKY PANKY
'82 LITTLE SEX, A
'84 FLAMINGO KID, THE

TONY IMI
CINEMATOGRAPHER
'80 FFOLKES
'81 SEA WOLVES, THE
'82 NIGHT CROSSING
'83 NATE & HAYES

JERROLD IMMEL
MUSIC
'81 DEATH HUNT
'82 MEGAFORCE

WILLIAM IMMERMAN
EXECUTIVE PRODUCER
'81 SOUTHERN COMFORT
'81 TAKE THIS JOB AND SHOVE IT*

LEONCIO IMPERIAL
EXECUTIVE PRODUCER
'83 BLIND RAGE*

MARK INDIG
LOCATIONS
'80 WINDOWS*
'81 BODY HEAT*
'81 FAN, THE
'83 BIG CHILL, THE*

MICHAEL INGBER
EXECUTIVE PRODUCER
'79 SOMETHING SHORT OF PARADISE

SYLVIA INGEMARSSON
EDITOR
'81 MONTENEGRO

MADELEINE INGLEHEARN
CHOREOGRAPHER
'83 WICKED LADY, THE

JOSEPH INGRAFFIA
2ND ASST. DIRECTOR
'80 USED CARS
'81 LEGEND OF THE LONE RANGER, THE
'81 WHOSE LIFE IS IT ANYWAY?*

PRECI INIEGO
CASTING
'83 YEAR OF LIVING DANGEROUSLY, THE*

FRANK INN
MISCELLANEOUS
'80 FOR THE LOVE OF BENJI
'80 OH! HEAVENLY DOG
'82 NATIONAL LAMPOON'S CLASS REUNION

JUANITA INN
MISCELLANEOUS
'80 OH! HEAVENLY DOG

JACQUES INNOCENTI
UNIT MANAGER
'84 UNTIL SEPTEMBER

DAVID INSLEY
CINEMATOGRAPHER
'81 POLYESTER

LANA INY
PUBLICIST
'82 PARADISE

JIMMY IOVINE
MISCELLANEOUS
'84 STREETS OF FIRE

PETER IOVINO
STILLS
'84 MUTANT*

JANE IREDALE
CASTING
'83 OUTSIDERS, THE*

JILL IRELAND
ASSOCIATE PRODUCER
'84 EVIL THAT MEN DO, THE*

JOHN IRVIN
DIRECTOR
'81 GHOST STORY
'81 DOGS OF WAR, THE
'84 CHAMPIONS

SAM IRVIN
PRODUCER
'82 FIRST TIME, THE
ASSOCIATE PRODUCER
'80 HOME MOVIES*
PRODUCTION MANAGER
'80 HOME MOVIES

FRANK IRVINE
EDITOR
'82 GREY FOX, THE

RICH IRVINE
EXECUTIVE PRODUCER
'80 WHY WOULD I LIE?*
'83 EDDIE AND THE CRUISERS*
'83 HEART LIKE A WHEEL*

THOMAS IRVINE
1ST ASST. DIRECTOR
'84 TERMINATOR, THE*

CONRAD IRVING
2ND ASST. DIRECTOR
'82 FORCED VENGEANCE

MARK IRWIN
CINEMATOGRAPHER
'79 BROOD, THE
'79 FAST COMPANY
'81 SCANNERS
'83 DEAD ZONE, THE
'83 VIDEODROME

LUCERO ISAAC
ART DIRECTOR
'82 MISSING*

BUD ISAACS
MISCELLANEOUS
'81 BLOOD BEACH

FRANK ISAACS
MISCELLANEOUS
'80 GALAXINA
'83 METALSTORM: THE DESTRUCTION OF JARED-SYN
'83 METALSTORM: THE DESTRUCTION OF JARED-SYN

JOHN ISAACS
HAIR
'79 10*
'80 LITTLE MISS MARKER*
'81 S.O.B.*
'83 CURSE OF THE PINK PANTHER
'84 MICKI AND MAUDE*

KARYN ISAACS
MISCELLANEOUS
'84 CHOOSE ME

DAN ISAACSON
MISCELLANEOUS
'83 STAYING ALIVE

JOAN ISAACSON
MAKEUP
'80 TERROR TRAIN*
'80 HOG WILD
'80 DEATH SHIP
'82 QUEST FOR FIRE*

MARIO ISCOVICH
ASSOCIATE PRODUCER
'79 RUNNER STUMBLES, THE
LOCATIONS
'84 2010

LENNY ISENBERG
PRODUCER
'80 CHEAPER TO KEEP HER

MARK ISHAM
MUSIC
'83 NEVER CRY WOLF
'84 MRS. SOFFEL

YOSHIYUKI ISHIDA
ART DIRECTOR
'82 CHALLENGE, THE
PRODUCTION DESIGNER
'82 CHALLENGE, THE

MITSUHARU ISHII
PRODUCER
'81 INCHON

KENNETH ISLEY
SOUND
'79 BOULEVARD NIGHTS*
'81 MAN WHO SAW TOMORROW, THE*

MONIQUE ISNARDON
EDITOR
'81 SUNDAY LOVERS*

ROBERT ISNARDON
EDITOR
'81 SUNDAY LOVERS*

FRED ISOLA
PROPS
'80 UNION CITY

BOB ISRAEL
PRODUCER
'84 BACHELOR PARTY*

DAVID ISRAEL
LOCATIONS
'81 FIRST MONDAY IN OCTOBER*
'83 INDEPENDENCE DAY

NANCY ISRAEL
ASSOCIATE PRODUCER
'84 NIGHT OF THE COMET*
PRODUCTION MANAGER
'83 VALLEY GIRL
'84 NIGHT OF THE COMET
1ST ASST. DIRECTOR
'83 VALLEY GIRL*

NEAL ISRAEL
DIRECTOR
'79 AMERICATHON
'84 BACHELOR PARTY
SCREENPLAY
'79 AMERICATHON*
'84 POLICE ACADEMY*
'84 BACHELOR PARTY*

NEIL ISRAEL
MISCELLANEOUS
'84 JOHNNY DANGEROUSLY

AUGUSTIN ITUARTE
ART DIRECTOR
'79 SUNBURN
PRODUCTION DESIGNER
'81 HIGH RISK

BETTE IVERSON
HAIR
'81 RAGGEDY MAN
'82 MISSING*
'83 BRAINSTORM*

GWEN IVESON
PRODUCTION MANAGER
'79 BROOD, THE
'83 VIDEODROME

DON IVEY
ART DIRECTOR
'81 HARDLY WORKING
'81 NOBODY'S PERFEKT
'82 LOVE CHILD
'83 BLUE SKIES AGAIN

JAMES IVORY
DIRECTOR
'79 EUROPEANS, THE
'80 QUARTET
'83 HEAT AND DUST
'84 BOSTONIANS, THE

DAVE IWERKS
MISCELLANEOUS
'82 TRON

CONNIE IZAY
MISCELLANEOUS
'80 INSIDE MOVES

IWONA IZDEBSKA
MISCELLANEOUS
'83 TO BE OR NOT TO BE

J

MICHAEL JABLOW
EDITOR
'81 MODERN PROBLEMS
'83 GET CRAZY*

SHONAGH JABOUR
MAKEUP
'79 BROOD, THE
'83 DEAD ZONE, THE
'83 VIDEODROME

CAROL ANN JACKSON
ASSISTANT EDITOR
'80 HUNTER, THE
'80 ORDINARY PEOPLE*
'84 SPLASH*

DEBRA DEVITO JACKSON
ASSISTANT EDITOR
'83 CAN SHE BAKE A CHERRY PIE?*

DOUG JACKSON
EDITOR
'83 FRIGHTMARE

FIONA JACKSON
CASTING
'79 MAN, A WOMAN AND A BANK, A*
2ND ASST. DIRECTOR
'80 CHANGELING, THE

JOE JACKSON
MUSIC
'84 MIKE'S MURDER*

LESLIE JACKSON
2ND ASST. DIRECTOR
'83 BUDDY SYSTEM, THE*

MARK JACKSON
SCREENPLAY
'80 EYES OF A STRANGER*

REG JACKSON
PUBLICIST
'80 HANGAR 18

REGGIE JACKSON
LOCATIONS
'84 PHILADELPHIA EXPERIMENT, THE*

ROBERT JACKSON
SOUND
'84 CHOOSE ME*

STEPHANIE JACKSON
MISCELLANEOUS
'80 SMALL CIRCLE OF FRIENDS, A

TONY JACKSON
SOUND
'79 SHOUT, THE
'82 MISSIONARY, THE

VEDA JACKSON
CHOREOGRAPHER
'82 JEKYLL AND HYDE
TOGETHER AGAIN*

MICHAEL JACOBI
ASSISTANT EDITOR
'79 APOCALYPSE NOW

ALLAN JACOBS
EDITOR
'79 LOVE AT FIRST BITE*
'81 DEATH HUNT*
'81 PURSUIT OF D.B. COOPER, THE*
'84 LASSITER*
'84 JOY OF SEX, THE*

DOUG JACOBS
MISCELLANEOUS
'83 PORKY'S II THE NEXT DAY

LILITH JACOBS
PROD. OFFICE COORD.
'80 JUST TELL ME WHAT YOU WANT*

NEWTON JACOBS
EXECUTIVE PRODUCER
'80 GALAXINA

RODGER JACOBS
MAKEUP
'80 MY BODYGUARD*
'81 ON THE RIGHT TRACK
'83 CLASS*
'84 SIXTEEN CANDLES*

RON JACOBS
ASSISTANT EDITOR
'83 SURVIVORS, THE*

RONALD JACOBS
PRODUCER
'81 ON THE RIGHT TRACK

SEAMAN JACOBS
SCREENPLAY
'80 OH GOD! BOOK II*

WILLIAM JACOBS
ASSISTANT EDITOR
'81 DEATH HUNT*
'81 KING OF THE MOUNTAIN*

JACK JACOBSEN
SOUND
'79 KRAMER VS. KRAMER
'79 WARRIORS, THE*
'80 GLORIA*
'81 ENDLESS LOVE
'81 FORT APACHE, THE BRONX
'83 JAWS 3-D
'83 TOUGH ENOUGH
'83 WITHOUT A TRACE
'84 COTTON CLUB, THE

VIRGINIA JACOBSEN
MAKEUP
'84 HOT DOG...THE MOVIE*

KISUNA JACOBSON
SCRIPT SUPERVISOR
'83 CHRISTINE
'84 REVENGE OF THE NERDS

TOM JACOBSON
ASSOCIATE PRODUCER
'80 ALLIGATOR
'83 FLASHDANCE*
'84 THIEF OF HEARTS
'84 TOP SECRET!
PRODUCTION MANAGER
'80 ALLIGATOR
'82 BEST FRIENDS
'84 THIEF OF HEARTS
UNIT PROD. MANAGER
'83 FLASHDANCE
UNIT MANAGER
'82 CAT PEOPLE*
LOCATIONS
'80 CAN'T STOP THE MUSIC*
MISCELLANEOUS
'79 AMERICAN GIGOLO

GORDON JACOBY
MISCELLANEOUS
'84 COTTON CLUB, THE

JOSEPH JACOBY
PRODUCER
'79 GREAT BANK HOAX, THE*
DIRECTOR
'79 GREAT BANK HOAX, THE
SCREENPLAY
'79 GREAT BANK HOAX, THE

NANCY PLATT JACOBY
EXEC IN CHARGE PROD
'81 HALLOWEEN II

NILO JACOPONI
MAKEUP
'79 BLOODLINE*
'81 INCHON*
'84 ONCE UPON A TIME IN AMERICA*

ANDREW JACQUEMIN
MUSIC SUPERVISOR
'82 MONTY PYTHON LIVE AT THE HOLLYWOOD BOWL

DENNY JAEGER
MUSIC
'83 HUNGER, THE*

ANDREA JAFFE
PUBLICIST
'81 TAPS*

GIB JAFFE
ASSISTANT EDITOR
'80 ROADIE
'82 ROCKY III*
MISCELLANEOUS
'84 SWING SHIFT

HERB JAFFE
PRODUCER
'79 TIME AFTER TIME
'82 JINXED
'83 LORDS OF DISCIPLINE, THE*
EXECUTIVE PRODUCER
'80 MOTEL HELL
'80 THOSE LIPS, THOSE EYES

HOWARD JAFFE
PRODUCER
'81 TAPS*

JANE SCHWARTZ JAFFE
ASSISTANT EDITOR
'83 MAX DUGAN RETURNS
'84 ADVENTURES OF BUCKAROO BANZAI ACROSS THE 8TH DIMENSION, THE*

LOUISE JAFFE
SCRIPT SUPERVISOR
'79 MOUNTAIN FAMILY ROBINSON
'80 NIJINSKY
'81 SPHINX
'81 ESCAPE FROM NEW YORK
'82 HALLOWEEN III: SEASON OF THE WITCH
'84 BEST DEFENSE
'84 ICE PIRATES, THE
'84 MEATBALLS PART II

MARK JAFFE
2ND ASST. DIRECTOR
'81 STRANGE BEHAVIOR

ROBERT JAFFE
PRODUCER
'80 MOTEL HELL*
SCREENPLAY
'80 MOTEL HELL*

ROBERT JAFFE
LOCATIONS
'81 TAPS
MISCELLANEOUS
'83 WITHOUT A TRACE

STANLEY JAFFE
PRODUCER
'79 KRAMER VS. KRAMER
'81 TAPS*
'83 WITHOUT A TRACE
DIRECTOR
'83 WITHOUT A TRACE
EXECUTIVE PRODUCER
'84 FIRSTBORN*

STEVEN-CHARLES JAFFE
PRODUCER
'80 MOTEL HELL*
'80 THOSE LIPS, THOSE EYES*
SCREENPLAY
'80 MOTEL HELL*
ASSOCIATE PRODUCER
'79 TIME AFTER TIME

JEFF JAFFEE
LOCATIONS
'82 ESCAPE ARTIST, THE*

HENRY JAGLOM
DIRECTOR
'83 CAN SHE BAKE A CHERRY PIE?
SCREENPLAY
'83 CAN SHE BAKE A CHERRY PIE?

MICHAEL JAGLOM
EXEC IN CHARGE PROD
'83 CAN SHE BAKE A CHERRY PIE?

DENNIS JAKOB
MISCELLANEOUS
'79 APOCALYPSE NOW

DON JAKOBY
SCREENPLAY
'83 BLUE THUNDER*

RAMIRO JALOMA
1ST ASST. DIRECTOR
'79 BOULEVARD NIGHTS

SATI JAMAL
2ND ASST. DIRECTOR
'81 BODY AND SOUL

ALLAN JAMES
UNIT MANAGER
'81 SUPERMAN II
1ST ASST. DIRECTOR
'79 BLOODLINE*
LOCATIONS
'80 NIJINSKY*
'83 PRIVATES ON PARADE
'84 TOP SECRET!*

BOB JAMES
MISCELLANEOUS
'83 DANIEL

CHARLES JAMES
COSTUME SUPERVISOR
'79 APOCALYPSE NOW

CINDY JAMES
MISCELLANEOUS
'79 GREAT SANTINI, THE
'80 BLACK MARBLE, THE
'83 SUBURBIA

DAVID JAMES
STILLS
'81 DOGS OF WAR, THE
'83 YELLOWBEARD
'83 YENTL
'84 ANOTHER COUNTRY
'84 ELECTRIC DREAMS

FREDERICK JAMES
SCREENPLAY
'80 HUMANOIDS FROM THE DEEP

JILL DEWOLFE JAMES
UNIT PUBLICIST
'81 ATLANTIC CITY

JOHN JAMES
LOCATIONS
'83 BLUE THUNDER*
'83 TABLE FOR FIVE*
'84 WINDY CITY

JOSEPH JAMES
MUSIC
'81 PRIEST OF LOVE

JOYCE JAMES
HAIR
'79 UNIDENTIFIED FLYING ODDBALL*
'80 WATCHER IN THE WOODS, THE*
'83 TRAIL OF THE PINK PANTHER*

KENT JAMES
COSTUMES
'81 CONDORMAN*

LOREN JAMES
STUNT COORDINATOR
'79 BUTCH AND SUNDANCE: THE EARLY YEARS
'81 RAGGEDY MAN

MAGGIE JAMES
SCRIPT SUPERVISOR
'79 STARTING OVER
'79 BELL JAR, THE
'79 NATURAL ENEMIES
'80 FIRST DEADLY SIN

RICHARD JAMES
ART DIRECTOR
'83 LOCAL HERO*
'83 SILKWOOD

SID JAMES
MISCELLANEOUS
'81 SO FINE

STEVE JAMES
STUNT COORDINATOR
'84 BROTHER FROM ANOTHER PLANET, THE*

TERRY JAMES
STUNT COORDINATOR
'81 STRIPES
'84 REVENGE OF THE NERDS

JERRY JAMESON
DIRECTOR
'80 RAISE THE TITANIC

COLIN JAMISON
HAIR
'79 DRACULA
'79 HANOVER STREET
'79 MURDER BY DECREE
'80 OH! HEAVENLY DOG
'81 OUTLAND
'82 FIVE DAYS ONE SUMMER
'83 YENTL
'84 SCANDALOUS
'84 INDIANA JONES AND THE TEMPLE OF DOOM

FRANCINE JAMISON
COSTUME SUPERVISOR
'83 MAN WHO WASN'T THERE, THE
'84 MEATBALLS PART II

PETER JAMISON
ART DIRECTOR
'79 OLD BOYFRIENDS
'80 BIG RED ONE, THE
PRODUCTION DESIGNER
'80 USED CARS
'81 ALL NIGHT LONG
'81 CONTINENTAL DIVIDE
'82 HALLOWEEN III: SEASON OF THE WITCH
'82 MISSING
'82 CHILLY SCENES OF WINTER
'84 BEST DEFENSE
'84 MIKE'S MURDER
'84 SWING SHIFT

STEVEN JANISZ
ASSISTANT EDITOR
'84 BIRDY*
'84 ELECTRIC DREAMS*

JOSEPH JANNI
PRODUCER
'79 YANKS*

LEO JANOS
UNIT PUBLICIST
'82 CANNERY ROW

MICHAEL JANOVER
SCREENPLAY
'81 HARDLY WORKING*
'84 PHILADELPHIA EXPERIMENT, THE*

ROGER JANS
STILLS
'80 BLUE LAGOON
'81 SATURDAY THE 14TH
'82 SUMMER LOVERS

CAROL SHAPIRO JANSON
PUBLICIST
'80 HEARTBEAT
'80 XANADU
UNIT PUBLICIST
'80 MY BODYGUARD
'81 BUDDY, BUDDY

MARIS JANSONS
KEY GRIP
'79 BROOD, THE
'79 FAST COMPANY
'83 DEAD ZONE, THE
'83 VIDEODROME
'84 RECKLESS*

BOB JANZ
MISCELLANEOUS
'80 HUNTER, THE

HENRI JAQUILLARD
PRODUCTION MANAGER
'80 PRIVATE BENJAMIN

JIM JARMUSCH
PRODUCER
'81 PERMANENT VACATION
DIRECTOR
'81 PERMANENT VACATION
'84 STRANGER THAN PARADISE
SCREENPLAY
'81 PERMANENT VACATION
'84 STRANGER THAN PARADISE
MUSIC
'81 PERMANENT VACATION*
EDITOR
'81 PERMANENT VACATION
'84 STRANGER THAN PARADISE*

MAURICE JARRE
MUSIC
'79 MAGICIAN OF LUBLIN, THE
'79 WINTER KILLS
'80 RESURRECTION
'80 AMERICAN SUCCESS COMPANY, THE
'80 BLACK MARBLE, THE
'80 LAST FLIGHT OF NOAH'S ARK,THE
'81 TAPS
'82 FIREFOX
'82 YOUNG DOCTORS IN LOVE
'82 DON'T CRY, IT'S ONLY THUNDER
'83 YEAR OF LIVING DANGEROUSLY, THE
'84 PASSAGE TO INDIA, A
'84 TOP SECRET!
'84 DREAMSCAPE

CHARLES JARROTT
DIRECTOR
'80 LAST FLIGHT OF NOAH'S ARK,THE
'81 CONDORMAN
'82 AMATEUR, THE

E. MICHAEL JARVIS
LOCATIONS
'84 RED DAWN*

JEFF JARVIS
SPECIAL EFFECTS
'80 ANY WHICH WAY YOU CAN*
'80 BRONCO BILLY
'84 FIRESTARTER*

GEN. SAMUEL JASKILKA USMC
MISCELLANEOUS
'81 INCHON

HEDAYAT JAVID
ASSOCIATE PRODUCER
'83 FRIGHTMARE*

MARYA DELIA JAVIER
PRODUCTION DESIGNER
'83 VALLEY GIRL
MISCELLANEOUS
'84 JOY OF SEX, THE

BARBARA JAVITZ
PROD. COORDINATOR
'81 HELL NIGHT

JOHN JAY
STILLS
'79 CLASS OF MISS MACMICHAEL, THE
'79 HANOVER STREET
'80 HUMAN FACTOR, THE

RICKY JAY
MISCELLANEOUS
'82 ESCAPE ARTIST, THE

DOROTHY JEAKINS

COSTUMES
'79 NORTH DALLAS FORTY
'79 LOVE AND BULLETS
'81 ON GOLDEN POND
'81 POSTMAN ALWAYS RINGS TWICE, THE

JEROME JEANNET

LOCATIONS
'80 TESS*

RUSSELL JEFFCOAT

STILLS
'82 SWAMP THING

LONA MARDOCK JEFFERS

MAKEUP
'84 JOY OF SEX, THE*

RAY JEFFERS

PROPS
'81 BLOOD BEACH

ROBERT JEFFORDS

1ST ASST. DIRECTOR
'83 BRAINSTORM*

HOWARD JEFFREY

PRODUCER
'81 LOOKER
EXECUTIVE PRODUCER
'80 DIVINE MADNESS
'82 JINXED
'83 TO BE OR NOT TO BE
ASSOCIATE PRODUCER
'80 NIJINSKY

DEAN JEFFRIES

STUNT COORDINATOR
'81 HONKY TONK FREEWAY

PHILIP JEFFRIES

PRODUCTION DESIGNER
'80 WHEN TIME RAN OUT
'81 CAVEMAN
'81 FIRST MONDAY IN OCTOBER
'82 OFFICER AND A GENTLEMAN, AN
'83 KISS ME GOODBYE
'84 MASS APPEAL

JEANNIE JEHA

PROD. COORDINATOR
'84 KARATE KID, THE

GREGORY JEIN

MISCELLANEOUS
'79 1941

WILLIAM JEKEL

EXECUTIVE PRODUCER
'80 BALTIMORE BULLET, THE*

HERB JELLINEK

EXEC IN CHARGE PROD
'82 NATIONAL LAMPOON'S CLASS REUNION
'82 YOUNG DOCTORS IN LOVE
'83 SILKWOOD
'84 FLAMINGO KID, THE
'84 IMPULSE

DAVID JENKINS

PRODUCTION DESIGNER
'82 I'M DANCING AS FAST AS I CAN

DOROTHY JENKINS

CASTING
'81 ON GOLDEN POND

ERIC JENKINS

EDITOR
'80 ALTERED STATES
'80 HEARTBEAT
'82 FAST TIMES AT RIDGEMONT HIGH
ASSISTANT EDITOR
'79 REAL LIFE

GEORGE JENKINS

PRODUCTION DESIGNER
'79 STARTING OVER
'79 CHINA SYNDROME, THE
'81 ROLLOVER
'81 POSTMAN ALWAYS RINGS TWICE, THE
'82 SOPHIE'S CHOICE

GORDON JENKINS

MUSIC
'80 FIRST DEADLY SIN

JANE JENKINS

CASTING
'80 IT'S MY TURN
'80 ON THE NICKEL
'82 HAMMETT*
'82 NIGHT SHIFT
'82 ESCAPE ARTIST, THE
'83 BLACK STALLION RETURNS, THE*
'83 BREATHLESS
'83 DEAD ZONE, THE*
'83 OCTOPUSSY*
'83 TABLE FOR FIVE
'84 BODY DOUBLE*
'84 COTTON CLUB, THE*
'84 DUNE*
'84 HARD TO HOLD*
'84 GRANDVIEW, U.S.A.*
'84 RED DAWN*

BOB JENNINGS

UNIT PUBLICIST
'81 DEADLY BLESSING

GRAHAME JENNINGS

EXECUTIVE PRODUCER
'84 HOTEL NEW HAMPSHIRE, THE*

GUNTHER JENNINGS

STUNT COORDINATOR
'82 JINXED
SPECIAL EFFECTS
'83 TABLE FOR FIVE
'84 WINDY CITY

JANE JENNINGS

PROPS
'83 ANGELO, MY LOVE

JOHN ROBERT JENNINGS

MISCELLANEOUS
'84 DREAMSCAPE

JOSEPH JENNINGS

ART DIRECTOR
'79 STAR TREK-THE MOTION PICTURE*
PRODUCTION DESIGNER
'82 STAR TREK II THE WRATH OF KHAN
'83 YELLOWBEARD
'84 JOHNNY DANGEROUSLY

MARIO JENNINGS

STILLS
'83 MAUSOLEUM

ELOIS JENNSEN

COSTUMES
'82 TRON*

ERIK JENSEN

MISCELLANEOUS
'84 GREMLINS

GARY JENSEN

STUNT COORDINATOR
'83 INDEPENDENCE DAY
'83 NIGHTMARES

GREG JENSEN

SPECIAL EFFECTS
'80 WHERE THE BUFFALO ROAM

HOWARD JENSEN

SPECIAL EFFECTS
'79 BEYOND THE POSEIDON ADVENTURE
'80 ROADIE*
'81 BODY HEAT
'81 TRUE CONFESSIONS
'82 ROCKY III
'82 HAMMETT*
'83 INDEPENDENCE DAY
'84 STREETS OF FIRE
SP. EFFECTS SUPERV.
'83 STAYING ALIVE
'83 HEART LIKE A WHEEL

RAYLAN JENSEN

EXECUTIVE PRODUCER
'83 JOYSTICKS*

JOHN JENSON
ART DIRECTOR
'83 SPACEHUNTER: ADVENTURES IN THE FORBIDDEN ZONE*

MARC JENY
2ND ASST. DIRECTOR
'84 AMERICAN DREAMER*

ROBERT JESSUP
CINEMATOGRAPHER
'80 BIG BRAWL, THE
'81 DEADLY BLESSING
'82 SILENT RAGE*
'82 SPLIT IMAGE

SANDRA JETTON
SCRIPT SUPERVISOR
'81 KNIGHTRIDERS

AUSTEN JEWELL
ASSOCIATE PRODUCER
'80 MOTEL HELL
UNIT PROD. MANAGER
'79 TIME AFTER TIME
'80 MOTEL HELL
'82 STAR TREK II THE WRATH OF KHAN
'83 TERMS OF ENDEARMENT*
'84 BEST DEFENSE*

ERIC JEWETT
1ST ASST. DIRECTOR
'82 PENITENTIARY II
'83 SUBURBIA
2ND ASST. DIRECTOR
'82 LAST AMERICAN VIRGIN, THE

NORMAN JEWISON
PRODUCER
'79 ...AND JUSTICE FOR ALL*
'82 BEST FRIENDS*
'84 ICEMAN*
'84 SOLDIER'S STORY, A*
DIRECTOR
'79 ...AND JUSTICE FOR ALL
'82 BEST FRIENDS
'84 SOLDIER'S STORY, A
EXECUTIVE PRODUCER
'81 DOGS OF WAR, THE*

ALBERT JEYTE
MAKEUP
'80 NUDE BOMB, THE
'81 ALL NIGHT LONG*
'81 GHOST STORY*

RUTH PRAWER JHABVALA
SCREENPLAY
'79 EUROPEANS, THE
'80 QUARTET
'83 HEAT AND DUST
'84 BOSTONIANS, THE

CESAR JIMENEZ
LOCATIONS
'84 ROMANCING THE STONE

MANUEL JIMENEZ
KEY GRIP
'84 HOT DOG...THE MOVIE

SURESH JINDAL
ASSOCIATE PRODUCER
'82 GANDHI

THOMAS JINGLES
ASSISTANT EDITOR
'80 STIR CRAZY

PETER JIRAS
LOCATIONS
'83 I AM THE CHEESE

ROBERT JIRAS
DIRECTOR
'83 I AM THE CHEESE
SCREENPLAY
'83 I AM THE CHEESE*
MAKEUP
'79 STARTING OVER*
'80 SIMON
'81 GHOST STORY*
'81 PRINCE OF THE CITY
'81 TAPS
'83 BRAINSTORM*

BILL JOBE
COSTUMES
'81 DEAD AND BURIED

PETER JOBIN
SCREENPLAY
'81 HAPPY BIRTHDAY TO ME*

CHARLES JOFFE
PRODUCER
'79 MANHATTAN
EXECUTIVE PRODUCER
'80 STARDUST MEMORIES*
'81 ARTHUR
'82 MIDSUMMER NIGHT'S SEX COMEDY, A
'83 ZELIG
'84 BROADWAY DANNY ROSE

ROLAND JOFFE
DIRECTOR
'84 KILLING FIELDS, THE

SVEIN JOHANSEN
MISCELLANEOUS
'80 EMPIRE STRIKES BACK, THE

INGRID JOHANSON
PROD. OFFICE COORD.
'79 ALAMBRISTA!*
'79 BOARDWALK
'82 YES, GIORGIO
'83 ANGELO, MY LOVE
'83 HUNGER, THE
'84 FALLING IN LOVE
'84 PLACES IN THE HEART
PROD. COORDINATOR
'84 RECKLESS

DAVID JOHN
SOUND
'83 BEYOND THE LIMIT
'83 DRESSER, THE

PRISCILLA JOHN
CASTING
'84 PASSAGE TO INDIA, A

TOM JOHN
PRODUCTION DESIGNER
'82 ZOOT SUIT

CAROLYN JOHNS
STILLS
'82 ROAD WARRIOR, THE

KRISTI JOHNS
ASSISTANT EDITOR
'82 MEGAFORCE*

ROY THOMAS JOHNS
MISCELLANEOUS
'82 ONE FROM THE HEART

ALAN JOHNSON
DIRECTOR
'83 TO BE OR NOT TO BE
ASSOCIATE PRODUCER
'81 HISTORY OF THE WORLD PART I*
CHOREOGRAPHER
'81 HISTORY OF THE WORLD PART I

B.J. JOHNSON
LOCATIONS
'79 HOT STUFF
'80 FINAL COUNTDOWN, THE*
'81 NOBODY'S PERFEKT
'82 LOVE CHILD
'83 BLUE SKIES AGAIN
'84 SPLASH*
MISCELLANEOUS
'83 SMOKEY AND THE BANDIT III

BARBARA JOHNSON
CASTING
'82 HAMMETT*
MISCELLANEOUS
'82 ESCAPE ARTIST, THE

BERNARD JOHNSON
COSTUMES
'82 HANKY PANKY

BRIAN JOHNSON
SPECIAL EFFECTS
'83 PIRATES OF PENZANCE, THE
SP. EFFECTS SUPERV.
'79 ALIEN
'81 DRAGONSLAYER
MISCELLANEOUS
'80 EMPIRE STRIKES BACK, THE
'84 NEVERENDING STORY, THE

CARLTON JOHNSON
CHOREOGRAPHER
'80 BLUES BROTHERS
'83 DOCTOR DETROIT

CHARLENE JOHNSON
HAIR
'79 C.H.O.M.P.S.

CHRISTOPHER JOHNSON
STILLS
'81 CATTLE ANNIE AND LITTLE BRITCHES

DENIS JOHNSON
PRODUCTION MANAGER
'79 HANOVER STREET
'80 AWAKENING, THE*
'81 OUTLAND

DENIS JOHNSON JR.
MISCELLANEOUS
'82 VICTOR/VICTORIA
'83 TRAIL OF THE PINK PANTHER

DIANE JOHNSON
HAIR
'79 HOT STUFF
'80 CADDYSHACK
'81 NOBODY'S PERFEKT*
'83 SMOKEY AND THE BANDIT III
'84 HARRY & SON

DIANE JOHNSON
SCREENPLAY
'80 SHINING, THE*

DON JOHNSON
SOUND
'79 JUST YOU AND ME KID
'79 SCAVENGER HUNT
'79 WHEN YOU COMIN' BACK, RED RYDER?
'82 FIREFOX
'82 HONKYTONK MAN
'82 JEKYLL AND HYDE TOGETHER AGAIN
'82 THINGS ARE TOUGH ALL OVER
'83 SUDDEN IMPACT

GEO. CLAYTON JOHNSON
SCREENPLAY
'83 TWILIGHT ZONE, THE MOVIE*

GERRY JOHNSON
SPECIAL EFFECTS
'80 OUTSIDER, THE

GRAY JOHNSON
2ND UNIT DIRECTOR
'79 LOVE AT FIRST BITE
STUNT COORDINATOR
'80 STUNT MAN, THE

GWEN JOHNSON
MISCELLANEOUS
'84 LAST STARFIGHTER, THE

HARLAN PETE JOHNSON
SPECIAL EFFECTS
'83 EDDIE MACON'S RUN

HOWARD JOHNSON
MISCELLANEOUS
'84 COTTON CLUB, THE

JACK JOHNSON
KEY GRIP
'80 SERIAL
'80 ANY WHICH WAY YOU CAN
'80 BRONCO BILLY
'82 FORCED VENGEANCE
'84 DREAMSCAPE*

JACK JOHNSON
PROPS
'79 HOT STUFF
'80 CADDYSHACK
'81 HARDLY WORKING
'81 NOBODY'S PERFEKT
'83 SMOKEY AND THE BANDIT III

JAMES JOHNSON
ASSISTANT EDITOR
'84 SONGWRITER*

JANET JOHNSON
PROD. COORDINATOR
'84 SILENT NIGHT, DEADLY NIGHT

JIM JOHNSON
PROPS
'84 PURPLE RAIN

JOANE JOHNSON
STILLS
'84 LAST NIGHT AT THE ALAMO*

JOE JOHNSON
ART DIRECTOR
'84 INDIANA JONES AND THE TEMPLE OF DOOM*

KEN JOHNSON
MISCELLANEOUS
'84 BIRDY

KENT JOHNSON
PROPS
'79 REMEMBER MY NAME
'80 FINAL COUNTDOWN, THE
'81 CHU CHU AND THE PHILLY FLASH
'81 MOMMIE DEAREST
'82 DEATHWISH II
'82 GREASE 2
'83 STAYING ALIVE
'83 CHRISTINE
'84 RHINESTONE

L.A. JOHNSON
PRODUCTION MANAGER
'82 HOME WORK

LAMONT JOHNSON
DIRECTOR
'81 CATTLE ANNIE AND LITTLE BRITCHES
'83 SPACEHUNTER: ADVENTURES IN THE FORBIDDEN ZONE

LARRY JOHNSON
SCRIPT SUPERVISOR
'84 IMPULSE

MARK JOHNSON
PRODUCER
'84 NATURAL, THE
EXECUTIVE PRODUCER
'82 DINER
1ST ASST. DIRECTOR
'80 FATSO
2ND ASST. DIRECTOR
'79 ESCAPE FROM ALCATRAZ*
'80 FOR THE LOVE OF BENJI*
MISCELLANEOUS
'80 CRUISING

MARY LEE JOHNSON
CO-PRODUCER
'81 FORT APACHE, THE BRONX*

MONICA JOHNSON
SCREENPLAY
'79 REAL LIFE*
'79 AMERICATHON*
'81 MODERN ROMANCE*
'82 JEKYLL AND HYDE TOGETHER AGAIN*

PAT JOHNSON
STUNT COORDINATOR
'80 BIG BRAWL, THE
'81 FORCE FIVE
MISCELLANEOUS
'84 KARATE KID, THE

PATRICIA JOHNSON
PUBLICIST
'84 POLICE ACADEMY
UNIT PUBLICIST
'79 MAGICIAN OF LUBLIN, THE*
'84 MRS. SOFFEL

RICHARD JOHNSON
SPECIAL EFFECTS
'79 OVER THE EDGE
'80 LITTLE DARLINGS
'81 HARD COUNTRY
'84 BEST DEFENSE*

RONDI JOHNSON
COSTUMES
'84 ICEMAN

RONDI JOHNSON
LOCATIONS
'80 CHANGELING, THE

SUSIE JOHNSON
MISCELLANEOUS
'81 HALLOWEEN II
'82 HALLOWEEN III: SEASON OF THE WITCH
'83 TESTAMENT

WALIS JOHNSON
ASSISTANT EDITOR
'84 BROTHER FROM ANOTHER PLANET, THE*

DALE JOHNSTON
MISCELLANEOUS
'82 LOVE CHILD

DANNY JOHNSTON
MISCELLANEOUS
'81 MY BLOODY VALENTINE

GERRY JOHNSTON
SPECIAL EFFECTS
'81 EXCALIBUR*
'83 EDUCATING RITA

JOE JOHNSTON
MISCELLANEOUS
'80 EMPIRE STRIKES BACK, THE
'83 RETURN OF THE JEDI

LARENE JOHNSTON
ASSISTANT EDITOR
'82 GREASE 2*

STEPHEN JOHNSTON
MISCELLANEOUS
'83 JOYSTICKS

ANNA HILL JOHNSTONE
COSTUMES
'79 GOING IN STYLE
'81 RAGTIME
'81 PRINCE OF THE CITY
'82 VERDICT, THE
'83 DANIEL
'83 NIGHT IN HEAVEN, A
'84 GARBO TALKS

RENEE JOHNSTONE
COSTUMES
'84 THIS IS SPINAL TAP

ALF JOINT
STUNT COORDINATOR
'81 SUPERMAN II*
'81 AMERICAN WEREWOLF IN LONDON, AN
'81 OUTLAND
'83 KEEP, THE
'84 SUPERGIRL

LANA JOKEL
EDITOR
'80 UNION CITY*

STAN JOLLEY
PRODUCTION DESIGNER
'79 AMERICATHON
'80 CADDYSHACK
'81 CATTLE ANNIE AND LITTLE BRITCHES
'81 TAPS*

SARA JOLLY
ASSISTANT EDITOR
'79 SHOUT, THE*

DARRELL JONAS
PROD. COORDINATOR
'80 HE KNOWS YOU'RE ALONE

AL JONES
STUNT COORDINATOR
'84 PURPLE RAIN

ALAN JONES
EDITOR
'83 TRAIL OF THE PINK PANTHER

ALAN JONES
MISCELLANEOUS
'84 DREAMSCAPE

ALLEN JONES
ART DIRECTOR
'82 DEATH VALLEY
MISCELLANEOUS
'80 FADE TO BLACK
'82 SEDUCTION, THE

AMY JONES
DIRECTOR
'83 LOVE LETTERS
SCREENPLAY
'83 LOVE LETTERS

BETSY JONES
COSTUMES
'79 BOARDWALK

BRYAN JONES
PRODUCTION DESIGNER
'84 THIS IS SPINAL TAP

CARO JONES
CASTING
'79 WHEN YOU COMIN' BACK, RED RYDER?
'80 FORMULA, THE*
'80 GONG SHOW MOVIE, THE
'80 OCTAGON, THE*
'82 SILENT RAGE
'82 FORCED VENGEANCE*
'83 CROSS CREEK
'84 KARATE KID, THE*

CINDY JONES
MISCELLANEOUS
'82 FIRST BLOOD

CLIFFORD JONES
EDITOR
'84 WINDY CITY

DAVID JONES
DIRECTOR
'83 BETRAYAL
2ND UNIT DIRECTOR
'80 FINAL COUNTDOWN, THE*

DENNIS JONES
ASSOCIATE PRODUCER
'84 ADVENTURES OF BUCKAROO BANZAI ACROSS THE 8TH DIMENSION,THE
'84 MRS. SOFFEL
PRODUCTION MANAGER
'82 POLTERGEIST
'83 TWILIGHT ZONE, THE MOVIE*
'84 MRS. SOFFEL
UNIT PROD. MANAGER
'81 RICH AND FAMOUS*
'84 ADVENTURES OF BUCKAROO BANZAI ACROSS THE 8TH DIMENSION,THE

DISLEY JONES
PRODUCTION DESIGNER
'79 LEGACY, THE

DON JONES
CINEMATOGRAPHER
'83 GOIN' ALL THE WAY
MISCELLANEOUS
'81 SMOKEY BITES THE DUST

DOUG JONES
STILLS
'80 ROADIE*

EARL JONES
HAIR
'84 PURPLE RAIN*

EVAN JONES
SCREENPLAY
'81 VICTORY*
'84 CHAMPIONS

GARY JONES
COSTUMES
'80 FIRST DEADLY SIN*

J.B. JONES
SPECIAL EFFECTS
'79 HOT STUFF
'81 FUNHOUSE, THE
'81 NOBODY'S PERFEKT
'82 LOVE CHILD
'83 SMOKEY AND THE BANDIT III
'83 NIGHT IN HEAVEN, A
'84 HARRY & SON
'84 WHERE THE BOYS ARE

JANE JONES
COSTUMES
'79 PRIZE FIGHTER, THE

JEFF JONES
ASSISTANT EDITOR
'80 INSIDE MOVES
'81 WHOSE LIFE IS IT ANYWAY?
'81 EARTHLING, THE*
'83 BLUE THUNDER

JIM JONES
MISCELLANEOUS
'80 COAL MINER'S DAUGHTER

L. DEAN JONES JR.
2ND ASST. DIRECTOR
'83 RIGHT STUFF, THE
'83 PRIVATE SCHOOL
'84 CITY HEAT*
'84 TIGHTROPE*

JUDI JONES
CASTING
'79 ROLLER BOOGIE*
'82 VICE SQUAD

KEN JONES
KEY GRIP
'81 PRIVATE LESSONS
'82 I'M DANCING AS FAST AS I CAN
'83 PRIVATE SCHOOL

KEN JONES
SPECIAL EFFECTS
'80 BATTLE BEYOND THE STARS*

LARRY JONES
EXECUTIVE PRODUCER
'83 OSTERMAN WEEKEND, THE*

LINDSEY JONES
PUBLICIST
'79 10
'81 S.O.B.
'83 CURSE OF THE PINK PANTHER*
'83 MAN WHO LOVED WOMEN, THE
'83 TRAIL OF THE PINK PANTHER
UNIT PUBLICIST
'84 MICKI AND MAUDE

MICHAEL JONES
SCREENPLAY
'84 MUTANT*

MIKE JONES
HAIR
'79 MOONRAKER*
'80 FFOLKES
'80 HOPSCOTCH*
'84 RAZOR'S EDGE, THE*

PERRY JONES
KEY GRIP
'83 SPRING BREAK

RALPH JONES
MUSIC
'83 LOVE LETTERS

RICARDO ROMERO JONES
MAKEUP
'80 PRIVATE BENJAMIN*

ROBERT JONES
EDITOR
'82 LOOKIN' TO GET OUT

ROBERT JONES
ART DIRECTOR
'79 STEVIE

ROBIN JONES
2ND ASST. DIRECTOR
'83 MY TUTOR

RON JONES
LOCATIONS
'84 GIVE MY REGARDS
TO BROAD STREET*

SALLY JONES
SCRIPT SUPERVISOR
'79 HANOVER STREET
'80 HEAVEN'S GATE*
'82 SENDER, THE
'84 BLAME IT ON RIO
'84 RAZOR'S EDGE, THE

TERRY JONES
DIRECTOR
'79 MONTY PYTHON'S LIFE OF BRIAN
'83 MONTY PYTHON'S
THE MEANING OF LIFE
SCREENPLAY
'79 MONTY PYTHON'S LIFE OF BRIAN*
'82 MONTY PYTHON LIVE AT
THE HOLLYWOOD BOWL*
'83 MONTY PYTHON'S
THE MEANING OF LIFE*

TONY JONES
MUSIC
'82 HOME WORK*

TREVOR JONES
MUSIC
'81 EXCALIBUR
'82 SENDER, THE
'82 DARK CRYSTAL, THE
'83 NATE & HAYES

VAN JONES
MISCELLANEOUS
'81 FOR YOUR EYES ONLY

VIVIAN JONES
SCRIPT SUPERVISOR
'82 PENITENTIARY II*

MEINIR JONES-LEWIS
HAIR
'80 NIJINSKY*

BO JONSSON
PRODUCER
'81 MONTENEGRO

VERA JORDACHE
MAKEUP
'83 SCREWBALLS*

ANNE JORDAN
PROD. SECRETARY
'84 SONGWRITER

DANNY JORDAN
KEY GRIP
'79 RAVAGERS
'81 THIEF
'82 OFFICER AND A GENTLEMAN, AN
'83 BAD BOYS*
'84 AGAINST ALL ODDS
'84 PURPLE RAIN

DAVE JORDAN
PROPS
'79 ALIEN
'81 AMERICAN WEREWOLF
IN LONDON, AN
'81 DOGS OF WAR, THE
'82 PINK FLOYD: THE WALL
'83 CURSE OF THE PINK PANTHER
'83 OCTOPUSSY
'83 TRAIL OF THE PINK PANTHER
'84 LASSITER

GLENN JORDAN
DIRECTOR
'81 ONLY WHEN I LAUGH
'83 BUDDY SYSTEM, THE
'84 MASS APPEAL

TIM JORDAN
ASSISTANT EDITOR
'79 SHOUT, THE*
'82 VENOM*

CONNIE JOSEFS
MISCELLANEOUS
'82 AMATEUR, THE

RUTH JOSEM
CASTING
'82 THAT CHAMPIONSHIP SEASON

DAVID JOSEPH
PRODUCER
'82 PIRATE MOVIE, THE

TEDDY JOSEPH
ASSOCIATE PRODUCER
'79 YANKS

EDDIE JOSEPHS
ASSISTANT EDITOR
'80 FAME*

RICK JOSEPHSON
SPECIAL EFFECTS
'83 CUJO
'84 SILENT NIGHT, DEADLY NIGHT

DRAGON JOSIPOVIC
UNIT MANAGER
'82 SOPHIE'S CHOICE*

JERRY JOST
SOUND
'79 TIME AFTER TIME
'80 FIRST FAMILY
'80 MOTEL HELL
'80 THOSE LIPS, THOSE EYES
'80 TOM HORN*
'82 SOME KIND OF HERO
'82 CANNERY ROW
'82 MY FAVORITE YEAR
'83 STAR CHAMBER
'84 BEST DEFENSE*
'84 JOHNNY DANGEROUSLY
'84 MICKI AND MAUDE
'84 RACING WITH THE MOON
'84 UNFAITHFULLY YOURS
'84 TEACHERS

LARRY JOST
SOUND
'79 NIGHTWING
'79 IN-LAWS, THE
'79 NORTH DALLAS FORTY
'80 ONE-TRICK PONY*
'81 HONKY TONK FREEWAY
'81 MOMMIE DEAREST
'81 ZORRO, THE GAY BLADE
'82 GREASE 2
'83 CROSS CREEK
'83 SILKWOOD
'84 LONELY GUY, THE*

JUHANI JOTUNI
UNIT MANAGER
'83 GORKY PARK

KRISTY JOURDAN
PROD. OFFICE COORD.
'81 STUDENT BODIES

GARY JULES JOUVENAT
PRODUCER
'82 OUT OF THE BLUE*

MICHAEL JOYCE
MISCELLANEOUS
'84 TERMINATOR, THE

ROBERT DWYER JOYCE
2ND ASST. DIRECTOR
'80 OUTSIDER, THE*

FLOYD JOYER
UNIT PROD. MANAGER
'79 GREAT SANTINI, THE*

TOM JOYNER
PRODUCTION MANAGER
'83 TENDER MERCIES
'83 TOUGH ENOUGH*
'84 AGAINST ALL ODDS*
'84 STARMAN
UNIT PROD. MANAGER
'79 MORE AMERICAN GRAFFITTI
'80 LAST MARRIED COUPLE
IN AMERICA, THE
'84 GRANDVIEW, U.S.A.
UNIT MANAGER
'80 BLUES BROTHERS*
1ST ASST. DIRECTOR
'80 ANY WHICH WAY YOU CAN
'80 BRONCO BILLY
'82 DON'T CRY, IT'S ONLY THUNDER

DENNIS JUBAN
MISCELLANEOUS
'79 APOCALYPSE NOW

JON JUBAN JR.
PROD. COORDINATOR
'82 DON'T CRY, IT'S ONLY THUNDER

LOPE JUBAN
PROD. COORDINATOR
'83 YEAR OF LIVING
DANGEROUSLY, THE*

LOPE JUBAN JR.
MISCELLANEOUS
'84 PURPLE HEARTS

PHIL JUDD
SOUND
'82 STARSTRUCK

RON JUDKINS
SOUND
'80 BATTLE BEYOND THE STARS
'81 SATURDAY THE 14TH
'82 LIAR'S MOON
'83 DEADLY FORCE
'84 CHOOSE ME*
'84 PURPLE HEARTS

DEANNE JUDSON
EXECUTIVE PRODUCER
'80 PROM NIGHT

JERRY JUHL
SCREENPLAY
'79 MUPPET MOVIE, THE*
'81 GREAT MUPPET CAPER, THE*

NANCY JULIBER
PROD. COORDINATOR
'82 Q: QUETZALCOATL

REMY JULIENNE
STUNT COORDINATOR
'81 CONDORMAN
'83 TRENCHCOAT
'84 UNTIL SEPTEMBER
MISCELLANEOUS
'81 FOR YOUR EYES ONLY
'83 OCTOPUSSY

CHRISTIAN JUNGBLUTH
LOCATIONS
'80 LADY VANISHES, THE*

ERIC JUPP
MUSIC
'79 TIM

SEYMOUR JURBIN
LOCATIONS
'79 PLAYERS

RANDY JURGENSEN
MISCELLANEOUS
'80 CRUISING

ANNIE JURGIELEWICZ
ASSOCIATE PRODUCER
'81 DOZENS, THE
PRODUCTION MANAGER
'81 DOZENS, THE

MARIO JURISIC
1ST ASST. DIRECTOR
'82 TEMPEST*

CHARLES JUROE
PUBLICIST
'81 FOR YOUR EYES ONLY
'83 OCTOPUSSY

MARTIN JUROW
CO-PRODUCER
'83 TERMS OF ENDEARMENT*

MAURICE JUSTEEN
MAKEUP
'81 BEYOND THE REEF

ANDREA JUSTIN
ASSISTANT EDITOR
'84 FALLING IN LOVE*

GEORGE JUSTIN
EXECUTIVE PRODUCER
'84 NO SMALL AFFAIR
EXEC IN CHARGE PROD
'81 ROLLOVER
PRODUCTION MANAGER
'81 ROLLOVER
UNIT PROD. MANAGER
'84 NO SMALL AFFAIR

SUSAN JUSTIN

MUSIC
'84 FINAL TERROR, THE

BILL JUSTIS

MUSIC
'79 VILLAIN, THE

CLAUDE JUTRA

DIRECTOR
'82 BY DESIGN
SCREENPLAY
'82 BY DESIGN*

ANDREE JUVILER

LOCATIONS
'80 COMPETITION, THE
'81 MODERN ROMANCE*

JOHN JYMPSON

EDITOR
'81 BEYOND THE REEF
'83 HIGH ROAD TO CHINA

K

PAULA KAATZ
COSTUME SUPERVISOR
'80 MY BODYGUARD

ROBERT KACHLER
MISCELLANEOUS
'83 STROKER ACE

GEORGE KACZENDER
DIRECTOR
'79 IN PRAISE OF OLDER WOMEN
EDITOR
'79 IN PRAISE OF OLDER WOMEN*

EDDIE KAFAFIAN
UNIT PUBLICIST
'84 TANK

JEREMY PAUL KAGAN
DIRECTOR
'82 CHOSEN, THE
'83 STING II, THE

MICHAEL KAGAN
PROD. COORDINATOR
'83 WICKED LADY, THE

JAMES KAGEL
MISCELLANEOUS
'81 DEAD AND BURIED
'81 ENTITY, THE
'81 HEARTBEEPS
'82 PARASITE

SAUL KAHAN
PUBLICIST
'79 HARDCORE
'79 1941
'80 BLUES BROTHERS
'82 BLADERUNNER
'82 NIGHT SHIFT
UNIT PUBLICIST
'79 MUPPET MOVIE, THE
'83 TWILIGHT ZONE, THE MOVIE*
'84 JOY OF SEX, THE

DAVID KAHLER
2ND ASST. DIRECTOR
'80 MIDNIGHT MADNESS*

KLAUS KAHLER
ASSOCIATE PRODUCER
'84 NEVERENDING STORY, THE

BLOSSOM KAHN
EXEC IN CHARGE PROD
'81 NIGHT THE LIGHTS WENT OUT IN GEORGIA, THE
'82 SEDUCTION, THE
'82 ZAPPED!

JOSEPH KAHN
PUBLICIST
'82 SPLIT IMAGE

MALCOLM KAHN
MISCELLANEOUS
'84 NATURAL, THE

MICHAEL KAHN
ASSOCIATE PRODUCER
'79 1941*
EDITOR
'79 ICE CASTLES*
'79 1941
'80 CLOSE ENCOUNTERS OF THE THIRD KIND SPECIAL EDITION
'80 USED CARS
'81 RAIDERS OF THE LOST ARK
'82 POLTERGEIST
'83 TABLE FOR FIVE
'83 TWILIGHT ZONE, THE MOVIE*
'84 FALLING IN LOVE
'84 INDIANA JONES AND THE TEMPLE OF DOOM

MILTON KAHN
PUBLICIST
'84 C.H.U.D.

SHELDON KAHN
EDITOR
'79 ELECTRIC HORSEMAN, THE
'80 PRIVATE BENJAMIN
'81 RICHARD PRYOR: LIVE ON THE SUNSET STRIP
'81 ABSENCE OF MALICE
'83 KISS ME GOODBYE
'84 GHOSTBUSTERS*
'84 UNFAITHFULLY YOURS

JIM KAIL
MAKEUP
'81 LAST CHASE, THE*
'82 YOUNG DOCTORS IN LOVE*
'84 STAR TREK III: THE SEARCH FOR SPOCK*
HAIR
'81 LAST CHASE, THE*

CONNIE KAISERMAN
ASSOCIATE PRODUCER
'79 EUROPEANS, THE
'80 QUARTET*
'83 HEAT AND DUST*
'84 BOSTONIANS, THE*

SUSAN KALINOWSKI
HAIR
'83 SWEET SIXTEEN

RICHARD KALK
MISCELLANEOUS
'79 ONION FIELD, THE
'80 BLACK MARBLE, THE

GARY KALKIN
PUBLICIST
'79 AMERICAN GIGOLO
'79 LAST EMBRACE
'84 BEST DEFENSE
UNIT PUBLICIST
'79 ESCAPE FROM ALCATRAZ
'80 SERIAL
'80 CAN'T STOP THE MUSIC
'80 NINE TO FIVE
'83 STAYING ALIVE
'83 TWO OF A KIND
'84 FLASHPOINT

ERRIKOS KALOUTAS
PROPS
'80 FOR THE LOVE OF BENJI

JAY KAMEN
EDITOR
'79 NORTH DALLAS FORTY
'82 SPLIT IMAGE

MICHAEL KAMEN
MUSIC
'81 POLYESTER*
'82 VENOM
'83 DEAD ZONE, THE

ROBERT MARK KAMEN
SCREENPLAY
'81 TAPS*
'82 SPLIT IMAGE*
'84 KARATE KID, THE

BERT KAMERMAN
ASSOCIATE PRODUCER
'81 HAND, THE*

LYNN KAMERN

UNIT MANAGER
'83 BLACK STALLION RETURNS, THE*

JOHN KANDER

MUSIC
'82 STILL OF THE NIGHT
'83 BLUE SKIES AGAIN
'84 PLACES IN THE HEART

ARTIE KANE

MUSIC
'80 NIGHT OF THE JUGGLER
'83 WRONG IS RIGHT

GEORGE KANE

MISCELLANEOUS
'82 LIAR'S MOON

JOHN KANE

PUBLICIST
'80 FAME
'81 WOLFEN
'83 TENDER MERCIES
UNIT PUBLICIST
'80 NIGHT OF THE JUGGLER
'81 NOBODY'S PERFEKT

JOSEPH KANE

MISCELLANEOUS
'84 SPLASH

MARY KANE

ASSOCIATE PRODUCER
'81 MS. 45*
PRODUCTION MANAGER
'81 MS. 45*

MICHAEL KANE

SCREENPLAY
'79 HOT STUFF*
'80 FOOLIN AROUND*
'81 SOUTHERN COMFORT*
'81 HARD COUNTRY
'81 LEGEND OF THE LONE RANGER, THE*
'83 ALL THE RIGHT MOVES
'84 BEAR, THE

MICHAEL KANE

2ND ASST. DIRECTOR
'79 GOLDENGIRL*

ROBERT KANE

SCREENPLAY
'79 VILLAIN, THE

THOMAS KANE

PRODUCTION MANAGER
'84 FLAMINGO KID, THE
UNIT PROD. MANAGER
'81 ONLY WHEN I LAUGH
1ST ASST. DIRECTOR
'79 KRAMER VS. KRAMER
'81 EYEWITNESS

WILLIAM KANE

PROPS
'79 NATURAL ENEMIES
'79 WARRIORS, THE
'80 DRESSED TO KILL
'80 TRIBUTE*
'81 NEIGHBORS
'82 SOUP FOR ONE

HARRIETTE KANEW

PROD. COORDINATOR
'79 NATURAL ENEMIES

JEFF KANEW

DIRECTOR
'79 NATURAL ENEMIES
'83 EDDIE MACON'S RUN
'84 REVENGE OF THE NERDS
SCREENPLAY
'79 NATURAL ENEMIES
'83 EDDIE MACON'S RUN
EDITOR
'79 NATURAL ENEMIES
'80 ORDINARY PEOPLE
'83 EDDIE MACON'S RUN

MAREK KANIEVSKA

DIRECTOR
'84 ANOTHER COUNTRY

ANTHONY KANT

ASSOCIATE PRODUCER
'83 ANGEL OF H.E.A.T.

HAL KANT

PRODUCER
'83 ANGEL OF H.E.A.T.*
EXECUTIVE PRODUCER
'83 ANGEL OF H.E.A.T.

NANCY KANTER

EDITOR
'84 LOVELESS, THE
ASSOCIATE EDITOR
'80 MELVIN AND HOWARD

ENID KANTOR

CASTING
'84 MUTANT*
PROD. COORDINATOR
'84 MUTANT

IGO KANTOR

PRODUCER
'81 HARDLY WORKING*
'84 MUTANT

BILL KAPLAN

SOUND
'79 OVER THE EDGE
'79 OLD BOYFRIENDS
'80 BLUES BROTHERS
'80 CARNY
'80 HEARTBEAT
'81 CONTINENTAL DIVIDE
'82 BEST LITTLE WHOREHOUSE IN TEXAS, THE
'83 DOCTOR DETROIT
'83 TWILIGHT ZONE, THE MOVIE*
'84 IRRECONCILABLE DIFFERENCES
'84 ROMANCING THE STONE
'84 TIGHTROPE

CINDY KAPLAN

ASSISTANT EDITOR
'81 REDS
'83 EASY MONEY*

GLENN KAPLAN

ASSISTANT EDITOR
'82 HANKY PANKY*
MISCELLANEOUS
'83 MAN WHO WASN'T THERE, THE

J. STEIN KAPLAN

ASSOCIATE PRODUCER
'84 FINAL TERROR, THE

JONATHAN KAPLAN

DIRECTOR
'79 OVER THE EDGE
'83 HEART LIKE A WHEEL

LARRY KAPLAN

PUBLICIST
'79 HAIR
'82 LITTLE SEX, A
'83 BIG CHILL, THE
UNIT PUBLICIST
'81 ENDLESS LOVE
'83 EDDIE AND THE CRUISERS

MICHAEL KAPLAN

COSTUMES
'82 BLADERUNNER*
'83 FLASHDANCE
'84 AGAINST ALL ODDS
'84 THIEF OF HEARTS
'84 AMERICAN DREAMER

SOL KAPLAN

MUSIC
'79 OVER THE EDGE

WENDY KAPLAN

SCRIPT SUPERVISOR
'79 PHANTASM*

STAVROS KAPLANIDIS

1ST ASST. DIRECTOR
'79 FEDORA*
2ND ASST. DIRECTOR
'80 FOR THE LOVE OF BENJI*
'82 SUMMER LOVERS*

ARNOLD KAPNICK

STILLS
'79 ON THE YARD

KARAN KAPOOR

STILLS
'84 BOSTONIANS, THE*

JOE KAPP

ASSOCIATE PRODUCER
'79 OVER THE EDGE*

DAVID KAPPES

ASSOCIATE PRODUCER
'83 JAWS 3-D
PRODUCTION MANAGER
'82 I'M DANCING AS FAST AS I CAN*
UNIT PROD. MANAGER
'83 JAWS 3-D

DANA KAPROFF

MUSIC
'79 WHEN A STRANGER CALLS
'80 BIG RED ONE, THE
'82 DEATH VALLEY
'83 GOLDEN SEAL, THE*

MICHAEL KARA

MISCELLANEOUS
'80 TRIBUTE

CHRIS KARAMANOS

LOCATIONS
'81 CANNONBALL RUN, THE
'82 MEGAFORCE

MILES KARAPIPERIS

ART DIRECTOR
'84 LITTLE DRUMMER GIRL, THE*

DEBRA KAREN

EDITOR
'79 MEATBALLS
'81 HAPPY BIRTHDAY TO ME

MICHAEL KAREN

ASSISTANT EDITOR
'79 MEATBALLS
'81 HAPPY BIRTHDAY TO ME*

LYNDA KARJOLA

PROD. COORDINATOR
'80 HEAVEN'S GATE*

LYNDA LEIGH KARJOLA

2ND ASST. DIRECTOR
'81 AMY*

FRED KARLIN

MUSIC
'79 RAVAGERS
'80 LOVING COUPLES

ARNOLD KARNICK

STILLS
'82 I, THE JURY

THOMAS KARNOWSKI

SCREENPLAY
'82 SWORD AND THE SORCERER, THE*
CO-PRODUCER
'82 SWORD AND THE SORCERER, THE*
PRODUCTION MANAGER
'82 SWORD AND THE SORCERER, THE*

BEVERLY KARP

PRODUCER
'81 MY DINNER WITH ANDRE*

GIDEON KARPOUSKY

MISCELLANEOUS
'83 METALSTORM: THE DESTRUCTION OF JARED-SYN

GARY KARR

ASSISTANT EDITOR
'80 HONEYSUCKLE ROSE*
'81 ROLLOVER

ATHAN KARRAS

MISCELLANEOUS
'81 POSTMAN ALWAYS RINGS TWICE, THE

MATIA KARRELL

1ST ASST. DIRECTOR
'82 ANDROID
'84 MAKING THE GRADE
2ND ASST. DIRECTOR
'80 SCHIZOID

ERIC KARSON

DIRECTOR
'80 OCTAGON, THE

JOHN KASARDA

ART DIRECTOR
'82 VERDICT, THE

LAWRENCE KASDAN

DIRECTOR
'81 BODY HEAT
'83 BIG CHILL, THE
SCREENPLAY
'80 EMPIRE STRIKES BACK, THE*
'81 RAIDERS OF THE LOST ARK
'81 BODY HEAT
'81 CONTINENTAL DIVIDE
'83 RETURN OF THE JEDI*
'83 BIG CHILL, THE*
EXECUTIVE PRODUCER
'83 BIG CHILL, THE*

MEG KASDAN

MISCELLANEOUS
'83 BIG CHILL, THE

AL KASHA

ASSOCIATE PRODUCER
'81 TAKE THIS JOB AND SHOVE IT*

PHYLLIS KASHA

CASTING
'79 BOARDWALK*
'83 LONELY LADY, THE*

AUDREY KASOFF

COSTUMES
'82 ANDROID*

DARYL KASS

ASSOCIATE PRODUCER
'83 JOYSTICKS*
PRODUCTION MANAGER
'83 JOYSTICKS

JEROME KASS

SCREENPLAY
'83 BLACK STALLION RETURNS, THE*

MARIO KASSAR

EXECUTIVE PRODUCER
'82 AMATEUR, THE*
'82 FIRST BLOOD*

AMY KASTENS

PUBLICIST
'81 RICH AND FAMOUS
'82 THAT CHAMPIONSHIP SEASON
'83 CLASS

ELLIOTT KASTNER

PRODUCER
'80 FFOLKES
'82 DEATH VALLEY
'83 MAN WOMAN AND CHILD*
'84 GARBO TALKS*
'84 OXFORD BLUES*
EXECUTIVE PRODUCER
'79 GOLDENGIRL
'80 FIRST DEADLY SIN*

MILTON KATSELAS
DIRECTOR
'79 WHEN YOU COMIN' BACK, RED RYDER?

ANDRES KATSIMITSOULIAS
LOCATIONS
'82 TEMPEST

CLIFFORD KATZ
EDITOR
'79 MOUNTAIN FAMILY ROBINSON*

DIANE KATZ
PROD. COORDINATOR
'79 SUNBURN
'81 CATTLE ANNIE AND LITTLE BRITCHES

GLORIA KATZ
PRODUCER
'84 BEST DEFENSE
SCREENPLAY
'84 BEST DEFENSE*
'84 INDIANA JONES AND THE TEMPLE OF DOOM*

MARTY KATZ
UNIT PROD. MANAGER
'83 HEART LIKE A WHEEL
MISCELLANEOUS
'83 HEART LIKE A WHEEL

MICHAEL KATZ
KEY GRIP
'79 REAL LIFE

NANCY KATZ
ASSISTANT EDITOR
'82 LITTLE SEX, A*
STILLS
'79 RICH KIDS
'82 THAT CHAMPIONSHIP SEASON*

RAY KATZ
EXECUTIVE PRODUCER
'84 RHINESTONE*

ROBIN KATZ
1ST ASST. DIRECTOR
'84 JUST THE WAY YOU ARE*

SHELLY KATZ
STILLS
'80 FOR THE LOVE OF BENJI

STEPHEN KATZ
ASSOCIATE PRODUCER
'83 PIRATES OF PENZANCE, THE*
CINEMATOGRAPHER
'80 BLUES BROTHERS
MISCELLANEOUS
'79 SILENT PARTNER, THE

VIRGINIA KATZ
ASSISTANT EDITOR
'81 ALL NIGHT LONG*
'83 CHRISTINE
'84 STARMAN*

GABRIEL KATZKA
PRODUCER
'79 BUTCH AND SUNDANCE: THE EARLY YEARS*
'81 BEAST WITHIN, THE*
'83 LORDS OF DISCIPLINE, THE*
EXECUTIVE PRODUCER
'79 METEOR*

JONATHAN KAUFER
DIRECTOR
'82 SOUP FOR ONE
SCREENPLAY
'82 SOUP FOR ONE

BILL KAUFMAN
MISCELLANEOUS
'80 ALLIGATOR

CHARLES KAUFMAN
PRODUCER
'80 MOTHER'S DAY*
DIRECTOR
'80 MOTHER'S DAY
SCREENPLAY
'80 MOTHER'S DAY*

CURT KAUFMAN
STILLS
'80 TRIBUTE
'82 SOUP FOR ONE

JIM KAUFMAN
UNIT PROD. MANAGER
'79 QUINTET
1ST ASST. DIRECTOR
'79 FAST COMPANY
'81 SCANNERS
'82 PARADISE
2ND ASST. DIRECTOR
'79 BLACK STALLION, THE*

LLOYD KAUFMAN
ASSOCIATE PRODUCER
'80 FINAL COUNTDOWN, THE
'80 MOTHER'S DAY*
UNIT PROD. MANAGER
'80 FINAL COUNTDOWN, THE

PHILIP KAUFMAN
DIRECTOR
'79 WANDERERS, THE
'83 RIGHT STUFF, THE
SCREENPLAY
'79 WANDERERS, THE*
'83 RIGHT STUFF, THE

RICHARD KAUFMAN
MISCELLANEOUS
'84 UNFAITHFULLY YOURS

ROBERT KAUFMAN
PRODUCER
'80 HOW TO BEAT THE HIGH COST OF LIVING*
SCREENPLAY
'79 LOVE AT FIRST BITE
'80 HOW TO BEAT THE HIGH COST OF LIVING
'80 NOTHING PERSONAL
'82 SPLIT IMAGE*
EXECUTIVE PRODUCER
'79 LOVE AT FIRST BITE*

ROSE KAUFMAN
SCREENPLAY
'79 WANDERERS, THE*

SANDRA KAUFMAN
ASSISTANT EDITOR
'80 UNION CITY*

SUSAN KAUFMAN
ART DIRECTOR
'80 HE KNOWS YOU'RE ALONE
PRODUCTION DESIGNER
'80 MOTHER'S DAY

ALAN KAUL
MISCELLANEOUS
'81 ROLLOVER

SINA KAUL
MISCELLANEOUS
'82 GANDHI

AIVAR KAULINS
PRODUCTION MANAGER
'84 RIDDLE OF THE SANDS

MARYTE KAVALIAUSKAS
SOUND
'83 EDDIE AND THE CRUISERS

SUSAN KAVESH
PROD. OFFICE COORD.
'83 STRANGE BREW

KEN KAWARAI
EXECUTIVE PRODUCER
'82 DON'T CRY, IT'S ONLY THUNDER*

GORDON KAY
MAKEUP
'83 HEAT AND DUST

ERNEST KAYE
ASSOCIATE PRODUCER
'83 MORTUARY*

JANICE KAYE
PUBLICIST
'83 CHRISTMAS STORY, A

JOHN KAYE
SCREENPLAY
'80 WHERE THE BUFFALO ROAM

NANCY KAYE
COSTUMES
'83 SCREWBALLS

NORA KAYE
PRODUCER
'80 NIJINSKY*
'81 PENNIES FROM HEAVEN*

SIMON KAYE
SOUND
'79 YANKS
'81 REDS*
'82 GANDHI
'82 VENOM*
'83 GORKY PARK
'83 NEVER SAY NEVER AGAIN
'83 PRIVATES ON PARADE
'84 INDIANA JONES AND THE TEMPLE OF DOOM*

STEPHANIE KAYE
HAIR
'79 AGATHA
'80 SATURN 3*
'80 ELEPHANT MAN, THE*
'80 LADY VANISHES, THE
'81 CLASH OF THE TITANS
'81 FOR YOUR EYES ONLY*
'83 NEVER SAY NEVER AGAIN*
'83 WICKED LADY, THE*
'84 LASSITER

ROBERT KAYLOR
DIRECTOR
'80 CARNY

JUDY KAYSER
PROD. SECRETARY
'84 CRACKERS

NICHOLAS KAZAN
SCREENPLAY
'82 FRANCES*

HOWARD KAZANJIAN
PRODUCER
'79 MORE AMERICAN GRAFFITTI
'83 RETURN OF THE JEDI
EXECUTIVE PRODUCER
'81 RAIDERS OF THE LOST ARK*

JEREMY KEABLE
MISCELLANEOUS
'83 DEAD ZONE, THE

DON KEACH
MISCELLANEOUS
'80 RAISE THE TITANIC

JAMES KEACH
SCREENPLAY
'80 LONG RIDERS, THE*
EXECUTIVE PRODUCER
'80 LONG RIDERS, THE*

STACY KEACH
SCREENPLAY
'80 LONG RIDERS, THE*
EXECUTIVE PRODUCER
'80 LONG RIDERS, THE*

JOHN KEAN
SOUND
'80 RESURRECTION
'81 RAGGEDY MAN
'81 ALL NIGHT LONG
'81 INCREDIBLE SHRINKING WOMAN, THE
'82 ZOOT SUIT

PETER KEAN
UNIT MANAGER
'79 EUROPEANS, THE

GENE KEARNEY
KEY GRIP
'80 HOPSCOTCH
'80 INSIDE MOVES
'80 URBAN COWBOY
'81 LEGEND OF THE LONE RANGER, THE
'82 CANNERY ROW
'82 DEATHWISH II
'82 E.T. THE EXTRA-TERRESTRIAL
'82 NIGHT SHIFT
'83 MAN WHO LOVED WOMEN, THE
'83 TWILIGHT ZONE, THE MOVIE*
'84 GHOSTBUSTERS*
'84 MIKE'S MURDER

GAIL KEARNS
PROD. OFFICE COORD.
'82 FIGHTING BACK
PROD. COORDINATOR
'84 ONCE UPON A TIME IN AMERICA

GINA KEARNS
HAIR
'80 USED CARS
'83 TWILIGHT ZONE, THE MOVIE*

MARY KEATS
HAIR
'78 DEER HUNTER, THE
'79 DREAMER
'79 10*
'80 RAGING BULL*
'80 HEAVEN'S GATE*
'81 CHARLIE CHAN AND THE CURSE OF THE DRAGON QUEEN*
'82 HAMMETT*
'82 YES, GIORGIO*

RICHARD KEEFE
ASSISTANT EDITOR
'81 RAGGEDY MAN*
'84 FIRESTARTER*

JAMES KEEFER
MISCELLANEOUS
'83 RETURN OF THE JEDI

CHUCK KEEHNE
COSTUMES
'79 APPLE DUMPLING GANG RIDES AGAIN, THE*
'79 NORTH AVENUE IRREGULARS, THE*

GUNNAR KEEL
2ND ASST. DIRECTOR
'83 BALLAD OF GREGORIO CORTEZ, THE

JAMES KEELER
HAIR
'79 LOST AND FOUND
'82 AMATEUR, THE
'83 STRANGE INVADERS

DOUG KEENAN
PROPS
'83 ALL THE RIGHT MOVES

SARA KEENE
PUBLICIST
'81 AMERICAN WEREWOLF IN LONDON, AN
'83 KRULL
'83 LORDS OF DISCIPLINE, THE
'83 NEVER SAY NEVER AGAIN

FRANK KEEVER
KEY GRIP
'79 LOVE AT FIRST BITE
'79 DOUBLE MCGUFFIN, THE
'81 RICHARD PRYOR: LIVE ON THE SUNSET STRIP*
'84 WINDY CITY

HARRIET KEHL
SCRIPT SUPERVISOR
'81 ON THE RIGHT TRACK
'83 BIG SCORE, THE

PAT KEHOE
1ST ASST. DIRECTOR
'79 RAVAGERS
'79 JUST YOU AND ME KID
'79 MAIN EVENT, THE*
'79 PRIZE FIGHTER, THE
'80 FINAL COUNTDOWN, THE
'81 SOUTHERN COMFORT
'82 POLTERGEIST
'82 THINGS ARE TOUGH ALL OVER
'83 BAD BOYS*
'83 TWILIGHT ZONE, THE MOVIE*
'84 CRIMES OF PASSION
'84 PHILADELPHIA EXPERIMENT, THE*

HANS-JURGEN KEIBACH
ART DIRECTOR
'80 FORMULA, THE

CLEMENS KEIFFENHEIM
2ND ASST. DIRECTOR
'79 BLOODLINE*
'82 FIVE DAYS ONE SUMMER*

LIZ KEIGLEY
CASTING
'80 BIG BRAWL, THE*
'80 HONEYSUCKLE ROSE*
'80 URBAN COWBOY*
'81 RAGGEDY MAN*
'81 DEADLY BLESSING*
'82 BEST LITTLE WHOREHOUSE IN TEXAS, THE*
'83 TERMS OF ENDEARMENT*
'83 TOUGH ENOUGH*
'84 CLOAK AND DAGGER*
'84 COUNTRY*
MISCELLANEOUS
'83 EDDIE MACON'S RUN

WARREN KEILLOR
SP. EFFECTS SUPERV.
'81 HAPPY BIRTHDAY TO ME*
MISCELLANEOUS
'80 PROM NIGHT

CATHERINE KELBER
EDITOR
'80 OUTSIDER, THE

PAM KELD
PROD. COORDINATOR
'84 PREPPIES

WILLIAM KELLARD
COSTUMES
'82 AMITYVILLE II: THE POSSESSION

ROGER KELLAWAY
MISCELLANEOUS
'83 BREATHLESS

CORD KELLER
SPECIAL EFFECTS
'80 HOME MOVIES

ELIZABETH HAAS KELLER
COSTUMES
'81 TUCK EVERLASTING

FREDERICK KING KELLER
DIRECTOR
'81 TUCK EVERLASTING
SCREENPLAY
'81 TUCK EVERLASTING*

HARRY KELLER
EDITOR
'80 STIR CRAZY
'81 STRIPES*
'82 HANKY PANKY
'83 MAN WHO WASN'T THERE, THE

MAX KELLER
PRODUCER
'81 DEADLY BLESSING*

MICHELINE KELLER
PRODUCER
'81 DEADLY BLESSING*

PATRICK KELLEY
EXECUTIVE PRODUCER
'79 LITTLE ROMANCE, A
'82 WORLD ACCORDING TO GARP, THE
'84 LITTLE DRUMMER GIRL, THE

MICHAEL KELLIBER
ASSISTANT EDITOR
'81 EXCALIBUR
'83 EDUCATING RITA

PHIL KELLISON
SP. EFFECTS SUPERV.
'81 MAN WHO SAW TOMORROW, THE
MISCELLANEOUS
'82 AIRPLANE II: THE SEQUEL

MARJORIE KELLOGG
SCREENPLAY
'79 BELL JAR, THE

BARBARA KELLY
MAKEUP
'81 SO FINE*
'84 BIRDY

BRIAN KELLY
EXECUTIVE PRODUCER
'82 BLADERUNNER*

CHRIS KELLY
PROPS
'79 HEARTLAND

CHRISTOPHER KELLY
ASSOCIATE EDITOR
'83 KEEP, THE

DAVID KELLY
2ND ASST. DIRECTOR
'84 MICKI AND MAUDE*

ERROL KELLY
ART DIRECTOR
'84 INDIANA JONES AND THE TEMPLE OF DOOM*

IAN KELLY
MISCELLANEOUS
'82 DARK CRYSTAL, THE
'84 ELECTRIC DREAMS

JAMES KELLY
CINEMATOGRAPHER
'80 HAPPY BIRTHDAY, GEMINI

JOHN KELLY
EDITOR
'80 MIDDLE AGE CRAZY

MARY JANE NOLAN KELLY
PROD. OFFICE COORD.
'82 SOUP FOR ONE
PROD. COORDINATOR
'81 BURNING, THE
'82 AUTHOR, AUTHOR
'83 WITHOUT A TRACE

MICHAEL KELLY
ASSOCIATE PRODUCER
'82 SWORD AND THE SORCERER, THE*
EDITOR
'82 HONKYTONK MAN*

MOIRA KELLY
PROD. OFFICE COORD.
'80 RAGING BULL*
PROD. COORDINATOR
'82 LITTLE SEX, A
MISCELLANEOUS
'84 CONAN THE DESTROYER

NANCY KELLY
LOCATIONS
'80 HUMANOIDS FROM THE DEEP

RICHARD KELLY
ASSISTANT EDITOR
'80 MIDDLE AGE CRAZY*

TERRY KELLY
ASSISTANT EDITOR
'84 PHILADELPHIA EXPERIMENT, THE

IRMI KELPINSKI
CASTING
'79 FEDORA

NICK KELSH
STILLS
'81 GALAXY OF TERROR

JOHN KEMENY
PRODUCER
'79 ICE CASTLES
'82 QUEST FOR FIRE*

LINDA KEMP
SCRIPT SUPERVISOR
'81 TARZAN, THE APE MAN

LOLA KEMP
HAIR
'80 STIR CRAZY
'83 MAN WHO WASN'T THERE, THE
'84 WOMAN IN RED, THE*
'84 MEATBALLS PART II

LYNDA KEMP

COSTUMES
'79 RUNNING
'80 NOTHING PERSONAL
'81 TICKET TO HEAVEN

ARTHUR KEMPEL

MUSIC
'81 GRADUATION DAY

JAN KEMPER

SCRIPT SUPERVISOR
'83 SCARFACE
'83 EDDIE MACON'S RUN
'84 COUNTRY
'84 TEACHERS

STEVE KEMPER

ASSISTANT EDITOR
'79 BUCK ROGERS*
'83 TWILIGHT ZONE, THE MOVIE*

VICTOR KEMPER

CINEMATOGRAPHER
'79 ...AND JUSTICE FOR ALL
'79 JERK, THE
'80 FINAL COUNTDOWN, THE
'80 XANADU
'80 NIGHT OF THE JUGGLER
'81 CHU CHU AND THE PHILLY FLASH
'81 FOUR SEASONS, THE
'82 AUTHOR, AUTHOR
'82 PARTNERS
'83 MR. MOM
'83 NATIONAL LAMPOON'S VACATION
'84 CLOAK AND DAGGER
'84 LONELY GUY, THE

RALPH KEMPLEN

EDITOR
'79 ESCAPE TO ATHENA
'81 GREAT MUPPET CAPER, THE
'82 DARK CRYSTAL, THE

PEARL KEMPTON

MISCELLANEOUS
'83 BREATHLESS
'84 AMERICAN DREAMER

PETER KENDALL

PROPS
'83 MAN FROM SNOWY RIVER, THE

ADAM KENNEDY

SCREENPLAY
'80 RAISE THE TITANIC

BROOKE KENNEDY

LOCATIONS
'79 KRAMER VS. KRAMER*
'82 LITTLE SEX, A

BYRON KENNEDY

PRODUCER
'82 ROAD WARRIOR, THE

CHRISTOPHER KENNEDY

ASSISTANT EDITOR
'84 LASSITER

JACK KENNEDY

KEY GRIP
'79 WARRIORS, THE
'80 FIRST DEADLY SIN

KATHLEEN KENNEDY

PRODUCER
'82 E.T. THE EXTRA-TERRESTRIAL*
EXECUTIVE PRODUCER
'84 GREMLINS*
ASSOCIATE PRODUCER
'82 POLTERGEIST
'83 TWILIGHT ZONE, THE MOVIE*
'84 INDIANA JONES
AND THE TEMPLE OF DOOM

LEON ISAAC KENNEDY

SCREENPLAY
'81 BODY AND SOUL
ASSOCIATE PRODUCER
'79 PENITENTIARY*

MAILLORY KENNEDY

CASTING
'81 MAN WHO SAW TOMORROW, THE*

PATRICK KENNEDY

EDITOR
'79 DREAMER*
'80 AIRPLANE
'83 MR. MOM

WILLIAM KENNEDY

SCREENPLAY
'84 COTTON CLUB, THE*

JEFF KENNEMORE

MAKEUP
'83 RUMBLEFISH*

ROBIN KENNETT

ASSISTANT EDITOR
'84 CHOOSE ME

BILL KENNEY

PRODUCTION DESIGNER
'80 CHANGE OF SEASONS, A
'80 MOUNTAIN MEN, THE
'81 BODY HEAT
'83 EDDIE MACON'S RUN
'83 TOUGH ENOUGH
'84 TANK
'84 WINDY CITY

DOUGLAS KENNEY

PRODUCER
'80 CADDYSHACK
SCREENPLAY
'80 CADDYSHACK*
EXECUTIVE PRODUCER
'81 MODERN PROBLEMS

MARIE KENNEY

SCRIPT SUPERVISOR
'79 NIGHTWING
'79 1941
'79 PROMISE, THE
'80 LOVING COUPLES
'80 OH GOD! BOOK II
'81 LEGEND OF THE LONE RANGER,THE
'81 TAPS
'82 MY FAVORITE YEAR
'83 CROSS CREEK
'84 CITY HEAT
'84 SWING SHIFT
'84 OH GOD, YOU DEVIL

CHRIS KENNY

PRODUCTION MANAGER
'84 SUPERGIRL*
UNIT MANAGER
'79 MOONRAKER*
'79 ESCAPE TO ATHENA

DOUG KENNY

LOCATIONS
'83 EDDIE AND THE CRUISERS

TONY KENRICK

SCREENPLAY
'81 NOBODY'S PERFEKT

BERNADINE KENT

CHOREOGRAPHER
'79 ELECTRIC HORSEMAN, THE

RODY KENT

CASTING
'84 PLACES IN THE HEART*

GARY KENWOOD

MISCELLANEOUS
'83 NEVER CRY WOLF

JOE KENWORTHY

SOUND
'81 SHARKEY'S MACHINE*
'81 KING OF THE MOUNTAIN
'81 PATERNITY*
'83 UNCOMMON VALOR
'84 RED DAWN

KATHY KENWORTHY
PROD. SECRETARY
'84 PROTOCOL

PAUL KENWORTHY
MISCELLANEOUS
'83 JAWS 3-D

WERNER KEPPLER
MAKEUP
'82 STAR TREK II
THE WRATH OF KHAN*
MISCELLANEOUS
'84 LAST STARFIGHTER, THE

HARRY KERAMIDAS
EDITOR
'84 CHILDREN OF THE CORN
ASSISTANT EDITOR
'81 BUSTIN' LOOSE*

RANDY KERBER
MUSIC SUPERVISOR
'80 DIVINE MADNESS*

BILL KERBY
SCREENPLAY
'79 ROSE, THE*

BLIEM KERN
ART DIRECTOR
'83 AMERICANA

DAVID KERN
EDITOR
'83 AMERICANA*
MISCELLANEOUS
'82 Q: QUETZALCOATL

ROBERT KERN JR.
EDITOR
'82 NIGHT SHIFT*

RONNI KERN
SCREENPLAY
'80 CHANGE OF SEASONS, A*

BRUCE KERNER
EXEC IN CHARGE PROD
'84 TERMINATOR, THE

PETER KERNOT
STILLS
'83 FINAL OPTION, THE*

JERRY KERNS
HAIR
'80 JAZZ SINGER, THE*

HUBIE KERNS JR.
STUNT COORDINATOR
'84 SPLASH*

NINA KEROVA
SCREENPLAY
'83 LIQUID SKY*
ASSOCIATE PRODUCER
'83 LIQUID SKY

MARY KERR
ART DIRECTOR
'80 NOTHING PERSONAL

LIZ KERRY
UNIT MANAGER
'84 FINDERS KEEPERS
PROD. COORDINATOR
'84 SHEENA

JOHN KERSHAW
SCREENPLAY
'83 LONELY LADY, THE*

DANA KERSHNER
MISCELLANEOUS
'84 RED DAWN

IRVIN KERSHNER
DIRECTOR
'80 EMPIRE STRIKES BACK, THE
'83 NEVER SAY NEVER AGAIN

STEVE KERSHOFF
MISCELLANEOUS
'79 MR. MIKE'S MONDO VIDEO

RISA KES
CASTING
'84 NEVERENDING STORY, THE*

MARCIA KESSELMAN
PROD. OFFICE COORD.
'80 MOTHER'S DAY*

TOM KESSENICH
KEY GRIP
'79 FAST BREAK
'80 IN GOD WE TRUST

STEVE KESTEN
PRODUCER
'83 AMITYVILLE 3D
EXECUTIVE PRODUCER
'84 CONAN THE DESTROYER
ASSOCIATE PRODUCER
'80 GLORIA
'80 NIGHT OF THE JUGGLER
'81 FOUR FRIENDS
'82 LITTLE SEX, A
PRODUCTION MANAGER
'80 GLORIA
UNIT PROD. MANAGER
'80 NIGHT OF THE JUGGLER
'81 FOUR FRIENDS*
'82 LITTLE SEX, A
'84 CONAN THE DESTROYER
MISCELLANEOUS
'79 ON THE YARD

JERRY KETCHAM
2ND ASST. DIRECTOR
'84 DREAMSCAPE*
LOCATIONS
'80 MY BODYGUARD

JAY KEUPER
ASSISTANT EDITOR
'80 FRIDAY THE 13TH
'81 FRIDAY THE 13TH PART TWO
'82 STRANGER IS WATCHING, A
'83 SPRING BREAK

ED KEYES
PROPS
'82 ZOOT SUIT

CHIRINE EL KHADEM
CINEMATOGRAPHER
'83 SMITHEREENS

GARY KIBBE
MISCELLANEOUS
'80 HEARTBEAT

MEREDITH KIBBEE
SCRIPT SUPERVISOR
'79 TOURIST TRAP

TOM KIBBEE
CASTING
'80 BORDERLINE*
'82 CREEPSHOW*

RIC KIDNEY
2ND ASST. DIRECTOR
'84 FIRESTARTER

JURGEN KIEBACH
ART DIRECTOR
'79 MAGICIAN OF LUBLIN, THE

TED KIERSCEY
MISCELLANEOUS
'79 BLACK HOLE, THE

FRITZ KIERSCH
DIRECTOR
'84 CHILDREN OF THE CORN

JAN KIESSER
CINEMATOGRAPHER
'84 CHOOSE ME
'84 PURPLE HEARTS
MISCELLANEOUS
'82 ENDANGERED SPECIES
'83 TABLE FOR FIVE
'84 MEATBALLS PART II

LIND KIFFE
2ND ASST. DIRECTOR
'83 REVENGE OF THE NINJA

KAROLYN KIISEL
COSTUMES
'83 GOIN' ALL THE WAY

CHERYL KILBORN
COSTUMES
'84 MARVIN AND TIGE*
MISCELLANEOUS
'84 TANK

LILLY KILVERT
ART DIRECTOR
'79 ALAMBRISTA!
PRODUCTION DESIGNER
'84 LOVELESS, THE

PAUL KIMATIAN
EXECUTIVE PRODUCER
'80 WITHOUT WARNING*
1ST ASST. DIRECTOR
'84 HOT DOG...THE MOVIE

LES KIMBER
ASSOCIATE PRODUCER
'82 MOTHER LODE
PRODUCTION MANAGER
'82 MOTHER LODE
'83 SUPERMAN III*
'84 FINDERS KEEPERS
UNIT PROD. MANAGER
'80 TOUCHED BY LOVE
'81 DEATH HUNT

JEFF KIMELMAN
EXECUTIVE PRODUCER
'83 RETURN OF THE ALIENS: THE DEADLY SPAWN*

ANNE KIMMEL
PRODUCER
'82 EATING RAOUL
'84 NOT FOR PUBLICATION

ANN KINDBERG
UNIT PROD. MANAGER
'83 INDEPENDENCE DAY
'84 BACHELOR PARTY

ALAN KING
PRODUCER
'81 CATTLE ANNIE AND LITTLE BRITCHES*
EXECUTIVE PRODUCER
'80 HAPPY BIRTHDAY, GEMINI
'81 WOLFEN

BARBARA KING
CASTING
'80 IDOLMAKER, THE*

DAVID KING
STILLS
'83 REVENGE OF THE NINJA*
'83 10 TO MIDNIGHT*

DENIS KING
MUSIC
'83 PRIVATES ON PARADE

ELIZABETH KING
ASSISTANT EDITOR
'83 MAUSOLEUM*

CHARLES KING III
SOUND
'80 SOMEWHERE IN TIME

JERRY KING
KEY GRIP
'80 COAST TO COAST
'80 LITTLE DARLINGS
'81 RICH AND FAMOUS
'81 HISTORY OF THE WORLD PART I
'82 YOUNG DOCTORS IN LOVE
'84 BEST DEFENSE*
'84 SPLASH*
'84 MASS APPEAL

JOEL KING
CINEMATOGRAPHER
'83 FRIGHTMARE
MISCELLANEOUS
'80 COAST TO COAST
'82 BEASTMASTER, THE
'82 OUT OF THE BLUE

JOYCE KING
SCRIPT SUPERVISOR
'79 BUDDY HOLLY STORY, THE
'82 SILENT RAGE
'82 NATIONAL LAMPOON'S CLASS REUNION
'83 D.C. CAB
'83 DOCTOR DETROIT
'84 SONGWRITER

JOYCE KOZY KING
ASSOCIATE PRODUCER
'82 IF YOU COULD SEE WHAT I HEAR
PRODUCTION MANAGER
'80 NOTHING PERSONAL
'81 LAST CHASE, THE
'82 IF YOU COULD SEE WHAT I HEAR

KATHLEEN KING
SOUND
'81 MS. 45

KEN KING
SOUND
'80 SCHIZOID
'81 HOWLING, THE
'83 SAVANNAH SMILES
'84 GREMLINS

LARRY KING
SCREENPLAY
'82 BEST LITTLE WHOREHOUSE IN TEXAS, THE*

NANCY KING
1ST ASST. DIRECTOR
'83 CHAINED HEAT
2ND ASST. DIRECTOR
'81 HOWLING, THE
'84 NOT FOR PUBLICATION*

PETER KING
HAIR
'83 DRAUGHTSMAN CONTRACT, THE*

PETER ROBB KING
MAKEUP
'81 INCHON*

PHILIPPA KING
PROD. COORDINATOR
'83 DEAD ZONE, THE

RAMSEY KING
CASTING
'79 SCAVENGER HUNT
'81 BEAST WITHIN, THE*

RICHARD KING
ASSISTANT EDITOR
'83 AMERICANA*
'83 I AM THE CHEESE

ROBB WILSON KING
ART DIRECTOR
'82 FRIDAY THE 13TH PART THREE IN 3D
'83 OSTERMAN WEEKEND, THE
PRODUCTION DESIGNER
'82 SWAMP THING
'83 LOSIN' IT
MISCELLANEOUS
'83 MAN WHO WASN'T THERE, THE

SANDY KING
SCRIPT SUPERVISOR
'80 LONG RIDERS, THE
'81 HARD COUNTRY
'81 THIEF
'83 RUMBLEFISH
'84 SIXTEEN CANDLES
'84 STARMAN

STEPHEN KING
SCREENPLAY
'82 CREEPSHOW

TERRY KING
SPECIAL EFFECTS
'82 I, THE JURY*

ZALMAN KING
EXECUTIVE PRODUCER
'80 ROADIE
'82 ENDANGERED SPECIES

BERNARD KINGHAM
MISCELLANEOUS
'81 GREAT MUPPET CAPER, THE

CLEVE KINGSTON
PROD. COORDINATOR
'84 SPLASH*

LINDA SONY KINNEY
PROD. COORDINATOR
'79 RAVAGERS
'79 PROMISES IN THE DARK
'82 LOOKIN' TO GET OUT
PROD. SECRETARY
'83 SUDDEN IMPACT
'84 CITY HEAT
'84 TIGHTROPE

SHARON KINNEY
CHOREOGRAPHER
'80 POPEYE*

TRISH KINNEY
SCRIPT SUPERVISOR
'81 LOOKER
'83 BLUE THUNDER
'84 GHOSTBUSTERS
'84 NO SMALL AFFAIR

ROBERT KINOSHITA
ART DIRECTOR
'80 GONG SHOW MOVIE, THE
'81 GOING APE!

RON KINWALD
2ND ASST. DIRECTOR
'82 SIX PACK*
'83 D.C. CAB*

RAY KINZER
KEY GRIP
'80 BLUES BROTHERS
'80 COAL MINER'S DAUGHTER
'81 RAGGEDY MAN
'83 EDDIE MACON'S RUN

MATTHEW KIPOIN
LOCATIONS
'84 SHEENA*

ROBERTA KIPP
ASSISTANT EDITOR
'81 LAST CHASE, THE*

PAT KIPPING
MISCELLANEOUS
'82 IF YOU COULD SEE WHAT I HEAR

SCOTT KIPSKER
MUSIC
'84 JOY OF SEX, THE*

GODFREY KIRBY
SOUND
'83 DRAUGHTSMAN CONTRACT, THE

TERRENCE KIRBY
PRODUCER
'84 CHILDREN OF THE CORN*

VAUNE KIRBY
ASSISTANT EDITOR
'84 SWING SHIFT

MICHAEL KIRCHBERGER
MISCELLANEOUS
'80 TIMES SQUARE

PATRICIA KIRCK
SCRIPT SUPERVISOR
'79 SAINT JACK
'79 GREAT BANK HOAX, THE*

JOHN KIRK
KEY GRIP
'80 RAISE THE TITANIC*

DOUGLAS KIRKLAND
STILLS
'79 LAST EMBRACE*

GEOFFREY KIRKLAND
ASSOCIATE PRODUCER
'80 FOXES*
PRODUCTION DESIGNER
'80 FAME
'82 SHOOT THE MOON
'83 RIGHT STUFF, THE
'84 BIRDY

JULIA KIRKLAND
COSTUME SUPERVISOR
'81 BEYOND THE REEF

LEILA KIRKPATRICK
PROD. SECRETARY
'83 LORDS OF DISCIPLINE, THE

SHARON KIRKPATRICK
STILLS
'80 HUMANOIDS FROM THE DEEP
SCRIPT SUPERVISOR
'80 BATTLE BEYOND THE STARS
'81 SMOKEY BITES THE DUST

GENE KIRKWOOD
PRODUCER
'80 IDOLMAKER, THE*
'83 GORKY PARK*
'83 NIGHT IN HEAVEN, A*
'83 KEEP, THE*
'84 POPE OF GREENWICH VILLAGE,

JAMES KIRKWOOD
SCREENPLAY
'82 SOME KIND OF HERO*
CO-PRODUCER
'82 SOME KIND OF HERO

SHELLEY KIRKWOOD
PUBLICIST
'84 POPE OF GREENWICH VILLAGE,THE*
UNIT PUBLICIST
'83 NIGHT IN HEAVEN, A*

HORST KIRSCHBERGER
MAKEUP
'84 NEVERENDING STORY, THE*

DAVID KIRSCHNER
SOUND
'84 STRANGERS KISS

STEVE KIRSHOFF
PROPS
'79 BOARDWALK
SPECIAL EFFECTS
'81 FRIDAY THE 13TH PART TWO
'84 PREPPIES

SAM KIRSON
MISCELLANEOUS
'84 CONAN THE DESTROYER

MICHAEL KISSAUN
2ND ASST. DIRECTOR
'83 TRENCHCOAT*

COLIN MICHAEL KITCHENS
2ND ASST. DIRECTOR
'83 NEVER CRY WOLF*

JOE KITE
SOUND
'80 TOM HORN*

MARTIN KITROSSER
SCREENPLAY
'82 FRIDAY THE 13TH PART THREE IN 3D*
SCRIPT SUPERVISOR
'80 FRIDAY THE 13TH
'81 DEADLY BLESSING
'81 FRIDAY THE 13TH PART TWO
'84 BEAT STREET

WILLIAM KITTREDGE
MISCELLANEOUS
'79 HEARTLAND

BRUCE KITZMEYER
ASSISTANT EDITOR
'80 HAPPY BIRTHDAY, GEMINI

R.J. KIZER
ASSOCIATE PRODUCER
'82 ANDROID
EDITOR
'80 BATTLE BEYOND THE STARS*
'81 GALAXY OF TERROR*
'82 ANDROID*
'83 TIMERIDER*

ROBERT KLANE
SCREENPLAY
'84 UNFAITHFULLY YOURS*

MICHAEL KLASTORIN
PUBLICIST
'82 SWAMP THING
UNIT PUBLICIST
'84 SONGWRITER

SEYMOUR KLATE
PRODUCTION DESIGNER
'80 SOMEWHERE IN TIME

LAWRENCE KLAUSNER
EXECUTIVE PRODUCER
'79 GREAT BANK HOAX, THE*

HAL KLEIN
PRODUCTION MANAGER
'79 LOVE AND BULLETS
'81 PURSUIT OF D.B. COOPER, THE

HILARY DOLE KLEIN
STILLS
'84 STONE BOY, THE

JORDAN KLEIN
MISCELLANEOUS
'84 SPLASH

MIKE KLEIN
ASSISTANT EDITOR
'80 IT'S MY TURN*
'83 SMOKEY AND THE BANDIT III

RAY KLEIN
SPECIAL EFFECTS
'80 RAGING BULL*
'84 OH GOD, YOU DEVIL

TINA KLEIN
MISCELLANEOUS
'83 MAUSOLEUM

MARSHA KLEINMAN
CASTING
'83 PRIVATE SCHOOL*
'84 OH GOD, YOU DEVIL
'84 MASS APPEAL

PETER KLEINOW
MISCELLANEOUS
'83 SPACEHUNTER: ADVENTURES IN THE FORBIDDEN ZONE
'84 TERMINATOR, THE

CARL KLEINSCHMITT
SCREENPLAY
'80 MIDDLE AGE CRAZY

RANDAL KLEISER
PRODUCER
'80 BLUE LAGOON
DIRECTOR
'80 BLUE LAGOON
'82 SUMMER LOVERS
'84 GRANDVIEW, U.S.A.
SCREENPLAY
'82 SUMMER LOVERS

RICHARD KLETTER
SCREENPLAY
'83 BLACK STALLION RETURNS, THE*
'83 NEVER CRY WOLF*

MAX KLEVEN
2ND ASST. DIRECTOR
'79 LOST AND FOUND
STUNT COORDINATOR
'80 CHANGELING, THE
'81 HAPPY BIRTHDAY TO ME
'83 FOOTLOOSE
'84 HOT DOG...THE MOVIE
'84 PROTOCOL

HENRY KLINE
PRODUCTION MANAGER
'83 TWO OF A KIND
'84 REVENGE OF THE NERDS

RICHARD KLINE
CINEMATOGRAPHER
'79 STAR TREK-THE MOTION PICTURE
'80 COMPETITION, THE
'80 TOUCHED BY LOVE
'81 BODY HEAT
'82 DEATHWISH II*
'83 BREATHLESS
'83 DEAL OF THE CENTURY
'83 MAN WOMAN AND CHILD
'84 ALL OF ME
'84 HARD TO HOLD
MISCELLANEOUS
'79 FIREPOWER

STEVE KLINE
SCREENPLAY
'80 BORDERLINE*

ELIZABETH KLING
ASSISTANT EDITOR
'84 POPE OF GREENWICH VILLAGE,

HOWARD KLING
PRODUCER
'81 TUCK EVERLASTING
EDITOR
'81 TUCK EVERLASTING*

MIKE KLINGBELL
MISCELLANEOUS
'81 HAPPY BIRTHDAY TO ME

TONY KLINGER
PRODUCER
'80 KIDS ARE ALL RIGHT, THE*

LYNZEE KLINGMAN
EDITOR
'80 GILDA LIVE*
'81 TRUE CONFESSIONS
'83 TWO OF A KIND*
MISCELLANEOUS
'79 HAIR
'84 PROTOCOL

DAEL KLIPPERSTEEN
ASSISTANT EDITOR
'79 SCAVENGER HUNT

HARRY KLOOSTER
PUBLICIST
'83 CHEECH AND CHONG'S STILL SMOKIN'

NANCY KLOPPER
CASTING
'81 MODERN PROBLEMS*
'81 MOMMIE DEAREST*
'82 OFFICER AND A GENTLEMAN, AN*
'83 RISKY BUSINESS
'83 DEAL OF THE CENTURY
'83 EDDIE AND THE CRUISERS
'83 KEEP, THE*
'84 AGAINST ALL ODDS
'84 MICKI AND MAUDE

ERIC KLOSTERMAN
LOCATIONS
'80 BALTIMORE BULLET, THE

GEORGES KLOTZ
EDITOR
'84 JUST THE WAY YOU ARE*

STEVEN KLOVES
SCREENPLAY
'84 RACING WITH THE MOON

LYNN KLUGMAN
MISCELLANEOUS
'79 MUPPET MOVIE, THE

JEFF KLUTZ
KEY GRIP
'83 REUBEN, REUBEN

STEVE KNAPMAN
LOCATIONS
'82 ROAD WARRIOR, THE

KATHLEEN KNAPP
CHOREOGRAPHER
'84 BACHELOR PARTY

PAM KNAPP
LOCATIONS
'82 BRAINWAVES

WILLIAM KNAPP
SPECIAL EFFECTS
'80 CARNY*

MICHAEL-JOHN KNATCHBULL
ASSOCIATE PRODUCER
'82 EVIL UNDER THE SUN
LOCATIONS
'83 DRESSER, THE
'83 KRULL*

NIKITA KNATZ
2ND UNIT DIRECTOR
'82 PERSONAL BEST
'84 FIRESTARTER*
MISCELLANEOUS
'82 BEASTMASTER, THE

DAVID KNEUSS
MISCELLANEOUS
'81 SO FINE

CHRISTOPHER KNIGHT
EXECUTIVE PRODUCER
'84 HOT DOG...THE MOVIE

DARIN KNIGHT
SOUND
'78 DEER HUNTER, THE
'79 PROMISES IN THE DARK
'80 CHEECH AND CHONG'S NEXT MOVIE
'80 HEAVEN'S GATE
'81 RICH AND FAMOUS
'81 HAND, THE
'82 DINER
'82 SECOND THOUGHTS
'83 SCARFACE
'83 KISS ME GOODBYE
'84 CITY HEAT
'84 CANNONBALL RUN II

EILEEN KNIGHT
CASTING
'81 S.O.B.*

JOHN KNIGHT
KEY GRIP
'83 STREAMERS

ROBIN KNIGHT
KEY GRIP
'81 HARD COUNTRY
'84 GRANDVIEW, U.S.A.
'84 AMERICAN DREAMER

TONGA KNIGHT
MAKEUP
'82 SWAMP THING

LEE KNIPPELBERG
2ND ASST. DIRECTOR
'80 PROM NIGHT

CHARLES KNODE
COSTUMES
'79 MONTY PYTHON'S LIFE OF BRIAN*
'82 BLADERUNNER*
'83 NEVER SAY NEVER AGAIN
PROPS
'82 MONTY PYTHON LIVE AT
THE HOLLYWOOD BOWL*

MARK KNOPFLER
MUSIC
'83 LOCAL HERO
'84 COMFORT AND JOY

EDDIE KNOTT
KEY GRIP
'79 HAIR
'79 HOT STUFF
'81 HARDLY WORKING
'83 PORKY'S II THE NEXT DAY

EDDIE KNOTT JR.
KEY GRIP
'81 FUNHOUSE, THE
'81 NOBODY'S PERFEKT
'82 LOVE CHILD
'83 SMOKEY AND THE BANDIT III
'83 BLUE SKIES AGAIN
'84 HARRY & SON
'84 WHERE THE BOYS ARE

ROBBIE KNOTT
SPECIAL EFFECTS
'79 BUDDY HOLLY STORY, THE
'79 MUPPET MOVIE, THE
'84 REPO MAN*

DEREK KNOWLER
PROPS
'79 LEGACY, THE
'83 PRIVATES ON PARADE

PHILIP KNOWLES
SPECIAL EFFECTS
'84 NEVERENDING STORY, THE

PETER KNOWLTON
MAKEUP
'82 EATING RAOUL
HAIR
'82 EATING RAOUL
MISCELLANEOUS
'83 CUJO

MICKEY KNOX
MISCELLANEOUS
'83 BREATHLESS
'84 BOLERO

SKIP KNOX
LOCATIONS
'84 TANK

JANET KNUTSEN
2ND ASST. DIRECTOR
'84 RHINESTONE*

MORNA KO
PROD. SECRETARY
'79 SAINT JACK

GEORGE KOBLASA
MISCELLANEOUS
'81 HAND, THE

STEPHEN KOBLICK
MISCELLANEOUS
'84 HOT DOG...THE MOVIE

RICHARD KOBRITZ
PRODUCER
'83 CHRISTINE

C.J. KOCH
SCREENPLAY
'83 YEAR OF
LIVING DANGEROUSLY, THE*

HOWARD KOCH
PRODUCER
'82 SOME KIND OF HERO
'82 AIRPLANE II: THE SEQUEL
EXECUTIVE PRODUCER
'81 DRAGONSLAYER

HOWARD KOCH JR.

PRODUCER
'80 IDOLMAKER, THE*
'81 HONKY TONK FREEWAY*
'83 GORKY PARK*
'83 NIGHT IN HEAVEN, A*
'83 KEEP, THE*
EXECUTIVE PRODUCER
'79 FRISCO KID, THE

KAREN KOCH

PRODUCTION MANAGER
'84 PARIS, TEXAS
PROD. OFFICE COORD.
'83 SILKWOOD*
PROD. COORDINATOR
'83 BALLAD OF GREGORIO CORTEZ, THE

KAREL KOCI

PROPS
'84 AMADEUS*

CHRIS. LUCIEN KOEFOED

ASSISTANT EDITOR
'82 STAR TREK II THE WRATH OF KHAN*
'83 UNCOMMON VALOR

KOELLE

MAKEUP
'80 XANADU*

FRED KOENEKAMP

CINEMATOGRAPHER
'79 AMITYVILLE HORROR, THE
'79 CHAMP, THE
'79 LOVE AND BULLETS
'80 FIRST FAMILY
'80 HUNTER, THE
'80 WHEN TIME RAN OUT
'81 FIRST MONDAY IN OCTOBER
'81 CARBON COPY
'82 YES, GIORGIO
'83 TWO OF A KIND
'83 WRONG IS RIGHT
'84 ADVENTURES OF BUCKAROO BANZAI ACROSS THE 8TH DIMENSION,THE

LAIRD KOENIG

SCREENPLAY
'79 BLOODLINE
'81 INCHON*

RICK KOFOED

ART DIRECTOR
'83 NATE & HAYES*

PHILIP KOHLER

PRODUCTION MANAGER
'81 FOR YOUR EYES ONLY*
'82 DARK CRYSTAL, THE
'83 OCTOPUSSY*
'84 KILLING FIELDS, THE*
LOCATIONS
'79 DRACULA*
'80 EMPIRE STRIKES BACK, THE
'81 SPHINX*

JOHN KOHN

PRODUCER
'84 RACING WITH THE MOON*
SCREENPLAY
'79 GOLDENGIRL

PETER KOHN

ASSOCIATE PRODUCER
'84 OXFORD BLUES*
UNIT MANAGER
'82 PINK FLOYD: THE WALL
1ST ASST. DIRECTOR
'84 OXFORD BLUES
2ND ASST. DIRECTOR
'80 AWAKENING, THE
'81 FRENCH LIEUTENANT'S WOMAN, THE
'83 CURSE OF THE PINK PANTHER*
'83 TRAIL OF THE PINK PANTHER*
'84 RIDDLE OF THE SANDS
LOCATIONS
'83 MONTY PYTHON'S THE MEANING OF LIFE
'84 GREYSTOKE: THE LEGEND OF TARZAN, LORD OF THE APES*

MICHAEL KOHNE

KEY GRIP
'79 MEATBALLS*
'80 NOTHING PERSONAL
'81 DEATH HUNT
'81 TICKET TO HEAVEN
'83 STRANGE BREW*

PANCHO KOHNER

PRODUCER
'79 LOVE AND BULLETS
'80 WHY WOULD I LIE?
'83 10 TO MIDNIGHT*
'84 EVIL THAT MEN DO, THE

KATHERINE KOLBERT

STILLS
'79 DAWN OF THE DEAD
'82 CREEPSHOW*

FRED KOLO

ART DIRECTOR
'82 I'M DANCING AS FAST AS I CAN

DAN KOLSRUD

ASSOCIATE PRODUCER
'83 SOMETHING WICKED THIS WAY COMES
1ST ASST. DIRECTOR
'80 COAL MINER'S DAUGHTER
'80 XANADU
'81 GHOST STORY*
'83 SOMETHING WICKED THIS WAY COMES
'83 GORKY PARK

STEPHEN KOLZAK

CASTING
'84 BACHELOR PARTY*

JAROMIR KOMAREK

STILLS
'84 AMADEUS*

J.W. KOMPARE

ASSISTANT EDITOR
'83 CHEECH AND CHONG'S STILL SMOKIN'*
'84 CHEECH AND CHONG'S THE CORSICAN BROTHERS*

APHRODITE KONDOS

COSTUMES
'81 ROAD GAMES
'82 PIRATE MOVIE, THE

FRANK KONIGSBERG

PRODUCER
'84 JOY OF SEX, THE

FAY KONKELL

SPECIAL EFFECTS
'81 ALL NIGHT LONG

STAVROS KONSTANTARAKOS

2ND ASST. DIRECTOR
'82 SUMMER LOVERS*

JOSEPH KONTRA

2ND ASST. DIRECTOR
'81 REDS*
'83 INDEPENDENCE DAY*

EDMOND KOONS

CINEMATOGRAPHER
'79 PERFECT COUPLE, A
'80 HEALTH
'81 MODERN PROBLEMS

DAVID KOONTZ

EXECUTIVE PRODUCER
'81 MOMMIE DEAREST*

WERNER KOOPMAN
MISCELLANEOUS
'80 SIMON

PATINKA KOPEC
MISCELLANEOUS
'84 UNFAITHFULLY YOURS

ARNOLD KOPELSON
PRODUCER
'80 FOOLIN AROUND
EXECUTIVE PRODUCER
'79 LEGACY, THE
'79 LOST AND FOUND
'80 NIGHT OF THE JUGGLER

NED KOPP
ASSOCIATE PRODUCER
'84 BIRDY
PRODUCTION MANAGER
'80 FOXES
'82 SHOOT THE MOON

CHARLES KOPPELMAN
MUSIC SUPERVISOR
'84 BEAR, THE*

ANNA KORDA
CASTING
'82 FIVE DAYS ONE SUMMER*
MISCELLANEOUS
'81 VICTORY

DAVID KORDA
ASSOCIATE PRODUCER
'79 SUNBURN
'81 CATTLE ANNIE
AND LITTLE BRITCHES

NICHOLAS VINCENT KORDA
ASSISTANT EDITOR
'79 BLACK HOLE, THE

MARIE KORDUS
ART DIRECTOR
'79 ROCK 'N ROLL HIGH SCHOOL

MIKE KORKKO
KEY GRIP
'82 LIAR'S MOON*

LORI KORNSPUN
ASSISTANT EDITOR
'84 BOSTONIANS, THE*

JOHN KOROGI
2ND ASST. DIRECTOR
'83 SAVANNAH SMILES

KATHLEEN KORTH
ASSISTANT EDITOR
'80 FOXES
'82 E.T. THE EXTRA-TERRESTRIAL

DAVID KOSH
2ND ASST. DIRECTOR
'80 MOTHER'S DAY

JERZY KOSINSKI
SCREENPLAY
'79 BEING THERE

RON KOSLOW
SCREENPLAY
'84 FIRSTBORN
CO-PRODUCER
'84 FIRSTBORN

JIM KOSNER
LOCATIONS
'84 RHINESTONE
MISCELLANEOUS
'84 RACING WITH THE MOON

ROBERT KOSTER
UNIT MANAGER
'79 BUTCH AND SUNDANCE:
THE EARLY YEARS

LARRY KOSTROFF
ASSOCIATE PRODUCER
'79 WHEN A STRANGER CALLS

SHO KOSUGI
MISCELLANEOUS
'83 REVENGE OF THE NINJA

JOHANN IWAN KOT
ART DIRECTOR
'84 NEVERENDING STORY, THE*

TED KOTCHEFF
PRODUCER
'82 SPLIT IMAGE
DIRECTOR
'79 NORTH DALLAS FORTY
'82 SPLIT IMAGE
'82 FIRST BLOOD
'83 UNCOMMON VALOR
SCREENPLAY
'79 NORTH DALLAS FORTY*
EXECUTIVE PRODUCER
'83 UNCOMMON VALOR

ALLAN KOTTER
SPECIAL EFFECTS
'79 BROOD, THE

JIM KOUF
SCREENPLAY
'83 CLASS*
'84 UP THE CREEK
'84 AMERICAN DREAMER*
ASSOCIATE PRODUCER
'83 CLASS*

LUCA KOUIMELIS
CASTING
'79 QUINTET
1ST ASST. DIRECTOR
'84 FINAL TERROR, THE
SCRIPT SUPERVISOR
'79 PERFECT COUPLE, A
'79 REMEMBER MY NAME
'80 ROADIE
'80 HEALTH
'80 POPEYE
'82 CAT PEOPLE
'82 COME BACK TO THE 5 & 10,
JIMMY DEAN, JIMMY DEAN
'82 ENDANGERED SPECIES
'82 48 HOURS
'83 STREAMERS
'83 CLASS
'84 STREETS OF FIRE

JOHN PETER KOUSAKIS
2ND ASST. DIRECTOR
'84 CANNONBALL RUN II*

KORNELL KOVACH
MUSIC
'81 MONTENEGRO

LASZLO KOVACS
CINEMATOGRAPHER
'79 RUNNER STUMBLES, THE
'79 BUTCH AND SUNDANCE:
THE EARLY YEARS
'80 HEARTBEAT
'80 INSIDE MOVES
'81 LEGEND OF THE LONE RANGER,THE
'82 FRANCES
'82 TOY, THE
'84 CRACKERS
'84 GHOSTBUSTERS
MISCELLANEOUS
'80 CLOSE ENCOUNTERS OF THE THIRD
KIND SPECIAL EDITION

JONATHAN KOVLER
EXECUTIVE PRODUCER
'79 REAL LIFE*

JAN KOWALSKI
1ST ASST. DIRECTOR
'81 BEYOND THE REEF

JOANNE KOZLOFF
MAKEUP
'84 ANGEL*

SARAH KOZLOFF
PROD. COORDINATOR
'80 UNION CITY

MICHAEL KOZOLL
SCREENPLAY
'82 FIRST BLOOD*

IVAN KRAL
MUSIC
'81 SUBWAY RIDERS*
MISCELLANEOUS
'82 DINER

JOEL KRAMER
STUNT COORDINATOR
'83 MAUSOLEUM

KAREN KRAMER
CASTING
'79 RUNNER STUMBLES, THE

LEE KRAMER
PRODUCER
'81 MAN WHO SAW TOMORROW, THE*
EXECUTIVE PRODUCER
'80 XANADU

LOUIS KRAMER
SOUND
'83 LOCAL HERO
'84 COMFORT AND JOY

RONNIE KRAMER
PROD. COORDINATOR
'80 HOPSCOTCH
PROD. SECRETARY
'79 CHINA SYNDROME, THE
'80 LITTLE DARLINGS

STANLEY KRAMER
PRODUCER
'79 RUNNER STUMBLES, THE
DIRECTOR
'79 RUNNER STUMBLES, THE

STEVE KRAMER
MISCELLANEOUS
'80 AIRPLANE

JONATHAN KRANE
EXECUTIVE PRODUCER
'83 CURSE OF THE PINK PANTHER
'83 MAN WHO LOVED WOMEN, THE
'83 TRAIL OF THE PINK PANTHER
'84 MICKI AND MAUDE*

JON KRANHOUSE
CINEMATOGRAPHER
'82 BRAINWAVES

DONALD KRANZE
EXECUTIVE PRODUCER
'81 PURSUIT OF D.B. COOPER, THE*
'82 NIGHT SHIFT

HILLARY JANE KRANZE
EDITOR
'81 ZORRO, THE GAY BLADE
ASSISTANT EDITOR
'80 DIVINE MADNESS

DICK KRATINA
CINEMATOGRAPHER
'79 FIREPOWER*
MISCELLANEOUS
'79 GREAT SANTINI, THE
'79 LAST EMBRACE
'80 CAN'T STOP THE MUSIC
'80 HERO AT LARGE

ROBIN KRAUSE
ASSOCIATE PRODUCER
'80 HOW TO BEAT
THE HIGH COST OF LIVING
STILLS
'79 LOVE AT FIRST BITE
'80 STUNT MAN, THE*

KENNETH KRAUSGILL
2ND ASST. DIRECTOR
'83 I AM THE CHEESE

CAROL KRAVETZ
CHOREOGRAPHER
'84 THIS IS SPINAL TAP
PROD. COORDINATOR
'84 CHAMPIONS

MICHAEL KRAVITZ
PRODUCER
'80 MOTHER'S DAY*
1ST ASST. DIRECTOR
'79 SOMETHING SHORT OF PARADISE

JAROSLAV KRCEK
MISCELLANEOUS
'84 AMADEUS

NEIL KREPELA
MISCELLANEOUS
'82 E.T. THE EXTRA-TERRESTRIAL
'84 2010

CARL KRESS
EDITOR
'79 MAN, A WOMAN AND A BANK, A
'79 METEOR
'80 HOPSCOTCH
'81 LOOKER
'83 STROKER ACE*
'84 CANNONBALL RUN II*

LYNN KRESSEL
CASTING
'81 PRIVATE LESSONS
'82 JEKYLL AND HYDE
TOGETHER AGAIN*
'83 PRIVATE SCHOOL*

JOHN KRETCHMER
1ST ASST. DIRECTOR
'84 PROTOCOL*
2ND ASST. DIRECTOR
'79 CHAPTER TWO
'79 IN-LAWS, THE
'80 DIVINE MADNESS
'80 HERO AT LARGE
'81 LOOKER
'82 I OUGHT TO BE IN PICTURES
'82 MAKING LOVE

MICHAEL KREVITT
KEY GRIP
'83 RISKY BUSINESS

STU KRIEGER
SCREENPLAY
'84 WHERE THE BOYS ARE*

STEVE KRISHOFF
MISCELLANEOUS
'84 C.H.U.D.

JONATHAN NOAH KRIVINE
ASSOCIATE PRODUCER
'82 ZAPPED!*

SERGE KRIZMAN
PRODUCTION DESIGNER
'79 LOVE AT FIRST BITE

CHUCK KRIZMANICH
MISCELLANEOUS
'79 MOUNTAIN FAMILY ROBINSON

JOAN KROC
EXECUTIVE PRODUCER
'84 MASS APPEAL

WOLF KROEGER
ASSOCIATE PRODUCER
'80 HEALTH*
ART DIRECTOR
'79 QUINTET
'79 IN PRAISE OF OLDER WOMEN
PRODUCTION DESIGNER
'80 POPEYE
'82 SPLIT IMAGE
'82 FIRST BLOOD
'83 STREAMERS

MARTY KROFFT
EXECUTIVE PRODUCER
'80 MIDDLE AGE CRAZY*

SID KROFFT
EXECUTIVE PRODUCER
'80 MIDDLE AGE CRAZY*

WILLIAM KRONICK
2ND UNIT DIRECTOR
'80 FLASH GORDON

BOBBI KRONOWITZ
PROD. COORDINATOR
'84 SPLASH*

JEREMY JOE KRONSBERG
DIRECTOR
'81 GOING APE!
SCREENPLAY
'81 GOING APE!

SANDY KROOPF
SCREENPLAY
'84 BIRDY*

LEE KROSSKOVE
KEY GRIP
'80 ON THE NICKEL
'81 BUSTIN' LOOSE*

BARRY KROST
EXECUTIVE PRODUCER
'79 WHEN A STRANGER CALLS*
'84 AMERICAN DREAMER

BILL KROYER
MISCELLANEOUS
'82 TRON

FRED KRUG
EXECUTIVE PRODUCER
'79 MOUNTAIN FAMILY ROBINSON

DON KRUGER
LOCATIONS
'79 ROSE, THE
'79 ELECTRIC HORSEMAN, THE
'80 URBAN COWBOY*
'82 CANNERY ROW

JOHN KRUIZE
SCREENPLAY
'84 MUTANT*

GABRIEL KRUKS
KEY GRIP
'80 FOXES
'83 NEVER CRY WOLF

WHITEY KRUMM
SPECIAL EFFECTS
'80 NUDE BOMB, THE*

LEE KRUSE
MAKEUP
'80 KIDNAPPING OF THE PRESIDENT, THE
MISCELLANEOUS
'80 KIDNAPPING OF THE PRESIDENT, THE

WILLIAM KRUZYKOWSKI
ASSISTANT EDITOR
'84 HARRY & SON*
'84 LITTLE DRUMMER GIRL, THE*

ANNA KSIELOPOLSKA
ASSISTANT EDITOR
'84 GIVE MY REGARDS TO BROAD STREET*

KAREN KUBECK
MAKEUP
'82 PARASITE
'83 PRIVATE SCHOOL*

YVONNE KUBIS
COSTUME SUPERVISOR
'81 EYE FOR AN EYE, AN

JAN KUBISTA
2ND ASST. DIRECTOR
'84 AMADEUS*

VICTOR KUBITSCHEK
MISCELLANEOUS
'80 MOTEL HELL
'81 HELL NIGHT

STANLEY KUBRICK
PRODUCER
'80 SHINING, THE
DIRECTOR
'80 SHINING, THE
SCREENPLAY
'80 SHINING, THE*

FRED KUCHNERT
MISCELLANEOUS
'79 BUDDY HOLLY STORY, THE

MICHELLE KUHAR
PROD. COORDINATOR
'81 RICHARD PRYOR: LIVE ON THE SUNSET STRIP
'82 TOY, THE

BERNIE KUKOFF
SCREENPLAY
'84 JOHNNY DANGEROUSLY*

BUZZ KULIK
DIRECTOR
'80 HUNTER, THE

AJIT KUMAR
1ST ASST. DIRECTOR
'84 PASSAGE TO INDIA, A*

DREW KUNIN
SOUND
'84 STRANGER THAN PARADISE*

HOWARD KUNIN
EDITOR
'79 ROLLER BOOGIE
MISCELLANEOUS
'80 FADE TO BLACK

GERLINDE KUNZ
MAKEUP
'84 LITTLE DRUMMER GIRL, THE*

PETER KUNZ
SPECIAL EFFECTS
'79 BOARDWALK
'83 ECHOES

HOWARD KUPERMAN
PRODUCER
'81 NIGHT THE LIGHTS WENT OUT IN GEORGIA, THE*

TONY KUPERSMITH
ART DIRECTOR
'84 MUTANT

LAWRENCE KUPPIN
EXECUTIVE PRODUCER
'81 ON THE RIGHT TRACK*

PETER KURAN
MISCELLANEOUS
'80 EMPIRE STRIKES BACK, THE
'82 CONAN THE BARBARIAN
'82 Q: QUETZALCOATL
'84 DREAMSCAPE

TED KURDYLA
LOCATIONS
'81 BLOW OUT
'84 C.H.U.D.*
MISCELLANEOUS
'84 ONCE UPON A TIME IN AMERICA

RON KURELO
MISCELLANEOUS
'84 POLICE ACADEMY

JOE KURI
PROPS
'79 BUCK ROGERS*
'80 FIRST FAMILY
'82 JINXED

MINDRY KURITA
PRODUCTION MANAGER
'81 INCHON*

JEFFREY KURLAND

COSTUMES
'81 FAN, THE*
'84 BROADWAY DANNY ROSE

JANE KURSON

EDITOR
'81 NEIGHBORS

PAUL KURTA

ASSOCIATE PRODUCER
'82 Q: QUETZALCOATL

DEBRA KURTZ

CASTING
'81 MODERN ROMANCE*

GARY KURTZ

PRODUCER
'80 EMPIRE STRIKES BACK, THE
'82 DARK CRYSTAL, THE*
2ND UNIT DIRECTOR
'82 DARK CRYSTAL, THE

KIM KURUMADA

EXECUTIVE PRODUCER
'84 MIKE'S MURDER
UNIT PROD. MANAGER
'84 MIKE'S MURDER
1ST ASST. DIRECTOR
'79 CHINA SYNDROME, THE
'79 PROMISES IN THE DARK
'80 URBAN COWBOY
'81 CONTINENTAL DIVIDE
'81 HAND, THE
'82 SOME KIND OF HERO

RON KURZ

SCREENPLAY
'81 FRIDAY THE 13TH PART TWO

DONALD KUSHNER

PRODUCER
'82 TRON

KEVIN KUTCHAVER

MISCELLANEOUS
'84 DREAMSCAPE

FELIX KUTLIK

1ST ASST. DIRECTOR
'81 SUBWAY RIDERS

LYNN KUWAHARA

LOCATIONS
'81 ...ALL THE MARBLES

RYU KUZE

STUNT COORDINATOR
'82 CHALLENGE, THE
MISCELLANEOUS
'82 CHALLENGE, THE

KAS KUZUI

PROD. COORDINATOR
'81 TATTOO

SANDRA KYBARTA

ART DIRECTOR
'83 SCREWBALLS

DAVID KYNOCH

STILLS
'79 PICNIC AT HANGING ROCK
'79 MY BRILLIANT CAREER

L

ANNE-MARIE L'HOTE
ASSISTANT EDITOR
'84 JUST THE WAY YOU ARE*

IAN LA FRENAIS
SCREENPLAY
'79 PRISONER OF ZENDA, THE*

CHARLES LA LOGGIA
PRODUCER
'81 FEAR NO EVIL*
EXECUTIVE PRODUCER
'81 FEAR NO EVIL

FRANK LA LOGGIA
PRODUCER
'81 FEAR NO EVIL*
DIRECTOR
'81 FEAR NO EVIL
SCREENPLAY
'81 FEAR NO EVIL
MUSIC
'81 FEAR NO EVIL*

PINA LA ROSA
ASSISTANT EDITOR
'83 YOR*

EMILE LA VIGNE
MAKEUP
'79 LOST AND FOUND*
'80 LAST MARRIED COUPLE IN AMERICA, THE*

PIERRE LABERGE
LOCATIONS
'84 ONCE UPON A TIME IN AMERICA*

IYA LABUNKA
PROD. COORDINATOR
'82 ANDROID
'83 LOVE LETTERS
'84 REPO MAN

DANIEL LACAMBRE
CINEMATOGRAPHER
'80 BATTLE BEYOND THE STARS
'80 HUMANOIDS FROM THE DEEP
'81 SATURDAY THE 14TH

GREG LACAVA
MAKEUP
'83 BLUE THUNDER
'84 GREMLINS
'84 SONGWRITER*

LILY LACAVA
SCRIPT SUPERVISOR
'84 STAR TREK III: THE SEARCH FOR SPOCK

CLAY LACEY
MISCELLANEOUS
'79 GREAT SANTINI, THE
'81 LAST CHASE, THE

RICHARD LACEY
SPECIAL EFFECTS
'81 SATURDAY THE 14TH

FRANCE LACHAPELLE
SCRIPT SUPERVISOR
'81 ATLANTIC CITY
'81 MY DINNER WITH ANDRE
'84 HOTEL NEW HAMPSHIRE, THE

EDWARD LACHMAN
CINEMATOGRAPHER
'80 UNION CITY
MISCELLANEOUS
'79 LAST EMBRACE

EDWARD LACHMAN JR.
CINEMATOGRAPHER
'79 SCALPEL

CLAY LACY
MISCELLANEOUS
'82 FIREFOX

BOB LADEN
MAKEUP
'82 WORLD ACCORDING TO GARP, THE
MISCELLANEOUS
'80 DRESSED TO KILL

TERRY LADIN
PROD. OFFICE COORD.
'79 BELL JAR, THE
'81 TATTOO
PROD. COORDINATOR
'82 SECOND THOUGHTS
'83 HEART LIKE A WHEEL

BARBARA LAFFEY
LOCATIONS
'79 LOST AND FOUND*

JEAN LAFLEUR
MISCELLANEOUS
'81 MY BLOODY VALENTINE

GAETAN LAFRANCE
STUNT COORDINATOR
'80 HOG WILD

CHARLES LAGUS
MISCELLANEOUS
'81 GREAT MUPPET CAPER, THE

MELISSA LAGUSIS M.D.
MISCELLANEOUS
'84 ICEMAN

FRANCES LAI
MUSIC
'81 BEYOND THE REEF

BOB LAIDLAW
MISCELLANEOUS
'84 ICEMAN

ROBERT LAIDLOW
MISCELLANEOUS
'81 LAST CHASE, THE

ROBERT LAING
PRODUCTION DESIGNER
'83 HIGH ROAD TO CHINA

MONTY LAIRD
MISCELLANEOUS
'79 APPLE DUMPLING GANG RIDES AGAIN, THE

MURDO LAIRD
MISCELLANEOUS
'83 RUMBLEFISH

BEN LAKE
MAKEUP
'82 ANNIE*

MICHAEL LAKE
MISCELLANEOUS
'83 MAN FROM SNOWY RIVER, THE

SAM LAKE
EXECUTIVE PRODUCER
'81 NESTING, THE*

MICHAEL LALLY
1ST ASST. DIRECTOR
'81 TARZAN, THE APE MAN*
2ND ASST. DIRECTOR
'84 LOVE STREAMS

GRACE LAM
PRODUCTION MANAGER
'82 FORCED VENGEANCE*

TONY LAMARCA
UNIT PROD. MANAGER
'82 TEMPEST
MISCELLANEOUS
'84 C.H.U.D.

IRENE LAMB
CASTING
'79 MURDER BY DECREE
'80 ROUGH CUT
'80 EMPIRE STRIKES BACK, THE*
'80 LADY VANISHES, THE*
'81 CLASH OF THE TITANS*
'81 TIME BANDITS
'82 MISSIONARY, THE
'83 ENIGMA*
'84 CHAMPIONS*

MARC LAMB
EDITOR
'84 MISUNDERSTOOD

ANN LAMBERT
COSTUMES
'82 DON'T CRY, IT'S ONLY THUNDER

ANN GRAY LAMBERT
COSTUMES
'82 POLTERGEIST

ELIZABETH LAMBERT
MAKEUP
'79 HOT STUFF*
'80 CADDYSHACK
'81 NOBODY'S PERFEKT
'83 SPRING BREAK
'83 SMOKEY AND THE BANDIT III*
'83 BLUE SKIES AGAIN
'84 HARRY & SON*
'84 WHERE THE BOYS ARE

ROBERT LAMBERT
EDITOR
'80 FINAL COUNTDOWN, THE
'82 BORDER, THE
'84 HOTEL NEW HAMPSHIRE, THE
2ND UNIT DIRECTOR
'80 FINAL COUNTDOWN, THE*
'82 BORDER, THE
'84 HOTEL NEW HAMPSHIRE, THE
MISCELLANEOUS
'81 DEAD AND BURIED

STEVEN LAMBERT
STUNT COORDINATOR
'83 REVENGE OF THE NINJA

BARBARA LAMBERTSON
LOCATIONS
'84 HOTEL NEW HAMPSHIRE, THE
MISCELLANEOUS
'81 POSTMAN ALWAYS RINGS TWICE, THE

JON JON LAMBON
COSTUMES
'82 SAFARI 3000

MAUREEN LAMBRAY
STILLS
'81 FAN, THE*
MISCELLANEOUS
'80 CARNY

ANGELO LAMBROU
MISCELLANEOUS
'82 TEMPEST

ASPA LAMBROU
PRODUCTION MANAGER
'79 FEDORA*
'80 FOR THE LOVE OF BENJI*
'81 FOR YOUR EYES ONLY*
'82 SUMMER LOVERS
'82 TEMPEST*
'84 LITTLE DRUMMER GIRL, THE*

SASH LAMEY
HAIR
'81 GALLIPOLI*

LEN LAMKIN
CINEMATOGRAPHER
'79 SCAVENGER HUNT

VAL LAMOND
CASTING
'83 NATE & HAYES*

MICHAEL LAMONT
ART DIRECTOR
'84 TOP SECRET!*

PETER LAMONT
ART DIRECTOR
'81 SPHINX
PRODUCTION DESIGNER
'81 FOR YOUR EYES ONLY
'83 OCTOPUSSY
'84 TOP SECRET!
MISCELLANEOUS
'79 MOONRAKER

LESLEY LAMONT-FISHER
MAKEUP
'84 PHAR LAP

BARBARA LAMPSON
HAIR
'81 PENNIES FROM HEAVEN*
'83 FOOTLOOSE
'83 MAX DUGAN RETURNS
'84 CITY HEAT
'84 CLOAK AND DAGGER

MICHALIS LAMRINOS
UNIT MANAGER
'81 FOR YOUR EYES ONLY*
LOCATIONS
'80 FOR THE LOVE OF BENJI
'81 FOR YOUR EYES ONLY*

BILL LANCASTER
SCREENPLAY
'82 THING, THE

CONI LANCASTER
PROD. COORDINATOR
'84 PHILADELPHIA EXPERIMENT, THE

ALISON LANCES
COSTUMES
'83 SMITHEREENS

JOHN LANCHBERY
MUSIC
'80 NIJINSKY

HAL LANDAKER
MISCELLANEOUS
'82 STAR TREK II THE WRATH OF KHAN
'84 STAR TREK III: THE SEARCH FOR SPOCK

EDIE LANDAU
PRODUCER
'80 HOPSCOTCH*
'82 CHOSEN, THE*

ELY LANDAU
PRODUCER
'80 HOPSCOTCH*
'82 CHOSEN, THE*

EMMANUELLE LANDE
ASSISTANT EDITOR
'83 EXPOSED*

IRVING LANDE
CASTING
'79 GREAT SANTINI, THE*

RICARDO LANDEROS
ASSISTANT EDITOR
'79 ROLLER BOOGIE*

HAL LANDERS
EXECUTIVE PRODUCER
'82 DEATHWISH II*

MICHAEL LANDES
PRODUCER
'83 BIG SCORE, THE*
EXECUTIVE PRODUCER
'83 I AM THE CHEESE*
'84 BOSTONIANS, THE*

GINO LANDI
CHOREOGRAPHER
'82 TEMPEST

EVAN LANDIS
ASSISTANT EDITOR
'83 STRANGE BREW*

JANE LANDIS
SOUND
'83 ANGELO, MY LOVE

JOHN LANDIS
PRODUCER
'83 TWILIGHT ZONE, THE MOVIE*
DIRECTOR
'80 BLUES BROTHERS
'81 AMERICAN WEREWOLF IN LONDON, AN
'83 TRADING PLACES
'83 TWILIGHT ZONE, THE MOVIE*
SCREENPLAY
'80 BLUES BROTHERS*
'81 AMERICAN WEREWOLF IN LONDON, AN
'83 TWILIGHT ZONE, THE MOVIE*

DOREEN LANDRY
PUBLICIST
'79 LOST AND FOUND
'80 ROUGH CUT
'80 SATURN 3
'82 SENDER, THE
'83 KEEP, THE
UNIT PUBLICIST
'81 DRAGONSLAYER

ALAN LANDSBURG
EXECUTIVE PRODUCER
'83 JAWS 3-D*
'83 PORKY'S II THE NEXT DAY*

ANDREW LANE
PRODUCER
'83 VALLEY GIRL*
'84 NIGHT OF THE COMET*
SCREENPLAY
'83 VALLEY GIRL*

BARBARA LANE
COSTUMES
'83 BEYOND THE LIMIT
'83 HEAT AND DUST
'84 LASSITER

DAVID LANE
2ND UNIT DIRECTOR
'83 SUPERMAN III
MISCELLANEOUS
'83 SUPERMAN III

DICK LANE
ASSISTANT EDITOR
'80 FORMULA, THE*

JOHN FRANCIS LANE
MISCELLANEOUS
'83 ANOTHER TIME, ANOTHER PLACE

LOU LANE
MAKEUP
'80 WILLIE & PHIL*

RICHARD LANE
EDITOR
'81 ...ALL THE MARBLES*
ASSISTANT EDITOR
'79 CHAMP, THE*

SHAREE LANE
MISCELLANEOUS
'83 STAYING ALIVE

STEVEN LANE
EXECUTIVE PRODUCER
'81 HOWLING, THE*

DAMIEN LANFRANCHI
ART DIRECTOR
'83 TRAIL OF THE PINK PANTHER*

JENNINGS LANG
PRODUCER
'79 CONCORDE-AIRPORT '79, THE
'80 LITTLE MISS MARKER
'80 NUDE BOMB, THE
'83 STING II, THE

RICHARD LANG
DIRECTOR
'80 CHANGE OF SEASONS, A
'80 MOUNTAIN MEN, THE

WILLIAM LANG
PRODUCTION MANAGER
'84 LITTLE DRUMMER GIRL, THE*
LOCATIONS
'81 EYE OF THE NEEDLE*
'82 SENDER, THE
'83 BRITANNIA HOSPITAL
'83 YENTL*
'84 GREYSTOKE: THE LEGEND OF TARZAN, LORD OF THE APES*

BRUCE LANGE
ASSISTANT EDITOR
'82 AMATEUR, THE*
'83 STRANGE BREW*
'84 MRS. SOFFEL

DAVID LANGE
PRODUCER
'83 I AM THE CHEESE
SCREENPLAY
'83 I AM THE CHEESE*

HARRY LANGE
ART DIRECTOR
'80 EMPIRE STRIKES BACK, THE*
PRODUCTION DESIGNER
'81 GREAT MUPPET CAPER, THE
'82 DARK CRYSTAL, THE
'83 MONTY PYTHON'S THE MEANING OF LIFE
MISCELLANEOUS
'81 SUPERMAN II

HENRY LANGE
PRODUCTION MANAGER
'81 SUNDAY LOVERS*
1ST ASST. DIRECTOR
'81 SUNDAY LOVERS*

JESSICA LANGE
PRODUCER
'84 COUNTRY*

MINELDA LANGE
MISCELLANEOUS
'83 I AM THE CHEESE

OWEN LANGEVIN
SOUND
'79 RUNNING*

BRUCE LANGHORNE
MUSIC
'80 MELVIN AND HOWARD

BARRY LANGLEY
1ST ASST. DIRECTOR
'81 DRAGONSLAYER
'83 PIRATES OF PENZANCE, THE
'84 TOP SECRET!

NORMAN LANGLEY
CINEMATOGRAPHER
'82 HOUSE OF THE LONG SHADOWS

YVES LANGLOIS
EDITOR
'82 QUEST FOR FIRE

P. KAREN LANGSHAW
MISCELLANEOUS
'83 OF UNKNOWN ORIGIN

BILL LANGSTROTH
STILLS
'82 IF YOU COULD SEE WHAT I HEAR*

STEVE LANNING
1ST ASST. DIRECTOR
'83 YENTL
2ND ASST. DIRECTOR
'79 CUBA*
'80 EMPIRE STRIKES BACK, THE*
'82 GANDHI

DORSE LANPHER
MISCELLANEOUS
'79 BLACK HOLE, THE

EDGAR LANSBURY
EXECUTIVE PRODUCER
'80 HE KNOWS YOU'RE ALONE*

ROSE LANSBURY
STILLS
'80 HE KNOWS YOU'RE ALONE

SHERRY LANSING
EXECUTIVE PRODUCER
'84 FIRSTBORN*

MICHAEL LANTIERI
SPECIAL EFFECTS
'83 FLASHDANCE
'84 THIEF OF HEARTS
'84 WOMAN IN RED, THE

ROBERT LANTOS
PRODUCER
'79 IN PRAISE OF OLDER WOMEN*
'82 PARADISE*

BEVERLY LANYON
PROPS
'82 SAFARI 3000

MICK LANZINO
HAIR
'81 KNIGHTRIDERS*

ROGER LAPAGE
ASSOCIATE PRODUCER
'82 ZAPPED!*

HARRY LAPHAM
SOUND
'83 CAN SHE BAKE A CHERRY PIE?
'83 ECHOES
'84 C.H.U.D.

JONATHAN LAPIDESE
ASSOCIATE EDITOR
'81 MODERN PROBLEMS
ASSISTANT EDITOR
'80 HEARTBEAT

STEVE LAPORTE
MAKEUP
'84 BEAR, THE

GARY LAPOTEN
PRODUCTION MANAGER
'82 EATING RAOUL
1ST ASST. DIRECTOR
'82 EATING RAOUL

DIANA LAPTOOK
LOCATIONS
'82 MIDSUMMER NIGHT'S SEX COMEDY, A*

ADOLFO LARA
KEY GRIP
'84 EVIL THAT MEN DO, THE

NATALIE LARDNER
ASSISTANT EDITOR
'84 BROTHER FROM ANOTHER PLANET, THE*

CHRIS LARGE
SOUND
'80 NOTHING PERSONAL

KEITH LARGE
LOCATIONS
'79 RUNNING*
'80 MIDDLE AGE CRAZY

EMILIO LARI
STILLS
'83 HIGH ROAD TO CHINA
'84 LASSITER

PETER LARKIN
PRODUCTION DESIGNER
'81 NEIGHBORS
'81 NIGHTHAWKS
'82 TOOTSIE
'83 REUBEN, REUBEN

GENE LARMON
MISCELLANEOUS
'82 TRON

STEVAN LARNER
CINEMATOGRAPHER
'79 GOLDENGIRL
'80 CADDYSHACK
'83 TWILIGHT ZONE, THE MOVIE*

CHARLES LAROCCA
KEY GRIP
'84 STONE BOY, THE

HENRY LARRECQ
ART DIRECTOR
'80 BLUES BROTHERS
'82 THING, THE

HUMBERTO LARRIVA
MUSIC
'84 REPO MAN*

RANDALL LARSEN
MISCELLANEOUS
'82 PARASITE

TAMBI LARSEN
ART DIRECTOR
'80 HEAVEN'S GATE*
PRODUCTION DESIGNER
'79 CIRCLE OF IRON

BOB LARSON
PRODUCER
'81 CONTINENTAL DIVIDE
EXECUTIVE PRODUCER
'80 COAL MINER'S DAUGHTER
'83 GORKY PARK

GAIL LARSON
MAKEUP
'81 GRADUATION DAY

GLEN LARSON
SCREENPLAY
'79 BUCK ROGERS*
EXECUTIVE PRODUCER
'79 BUCK ROGERS

GREY LARSON
MUSIC
'81 TUCK EVERLASTING*

JACK LARSON
ASSOCIATE PRODUCER
'84 MIKE'S MURDER

JAMES LARUE
1ST ASST. DIRECTOR
'84 NIGHTMARE ON ELM STREET, A

JIM LARUE
SOUND
'79 AMERICATHON
'82 TRON

LOUIS LARUSSO II
SCREENPLAY
'81 BEYOND THE REEF*

ROBERT LASANKA
CASTING
'79 CONCORDE-AIRPORT '79, THE*
'80 RESURRECTION*
'80 LITTLE MISS MARKER*
'80 NUDE BOMB, THE*

JASON LASKAY
ASSOCIATE PRODUCER
'84 RAZOR'S EDGE, THE

ALEX LASKER
SCREENPLAY
'82 FIREFOX*

DENNIS LASKER
ASSOCIATE PRODUCER
'84 ICE PIRATES, THE

LAWRENCE LASKER
SCREENPLAY
'83 WAR GAMES*

GENE LASKO
PRODUCER
'81 FOUR FRIENDS*
2ND UNIT DIRECTOR
'81 FOUR FRIENDS

WILLIAM LASKY
2ND ASST. DIRECTOR
'79 AMERICATHON*

WALTER LASSALLY
CINEMATOGRAPHER
'79 GREAT BANK HOAX, THE
'79 SOMETHING SHORT OF PARADISE
'83 HEAT AND DUST
'83 PRIVATE SCHOOL
'84 BOSTONIANS, THE

CARLO LASTRICATI
1ST ASST. DIRECTOR
'79 LITTLE ROMANCE, A

ANDREW LASZLO
CINEMATOGRAPHER
'79 WARRIORS, THE
'81 SOUTHERN COMFORT
'81 FUNHOUSE, THE
'82 FIRST BLOOD
'82 I, THE JURY
'84 STREETS OF FIRE
'84 THIEF OF HEARTS

AARON LATHAM
SCREENPLAY
'80 URBAN COWBOY*

STAN LATHAN
DIRECTOR
'84 BEAT STREET
2ND UNIT DIRECTOR
'83 RICHARD PRYOR: HERE AND NOW

PHILIP LATHROP
CINEMATOGRAPHER
'79 CONCORDE-AIRPORT '79, THE
'80 CHANGE OF SEASONS, A
'80 FOOLIN AROUND
'80 LITTLE MISS MARKER
'80 LOVING COUPLES
'81 ALL NIGHT LONG
'82 JEKYLL AND HYDE TOGETHER AGAIN
'82 NATIONAL LAMPOON'S CLASS REUNION
MISCELLANEOUS
'82 HAMMETT

MARC LAUB
EDITOR
'80 HONEYSUCKLE ROSE*
'81 FOUR FRIENDS*
'82 HAMMETT*

KEN LAUBER
MUSIC
'82 CHILLY SCENES OF WINTER

ALAIN LAUDE
PROPS
'80 QUARTET
'84 UNTIL SEPTEMBER

MARCEL LAUDE
PROPS
'80 TESS

DIDIER LAUERGNE
MAKEUP
'80 TESS

MICHAEL LAUGHLIN
DIRECTOR
'81 STRANGE BEHAVIOR
'83 STRANGE INVADERS
SCREENPLAY
'81 STRANGE BEHAVIOR*
'83 STRANGE INVADERS*

BILLIE LAUGHRIDE
HAIR
'79 WHEN A STRANGER CALLS*

CLAUDETTE LAURENCELLE
PROD. COORDINATOR
'83 NEVER CRY WOLF*

HENRI LAURENT
MISCELLANEOUS
'84 CHEECH AND CHONG'S THE CORSICAN BROTHERS

JEAN-CLAUDE LAUREUX
SOUND
'81 ATLANTIC CITY
'81 MY DINNER WITH ANDRE

PETER LAUTERMAN
PROPS
'79 BROOD, THE
'79 FAST COMPANY
'83 DEAD ZONE, THE
'83 VIDEODROME

MARJORIE LAVELLY
SCRIPT SUPERVISOR
'79 MURDER BY DECREE
'79 STEVIE

PETER LAVENDER
MISCELLANEOUS
'80 KIDNAPPING OF THE PRESIDENT, THE

AL LAVERDE
KEY GRIP
'82 THAT CHAMPIONSHIP SEASON
'83 BIG CHILL, THE
'84 CHOOSE ME
'84 RACING WITH THE MOON

EMILE LAVIGNE
MAKEUP
'80 DEFIANCE*

TOM LAVIN
MUSIC
'82 OUT OF THE BLUE

GENE LAW
1ST ASST. DIRECTOR
'80 WHERE THE BUFFALO ROAM
'81 MODERN PROBLEMS

BRUCE LAWHEAD
LOCATIONS
'80 FIRST FAMILY

MICHAEL LAWLER
MISCELLANEOUS
'81 LOOKER

JOHN LAWLESS
ART DIRECTOR
'81 NESTING, THE
'84 OVER THE BROOKLYN BRIDGE

LOUIS LAWLESS
KEY GRIP
'82 PENITENTIARY II

BOB LAWRENCE
MAKEUP
'81 REDS*

BRIAN LAWRENCE
1ST ASST. DIRECTOR
'82 HOUSE OF THE LONG SHADOWS*

JEROME LAWRENCE
SCREENPLAY
'81 FIRST MONDAY IN OCTOBER*

JOEL DAVID LAWRENCE
PRODUCTION DESIGNER
'81 FORCE FIVE

PETER LAWRENCE
SCREENPLAY
'81 BURNING, THE*

RICHARD LAWRENCE
ART DIRECTOR
'80 MIDNIGHT MADNESS*
'81 FORCE FIVE
'83 RIGHT STUFF, THE*
'83 SOMETHING WICKED THIS WAY COMES*
'84 AGAINST ALL ODDS

ROBERT LAWRENCE
EDITOR
'83 EXPOSED*
'83 NEVER SAY NEVER AGAIN

SANDY LAWRENCE
PROD. COORDINATOR
'81 RICH AND FAMOUS*
PROD. SECRETARY
'80 FORMULA, THE

NICK LAWS
1ST ASST. DIRECTOR
'84 PASSAGE TO INDIA, A*

DEBORAH LAWSON
LOCATIONS
'83 CUJO

PETA LAWSON
PROD. COORDINATOR
'84 PHAR LAP

TONY LAWSON
EDITOR
'81 DRAGONSLAYER
'84 BOUNTY, THE

JENNIFER LAX
COSTUMES
'83 ECHOES
'84 C.H.U.D.
PROPS
'84 ALPHABET CITY

CHARLES LAYTON
PRODUCTION MANAGER
'82 CREEPSHOW
1ST ASST. DIRECTOR
'81 FRIDAY THE 13TH PART TWO

JOE LAYTON
DIRECTOR
'81 RICHARD PRYOR: LIVE ON THE SUNSET STRIP
EXECUTIVE PRODUCER
'82 ANNIE
MISCELLANEOUS
'82 ANNIE

DAVID LAZAR
PRODUCER
'81 GREAT MUPPET CAPER, THE*
CO-PRODUCER
'79 MUPPET MOVIE, THE

IRVING PAUL LAZAR
EXECUTIVE PRODUCER
'81 NEIGHBORS*

WENDI LAZAR
ASSOCIATE PRODUCER
'81 ROLLOVER

WENDY LAZAR-PILLOT
LOCATIONS
'81 ARTHUR

LES LAZAROWITZ
SOUND
'79 LAST EMBRACE
'79 VOICES*
'80 RAGING BULL*
'80 TIMES SQUARE
'81 SO FINE
'81 NEIGHBORS*
'81 NIGHTHAWKS
'82 AUTHOR, AUTHOR
'82 TOOTSIE
'83 EASY MONEY
'83 KING OF COMEDY, THE
'83 NIGHT IN HEAVEN, A
'84 FALLING IN LOVE

PAUL LAZARUS III
PRODUCER
'79 HANOVER STREET
'82 BARBAROSA

HEINZ LAZEK
EXECUTIVE PRODUCER
'79 FIFTH MUSKETEER, THE

DAVID LAZER
EXECUTIVE PRODUCER
'82 DARK CRYSTAL, THE

LOUIS LAZZARA
MAKEUP
'84 MUTANT*

GREG LAZZARO
LOCATIONS
'80 CHEAPER TO KEEP HER

CLAUDE LE COMTE
CINEMATOGRAPHER
'81 SUNDAY LOVERS*
'84 JUST THE WAY YOU ARE

GARY LE MEL
MUSIC SUPERVISOR
'79 MAIN EVENT, THE

DON LE PAGE
MAKEUP
'79 MORE AMERICAN GRAFFITTI
'82 SHOOT THE MOON*

RICHARD LEA
SPECIAL EFFECTS
'80 NUDE BOMB, THE*
'84 SWING SHIFT*

ROGER MURRAY LEACH
ART DIRECTOR
'84 KILLING FIELDS, THE*

WILFORD LEACH
DIRECTOR
'83 PIRATES OF PENZANCE, THE
SCREENPLAY
'83 PIRATES OF PENZANCE, THE

ROBERT LEADER
ASSISTANT EDITOR
'81 FUNHOUSE, THE

DAVID LEAN
DIRECTOR
'84 PASSAGE TO INDIA, A
SCREENPLAY
'84 PASSAGE TO INDIA, A
EDITOR
'84 PASSAGE TO INDIA, A

RICHARD LEARMAN
UNIT PROD. MANAGER
'83 SOMETHING WICKED THIS WAY COMES
1ST ASST. DIRECTOR
'80 HUNTER, THE
'80 LAST FLIGHT OF NOAH'S ARK, THE
'81 STRIPES
'81 CONDORMAN
'81 PURSUIT OF D.B. COOPER, THE

DERRICK LEATHER
SOUND
'79 ALIEN

BOOTS LEBARON
PUBLICIST
'83 CUJO

CHRISTOPHER LEBENZON
EDITOR
'81 WOLFEN*
ASSISTANT EDITOR
'82 ONE FROM THE HEART
'83 OUTSIDERS, THE

JACK LEBER
ASSISTANT EDITOR
'80 TOUCHED BY LOVE

MAURICE LEBLANC
PROPS
'80 TERROR TRAIN

PAUL LEBLANC
MAKEUP
'83 BLACK STALLION RETURNS, THE
'84 AMADEUS
HAIR
'79 BLACK STALLION, THE
'79 MORE AMERICAN GRAFFITTI
'81 DEATH HUNT
'82 SHOOT THE MOON*
'83 BLACK STALLION RETURNS, THE
'84 BIRDY
'84 PLACES IN THE HEART
'84 MRS. SOFFEL
MISCELLANEOUS
'84 AMADEUS

JAMES LEBOVITZ
MISCELLANEOUS
'81 PERMANENT VACATION

ARMAND LEBOWITZ
EDITOR
'82 Q: QUETZALCOATL

MICHAEL LEBOWITZ
PRODUCER
'79 FAST COMPANY*

HECTOR LOPEZ LECHUGA
ASSOCIATE PRODUCER
'84 UNDER THE VOLCANO*

ROBERT LECKY
EXEC IN CHARGE PROD
'79 LOVE AT FIRST BITE

ROGER LECLAIR
STILLS
'82 DON'T CRY, IT'S ONLY THUNDER
'83 SWEET SIXTEEN

ROGER LECLAIRE
MISCELLANEOUS
'80 CAN'T STOP THE MUSIC

PIERRE-LOUIS LECOUER
ASSISTANT EDITOR
'80 TESS*

ED LEDDING
1ST ASST. DIRECTOR
'79 OVER THE EDGE
'79 WHEN A STRANGER CALLS
'80 ROADIE

DEBORAH LEDENDECKER
SCRIPT SUPERVISOR
'80 MANIAC

MIMI LEDER
SCRIPT SUPERVISOR
'80 BORDERLINE*

JOSEPH LEDERER
STILLS
'82 FIRST BLOOD
'83 RUNNING BRAVE

MAGGIE LEDERER
LOCATIONS
'83 SMITHEREENS

RICHARD LEDERER
PRODUCER
'80 HOLLYWOOD KNIGHTS, THE

BOB LEDERMAN
ASSISTANT EDITOR
'82 PERSONAL BEST*
'83 FLASHDANCE*

PATRICIA LEDFORD
LOCATIONS
'84 STARMAN*

CHRIS LEE
HAIR
'79 AMERICAN GIGOLO
'79 AMITYVILLE HORROR, THE
'79 APPLE DUMPLING GANG RIDES AGAIN, THE
'80 JAZZ SINGER, THE*
'80 LONG RIDERS, THE
'81 AMY
'81 CONTINENTAL DIVIDE
'81 ENTITY, THE

DANNY LEE
SPECIAL EFFECTS
'79 APPLE DUMPLING GANG RIDES AGAIN, THE*
'79 NORTH AVENUE IRREGULARS, THE*
'80 LAST FLIGHT OF NOAH'S ARK, THE*
'80 MIDNIGHT MADNESS
'81 AMY
'81 DEVIL AND MAX DEVLIN, THE*
MISCELLANEOUS
'79 BLACK HOLE, THE
'80 WATCHER IN THE WOODS, THE

DAVID LEE
SOUND
'79 SILENT PARTNER, THE
'79 MAN, A WOMAN AND A BANK, A
'80 MIDDLE AGE CRAZY
'80 TRIBUTE
'83 STRANGE BREW
'84 POLICE ACADEMY
'84 MRS. SOFFEL

DENNIS LEE
MISCELLANEOUS
'84 C.H.U.D.

EUGENE LEE
PRODUCTION DESIGNER
'79 MR. MIKE'S MONDO VIDEO*
'80 GILDA LIVE*
'83 EASY MONEY

FRANNE LEE
PRODUCTION DESIGNER
'79 MR. MIKE'S MONDO VIDEO*
COSTUMES
'80 GILDA LIVE*
'83 BABY IT'S YOU

JANICE LEE
MISCELLANEOUS
'81 HONKY TONK FREEWAY

KENNY LEE
MISCELLANEOUS
'79 ELECTRIC HORSEMAN, THE
'80 BRUBAKER
'81 LEGEND OF THE LONE RANGER, THE

KEVIN LEE
ASSISTANT EDITOR
'82 HANKY PANKY*

NORMA LEE
HAIR
'83 DOCTOR DETROIT*

PETER LEE
MISCELLANEOUS
'81 HONKY TONK FREEWAY

PHILIP LEE
PROPS
'82 FORCED VENGEANCE*

PIO LEE
EXECUTIVE PRODUCER
'83 BLIND RAGE*

RICHARD LEE
KEY GRIP
'80 ROUGH CUT

ROBERT LEE
SCREENPLAY
'81 FIRST MONDAY IN OCTOBER*

ROBERT LEE
MISCELLANEOUS
'81 HAND, THE

SE HYUNG LEE
LOCATIONS
'81 INCHON*

SUNG KU LEE
MISCELLANEOUS
'81 INCHON

JERRY LEEDS
1ST ASST. DIRECTOR
'82 STRANGER IS WATCHING, A*

MICHAEL LEESON
SCREENPLAY
'83 SURVIVORS, THE

GERRY BEEKER LEETCH
HAIR
'79 BUDDY HOLLY STORY, THE*
'83 TERMS OF ENDEARMENT*

TOM LEETCH
PRODUCER
'82 NIGHT CROSSING
CO-PRODUCER
'79 APPLE DUMPLING GANG RIDES AGAIN, THE
'79 NORTH AVENUE IRREGULARS, THE
'80 WATCHER IN THE WOODS, THE
UNIT PROD. MANAGER
'79 APPLE DUMPLING GANG RIDES AGAIN, THE

DOMINIQUE LEFEVRE
PROD. SECRETARY
'80 FIENDISH PLOT OF DR. FU MANCHU, THE

SUE LEFTON
CHOREOGRAPHER
'80 TESS

AL LEGGET
PROPS
'80 HUNTER, THE

STEVEN LEGLER
ART DIRECTOR
'81 HELL NIGHT
PRODUCTION DESIGNER
'84 CHOOSE ME

MICHEL LEGRAND
MUSIC
'80 HUNTER, THE
'80 MOUNTAIN MEN, THE
'81 ATLANTIC CITY
'82 BEST FRIENDS
'83 NEVER SAY NEVER AGAIN
'83 YENTL

JOHN LEHANE
LOCATIONS
'84 CRACKERS

AL LEHMAN
COSTUMES
'80 WHY WOULD I LIE?

TOIVO LEHMUSVIRTA
UNIT MANAGER
'81 REDS

SHARI LEIBOWITZ
PROD. OFFICE COORD.
'79 WINTER KILLS
'80 SIMON
'81 BLOW OUT
'81 FOUR SEASONS, THE
'83 SCARFACE
'83 KISS ME GOODBYE
PROD. COORDINATOR
'84 BODY DOUBLE

JERRY LEIDER
PRODUCER
'80 JAZZ SINGER, THE
'83 TRENCHCOAT

R. ALLEN LEIDER
PUBLICIST
'81 NESTING, THE

CHERYL LEIGH
SCRIPT SUPERVISOR
'81 GREAT MUPPET CAPER, THE
'82 DARK CRYSTAL, THE

JOAN LEIGH
PROPS
'83 LIQUID SKY

MITCH LEIGH
EXECUTIVE PRODUCER
'83 SPRING BREAK*

NORMAN LEIGH
CINEMATOGRAPHER
'80 SCHIZOID
'83 DEADLY FORCE*

WARREN LEIGHT
SCREENPLAY
'80 MOTHER'S DAY*

ROBERT LEIGHTON
MISCELLANEOUS
'84 THIS IS SPINAL TAP

TED LEIGHTON
SCREENPLAY
'80 HUNTER, THE*

WARNER LEIGHTON
EDITOR
'79 C.H.O.M.P.S.*

RAYMOND LEIN
SPECIAL EFFECTS
'80 CHEAPER TO KEEP HER

BARRY LEIRER
ASSISTANT EDITOR
'82 LOVE AND MONEY
'84 POPE OF GREENWICH VILLAGE,THE*

FREDDIE LEITENSDORFER
KEY GRIP
'84 MOSCOW ON THE HUDSON*
'84 LITTLE DRUMMER GIRL, THE

ED LEITER
MISCELLANEOUS
'81 MS. 45

RICHARD LEITERMAN
CINEMATOGRAPHER
'81 TICKET TO HEAVEN
'82 MOTHER LODE
MISCELLANEOUS
'81 DEATH HUNT

PAUL LEMARINEL
MAKEUP
'84 JUST THE WAY YOU ARE*

STEPHEN LEMAY
SCREENPLAY
'80 HOME MOVIES*

TOIVO LEMBER
2ND ASST. DIRECTOR
'82 ROAD WARRIOR, THE
LOCATIONS
'79 MY BRILLIANT CAREER

ESTELLE LEMIEUX
UNIT MANAGER
'81 HAPPY BIRTHDAY TO ME
'84 HOTEL NEW HAMPSHIRE, THE

RAYMOND LEMOIGNE
PROPS
'83 HANNA K

MAX LEMON
EDITOR
'79 PICNIC AT HANGING ROCK

RUSTY LEMORANDE
PRODUCER
'84 ELECTRIC DREAMS*
SCREENPLAY
'84 ELECTRIC DREAMS
EXEC IN CHARGE PROD
'80 DIE LAUGHING
CO-PRODUCER
'83 YENTL

TONI LEMOS
LOCATIONS
'81 DEAD AND BURIED
MISCELLANEOUS
'84 RACING WITH THE MOON

MANFRED LENERT
LOCATIONS
'84 RIDDLE OF THE SANDS*

MICHAEL LENNICK
MISCELLANEOUS
'83 VIDEODROME

HELEN LENNOX
HAIR
'80 MIRROR CRACK'D, THE

JOHN THOMAS LENOX
EXECUTIVE PRODUCER
'84 SPLASH
PRODUCTION MANAGER
'84 SPLASH

TERRY LENS
PRODUCTION MANAGER
'81 NIGHTHAWKS*
LOCATIONS
'83 YELLOWBEARD

MIKLOS LENTE
CINEMATOGRAPHER
'79 IN PRAISE OF OLDER WOMEN
'81 HAPPY BIRTHDAY TO ME
'83 SCREWBALLS

MASSIMO LENTINI
PRODUCTION DESIGNER
'83 1990: THE BRONX WARRIORS
COSTUMES
'83 1990: THE BRONX WARRIORS

LEONARD
HAIR
'80 SHINING, THE
'84 BOUNTY, THE

TERRY LEONARD
2ND UNIT DIRECTOR
'80 USED CARS
'82 CONAN THE BARBARIAN
'83 BLUE THUNDER*
'84 ROMANCING THE STONE
'84 RED DAWN
STUNT COORDINATOR
'79 APOCALYPSE NOW
'79 CIRCLE OF IRON
'79 1941
'80 MOUNTAIN MEN, THE
'80 MY BODYGUARD
'80 USED CARS
'82 CONAN THE BARBARIAN
'82 HAMMETT
'83 CHRISTINE
'84 GREMLINS
'84 ROMANCING THE STONE*
'84 STARMAN
'84 RED DAWN
MISCELLANEOUS
'83 EASY MONEY

ARTHUR LEONARDI
MISCELLANEOUS
'83 TRAIL OF THE PINK PANTHER

JOHN LEONE
SCREENPLAY
'83 TOUGH ENOUGH

MARIO LEONE
ASSISTANT EDITOR
'81 DEATH HUNT*

MICHAEL LEONE
EXECUTIVE PRODUCER
'79 FORCE OF ONE, A
'80 OCTAGON, THE*
'81 CHARLIE CHAN AND THE CURSE OF THE DRAGON QUEEN*
'81 ENTITY, THE*
'82 I, THE JURY*
'83 TOUGH ENOUGH*

SERGIO LEONE
DIRECTOR
'84 ONCE UPON A TIME IN AMERICA
SCREENPLAY
'84 ONCE UPON A TIME IN AMERICA*

MATTHEW LEONETTI
CINEMATOGRAPHER
'79 BREAKING AWAY
'80 RAISE THE TITANIC
'81 EYEWITNESS
'82 FAST TIMES AT RIDGEMONT HIGH
'82 POLTERGEIST
'83 BUDDY SYSTEM, THE
'84 ICE PIRATES, THE
'84 SONGWRITER

STRATTON LEOPOLD
LOCATIONS
'80 HOPSCOTCH*
'83 BIG CHILL, THE*
MISCELLANEOUS
'84 TANK

BERYL LERMAN
MAKEUP
'81 AMERICAN WEREWOLF IN LONDON, AN*
'81 EYE OF THE NEEDLE*
'83 KEEP, THE*

DAN LERNER
MISCELLANEOUS
'83 STAYING ALIVE
'83 DEAL OF THE CENTURY
'84 AGAINST ALL ODDS

FRED LERNER
2ND UNIT DIRECTOR
'84 GRANDVIEW, U.S.A.
STUNT COORDINATOR
'84 GRANDVIEW, U.S.A.

STUART LERNER M.D.
MISCELLANEOUS
'81 HAND, THE

ROCCO LERRO
1ST ASST. DIRECTOR
'83 1990: THE BRONX WARRIORS*

MICHAEL LESSON
SCREENPLAY
'82 JEKYLL AND HYDE TOGETHER AGAIN*

DAVID LESTER
2ND ASST. DIRECTOR
'82 MEGAFORCE*

MARK LESTER
DIRECTOR
'79 ROLLER BOOGIE
'84 FIRESTARTER
EXECUTIVE PRODUCER
'81 FUNHOUSE, THE*

RICHARD LESTER
DIRECTOR
'79 BUTCH AND SUNDANCE: THE EARLY YEARS
'79 CUBA
'81 SUPERMAN II
'83 SUPERMAN III
'84 FINDERS KEEPERS
EXECUTIVE PRODUCER
'84 FINDERS KEEPERS

HENRY LETANG
CHOREOGRAPHER
'84 COTTON CLUB, THE*

PHIL LETO
HAIR
'79 BELL JAR, THE
'79 GOING IN STYLE
'79 WANDERERS, THE
'80 JUST TELL ME WHAT YOU WANT
'81 GHOST STORY
'81 PRINCE OF THE CITY
'82 THAT CHAMPIONSHIP SEASON
'84 TANK*

MAY LEUNG
LOCATIONS
'84 INDIANA JONES AND THE TEMPLE OF DOOM*

THOMAS LEUNG
ASSISTANT EDITOR
'79 GAME OF DEATH*

RENATE LEUSCHNER
HAIR
'80 CHANGELING, THE*
'84 RHINESTONE*

ANGELO LEUZZI
PROPS
'83 STRANGE INVADERS*
'83 I AM THE CHEESE

SCOTT LEVA

STUNT COORDINATOR
'80 MOTHER'S DAY
'83 HOUSE ON SORORITY ROW

MISCELLANEOUS
'80 MOTHER'S DAY

ALEX LEVAC

STILLS
'80 SCHIZOID
'81 SMOKEY BITES THE DUST

SYLVESTER LEVAY

MUSIC
'84 WHERE THE BOYS ARE
'84 BODY ROCK

BORIS LEVEN

PRODUCTION DESIGNER
'83 KING OF COMEDY, THE

JOHN LEVENBERGER

PROPS
'79 SHOUT, THE*
'81 SHOCK TREATMENT
'81 CHARIOTS OF FIRE
'83 SUPERMAN III*
'83 BRITANNIA HOSPITAL

ELLEN LEVENE

PUBLICIST
'82 FIGHTING BACK
'82 VERDICT, THE
'83 ALL THE RIGHT MOVES
'83 DANIEL
'84 FLAMINGO KID, THE

UNIT PUBLICIST
'81 ARTHUR
'82 DEATHTRAP

CHERYL LEVENSON

PROPS
'82 BUTTERFLY

FRANK LEVERING

SCREENPLAY
'82 PARASITE*

ADRIANNE LEVESQUE

COSTUME SUPERVISOR
'79 OVER THE EDGE

MICHAEL LEVESQUE

ART DIRECTOR
'80 BORDERLINE
'80 FOXES
'82 BARBAROSA

SCHMULICK LEVI

KEY GRIP
'79 MAGICIAN OF LUBLIN, THE
'81 ENTER THE NINJA

MERINA LEVIKOVA-NEYMAN

PRODUCTION DESIGNER
'83 LIQUID SKY

COSTUMES
'83 LIQUID SKY

ALEXANDRA LEVILOFF

ASSISTANT EDITOR
'82 PARTNERS
'83 BLUE SKIES AGAIN*

DELORES LEVIN

SCRIPT SUPERVISOR
'79 IN-LAWS, THE

DON LEVIN

EXECUTIVE PRODUCER
'83 LOVE LETTERS*
'84 ANGEL*

JERRY LEVIN

MISCELLANEOUS
'79 ...AND JUSTICE FOR ALL

LAURIE LEVIN

MISCELLANEOUS
'82 BARBAROSA

SIDNEY LEVIN

EDITOR
'79 NORMA RAE
'80 WHOLLY MOSES!
'81 BACK ROADS
'82 I OUGHT TO BE IN PICTURES
'83 CROSS CREEK
'84 RIVER, THE

2ND UNIT DIRECTOR
'83 CROSS CREEK

MISCELLANEOUS
'80 HERO AT LARGE

SY LEVIN

LOCATIONS
'84 HARDBODIES

ALAN LEVINE

ASSOCIATE PRODUCER
'79 PROPHECY

PRODUCTION MANAGER
'81 ESCAPE FROM NEW YORK
'82 NIGHT SHIFT
'83 MAN WHO LOVED WOMEN, THE
'84 MICKI AND MAUDE

UNIT PROD. MANAGER
'79 PROPHECY
'80 ISLAND, THE
'82 CHALLENGE, THE*

ALAN LEVINE

STILLS
'83 10 TO MIDNIGHT*

DARRYL LEVINE

COSTUME SUPERVISOR
'83 CHRISTINE

HOLLY LEVINE

PUBLICIST
'80 TERROR TRAIN

JOSEPH LEVINE

PRODUCER
'81 TATTOO*

RICHARD LEVINE

PRODUCER
'81 TATTOO*

ROBERT LEVINE

EXECUTIVE PRODUCER
'82 THAT CHAMPIONSHIP SEASON

PUBLICIST
'84 ROMANCING THE STONE

STEVEN LEVINE

PROPS
'80 AIRPLANE
'81 HARD COUNTRY
'84 ALL OF ME

BRYAN LEVINGE

2ND ASST. DIRECTOR
'79 GAME OF DEATH*

ART LEVINSON

ASSOCIATE PRODUCER
'79 BREAKING AWAY
'82 MY FAVORITE YEAR
'83 MR. MOM*
'84 RACING WITH THE MOON
'84 TEACHERS

PRODUCTION MANAGER
'84 RACING WITH THE MOON

UNIT PROD. MANAGER
'79 BREAKING AWAY
'83 MR. MOM
'84 TEACHERS

UNIT MANAGER
'82 MY FAVORITE YEAR*

BARRY LEVINSON

DIRECTOR
'82 DINER
'84 NATURAL, THE

SCREENPLAY
'79 ...AND JUSTICE FOR ALL*
'80 INSIDE MOVES*
'82 BEST FRIENDS*
'82 DINER
'84 UNFAITHFULLY YOURS*

HAL LEVINSON

ASSISTANT EDITOR
'80 JUST TELL ME WHAT YOU WANT

MAUREEN LEVITT

ASSISTANT EDITOR
'82 GREY FOX, THE

MELANIE LEVITT
MAKEUP
'79 FORCE OF ONE, A*
'83 TWILIGHT ZONE, THE MOVIE*

ARIEL LEVY
PRODUCTION MANAGER
'81 SPHINX*
'82 DEATH VALLEY
1ST ASST. DIRECTOR
'79 MURDER BY DECREE
'80 NIJINSKY*

AUDREY LEVY
HAIR
'84 ALL OF ME*
'84 LAST STARFIGHTER, THE

DONALD LEVY
PUBLICIST
'82 NATIONAL LAMPOON'S CLASS REUNION
'82 POLTERGEIST
'83 BRAINSTORM*
'84 ICEMAN
UNIT PUBLICIST
'79 MAN, A WOMAN AND A BANK, A
'84 SOLDIER'S STORY, A
'84 2010

FRANKLIN LEVY
EXECUTIVE PRODUCER
'81 NIGHTHAWKS*

GAD LEVY
PRODUCTION MANAGER
'79 CIRCLE OF IRON

GADY LEVY
LOCATIONS
'82 PARADISE

GENE LEVY
EXECUTIVE PRODUCER
'84 STREETS OF FIRE
UNIT PROD. MANAGER
'80 LONG RIDERS, THE
'81 SOUTHERN COMFORT
'81 THIEF
'82 48 HOURS
'84 STREETS OF FIRE

GERRY LEVY
PRODUCTION MANAGER
'83 OCTOPUSSY*
UNIT MANAGER
'82 GANDHI*
LOCATIONS
'82 FIVE DAYS ONE SUMMER
'83 HUNGER, THE*

JULES LEVY
PRODUCER
'82 SAFARI 3000*

LOREN LEVY
PROPS
'82 STRANGER IS WATCHING, A

LYNDA LEVY
PUBLICIST
'79 LEGACY, THE
'84 OXFORD BLUES
UNIT PUBLICIST
'81 OUTLAND

MARVIN LEVY
PUBLICIST
'80 CLOSE ENCOUNTERS OF THE THIRD KIND SPECIAL EDITION*

NISSIM LEVY
1ST ASST. DIRECTOR
'79 CIRCLE OF IRON
'84 BEST DEFENSE*

ROBERT LEVY
ASSOCIATE PRODUCER
'82 SAFARI 3000

SAMUEL LEVY
KEY GRIP
'83 REVENGE OF THE NINJA

DENNIS LEW
ASSISTANT EDITOR
'79 FRISCO KID, THE*
'80 JAZZ SINGER, THE*
'81 TAPS

ROBERT LEWINE
STILLS
'83 SPRING BREAK*

CANDY LEWIS
MISCELLANEOUS
'82 ZAPPED!

CARI LEWIS
ASSISTANT EDITOR
'84 FLASHPOINT*

CHARLES LEWIS
SOUND
'79 MUPPET MOVIE, THE

DENNIS LEWIS
KEY GRIP
'80 SHINING, THE

EDWARD LEWIS
PRODUCER
'82 MISSING*
'84 CRACKERS*
'84 RIVER, THE*

GARRETT LEWIS
PRODUCTION DESIGNER
'80 OH! HEAVENLY DOG

GREGORY LEWIS
MAKEUP
'79 PENITENTIARY

HEDGEMON LEWIS
MISCELLANEOUS
'79 MAIN EVENT, THE

HERMAN LEWIS
SOUND
'79 BEYOND THE POSEIDON ADVENTURE
'80 WHEN TIME RAN OUT

JERRY LEWIS
DIRECTOR
'81 HARDLY WORKING
SCREENPLAY
'81 HARDLY WORKING*

JOE LEWIS
MISCELLANEOUS
'79 CIRCLE OF IRON

MARK LEWIS
MISCELLANEOUS
'84 REPO MAN

MARSHA LEWIS
HAIR
'81 FOR YOUR EYES ONLY*
'82 MOONLIGHTING

MICHAEL LEWIS
MUSIC
'79 LEGACY, THE
'80 FFOLKES
'81 SPHINX
'82 YES, GIORGIO

MILDRED LEWIS
PRODUCER
'82 MISSING*

NANCY LEWIS
PROD. OFFICE COORD.
'82 MONTY PYTHON LIVE AT THE HOLLYWOOD BOWL

PAUL LEWIS
EXECUTIVE PRODUCER
'82 OUT OF THE BLUE
EXEC IN CHARGE PROD
'82 SILENT RAGE
ASSOCIATE PRODUCER
'80 STUNT MAN, THE
UNIT PROD. MANAGER
'82 SILENT RAGE

RHEA LEWIS
SCRIPT SUPERVISOR
'80 HUMANOIDS FROM THE DEEP
MISCELLANEOUS
'83 LOSIN' IT

ROBERT LEWIS
PROD. COORDINATOR
'83 MAUSOLEUM*

TERRY LEWIS
PROPS
'79 CHINA SYNDROME, THE
'79 NORTH DALLAS FORTY
'81 HONKY TONK FREEWAY
'82 BLADERUNNER
'83 TERMS OF ENDEARMENT

W. MICHAEL LEWIS
MUSIC
'81 BODY AND SOUL
'81 ENTER THE NINJA*
'83 BALLAD OF GREGORIO CORTEZ, THE*
'83 MY TUTOR

PIERRE LHOMME
CINEMATOGRAPHER
'80 QUARTET

SHIRLEY LIBBY
STILLS
'80 PRIVATE EYES, THE
'84 MARVIN AND TIGE

HERWIG LIBOWITZKY
ART DIRECTOR
'79 PRISONER OF ZENDA, THE

PINSEROSA LIBRE
CASTING
'83 YEAR OF LIVING DANGEROUSLY, THE*

NICOLAI LICARET
MISCELLANEOUS
'83 ANGELO, MY LOVE

LOU LICHTENFIELD
MISCELLANEOUS
'80 FLASH GORDON

LUCIE LICHTIG
SCRIPT SUPERVISOR
'79 LITTLE ROMANCE, A

GARY LIDDIARD
MAKEUP
'79 BUTCH AND SUNDANCE: THE EARLY YEARS*
'79 ELECTRIC HORSEMAN, THE*
'80 BRUBAKER
'80 ORDINARY PEOPLE
'81 RICH AND FAMOUS*
'81 ALL NIGHT LONG*
'83 ROMANTIC COMEDY
'83 SOMETHING WICKED THIS WAY COMES*
'84 BEST DEFENSE*
'84 MICKI AND MAUDE*
'84 NATURAL, THE*
'84 UNFAITHFULLY YOURS

KEITH LIDDIARD
ART DIRECTOR
'84 RIDDLE OF THE SANDS*

RICHARD LIEBEGOTT
PROD. SECRETARY
'79 FRISCO KID, THE
MISCELLANEOUS
'83 STROKER ACE

PHILIP LIEBERMAN PHD
MISCELLANEOUS
'84 ICEMAN

TERRY LIEBLING
CASTING
'79 APOCALYPSE NOW*
'79 MORE AMERICAN GRAFFITTI*
'80 BRUBAKER
'80 EMPIRE STRIKES BACK, THE*
'80 HIDE IN PLAIN SIGHT*
'80 NINE TO FIVE
'81 SHARKEY'S MACHINE
'81 PATERNITY
'81 POSTMAN ALWAYS RINGS TWICE, THE
'82 BEST LITTLE WHOREHOUSE IN TEXAS, THE*
'82 I'M DANCING AS FAST AS I CAN
'83 TO BE OR NOT TO BE
'84 ADVENTURES OF BUCKAROO BANZAI ACROSS THE 8TH DIMENSION, THE

ERIC LIEBOWITZ
STILLS
'83 ECHOES

WEILAND LIEBSKI
1ST ASST. DIRECTOR
'79 AVALANCHE EXPRESS
'79 FEDORA*

MAGGIE LIESTON
MAKEUP
'79 MONTY PYTHON'S LIFE OF BRIAN*
HAIR
'79 MONTY PYTHON'S LIFE OF BRIAN*

YISRAEL LIFSCHUTZ
MISCELLANEOUS
'82 CHOSEN, THE

ROBERT LIFTON
PRODUCER
'83 EDDIE AND THE CRUISERS*

JAMES LIGGAT
CASTING
'80 SHINING, THE

GRAHAM LIGHT
MISCELLANEOUS
'79 FAST COMPANY

RICHARD LIGHTSTONE
SOUND
'79 MEATBALLS
'81 DEATH HUNT
'81 HAPPY BIRTHDAY TO ME
'83 SPACEHUNTER: ADVENTURES IN THE FORBIDDEN ZONE
'84 LOVE STREAMS*
'84 TERMINATOR, THE

BILL LILES
MISCELLANEOUS
'82 ESCAPE ARTIST, THE

JAMES LILES
MISCELLANEOUS
'79 CHINA SYNDROME, THE
'80 WHOLLY MOSES!
'81 UNDER THE RAINBOW

MITCH LILLIAN
KEY GRIP
'84 MARVIN AND TIGE

STEPHEN LILLIS
1ST ASST. DIRECTOR
'81 FEAR NO EVIL
LOCATIONS
'84 WEEKEND PASS

STEPHEN LIM
1ST ASST. DIRECTOR
'83 HEART LIKE A WHEEL
'84 FLAMINGO KID, THE

MIGUEL LIMA
PRODUCTION MANAGER
'83 YELLOWBEARD*

MELVIN LIND
2ND ASST. DIRECTOR
'79 MONTY PYTHON'S LIFE OF BRIAN
'81 CHARIOTS OF FIRE*
'83 BEYOND THE LIMIT
'83 LOCAL HERO*
'84 SUPERGIRL*

DONNA LINDEMANN
PROD. SECRETARY
'84 BIRDY*

JOHN LINDER
KEY GRIP
'79 BREAKING AWAY
'82 FAST TIMES AT RIDGEMONT HIGH
'82 POLTERGEIST
'83 BUDDY SYSTEM, THE
'84 SONGWRITER

JOHN LINDER JR.
KEY GRIP
'84 ICE PIRATES, THE

SHARON LINDER
HAIR
'84 RUNAWAY

STU LINDER
EDITOR
'80 FIRST FAMILY
'80 MY BODYGUARD
'82 SIX WEEKS
'82 DINER
'84 NATURAL, THE

HAL LINDERS
MISCELLANEOUS
'82 VICE SQUAD

MICHAEL LINDGREN
LOCATIONS
'82 MIDSUMMER NIGHT'S SEX COMEDY, A*
MISCELLANEOUS
'84 FLAMINGO KID, THE

WIM LINDNER
MISCELLANEOUS
'80 ROUGH CUT

BRIAN LINDQUIST
PUBLICIST
'81 STRIPES
UNIT PUBLICIST
'84 WHERE THE BOYS ARE
MISCELLANEOUS
'82 SUMMER LOVERS

KATE LINDSAY
COSTUMES
'83 ANGEL OF H.E.A.T.

ROBERT LINDSAY
CINEMATOGRAPHER
'80 MANIAC

MORT LINDSEY
MUSIC
'79 REAL LIFE

BEA LINDZON
MISCELLANEOUS
'81 SOUTHERN COMFORT

STEPHEN LINEWEAVER
ART DIRECTOR
'84 BROTHER FROM ANOTHER PLANET, THE
'84 ALPHABET CITY*
SP. EFFECTS SUPERV.
'84 ALPHABET CITY

JAMES LING
EDITOR
'81 TARZAN, THE APE MAN

ANDRE LINK
PRODUCER
'81 HAPPY BIRTHDAY TO ME*
'81 MY BLOODY VALENTINE*
'83 SPACEHUNTER: ADVENTURES IN THE FORBIDDEN ZONE*
EXECUTIVE PRODUCER
'79 MEATBALLS*

DARRYL LINKOW
SOUND
'81 GRADUATION DAY

LINDA LINN
PROPS
'83 VALLEY GIRL

ART LINSON
PRODUCER
'80 MELVIN AND HOWARD*
'80 WHERE THE BUFFALO ROAM
'82 FAST TIMES AT RIDGEMONT HIGH*
DIRECTOR
'80 WHERE THE BUFFALO ROAM

PHILLIP LINSON
ASSISTANT EDITOR
'84 FRIDAY THE 13TH PART IV THE FINAL CHAPTER*

KEN LINTOTT
MAKEUP
'80 NIJINSKY
'82 MISSIONARY, THE
'83 GORKY PARK*

MARK LIONE
ASSISTANT EDITOR
'81 SATURDAY THE 14TH*

STEVE LIPETZ
2ND ASST. DIRECTOR
'81 FEAR NO EVIL*

DAVID LIPMAN
2ND ASST. DIRECTOR
'84 BREAKIN 2 ELECTRIC BOOGALOO*

STUART LIPPMAN
SCRIPT SUPERVISOR
'79 AMERICATHON

ART LIPSCHULTZ
PROPS
'78 DEER HUNTER, THE*
'81 BEAST WITHIN, THE
'82 SIX PACK
'84 REVENGE OF THE NERDS

HOWARD LIPSON
EXECUTIVE PRODUCER
'82 PARADISE*
ASSOCIATE PRODUCER
'79 IN PRAISE OF OLDER WOMEN

MARK LIPSON
ASSOCIATE PRODUCER
'84 CHILDREN OF THE CORN

AARON LIPSTADT
DIRECTOR
'82 ANDROID
PRODUCTION MANAGER
'81 GALAXY OF TERROR
MISCELLANEOUS
'81 SATURDAY THE 14TH

HOWARD LIPSTONE
EXECUTIVE PRODUCER
'83 JAWS 3-D*

MARCI LIROFF
CASTING
'82 SIX WEEKS*
'83 RUNNING BRAVE*
'83 ALL THE RIGHT MOVES*
'83 CHRISTMAS STORY, A*
'83 FOOTLOOSE*
'83 KISS ME GOODBYE*
'83 PORKY'S II THE NEXT DAY*
'83 TWILIGHT ZONE, THE MOVIE*
'84 JOHNNY DANGEROUSLY*
'84 INDIANA JONES AND THE TEMPLE OF DOOM*

STEVE LISBERGER
DIRECTOR
'82 TRON
SCREENPLAY
'82 TRON
MISCELLANEOUS
'82 TRON

GAETANO LISI
2ND ASST. DIRECTOR
'81 SO FINE*
LOCATIONS
'81 PRINCE OF THE CITY
'84 COTTON CLUB, THE*
2ND UNIT DIRECTOR
'80 GLORIA

TOM LISI
LOCATIONS
'80 GLORIA*
'80 NIGHT OF THE JUGGLER

DAVID LISTER
LOCATIONS
'79 BLACK STALLION, THE*

HELEN LISTON
LOCATIONS
'81 ROAD GAMES

FRANK LISZCAK
SPECIAL EFFECTS
'82 I, THE JURY*

RUDY LISZCAK
SPECIAL EFFECTS
'80 SMALL CIRCLE OF FRIENDS, A*

MARTI LITIS
MISCELLANEOUS
'81 HARD COUNTRY

ROBERT LITTELL
SCREENPLAY
'82 AMATEUR, THE*

GEORGE LITTLE
COSTUME SUPERVISOR
'83 UNCOMMON VALOR*
'84 RED DAWN

LAURA LITTLE
PROD. OFFICE COORD.
'80 MANIAC*

CAROL LITTLETON
EDITOR
'80 ROADIE*
'81 BODY HEAT
'82 E.T. THE EXTRA-TERRESTRIAL
'83 BIG CHILL, THE
'84 PLACES IN THE HEART

LYNNE LITTMAN
PRODUCER
'83 TESTAMENT*
DIRECTOR
'83 TESTAMENT

GEORGE LITTO
PRODUCER
'79 OVER THE EDGE
'80 DRESSED TO KILL
'81 BLOW OUT

SYDNEY LITWACK
ART DIRECTOR
'79 GOLDENGIRL
'81 WHOSE LIFE IS IT ANYWAY?
'83 BLUE THUNDER
'84 PLACES IN THE HEART

JOSEPH LIUZZI
LOCATIONS
'84 TERMINATOR, THE

DAVID LIVINGSTON
EXEC IN CHARGE PROD
'83 GOLDEN SEAL, THE
UNIT PROD. MANAGER
'83 GOLDEN SEAL, THE

DOC LIVINGSTON
UNIT PUBLICIST
'83 SWEET SIXTEEN*

HAROLD LIVINGSTON
SCREENPLAY
'79 STAR TREK-THE MOTION PICTURE

LINDA LIVINGSTON
MISCELLANEOUS
'80 CHEECH AND CHONG'S NEXT MOVIE

MARGARET LIVINGSTON
PROD. SECRETARY
'80 CHANGELING, THE

VICTOR LIVINOSTON
ASSISTANT EDITOR
'83 RIGHT STUFF, THE*

CHRIS LLOYD
ASSISTANT EDITOR
'79 CIRCLE OF IRON*

EUAN LLOYD
PRODUCER
'81 SEA WOLVES, THE
'83 FINAL OPTION, THE

JAN LLOYD
1ST ASST. DIRECTOR
'81 HARD COUNTRY
'82 NIGHT SHIFT
'84 SPLASH

JOHN LLOYD
ART DIRECTOR
'81 RAGGEDY MAN
PRODUCTION DESIGNER
'79 BELL JAR, THE
'79 PRISONER OF ZENDA, THE
'80 BLUES BROTHERS
'82 THING, THE
'83 D.C. CAB
'84 CRACKERS

MICHAEL LLOYD
MISCELLANEOUS
'83 SOMETHING WICKED
THIS WAY COMES
'84 COUNTRY

MICHAEL LLOYD
MUSIC
'83 TOUGH ENOUGH*

PETER LLOYD
MISCELLANEOUS
'82 TRON
'82 TRON

RUSSELL LLOYD
EDITOR
'80 FIENDISH PLOT OF
DR. FU MANCHU, THE
'80 LADY VANISHES, THE

TED LLOYD
ASSOCIATE PRODUCER
'79 LEGACY, THE
MISCELLANEOUS
'80 FFOLKES
'81 DOGS OF WAR, THE
'83 NATE & HAYES

TOM LLOYD
MAKEUP
'82 TOY, THE*

TONY LLOYD
MAKEUP
'79 BEYOND THE POSEIDON ADVENTURE*
'80 DRESSED TO KILL*
'81 BUSTIN' LOOSE*
'81 HAND, THE
'81 VICTORY*
'82 DEATHTRAP*
'83 RICHARD PRYOR: HERE AND NOW
'83 BEYOND THE LIMIT*
'84 BLAME IT ON RIO
HAIR
'80 DRESSED TO KILL*

WARREN LLOYD
MISCELLANEOUS
'81 EARTHLING, THE

BRENDA LOADER
SCRIPT SUPERVISOR
'79 MONTY PYTHON'S LIFE OF BRIAN
'84 GIVE MY REGARDS
TO BROAD STREET

MICHAEL LOBELL
PRODUCER
'79 DREAMER
'80 WINDOWS
'81 SO FINE

BENJAMIN LOBO
CINEMATOGRAPHER
'83 BLIND RAGE

RICHARD LOCHTE
SCREENPLAY
'79 ESCAPE TO ATHENA*

MIKE LOCKEY

HAIR
- '81 RAIDERS OF THE LOST ARK*
- '81 SHOCK TREATMENT*
- '83 BEYOND THE LIMIT
- '83 LORDS OF DISCIPLINE, THE
- '84 RAZOR'S EDGE, THE*
- '84 RIDDLE OF THE SANDS

BOB LOCKWOOD

2ND UNIT DIRECTOR
- '81 DEATH HUNT*

RUSSELL LODGE

2ND ASST. DIRECTOR
- '84 KIPPERBANG*

JOE LODUCA

MUSIC
- '83 EVIL DEAD, THE

DILMA LOES

MISCELLANEOUS
- '84 BLAME IT ON RIO

DAGMAR LOESCH

HAIR
- '81 SOUTHERN COMFORT
- '82 48 HOURS
- '84 STREETS OF FIRE

STEPHEN LOFARO

1ST ASST. DIRECTOR
- '83 PRIVATE SCHOOL

2ND ASST. DIRECTOR
- '79 MORE AMERICAN GRAFFITTI
- '79 PROMISE, THE
- '80 DIE LAUGHING
- '80 LAST MARRIED COUPLE IN AMERICA, THE
- '81 NOBODY'S PERFEKT

THOMAS LOFARO

UNIT PROD. MANAGER
- '79 PROMISE, THE

1ST ASST. DIRECTOR
- '79 MORE AMERICAN GRAFFITTI
- '79 PROMISE, THE
- '80 LAST MARRIED COUPLE IN AMERICA, THE
- '80 OH GOD! BOOK II
- '81 FIRST MONDAY IN OCTOBER
- '82 PARTNERS
- '84 CHAMPIONS*
- '84 DREAMSCAPE*

2ND ASST. DIRECTOR
- '79 DOUBLE MCGUFFIN, THE

GIOVANNI LOFFREDA

UNIT MANAGER
- '83 YOR

CAREY LOFTIN

STUNT COORDINATOR
- '78 DEER HUNTER, THE*
- '79 CHINA SYNDROME, THE*
- '79 PROMISE, THE
- '80 RESURRECTION
- '80 FOOLIN AROUND
- '81 BLOW OUT
- '83 DEAD ZONE, THE*

BOB LOGAN

MISCELLANEOUS
- '81 SMOKEY BITES THE DUST

BRUCE LOGAN

CINEMATOGRAPHER
- '81 INCREDIBLE SHRINKING WOMAN, THE
- '82 TRON

SPECIAL EFFECTS
- '79 AVALANCHE EXPRESS*

MISCELLANEOUS
- '80 AIRPLANE
- '81 INCREDIBLE SHRINKING WOMAN, THE
- '83 DEAL OF THE CENTURY

GARY LOGAN

MUSIC
- '80 HUMAN FACTOR, THE*

KATHY LOGAN

MAKEUP
- '79 REAL LIFE
- '81 SATURDAY THE 14TH
- '83 LOVE LETTERS

RICHARD LOGAN

MUSIC
- '80 HUMAN FACTOR, THE*

JOHN LOGGIA

SPECIAL EFFECTS
- '82 FIRST TIME, THE

AUGIE LOHMAN

SPECIAL EFFECTS
- '79 ELECTRIC HORSEMAN, THE
- '79 WINTER KILLS

PAUL LOHMANN

CINEMATOGRAPHER
- '79 NORTH DALLAS FORTY
- '79 TIME AFTER TIME
- '79 METEOR
- '80 HIDE IN PLAIN SIGHT
- '81 CHARLIE CHAN AND THE CURSE OF THE DRAGON QUEEN
- '81 LOOKER
- '81 MOMMIE DEAREST
- '82 ENDANGERED SPECIES

HARRY LOJEWSKI

MUSIC SUPERVISOR
- '79 VOICES
- '82 DINER
- '82 YES, GIORGIO

PAUL LOMANTAGNE

LOCATIONS
- '80 TERROR TRAIN

RAOUL LOMAS

CINEMATOGRAPHER
- '84 CHILDREN OF THE CORN

JOE LOMBARDI

SPECIAL EFFECTS
- '79 APOCALYPSE NOW*
- '80 SMALL CIRCLE OF FRIENDS, A*
- '81 ENTITY, THE
- '81 DOGS OF WAR, THE
- '82 HAMMETT*
- '82 HANKY PANKY*

SP. EFFECTS SUPERV.
- '83 UNCOMMON VALOR

STEVE LOMBARDI

PROPS
- '81 SOUTHERN COMFORT

SPECIAL EFFECTS
- '80 LONG RIDERS, THE*

MARK LOMBARDO

ASSOCIATE PRODUCER
- '84 MISUNDERSTOOD

PRODUCTION MANAGER
- '84 PROTOCOL*

TONY LOMBARDO

EDITOR
- '79 PERFECT COUPLE, A
- '80 HEALTH*
- '80 POPEYE

ASSISTANT EDITOR
- '81 CHEECH AND CHONG'S NICE DREAMS*

DANIEL LOMINO

ART DIRECTOR
- '80 CLOSE ENCOUNTERS OF THE THIRD KIND SPECIAL EDITION
- '82 FAST TIMES AT RIDGEMONT HIGH

PRODUCTION DESIGNER
- '81 BUDDY, BUDDY
- '81 CHU CHU AND THE PHILLY FLASH
- '83 CHRISTINE
- '84 STARMAN

ULLI LOMMEL

PRODUCER
- '82 BRAINWAVES

DIRECTOR
- '82 BRAINWAVES

SCREENPLAY
- '82 BRAINWAVES

BRITT LOMOND
UNIT PROD. MANAGER
'80 SOMEWHERE IN TIME
1ST ASST. DIRECTOR
'84 PURPLE RAIN*

RICHARD LONCRAINE
DIRECTOR
'82 MISSIONARY, THE

ANDREW LONDON
SOUND
'80 TWINKLE TWINKLE "KILLER" KANE*
EDITOR
'83 PSYCHO II
'84 CLOAK AND DAGGER
MISCELLANEOUS
'81 WOLFEN

JOHN LONDON
KEY GRIP
'82 48 HOURS
'83 GET CRAZY
'84 KARATE KID, THE

MELODY LONDON
EDITOR
'84 STRANGER THAN PARADISE*

DANNE LONG
HAIR
'81 CATTLE ANNIE
AND LITTLE BRITCHES*

DOROTHEA LONG
HAIR
'80 OCTAGON, THE
'81 BUDDY, BUDDY
'81 CHU CHU AND THE PHILLY FLASH
'82 FORCED VENGEANCE
'82 MEGAFORCE
'83 STAR CHAMBER

JIM LONG
2ND ASST. DIRECTOR
'79 FAST COMPANY

KATHLEEN LONG
PROD. COORDINATOR
'84 MASS APPEAL

NATE LONG
2ND UNIT DIRECTOR
'79 OVER THE EDGE
'82 TEX
STUNT COORDINATOR
'82 TEX

BRIAN LONGBOTHAM
MISCELLANEOUS
'80 WATCHER IN THE WOODS, THE

GRAHAM LONGHURST
SPECIAL EFFECTS
'80 ELEPHANT MAN, THE
'82 PINK FLOYD: THE WALL*
'83 HUNGER, THE

SUSAN LONGMIRE
ART DIRECTOR
'79 RUNNING
PRODUCTION DESIGNER
'81 TICKET TO HEAVEN

JOHN LONGMUIR
1ST ASST. DIRECTOR
'79 BLOODLINE*

JOE LONGO
PROPS
'81 FIRST MONDAY IN OCTOBER
'82 STAR TREK II
THE WRATH OF KHAN
'84 STAR TREK III:
THE SEARCH FOR SPOCK

PETER LONSDALE
ASSISTANT EDITOR
'84 FIRSTBORN*

VIVIENNE LOOBOSH
PRODUCER
'81 TICKET TO HEAVEN

RICH LOOK
MUSIC
'80 HAPPY BIRTHDAY, GEMINI*

LEN LOOKABAUGH
KEY GRIP
'79 RUNNER STUMBLES, THE
'79 BUTCH AND SUNDANCE:
THE EARLY YEARS
'80 HEARTBEAT
'80 HOW TO BEAT
THE HIGH COST OF LIVING
'81 ON GOLDEN POND
'81 POSTMAN ALWAYS
RINGS TWICE, THE
'82 FRANCES
'82 TOY, THE
'83 STAR 80
'84 CRACKERS
'84 THIEF OF HEARTS
'84 WOMAN IN RED, THE

DIANA LOOMIS
SCRIPT SUPERVISOR
'79 BUCK ROGERS*

STEPHEN LOOMIS
COSTUMES
'80 FOG, THE*
'81 BUSTIN' LOOSE*
'81 ESCAPE FROM NEW YORK

MICHAEL LOONEY
2ND ASST. DIRECTOR
'80 LOVING COUPLES*
'81 MODERN ROMANCE
'84 NO SMALL AFFAIR
'84 SWING SHIFT

IRA LOONSTEIN
PRODUCTION MANAGER
'79 WINTER KILLS*
UNIT PROD. MANAGER
'79 ROSE, THE
'80 UP THE ACADEMY
'81 RICH AND FAMOUS*
UNIT MANAGER
'78 DEER HUNTER, THE*
LOCATIONS
'84 ICE PIRATES, THE

LARS LOOSCHEN
STILLS
'79 FEDORA

WILLIAM LOOSE
MUSIC
'81 MAN WHO SAW TOMORROW, THE*

BARBARA LOPEZ
HAIR
'84 BEVERLY HILLS COP

CHAYO LOPEZ
PROD. COORDINATOR
'81 CAVEMAN*

DANIEL LOPEZ
MISCELLANEOUS
'84 EVIL THAT MEN DO, THE

ENRIQUE LOPEZ
SOUND
'80 EYES OF A STRANGER

GINETTE ANGOSSE LOPEZ
2ND ASST. DIRECTOR
'79 HURRICANE*

HECTOR LOPEZ
MISCELLANEOUS
'79 PLAYERS

SANTO LOQUASTO
PRODUCTION DESIGNER
'81 SO FINE
'81 FAN, THE
'84 FALLING IN LOVE
COSTUMES
'80 SIMON
'80 STARDUST MEMORIES
'82 MIDSUMMER NIGHT'S
SEX COMEDY, A
'83 ZELIG

ROSEMARY LORD
PUBLICIST
'79 ICE CASTLES

SUZANNE LORE
PROD. OFFICE COORD.
'83 CHRISTMAS STORY, A
PROD. COORDINATOR
'80 CHANGELING, THE
'80 TRIBUTE
'82 AMATEUR, THE
'84 POLICE ACADEMY

TONY LOREE
1ST ASST. DIRECTOR
'83 SWEET SIXTEEN

SAM LORENO
PROPS
'82 BORDER, THE*

BARBARA LORENZ
HAIR
'79 JERK, THE
'79 SUNBURN
'80 CHEECH AND CHONG'S NEXT MOVIE
'81 CHEECH AND CHONG'S NICE DREAMS
'81 HONKY TONK FREEWAY*
'82 BEST LITTLE WHOREHOUSE IN TEXAS, THE*
'82 ONE FROM THE HEART
'83 STAYING ALIVE
'83 GET CRAZY
'83 TWO OF A KIND*
'84 RHINESTONE*

MICHAEL LORENZ
MAKEUP
'80 SERIAL*
'84 JOHNNY DANGEROUSLY*

VANCE LORENZINI
ART DIRECTOR
'81 EYE FOR AN EYE, AN
'83 LOSIN' IT

SAM LORENZO SR.
PROPS
'83 INDEPENDENCE DAY

ALAN LORIMER
SPECIAL EFFECTS
'81 CHEECH AND CHONG'S NICE DREAMS
'82 I OUGHT TO BE IN PICTURES
'83 MAX DUGAN RETURNS
'83 TWO OF A KIND

LYNN LORING
PRODUCER
'83 MR. MOM*

PHIL LORY
SPECIAL EFFECTS
'82 TOY, THE

LOS FOLKLORISTAS
MUSIC
'84 EL NORTE

GAVRIK LOSEY
PRODUCER
'79 AGATHA*

CHRISTINE LOSS
STILLS
'79 ROCKY II*
'80 RAGING BULL*
'81 ...ALL THE MARBLES
'81 TRUE CONFESSIONS
'82 ROCKY III
'82 FORCED VENGEANCE*
'82 YES, GIORGIO*
'83 BRAINSTORM*
'83 TABLE FOR FIVE

STAN LOTH
MISCELLANEOUS
'83 JAWS 3-D

LEO LOTITO
MAKEUP
'79 OVER THE EDGE
'80 COMPETITION, THE*
'80 WHEN TIME RAN OUT*
'81 BLOW OUT*

LEO LOTITO JR.
MAKEUP
'80 HONEYSUCKLE ROSE*

EVAN LOTTMAN
EDITOR
'79 SEDUCTION OF JOE TYNAN, THE
'79 ON THE YARD
'80 HONEYSUCKLE ROSE*
'81 ROLLOVER
'82 SOPHIE'S CHOICE

DAVID LOUGHERY
SCREENPLAY
'84 DREAMSCAPE*

KIMBERLY LOUIS
MISCELLANEOUS
'84 FLAMINGO KID, THE

MANVEL LOUIS
MISCELLANEOUS
'80 RAISE THE TITANIC
'83 YELLOWBEARD

R.J. LOUIS
EXECUTIVE PRODUCER
'84 KARATE KID, THE
ASSOCIATE PRODUCER
'80 IDOLMAKER, THE*
PRODUCTION MANAGER
'80 IDOLMAKER, THE
UNIT PROD. MANAGER
'82 JEKYLL AND HYDE TOGETHER AGAIN

GENE LOURIE
ART DIRECTOR
'80 BRONCO BILLY

TOBY LOVALLO
2ND ASST. DIRECTOR
'79 BEING THERE
'79 VILLAIN, THE*
'80 BIG BRAWL, THE
'80 THOSE LIPS, THOSE EYES

DEBORAH LOVE
2ND ASST. DIRECTOR
'82 48 HOURS
'83 JAWS 3-D
'84 STREETS OF FIRE

DENNIE LOVE
2ND ASST. DIRECTOR
'82 JINXED*

RICHARD LOVE
PRODUCTION MANAGER
'79 MR. MIKE'S MONDO VIDEO*

SANDI LOVE
COSTUMES
'83 MAN WHO WASN'T THERE, THE
'84 MEATBALLS PART II
COSTUME SUPERVISOR
'82 FRIDAY THE 13TH PART THREE IN 3D

STEVEN LOVE
2ND ASST. DIRECTOR
'84 ALPHABET CITY*

SUE LOVE
HAIR
'84 OXFORD BLUES

SYLVIA LOVEGREN
PROD. COORDINATOR
'84 TANK

RAY LOVEJOY
EDITOR
'80 SHINING, THE
'83 DRESSER, THE
'83 KRULL
'84 SHEENA

STEPHEN LOVEJOY
ASSISTANT EDITOR
'81 HISTORY OF THE WORLD PART I*
'83 BLUE SKIES AGAIN*
'84 ICEMAN*

JOHN LOVELADY
MISCELLANEOUS
'79 MUPPET MOVIE, THE

JAMES LOVELETT
STUNT COORDINATOR
'80 TIMES SQUARE*
'81 FAN, THE

DYSON LOVELL
PRODUCER
'79 CHAMP, THE
'81 ENDLESS LOVE
EXECUTIVE PRODUCER
'84 COTTON CLUB, THE

JUDY LOVELL
MAKEUP
'81 GALLIPOLI
'81 EARTHLING, THE
'83 YEAR OF LIVING DANGEROUSLY, THE
HAIR
'81 EARTHLING, THE
MISCELLANEOUS
'83 YEAR OF LIVING DANGEROUSLY, THE

PATRICIA LOVELL
PRODUCER
'81 GALLIPOLI*
EXECUTIVE PRODUCER
'79 PICNIC AT HANGING ROCK

CHARLIE LOVENTHAL
DIRECTOR
'82 FIRST TIME, THE
SCREENPLAY
'80 HOME MOVIES*
'82 FIRST TIME, THE*
CASTING
'80 HOME MOVIES

LAURIE LOVERDE
HAIR
'83 10 TO MIDNIGHT

LYNN LEWIS LOVETT
SCRIPT SUPERVISOR
'79 ALL THAT JAZZ*
'80 ONE-TRICK PONY
'80 WILLIE & PHIL
'81 ENDLESS LOVE
'81 NEIGHBORS
'84 COTTON CLUB, THE

ROBERT LOVETT
EDITOR
'82 HAMMETT*
'83 GOLDEN SEAL, THE
'84 COTTON CLUB, THE*

JACK LOVICK
MISCELLANEOUS
'83 MAN FROM SNOWY RIVER, THE

TOM LOVITER
MISCELLANEOUS
'81 SCANNERS

B. LOVITT
EDITOR
'79 FORCE OF ONE, A

BERT LOVITT
EDITOR
'81 BEAST WITHIN, THE*

DAVID LOWE
CO-PRODUCER
'82 FIGHTING BACK*

GARY LOWE
2ND ASST. DIRECTOR
'84 NIGHT OF THE COMET

MICHELLE LOWE
MAKEUP
'79 TIM
HAIR
'79 TIM

DANIEL LOWENTHAL
EDITOR
'80 MOTHER'S DAY
'83 BIG SCORE, THE
MISCELLANEOUS
'84 FRIDAY THE 13TH PART IV THE FINAL CHAPTER

WOLF LOWENTHAL
SCREENPLAY
'81 COMIN' AT YA!*

TONY LOWER
EDITOR
'83 RUNNING BRAVE*

BUCKETS LOWERY
MISCELLANEOUS
'83 PORKY'S II THE NEXT DAY

KEITH LOWES
ASSISTANT EDITOR
'83 MONTY PYTHON'S THE MEANING OF LIFE*

JACK LOWIN
2ND UNIT DIRECTOR
'84 TOP SECRET!

DICK LOWRY
DIRECTOR
'83 SMOKEY AND THE BANDIT III

HUNT LOWRY
PRODUCER
'83 GET CRAZY
'84 TOP SECRET!*
ASSOCIATE PRODUCER
'80 AIRPLANE
CO-PRODUCER
'80 HUMANOIDS FROM THE DEEP

WILLIAM LOWRY SR.
KEY GRIP
'81 NIGHT THE LIGHTS WENT OUT IN GEORGIA, THE

MALCOLM LUBLINER
MISCELLANEOUS
'81 BLOOD BEACH

BLAKE LUCAS
MISCELLANEOUS
'84 CHEECH AND CHONG'S THE CORSICAN BROTHERS

GEORGE LUCAS
SCREENPLAY
'83 RETURN OF THE JEDI*
EXECUTIVE PRODUCER
'79 MORE AMERICAN GRAFFITTI
'80 EMPIRE STRIKES BACK, THE
'81 RAIDERS OF THE LOST ARK*
'83 RETURN OF THE JEDI
'84 INDIANA JONES AND THE TEMPLE OF DOOM*

JIM LUCAS
MISCELLANEOUS
'81 ESCAPE FROM NEW YORK
'81 HONKY TONK FREEWAY

MARCIA LUCAS
EDITOR
'83 RETURN OF THE JEDI*

TOM LUCAS
MAKEUP
'83 BREATHLESS
'84 HARD TO HOLD

DEBORAH LUCCHESI
CASTING
'84 IRRECONCILABLE DIFFERENCES*
'84 IMPULSE*

ENRICO LUCHERINI
PUBLICIST
'83 YOR

BILL LUCIANO
ASSISTANT EDITOR
'79 BUCK ROGERS*

MICHAEL LUCIANO
EDITOR
'81 STRIPES*
'81 HARDLY WORKING
MISCELLANEOUS
'81 TAPS

TONY LUCIBELLO
1ST ASST. DIRECTOR
'79 LOST AND FOUND
'83 SPACEHUNTER: ADVENTURES IN THE FORBIDDEN ZONE

PAULO LUCIDI
UNIT MANAGER
'80 POPEYE

GLENN LUDLOW
LOCATIONS
'83 RUNNING BRAVE*

KURT LUEDTKE
SCREENPLAY
'81 ABSENCE OF MALICE

CHRISTINE LUESCHER
MISCELLANEOUS
'83 NEVER CRY WOLF

JOHN LUGAR
ASSOCIATE PRODUCER
'81 LOOKER

RUTH LUGO
PROD. SECRETARY
'80 GUYANA: CULT OF THE DAMNED

JOE LUIZZI
LOCATIONS
'84 PHILADELPHIA EXPERIMENT,THE*

BILL LUKATHER
UNIT MANAGER
'78 DEER HUNTER, THE*

SIDNEY LUMET
PRODUCER
'80 JUST TELL ME WHAT YOU WANT*
DIRECTOR
'80 JUST TELL ME WHAT YOU WANT
'81 PRINCE OF THE CITY
'82 DEATHTRAP
'82 VERDICT, THE
'83 DANIEL
'84 GARBO TALKS
SCREENPLAY
'81 PRINCE OF THE CITY*
EXECUTIVE PRODUCER
'83 DANIEL*

ANG KOK LUN
PROD. COORDINATOR
'83 BLIND RAGE*

JAN-ERIC LUNDBERG
SOUND
'81 MONTENEGRO

KERT LUNDELL
ART DIRECTOR
'81 THEY ALL LAUGHED

KURT LUNDELL
MISCELLANEOUS
'79 FISH THAT SAVED PITTSBURGH,THE

SVEN LUNDEN
MAKEUP
'81 MONTENEGRO

KAREN LUNER
COSTUMES
'84 LOVELESS, THE

JOHN LUOFF
2ND ASST. DIRECTOR
'83 EXPOSED*

GUY LUONGO
UNIT PROD. MANAGER
'79 BLOODLINE*
MISCELLANEOUS
'81 INCHON

MARSHALL LUPO
ASSOCIATE PRODUCER
'81 COMIN' AT YA!

TOM LUPO
STUNT COORDINATOR
'80 HANGAR 18*
MISCELLANEOUS
'79 AVALANCHE EXPRESS

DAN LUPOVITZ
2ND ASST. DIRECTOR
'83 LOSIN' IT

TONY LURASCHI
DIRECTOR
'80 OUTSIDER, THE
SCREENPLAY
'80 OUTSIDER, THE

JOHN LURIE
MUSIC
'81 PERMANENT VACATION*
'81 SUBWAY RIDERS*
'84 STRANGER THAN PARADISE

TOM LUSE
LOCATIONS
'84 BEAR, THE*

SKIP LUSK
EDITOR
'83 REUBEN, REUBEN
ASSISTANT EDITOR
'81 BUSTIN' LOOSE*

KOOL LUSKY
LOCATIONS
'82 EATING RAOUL*

ADELE LUSTIG
PROD. COORDINATOR
'79 PHANTASM

WILLIAM LUSTIG
PRODUCER
'80 MANIAC*
DIRECTOR
'80 MANIAC

ELLEN LUTTER
COSTUMES
'80 MOTHER'S DAY
'81 FRIDAY THE 13TH PART TWO

GEORGE LUXENBERG
PROPS
'80 THOSE LIPS, THOSE EYES*

ENRICO LUZZI
COSTUMES
'83 YOR

JOHN LVOFF
2ND ASST. DIRECTOR
'84 UNTIL SEPTEMBER

EUSTACE LYCETT
SPECIAL EFFECTS
'79 NORTH AVENUE IRREGULARS, THE*
'80 LAST FLIGHT
OF NOAH'S ARK, THE*
MISCELLANEOUS
'79 BLACK HOLE, THE

BILL LYDAY JR.
UNIT PUBLICIST
'79 DOUBLE MCGUFFIN, THE

CRAIG LYMAN
MAKEUP
'84 COTTON CLUB, THE

DANA LYMAN
COSTUMES
'83 SUBURBIA

DAVID LYNCH
DIRECTOR
'80 ELEPHANT MAN, THE
'84 DUNE
SCREENPLAY
'80 ELEPHANT MAN, THE*
'84 DUNE

DORIS LYNCH
COSTUMES
'80 STEEL*

MICHAEL LYNCH
CASTING
'83 NATE & HAYES*

PAUL LYNCH
DIRECTOR
'80 PROM NIGHT

ADRIAN LYNE

DIRECTOR
'80 FOXES
'83 FLASHDANCE

JOANNA LYNES

ASSISTANT EDITOR
'79 TIM

DIANA LYNN

STILLS
'83 DEADLY FORCE
'84 ANGEL

DORIS LYNN

COSTUMES
'80 FADE TO BLACK

ROBERT LYNN

LOCATIONS
'80 FIENDISH PLOT OF DR. FU MANCHU, THE
2ND UNIT DIRECTOR
'81 SUPERMAN II*

GILLIAN LYNNE

MISCELLANEOUS
'83 YENTL

JEFF LYNNE

MUSIC
'80 XANADU*

SHERRYI LYNNE

MISCELLANEOUS
'83 EDDIE AND THE CRUISERS

AGGIE LYON

COSTUMES
'80 BIG BRAWL, THE

JOHN LYON

MISCELLANEOUS
'83 EDDIE AND THE CRUISERS

MARK ROBERT LYON

2ND ASST. DIRECTOR
'81 BEAST WITHIN, THE

RACHEL LYON

PRODUCER
'80 TELL ME A RIDDLE*

JACK LYONS

PUBLICIST
'79 RUNNER STUMBLES, THE
'82 VICE SQUAD
UNIT PUBLICIST
'81 HARD COUNTRY
'83 DEADLY FORCE
'84 LAST STARFIGHTER, THE

ROGER LYONS

1ST ASST. DIRECTOR
'83 LORDS OF DISCIPLINE, THE*

DEAN STEPHEN LYRAS

2ND ASST. DIRECTOR
'81 GHOST STORY*
'81 HEARTBEEPS

ALEV LYTLE

SCREENPLAY
'80 TELL ME A RIDDLE*

BILL LYTLE

CASTING
'82 FRIDAY THE 13TH PART THREE IN 3D*

JOHN LYTLE

UNIT PROD. MANAGER
'81 UNDER THE RAINBOW
LOCATIONS
'79 BUDDY HOLLY STORY, THE
'83 MAN WHO WASN'T THERE, THE
'84 FRIDAY THE 13TH PART IV THE FINAL CHAPTER

M

GARY MAAS
STUNT COORDINATOR
'83 PORKY'S II THE NEXT DAY*
MISCELLANEOUS
'83 PORKY'S II THE NEXT DAY

MOSS MABRY
COSTUMES
'79 SUNBURN
'80 TOUCHED BY LOVE
'81 CONTINENTAL DIVIDE
'81 CARBON COPY
'82 TOY, THE

G. MAC BROWN
ASSOCIATE PRODUCER
'83 I AM THE CHEESE

GALT MACDERMOT
MUSIC
'79 HAIR*

DON MACDONALD
ASSOCIATE PRODUCER
'80 CADDYSHACK
'80 DIE LAUGHING

MICHAEL MACDONALD
UNIT MANAGER
'84 MRS. SOFFEL*
LOCATIONS
'83 CHRISTMAS STORY, A*

PETER MACDONALD
2ND UNIT DIRECTOR
'80 EMPIRE STRIKES BACK, THE*
'81 DRAGONSLAYER
'81 EXCALIBUR
MISCELLANEOUS
'81 EXCALIBUR

RICHARD MACDONALD
PRODUCTION DESIGNER
'79 ROSE, THE
'79 ...AND JUSTICE FOR ALL
'80 ALTERED STATES
'82 CANNERY ROW
'83 SOMETHING WICKED THIS WAY COMES
'84 ELECTRIC DREAMS
'84 SUPERGIRL
'84 TEACHERS

ROBERT MACDONALD
SPECIAL EFFECTS
'80 FIRST FAMILY
'80 WHEN TIME RAN OUT*
'82 YES, GIORGIO*

ROBERT MACDONALD SR.
SP. EFFECTS SUPERV.
'84 GREMLINS

ROBERT MACDONALD JR.
SPECIAL EFFECTS
'82 YES, GIORGIO*

SCOTT MACDONOUGH
PUBLICIST
'80 WINDOWS
UNIT PUBLICIST
'79 MANHATTAN
'81 BACK ROADS

HEATHER JO MACDOUGALL
ASSISTANT EDITOR
'84 HARD TO HOLD*

FRANCHETTE MACE
ASSOCIATE PRODUCER
'84 FLASHPOINT*

MAX MACGREGOR
2ND ASST. DIRECTOR
'83 HERCULES

PETER MACGREGOR-SCOTT
PRODUCER
'83 CHEECH AND CHONG'S STILL SMOKIN'
'84 CHEECH AND CHONG'S THE CORSICAN BROTHERS
ASSOCIATE PRODUCER
'79 JERK, THE
'79 PRISONER OF ZENDA, THE
'80 CHEECH AND CHONG'S NEXT MOVIE
CO-PRODUCER
'82 BEST LITTLE WHOREHOUSE IN TEXAS, THE
'84 REVENGE OF THE NERDS
PRODUCTION MANAGER
'79 JERK, THE
'80 CHEECH AND CHONG'S NEXT MOVIE
'82 BEST LITTLE WHOREHOUSE IN TEXAS, THE

BETSY MACGRUDER
1ST ASST. DIRECTOR
'84 REPO MAN
PROD. COORDINATOR
'80 BATTLE BEYOND THE STARS*

CHINA MACHADO
MISCELLANEOUS
'79 LOVE AT FIRST BITE

NEIL MACHLIS
ASSOCIATE PRODUCER
'80 CAN'T STOP THE MUSIC
'80 STEEL
'81 MOMMIE DEAREST
'82 GREASE 2
'83 CUJO
'84 JOHNNY DANGEROUSLY
'84 2010*
UNIT PROD. MANAGER
'79 AMERICAN GIGOLO
'80 CAN'T STOP THE MUSIC*
'80 STEEL
'81 MOMMIE DEAREST
'82 GREASE 2
'83 CUJO
'84 JOHNNY DANGEROUSLY
'84 2010

MIREILLE MACHU
ASSISTANT EDITOR
'82 LOOKIN' TO GET OUT*

HAMISH MACINNES
MISCELLANEOUS
'82 FIVE DAYS ONE SUMMER

STEPHEN MACK
EDITOR
'83 ANGELO, MY LOVE

TOM MACK
1ST ASST. DIRECTOR
'79 ONION FIELD, THE
'80 BLACK MARBLE, THE
'81 TAPS
'81 TRUE CONFESSIONS
'83 SURVIVORS, THE
'83 BAD BOYS*
'84 AGAINST ALL ODDS
'84 FALLING IN LOVE
'84 AMERICAN DREAMER*

D. LYNNE MACKAY

COSTUMES
'80 HAPPY BIRTHDAY, GEMINI

JOHN MACKENZIE

DIRECTOR
'83 BEYOND THE LIMIT

FLETCHER MACKEY

ART DIRECTOR
'84 LAST NIGHT AT THE ALAMO

BOB MACKIE

COSTUMES
'79 VILLAIN, THE*
'80 SMOKEY AND THE BANDIT II
'81 ...ALL THE MARBLES
'81 CHU CHU AND THE PHILLY FLASH*
'81 PENNIES FROM HEAVEN
'83 STAYING ALIVE*
'83 MAX DUGAN RETURNS

WOODS MACKINTOSH

ART DIRECTOR
'80 ONE-TRICK PONY
'82 WORLD ACCORDING TO GARP, THE
PRODUCTION DESIGNER
'80 FIRST DEADLY SIN
'83 JAWS 3-D

MARY LOU MACLAURY

1ST ASST. DIRECTOR
'83 ANGEL OF H.E.A.T.*
2ND ASST. DIRECTOR
'80 LONG RIDERS, THE

MICHAEL MACLAVERTY

ASSISTANT EDITOR
'79 RUNNING

GUS MACLEAN

2ND ASST. DIRECTOR
'84 COMFORT AND JOY

STEPHEN MACLEAN

SCREENPLAY
'82 STARSTRUCK
ASSOCIATE PRODUCER
'82 STARSTRUCK

DAVID MACLEOD

2ND ASST. DIRECTOR
'80 TERROR TRAIN
'81 DEATH HUNT

DOUG MACLEON

LOCATIONS
'84 FINDERS KEEPERS

DAVID MACMILLAN

SOUND
'83 RIGHT STUFF, THE
'84 BIRDY

KENNETH MACMILLAN

CHOREOGRAPHER
'80 NIJINSKY*

IAN MACNAUGHTON

DIRECTOR
'82 MONTY PYTHON LIVE AT THE HOLLYWOOD BOWL*

LILLIAN MACNEILL

SCRIPT SUPERVISOR
'80 HERO AT LARGE
'81 ROLLOVER
'81 FORT APACHE, THE BRONX
'81 NIGHT THE LIGHTS WENT OUT IN GEORGIA, THE
'82 SOPHIE'S CHOICE
'83 ALL THE RIGHT MOVES
'84 MOSCOW ON THE HUDSON

EARL MACRAUCH

SCREENPLAY
'82 STRANGER IS WATCHING, A*
'84 ADVENTURES OF BUCKAROO BANZAI ACROSS THE 8TH DIMENSION, THE

BILL MACSEMS

PROPS
'79 CHAPTER TWO
'79 10
'80 HERO AT LARGE
'80 HIDE IN PLAIN SIGHT
'80 PRIVATE BENJAMIN
'81 ONLY WHEN I LAUGH
'81 THIEF
'82 YES, GIORGIO
'83 BUDDY SYSTEM, THE
'84 MASS APPEAL

CLAIRE MACTAGUE

PROD. COORDINATOR
'79 RUNNER STUMBLES, THE
'80 STIR CRAZY
'80 THOSE LIPS, THOSE EYES
'83 STAR CHAMBER
'83 TWO OF A KIND
'84 UNFAITHFULLY YOURS

JOSEPH MADALENA

PRODUCTION MANAGER
'84 CHILDREN OF THE CORN

BETTY PECHA MADDEN

COSTUMES
'82 BEASTMASTER, THE
'83 DEADLY FORCE

IAN MADDEN

1ST ASST. DIRECTOR
'84 COMFORT AND JOY

TERRY MADDEN

2ND ASST. DIRECTOR
'81 CLASH OF THE TITANS*
'81 FOR YOUR EYES ONLY*
'81 DOGS OF WAR, THE*
'82 FIVE DAYS ONE SUMMER*
'83 OCTOPUSSY*

MARILYN MADDEROM

ASSISTANT EDITOR
'79 ELECTRIC HORSEMAN, THE
'80 ORDINARY PEOPLE*
'83 STAR 80

DIANA MADDOX

SCREENPLAY
'80 CHANGELING, THE*
'82 AMATEUR, THE*

JOE MADELENA

LOCATIONS
'84 ANGEL

ROBERT MADERO

PRODUCER
'83 MAUSOLEUM*
SCREENPLAY
'83 MAUSOLEUM*

DOUGLAS MADISON

PROPS
'79 APOCALYPSE NOW
'80 STUNT MAN, THE
'80 MELVIN AND HOWARD*
'80 MIDDLE AGE CRAZY
'82 HAMMETT*
'82 SECOND THOUGHTS
'83 RUMBLEFISH
'83 OSTERMAN WEEKEND, THE
'83 OUTSIDERS, THE
'83 UNCOMMON VALOR

JERRY MADORE

KEY GRIP
'80 HANGAR 18

HARRY MADSEN

STUNT COORDINATOR
'79 BOARDWALK
'81 FOUR FRIENDS
'83 BABY IT'S YOU
'83 ECHOES
'84 FLAMINGO KID, THE
'84 ALPHABET CITY
'84 C.H.U.D.

SHIRLEY MAE

MAKEUP
'79 PHANTASM

GEORGE MAEKO

SCREENPLAY
'81 DOGS OF WAR, THE*

KEIS MAES

MAKEUP
'84 UNDER THE VOLCANO*
HAIR
'84 UNDER THE VOLCANO*

BUD MAFFETT

SOUND
'79 FISH THAT SAVED PITTSBURGH, THE
'79 HARDCORE
'79 NORTH AVENUE IRREGULARS, THE
'81 RICHARD PRYOR: LIVE ON THE SUNSET STRIP*

HENRY MAFFETT

SOUND
'79 APPLE DUMPLING GANG RIDES AGAIN, THE
'79 BLACK HOLE, THE
'80 HERBIE GOES BANANAS
'80 LAST FLIGHT OF NOAH'S ARK,THE
'81 AMY
'82 TEX

ITZHAK MAGAL

SOUND
'82 ZAPPED!*

MIKE MAGGI

MAKEUP
'79 STARTING OVER*
'79 NATURAL ENEMIES
'79 WARRIORS, THE
'80 FIRST DEADLY SIN
'81 ROLLOVER*
'82 SOPHIE'S CHOICE
'83 STROKER ACE*

MICHAEL MAGILL

ASSISTANT EDITOR
'84 AMADEUS*

JEAN MARC MAGNAN

ASSISTANT EDITOR
'81 GAS*

RENATA MAGNANTI

HAIR
'84 ONCE UPON A TIME IN AMERICA*

ALBERT MAGNOLI

DIRECTOR
'84 PURPLE RAIN
SCREENPLAY
'84 PURPLE RAIN*
EDITOR
'84 PURPLE RAIN*
'84 RECKLESS

VIC MAGNOTTA

STUNT COORDINATOR
'79 VOICES
'79 WANDERERS, THE
'80 SIMON
'80 DRESSED TO KILL
'81 RAGTIME
'81 ROLLOVER
'81 ENDLESS LOVE
'81 FORT APACHE, THE BRONX
'82 STRANGER IS WATCHING, A
'82 AMITYVILLE II: THE POSSESSION
'82 FIGHTING BACK*
'82 WORLD ACCORDING TO GARP, THE
'83 EASY MONEY
'83 I AM THE CHEESE
'84 BOUNTY, THE
'84 COTTON CLUB, THE
'84 FIRSTBORN*
'84 BEAT STREET
'84 SPLASH*

BETSY MAGRUDER

1ST ASST. DIRECTOR
'84 TERMINATOR, THE*
2ND ASST. DIRECTOR
'81 GALAXY OF TERROR
'82 SEDUCTION, THE
'82 PARASITE

ALICE MAGUIRE

PROPS
'80 FRIDAY THE 13TH

C.J. MAGUIRE

PROPS
'83 FOOTLOOSE
'83 JAWS 3-D

DENNIS MAGUIRE

2ND ASST. DIRECTOR
'84 PROTOCOL*

PAUL MAGWOOD

2ND ASST. DIRECTOR
'79 TIME AFTER TIME
'80 COMPETITION, THE*
'84 MASS APPEAL*

TATIANA MAHAILOFF

SCRIPT SUPERVISOR
'79 MEATBALLS

BOB MAHARIS

LOCATIONS
'82 THINGS ARE TOUGH ALL OVER
'84 REVENGE OF THE NERDS

"FAST" EDDIE MAHLER

SOUND
'80 CHEAPER TO KEEP HER
'80 IN GOD WE TRUST

ZDENEK MAHLER

MISCELLANEOUS
'84 AMADEUS

TOM MAHONEY

CHOREOGRAPHER
'80 AIRPLANE

RICHARD MAIBAUM

SCREENPLAY
'81 FOR YOUR EYES ONLY*
'83 OCTOPUSSY*

ROBERT MAIER

PRODUCTION MANAGER
'81 POLYESTER
'83 HOUSE ON SORORITY ROW
MISCELLANEOUS
'81 POLYESTER

PAUL MAIGRET

PRODUCTION MANAGER
'80 TESS

DAVID MAIN

CO-PRODUCER
'80 NOTHING PERSONAL

DENNIS MAITLAND

SOUND
'79 ...AND JUSTICE FOR ALL
'80 GLORIA*
'80 WILLIE & PHIL
'80 NIGHT OF THE JUGGLER
'81 ROLLOVER
'81 CHU CHU AND THE PHILLY FLASH
'81 TATTOO
'81 WOLFEN
'82 TEMPEST
'83 SURVIVORS, THE
'84 MOSCOW ON THE HUDSON

SCOTT MAITLAND

1ST ASST. DIRECTOR
'81 THIEF*
'83 CLASS*
'83 JAWS 3-D*
'83 KING OF COMEDY, THE
'83 NEVER CRY WOLF*
'84 MRS. SOFFEL*

LEE MAJORS

EXECUTIVE PRODUCER
'80 STEEL

DUSAN MAKEVEJEV

DIRECTOR
'81 MONTENEGRO
SCREENPLAY
'81 MONTENEGRO

HARRY MAKIN

CINEMATOGRAPHER
'82 IF YOU COULD SEE WHAT I HEAR

PETR MAKOVICKA

2ND ASST. DIRECTOR
'84 AMADEUS*

CONSTANTINE MAKRIS
KEY GRIP
'79 HEARTLAND

PHILIP MALAMUTH
ASSISTANT EDITOR
'83 FRIGHTMARE*

MARIE-CHRISTINE MALBERT
PUBLICIST
'83 EXPOSED*

ROB MALENFANT
1ST ASST. DIRECTOR
'80 HAPPY BIRTHDAY, GEMINI
2ND UNIT DIRECTOR
'80 HAPPY BIRTHDAY, GEMINI

SUSAN MALERSTEIN
SCRIPT SUPERVISOR
'83 OSTERMAN WEEKEND, THE
'83 SUBURBIA
'84 FRIDAY THE 13TH PART IV THE FINAL CHAPTER

ARTI MALESCI
STUNT COORDINATOR
'83 SPRING BREAK

ALAN MALEY
MISCELLANEOUS
'81 DRAGONSLAYER

NICK MALEY
MISCELLANEOUS
'83 BRITANNIA HOSPITAL
'83 KRULL

MARTIN MALIVOIRE
SPECIAL EFFECTS
'82 IF YOU COULD SEE WHAT I HEAR
'82 PORKY'S
'82 QUEST FOR FIRE
'83 CHRISTMAS STORY, A
MISCELLANEOUS
'83 STRANGE INVADERS

JACK MALKEN
MUSIC
'81 NESTING, THE*

BARRY MALKIN
EDITOR
'79 LAST EMBRACE
'80 ONE-TRICK PONY*
'80 WINDOWS
'81 FOUR FRIENDS*
'83 RUMBLEFISH
'84 COTTON CLUB, THE*
MISCELLANEOUS
'82 HAMMETT

RICHARD MALL
KEY GRIP
'84 BACHELOR PARTY*

JOANNE MALLAS
PRODUCTION MANAGER
'83 ANGELO, MY LOVE

LOUIS MALLE
DIRECTOR
'81 ATLANTIC CITY
'81 MY DINNER WITH ANDRE
'84 CRACKERS

VINCENT MALLE
ASSOCIATE PRODUCER
'84 UNTIL SEPTEMBER
PROD. COORDINATOR
'81 ATLANTIC CITY

BRUCE MALLEN
EXECUTIVE PRODUCER
'82 PARADISE*

BILL MALLEY
PRODUCTION DESIGNER
'80 DEFIANCE
'80 TWINKLE TWINKLE "KILLER" KANE*
'81 MOMMIE DEAREST
'83 STAR CHAMBER
'83 DEAL OF THE CENTURY
'84 PROTOCOL

BRUCE MALMUTH
DIRECTOR
'81 NIGHTHAWKS
'83 MAN WHO WASN'T THERE, THE

JEANNE MALONE
COSTUME SUPERVISOR
'81 MODERN PROBLEMS

LEIGH MALONE
ART DIRECTOR
'81 GREAT MUPPET CAPER, THE*
MISCELLANEOUS
'79 MUPPET MOVIE, THE

SHEREEN MALONEY
ASSISTANT EDITOR
'81 STRANGE BEHAVIOR

DAVID MALTBY
LOCATIONS
'80 OH! HEAVENLY DOG

ANTONIO MALTEMPO
MAKEUP
'83 1990: THE BRONX WARRIORS*

MAMADE
CASTING
'82 QUEST FOR FIRE*
'83 ENIGMA*
'84 CHEECH AND CHONG'S THE CORSICAN BROTHERS
'84 UNTIL SEPTEMBER*
'84 AMERICAN DREAMER*

MARLA MAMALIS
MAKEUP
'80 HUMANOIDS FROM THE DEEP
HAIR
'80 HUMANOIDS FROM THE DEEP

DAVID MAMET
SCREENPLAY
'81 POSTMAN ALWAYS RINGS TWICE, THE
'82 VERDICT, THE

BOB MANAHAN
CASTING
'81 FORCE FIVE

GEORGE MANASSE
PRODUCER
'80 HE KNOWS YOU'RE ALONE
PRODUCTION MANAGER
'79 BELL JAR, THE
'80 TRIBUTE*
'81 NEIGHBORS
'83 PORKY'S II THE NEXT DAY

VERONICA MANCHOT
ASSISTANT EDITOR
'79 AVALANCHE EXPRESS*

JORGE MANCILLA
MISCELLANEOUS
'83 UNDER FIRE

CLAUDIO MANCINI
EXECUTIVE PRODUCER
'84 ONCE UPON A TIME IN AMERICA

HENRY MANCINI
MUSIC
'79 NIGHTWING
'79 PRISONER OF ZENDA, THE
'79 10
'80 CHANGE OF SEASONS, A
'80 LITTLE MISS MARKER
'81 S.O.B.
'81 BACK ROADS
'81 CONDORMAN
'81 MOMMIE DEAREST
'82 VICTOR/VICTORIA
'82 SECOND THOUGHTS
'83 CURSE OF THE PINK PANTHER
'83 MAN WHO LOVED WOMEN, THE
'83 TRAIL OF THE PINK PANTHER
'84 HARRY & SON

FRANK MANCUSO JR.
PRODUCER
'82 FRIDAY THE 13TH PART THREE IN 3D
'83 MAN WHO WASN'T THERE, THE
'84 FRIDAY THE 13TH PART IV THE FINAL CHAPTER
ASSOCIATE PRODUCER
'81 FRIDAY THE 13TH PART TWO

JOHNNY MANDEL

MUSIC
'79 AGATHA
'80 BALTIMORE BULLET, THE
'80 CADDYSHACK
'82 DEATHTRAP
'82 LOOKIN' TO GET OUT
'82 VERDICT, THE

MISCELLANEOUS
'82 SOUP FOR ONE
'83 STAYING ALIVE

LORING MANDEL

SCREENPLAY
'79 PROMISES IN THE DARK
'84 LITTLE DRUMMER GIRL, THE

ROBERT MANDEL

DIRECTOR
'83 INDEPENDENCE DAY

BABALOO MANDELL

SCREENPLAY
'82 NIGHT SHIFT*
'84 SPLASH*

JOHN MANDELL

MUSIC
'79 BEING THERE

KAY MANDER

SCRIPT SUPERVISOR
'80 HUMAN FACTOR, THE

TOMMIE MANDERSON

MAKEUP
'79 ALIEN
'80 QUARTET*
'83 LOCAL HERO
'84 KILLING FIELDS, THE
'84 SCANDALOUS*

FRITZ MANES

PRODUCER
'80 ANY WHICH WAY YOU CAN
'84 CITY HEAT
'84 TIGHTROPE*

EXECUTIVE PRODUCER
'82 FIREFOX
'82 HONKYTONK MAN
'83 SUDDEN IMPACT

ASSOCIATE PRODUCER
'79 ESCAPE FROM ALCATRAZ
'80 BRONCO BILLY

UNIT PROD. MANAGER
'82 FIREFOX*
'84 CITY HEAT
'84 TIGHTROPE

2ND ASST. DIRECTOR
'80 ANY WHICH WAY YOU CAN*
'80 BRONCO BILLY*

HARRY MANFREDINI

MUSIC
'80 FRIDAY THE 13TH
'81 FRIDAY THE 13TH PART TWO
'82 SWAMP THING
'82 FRIDAY THE 13TH PART THREE IN 3D
'83 SPRING BREAK
'84 FRIDAY THE 13TH PART IV THE FINAL CHAPTER

RITA MANGAT

ASSOCIATE PRODUCER
'83 HEAT AND DUST*

DEE MANGES

MAKEUP
'82 SIX PACK

JOSEPH MANGINE

CINEMATOGRAPHER
'80 ALLIGATOR
'80 MOTHER'S DAY
'82 SWORD AND THE SORCERER, THE
'84 EXTERMINATOR II*

JIM MANIOLAS

1ST ASST. DIRECTOR
'79 EUROPEANS, THE

ANNIE MANISCALCO

MAKEUP
'83 LOSIN' IT*
'84 PHILADELPHIA EXPERIMENT, THE

ISIDORE MANKOFSKY

CINEMATOGRAPHER
'79 MUPPET MOVIE, THE
'80 SOMEWHERE IN TIME
'80 JAZZ SINGER, THE

MISCELLANEOUS
'83 TRENCHCOAT

PETER MANLEY

ASSOCIATE PRODUCER
'84 GIVE MY REGARDS TO BROAD STREET

PRODUCTION MANAGER
'83 HEAT AND DUST
'83 HIGH ROAD TO CHINA*

MAX MANLOVE

PROD. COORDINATOR
'81 MODERN ROMANCE
'84 HARRY & SON

PROD. SECRETARY
'81 BUSTIN' LOOSE*
'81 CONTINENTAL DIVIDE

ANITA MANN

CHOREOGRAPHER
'81 GREAT MUPPET CAPER, THE

CHARLES MANN

MISCELLANEOUS
'79 YANKS

CORRINE MANN

CO-PRODUCER
'80 CHEAPER TO KEEP HER

DELBERT MANN

DIRECTOR
'82 NIGHT CROSSING

EARL MANN

2ND ASST. DIRECTOR
'80 CHEAPER TO KEEP HER*

MICHAEL MANN

DIRECTOR
'81 THIEF
'83 KEEP, THE

SCREENPLAY
'81 THIEF
'83 KEEP, THE

EXECUTIVE PRODUCER
'81 THIEF

PAMELA MANN

SCRIPT SUPERVISOR
'80 EMPIRE STRIKES BACK, THE*
'81 RAIDERS OF THE LOST ARK
'81 AMERICAN WEREWOLF IN LONDON, AN

SHARON MANN

2ND ASST. DIRECTOR
'83 STAYING ALIVE*
'84 FRIDAY THE 13TH PART IV THE FINAL CHAPTER*

STANLEY MANN

SCREENPLAY
'79 CIRCLE OF IRON*
'79 METEOR*
'81 EYE OF THE NEEDLE
'84 FIRESTARTER
'84 CONAN THE DESTROYER

TED MANN

EXECUTIVE PRODUCER
'80 BRUBAKER
'83 KRULL

THOMAS MANN

PRODUCTION MANAGER
'80 HUMANOIDS FROM THE DEEP

BOB MANNING

PRODUCTION MANAGER
'84 ANGEL
'84 CRIMES OF PASSION
'84 BEAR, THE

COLIN MANNING
KEY GRIP
'80 NIJINSKY

EDWARD MANNING
MISCELLANEOUS
'84 DREAMSCAPE

MICHELLE MANNING
ASSOCIATE PRODUCER
'84 SIXTEEN CANDLES*

RITA MANNING
MISCELLANEOUS
'83 BREATHLESS

SHEILA MANNING
CASTING
'80 PROM NIGHT*
'80 GALAXINA

WILLIAM MANNING
KEY GRIP
'84 WEEKEND PASS

DEBORAH MANNIS
ASSOCIATE PRODUCER
'82 THINGS ARE TOUGH ALL OVER*

JOSEPH MANNIS
EXECUTIVE PRODUCER
'83 CHEECH AND CHONG'S STILL SMOKIN'
'84 CHEECH AND CHONG'S THE CORSICAN BROTHERS*

BOBBIE MANNIX
COSTUMES
'79 WARRIORS, THE*
'80 LONG RIDERS, THE
'80 XANADU

CARL MANOOGIAN
KEY GRIP
'79 CONCORDE-AIRPORT '79, THE
'80 CHANGE OF SEASONS, A
'80 FOOLIN AROUND
'80 LITTLE MISS MARKER
'80 LOVING COUPLES
'81 ALL NIGHT LONG
'81 BUSTIN' LOOSE*
'82 HAMMETT*
'82 JEKYLL AND HYDE TOGETHER AGAIN
'82 NATIONAL LAMPOON'S CLASS REUNION
'84 JOHNNY DANGEROUSLY

PETER MANOOGIAN
PRODUCTION MANAGER
'83 METALSTORM: THE DESTRUCTION OF JARED-SYN*
1ST ASST. DIRECTOR
'81 GALAXY OF TERROR
'82 SEDUCTION, THE
'82 PARASITE
'83 METALSTORM: THE DESTRUCTION OF JARED-SYN

MARK MANOS
ASSISTANT EDITOR
'84 NOT FOR PUBLICATION

MONI MANSANO
MAKEUP
'79 CIRCLE OF IRON*
'79 MAGICIAN OF LUBLIN, THE
'83 REVENGE OF THE NINJA
'84 BREAKIN 2 ELECTRIC BOOGALOO
HAIR
'79 MAGICIAN OF LUBLIN, THE
'83 REVENGE OF THE NINJA
'84 BREAKIN 2 ELECTRIC BOOGALOO

JOHN MANSBRIDGE
ART DIRECTOR
'79 APPLE DUMPLING GANG RIDES AGAIN, THE*
'79 BLACK HOLE, THE*
'79 NORTH AVENUE IRREGULARS, THE*
'80 HERBIE GOES BANANAS*
'80 LAST FLIGHT OF NOAH'S ARK,THE
'80 MIDNIGHT MADNESS*
'81 AMY*
'81 DEVIL AND MAX DEVLIN, THE*
'82 TEX
'82 TRON*
'83 SOMETHING WICKED THIS WAY COMES*
'83 TRENCHCOAT
'84 COUNTRY
'84 SPLASH
MISCELLANEOUS
'80 WATCHER IN THE WOODS, THE

MARK MANSBRIDGE
ART DIRECTOR
'81 AMY*
'83 MAN WITH TWO BRAINS, THE

ALAN MANSER
ART DIRECTOR
'80 RAGING BULL*

SIMON MANSES
MISCELLANEOUS
'81 KNIGHTRIDERS

DAVID MANSFIELD
MUSIC
'80 HEAVEN'S GATE

DAVID MANSON
EXECUTIVE PRODUCER
'84 BIRDY

LOFTI MANSOURI
MISCELLANEOUS
'82 YES, GIORGIO

COSTA MANTIS
1ST ASST. DIRECTOR
'80 HE KNOWS YOU'RE ALONE

MARCUS MANTON
EDITOR
'84 BREAKIN 2 ELECTRIC BOOGALOO

DOV MAOZ
LOCATIONS
'83 TABLE FOR FIVE*

MAREVA MAPUHI
PROD. SECRETARY
'81 BEYOND THE REEF

FLOR MARAJAS
MISCELLANEOUS
'84 PURPLE HEARTS

DON MARANDO
MAKEUP
'79 GOING IN STYLE*

ALFRED MARAZZI
MAKEUP
'81 SO FINE*

TERRY MARCEL
2ND UNIT DIRECTOR
'83 CURSE OF THE PINK PANTHER
'83 TRAIL OF THE PINK PANTHER

CANDY MARCELLINO
SCRIPT SUPERVISOR
'81 CONTINENTAL DIVIDE
'81 HALLOWEEN II
'82 THING, THE

ALFREDO MARCHETTI
KEY GRIP
'82 ONE FROM THE HEART*

DOROTHY MARCHINI
PRODUCTION MANAGER
'81 RAIDERS OF THE LOST ARK*

NICK MARCK
2ND ASST. DIRECTOR
'79 RUNNER STUMBLES, THE
'79 10*
'80 CARNY
'80 HONEYSUCKLE ROSE
'81 POSTMAN ALWAYS RINGS TWICE, THE

DAVID MARCONI
MISCELLANEOUS
'83 RUMBLEFISH

ROBERT MARCUCCI
PRODUCER
'84 RAZOR'S EDGE, THE*
MISCELLANEOUS
'80 IDOLMAKER, THE

ALEXANDRE MARCUS
MAKEUP
'81 SUNDAY LOVERS*

GARY MARCUS
2ND ASST. DIRECTOR
'84 ALPHABET CITY*

IRWIN MARCUS
2ND ASST. DIRECTOR
'84 CHAMPIONS*
'84 THIS IS SPINAL TAP
'84 JOY OF SEX, THE

LAWRENCE MARCUS
SCREENPLAY
'80 STUNT MAN, THE

PAUL MARCUS
LOCATIONS
'84 BROTHER FROM ANOTHER PLANET, THE

PAULA MARCUS
2ND ASST. DIRECTOR
'79 OVER THE EDGE
'80 STUNT MAN, THE

RICHARD MARCUS
ASSOCIATE PRODUCER
'82 PARASITE*

SHIRLEY MARCUS
PROD. OFFICE COORD.
'79 CHAPTER TWO
'80 DRESSED TO KILL
'80 FIRST DEADLY SIN
'81 ONLY WHEN I LAUGH
PROD. COORDINATOR
'79 DOUBLE MCGUFFIN, THE
'82 I, THE JURY*

GRAEME MARDELL
KEY GRIP
'81 ROAD GAMES
'81 EARTHLING, THE
'82 ROAD WARRIOR, THE
'84 BOUNTY, THE

RICHARD MARDEN
EDITOR
'80 SATURN 3
'80 MIRROR CRACK'D, THE
'82 EVIL UNDER THE SUN
'84 BLAME IT ON RIO*

LINDA MARDER
ART DIRECTOR
'79 REAL LIFE*

SUSAN MARGARET
CASTING
'81 MAN WHO SAW TOMORROW, THE*

GEORGE MARGELLOS
2ND ASST. DIRECTOR
'79 MAN, A WOMAN AND A BANK, A

JIM MARGELLOS
PRODUCTION MANAGER
'80 CHANGELING, THE
'84 POLICE ACADEMY

ANTONELLA MARGHERITI
MISCELLANEOUS
'83 YOR

EDWARD MARGHERITI
SPECIAL EFFECTS
'83 YOR*

TONY MARGHERITI
SPECIAL EFFECTS
'83 YOR*

STUART MARGOLIN
SCREENPLAY
'79 MAN, A WOMAN AND A BANK, A*

MICHAEL MARGULIES
CINEMATOGRAPHER
'80 MY BODYGUARD
'82 SIX WEEKS
'84 POLICE ACADEMY

ROBIN MARIA
PROD. COORDINATOR
'82 SPLIT IMAGE

JACQUELINE MARIANI
ASSISTANT EDITOR
'80 TESS*

MICHAEL MARIANI
MISCELLANEOUS
'83 ANGEL OF H.E.A.T.

IRENE MARIANO
CASTING
'80 CARNY*
'84 LAST STARFIGHTER, THE*
'84 TANK*

MARTIN MARIAS
PROPS
'79 WHEN A STRANGER CALLS

CAROLE MARIE
PROD. SECRETARY
'83 LONE WOLF MCQUADE

SALAH MARIE
ART DIRECTOR
'80 AWAKENING, THE*

LOUIS MARIE-FRANCE
COSTUMES
'84 PURPLE RAIN*

VAUGHN MARIE-FRANCE
COSTUMES
'84 PURPLE RAIN*

BOJANA MARIJAN
MISCELLANEOUS
'81 MONTENEGRO

ANDREW PETER MARIN
SCREENPLAY
'80 HOG WILD

CARL MARIN
HAIR
'83 HERCULES

CHEECH MARIN
SCREENPLAY
'80 CHEECH AND CHONG'S NEXT MOVIE*
'81 CHEECH AND CHONG'S NICE DREAMS*
'82 THINGS ARE TOUGH ALL OVER*
'83 CHEECH AND CHONG'S STILL SMOKIN'*
'84 CHEECH AND CHONG'S THE CORSICAN BROTHERS*

JESUS MARIN
1ST ASST. DIRECTOR
'83 UNDER FIRE*

RIKKI MARIN
ASSOCIATE PRODUCER
'83 CHEECH AND CHONG'S STILL SMOKIN'*
'84 CHEECH AND CHONG'S THE CORSICAN BROTHERS*

LORENZO MARINELLI
EDITOR
'80 MANIAC

JACK MARINO
PROPS
'79 JUST YOU AND ME KID
'80 ISLAND, THE
'81 HISTORY OF THE WORLD PART I

ANNE MARISSE
SCREENPLAY
'81 GRADUATION DAY*

GORDON MARK
UNIT MANAGER
'84 RUNAWAY
1ST ASST. DIRECTOR
'83 GOLDEN SEAL, THE
LOCATIONS
'79 MAN, A WOMAN AND A BANK, A
'82 FIRST BLOOD
'82 MOTHER LODE
'83 STAR 80

MARY ELLEN MARK
MISCELLANEOUS
'83 SILKWOOD

STANLEY MARK
EXEC IN CHARGE PROD
'80 FIRST DEADLY SIN
ASSOCIATE PRODUCER
'82 DEATH VALLEY

STEPHEN MARK
ASSISTANT EDITOR
'81 ENDLESS LOVE
'81 HONKY TONK FREEWAY*
'84 COUNTRY

LT. COL. JOHN MARKANTON
MISCELLANEOUS
'81 SOUTHERN COMFORT

BILL MARKE
SOUND
'83 AMERICANA*

DONN MARKEL
MAKEUP
'83 BALLAD OF GREGORIO CORTEZ, THE
HAIR
'83 BALLAD OF GREGORIO CORTEZ, THE

MARSHALL MARKER
STILLS
'79 ICE CASTLES
'80 FOOLIN AROUND
'80 MIDDLE AGE CRAZY*
'80 THOSE LIPS, THOSE EYES
'81 HARDLY WORKING

PATRICK MARKEY
LOCATIONS
'80 BRUBAKER
'80 ORDINARY PEOPLE
'81 THIEF*

PETER MARKLE
DIRECTOR
'84 HOT DOG...THE MOVIE

EDWARD MARKLEY
UNIT PROD. MANAGER
'79 BUCK ROGERS*
1ST ASST. DIRECTOR
'79 GREAT SANTINI, THE*

ROBERT MARKOWITZ
DIRECTOR
'79 VOICES

BEAU MARKS
1ST ASST. DIRECTOR
'81 PRIVATE LESSONS*
'83 TIMERIDER
'84 IMPULSE
2ND ASST. DIRECTOR
'79 FISH THAT SAVED PITTSBURGH,THE*

EDDIE MARKS
COSTUMES
'81 TAPS
COSTUME SUPERVISOR
'80 MELVIN AND HOWARD*
'80 WHERE THE BUFFALO ROAM*
'84 REVENGE OF THE NERDS

ELLIOTT MARKS
STILLS
'79 RUNNER STUMBLES, THE
'79 CHAMP, THE*
'79 VILLAIN, THE
'80 CAN'T STOP THE MUSIC
'80 FORMULA, THE*
'80 MELVIN AND HOWARD
'80 URBAN COWBOY*
'81 RICH AND FAMOUS
'81 DEAD AND BURIED
'81 HISTORY OF THE WORLD PART I
'82 SHOOT THE MOON
'82 SIX WEEKS
'82 ANNIE
'83 NATIONAL LAMPOON'S VACATION
'84 AGAINST ALL ODDS
'84 BEST DEFENSE*
'84 COUNTRY*

J. DAVID MARKS
EXECUTIVE PRODUCER
'81 TAKE THIS JOB AND SHOVE IT*

JEFF MARKS
STILLS
'84 INDIANA JONES AND THE TEMPLE OF DOOM*

JULIAN MARKS
1ST ASST. DIRECTOR
'81 MY BLOODY VALENTINE*

MAURICE MARKS
2ND ASST. DIRECTOR
'80 HOPSCOTCH*
'81 BUDDY, BUDDY*

RICHARD MARKS
EDITOR
'79 APOCALYPSE NOW*
'81 HAND, THE
'81 PENNIES FROM HEAVEN
'83 MAX DUGAN RETURNS
'83 TERMS OF ENDEARMENT
'84 ADVENTURES OF BUCKAROO BANZAI ACROSS THE 8TH DIMENSION, THE*

WILLIAM MARKY
SOUND
'80 GONG SHOW MOVIE, THE

SANDRA ULOSEVICH MARLEY
SCRIPT SUPERVISOR
'82 AMATEUR, THE
'83 PORKY'S II THE NEXT DAY

STEVEN MARLO
MISCELLANEOUS
'79 BEYOND THE POSEIDON ADVENTURE

MARC MARMIER
PROPS
'84 JUST THE WAY YOU ARE*

LISA MARMON
2ND ASST. DIRECTOR
'80 ALLIGATOR
'80 XANADU*
'81 RAGGEDY MAN
'82 TRON
'82 ZOOT SUIT
'83 SOMETHING WICKED THIS WAY COMES
'83 PSYCHO II

RICHARD MARQUAND
DIRECTOR
'79 LEGACY, THE
'81 EYE OF THE NEEDLE
'83 RETURN OF THE JEDI
'84 UNTIL SEPTEMBER

TONY MARRERO
HAIR
'82 SWAMP THING
'82 TOOTSIE*
'84 FIRSTBORN

EDWARD MARRITZ
MISCELLANEOUS
'79 HEARTLAND

ARMENIO MARRONI
HAIR
'83 1990: THE BRONX WARRIORS

ENNIO MARRONI
HAIR
'79 HURRICANE
'82 FIGHTING BACK

DEBORAH MARRS
2ND ASST. DIRECTOR
'82 FIGHTING BACK*
'84 NOT FOR PUBLICATION*

MICHELE MARSALA
PRODUCER
'83 YOR

KEN MARSCHALL
MISCELLANEOUS
'84 TERMINATOR, THE

JAMES MARSH
ASSISTANT EDITOR
'84 RIDDLE OF THE SANDS

LINDA MARSH
CASTING
'84 CRIMES OF PASSION

RAY MARSH
1ST ASST. DIRECTOR
'81 NIGHT THE LIGHTS WENT OUT IN GEORGIA, THE

SANDRA MARSH
PRODUCER
'84 FINDERS KEEPERS*

STEPHEN MARSH
ART DIRECTOR
'84 ANGEL
'84 CRIMES OF PASSION

TERENCE MARSH
PRODUCER
'84 FINDERS KEEPERS*
SCREENPLAY
'84 FINDERS KEEPERS*
PRODUCTION DESIGNER
'79 FRISCO KID, THE
'81 SPHINX
'81 ABSENCE OF MALICE
'81 SUNDAY LOVERS
'83 TO BE OR NOT TO BE
'84 FINDERS KEEPERS

BOB MARSHAK
STILLS
'84 BROTHER FROM ANOTHER PLANET, THE

ALAN MARSHALL
PRODUCER
'80 FAME*
'82 SHOOT THE MOON
'82 PINK FLOYD: THE WALL
'84 ANOTHER COUNTRY
'84 BIRDY

ALAN MARSHALL
MAKEUP
'83 10 TO MIDNIGHT
'84 EVIL THAT MEN DO, THE

BRIAN MARSHALL
SOUND
'79 PRISONER OF ZENDA, THE*

DIANE MARSHALL
MISCELLANEOUS
'82 FIRST BLOOD

FRANK MARSHALL
PRODUCER
'81 RAIDERS OF THE LOST ARK
'82 POLTERGEIST*
EXECUTIVE PRODUCER
'79 WARRIORS, THE
'83 TWILIGHT ZONE, THE MOVIE
'84 GREMLINS*
'84 INDIANA JONES AND THE TEMPLE OF DOOM*
2ND UNIT DIRECTOR
'84 INDIANA JONES AND THE TEMPLE OF DOOM*
MISCELLANEOUS
'82 E.T. THE EXTRA-TERRESTRIAL

GARRY MARSHALL
DIRECTOR
'82 YOUNG DOCTORS IN LOVE
'84 FLAMINGO KID, THE
SCREENPLAY
'84 FLAMINGO KID, THE*
EXECUTIVE PRODUCER
'82 YOUNG DOCTORS IN LOVE

GARTH MARSHALL
SOUND
'79 MONTY PYTHON'S LIFE OF BRIAN
'81 TIME BANDITS
'83 MONTY PYTHON'S THE MEANING OF LIFE

JOHN MARSHALL
2ND ASST. DIRECTOR
'84 FLASHPOINT

KELLY MARSHALL
PROD. COORDINATOR
'79 BUDDY HOLLY STORY, THE
'81 UNDER THE RAINBOW*

LORI MARSHALL
MISCELLANEOUS
'84 FLAMINGO KID, THE

NEAL MARSHALL
SCREENPLAY
'84 FLAMINGO KID, THE*

ROBERT MARSHALL
STILLS
'84 KIPPERBANG

JACK MARSTON
MISCELLANEOUS
'83 FRIGHTMARE

ANN MARTIN
ASSISTANT EDITOR
'84 2010*

BARBARA MARTIN
MISCELLANEOUS
'84 DREAMSCAPE

BILL MARTIN
ASSISTANT EDITOR
'79 BUCK ROGERS*

BILL MARTIN
1ST ASST. DIRECTOR
'79 GOLDENGIRL

DALE MARTIN
SPECIAL EFFECTS
'81 HAND, THE*
'84 TANK*
'84 RED DAWN*
SP. EFFECTS SUPERV.
'82 E.T. THE EXTRA-TERRESTRIAL
'83 SPACEHUNTER: ADVENTURES IN THE FORBIDDEN ZONE

DORIS MARTIN
SCRIPT SUPERVISOR
'81 SUPERMAN II*
'84 SUPERGIRL*

GARY MARTIN
PROPS
'80 MANIAC*

GEORGE MARTIN
ASSISTANT EDITOR
'81 HISTORY OF THE WORLD PART I*
'81 INCHON*
'83 SPACEHUNTER: ADVENTURES IN THE FORBIDDEN ZONE*

GEORGE MARTIN
MUSIC
'81 HONKY TONK FREEWAY*
MISCELLANEOUS
'84 GIVE MY REGARDS TO BROAD STREET

JACKIE MARTIN
MISCELLANEOUS
'80 BLACK MARBLE, THE
'83 CUJO

KIMBERLY MARTIN
PROD. OFFICE COORD.
'80 MOTHER'S DAY*

MARDIK MARTIN
SCREENPLAY
'80 RAGING BULL*

MICHAEL MARTIN
MUSIC
'79 ALAMBRISTA!

SAM MARTIN
CINEMATOGRAPHER
'81 BEYOND THE REEF

STEVE MARTIN
SCREENPLAY
'79 JERK, THE*
'82 DEAD MEN DON'T WEAR PLAID*
'83 MAN WITH TWO BRAINS, THE*

STEVE MARTIN
MISCELLANEOUS
'81 HONKY TONK FREEWAY

TERRI MARTIN
PROD. COORDINATOR
'82 SWORD AND THE SORCERER, THE*
'84 NOT FOR PUBLICATION*

TERRY MARTIN
STUNT COORDINATOR
'80 PROM NIGHT
'82 IF YOU COULD SEE WHAT I HEAR*

VICTORIA MARTIN
ASSISTANT EDITOR
'83 STAYING ALIVE*

JOHN MARTINELLI
EDITOR
'81 HARD COUNTRY

SERGIO MARTINELLI
MISCELLANEOUS
'79 HURRICANE

AL MARTINEZ
ASSISTANT EDITOR
'84 EL NORTE

FRANK MARTINEZ
2ND ASST. DIRECTOR
'80 BATTLE BEYOND THE STARS*

LEO MARTINEZ
MISCELLANEOUS
'81 ENTER THE NINJA

LOUISE MARTINEZ
COSTUMES
'83 LIANNA

RONALD MARTINEZ
1ST ASST. DIRECTOR
'80 LITTLE MISS MARKER

PASQUALE MARTINO
MISCELLANEOUS
'82 TEMPEST

PAUL MARTINO
ASSOCIATE PRODUCER
'80 ONE-TRICK PONY
CASTING
'79 RICH KIDS
'79 HEARTLAND
'80 ONE-TRICK PONY

JACK MARTY
ART DIRECTOR
'82 SILENT RAGE
'82 SPLIT IMAGE
PRODUCTION DESIGNER
'81 DEADLY BLESSING

IRA MARVIN
UNIT PROD. MANAGER
'83 TERMS OF ENDEARMENT*
MISCELLANEOUS
'84 SPLASH

MIKE MARVIN
SCREENPLAY
'82 SIX PACK*
'84 HOT DOG...THE MOVIE
CO-PRODUCER
'84 HOT DOG...THE MOVIE
MISCELLANEOUS
'84 HOT DOG...THE MOVIE

ANDREW MARX
PUBLICIST
'83 LONE WOLF MCQUADE
'84 TERMINATOR, THE
UNIT PUBLICIST
'84 UP THE CREEK

MICHELLE MARX
1ST ASST. DIRECTOR
'81 DOGS OF WAR, THE*

RICHARD MARX
ASSOCIATE EDITOR
'84 EVIL THAT MEN DO, THE
ASSISTANT EDITOR
'83 10 TO MIDNIGHT

RICK MARX
SCREENPLAY
'84 PREPPIES*

PASCAL MARZINE
ASSISTANT EDITOR
'84 CHEECH AND CHONG'S THE CORSICAN BROTHERS*

MASARONE
HAIR
'81 FAN, THE

MICHAEL MASCHIO
PRODUCTION MANAGER
'82 BORDER, THE*
'84 IMPULSE
LOCATIONS
'79 SCAVENGER HUNT
'81 THIEF*

TOM MASCHLER
ASSOCIATE PRODUCER
'81 FRENCH LIEUTENANT'S WOMAN,THE*

MARCELLO MASCIOCCHI
CINEMATOGRAPHER
'83 YOR

ARTHUR MASLANSKY
EXECUTIVE PRODUCER
'83 METALSTORM: THE DESTRUCTION OF JARED-SYN*

MICHAEL MASLANSKY
PUBLICIST
'83 FOOTLOOSE

PAUL MASLANSKY
PRODUCER
'79 CIRCLE OF IRON*
'82 LOVE CHILD
'84 POLICE ACADEMY
EXECUTIVE PRODUCER
'79 VILLAIN, THE
'79 HOT STUFF
ASSOCIATE PRODUCER
'79 SCAVENGER HUNT
CO-PRODUCER
'79 WHEN YOU COMIN' BACK, RED RYDER?

CANDIS MASON
SCRIPT SUPERVISOR
'84 FIRESTARTER

EISHA MASON
2ND ASST. DIRECTOR
'82 PENITENTIARY II*

FRANK MASON
MISCELLANEOUS
'83 ECHOES

JOHN MASON
SOUND
'83 EVIL DEAD, THE
'84 FINAL TERROR, THE

PETER MASON
MISCELLANEOUS
'81 VICTORY

VALORIE MASSALAS
CASTING
'83 TWO OF A KIND*

WALTER MASSI
UNIT MANAGER
'84 ONCE UPON A TIME IN AMERICA

NICK MASTANDREA
ASSISTANT EDITOR
'81 KNIGHTRIDERS*
KEY GRIP
'79 DAWN OF THE DEAD*
'81 KNIGHTRIDERS
'82 CREEPSHOW

ANTHONY MASTERS
PRODUCTION DESIGNER
'84 DUNE

BILL MASTERS
KEY GRIP
'80 MIDDLE AGE CRAZY*

GEORGE MASTERS
MAKEUP
'79 VILLAIN, THE*
'80 MIDDLE AGE CRAZY*
MISCELLANEOUS
'82 TOOTSIE

RUBEN MASTERS
ART DIRECTOR
'81 MS. 45

PETER MASTERSON
SCREENPLAY
'82 BEST LITTLE WHOREHOUSE IN TEXAS, THE*

ARMAND MASTROIANNI
DIRECTOR
'80 HE KNOWS YOU'RE ALONE

ANTONIO MATA
PROPS
'81 CAVEMAN
'82 MISSING*
'83 UNDER FIRE
'84 ROMANCING THE STONE*
'84 EVIL THAT MEN DO, THE

WENDE PHIFER MATE
ASSISTANT EDITOR
'84 BEAT STREET*

BARBARA MATERA
MISCELLANEOUS
'82 EVIL UNDER THE SUN

GEORGE MATHER
ASSOCIATE PRODUCER
'80 GALAXINA

LINDA MATHESON
COSTUMES
'80 MIDDLE AGE CRAZY*

RICHARD MATHESON
SCREENPLAY
'80 SOMEWHERE IN TIME
'83 JAWS 3-D*
'83 TWILIGHT ZONE, THE MOVIE*

MICHAEL MATHEWS
CINEMATOGRAPHER
'81 TUCK EVERLASTING
EDITOR
'81 TUCK EVERLASTING*

STEVE MATHIS
SCREENPLAY
'80 WITHOUT WARNING*

ANNE MATHISEN
PROD. SECRETARY
'82 BY DESIGN*

MELISSA MATHISON
SCREENPLAY
'79 BLACK STALLION, THE*
'82 E.T. THE EXTRA-TERRESTRIAL
'82 ESCAPE ARTIST, THE*
ASSOCIATE PRODUCER
'82 E.T. THE EXTRA-TERRESTRIAL

KAZU MATSUI
MISCELLANEOUS
'81 SOUTHERN COMFORT

MANIZIO MATTEI
LOCATIONS
'83 HANNA K*

ALEX MATTER
SCREENPLAY
'82 SIX PACK*

MICHAEL MATTESON
KEY GRIP
'83 TESTAMENT

CHARLES MATTHAU
ASSOCIATE PRODUCER
'81 BUDDY, BUDDY
'81 FIRST MONDAY IN OCTOBER
'82 I OUGHT TO BE IN PICTURES*

WALTER MATTHAU
EXECUTIVE PRODUCER
'80 LITTLE MISS MARKER

DON MATTHEWS
SOUND
'80 ON THE NICKEL
'81 CHEECH AND CHONG'S NICE DREAMS

MARILYN MATTHEWS
COSTUME SUPERVISOR
'80 CHEAPER TO KEEP HER

MITCH MATTHEWS
CASTING
'82 ROAD WARRIOR, THE
'83 MAN FROM SNOWY RIVER, THE

VERNLIN MATTHEWS
KEY GRIP
'80 CHEAPER TO KEEP HER

PETER MATTHIESSEN
MISCELLANEOUS
'83 NEVER CRY WOLF

DAVID MATTINGLY
MISCELLANEOUS
'80 MIDNIGHT MADNESS
'80 WATCHER IN THE WOODS, THE
'81 DEVIL AND MAX DEVLIN, THE

BRUCE MATTOX
SPECIAL EFFECTS
'82 CANNERY ROW*
'84 MIKE'S MURDER

DENVER MATTSON
STUNT COORDINATOR
'79 MAIN EVENT, THE

HERTA MATULA
HAIR
'79 FIFTH MUSKETEER, THE*

BETSY MATURO
ASSISTANT EDITOR
'80 TIMES SQUARE

MEL MATZ
UNIT PROD. MANAGER
'81 FOUR SEASONS, THE

PETER MATZ
MUSIC
'79 PRIZE FIGHTER, THE
'80 PRIVATE EYES, THE

PATRICIA MATZFORFF
PROD. COORDINATOR
'81 ABSENCE OF MALICE

CHRIS MAUDSON
2ND ASST. DIRECTOR
'82 STARSTRUCK*

DANNY MAUGHON
LOCATIONS
'84 MARVIN AND TIGE

RANDI MAURER
PROD. COORDINATOR
'80 ALLIGATOR

CYNTHIA MAURIZIO
ASSISTANT EDITOR
'79 WANDERERS, THE

RODGER MAUS
ART DIRECTOR
'80 HERBIE GOES BANANAS*
PRODUCTION DESIGNER
'79 10
'81 S.O.B.
'82 VICTOR/VICTORIA
'83 BUDDY SYSTEM, THE
'83 MAN WHO LOVED WOMEN, THE
'83 TRENCHCOAT
'84 MICKI AND MAUDE

MICHAEL MAVROMATIS
MISCELLANEOUS
'81 GALLIPOLI

JACK MAXSTED
ART DIRECTOR
'79 ARABIAN ADVENTURE

FRANCESCA MAXWELL
MAKEUP
'82 SEDUCTION, THE
'84 DREAMSCAPE

GARY MAXWELL
1ST ASST. DIRECTOR
'79 MOUNTAIN FAMILY ROBINSON

RICHARD MAXWELL
SCREENPLAY
'82 CHALLENGE, THE*

RONALD MAXWELL
DIRECTOR
'80 LITTLE DARLINGS
'81 NIGHT THE LIGHTS WENT OUT IN GEORGIA, THE

BILLY MAY
MUSIC
'81 PENNIES FROM HEAVEN*

BOB MAY
MISCELLANEOUS
'81 HARDLY WORKING

BRIAN MAY
MUSIC
'81 GALLIPOLI
'81 ROAD GAMES
'84 CLOAK AND DAGGER

MARLANA MAY
MAKEUP
'81 FUNHOUSE, THE
'81 HARDLY WORKING*

MIKE MAY
PROPS
'81 ESCAPE FROM NEW YORK

TOM MAY
KEY GRIP
'79 PROPHECY
'80 RESURRECTION
'80 CARNY
'80 UP THE ACADEMY
'81 S.O.B.
'81 SOUTHERN COMFORT
'81 BUDDY, BUDDY
'81 PURSUIT OF D.B. COOPER, THE*
'83 STAR CHAMBER
'83 STAYING ALIVE
'83 UNCOMMON VALOR
'84 2010

JO ANN MAY-PAVEY
PROD. OFFICE COORD.
'81 TRUE CONFESSIONS
PROD. COORDINATOR
'82 ROCKY III
'83 RIGHT STUFF, THE

RUSS MAYBERRY
DIRECTOR
'79 UNIDENTIFIED FLYING ODDBALL

PAUL MAYERSBERG
SCREENPLAY
'83 MERRY CHRISTMAS,MR. LAWRENCE*

LEE MAYES
LOCATIONS
'83 BALLAD OF GREGORIO CORTEZ,THE
'83 SILKWOOD
'84 PLACES IN THE HEART

WENDELL MAYES
SCREENPLAY
'79 LOVE AND BULLETS
'82 MONSIGNOR*

TONY MAYLAM
DIRECTOR
'81 BURNING, THE
'84 RIDDLE OF THE SANDS
SCREENPLAY
'84 RIDDLE OF THE SANDS*

LESLIE MAYLATH
ASSOCIATE PRODUCER
'81 HARDLY WORKING*

BERNARD MAZAUVIC
PRODUCTION MANAGER
'80 NIJINSKY*
'83 CURSE OF THE PINK PANTHER*
'83 TRAIL OF THE PINK PANTHER

CAROLINE MAZAUVIC
CASTING
'83 TRAIL OF THE PINK PANTHER*

ADEL MAZEN
ART DIRECTOR
'79 PENITENTIARY

FRANK MAZOLLA
EDITOR
'79 FISH THAT SAVED PITTSBURGH,THE*

IRWIN MAZUR
MUSIC SUPERVISOR
'84 HARDBODIES*

PAULA MAZUR
2ND ASST. DIRECTOR
'81 NEIGHBORS*

PAUL MAZURSKY
PRODUCER
'80 WILLIE & PHIL*
'82 TEMPEST
'84 MOSCOW ON THE HUDSON
DIRECTOR
'80 WILLIE & PHIL
'82 TEMPEST
'84 MOSCOW ON THE HUDSON
SCREENPLAY
'80 WILLIE & PHIL
'82 TEMPEST*
'84 MOSCOW ON THE HUDSON*

ROY MAZZA
PROD. COORDINATOR
'82 MAKING LOVE

RUBEN MAZZINI
ASSISTANT EDITOR
'80 LOVING COUPLES*

CARL MAZZOCONE
LOCATIONS
'83 JAWS 3-D

CARL MAZZOCONE
MISCELLANEOUS
'84 STARMAN

EUGENE MAZZOLA
1ST ASST. DIRECTOR
'83 BRAINSTORM*

JIM MAZZOLA
PROPS
'79 LAST EMBRACE
'80 STARDUST MEMORIES
'80 WINDOWS
'81 SO FINE
'81 ARTHUR
'81 TATTOO*
'82 MIDSUMMER NIGHT'S SEX COMEDY, A
'83 ZELIG
'84 BROADWAY DANNY ROSE

JOHN MAZZOLA
KEY GRIP
'80 TRIBUTE*

RICHARD MAZZOLA
ASSISTANT EDITOR
'79 OVER THE EDGE

RICHARD MAZZOLA
KEY GRIP
'84 FLASHPOINT

TOM MAZZOLA
ART DIRECTOR
'82 PENITENTIARY II

MICKEY MCAFEE
ASSISTANT EDITOR
'79 FIVE DAYS FROM HOME

DON MCALPINE
CINEMATOGRAPHER
'79 MY BRILLIANT CAREER
'81 EARTHLING, THE
'82 TEMPEST
'82 DON'T CRY, IT'S ONLY THUNDER
'83 BLUE SKIES AGAIN
'84 HARRY & SON
'84 MOSCOW ON THE HUDSON

NANCY MCARDLE
COSTUME SUPERVISOR
'80 MELVIN AND HOWARD*
'81 ENTITY, THE
'82 SECOND THOUGHTS*

DAVID MCAREE
LOCATIONS
'83 RUNNING BRAVE*

VIVIAN MCATEER
HAIR
'79 HARDCORE
'80 FATSO
'80 HEARTBEAT
'81 BLOW OUT*
'81 HISTORY OF THE WORLD PART I
'81 TRUE CONFESSIONS*
'82 ROCKY III
'83 BREATHLESS*
'84 HARD TO HOLD
'84 JOHNNY DANGEROUSLY*
'84 2010

TIM MCAVOY
ASSISTANT EDITOR
'79 JUST YOU AND ME KID
'80 SMALL CIRCLE OF FRIENDS, A
'80 IT'S MY TURN*

CHRIS MCBEE
HAIR
'80 NUDE BOMB, THE

CAROL MCBRIDE
ASSISTANT EDITOR
'83 VIDEODROME*

IAN MCBRIDE
ASSISTANT EDITOR
'80 PROM NIGHT*

JIM MCBRIDE
DIRECTOR
'83 BREATHLESS
SCREENPLAY
'83 BREATHLESS*

JOSEPH MCBRIDE
SCREENPLAY
'79 ROCK 'N ROLL HIGH SCHOOL*

BRUCE MCBROOM
STILLS
'79 10
'80 FIENDISH PLOT OF DR. FU MANCHU, THE
'81 S.O.B.*
'82 CANNERY ROW
'82 E.T. THE EXTRA-TERRESTRIAL
'82 48 HOURS
'82 POLTERGEIST
'83 UNDER FIRE
'84 ADVENTURES OF BUCKAROO BANZAI ACROSS THE 8TH DIMENSION, THE
'84 HARD TO HOLD
'84 RUNAWAY
'84 2010

JIM MCCABE
LOCATIONS
'82 FORCED VENGEANCE
'82 MY FAVORITE YEAR*
'84 IMPULSE

STEPHEN MCCABE
ART DIRECTOR
'81 MY DINNER WITH ANDRE

ROBERT MCCALL
ART DIRECTOR
'79 BLACK HOLE, THE*

RICHARD MCCALLUM
EXECUTIVE PRODUCER
'81 PENNIES FROM HEAVEN

RICK MCCALLUM
ASSOCIATE PRODUCER
'82 I OUGHT TO BE IN PICTURES*

CAPT. BRENDAN MCCANN
MISCELLANEOUS
'80 OUTSIDER, THE

HANK MCCANN
CASTING
'79 WINTER KILLS*
'81 PENNIES FROM HEAVEN*
'83 MAN WOMAN AND CHILD
'83 MAX DUGAN RETURNS
'84 HOT DOG...THE MOVIE

JANE MCCANN
MISCELLANEOUS
'83 LOSIN' IT

MICKEY MCCARDLE
UNIT PROD. MANAGER
'80 STIR CRAZY
'82 HANKY PANKY*
1ST ASST. DIRECTOR
'79 10
'83 MAN WHO LOVED WOMEN, THE
'84 MICKI AND MAUDE

BOB MCCARRON
MAKEUP
'83 NATE & HAYES
MISCELLANEOUS
'82 ROAD WARRIOR, THE
'83 NATE & HAYES
'83 YEAR OF LIVING DANGEROUSLY, THE

ROBERT MCCART
2ND ASST. DIRECTOR
'79 BLACK STALLION, THE*
'81 ATLANTIC CITY*

JO MCCARTHY
HAIR
'80 CHEAPER TO KEEP HER
'80 FORMULA, THE
'82 SIX WEEKS*
'83 PSYCHO II
'84 BEST DEFENSE*

KYLE MCCARTHY
LOCATIONS
'81 ENDLESS LOVE

MARY-JANE MCCARTHY
COSTUMES
'82 PARADISE*

PENNY MCCARTHY
PROD. OFFICE COORD.
'82 ESCAPE ARTIST, THE*
PROD. COORDINATOR
'84 MIKE'S MURDER

PETER MCCARTHY
PRODUCER
'84 REPO MAN*

PAUL MCCARTNEY
SCREENPLAY
'84 GIVE MY REGARDS TO BROAD STREET
MUSIC
'84 GIVE MY REGARDS TO BROAD STREET

BRIGITTE MCCAUGHRY
MAKEUP
'81 SCANNERS

CONNIE MCCAULEY
ASSOCIATE PRODUCER
'84 MASS APPEAL*

DANIEL MCCAULEY
UNIT PROD. MANAGER
'80 HERBIE GOES BANANAS
'81 MODERN ROMANCE*
1ST ASST. DIRECTOR
'79 METEOR
'79 SCAVENGER HUNT*
'79 STAR TREK-THE MOTION PICTURE
'80 STIR CRAZY
'81 ZORRO, THE GAY BLADE*
'82 JINXED
'83 BLUE THUNDER*
'84 UP THE CREEK

KIRBY MCCAULEY
EXECUTIVE PRODUCER
'83 CHRISTINE*

MATTHEW MCCAULEY
MUSIC
'80 MIDDLE AGE CRAZY

TIM MCCAULEY
MUSIC
'83 SCREWBALLS

RON MCCAUSLAND
KEY GRIP
'80 ALLIGATOR
'82 PARASITE
'83 CHAINED HEAT
'83 METALSTORM: THE DESTRUCTION OF JARED-SYN
'83 MY TUTOR
'84 PHILADELPHIA EXPERIMENT, THE

BOOKER MCCLAY
PUBLICIST
'83 STING II, THE
'84 AGAINST ALL ODDS

LISA MCCLELLAND
PROD. COORDINATOR
'84 MRS. SOFFEL*

KEVIN MCCLORY
EXECUTIVE PRODUCER
'83 NEVER SAY NEVER AGAIN

CARLA MCCLOSKEY
2ND ASST. DIRECTOR
'79 FORCE OF ONE, A*

LARRY MCCONKEY
MISCELLANEOUS
'84 BIRDY

HILTON MCCONNICO
PRODUCTION DESIGNER
'84 UNTIL SEPTEMBER

PAT MCCORKLE
CASTING
'83 ALL THE RIGHT MOVES*
'84 FALLING IN LOVE*
'84 SPLASH*

ROBERT MCCORMACK
MISCELLANEOUS
'79 MUPPET MOVIE, THE

KEVIN MCCORMICK
EXECUTIVE PRODUCER
'80 TIMES SQUARE*
'81 FAN, THE

PAT MCCORMICK
SCREENPLAY
'81 UNDER THE RAINBOW*

PATRICK MCCORMICK
PRODUCTION MANAGER
'84 MOSCOW ON THE HUDSON
UNIT PROD. MANAGER
'84 GHOSTBUSTERS
'84 FIRSTBORN

TIMAREE MCCORMICK
COSTUMES
'81 GALAXY OF TERROR

TERRENCE MCCORRY
ART DIRECTOR
'84 ALPHABET CITY*

JIM MCCOY
MAKEUP
'80 CAN'T STOP THE MUSIC*
'80 HOPSCOTCH*
'81 STRIPES*
'82 STAR TREK II THE WRATH OF KHAN*
'84 STAR TREK III: THE SEARCH FOR SPOCK*

MICHAEL MCCRACKEN
MAKEUP
'83 PSYCHO II*
MISCELLANEOUS
'81 HEARTBEEPS
'83 TWILIGHT ZONE, THE MOVIE

MICHAEL JOHN MCCRACKEN
MISCELLANEOUS
'84 ICE PIRATES, THE

MICHAEL SHAWN MCCRACKEN
MISCELLANEOUS
'84 ICE PIRATES, THE

JOHN MCCRAW
STILLS
'82 LIAR'S MOON*

TOM MCCRORY
1ST ASST. DIRECTOR
'79 BLACK HOLE, THE
'81 ...ALL THE MARBLES*

CAROL MCCULLOUGH
STILLS
'79 WHEN A STRANGER CALLS
'81 POSTMAN ALWAYS RINGS TWICE, THE
'82 OFFICER AND A GENTLEMAN, AN
'83 BREATHLESS
'84 IRRECONCILABLE DIFFERENCES

J.J. MCCULLOUGH
MISCELLANEOUS
'83 NEVER CRY WOLF

CASS MCCUNE
PROD. COORDINATOR
'79 AVALANCHE EXPRESS

GRANT MCCUNE
MISCELLANEOUS
'79 STAR TREK-THE MOTION PICTURE
'82 FIREFOX

PATT MCCURDY
PROD. COORDINATOR
'81 PURSUIT OF D.B. COOPER, THE*
'83 UNDER FIRE*

DON MCCUTCHEON
2ND ASST. DIRECTOR
'79 RUNNING*
LOCATIONS
'80 HAPPY BIRTHDAY, GEMINI

BLANCHE MCDERMAID
SCRIPT SUPERVISOR
'79 BLACK STALLION, THE
'82 PORKY'S
'83 STRANGE INVADERS*
'83 CHRISTMAS STORY, A

BEVERLY MCDERMOTT
CASTING
'81 HARDLY WORKING
'84 WHERE THE BOYS ARE*

DEBRA MCDERMOTT
ASSOCIATE EDITOR
'84 AMADEUS

MARGARITA MCDERMOTT
PROD. SECRETARY
'79 JAGUAR LIVES

PAT MCDERMOTT
HAIR
'81 RAIDERS OF THE LOST ARK*
'81 SUPERMAN II*
'83 RETURN OF THE JEDI
'83 BRITANNIA HOSPITAL
'83 EDUCATING RITA
'84 SUPERGIRL

BOB MCDONALD
SPECIAL EFFECTS
'80 FOOLIN AROUND

DOUG MCDONALD
PROPS
'83 CHAINED HEAT

HOLLY MCDONALD
PROPS
'84 FIRESTARTER*

JOCELYN MCDONALD
HAIR
'80 KIDNAPPING OF THE PRESIDENT, THE

MAXIE MCDONALD
PROPS
'84 ANOTHER COUNTRY

MORI MCDONALD
SCRIPT SUPERVISOR
'83 FRIGHTMARE

PRISCILLA MCDONALD
PUBLICIST
'82 LAST AMERICAN VIRGIN, THE
'84 LOVE STREAMS

ANNA MCDONNELL
MISCELLANEOUS
'84 RED DAWN

JEANNE MCDONNELL
ART DIRECTOR
'83 LIANNA

SCOTT MCDONOUGH
PUBLICIST
'79 CHAPTER TWO
'82 I, THE JURY

AMY MCELHENNEY
PROD. SECRETARY
'80 BLUES BROTHERS
'81 ALL NIGHT LONG
'83 STING II, THE
'83 NATIONAL LAMPOON'S VACATION

HAL MCELROY
PRODUCER
'79 PICNIC AT HANGING ROCK*

JAMES MCELROY
PRODUCER
'79 PICNIC AT HANGING ROCK*
'83 YEAR OF LIVING DANGEROUSLY, THE

WILLIAM MCEUEN
PRODUCER
'79 JERK, THE*
'82 DEAD MEN DON'T WEAR PLAID*
'83 MAN WITH TWO BRAINS, THE*
EXECUTIVE PRODUCER
'84 LONELY GUY, THE

STEPHEN MCEVEETY
2ND ASST. DIRECTOR
'80 HERBIE GOES BANANAS*
'81 DEVIL AND MAX DEVLIN, THE*
'81 FORCE FIVE
'81 ZORRO, THE GAY BLADE*

VINCENT MCEVEETY
DIRECTOR
'79 APPLE DUMPLING GANG RIDES AGAIN, THE
'80 HERBIE GOES BANANAS
'81 AMY

CARLOS MCEVILLY
MISCELLANEOUS
'83 TIMERIDER

JACKIE MCEVOY
PROD. OFFICE COORD.
'84 BEAT STREET*

ROBERT MCEWEN
UNIT PUBLICIST
'80 KIDNAPPING OF THE PRESIDENT,THE

ANNE MCFADYEN
HAIR
'81 EXCALIBUR
'84 COMFORT AND JOY

GAVIN MCFADYEN
ASSOCIATE PRODUCER
'83 KEEP, THE*

MARIE MCFERRAN
PROD. SECRETARY
'80 OUTSIDER, THE*

BRIAN MCFRANKISH
1ST ASST. DIRECTOR
'83 BRAINSTORM*

MARK MCGANN
2ND ASST. DIRECTOR
'81 NEIGHBORS*
'82 AUTHOR, AUTHOR
'82 DEATHTRAP
'82 YES, GIORGIO*
'84 FLAMINGO KID, THE*

DAVID MCGIFFERT
1ST ASST. DIRECTOR
'79 REAL LIFE
'80 HIDE IN PLAIN SIGHT
'80 HONEYSUCKLE ROSE
'80 IT'S MY TURN
'81 ABSENCE OF MALICE
'82 OFFICER AND A GENTLEMAN, AN
'82 TOOTSIE
'83 BRAINSTORM*
'84 HARRY & SON
'84 SONGWRITER

JOSEPH MCGILL
HAIR
'79 PRIZE FIGHTER, THE*

GEORGE MCGINNIS
MISCELLANEOUS
'79 BLACK HOLE, THE

MARY MCGLONE
ASSISTANT EDITOR
'80 BORDERLINE
'83 GORKY PARK
'83 INDEPENDENCE DAY*

NANCY MCGOVERN
STILLS
'82 HOME WORK

ANN MCGOWAN
MAKEUP
'79 MOUNTAIN FAMILY ROBINSON

DONISA MCGOWAN
HAIR
'81 FUNHOUSE, THE
'81 HARDLY WORKING*

LINDA MCGOWAN
LOCATIONS
'79 CHAMP, THE

MICHAEL MCGOWAN
MISCELLANEOUS
'81 NIGHT THE LIGHTS WENT OUT IN GEORGIA, THE

JAMES MCGRATH
KEY GRIP
'81 NEIGHBORS
'81 THEY ALL LAUGHED

MICHAEL MCGRATH
MISCELLANEOUS
'84 RACING WITH THE MOON

JOHN MCGRAW
PRODUCTION DESIGNER
'82 MONTY PYTHON LIVE AT THE HOLLYWOOD BOWL*

JOHN MCGREEVEY
SCREENPLAY
'82 NIGHT CROSSING

MIKE MCGREEVY
KEY GRIP
'80 FATSO

GAIL MCGREGOR
PUBLICIST
'79 FAST COMPANY

THOMAS MCGUANE
SCREENPLAY
'80 TOM HORN*

DAVID MCHUGH
MUSIC
'81 NOBODY'S PERFEKT
'84 MOSCOW ON THE HUDSON

NAISH MCHUGH
MISCELLANEOUS
'84 MRS. SOFFEL

PETER MCINTOSH
PRODUCTION MANAGER
'83 EASY MONEY*
'83 KISS ME GOODBYE
'84 BEAT STREET
LOCATIONS
'79 VOICES
'81 RICH AND FAMOUS*

RAY MCINTYER
MISCELLANEOUS
'83 MAUSOLEUM

ALASTAIR MCINTYRE
EDITOR
'80 TESS*

CRAIG MCKAY
EDITOR
'80 MELVIN AND HOWARD
'81 REDS*
'84 SWING SHIFT

DON MCKAYLE
CHOREOGRAPHER
'80 JAZZ SINGER, THE

MICHAEL MCKEAN
SCREENPLAY
'84 THIS IS SPINAL TAP*
MUSIC
'84 THIS IS SPINAL TAP*

DOW MCKEEVER
LOCATIONS
'82 STILL OF THE NIGHT*

BERNARD MCKENNA
SCREENPLAY
'83 YELLOWBEARD*

DOUGLAS MCKENNA
ASSOCIATE PRODUCER
'83 LIANNA*

SHERRY MCKENNA
MISCELLANEOUS
'84 LAST STARFIGHTER, THE

BOB MCKENZIE
KEY GRIP
'81 ON THE RIGHT TRACK

LES MCKENZIE
SOUND
'79 TIM

DOUGLAS MCKEOWN
DIRECTOR
'83 RETURN OF THE ALIENS: THE DEADLY SPAWN
SCREENPLAY
'83 RETURN OF THE ALIENS: THE DEADLY SPAWN

PATRICIA MCKIERNAN
COSTUMES
'81 DEADLY BLESSING

TOM MCKINLEY
COSTUMES
'81 FAN, THE*

GAVIN MCKINNEY
MISCELLANEOUS
'84 SPLASH

JOE MCKINNEY
MAKEUP
'79 ESCAPE FROM ALCATRAZ
'80 ANY WHICH WAY YOU CAN

W.R. MCKINNEY
SCREENPLAY
'84 TEACHERS

LYN MCKISSICK
COSTUMES
'82 LIAR'S MOON*
SCRIPT SUPERVISOR
'81 STUDENT BODIES
'82 ANDROID
'83 CHAINED HEAT
'83 SAVANNAH SMILES
'84 CRIMES OF PASSION*
'84 PURPLE RAIN

ANDREW MCLAGLEN
DIRECTOR
'80 FFOLKES
'81 SEA WOLVES, THE

WOODROW MCLAIN
MISCELLANEOUS
'81 INCHON

GARY MCLARTY
STUNT COORDINATOR
'80 BLUES BROTHERS
'80 COAST TO COAST*
'83 TWILIGHT ZONE, THE MOVIE*
'84 BEVERLY HILLS COP

BILL MCLAUGHLIN
PROPS
'84 UP THE CREEK

CHRIS MCLAUGHLIN
SOUND
'79 ROSE, THE*
'79 REMEMBER MY NAME*
'80 SMALL CIRCLE OF FRIENDS, A*
'80 LONG RIDERS, THE*
'81 TRUE CONFESSIONS*
'82 ESCAPE ARTIST, THE*
'84 NATURAL, THE*

GREGG MCLAUGHLIN
EDITOR
'79 BLACK HOLE, THE
'81 AMY

IRVINE MCLAUGHLIN
KEY GRIP
'82 DON'T CRY, IT'S ONLY THUNDER

WAYNE MCLAUGHLIN
PROPS
'82 BY DESIGN
'83 NEVER CRY WOLF*

MICHAEL MCLAVERTY
EDITOR
'80 KIDNAPPING OF THE PRESIDENT, THE

BOB MCLEAN
KEY GRIP
'80 ORDINARY PEOPLE*

DWAYNE MCLEAN
STUNT COORDINATOR
'81 MY BLOODY VALENTINE
'82 PORKY'S

MICHAEL MCLEAN
CASTING
'80 BALTIMORE BULLET, THE
'80 FLASH GORDON*
'81 BEYOND THE REEF
'83 OSTERMAN WEEKEND, THE
'83 TOUGH ENOUGH*
'83 YELLOWBEARD

NICK MCLEAN
CINEMATOGRAPHER
'83 STAYING ALIVE
'83 STROKER ACE
'84 CITY HEAT
'84 CANNONBALL RUN II

GORDON MCLENDON
EXECUTIVE PRODUCER
'81 VICTORY

PETER MCLENNAN
MISCELLANEOUS
'82 MOTHER LODE

SCOTT MCLENNAN
EDITOR
'81 MAN WHO SAW TOMORROW, THE*

ANNE MCLEOD
SCRIPT SUPERVISOR
'81 ROAD GAMES

DAVID MCLEOD
ASSOCIATE PRODUCER
'81 REDS
1ST ASST. DIRECTOR
'83 STRANGE BREW*
2ND ASST. DIRECTOR
'83 STRANGE INVADERS

DOUG MCLEOD
UNIT MANAGER
'83 SUPERMAN III*

JOHN MCLEOD
MUSIC
'83 ANOTHER TIME, ANOTHER PLACE

MARY MCLEOD
COSTUMES
'82 PORKY'S*
'83 CHRISTMAS STORY, A
'83 PORKY'S II THE NEXT DAY

NED MCLEOD
LOCATIONS
'81 ABSENCE OF MALICE

SANDY MCLEOD
SCRIPT SUPERVISOR
'79 RICH KIDS
'79 SEDUCTION OF JOE TYNAN, THE
'79 LAST EMBRACE
'80 TIMES SQUARE

TOMMY MCLOUGHLIN
MISCELLANEOUS
'80 DIVINE MADNESS

KATE MCMAHON
PROD. COORDINATOR
'84 HARDBODIES*

MARILYN MCMAHON
ASSISTANT EDITOR
'81 BLOOD BEACH*

PATRICK MCMAHON
EDITOR
'83 STRANGE BREW

W. THOMAS MCMAHON
EXECUTIVE PRODUCER
'83 HOUSE ON SORORITY ROW*

JEFF MCMANUS
PROPS
'83 LOCAL HERO*

DAVID MCMILLAN
SOUND
'79 MORE AMERICAN GRAFFITTI
'80 DIE LAUGHING
'80 TELL ME A RIDDLE
'82 SHOOT THE MOON
'84 INDIANA JONES AND THE TEMPLE OF DOOM*

IAN MCMILLAN
CINEMATOGRAPHER
'84 GIVE MY REGARDS TO BROAD STREET

LAIRD MCMURRAY
PROPS
'84 JUST THE WAY YOU ARE*

ERNEST MCNABB
MISCELLANEOUS
'83 SPACEHUNTER: ADVENTURES IN THE FORBIDDEN ZONE

LOLA "SKIP" MCNALLEY
HAIR
'79 BEYOND THE POSEIDON ADVENTURE*
'79 NORMA RAE
'80 THOSE LIPS, THOSE EYES
'81 CUTTER'S WAY
'82 CANNERY ROW
'82 E.T. THE EXTRA-TERRESTRIAL
'82 ESCAPE ARTIST, THE
'82 CHILLY SCENES OF WINTER
'84 ICE PIRATES, THE*
'84 RED DAWN

TIM MCNALLY
MAKEUP
'79 BOULEVARD NIGHTS*
'83 RUMBLEFISH*

JACKIE MCNAMARA
CASTING
'82 BRAINWAVES*
'83 SMOKEY AND THE BANDIT III
'83 PSYCHO II

JAMES MCNAMARA
PRODUCER
'81 HARDLY WORKING*

GARY MCNETT
LOCATIONS
'82 LAST AMERICAN VIRGIN, THE

RALPH MCQUARRIE
MISCELLANEOUS
'80 EMPIRE STRIKES BACK, THE
'82 E.T. THE EXTRA-TERRESTRIAL

STEVE MCQUEEN
EXECUTIVE PRODUCER
'80 TOM HORN

EDWARD MCQUEEN-MASON
EDITOR
'81 ROAD GAMES

PETER MCQUILLAN
ASSOCIATE PRODUCER
'83 SCREWBALLS*

ROBERT MCRAE
KEY GRIP
'84 KILLING FIELDS, THE

VIVIAN MCRAE
CASTING
'79 BOULEVARD NIGHTS

GREIG MCRITCHIE
ASSISTANT EDITOR
'80 USED CARS
'81 MOMMIE DEAREST
'82 MONSIGNOR*

ROSEMARIE MCSHERRY
ART DIRECTOR
'83 OF UNKNOWN ORIGIN

DENNIS MCTAGGERT
ASSISTANT EDITOR
'83 BRITANNIA HOSPITAL*
'83 LORDS OF DISCIPLINE, THE
'84 RAZOR'S EDGE, THE

RICHARD MCWHORTER
ASSOCIATE PRODUCER
'79 BLOODLINE
'82 DEAD MEN DON'T WEAR PLAID
'82 LOVE AND MONEY
'84 TANK
PRODUCTION MANAGER
'83 TABLE FOR FIVE
UNIT PROD. MANAGER
'82 DEAD MEN DON'T WEAR PLAID
'82 LOVE AND MONEY
'84 TANK

DEBBIE MCWILLIAMS
CASTING
'81 SHOCK TREATMENT*
'81 SUPERMAN II*
'81 AMERICAN WEREWOLF
IN LONDON, AN*
'81 DRAGONSLAYER*
'81 FOR YOUR EYES ONLY*
'82 MOONLIGHTING
'83 SUPERMAN III*
'83 OCTOPUSSY*
'83 PIRATES OF PENZANCE, THE*
'84 BOUNTY, THE
'84 SCANDALOUS
'84 FINDERS KEEPERS*

JOY MCWILLIAMS
MISCELLANEOUS
'82 SECOND THOUGHTS

SYD MEAD
MISCELLANEOUS
'82 BLADERUNNER
'82 TRON
'84 2010

JANE MEADE
MAKEUP
'83 SCREWBALLS*

PHILIP MEADOR
MISCELLANEOUS
'84 COUNTRY
'84 SPLASH

JOE MEALY
STILLS
'83 GOIN' ALL THE WAY

PIER ANTONIO MECACCI
MAKEUP
'81 SUNDAY LOVERS*
'83 TRENCHCOAT*

PATRICK MECHIER
LOCATIONS
'80 PRIVATE BENJAMIN*

PETER MEDAK
DIRECTOR
'80 CHANGELING, THE
'81 ZORRO, THE GAY BLADE

DEREK MEDDINGS
SPECIAL EFFECTS
'81 FOR YOUR EYES ONLY
MISCELLANEOUS
'79 MOONRAKER
'81 SUPERMAN II
'83 KRULL
'84 SUPERGIRL

JIMMY MEDEARIS
MISCELLANEOUS
'80 STIR CRAZY
'80 LONG RIDERS, THE
'80 MOUNTAIN MEN, THE
'81 CUTTER'S WAY
'82 HONKYTONK MAN

RONALD MEDICO
EDITOR
'80 ALLIGATOR*

ENRICO MEDIOLI
SCREENPLAY
'84 ONCE UPON A TIME IN AMERICA*

JOE MEDJUCK
ASSOCIATE PRODUCER
'81 STRIPES
'84 GHOSTBUSTERS*

BIG BOY MEDLIN
SCREENPLAY
'80 ROADIE*

MARK MEDOFF
SCREENPLAY
'79 WHEN YOU COMIN' BACK,
RED RYDER?

VINCENZO MEDUSA
ART DIRECTOR
'83 PIRANHA II: THE SPAWNING*

LISA MEECHAN
PROD. SECRETARY
'84 FLASHPOINT

MIKE MEEHAN
LOCATIONS
'80 COAST TO COAST
'82 GREASE 2
'84 HARD TO HOLD

THOMAS MEEHAN
SCREENPLAY
'83 TO BE OR NOT TO BE*

DAVID MEEKS
MISCELLANEOUS
'83 REUBEN, REUBEN

PHIL MEHEUX
CINEMATOGRAPHER
'81 FINAL CONFLICT, THE*
'83 BEYOND THE LIMIT
'83 FINAL OPTION, THE

JOHN MEIER
STUNT COORDINATOR
'83 PRIVATE SCHOOL

ROLF MEIER
UNIT MANAGER
'79 MAGICIAN OF LUBLIN, THE

JOHN MEIGHEN
ART DIRECTOR
'84 HOTEL NEW HAMPSHIRE, THE

CAROL MEIKLE
HAIR
'79 JUST YOU AND ME KID
'80 DIVINE MADNESS*
'81 MODERN ROMANCE
'82 I OUGHT TO BE IN PICTURES*
'82 PARTNERS

GINETTE MEJINSKY
UNIT MANAGER
'80 OUTSIDER, THE

RICHARD MELECKIAN
MISCELLANEOUS
'84 RIVER, THE

GIL MELLE
MUSIC
'80 BORDERLINE
'81 BLOOD BEACH
'81 LAST CHASE, THE

DANIEL MELNICK
PRODUCER
'80 FIRST FAMILY
'82 MAKING LOVE*
EXECUTIVE PRODUCER
'79 ALL THAT JAZZ
'80 ALTERED STATES
'83 FOOTLOOSE
'84 UNFAITHFULLY YOURS

GAIL MELNICK
CASTING
'80 AMERICAN SUCCESS COMPANY,THE*
'80 STEEL
'81 NOBODY'S PERFEKT

MARK MELNICK
EDITOR
'83 UNCOMMON VALOR
ASSISTANT EDITOR
'81 PURSUIT OF D.B. COOPER, THE*
MISCELLANEOUS
'83 STAYING ALIVE

BENJAMIN MELNIKER
PRODUCER
'82 SWAMP THING*

BARRIE MELROSE
PRODUCTION MANAGER
'79 CUBA*
'84 KILLING FIELDS, THE*
LOCATIONS
'79 UNIDENTIFIED FLYING ODDBALL
MISCELLANEOUS
'82 EVIL UNDER THE SUN
'83 YENTL
'84 PASSAGE TO INDIA, A

MAXWELL MELTZER
MISCELLANEOUS
'83 CHAINED HEAT

MICHAEL MELTZER
PRODUCER
'84 UP THE CREEK

MICHAEL MELVION
MUSIC
'81 KING OF THE MOUNTAIN

DANI BEN MENACHEM
UNIT MANAGER
'84 SHEENA

MARTIN MENARD
HAIR
'83 OF UNKNOWN ORIGIN*

ROBERT MENDELSOHN
PRODUCTION MANAGER
'79 ONION FIELD, THE

GEORGE MENDELUK
PRODUCER
'80 KIDNAPPING OF THE PRESIDENT, THE*
DIRECTOR
'80 KIDNAPPING OF THE PRESIDENT, THE

JOY MENDENHALL
PROD. SECRETARY
'84 SILENT NIGHT, DEADLY NIGHT

MAX MENDES
LOCATIONS
'80 BORDERLINE
'83 HEART LIKE A WHEEL*

ANTHONY MENDLESON
COSTUMES
'79 GREAT TRAIN ROBBERY, THE
'80 ROUGH CUT*
'81 DRAGONSLAYER
'83 KRULL
'83 KEEP, THE

HECTOR MENDOZA
STILLS
'83 FRIGHTMARE*

JAIME MENDOZA-NAVA
MUSIC
'83 MAUSOLEUM

CHRIS MENGES
CINEMATOGRAPHER
'83 LOCAL HERO
'84 COMFORT AND JOY
'84 KILLING FIELDS, THE
MISCELLANEOUS
'80 EMPIRE STRIKES BACK, THE

MARCELLO MENICONI
MAKEUP
'84 MISUNDERSTOOD

FRANK MENKE
SCREENPLAY
'84 MARVIN AND TIGE*

RAYMOND MENMUIR
ASSOCIATE PRODUCER
'83 FINAL OPTION, THE

GAIL MILLER MENSCHEL
SCRIPT SUPERVISOR
'81 DOZENS, THE

DAVID MENTEER
1ST ASST. DIRECTOR
'79 PRISONER OF ZENDA, THE*

RUSSELL MENZER
ART DIRECTOR
'80 WHEN TIME RAN OUT

ERIC MEOLA
STILLS
'83 ALL THE RIGHT MOVES*

VIVIEN MEPHAN
MAKEUP
'83 MAN FROM SNOWY RIVER, THE

CAROL MERCATORIS
HAIR
'80 CAN'T STOP THE MUSIC*

GLENN MERCER
MUSIC
'83 SMITHEREENS*

RAY MERCER JR.
PROPS
'79 BEING THERE
'79 PROPHECY
'81 POSTMAN ALWAYS RINGS TWICE, THE
'82 FRANCES
'84 SOLDIER'S STORY, A

RAY MERCER
PROPS
'84 SWING SHIFT

SAM MERCER
LOCATIONS
'81 STRIPES*
'82 ESCAPE ARTIST, THE*
'82 SECOND THOUGHTS
'83 NATIONAL LAMPOON'S VACATION*
'84 PROTOCOL*
'84 SWING SHIFT
'84 OH GOD, YOU DEVIL

ISMAIL MERCHANT
PRODUCER
'79 EUROPEANS, THE
'80 QUARTET
'83 HEAT AND DUST
'84 BOSTONIANS, THE

JOE MERCURIO
SPECIAL EFFECTS
'79 NORTH DALLAS FORTY
'80 SERIAL
'81 FIRST MONDAY IN OCTOBER
'81 MOMMIE DEAREST
'82 48 HOURS
'82 OFFICER AND A GENTLEMAN, AN
'84 AGAINST ALL ODDS

BILL MEREDITH
SOUND
'81 NESTING, THE

LEWIS MERESTEIN
MUSIC SUPERVISOR
'82 VICE SQUAD*

JOAN MERLO
PROD. OFFICE COORD.
'83 BAD BOYS

BARRY MERRELLS
PROPS
'80 TOUCHED BY LOVE

DAVID MERRICK
PRODUCER
'80 ROUGH CUT

DOUGLAS MERRIFIELD
MISCELLANEOUS
'84 THIEF OF HEARTS

DON MERRITT
SOUND
'79 PERFECT COUPLE, A*
'80 HEALTH*

JOHN MERRITT
EDITOR
'81 EXCALIBUR

MARION MERTES
SCRIPT SUPERVISOR
'83 LONELY LADY, THE

MICHAEL MERTINEIT
2ND ASST. DIRECTOR
'80 LADY VANISHES, THE

JANET MERWIN
SCRIPT SUPERVISOR
'79 HEARTLAND
'83 EDDIE AND THE CRUISERS
'83 JAWS 3-D

WILLIAM MESHOVER
ASSISTANT EDITOR
'79 GOING IN STYLE*
'79 TIME AFTER TIME*
'80 SMOKEY AND THE BANDIT II*
'81 CANNONBALL RUN, THE*
'83 INDEPENDENCE DAY*
'83 TWILIGHT ZONE, THE MOVIE*
'84 ROMANCING THE STONE*

PHILIP FRANK MESSINA
SCREENPLAY
'83 BRAINSTORM*

ROBERTO MESSINA
STUNT COORDINATOR
'80 POPEYE

CARL MESTERTON
1ST ASST. DIRECTOR
'81 REDS*

EVA MESZAROS
PRODUCTION MANAGER
'80 NIJINSKY*
'81 SPHINX*

BURT METCALF
MISCELLANEOUS
'79 MOUNTAIN FAMILY ROBINSON

MARK METCALF
PRODUCER
'82 CHILLY SCENES OF WINTER*

KEN METCALFE
LOCATIONS
'81 ENTER THE NINJA

JULIUS METOYER JR.
MISCELLANEOUS
'82 PENITENTIARY II

HANS METZ
SPECIAL EFFECTS
'82 THINGS ARE TOUGH ALL OVER*
MISCELLANEOUS
'84 SPLASH

REXFORD METZ
CINEMATOGRAPHER
'80 SERIAL
'82 FORCED VENGEANCE
MISCELLANEOUS
'80 RAISE THE TITANIC
'82 SIX PACK
'82 ANNIE
'82 NIGHT CROSSING
'83 D.C. CAB
'83 DOCTOR DETROIT
'83 TABLE FOR FIVE

ALAN METZGER
CINEMATOGRAPHER
'79 ON THE YARD
'79 VOICES
'80 GILDA LIVE*

BONNIE METZGER
UNIT PUBLICIST
'84 PURPLE RAIN

DOUG METZGER
2ND ASST. DIRECTOR
'83 NIGHTMARES
'83 TRENCHCOAT*
'84 SPLASH*

JOAN METZGER
ASSISTANT EDITOR
'80 ONE-TRICK PONY*

SUSAN BROCKMAN METZGER
UNIT PUBLICIST
'84 GARBO TALKS

CHARLENE MEYER
PROD. SECRETARY
'80 HANGAR 18

DIETER MEYER
PRODUCTION MANAGER
'79 FEDORA*
'80 FORMULA, THE*
'82 FIREFOX
'82 NIGHT CROSSING
MISCELLANEOUS
'84 LITTLE DRUMMER GIRL, THE

JOHN MEYER
SCREENPLAY
'84 NOT FOR PUBLICATION*

MUFFIE MEYER
EDITOR
'80 GILDA LIVE*

NANCY MEYER
PROD. COORDINATOR
'80 RAISE THE TITANIC

NICHOLAS MEYER
DIRECTOR
'79 TIME AFTER TIME
'82 STAR TREK II
THE WRATH OF KHAN
SCREENPLAY
'79 TIME AFTER TIME

RICHARD MEYER
EDITOR
'82 SILENT RAGE
'82 NATIONAL LAMPOON'S
CLASS REUNION*
ASSISTANT EDITOR
'84 AGAINST ALL ODDS*

ROSLYN MEYER
ASSOCIATE PRODUCER
'80 EYES OF A STRANGER

CHARLES MEYERS
1ST ASST. DIRECTOR
'82 LOOKIN' TO GET OUT

ERIC MEYERS
PUBLICIST
'82 WORLD ACCORDING TO GARP, THE
UNIT PUBLICIST
'82 SOUP FOR ONE

ETHEL JOHNSON MEYERS
MISCELLANEOUS
'83 ECHOES

JERRY MEYERS
MISCELLANEOUS
'83 LOSIN' IT

KIM MEYERS
PROD. OFFICE COORD.
'82 SWAMP THING*

LANNY MEYERS
MUSIC
'82 FIRST TIME, THE

NANCY MEYERS
PRODUCER
'80 PRIVATE BENJAMIN*
SCREENPLAY
'80 PRIVATE BENJAMIN*
'84 IRRECONCILABLE DIFFERENCES*
EXECUTIVE PRODUCER
'84 IRRECONCILABLE DIFFERENCES

JOHN MEZA
LOCATIONS
'79 BOULEVARD NIGHTS

AL MIAN
SOUND
'79 WARRIORS, THE*
'80 DEFIANCE*
'81 REDS*

TONY MICHAELAS
2ND ASST. DIRECTOR
'82 TEMPEST*

BARBARA MICHAELS
UNIT PROD. MANAGER
'79 WHEN A STRANGER CALLS
1ST ASST. DIRECTOR
'83 10 TO MIDNIGHT

INGRID MICHAELS
PROD. COORDINATOR
'83 SAVANNAH SMILES

J. MICHAELS
EDITOR
'80 UNION CITY*

JOEL MICHAELS
PRODUCER
'79 SILENT PARTNER, THE*
'80 CHANGELING, THE*
'80 TRIBUTE*
'82 AMATEUR, THE*
'84 PHILADELPHIA EXPERIMENT,THE*
EXECUTIVE PRODUCER
'83 LOSIN' IT*

LORNE MICHAELS
PRODUCER
'80 GILDA LIVE
SCREENPLAY
'80 GILDA LIVE*
EXECUTIVE PRODUCER
'79 MR. MIKE'S MONDO VIDEO

RICHARD MICHAELS
DIRECTOR
'83 BLUE SKIES AGAIN

DEBRA MICHAELSON
2ND ASST. DIRECTOR
'81 NIGHT THE LIGHTS WENT OUT IN GEORGIA, THE
'83 BREATHLESS
'84 MASS APPEAL*
PROD. COORDINATOR
'79 TOURIST TRAP

HAROLD MICHELSON
ART DIRECTOR
'80 CAN'T STOP THE MUSIC
'81 MOMMIE DEAREST
'83 TERMS OF ENDEARMENT
PRODUCTION DESIGNER
'79 STAR TREK-THE MOTION PICTURE
'81 HISTORY OF THE WORLD PART I

DIANA MICHENER
STILLS
'81 MY DINNER WITH ANDRE

KEITH MICHL
ART DIRECTOR
'79 ROLLER BOOGIE

ANAMARIE MICHNEVICH
ART DIRECTOR
'84 RECKLESS

JACK MICHON
ASSISTANT EDITOR
'79 NORTH DALLAS FORTY

TOM MICKEL
LOCATIONS
'79 REAL LIFE*

DAVID MIDDLEMAS
PRODUCTION MANAGER
'79 FIREPOWER*
'84 BOUNTY, THE*

MALCOLM MIDDLETON
ART DIRECTOR
'79 HANOVER STREET*
'81 OUTLAND
'84 RAZOR'S EDGE, THE
'84 SHEENA
PRODUCTION DESIGNER
'82 SENDER, THE

MICHAEL MIDDLETON
STILLS
'82 HONKYTONK MAN

WENDY MIDENER
MISCELLANEOUS
'80 EMPIRE STRIKES BACK, THE

MICHAEL MIDLAM
1ST ASST. DIRECTOR
'79 TIM

BETTE MIDLER
SCREENPLAY
'80 DIVINE MADNESS*

KATHLEEN MIFSUD
MAKEUP
'80 PROM NIGHT

PIERRE MIGNOT
CINEMATOGRAPHER
'82 COME BACK TO THE 5 & 10, JIMMY DEAN, JIMMY DEAN
'83 STREAMERS

GEORGE MIHALKA
DIRECTOR
'81 MY BLOODY VALENTINE

PIROSKA MIHALKA
STILLS
'81 HAPPY BIRTHDAY TO ME
'81 MY BLOODY VALENTINE
'83 OF UNKNOWN ORIGIN

GINA MILANO
MISCELLANEOUS
'83 DOCTOR DETROIT

JODY MILANO
PROD. COORDINATOR
'84 NOT FOR PUBLICATION*

NINO MILANO
PRODUCTION MANAGER
'81 COMIN' AT YA!

SUSAN MILANO
ASSISTANT EDITOR
'79 MR. MIKE'S MONDO VIDEO

ARNON MILCHAN
PRODUCER
'83 KING OF COMEDY, THE
'84 ONCE UPON A TIME IN AMERICA

MICHAEL MILEHAM
MISCELLANEOUS
'83 LONELY LADY, THE

ANN MILES
HAIR
'80 UNION CITY

CHRISTOPHER MILES
PRODUCER
'81 PRIEST OF LOVE*
DIRECTOR
'81 PRIEST OF LOVE

JOHN MILES
PRODUCTION DESIGNER
'82 MONTY PYTHON LIVE AT
THE HOLLYWOOD BOWL*

JULIA MILES
EXECUTIVE PRODUCER
'81 FOUR FRIENDS*

T. STEPHEN MILES
COSTUMES
'83 YELLOWBEARD

TERRY MILES
MAKEUP
'81 FOUR SEASONS, THE*

NICK MILETI
PRODUCER
'83 STREAMERS*

GENE MILFORD
EDITOR
'81 INCHON

MICHAEL MILGROM
PROPS
'80 BLUES BROTHERS
'81 HEARTBEEPS
'82 MISSING*
'83 TWILIGHT ZONE, THE MOVIE*

CHARLES MILHAUPT
ASSOCIATE PRODUCER
'84 ICEMAN
'84 SOLDIER'S STORY, A
PROD. COORDINATOR
'79 ...AND JUSTICE FOR ALL

JOHN MILIUS
PRODUCER
'83 UNCOMMON VALOR*
DIRECTOR
'82 CONAN THE BARBARIAN
'84 RED DAWN
SCREENPLAY
'79 APOCALYPSE NOW*
'82 CONAN THE BARBARIAN*
'84 RED DAWN*
EXECUTIVE PRODUCER
'79 HARDCORE
'79 1941
'80 USED CARS*
MISCELLANEOUS
'83 LONE WOLF MCQUADE

EDWARD MILKIS
PRODUCER
'82 BEST LITTLE WHOREHOUSE
IN TEXAS, THE*

ED MILKOVICH
1ST ASST. DIRECTOR
'81 FORCE FIVE
'82 FRANCES*
2ND ASST. DIRECTOR
'79 RAVAGERS
'79 JERK, THE
'79 MAIN EVENT, THE
'80 FINAL COUNTDOWN, THE*
'80 TOM HORN

HENRY MILLAR
SPECIAL EFFECTS
'79 JERK, THE
'80 CHANGE OF SEASONS, A*
'80 HOW TO BEAT
THE HIGH COST OF LIVING
'81 GOING APE!
'84 ADVENTURES OF BUCKAROO BANZAI
ACROSS THE 8TH DIMENSION,THE*
'84 UNFAITHFULLY YOURS
SP. EFFECTS SUPERV.
'84 2010

HENRY MILLAR JR.
SPECIAL EFFECTS
'79 CHINA SYNDROME, THE
'81 GHOST STORY
'82 SIX PACK
'83 STAR CHAMBER
'83 STAR 80*
SP. EFFECTS SUPERV.
'79 FRISCO KID, THE

MIKE MILLAR
SPECIAL EFFECTS
'80 CHANGE OF SEASONS, A*

STUART MILLAR
EXECUTIVE PRODUCER
'82 SHOOT THE MOON*

ALAN MILLER
EDITOR
'79 MR. MIKE'S MONDO VIDEO*

ANDREW MILLER
SPECIAL EFFECTS
'81 HAND, THE*

ANN MILLER
PROPS
'82 STILL OF THE NIGHT

BARBARA MILLER
CASTING
'80 BIG RED ONE, THE*
'80 CARNY*
'81 S.O.B.*
'82 LOVE AND MONEY
'84 LAST STARFIGHTER, THE*
'84 TANK*

BILLY MILLER
KEY GRIP
'79 RICH KIDS
'79 LAST EMBRACE
'80 SIMON
'80 CRUISING
'81 SO FINE
'81 PRINCE OF THE CITY
'81 WOLFEN
'82 I, THE JURY
'83 DANIEL
'83 LOVESICK
'83 TERMS OF ENDEARMENT
'84 GARBO TALKS

BRUCE MILLER
PROPS
'82 CREEPSHOW

BURTON MILLER
COSTUMES
'79 CONCORDE-AIRPORT '79, THE
'80 NUDE BOMB, THE
'83 STING II, THE

CHARLES MILLER
LOCATIONS
'84 COTTON CLUB, THE*

CHRISTOPHER MILLER
2ND ASST. DIRECTOR
'79 BLACK HOLE, THE*
'80 HERBIE GOES BANANAS*
'80 LAST FLIGHT
OF NOAH'S ARK, THE*
'81 DEVIL AND MAX DEVLIN, THE*
'82 TEX

DANA MILLER
ASSOCIATE PRODUCER
'84 HARD TO HOLD*

DAVID MILLER
MISCELLANEOUS
'82 BEASTMASTER, THE
'84 NIGHTMARE ON ELM STREET, A
'84 NIGHT OF THE COMET
'84 MUTANT

DEE MILLER
CASTING
'79 CHAMP, THE*
'83 BLUE SKIES AGAIN*
'83 PORKY'S II THE NEXT DAY*

DR. MAYNARD MILLER
MISCELLANEOUS
'82 THING, THE

GEORGE MILLER
DIRECTOR
'82 ROAD WARRIOR, THE
'83 TWILIGHT ZONE, THE MOVIE*
SCREENPLAY
'82 ROAD WARRIOR, THE*

GEORGE MILLER
DIRECTOR
'83 MAN FROM SNOWY RIVER, THE

GERALYN MILLER
PROD. OFFICE COORD.
'81 ON GOLDEN POND

HARVEY MILLER
PRODUCER
'80 PRIVATE BENJAMIN*
SCREENPLAY
'80 PRIVATE BENJAMIN*
'82 JEKYLL AND HYDE TOGETHER AGAIN*
'84 CANNONBALL RUN II*
EXECUTIVE PRODUCER
'81 STUDENT BODIES*

HARRY MILLER III
EDITOR
'84 WEEKEND PASS

JASON MILLER
DIRECTOR
'82 THAT CHAMPIONSHIP SEASON
SCREENPLAY
'82 THAT CHAMPIONSHIP SEASON

JAY MILLER
PROPS
'79 BUCK ROGERS*

KARL MILLER
SPECIAL EFFECTS
'80 MELVIN AND HOWARD
'81 CONTINENTAL DIVIDE

KARL LEWIS MILLER
MISCELLANEOUS
'79 AMITYVILLE HORROR, THE
'80 KIDNAPPING OF THE PRESIDENT, THE
'81 EYEWITNESS
'83 CUJO
'84 BODY DOUBLE
'84 DREAMSCAPE

KEN MILLER
ASSISTANT EDITOR
'81 HARD COUNTRY

KEN MILLER
KEY GRIP
'81 BLOOD BEACH
'81 DEAD AND BURIED
'82 VICE SQUAD

LAWRENCE MILLER
ART DIRECTOR
'83 KING OF COMEDY, THE*
PRODUCTION DESIGNER
'84 FLAMINGO KID, THE

MARILYN SUZANNE MILLER
SCREENPLAY
'80 GILDA LIVE*

MARK MILLER
SCREENPLAY
'83 SAVANNAH SMILES

MELISSA MILLER
SCREENPLAY
'80 OH GOD! BOOK II*

MICHAEL MILLER
DIRECTOR
'82 SILENT RAGE
'82 NATIONAL LAMPOON'S CLASS REUNION

MICHAEL MILLER
ASSISTANT EDITOR
'79 MANHATTAN
'80 STARDUST MEMORIES
'82 LITTLE SEX, A*

MICHAEL MILLER
KEY GRIP
'80 GILDA LIVE
'82 TOOTSIE*
'83 LET'S SPEND THE NIGHT TOGETHER*
'84 FLAMINGO KID, THE

MURRAY MILLER
LOCATIONS
'79 BOARDWALK
'80 JUST TELL ME WHAT YOU WANT

ROBERT MILLER
KEY GRIP
'80 RAGING BULL*

ROBERT MILLER SR.
KEY GRIP
'84 COUNTRY

ROBERT ELLIS MILLER
DIRECTOR
'80 BALTIMORE BULLET, THE
'83 REUBEN, REUBEN

ROBIN MILLER
PROPS
'83 TESTAMENT
'84 CHILDREN OF THE CORN
'84 CRIMES OF PASSION

RON MILLER
PRODUCER
'79 APPLE DUMPLING GANG RIDES AGAIN, THE
'79 BLACK HOLE, THE
'79 UNIDENTIFIED FLYING ODDBALL
'79 NORTH AVENUE IRREGULARS, THE
'80 HERBIE GOES BANANAS
'80 LAST FLIGHT OF NOAH'S ARK, THE
'80 MIDNIGHT MADNESS
'80 WATCHER IN THE WOODS, THE
EXECUTIVE PRODUCER
'81 CONDORMAN
'81 DEVIL AND MAX DEVLIN, THE
'82 TEX
'82 TRON
'82 NIGHT CROSSING
'83 NEVER CRY WOLF

SCOTT MILLER
MISCELLANEOUS
'80 CHANGE OF SEASONS, A

SHERRIE MILLER
CHOREOGRAPHER
'83 GOIN' ALL THE WAY

STAN MILLER
SOUND
'82 MONTY PYTHON LIVE AT THE HOLLYWOOD BOWL

STEPHEN MILLER
PRODUCER
'81 MY BLOODY VALENTINE*
EXECUTIVE PRODUCER
'80 HOG WILD*

STEVE MILLER
PROPS
'81 BURNING, THE
MISCELLANEOUS
'83 JAWS 3-D

SUE MILLER
COSTUMES
'84 FINAL TERROR, THE

THOMAS MILLER
PRODUCER
'82 BEST LITTLE WHOREHOUSE

TOM MILLER
PUBLICIST
'83 EASY MONEY
'84 HARRY & SON
UNIT PUBLICIST
'79 BOARDWALK
'81 SO FINE
'81 BLOW OUT
'81 TATTOO
'84 COTTON CLUB, THE

TOM MILLER
MAKEUP
'81 NIGHT THE LIGHTS WENT OUT IN GEORGIA, THE

VICTOR MILLER
SCREENPLAY
'80 FRIDAY THE 13TH
'82 STRANGER IS WATCHING, A*

WANDA MILLER
MAKEUP
'83 REUBEN, REUBEN*

RITA MILLER-GRANT
PROD. COORDINATOR
'84 GHOSTBUSTERS*

ANN MILLGATE
ASSISTANT EDITOR
'79 GOLDENGIRL
'80 COAST TO COAST*

BILL MILLIE
CHOREOGRAPHER
'80 FORMULA, THE

BILL MILLION
MUSIC
'83 SMITHEREENS*

ANN MILLS
EDITOR
'82 NATIONAL LAMPOON'S CLASS REUNION*
ASSISTANT EDITOR
'82 SILENT RAGE*

BILL MILLS
MAKEUP
'80 FINAL COUNTDOWN, THE

BOB MILLS
MAKEUP
'79 ICE CASTLES
'79 ONION FIELD, THE
'79 PLAYERS
'79 WHEN A STRANGER CALLS
'80 BLACK MARBLE, THE
'80 COAST TO COAST*
'81 BACK ROADS
'82 YES, GIORGIO*
'83 EDDIE MACON'S RUN
'84 JOHNNY DANGEROUSLY*
'84 PLACES IN THE HEART
'84 THIEF OF HEARTS
'84 AMERICAN DREAMER

JOHN MILLS
PROPS
'84 KIPPERBANG

RICHARD MILLS
MAKEUP
'79 STEVIE
'80 FLASH GORDON*
'81 RAIDERS OF THE LOST ARK*
'81 DOGS OF WAR, THE*
'83 WICKED LADY, THE*
'83 KEEP, THE*

SUSAN MILLS
HAIR
'83 RUMBLEFISH*

JOHN MILLS-COCKLE
MUSIC
'80 TERROR TRAIN

BOB MILMAN
UNIT MANAGER
'80 HE KNOWS YOU'RE ALONE

OVRY MILNSHTEIN
2ND ASST. DIRECTOR
'83 HANNA K*

DOUGLAS MILSOME
MISCELLANEOUS
'80 SHINING, THE

CLIVE MILTON
LOCATIONS
'84 HOT DOG...THE MOVIE

H.A. MILTON
SCREENPLAY
'83 PIRANHA II: THE SPAWNING

SIMON MILTON
ASSISTANT EDITOR
'83 MONTY PYTHON'S THE MEANING OF LIFE*

SERGIO MIMMS
2ND ASST. DIRECTOR
'79 PENITENTIARY*

ROGER MINAMI
CHOREOGRAPHER
'83 SPRING BREAK

AMY MINASSIAN
MAKEUP
'83 REUBEN, REUBEN*
HAIR
'83 REUBEN, REUBEN*

MIKE MINER
PROPS
'80 FOOLIN AROUND

STEVE MINER
PRODUCER
'81 FRIDAY THE 13TH PART TWO
DIRECTOR
'81 FRIDAY THE 13TH PART TWO
'82 FRIDAY THE 13TH PART THREE IN 3D
ASSOCIATE PRODUCER
'80 FRIDAY THE 13TH
UNIT PROD. MANAGER
'80 FRIDAY THE 13TH

DICK MINGALONE
MISCELLANEOUS
'79 FISH THAT SAVED PITTSBURGH, THE

CHERI MINNS
MAKEUP
'81 KING OF THE MOUNTAIN
'82 FRIDAY THE 13TH PART THREE IN 3D
'83 MAN WHO WASN'T THERE, THE
'84 WINDY CITY
'84 MEATBALLS PART II

BOB MINOR
MISCELLANEOUS
'81 BODY AND SOUL

MICHAEL MINOR
MISCELLANEOUS
'82 BEASTMASTER, THE

MIKE MINOR
ART DIRECTOR
'81 MAN WHO SAW TOMORROW, THE

CHARLES MINSKY
MISCELLANEOUS
'83 TESTAMENT

BARBARA MINSTER
HAIR
'79 STAR TREK-THE MOTION PICTURE

LISA MIONE
CASTING
'80 BATTLE BEYOND THE STARS
'81 GALAXY OF TERROR

SERGIO MIONI
STUNT COORDINATOR
'83 BLACK STALLION RETURNS, THE

ALFREDO MIRABILE
PRODUCTION MANAGER
'79 KILLER FISH*

GRACIELA MIRAMONTES
PROD. COORDINATOR
'81 CAVEMAN*

ANDREW MIRISCH
EXECUTIVE PRODUCER
'83 NIGHTMARES*
ASSOCIATE PRODUCER
'79 BUCK ROGERS*

LAWRENCE MIRISCH
2ND ASST. DIRECTOR
'81 WHOSE LIFE IS IT ANYWAY?*

MARVIN MIRISCH
EXECUTIVE PRODUCER
'79 DRACULA
'83 ROMANTIC COMEDY

WALTER MIRISCH
PRODUCER
'79 DRACULA
'79 PRISONER OF ZENDA, THE
'83 ROMANTIC COMEDY*

STEVEN MIRKOVICH
ASSISTANT EDITOR
'79 TIME AFTER TIME*
'80 SMOKEY AND THE BANDIT II*
'80 WILLIE & PHIL
'81 CANNONBALL RUN, THE*
'81 PATERNITY
'82 TEMPEST

ELLEN MIROJNICK
COSTUMES
'84 FLAMINGO KID, THE
'84 RECKLESS

CHRISTOPHER MISIANO
KEY GRIP
'81 BURNING, THE

ERNEST MISKO
COSTUMES
'81 HAND, THE
COSTUME SUPERVISOR
'82 SUMMER LOVERS
'84 SONGWRITER*

MICHAEL MISLOVE
MISCELLANEOUS
'79 AMERICATHON

RENEE MISSEL
PRODUCER
'80 RESURRECTION*
EXECUTIVE PRODUCER
'79 MAIN EVENT, THE*

ALISTAIR MITCHELL
MAKEUP
'80 WITHOUT WARNING

DAVID MITCHELL
ART DIRECTOR
'79 RICH KIDS
PRODUCTION DESIGNER
'80 ONE-TRICK PONY
'81 MY DINNER WITH ANDRE

GAVIN MITCHELL
ART DIRECTOR
'82 IF YOU COULD SEE WHAT I HEAR
'83 CHRISTMAS STORY, A

GREGG MITCHELL
HAIR
'80 SOMEWHERE IN TIME*

J.L. MITCHELL
MISCELLANEOUS
'80 AIRPLANE

JAMES MITCHELL
EDITOR
'79 HANOVER STREET
'80 FADE TO BLACK
'80 GONG SHOW MOVIE, THE
'83 STAR CHAMBER
'84 2010
MISCELLANEOUS
'79 ROCKY II

JOHN MITCHELL
SOUND
'79 LOST AND FOUND
'79 MURDER BY DECREE
'80 RAISE THE TITANIC*
'80 ROUGH CUT
'80 MIRROR CRACK'D, THE
'82 EVIL UNDER THE SUN*
'84 BOUNTY, THE
'84 PASSAGE TO INDIA, A

JULIAN MITCHELL
SCREENPLAY
'84 ANOTHER COUNTRY

MAMIE MITCHELL
SCRIPT SUPERVISOR
'84 MARVIN AND TIGE

MARTHA MITCHELL
SCRIPT SUPERVISOR
'83 LIQUID SKY

PAT MITCHELL
SOUND
'80 HOW TO BEAT
THE HIGH COST OF LIVING
'81 SUNDAY LOVERS*
'82 PARTNERS
'84 JOY OF SEX, THE

PHYLLIS MITCHELL
PROD. SECRETARY
'84 BEAT STREET

RICK MITCHELL
ASSISTANT EDITOR
'79 STAR TREK-THE MOTION PICTURE*
'82 SWAMP THING

VERA MITCHELL
HAIR
'84 PASSAGE TO INDIA, A*

VICTORIA MITCHELL
CASTING
'79 RUNNING*
'81 LAST CHASE, THE

ELIZABETH MITCHIE
MAKEUP
'79 PICNIC AT HANGING ROCK*

BEN EDWARD MITZNER
PRODUCTION DESIGNER
'82 TRON

DEAN EDWARD MITZNER
PRODUCTION DESIGNER
'79 1941
'80 NINE TO FIVE
'81 LOOKER
'82 NATIONAL LAMPOON'S
CLASS REUNION
'83 MAN WOMAN AND CHILD
'83 NIGHTMARES

BILL MIZEL
2ND ASST. DIRECTOR
'84 SHEENA*

JOHN MOAR
HAIR
'84 FINDERS KEEPERS

PATRICIA MOCK
CASTING
'81 BACK ROADS
'82 CHALLENGE, THE*
'83 SURVIVORS, THE*

PHILIPPE MODAVE
EXECUTIVE PRODUCER
'80 OUTSIDER, THE

PHILLIPE MODAVE
PRODUCTION MANAGER
'81 CONDORMAN*
'84 AMERICAN DREAMER*
LOCATIONS
'79 MOONRAKER*

MIKE MODER

PRODUCER
'82 SUMMER LOVERS
EXECUTIVE PRODUCER
'81 THEY ALL LAUGHED
'84 BEVERLY HILLS COP
'84 SONGWRITER
UNIT PROD. MANAGER
'84 BEVERLY HILLS COP
'84 SONGWRITER
1ST ASST. DIRECTOR
'82 SUMMER LOVERS
MISCELLANEOUS
'80 LOVING COUPLES

PAUL MOEN

2ND ASST. DIRECTOR
'79 1941*
'80 CAN'T STOP THE MUSIC
'80 INSIDE MOVES
'80 MOUNTAIN MEN, THE
'81 SHARKEY'S MACHINE*
'81 ...ALL THE MARBLES*
'82 LOOKIN' TO GET OUT
'82 TOY, THE*
'83 SUDDEN IMPACT
'84 TIGHTROPE*
'84 FRIDAY THE 13TH PART IV THE FINAL CHAPTER*

MARK MOFFATT

MISCELLANEOUS
'82 STARSTRUCK

RAY MOGGIO

LOCATIONS
'84 RED DAWN*

AVI MOGRABI

2ND ASST. DIRECTOR
'83 HANNA K*

SHLOMO MOGRABI

PRODUCTION MANAGER
'84 LITTLE DRUMMER GIRL, THE*
MISCELLANEOUS
'84 BEST DEFENSE

AHMED SAMI MOHAMED

LOCATIONS
'83 TABLE FOR FIVE*

ARLINE MOHR

ASSOCIATE PRODUCER
'83 MAUSOLEUM*

JOHN MOIO

2ND UNIT DIRECTOR
'83 TWO OF A KIND
STUNT COORDINATOR
'80 BORDERLINE
'80 WHERE THE BUFFALO ROAM
'81 HARD COUNTRY
'82 FAST TIMES AT RIDGEMONT HIGH
'82 ZAPPED!*
'84 JOHNNY DANGEROUSLY

NUALA MOISELLE

CASTING
'83 EDUCATING RITA*

JULIE MOLDO

PROD. COORDINATOR
'82 HOME WORK

GERALD MOLEN

UNIT PROD. MANAGER
'81 POSTMAN ALWAYS RINGS TWICE, THE
'82 TOOTSIE
'83 LET'S SPEND THE NIGHT TOGETHER
'84 SOLDIER'S STORY, A

RON MOLER

PRODUCER
'84 BACHELOR PARTY*

BUD MOLIN

EDITOR
'79 BLOODLINE
'79 JERK, THE*
'80 UP THE ACADEMY*
'82 DEAD MEN DON'T WEAR PLAID
'83 MAN WITH TWO BRAINS, THE
'84 ALL OF ME
2ND UNIT DIRECTOR
'80 UP THE ACADEMY

CATHERINE MOLINARO

2ND ASST. DIRECTOR
'84 JUST THE WAY YOU ARE*

EDOUARD MOLINARO

DIRECTOR
'81 SUNDAY LOVERS*
'84 JUST THE WAY YOU ARE

DAVID MOLL

PROPS
'79 FAST BREAK
'80 LOVING COUPLES
'81 RICH AND FAMOUS
'84 GRANDVIEW, U.S.A.
'84 AMERICAN DREAMER

FRED MOLLIN

MUSIC
'79 FAST COMPANY

ANDREW MOLLO

MISCELLANEOUS
'83 KEEP, THE

JOHN MOLLO

COSTUMES
'79 ALIEN
'80 EMPIRE STRIKES BACK, THE
'81 OUTLAND
'82 GANDHI*
'83 LORDS OF DISCIPLINE, THE
'84 GREYSTOKE: THE LEGEND OF TARZAN, LORD OF THE APES*
MISCELLANEOUS
'83 PRIVATES ON PARADE

MIKE MOLLOY

CINEMATOGRAPHER
'79 SHOUT, THE
'80 HUMAN FACTOR, THE
'80 KIDNAPPING OF THE PRESIDENT, THE
'81 SHOCK TREATMENT

MICHAEL MOLLY

ART DIRECTOR
'80 STARDUST MEMORIES
'81 THIEF*
'82 STILL OF THE NIGHT
'84 MOSCOW ON THE HUDSON*

JIM MOLONEY

SCREENPLAY
'80 FIENDISH PLOT OF DR. FU MANCHU, THE*

KAY MOLYNEAUX

LOCATIONS
'79 GOLDENGIRL
'80 NINE TO FIVE

JAMES MOMEL

CINEMATOGRAPHER
'81 MS. 45

DIANA MONA

MAKEUP
'83 HOUSE ON SORORITY ROW
HAIR
'83 HOUSE ON SORORITY ROW

NIC MONAT

2ND ASST. DIRECTOR
'82 SAFARI 3000

E.H.B. "CHIP" MONCK

MISCELLANEOUS
'80 DIVINE MADNESS

ANDREW MONDSHEIN

EDITOR
'84 GARBO TALKS
ASSISTANT EDITOR
'83 DANIEL

E.C. MONELL

ASSOCIATE PRODUCER
'83 OSTERMAN WEEKEND, THE*

MARY-ANN MONFORTON
COSTUMES
'82 FIRST TIME, THE

VINCENT MONGOL
SCREENPLAY
'83 CHAINED HEAT*

KARAN MONKOUSE
PROPS
'84 PHAR LAP

NICK MONKS
ASSISTANT EDITOR
'80 HOPSCOTCH*

EVA MONLEY
ASSOCIATE PRODUCER
'79 PROMISE, THE
'84 CHAMPIONS

MARK MONSKY
MISCELLANEOUS
'81 EYEWITNESS

SERGIO MONTANARI
EDITOR
'79 STARCRASH

LINDA MONTANTI
2ND ASST. DIRECTOR
'83 TRADING PLACES*

JOHN MONTE
STILLS
'79 BEYOND THE POSEIDON ADVENTURE
'79 CHAPTER TWO
'80 AIRPLANE
'80 BORDERLINE
'80 WHEN TIME RAN OUT
'81 BODY HEAT*
'81 HARD COUNTRY
'81 PURSUIT OF D.B. COOPER, THE*
'82 ZOOT SUIT

LISA MONTELEONE
MAKEUP
'81 MS. 45

GLORIA MONTEMAYOR
HAIR
'79 BLACK HOLE, THE
'80 HERBIE GOES BANANAS
'80 MIDNIGHT MADNESS
'81 DEVIL AND MAX DEVLIN, THE
'81 MODERN PROBLEMS

ELBA MONTES
MISCELLANEOUS
'84 CRACKERS

ANN MONTESANTO
HAIR
'81 FEAR NO EVIL*

CHERI MONTESANTO
MAKEUP
'81 FEAR NO EVIL*

FRANK MONTESANTO
HAIR
'81 FEAR NO EVIL*

ANDREW MONTGOMERY
2ND ASST. DIRECTOR
'81 EXCALIBUR*
'84 KIPPERBANG*

MICHAEL MONTGOMERY
MISCELLANEOUS
'82 VICE SQUAD

MONTY MONTGOMERY
DIRECTOR
'84 LOVELESS, THE*
SCREENPLAY
'84 LOVELESS, THE*

PAULA MONTGOMERY
PROD. COORDINATOR
'80 IT'S MY TURN

VINCENT MONTON
CINEMATOGRAPHER
'81 ROAD GAMES

EDWARD MONTORO
EXECUTIVE PRODUCER
'84 MUTANT*

SARAH MONZANI
MAKEUP
'82 SENDER, THE
'82 QUEST FOR FIRE*
'84 ANOTHER COUNTRY
HAIR
'79 ALIEN

DON MOODY
2ND ASST. DIRECTOR
'83 PORKY'S II THE NEXT DAY*

TRICIA MOODY
MISCELLANEOUS
'81 SMOKEY BITES THE DUST

SUN MYUNG MOON
MISCELLANEOUS
'81 INCHON

PAUL MOONEY
MISCELLANEOUS
'81 RICHARD PRYOR: LIVE ON THE SUNSET STRIP

HANK MOONJEAN
PRODUCER
'80 SMOKEY AND THE BANDIT II
'81 SHARKEY'S MACHINE
'81 INCREDIBLE SHRINKING WOMAN, THE
'81 PATERNITY*
'83 STROKER ACE

DENNY MOORADIAN
KEY GRIP
'84 MUTANT

JUDY MOORADIAN
ASSOCIATE PRODUCER
'84 HARDBODIES

JUDY MOORCROFT
COSTUMES
'79 EUROPEANS, THE
'79 MURDER BY DECREE
'80 QUARTET
'81 SPHINX
'83 YENTL
'84 KILLING FIELDS, THE
'84 PASSAGE TO INDIA, A

CHARLES MOORE
MISCELLANEOUS
'82 HALLOWEEN III: SEASON OF THE WITCH

DUDLEY MOORE
MUSIC
'82 SIX WEEKS

FRAN MOORE
PUBLICIST
'82 STARSTRUCK

FREDERICK MOORE
CINEMATOGRAPHER
'83 MAN WHO WASN'T THERE, THE

JAY MOORE
ART DIRECTOR
'79 WANDERERS, THE
'80 JUST TELL ME WHAT YOU WANT
'83 SURVIVORS, THE

JOHN MOORE
ART DIRECTOR
'82 SOPHIE'S CHOICE
'84 GHOSTBUSTERS*

JOSEPH MOORE
2ND ASST. DIRECTOR
'79 BLACK HOLE, THE*
'80 STIR CRAZY*
'81 ZORRO, THE GAY BLADE*
'82 JINXED*
'83 MAN WHO LOVED WOMEN, THE*
'83 TWO OF A KIND
'84 MICKI AND MAUDE*

KATHERINE MOORE
PUBLICIST
'83 UNDER FIRE

LAUREL MOORE
STILLS
'80 BIG RED ONE, THE
'81 HOWLING, THE
'82 SEDUCTION, THE
'82 FRIDAY THE 13TH PART THREE IN 3D
'83 MAN WHO WASN'T THERE, THE
'84 MEATBALLS PART II

M. MICHAEL MOORE
1ST ASST. DIRECTOR
'79 ELECTRIC HORSEMAN, THE

MICHAEL MOORE
2ND UNIT DIRECTOR
'80 CHANGE OF SEASONS, A
'81 RAIDERS OF THE LOST ARK
'81 ZORRO, THE GAY BLADE
'82 SIX PACK
'83 NEVER SAY NEVER AGAIN
'84 INDIANA JONES AND THE TEMPLE OF DOOM*
'84 LITTLE DRUMMER GIRL, THE

MICHAEL MOORE
ART DIRECTOR
'82 STAR TREK II THE WRATH OF KHAN

MICHAEL MOORE
SOUND
'79 REAL LIFE
'79 ROCK 'N ROLL HIGH SCHOOL

MICHAEL MOORE
MISCELLANEOUS
'82 QUEST FOR FIRE

MICKEY MOORE
2ND UNIT DIRECTOR
'80 RAISE THE TITANIC

MILLIE MOORE
EDITOR
'80 THOSE LIPS, THOSE EYES
'82 HALLOWEEN III: SEASON OF THE WITCH

MORGAN MOORE
PUBLICIST
'80 USED CARS
UNIT PUBLICIST
'83 MAN WITH TWO BRAINS, THE

PATRICK MOORE
EDITOR
'84 OXFORD BLUES
ASSISTANT EDITOR
'80 ELEPHANT MAN, THE
'83 PIRATES OF PENZANCE, THE
'84 GREYSTOKE: THE LEGEND OF TARZAN, LORD OF THE APES

RANDY MOORE
ART DIRECTOR
'83 SUBURBIA

RICHARD MOORE
DIRECTOR
'79 CIRCLE OF IRON

RICHARD MOORE
ASSOCIATE PRODUCER
'83 STRANGE INVADERS*

RICHARD MOORE
CINEMATOGRAPHER
'82 ANNIE

ROBERT MOORE
KEY GRIP
'78 DEER HUNTER, THE
'79 ROSE, THE
'79 PROMISES IN THE DARK
'79 WINTER KILLS
'80 STIR CRAZY
80 LAST MARRIED COUPLE IN AMERICA, THE
'80 OH GOD! BOOK II
'82 ONE FROM THE HEART*

ROBERT MOORE
DIRECTOR
'79 CHAPTER TWO

ROBIN MOORE
SCREENPLAY
'81 INCHON*

ROY MOORE
SCREENPLAY
'81 LAST CHASE, THE*

SAM MOORE
PROPS
'79 BEYOND THE POSEIDON ADVENTURE
'80 OCTAGON, THE
'80 WHEN TIME RAN OUT
'81 RICHARD PRYOR: LIVE ON THE SUNSET STRIP
'81 CHARLIE CHAN AND THE CURSE OF THE DRAGON QUEEN
'82 DEAD MEN DON'T WEAR PLAID
'84 ICE PIRATES, THE
'84 JOHNNY DANGEROUSLY

SAM MOORE
ASSISTANT EDITOR
'81 ...ALL THE MARBLES*

STEPHANIE MOORE
LOCATIONS
'83 BAD BOYS*

STEVE MOORE
ASSOCIATE EDITOR
'79 DOUBLE MCGUFFIN, THE
ASSISTANT EDITOR
'80 OH! HEAVENLY DOG*
MISCELLANEOUS
'80 MIDDLE AGE CRAZY

SUSANNA MOORE
PRODUCTION DESIGNER
'81 STRANGE BEHAVIOR
'83 STRANGE INVADERS
COSTUMES
'83 STRANGE INVADERS

TED MOORE
CINEMATOGRAPHER
'81 CLASH OF THE TITANS
'81 PRIEST OF LOVE

TOM MOORE
ASSISTANT EDITOR
'84 RED DAWN*

WILLIAM MOORE
SCREENPLAY
'79 FIVE DAYS FROM HOME

VAHAN MOOSEKIAN
LOCATIONS
'81 LOOKER

PHILIPPE MORA
DIRECTOR
'81 BEAST WITHIN, THE

RENATO MORADO
STUNT COORDINATOR
'84 PURPLE HEARTS

JACQUE MORALI
PRODUCER
'80 CAN'T STOP THE MUSIC*
MUSIC
'80 CAN'T STOP THE MUSIC

MARTHA MORAN
MISCELLANEOUS
'83 RUNNING BRAVE

MIKE MORAN
MUSIC
'82 MISSIONARY, THE
'83 BETRAYAL*

PAT MORAN
CASTING
'81 POLYESTER

RICHARD MORAN
KEY GRIP
'79 CHAPTER TWO*
'79 IN-LAWS, THE
'79 JUST YOU AND ME KID
'80 SEEMS LIKE OLD TIMES
'80 HERO AT LARGE
'80 PRIVATE BENJAMIN
'81 ONLY WHEN I LAUGH
'82 I OUGHT TO BE IN PICTURES
'82 MAKING LOVE
'83 ROMANTIC COMEDY
'83 MAX DUGAN RETURNS
'84 GREMLINS
'84 UNFAITHFULLY YOURS
'84 TEACHERS

RICK MORANIS
DIRECTOR
'83 STRANGE BREW*
SCREENPLAY
'83 STRANGE BREW*

IVAN MORAVEC
MISCELLANEOUS
'84 AMADEUS

MURIEL MOREAU
ASSISTANT EDITOR
'84 JUST THE WAY YOU ARE*

ROBERT MOREHEAD
STILLS
'79 TIM

GEORGE MORFOGEN
PRODUCER
'81 THEY ALL LAUGHED*
ASSOCIATE PRODUCER
'79 SAINT JACK

ANDRE MORGAN
SCREENPLAY
'82 MEGAFORCE*
EXECUTIVE PRODUCER
'84 LASSITER*
'84 CANNONBALL RUN II*
EXEC IN CHARGE PROD
'80 BIG BRAWL, THE
ASSOCIATE PRODUCER
'79 GAME OF DEATH
MISCELLANEOUS
'81 CANNONBALL RUN, THE

BILL MORGAN
MAKEUP
'81 DEATH HUNT

BOB MORGAN
PUBLICIST
'79 ONION FIELD, THE

DON MORGAN
PUBLICIST
'79 CHAMP, THE
'80 FORMULA, THE
UNIT PUBLICIST
'80 HERO AT LARGE

DONALD MORGAN
CINEMATOGRAPHER
'80 USED CARS
'83 CHRISTINE
'84 STARMAN
'84 MEATBALLS PART II

DONALD MORGAN
KEY GRIP
'80 FADE TO BLACK

LYNN MORGAN
2ND ASST. DIRECTOR
'79 PRIZE FIGHTER, THE
'79 WHEN A STRANGER CALLS

MARILYSE MORGAN
PROD. COORDINATOR
'84 LASSITER

RILEY MORGAN
PROPS
'82 BEASTMASTER, THE*
'82 ZAPPED!*
'83 JOYSTICKS

TONI MORGAN
ASSISTANT EDITOR
'80 HOPSCOTCH*

MORGANA
SCRIPT SUPERVISOR
'80 SERIAL
'81 KING OF THE MOUNTAIN

ALBERT MORIANI
EDITOR
'83 YOR

BRUCE MORIARTY
2ND ASST. DIRECTOR
'81 TICKET TO HEAVEN

BRUCE MORIARTY
MISCELLANEOUS
'83 BLACK STALLION RETURNS, THE

DON MORIARTY
ASSOCIATE PRODUCER
'81 ZORRO, THE GAY BLADE*

JIM MORIARTY
PROD. COORDINATOR
'83 RICHARD PRYOR: HERE AND NOW

KEVIN MORIARTY
LOCATIONS
'81 EXCALIBUR

NORMA MORICEAU
COSTUMES
'82 ROAD WARRIOR, THE
'83 NATE & HAYES

GERALD MORIN
1ST ASST. DIRECTOR
'83 LONELY LADY, THE
LOCATIONS
'82 YES, GIORGIO*

PATRICK MORIN
STILLS
'79 MOONRAKER

PHIL MORINI
2ND ASST. DIRECTOR
'82 ANNIE*

RUTH MORLEY
COSTUMES
'79 KRAMER VS. KRAMER
'80 LITTLE MISS MARKER
'82 CHOSEN, THE
'82 HAMMETT
'82 I OUGHT TO BE IN PICTURES
'82 ONE FROM THE HEART
'82 TOOTSIE

TED MORLEY
PRODUCTION MANAGER
'84 BOSTONIANS, THE
1ST ASST. DIRECTOR
'79 FIREPOWER
'79 PRISONER OF ZENDA, THE*
'83 BETRAYAL
'83 YELLOWBEARD*
2ND ASST. DIRECTOR
'81 EXCALIBUR*

GIORGIO MORODER
MUSIC
'79 AMERICAN GIGOLO
'80 FOXES
'82 CAT PEOPLE
'83 SCARFACE
'83 D.C. CAB
'84 ELECTRIC DREAMS
'84 NEVERENDING STORY, THE*

BOB MORONES
CASTING
'84 EL NORTE

GIANNI MOROSI
MAKEUP
'81 INCHON*

ENNIO MORRICONE
MUSIC
'79 BLOODLINE
'80 ISLAND, THE
'80 WINDOWS
'81 SO FINE
'82 BUTTERFLY
'82 THING, THE
'84 ONCE UPON A TIME IN AMERICA

BRIAN MORRIS
PRODUCTION DESIGNER
'79 YANKS
'82 PINK FLOYD: THE WALL
'82 QUEST FOR FIRE*
'83 HUNGER, THE
'84 ANOTHER COUNTRY

DESMOND MORRIS
MISCELLANEOUS
'82 QUEST FOR FIRE

ELIZABETH MORRIS
UNIT PUBLICIST
'81 HAPPY BIRTHDAY TO ME

JOHN MORRIS
MUSIC
'79 IN-LAWS, THE
'80 ELEPHANT MAN, THE
'80 IN GOD WE TRUST
'81 HISTORY OF THE WORLD PART I
'83 TO BE OR NOT TO BE
'83 YELLOWBEARD
'84 JOHNNY DANGEROUSLY
'84 WOMAN IN RED, THE

JOHN MORRIS
SPECIAL EFFECTS
'80 FFOLKES

KATE MORRIS
MISCELLANEOUS
'81 DEAD AND BURIED
'84 MISUNDERSTOOD

KATHY MORRIS
PROD. COORDINATOR
'79 JAGUAR LIVES

MICKEY MORRIS
MAKEUP
'80 HUMAN FACTOR, THE

OSWALD MORRIS
CINEMATOGRAPHER
'80 JUST TELL ME WHAT YOU WANT
'81 GREAT MUPPET CAPER, THE
'82 DARK CRYSTAL, THE

REDMOND MORRIS
PRODUCTION MANAGER
'83 GORKY PARK
'83 PRIVATES ON PARADE
UNIT MANAGER
'81 FOR YOUR EYES ONLY*
LOCATIONS
'79 AGATHA*
'79 YANKS
'81 FOR YOUR EYES ONLY*
'81 REDS

REGINALD MORRIS
CINEMATOGRAPHER
'79 MURDER BY DECREE
'80 MIDDLE AGE CRAZY
'80 TRIBUTE
'82 PORKY'S
'83 CHRISTMAS STORY, A
'83 PORKY'S II THE NEXT DAY

THAINE MORRIS
MISCELLANEOUS
'81 DRAGONSLAYER
'83 RETURN OF THE JEDI
'84 2010

JOHN MORRISEY
ASSISTANT EDITOR
'83 SUDDEN IMPACT
'84 TIGHTROPE

KEN MORRISEY
ASSISTANT EDITOR
'79 AVALANCHE EXPRESS*
'81 FOUR SEASONS, THE*
'82 I, THE JURY*

BECKY MORRISON
CO-PRODUCER
'81 FEAR NO EVIL

LARRY MORRISON
ASSISTANT EDITOR
'82 FRIDAY THE 13TH PART THREE IN 3D
'84 BLAME IT ON RIO

FRANK MORRISS
EDITOR
'80 INSIDE MOVES
'81 WHOSE LIFE IS IT ANYWAY?
'81 EARTHLING, THE
'83 BLUE THUNDER*
'84 ROMANCING THE STONE*

ANDREW MORSE
2ND ASST. DIRECTOR
'82 PIRATE MOVIE, THE

TERRY MORSE
PRODUCTION MANAGER
'80 BIG BRAWL, THE

TERRY MORSE JR.
PRODUCER
'80 BIG BRAWL, THE*

SUSAN MORSE
EDITOR
'79 MANHATTAN
'80 STARDUST MEMORIES
'81 ARTHUR
'82 MIDSUMMER NIGHT'S SEX COMEDY, A
'83 ZELIG
'84 BROADWAY DANNY ROSE

DON MORSKI
PROPS
'80 ALLIGATOR

GUSTAVE MORTENSEN
SOUND
'79 VOICES*

CINDY MORTON
LOCATIONS
'83 CHRISTMAS STORY, A*

GARY MORTON
EXECUTIVE PRODUCER
'83 ALL THE RIGHT MOVES

ROB MORTON
SCREENPLAY
'84 SWING SHIFT

JOEL MORWOOD
ASSOCIATE PRODUCER
'80 JAZZ SINGER, THE
'83 TRENCHCOAT

JOE MOSCA
ASSISTANT EDITOR
'80 PRIVATE BENJAMIN
'81 RICHARD PRYOR: LIVE ON THE SUNSET STRIP*
'81 ABSENCE OF MALICE
'84 GHOSTBUSTERS*

MIKE MOSCHELLA
MAKEUP
'79 C.H.O.M.P.S.
'80 ROADIE
'81 FORCE FIVE

JERRY MOSELEY
MUSIC
'83 FRIGHTMARE

DICK MOSES
PRODUCTION MANAGER
'80 DEFIANCE*
'83 TOUGH ENOUGH*
UNIT PROD. MANAGER
'81 HONKY TONK FREEWAY*

GILBERT MOSES
DIRECTOR
'79 FISH THAT SAVED PITTSBURGH, THE

RICHARD MOSES
SCREENPLAY
'81 ON THE RIGHT TRACK*
CO-PRODUCER
'81 ON THE RIGHT TRACK*

WILBUR MOSIER
PRODUCTION MANAGER
'79 CONCORDE-AIRPORT '79, THE*
'81 MODERN PROBLEMS
UNIT PROD. MANAGER
'79 BUTCH AND SUNDANCE: THE EARLY YEARS

RICH MOSKAL
LOCATIONS
'84 GRANDVIEW, U.S.A.

BARRY MOSS
CASTING
'80 FRIDAY THE 13TH*
'81 ENDLESS LOVE*
'82 STRANGER IS WATCHING, A*
'83 SPRING BREAK*
MISCELLANEOUS
'84 COTTON CLUB, THE

GERALD MOSS
PROPS
'80 SOMEWHERE IN TIME
'81 ALL NIGHT LONG
'81 CONTINENTAL DIVIDE
'82 BEST LITTLE WHOREHOUSE IN TEXAS, THE
'84 MIKE'S MURDER
'84 THIEF OF HEARTS

NED MOSS
UNIT PUBLICIST
'80 HOW TO BEAT THE HIGH COST OF LIVING*

OLIVER MOSS
SOUND
'80 HOPSCOTCH*

PETER MOSS
CINEMATOGRAPHER
'84 FLASHPOINT

GEORGE MOSSMAN
MISCELLANEOUS
'83 WICKED LADY, THE
'84 GREYSTOKE: THE LEGEND OF TARZAN, LORD OF THE APES

TEDDY MOSSMAN
PROPS
'80 OH! HEAVENLY DOG*
'81 HAND, THE

JEFF MOST
STUNT COORDINATOR
'83 LIQUID SKY*

NANCY MOTT
MISCELLANEOUS
'83 LOSIN' IT

TOMMASO MOTTOLA
2ND ASST. DIRECTOR
'84 AMADEUS*

PAT MOTYKA
SCRIPT SUPERVISOR
'84 SILENT NIGHT, DEADLY NIGHT

FRANCOIS MOULLIN
2ND ASST. DIRECTOR
'79 FIREPOWER*
'82 SHOOT THE MOON
'83 MAN WOMAN AND CHILD*

ROBIN MOUNSEY
MISCELLANEOUS
'84 ICEMAN

EUNICE MOUNTJOY
ASSOCIATE EDITOR
'84 PASSAGE TO INDIA, A
ASSISTANT EDITOR
'81 BEYOND THE REEF*

EDGARD MOURINO
STUNT COORDINATOR
'84 SPLASH*

IBRAHIM MOUSSA
MISCELLANEOUS
'83 EXPOSED

ALAN MOYLE
DIRECTOR
'80 TIMES SQUARE

MILAN MRDJENOVICH
ASSOCIATE PRODUCER
'81 EYE FOR AN EYE, AN*

JERRY MUCHWEILLER
MAKEUP
'81 BODY AND SOUL

JEAN-PAUL MUGEL
SOUND
'81 SUNDAY LOVERS*
'84 PARIS, TEXAS

JEAN MUIR
COSTUMES
'83 BETRAYAL*

ISABEL MULA
SCRIPT SUPERVISOR
'79 JAGUAR LIVES

TERENCE MULCAHY
SCREENPLAY
'84 NO SMALL AFFAIR*

WALT MULCONERY
EDITOR
'83 FLASHDANCE*
'84 KARATE KID, THE*

DOMINIC MULDOWNEY
MUSIC
'83 BETRAYAL*

SHIRLEY MULDOWNEY
MISCELLANEOUS
'83 HEART LIKE A WHEEL

THOMAS MULHEARN
MISCELLANEOUS
'81 FORT APACHE, THE BRONX

GEORGE MULHOLLAND
SOUND
'79 BLACK STALLION, THE*

ANDREW MULKANI
KEY GRIP
'79 MEATBALLS*
'83 STRANGE BREW*

WANDA MULL
PRODUCTION MANAGER
'83 NEVER CRY WOLF*

BOB MULLEN
ASSISTANT EDITOR
'81 SUPERMAN II

JUDITH ATWELL MULLEN
PROD. COORDINATOR
'80 OH! HEAVENLY DOG
PROD. SECRETARY
'79 LITTLE ROMANCE, A

MARJORIE MULLEN
SCRIPT SUPERVISOR
'81 FIRST MONDAY IN OCTOBER

MELINDA MULLEN
UNIT PUBLICIST
'82 YES, GIORGIO

ERIC MULLER
MAKEUP
'79 LITTLE ROMANCE, A*

FREDERICK MULLER
ASSOCIATE PRODUCER
'83 HIGH ROAD TO CHINA
'84 LASSITER

ROBBY MULLER
CINEMATOGRAPHER
'79 SAINT JACK
'80 HONEYSUCKLE ROSE
'81 THEY ALL LAUGHED
'84 PARIS, TEXAS
'84 REPO MAN
'84 BODY ROCK

ROBERT MULLIGAN
PRODUCER
'83 KISS ME GOODBYE
DIRECTOR
'83 KISS ME GOODBYE

PATRICK MULLINS
ASSISTANT EDITOR
'82 FIGHTING BACK

PETER MULLINS
PRODUCTION DESIGNER
'81 DOGS OF WAR, THE
'83 CURSE OF THE PINK PANTHER
'83 TRAIL OF THE PINK PANTHER
'84 LASSITER
'84 SCANDALOUS

CHARLES MULVEHILL
PRODUCER
'81 POSTMAN ALWAYS RINGS TWICE, THE*
ASSOCIATE PRODUCER
'79 BEING THERE
'82 FRANCES
'84 SWING SHIFT
PRODUCTION MANAGER
'79 BEING THERE
UNIT PROD. MANAGER
'84 SWING SHIFT
UNIT MANAGER
'82 FRANCES

MUKY MUNKACSI
STILLS
'79 ...AND JUSTICE FOR ALL*
'80 NIGHT OF THE JUGGLER
'81 RAGTIME*
'81 EYEWITNESS
'82 STILL OF THE NIGHT

RANDY MUNKACSI
STILLS
'79 BELL JAR, THE
'80 FIRST DEADLY SIN
'81 PATERNITY*
'82 WORLD ACCORDING TO GARP, THE
'83 SURVIVORS, THE
'84 LONELY GUY, THE*

WILLIAM MUNNS
MISCELLANEOUS
'82 SWAMP THING
'82 BEASTMASTER, THE
'83 ANGEL OF H.E.A.T.

MANUEL MUNOZ
1ST ASST. DIRECTOR
'84 UNDER THE VOLCANO

CHRIS MUNRO
SOUND
'84 OXFORD BLUES

CLARK MUNRO
PROPS
'81 GALLIPOLI
'83 YEAR OF LIVING DANGEROUSLY, THE

GORDON MUNRO
MISCELLANEOUS
'81 TATTOO

JAMES MURAKAMI
DIRECTOR
'80 BATTLE BEYOND THE STARS
ART DIRECTOR
'82 ESCAPE ARTIST, THE*
'83 WAR GAMES
'84 BEVERLY HILLS COP
'84 NATURAL, THE*
'84 JOY OF SEX, THE

WALTER MURCH
EDITOR
'79 APOCALYPSE NOW*
MISCELLANEOUS
'79 APOCALYPSE NOW

BOB MURDOCK
PROPS
'80 LAST MARRIED COUPLE IN AMERICA, THE

DENNIS MUREN
SPECIAL EFFECTS
'81 DRAGONSLAYER
MISCELLANEOUS
'80 EMPIRE STRIKES BACK, THE
'81 DRAGONSLAYER
'82 E.T. THE EXTRA-TERRESTRIAL
'83 RETURN OF THE JEDI
'84 INDIANA JONES AND THE TEMPLE OF DOOM

MELANIE MUROFF
STILLS
'80 EYES OF A STRANGER*

ANNE MURPHY
2ND ASST. DIRECTOR
'81 MY BLOODY VALENTINE
'84 HOTEL NEW HAMPSHIRE, THE

BILL MURPHY
2ND ASST. DIRECTOR
'80 EYES OF A STRANGER

BRIANNE MURPHY
CINEMATOGRAPHER
'80 FATSO

BRIDGET MURPHY
PROD. OFFICE COORD.
'82 FIRST BLOOD
PROD. COORDINATOR
'79 SCAVENGER HUNT*
'80 COMPETITION, THE
'83 CHRISTINE

DAVID MURPHY
COSTUME SUPERVISOR
'84 SCANDALOUS
MISCELLANEOUS
'81 HISTORY OF THE WORLD PART I

DENNIS MURPHY
CO-PRODUCER
'81 FRIDAY THE 13TH PART TWO
2ND ASST. DIRECTOR
'79 BELL JAR, THE*
'79 BOARDWALK
'82 Q: QUETZALCOATL*

FRED MURPHY
CINEMATOGRAPHER
'79 HEARTLAND
'80 TELL ME A RIDDLE
'82 Q: QUETZALCOATL
'83 EDDIE AND THE CRUISERS

KAREN MURPHY
PRODUCER
'84 THIS IS SPINAL TAP

MAUREEN MURPHY
PROD. SECRETARY
'84 BIRDY*

MICHAEL MURPHY
EXECUTIVE PRODUCER
'83 OSTERMAN WEEKEND, THE*

PHILIP MURPHY
UNIT MANAGER
'84 OVER THE BROOKLYN BRIDGE

RICHARD MURPHY
SCREENPLAY
'80 KIDNAPPING OF THE PRESIDENT, THE

RICHARD MURPHY
SOUND
'80 FRIDAY THE 13TH
'81 FRIDAY THE 13TH PART TWO

WALTER MURPHY
MISCELLANEOUS
'84 RHINESTONE

BILL MURRAY
SCREENPLAY
'84 RAZOR'S EDGE, THE*

CHRIS MURRAY
SPECIAL EFFECTS
'81 GALLIPOLI*

CHUCK MURRAY
PRODUCTION MANAGER
'79 10
UNIT PROD. MANAGER
'81 GOING APE!

FORREST MURRAY
1ST ASST. DIRECTOR
'83 CAN SHE BAKE A CHERRY PIE?

GRAEME MURRAY
ART DIRECTOR
'83 NEVER CRY WOLF

JAMES "RIP" MURRAY
2ND ASST. DIRECTOR
'83 SUBURBIA

JOHN MURRAY
KEY GRIP
'79 AMITYVILLE HORROR, THE
'80 HUNTER, THE
'81 RICHARD PRYOR: LIVE ON THE SUNSET STRIP*
'81 FIRST MONDAY IN OCTOBER
'82 YES, GIORGIO*
'83 TWO OF A KIND
'83 WRONG IS RIGHT
'84 ADVENTURES OF BUCKAROO BANZAI ACROSS THE 8TH DIMENSION,THE

KAREN MURRAY
2ND ASST. DIRECTOR
'79 10*

MICHAEL MURRAY
1ST ASST. DIRECTOR
'83 LORDS OF DISCIPLINE, THE*
2ND ASST. DIRECTOR
'81 SHOCK TREATMENT
'81 AMERICAN WEREWOLF IN LONDON, AN
'83 BRITANNIA HOSPITAL

WILLIAM MURRAY
2ND ASST. DIRECTOR
'84 REPO MAN

ROGER MURRAY-LEACH
PRODUCTION DESIGNER
'83 LOCAL HERO

PETER MURTON
PRODUCTION DESIGNER
'79 DRACULA
'81 SUPERMAN II*
'83 SUPERMAN III
'84 SHEENA

THOMAS MURTON
MISCELLANEOUS
'80 BRUBAKER

ISIDOR MUSALEM
2ND ASST. DIRECTOR
'84 BEST DEFENSE*

LOUIS MUSCATE
2ND ASST. DIRECTOR
'80 LAST FLIGHT OF NOAH'S ARK, THE*
'80 OCTAGON, THE
'81 EYE FOR AN EYE, AN*
'81 PURSUIT OF D.B. COOPER, THE*

LEWIS MUSLIN
ASSISTANT EDITOR
'83 PRIVATES ON PARADE

CHARLES MUSSER
MISCELLANEOUS
'81 RAGTIME

NANCY MUSSER
SCRIPT SUPERVISOR
'84 ALPHABET CITY

GLORIA MUSSETTA
COSTUMES
'83 TRENCHCOAT

TOBY MUSSMAN
LOCATIONS
'80 GALAXINA*
'83 MY TUTOR

JOHN MUTO
PRODUCTION DESIGNER
'84 NIGHT OF THE COMET
MISCELLANEOUS
'83 STRANGE INVADERS

FLOYD MUTRUX
DIRECTOR
'80 HOLLYWOOD KNIGHTS, THE
SCREENPLAY
'80 HOLLYWOOD KNIGHTS, THE

GAIL MUTRUX
ASSOCIATE PRODUCER
'79 PROMISES IN THE DARK

RON MUTZ
ASSOCIATE PRODUCER
'80 UNION CITY

TOM MWANGI
2ND ASST. DIRECTOR
'84 SHEENA*

BILLY MYATT
SPECIAL EFFECTS
'80 USED CARS
'84 ROMANCING THE STONE*

BARBARA MYERHOFF
MISCELLANEOUS
'83 TESTAMENT

CHUCK MYERS
UNIT PROD. MANAGER
'79 1941*
1ST ASST. DIRECTOR
'80 BORDERLINE
'80 CLOSE ENCOUNTERS OF THE THIRD KIND SPECIAL EDITION
'81 ...ALL THE MARBLES*
'83 RIGHT STUFF, THE
'83 LET'S SPEND THE NIGHT TOGETHER
'84 NO SMALL AFFAIR
'84 SWING SHIFT

DAVID MYERS
CINEMATOGRAPHER
'80 ROADIE
'80 DIE LAUGHING
'82 ZOOT SUIT
'83 DEADLY FORCE*

ED MYERS
MISCELLANEOUS
'84 MARVIN AND TIGE

ERIC MYERS
PUBLICIST
'81 HONKY TONK FREEWAY
'83 TRADING PLACES
'83 UNCOMMON VALOR
UNIT PUBLICIST
'84 FALLING IN LOVE

JULIAN MYERS
PUBLICIST
'80 DEFIANCE*

KEN MYERS
MISCELLANEOUS
'84 FINAL TERROR, THE

RUTH MYERS

COSTUMES
'79 ...AND JUSTICE FOR ALL
'79 MAIN EVENT, THE
'80 ALTERED STATES
'80 COMPETITION, THE
'80 IN GOD WE TRUST
'80 IT'S MY TURN
'81 FIRST MONDAY IN OCTOBER
'81 SUNDAY LOVERS*
'82 CANNERY ROW
'83 SOMETHING WICKED THIS WAY COMES
'84 ELECTRIC DREAMS
'84 WOMAN IN RED, THE
'84 TEACHERS

STANLEY MYERS

MUSIC
'78 DEER HUNTER, THE
'79 CLASS OF MISS MACMICHAEL,THE
'80 WATCHER IN THE WOODS, THE
'82 MOONLIGHTING
'83 BEYOND THE LIMIT

STEVEN MYERS

ASSISTANT EDITOR
'84 REPO MAN*

STEVIE MYERS

MISCELLANEOUS
'79 VILLAIN, THE
'80 WHOLLY MOSES!
'82 BEST LITTLE WHOREHOUSE IN TEXAS, THE
'84 WOMAN IN RED, THE

TONI MYERS

EDITOR
'82 BY DESIGN

ALAN MYERSON

DIRECTOR
'81 PRIVATE LESSONS

BENT MYGGEN

MUSIC
'81 SMOKEY BITES THE DUST

JOHN MYHERS

SCREENPLAY
'79 PRIZE FIGHTER, THE*
'80 PRIVATE EYES, THE*

FREDRIC MYROW

MUSIC
'79 PHANTASM*
'80 ON THE NICKEL

N

HISAO NABESHIMA
CASTING
'82 CHALLENGE, THE*
1ST ASST. DIRECTOR
'82 CHALLENGE, THE*

FRANCOIS NADAL
MISCELLANEOUS
'80 TESS

JESS NADELMAN
LOCATIONS
'79 FORCE OF ONE, A

NADIA
MAKEUP
'80 HERBIE GOES BANANAS*
'81 DEVIL AND MAX DEVLIN, THE*

BUDDY NADLER
2ND ASST. DIRECTOR
'79 FISH THAT SAVED PITTSBURGH, THE*

DEBORAH NADOOLMAN
COSTUMES
'79 1941
'80 BLUES BROTHERS
'81 RAIDERS OF THE LOST ARK
'81 AMERICAN WEREWOLF IN LONDON, AN
'83 TRADING PLACES
'83 TWILIGHT ZONE, THE MOVIE
'84 CRACKERS

JEANETTE NAE
SCRIPT SUPERVISOR
'79 MAGICIAN OF LUBLIN, THE

WALLY NAGHTIN
MISCELLANEOUS
'84 HOTEL NEW HAMPSHIRE, THE

JENNIFER NAIRN-SMITH
MISCELLANEOUS
'80 IDOLMAKER, THE

RAIJIN NAKAHATA
SCRIPT SUPERVISOR
'83 MERRY CHRISTMAS, MR. LAWRENCE

DESMOND NAKANO
SCREENPLAY
'79 BOULEVARD NIGHTS
'84 BODY ROCK

AKIRA NAKAYAMA
STILLS
'81 INCHON*

STEVEN NALEVANSKY
PRODUCER
'81 BLOOD BEACH

MARTY NALLAN
KEY GRIP
'79 ALL THAT JAZZ
'79 NATURAL ENEMIES
'80 FAME
'81 ROLLOVER

ARTHUR NAMES
SOUND
'80 ALLIGATOR
'80 MIDNIGHT MADNESS

HERB NANAS
MISCELLANEOUS
'82 FIRST BLOOD

MICHAEL NANKIN
DIRECTOR
'80 MIDNIGHT MADNESS*
SCREENPLAY
'80 MIDNIGHT MADNESS*
CO-PRODUCER
'80 MIDNIGHT MADNESS*

LUIGI NANNERINI
MISCELLANEOUS
'79 STARCRASH

J. CRAIG NANNOS
MISCELLANEOUS
'81 TAPS

MARCUS NANTON
EDITOR
'84 EXTERMINATOR II*

HARRY NAP
PRODUCTION MANAGER
'84 NEVERENDING STORY, THE

ANNIE NAP-OLEON
PROD. COORDINATOR
'84 NEVERENDING STORY, THE

JOE NAPOLITANO
1ST ASST. DIRECTOR
'80 FIRST DEADLY SIN
'81 BLOW OUT
'83 SCARFACE*
'84 BODY DOUBLE
'84 POPE OF GREENWICH VILLAGE,THE

GARY NARDINO
EXECUTIVE PRODUCER
'84 STAR TREK III: THE SEARCH FOR SPOCK

HIRO NARITA
CINEMATOGRAPHER
'83 NEVER CRY WOLF

SILVIO NARIZZANO
DIRECTOR
'79 CLASS OF MISS MACMICHAEL, THE

BOONE NARR
MISCELLANEOUS
'80 ANY WHICH WAY YOU CAN
'82 BEASTMASTER, THE
'82 PARADISE

SCOTT NARRIE
LOCATIONS
'81 FEAR NO EVIL

TOICHIRO NARUSHIMA
CINEMATOGRAPHER
'83 MERRY CHRISTMAS, MR. LAWRENCE

RON NARY
SPECIAL EFFECTS
'82 ZAPPED!*

ANNALISA NASALLA-ROCCA
COSTUMES
'84 SHEENA

MARCIA NASATIR
EXECUTIVE PRODUCER
'83 BIG CHILL, THE*

NANCY NASH
PUBLICIST
'82 FORCED VENGEANCE*

PHIL NASO
HAIR
'79 VOICES
'81 REDS*

NICK NASS
STILLS
'83 SAVANNAH SMILES

GEORGE NASSER
PRODUCTION MANAGER
'84 LITTLE DRUMMER GIRL, THE*

RIAD NASSER
2ND ASST. DIRECTOR
'83 HANNA K*

CONSTANT NATALE
HAIR
'81 SCANNERS
'81 GAS
'83 VIDEODROME*
'83 OF UNKNOWN ORIGIN*

GERMANO NATALI
SPECIAL EFFECTS
'79 STARCRASH*

HERMAN NATHAN
SPECIAL EFFECTS
'83 HERCULES

MICHAEL NATHANSON
EXEC IN CHARGE PROD
'84 ADVENTURES OF BUCKAROO BANZAI ACROSS THE 8TH DIMENSION, THE

HERTZ NATIV
MAKEUP
'84 JUST THE WAY YOU ARE*

FEDERICO NATIVIDAD
ASSISTANT EDITOR
'83 YEAR OF LIVING DANGEROUSLY, THE*

TOTO NATIVIDAD
ASSISTANT EDITOR
'84 PURPLE HEARTS*

RICK NATKIN
SCREENPLAY
'80 NIGHT OF THE JUGGLER*
'84 PURPLE HEARTS*
ASSOCIATE PRODUCER
'84 PURPLE HEARTS

JAMES NAU
ASSISTANT EDITOR
'84 GARBO TALKS

BECKY NAUERT
ASSISTANT EDITOR
'79 TOURIST TRAP*

DEIDRE NAUGHTON
COSTUMES
'79 PENITENTIARY*

GREGORY NAVA
DIRECTOR
'84 EL NORTE
SCREENPLAY
'84 EL NORTE*
MISCELLANEOUS
'84 EL NORTE

AURELIO NAVARRO
PRODUCTION MANAGER
'81 ENTER THE NINJA

BERTA NAVARRO
UNIT PROD. MANAGER
'84 EL NORTE*

WILLIE NAVARRO
ASSISTANT EDITOR
'79 DREAMER*
'80 BRUBAKER*

REN NAVEZ
2ND ASST. DIRECTOR
'83 BLACK STALLION RETURNS, THE

DEEPAK NAYER
UNIT MANAGER
'83 HEAT AND DUST

MATTHEW NAYTHONS
MISCELLANEOUS
'83 UNDER FIRE

BEV NEAL
ASSISTANT EDITOR
'83 RUNNING BRAVE

ROBIN NEAL
MAKEUP
'83 CUJO
'84 FRIDAY THE 13TH PART IV THE FINAL CHAPTER

MICHAEL NEALE
LOCATIONS
'80 GALAXINA*
'82 NIGHT SHIFT*
'83 MR. MOM
'84 ADVENTURES OF BUCKAROO BANZAI ACROSS THE 8TH DIMENSION, THE

JUD NEALON
ASSISTANT EDITOR
'79 GOING IN STYLE*
'80 ANY WHICH WAY YOU CAN
'80 UP THE ACADEMY

CAROLINE NEAME
PROD. SECRETARY
'79 STEVIE
LOCATIONS
'81 CHARIOTS OF FIRE*

RONALD NEAME
DIRECTOR
'79 METEOR
'80 HOPSCOTCH
'81 FIRST MONDAY IN OCTOBER

HAROD NEBENZAL
PROD. COORDINATOR
'79 FEDORA

LARRY NEBER
MISCELLANEOUS
'83 UNCOMMON VALOR

PRISCILLA NEDD
EDITOR
'83 EDDIE AND THE CRUISERS
'84 FLAMINGO KID, THE
'84 NO SMALL AFFAIR*
ASSISTANT EDITOR
'79 AMERICAN GIGOLO

UDI NEDIVI
MISCELLANEOUS
'83 LONE WOLF MCQUADE
'84 SHEENA

HAL NEEDHAM
DIRECTOR
'79 VILLAIN, THE
'80 SMOKEY AND THE BANDIT II
'81 CANNONBALL RUN, THE
'82 MEGAFORCE
'83 STROKER ACE
'84 CANNONBALL RUN II
SCREENPLAY
'82 MEGAFORCE*
'83 STROKER ACE*
'84 CANNONBALL RUN II*

TERRY NEEDHAM
1ST ASST. DIRECTOR
'83 BRITANNIA HOSPITAL*
2ND ASST. DIRECTOR
'79 FIFTH MUSKETEER, THE
'80 SHINING, THE*
'80 FFOLKES*
'80 FLASH GORDON*
'80 HEAVEN'S GATE*
LOCATIONS
'81 RAGTIME*
'81 DOGS OF WAR, THE*
'84 SUPERGIRL
MISCELLANEOUS
'81 HISTORY OF THE WORLD PART I

BEALA NEEL
ART DIRECTOR
'81 ...ALL THE MARBLES

JOSHUA NEFSKY
STILLS
'79 MEATBALLS

TRACY NEFTZGER
KEY GRIP
'81 GALAXY OF TERROR
'82 SWORD AND THE SORCERER, THE
'82 ANDROID
'82 EATING RAOUL
'82 LAST AMERICAN VIRGIN, THE
'83 SUBURBIA
'84 NOT FOR PUBLICATION*

ZELJKO "JOCKO" NEGOVETIC
MISCELLANEOUS
'84 RIVER, THE

ALFONSO LOPEZ NEGRETE
ASSOCIATE PRODUCER
'80 GUYANA: CULT OF THE DAMNED

BILLY NEIGHBORS
MISCELLANEOUS
'84 BEAR, THE

DEBRA NEIL
ASSISTANT EDITOR
'84 CHILDREN OF THE CORN

STEVE NEIL
MISCELLANEOUS
'80 BATTLE BEYOND THE STARS
'81 SATURDAY THE 14TH

VE NEILL
MAKEUP
'79 STAR TREK-THE MOTION PICTURE*
'79 TOURIST TRAP
'80 NINE TO FIVE*
'81 INCREDIBLE SHRINKING WOMAN, THE
'82 SWORD AND THE SORCERER, THE
'82 MONTY PYTHON LIVE AT THE HOLLYWOOD BOWL*

CLAUDE NEJAR
ASSOCIATE PRODUCER
'82 QUEST FOR FIRE*

ARGYLE NELSON
EDITOR
'80 NIGHT OF THE JUGGLER
'81 BUDDY, BUDDY
'81 CHU CHU AND THE PHILLY FLASH
'83 SOMETHING WICKED THIS WAY COMES*

B.J. NELSON
SCREENPLAY
'83 LONE WOLF MCQUADE

BILL NELSON
SOUND
'80 DEFIANCE*
'81 MODERN ROMANCE
'82 FRIDAY THE 13TH PART THREE IN 3D
'82 MOTHER LODE
'83 MAN WHO WASN'T THERE, THE
'84 MEATBALLS PART II

BOB NELSON
ART DIRECTOR
'82 SHOOT THE MOON

DANNI NELSON
HAIR
'79 BOARDWALK
'83 ECHOES

DOUG NELSON
MUSIC
'83 RICHARD PRYOR: HERE AND NOW

DOUG NELSON
MISCELLANEOUS
'82 VICE SQUAD

ERIK NELSON
PROPS
'79 BOULEVARD NIGHTS
'80 IT'S MY TURN
'80 MY BODYGUARD
'81 BLOW OUT
'81 MODERN ROMANCE
'82 OFFICER AND A GENTLEMAN, AN
'83 SPACEHUNTER: ADVENTURES IN THE FORBIDDEN ZONE
'83 HEART LIKE A WHEEL
'84 ADVENTURES OF BUCKAROO BANZAI ACROSS THE 8TH DIMENSION,THE

GARY NELSON
DIRECTOR
'79 BLACK HOLE, THE

JAMES NELSON
PRODUCER
'80 BORDERLINE
ASSOCIATE PRODUCER
'79 CHINA SYNDROME, THE
UNIT PROD. MANAGER
'79 CHINA SYNDROME, THE

JEFFREY NELSON
PRODUCER
'80 RETURN OF THE SECAUCUS SEVEN, THE*
'83 LIANNA*

KRISTEN NELSON
COSTUMES
'81 STUDENT BODIES
'82 LIAR'S MOON*
'83 MY TUTOR
'83 JOYSTICKS*

LLOYD NELSON
SCRIPT SUPERVISOR
'79 ESCAPE FROM ALCATRAZ
'80 ANY WHICH WAY YOU CAN
'80 BRONCO BILLY
'80 CHANGE OF SEASONS, A
'81 STRIPES
'82 FIREFOX
'82 HAMMETT*
'82 HONKYTONK MAN
'83 SUDDEN IMPACT
'83 OUTSIDERS, THE
'84 TIGHTROPE

MACK NELSON
HAIR
'81 EYE OF THE NEEDLE*

MIRIAM NELSON
CHOREOGRAPHER
'79 BUCK ROGERS

RALPH NELSON
STILLS
'80 RAISE THE TITANIC
'80 MOUNTAIN MEN, THE
'81 S.O.B.*
'81 LOOKER
'82 JINXED
'83 TWILIGHT ZONE, THE MOVIE*
'83 WAR GAMES
'84 BODY DOUBLE
'84 KARATE KID, THE

RALPH NELSON JR.
STILLS
'79 BUTCH AND SUNDANCE: THE EARLY YEARS
'80 HERO AT LARGE
'80 HIDE IN PLAIN SIGHT*
'80 NINE TO FIVE
'83 MR. MOM
'84 BIRDY*
'84 GREMLINS
'84 INDIANA JONES AND THE TEMPLE OF DOOM*

SANDY NELSON
SCRIPT SUPERVISOR
'79 BLACK HOLE, THE
'80 BORDERLINE*
LOCATIONS
'84 GARBO TALKS*

STEVE NELSON
SOUND
'84 NIGHT OF THE COMET
'84 REPO MAN

TERRY NELSON
ASSOCIATE PRODUCER
'80 MELVIN AND HOWARD
'80 XANADU
'81 RAGGEDY MAN
'82 MISSING
'83 CROSS CREEK
PRODUCTION MANAGER
'83 CROSS CREEK
UNIT PROD. MANAGER
'80 MELVIN AND HOWARD
'80 XANADU
'81 RAGGEDY MAN

THOMAS NELSON
SOUND
'84 RECKLESS

WALLY NELSON
ASSISTANT EDITOR
'83 NEVER SAY NEVER AGAIN

GERHARD NEMETZ
MAKEUP
'82 NIGHT CROSSING*
HAIR
'82 NIGHT CROSSING*

MICHAEL NEMIRSKY
ART DIRECTOR
'83 SPACEHUNTER: ADVENTURES IN THE FORBIDDEN ZONE*

RILDO NENEZES
MISCELLANEOUS
'84 KARATE KID, THE

FLORENCE NERLINGER
PROD. OFFICE COORD.
'79 RICH KIDS
PROD. COORDINATOR
'80 FINAL COUNTDOWN, THE
'81 RICH AND FAMOUS*
'82 HANKY PANKY
'82 NIGHT SHIFT*

JANE NERLINGER
PROD. OFFICE COORD.
'81 SO FINE

MARCO NERO
STILLS
'81 NESTING, THE
'84 PREPPIES

EMIL NERODA
SOUND
'79 SCALPEL

ROBERT NESE
STILLS
'79 C.H.O.M.P.S.*
'79 GOLDENGIRL

DICKEY NESENGER
SCRIPT SUPERVISOR
'79 NORTH DALLAS FORTY

RAMI NESHER
MISCELLANEOUS
'84 SHEENA

LAWRENCE NESIS
ASSOCIATE PRODUCER
'79 MEATBALLS
'81 ATLANTIC CITY*
'81 HAPPY BIRTHDAY TO ME
'81 MY BLOODY VALENTINE
'81 VIDEODROME

MICHAEL NESMITH
SCREENPLAY
'83 TIMERIDER*
EXECUTIVE PRODUCER
'83 TIMERIDER
'84 REPO MAN
MUSIC
'83 TIMERIDER

ROBERT NESSLIN
EXECUTIVE PRODUCER
'81 TUCK EVERLASTING

GEOFFREY NETHERCOTT
EXECUTIVE PRODUCER
'83 MERRY CHRISTMAS, MR. LAWRENCE*

BEN NETT
SCREENPLAY
'80 WITHOUT WARNING*

BRAD NEUFELD
ASSOCIATE PRODUCER
'81 FUNHOUSE, THE

GLENN NEUFELD
STILLS
'83 FRIGHTMARE*
PROPS
'83 FRIGHTMARE

MACE NEUFELD
PRODUCER
'79 FRISCO KID, THE
EXECUTIVE PRODUCER
'81 FUNHOUSE, THE*
ASSOCIATE PRODUCER
'81 FINAL CONFLICT, THE*

STANLEY NEUFIELD
PRODUCTION MANAGER
'79 FIREPOWER*

STUART NEUMAN
LOCATIONS
'82 AMATEUR, THE*

KURT NEUMANN
ASSOCIATE PRODUCER
'82 CANNERY ROW
'82 MONSIGNOR
'83 STAR CHAMBER*
'84 HARD TO HOLD*
PRODUCTION MANAGER
'79 MUPPET MOVIE, THE
'82 MONSIGNOR
'84 HARD TO HOLD
UNIT PROD. MANAGER
'80 OH GOD! BOOK II
'82 CANNERY ROW
'83 STAR CHAMBER

STUART NEUMANN
2ND ASST. DIRECTOR
'82 ZAPPED!*
LOCATIONS
'81 FIRST MONDAY IN OCTOBER*
'82 BEST FRIENDS*
'84 PROTOCOL*

WILLIE PAUL NEUNER
SPECIAL EFFECTS
'79 LOVE AND BULLETS*

THOMAS NEUWIRTH
MISCELLANEOUS
'82 FIRST BLOOD

ROBERT NEW
CINEMATOGRAPHER
'80 PROM NIGHT

BASIL NEWALL
MAKEUP
'79 MAN, A WOMAN AND A BANK, A*
'79 GREAT TRAIN ROBBERY, THE*
'81 CLASH OF THE TITANS*
'81 EXCALIBUR*
'82 VENOM

PETER NEWARD
CINEMATOGRAPHER
'80 KIDS ARE ALL RIGHT, THE*

CHRIS NEWBERRY
EDITOR
'81 SUNDAY LOVERS*

NORMAN NEWBERRY
ART DIRECTOR
'79 WINTER KILLS
'81 GHOST STORY
'81 HISTORY OF THE WORLD PART I
'82 BEST LITTLE WHOREHOUSE IN TEXAS, THE
'83 STAYING ALIVE
'83 TABLE FOR FIVE
'84 RIVER, THE

PIP NEWBERRY
COSTUMES
'83 LOCAL HERO*
'84 OXFORD BLUES

IRA NEWBORN
MUSIC
'81 ALL NIGHT LONG*
'84 SIXTEEN CANDLES
MUSIC SUPERVISOR
'80 BLUES BROTHERS

LAURIE NEWBOUND
SCRIPT SUPERVISOR
'80 HOME MOVIES*

J.R. NEWCOM
ASSISTANT EDITOR
'81 EARTHLING, THE*

PAT NEWCOMB
PUBLICIST
'82 SHOOT THE MOON*

MIKE NEWELL
DIRECTOR
'80 AWAKENING, THE

MURRAY NEWEY
1ST ASST. DIRECTOR
'81 STRANGE BEHAVIOR
'82 PIRATE MOVIE, THE
'83 MAN FROM SNOWY RIVER, THE
'84 PHAR LAP

MARY ANN NEWFIELD
SCRIPT SUPERVISOR
'79 AMITYVILLE HORROR, THE
'81 SOUTHERN COMFORT
'82 OFFICER AND A GENTLEMAN, AN

CHASE NEWHART
2ND ASST. DIRECTOR
'80 IN GOD WE TRUST*
'80 WHY WOULD I LIE?*

CHARLES NEWIRTH
UNIT PROD. MANAGER
'82 PARASITE
LOCATIONS
'82 SEDUCTION, THE
'84 THIEF OF HEARTS*

DALE NEWKIRK
SPECIAL EFFECTS
'80 BLACK MARBLE, THE
'82 PERSONAL BEST

CHRIS NEWMAN
SOUND
'79 ALL THAT JAZZ*
'79 HAIR
'79 WINTER KILLS
'80 FAME
'80 ONE-TRICK PONY*
'80 WINDOWS
'81 RAGTIME
'81 FAN, THE
'82 SOPHIE'S CHOICE
'82 SOUP FOR ONE
'82 WORLD ACCORDING TO GARP, THE
'83 DANIEL
'84 AMADEUS
'84 BEAT STREET

CHRIS NEWMAN
1ST ASST. DIRECTOR
'84 FINDERS KEEPERS
2ND ASST. DIRECTOR
'81 FINAL CONFLICT, THE*
'81 GREAT MUPPET CAPER, THE
'82 DARK CRYSTAL, THE
'83 SUPERMAN III*
'84 SUPERGIRL*

DAN NEWMAN
SOUND
'83 ANGEL OF H.E.A.T.*

DAVID NEWMAN
SCREENPLAY
'81 SUPERMAN II*
'82 JINXED*
'83 SUPERMAN III*
'84 SHEENA*

DAVID NEWMAN
2ND ASST. DIRECTOR
'83 ANGEL OF H.E.A.T.

DON NEWMAN
MISCELLANEOUS
'84 ANGEL

DONALD NEWMAN
1ST ASST. DIRECTOR
'84 THIS IS SPINAL TAP
2ND ASST. DIRECTOR
'80 MIDNIGHT MADNESS*
'81 STRIPES*

EVE NEWMAN
EDITOR
'80 LITTLE MISS MARKER
'84 NO SMALL AFFAIR*

JAN NEWMAN
MAKEUP
'79 FAST COMPANY
'80 TOUCHED BY LOVE*

LESLIE NEWMAN
SCREENPLAY
'81 SUPERMAN II*
'83 SUPERMAN III*

MARK NEWMAN
ASSISTANT EDITOR
'84 JOY OF SEX, THE

PAT NEWMAN
KEY GRIP
'80 KIDS ARE ALL RIGHT, THE

PAUL NEWMAN
PRODUCER
'84 HARRY & SON*
DIRECTOR
'84 HARRY & SON
SCREENPLAY
'84 HARRY & SON*

PETER NEWMAN
MISCELLANEOUS
'82 COME BACK TO THE 5 & 10, JIMMY DEAN, JIMMY DEAN

PHYLLIS NEWMAN
MAKEUP
'82 BY DESIGN
'82 FIRST BLOOD*
'82 MOTHER LODE*
'82 OUT OF THE BLUE
'83 RUNNING BRAVE

RANDY NEWMAN
MUSIC
'81 RAGTIME
'84 NATURAL, THE

THOMAS NEWMAN
MUSIC
'84 RECKLESS
'84 REVENGE OF THE NERDS
'84 GRANDVIEW, U.S.A.

WALTER NEWMAN
SCREENPLAY
'79 CHAMP, THE

CATHY NEWPORT
SCRIPT SUPERVISOR
'81 RICHARD PRYOR: LIVE ON THE SUNSET STRIP*

JAMES WILLIAM NEWPORT
PRODUCTION DESIGNER
'79 OVER THE EDGE
'81 CHEECH AND CHONG'S NICE DREAMS
'83 HEART LIKE A WHEEL
'84 MEATBALLS PART II

JIM NEWPORT
MISCELLANEOUS
'82 ZAPPED!

KATHLEEN NEWPORT
SCRIPT SUPERVISOR
'81 PATERNITY
'82 FRIDAY THE 13TH PART THREE IN 3D
'83 GET CRAZY

CHRISTY ANN NEWQUIST
MAKEUP
'84 CRIMES OF PASSION

DAVE NEWTON
PROPS
'83 MONTY PYTHON'S THE MEANING OF LIFE*

MARVIN NEWTON
STILLS
'79 AMERICATHON
'80 WHY WOULD I LIE?

JOANNA NEY
PUBLICIST
'79 GOING IN STYLE
'81 ROLLOVER
'81 EYEWITNESS
UNIT PUBLICIST
'79 PLAYERS

YURI NEYMAN
CINEMATOGRAPHER
'83 LIQUID SKY
SPECIAL EFFECTS
'83 LIQUID SKY

DAVID NG
ART DIRECTOR
'79 SAINT JACK

GEORGE NICE
PRODUCER
'83 ECHOES*

ALLAN NICHOLLS
SCREENPLAY
'79 PERFECT COUPLE, A*
ASSOCIATE PRODUCER
'79 QUINTET
PRODUCTION MANAGER
'83 STREAMERS
1ST ASST. DIRECTOR
'83 STREAMERS

BOB NICHOLS
ASSISTANT EDITOR
'84 BEAT STREET*

CONNIE NICHOLS
HAIR
'79 CONCORDE-AIRPORT '79, THE
'80 LITTLE MISS MARKER*
'81 BLOOD BEACH
'81 PENNIES FROM HEAVEN*
'84 JOHNNY DANGEROUSLY*

DAVID NICHOLS
ASSOCIATE PRODUCER
'79 AMERICATHON
'80 IDOLMAKER, THE*
ART DIRECTOR
'82 SWAMP THING
PRODUCTION DESIGNER
'83 TESTAMENT

DAVID NICHOLS
2ND ASST. DIRECTOR
'83 HEAT AND DUST

MIKE NICHOLS
PRODUCER
'83 SILKWOOD*
DIRECTOR
'80 GILDA LIVE
'83 SILKWOOD

PETER NICHOLS
SCREENPLAY
'83 PRIVATES ON PARADE

AL NICHOLSON
1ST ASST. DIRECTOR
'79 C.H.O.M.P.S.
'84 COUNTRY

BRUCE NICHOLSON
MISCELLANEOUS
'84 NEVERENDING STORY, THE
'84 INDIANA JONES AND THE TEMPLE OF DOOM

CHRISTINE NICHOLSON
COSTUMES
'80 SCHIZOID

DAVID NICHOLSON
EDITOR
'79 RUNNING

GEORGE NICHOLSON
EDITOR
'79 GOLDENGIRL
'80 COAST TO COAST

JAMES NICHOLSON
1ST ASST. DIRECTOR
'79 NORMA RAE

LESLEY LYNN NICHOLSON
COSTUMES
'82 PARASITE

SAM NICHOLSON
MISCELLANEOUS
'80 WATCHER IN THE WOODS, THE
'83 TWO OF A KIND

TONY NICHOLSON
PROPS
'80 OUTSIDER, THE

WALLY NICITA
CASTING
'80 CADDYSHACK
'80 DIE LAUGHING
'80 PRIVATE BENJAMIN*
'81 BODY HEAT
'81 WHOSE LIFE IS IT ANYWAY?
'81 GOING APE!
'82 LOVE CHILD
'82 MISSING
'83 BIG CHILL, THE
'83 DOCTOR DETROIT
'83 UNDER FIRE
'83 WAR GAMES
'84 BLAME IT ON RIO*
'84 ELECTRIC DREAMS*
'84 IRRECONCILABLE DIFFERENCES*
'84 MIKE'S MURDER
'84 RACING WITH THE MOON
'84 IMPULSE*
'84 AMERICAN DREAMER*

JIMMY NICKERSON
STUNT COORDINATOR
'79 ROCKY II
'80 RAGING BULL
'83 TOUGH ENOUGH

DAVID NICKSAY
PRODUCER
'84 MRS. SOFFEL*
ASSOCIATE PRODUCER
'82 I'M DANCING AS FAST AS I CAN
PRODUCTION MANAGER
'82 I'M DANCING AS FAST AS I CAN*

STEVE NICOLAIDES
PRODUCTION MANAGER
'82 SENDER, THE

PAUL NICOLAS
DIRECTOR
'83 CHAINED HEAT
SCREENPLAY
'83 CHAINED HEAT*

JOHN NICOLELLA
PRODUCER
'83 EASY MONEY
EXECUTIVE PRODUCER
'80 TIMES SQUARE*
ASSOCIATE PRODUCER
'79 LAST EMBRACE
'80 WINDOWS
'81 FAN, THE*
PRODUCTION MANAGER
'83 CURSE OF THE PINK PANTHER*
UNIT PROD. MANAGER
'80 WINDOWS
2ND UNIT DIRECTOR
'80 TIMES SQUARE*

MICHAEL NICOLINI
PRODUCTION MANAGER
'80 OH! HEAVENLY DOG*

MICHEL NICOLINI
UNIT MANAGER
'79 LITTLE ROMANCE, A*

HEINER NIEHAUS
MAKEUP
'84 NEVERENDING STORY, THE*

LENNIE NIEHAUS
MUSIC
'84 CITY HEAT
'84 TIGHTROPE

TRISH NIEHAUS
PROD. SECRETARY
'84 RIVER, THE*

TIM NIELSEN
EXECUTIVE PRODUCER
'82 BRAINWAVES*

BRENDA NIELSON
SCREENPLAY
'82 OUT OF THE BLUE*

DAVID NIEMAN
MISCELLANEOUS
'82 FIREFOX

LISA NIEMI
CHOREOGRAPHER
'84 GRANDVIEW, U.S.A.*

CYNTHIA NIGH
PROD. SECRETARY
'83 TWILIGHT ZONE, THE MOVIE*

JEFF NIGHTBYRD
LOCATIONS
'80 ROADIE

GOVIND NIHALANI
2ND UNIT DIRECTOR
'82 GANDHI

VASLAV NIJINSKY
CHOREOGRAPHER
'80 NIJINSKY*

HARRY NILSSON
MUSIC
'80 POPEYE

LEONARD NIMOY
DIRECTOR
'84 STAR TREK III:
THE SEARCH FOR SPOCK

BILL NIPPER
SPECIAL EFFECTS
'82 I, THE JURY*

DENNIS NISBETT
SOUND
'79 ARABIAN ADVENTURE

THEO NISCHWITZ
MISCELLANEOUS
'79 FEDORA

JOHN FORREST NISS
MISCELLANEOUS
'80 HANGAR 18

JACK NITZSCHE
MUSIC
'79 HARDCORE
'79 WHEN YOU COMIN' BACK,
RED RYDER?
'80 CRUISING
'80 HEARTBEAT
'81 CUTTER'S WAY
'82 CANNERY ROW
'82 OFFICER AND A GENTLEMAN, AN
'82 PERSONAL BEST*
'83 BREATHLESS
'83 WITHOUT A TRACE
'84 RAZOR'S EDGE, THE
'84 STARMAN
'84 WINDY CITY

DAVID NIVEN JR.
PRODUCER
'79 ESCAPE TO ATHENA*
'82 MONSIGNOR*

CHRIS NIXON
PUBLICIST
'80 AWAKENING, THE

FRANKIE NIXON
SCRIPT SUPERVISOR
'84 CHILDREN OF THE CORN*
'84 CRIMES OF PASSION*

BERNARD NOBEL
SOUND
'83 SMITHEREENS*

NIGEL NOBLE
SOUND
'84 OVER THE BROOKLYN BRIDGE

PEPITA NOBLE
ASSOCIATE EDITOR
'79 BOARDWALK

THOM NOBLE
EDITOR
'79 BOARDWALK
'81 TATTOO
'84 RED DAWN
MISCELLANEOUS
'79 NORTH DALLAS FORTY
'82 FIRST BLOOD

BURT NODELLA
MISCELLANEOUS
'80 JAZZ SINGER, THE

MATTHEW NODELLA
LOCATIONS
'80 JAZZ SINGER, THE

BARRY NOLAN
MISCELLANEOUS
'84 DUNE
'84 CONAN THE DESTROYER
'84 MEATBALLS PART II

BOB NOLAN
SPECIAL EFFECTS
'80 SEEMS LIKE OLD TIMES

LELAND NOLAN
PRODUCER
'80 FIENDISH PLOT
OF DR. FU MANCHU, THE*

STEPHANIE NOLAN
ASSISTANT EDITOR
'82 OUT OF THE BLUE*

RANDY NOLEN
MISCELLANEOUS
'81 HELL NIGHT
'83 MORTUARY
'84 UNDER THE VOLCANO
'84 FRIDAY THE 13TH PART
IV THE FINAL CHAPTER

AILEEN NOLLMAN
SCRIPT SUPERVISOR
'82 DEATHWISH II

MIKE NOMAD
MISCELLANEOUS
'84 SPLASH

ERIC VAN HAREN NOMAN
MISCELLANEOUS
'79 HANOVER STREET
'81 FRIDAY THE 13TH PART TWO
'83 MAN WHO WASN'T THERE, THE

MAURO NONNIS
ASSISTANT EDITOR
'83 1990: THE BRONX WARRIORS*

RICHARD NORD
<u>ASSISTANT EDITOR</u>
'82 MIDSUMMER NIGHT'S SEX COMEDY, A
'83 ZELIG*
'84 BROADWAY DANNY ROSE*

NEIL NORDLINGER
<u>MISCELLANEOUS</u>
'83 JAWS 3-D

GUS NORIN
<u>MAKEUP</u>
'80 WHOLLY MOSES!*

JOHN NORIN
<u>MAKEUP</u>
'80 OH GOD! BOOK II*
'82 PARTNERS*

ROBERT NORIN
<u>MAKEUP</u>
'80 FATSO
'80 WHOLLY MOSES!*
'81 HISTORY OF THE WORLD PART I
'82 DEATH VALLEY
<u>MISCELLANEOUS</u>
'80 CRUISING

PETER NORMAN
<u>CINEMATOGRAPHER</u>
'80 GILDA LIVE*
<u>2ND UNIT DIRECTOR</u>
'83 SURVIVORS, THE
<u>MISCELLANEOUS</u>
'81 NIGHTHAWKS
'84 MRS. SOFFEL

RON NORMAN
<u>PRODUCTION MANAGER</u>
'82 BRAINWAVES

AARON NORRIS
<u>ASSOCIATE PRODUCER</u>
'82 SILENT RAGE
'83 LONE WOLF MCQUADE*
<u>STUNT COORDINATOR</u>
'79 FORCE OF ONE, A
'80 OCTAGON, THE
'81 EYE FOR AN EYE, AN
'82 SILENT RAGE
'82 FORCED VENGEANCE
'83 LONE WOLF MCQUADE
<u>MISCELLANEOUS</u>
'79 FORCE OF ONE, A
'80 OCTAGON, THE

CHUCK NORRIS
<u>MISCELLANEOUS</u>
'79 FORCE OF ONE, A
'80 OCTAGON, THE

GEORGE NORRIS
<u>EDITOR</u>
'80 HE KNOWS YOU'RE ALONE
'84 EXTERMINATOR II*

GLORIA NORRIS
<u>SCREENPLAY</u>
'80 HOME MOVIES*
<u>SCRIPT SUPERVISOR</u>
'80 HOME MOVIES*

PATRICIA NORRIS
<u>COSTUMES</u>
'79 FISH THAT SAVED PITTSBURGH, THE
'80 BALTIMORE BULLET, THE
'80 ELEPHANT MAN, THE
'80 FATSO
'80 HEARTBEAT
'81 FOUR FRIENDS
'81 HISTORY OF THE WORLD PART I
'82 FRANCES
'82 VICTOR/VICTORIA
'83 SCARFACE
'83 STAR CHAMBER
'84 JOHNNY DANGEROUSLY
'84 MICKI AND MAUDE
'84 RACING WITH THE MOON
'84 2010

PATRICK NORRIS
<u>COSTUMES</u>
'80 ON THE NICKEL

ALEX NORTH
<u>MUSIC</u>
'80 CARNY
'81 DRAGONSLAYER
'84 UNDER THE VOLCANO

EDMUND NORTH
<u>SCREENPLAY</u>
'79 METEOR*

REX NORTH
<u>KEY GRIP</u>
'83 TIMERIDER

CHARLES NORTHCOTE
<u>MISCELLANEOUS</u>
'83 CHRISTMAS STORY, A

B.W.L. NORTON
<u>DIRECTOR</u>
'79 MORE AMERICAN GRAFFITTI
<u>SCREENPLAY</u>
'79 MORE AMERICAN GRAFFITTI
'83 LOSIN' IT

BETSY NORTON
<u>SCRIPT SUPERVISOR</u>
'79 RUNNER STUMBLES, THE
'79 GREAT SANTINI, THE
'79 HARDCORE
'79 SCAVENGER HUNT
'80 INSIDE MOVES
'80 MY BODYGUARD
'81 HISTORY OF THE WORLD PART I
'81 WHOSE LIFE IS IT ANYWAY?
'82 SIX WEEKS
'82 DINER
'82 TOY, THE
'82 ESCAPE ARTIST, THE
'84 IRRECONCILABLE DIFFERENCES
'84 RIVER, THE
'84 UNFAITHFULLY YOURS
'84 WINDY CITY

CHARLES NORTON
<u>UNIT PROD. MANAGER</u>
'83 MAUSOLEUM
<u>1ST ASST. DIRECTOR</u>
'83 MAUSOLEUM

ESCOTT NORTON
<u>PROPS</u>
'81 GRADUATION DAY

ROSANNA NORTON
<u>COSTUMES</u>
'80 STUNT MAN, THE
'80 AIRPLANE
'82 TRON*
'82 CHILLY SCENES OF WINTER
'83 GET CRAZY
'84 HARD TO HOLD

BILL NORTON SR.
<u>SCREENPLAY</u>
'80 NIGHT OF THE JUGGLER*

THOMAS NORTON
<u>MISCELLANEOUS</u>
'82 STILL OF THE NIGHT

BERNADETTE NORWICKI
<u>PROD. SECRETARY</u>
'83 BLACK STALLION RETURNS, THE*

JACQUE NOSCO
<u>SOUND</u>
'80 BALTIMORE BULLET, THE

NOEL NOSSECK
<u>DIRECTOR</u>
'79 DREAMER
'81 KING OF THE MOUNTAIN

BLAISE NOTO
<u>UNIT PUBLICIST</u>
'83 BREATHLESS

BLAINE NOVAK
PRODUCER
'81 THEY ALL LAUGHED*
SCREENPLAY
'84 STRANGERS KISS*

DAVID NOVEK
UNIT PUBLICIST
'82 QUEST FOR FIRE

DON NOVELLO
SCREENPLAY
'80 GILDA LIVE*

ANGELO NOVI
STILLS
'84 ONCE UPON A TIME IN AMERICA

ED NOVICK
SOUND
'83 LIQUID SKY*

CHRISTOPHER NOWAK
ART DIRECTOR
'81 FORT APACHE, THE BRONX
'82 HANKY PANKY

DAVID NOWELL
MISCELLANEOUS
'79 VILLAIN, THE

JAMES NOWNES
EDITOR
'82 PENITENTIARY II

ARIELLE NOYER
ASSISTANT EDITOR
'80 TESS*
'84 JUST THE WAY YOU ARE*

MICHAEL NOZIK
2ND ASST. DIRECTOR
'81 DOZENS, THE
LOCATIONS
'83 BABY IT'S YOU*
'84 RECKLESS

PAUL NUCKLES
STUNT COORDINATOR
'84 PLACES IN THE HEART

TY NUH
MISCELLANEOUS
'81 DEAD AND BURIED

GRAFTON NUNES
PRODUCER
'84 LOVELESS, THE*

PAQUITA NUNEZ
HAIR
'80 ISLAND, THE
'81 SPHINX*

C. DENEEN NUNLEY
PROPS
'81 STUDENT BODIES

DON NUNLEY
PRODUCTION DESIGNER
'81 STUDENT BODIES
PROPS
'79 AMITYVILLE HORROR, THE
'80 RESURRECTION
'80 STIR CRAZY
'80 HOW TO BEAT THE HIGH COST OF LIVING
'81 SUNDAY LOVERS
'83 EDDIE MACON'S RUN*
'84 WOMAN IN RED, THE

FRANK NURRE
LOCATIONS
'80 CHANGE OF SEASONS, A

ADOLF NURSCHINGER
PROPS
'84 LITTLE DRUMMER GIRL, THE

JOHN NUTH
ASSISTANT EDITOR
'81 BEYOND THE REEF*

NANCY NUTTALL
MISCELLANEOUS
'81 SATURDAY THE 14TH

GERALD NUTTING
ASSOCIATE PRODUCER
'81 S.O.B.
'82 VICTOR/VICTORIA
'83 CURSE OF THE PINK PANTHER
'83 MAN WHO LOVED WOMEN, THE
'83 TRAIL OF THE PINK PANTHER

BRUNO NUYTTEN
CINEMATOGRAPHER
'80 BRUBAKER

DAN NYBERG
PRODUCTION MANAGER
'80 PROM NIGHT
2ND UNIT DIRECTOR
'80 PROM NIGHT*

BEN NYE
MAKEUP
'80 HEAVEN'S GATE

BEN NYE II
MAKEUP
'79 MUPPET MOVIE, THE
'79 10*
'82 CHILLY SCENES OF WINTER
'83 TERMS OF ENDEARMENT

BEN NYE JR.
MAKEUP
'81 CUTTER'S WAY
'82 SIX WEEKS*
'84 BEVERLY HILLS COP*
'84 RHINESTONE*

SVEN NYKVIST
CINEMATOGRAPHER
'79 STARTING OVER
'79 HURRICANE
'80 WILLIE & PHIL
'81 POSTMAN ALWAYS RINGS TWICE, THE
'82 CANNERY ROW
'83 STAR 80

MICHAEL NYMAN
MUSIC
'83 DRAUGHTSMAN CONTRACT, THE

RON NYSWANER
SCREENPLAY
'83 SMITHEREENS*
'84 MRS. SOFFEL

O

DAN O'BANNON
SCREENPLAY
'79 ALIEN
'81 DEAD AND BURIED*
'83 BLUE THUNDER*
MISCELLANEOUS
'79 ALIEN

ROBERT O'BRADOVICH
MAKEUP
'79 WANDERERS, THE

PETER O'BRIAN
PRODUCER
'79 FAST COMPANY*
'82 GREY FOX, THE

BERNADETTE O'BRIEN
COSTUMES
'82 VICE SQUAD

CATHERINE O'BRIEN
PUBLICIST
'80 HUMAN FACTOR, THE*
'83 BRITANNIA HOSPITAL
UNIT PUBLICIST
'79 ARABIAN ADVENTURE

DEAN O'BRIEN
UNIT PROD. MANAGER
'82 THINGS ARE TOUGH ALL OVER*
'83 WRONG IS RIGHT*

DENIS O'BRIEN
EXECUTIVE PRODUCER
'79 MONTY PYTHON'S LIFE OF BRIAN*
'81 TIME BANDITS*
'82 MISSIONARY, THE*
'82 MONTY PYTHON LIVE AT THE HOLLYWOOD BOWL*
'83 PRIVATES ON PARADE*

FRANCIS O'BRIEN
EXECUTIVE PRODUCER
'81 GALLIPOLI

RICHARD O'BRIEN
SCREENPLAY
'81 SHOCK TREATMENT*
MUSIC
'81 SHOCK TREATMENT*

WILLIAM O'BRIEN
ART DIRECTOR
'79 1941
'82 CANNERY ROW

KEVIN O'CALLAGHAN
MISCELLANEOUS
'84 FLAMINGO KID, THE

C.R. O'CHRISTOPHER
SCREENPLAY
'81 LAST CHASE, THE*

CAROL O'CONNELL
HAIR
'80 HOPSCOTCH*
'81 STRIPES
'82 MY FAVORITE YEAR*

SUSAN O'CONNELL
PRODUCER
'80 TELL ME A RIDDLE*

THOMAS O'CONNELL
MISCELLANEOUS
'83 JOYSTICKS

DENNIS O'CONNOR
ASSOCIATE EDITOR
'84 C.H.U.D.

PAT O'CONNOR
PROPS
'79 AMERICAN GIGOLO
'80 SEEMS LIKE OLD TIMES
'80 CAN'T STOP THE MUSIC
'83 DOCTOR DETROIT
'84 RACING WITH THE MOON

PETER O'CONNOR
SOUND
'82 HOUSE OF THE LONG SHADOWS

RICHARD O'CONNOR
EXEC IN CHARGE PROD
'79 MUPPET MOVIE, THE
'80 RAISE THE TITANIC
'80 BORDERLINE
'81 HARD COUNTRY
'81 LEGEND OF THE LONE RANGER, THE
'81 ON GOLDEN POND
'82 BARBAROSA
MISCELLANEOUS
'81 GREAT MUPPET CAPER, THE

DENISE O'DELL
PROD. COORDINATOR
'79 CUBA
MISCELLANEOUS
'82 EVIL UNDER THE SUN

DENNIS O'DELL
EXECUTIVE PRODUCER
'79 CUBA
'80 HEAVEN'S GATE*
PRODUCTION MANAGER
'80 HEAVEN'S GATE*

JERRY O'DELL
MAKEUP
'79 HOT STUFF*
'80 CHEECH AND CHONG'S NEXT MOVIE
'80 OH GOD! BOOK II*
'81 HONKY TONK FREEWAY*
'82 OFFICER AND A GENTLEMAN, AN
'83 DOCTOR DETROIT*
'84 SWING SHIFT*

MICHAEL O'DONOGHUE
PRODUCER
'79 MR. MIKE'S MONDO VIDEO
DIRECTOR
'79 MR. MIKE'S MONDO VIDEO
SCREENPLAY
'79 MR. MIKE'S MONDO VIDEO*
'80 GILDA LIVE*

PATRICIA O'DONOHUE
MISCELLANEOUS
'80 STIR CRAZY

DANNY O'DONOVAN
PRODUCER
'79 GOLDENGIRL

EDWIN O'DONOVAN
ART DIRECTOR
'79 HARDCORE
'80 RESURRECTION
'81 HONKY TONK FREEWAY

JAMES O'FALLON
ASSOCIATE PRODUCER
'83 RISKY BUSINESS

DENNIS O'FLAHERTY
SCREENPLAY
'82 HAMMETT*

JOE O'HAR
ASSOCIATE PRODUCER
'81 HAND, THE*
LOCATIONS
'80 CLOSE ENCOUNTERS OF THE THIRD KIND SPECIAL EDITION
'81 HAND, THE
'82 FRANCES
'82 PARTNERS
'83 BREATHLESS
'84 RIVER, THE*
'84 BEAR, THE*

PAM O'HAR
LOCATIONS
'79 AMERICATHON

CORKY O'HARA
EDITOR
'80 HOME MOVIES
'80 EXTERMINATOR, THE

JOCK O'MAHONEY
STUNT COORDINATOR
'81 TARZAN, THE APE MAN

DAVID O'MALLEY
SCREENPLAY
'82 BOOGENS, THE*

SUZANNE O'MALLEY
SCREENPLAY
'83 PRIVATE SCHOOL*

C. TIMOTHY O'MEARA
EDITOR
'79 ROSE, THE*
'79 GOING IN STYLE*
'82 CONAN THE BARBARIAN
'84 LAST STARFIGHTER, THE

EMMITT-LEON O'NEIL
2ND ASST. DIRECTOR
'80 WHEN TIME RAN OUT*
'81 S.O.B.
'81 INCREDIBLE SHRINKING WOMAN, THE
'81 PENNIES FROM HEAVEN*
'82 BEST LITTLE WHOREHOUSE IN TEXAS, THE*
'82 NATIONAL LAMPOON'S CLASS REUNION*
'83 ALL THE RIGHT MOVES
'84 OH GOD, YOU DEVIL

ROBERT VINCENT O'NEIL
DIRECTOR
'84 ANGEL
SCREENPLAY
'80 BALTIMORE BULLET, THE*
'82 VICE SQUAD*
'83 DEADLY FORCE*
'84 ANGEL*

FRANK O'NEILL
MISCELLANEOUS
'79 NORTH DALLAS FORTY

INSPECTOR O'NEILL
MISCELLANEOUS
'80 OUTSIDER, THE

TERENCE O'NEILL
EXECUTIVE PRODUCER
'81 MOMMIE DEAREST*

TERESA O'NEILL
PROD. COORDINATOR
'84 CHOOSE ME

DOUG O'NEONS
MISCELLANEOUS
'84 CHILDREN OF THE CORN

CHARLIE O'REILLY
MISCELLANEOUS
'79 ON THE YARD

MICHAEL O'REILLY
MISCELLANEOUS
'79 MY BRILLIANT CAREER

PATRICIA O'REILLY
PUBLICIST
'83 SUPERMAN III*

P.J. O'ROURKE
SCREENPLAY
'83 EASY MONEY*

STEPHEN O'ROURKE
EXECUTIVE PRODUCER
'82 PINK FLOYD: THE WALL

GRANIA O'SHANNON
UNIT MANAGER
'82 GANDHI*
LOCATIONS
'83 EDUCATING RITA

SAM O'STEEN
EDITOR
'79 HURRICANE
'82 AMITYVILLE II: THE POSSESSION
'83 SILKWOOD

MICHAEL O'SULLIVAN
ART DIRECTOR
'84 NOT FOR PUBLICATION*

WILLIAM O'SULLIVAN
PRODUCTION MANAGER
'80 HUNTER, THE
UNIT PROD. MANAGER
'82 ANNIE*

STANLEY O'TOOLE
PRODUCER
'80 NIJINSKY*
'81 SPHINX
EXECUTIVE PRODUCER
'81 OUTLAND

BILL OAKES
EXECUTIVE PRODUCER
'82 GREASE 2
'83 STAYING ALIVE
ASSOCIATE PRODUCER
'80 TIMES SQUARE
'81 FAN, THE*

HERBERT OAKES
EXECUTIVE PRODUCER
'83 EDUCATING RITA

HUGH OAKS
MISCELLANEOUS
'82 FIRST BLOOD

BRYAN OATES
ASSISTANT EDITOR
'81 HONKY TONK FREEWAY*
'84 KILLING FIELDS, THE*

JOHN OATES
PROPS
'82 AUTHOR, AUTHOR*
'82 DEATHTRAP
'84 POPE OF GREENWICH VILLAGE,THE

JOHN OATES JR.
PROPS
'82 LITTLE SEX, A

ARION OBER
MUSIC
'82 EATING RAOUL
MUSIC SUPERVISOR
'80 GALAXINA

TOM OBLAK
STUNT COORDINATOR
'82 BRAINWAVES

CAROL ANN OBLATH
ASSOCIATE EDITOR
'83 BREATHLESS

DAVID OBST
EXECUTIVE PRODUCER
'84 REVENGE OF THE NERDS*

LYNDA ROSEN OBST
ASSOCIATE PRODUCER
'83 FLASHDANCE*

RICHARD OCEAN
MISCELLANEOUS
'84 THIS IS SPINAL TAP

DAVID OCHOA
EXECUTIVE PRODUCER
'83 BALLAD OF GREGORIO CORTEZ, THE*

JOSE MARIA OCHOA
1ST ASST. DIRECTOR
'84 ROMANCING THE STONE*
'84 EVIL THAT MEN DO, THE*

KAAREN OCHOA
SCRIPT SUPERVISOR
'83 BALLAD OF GREGORIO CORTEZ, THE

MICHAEL OCHS
MISCELLANEOUS
'83 LOSIN' IT

DAVID ODELL
SCREENPLAY
'82 DARK CRYSTAL, THE
'83 NATE & HAYES*
'84 SUPERGIRL

JACQUES OFFENBACH
MUSIC
'84 HOTEL NEW HAMPSHIRE, THE

GOLDA OFFENHEIM
PROD. COORDINATOR
'81 RAGTIME
'84 DUNE

JENNIFER OGDEN
ASSOCIATE PRODUCER
'84 GARBO TALKS
PRODUCTION MANAGER
'83 DANIEL
UNIT PROD. MANAGER
'82 DEATHTRAP
'84 GARBO TALKS
UNIT MANAGER
'82 VERDICT, THE
PROD. OFFICE COORD.
'79 MANHATTAN
'80 CRUISING
'80 JUST TELL ME WHAT YOU WANT*
'81 PRINCE OF THE CITY
MISCELLANEOUS
'80 GILDA LIVE

RITA OGDEN
MAKEUP
'81 ATLANTIC CITY
'82 DON'T CRY, IT'S ONLY THUNDER*
'83 TIMERIDER
'84 NOT FOR PUBLICATION*
HAIR
'81 ATLANTIC CITY
'83 TIMERIDER
'84 NOT FOR PUBLICATION*

TERRY OGISU
EXECUTIVE PRODUCER
'82 DON'T CRY, IT'S ONLY THUNDER*

KAN OGURO
COSTUMES
'81 TATTOO*
HAIR
'81 TATTOO*
PROPS
'81 TATTOO*

JILL OHANNESON
COSTUMES
'83 SWEET SIXTEEN

BERTIL OHLSSON
EXECUTIVE PRODUCER
'84 AMADEUS*

KIJURO OHTA
UNIT PROD. MANAGER
'82 CHALLENGE, THE*

DARRYN OKADA
KEY GRIP
'83 FRIGHTMARE

OLDRICH OKAJ
MISCELLANEOUS
'83 YENTL

GERALD OKAMURA
MISCELLANEOUS
'82 SWORD AND THE SORCERER, THE

KOZO OKAZAKI
CINEMATOGRAPHER
'82 CHALLENGE, THE

MOHAMED ALI EL OKBY
2ND ASST. DIRECTOR
'84 MISUNDERSTOOD

MARC OKRAND
MISCELLANEOUS
'84 STAR TREK III: THE SEARCH FOR SPOCK

CHARLES OKUN
PRODUCER
'83 LOVESICK
EXECUTIVE PRODUCER
'80 HEAVEN'S GATE*
PRODUCTION MANAGER
'80 HEAVEN'S GATE*
'83 LOVESICK
1ST ASST. DIRECTOR
'78 DEER HUNTER, THE
'81 LEGEND OF THE LONE RANGER, THE
'82 SOUP FOR ONE

JEFFREY OKUN
MISCELLANEOUS
'84 LAST STARFIGHTER, THE

CLIFFE OLAND
ASSISTANT EDITOR
'79 NORMA RAE*

MIKE OLDFIELD
MUSIC
'84 KILLING FIELDS, THE

MICHAEL OLEKSINSKI
ASSISTANT EDITOR
'83 SUBURBIA

S. RODGER OLENICOFF
CO-PRODUCER
'79 ICE CASTLES

JOEL OLIANSKY
DIRECTOR
'80 COMPETITION, THE
SCREENPLAY
'80 COMPETITION, THE

ALAN OLINEY
2ND UNIT DIRECTOR
'83 D.C. CAB*
STUNT COORDINATOR
'83 D.C. CAB
'84 KARATE KID, THE

JACK OLIVER
UNIT PROD. MANAGER
'81 TARZAN, THE APE MAN
1ST ASST. DIRECTOR
'81 TARZAN, THE APE MAN*

JOHNNY OLIVER
MISCELLANEOUS
'82 NATIONAL LAMPOON'S CLASS REUNION

POM OLIVER
PROD. SECRETARY
'79 PICNIC AT HANGING ROCK

ROBIN OLIVER
2ND ASST. DIRECTOR
'80 GALAXINA

STEPHEN OLIVER
SCREENPLAY
'79 SUNBURN*

TOMMY OLIVER
MISCELLANEOUS
'83 TENDER MERCIES

GERALD OLIVIER
MISCELLANEOUS
'83 HERCULES

MARTY OLLSTEIN
CINEMATOGRAPHER
'79 PENITENTIARY

FRANCOIS OLMET
2ND ASST. DIRECTOR
'79 RUNNING*

EDWARD JAMES OLMOS
ASSOCIATE PRODUCER
'83 BALLAD OF GREGORIO CORTEZ, THE*
MUSIC
'83 BALLAD OF GREGORIO CORTEZ, THE*

CARL OLSEN
PRODUCTION MANAGER
'84 FLASHPOINT
1ST ASST. DIRECTOR
'79 FAST BREAK
'80 LOVING COUPLES

GERALD OLSON
ASSOCIATE PRODUCER
'82 SWORD AND THE SORCERER, THE*
'84 REPO MAN
1ST ASST. DIRECTOR
'79 ROCK 'N ROLL HIGH SCHOOL

OMAR
HAIR
'81 BUSTIN' LOOSE*

WOODY OMENS
CINEMATOGRAPHER
'81 HISTORY OF THE WORLD PART I

MIROSLAV ONDRICEK
CINEMATOGRAPHER
'79 HAIR
'81 RAGTIME
'82 WORLD ACCORDING TO GARP, THE
'83 SILKWOOD
'84 AMADEUS

LORITA ONG
COSTUME SUPERVISOR
'79 SAINT JACK*

ROBERTO ONORATI
PRODUCTION MANAGER
'83 YOR*

AL ONORATO
CASTING
'82 SWORD AND THE SORCERER, THE*

PAUL ONORATO
CINEMATOGRAPHER
'79 TIM

MAUDE ONSLOW
HAIR
'79 LEGACY, THE

KOMSON OPASSATHAVORN
PROD. COORDINATOR
'83 UNCOMMON VALOR

DANNY OPATOSHU
SCREENPLAY
'83 GET CRAZY*

MARK OPER
2ND ASST. DIRECTOR
'80 BATTLE BEYOND THE STARS*

JONATHAN OPPENHEIM
ASSISTANT EDITOR
'81 ARTHUR*

BARRY OPPER
EXECUTIVE PRODUCER
'82 ANDROID*

DON OPPER
SCREENPLAY
'82 ANDROID*
PROD. COORDINATOR
'81 GALAXY OF TERROR

JEANINE OPPEWALL
ART DIRECTOR
'83 TENDER MERCIES
'83 LOVE LETTERS
MISCELLANEOUS
'79 HARDCORE

ERIC ORBOM
MISCELLANEOUS
'83 BREATHLESS

LORETTA ORDEWER
PROD. OFFICE COORD.
'82 GANDHI
PROD. COORDINATOR
'83 HUNGER, THE
'84 BOUNTY, THE
PROD. SECRETARY
'79 GREAT TRAIN ROBBERY, THE
'80 ELEPHANT MAN, THE

ARNOLD ORGOLINI
PRODUCER
'79 METEOR*

ORLANDO
STILLS
'79 ROCKY II*
'79 BOULEVARD NIGHTS*
'79 SCAVENGER HUNT
'80 CHEAPER TO KEEP HER*
'80 USED CARS
'81 BUDDY, BUDDY
'81 CHU CHU AND THE PHILLY FLASH
'81 HAND, THE
'81 ONLY WHEN I LAUGH
'82 YOUNG DOCTORS IN LOVE
'84 IMPULSE

JOE ORLANDO
MISCELLANEOUS
'84 NOT FOR PUBLICATION

MICHAEL ORLANDO
MISCELLANEOUS
'78 DEER HUNTER, THE

KATHERINE ORLOFF
UNIT PUBLICIST
'79 TIME AFTER TIME

CHARLES ORME
ASSOCIATE PRODUCER
'81 OUTLAND

ALAN ORMSBY
SCREENPLAY
'80 MY BODYGUARD
'82 CAT PEOPLE
'83 PORKY'S II THE NEXT DAY*

ARTHUR ORNITZ
CINEMATOGRAPHER
'81 TATTOO
'82 CHOSEN, THE
'82 HANKY PANKY

KIM ORNITZ
SOUND
'80 CRUISING
'82 STRANGER IS WATCHING, A
'82 AMITYVILLE II: THE POSSESSION
'82 I, THE JURY
'83 SPRING BREAK

DAVID ORNSTEIN
ASSISTANT EDITOR
'79 ROLLER BOOGIE*
'80 FADE TO BLACK*
'82 SEDUCTION, THE*

MICHAEL ORNSTEIN
ASSOCIATE EDITOR
'81 HALLOWEEN II
ASSISTANT EDITOR
'81 MODERN ROMANCE

ESTER OROPEZA
MAKEUP
'83 UNDER FIRE*

RON OROVER
STILLS
'83 RIGHT STUFF, THE

DENIS GORDON ORR
ART DIRECTOR
'79 CUBA

MONA ORR
HAIR
'80 RAGING BULL*

ERNIE ORSATTI
2ND UNIT DIRECTOR
'84 EVIL THAT MEN DO, THE
STUNT COORDINATOR
'82 DEAD MEN DON'T WEAR PLAID
'82 DEATHWISH II*
'83 10 TO MIDNIGHT

JOSE LUIS ORTEGA
SCRIPT SUPERVISOR
'80 OCTAGON, THE*
'84 EVIL THAT MEN DO, THE

KENNY ORTEGA
CHOREOGRAPHER
'80 XANADU*

SERGIO ORTEGA
ASSISTANT EDITOR
'81 CATTLE ANNIE
AND LITTLE BRITCHES*
'83 UNDER FIRE

AURELIO ORTIZ
PRODUCTION MANAGER
'83 UNDER FIRE

ARNO ORTMAIER
PRODUCTION MANAGER
'84 LITTLE DRUMMER GIRL, THE*
UNIT PROD. MANAGER
'84 MOSCOW ON THE HUDSON

RIZ ORTOLANI
MUSIC
'79 FIFTH MUSKETEER, THE

STEFANO ORTOLANI
ART DIRECTOR
'82 MONSIGNOR

PETER ORTON
SCREENPLAY
'84 MUTANT*

DANDA ORTONA
COSTUMES
'83 BLACK STALLION RETURNS, THE

ROBERT ORTWIN
UNIT PROD. MANAGER
'80 WHY WOULD I LIE?*
LOCATIONS
'81 SUNDAY LOVERS
'83 10 TO MIDNIGHT

BARRIE OSBORNE
ASSOCIATE PRODUCER
'83 BIG CHILL, THE
PRODUCTION MANAGER
'79 APOCALYPSE NOW*
'83 OCTOPUSSY*
UNIT PROD. MANAGER
'80 SMALL CIRCLE OF FRIENDS, A
'81 CUTTER'S WAY
'82 ESCAPE ARTIST, THE
'83 BIG CHILL, THE
2ND ASST. DIRECTOR
'79 CHINA SYNDROME, THE
MISCELLANEOUS
'84 COTTON CLUB, THE

MAUREEN OSBORNE-BEALL
PROD. COORDINATOR
'81 CANNONBALL RUN, THE
'82 MEGAFORCE

EIKO OSHIMA
EXECUTIVE PRODUCER
'83 MERRY CHRISTMAS,
MR. LAWRENCE*

NAGISA OSHIMA
DIRECTOR
'83 MERRY CHRISTMAS,
MR. LAWRENCE
SCREENPLAY
'83 MERRY CHRISTMAS,
MR. LAWRENCE*

TOMOYO OSHIMA
EDITOR
'83 MERRY CHRISTMAS, MR. LAWRENCE

IRVING OSHMAN
MISCELLANEOUS
'81 PRIVATE LESSONS

CLIFF OSMOND
ASSOCIATE PRODUCER
'82 BOOGENS, THE*

HORST OSTERKAMP
ASSOCIATE PRODUCER
'83 MAUSOLEUM*

ALBERT OSTERMAIER
MISCELLANEOUS
'79 HAIR

BOB OSTERMAN
MAKEUP
'83 STING II, THE*

BEN OTICO
SPECIAL EFFECTS
'81 ENTER THE NINJA

RON OTTESON
SPECIAL EFFECTS
'80 GLORIA*
'80 NIGHT OF THE JUGGLER*
'81 WOLFEN*
SP. EFFECTS SUPERV.
'81 HAPPY BIRTHDAY TO ME*

H. BUD OTTO
SCRIPT SUPERVISOR
'79 NORMA RAE
'79 10
'81 S.O.B.
'81 ENTITY, THE
'83 MAN WOMAN AND CHILD
'83 MR. MOM
'83 WAR GAMES
'84 ADVENTURES OF BUCKAROO BANZAI
ACROSS THE 8TH DIMENSION, THE

JEAN-PAUL OUELLETTE
2ND UNIT DIRECTOR
'84 TERMINATOR, THE*

FRANCOIS OUIMET
UNIT MANAGER
'83 OF UNKNOWN ORIGIN
2ND ASST. DIRECTOR
'81 HAPPY BIRTHDAY TO ME

ANDREW OVERHALTZER
SPECIAL EFFECTS
'81 TAPS*

E. ANN OVERMAN
PROD. COORDINATOR
'83 10 TO MIDNIGHT*

AL OVERTON
SOUND
'81 PENNIES FROM HEAVEN
'82 JINXED

AL OVERTON JR.

SOUND
'79 ELECTRIC HORSEMAN, THE
'80 SEEMS LIKE OLD TIMES
'80 FATSO
'80 HUNTER, THE
'81 PURSUIT OF D.B. COOPER, THE*
'82 I OUGHT TO BE IN PICTURES
'82 NIGHT SHIFT
'83 ROMANTIC COMEDY
'83 FOOTLOOSE
'83 MAX DUGAN RETURNS
'83 MR. MOM
'84 PROTOCOL
'84 REVENGE OF THE NERDS

AL OVERTON SR.

SOUND
'81 BEAST WITHIN, THE

TOM OVERTON

SOUND
'79 CHAPTER TWO
'79 STAR TREK-THE MOTION PICTURE
'80 AIRPLANE
'80 HERO AT LARGE
'80 JAZZ SINGER, THE
'81 ONLY WHEN I LAUGH
'82 AIRPLANE II: THE SEQUEL
'82 DEATHWISH II
'82 FAST TIMES AT RIDGEMONT HIGH
'84 SWING SHIFT
'84 WOMAN IN RED, THE

JESSICA OVERWISE

CASTING
'80 PRIVATE BENJAMIN*
'84 UP THE CREEK*

PETER OWEN

MISCELLANEOUS
'83 DRAUGHTSMAN CONTRACT, THE

COLLEEN OWENS

HAIR
'82 BEST LITTLE WHOREHOUSE IN TEXAS, THE*

WILLIAM OWENS

UNIT PROD. MANAGER
'81 DEAD AND BURIED

RON OXLEY

MISCELLANEOUS
'81 CONTINENTAL DIVIDE
'82 CAT PEOPLE
'84 EL NORTE

DAVID OYSTER

MISCELLANEOUS
'81 CONTINENTAL DIVIDE

FRANK OZ

PRODUCER
'81 GREAT MUPPET CAPER, THE*
DIRECTOR
'82 DARK CRYSTAL, THE*
MISCELLANEOUS
'79 MUPPET MOVIE, THE

BOB OZMANS

STUNT COORDINATOR
'84 EL NORTE

VENITA OZOLS

2ND ASST. DIRECTOR
'80 SEEMS LIKE OLD TIMES
'80 XANADU*
'81 ON GOLDEN POND
'82 GREASE 2*
'84 ICE PIRATES, THE*

P

JOSEPH PACELLI
PRODUCTION DESIGNER
'84 STONE BOY, THE

LOU PACIOCCO
EXECUTIVE PRODUCER
'83 CHAINED HEAT*

JOHN PACKARD
ASSOCIATE PRODUCER
'80 MANIAC

SHIRLEY PADGETT
HAIR
'80 IDOLMAKER, THE
'82 SIX WEEKS*
'82 BLADERUNNER
'83 ROMANTIC COMEDY
'83 OSTERMAN WEEKEND, THE*
'84 BEST DEFENSE*
'84 MICKI AND MAUDE*
'84 UNFAITHFULLY YOURS

NINA PADOVANO
COSTUME SUPERVISOR
'84 BACHELOR PARTY

EDWARD PADULA
MISCELLANEOUS
'84 COTTON CLUB, THE

ANTHONY PAGE
DIRECTOR
'80 LADY VANISHES, THE

GRANT PAGE
STUNT COORDINATOR
'81 ROAD GAMES
'82 PIRATE MOVIE, THE

JIMMY PAGE
MUSIC
'82 DEATHWISH II

KEVIN PAGE
MISCELLANEOUS
'83 SUBURBIA

PAMELA PAGE
ASSISTANT EDITOR
'80 HOME MOVIES*

SHEILA PAGE
SCRIPT SUPERVISOR
'82 STRANGER IS WATCHING, A
'82 AMITYVILLE II: THE POSSESSION
'83 SURVIVORS, THE
'83 KING OF COMEDY, THE*
'83 I AM THE CHEESE

MARVIN PAIGE
CASTING
'79 C.H.O.M.P.S.
'79 STAR TREK-THE MOTION PICTURE

JASON PAIKOWSKY
UNIT MANAGER
'84 JUST THE WAY YOU ARE*

EMILY PAINE
ASSISTANT EDITOR
'79 ALL THAT JAZZ*
'81 NIGHT THE LIGHTS WENT OUT IN GEORGIA, THE
'83 TENDER MERCIES
'83 TRADING PLACES*

CHARLENE PAINTER
CHOREOGRAPHER
'84 PROTOCOL

CHUCK PAINTER
PUBLICIST
'83 LONELY LADY, THE
UNIT PUBLICIST
'83 TABLE FOR FIVE

ALAN PAKULA
PRODUCER
'79 STARTING OVER*
'82 SOPHIE'S CHOICE*
DIRECTOR
'79 STARTING OVER
'81 ROLLOVER
'82 SOPHIE'S CHOICE
SCREENPLAY
'82 SOPHIE'S CHOICE

LAZLO PAL
MISCELLANEOUS
'83 HEART LIKE A WHEEL

JOANNE PALACE
COSTUMES
'84 PHILADELPHIA EXPERIMENT, THE
COSTUME SUPERVISOR
'83 LOSIN' IT

ALFONSE PALERMO
CHOREOGRAPHER
'81 TRUE CONFESSIONS

ALAN PALEY
ASSOCIATE EDITOR
'79 HANOVER STREET

STEPHEN PALEY
MISCELLANEOUS
'83 BREATHLESS

MICHAEL PALIN
PRODUCER
'82 MISSIONARY, THE*
SCREENPLAY
'79 MONTY PYTHON'S LIFE OF BRIAN*
'81 TIME BANDITS*
'82 MISSIONARY, THE
'82 MONTY PYTHON LIVE AT THE HOLLYWOOD BOWL*
'83 MONTY PYTHON'S THE MEANING OF LIFE*

JACK PALINKAS
KEY GRIP
'80 STUNT MAN, THE

YANIKO PALIS
PROD. COORDINATOR
'81 MY BLOODY VALENTINE*

AUGUSTO PALISOC
PROD. COORDINATOR
'83 BLIND RAGE*

LARRY PALL
2ND UNIT DIRECTOR
'83 STRANGE BREW

ROSPO PALLENBERG
SCREENPLAY
'81 EXCALIBUR*

RICCARDO PALLOTTINI
MISCELLANEOUS
'79 KILLER FISH

CHERI PALMER
PROD. COORDINATOR
'84 ANGEL

FRANK PALMER

KEY GRIP
'81 ESCAPE FROM NEW YORK

GREGORY PALMER

2ND ASST. DIRECTOR
'82 BEST FRIENDS*
MISCELLANEOUS
'84 ICEMAN

JERRY PALMER

ART DIRECTOR
'83 GOIN' ALL THE WAY

JOHN PALMER

ASSOCIATE PRODUCER
'81 CLASH OF THE TITANS
PRODUCTION MANAGER
'82 FIVE DAYS ONE SUMMER*

KEITH PALMER

EDITOR
'83 LONELY LADY, THE

NORMAN PALMER

EDITOR
'80 MIDNIGHT MADNESS*

PATRICK PALMER

PRODUCER
'79 ...AND JUSTICE FOR ALL*
'82 BEST FRIENDS*
'84 ICEMAN*
'84 SOLDIER'S STORY, A*
EXECUTIVE PRODUCER
'81 DOGS OF WAR, THE*

DANTE PALMERI

MAKEUP
'80 FOG, THE
'83 LOSIN' IT*

NATALIE PALMERI

HAIR
'83 LOSIN' IT*

CONRAD PALMISANO

2ND UNIT DIRECTOR
'82 FIRST BLOOD
'83 HEART LIKE A WHEEL
'83 UNCOMMON VALOR
STUNT COORDINATOR
'79 BREAKING AWAY
'79 JERK, THE
'80 ROADIE
'80 AIRPLANE
'80 ALLIGATOR
'81 HEARTBEEPS
'81 NIGHT THE LIGHTS WENT OUT IN GEORGIA, THE
'81 WHOSE LIFE IS IT ANYWAY?
'82 SPLIT IMAGE
'82 ENDANGERED SPECIES*
'82 FIRST BLOOD
'82 ONE FROM THE HEART
'83 CUJO
'83 UNCOMMON VALOR

LILIA PALOMINO

MAKEUP
'83 YELLOWBEARD*

STEFANO PALTRINIERI

ART DIRECTOR
'83 PIRANHA II: THE SPAWNING*

BRUCE PALTROW

PRODUCER
'82 LITTLE SEX, A*
DIRECTOR
'82 LITTLE SEX, A

DENNIS PALUMBO

SCREENPLAY
'82 MY FAVORITE YEAR*

AGNESE PANAROTTO

HAIR
'83 YOR

EDIE PANDA

HAIR
'79 BEING THERE*
'79 ONION FIELD, THE
'79 WHEN A STRANGER CALLS*
'80 CLOSE ENCOUNTERS OF THE THIRD KIND SPECIAL EDITION
'81 THIEF*
'83 SOMETHING WICKED THIS WAY COMES

MICHELLE PANELLI

ASSOCIATE PRODUCER
'83 TWO OF A KIND*

MICHAEL PANGRAZIO

MISCELLANEOUS
'82 E.T. THE EXTRA-TERRESTRIAL
'83 RETURN OF THE JEDI
'84 NEVERENDING STORY, THE
'84 INDIANA JONES AND THE TEMPLE OF DOOM

BILL PANKOW

EDITOR
'84 BODY DOUBLE*
ASSISTANT EDITOR
'79 KRAMER VS. KRAMER
'80 DRESSED TO KILL
'82 STILL OF THE NIGHT
'83 SCARFACE

MIKE PANTAGES

KEY GRIP
'81 EYE FOR AN EYE, AN

WILLIAM PANZER

PRODUCER
'80 STEEL*
'83 OSTERMAN WEEKEND, THE*

LESLIE PAONESSA

ASSOCIATE PRODUCER
'81 HAND, THE*

DIMITRI PAPACONSTANDIS

MISCELLANEOUS
'82 SUMMER LOVERS

MICHAEL PAPALE

MISCELLANEOUS
'83 VALLEY GIRL
'84 JOY OF SEX, THE

PETE PAPANICKOLAS

KEY GRIP
'81 ...ALL THE MARBLES
'82 AIRPLANE II: THE SEQUEL
'82 HAMMETT*

VANGELIS PAPATHANASSIOU

MUSIC
'81 CHARIOTS OF FIRE
'82 BLADERUNNER
'82 MISSING
'84 BOUNTY, THE

CONNIE PAPINEAU

SCRIPT SUPERVISOR
'84 BACHELOR PARTY
'84 PHILADELPHIA EXPERIMENT, THE

PHEDON PAPMICHAEL

ART DIRECTOR
'84 LOVE STREAMS

JOSEPH PAPP

PRODUCER
'83 PIRATES OF PENZANCE, THE

GEORGE PAPPAS

PRODUCER
'80 FIRST DEADLY SIN*

STUART PAPPE

EDITOR
'79 WANDERERS, THE*
'80 CARNY
'83 CLASS*
'84 SONGWRITER

ROGER PARADISO

PRODUCTION MANAGER
'84 RHINESTONE
LOCATIONS
'81 ONLY WHEN I LAUGH
'82 ANNIE
'83 LOVESICK
'83 TWO OF A KIND*

PETER PARASHELES

EDITOR
'83 NEVER CRY WOLF*

B.J. PARDO

HAIR
'80 JAZZ SINGER, THE*
'82 SECOND THOUGHTS*

ROLF PARDULA
SOUND
'80 HE KNOWS YOU'RE ALONE
'80 MOTHER'S DAY

DANIEL PAREDES
COSTUMES
'79 AMERICATHON
'82 CAT PEOPLE
'84 ICE PIRATES, THE

GAIL PARENT
SCREENPLAY
'79 MAIN EVENT, THE*

PAULO PARENTE
PRODUCTION MANAGER
'79 KILLER FISH*

JEFF PARGUER
CASTING
'82 PERSONAL BEST

IRVING PARHAM
ASSOCIATE PRODUCER
'79 PENITENTIARY*
LOCATIONS
'82 PENITENTIARY II

JOSEPH PARIS
HAIR
'80 FIRST DEADLY SIN

MARC LUDOVIC PARIS
HAIR
'80 TESS

MARIE MADELEINE PARIS
MAKEUP
'83 ENIGMA*

MICHAEL PARIS
STILLS
'81 PRIVATE LESSONS
'82 VICE SQUAD
'83 PRIVATE SCHOOL*
'84 PHILADELPHIA EXPERIMENT, THE*

ANDY PARK
MISCELLANEOUS
'84 COMFORT AND JOY

IAN PARK
KEY GRIP
'82 PIRATE MOVIE, THE

YOUNG SIL PARK
PRODUCTION MANAGER
'81 INCHON*

ALAN PARKER
DIRECTOR
'80 FAME
'82 SHOOT THE MOON
'82 PINK FLOYD: THE WALL
'84 BIRDY

ALAN PARKER
MUSIC
'83 JAWS 3-D

BARBARA PARKER
SCRIPT SUPERVISOR
'83 NEVER CRY WOLF

BERNADETTE PARKER
HAIR
'84 NATURAL, THE

DAVID PARKER
SOUND
'80 ISLAND, THE*
'83 RUMBLEFISH
STILLS
'83 MAN FROM SNOWY RIVER, THE
'84 PHAR LAP

DICK PARKER
SPECIAL EFFECTS
'82 TEMPEST*

ED PARKER
MISCELLANEOUS
'83 CURSE OF THE PINK PANTHER

FRANK PARKER
PROPS
'82 OUT OF THE BLUE

JAMES PARKER
2ND ASST. DIRECTOR
'81 ROAD GAMES

JANICE PARKER
ASSISTANT EDITOR
'79 ROCKY II*
'80 SMOKEY AND THE BANDIT II*
'81 SHARKEY'S MACHINE*
'81 CANNONBALL RUN, THE*
'83 STROKER ACE*
'84 CANNONBALL RUN II*

JUDE PARKER
2ND ASST. DIRECTOR
'81 SATURDAY THE 14TH

RICHARD PARKER
SPECIAL EFFECTS
'79 LOVE AND BULLETS*
'80 FIENDISH PLOT
OF DR. FU MANCHU, THE

RICK PARKER
MISCELLANEOUS
'84 MRS. SOFFEL

SCOTT PARKER
SCREENPLAY
'80 DIE LAUGHING*
'80 HE KNOWS YOU'RE ALONE

WALTER PARKES
SCREENPLAY
'83 WAR GAMES*

ROD PARKHURST
MISCELLANEOUS
'82 FIRST BLOOD

BOB PARKINSON
PRODUCER
'83 RICHARD PRYOR: HERE AND NOW*

DOROTHY PARKINSON
MISCELLANEOUS
'79 VILLAIN, THE

PETER PARKS
MISCELLANEOUS
'80 SATURN 3

STAN PARKS
SPECIAL EFFECTS
'80 HEAVEN'S GATE*
'83 SCARFACE*
SP. EFFECTS SUPERV.
'84 RIVER, THE*

BARRY PARNELL
ASSOCIATE PRODUCER
'81 INCREDIBLE SHRINKING
WOMAN, THE*

BILL PARNELL
ASSISTANT EDITOR
'80 FIENDISH PLOT
OF DR. FU MANCHU, THE

LARRY PARR
ASSOCIATE PRODUCER
'83 MERRY CHRISTMAS,MR. LAWRENCE*

ANTONIO PARRA
SPECIAL EFFECTS
'79 CUBA

ROBERT PARRA
2ND ASST. DIRECTOR
'79 CUBA*
'79 JAGUAR LIVES

KARL PARRICK
LOCATIONS
'81 UNDER THE RAINBOW*

LYNN PARRICK
LOCATIONS
'81 UNDER THE RAINBOW*

ANSELMO PARRINELLO
MISCELLANEOUS
'84 DUNE

MICHAEL PARRINELLO
UNIT MANAGER
'81 BEYOND THE REEF

DENNIS PARRISH
PROPS
'79 BLOODLINE
'79 JERK, THE
'80 CHEECH AND CHONG'S NEXT MOVIE
'81 LEGEND OF THE LONE RANGER, THE
'81 PENNIES FROM HEAVEN
'82 I OUGHT TO BE IN PICTURES
'82 NIGHT SHIFT
'83 MAN WITH TWO BRAINS, THE
'83 MAX DUGAN RETURNS
'83 TO BE OR NOT TO BE
'84 PROTOCOL
'84 RED DAWN

GIL PARRONDO
PRODUCTION DESIGNER
'79 CUBA

CLIVE PARSONS
PRODUCER
'83 BRITANNIA HOSPITAL*
'84 COMFORT AND JOY*

LINDSLEY PARSONS III
2ND ASST. DIRECTOR
'79 BEYOND THE POSEIDON ADVENTURE

LINDSEY PARSONS JR.
EXEC IN CHARGE PROD
'79 STAR TREK-THE MOTION PICTURE

MIKE PARSONS
PROPS
'81 DEADLY BLESSING
'82 SILENT RAGE
'82 SPLIT IMAGE
'83 TENDER MERCIES

JENNIFER JACKSON PART
CASTING
'81 PURSUIT OF D.B. COOPER, THE*

P.N. PARTHASARATHY
MISCELLANEOUS
'84 PASSAGE TO INDIA, A

GEORGE PARTLETON
MAKEUP
'82 HOUSE OF THE LONG SHADOWS

DOLLY PARTON
MUSIC
'84 RHINESTONE
MUSIC SUPERVISOR
'84 RHINESTONE*

REG PARTON
STUNT COORDINATOR
'80 MIDNIGHT MADNESS

REGGIE PARTON
MISCELLANEOUS
'82 SWORD AND THE SORCERER, THE

TED PARVIN
MISCELLANEOUS
'84 ROMANCING THE STONE

THEODORE PARVIN
PRODUCER
'79 METEOR*
PRODUCTION MANAGER
'81 CAVEMAN*

JULIA PASCAL
LOCATIONS
'81 LAST CHASE, THE*
MISCELLANEOUS
'81 DOGS OF WAR, THE

AGOSTINO PASCARELLA
KEY GRIP
'83 LONELY LADY, THE

JOANNE PASCUITO
CASTING
'83 CHRISTMAS STORY, A*

PETER PASSAS
MISCELLANEOUS
'82 I, THE JURY

IVAN PASSER
DIRECTOR
'81 CUTTER'S WAY

PETER PASTORELLI
LOCATIONS
'83 HUNGER, THE*

TOM PATCHETT
SCREENPLAY
'80 UP THE ACADEMY*
'81 GREAT MUPPET CAPER, THE*

FELIPPA PATE
CASTING
'79 TIM

MICHAEL PATE
PRODUCER
'79 TIM
DIRECTOR
'79 TIM
SCREENPLAY
'79 TIM

TONY PATERSON
EDITOR
'84 PHAR LAP

ALAN PATILLO
ASSOCIATE EDITOR
'82 GANDHI

WALTER PATRIARCA
ART DIRECTOR
'83 YOR

JENNY PATRICK
MISCELLANEOUS
'80 TESS
'81 EYE OF THE NEEDLE

VINCENT PATRICK
SCREENPLAY
'84 POPE OF GREENWICH VILLAGE,THE

BASILIO PATRIZI
PROPS
'83 YOR

MARCIA PATTEN
COSTUME SUPERVISOR
'81 BURNING, THE

BRUCE PATTERSON
PROD. OFFICE COORD.
'82 TOOTSIE

LORNE PATTERSON
MISCELLANEOUS
'83 RETURN OF THE JEDI

RAYMOND PATTERSON
CHOREOGRAPHER
'82 FIRST TIME, THE

ALAN PATTILLO

EDITOR
'79 GAME OF DEATH

EDNA RUTH PAUL

EDITOR
'81 FEAR NO EVIL
'83 EVIL DEAD, THE

KEN PAUL

PUBLICIST
'83 MERRY CHRISTMAS,MR. LAWRENCE

VICTOR PAUL

STUNT COORDINATOR
'80 BALTIMORE BULLET, THE
'82 MY FAVORITE YEAR
'84 CLOAK AND DAGGER
'84 RACING WITH THE MOON

WILLIAM PAUL

EXECUTIVE PRODUCER
'80 TWINKLE TWINKLE "KILLER" KANE

TODD PAULIN

LOCATIONS
'82 CAT PEOPLE*

LAWRENCE PAULL

PRODUCTION DESIGNER
'80 HOW TO BEAT THE HIGH COST OF LIVING
'80 IN GOD WE TRUST
'82 BLADERUNNER
'83 DOCTOR DETROIT
'84 ROMANCING THE STONE

DAVID PAULSEN

DIRECTOR
'80 SCHIZOID
SCREENPLAY
'80 SCHIZOID

PAUL PAV

LOCATIONS
'79 HARDCORE
'79 IN-LAWS, THE
'80 ALTERED STATES
'80 HUNTER, THE
'81 RICH AND FAMOUS*
'82 POLTERGEIST
'83 ROMANTIC COMEDY*
'83 BRAINSTORM
'84 GHOSTBUSTERS*
'84 STARMAN*

CLARK PAYLOW

PRODUCER
'83 SAVANNAH SMILES
EXECUTIVE PRODUCER
'81 HAND, THE
ASSOCIATE PRODUCER
'80 CLOSE ENCOUNTERS OF THE THIRD KIND SPECIAL EDITION
PRODUCTION MANAGER
'81 HAND, THE
UNIT PROD. MANAGER
'80 CLOSE ENCOUNTERS OF THE THIRD KIND SPECIAL EDITION
1ST ASST. DIRECTOR
'82 DEATH VALLEY*

ALLEN PAYNE

HAIR
'80 INSIDE MOVES
'82 I OUGHT TO BE IN PICTURES*

BARRIE PAYNE

STILLS
'80 HOPSCOTCH*
'84 RIDDLE OF THE SANDS

BRIAN PAYNE

PROPS
'82 QUEST FOR FIRE
'83 MONTY PYTHON'S THE MEANING OF LIFE*
'84 TOP SECRET!

DAVID PAYNE

PRODUCER
'83 DRAUGHTSMAN CONTRACT, THE

ELROY PAYNE

MISCELLANEOUS
'82 SWORD AND THE SORCERER, THE

GARRY PAYNE

MISCELLANEOUS
'84 CONAN THE DESTROYER

HAROLD PAYNE

MUSIC
'84 JOY OF SEX, THE*

JOHN PAYNE

KEY GRIP
'80 AWAKENING, THE
'83 FINAL OPTION, THE

LOGAN PAYNE

MISCELLANEOUS
'84 NATURAL, THE

MICHELE PAYNE

MAKEUP
'84 THIS IS SPINAL TAP
HAIR
'84 THIS IS SPINAL TAP

ROBERT PAYNTER

CINEMATOGRAPHER
'79 FIREPOWER*
'81 SUPERMAN II*
'81 AMERICAN WEREWOLF IN LONDON, AN
'81 FINAL CONFLICT, THE*
'83 SUPERMAN III
'83 TRADING PLACES
MISCELLANEOUS
'80 SATURN 3

BRIAN PEACHEY

ASSISTANT EDITOR
'79 YANKS

CATHERINE PEACOCK

ASSISTANT EDITOR
'81 THEY ALL LAUGHED*

TONI PEACOCK

ASSISTANT EDITOR
'80 MOTHER'S DAY*

BARRY PEAKE

STILLS
'79 AVALANCHE EXPRESS
'80 AWAKENING, THE*
'81 AMERICAN WEREWOLF IN LONDON, AN
'82 PIRATE MOVIE, THE
'83 DRESSER, THE
'84 SCANDALOUS

CHRISTOPHER PEARCE

EXEC IN CHARGE PROD
'82 THAT CHAMPIONSHIP SEASON
'83 REVENGE OF THE NINJA
'83 10 TO MIDNIGHT
ASSOCIATE PRODUCER
'80 SCHIZOID
'84 OVER THE BROOKLYN BRIDGE
UNIT PROD. MANAGER
'84 BREAKIN 2 ELECTRIC BOOGALOO
'84 LOVE STREAMS*
MISCELLANEOUS
'82 DEATHWISH II

GLADYS PEARCE

PROD. COORDINATOR
'83 NEVER SAY NEVER AGAIN

HAYDEN PEARCE

ART DIRECTOR
'83 ANOTHER TIME, ANOTHER PLACE

JILL PEARCE

CASTING
'79 JAGUAR LIVES*

JOE PEARCE

STILLS
'81 DRAGONSLAYER*

RICHARD PEARCE
DIRECTOR
'79 HEARTLAND
'84 COUNTRY

TERRY PEARCE
2ND ASST. DIRECTOR
'79 CLASS OF MISS MACMICHAEL, THE
'83 NATE & HAYES*

DANIEL PEARL
CINEMATOGRAPHER
'82 ZAPPED!

DOROTHY PEARL
MAKEUP
'79 RAVAGERS*
'80 MELVIN AND HOWARD
'80 WHERE THE BUFFALO ROAM
'81 ABSENCE OF MALICE*
'81 POSTMAN ALWAYS RINGS TWICE, THE
'82 FRANCES
'82 POLTERGEIST
'82 TOOTSIE*
'84 AGAINST ALL ODDS
MISCELLANEOUS
'82 TOOTSIE

HERB PEARL
MISCELLANEOUS
'80 MOUNTAIN MEN, THE

LINDA PEARL
ART DIRECTOR
'81 PRIVATE LESSONS
'83 TESTAMENT
'83 TIMERIDER
'83 MY TUTOR

MEL PEARL
EXECUTIVE PRODUCER
'83 LOVE LETTERS*
'84 ANGEL*

NAN PEARLMAN
CO-PRODUCER
'80 HE KNOWS YOU'RE ALONE*

VICTORIA "PINKY" PEARMAN
PROD. COORDINATOR
'84 CHILDREN OF THE CORN

BILL PEARSON
MISCELLANEOUS
'79 ALIEN

DURK PEARSON
MISCELLANEOUS
'82 FIREFOX

SANDRA PEARSON
SCRIPT SUPERVISOR
'82 MONTY PYTHON LIVE AT THE HOLLYWOOD BOWL

MICHAEL PECAS
1ST ASST. DIRECTOR
'81 SUNDAY LOVERS*

CHARLES PECK
CASTING
'81 BUDDY, BUDDY*

KIMI PECK
SCREENPLAY
'80 LITTLE DARLINGS*
ASSOCIATE PRODUCER
'80 LITTLE DARLINGS

RON PECK
2ND ASST. DIRECTOR
'84 BOSTONIANS, THE

SAM PECKINPAH
DIRECTOR
'83 OSTERMAN WEEKEND, THE

LILLA PEDERSON
EDITOR
'80 CHANGELING, THE

MARINA PEDRAZA
HAIR
'79 ELECTRIC HORSEMAN, THE
'79 PLAYERS
'80 STUNT MAN, THE
'80 BRUBAKER
'80 HOW TO BEAT THE HIGH COST OF LIVING*
'81 KING OF THE MOUNTAIN
'81 ZORRO, THE GAY BLADE*
'82 OFFICER AND A GENTLEMAN, AN
'82 YOUNG DOCTORS IN LOVE*
'84 AGAINST ALL ODDS
'84 STARMAN

MIGUEL PEDREGOSA
STUNT COORDINATOR
'79 HURRICANE
'84 CONAN THE DESTROYER*

LARRY PEERCE
DIRECTOR
'79 BELL JAR, THE
'80 WHY WOULD I LIE?
'82 LOVE CHILD
'84 HARD TO HOLD

BARBARA PEETERS
DIRECTOR
'80 HUMANOIDS FROM THE DEEP

REGGIE PEIRCE
PROPS
'81 INCREDIBLE SHRINKING WOMAN, THE*

RANJIT PEIRIS
1ST ASST. DIRECTOR
'84 INDIANA JONES AND THE TEMPLE OF DOOM*

HAZEL PEISER
ART DIRECTOR
'79 CLASS OF MISS MACMICHAEL, THE
PRODUCTION DESIGNER
'84 RIDDLE OF THE SANDS

PAMELA PEITZMAN
MAKEUP
'81 HELL NIGHT
'81 TAKE THIS JOB AND SHOVE IT
'83 SUBURBIA
'84 BACHELOR PARTY
HAIR
'81 TAKE THIS JOB AND SHOVE IT
'83 SUBURBIA
'84 BACHELOR PARTY

BOBBY PELHAM
HAIR
'79 PRIZE FIGHTER, THE*

JACQUES PELLEGRIN
1ST ASST. DIRECTOR
'83 MAN WOMAN AND CHILD*

DIANA PELLEGRINI
ASSOCIATE EDITOR
'79 BLACK STALLION, THE*

PAUL RONALD PELLET
STILLS
'84 MISUNDERSTOOD

MARK PELTZER
PROPS
'82 FIGHTING BACK

THOMAS PENICK
ASSISTANT EDITOR
'80 ALTERED STATES*

ARTHUR PENN
PRODUCER
'81 FOUR FRIENDS*
DIRECTOR
'81 FOUR FRIENDS

BOB PENN

STILLS
'79 ALIEN
'79 DRACULA
'80 FLASH GORDON
'81 RAGTIME*
'82 SENDER, THE
'82 CONAN THE BARBARIAN*
'82 EVIL UNDER THE SUN
'83 NEVER SAY NEVER AGAIN
'83 PIRATES OF PENZANCE, THE
'84 FIRESTARTER
'84 SUPERGIRL

PAT PENNELEGION

UNIT MANAGER
'84 CHAMPIONS
PROD. SECRETARY
'80 SHINING, THE*

CHUCK PENNELL

MUSIC
'84 LAST NIGHT AT THE ALAMO*

EAGLE PENNELL

PRODUCER
'84 LAST NIGHT AT THE ALAMO*
DIRECTOR
'84 LAST NIGHT AT THE ALAMO
EDITOR
'84 LAST NIGHT AT THE ALAMO*

CARL PENNER

MISCELLANEOUS
'79 MOUNTAIN FAMILY ROBINSON

BARBARA PENSIERO

PROD. SECRETARY
'84 RIVER, THE*

DAVID PEOPLES

SCREENPLAY
'82 BLADERUNNER*

LEO PEPIN

LOCATIONS
'80 IN GOD WE TRUST

KEN PEPIOT

SPECIAL EFFECTS
'79 GREAT SANTINI, THE
'80 HEAVEN'S GATE*
'81 INCHON*
'82 DEATHWISH II
'83 SCARFACE*
'83 RIGHT STUFF, THE
'84 BEVERLY HILLS COP
SP. EFFECTS SUPERV.
'84 RIVER, THE*

GEORGE PEPPARD

PRODUCER
'79 FIVE DAYS FROM HOME
DIRECTOR
'79 FIVE DAYS FROM HOME

DIANE PEPPER

HAIR
'80 IT'S MY TURN*
'82 LOOKIN' TO GET OUT

JOHN PEPPER

2ND ASST. DIRECTOR
'79 LITTLE ROMANCE, A*
'82 WORLD ACCORDING TO GARP, THE*
'84 GHOSTBUSTERS*

PAUL PEPPERMAN

PRODUCER
'82 BEASTMASTER, THE*
SCREENPLAY
'82 BEASTMASTER, THE*
CO-PRODUCER
'79 PHANTASM
SPECIAL EFFECTS
'79 PHANTASM

GEORGE PEPPIATT

PROPS
'83 LORDS OF DISCIPLINE, THE*

VINCENT PERANIO

ART DIRECTOR
'79 PRIZE FIGHTER, THE
'80 PRIVATE EYES, THE
'83 HOUSE ON SORORITY ROW
PRODUCTION DESIGNER
'81 POLYESTER

EDWARD PERCHALUK

PUBLICIST
'80 MANIAC

DANIELLE PEREDEZ

COSTUMES
'81 RICHARD PRYOR: LIVE ON THE SUNSET STRIP

SID PERELL

MAKEUP
'79 PRIZE FIGHTER, THE
'80 HOW TO BEAT THE HIGH COST OF LIVING*
'80 PRIVATE EYES, THE

ASOKA PERERA

UNIT MANAGER
'84 INDIANA JONES AND THE TEMPLE OF DOOM

FERNANDO PEREZ

SPECIAL EFFECTS
'79 FIFTH MUSKETEER, THE*
'82 TEMPEST*

GRACIANO PEREZ

KEY GRIP
'82 MISSING
'83 UNDER FIRE

JOSE PEREZ

MAKEUP
'79 PICNIC AT HANGING ROCK*

JUNE PERFIT

EXECUTIVE PRODUCER
'83 SWEET SIXTEEN*

MARTIN PERFIT

EXECUTIVE PRODUCER
'83 SWEET SIXTEEN*

ANDRE PERGAMENT

MISCELLANEOUS
'83 ENIGMA

ROBERT PERGAMENT

ASSISTANT EDITOR
'79 10*
'80 AMERICAN SUCCESS COMPANY, THE*
'81 S.O.B.*
'82 VICTOR/VICTORIA
'83 MAN WHO LOVED WOMEN, THE*
'83 PRIVATE SCHOOL*
'84 MICKI AND MAUDE*

JAMES PERGOLA

CINEMATOGRAPHER
'79 HOT STUFF
'81 HARDLY WORKING
'81 NOBODY'S PERFEKT
'82 SENDER, THE*
'82 LOVE CHILD
'83 SMOKEY AND THE BANDIT III
MISCELLANEOUS
'80 CADDYSHACK
'84 HARRY & SON

TAMI PERI-PORATH

STILLS
'82 LAST AMERICAN VIRGIN, THE

SUZANA PERIC

ASSISTANT EDITOR
'82 HAMMETT*

MICHAEL PERILSTEIN

MUSIC
'83 RETURN OF THE ALIENS: THE DEADLY SPAWN

ZORAN PERISIC

MISCELLANEOUS
'81 SUPERMAN II

GEORGE PERKINS

ASSOCIATE PRODUCER
'83 JOYSTICKS*
1ST ASST. DIRECTOR
'83 JOYSTICKS

HAYWARD PERKINS
PROPS
'80 WITHOUT WARNING

JAY PERLMAN
MISCELLANEOUS
'81 NESTING, THE

DAVID PERLMUTTER
PRODUCER
'80 NOTHING PERSONAL
EXECUTIVE PRODUCER
'79 FAST COMPANY

BRUCE PERLSTEIN
ASSISTANT EDITOR
'82 BRAINWAVES*

DAVID PERMUT
EXECUTIVE PRODUCER
'82 FIGHTING BACK*

FRANCIS PERNET
UNIT MANAGER
'80 FIENDISH PLOT OF DR. FU MANCHU, THE*

JACQUELINE PERPERE
MISCELLANEOUS
'84 RAZOR'S EDGE, THE

DAN PERRI
MISCELLANEOUS
'79 DOUBLE MCGUFFIN, THE

RALPH PERRI
KEY GRIP
'81 MY DINNER WITH ANDRE

RENEE PERRIN
LOCATIONS
'82 CAT PEOPLE*

JOSETTE PERROTTA
UNIT MANAGER
'80 HOG WILD
'82 PORKY'S

OLIVIER PERROY
EXECUTIVE PRODUCER
'79 KILLER FISH*

DAN PERRY
EDITOR
'83 ECHOES

DON PERRY
MUSIC SUPERVISOR
'82 BOOGENS, THE
'83 RUNNING BRAVE

EMILY PERRY
PROPS
'81 TRUE CONFESSIONS
'83 RIGHT STUFF, THE*

FRANK PERRY
DIRECTOR
'81 MOMMIE DEAREST
'82 MONSIGNOR
SCREENPLAY
'81 MOMMIE DEAREST*

JOHN PERRY
COSTUMES
'84 IMPULSE
COSTUME SUPERVISOR
'82 YOUNG DOCTORS IN LOVE

KAREN PERRY
COSTUMES
'84 BROTHER FROM ANOTHER PLANET, THE

PENNY PERRY
CASTING
'79 JERK, THE*
'79 WHEN A STRANGER CALLS
'80 COAST TO COAST
'80 FOXES*
'80 IDOLMAKER, THE*
'80 ORDINARY PEOPLE
'81 CATTLE ANNIE AND LITTLE BRITCHES
'82 DEAD MEN DON'T WEAR PLAID
'83 REUBEN, REUBEN*
'83 STAR CHAMBER
'83 STING II, THE
'83 NATE & HAYES*
'83 GOLDEN SEAL, THE
'83 LOCAL HERO*
'84 ALL OF ME
'84 NEVERENDING STORY, THE*
'84 STONE BOY, THE
'84 2010

RICHARD PERRY
MISCELLANEOUS
'79 VOICES

SIMON PERRY
PRODUCER
'83 ANOTHER TIME, ANOTHER PLACE

STEVE PERRY
ASSOCIATE PRODUCER
'83 SUDDEN IMPACT
UNIT PROD. MANAGER
'82 FIREFOX*
'82 HONKYTONK MAN
'83 SUDDEN IMPACT
1ST ASST. DIRECTOR
'79 1941*
'80 MOUNTAIN MEN, THE
'80 ORDINARY PEOPLE
'81 MODERN ROMANCE
'82 FIREFOX*
'83 WRONG IS RIGHT*

DIAN PERRYMAN
PRODUCTION DESIGNER
'84 SILENT NIGHT, DEADLY NIGHT

CAROL PERSHING
HAIR
'84 SPLASH*

BILL PERSKY
DIRECTOR
'80 SERIAL

LESTER PERSKY
PRODUCER
'79 HAIR*
'79 YANKS*

CHARLES PERSONS
2ND ASST. DIRECTOR
'80 CADDYSHACK

ELLEN PERSONS
PROD. COORDINATOR
'79 HOT STUFF

SONNY PERSONS
PRODUCTION MANAGER
'81 HARDLY WORKING*
2ND ASST. DIRECTOR
'79 HOT STUFF

ALLEN PERSSELIN
EDITOR
'82 HOME WORK

LUCIANO PESCIAROLI
PRODUCTION MANAGER
'80 NIJINSKY*

GABRIELLA PESCUCCI
COSTUMES
'84 ONCE UPON A TIME IN AMERICA

ALEXANDER PESKANOV
MUSIC
'80 HE KNOWS YOU'RE ALONE*

MARK PESKANOV
MUSIC
'80 HE KNOWS YOU'RE ALONE*

SANTA PESTONJI
MISCELLANEOUS
'84 KILLING FIELDS, THE

LORENA PETANI
PROD. OFFICE COORD.
'83 BIG SCORE, THE

JOAN PETCH
HAIR
'82 PIRATE MOVIE, THE

DON PETERMAN

CINEMATOGRAPHER
'79 WHEN A STRANGER CALLS
'81 RICH AND FAMOUS
'81 KING OF THE MOUNTAIN
'82 YOUNG DOCTORS IN LOVE
'83 FLASHDANCE
'83 KISS ME GOODBYE
'84 BEST DEFENSE
'84 SPLASH
'84 MASS APPEAL

BARRY PETERS

EDITOR
'79 ARABIAN ADVENTURE

CHARLIE PETERS

SCREENPLAY
'81 PATERNITY
'83 KISS ME GOODBYE
'84 BLAME IT ON RIO*

JON PETERS

PRODUCER
'79 MAIN EVENT, THE*
'82 SIX WEEKS*
EXECUTIVE PRODUCER
'80 CADDYSHACK
'80 DIE LAUGHING
'81 AMERICAN WEREWOLF IN LONDON, AN*
'82 MISSING*
'83 D.C. CAB*
'83 FLASHDANCE*

KENNETH PETERS

SCREENPLAY
'82 VICE SQUAD*

PAUL PETERS

ART DIRECTOR
'79 BUCK ROGERS
'83 STROKER ACE
PRODUCTION DESIGNER
'80 ROADIE
'82 SECOND THOUGHTS

ROBERT PETERS

SPECIAL EFFECTS
'80 PRIVATE BENJAMIN

DAN PETERSON

LOCATIONS
'82 BEASTMASTER, THE
STUNT COORDINATOR
'83 OCTOPUSSY*

DEBBIE PETERSON

PROD. SECRETARY
'84 CONAN THE DESTROYER*

EILEEN PETERSON

PUBLICIST
'79 CHINA SYNDROME, THE

LORNE PETERSON

MISCELLANEOUS
'80 EMPIRE STRIKES BACK, THE
'82 E.T. THE EXTRA-TERRESTRIAL
'84 INDIANA JONES AND THE TEMPLE OF DOOM

MAURICE PETERSON

SCREENPLAY
'82 HOME WORK*

OSCAR PETERSON

MUSIC
'79 SILENT PARTNER, THE

PETE PETERSON

MISCELLANEOUS
'79 BEYOND THE POSEIDON ADVENTURE

ROY PETERSON

ASSISTANT EDITOR
'81 CAVEMAN*

WOLFGANG PETERSON

DIRECTOR
'84 NEVERENDING STORY, THE
SCREENPLAY
'84 NEVERENDING STORY, THE*

HAZEL PETHIG

COSTUMES
'79 MONTY PYTHON'S LIFE OF BRIAN*

PETRA

EDITOR
'81 STRANGE BEHAVIOR

HELGA PETRASHEVICH

SCRIPT SUPERVISOR
'79 SOMETHING SHORT OF PARADISE

DANIEL PETRIE

DIRECTOR
'80 RESURRECTION
'81 FORT APACHE, THE BRONX
'82 SIX PACK

DANIEL PETRIE JR.

SCREENPLAY
'84 BEVERLY HILLS COP

ROBERT PETROFF

SOUND
'83 HERCULES

MISCHA PETRON

ART DIRECTOR
'84 EXTERMINATOR II*

BILL PETROTTA

PROPS
'79 VILLAIN, THE
'80 WHOLLY MOSES!
'81 CHEECH AND CHONG'S NICE DREAMS
'82 MEGAFORCE
'83 STROKER ACE
'84 CANNONBALL RUN II

VICTOR PETROTTA

PROPS
'79 FRISCO KID, THE
'80 COAL MINER'S DAUGHTER
'80 XANADU
'81 RAGGEDY MAN
'82 CAT PEOPLE

JOE PETRUCCIO JR.

PROPS
'83 EDDIE AND THE CRUISERS

SUZANNE PETTIT

EDITOR
'80 TELL ME A RIDDLE
'83 TESTAMENT
'83 TIMERIDER*

DEE DEE PETTY

HAIR
'83 OUTSIDERS, THE

JACK PETTY

MAKEUP
'80 USED CARS*
'83 OUTSIDERS, THE

KATHRYN PETTY

ASSOCIATE PRODUCER
'83 LONE WOLF MCQUADE*

JOHN PEVERALL

PRODUCER
'78 DEER HUNTER, THE*

TOM PEVSNER

ASSOCIATE PRODUCER
'79 DRACULA
'81 FOR YOUR EYES ONLY
'83 OCTOPUSSY

ALAIN PEYROLLAZ

2ND ASST. DIRECTOR
'84 CHEECH AND CHONG'S THE CORSICAN BROTHERS

MICHAEL PEYSER

ASSOCIATE PRODUCER
'82 MIDSUMMER NIGHT'S SEX COMEDY, A
'83 ZELIG
'84 BROADWAY DANNY ROSE
PRODUCTION MANAGER
'80 STARDUST MEMORIES
'81 ARTHUR
'83 ZELIG
MISCELLANEOUS
'79 MANHATTAN

PETER PEYTON
ASSOCIATE PRODUCER
'82 PERSONAL BEST

STEVE PEYTON
MISCELLANEOUS
'83 MAUSOLEUM

ANDREW PFEFFER
EXECUTIVE PRODUCER
'81 ENTITY, THE*
'82 I, THE JURY*
'83 TOUGH ENOUGH*

CAROLYN PFEIFFER
PRODUCER
'80 ROADIE
'82 ENDANGERED SPECIES
'84 CHOOSE ME*

JACK PHELAN
PRODUCTION MANAGER
'81 EXCALIBUR
'83 EDUCATING RITA

KEN PHELPS
KEY GRIP
'84 INDIANA JONES AND THE TEMPLE OF DOOM

TIM PHELPS
MISCELLANEOUS
'80 HONEYSUCKLE ROSE

WIN PHELPS
UNIT MANAGER
'83 OSTERMAN WEEKEND, THE
1ST ASST. DIRECTOR
'79 ...AND JUSTICE FOR ALL
'80 HERBIE GOES BANANAS
'82 BEST FRIENDS
'82 DINER*
'82 ZOOT SUIT

WENDI PHIFER
MISCELLANEOUS
'82 STILL OF THE NIGHT

JACK PHILBRICK
2ND ASST. DIRECTOR
'83 CHRISTINE

BOB PHILIPPE
MAKEUP
'80 SMALL CIRCLE OF FRIENDS, A*

LEE PHILIPS
DIRECTOR
'81 ON THE RIGHT TRACK

ARLENE PHILLIPS
CHOREOGRAPHER
'79 ESCAPE TO ATHENA
'80 CAN'T STOP THE MUSIC
'81 FAN, THE
'82 ANNIE
'83 MONTY PYTHON'S THE MEANING OF LIFE
MISCELLANEOUS
'80 CAN'T STOP THE MUSIC
'80 CAN'T STOP THE MUSIC
'82 ANNIE

BILL PHILLIPS
SCREENPLAY
'83 CHRISTINE

DAVID PHILLIPS
PROPS
'80 DEATH SHIP*

DON PHILLIPS
PRODUCER
'80 MELVIN AND HOWARD*

DON PHILLIPS
CASTING
'82 FAST TIMES AT RIDGEMONT HIGH*

FRANK PHILLIPS
CINEMATOGRAPHER
'79 APPLE DUMPLING GANG RIDES AGAIN, THE
'79 BLACK HOLE, THE
'80 HERBIE GOES BANANAS
'80 MIDNIGHT MADNESS
'81 GOING APE!

FRED PHILLIPS
MAKEUP
'79 STAR TREK-THE MOTION PICTURE*
'79 WHEN YOU COMIN' BACK, RED RYDER?
'81 UNDER THE RAINBOW

GEORGE PHILLIPS
MISCELLANEOUS
'80 COAST TO COAST

JANNA PHILLIPS
MAKEUP
'79 STAR TREK-THE MOTION PICTURE*
'82 MEGAFORCE*

JOAN PHILLIPS
HAIR
'80 AIRPLANE
'81 NIGHT THE LIGHTS WENT OUT IN GEORGIA, THE

ALEX PHILLIPS JR.
CINEMATOGRAPHER
'79 SUNBURN
'80 FADE TO BLACK
'81 HIGH RISK

JULIA PHILLIPS
PRODUCER
'80 CLOSE ENCOUNTERS OF THE THIRD KIND SPECIAL EDITION*

KIM PHILLIPS
HAIR
'84 FRIDAY THE 13TH PART IV THE FINAL CHAPTER

LLOYD PHILLIPS
PRODUCER
'83 NATE & HAYES*

MARILYN PHILLIPS
HAIR
'79 SCAVENGER HUNT

MICHAEL PHILLIPS
PRODUCER
'80 CLOSE ENCOUNTERS OF THE THIRD KIND SPECIAL EDITION*
'81 HEARTBEEPS
'82 CANNERY ROW
'84 FLAMINGO KID, THE

MICHAEL PHILLIPS
LOCATIONS
'82 SPLIT IMAGE

RON PHILLIPS
STILLS
'80 BIG BRAWL, THE
'80 URBAN COWBOY*
'81 BODY HEAT*
'82 SPLIT IMAGE
'83 CROSS CREEK
'83 INDEPENDENCE DAY*
'83 JAWS 3-D
'83 LONE WOLF MCQUADE
'83 TENDER MERCIES
'84 HARRY & SON
'84 SOLDIER'S STORY, A
'84 WHERE THE BOYS ARE

STU PHILLIPS
MUSIC
'79 BUCK ROGERS

TOBY PHILLIPS
MISCELLANEOUS
'83 YENTL
'84 BOUNTY, THE

WILLIAM PHILLIPS
ASSOCIATE PRODUCER
'82 STAR TREK II THE WRATH OF KHAN

TIM PHILO
CINEMATOGRAPHER
'83 EVIL DEAD, THE

DAVID PHILOSOPH
MISCELLANEOUS
'82 PARADISE

DAVID PHINNEY
ASSOCIATE PRODUCER
'79 BUCK ROGERS*

JACKI PHIPPS
LOCATIONS
'83 TOUGH ENOUGH

KEVIN PHIPPS
ART DIRECTOR
'84 CONAN THE DESTROYER*

KIERON PHIPPS
2ND ASST. DIRECTOR
'80 HOPSCOTCH*
'81 FINAL CONFLICT, THE*
'82 PINK FLOYD: THE WALL
'83 CURSE OF THE PINK PANTHER*
'83 TRAIL OF THE PINK PANTHER*
'83 KEEP, THE*
'84 GREYSTOKE: THE LEGEND OF TARZAN, LORD OF THE APES*

DOMINIQUE PIAT
SCRIPT SUPERVISOR
'84 JUST THE WAY YOU ARE*

ROBERTO D'ETTORE PIAZZOLI
CINEMATOGRAPHER
'83 PIRANHA II: THE SPAWNING
MISCELLANEOUS
'83 PIRANHA II: THE SPAWNING

JEAN LOUIS PICAVET
CINEMATOGRAPHER
'83 ENIGMA

PIERO PICCIONI
MUSIC
'82 FIGHTING BACK

CHARLEY PICERNI
STUNT COORDINATOR
'80 PRIVATE EYES, THE

SHERRY PICHON
PROD. COORDINATOR
'80 CHEAPER TO KEEP HER

STEVE PICKARD
ASSISTANT EDITOR
'79 HANOVER STREET*

ULRICH PICKARDT
MISCELLANEOUS
'83 EXPOSED

DAVID PICKER
PRODUCER
'79 BLOODLINE*
'79 JERK, THE*
'82 DEAD MEN DON'T WEAR PLAID*
'83 MAN WITH TWO BRAINS, THE*
'84 BEAT STREET*

ROBERN PICKERING
MAKEUP
'83 MERRY CHRISTMAS,MR. LAWRENCE*

MIKE PICKWOAD
ART DIRECTOR
'82 HOUSE OF THE LONG SHADOWS

DON PICTON
ART DIRECTOR
'81 CLASH OF THE TITANS*

JULIO PIEDRA
MAKEUP
'83 ECHOES*

BUD PIEFER
PROPS
'78 DEER HUNTER, THE*

BART PIERCE
MISCELLANEOUS
'83 EVIL DEAD, THE

BILL PIERCE
PROPS
'82 MONTY PYTHON LIVE AT THE HOLLYWOOD BOWL*

TONY PIERCE-ROBERTS
CINEMATOGRAPHER
'84 KIPPERBANG

ERIC PIERRE
MAKEUP
'84 UNTIL SEPTEMBER

HENRY PIERSIG
SPECIAL EFFECTS
'83 STRANGE BREW*

FRANK PIERSON
LOCATIONS
'83 SCARFACE*
'84 BODY DOUBLE*

TOM PIERSON
MUSIC
'79 QUINTET
MISCELLANEOUS
'80 POPEYE

DENNIS PIES
MISCELLANEOUS
'84 DREAMSCAPE

BARBARA PIETERS
PROD. COORDINATOR
'79 AMITYVILLE HORROR, THE

DENNIS PIKE
MISCELLANEOUS
'79 BROOD, THE
'81 SCANNERS

DON PIKE
2ND UNIT DIRECTOR
'82 I, THE JURY
STUNT COORDINATOR
'82 I, THE JURY

KELVIN PIKE
CINEMATOGRAPHER
'83 DRESSER, THE

KEVIN PIKE
SPECIAL EFFECTS
'84 MRS. SOFFEL*
SP. EFFECTS SUPERV.
'84 INDIANA JONES AND THE TEMPLE OF DOOM

JAMES PILCHER
SOUND
'79 RUNNER STUMBLES, THE
'80 CHANGELING, THE*
'81 NIGHT THE LIGHTS WENT OUT IN GEORGIA, THE
'84 PLACES IN THE HEART

SUSAN PILE
PUBLICIST
'79 FRISCO KID, THE
'80 SOMEWHERE IN TIME
UNIT PUBLICIST
'80 MELVIN AND HOWARD

JACQUES PINARD
UNIT MANAGER
'80 DEATH SHIP

DENISE PINCKLEY
PROD. OFFICE COORD.
'81 FRIDAY THE 13TH PART TWO
'84 ALPHABET CITY

ED PINE
PUBLICIST
'84 STAR TREK III: THE SEARCH FOR SPOCK
UNIT PUBLICIST
'84 THIEF OF HEARTS
'84 RED DAWN

HOWARD PINE
EXECUTIVE PRODUCER
'80 COMPETITION, THE
'83 SURVIVORS, THE
UNIT PROD. MANAGER
'80 COMPETITION, THE
'83 SURVIVORS, THE*
'84 KARATE KID, THE
MISCELLANEOUS
'82 ANNIE

TINA PINE
SCREENPLAY
'81 ON THE RIGHT TRACK*
CO-PRODUCER
'81 ON THE RIGHT TRACK*

PINK FLOYD
MUSIC
'82 PINK FLOYD: THE WALL

CRAIG PINKARD
PRODUCTION MANAGER
'84 ELECTRIC DREAMS

HELGO PINNOW
COSTUMES
'80 AMERICAN SUCCESS COMPANY, THE*

EFREN PINON
DIRECTOR
'83 BLIND RAGE

JACQUELINE PINON
COSTUMES
'84 MUTANT

MARTHA PINSON
SCRIPT SUPERVISOR
'80 DRESSED TO KILL
'81 RAGTIME
'81 PRINCE OF THE CITY
'82 AUTHOR, AUTHOR
'82 DEATHTRAP
'83 DANIEL
'83 WITHOUT A TRACE
'84 FLAMINGO KID, THE
'84 GARBO TALKS

HAROLD PINTER
SCREENPLAY
'81 FRENCH LIEUTENANT'S WOMAN, THE
'83 BETRAYAL

HERBERT PINTER
ART DIRECTOR
'81 GALLIPOLI
'83 YEAR OF LIVING DANGEROUSLY, THE

TOMISLAV PINTER
CINEMATOGRAPHER
'81 MONTENEGRO

DEBBIE PINTHUS
2ND ASST. DIRECTOR
'83 CHAINED HEAT
'83 METALSTORM: THE DESTRUCTION OF JARED-SYN

ERNEST PINTOFF
DIRECTOR
'79 JAGUAR LIVES

MARK PIPER
UNIT MANAGER
'79 TIM
2ND ASST. DIRECTOR
'80 BLUE LAGOON

MARIO PISANI
PRODUCTION MANAGER
'81 SO FINE
'82 YES, GIORGIO
'83 KRULL*
MISCELLANEOUS
'81 CLASH OF THE TITANS

ADRIANO PISCHIUTTA
SPECIAL EFFECTS
'82 TEMPEST*

EDWARD PISONI
ART DIRECTOR
'80 CRUISING
'81 ENDLESS LOVE
'81 PRINCE OF THE CITY
'82 DEATHTRAP
'83 KING OF COMEDY, THE*
'84 MRS. SOFFEL*
PRODUCTION DESIGNER
'82 VERDICT, THE

THEODOR PISTEK
COSTUMES
'84 AMADEUS

RUDY PISUENA
STILLS
'83 BLIND RAGE

MICHAEL PITALO
CASTING
'82 TOY, THE*

DEAN PITCHFORD
SCREENPLAY
'83 FOOTLOOSE

JULIE PITKANEN
SCRIPT SUPERVISOR
'79 ELECTRIC HORSEMAN, THE
'80 BRUBAKER
'80 COMPETITION, THE
'80 HIDE IN PLAIN SIGHT
'80 ORDINARY PEOPLE
'81 RICH AND FAMOUS
'82 ROCKY III
'82 YES, GIORGIO
'82 SECOND THOUGHTS
'83 STAYING ALIVE
'83 BREATHLESS
'83 KISS ME GOODBYE
'83 TWO OF A KIND
'84 JOHNNY DANGEROUSLY
'84 RHINESTONE

PATSY PITTS
SCRIPT SUPERVISOR
'80 SCHIZOID

LOUIS PITZELE
1ST ASST. DIRECTOR
'80 PRIVATE BENJAMIN*

LARRY PIZER
CINEMATOGRAPHER
'79 EUROPEANS, THE
'81 CATTLE ANNIE AND LITTLE BRITCHES
'83 TIMERIDER

ALLAN PLACKO
MISCELLANEOUS
'81 TARZAN, THE APE MAN

BREN PLAISTOWE
HAIR
'79 LOVE AT FIRST BITE
'80 HUNTER, THE
'84 GRANDVIEW, U.S.A.*

LOIS PLANCO
CASTING
'80 HAPPY BIRTHDAY, GEMINI
'82 MY FAVORITE YEAR*
'82 QUEST FOR FIRE*
'83 EXPOSED*
'84 COTTON CLUB, THE*
'84 BACHELOR PARTY*

OTTO PLASCHKES
EXECUTIVE PRODUCER
'80 HOPSCOTCH

GARY PLATEK
MISCELLANEOUS
'83 AMITYVILLE 3D

ALAN PLATER
SCREENPLAY
'81 PRIEST OF LOVE

POLLY PLATT
PRODUCTION DESIGNER
'82 YOUNG DOCTORS IN LOVE
'83 MAN WITH TWO BRAINS, THE
'83 TERMS OF ENDEARMENT

DIANA PLESANTS
LOCATIONS
'84 MAKING THE GRADE*

MIMIS PLIVOURIS
PROPS
'82 SUMMER LOVERS

MICHAEL PLOOG
MISCELLANEOUS
'82 SECOND THOUGHTS

HUNG KIM PO
MISCELLANEOUS
'79 GAME OF DEATH

AMOS POE
PRODUCER
'81 SUBWAY RIDERS*
DIRECTOR
'81 SUBWAY RIDERS
'84 ALPHABET CITY
SCREENPLAY
'81 SUBWAY RIDERS
'84 ALPHABET CITY*
EDITOR
'81 SUBWAY RIDERS*

STEPHEN POE
PRODUCER
'84 MEATBALLS PART II*

FERDINANDO POGGI
STUNT COORDINATOR
'81 CLASH OF THE TITANS

S. LEE POGOSTIN
SCREENPLAY
'83 HIGH ROAD TO CHINA*

SIDNEY POITIER
DIRECTOR
'80 STIR CRAZY
'82 HANKY PANKY

BARBARA POKRAS
EDITOR
'82 DON'T CRY,IT'S ONLY THUNDER*

HAL POLAIRE
ASSOCIATE PRODUCER
'80 RAGING BULL*
UNIT PROD. MANAGER
'83 CLASS

MICHAEL POLAIRE
LOCATIONS
'83 RIGHT STUFF, THE

CAROL POLAKOFF
1ST ASST. DIRECTOR
'83 ECHOES
2ND ASST. DIRECTOR
'80 FOXES

MICHAEL POLAKOW
ASSISTANT EDITOR
'79 LITTLE ROMANCE, A*
'80 NIJINSKY

MARIAN POLAN
MISCELLANEOUS
'81 NOBODY'S PERFEKT

ROMAN POLANSKI
DIRECTOR
'80 TESS
SCREENPLAY
'80 TESS*

BASIL POLEDOURIS
MUSIC
'80 BLUE LAGOON
'82 SUMMER LOVERS
'82 CONAN THE BARBARIAN
'84 MAKING THE GRADE
'84 PROTOCOL
'84 CONAN THE DESTROYER
'84 RED DAWN

TIBOR POLGAR
MUSIC
'79 IN PRAISE OF OLDER WOMEN

PAM POLIFRONI
CASTING
'82 TEX*
'82 TRON
'83 SOMETHING WICKED THIS WAY COMES*
'83 TRENCHCOAT*

PETER POLITANOFF
ART DIRECTOR
'81 BURNING, THE

STEVE POLIVKA
ASSISTANT EDITOR
'79 MUPPET MOVIE, THE
'79 FORCE OF ONE, A
'80 SERIAL
'81 GOING APE!
'82 CHALLENGE, THE

MILBRY POLK
MISCELLANEOUS
'81 ROLLOVER

ROBERT POLK
MUSIC
'84 BACHELOR PARTY

GEORGE POLKINGHORNE
MISCELLANEOUS
'80 CLOSE ENCOUNTERS OF THE THIRD KIND SPECIAL EDITION

MARTIN POLL
PRODUCER
'81 NIGHTHAWKS

BERNIE POLLACK
COSTUMES
'79 ELECTRIC HORSEMAN, THE
'80 MOTEL HELL*
'80 ORDINARY PEOPLE
'81 ABSENCE OF MALICE
'84 NATURAL, THE*

BETSY POLLACK
PRODUCTION MANAGER
'83 SWEET SIXTEEN
1ST ASST. DIRECTOR
'84 ANGEL

HEDY POLLACK
MAKEUP
'84 NEVERENDING STORY, THE*

PATSY POLLACK
CASTING
'79 SHOUT, THE*
'81 FRENCH LIEUTENANT'S WOMAN, THE
'81 REDS*
'83 BRITANNIA HOSPITAL
'83 KRULL
'84 GREYSTOKE: THE LEGEND OF TARZAN, LORD OF THE APES

SYDNEY POLLACK
PRODUCER
'81 ABSENCE OF MALICE
'82 TOOTSIE*
'84 SONGWRITER
DIRECTOR
'79 ELECTRIC HORSEMAN, THE
'81 ABSENCE OF MALICE
'82 TOOTSIE
EXECUTIVE PRODUCER
'80 HONEYSUCKLE ROSE

PAUL POLLARD
SPECIAL EFFECTS
'79 PRISONER OF ZENDA, THE

SAM POLLARD
EDITOR
'81 BODY AND SOUL*

GIUSEPPE POLLINI
1ST ASST. DIRECTOR
'79 KILLER FISH*

GUY POLNEMUS

STILLS
'80 MOTHER'S DAY

MICHAEL POLOKAW

ASSISTANT EDITOR
'80 HEAVEN'S GATE*

ABRAHAM POLONSKY

SCREENPLAY
'79 AVALANCHE EXPRESS
'82 MONSIGNOR*

SONYA POLONSKY

EDITOR
'83 BABY IT'S YOU
ASSISTANT EDITOR
'80 RAGING BULL

COLIN POLSON

HAIR
'82 SAFARI 3000

GUY POLZEL

KEY GRIP
'79 NORTH DALLAS FORTY
'79 TIME AFTER TIME
'81 CHARLIE CHAN AND THE CURSE OF THE DRAGON QUEEN
'81 LOOKER
'81 MOMMIE DEAREST
'82 ENDANGERED SPECIES

JOHN POMMER

EXEC IN CHARGE PROD
'79 GREAT SANTINI, THE
ASSOCIATE PRODUCER
'80 ROADIE
PRODUCTION MANAGER
'80 ROADIE

CHESTER POMPEI

MISCELLANEOUS
'83 MORTUARY

LYLE PONCHER

EXECUTIVE PRODUCER
'82 CHALLENGE, THE

JOHN PONCHOCK

EXECUTIVE PRODUCER
'83 HOUSE ON SORORITY ROW*

DARRYL PONICSAN

SCREENPLAY
'81 TAPS*

ALEX PONTI

PRODUCER
'79 KILLER FISH

DUANE POOLE

SCREENPLAY
'79 C.H.O.M.P.S.*

FRANK POPE

SPECIAL EFFECTS
'82 EATING RAOUL

THOMAS POPE

SCREENPLAY
'83 LORDS OF DISCIPLINE, THE*

JACK POPIN

PRODUCTION DESIGNER
'79 GREAT SANTINI, THE

ANNE POPISCHIL

MAKEUP
'81 STRANGE BEHAVIOR
HAIR
'81 STRANGE BEHAVIOR
'83 BABY IT'S YOU

JACK POPLIN

ART DIRECTOR
'83 CLASS

MIKE POPOVICH

KEY GRIP
'82 ZAPPED!

CLAUDIA PORCELLA

MAKEUP
'81 SUBWAY RIDERS

EMMA PORTEOUS

COSTUMES
'80 LADY VANISHES, THE
'80 WATCHER IN THE WOODS, THE
'81 CLASH OF THE TITANS
'81 DOGS OF WAR, THE
'82 FIVE DAYS ONE SUMMER
'83 OCTOPUSSY
'84 SUPERGIRL
'84 TOP SECRET!

BOBBY PORTER

STUNT COORDINATOR
'82 TOY, THE

COLE PORTER

MUSIC
'82 EVIL UNDER THE SUN

JILL PORTER

MAKEUP
'79 MY BRILLIANT CAREER

RICK PORTER

STILLS
'79 BROOD, THE
'79 FAST COMPANY
'83 DEAD ZONE, THE
'83 VIDEODROME

STEVE POSEY

CINEMATOGRAPHER
'82 PENITENTIARY II
MISCELLANEOUS
'79 PENITENTIARY
'82 SWORD AND THE SORCERER, THE

SUZEN POSHEK

MAKEUP
'81 BURNING, THE
HAIR
'81 BURNING, THE

JOHN POSIMATO

PROPS
'83 ECHOES*

AUGUSTO POSSANZA

SPECIAL EFFECTS
'79 KILLER FISH*

DON POST

MISCELLANEOUS
'81 HALLOWEEN II
'82 HALLOWEEN III: SEASON OF THE WITCH

MIKE POST

MUSIC
'83 RUNNING BRAVE
MUSIC SUPERVISOR
'84 RHINESTONE*
MISCELLANEOUS
'84 RHINESTONE

MYRNA POST

PUBLICIST
'80 DEFIANCE*

STEVEN POSTER

CINEMATOGRAPHER
'81 BLOOD BEACH
'81 DEAD AND BURIED
'83 SPRING BREAK
'83 STRANGE BREW
'83 TESTAMENT
MISCELLANEOUS
'80 CLOSE ENCOUNTERS OF THE THIRD KIND SPECIAL EDITION
'82 BEST LITTLE WHOREHOUSE IN TEXAS, THE
'82 BLADERUNNER

GIORGIO POSTIGLIONE

ART DIRECTOR
'79 HURRICANE
'83 AMITYVILLE 3D
'84 FIRESTARTER

TONY POSTON
KEY GRIP
'80 BIG BRAWL, THE
'80 FOR THE LOVE OF BENJI
'81 DEADLY BLESSING
'82 SILENT RAGE
'82 SPLIT IMAGE
'83 LONE WOLF MCQUADE

DENNIS POTTER
SCREENPLAY
'81 PENNIES FROM HEAVEN
'83 GORKY PARK

JAMES POTTER
MISCELLANEOUS
'84 EVIL THAT MEN DO, THE

MARK POTTER JR.
ASSISTANT EDITOR
'79 EUROPEANS, THE

MARK POTTER
EDITOR
'84 BOSTONIANS, THE*
ASSISTANT EDITOR
'80 QUARTET
'83 HEAT AND DUST

STEVE POTTER
ASSISTANT EDITOR
'79 HOT STUFF
'80 DIE LAUGHING
'81 NOBODY'S PERFEKT
'82 SECOND THOUGHTS
'83 CUJO

HARRY POTTLE
PRODUCTION DESIGNER
'79 MURDER BY DECREE

MARILYN POUCHER
2ND ASST. DIRECTOR
'82 FRIDAY THE 13TH PART THREE IN 3D
HAIR
'83 TESTAMENT

MARIE-FRANCE POULIZAC
ASSISTANT EDITOR
'84 UNTIL SEPTEMBER

JON POVILL
ASSOCIATE PRODUCER
'79 STAR TREK-THE MOTION PICTURE

STEVE POWDER
MUSIC
'83 PIRANHA II: THE SPAWNING

ANDY POWELL
1ST ASST. DIRECTOR
'83 DRAUGHTSMAN CONTRACT, THE

ANTHONY POWELL
COSTUMES
'80 TESS
'81 PRIEST OF LOVE
'82 EVIL UNDER THE SUN
'84 INDIANA JONES AND THE TEMPLE OF DOOM

EDDIE POWELL
STUNT COORDINATOR
'79 DRACULA

ELLEN POWELL
HAIR
'83 TWILIGHT ZONE, THE MOVIE*

IVOR POWELL
ASSOCIATE PRODUCER
'79 ALIEN
'82 BLADERUNNER

JOE POWELL
STUNT COORDINATOR
'84 TOP SECRET!

LAMBERT POWELL
SPECIAL EFFECTS
'80 JAZZ SINGER, THE

LARRY POWELL
PRODUCTION MANAGER
'82 FORCED VENGEANCE*
UNIT PROD. MANAGER
'80 ANY WHICH WAY YOU CAN
'80 BRONCO BILLY
MISCELLANEOUS
'83 RIGHT STUFF, THE

PETER POWELL
SCREENPLAY
'80 FINAL COUNTDOWN, THE*

ZAKIYA POWELL
PUBLICIST
'83 HEAT AND DUST
'84 COMFORT AND JOY
UNIT PUBLICIST
'84 BOSTONIANS, THE

DEANN POWER
HAIR
'84 LOVE STREAMS

DEREK POWER
PRODUCER
'81 FUNHOUSE, THE*

PAMELA POWER
EDITOR
'83 HUNGER, THE

PAUL POWER
MISCELLANEOUS
'80 CHEECH AND CHONG'S NEXT MOVIE

KAYE POWNALL
HAIR
'79 CHAMP, THE*
'79 CHINA SYNDROME, THE
'79 MAIN EVENT, THE
'80 BLACK MARBLE, THE
'80 HONEYSUCKLE ROSE*
'80 LAST MARRIED COUPLE IN AMERICA, THE*
'80 NINE TO FIVE*
'81 ROLLOVER*
'81 ALL NIGHT LONG*
'83 BRAINSTORM*
'83 DEAL OF THE CENTURY
'83 TABLE FOR FIVE
'83 TERMS OF ENDEARMENT*
'83 WICKED LADY, THE*
'84 ALL OF ME*

HOWARD POYOUROW
MISCELLANEOUS
'80 SEEMS LIKE OLD TIMES
'81 ONLY WHEN I LAUGH

LILY POYSER
UNIT PUBLICIST
'80 NIJINSKY

EMILY PRAGER
SCREENPLAY
'79 MR. MIKE'S MONDO VIDEO*

CATE PRAGGASTIS
CASTING
'84 PHILADELPHIA EXPERIMENT, THE*

MARY PRANGE
ASSISTANT EDITOR
'84 TANK

THOMAS PRATE JR.
KEY GRIP
'82 SOPHIE'S CHOICE
'82 STILL OF THE NIGHT
'83 JAWS 3-D
'84 FALLING IN LOVE
'84 PLACES IN THE HEART

ANTHONY PRATT
PRODUCTION DESIGNER
'81 EXCALIBUR
'84 GIVE MY REGARDS TO BROAD STREET

CHARLES PRATT
PRODUCER
'79 GREAT SANTINI, THE

DONA PRATT
STILLS
'80 EYES OF A STRANGER*

ROGER PRATT
CINEMATOGRAPHER
'82 SENDER, THE*

LT. COMM. RAY PRATTE
MISCELLANEOUS
'80 ISLAND, THE

JACQUES PRAYER
STILLS
'83 EXPOSED*
'84 JUST THE WAY YOU ARE*

YVETTE PRAYER
PROD. SECRETARY
'84 CHEECH AND CHONG'S THE CORSICAN BROTHERS*

MICHAEL PREECE
DIRECTOR
'79 PRIZE FIGHTER, THE

DENIS PREGNOLATO
ASSOCIATE PRODUCER
'84 WHERE THE BOYS ARE

OTTO PREMINGER
PRODUCER
'80 HUMAN FACTOR, THE
DIRECTOR
'80 HUMAN FACTOR, THE

BONNIE PRENDERGAST
SCRIPT SUPERVISOR
'79 STAR TREK-THE MOTION PICTURE
'80 FIRST FAMILY
'81 SUNDAY LOVERS

VINCENT PRENTICE
MAKEUP
'81 DEAD AND BURIED*
'81 HEARTBEEPS*

COLIN PRESCOT
MISCELLANEOUS
'83 SUPERMAN III

BOB PRESNER
MISCELLANEOUS
'81 MY BLOODY VALENTINE

ROBERTA PRESSER
PROD. OFFICE COORD.
'80 HE KNOWS YOU'RE ALONE

ANDREW PRESSMAN
ASSISTANT EDITOR
'83 EXPOSED*

EDWARD PRESSMAN
PRODUCER
'79 OLD BOYFRIENDS*
'81 HAND, THE
EXECUTIVE PRODUCER
'80 HEARTBEAT*
'82 CONAN THE BARBARIAN*
'83 PIRATES OF PENZANCE, THE

MICHAEL PRESSMAN
PRODUCER
'80 THOSE LIPS, THOSE EYES*
DIRECTOR
'79 BOULEVARD NIGHTS
'80 THOSE LIPS, THOSE EYES
'82 SOME KIND OF HERO
'83 DOCTOR DETROIT

DAVID PRESTON
SCREENPLAY
'83 SPACEHUNTER: ADVENTURES IN THE FORBIDDEN ZONE*

DON PRESTON
MUSIC
'82 ANDROID

EARL PRESTON
ART DIRECTOR
'79 BLACK STALLION, THE*
PRODUCTION DESIGNER
'81 HAPPY BIRTHDAY TO ME

MICHAEL PRESTON
KEY GRIP
'84 BROTHER FROM ANOTHER PLANET, THE

SIMON PRESTON
MISCELLANEOUS
'84 AMADEUS

SUSANNA PRESTON
SCRIPT SUPERVISOR
'80 CADDYSHACK
'81 FUNHOUSE, THE
'81 HARDLY WORKING
'83 BLUE SKIES AGAIN
'83 NIGHT IN HEAVEN, A
'83 TOUGH ENOUGH
'84 WHERE THE BOYS ARE
'84 SPLASH*

WARD PRESTON
PRODUCTION DESIGNER
'80 AIRPLANE
'80 STEEL
'82 THAT CHAMPIONSHIP SEASON
'84 PURPLE RAIN

ALAN PRICE
MUSIC
'83 BRITANNIA HOSPITAL

DARIA PRICE
SCREENPLAY
'81 NESTING, THE*
SCRIPT SUPERVISOR
'83 STRANGE INVADERS*

FRED PRICE
ART DIRECTOR
'79 GOING IN STYLE*
'83 PORKY'S II THE NEXT DAY

GEORGE PRICE
MUSIC
'80 GUYANA: CULT OF THE DAMNED*
MISCELLANEOUS
'84 MUTANT

JEFFREY PRICE
SCREENPLAY
'83 TRENCHCOAT*

MARTIN PRICE
ART DIRECTOR
'84 BACHELOR PARTY*

PETER PRICE
PRODUCTION MANAGER
'80 HEAVEN'S GATE*
MISCELLANEOUS
'80 KIDS ARE ALL RIGHT, THE

SAM PRICE
SPECIAL EFFECTS
'79 LOVE AND BULLETS*
'80 HEAVEN'S GATE*
'81 CHARLIE CHAN AND THE CURSE OF THE DRAGON QUEEN*

STEPHEN PRICE
ASSISTANT EDITOR
'81 STRIPES*

CLEA PRICETTI
SCRIPT SUPERVISOR
'81 NESTING, THE

JAMES PRICH
2ND ASST. DIRECTOR
'81 SUNDAY LOVERS

SORIN PRICOPIE
STUNT COORDINATOR
'81 BEAST WITHIN, THE

JACK PRIESTLEY
CINEMATOGRAPHER
'80 FIRST DEADLY SIN

TOM PRIESTLEY JR.
CINEMATOGRAPHER
'84 BEAT STREET

TOM PRIESTLEY
EDITOR
'79 LOVE AND BULLETS*
'80 TESS*
'80 TIMES SQUARE
'83 ANOTHER TIME, ANOTHER PLACE

BERNARD PRIM
STILLS
'80 TESS

ROBERT PRIMES
MISCELLANEOUS
'83 RUMBLEFISH

BARRY PRIMUS
2ND UNIT DIRECTOR
'79 ROSE, THE

JON PATRICK PRINCE
STILLS
'82 SWORD AND THE SORCERER, THE

RICHARD PRINCE
UNIT PROD. MANAGER
'82 PERSONAL BEST*
2ND ASST. DIRECTOR
'80 MY BODYGUARD
'83 RISKY BUSINESS*
'83 UNCOMMON VALOR*

CARL PRINCI
MISCELLANEOUS
'79 10

MARK PRINCI
MISCELLANEOUS
'79 KILLER FISH

GIULANO PRINCIPATO
UNIT MANAGER
'83 PIRANHA II: THE SPAWNING

JIM PRINE
MISCELLANEOUS
'80 LAST FLIGHT OF NOAH'S ARK, THE

DAVID PRINGLE
ASSOCIATE PRODUCER
'84 EVIL THAT MEN DO, THE*
MISCELLANEOUS
'84 EVIL THAT MEN DO, THE

FRANK PRINZI
KEY GRIP
'84 STRANGER THAN PARADISE

PECK PRIOR
ASSISTANT EDITOR
'83 FOOTLOOSE*
'84 PROTOCOL*

BONNIE PRIORE
MAKEUP
'82 CREEPSHOW

ANNE PRITCHARD
PRODUCTION DESIGNER
'79 MAN, A WOMAN AND A BANK, A
'81 ATLANTIC CITY
'83 OF UNKNOWN ORIGIN
MISCELLANEOUS
'82 BEST FRIENDS

JUDITH PRITCHARD
PROD. COORDINATOR
'83 OSTERMAN WEEKEND, THE*
'84 GRANDVIEW, U.S.A.

SUSAN PEREZ PRITCHARD
COSTUMES
'83 HOUSE ON SORORITY ROW

TERRY PRITCHARD
ART DIRECTOR
'81 FRENCH LIEUTENANT'S WOMAN, THE*
'83 BEYOND THE LIMIT*
'84 RIDDLE OF THE SANDS*
PRODUCTION DESIGNER
'84 OXFORD BLUES

BOB PRITCHETT
HAIR
'81 HAPPY BIRTHDAY TO ME
'84 HOTEL NEW HAMPSHIRE, THE*

JOHN PRITCHETT
SOUND
'83 STREAMERS

JAMES PROCTOR
SCREENPLAY
'79 DREAMER*

PAT PROFT
SCREENPLAY
'84 POLICE ACADEMY*
'84 BACHELOR PARTY*
MISCELLANEOUS
'84 JOHNNY DANGEROUSLY

MELISSA PROPHET
ASSOCIATE PRODUCER
'84 COTTON CLUB, THE

TOM PROPHET
KEY GRIP
'80 HEALTH

TOM PROPHET JR.
KEY GRIP
'79 CHINA SYNDROME, THE
'79 PERFECT COUPLE, A
'80 MY BODYGUARD*
'81 MODERN PROBLEMS

CHIP PROSER
SCREENPLAY
'84 ICEMAN*

JAMES PROSER
ASSISTANT EDITOR
'80 MANIAC
1ST ASST. DIRECTOR
'80 MOTHER'S DAY
LOCATIONS
'80 MOTHER'S DAY

JANE PROSNIT
PROD. COORDINATOR
'80 INSIDE MOVES
'81 ENTITY, THE
'82 SIX WEEKS
'83 MAN WOMAN AND CHILD
'84 ALL OF ME
'84 MICKI AND MAUDE

JUAN CLEMENTE PROSPER
LOCATIONS
'79 JAGUAR LIVES

TODD PROST
HAIR
'84 PURPLE RAIN*

FRANCOIS PROTAT
CINEMATOGRAPHER
'83 RUNNING BRAVE

WALLEY PROTZ
MISCELLANEOUS
'79 FAST COMPANY

MICHEL PROULX
ART DIRECTOR
'80 DEATH SHIP*

DAVID PROVAL
MISCELLANEOUS
'83 D.C. CAB

RICK PROVENZANO
HAIR
'80 LAST MARRIED COUPLE IN AMERICA, THE*
'84 ICE PIRATES, THE*

ROBERT PROVENZANO
PROPS
'84 OVER THE BROOKLYN BRIDGE*

LYNETTE PRUCHA
PROD. COORDINATOR
'84 WEEKEND PASS
PROD. SECRETARY
'83 MY TUTOR

RICHARD PRYOR

PRODUCER
'81 RICHARD PRYOR: LIVE ON THE SUNSET STRIP
'81 BUSTIN' LOOSE*

DIRECTOR
'83 RICHARD PRYOR: HERE AND NOW

SCREENPLAY
'81 RICHARD PRYOR: LIVE ON THE SUNSET STRIP
'83 RICHARD PRYOR: HERE AND NOW

PETER PRZYGODDA

EDITOR
'84 PARIS, TEXAS

ALDO PUCCINI

SPECIAL EFFECTS
'79 HURRICANE*

CARLOS PUENTE

ASSISTANT EDITOR
'81 CAVEMAN*

TONY PUEO

COSTUMES
'79 FIFTH MUSKETEER, THE

MAJOR-GEN. LEWIS PUGH

MISCELLANEOUS
'81 SEA WOLVES, THE

ROGER PUGLIESE

2ND ASST. DIRECTOR
'83 HUNGER, THE*
'84 GRANDVIEW, U.S.A.

JAMES PULLEN

MISCELLANEOUS
'84 PLACES IN THE HEART

ROGER PULVERS

MISCELLANEOUS
'83 MERRY CHRISTMAS,MR. LAWRENCE

EVELYN PURCELL

2ND UNIT DIRECTOR
'80 MELVIN AND HOWARD
'84 SWING SHIFT

GLYNN PURCELL

1ST ASST. DIRECTOR
'82 HOUSE OF THE LONG SHADOWS*

JULIE PURCELL

HAIR
'83 CUJO

STEVE PURCELL

SPECIAL EFFECTS
'83 RISKY BUSINESS

RON PURDIE

PRODUCTION MANAGER
'83 FINAL OPTION, THE
'84 SCANDALOUS

1ST ASST. DIRECTOR
'83 WICKED LADY, THE

DEBBIE PUTNAM

LOCATIONS
'83 REUBEN, REUBEN

DAVID PUTTNAM

PRODUCER
'80 FOXES*
'81 CHARIOTS OF FIRE
'83 LOCAL HERO
'84 KILLING FIELDS, THE

EXECUTIVE PRODUCER
'84 KIPPERBANG

MARIO PUZO

SCREENPLAY
'81 SUPERMAN II*

TREVOR PYKE

SOUND
'84 NEVERENDING STORY, THE*

LILLIAN PYLES

PROD. OFFICE COORD.
'84 COTTON CLUB, THE

ALBERT PYUM

DIRECTOR
'82 SWORD AND THE SORCERER, THE

SCREENPLAY
'82 SWORD AND THE SORCERER, THE*

Q

DAVID QUAID
CINEMATOGRAPHER
'83 NIGHT IN HEAVEN, A
'83 I AM THE CHEESE

GIANNI QUARANTA
ART DIRECTOR
'82 TEMPEST*

AARON QUARLES
HAIR
'84 RECKLESS

QUEEN
MUSIC
'80 FLASH GORDON*

GERMAN QUEJIDO
PROPS
'79 CUBA

RON QUELCH
PROPS
'79 GREAT TRAIN ROBBERY, THE

CHANTAL QUESMARD
PROD. SECRETARY
'84 JUST THE WAY YOU ARE*

JOHN QUESTED
EXECUTIVE PRODUCER
'79 SUNBURN*

ROBERTO QUEZADA
ASSISTANT EDITOR
'79 PHANTASM*
MISCELLANEOUS
'82 BEASTMASTER, THE

KEVIN QUIBELL
SPECIAL EFFECTS
'80 HEAVEN'S GATE*
'84 GRANDVIEW, U.S.A.*

JENNY QUIGLEY
SCRIPT SUPERVISOR
'82 PIRATE MOVIE, THE

LUKE QUIGLEY
KEY GRIP
'83 BEYOND THE LIMIT

RONALD QUIGLEY
LOCATIONS
'81 PENNIES FROM HEAVEN
'83 MAN WHO LOVED WOMEN, THE
'84 MICKI AND MAUDE

JOHN QUILL
PRODUCER
'79 NATURAL ENEMIES
PRODUCTION MANAGER
'80 HAPPY BIRTHDAY, GEMINI

SARAH QUILL
STILLS
'82 HOUSE OF THE LONG SHADOWS

RICHARD QUINE
DIRECTOR
'79 PRISONER OF ZENDA, THE

SHIRL QUINLAN
COSTUMES
'79 PHANTASM

JOE QUINLIVAN
SPECIAL EFFECTS
'80 WITHOUT WARNING
'80 SCHIZOID
'83 REVENGE OF THE NINJA
'83 METALSTORM: THE DESTRUCTION OF JARED-SYN
SP. EFFECTS SUPERV.
'83 SAVANNAH SMILES

ED QUINN
KEY GRIP
'79 RUNNING*
'79 WANDERERS, THE
'80 RAGING BULL*
'80 DRESSED TO KILL
'81 RAGTIME
'81 NIGHTHAWKS
'82 WORLD ACCORDING TO GARP, THE
'83 HUNGER, THE
'83 SILKWOOD
'84 POPE OF GREENWICH VILLAGE,THE

JAMES QUINN
1ST ASST. DIRECTOR
'80 UP THE ACADEMY
'81 RICH AND FAMOUS
'81 REDS*
'83 KISS ME GOODBYE
'84 CRACKERS
'84 GREMLINS

ROBERT QUINN
ART DIRECTOR
'80 HEALTH

SPENCER QUINN
LOCATIONS
'79 BEING THERE
'82 SIX WEEKS*

LEE QUINONES
MISCELLANEOUS
'83 SMITHEREENS

ANA MARIA QUINTANA
SCRIPT SUPERVISOR
'79 BREAKING AWAY
'79 BUTCH AND SUNDANCE: THE EARLY YEARS
'80 FORMULA, THE
'80 HOW TO BEAT THE HIGH COST OF LIVING
'81 ZORRO, THE GAY BLADE
'82 BLADERUNNER
'83 BRAINSTORM
'83 UNDER FIRE
'84 NATURAL, THE

GENE QUINTANO
PRODUCER
'84 MAKING THE GRADE
SCREENPLAY
'81 COMIN' AT YA!*
'84 MAKING THE GRADE
EXECUTIVE PRODUCER
'81 COMIN' AT YA!*

JACQUES QUINTERNET
LOCATIONS
'80 QUARTET

JUAN QUIRNO

STILLS
'80 QUARTET

MARTIN QUIROZ

SOUND
'79 ALAMBRISTA!

RAY QUIROZ

SCRIPT SUPERVISOR
'79 APOCALYPSE NOW*
'79 FAST BREAK
'80 RAISE THE TITANIC
'80 STIR CRAZY
'80 FOOLIN AROUND
'80 TOM HORN
'81 PENNIES FROM HEAVEN
'82 I OUGHT TO BE IN PICTURES
'82 NIGHT SHIFT
'82 PERSONAL BEST
'83 MAX DUGAN RETURNS

LYNDELL QUIYOU

HAIR
'80 GILDA LIVE
'81 BLOW OUT*
'83 BIG CHILL, THE
'83 KING OF COMEDY, THE
'84 COTTON CLUB, THE
'84 FALLING IN LOVE*

R

JANE RAAB
PROD. OFFICE COORD.
'83 STRANGE INVADERS
'84 POPE OF GREENWICH VILLAGE,THE
PROD. COORDINATOR
'84 SPLASH*

DAVID RABE
SCREENPLAY
'82 I'M DANCING AS FAST AS I CAN
'83 STREAMERS
EXECUTIVE PRODUCER
'82 I'M DANCING AS FAST AS I CAN

LINDA RABIN
PROD. SECRETARY
'84 INDIANA JONES
AND THE TEMPLE OF DOOM*

APOLINAR RABINAL
PRODUCTION MANAGER
'83 NEVER SAY NEVER AGAIN*

ALEC RABINOWITZ
ASSOCIATE PRODUCER
'83 HOUSE ON SORORITY ROW

HARRY RABINOWITZ
MISCELLANEOUS
'84 ELECTRIC DREAMS

MORTON RABINOWITZ
PRODUCTION DESIGNER
'81 FUNHOUSE, THE

AMY RABINS
MISCELLANEOUS
'82 SEDUCTION, THE
'84 DREAMSCAPE

LEWIS RABKIN
MAKEUP
'82 SAFARI 3000

HAROLD RABUSE
KEY GRIP
'80 LONG RIDERS, THE
'82 BORDER, THE
'83 FOOTLOOSE

LOUIS RACE
1ST ASST. DIRECTOR
'84 INDIANA JONES
AND THE TEMPLE OF DOOM*
2ND ASST. DIRECTOR
'79 PRISONER OF ZENDA, THE*
'80 BLACK MARBLE, THE*
'83 SURVIVORS, THE*

BURANEE RACHJAIBUN
2ND ASST. DIRECTOR
'84 KILLING FIELDS, THE*

LEWIS RACHMIL
PRODUCER
'83 FOOTLOOSE*
ASSOCIATE PRODUCER
'84 PROTOCOL

MICHAEL RACHMIL
PRODUCER
'84 RUNAWAY
ASSOCIATE PRODUCER
'79 HANOVER STREET*
'80 TOM HORN*
'81 DEAD AND BURIED
PRODUCTION MANAGER
'83 HIGH ROAD TO CHINA*
UNIT PROD. MANAGER
'80 TOM HORN

FRANK RACITI
ASSISTANT EDITOR
'80 IDOLMAKER, THE

CHIP RADAELLI
ART DIRECTOR
'80 HANGAR 18

MARK RADCLIFFE
PRODUCTION MANAGER
'79 ROCK 'N ROLL HIGH SCHOOL
2ND ASST. DIRECTOR
'82 ESCAPE ARTIST, THE*
'83 RUMBLEFISH
'84 PROTOCOL*
LOCATIONS
'81 CUTTER'S WAY

MICHAEL RADFORD
DIRECTOR
'83 ANOTHER TIME, ANOTHER PLACE
SCREENPLAY
'83 ANOTHER TIME, ANOTHER PLACE

SHAYNE RADFORD
HAIR
'83 NATE & HAYES

ANUAR RADIN
PRODUCTION MANAGER
'81 HIGH RISK

GILDA RADNER
SCREENPLAY
'80 GILDA LIVE*

ZANE RADNEY
UNIT PROD. MANAGER
'83 NIGHTMARES

ROBERT RADNITZ
PRODUCER
'83 CROSS CREEK

JAMES RADO
MUSIC
'79 HAIR*

TOM RAEBURN
PROPS
'80 HOPSCOTCH*
'83 DRAUGHTSMAN CONTRACT, THE*

BOB RAFELSON
PRODUCER
'81 POSTMAN ALWAYS
RINGS TWICE, THE*
DIRECTOR
'81 POSTMAN ALWAYS
RINGS TWICE, THE

TOBY RAFELSON
ART DIRECTOR
'83 UNDER FIRE*
PRODUCTION DESIGNER
'80 MELVIN AND HOWARD
'82 BORDER, THE

JOSEPH RAFFILL
PRODUCER
'81 HIGH RISK*
LOCATIONS
'84 PHILADELPHIA EXPERIMENT, THE*

STEWART RAFFILL

DIRECTOR
'81 HIGH RISK
'84 ICE PIRATES, THE
'84 PHILADELPHIA EXPERIMENT, THE
SCREENPLAY
'81 HIGH RISK
'84 ICE PIRATES, THE*

LEE RAFNER

PRODUCTION MANAGER
'80 BLACK MARBLE, THE
'81 EYE FOR AN EYE, AN

JAMES RAGAN

1ST ASST. DIRECTOR
'82 ENDANGERED SPECIES

PINKI RAGAN

PROD. COORDINATOR
'84 REVENGE OF THE NERDS

SUSAN RAGAN

STILLS
'81 BODY AND SOUL

OSMAN RAGHEB

MISCELLANEOUS
'80 AMERICAN SUCCESS COMPANY,THE

JENNIE RAGLAN

PROD. SECRETARY
'81 CHARIOTS OF FIRE

ROBERT RAGLAND

MUSIC
'79 MOUNTAIN FAMILY ROBINSON
'79 JAGUAR LIVES
'82 BRAINWAVES
'82 Q: QUETZALCOATL
'83 10 TO MIDNIGHT

GEROME RAGNI

MUSIC
'79 HAIR*

RICHARD RAGUSE

SOUND
'79 ICE CASTLES*

CRAIG RAICHE

PROPS
'79 OVER THE EDGE
'80 LONG RIDERS, THE
'82 48 HOURS
'82 POLTERGEIST
'83 TWILIGHT ZONE, THE MOVIE*
'84 STREETS OF FIRE*

SAMUEL RAIMI

DIRECTOR
'83 EVIL DEAD, THE
SCREENPLAY
'83 EVIL DEAD, THE
EXECUTIVE PRODUCER
'83 EVIL DEAD, THE*

JIMMY RAITT

PROPS
'79 ALL THAT JAZZ
'80 CRUISING*
'81 ENDLESS LOVE
'81 FORT APACHE, THE BRONX
'81 WOLFEN
'82 TOOTSIE
'83 DANIEL
'83 KING OF COMEDY, THE
'83 TRADING PLACES
'84 COTTON CLUB, THE
'84 FALLING IN LOVE

PEGGY RAJSKI

PRODUCER
'84 BROTHER FROM
ANOTHER PLANET, THE*
PRODUCTION MANAGER
'83 LIANNA
'84 BROTHER FROM
ANOTHER PLANET, THE

ALVIN RAKOFF

DIRECTOR
'80 DEATH SHIP

KEN RALSTON

MISCELLANEOUS
'81 DRAGONSLAYER
'82 STAR TREK II
THE WRATH OF KHAN
'83 RETURN OF THE JEDI
'84 STAR TREK III:
THE SEARCH FOR SPOCK

BOB RAMAE

ASSISTANT EDITOR
'80 FORMULA, THE*
'81 RICH AND FAMOUS
'82 FORCED VENGEANCE

CARLO RAMBALDI

MISCELLANEOUS
'79 NIGHTWING
'79 ALIEN
'80 CLOSE ENCOUNTERS OF THE THIRD
KIND SPECIAL EDITION
'81 HAND, THE
'82 E.T. THE EXTRA-TERRESTRIAL
'84 DUNE
'84 CONAN THE DESTROYER

PAT RAMBAUT

SCRIPT SUPERVISOR
'82 MOONLIGHTING
'84 COMFORT AND JOY

AL RAMIREZ

SOUND
'83 JOYSTICKS

DAVID RAMIREZ

EDITOR
'82 BARBAROSA*
'83 CHEECH AND CHONG'S
STILL SMOKIN'*
ASSISTANT EDITOR
'80 BLUES BROTHERS*

STEVEN RAMIREZ

ASSISTANT EDITOR
'80 OCTAGON, THE*
'83 TOUGH ENOUGH

HAROLD RAMIS

DIRECTOR
'80 CADDYSHACK
'83 NATIONAL LAMPOON'S VACATION
SCREENPLAY
'79 MEATBALLS*
'80 CADDYSHACK*
'81 STRIPES*
'84 GHOSTBUSTERS*

PHIL RAMONE

EXECUTIVE PRODUCER
'84 BODY ROCK*
MUSIC SUPERVISOR
'83 FLASHDANCE
MISCELLANEOUS
'80 ONE-TRICK PONY

SUSIE RAMOS

STILLS
'80 HANGAR 18

VIC RAMOS

EXECUTIVE PRODUCER
'82 LIAR'S MOON*
CASTING
'79 APOCALYPSE NOW*
'79 BLACK STALLION, THE*
'79 HARDCORE
'79 OVER THE EDGE
'80 BLUE LAGOON
'80 DRESSED TO KILL
'80 GLORIA
'80 MY BODYGUARD
'81 THIEF

TODD RAMSAY

EDITOR
'79 STAR TREK-THE MOTION PICTURE
'81 ESCAPE FROM NEW YORK
'82 THING, THE

RAMSEY

HAIR
'84 MICKI AND MAUDE*
'84 IMPULSE

JOHN RAMSEY

KEY GRIP
'84 SWING SHIFT

TOM RAMSEY

KEY GRIP
'79 REMEMBER MY NAME
'80 BORDERLINE
'80 MELVIN AND HOWARD
'80 WHERE THE BUFFALO ROAM
'81 MAN WHO SAW TOMORROW, THE
'83 HEART LIKE A WHEEL

FRED RAMSON

KEY GRIP
'82 OUT OF THE BLUE

TOM RAND

COSTUMES
'81 FRENCH LIEUTENANT'S WOMAN, THE
'83 PIRATES OF PENZANCE, THE

JASON RANDAL

STUNT COORDINATOR
'82 OFFICER AND A GENTLEMAN, AN

BILL RANDALL

SOUND
'80 HOLLYWOOD KNIGHTS, THE
'81 BLOOD BEACH
'81 DEAD AND BURIED
'81 LEGEND OF THE LONE RANGER,THE
'81 TARZAN, THE APE MAN
'84 BOLERO

BILL RANDALL SR.

SOUND
'82 NATIONAL LAMPOON'S CLASS REUNION

CORKY RANDALL

MISCELLANEOUS
'79 BLACK STALLION, THE
'83 BLACK STALLION RETURNS, THE

GLENN RANDALL

2ND UNIT DIRECTOR
'82 E.T. THE EXTRA-TERRESTRIAL
'84 INDIANA JONES AND THE TEMPLE OF DOOM*
STUNT COORDINATOR
'79 BLACK STALLION, THE
'81 RAIDERS OF THE LOST ARK
'83 RETURN OF THE JEDI
'84 INDIANA JONES AND THE TEMPLE OF DOOM*

GLENN RANDALL JR.

2ND UNIT DIRECTOR
'84 FIRESTARTER*
'84 MRS. SOFFEL*
STUNT COORDINATOR
'81 GHOST STORY
'82 POLTERGEIST
'84 FIRESTARTER
'84 MRS. SOFFEL

JUNE RANDALL

SCRIPT SUPERVISOR
'80 SHINING, THE
'80 FLASH GORDON
'80 DEATH SHIP
'81 OUTLAND
'82 GANDHI
'84 BOUNTY, THE

MICHAEL RANDALL

HAIR
'82 SPLIT IMAGE*

SHAWN RANDALL

SCREENPLAY
'83 LONELY LADY, THE*

ANTHONY RANDEL

MISCELLANEOUS
'81 SATURDAY THE 14TH
'81 GALAXY OF TERROR
'81 GALAXY OF TERROR

LIZA RANDOL

ASSISTANT EDITOR
'83 WAR GAMES
'84 NATURAL, THE

GINNY RANDOLPH

ART DIRECTOR
'84 STRANGERS KISS

IDA RANDOM

ART DIRECTOR
'82 FRANCES
PRODUCTION DESIGNER
'83 BIG CHILL, THE
'84 BODY DOUBLE
'84 IRRECONCILABLE DIFFERENCES

ALEJANDRO RANGEL

KEY GRIP
'84 EL NORTE*

GERMINAL RANGEL

MISCELLANEOUS
'82 EVIL UNDER THE SUN

MARTIN RANSOHOFF

PRODUCER
'79 NIGHTWING
'79 WANDERERS, THE
'80 CHANGE OF SEASONS, A
'82 HANKY PANKY
'83 CLASS

PETER RANSOHOFF

ASSISTANT EDITOR
'80 MOUNTAIN MEN, THE*
'81 STRIPES*
'83 CLASS
'83 SAVANNAH SMILES

SCOTT RANSOM

MISCELLANEOUS
'83 GOLDEN SEAL, THE

ARUNDHATI RAO

1ST ASST. DIRECTOR
'84 PASSAGE TO INDIA, A*

LARRY RAPAPORT

UNIT PROD. MANAGER
'83 STAR 80*
LOCATIONS
'80 IT'S MY TURN*
'81 THIEF*

RON RAPIEL

LOCATIONS
'79 10*

JOE RAPOSO

MUSIC
'81 GREAT MUPPET CAPER, THE

ANNE RAPP

SCRIPT SUPERVISOR
'83 LONE WOLF MCQUADE
'83 TENDER MERCIES
'84 PLACES IN THE HEART
'84 THIS IS SPINAL TAP

LARRY RAPPAPORT

LOCATIONS
'84 WOMAN IN RED, THE*

MICHELE RAPPAPORT

PRODUCER
'79 OLD BOYFRIENDS*

JUDITH RASCOE

SCREENPLAY
'81 ENDLESS LOVE

MAGGIE RASH

2ND ASST. DIRECTOR
'81 UNDER THE RAINBOW*

STEVE RASH

DIRECTOR
'79 BUDDY HOLLY STORY, THE
'81 UNDER THE RAINBOW

LENNA RASHKOVSKY-KALEVA

MAKEUP
'83 LIQUID SKY

LAURIE RASKIN

STILLS
'81 TICKET TO HEAVEN

JEAN-PIERRE RASSAM

ASSOCIATE PRODUCER
'80 TESS

JAMES RATHBUN

PROPS
'82 HALLOWEEN III: SEASON OF THE WITCH*

CRISTI JANAKI RATHOD

MISCELLANEOUS
'84 INDIANA JONES AND THE TEMPLE OF DOOM

ERIC RATTRAY

EXEC IN CHARGE PROD
'84 TOP SECRET!
ASSOCIATE PRODUCER
'80 SATURN 3
'81 DRAGONSLAYER
'83 BETRAYAL
2ND UNIT DIRECTOR
'80 SATURN 3

GORDON RATTRAY

ART DIRECTOR
'79 MOUNTAIN FAMILY ROBINSON

LAIRD RATTRAY

PROPS
'79 MOUNTAIN FAMILY ROBINSON

ELLEN RAUCH

2ND ASST. DIRECTOR
'81 SO FINE*
'82 FIGHTING BACK*
'83 EDDIE MACON'S RUN

MIKE RAUCH

PRODUCTION MANAGER
'79 ON THE YARD
UNIT PROD. MANAGER
'83 EDDIE MACON'S RUN
1ST ASST. DIRECTOR
'79 GOING IN STYLE
'79 LAST EMBRACE
'79 VOICES
'80 SIMON
'80 DRESSED TO KILL
MISCELLANEOUS
'84 COTTON CLUB, THE

GRETCHEN RAV

PROPS
'81 ATLANTIC CITY

IRVING RAVETCH

SCREENPLAY
'79 NORMA RAE*

BRIAN RAVOK

EDITOR
'80 PROM NIGHT
'83 SCREWBALLS

DENNON RAWLES

CHOREOGRAPHER
'83 STAYING ALIVE*

SAHBER RAWLES

CHOREOGRAPHER
'83 STAYING ALIVE*

KAY RAWLINGS

SCRIPT SUPERVISOR
'79 FIFTH MUSKETEER, THE
'80 EMPIRE STRIKES BACK, THE*
'80 LADY VANISHES, THE

TERRY RAWLINGS

EDITOR
'79 ALIEN
'80 AWAKENING, THE
'81 CHARIOTS OF FIRE
'82 BLADERUNNER
'83 YENTL

ALAN RAWLINS

KEY GRIP
'84 BEAR, THE

DAVID RAWLINS

EDITOR
'79 CHINA SYNDROME, THE
'80 URBAN COWBOY
'82 SOUP FOR ONE
'83 OSTERMAN WEEKEND, THE*
'84 FIRESTARTER*

PHIL RAWLINS

ASSOCIATE PRODUCER
'80 FIRST FAMILY*
UNIT PROD. MANAGER
'79 STAR TREK-THE MOTION PICTURE
'80 FIRST FAMILY
'83 BLUE THUNDER*
'83 KISS ME GOODBYE
'84 GREMLINS

STRATTON RAWSON

SCREENPLAY
'81 TUCK EVERLASTING*
LOCATIONS
'84 NATURAL, THE*

DAVID RAY

EDITOR
'80 ONE-TRICK PONY*
'83 SCARFACE*
ASSOCIATE EDITOR
'79 ALL THAT JAZZ
ASSISTANT EDITOR
'80 SIMON*

JOHANNA RAY

CASTING
'81 HELL NIGHT
'82 SEDUCTION, THE
'82 PARASITE
'83 METALSTORM: THE DESTRUCTION OF JARED-SYN*
'83 FRIGHTMARE*
'84 FIRESTARTER
'84 DREAMSCAPE

JOSEPH RAY

2ND ASST. DIRECTOR
'79 ALL THAT JAZZ
'79 HAIR*
'81 ROLLOVER
'81 FORT APACHE, THE BRONX
'82 SOPHIE'S CHOICE
'83 TRADING PLACES*
'84 MOSCOW ON THE HUDSON

KIMBERLY RAY

ASSISTANT EDITOR
'81 HALLOWEEN II*
'82 THING, THE*
'84 MIKE'S MURDER*

LINDA RAY

SCRIPT SUPERVISOR
'79 TIM
'82 ROAD WARRIOR, THE

TONY RAY

PRODUCER
'80 WILLIE & PHIL*
EXECUTIVE PRODUCER
'79 ROSE, THE
UNIT PROD. MANAGER
'80 WILLIE & PHIL
'82 SOUP FOR ONE
'83 WITHOUT A TRACE

MICHELE RAY-GAVRAS

EXECUTIVE PRODUCER
'83 HANNA K

BASIL RAYBURN

ASSOCIATE PRODUCER
'83 LORDS OF DISCIPLINE, THE
MISCELLANEOUS
'79 LOVE AND BULLETS
'80 WATCHER IN THE WOODS, THE
'84 ELECTRIC DREAMS

JANE RAYLEIGH

PROD. SECRETARY
'84 CONAN THE DESTROYER*

TOM RAZZANO

UNIT MANAGER
'83 DANIEL
2ND ASST. DIRECTOR
'84 RECKLESS
LOCATIONS
'83 BABY IT'S YOU*

KAREN REA
CASTING
'79 MAIN EVENT, THE*
'80 HONEYSUCKLE ROSE*
'80 OH GOD! BOOK II
'81 STRIPES
'81 PURSUIT OF D.B. COOPER, THE*
'82 NATIONAL LAMPOON'S CLASS REUNION
'83 SPACEHUNTER: ADVENTURES IN THE FORBIDDEN ZONE
'83 CHRISTINE
'83 WRONG IS RIGHT
'84 GHOSTBUSTERS*
'84 NO SMALL AFFAIR
'84 ROMANCING THE STONE*

MICHAEL REA
ASSISTANT EDITOR
'83 DEAD ZONE, THE*
'83 VIDEODROME*

PETER REA
PRODUCER
'84 GRANDVIEW, U.S.A.*

RUDY REACHI
PROPS
'80 HOLLYWOOD KNIGHTS, THE
'84 ROMANCING THE STONE*

ADRIENNE READ
SCRIPT SUPERVISOR
'82 STARSTRUCK

TONY READING
ART DIRECTOR
'81 RAGTIME*
'83 KRULL*

SCOTT JON READWINE
MAKEUP
'82 VICE SQUAD
'83 DEADLY FORCE

CRAIG REARDON
MISCELLANEOUS
'81 STRANGE BEHAVIOR
'82 E.T. THE EXTRA-TERRESTRIAL
'82 POLTERGEIST
'83 TWILIGHT ZONE, THE MOVIE
'83 TWILIGHT ZONE, THE MOVIE
'84 DREAMSCAPE

BARRY REBO
CINEMATOGRAPHER
'79 MR. MIKE'S MONDO VIDEO

RAY RECHT
ART DIRECTOR
'82 AMITYVILLE II: THE POSSESSION

BILLY RECORD
KEY GRIP
'83 AMERICANA

RON RECORD
KEY GRIP
'79 OVER THE EDGE*

ROBERT REDDING
MAKEUP
'82 SUMMER LOVERS*

DON REDDY
CINEMATOGRAPHER
'79 DOUBLE MCGUFFIN, THE
'80 FOR THE LOVE OF BENJI
'80 OH! HEAVENLY DOG

ROBERT REDFORD
DIRECTOR
'80 ORDINARY PEOPLE

VAN REDIN
STILLS
'84 SONGWRITER*

ANTHONY REDMAN
EDITOR
'81 EYE FOR AN EYE, AN
'81 INCREDIBLE SHRINKING WOMAN, THE*
'83 LONE WOLF MCQUADE

DAVID REDPATH
MISCELLANEOUS
'84 SHEENA

JAMES REECE
PROPS
'80 HANGAR 18
'83 REVENGE OF THE NINJA

CLIVE REED
1ST ASST. DIRECTOR
'83 YELLOWBEARD*

DON REED
2ND ASST. DIRECTOR
'84 PREPPIES

HAL REED
PRODUCTION MANAGER
'81 HARDLY WORKING*

MARCIA REED
STILLS
'79 MUPPET MOVIE, THE*
'80 ORDINARY PEOPLE
'81 HEARTBEEPS
'82 ENDANGERED SPECIES*
'83 SUDDEN IMPACT
'83 GET CRAZY
'83 KISS ME GOODBYE
'83 WRONG IS RIGHT
'84 CITY HEAT
'84 TIGHTROPE

STAN REED
KEY GRIP
'82 TRON

TIM REED
2ND ASST. DIRECTOR
'84 CHAMPIONS*
'84 SCANDALOUS*

MARK REEDALL
MAKEUP
'80 BORDERLINE
'80 COAL MINER'S DAUGHTER
'80 NINE TO FIVE*
'81 RAGGEDY MAN
'82 MISSING
'84 MIKE'S MURDER

JERRY REES
MISCELLANEOUS
'82 TRON

CONNIE REEVE
MAKEUP
'81 CLASH OF THE TITANS*

DANIS REGAL
PROD. COORDINATOR
'83 LIANNA*
'84 CLOAK AND DAGGER

CHRIS REGAN
MISCELLANEOUS
'82 ZAPPED!

PEGGY REGAN
MISCELLANEOUS
'82 ZAPPED!

RUSS REGAN
MUSIC SUPERVISOR
'84 BREAKIN 2 ELECTRIC BOOGALOO

RUTH REGINA
MAKEUP
'81 HARDLY WORKING*

JANE REHM
COSTUME SUPERVISOR
'81 HALLOWEEN II
'82 HALLOWEEN III: SEASON OF THE WITCH

BOB REHME
EXECUTIVE PRODUCER
'81 EYE FOR AN EYE, AN
'82 VICE SQUAD*

JOE REICH
CASTING
'82 BEASTMASTER, THE
'84 WHERE THE BOYS ARE*

STEPHANIE REICHEL
ART DIRECTOR
'82 FIRST BLOOD

STEPHEN REICHEL
PRODUCTION MANAGER
'82 QUEST FOR FIRE*

BILL REICHERT
STILLS
'82 BEASTMASTER, THE

JULIE REICHERT
SCREENPLAY
'84 BREAKIN 2 ELECTRIC BOOGALOO*

MARK REICHERT
DIRECTOR
'80 UNION CITY
SCREENPLAY
'80 UNION CITY

DAR REID
LOCATIONS
'81 GOING APE!

JENNY REID
SCRIPT SUPERVISOR
'82 PINK FLOYD: THE WALL
'84 OXFORD BLUES

JULIE REID
PROD. SECRETARY
'81 BUSTIN' LOOSE*

MARCIA REIDER
CASTING
'84 SILENT NIGHT, DEADLY NIGHT*
MISCELLANEOUS
'84 SILENT NIGHT, DEADLY NIGHT

JOSEPH REIDY
1ST ASST. DIRECTOR
'83 AMITYVILLE 3D
2ND ASST. DIRECTOR
'81 RICH AND FAMOUS*
'81 EYEWITNESS
'81 NIGHTHAWKS
'82 I'M DANCING AS FAST AS I CAN*
'82 LITTLE SEX, A*
'82 TOOTSIE
'82 SECOND THOUGHTS
'83 SURVIVORS, THE*

ROBERT REIFF
STILLS
'84 PURPLE RAIN

JAMES REIGLE
SCREENPLAY
'82 ANDROID*

JEAN BURT REILLY
HAIR
'79 ROCKY II
'80 RAGING BULL*
'80 ORDINARY PEOPLE*
'81 TRUE CONFESSIONS*

THOMAS REILLY
1ST ASST. DIRECTOR
'83 LOVESICK
'83 ZELIG*
'84 BROADWAY DANNY ROSE
2ND ASST. DIRECTOR
'81 ARTHUR
'82 SOUP FOR ONE
'82 MIDSUMMER NIGHT'S SEX COMEDY, A*

BOB REILY
SPECIAL EFFECTS
'79 SEDUCTION OF JOE TYNAN, THE

KEN REIMER
STILLS
'81 FEAR NO EVIL

RICHARD REINBERG
EXECUTIVE PRODUCER
'82 PENITENTIARY II*

CARL REINER
DIRECTOR
'79 JERK, THE
'82 DEAD MEN DON'T WEAR PLAID
'83 MAN WITH TWO BRAINS, THE
'84 ALL OF ME
SCREENPLAY
'82 DEAD MEN DON'T WEAR PLAID*
'83 MAN WITH TWO BRAINS, THE*

ROB REINER
DIRECTOR
'84 THIS IS SPINAL TAP
SCREENPLAY
'84 THIS IS SPINAL TAP*
MUSIC
'84 THIS IS SPINAL TAP*

WALDOMIRO REIS
SPECIAL EFFECTS
'79 KILLER FISH*

DOLF REIST
STILLS
'82 FIVE DAYS ONE SUMMER*

KAREL REISZ
DIRECTOR
'81 FRENCH LIEUTENANT'S WOMAN, THE

ROBERT REITANO
EDITOR
'83 EASY MONEY*

IVAN REITMAN
PRODUCER
'81 STRIPES*
'84 GHOSTBUSTERS
DIRECTOR
'79 MEATBALLS
'81 STRIPES
'84 GHOSTBUSTERS
EXECUTIVE PRODUCER
'83 SPACEHUNTER: ADVENTURES IN THE FORBIDDEN ZONE

SIMON RELPH
PRODUCER
'83 PRIVATES ON PARADE
EXECUTIVE PRODUCER
'81 REDS*
1ST ASST. DIRECTOR
'79 YANKS
'81 REDS*
MISCELLANEOUS
'79 YANKS

ROBERT RELYEA
ASSOCIATE PRODUCER
'84 BLAME IT ON RIO
PRODUCTION MANAGER
'84 BLAME IT ON RIO*

PAT REMBAUT
SCRIPT SUPERVISOR
'79 CLASS OF MISS MACMICHAEL, THE

JAY REMER
PUBLICIST
'79 WANDERERS, THE
'80 FIRST DEADLY SIN

RICHARD REMIAS
MISCELLANEOUS
'81 ENTER THE NINJA

BARBARA REMSEN
CASTING
'84 NOT FOR PUBLICATION*
'84 BEAR, THE

DIEMUT REMY
COSTUMES
'84 NEVERENDING STORY, THE

MORGAN RENARD
STILLS
'80 ALTERED STATES
'80 INSIDE MOVES
'82 TOY, THE
'83 LONELY LADY, THE*
'83 TWILIGHT ZONE, THE MOVIE*
'84 CRACKERS
'82 HAMMETT*

MADELYN RENEE
MISCELLANEOUS
'82 YES, GIORGIO

JEFF RENFROW
KEY GRIP
'83 BAD BOYS*

GRETCHEN RENNELL
CASTING
'81 REDS*
'83 FLASHDANCE
'84 COTTON CLUB, THE*
'84 THIEF OF HEARTS

JOHN RENTSCH
PUBLICIST
'84 CHAMPIONS*

JOE RENZETTI
MUSIC
'80 FATSO
'80 EXTERMINATOR, THE
'81 DEAD AND BURIED
'81 UNDER THE RAINBOW
MISCELLANEOUS
'79 BUDDY HOLLY STORY, THE

MAGGIE RENZI
PRODUCER
'83 LIANNA*
'84 BROTHER FROM ANOTHER PLANET, THE*
ASSISTANT EDITOR
'80 RETURN OF THE SECAUCUS SEVEN, THE*
UNIT MANAGER
'80 RETURN OF THE SECAUCUS SEVEN, THE
'83 LIANNA
'84 BROTHER FROM ANOTHER PLANET, THE
LOCATIONS
'83 LIANNA*

MARTA RENZI
CHOREOGRAPHER
'83 LIANNA

GAYNE RESCHER
CINEMATOGRAPHER
'82 STAR TREK II THE WRATH OF KHAN

PATRICIA RESNICK
SCREENPLAY
'79 QUINTET*
'80 NINE TO FIVE*

LINDA RESSEL
CASTING
'79 MEATBALLS*

TODD RETHERFORD
MISCELLANEOUS
'81 AMY

DANNY RETZ
ASSISTANT EDITOR
'84 MUTANT*

FLORENT RETZ
ASSISTANT EDITOR
'79 ROLLER BOOGIE*
'80 FADE TO BLACK*

OTTO RETZER
LOCATIONS
'79 FIFTH MUSKETEER, THE

EFRAIM REUVENI
ASSISTANT EDITOR
'82 YOUNG DOCTORS IN LOVE*

LARRY REVENE
CINEMATOGRAPHER
'84 PREPPIES

FRED REXER
MISCELLANEOUS
'84 RED DAWN

EDITH REY
SCREENPLAY
'83 SPACEHUNTER: ADVENTURES IN THE FORBIDDEN ZONE*

CECILIA REYES
ASSISTANT EDITOR
'83 JAWS 3-D
'84 OH GOD, YOU DEVIL

LUIS REYES
PUBLICIST
'84 LONELY GUY, THE

DREAS REYNECKER
MISCELLANEOUS
'84 GREYSTOKE: THE LEGEND OF TARZAN, LORD OF THE APES

MARY-JANE REYNER
COSTUME SUPERVISOR
'84 COMFORT AND JOY*

BURT REYNOLDS
DIRECTOR
'81 SHARKEY'S MACHINE

CARL REYNOLDS
ASSOCIATE PRODUCER
'81 FEAR NO EVIL*

DON REYNOLDS
SOUND
'83 NATE & HAYES

JONATHAN REYNOLDS
SCREENPLAY
'84 MICKI AND MAUDE

KEVIN REYNOLDS
SCREENPLAY
'84 RED DAWN*

LYNN REYNOLDS
MAKEUP
'79 TIME AFTER TIME

NORMAN REYNOLDS
PRODUCTION DESIGNER
'80 EMPIRE STRIKES BACK, THE
'81 RAIDERS OF THE LOST ARK
'83 RETURN OF THE JEDI

PAUL REYNOLDS
MISCELLANEOUS
'81 TARZAN, THE APE MAN

SHARRON REYNOLDS
SCRIPT SUPERVISOR
'82 EATING RAOUL
'83 METALSTORM: THE DESTRUCTION OF JARED-SYN
'83 LOVE LETTERS
'84 ANGEL
'84 REPO MAN*
PROD. COORDINATOR
'80 FADE TO BLACK
'81 TAKE THIS JOB AND SHOVE IT

SIMONE REYNOLDS
CASTING
'84 GIVE MY REGARDS TO BROAD STREET

WILLIAM REYNOLDS

EDITOR
'79 LITTLE ROMANCE, A
'79 OLD BOYFRIENDS
'80 HEAVEN'S GATE*
'80 NIJINSKY
'82 AUTHOR, AUTHOR
'82 MAKING LOVE
'83 YELLOWBEARD
'84 LONELY GUY, THE*
'84 LITTLE DRUMMER GIRL, THE

MISCELLANEOUS
'80 HEAVEN'S GATE

WILLIAM REYNOLDS

MAKEUP
'80 ON THE NICKEL

HARRY REZ

KEY GRIP
'79 NIGHTWING
'79 ONION FIELD, THE
'80 ROADIE
'83 MAN WHO WASN'T THERE, THE

STEVE REZ III

KEY GRIP
'82 FRIDAY THE 13TH PART THREE IN 3D

STEVE RHEA

LOCATIONS
'84 PHILADELPHIA EXPERIMENT, THE*

DANA RHEAUME

MISCELLANEOUS
'83 METALSTORM: THE DESTRUCTION OF JARED-SYN

DELWYN RHEAUME

SPECIAL EFFECTS
'79 AMITYVILLE HORROR, THE
'81 BLOOD BEACH

JUDITH RHEINER

PUBLICIST
'82 DINER
'83 BLUE SKIES AGAIN

UNIT PUBLICIST
'84 IRRECONCILABLE DIFFERENCES

JOHN RHODE

LOCATIONS
'82 PARASITE

PHILIP RHODES

MAKEUP
'82 DEATHWISH II

SHARI RHODES

CASTING
'80 BIG BRAWL, THE*
'80 CLOSE ENCOUNTERS OF THE THIRD KIND SPECIAL EDITION*
'80 URBAN COWBOY*
'81 RAGGEDY MAN*
'81 DEADLY BLESSING*
'82 BARBAROSA*
'82 BEST LITTLE WHOREHOUSE IN TEXAS, THE*
'83 TENDER MERCIES
'83 TERMS OF ENDEARMENT*
'83 TOUGH ENOUGH*

TED RHODES

KEY GRIP
'81 STUDENT BODIES

PAUL RHUDY

ART DIRECTOR
'84 MARVIN AND TIGE*

CRAIG LAURENCE RICE

1ST ASST. DIRECTOR
'84 BROTHER FROM ANOTHER PLANET, THE

2ND ASST. DIRECTOR
'82 PENITENTIARY II*

HEIDI RICE

SCRIPT SUPERVISOR
'84 LAST NIGHT AT THE ALAMO

JOHN RICE

SCRIPT SUPERVISOR
'79 DAWN OF THE DEAD

MILT RICE

SPECIAL EFFECTS
'79 NIGHTWING
'79 IN-LAWS, THE
'80 STUNT MAN, THE
'80 URBAN COWBOY
'81 BUDDY, BUDDY

DAVID LOWELL RICH

DIRECTOR
'79 CONCORDE-AIRPORT '79, THE
'81 CHU CHU AND THE PHILLY FLASH

GARY RICH

SOUND
'80 MANIAC
'81 BURNING, THE
'84 FRIDAY THE 13TH PART IV THE FINAL CHAPTER

JAMES RICH JR.

CO-PRODUCER
'82 MONTY PYTHON LIVE AT THE HOLLYWOOD BOWL

RAY RICH

KEY GRIP
'80 CLOSE ENCOUNTERS OF THE THIRD KIND SPECIAL EDITION

SHIRLEY RICH

CASTING
'79 KRAMER VS. KRAMER
'80 FORMULA, THE*
'84 FIRSTBORN

MISCELLANEOUS
'82 DEATH VALLEY

JEFFERSON RICHARD

PRODUCTION MANAGER
'80 WITHOUT WARNING

MISCELLANEOUS
'82 BUTTERFLY

BOB RICHARDS

PROPS
'80 BLACK MARBLE, THE

DICK RICHARDS

PRODUCER
'82 TOOTSIE*

DIRECTOR
'82 DEATH VALLEY
'83 MAN WOMAN AND CHILD

KY RICHARDS III

LOCATIONS
'79 REAL LIFE*

JACK RICHARDS

CINEMATOGRAPHER
'81 BEAST WITHIN, THE
'81 ON THE RIGHT TRACK

JOHN RICHARDS

SOUND
'82 EVIL UNDER THE SUN*

MARTIN RICHARDS

PRODUCER
'81 FORT APACHE, THE BRONX*

MARY RICHARDS

PROD. SECRETARY
'81 SPHINX
'83 LOCAL HERO
'84 GREYSTOKE: THE LEGEND OF TARZAN, LORD OF THE APES

SIOUX RICHARDS

SCRIPT SUPERVISOR
'83 BAD BOYS

BARRY RICHARDSON

HAIR
'81 AMERICAN WEREWOLF IN LONDON, AN
'81 REDS*
'82 PINK FLOYD: THE WALL*
'84 GREYSTOKE: THE LEGEND OF TARZAN, LORD OF THE APES
'84 LITTLE DRUMMER GIRL, THE

ED RICHARDSON

ART DIRECTOR
'79 AMERICAN GIGOLO
'79 DOUBLE MCGUFFIN, THE
'82 CAT PEOPLE
'83 SCARFACE
'84 THIEF OF HEARTS
PRODUCTION DESIGNER
'81 HARD COUNTRY
'81 MODERN ROMANCE

GEOFF RICHARDSON

KEY GRIP
'83 MAN FROM SNOWY RIVER, THE

GEORGE RICHARDSON

ART DIRECTOR
'80 NIJINSKY*
'80 OH! HEAVENLY DOG
'83 HIGH ROAD TO CHINA

GILLIAN RICHARDSON

SCRIPT SUPERVISOR
'83 DEAD ZONE, THE
'83 VIDEODROME

HENRY RICHARDSON

EDITOR
'83 OCTOPUSSY*

HENRY RICHARDSON

MISCELLANEOUS
'80 KIDNAPPING OF THE PRESIDENT, THE

JIM RICHARDSON

LOCATIONS
'80 DEFIANCE*

JOHN RICHARDSON

SPECIAL EFFECTS
'79 ESCAPE TO ATHENA
'80 WATCHER IN THE WOODS, THE
'82 FIVE DAYS ONE SUMMER
'83 OCTOPUSSY
MISCELLANEOUS
'80 FFOLKES
'80 FFOLKES

LARRY RICHARDSON

ASSISTANT EDITOR
'83 NATE & HAYES
'84 KIPPERBANG*

TANGERINE RICHARDSON

SCRIPT SUPERVISOR
'79 C.H.O.M.P.S.

TONY RICHARDSON

DIRECTOR
'82 BORDER, THE
'84 HOTEL NEW HAMPSHIRE, THE
SCREENPLAY
'84 HOTEL NEW HAMPSHIRE, THE

BILL RICHERT

STILLS
'82 ZAPPED!

WILLIAM RICHERT

DIRECTOR
'79 WINTER KILLS
'80 AMERICAN SUCCESS COMPANY,THE
SCREENPLAY
'79 WINTER KILLS
'80 AMERICAN SUCCESS COMPANY,THE*

SYLVIE RICHEZ

PROD. SECRETARY
'80 QUARTET

ANTHONY RICHMOND

CINEMATOGRAPHER
'80 AMERICAN SUCCESS COMPANY,THE
'80 KIDS ARE ALL RIGHT, THE*
MISCELLANEOUS
'79 LOVE AND BULLETS

ILENE RICHMOND

PUBLICIST
'81 UNDER THE RAINBOW

JEANNE RICHMOND

MAKEUP
'79 EUROPEANS, THE*
'84 RIDDLE OF THE SANDS
'84 BOSTONIANS, THE

TED RICHMOND

PRODUCER
'79 FIFTH MUSKETEER, THE

TOM RICHMOND

CINEMATOGRAPHER
'84 HARDBODIES

GABY RICHTER

MISCELLANEOUS
'84 NEVERENDING STORY, THE

FRANK RICHTER JR.

SOUND
'81 ON THE RIGHT TRACK

W.D. RICHTER

PRODUCER
'84 ADVENTURES OF BUCKAROO BANZAI ACROSS THE 8TH DIMENSION, THE*
DIRECTOR
'84 ADVENTURES OF BUCKAROO BANZAI ACROSS THE 8TH DIMENSION, THE
SCREENPLAY
'79 DRACULA
'80 BRUBAKER
'81 ALL NIGHT LONG

RICHARD RICHTSFELD

SPECIAL EFFECTS
'80 AMERICAN SUCCESS COMPANY, THE
SP. EFFECTS SUPERV.
'79 BLOODLINE

FRANK RICHWOOD

ART DIRECTOR
'84 NO SMALL AFFAIR
'84 RHINESTONE

JOCELYN RICKARDS

COSTUMES
'81 CHARLIE CHAN AND THE CURSE OF THE DRAGON QUEEN

GREG RICKETSON

PRODUCTION MANAGER
'81 ROAD GAMES*
UNIT MANAGER
'81 EARTHLING, THE

TOM RICKMAN

SCREENPLAY
'80 COAL MINER'S DAUGHTER

NELSON RIDDLE

MUSIC
'80 GUYANA: CULT OF THE DAMNED*

CRAIG RIDENOUR

ASSISTANT EDITOR
'84 STARMAN*

SHARON RIDGEWAY

SCRIPT SUPERVISOR
'81 BURNING, THE

ANTHONY RIDIO

CO-PRODUCER
'84 FINAL TERROR, THE*
2ND ASST. DIRECTOR
'84 FINAL TERROR, THE

LAURIE RIDLEY

STILLS
'79 GREAT TRAIN ROBBERY, THE*
'80 ROUGH CUT
'81 DRAGONSLAYER*
'84 BEST DEFENSE*
'84 TOP SECRET!

CHRIS RIDSDALE
ASSISTANT EDITOR
'79 DRACULA
'81 FRENCH LIEUTENANT'S WOMAN, THE*

RIC RIELDS
ASSISTANT EDITOR
'84 MIKE'S MURDER*

ROBERT RIGER
2ND UNIT DIRECTOR
'81 VICTORY

JIM BISHOP RIGGIO
1ST ASST. DIRECTOR
'81 TATTOO*

JOSEPH RIGGIO
KEY GRIP
'79 PRISONER OF ZENDA, THE*
'80 NUDE BOMB, THE

RITA RIGGS
COSTUMES
'80 IDOLMAKER, THE
'81 CATTLE ANNIE AND LITTLE BRITCHES
'82 YES, GIORGIO*
'83 DEAL OF THE CENTURY
COSTUME SUPERVISOR
'82 OFFICER AND A GENTLEMAN, AN*

KERRY RIKE
KEY GRIP
'83 TENDER MERCIES

LAURIE RILEY
COSTUME SUPERVISOR
'82 OFFICER AND A GENTLEMAN, AN*

LAURIN RINDER
MUSIC
'81 ENTER THE NINJA*

KLAUS RINGEL
PROPS
'84 MOSCOW ON THE HUDSON*

BOB RINGWOOD
ART DIRECTOR
'83 DRAUGHTSMAN CONTRACT, THE
COSTUMES
'81 EXCALIBUR
'84 DUNE

KEN RINKER
MISCELLANEOUS
'84 PLACES IN THE HEART

ALAN RINZLER
ASSOCIATE PRODUCER
'84 SHEENA*

TONI-CONCHITA RIOS
PROD. OFFICE COORD.
'84 EL NORTE
MISCELLANEOUS
'84 EL NORTE

HILLARY ANNE RIPPS
ASSOCIATE PRODUCER
'82 SIX WEEKS

MICHAEL RIPPS
EDITOR
'84 STREETS OF FIRE*
ASSOCIATE EDITOR
'83 WAR GAMES
ASSISTANT EDITOR
'81 GHOST STORY

SARA RISHER
ASSOCIATE PRODUCER
'81 POLYESTER
'82 FIRST TIME, THE
CO-PRODUCER
'84 NIGHTMARE ON ELM STREET, A

CLAUDE RISI
1ST ASST. DIRECTOR
'81 SUNDAY LOVERS*

DINO RISI
DIRECTOR
'81 SUNDAY LOVERS*

GEORGE RISKO
MISCELLANEOUS
'81 ENTITY, THE

BRIAN RISLEY
PUBLICIST
'84 BROTHER FROM ANOTHER PLANET, THE

EDWARD RISSIEN
EXECUTIVE PRODUCER
'79 SAINT JACK*

DANTON RISSNER
PRODUCER
'80 UP THE ACADEMY*

BARBARA RITCHIE
HAIR
'80 EMPIRE STRIKES BACK, THE
'81 DRAGONSLAYER*
'83 DRESSER, THE
'83 KRULL
'83 KEEP, THE

MICHAEL RITCHIE
PRODUCER
'80 DIVINE MADNESS
DIRECTOR
'80 DIVINE MADNESS
'80 ISLAND, THE
'83 SURVIVORS, THE

MARTIN RITT
DIRECTOR
'79 NORMA RAE
'81 BACK ROADS
'83 CROSS CREEK

JEREMY RITZER
CASTING
'79 ALL THAT JAZZ*
'79 GOING IN STYLE*
'79 HAIR*
'79 ON THE YARD*
'79 WARRIORS, THE*
'80 ALTERED STATES*
'80 CAN'T STOP THE MUSIC*
'80 DEFIANCE*
'80 FAME*
'80 THOSE LIPS, THOSE EYES*
'81 RICH AND FAMOUS*
'81 SO FINE*
'81 ARTHUR*
'81 EYEWITNESS*
'81 FOUR SEASONS, THE*
'81 TATTOO*
'82 ANNIE*
'82 LITTLE SEX, A*
'83 STAR 80*
'83 AMITYVILLE 3D*
'83 BAD BOYS*
'84 HOTEL NEW HAMPSHIRE, THE*
'84 PLACES IN THE HEART*

J. MICHAEL RIVA
ART DIRECTOR
'80 BRUBAKER
'80 ORDINARY PEOPLE*
PRODUCTION DESIGNER
'81 HALLOWEEN II
'81 HAND, THE
'83 BAD BOYS
'84 ADVENTURES OF BUCKAROO BANZAI ACROSS THE 8TH DIMENSION, THE

STELLA RIVERS
HAIR
'79 ARABIAN ADVENTURE

WILLIAM RIVERS
MISCELLANEOUS
'82 BEASTMASTER, THE

PHILLIPPE RIVIER
2ND ASST. DIRECTOR
'81 NESTING, THE

MARC RIVIERE
1ST ASST. DIRECTOR
'84 JUST THE WAY YOU ARE*

STEPHEN RIVKIN
EDITOR
'84 HOT DOG...THE MOVIE

WALTER RIZZATI
MUSIC
'83 1990: THE BRONX WARRIORS

ANGELO RIZZI
PROPS
'79 FEDORA*

NEIL ROACH
CINEMATOGRAPHER
'82 SILENT RAGE*
MISCELLANEOUS
'80 ISLAND, THE

PATRICK ROARK
EDITOR
'82 MEGAFORCE*

PETER ROBB-KING
MAKEUP
'79 DRACULA
'79 HANOVER STREET
'79 MURDER BY DECREE
'81 OUTLAND

DEREK ROBBINS
PUBLICIST
'81 RAIDERS OF THE LOST ARK
'83 FINAL OPTION, THE

DICK ROBBINS
SCREENPLAY
'79 C.H.O.M.P.S.*

MATTHEW ROBBINS
DIRECTOR
'81 DRAGONSLAYER
SCREENPLAY
'81 DRAGONSLAYER*

RABBI STEVEN ROBBINS
MISCELLANEOUS
'79 FRISCO KID, THE

RICHARD ROBBINS
MUSIC
'79 EUROPEANS, THE
'80 QUARTET
'83 HEAT AND DUST
'84 BOSTONIANS, THE

JOHN ROBERDEAU
EXECUTIVE PRODUCER
'83 STREAMERS*

CHARLENE ROBERSON
MAKEUP
'80 CARNY*
'80 FOOLIN AROUND
'80 LOVING COUPLES*
'82 BARBAROSA*
'84 TANK

JAMES ROBERSON
CINEMATOGRAPHER
'79 MOUNTAIN FAMILY ROBINSON

LORRAINE ROBERSON
HAIR
'80 SMOKEY AND THE BANDIT II*
'80 COAL MINER'S DAUGHTER
'81 INCREDIBLE SHRINKING WOMAN, THE*
'82 BEST LITTLE WHOREHOUSE IN TEXAS, THE*

LUIS ROBERT
MISCELLANEOUS
'81 CLASH OF THE TITANS

MICHELE ROBERT-LAUUAC
ASSISTANT EDITOR
'83 HANNA K*

FRANCESCA ROBERTI
SCRIPT SUPERVISOR
'79 BLOODLINE*
'81 SO FINE*
'82 MONSIGNOR

BEN ROBERTS
SCREENPLAY
'81 LEGEND OF THE LONE RANGER, THE*

BOBBY ROBERTS
EXECUTIVE PRODUCER
'82 DEATHWISH II*

BRUCE ROBERTS
MUSIC
'82 JINXED*

BYRON ROBERTS
CO-PRODUCER
'80 GONG SHOW MOVIE, THE
UNIT PROD. MANAGER
'80 GONG SHOW MOVIE, THE

DAN ROBERTS
PROPS
'81 THEY ALL LAUGHED*

DEBORAH ROBERTS
ASSISTANT EDITOR
'82 HAMMETT*
'83 MAN WHO LOVED WOMEN, THE*
'84 MICKI AND MAUDE*

DON ROBERTS
UNIT PROD. MANAGER
'80 LITTLE MISS MARKER
'81 HEARTBEEPS*
1ST ASST. DIRECTOR
'82 NIGHT CROSSING
'84 TANK

JOE ROBERTS
SCREENPLAY
'83 MY TUTOR

JOHN ROBERTS
ART DIRECTOR
'80 MIRROR CRACK'D, THE

LARRY ROBERTS
SPECIAL EFFECTS
'80 INSIDE MOVES
'81 RICH AND FAMOUS
'81 KNIGHTRIDERS
'84 CRACKERS

LT. COL. GEORGE ROBERTS
MISCELLANEOUS
'79 YANKS

MARTIN ROBERTS
PUBLICIST
'80 ALLIGATOR

PAMELA ROBERTS
CASTING
'83 STRANGE BREW

PETER ROBERTS
STILLS
'84 HARDBODIES

RANDY ROBERTS
EDITOR
'79 PLAYERS
'80 SMALL CIRCLE OF FRIENDS, A
'82 HAMMETT*
'82 ONE FROM THE HEART*
'83 JAWS 3-D*
MISCELLANEOUS
'84 OH GOD, YOU DEVIL

ROBBE ROBERTS
EDITOR
'81 PURSUIT OF D.B. COOPER, THE*
MISCELLANEOUS
'81 CATTLE ANNIE AND LITTLE BRITCHES

ROOSEVELT ROBERTS
KEY GRIP
'79 BOARDWALK
'79 GREAT BANK HOAX, THE
'80 UNION CITY

SELWYN ROBERTS
1ST ASST. DIRECTOR
'84 GIVE MY REGARDS TO BROAD STREET

TONY PIERCE ROBERTS
CINEMATOGRAPHER
'82 MOONLIGHTING

WILLIAM ROBERTS
SCREENPLAY
'81 LEGEND OF THE LONE RANGER, THE*
'83 10 TO MIDNIGHT

ERIC ROBERTSON
MUSIC
'82 IF YOU COULD SEE WHAT I HEAR

LARRY ROBERTSON
PROPS
'79 GREAT BANK HOAX, THE

PATTIE ROBERTSON
SCRIPT SUPERVISOR
'80 CHANGELING, THE
'82 FIRST BLOOD

R.J. ROBERTSON
MISCELLANEOUS
'84 DREAMSCAPE

ROBBIE ROBERTSON
PRODUCER
'80 CARNY
MUSIC SUPERVISOR
'83 KING OF COMEDY, THE

HELEN ROBIN
PROD. COORDINATOR
'81 ARTHUR
'82 MIDSUMMER NIGHT'S SEX COMEDY, A
'83 ZELIG
'84 BROADWAY DANNY ROSE

STEPHEN ROBINETTE
HAIR
'84 ADVENTURES OF BUCKAROO BANZAI ACROSS THE 8TH DIMENSION,THE
'84 AMERICAN DREAMER

JOHN ROBINS
SCREENPLAY
'80 DEATH SHIP

VAL ROBINS
ASSOCIATE PRODUCER
'80 HUMAN FACTOR, THE*
MISCELLANEOUS
'80 HUMAN FACTOR, THE

AMY ROBINSON
PRODUCER
'82 CHILLY SCENES OF WINTER*
'83 BABY IT'S YOU*

BRUCE ROBINSON
SCREENPLAY
'84 KILLING FIELDS, THE

CLIFFORD ROBINSON
ART DIRECTOR
'84 PASSAGE TO INDIA, A*

CLINT ROBINSON
PROPS
'81 BUSTIN' LOOSE*

DAR ROBINSON
2ND UNIT DIRECTOR
'84 ICEMAN
STUNT COORDINATOR
'81 NIGHTHAWKS
'84 FIRSTBORN*

DAVID ROBINSON
UNIT MANAGER
'84 JUST THE WAY YOU ARE*

DON ROBINSON
KEY GRIP
'82 HOME WORK

GLEN ROBINSON
SPECIAL EFFECTS
'79 HURRICANE*
'79 METEOR*
'81 PENNIES FROM HEAVEN
'82 DEAD MEN DON'T WEAR PLAID
SP. EFFECTS SUPERV.
'82 AMITYVILLE II: THE POSSESSION

GORDON ROBINSON
1ST ASST. DIRECTOR
'79 MEATBALLS

JAMES ROBINSON
EXECUTIVE PRODUCER
'84 STONE BOY, THE

JANE ROBINSON
COSTUMES
'82 MOONLIGHTING
'83 BETRAYAL*

JOYCE ROBINSON
CASTING
'79 CHAMP, THE*
'79 FORCE OF ONE, A*
'80 DEFIANCE*
'80 HERO AT LARGE*
'80 IN GOD WE TRUST*
'81 CLASH OF THE TITANS*

KATHY ROBINSON
COSTUME SUPERVISOR
'80 EYES OF A STRANGER

KEN ROBINSON
EDITOR
'84 PURPLE RAIN*

LARRY ROBINSON
MISCELLANEOUS
'79 1941
'80 CLOSE ENCOUNTERS OF THE THIRD KIND SPECIAL EDITION

MILTON ROBINSON
SOUND
'84 STONE BOY, THE*

PHIL ALDEN ROBINSON
SCREENPLAY
'84 ALL OF ME
'84 RHINESTONE*
ASSOCIATE PRODUCER
'84 ALL OF ME

REECE ROBINSON
SPECIAL EFFECTS
'81 ROAD GAMES

RICHARD ROBINSON
STILLS
'81 SHARKEY'S MACHINE
'81 CANNONBALL RUN, THE
'81 INCREDIBLE SHRINKING WOMAN, THE
'81 PATERNITY*
'83 FOOTLOOSE
'84 BEVERLY HILLS COP
'84 THIEF OF HEARTS

ROBBIE ROBINSON
STILLS
'82 BEST LITTLE WHOREHOUSE IN TEXAS, THE
'84 MASS APPEAL
MISCELLANEOUS
'83 STAYING ALIVE

TERRY ROBINSON
PROD. SECRETARY
'79 JERK, THE

TRISH ROBINSON
CASTING
'84 FINDERS KEEPERS*

ROGER ROBLES
STILLS
'81 ENTER THE NINJA

GEORGE ROBOTHAM
STUNT COORDINATOR
'79 PRISONER OF ZENDA, THE

MARK ROBSON
PRODUCER
'79 AVALANCHE EXPRESS
DIRECTOR
'79 AVALANCHE EXPRESS

MARIA CRISTINA ROCCA
MAKEUP
'82 FIGHTING BACK

ORIETTA NASALI ROCCA
COSTUMES
'81 SUNDAY LOVERS*

MANLIO ROCCHETTI
MAKEUP
'84 ONCE UPON A TIME IN AMERICA*

ART ROCHESTER
SOUND
'80 HONEYSUCKLE ROSE
'81 POSTMAN ALWAYS RINGS TWICE, THE
'82 BORDER, THE
'82 POLTERGEIST
'83 BAD BOYS
'83 BRAINSTORM
'84 MISUNDERSTOOD
'84 NO SMALL AFFAIR
'84 SONGWRITER

LUIGI ROCHETTI
MAKEUP
'83 LONELY LADY, THE*
'84 DUNE*
'84 CONAN THE DESTROYER

NONI ROCK
LOCATIONS
'79 KRAMER VS. KRAMER*
'81 FORT APACHE, THE BRONX

JILL ROCKOW
MISCELLANEOUS
'81 GRADUATION DAY
'83 FRIGHTMARE

JANIS ROCKWELL-STRONG
PROD. COORDINATOR
'84 FIRESTARTER

ROB RODA
PROD. COORDINATOR
'84 HARDBODIES*

ROBERT RODA
2ND ASST. DIRECTOR
'84 TERMINATOR, THE

FRANC RODDAM
DIRECTOR
'83 LORDS OF DISCIPLINE, THE

GENE RODDENBERRY
PRODUCER
'79 STAR TREK-THE MOTION PICTURE
MISCELLANEOUS
'84 STAR TREK III: THE SEARCH FOR SPOCK

JOHN RODDICK
2ND ASST. DIRECTOR
'81 KNIGHTRIDERS*

SALLY RODDY
SCRIPT SUPERVISOR
'79 FIVE DAYS FROM HOME

DONALD RODE
EDITOR
'84 TANK

DIANE RODERICK
STILLS
'84 NIGHT OF THE COMET

ALAN RODERICK-JONES
ART DIRECTOR
'81 TARZAN, THE APE MAN
PRODUCTION DESIGNER
'83 DEADLY FORCE
'84 BOLERO

JOSE LOPEZ RODERO
ASSOCIATE PRODUCER
'82 AMITYVILLE II: THE POSSESSION
'84 DUNE
1ST ASST. DIRECTOR
'79 HURRICANE
'81 SPHINX
'82 FIGHTING BACK
'84 DUNE

KUKI LOPEZ RODERO
1ST ASST. DIRECTOR
'79 JAGUAR LIVES
'81 REDS*
MISCELLANEOUS
'84 CONAN THE DESTROYER

PEPE LOPEZ RODERO
1ST ASST. DIRECTOR
'82 CONAN THE BARBARIAN

AGGIE GUERRARD RODGERS
COSTUMES
'79 MORE AMERICAN GRAFFITTI
'83 RETURN OF THE JEDI*
'84 ADVENTURES OF BUCKAROO BANZAI ACROSS THE 8TH DIMENSION,

MARY RODGERS
SCREENPLAY
'81 DEVIL AND MAX DEVLIN, THE

MIC RODGERS
STUNT COORDINATOR
'84 RECKLESS

NILE RODGERS
MUSIC
'82 SOUP FOR ONE*
'84 ALPHABET CITY

NILOS RODIS-JAMERO
COSTUMES
'83 RETURN OF THE JEDI*

NANCY RODMAN
CASTING
'80 OCTAGON, THE*

VICTOR RODRIGUE
STILLS
'79 LITTLE ROMANCE, A

CARLOS RODRIGUEZ
UNIT PROD. MANAGER
'84 ROMANCING THE STONE*

JUAN RODRIGUEZ
SOUND
'79 MR. MIKE'S MONDO VIDEO*

XAVIER RODRIGUEZ
ART DIRECTOR
'83 BEYOND THE LIMIT*

BART ROE
2ND ASST. DIRECTOR
'79 ELECTRIC HORSEMAN, THE

BOB ROE
2ND ASST. DIRECTOR
'81 SOUTHERN COMFORT
'82 POLTERGEIST
'82 THINGS ARE TOUGH ALL OVER
'83 BAD BOYS*
'84 MARVIN AND TIGE

JACK ROE
PRODUCTION MANAGER
'81 LOOKER
UNIT PROD. MANAGER
'80 DIVINE MADNESS
'84 PROTOCOL
1ST ASST. DIRECTOR
'79 CHAPTER TWO
'79 IN-LAWS, THE
'80 DIVINE MADNESS
'80 HERO AT LARGE
'82 I OUGHT TO BE IN PICTURES
'82 MAKING LOVE
'83 ROMANTIC COMEDY
'83 MAX DUGAN RETURNS
'84 LONELY GUY, THE

KATHY KENWORTHY ROE
PROD. COORDINATOR
'84 WOMAN IN RED, THE

WALDO ROEG
2ND ASST. DIRECTOR
'80 ROUGH CUT*

AL ROELOFS
ART DIRECTOR
'79 BLACK HOLE, THE*
'82 TRON*

JOSH ROGAN
SCREENPLAY
'83 TWILIGHT ZONE, THE MOVIE*

JOHN ROGER
MISCELLANEOUS
'80 HOW TO BEAT THE HIGH COST OF LIVING

DAVE ROGERS
MISCELLANEOUS
'81 CATTLE ANNIE AND LITTLE BRITCHES

JAIME ROGERS
CHOREOGRAPHER
'79 AMERICATHON
'80 WHOLLY MOSES!

JOHN ROGERS
PRODUCTION MANAGER
'80 HOW TO BEAT THE HIGH COST OF LIVING
UNIT PROD. MANAGER
'82 BLADERUNNER

MICHAEL ROGERS
SCREENPLAY
'79 KILLER FISH

NOEL ROGERS
ASSISTANT EDITOR
'79 CIRCLE OF IRON*

STEVE ROGERS
SOUND
'83 HOUSE ON SORORITY ROW

CHARLES ROGGERO
EDITOR
'81 POLYESTER

ED ROGINSKI
UNIT PUBLICIST
'80 WHOLLY MOSES!

ELISE ROHDEN
PROD. OFFICE COORD.
'82 ESCAPE ARTIST, THE*
PROD. COORDINATOR
'79 BREAKING AWAY
'80 SMALL CIRCLE OF FRIENDS, A*
'81 CUTTER'S WAY
'83 BIG CHILL, THE
'83 CROSS CREEK

DANIELE ROHRBACH
PROD. COORDINATOR
'81 SCANNERS
'81 GAS
'84 HOTEL NEW HAMPSHIRE, THE

GUNTHAR ROHRBACK
CO-PRODUCER
'84 NEVERENDING STORY, THE

CASEY ROHRS
ASSISTANT EDITOR
'82 BORDER, THE

OWEN ROIZMAN
CINEMATOGRAPHER
'79 ELECTRIC HORSEMAN, THE
'80 BLACK MARBLE, THE
'81 ABSENCE OF MALICE
'81 TAPS
'81 TRUE CONFESSIONS
'82 TOOTSIE

MAURICIO ROJAS
MISCELLANEOUS
'84 UNDER THE VOLCANO

MINI ROJAS
CINEMATOGRAPHER
'80 EYES OF A STRANGER

CLIFF ROLAND
STILLS
'83 RICHARD PRYOR: HERE AND NOW

LORINDA ROLAND
MISCELLANEOUS
'81 WHOSE LIFE IS IT ANYWAY?

RITA ROLAND
EDITOR
'80 RESURRECTION
'81 FORT APACHE, THE BRONX
'82 SIX PACK

SANDRA WEINTRAUB ROLAND
SCREENPLAY
'83 HIGH ROAD TO CHINA*

TOM ROLF
EDITOR
'79 HARDCORE
'79 PROPHECY
'80 HEAVEN'S GATE*
'81 GHOST STORY
'83 RIGHT STUFF, THE*
'83 WAR GAMES
'84 THIEF OF HEARTS

HELEN ROLLAND
CASTING
'82 PIRATE MOVIE, THE

JACOB ROLLING
KEY GRIP
'81 ATLANTIC CITY

JACK ROLLINS
EXECUTIVE PRODUCER
'80 STARDUST MEMORIES*

ROBERT ROLSKY
2ND ASST. DIRECTOR
'84 CRIMES OF PASSION

JULIE ROMAN
ASSISTANT EDITOR
'84 AMADEUS*

TIMOTEA NEVADO ROMAN
MISCELLANEOUS
'84 CONAN THE DESTROYER

TONY ROMAN
ART DIRECTOR
'80 NIJINSKY*

NICHOLAS ROMANAC
ART DIRECTOR
'83 SPRING BREAK
PROPS
'81 FUNHOUSE, THE

MARK ROMANEK
2ND ASST. DIRECTOR
'80 HOME MOVIES

GEORGE ROMANIS
MISCELLANEOUS
'84 OXFORD BLUES

PATRICK ROMANO
MISCELLANEOUS
'84 KARATE KID, THE

ROBIN ROMANO
1ST ASST. DIRECTOR
'83 SMITHEREENS*

ANDY ROMANOFF
MISCELLANEOUS
'82 BEST LITTLE WHOREHOUSE IN TEXAS, THE

ALEX ROMERO
CHOREOGRAPHER
'79 FRISCO KID, THE
'79 LOVE AT FIRST BITE
'81 ZORRO, THE GAY BLADE
MISCELLANEOUS
'80 XANADU

GEORGE ROMERO
DIRECTOR
'79 DAWN OF THE DEAD
'81 KNIGHTRIDERS
'82 CREEPSHOW
SCREENPLAY
'79 DAWN OF THE DEAD
'81 KNIGHTRIDERS
EDITOR
'79 DAWN OF THE DEAD
'81 KNIGHTRIDERS*
'82 CREEPSHOW*

PETER ROMERO
ART DIRECTOR
'80 LONG RIDERS, THE
'83 RIGHT STUFF, THE*

ROBERT ROMERO
1ST ASST. DIRECTOR
'84 EL NORTE*

TONY ROMERO
SOUND
'81 SOUTHERN COMFORT*

ROSA PEREZ ROMO
SCRIPT SUPERVISOR
'84 EL NORTE*

TAL RON
LOCATIONS
'83 HANNA K*

LACI RONAY
PRODUCTION MANAGER
'79 PRISONER OF ZENDA, THE
LOCATIONS
'80 HOPSCOTCH*

BARBARA RONCI
HAIR
'80 RESURRECTION
'84 MASS APPEAL

REID RONDELL
STUNT COORDINATOR
'81 CAVEMAN*
'83 ALL THE RIGHT MOVES
'84 NO SMALL AFFAIR
'84 STAR TREK III: THE SEARCH FOR SPOCK*

RIC RONDELL
PRODUCTION MANAGER
'83 CURSE OF THE PINK PANTHER*
UNIT PROD. MANAGER
'83 PRIVATE SCHOOL
2ND UNIT DIRECTOR
'83 PRIVATE SCHOOL

GEORGE RONDO
MISCELLANEOUS
'79 CHAPTER TWO

DAVID RONNE
SOUND
'79 BUTCH AND SUNDANCE: THE EARLY YEARS
'79 MAIN EVENT, THE
'80 MELVIN AND HOWARD
'80 TOUCHED BY LOVE
'81 ON GOLDEN POND
'81 THIEF
'82 FRANCES
'83 STAR 80
'83 MAN WOMAN AND CHILD
'84 CRACKERS
'84 RIVER, THE

ROBERT ROONEY
PUBLICIST
'79 WINTER KILLS
UNIT PUBLICIST
'80 WHY WOULD I LIE?

FRED ROOS
PRODUCER
'79 BLACK STALLION, THE*
'82 HAMMETT*
'82 ONE FROM THE HEART*
'83 RUMBLEFISH*
'83 BLACK STALLION RETURNS, THE*
'83 OUTSIDERS, THE*
EXECUTIVE PRODUCER
'82 ESCAPE ARTIST, THE*
CO-PRODUCER
'79 APOCALYPSE NOW*
'84 COTTON CLUB, THE*

GINA ROOSE
ASSISTANT EDITOR
'80 SIMON*
'80 ONE-TRICK PONY*
'81 BLOW OUT
'82 COME BACK TO THE 5 & 10, JIMMY DEAN, JIMMY DEAN*
'83 EASY MONEY*

RONALD ROOSE
EDITOR
'79 WANDERERS, THE*
'82 WORLD ACCORDING TO GARP, THE*
'83 EASY MONEY*

ROBERT ROOY
1ST ASST. DIRECTOR
'83 OSTERMAN WEEKEND, THE
2ND ASST. DIRECTOR
'82 DINER
'82 ENDANGERED SPECIES*

CLIFF ROQUEMORE
CASTING
'81 BODY AND SOUL
PRODUCTION MANAGER
'82 PENITENTIARY II*

FRAN ROSATI
PRODUCER
'81 LAST CHASE, THE*

GREG ROSATTI
MISCELLANEOUS
'82 ZOOT SUIT

BEN ROSCOLONE
KEY GRIP
'80 FOG, THE
'84 DREAMSCAPE*

ALEX ROSE
PRODUCER
'79 NORMA RAE*

BOB ROSE
KEY GRIP
'79 ELECTRIC HORSEMAN, THE
'80 ALTERED STATES
'80 BLACK MARBLE, THE
'81 ABSENCE OF MALICE
'81 TAPS
'81 TRUE CONFESSIONS
'82 TOOTSIE*

DAVID ROSE
2ND ASST. DIRECTOR
'83 GOLDEN SEAL, THE
'84 RUNAWAY

JACK ROSE
SCREENPLAY
'79 LOST AND FOUND*
'81 GREAT MUPPET CAPER, THE*

LES ROSE
DIRECTOR
'80 HOG WILD
'81 GAS

MICKEY ROSE
DIRECTOR
'81 STUDENT BODIES
SCREENPLAY
'81 STUDENT BODIES

NORMA ROSE
PROD. COORDINATOR
'80 KIDNAPPING OF THE PRESIDENT, THE

PAUL ROSE
2ND ASST. DIRECTOR
'82 LOVE CHILD
'84 MASS APPEAL*

PENNY ROSE
COSTUMES
'82 QUEST FOR FIRE*
'83 LOCAL HERO*
COSTUME SUPERVISOR
'84 ANOTHER COUNTRY

REGINALD ROSE
SCREENPLAY
'81 SEA WOLVES, THE
'81 WHOSE LIFE IS IT ANYWAY?*
'83 FINAL OPTION, THE

SIDNEY ROSE
EXECUTIVE PRODUCER
'80 KIDS ARE ALL RIGHT, THE

DARRI ROSEBOROUGH
HAIR
'84 ANGEL

JEB ROSEBROOK
SCREENPLAY
'79 BLACK HOLE, THE*

REID ROSEFELT
PUBLICIST
'81 KNIGHTRIDERS*

CLIFFORD ROSEMAN
LOCATIONS
'84 ELECTRIC DREAMS*

HILTON ROSEMARIN
PROPS
'83 RUNNING BRAVE

CHARLES ROSEN
PRODUCTION DESIGNER
'79 LAST EMBRACE
'79 MAIN EVENT, THE
'80 INSIDE MOVES
'81 ENTITY, THE
'82 MY FAVORITE YEAR
'82 TOY, THE
'83 FLASHDANCE
'84 RIVER, THE

DEBORAH ROSEN
PUBLICIST
'82 FRANCES
'82 JEKYLL AND HYDE TOGETHER AGAIN
UNIT PUBLICIST
'83 BUDDY SYSTEM, THE
'83 WITHOUT A TRACE
'84 UNFAITHFULLY YOURS

EDWARD ROSEN
EXECUTIVE PRODUCER
'79 AMERICATHON

GARY ROSEN
ASSISTANT EDITOR
'81 INCREDIBLE SHRINKING WOMAN, THE*

ROBERT ROSEN
PRODUCER
'79 PROPHECY
'81 GOING APE!
'82 CHALLENGE, THE*

HENRY ROSENBAUM
SCREENPLAY
'82 HANKY PANKY*
'83 GET CRAZY*
ASSOCIATE PRODUCER
'82 HANKY PANKY*

MARK ROSENBAUM
ASSOCIATE EDITOR
'84 SILENT NIGHT, DEADLY NIGHT
ASSISTANT EDITOR
'80 HANGAR 18

BARRY ROSENBERG
MISCELLANEOUS
'79 GREAT BANK HOAX, THE

BENJY ROSENBERG
ASSOCIATE PRODUCER
'84 POPE OF GREENWICH VILLAGE,THE
1ST ASST. DIRECTOR
'79 SCAVENGER HUNT*
'81 SHARKEY'S MACHINE
'81 HONKY TONK FREEWAY
'81 PATERNITY
2ND ASST. DIRECTOR
'79 AMITYVILLE HORROR, THE
'79 LOVE AND BULLETS

C.A. ROSENBERG
SCREENPLAY
'80 MANIAC*

EDDY ROSENBERG
MISCELLANEOUS
'82 PORKY'S

FRED ROSENBERG
MISCELLANEOUS
'81 SMOKEY BITES THE DUST

JEANNE ROSENBERG
SCRIPT SUPERVISOR
'79 ROCK 'N ROLL HIGH SCHOOL
'79 ROLLER BOOGIE*
'80 FOG, THE
'81 HOWLING, THE
'82 BEASTMASTER, THE
'82 VICE SQUAD
'83 DEADLY FORCE

JEANNE ROSENBERG
SCREENPLAY
'79 BLACK STALLION, THE*

MARION ROSENBERG
ASSOCIATE PRODUCER
'78 DEER HUNTER, THE*

MICHAEL ROSENBERG
EXECUTIVE PRODUCER
'80 TELL ME A RIDDLE

PHILIP ROSENBERG
PRODUCTION DESIGNER
'79 ALL THAT JAZZ
'81 EYEWITNESS
'82 SOUP FOR ONE
'83 DANIEL
'83 LOVESICK
'84 GARBO TALKS

RICH ROSENBERG
LOCATIONS
'84 LONELY GUY, THE

RICK ROSENBERG
PRODUCER
'80 HIDE IN PLAIN SIGHT*

STUART ROSENBERG
DIRECTOR
'79 AMITYVILLE HORROR, THE
'79 LOVE AND BULLETS
'80 BRUBAKER
'84 POPE OF GREENWICH VILLAGE,THE

MICHAEL ROSENBLATT
EXECUTIVE PRODUCER
'83 VALLEY GIRL*
'84 NIGHT OF THE COMET*
'84 ALPHABET CITY*

SHARON ROSENBLATT
MAKEUP
'83 GOIN' ALL THE WAY*

STEVE ROSENBLOOM
2ND ASST. DIRECTOR
'84 UP THE CREEK*

IRVING ROSENBLUM
EDITOR
'79 FRISCO KID, THE*
'81 ...ALL THE MARBLES*
'82 FORCED VENGEANCE

RALPH ROSENBLUM
PRODUCER
'79 GREAT BANK HOAX, THE*
EDITOR
'79 GREAT BANK HOAX, THE
MISCELLANEOUS
'84 MARVIN AND TIGE

STEVEN ROSENBLUM
ASSISTANT EDITOR
'82 SOME KIND OF HERO
'82 LIAR'S MOON*
'84 IMPULSE*

BARRY ROSENBUSH
ASSOCIATE PRODUCER
'83 NIGHT IN HEAVEN, A
MISCELLANEOUS
'80 IDOLMAKER, THE

HILARY ROSENFELD
COSTUMES
'79 RICH KIDS
'79 HEARTLAND
'80 ONE-TRICK PONY
'81 EYEWITNESS
'83 BALLAD OF GREGORIO CORTEZ, THE

SCOTT ROSENFELT
PRODUCTION MANAGER
'80 GALAXINA

JAMES ROSENFIELD
LOCATIONS
'80 CARNY
'81 ON GOLDEN POND

JASON ROSENFIELD
EDITOR
'82 COME BACK TO THE 5 & 10, JIMMY DEAN, JIMMY DEAN

JOHN ROSENGRANT
MISCELLANEOUS
'83 METALSTORM: THE DESTRUCTION OF JARED-SYN

HOWARD ROSENMAN
PRODUCER
'80 RESURRECTION*
EXECUTIVE PRODUCER
'79 MAIN EVENT, THE*

LEONARD ROSENMAN
MUSIC
'79 PROMISES IN THE DARK
'79 PROPHECY
'80 HIDE IN PLAIN SIGHT
'82 MAKING LOVE
'83 CROSS CREEK
MISCELLANEOUS
'80 JAZZ SINGER, THE

IRA ROSENSTEIN
LOCATIONS
'83 BUDDY SYSTEM, THE

ROBERT ROSENSTONE
MISCELLANEOUS
'81 REDS

JACK ROSENTHAL
SCREENPLAY
'83 YENTL*
'84 KIPPERBANG

JACK ROSENTHAL
ASSOCIATE PRODUCER
'81 CONTINENTAL DIVIDE*

JOEL ROSENTHAL
ASSISTANT EDITOR
'82 FIRST TIME, THE

JUDY ROSENTHAL
SCRIPT SUPERVISOR
'79 LOVE AT FIRST BITE
'79 FORCE OF ONE, A
'79 DOUBLE MCGUFFIN, THE
'80 FATSO
'80 UP THE ACADEMY

LAURENCE ROSENTHAL
MUSIC
'79 METEOR
'81 CLASH OF THE TITANS
'83 EASY MONEY
'83 HEART LIKE A WHEEL

LAWRENCE ROSENTHAL
EXECUTIVE PRODUCER
'82 FIRST TIME, THE*

MICHAEL ROSENTHAL
ASSISTANT EDITOR
'83 NEVER CRY WOLF*

RICHARD ROSENTHAL
DIRECTOR
'81 HALLOWEEN II
'83 BAD BOYS
'84 AMERICAN DREAMER

ROBERT ROSENTHAL
DIRECTOR
'82 ZAPPED!
SCREENPLAY
'82 ZAPPED!*

ZADE ROSENTHAL
STILLS
'81 DEADLY BLESSING
'83 TERMS OF ENDEARMENT
'83 TOUGH ENOUGH
'83 SILKWOOD
'84 PLACES IN THE HEART

CHARLES ROSHER
CINEMATOGRAPHER
'79 NIGHTWING
'79 ONION FIELD, THE
'83 INDEPENDENCE DAY

CHARLES ROSHER JR.
CINEMATOGRAPHER
'81 HEARTBEEPS

ARIEL ROSHKO
ART DIRECTOR
'84 BEST DEFENSE*
'84 LITTLE DRUMMER GIRL, THE*

MARK ROSMAN
PRODUCER
'83 HOUSE ON SORORITY ROW*
DIRECTOR
'83 HOUSE ON SORORITY ROW
SCREENPLAY
'83 HOUSE ON SORORITY ROW
ASSOCIATE PRODUCER
'80 HOME MOVIES*
1ST ASST. DIRECTOR
'80 HOME MOVIES

JUDI ROSNER
PROD. OFFICE COORD.
'82 CREEPSHOW
PROD. COORDINATOR
'81 BLOOD BEACH
'81 HISTORY OF THE WORLD PART I
'84 ADVENTURES OF BUCKAROO BANZAI ACROSS THE 8TH DIMENSION,THE
PROD. SECRETARY
'79 BOULEVARD NIGHTS

ANGIE ROSS
EDITOR
'79 JAGUAR LIVES

ARNOLD ROSS
PRODUCTION MANAGER
'79 FIREPOWER*
'83 NEVER SAY NEVER AGAIN*
'84 BOUNTY, THE*
LOCATIONS
'83 WICKED LADY, THE*

BOB ROSS
STILLS
'79 NATURAL ENEMIES

BRIAN ROSS
LOCATIONS
'80 KIDNAPPING OF THE PRESIDENT, THE
'83 RUNNING BRAVE*

CARY ROSS
LOCATIONS
'81 HAPPY BIRTHDAY TO ME

ELEANOR ROSS
CASTING
'82 SUMMER LOVERS*

GLENNA ROSS
SCRIPT SUPERVISOR
'80 EXTERMINATOR, THE

HERBERT ROSS
PRODUCER
'81 PENNIES FROM HEAVEN*
'82 I OUGHT TO BE IN PICTURES*
'83 MAX DUGAN RETURNS*
DIRECTOR
'80 NIJINSKY
'81 PENNIES FROM HEAVEN
'82 I OUGHT TO BE IN PICTURES
'83 FOOTLOOSE
'83 MAX DUGAN RETURNS
'84 PROTOCOL

JUDITH ROSS
SCREENPLAY
'79 RICH KIDS

MARCIA ROSS
CASTING
'83 CUJO*
'83 LONE WOLF MCQUADE*
'84 STREETS OF FIRE*

MICHAEL ROSS
PROPS
'79 MAIN EVENT, THE
'80 LITTLE DARLINGS
'83 BREATHLESS
'84 AMADEUS*

REBECCA ROSS
ASSISTANT EDITOR
'81 HONKY TONK FREEWAY*

SHARYN LESLIE ROSS
EDITOR
'83 LIQUID SKY

STEPHEN ROSS
2ND ASST. DIRECTOR
'80 FRIDAY THE 13TH

WALLY ROSS
MISCELLANEOUS
'81 HONKY TONK FREEWAY

GRAZIA ROSSE
HAIR
'81 THEY ALL LAUGHED*

GIL ROSSELLINI
2ND ASST. DIRECTOR
'83 LONELY LADY, THE*

CINZIA ROSSI
SOUND
'83 YOR

RICHARD ROSSI
ASSISTANT EDITOR
'84 FALLING IN LOVE*

DANNY ROSSNER
PRODUCTION MANAGER
'81 MY BLOODY VALENTINE

EDWARD ROSSON
CINEMATOGRAPHER
'79 LOVE AT FIRST BITE

KAREN ROSTON
COSTUMES
'79 MR. MIKE'S MONDO VIDEO
'80 GILDA LIVE*

NINO ROTA
MUSIC
'79 HURRICANE

ANN ROTH
COSTUMES
'79 HAIR
'79 PROMISES IN THE DARK
'80 DRESSED TO KILL
'80 ISLAND, THE
'80 NINE TO FIVE
'81 ROLLOVER
'81 BLOW OUT*
'81 HONKY TONK FREEWAY
'81 ONLY WHEN I LAUGH
'82 WORLD ACCORDING TO GARP, THE
'83 SURVIVORS, THE
'83 MAN WHO LOVED WOMEN, THE*
'83 SILKWOOD
'84 PLACES IN THE HEART

ANNA ROTH
ASSOCIATE PRODUCER
'83 UNDER FIRE
2ND ASST. DIRECTOR
'82 MISSING

DENA ROTH
ART DIRECTOR
'82 LIAR'S MOON*
ASSISTANT EDITOR
'79 PHANTASM*
SCRIPT SUPERVISOR
'79 PHANTASM*

ERIC ROTH
SCREENPLAY
'79 CONCORDE-AIRPORT '79, THE

JAY ROTH
MISCELLANEOUS
'82 ANDROID

JOE ROTH
PRODUCER
'79 AMERICATHON
'84 STONE BOY, THE*
'84 FINAL TERROR, THE
EXECUTIVE PRODUCER
'84 BACHELOR PARTY

PATRICIA ROTH
SCRIPT SUPERVISOR
'81 TUCK EVERLASTING

PETER ROTH
ART DIRECTOR
'84 MOSCOW ON THE HUDSON*

RICHARD ROTH
PRODUCER
'81 OUTLAND

STEPHEN ROTH
PRODUCER
'82 PARADISE*
EXECUTIVE PRODUCER
'79 IN PRAISE OF OLDER WOMEN*

ROBERT ROTHBARD
LOCATIONS
'82 FIGHTING BACK
'84 ONCE UPON A TIME IN AMERICA*

PAUL ROTHCHILD
MUSIC
'79 ROSE, THE

CAPRICE ROTHE
MISCELLANEOUS
'82 E.T. THE EXTRA-TERRESTRIAL

N.A. ROTHENBERG, D.V.M.
MISCELLANEOUS
'80 FOR THE LOVE OF BENJI

WARREN ROTHENBERGER
MISCELLANEOUS
'81 ONLY WHEN I LAUGH

ED ROTHKOWITZ
ASSOCIATE PRODUCER
'80 KIDS ARE ALL RIGHT, THE*
EDITOR
'80 KIDS ARE ALL RIGHT, THE

CONRAD ROTHMAN
SPECIAL EFFECTS
'81 EARTHLING, THE

MARION ROTHMAN
EDITOR
'79 STARTING OVER
'81 ALL NIGHT LONG
'83 CHRISTINE
'84 STARMAN

MIMI ROTHMAN
PROD. COORDINATOR
'81 NIGHT THE LIGHTS WENT OUT IN GEORGIA, THE

MOSES ROTHMAN
EXECUTIVE PRODUCER
'80 FFOLKES

RICHARD ROTHSCHILD
1ST ASST. DIRECTOR
'80 USED CARS
'81 CHARLIE CHAN AND THE CURSE OF THE DRAGON QUEEN
'83 TENDER MERCIES

RICHARD ROTHSTEIN
SCREENPLAY
'82 DEATH VALLEY
CO-PRODUCER
'82 DEATH VALLEY*

ROGER ROTHSTEIN
PRODUCER
'81 ONLY WHEN I LAUGH*
'83 TWO OF A KIND*
EXECUTIVE PRODUCER
'79 CHAPTER TWO
'80 SEEMS LIKE OLD TIMES
'82 I OUGHT TO BE IN PICTURES
'83 MAX DUGAN RETURNS
ASSOCIATE PRODUCER
'80 HERO AT LARGE
UNIT PROD. MANAGER
'79 CHAPTER TWO
'80 SEEMS LIKE OLD TIMES
'80 HERO AT LARGE
'82 I OUGHT TO BE IN PICTURES
'83 MAX DUGAN RETURNS

JOHN ROTHWELL
PUBLICIST
'79 STAR TREK-THE MOTION PICTURE*

STEPHEN ROTTER
EDITOR
'82 WORLD ACCORDING TO GARP, THE*
'83 RIGHT STUFF, THE*

NICK ROTUNDO
ASSISTANT EDITOR
'81 LAST CHASE, THE*

GIUSEPPE ROTUNNO
CINEMATOGRAPHER
'79 ALL THAT JAZZ
'80 POPEYE
'81 ROLLOVER
'82 FIVE DAYS ONE SUMMER
'84 AMERICAN DREAMER

VACLAV ROUHA
PRODUCTION MANAGER
'84 AMADEUS*

BARBARA ROUSE
MAKEUP
'81 MY DINNER WITH ANDRE

CHRISTOPHER ROUSE
ASSISTANT EDITOR
'82 LOOKIN' TO GET OUT*

KEITH ROUSE
ASSOCIATE PRODUCER
'81 MY DINNER WITH ANDRE*
ASSISTANT EDITOR
'81 MY DINNER WITH ANDRE*

FRANK ROUSSEAU
MISCELLANEOUS
'84 TANK

PATRICK ROUSSEAU
SOUND
'81 GAS
'84 HOTEL NEW HAMPSHIRE, THE

ANNICK ROUSSET-ROUARD
ASSISTANT EDITOR
'79 LITTLE ROMANCE, A*

YVES ROUSSET-ROUARD
PRODUCER
'79 LITTLE ROMANCE, A*

MAY ROUTH
COSTUMES
'79 BEING THERE
'80 FIRST FAMILY
'81 GHOST STORY
'82 MY FAVORITE YEAR
'84 SPLASH

CHARLES ROVEN
PRODUCER
'83 HEART LIKE A WHEEL

DIANA ROWAN
CASTING
'83 MERRY CHRISTMAS, MR. LAWRENCE*

URSALA-DENINE ROWAN
ASSISTANT EDITOR
'80 HONEYSUCKLE ROSE*

JACK ROWAND
STILLS
'82 PORKY'S
'83 SCREWBALLS

CONNIE ROWBOTHAM
PROD. SECRETARY
'84 TEACHERS

BILL ROWE
SOUND
'82 EVIL UNDER THE SUN*

CLINT ROWE
MISCELLANEOUS
'82 HALLOWEEN III: SEASON OF THE WITCH
'82 THING, THE

TOM ROWE
SCREENPLAY
'81 TARZAN, THE APE MAN*

GAIL ROWELL
HAIR
'81 PURSUIT OF D.B. COOPER, THE*

KATHLEEN ROWELL
SCREENPLAY
'84 JOY OF SEX, THE*

KATHLEEN KNUTSEN ROWELL
SCREENPLAY
'83 OUTSIDERS, THE

LAURA ROWELL
HAIR
'84 BEAR, THE

BRUCE ROWLAND
MUSIC
'83 MAN FROM SNOWY RIVER, THE
'84 PHAR LAP

GEOFF ROWLANDS
ASSISTANT EDITOR
'80 CLOSE ENCOUNTERS OF THE THIRD KIND SPECIAL EDITION*

CHARLES ROWLEY
MISCELLANEOUS
'81 NOBODY'S PERFEKT
'83 BLUE SKIES AGAIN

CHUCK ROWLEY
LOCATIONS
'84 HARRY & SON

FRAN ROY
ASSOCIATE PRODUCER
'81 ALL NIGHT LONG*

GLENDA ROY
PUBLICIST
'82 BY DESIGN*
UNIT PUBLICIST
'82 IF YOU COULD SEE WHAT I HEAR

HOGUETTE ROY
HAIR
'80 TERROR TRAIN
'81 MY BLOODY VALENTINE

MARTHA ROYALL
MISCELLANEOUS
'79 ...AND JUSTICE FOR ALL

BRON ROYLANCE
MAKEUP
'79 10*
'82 CANNERY ROW*

JAYNE ROYLE
MAKEUP
'80 FLASH GORDON*
'81 DRAGONSLAYER*

MIKLOS ROZSA
MUSIC
'79 FEDORA
'79 LAST EMBRACE
'79 TIME AFTER TIME
'81 EYE OF THE NEEDLE
'82 DEAD MEN DON'T WEAR PLAID

AL RUBAN
EXECUTIVE PRODUCER
'84 LOVE STREAMS
EXEC IN CHARGE PROD
'82 SWAMP THING
CINEMATOGRAPHER
'84 LOVE STREAMS
UNIT PROD. MANAGER
'84 LOVE STREAMS*

MARC REID RUBEL
SCREENPLAY
'80 XANADU*

PAUL RUBELL
EDITOR
'84 STONE BOY, THE
'84 FINAL TERROR, THE*
ASSISTANT EDITOR
'80 CHANGELING, THE*

BINNIE RUBEN
LOCATIONS
'84 BACHELOR PARTY

JOSEPH RUBEN
DIRECTOR
'84 DREAMSCAPE
SCREENPLAY
'84 DREAMSCAPE*

BRUCE RUBIN
SCREENPLAY
'82 ZAPPED!*
2ND UNIT DIRECTOR
'82 ZAPPED!

FRANK RUBIN
PRODUCER
'83 GOIN' ALL THE WAY*

GLYNN RUBIN
STUNT COORDINATOR
'80 PRIVATE BENJAMIN

JANICE RUBIN
STILLS
'82 LIAR'S MOON*

JUDITH RUBIN
PROD. SECRETARY
'84 JUST THE WAY YOU ARE*

LANCE RUBIN
MUSIC
'80 MOTEL HELL
'81 HAPPY BIRTHDAY TO ME*
'81 MODERN ROMANCE

MANN RUBIN
SCREENPLAY
'80 FIRST DEADLY SIN

MICHAEL RUBIN
MISCELLANEOUS
'80 RETURN OF THE SECAUCUS SEVEN, THE

RICHARD RUBIN
PROPS
'79 STAR TREK-THE MOTION PICTURE
'80 NINE TO FIVE
'80 THOSE LIPS, THOSE EYES*
'81 MODERN PROBLEMS
'83 KISS ME GOODBYE
'84 UNFAITHFULLY YOURS

STELLA RUBIN
PROD. SECRETARY
'81 HIGH RISK*

STEVEN RUBIN
PUBLICIST
'82 ENDANGERED SPECIES
'83 SPACEHUNTER: ADVENTURES IN THE FORBIDDEN ZONE
UNIT PUBLICIST
'83 PORKY'S II THE NEXT DAY

DOLORES RUBIN-LEVIN
SCRIPT SUPERVISOR
'81 CHU CHU AND THE PHILLY FLASH

MICHEL RUBINI
MUSIC
'83 HUNGER, THE*

ARTHUR RUBINSTEIN
MUSIC
'79 GREAT BANK HOAX, THE
'81 ON THE RIGHT TRACK
'81 WHOSE LIFE IS IT ANYWAY?
'83 BLUE THUNDER
'83 DEAL OF THE CENTURY
'83 WAR GAMES

DONALD RUBINSTEIN
MUSIC
'81 KNIGHTRIDERS

KEITH RUBINSTEIN
ASSOCIATE PRODUCER
'83 DEADLY FORCE

KEITH RUBINSTEIN
MUSIC SUPERVISOR
'82 VICE SQUAD*

MARLENE RUBINSTEIN
MISCELLANEOUS
'84 CANNONBALL RUN II

RICHARD RUBINSTEIN
PRODUCER
'79 DAWN OF THE DEAD
'81 KNIGHTRIDERS
'82 CREEPSHOW

TONY RUBIO
PRODUCTION MANAGER
'83 YELLOWBEARD*
2ND ASST. DIRECTOR
'81 HIGH RISK
MISCELLANEOUS
'83 AMITYVILLE 3D

ALBERT RUDDY
PRODUCER
'81 CANNONBALL RUN, THE
'82 MEGAFORCE
'84 LASSITER
'84 CANNONBALL RUN II
SCREENPLAY
'82 MEGAFORCE*
'84 CANNONBALL RUN II*
EXECUTIVE PRODUCER
'81 DEATH HUNT*

SCOTT RUDIN
PRODUCER
'82 I'M DANCING AS FAST AS I CAN*
'84 RECKLESS*
'84 MRS. SOFFEL*
CASTING
'79 LAST EMBRACE
'79 WANDERERS, THE
'80 RESURRECTION*
'80 SIMON
'80 HIDE IN PLAIN SIGHT*

NORMAN RUDMAN
EXECUTIVE PRODUCER
'80 BALTIMORE BULLET, THE*

GENE RUDOLF
PRODUCTION DESIGNER
'80 RAGING BULL
'81 NIGHT THE LIGHTS WENT OUT IN GEORGIA, THE
'82 AUTHOR, AUTHOR
'83 TRADING PLACES
MISCELLANEOUS
'80 RAGING BULL
'82 DINER
'83 RIGHT STUFF, THE
'84 AGAINST ALL ODDS

ALAN RUDOLPH
DIRECTOR
'79 REMEMBER MY NAME
'80 ROADIE
'82 ENDANGERED SPECIES
'84 CHOOSE ME
'84 SONGWRITER
SCREENPLAY
'79 REMEMBER MY NAME
'82 ENDANGERED SPECIES*
'84 CHOOSE ME

JOYCE RUDOLPH
STILLS
'82 I'M DANCING AS FAST AS I CAN
'84 CHOOSE ME
'84 SONGWRITER*
'84 TERMINATOR, THE

ALTON RUFF
CHOREOGRAPHER
'83 STING II, THE

CHERI RUFF
HAIR
'79 VILLAIN, THE*
'80 RAISE THE TITANIC*
'80 CHANGE OF SEASONS, A*
'80 LOVING COUPLES*
'82 JEKYLL AND HYDE TOGETHER AGAIN
'83 INDEPENDENCE DAY
'83 TO BE OR NOT TO BE
'83 TWILIGHT ZONE, THE MOVIE*
'84 GREMLINS
'84 KARATE KID, THE

JOSEPH RUFFALO
PRODUCER
'84 PURPLE RAIN*

EVA RUGGIERO
EDITOR
'80 MOUNTAIN MEN, THE
'81 STRIPES*
'83 SAVANNAH SMILES

PETE RUGOLO
MUSIC
'81 CHU CHU AND THE PHILLY FLASH

JEAN-PIERRE RUH
SOUND
'79 SAINT JACK
'80 TESS
'84 ONCE UPON A TIME IN AMERICA

FRANCISCO RUIZ
LOCATIONS
'84 BOLERO

JUAN RUIZ-ANCHIA
CINEMATOGRAPHER
'84 STONE BOY, THE

MARIBEL RUIZ-CAPILLAS
SCRIPT SUPERVISOR
'84 BOLERO

JEANNE RUMMANS
SCRIPT SUPERVISOR
'83 ANGEL OF H.E.A.T.

ERIC RUMSEY
SPECIAL EFFECTS
'84 CHILDREN OF THE CORN

LOUISE RUNDELL
MAKEUP
'81 GAS
'81 MY BLOODY VALENTINE

PETER RUNFOLO
PRODUCTION MANAGER
'83 STRANGE INVADERS*
UNIT PROD. MANAGER
'79 VOICES

WERNER RUNGE
PROPS
'84 NEVERENDING STORY, THE*

MIKE RUNYARD
MISCELLANEOUS
'83 NEVER SAY NEVER AGAIN

JOHN RUPKALVIS
MISCELLANEOUS
'83 METALSTORM: THE DESTRUCTION OF JARED-SYN
'83 METALSTORM: THE DESTRUCTION OF JARED-SYN

JOHN RUSAC
STILLS
'81 BURNING, THE*

JEREMIAH RUSCONI
ART DIRECTOR
'79 EUROPEANS, THE

ROBIN RUSE-RINEHART
2ND ASST. DIRECTOR
'79 SAINT JACK*

ALICE RUSH
COSTUME SUPERVISOR
'79 AMERICAN GIGOLO

DON RUSH
SOUND
'80 DIVINE MADNESS

RICHARD RUSH
PRODUCER
'80 STUNT MAN, THE
DIRECTOR
'80 STUNT MAN, THE

NANCY RUSHLOW
MISCELLANEOUS
'83 GET CRAZY

SUSAN RUSKIN
ASSOCIATE PRODUCER
'84 WOMAN IN RED, THE*

CHUCK RUSSELL
SCREENPLAY
'84 DREAMSCAPE*
EXECUTIVE PRODUCER
'81 HELL NIGHT*
'82 SEDUCTION, THE*
ASSOCIATE PRODUCER
'84 BODY ROCK
'84 DREAMSCAPE

JIM BOB RUSSELL
STILLS
'80 OH! HEAVENLY DOG

KEN RUSSELL
DIRECTOR
'80 ALTERED STATES
'84 CRIMES OF PASSION

LANE RUSSELL
ASSISTANT EDITOR
'83 DEADLY FORCE*

MIKE RUSSELL
PUBLICIST
'79 HANOVER STREET
UNIT PUBLICIST
'81 DOGS OF WAR, THE
'83 BEYOND THE LIMIT

SHIRLEY RUSSELL
PRODUCTION DESIGNER
'79 AGATHA
COSTUMES
'79 CUBA
'79 YANKS
'81 REDS
'84 GREYSTOKE: THE LEGEND OF TARZAN, LORD OF THE APES*
'84 RAZOR'S EDGE, THE

TANYA RUSSELL
STUNT COORDINATOR
'79 LAST EMBRACE*

WILBUR RUSSELL
PROPS
'79 BLACK HOLE, THE
'82 TRON
'84 SPLASH*

WILLY RUSSELL
SCREENPLAY
'83 EDUCATING RITA

JEAN-LUC RUSSIER
MAKEUP
'84 JUST THE WAY YOU ARE*

AARON RUSSO
PRODUCER
'79 ROSE, THE*
'82 PARTNERS
'83 TRADING PLACES
'84 TEACHERS

IRWIN RUSSO
EXECUTIVE PRODUCER
'84 TEACHERS
ASSOCIATE PRODUCER
'83 TRADING PLACES*

JOE RUSSO
ART DIRECTOR
'82 BEST FRIENDS

JOSAN RUSSO
ART DIRECTOR
'80 CARNY
'84 ICEMAN*

SALVATORE RUSSO
COSTUMES
'79 KILLER FISH*

BRIAN RUST
MISCELLANEOUS
'80 SHINING, THE

WAYNE RUST
HAIR
'81 ALL NIGHT LONG*

DIANA RUSTON
SOUND
'83 ANOTHER TIME, ANOTHER PLACE

FRANK RUSZCZYNSKI
2ND ASST. DIRECTOR
'83 OF UNKNOWN ORIGIN*

MICHAEL RUTHERFORD
MUSIC
'79 SHOUT, THE*

CHANDRAN RUTNAM
PROD. COORDINATOR
'81 TARZAN, THE APE MAN
MISCELLANEOUS
'84 INDIANA JONES AND THE TEMPLE OF DOOM

ALFREDO RUVALCABA
STILLS
'81 ZORRO, THE GAY BLADE
'84 ROMANCING THE STONE*
'84 EVIL THAT MEN DO, THE

RODOLFO RUZZA
PROPS
'83 1990: THE BRONX WARRIORS*

GUISEPPE RUZZOLINI
CINEMATOGRAPHER
'84 FIRESTARTER

CHRIS RYAN
2ND ASST. DIRECTOR
'84 ICE PIRATES, THE*
'84 JOHNNY DANGEROUSLY*
'84 RHINESTONE*

CHRISTOPHER RYAN
COSTUMES
'82 GREY FOX, THE
'84 POLICE ACADEMY

GEOFFREY RYAN
LOCATIONS
'84 LAST STARFIGHTER, THE

JOHN RYAN
PRODUCER
'80 KIDNAPPING OF THE PRESIDENT, THE*

KEN RYAN
ART DIRECTOR
'80 HUMAN FACTOR, THE

KENNETH RYAN
ASSOCIATE PRODUCER
'83 LET'S SPEND THE NIGHT TOGETHER

LATA RYAN
PROD. COORDINATOR
'79 1941
'84 INDIANA JONES AND THE TEMPLE OF DOOM
PROD. SECRETARY
'79 WHEN YOU COMIN' BACK, RED RYDER?

PATTY RYAN
CASTING
'82 BRAINWAVES*

PAUL RYAN
CINEMATOGRAPHER
'84 HOT DOG...THE MOVIE

ROBIN RYAN
STILLS
'81 EYE FOR AN EYE, AN

TERRY RYAN
COSTUMES
'82 STARSTRUCK*
'83 YEAR OF LIVING DANGEROUSLY,THE
COSTUME SUPERVISOR
'81 GALLIPOLI

TIM RYAN
KEY GRIP
'83 STROKER ACE
'83 BRAINSTORM
'84 CANNONBALL RUN II

HARI RYATT
ASSISTANT EDITOR
'82 LIAR'S MOON*

GARY RYBAR
MISCELLANEOUS
'79 BREAKING AWAY

CAROL RYDALL
MISCELLANEOUS
'79 ESCAPE FROM ALCATRAZ

MARK RYDELL
DIRECTOR
'79 ROSE, THE
'81 ON GOLDEN POND
'84 RIVER, THE

DIANE RYDER
ASSISTANT EDITOR
'83 MONTY PYTHON'S THE MEANING OF LIFE*

ARDEN RYSHPAN
CASTING
'82 QUEST FOR FIRE*

S

MARIO CABRAL E SA
UNIT MANAGER
'81 SEA WOLVES, THE

ROBERT SAAD
MISCELLANEOUS
'84 POLICE ACADEMY

ERIC SAARINEN
CINEMATOGRAPHER
'79 REAL LIFE
'81 MODERN ROMANCE
'83 GOLDEN SEAL, THE
MISCELLANEOUS
'79 FORCE OF ONE, A

SHIMON SABAH
KEY GRIP
'79 CIRCLE OF IRON
'84 BEST DEFENSE*

JAMES SABAT
SOUND
'79 SEDUCTION OF JOE TYNAN, THE
'79 STARTING OVER
'79 GOING IN STYLE
'79 MANHATTAN
'79 DOUBLE MCGUFFIN, THE
'80 STARDUST MEMORIES
'80 JUST TELL ME WHAT YOU WANT
'81 ARTHUR
'81 PRINCE OF THE CITY
'82 DEATHTRAP
'82 MIDSUMMER NIGHT'S SEX COMEDY, A
'82 VERDICT, THE
'83 EXPOSED*
'83 TRADING PLACES
'83 ZELIG
'84 BROADWAY DANNY ROSE
'84 LONELY GUY, THE*
'84 GARBO TALKS
'84 POPE OF GREENWICH VILLAGE,THE

DANILO SABATINI
MISCELLANEOUS
'80 NIJINSKY

ANTHONY SABATINO
PRODUCTION DESIGNER
'83 RICHARD PRYOR: HERE AND NOW*

ENRICO SABBATINI
COSTUMES
'79 BLOODLINE

FRED SABINE
STILLS
'84 ALL OF ME
'84 LONELY GUY, THE*

PETER SABITSON
MISCELLANEOUS
'82 Q: QUETZALCOATL

DARDANO SACCHETTI
SCREENPLAY
'83 1990: THE BRONX WARRIORS*

THOMAS SACCIO
PROPS
'79 BELL JAR, THE
'79 KRAMER VS. KRAMER
'80 RAGING BULL*
'80 ONE-TRICK PONY
'81 FAN, THE
'82 WORLD ACCORDING TO GARP, THE
'83 EASY MONEY
'83 WITHOUT A TRACE
'84 FIRSTBORN
'84 BEAT STREET

TOM SACHS
PRODUCER
'80 LADY VANISHES, THE

WILLIAM SACHS
PRODUCER
'84 EXTERMINATOR II*
DIRECTOR
'80 GALAXINA
SCREENPLAY
'80 GALAXINA
'84 EXTERMINATOR II*

JESSICA SACK
ART DIRECTOR
'80 EYES OF A STRANGER

DANIEL SACKHEIM
ASSISTANT EDITOR
'82 TOY, THE*
'84 LOVE STREAMS*
'84 NO SMALL AFFAIR*

WILLIAM SACKHEIM
PRODUCER
'79 IN-LAWS, THE*
'80 COMPETITION, THE
'83 SURVIVORS, THE
'84 NO SMALL AFFAIR
SCREENPLAY
'82 FIRST BLOOD*

HOWARD SACKLER
SCREENPLAY
'79 SAINT JACK*

EZRA SACKS
SCREENPLAY
'80 SMALL CIRCLE OF FRIENDS, A

NINA SADEK
MISCELLANEOUS
'83 HOUSE ON SORORITY ROW

MARTIN JAY SADOFF
EDITOR
'81 GRADUATION DAY
MISCELLANEOUS
'82 FRIDAY THE 13TH PART THREE IN 3D

AARON SADOVNICK
ASSOCIATE PRODUCER
'82 OUT OF THE BLUE

ROBIN SAENS
MISCELLANEOUS
'83 CHRISTINE

EDDIE SAETA
ASSOCIATE PRODUCER
'81 ...ALL THE MARBLES*
PRODUCTION MANAGER
'81 ...ALL THE MARBLES
MISCELLANEOUS
'79 GOLDENGIRL

CRAIG SAFAN
MUSIC
'80 FADE TO BLACK
'83 NIGHTMARES
'84 LAST STARFIGHTER, THE
MISCELLANEOUS
'81 THIEF

DON SAFRAN
PUBLICIST
'81 LEGEND OF THE LONE RANGER, THE

DON SAFRAN
SCREENPLAY
'82 HOME WORK*
ASSOCIATE PRODUCER
'82 HOME WORK

MARTIN SAGARABARRIA
MISCELLANEOUS
'81 ENTER THE NINJA

RAY SAGER
1ST ASST. DIRECTOR
'80 TERROR TRAIN
'81 MY BLOODY VALENTINE*
2ND UNIT DIRECTOR
'81 MY BLOODY VALENTINE

RIC SAGLIANI
MAKEUP
'82 DEAD MEN DON'T WEAR PLAID*
'83 MAN WITH TWO BRAINS, THE*
'83 MR. MOM
'84 ALL OF ME*
'84 LONELY GUY, THE*

MICHAEL SAHL
MISCELLANEOUS
'80 UNION CITY

PETER SAINSBURY
MISCELLANEOUS
'83 DRAUGHTSMAN CONTRACT, THE

FLAVIE SAINTS
SCRIPT SUPERVISOR
'81 BEYOND THE REEF

VINCENT SAIZIS
CINEMATOGRAPHER
'79 RAVAGERS
MISCELLANEOUS
'80 BRUBAKER

MATSUSABURO SAKAGUCHI
ASSOCIATE PRODUCER
'81 INCHON

RYUICHI SAKAMOTO
MUSIC
'83 MERRY CHRISTMAS, MR. LAWRENCE

SAUL SALADOW
ASSISTANT EDITOR
'79 FRISCO KID, THE*
'79 HANOVER STREET*
'80 BLACK MARBLE, THE
'80 FIRST FAMILY*
'81 RICHARD PRYOR: LIVE ON THE SUNSET STRIP*
'83 KISS ME GOODBYE*
'84 GHOSTBUSTERS*
'84 UNFAITHFULLY YOURS*

REY SALAMAT
MAKEUP
'83 BLIND RAGE

F. SALAMON
STUNT COORDINATOR
'82 TEMPEST*

MIKE SALAMUNOVICH
UNIT PROD. MANAGER
'80 WHEN TIME RAN OUT
1ST ASST. DIRECTOR
'79 BEYOND THE POSEIDON ADVENTURE
'81 CHU CHU AND THE PHILLY FLASH

RONALD SALAND
PRODUCER
'79 AMITYVILLE HORROR, THE*
'81 NIGHT THE LIGHTS WENT OUT IN GEORGIA, THE*

CHARLES SALDANA
KEY GRIP
'79 DREAMER
'79 ESCAPE FROM ALCATRAZ
'81 BEAST WITHIN, THE
'81 INCHON
'82 FIREFOX
'82 HONKYTONK MAN
'82 THINGS ARE TOUGH ALL OVER
'83 SUDDEN IMPACT
'83 ALL THE RIGHT MOVES
'83 BAD BOYS*
'84 CITY HEAT
'84 TIGHTROPE

NANCY SALES
ASSISTANT EDITOR
'79 ROCKY II*
'79 HANOVER STREET*
'80 FIRST FAMILY*

ILYA SALKIND
EXECUTIVE PRODUCER
'81 SUPERMAN II
'83 SUPERMAN III
'84 SUPERGIRL

JOSE JOAQUIM SALLES
1ST ASST. DIRECTOR
'84 BLAME IT ON RIO*

ROBERT SALLIN
PRODUCER
'82 STAR TREK II THE WRATH OF KHAN

NORMAN SALLING
COSTUMES
'80 ROUGH CUT*
'81 SHARKEY'S MACHINE
'83 STROKER ACE
'83 MAN WHO LOVED WOMEN, THE*
'84 CITY HEAT
COSTUME SUPERVISOR
'80 SMOKEY AND THE BANDIT II
'81 CANNONBALL RUN, THE
'84 CANNONBALL RUN II

MICHEL SALLIOUTI
1ST ASST. DIRECTOR
'79 KILLER FISH*

ROGER SALLOCH
SCRIPT SUPERVISOR
'83 HANNA K*

KEN SALLOWS
ASSISTANT EDITOR
'83 MAN FROM SNOWY RIVER, THE

CHARLES SALMON
PRODUCTION MANAGER
'84 GIVE MY REGARDS TO BROAD STREET

SCOTT SALMON
CHOREOGRAPHER
'80 STIR CRAZY
'80 LAST MARRIED COUPLE IN AMERICA, THE

LORIN SALOB
PRODUCTION MANAGER
'84 RUNAWAY
1ST ASST. DIRECTOR
'82 TRON
'82 CHILLY SCENES OF WINTER

CAROL LYNN SALONEN
MISCELLANEOUS
'83 SAVANNAH SMILES

J.J. SALTER
SCREENPLAY
'84 JOY OF SEX, THE*

HARRY SALTZMAN
EXECUTIVE PRODUCER
'80 NIJINSKY

RUGGERO SALVADORI
1ST ASST. DIRECTOR
'83 PIRANHA II: THE SPAWNING

SERGIO SALVATI
CINEMATOGRAPHER
'83 1990: THE BRONX WARRIORS

VLADIMIRO SALVATORE
KEY GRIP
'80 POPEYE*
'83 BLACK STALLION RETURNS, THE

DAVID SALVEN

EXEC IN CHARGE PROD
'81 ENTITY, THE
'82 SIX WEEKS
'83 MAN WOMAN AND CHILD
'84 ALL OF ME
ASSOCIATE PRODUCER
'79 FISH THAT SAVED PITTSBURGH, THE
'83 DEAL OF THE CENTURY
PRODUCTION MANAGER
'81 ENTITY, THE
'82 SIX WEEKS
UNIT PROD. MANAGER
'79 FISH THAT SAVED PITTSBURGH, THE
'80 INSIDE MOVES
'83 DEAL OF THE CENTURY
'83 MAN WOMAN AND CHILD
'84 ALL OF ME

DAVID SALVEN JR.

LOCATIONS
'83 DEAL OF THE CENTURY*
'83 MAN WOMAN AND CHILD
'84 ALL OF ME

FEDERICO SALZMANN

ASSISTANT EDITOR
'81 ATLANTIC CITY

UMBERTO SAMBUCO

PRODUCTION MANAGER
'81 SUNDAY LOVERS*
'83 PIRANHA II: THE SPAWNING
'84 MISUNDERSTOOD*
UNIT MANAGER
'81 FOR YOUR EYES ONLY*
LOCATIONS
'81 FOR YOUR EYES ONLY*

RUTH SAMET

PUBLICIST
'83 INDEPENDENCE DAY

AHMED SAMI

PRODUCTION MANAGER
'80 AWAKENING, THE*
'81 GALLIPOLI*

PETER SAMISH

ART DIRECTOR
'79 ...AND JUSTICE FOR ALL

JUNE SAMSON

SCRIPT SUPERVISOR
'78 DEER HUNTER, THE
'79 ...AND JUSTICE FOR ALL
'80 HEAVEN'S GATE*
'80 MOUNTAIN MEN, THE
'81 HONKY TONK FREEWAY
'81 ONLY WHEN I LAUGH
'82 CHALLENGE, THE
'82 THINGS ARE TOUGH ALL OVER
'83 MAN WITH TWO BRAINS, THE
'84 AGAINST ALL ODDS

KIM SAMSON

HAIR
'84 SWING SHIFT*
'84 WINDY CITY

WALLY SAMSON

UNIT PROD. MANAGER
'80 HONEYSUCKLE ROSE
'81 BACK ROADS
'83 TABLE FOR FIVE
'84 WINDY CITY

MARTIN SAMUEL

HAIR
'79 EUROPEANS, THE
'80 IT'S MY TURN*
'80 XANADU*
'81 FIRST MONDAY IN OCTOBER
'82 SHOOT THE MOON*
'82 I'M DANCING AS FAST AS I CAN
'82 PINK FLOYD: THE WALL*

PETER SAMUELSON

PRODUCER
'79 MAN, A WOMAN AND A BANK, A*
'84 REVENGE OF THE NERDS*

PACO GARCIA SAN JOSE

SPECIAL EFFECTS
'79 LOVE AND BULLETS*

CONNIE SANCHEZ

PROD. COORDINATOR
'83 10 TO MIDNIGHT*

JOSE ANTONIO SANCHEZ

MAKEUP
'79 CUBA
'80 ISLAND, THE*
'81 SPHINX*
'82 CONAN THE BARBARIAN
'84 FIRESTARTER*
HAIR
'82 CONAN THE BARBARIAN

LUIS SANCHEZ

MISCELLANEOUS
'84 ROMANCING THE STONE

PAUL SANCHEZ

MAKEUP
'80 SOMEWHERE IN TIME*

TERESA SANCHEZ

MAKEUP
'84 UNDER THE VOLCANO*
HAIR
'84 UNDER THE VOLCANO*

VICKI SANCHEZ

COSTUMES
'79 CHAPTER TWO
'80 LAST MARRIED COUPLE IN AMERICA, THE*
'80 OH GOD! BOOK II
'81 BLOW OUT*
'82 BORDER, THE
'83 TABLE FOR FIVE

DAN SANDBURG

EXECUTIVE PRODUCER
'82 Q: QUETZALCOATL*

KIRK SANDBURG

MISCELLANEOUS
'84 UP THE CREEK

JACK SANDEEN

COSTUMES
'81 AMY
COSTUME SUPERVISOR
'80 HERBIE GOES BANANAS
'80 LAST FLIGHT OF NOAH'S ARK, THE
'80 MIDNIGHT MADNESS
'82 TEX
'84 COUNTRY

WILLIAM SANDELL

ART DIRECTOR
'79 PROMISE, THE
'81 BLOOD BEACH
'81 DEAD AND BURIED*
PRODUCTION DESIGNER
'82 AIRPLANE II: THE SEQUEL

ANDREW SANDERS

ART DIRECTOR
'81 SHOCK TREATMENT
'83 MERRY CHRISTMAS, MR. LAWRENCE
'83 PRIVATES ON PARADE*

DAVID SANDERS

STUNT COORDINATOR
'81 STUDENT BODIES
'82 LIAR'S MOON

DON SANDERS

SOUND
'82 SWORD AND THE SORCERER, THE
'83 MORTUARY*

JACK FROST SANDERS

PRODUCER
'81 KING OF THE MOUNTAIN
EXECUTIVE PRODUCER
'84 WOMAN IN RED, THE
PRODUCTION MANAGER
'81 BLOOD BEACH
'83 TO BE OR NOT TO BE
'84 WOMAN IN RED, THE
1ST ASST. DIRECTOR
'79 BUTCH AND SUNDANCE: THE EARLY YEARS
'79 PLAYERS*
'82 AIRPLANE II: THE SEQUEL
'82 BEST LITTLE WHOREHOUSE IN TEXAS, THE
MISCELLANEOUS
'83 TO BE OR NOT TO BE

RONALD SANDERS

EDITOR
'79 FAST COMPANY
'81 SCANNERS
'83 DEAD ZONE, THE
'83 VIDEODROME
'84 FIRESTARTER*

TIM SANDERS

PRODUCTION MANAGER
'83 YEAR OF LIVING DANGEROUSLY, THE

DAVID SANDERSON

MISCELLANEOUS
'79 PICNIC AT HANGING ROCK

PHIL SANDERSON

ASSISTANT EDITOR
'81 RAIDERS OF THE LOST ARK*
'83 KEEP, THE
'84 SHEENA*

BARRY SANDLER

PRODUCER
'84 CRIMES OF PASSION
SCREENPLAY
'80 MIRROR CRACK'D, THE*
'82 MAKING LOVE
'84 CRIMES OF PASSION
ASSOCIATE PRODUCER
'82 MAKING LOVE*

ROGER SANDLER

STILLS
'83 OSTERMAN WEEKEND, THE

TERRIL SANDLIN

HAIR
'82 BUTTERFLY

JAY SANDRICH

DIRECTOR
'80 SEEMS LIKE OLD TIMES

RICHARD SANDS

KEY GRIP
'84 BACHELOR PARTY*

TIBOR SANDS

MISCELLANEOUS
'83 AMITYVILLE 3D

SHERRIE SANET

ASSISTANT EDITOR
'82 SPLIT IMAGE

CARMEN SANFORD

LOCATIONS
'79 PENITENTIARY*

CHUCK SANFORD

2ND ASST. DIRECTOR
'80 NUDE BOMB, THE

DONALD SANFORD

SCREENPLAY
'79 RAVAGERS

HELEN SANFORD

SCREENPLAY
'83 ANGEL OF H.E.A.T.

JONATHAN SANGER

PRODUCER
'80 ELEPHANT MAN, THE
'82 FRANCES
ASSOCIATE PRODUCER
'79 FORCE OF ONE, A
'80 FATSO
UNIT PROD. MANAGER
'79 FORCE OF ONE, A
'80 FATSO

JIMMY SANGSTER

SCREENPLAY
'79 LEGACY, THE*

MIKIO SANKEY

MISCELLANEOUS
'83 REVENGE OF THE NINJA

ALDO SANTARELLI

UNIT MANAGER
'79 KILLER FISH*

JOHN SANTI

1ST ASST. DIRECTOR
'83 HERCULES

JOE SANTLEY

PUBLICIST
'84 CHILDREN OF THE CORN
UNIT PUBLICIST
'79 SCAVENGER HUNT
'81 TAKE THIS JOB AND SHOVE IT

LUCA SANTOLINI

PROD. SECRETARY
'83 1990: THE BRONX WARRIORS*

CARL SANTORO

MISCELLANEOUS
'83 RETURN OF THE ALIENS: THE DEADLY SPAWN

DANNY SANTOS

COSTUME SUPERVISOR
'81 ENTER THE NINJA*

ELVIE SANTOS

COSTUME SUPERVISOR
'81 ENTER THE NINJA*

JOHN SANTUCCI

MISCELLANEOUS
'81 THIEF

FRANCISCA NUNEZ SANZ

HAIR
'84 FIRESTARTER

PETER SAPHIER

EXECUTIVE PRODUCER
'83 EDDIE MACON'S RUN
CO-PRODUCER
'83 SCARFACE

RICHARD SARAFIAN

DIRECTOR
'79 SUNBURN
'84 BEAR, THE

FRANK SARAFINE

MISCELLANEOUS
'82 TRON

GIANNI SARAGO

MISCELLANEOUS
'83 LONELY LADY, THE

MICHAEL SARAO

2ND ASST. DIRECTOR
'83 OF UNKNOWN ORIGIN*

PASQUALE SARAO

SPECIAL EFFECTS
'83 1990: THE BRONX WARRIORS*

PHILIPPE SARDE

MUSIC
'80 TESS
'81 GHOST STORY
'82 QUEST FOR FIRE
'83 LOVESICK

BILL SARDELL

ART DIRECTOR
'80 SERIAL

SYLVIA SARDU

HAIR
'83 STING II, THE*

ALVIN SARGEANT

SCREENPLAY
'80 ORDINARY PEOPLE

JOSEPH SARGENT

DIRECTOR
'79 GOLDENGIRL
'80 COAST TO COAST
'83 NIGHTMARES

LIA SARGENT
MISCELLANEOUS
'79 GOLDENGIRL

RALPH SARIEGO
UNIT PROD. MANAGER
'82 TRON

ART SARNO
PUBLICIST
'80 AIRPLANE
'81 LOOKER
UNIT PUBLICIST
'80 HUNTER, THE
'81 CANNONBALL RUN, THE*

ART SARNO JR.
PUBLICIST
'80 FOOLIN AROUND

JAMES SARZOTTI
MAKEUP
'83 BABY IT'S YOU
'83 LIANNA
'84 RECKLESS
HAIR
'83 LIANNA

KYOJI SASAKI
PROPS
'82 CHALLENGE, THE

PETER SASDY
DIRECTOR
'83 LONELY LADY, THE

STEPHEN SASSEN
2ND ASST. DIRECTOR
'81 PRIVATE LESSONS
'83 TIMERIDER

JACKIE SAUNDERS
SCRIPT SUPERVISOR
'80 PRIVATE EYES, THE
'80 HANGAR 18
'82 I'M DANCING AS FAST AS I CAN
'82 DON'T CRY, IT'S ONLY THUNDER
'83 CUJO
'84 CHAMPIONS*

JUDITH SAUNDERS
SCRIPT SUPERVISOR
'82 LAST AMERICAN VIRGIN, THE
'82 ZAPPED!

RUSSELL SAUNDERS
PRODUCTION MANAGER
'81 STRIPES
UNIT PROD. MANAGER
'79 AMITYVILLE HORROR, THE

TERENCE SAUNDERS
SPECIAL EFFECTS
'81 FOUR SEASONS, THE*
MISCELLANEOUS
'79 BLACK HOLE, THE
'79 BLACK HOLE, THE

LIAM SAURIN
SOUND
'83 EDUCATING RITA*

GAUDELINE SAURIOL
COSTUMES
'81 GAS

ROBERT SAUSSIER
UNIT MANAGER
'79 MOONRAKER*

HAL SAVAGE
ASSOCIATE PRODUCER
'82 BY DESIGN*

PETER SAVAGE
ASSOCIATE PRODUCER
'80 RAGING BULL*

JEAN SAVARD
UNIT MANAGER
'81 SCANNERS
'81 GAS

PHIL SAVATH
SCREENPLAY
'79 FAST COMPANY*

CARLO SAVINA
MUSIC
'81 COMIN' AT YA!

TOM SAVINI
STUNT COORDINATOR
'80 FRIDAY THE 13TH
SPECIAL EFFECTS
'80 FRIDAY THE 13TH
MISCELLANEOUS
'79 DAWN OF THE DEAD
'80 EYES OF A STRANGER
'80 MANIAC
'81 BURNING, THE
'81 BURNING, THE
'82 CREEPSHOW
'84 FRIDAY THE 13TH PART IV THE FINAL CHAPTER

JILL SAVITT
ASSISTANT EDITOR
'84 PLACES IN THE HEART*

JOHN SAVKA
KEY GRIP
'82 BEASTMASTER, THE
'83 SWEET SIXTEEN
'84 ANGEL
'84 CHILDREN OF THE CORN
'84 FRIDAY THE 13TH PART IV THE FINAL CHAPTER

MARC SAVOY
MISCELLANEOUS
'81 SOUTHERN COMFORT

KATINA SAVVIDIS
CHOREOGRAPHER
'80 LONG RIDERS, THE

GEORGE SAWAYA
STUNT COORDINATOR
'79 CONCORDE-AIRPORT '79, THE

MARK SAWICKI
MISCELLANEOUS
'81 SATURDAY THE 14TH
'81 GALAXY OF TERROR

RICHARD SAWYER
ART DIRECTOR
'80 MELVIN AND HOWARD
'81 HAND, THE
'82 BORDER, THE
'83 TWILIGHT ZONE, THE MOVIE*
PRODUCTION DESIGNER
'80 WHERE THE BUFFALO ROAM
'82 THINGS ARE TOUGH ALL OVER
MISCELLANEOUS
'84 BACHELOR PARTY

WILLIAM SAWYER
EDITOR
'79 REMEMBER MY NAME*

ERNIE SAWYERS
PROPS
'79 BUDDY HOLLY STORY, THE
'81 UNDER THE RAINBOW
MISCELLANEOUS
'84 FIRESTARTER

ERNIE SAWYERS JR.
PROPS
'79 SCAVENGER HUNT
SCRIPT SUPERVISOR
'81 UNDER THE RAINBOW

CAROLINE SAX
SCRIPT SUPERVISOR
'83 DRESSER, THE
'84 SHEENA
'84 BOSTONIANS, THE

JOHN SAXTON
SCREENPLAY
'81 HAPPY BIRTHDAY TO ME*

MICHAEL SAXTON
ASSISTANT EDITOR
'79 SHOUT, THE*

JOHN SAYLES
DIRECTOR
'80 RETURN OF THE SECAUCUS SEVEN, THE
'83 BABY IT'S YOU
'83 LIANNA
'84 BROTHER FROM ANOTHER PLANET, THE
SCREENPLAY
'80 RETURN OF THE SECAUCUS SEVEN, THE
'80 ALLIGATOR
'80 BATTLE BEYOND THE STARS
'81 HOWLING, THE*
'82 CHALLENGE, THE*
'83 BABY IT'S YOU
'83 LIANNA
'84 BROTHER FROM ANOTHER PLANET, THE
EDITOR
'80 RETURN OF THE SECAUCUS SEVEN, THE
'83 LIANNA
'84 BROTHER FROM ANOTHER PLANET, THE

AMY SAYRES
LOCATIONS
'81 THEY ALL LAUGHED*
'83 KING OF COMEDY, THE

JAMES SBARDELLATI
1ST ASST. DIRECTOR
'80 BATTLE BEYOND THE STARS
'80 HUMANOIDS FROM THE DEEP
'82 BEASTMASTER, THE
2ND UNIT DIRECTOR
'80 HUMANOIDS FROM THE DEEP

ARNOLD SCAASI
COSTUMES
'80 LOVING COUPLES*
'83 KISS ME GOODBYE

T. CARLYLE SCALES
EXECUTIVE PRODUCER
'79 GREAT BANK HOAX, THE*

ROY SCAMMELL
STUNT COORDINATOR
'79 ALIEN
'80 SATURN 3
'82 VENOM
'84 GREYSTOKE: THE LEGEND OF TARZAN, LORD OF THE APES
'84 SHEENA
'84 GIVE MY REGARDS TO BROAD STREET

SUSAN SCANLAN
CHOREOGRAPHER
'84 BODY ROCK

STEPHEN SCANLON
SOUND
'80 SIMON
'83 LOVESICK

GERALD SCARFE
MISCELLANEOUS
'82 PINK FLOYD: THE WALL

FERDINANDO SCARFIOTTI
MISCELLANEOUS
'79 AMERICAN GIGOLO
'81 HONKY TONK FREEWAY
'82 CAT PEOPLE
'83 SCARFACE
'84 THIEF OF HEARTS

ROBERTA SHERRY SCELZA
SCRIPT SUPERVISOR
'81 FOUR SEASONS, THE

DAVID SCHACKER
CASTING
'82 LIAR'S MOON*

JULIE SCHAEFER
COSTUMES
'83 FRIGHTMARE

STAN SCHAEFER
CASTING
'82 ANDROID

STEPHEN SCHAEFER
UNIT PUBLICIST
'80 TIMES SQUARE

MARTIN SCHAER
MISCELLANEOUS
'83 MAN WHO LOVED WOMEN, THE

HAL SCHAFFEL
UNIT PROD. MANAGER
'79 MAIN EVENT, THE*

ROBERT SCHAFFEL
PRODUCER
'82 LOOKIN' TO GET OUT
'83 TABLE FOR FIVE

KARL SCHAFFER
MISCELLANEOUS
'79 AVALANCHE EXPRESS

FRANKLIN SCHAFFNER
DIRECTOR
'81 SPHINX
'82 YES, GIORGIO
EXECUTIVE PRODUCER
'81 SPHINX

MAURY SCHALLACK
MISCELLANEOUS
'80 BATTLE BEYOND THE STARS

KARL SCHAPER
PRODUCTION MANAGER
'80 FORMULA, THE*

DAVID SCHARF
MISCELLANEOUS
'82 BLADERUNNER

RICHARD SCHARF
MAKEUP
'80 DIE LAUGHING

LEE SCHATTINO
PROPS
'83 SMITHEREENS*

JERRY SCHATZBERG
DIRECTOR
'84 MISUNDERSTOOD
'84 NO SMALL AFFAIR

JEFFREY SCHECHTMAN
PRODUCER
'83 PIRANHA II: THE SPAWNING*
'84 BODY ROCK

WILL SCHECK
PROPS
'81 NESTING, THE

HANNAH SCHEEL
SCRIPT SUPERVISOR
'79 ONION FIELD, THE
'79 WINTER KILLS
'80 RAGING BULL
'81 BLOW OUT
'81 TRUE CONFESSIONS
'82 CHILLY SCENES OF WINTER
'83 KING OF COMEDY, THE*

JOHN SCHEELE
MISCELLANEOUS
'82 TRON

K.C. SCHEIBEL
ART DIRECTOR
'82 ANDROID*

CYNTHIA SCHEIDER
EDITOR
'79 BREAKING AWAY
'81 EYEWITNESS
'82 CHILLY SCENES OF WINTER
'83 WITHOUT A TRACE

STEFAAN SCHEIDER
1ST ASST. DIRECTOR
'84 MOSCOW ON THE HUDSON*

ANDREW SCHEINMAN
PRODUCER
'80 MOUNTAIN MEN, THE*
CO-PRODUCER
'80 AWAKENING, THE*

MAURICE SCHELL
ASSISTANT EDITOR
'79 LAST EMBRACE

HENNING SCHELLERUP
CINEMATOGRAPHER
'84 SILENT NIGHT, DEADLY NIGHT
2ND UNIT DIRECTOR
'80 HANGAR 18
MISCELLANEOUS
'84 NIGHTMARE ON ELM STREET, A

FRED SCHEPISI
DIRECTOR
'82 BARBAROSA
'84 ICEMAN

KARL SCHERER
SOUND
'80 CHANGELING, THE*

WERNER SCHERER
HAIR
'80 STARDUST MEMORIES

EDGAR SCHERICK
PRODUCER
'80 AMERICAN SUCCESS COMPANY,THE*
'82 I'M DANCING AS FAST AS I CAN*
'84 RECKLESS*
'84 MRS. SOFFEL*
EXECUTIVE PRODUCER
'82 SHOOT THE MOON*

GREGORY SCHERICK
ASSISTANT EDITOR
'84 PROTOCOL*

GERHARD SCHEVRICH
ASSOCIATE PRODUCER
'83 CHAINED HEAT*

ELLIOT SCHICK
PRODUCER
'81 EARTHLING, THE*
EXEC IN CHARGE PROD
'78 DEER HUNTER, THE
'83 BLUE SKIES AGAIN
UNIT PROD. MANAGER
'83 BLUE SKIES AGAIN
'84 RED DAWN

SANDRA SCHIECK
ASSOCIATE PRODUCER
'84 NIGHT OF THE COMET*

PAUL SCHIFF
1ST ASST. DIRECTOR
'83 HOUSE ON SORORITY ROW

ROBERT SCHIFFER
MAKEUP
'79 APPLE DUMPLING GANG RIDES AGAIN, THE
'79 BLACK HOLE, THE
'79 NORTH AVENUE IRREGULARS, THE
'80 HERBIE GOES BANANAS*
'80 LAST FLIGHT OF NOAH'S ARK,THE
'80 MIDNIGHT MADNESS
'81 AMY
'81 CONDORMAN
'81 DEVIL AND MAX DEVLIN, THE*
'82 TEX
'82 TRON
'83 TRENCHCOAT*
'84 COUNTRY
'84 SPLASH
MISCELLANEOUS
'83 SOMETHING WICKED THIS WAY COMES

LALO SCHIFRIN
MUSIC
'79 AMITYVILLE HORROR, THE
'79 BOULEVARD NIGHTS
'79 CONCORDE-AIRPORT '79, THE
'79 ESCAPE TO ATHENA
'79 LOVE AND BULLETS
'80 SERIAL
'80 BIG BRAWL, THE
'80 BRUBAKER
'80 COMPETITION, THE
'80 NUDE BOMB, THE
'80 WHEN TIME RAN OUT
'81 BUDDY, BUDDY
'81 CAVEMAN
'82 SEDUCTION, THE
'82 STRANGER IS WATCHING, A
'82 AMITYVILLE II: THE POSSESSION
'83 STING II, THE
'83 SUDDEN IMPACT
'83 DOCTOR DETROIT
'83 OSTERMAN WEEKEND, THE
'84 TANK

JOEL SCHILLER
PRODUCTION DESIGNER
'79 BUDDY HOLLY STORY, THE
'79 ICE CASTLES
'79 MUPPET MOVIE, THE
'80 SMALL CIRCLE OF FRIENDS, A
'80 HONEYSUCKLE ROSE
'81 CHARLIE CHAN AND THE CURSE OF THE DRAGON QUEEN
'82 MEGAFORCE
'84 MISUNDERSTOOD
'84 SONGWRITER

MARK SCHILZ
1ST ASST. DIRECTOR
'83 TRENCHCOAT*

BUD SCHINDLER
KEY GRIP
'82 MEGAFORCE

PETER SCHINDLER
ASSOCIATE PRODUCER
'82 FRIDAY THE 13TH PART THREE IN 3D
1ST ASST. DIRECTOR
'80 TELL ME A RIDDLE
2ND ASST. DIRECTOR
'80 ALTERED STATES
'80 FOOLIN' AROUND

GUS SCHIRMER
CASTING
'79 MUPPET MOVIE, THE

MURRAY SCHISGAL
SCREENPLAY
'82 TOOTSIE*

JOHN SCHLESINGER
DIRECTOR
'79 YANKS
'81 HONKY TONK FREEWAY

MARLA DENISE SCHLOM
COSTUME SUPERVISOR
'84 WHERE THE BOYS ARE

MARSHALL SCHLOM
SCRIPT SUPERVISOR
'79 CHINA SYNDROME, THE
'79 PROMISES IN THE DARK
'80 CHEECH AND CHONG'S NEXT MOVIE
'80 ISLAND, THE
'80 NINE TO FIVE
'81 MOMMIE DEAREST
'81 ON GOLDEN POND
'82 ANNIE
'82 BEST LITTLE WHOREHOUSE IN TEXAS, THE
'83 SILKWOOD
'84 MIKE'S MURDER
'84 2010

HANK SCHLOSS
MISCELLANEOUS
'79 MOUNTAIN FAMILY ROBINSON

ROBERTO SCHLOSSER
1ST ASST. DIRECTOR
'80 GUYANA: CULT OF THE DAMNED

HAL SCHLUETER
LOCATIONS
'82 CHILLY SCENES OF WINTER

ARNE SCHMIDT
ASSOCIATE PRODUCER
'83 HEART LIKE A WHEEL
1ST ASST. DIRECTOR
'80 AIRPLANE
'80 BIG RED ONE, THE
'82 HAMMETT*
'82 ONE FROM THE HEART
'84 FLASHPOINT*
'84 RUNAWAY
'84 RED DAWN

ARTHUR SCHMIDT
EDITOR
'79 FISH THAT
SAVED PITTSBURGH, THE*
'80 COAL MINER'S DAUGHTER
'82 ESCAPE ARTIST, THE
'83 BUDDY SYSTEM, THE
'84 FIRSTBORN

CARL SCHMIDT
MISCELLANEOUS
'81 INCHON

JAN SCHMIDT
2ND UNIT DIRECTOR
'84 AMADEUS

KIM SCHMIDT
SCRIPT SUPERVISOR
'79 GAME OF DEATH

MARLENE SCHMIDT
PRODUCER
'83 MORTUARY*
SCREENPLAY
'83 MORTUARY*

DAVID SCHMOELLER
DIRECTOR
'79 TOURIST TRAP
'82 SEDUCTION, THE
SCREENPLAY
'79 TOURIST TRAP*
'82 SEDUCTION, THE

ANNE SCHNEE
ASSISTANT EDITOR
'84 PARIS, TEXAS

CHARLES SCHNEER
PRODUCER
'81 CLASH OF THE TITANS*

SCOTT SCHNEID
EXECUTIVE PRODUCER
'84 SILENT NIGHT, DEADLY NIGHT

BARRY SCHNEIDER
SCREENPLAY
'79 ROLLER BOOGIE
'81 TAKE THIS JOB AND SHOVE IT
'83 DEADLY FORCE*

BOB SCHNEIDER
UNIT PROD. MANAGER
'80 IT'S MY TURN
'82 OFFICER AND A GENTLEMAN, AN

DANIEL SCHNEIDER
LOCATIONS
'81 BODY HEAT*

GILLE SCHNEIDER
ASSISTANT EDITOR
'79 LITTLE ROMANCE, A*
LOCATIONS
'83 EXPOSED*

HAROLD SCHNEIDER
PRODUCER
'81 ENTITY, THE
'83 WAR GAMES

DAVID SCHNEIDERMAN
SOUND
'84 WHERE THE BOYS ARE

WALLY SCHNEIDERMAN
MAKEUP
'79 SHOUT, THE
'79 AGATHA
'79 YANKS
'80 ELEPHANT MAN, THE
'80 NOTHING PERSONAL*
'81 EYE OF THE NEEDLE*
'83 YENTL
MISCELLANEOUS
'80 ELEPHANT MAN, THE

STEVE SCHOENBERG
ASSISTANT EDITOR
'82 SILENT RAGE*
'84 HOT DOG...THE MOVIE

MICHAEL SCHOENBRUN
UNIT PROD. MANAGER
'84 STAR TREK III:
THE SEARCH FOR SPOCK

BRENT SCHOENFELD
EDITOR
'82 BUTTERFLY
ASSISTANT EDITOR
'83 HEART LIKE A WHEEL

DON SCHOENFELD
MAKEUP
'79 BEYOND THE POSEIDON ADVENTURE*
'79 CHINA SYNDROME, THE*

JOHN SCHOFIELD
UNIT PROD. MANAGER
'84 ROMANCING THE STONE*

KIM SCHOLES
MUSIC
'81 NESTING, THE*

ART SCHOLL
MISCELLANEOUS
'81 PURSUIT OF D.B. COOPER, THE

EVA MARIE SCHONECKER
2ND ASST. DIRECTOR
'80 FORMULA, THE*

SKIP SCHOOLNIK
EDITOR
'81 BODY AND SOUL*
'81 HALLOWEEN II*
'82 MEGAFORCE*

THELMA SCHOONMAKER
EDITOR
'80 RAGING BULL
'83 KING OF COMEDY, THE
MISCELLANEOUS
'83 KING OF COMEDY, THE

JAMES SCHOPPE
ART DIRECTOR
'79 ROSE, THE
'79 BEING THERE
'80 STUNT MAN, THE
'80 WHY WOULD I LIE?
'82 SOME KIND OF HERO
'82 LOOKIN' TO GET OUT
'83 RETURN OF THE JEDI*
PRODUCTION DESIGNER
'80 OCTAGON, THE
'83 UNCOMMON VALOR
'84 REVENGE OF THE NERDS

BARRY SCHRADER
MUSIC
'81 GALAXY OF TERROR

LEONARD SCHRADER
SCREENPLAY
'79 OLD BOYFRIENDS*

PAUL SCHRADER

DIRECTOR
'79 AMERICAN GIGOLO
'79 HARDCORE
'82 CAT PEOPLE
SCREENPLAY
'79 AMERICAN GIGOLO
'79 HARDCORE
'79 OLD BOYFRIENDS*
'80 RAGING BULL*
EXECUTIVE PRODUCER
'79 OLD BOYFRIENDS

SHELDON SCHRAGER

EXECUTIVE PRODUCER
'79 PROMISES IN THE DARK
UNIT PROD. MANAGER
'79 PROMISES IN THE DARK

CHARLES SCHRAM

MAKEUP
'79 BEING THERE*
'80 FIRST FAMILY
'81 CHARLIE CHAN AND THE CURSE OF THE DRAGON QUEEN*
'81 MOMMIE DEAREST*
'82 GREASE 2

AMY SCHREIBER

CASTING
'80 HANGAR 18

MYRL SCHREIBMAN

PRODUCER
'83 ANGEL OF H.E.A.T.*
DIRECTOR
'83 ANGEL OF H.E.A.T.
PRODUCTION DESIGNER
'83 ANGEL OF H.E.A.T.

ELAINE SCHREYECK

SCRIPT SUPERVISOR
'79 MOONRAKER
'80 HOPSCOTCH
'80 MIRROR CRACK'D, THE
'81 SUPERMAN II*
'81 FOR YOUR EYES ONLY
'82 EVIL UNDER THE SUN
'83 CURSE OF THE PINK PANTHER
'83 OCTOPUSSY
'83 TRAIL OF THE PINK PANTHER

EARL SCHRIVER

MISCELLANEOUS
'81 KNIGHTRIDERS

RICHARD SCHRODER

2ND ASST. DIRECTOR
'82 BLADERUNNER*

MICHAEL SCHROEDER

1ST ASST. DIRECTOR
'83 REVENGE OF THE NINJA*

SABINE SCHROTH

CASTING
'84 MOSCOW ON THE HUDSON*

SANDRA SCHULBERG

ASSOCIATE PRODUCER
'79 ALAMBRISTA!*

BLANCHE SCHULER

MAKEUP
'82 PARADISE

FRED SCHULER

CINEMATOGRAPHER
'80 STIR CRAZY
'80 GLORIA
'81 ARTHUR
'82 SOUP FOR ONE
'82 LOVE AND MONEY
'83 AMITYVILLE 3D
'83 EASY MONEY
'83 KING OF COMEDY, THE
'84 WOMAN IN RED, THE

ARNOLD SCHULKES

2ND ASST. DIRECTOR
'79 SHOUT, THE

ARNOLD SCHULMAN

SCREENPLAY
'79 PLAYERS

CHARLES SCHULTHIES

SPECIAL EFFECTS
'81 WHOSE LIFE IS IT ANYWAY?
'82 DINER
'82 MY FAVORITE YEAR

CHARLES SCHULTHIES JR.

SPECIAL EFFECTS
'84 TEACHERS

ALAN SCHULTZ

ASSISTANT EDITOR
'81 HELL NIGHT*
'82 SEDUCTION, THE*

BARBARA SCHULTZ

EXECUTIVE PRODUCER
'79 ALAMBRISTA!

CHARLES SCHULTZ

EXECUTIVE PRODUCER
'84 SOLDIER'S STORY, A

DENNIS SCHULTZ

MISCELLANEOUS
'83 SPACEHUNTER: ADVENTURES IN THE FORBIDDEN ZONE

GAYLIN SCHULTZ

KEY GRIP
'79 ...AND JUSTICE FOR ALL
'79 JERK, THE
'80 FINAL COUNTDOWN, THE
'80 XANADU
'81 CHU CHU AND THE PHILLY FLASH
'81 FOUR SEASONS, THE
'82 PARTNERS
'82 ZOOT SUIT
'83 MR. MOM
'83 NATIONAL LAMPOON'S VACATION
'84 CLOAK AND DAGGER
'84 LONELY GUY, THE*

JAY SCHULTZ

EXECUTIVE PRODUCER
'82 PENITENTIARY II*

LUCIA SCHULTZ

PROD. COORDINATOR
'80 HUMANOIDS FROM THE DEEP

MICHAEL SCHULTZ

DIRECTOR
'79 SCAVENGER HUNT
'81 CARBON COPY

WIELAND SCHULZ-KEIL

PRODUCER
'84 UNDER THE VOLCANO*

ANNE SCHUMACHER

MISCELLANEOUS
'84 WEEKEND PASS

ISABELLE SCHUMACHER

HAIR
'84 JUST THE WAY YOU ARE*

JOEL SCHUMACHER

DIRECTOR
'81 INCREDIBLE SHRINKING WOMAN, THE
'83 D.C. CAB
SCREENPLAY
'83 D.C. CAB

MARTHA SCHUMACHER

ASSOCIATE PRODUCER
'84 FIRESTARTER

ROGER SCHUMACHER

MISCELLANEOUS
'83 TWO OF A KIND
'84 ALL OF ME

FRAN SCHUSTER

EXECUTIVE PRODUCER
'82 ZAPPED!*

HOWARD SCHUSTER

EXECUTIVE PRODUCER
'82 ZAPPED!*

MARTIN SCHUTE
CO-PRODUCER
'84 SCANDALOUS

ERIC SCHWAB
LOCATIONS
'84 BODY DOUBLE*

AL SCHWARTZ
SCREENPLAY
'82 LOOKIN' TO GET OUT*

ALBERT SCHWARTZ
PRODUCER
'83 BIG SCORE, THE*
EXECUTIVE PRODUCER
'83 I AM THE CHEESE*
'84 BOSTONIANS, THE*

ANDREW SCHWARTZ
STILLS
'81 CAVEMAN

BERNARD SCHWARTZ
PRODUCER
'80 COAL MINER'S DAUGHTER
EXECUTIVE PRODUCER
'81 ROAD GAMES
'83 PSYCHO II

DAVID SCHWARTZ
LOCATIONS
'83 TRADING PLACES

DEBBIE SCHWARTZ
ASSISTANT EDITOR
'82 BRAINWAVES*

GIL SCHWARTZ
KEY GRIP
'79 PRIZE FIGHTER, THE
'80 PRIVATE EYES, THE

HAL SCHWARTZ
ASSOCIATE PRODUCER
'81 GRADUATION DAY
1ST ASST. DIRECTOR
'81 GRADUATION DAY

HOWARD SCHWARTZ
CINEMATOGRAPHER
'81 DEVIL AND MAX DEVLIN, THE

IRVING SCHWARTZ
ASSOCIATE PRODUCER
'83 BIG SCORE, THE

JANE SCHWARTZ
ASSISTANT EDITOR
'82 HOME WORK*

MARTIN SCHWARTZ
MUSIC SUPERVISOR
'84 REVENGE OF THE NERDS

MARTY SCHWARTZ
2ND ASST. DIRECTOR
'82 MEGAFORCE*
LOCATIONS
'81 FORCE FIVE

MURRAY SCHWARTZ
UNIT PROD. MANAGER
'81 PENNIES FROM HEAVEN
'83 FOOTLOOSE

NORMAN SCHWARTZ
MISCELLANEOUS
'79 HURRICANE

ROBERT SCHWARTZ
KEY GRIP
'79 MR. MIKE'S MONDO VIDEO

RUSSEL SCHWARTZ
ASSOCIATE PRODUCER
'81 THEY ALL LAUGHED

STEPHEN SCHWARTZ
MUSIC
'83 ECHOES

TERI SCHWARTZ
UNIT PROD. MANAGER
'84 CRACKERS

TOM SCHWARTZ
MISCELLANEOUS
'81 SCANNERS
'81 HELL NIGHT

LOU SCHWARTZBERG
MISCELLANEOUS
'80 ALTERED STATES

JACK SCHWARTZMAN
PRODUCER
'83 NEVER SAY NEVER AGAIN
EXECUTIVE PRODUCER
'79 BEING THERE
'83 I AM THE CHEESE*

RONALD SCHWARY
PRODUCER
'80 ORDINARY PEOPLE
'83 LET'S SPEND THE NIGHT TOGETHER
'84 SOLDIER'S STORY, A*
EXECUTIVE PRODUCER
'81 ABSENCE OF MALICE
ASSOCIATE PRODUCER
'79 ELECTRIC HORSEMAN, THE
PRODUCTION MANAGER
'79 ELECTRIC HORSEMAN, THE
'81 ABSENCE OF MALICE
UNIT PROD. MANAGER
'80 ORDINARY PEOPLE
MISCELLANEOUS
'80 CLOSE ENCOUNTERS OF THE THIRD KIND SPECIAL EDITION

ILSE SCHWARZWALD
PROD. COORDINATOR
'84 LITTLE DRUMMER GIRL, THE
PROD. SECRETARY
'84 NEVERENDING STORY, THE*

ANNE SCHWEBEL
PUBLICIST
'82 ONE FROM THE HEART

ALBERT SCHWINGES
PRODUCTION MANAGER
'80 LADY VANISHES, THE*

TOM SCHWOEGLER
MISCELLANEOUS
'79 BREAKING AWAY

BOB SCIPO
MISCELLANEOUS
'80 FLASH GORDON

LASZLO SCLVALSK
STILLS
'79 BLACK STALLION, THE

PETE SCOPPA
1ST ASST. DIRECTOR
'79 WINTER KILLS

MARTIN SCORSESE
DIRECTOR
'80 RAGING BULL
'83 KING OF COMEDY, THE

ALLAN SCOTT
SCREENPLAY
'80 AWAKENING, THE*

BILL SCOTT
ASSOCIATE PRODUCER
'84 HOTEL NEW HAMPSHIRE, THE*
1ST ASST. DIRECTOR
'80 HEARTBEAT
'82 TOY, THE
'84 HOTEL NEW HAMPSHIRE, THE

BRAD SCOTT
KEY GRIP
'83 GOIN' ALL THE WAY

CAROL SCOTT
MISCELLANEOUS
'80 CARNY

DAVID SCOTT
PROPS
'82 CHILLY SCENES OF WINTER

DEBORAH SCOTT
COSTUMES
'82 E.T. THE EXTRA-TERRESTRIAL

DUNCAN SCOTT
2ND ASST. DIRECTOR
'83 ZELIG*

ELLIOT SCOTT
PRODUCTION DESIGNER
'79 ARABIAN ADVENTURE
'79 FIFTH MUSKETEER, THE
'80 WATCHER IN THE WOODS, THE
'81 DRAGONSLAYER
'82 EVIL UNDER THE SUN
'83 PIRATES OF PENZANCE, THE
'84 INDIANA JONES AND THE TEMPLE OF DOOM

GARY SCOTT
MUSIC
'83 DEADLY FORCE

GORDON SCOTT
EXEC IN CHARGE PROD
'79 HANOVER STREET

J.C. SCOTT
ASSOCIATE PRODUCER
'82 SENDER, THE*

JAN SCOTT
ART DIRECTOR
'80 LOVING COUPLES
PRODUCTION DESIGNER
'81 RICH AND FAMOUS
'84 GRANDVIEW, U.S.A.

JANE SCOTT
ASSOCIATE PRODUCER
'79 MY BRILLIANT CAREER
MISCELLANEOUS
'79 MY BRILLIANT CAREER

JILL SCOTT
ART DIRECTOR
'80 MIDDLE AGE CRAZY
'81 TICKET TO HEAVEN

JOHN SCOTT
MUSIC
'79 NORTH DALLAS FORTY
'80 FINAL COUNTDOWN, THE
'83 YOR
'84 GREYSTOKE: THE LEGEND OF TARZAN, LORD OF THE APES
MISCELLANEOUS
'81 DEATH HUNT
'83 DEAD ZONE, THE

MARTHA SCOTT
PRODUCER
'81 FIRST MONDAY IN OCTOBER*

MARY SCOTT
ASSISTANT EDITOR
'79 NIGHTWING
'79 AMERICATHON
'80 WHY WOULD I LIE?
'81 LOOKER
'83 ROMANTIC COMEDY

MICKEY SCOTT
MAKEUP
'81 THEY ALL LAUGHED*
'83 BIG CHILL, THE*
'84 FALLING IN LOVE*
'84 FLAMINGO KID, THE*

NICOLE SCOTT
1ST ASST. DIRECTOR
'81 SATURDAY THE 14TH
PROD. COORDINATOR
'81 SATURDAY THE 14TH
MISCELLANEOUS
'83 METALSTORM: THE DESTRUCTION OF JARED-SYN

OZ SCOTT
DIRECTOR
'81 BUSTIN' LOOSE

PETER SCOTT
1ST ASST. DIRECTOR
'84 CHEECH AND CHONG'S THE CORSICAN BROTHERS*

RIDLEY SCOTT
DIRECTOR
'79 ALIEN
'82 BLADERUNNER

TOM SCOTT
MUSIC
'80 STIR CRAZY
'82 HANKY PANKY
'84 HARD TO HOLD*

TONY SCOTT
DIRECTOR
'83 HUNGER, THE

WALTER SCOTT
2ND UNIT DIRECTOR
'80 HIDE IN PLAIN SIGHT
STUNT COORDINATOR
'81 ON GOLDEN POND
'81 THIEF
'82 CAT PEOPLE
'82 YOUNG DOCTORS IN LOVE
'84 THIEF OF HEARTS

WILLIAM SCOTT
1ST ASST. DIRECTOR
'80 CARNY
'81 POSTMAN ALWAYS RINGS TWICE, THE
'82 FRANCES*
'84 WINDY CITY
2ND ASST. DIRECTOR
'79 WINTER KILLS

JAMES SCRIBNER
MAKEUP
'83 SOMETHING WICKED THIS WAY COMES*
'83 NIGHTMARES

JOE SCULLY
CASTING
'79 MAN, A WOMAN AND A BANK, A*
'80 MIDDLE AGE CRAZY
'82 DEATHWISH II*
MISCELLANEOUS
'82 DEATH VALLEY

MARIO SCUTTI
MAKEUP
'83 YOR
'84 DUNE*

ANDREW SCHWARTZ
STILLS
'83 EXPOSED*

STEVE SEAGAL
MISCELLANEOUS
'82 CHALLENGE, THE

MALCOLM SEAGRAVE
MUSIC
'79 PHANTASM*

ADELINE LEONARD SEAKWOOD
PROD. OFFICE COORD.
'79 STARTING OVER
'82 ANNIE*
'83 LOVESICK
'83 TRADING PLACES
PROD. COORDINATOR
'81 WOLFEN

JOHN SEAKWOOD
STILLS
'84 BEAT STREET*

DAVID SEAL

KEY GRIP
'81 GRADUATION DAY

GARY SEAL

ASSISTANT EDITOR
'84 LAST NIGHT AT THE ALAMO

JOHN SEALE

MISCELLANEOUS
'83 YEAR OF LIVING DANGEROUSLY, THE

PETER SEAMAN

SCREENPLAY
'83 TRENCHCOAT*

CLIFFORD SEARCY

MISCELLANEOUS
'84 DREAMSCAPE

B.J. SEARS

ASSISTANT EDITOR
'81 STUDENT BODIES

ERIC SEARS

ASSISTANT EDITOR
'79 CHAMP, THE*
'80 JAZZ SINGER, THE*

JONATHAN SEAY

MISCELLANEOUS
'81 FEAR NO EVIL
'84 ICE PIRATES, THE
'84 ICE PIRATES, THE
'84 PHILADELPHIA EXPERIMENT, THE

LOREY SEBASTIAN

STILLS
'79 BOARDWALK
'81 SO FINE
'81 NEIGHBORS*
'82 AUTHOR, AUTHOR
'83 DANIEL
'83 KING OF COMEDY, THE
'83 LOVESICK
'84 FALLING IN LOVE
'84 ICEMAN*

KIM SECRIST

EDITOR
'83 TIMERIDER*
'84 THIS IS SPINAL TAP*
ASSISTANT EDITOR
'83 MAUSOLEUM*

LARRY SECRIST

STILLS
'84 FRIDAY THE 13TH PART IV THE FINAL CHAPTER
MISCELLANEOUS
'83 MAN WHO WASN'T THERE, THE

WOLF SEEBERG

SOUND
'84 HOT DOG...THE MOVIE

JOSEPH SEFEL

EXECUTIVE PRODUCER
'80 KIDNAPPING OF THE PRESIDENT, THE

ERICH SEGAL

SCREENPLAY
'80 CHANGE OF SEASONS, A*
'83 MAN WOMAN AND CHILD*

FRED SEGAL

SCREENPLAY
'80 CHANGE OF SEASONS, A*

JERRY SEGAL

SCREENPLAY
'80 DIE LAUGHING*
MUSIC
'80 DIE LAUGHING*

MARION SEGAL

EDITOR
'81 CARBON COPY
ASSOCIATE EDITOR
'80 LAST MARRIED COUPLE IN AMERICA, THE

YOSSI SEGAL

1ST ASST. DIRECTOR
'83 SMITHEREENS*

THOMAS SEID

ASSISTANT EDITOR
'80 FIRST DEADLY SIN*

TAKASHI SEIDA

STILLS
'82 QUEST FOR FIRE
'83 SPACEHUNTER: ADVENTURES IN THE FORBIDDEN ZONE
'84 FINDERS KEEPERS

ARTHUR SEIDELMAN

DIRECTOR
'83 ECHOES

JAMES SEIDELMAN

ASSISTANT EDITOR
'79 BUDDY HOLLY STORY, THE
'80 COMPETITION, THE*
'80 IN GOD WE TRUST
'83 D.C. CAB
'84 GHOSTBUSTERS*

SUSAN SEIDELMAN

PRODUCER
'83 SMITHEREENS
DIRECTOR
'83 SMITHEREENS
EDITOR
'83 SMITHEREENS

ROBERT SEIDMAN

MISCELLANEOUS
'84 ALPHABET CITY

TOM SEIDMAN

2ND ASST. DIRECTOR
'81 RICH AND FAMOUS*
'81 REDS*
'82 HONKYTONK MAN
'82 NATIONAL LAMPOON'S CLASS REUNION*
'83 WRONG IS RIGHT*

JANE SEIGEL

2ND ASST. DIRECTOR
'83 RISKY BUSINESS*

CHRISTOPHER SEITER

PRODUCTION MANAGER
'80 BORDERLINE
UNIT PROD. MANAGER
'79 BLACK HOLE, THE
'79 NORTH AVENUE IRREGULARS, THE
1ST ASST. DIRECTOR
'79 NORTH AVENUE IRREGULARS, THE

LEON SEITH

EDITOR
'80 FOR THE LOVE OF BENJI

BERNARD SEITZ

1ST ASST. DIRECTOR
'84 AMERICAN DREAMER*

JANE SEITZ

EDITOR
'84 NEVERENDING STORY, THE

JACK SEKELY

EDITOR
'80 MIDNIGHT MADNESS*

DIANE SELETOS

MISCELLANEOUS
'83 MORTUARY

TIMUCIN SELGUR

EXEC IN CHARGE PROD
'83 YOR

ARNAUD SELIGNAC

STILLS
'81 EXCALIBUR

STEVE SELIY

LOCATIONS
'84 MRS. SOFFEL*

ARLENE SELLERS
PRODUCER
'79 CUBA*
'83 BLUE SKIES AGAIN*
'84 IRRECONCILABLE DIFFERENCES*
'84 SCANDALOUS*
EXECUTIVE PRODUCER
'80 LADY VANISHES, THE*
'84 SWING SHIFT*

ARTHUR SELLERS
SCREENPLAY
'81 MODERN PROBLEMS*

KEVIN SELLERS
SCREENPLAY
'83 BLUE SKIES AGAIN

BILL SELLIER
STILLS
'84 SILENT NIGHT, DEADLY NIGHT

CHARLES SELLIER JR.
PRODUCER
'80 HANGAR 18
'82 BOOGENS, THE
DIRECTOR
'84 SILENT NIGHT, DEADLY NIGHT

BRENT SELLSTROM
MISCELLANEOUS
'81 LOOKER

DAVID SELTZER
SCREENPLAY
'79 PROPHECY
'82 SIX WEEKS
'83 TABLE FOR FIVE

ISADOR SELTZER
MISCELLANEOUS
'81 TATTOO

MARY SELWAY
CASTING
'79 SHOUT, THE*
'79 AGATHA
'79 ALIEN*
'79 DRACULA
'79 HANOVER STREET
'79 GREAT TRAIN ROBBERY, THE
'80 AWAKENING, THE
'80 FLASH GORDON*
'80 TESS
'81 RAIDERS OF THE LOST ARK*
'81 EXCALIBUR
'81 OUTLAND
'82 SENDER, THE*
'82 FIREFOX*
'82 FIVE DAYS ONE SUMMER*
'82 VICTOR/VICTORIA
'83 BEYOND THE LIMIT*
'83 CURSE OF THE PINK PANTHER
'83 GORKY PARK*
'83 RETURN OF THE JEDI
'83 TRAIL OF THE PINK PANTHER*
'84 INDIANA JONES
AND THE TEMPLE OF DOOM*
'84 TOP SECRET!*

JULIE SELZER
CASTING
'84 MAKING THE GRADE*

JOYCE SELZNICK
CASTING
'79 BUDDY HOLLY STORY, THE

GEORGE HERBERT SEMEL MD
MISCELLANEOUS
'79 PROMISE, THE

STEPHEN SEMEL
ASSOCIATE EDITOR
'80 GALAXINA
ASSISTANT EDITOR
'82 ESCAPE ARTIST, THE
'83 BUDDY SYSTEM, THE

JULIAN SEMILIAN
EDITOR
'82 DEATHWISH II*
ASSISTANT EDITOR
'80 MOTEL HELL

MAILE SEMITOKOL
LOCATIONS
'81 RAIDERS OF THE LOST ARK*

DEAN SEMLER
CINEMATOGRAPHER
'82 ROAD WARRIOR, THE
MISCELLANEOUS
'81 EARTHLING, THE

DIEGO GOMEZ SEMPERE
PRODUCTION MANAGER
'79 CUBA*

LORENZO SEMPLE JR.
SCREENPLAY
'79 HURRICANE
'80 FLASH GORDON
'83 NEVER SAY NEVER AGAIN
'84 SHEENA*
EXECUTIVE PRODUCER
'79 HURRICANE

SCOTT SENECHAL
SOUND
'84 COUNTRY*

ANNA SENIOR
COSTUMES
'79 MY BRILLIANT CAREER
'84 PHAR LAP

LORRAINE SENNA
2ND ASST. DIRECTOR
'80 SOMEWHERE IN TIME
'80 DEFIANCE*

JACK SENTER
ART DIRECTOR
'83 MAN WHO LOVED WOMEN, THE
'84 MICKI AND MAUDE
PRODUCTION DESIGNER
'81 MODERN PROBLEMS

LEILA SEPPANEN
HAIR
'80 NOTHING PERSONAL

RANDY SER
ART DIRECTOR
'83 MORTUARY
PROPS
'84 WEEKEND PASS

ERIC SERENA
HAIR
'81 LOOKER*

TIIU SERENANDER
STILLS
'81 MONTENEGRO

EVA SERENY
STILLS
'82 FIVE DAYS ONE SUMMER*

MICHAEL SERESIN
ASSOCIATE PRODUCER
'80 FOXES*
CINEMATOGRAPHER
'80 FAME
'82 SHOOT THE MOON
'84 BIRDY

LINDA SERIJAN
COSTUME SUPERVISOR
'80 SMALL CIRCLE OF FRIENDS, A

PAUL SERMONS
2ND ASST. DIRECTOR
'84 TANK*

PINO SERPE
MISCELLANEOUS
'79 MAGICIAN OF LUBLIN, THE

BEVERLY SETLOWE
PROD. COORDINATOR
'81 MODERN PROBLEMS
'83 ROMANTIC COMEDY

JEROME SEVEN
MISCELLANEOUS
'81 FEAR NO EVIL

JOHN SEXTON
PRODUCER
'84 PHAR LAP

TIM SEXTON
MUSIC SUPERVISOR
'84 BACHELOR PARTY*

GARY SEYBERT
PROPS
'80 HEARTBEAT
'81 FOUR SEASONS, THE
'82 LOVE AND MONEY

MONIQUE SEYLER
PROD. COORDINATOR
'83 LIANNA*

JULIAN SEYMOUR
EXECUTIVE PRODUCER
'84 ANOTHER COUNTRY*

MICHAEL SEYMOUR
PRODUCTION DESIGNER
'79 ALIEN
MISCELLANEOUS
'81 GHOST STORY

DAVID SHABER

SCREENPLAY
'79 LAST EMBRACE
'79 WARRIORS, THE*
'80 THOSE LIPS, THOSE EYES
'81 ROLLOVER
'81 NIGHTHAWKS

ELIZABETH SHAFER

SCRIPT SUPERVISOR
'80 RETURN OF THE SECAUCUS SEVEN, THE

MARTIN SHAFER

PRODUCER
'80 MOUNTAIN MEN, THE*
'81 MODERN ROMANCE*
CO-PRODUCER
'80 AWAKENING, THE*

ANTHONY SHAFFER

SCREENPLAY
'82 EVIL UNDER THE SUN

PAUL SHAFFER

SCREENPLAY
'80 GILDA LIVE*
MUSIC SUPERVISOR
'79 MR. MIKE'S MONDO VIDEO

PETER SHAFFER

SCREENPLAY
'84 AMADEUS

RITA SHAFFER

MISCELLANEOUS
'79 QUINTET

MOHAMED SHAFI

PRODUCTION MANAGER
'81 SEA WOLVES, THE*

STEVE SHAGAN

PRODUCER
'80 FORMULA, THE
SCREENPLAY
'79 NIGHTWING*
'80 FORMULA, THE

RICK SHAINE

EDITOR
'80 EYES OF A STRANGER
'83 EASY MONEY*
'84 NIGHTMARE ON ELM STREET, A

MICHAEL SHAMBERG

PRODUCER
'80 HEARTBEAT*
'81 MODERN PROBLEMS*
'83 BIG CHILL, THE

JACK SHAMPAN

ART DIRECTOR
'83 YELLOWBEARD

ELLEN ROME SHANAHAN

COSTUMES
'84 WEEKEND PASS

JOHN HERMAN SHANER

PRODUCER
'80 LAST MARRIED COUPLE IN AMERICA, THE*
SCREENPLAY
'80 LAST MARRIED COUPLE IN AMERICA, THE

JEFF SHANK

ASSISTANT EDITOR
'80 BATTLE BEYOND THE STARS*

RAVI SHANKAR

MUSIC
'82 GANDHI

MARK SHANKER

PRODUCER
'80 FIRST DEADLY SIN*

LINDA SHANKLIN

SCRIPT SUPERVISOR
'80 MOTEL HELL

SUSAN SHANKS

ASSISTANT EDITOR
'80 TERROR TRAIN

JOHN SHANNON

STILLS
'79 AMERICAN GIGOLO
'79 FRISCO KID, THE
'79 MUPPET MOVIE, THE*
'79 WINTER KILLS
'80 ANY WHICH WAY YOU CAN
'80 BRONCO BILLY
'80 PRIVATE BENJAMIN
'81 PURSUIT OF D.B. COOPER, THE*
'82 BEST FRIENDS
'82 CAT PEOPLE
'82 FIREFOX
'83 STROKER ACE
'83 FLASHDANCE
'83 MAN WOMAN AND CHILD*
'84 PROTOCOL
'84 STAR TREK III: THE SEARCH FOR SPOCK
'84 SWING SHIFT
'84 RED DAWN

ALAN SHAPIRO

MISCELLANEOUS
'83 HOUSE ON SORORITY ROW

ALBERT SHAPIRO

1ST ASST. DIRECTOR
'81 GOING APE!
'82 FAST TIMES AT RIDGEMONT HIGH
'83 FLASHDANCE
'83 TERMS OF ENDEARMENT
'84 ALL OF ME
'84 MIKE'S MURDER
2ND ASST. DIRECTOR
'79 C.H.O.M.P.S.
'79 PROMISES IN THE DARK
'80 URBAN COWBOY

BARBARA SHAPIRO

CASTING
'83 LIANNA
'84 BROTHER FROM ANOTHER PLANET, THE

BOBBY SHAPIRO

EDITOR
'84 WHERE THE BOYS ARE*
ASSISTANT EDITOR
'84 NO SMALL AFFAIR*

GEORGE SHAPIRO

PRODUCER
'80 IN GOD WE TRUST*

HARVEY SHAPIRO

LOCATIONS
'83 NIGHT IN HEAVEN, A

JERRY SHAPIRO

1ST ASST. DIRECTOR
'82 I, THE JURY

KEN SHAPIRO

DIRECTOR
'81 MODERN PROBLEMS
SCREENPLAY
'81 MODERN PROBLEMS*

LINDA SHAPIRO

PUBLICIST
'79 SILENT PARTNER, THE

MELVIN SHAPIRO

EDITOR
'79 ICE CASTLES*
'84 NO SMALL AFFAIR*
'84 WHERE THE BOYS ARE*

MELVIN SHAPIRO

ASSOCIATE PRODUCER
'81 STUDENT BODIES

STANLEY SHAPIRO

PRODUCER
'81 CARBON COPY*

IRENE SHARAFF
COSTUMES
'81 MOMMIE DEAREST

BECKY SHARGO
MUSIC SUPERVISOR
'83 FOOTLOOSE
'83 MAN WHO WASN'T THERE, THE

HAIM SHARIR
UNIT PROD. MANAGER
'84 BEST DEFENSE*

BRUCE SHARMAN
ASSOCIATE PRODUCER
'81 GREAT MUPPET CAPER, THE
'82 DARK CRYSTAL, THE
MISCELLANEOUS
'80 EMPIRE STRIKES BACK, THE

JIM SHARMAN
DIRECTOR
'81 SHOCK TREATMENT
SCREENPLAY
'81 SHOCK TREATMENT*

STEPHEN SHARMAT
EXECUTIVE PRODUCER
'81 EARTHLING, THE

ALAN SHARP
SCREENPLAY
'83 OSTERMAN WEEKEND, THE

ARCHIE SHARP
ART DIRECTOR
'79 DREAMER

IAN SHARP
DIRECTOR
'83 FINAL OPTION, THE

LINDA SHARP
HAIR
'83 LONE WOLF MCQUADE

PAMELA SHARP
ASSISTANT EDITOR
'79 DREAMER*
'80 BRUBAKER*
'83 TWO OF A KIND*

RICK SHARP
MAKEUP
'79 CONCORDE-AIRPORT '79, THE*
'80 SMOKEY AND THE BANDIT II*
'80 LITTLE MISS MARKER*
'80 XANADU*
'81 S.O.B.*
'81 FIRST MONDAY IN OCTOBER*
'81 GHOST STORY*
'82 SHOOT THE MOON*
'82 THINGS ARE TOUGH ALL OVER
'83 FLASHDANCE
'83 GET CRAZY*
'83 KISS ME GOODBYE
'83 MAN WHO LOVED WOMEN, THE*
'84 MICKI AND MAUDE*
'84 IMPULSE

DON SHARPLESS
SOUND
'79 GOLDENGIRL
'80 LAST MARRIED COUPLE IN AMERICA, THE
'80 OH GOD! BOOK II
'81 S.O.B.
'81 BUDDY, BUDDY
'82 FORCED VENGEANCE
'83 MAN WHO LOVED WOMEN, THE

IVAN SHARROCK
SOUND
'80 FLASH GORDON
'81 AMERICAN WEREWOLF IN LONDON, AN
'81 DOGS OF WAR, THE
'83 KRULL
'84 GREYSTOKE: THE LEGEND OF TARZAN, LORD OF THE APES

KEITH SHARTLE
PROD. COORDINATOR
'83 DEAL OF THE CENTURY

JERRY SHATZBERG
DIRECTOR
'79 SEDUCTION OF JOE TYNAN, THE
'80 HONEYSUCKLE ROSE

ANNE SHAW
PROD. COORDINATOR
'79 MAIN EVENT, THE
'81 VICTORY*
'84 UNDER THE VOLCANO*

DEBORAH SHAW
MISCELLANEOUS
'80 RETURN OF THE SECAUCUS SEVEN, THE

DENNIS SHAW
2ND ASST. DIRECTOR
'84 UNDER THE VOLCANO

FRANK SHAW
SCREENPLAY
'79 FRISCO KID, THE*

IAN SHAW
MUSIC
'84 PREPPIES

JEAN EVENSEN SHAW
MISCELLANEOUS
'80 COMPETITION, THE
'80 COMPETITION, THE

TOM SHAW JR.
PROPS
'81 VICTORY
'82 HAMMETT*
'82 ONE FROM THE HEART

KAREN SHAW
PROD. SECRETARY
'84 GREMLINS

LARRY SHAW
STILLS
'84 LOVE STREAMS*

LINDY SHAW
MAKEUP
'83 PRIVATES ON PARADE*

MARK SHAW
ASSISTANT EDITOR
'81 SO FINE

PAULA SHAW
LOCATIONS
'84 CITY HEAT

PENELOPE SHAW
ASSISTANT EDITOR
'80 HEAVEN'S GATE*
'84 DUNE

PETER SHAW
PRODUCER
'83 ENIGMA
'84 CHAMPIONS

PHILIP SHAW
EDITOR
'81 SUNDAY LOVERS*

RODGER SHAW
MISCELLANEOUS
'84 GREYSTOKE: THE LEGEND OF TARZAN, LORD OF THE APES

ROSE TOBIAS SHAW
CASTING
'80 AMERICAN SUCCESS COMPANY,THE*
'80 NIJINSKY
'80 OH! HEAVENLY DOG*
'80 HUMAN FACTOR, THE
'81 SEA WOLVES, THE
'81 VICTORY
'83 HIGH ROAD TO CHINA
'83 LONELY LADY, THE*
'84 LASSITER

SAM SHAW
EXECUTIVE PRODUCER
'80 GLORIA
MISCELLANEOUS
'84 LOVE STREAMS

SANDY SHAW
MISCELLANEOUS
'82 FIREFOX

SHIRLEY SHAW
ASSISTANT EDITOR
'80 AWAKENING, THE*

SUSAN SHAW
CASTING
'81 CUTTER'S WAY
'82 HALLOWEEN III: SEASON OF THE WITCH

TOM SHAW
ASSOCIATE PRODUCER
'80 TWINKLE TWINKLE "KILLER" KANE
UNIT PROD. MANAGER
'79 MAIN EVENT, THE*
'81 VICTORY
UNIT MANAGER
'81 TARZAN, THE APE MAN
1ST ASST. DIRECTOR
'80 TWINKLE TWINKLE "KILLER" KANE
PROPS
'80 WHERE THE BUFFALO ROAM
'83 GET CRAZY
MISCELLANEOUS
'84 UNDER THE VOLCANO

ALLEN SHAWN
MUSIC
'81 MY DINNER WITH ANDRE

WALLACE SHAWN
SCREENPLAY
'81 MY DINNER WITH ANDRE*

CHERYL SHAWVER
MISCELLANEOUS
'83 CROSS CREEK

ROBERT SHAYE
PRODUCER
'84 NIGHTMARE ON ELM STREET, A
EXECUTIVE PRODUCER
'81 POLYESTER
'82 FIRST TIME, THE*

LINDA SHAYNE
SCREENPLAY
'83 SCREWBALLS*
EXECUTIVE PRODUCER
'83 SCREWBALLS*

KATHY SHEA
ASSOCIATE PRODUCER
'83 STROKER ACE

HARRY SHEARER
SCREENPLAY
'79 REAL LIFE*
'84 THIS IS SPINAL TAP*
MUSIC
'84 THIS IS SPINAL TAP*

JACQUELINE SHEARER
1ST ASST. DIRECTOR
'81 DOZENS, THE

ROGER SHEARMAN
CINEMATOGRAPHER
'79 FORCE OF ONE, A
'80 STEEL
'81 EYE FOR AN EYE, AN
'83 LONE WOLF MCQUADE
MISCELLANEOUS
'79 JUST YOU AND ME KID
'82 I OUGHT TO BE IN PICTURES
'84 COUNTRY
'84 UP THE CREEK

RONALD SHEDLO
PRODUCER
'81 BACK ROADS

ANNABELLE SHEEHAN
ASSISTANT EDITOR
'82 ROAD WARRIOR, THE*

LINDA SHEEHY
PROD. COORDINATOR
'83 SPACEHUNTER: ADVENTURES IN THE FORBIDDEN ZONE*

ROBERT SHEERER
DIRECTOR
'80 HOW TO BEAT THE HIGH COST OF LIVING

ANDREW SHEINMAN
PRODUCER
'81 MODERN ROMANCE*

RIKI SHELACH
1ST ASST. DIRECTOR
'79 MAGICIAN OF LUBLIN, THE

DON SHELDON
HAIR
'79 BEYOND THE POSEIDON ADVENTURE*

TED SHELL
PRODUCTION DESIGNER
'79 C.H.O.M.P.S.

BOB SHELLEY
SPECIAL EFFECTS
'79 PRIZE FIGHTER, THE*
'81 NIGHT THE LIGHTS WENT OUT IN GEORGIA, THE
'83 BAD BOYS
'83 BIG SCORE, THE*

BOB SHELLEY JR.
SPECIAL EFFECTS
'83 BIG SCORE, THE*
'84 MAKING THE GRADE

WOODY SHELP
MISCELLANEOUS
'82 EVIL UNDER THE SUN

RON SHELTON
SCREENPLAY
'83 UNDER FIRE*
ASSOCIATE PRODUCER
'81 PURSUIT OF D.B. COOPER, THE
2ND UNIT DIRECTOR
'83 UNDER FIRE

VINCENT "BUD" SHELTON
PROPS
'80 JAZZ SINGER, THE
'80 MOUNTAIN MEN, THE

AHARON SHEMI
2ND UNIT DIRECTOR
'82 PARADISE

WALTER SHENSON
PRODUCER
'83 REUBEN, REUBEN

ALBERT SHEPARD
ASSOCIATE PRODUCER
'82 PENITENTIARY II*
CO-PRODUCER
'79 PENITENTIARY*

DODIE SHEPARD
COSTUME SUPERVISOR
'81 ON THE RIGHT TRACK

SAM SHEPARD
SCREENPLAY
'84 PARIS, TEXAS

BILL SHEPHARD
CASTING
'84 COUNTRY*
'84 SPLASH*

DYLAN SHEPHARD
KEY GRIP
'79 ROLLER BOOGIE
'80 WITHOUT WARNING
'80 GALAXINA
'80 SCHIZOID
'83 ANGEL OF H.E.A.T.
'83 10 TO MIDNIGHT
'84 TERMINATOR, THE

DAVID SHEPHERD
1ST ASST. DIRECTOR
'82 IF YOU COULD SEE WHAT I HEAR
'83 STRANGE INVADERS*
2ND ASST. DIRECTOR
'79 MEATBALLS

JEAN SHEPHERD
SCREENPLAY
'83 CHRISTMAS STORY, A*

PETER SHEPHERD
EXEC IN CHARGE PROD
'83 PIRANHA II: THE SPAWNING

RICHARD SHEPHERD
PRODUCER
'83 HUNGER, THE

ROBERT SHEPHERD
MISCELLANEOUS
'82 FIREFOX

CAROLE BRODY SHEPPARD
SCRIPT SUPERVISOR
'82 LITTLE SEX, A

WERNER SHERER
HAIR
'81 SO FINE*
'82 AMITYVILLE II: THE POSSESSION
'83 SURVIVORS, THE
'83 CROSS CREEK

MICHAEL SHERIDAN
EDITOR
'79 CHAMP, THE
'81 ENDLESS LOVE

STEVE SHERIDAN
KEY GRIP
'82 IF YOU COULD SEE WHAT I HEAR

DAVID SHERLOCK
MISCELLANEOUS
'83 YELLOWBEARD

JERRY SHERLOCK
PRODUCER
'81 CHARLIE CHAN AND THE CURSE OF THE DRAGON QUEEN

FRANCINE SHERMAINE
HAIR
'80 WHOLLY MOSES!*

AARON SHERMAN
MISCELLANEOUS
'84 ANOTHER COUNTRY

ERIC SHERMAN
MISCELLANEOUS
'80 WHERE THE BUFFALO ROAM
'81 GOING APE!

GARY SHERMAN
DIRECTOR
'81 DEAD AND BURIED
'82 VICE SQUAD

ROBERT SHERMAN
PRODUCER
'84 OH GOD, YOU DEVIL

ROGER SHERMAN
MISCELLANEOUS
'80 WHERE THE BUFFALO ROAM

SHALOM SHERMAN
MISCELLANEOUS
'80 TELL ME A RIDDLE

STANFORD SHERMAN
SCREENPLAY
'80 ANY WHICH WAY YOU CAN
'83 KRULL
'83 MAN WHO WASN'T THERE, THE
'84 ICE PIRATES, THE*

TOM SHEROHMAN
SCREENPLAY
'81 MODERN PROBLEMS*

BETTY SHERRIFF
HAIR
'79 UNIDENTIFIED FLYING ODDBALL*

BILLY SHERRILL
MUSIC
'81 TAKE THIS JOB AND SHOVE IT

JOHN SHERROD
2ND UNIT DIRECTOR
'79 PENITENTIARY
'82 PENITENTIARY II
STUNT COORDINATOR
'79 PENITENTIARY
'82 FRIDAY THE 13TH PART THREE IN 3D
'82 PENITENTIARY II
'83 MAN WHO WASN'T THERE, THE
'83 BIG SCORE, THE
'84 FRIDAY THE 13TH PART IV THE FINAL CHAPTER
'84 MEATBALLS PART II

DAVID SHERWIN
SCREENPLAY
'83 BRITANNIA HOSPITAL

JIM SHERWOOD
MISCELLANEOUS
'80 COAST TO COAST

STEWART SHERWOOD
MISCELLANEOUS
'83 DEAD ZONE, THE

RHONDA SHEVACK
MISCELLANEOUS
'82 LIAR'S MOON

STEVE SHEWCHUCK
PROPS
'79 SILENT PARTNER, THE
'80 TRIBUTE*

PETER SHEWCHUK
SOUND
'82 AMATEUR, THE
'83 STRANGE INVADERS

SALLY SHEWRING
PROD. COORDINATOR
'82 PINK FLOYD: THE WALL

IAN SHIEBEL
PROPS
'83 METALSTORM: THE DESTRUCTION OF JARED-SYN

CATHERINE SHIELDS
ASSISTANT EDITOR
'83 TIMERIDER*

TONY SHIELDS
MISCELLANEOUS
'80 USED CARS
'82 SWORD AND THE SORCERER, THE

JEROME SHIELL
MISCELLANEOUS
'84 IRRECONCILABLE DIFFERENCES

FRANCINE SHIFFER
MAKEUP
'84 SCANDALOUS*

ELAINE SHINDELL
PROD. OFFICE COORD.
'81 PATERNITY

WILFRED SHINGLETON
PRODUCTION DESIGNER
'80 LADY VANISHES, THE
'81 EYE OF THE NEEDLE
'83 HEAT AND DUST

TED SHINNEMAN
KEY GRIP
'79 SCAVENGER HUNT

TRUDY SHIP
ASSISTANT EDITOR
'79 SEDUCTION OF JOE TYNAN, THE
'81 FAN, THE
'84 FALLING IN LOVE*

ARTHUR SHIPPEE
PROPS
'80 FATSO
'83 TABLE FOR FIVE

ARTHUR SHIPPEE JR.
PROPS
'82 LOOKIN' TO GET OUT
'84 WINDY CITY

MASAICHI SHIRAI
2ND ASST. DIRECTOR
'82 CHALLENGE, THE*

TAKASHI SHIRAI
LOCATIONS
'83 MERRY CHRISTMAS, MR. LAWRENCE

DAVID SHIRE
MUSIC
'79 FAST BREAK*
'79 NORMA RAE
'79 PROMISE, THE
'79 OLD BOYFRIENDS
'81 NIGHT THE LIGHTS WENT OUT IN GEORGIA, THE
'81 ONLY WHEN I LAUGH
'81 PATERNITY
'82 WORLD ACCORDING TO GARP, THE
'83 MAX DUGAN RETURNS
'84 2010
'84 OH GOD, YOU DEVIL

JOHN SHIRLEY
EDITOR
'83 NATE & HAYES
'84 KIPPERBANG

MICKEY SHIRRARD
COSTUMES
'79 AVALANCHE EXPRESS

MARK SHIVAS
PRODUCER
'82 MOONLIGHTING*

SHELDON SHKOLNIK
MUSIC
'80 TELL ME A RIDDLE

JOANNE SHOE
SCRIPT SUPERVISOR
'82 CREEPSHOW

STEVEN SHOENBERG
ASSISTANT EDITOR
'82 NATIONAL LAMPOON'S CLASS REUNION*

JACK SHOLDER
EDITOR
'81 BURNING, THE

MICHAL SHOOB
SCREENPLAY
'82 PARASITE*

BRENDA SHOPHER
HAIR
'84 MUTANT

HOWARD SHORE
MUSIC
'79 BROOD, THE
'81 SCANNERS
'83 VIDEODROME

HOWARD SHORE
MISCELLANEOUS
'81 MAN WHO SAW TOMORROW, THE

KATHY SHORKEY
MAKEUP
'83 METALSTORM: THE DESTRUCTION OF JARED-SYN*
'84 ANGEL*

CHRIS SHORT
2ND ASST. DIRECTOR
'83 NATE & HAYES*

ROBERT SHORT
MISCELLANEOUS
'80 ALLIGATOR

SKIP SHORT
PRODUCER
'84 FLASHPOINT

MARTIN SHORTAL
MISCELLANEOUS
'81 OUTLAND

MURRAY SHOSTAK
PRODUCER
'81 DEATH HUNT

MARK SHOSTROM
MISCELLANEOUS
'83 DEADLY FORCE

JAMIE SHOURT
MISCELLANEOUS
'81 HEARTBEEPS

TOM SHOUSE
MISCELLANEOUS
'81 BODY AND SOUL
'81 GALAXY OF TERROR

GAIL SHOWALTER
ASSOCIATE EDITOR
'81 BURNING, THE
ASSISTANT EDITOR
'80 HONEYSUCKLE ROSE*

BUD SHRAKE
SCREENPLAY
'79 NIGHTWING*
'80 TOM HORN*
'84 SONGWRITER

BARBARA SHRIER
PROD. OFFICE COORD.
'81 ATLANTIC CITY
PROD. COORDINATOR
'82 QUEST FOR FIRE

DENNIS SHRYACK
SCREENPLAY
'84 FLASHPOINT*

ROBERT SHUE
2ND ASST. DIRECTOR
'81 ...ALL THE MARBLES*

ROBERT SHUGRUE
EDITOR
'80 RAISE THE TITANIC*
'84 STAR TREK III: THE SEARCH FOR SPOCK

ROBERT SHULENBERG
PRODUCTION DESIGNER
'82 EATING RAOUL
'84 NOT FOR PUBLICATION

BLANCHE SHULER
MAKEUP
'80 BIG RED ONE, THE
HAIR
'80 BIG RED ONE, THE

LAUREN SHULER
PRODUCER
'83 MR. MOM*

JENNIFER SHULL

CASTING
'79 CHAPTER TWO
'79 ELECTRIC HORSEMAN, THE
'79 HOT STUFF
'80 SEEMS LIKE OLD TIMES
'80 SOMEWHERE IN TIME
'80 COMPETITION, THE
'80 HUNTER, THE
'80 TOUCHED BY LOVE
'81 ONLY WHEN I LAUGH
'82 CANNERY ROW
'82 FRANCES
'82 I OUGHT TO BE IN PICTURES
'82 ONE FROM THE HEART
'82 YES, GIORGIO*
'83 NEVER CRY WOLF
'84 RAZOR'S EDGE, THE*
'84 STARMAN

BOB SHULMAN

KEY GRIP
'80 FRIDAY THE 13TH

MARCIA SHULMAN

CASTING
'83 CHRISTMAS STORY, A*

IRA SHUMAN

2ND ASST. DIRECTOR
'81 BACK ROADS

ALICE SHURE

ASSOCIATE PRODUCER
'83 WITHOUT A TRACE
'84 FIRSTBORN

GARY SHUSETT

CO-PRODUCER
'84 FINAL TERROR, THE*

RONALD SHUSETT

PRODUCER
'81 DEAD AND BURIED*
SCREENPLAY
'81 DEAD AND BURIED*
'84 FINAL TERROR, THE*
EXECUTIVE PRODUCER
'79 ALIEN

ROSIE SHUSTER

SCREENPLAY
'80 GILDA LIVE*

MARTIN SHUTE

EXECUTIVE PRODUCER
'81 WHOSE LIFE IS IT ANYWAY?*

CHARLES SHYER

PRODUCER
'80 PRIVATE BENJAMIN*
DIRECTOR
'84 IRRECONCILABLE DIFFERENCES
SCREENPLAY
'80 PRIVATE BENJAMIN*
'84 IRRECONCILABLE DIFFERENCES*

MICHAEL SIBLEY

MISCELLANEOUS
'83 LONE WOLF MCQUADE

GAIL SICILIA

UNIT PUBLICIST
'82 MIDSUMMER NIGHT'S SEX COMEDY, A
'83 ZELIG
MISCELLANEOUS
'83 ZELIG
'84 BROADWAY DANNY ROSE

JAMES SICKE

SCREENPLAY
'83 REVENGE OF THE NINJA

JOHN SIDDALL

ART DIRECTOR
'81 DOGS OF WAR, THE*
'84 SCANDALOUS*

ROBERT SIDELL

MAKEUP
'81 BODY HEAT
'82 E.T. THE EXTRA-TERRESTRIAL
'83 LONE WOLF MCQUADE
'83 OSTERMAN WEEKEND, THE
'84 RHINESTONE*

FREDERIC SIDEWATER

ASSOCIATE PRODUCER
'81 RAGTIME

BARRY SIEGEL

SCREENPLAY
'80 WINDOWS

CAROL SIEGEL

ASSOCIATE PRODUCER
'82 JINXED*

DAVID SIEGEL

LOCATIONS
'83 EXPOSED*
MISCELLANEOUS
'83 MAN WHO WASN'T THERE, THE

DAVID SIEGEL

ASSISTANT EDITOR
'84 FIRSTBORN*

DON SIEGEL

PRODUCER
'79 ESCAPE FROM ALCATRAZ
DIRECTOR
'79 ESCAPE FROM ALCATRAZ
'80 ROUGH CUT
'82 JINXED

DIETMAR SIEGERT

1ST ASST. DIRECTOR
'80 AMERICAN SUCCESS COMPANY,THE

NANETTE SIEGERT

PROD. OFFICE COORD.
'78 DEER HUNTER, THE
PROD. COORDINATOR
'79 10
'80 HEAVEN'S GATE*
'81 HONKY TONK FREEWAY
'82 NIGHT SHIFT*

MARC SIEGLER

SCREENPLAY
'81 GALAXY OF TERROR*
CO-PRODUCER
'81 GALAXY OF TERROR

JOE SIERRA

LOCATIONS
'83 LONE WOLF MCQUADE

CHRIS SIEVERNICH

PRODUCER
'84 PARIS, TEXAS*
EXECUTIVE PRODUCER
'84 PARIS, TEXAS

LILYAN SIEVERNICH

PROD. OFFICE COORD.
'84 PARIS, TEXAS*

ILLE SIEVERS

COSTUME SUPERVISOR
'82 NIGHT CROSSING
'84 LITTLE DRUMMER GIRL, THE

JAMES SIGNORELLI

DIRECTOR
'83 EASY MONEY

SERGE SILBERMAN

EXECUTIVE PRODUCER
'83 EXPOSED

PETER SILBERMANN

PUBLICIST
'80 TOUCHED BY LOVE
'81 BODY HEAT
'82 LOOKIN' TO GET OUT*
'83 CHRISTINE
UNIT PUBLICIST
'81 CAVEMAN

JUDY SILBERSTEIN
ASSISTANT EDITOR
'84 C.H.U.D.*

DRAKE SILLIMAN
EDITOR
'83 SWEET SIXTEEN

STIRLING SILLIPHANT
SCREENPLAY
'79 CIRCLE OF IRON*
'80 WHEN TIME RAN OUT*

KATHY SILVA
CASTING
'79 CHAMP, THE*

DAVID SILVAN
MISCELLANEOUS
'80 GUYANA: CULT OF THE DAMNED

AL SILVANI
MISCELLANEOUS
'79 ROCKY II
'80 RAGING BULL

DAVID SILVER
ASSOCIATE PRODUCER
'83 ROMANTIC COMEDY
UNIT PROD. MANAGER
'79 IN-LAWS, THE
'80 ALTERED STATES
'80 PRIVATE BENJAMIN
'83 ROMANTIC COMEDY
1ST ASST. DIRECTOR
'79 CHAMP, THE

JEFFREY SILVER
PRODUCTION MANAGER
'84 EXTERMINATOR II
1ST ASST. DIRECTOR
'83 ANGELO, MY LOVE*
'83 I AM THE CHEESE
LOCATIONS
'79 GOING IN STYLE
'80 DRESSED TO KILL
'82 AMITYVILLE II: THE POSSESSION

JESSE SILVER
MISCELLANEOUS
'83 SOMETHING WICKED
THIS WAY COMES

JOAN MICKLIN SILVER
PRODUCER
'79 ON THE YARD
DIRECTOR
'82 CHILLY SCENES OF WINTER
SCREENPLAY
'82 CHILLY SCENES OF WINTER

JOEL SILVER
PRODUCER
'82 48 HOURS*
'84 STREETS OF FIRE*
EXECUTIVE PRODUCER
'82 JEKYLL AND HYDE
TOGETHER AGAIN
ASSOCIATE PRODUCER
'79 WARRIORS, THE
CO-PRODUCER
'80 XANADU

RAPHAEL SILVER
DIRECTOR
'79 ON THE YARD

TONY SILVER
MISCELLANEOUS
'80 RESURRECTION

KARL SILVERA
MAKEUP
'82 PERSONAL BEST*

JUDITH SILVERMAN
MAKEUP
'82 FORCED VENGEANCE

LOUIS SILVERMAN
EXECUTIVE PRODUCER
'82 BY DESIGN

RON SILVERMAN
PRODUCER
'80 BRUBAKER
'83 KRULL

STANLEY SILVERMAN
MUSIC
'80 SIMON
'81 EYEWITNESS
'82 I'M DANCING AS FAST AS I CAN

LOUIS SILVERSTEIN
PRODUCER
'83 STRANGE BREW

RICHARD JAY SILVERSTHORN
MAKEUP
'81 FEAR NO EVIL*

ALAN SILVESTRI
MUSIC
'84 ROMANCING THE STONE

FRANCA SILVI
ASSISTANT EDITOR
'81 INCHON*

ROBERTO SILVI
EDITOR
'80 TWINKLE TWINKLE "KILLER" KANE*
'81 VICTORY
'83 PIRANHA II: THE SPAWNING
'83 OF UNKNOWN ORIGIN
'84 UNDER THE VOLCANO

DIANE SIMARD
MAKEUP
'84 HOTEL NEW HAMPSHIRE, THE*

CARLO SIMI
ART DIRECTOR
'84 ONCE UPON A TIME IN AMERICA*

MARGERY SIMKIN
CASTING
'82 PINK FLOYD: THE WALL*
'82 TEX*
'83 BABY IT'S YOU
'83 TESTAMENT
'84 BEVERLY HILLS COP*
'84 FLAMINGO KID, THE
'84 RECKLESS
'84 MRS. SOFFEL*
MISCELLANEOUS
'80 TIMES SQUARE

ALAN SIMMONDS
CO-PRODUCER
'81 TICKET TO HEAVEN
1ST ASST. DIRECTOR
'79 RUNNING
'79 SILENT PARTNER, THE

BOB SIMMONS
ASSOCIATE PRODUCER
'83 SUPERMAN III
STUNT COORDINATOR
'79 MOONRAKER
MISCELLANEOUS
'81 SEA WOLVES, THE
'81 FOR YOUR EYES ONLY
'81 FOR YOUR EYES ONLY
'83 FINAL OPTION, THE
'83 OCTOPUSSY

BRIAN SIMMONS
SOUND
'80 AWAKENING, THE
'83 BETRAYAL
'83 YELLOWBEARD*
'84 SHEENA

DAVID SIMMONS
ASSISTANT EDITOR
'79 ...AND JUSTICE FOR ALL
'80 CAN'T STOP THE MUSIC
'80 POPEYE*
'82 BEST LITTLE WHOREHOUSE
IN TEXAS, THE*

DON SIMMONS
CASTING
'84 PREPPIES

JEF SIMMONS
MAKEUP
'83 CHEECH AND CHONG'S STILL SMOKIN'
'84 CHEECH AND CHONG'S THE CORSICAN BROTHERS
HAIR
'84 CHEECH AND CHONG'S THE CORSICAN BROTHERS

MATTY SIMMONS
PRODUCER
'82 NATIONAL LAMPOON'S CLASS REUNION
'83 NATIONAL LAMPOON'S VACATION

PAUL SIMMONS
COSTUMES
'82 SWAMP THING*

RUDD SIMMONS
LOCATIONS
'84 NOT FOR PUBLICATION*

BOB SIMON
2ND ASST. DIRECTOR
'82 STRANGER IS WATCHING, A

BRUCE SIMON
2ND ASST. DIRECTOR
'84 MUTANT

KAREN SIMON
PROPS
'80 EYES OF A STRANGER

MELVIN SIMON
EXECUTIVE PRODUCER
'79 RUNNER STUMBLES, THE
'79 WHEN A STRANGER CALLS*
'79 WHEN YOU COMIN' BACK, RED RYDER?
'80 STUNT MAN, THE
'80 MY BODYGUARD
'81 CHU CHU AND THE PHILLY FLASH
'81 ZORRO, THE GAY BLADE
'82 PORKY'S*
'83 PORKY'S II THE NEXT DAY*

NEIL SIMON
PRODUCER
'81 ONLY WHEN I LAUGH*
'82 I OUGHT TO BE IN PICTURES*
'83 MAX DUGAN RETURNS*
SCREENPLAY
'79 CHAPTER TWO
'80 SEEMS LIKE OLD TIMES
'81 ONLY WHEN I LAUGH
'82 I OUGHT TO BE IN PICTURES
'83 MAX DUGAN RETURNS

PAUL SIMON
SCREENPLAY
'80 ONE-TRICK PONY
MUSIC
'80 ONE-TRICK PONY

ROGER SIMON
SCREENPLAY
'81 BUSTIN' LOOSE

JAMES SIMONS
1ST ASST. DIRECTOR
'84 MASS APPEAL
2ND ASST. DIRECTOR
'80 PRIVATE EYES, THE
'81 UNDER THE RAINBOW*

ROGER SIMONS
1ST ASST. DIRECTOR
'80 SATURN 3
'81 SHOCK TREATMENT
'81 EYE OF THE NEEDLE
'82 SENDER, THE*
'83 BRITANNIA HOSPITAL*
'83 KEEP, THE*
'84 ELECTRIC DREAMS

ROGER SIMONS
MISCELLANEOUS
'83 KEEP, THE

M.H. SIMONSONS
PRODUCER
'83 CAN SHE BAKE A CHERRY PIE?

BILLY SIMPSON
KEY GRIP
'81 GHOST STORY
'81 HEARTBEEPS

CLAIRE SIMPSON
EDITOR
'84 C.H.U.D.

DON SIMPSON
PRODUCER
'83 FLASHDANCE*
'84 BEVERLY HILLS COP*
'84 THIEF OF HEARTS*

FRANK SIMPSON
2ND ASST. DIRECTOR
'79 BELL JAR, THE*
LOCATIONS
'79 STARTING OVER

NORMAND SIMPSON
PROPS
'79 IN PRAISE OF OLDER WOMEN
'80 DEATH SHIP*

PETER SIMPSON
PRODUCER
'80 PROM NIGHT

RICHARD SIMPSON
ASSOCIATE PRODUCER
'80 PROM NIGHT

TOM SIMPSON
MISCELLANEOUS
'83 SAVANNAH SMILES

ALAN SIMS
MISCELLANEOUS
'84 FRIDAY THE 13TH PART IV THE FINAL CHAPTER

JEANIE SIMS
MISCELLANEOUS
'83 SOMETHING WICKED THIS WAY COMES

FRANK SINATRA
EXECUTIVE PRODUCER
'80 FIRST DEADLY SIN*

JAMES SINGELIS
ART DIRECTOR
'84 ONCE UPON A TIME IN AMERICA*

ABBY SINGER
PRODUCTION MANAGER
'82 LITTLE SEX, A

BRUCE SINGER
SCREENPLAY
'84 MEATBALLS PART II

CAREN SINGER
PRODUCTION MANAGER
'81 SMOKEY BITES THE DUST
'83 METALSTORM: THE DESTRUCTION OF JARED-SYN*
1ST ASST. DIRECTOR
'80 WITHOUT WARNING
'80 SCHIZOID
2ND ASST. DIRECTOR
'79 ROCK 'N ROLL HIGH SCHOOL

GEORGE SINGER JR.
KEY GRIP
'79 PHANTASM

LARRY SINGER
STILLS
'83 HOUSE ON SORORITY ROW

ROBERT SINGER
PRODUCER
'83 CUJO*
'83 INDEPENDENCE DAY*

PARKIE SINGH
ASSISTANT EDITOR
'79 PROMISE, THE

VINCENT SINGLETARY
CINEMATOGRAPHER
'83 RICHARD PRYOR: HERE AND NOW

RALPH SINGLETON
PRODUCTION MANAGER
'81 HISTORY OF THE WORLD PART I
'82 ONE FROM THE HEART*
UNIT PROD. MANAGER
'83 EXPOSED
1ST ASST. DIRECTOR
'79 SEDUCTION OF JOE TYNAN, THE
2ND ASST. DIRECTOR
'83 TESTAMENT*
MISCELLANEOUS
'83 EXPOSED

TOBI SINGLETON
PROD. COORDINATOR
'79 GREAT SANTINI, THE
'80 ROADIE

MITCHELL SINOWAY
ASSISTANT EDITOR
'80 CHANGELING, THE*
'83 FLASHDANCE*

DAN SIRETTA
CHOREOGRAPHER
'80 THOSE LIPS, THOSE EYES

BOB SIRUCEK
MISCELLANEOUS
'79 HEARTLAND

ROSEMARY ANNE SISSON
SCREENPLAY
'80 WATCHER IN THE WOODS, THE*

JOHN SISTRUNK
STUNT COORDINATOR
'83 MY TUTOR
'84 WEEKEND PASS

WILLIAM SIVEL
SOUND
'81 CONDORMAN

BRAD SIX
MISCELLANEOUS
'83 ANGEL OF H.E.A.T.

JANICE SIZEMORE
PRODUCTION MANAGER
'80 UNION CITY

PER SJOSTEDT
PRODUCTION MANAGER
'84 PREPPIES

MONA SKAGER
ASSOCIATE PRODUCER
'79 APOCALYPSE NOW
'82 HAMMETT
'82 ONE FROM THE HEART
LOCATIONS
'82 HAMMETT*

COLIN SKEAPING
STUNT COORDINATOR
'81 GREAT MUPPET CAPER, THE
'82 SENDER, THE

DAVID SKEPNER
MISCELLANEOUS
'80 COAL MINER'S DAUGHTER

ANN SKINNER
SCRIPT SUPERVISOR
'79 SHOUT, THE
'79 BOARDWALK

JEAN SKINNER
SCRIPT SUPERVISOR
'79 CIRCLE OF IRON
'79 GREAT TRAIN ROBBERY, THE
'81 EXCALIBUR

KAL SKINNER
MISCELLANEOUS
'82 BARBAROSA

JERZY SKOLIMOWSKI
PRODUCER
'82 MOONLIGHTING*
DIRECTOR
'79 SHOUT, THE
'82 MOONLIGHTING
SCREENPLAY
'79 SHOUT, THE*
'82 MOONLIGHTING

KAREL SKOP
MISCELLANEOUS
'83 YENTL

DENNIS SKOTAK
MISCELLANEOUS
'80 BATTLE BEYOND THE STARS
'81 GALAXY OF TERROR

ROBERT SKOTAK
PRODUCTION DESIGNER
'81 GALAXY OF TERROR*

ROBERT SKOTAK
MISCELLANEOUS
'83 STRANGE INVADERS

CHARLES SKOURAS
PRODUCTION MANAGER
'82 ANDROID

CHARLES SKOURAS III
ASSOCIATE PRODUCER
'83 LOVE LETTERS
PRODUCTION MANAGER
'83 LOVE LETTERS
PROD. COORDINATOR
'80 BATTLE BEYOND THE STARS*

DANNY SKUNDRIC
PROPS
'81 OUTLAND

BERNARD SLADE
SCREENPLAY
'80 TRIBUTE
'83 ROMANTIC COMEDY

KATHY SLAKEY
2ND ASST. DIRECTOR
'80 LOVING COUPLES*

FRED SLARK
PRODUCTION MANAGER
'83 ANGEL OF H.E.A.T.
UNIT PROD. MANAGER
'84 ICE PIRATES, THE

FRANKIE SLATER
UNIT PUBLICIST
'81 MODERN ROMANCE

MARK SLATER
2ND ASST. DIRECTOR
'80 EXTERMINATOR, THE

MARY JO SLATER
CASTING
'79 NATURAL ENEMIES

TANDI SLATER
PROD. OFFICE COORD.
'84 BEAR, THE

PAUL SLAUGHTER
STILLS
'84 HOT DOG...THE MOVIE

SYD SLEMBRIDGE
MISCELLANEOUS
'83 LONE WOLF MCQUADE

DONALD SLEMP
ASSISTANT EDITOR
'79 LOVE AT FIRST BITE*

BARBARA SLIFKA
PROD. SECRETARY
'82 PARASITE

HARRY EVANS SLOAN
EXECUTIVE PRODUCER
'81 ON THE RIGHT TRACK*

LINDA SLOAN
MISCELLANEOUS
'80 EYES OF A STRANGER

MICHAEL SLOAN
MISCELLANEOUS
'84 EXTERMINATOR II

PHIL SLOAN
KEY GRIP
'80 HUMANOIDS FROM THE DEEP

DOREEN SLOANE
SCRIPT SUPERVISOR
'79 ARABIAN ADVENTURE

JULIE SLOANE
ASSISTANT EDITOR
'80 SIMON*

BILL SLOBODIAN
ASSOCIATE PRODUCER
'84 PREPPIES

DOUGLAS SLOCOMBE
CINEMATOGRAPHER
'79 LOST AND FOUND
'80 NIJINSKY
'80 LADY VANISHES, THE
'81 RAIDERS OF THE LOST ARK
'83 NEVER SAY NEVER AGAIN
'83 PIRATES OF PENZANCE, THE
'84 INDIANA JONES AND THE TEMPLE OF DOOM
MISCELLANEOUS
'80 CLOSE ENCOUNTERS OF THE THIRD KIND SPECIAL EDITION

TOM SLOCUM
MUSIC
'81 CATTLE ANNIE AND LITTLE BRITCHES*

GENE SLOTT
EXECUTIVE PRODUCER
'81 LAST CHASE, THE

VALLI SLUTSKI
MAKEUP
'81 TICKET TO HEAVEN

STEFNA SMAL
ASSISTANT EDITOR
'80 FAME*
'82 SHOOT THE MOON*

DEBRA JACKSON SMALL
ASSISTANT EDITOR
'83 BIG SCORE, THE

HOWARD SMALL
MISCELLANEOUS
'82 MEGAFORCE

JOANNE SMALL
SCRIPT SUPERVISOR
'84 OVER THE BROOKLYN BRIDGE

JOHN SMALL
MISCELLANEOUS
'79 METEOR

MICHAEL SMALL
MUSIC
'79 GOING IN STYLE
'80 THOSE LIPS, THOSE EYES
'81 ROLLOVER
'81 CONTINENTAL DIVIDE
'81 POSTMAN ALWAYS RINGS TWICE, THE
'83 STAR CHAMBER
'84 FIRSTBORN

JEANETTE SMALLWOOD
HAIR
'83 FINAL OPTION, THE

NEVILLE SMALLWOOD
MAKEUP
'79 LEGACY, THE
'80 LADY VANISHES, THE
'81 SEA WOLVES, THE
'81 DOGS OF WAR, THE*
'83 FINAL OPTION, THE
'83 YELLOWBEARD*

BOB SMALLY
2ND ASST. DIRECTOR
'79 BUDDY HOLLY STORY, THE

YURI SMALTZOFF
MISCELLANEOUS
'80 BLACK MARBLE, THE

TONY SMART
STUNT COORDINATOR
'83 HIGH ROAD TO CHINA
'84 NEVERENDING STORY, THE

ROBERT SMAWLEY
1ST ASST. DIRECTOR
'81 UNDER THE RAINBOW

BRUCE SMEATON
MUSIC
'79 CIRCLE OF IRON
'79 PICNIC AT HANGING ROCK
'82 BARBAROSA
'84 ICEMAN

GUGLIELMO SMERALDI
PROD. SECRETARY
'83 1990: THE BRONX WARRIORS*

CAROL JEAN SMETANA
2ND ASST. DIRECTOR
'80 MELVIN AND HOWARD*
'84 NATURAL, THE*
'84 RED DAWN*

DON SMETZER
STILLS
'79 DOUBLE MCGUFFIN, THE
'80 COAL MINER'S DAUGHTER*
'80 UP THE ACADEMY
'81 STRIPES
'82 CHALLENGE, THE
'82 ESCAPE ARTIST, THE*
'83 BAD BOYS*
'84 GRANDVIEW, U.S.A.

JACK SMIGHT
DIRECTOR
'79 FAST BREAK
'80 LOVING COUPLES

KIM SMILEY JR.
PUBLICIST
'84 MUTANT

DAVID SMILOW
SCREENPLAY
'83 SPRING BREAK

DAVID SMIRNOFF
UNIT PROD. MANAGER
'80 BALTIMORE BULLET, THE

ADRIAN SMITH
ART DIRECTOR
'84 GIVE MY REGARDS TO BROAD STREET

AL SMITH
MISCELLANEOUS
'80 TERROR TRAIN

ALLEN SMITH
PRODUCTION DESIGNER
'79 ESCAPE FROM ALCATRAZ

ANDREW SMITH
SCREENPLAY
'79 MAIN EVENT, THE*

ANNICK SMITH
EXECUTIVE PRODUCER
'79 HEARTLAND

BABETTE SMITH
PUBLICIST
'83 YEAR OF LIVING DANGEROUSLY, THE

BILLY RAY SMITH
PRODUCTION MANAGER
'84 PHILADELPHIA EXPERIMENT, THE

BITTY O'SULLIVAN SMITH
ASSISTANT EDITOR
'84 HARRY & SON*

BOBBI SMITH
LOCATIONS
'80 HEARTBEAT*

BOBBIE SMITH
HAIR
'79 PRISONER OF ZENDA, THE*
'80 WATCHER IN THE WOODS, THE*
'81 SUPERMAN II*
'81 DRAGONSLAYER*
'82 VICTOR/VICTORIA
'83 SUPERMAN III*
'83 TRAIL OF THE PINK PANTHER*

BUD SMITH
ASSOCIATE PRODUCER
'84 KARATE KID, THE
EDITOR
'80 CRUISING
'82 CAT PEOPLE
'82 PERSONAL BEST
'83 DEAL OF THE CENTURY
'83 FLASHDANCE*
'84 KARATE KID, THE*
2ND UNIT DIRECTOR
'82 CAT PEOPLE

C.M. SMITH
MISCELLANEOUS
'83 NEVER CRY WOLF

CABELL SMITH
SOUND
'80 IT'S MY TURN*

CAROLE SMITH
PROD. OFFICE COORD.
'84 LOVE STREAMS

CHRISTINA SMITH
MAKEUP
'80 HOLLYWOOD KNIGHTS, THE
'81 MODERN ROMANCE
'82 FIREFOX
'82 PERSONAL BEST*
'83 WRONG IS RIGHT
'84 NO SMALL AFFAIR

CLIVE SMITH
MUSIC
'83 LIQUID SKY*

COURTNEY SMITH
PRODUCER
'79 FAST COMPANY*
SCREENPLAY
'79 FAST COMPANY*

CRAIG SMITH
MAKEUP
'80 XANADU*

DEAN SMITH
STUNT COORDINATOR
'84 LONELY GUY, THE

DEBBIE SMITH
PROD. COORDINATOR
'80 CARNY
'81 S.O.B.
'84 LAST STARFIGHTER, THE

DICK SMITH
MISCELLANEOUS
'78 DEER HUNTER, THE
'80 ALTERED STATES
'81 SCANNERS
'81 GHOST STORY
'81 NIGHTHAWKS
'83 HUNGER, THE
'84 AMADEUS
'84 STARMAN

DONNA SMITH
PRODUCTION MANAGER
'84 TERMINATOR, THE
PROD. OFFICE COORD.
'80 RAGING BULL*
MISCELLANEOUS
'84 RECKLESS

DOYLE SMITH
CINEMATOGRAPHER
'84 LOVELESS, THE

DUSTIN SMITH
KEY GRIP
'84 OVER THE BROOKLYN BRIDGE

ELAINE SMITH
PROD. COORDINATOR
'80 PRIVATE EYES, THE
LOCATIONS
'84 MUTANT

FRANK SMITH
ART DIRECTOR
'79 APPLE DUMPLING GANG RIDES AGAIN, THE*

GILL SMITH
ASSISTANT EDITOR
'80 SHINING, THE*
'83 KRULL*

GREG SMITH
CHOREOGRAPHER
'82 JEKYLL AND HYDE TOGETHER AGAIN*

HOWARD SMITH
PRODUCER
'81 NIGHT THE LIGHTS WENT OUT IN GEORGIA, THE*
'84 RHINESTONE*

HOWARD SMITH
EDITOR
'82 TEX
'83 TWILIGHT ZONE, THE MOVIE*

IAIN SMITH
ASSOCIATE PRODUCER
'83 LOCAL HERO
'84 KILLING FIELDS, THE
LOCATIONS
'81 CHARIOTS OF FIRE*

IRA SMITH
PRODUCER
'82 AMITYVILLE II: THE POSSESSION*

IRBY SMITH
1ST ASST. DIRECTOR
'80 CHANGELING, THE
'80 HOW TO BEAT THE HIGH COST OF LIVING
'81 DEVIL AND MAX DEVLIN, THE
'82 BORDER, THE
'82 TEMPEST*

JACK SMITH
LOCATIONS
'81 HOWLING, THE

JACQUELINE SMITH
ASSISTANT EDITOR
'82 CAT PEOPLE

JANET LEE SMITH
PROD. COORDINATOR
'82 FRIDAY THE 13TH PART THREE IN 3D
'84 MEATBALLS PART II
MISCELLANEOUS
'83 MAN WHO WASN'T THERE, THE
'84 FRIDAY THE 13TH PART IV THE FINAL CHAPTER

JEFF SMITH
KEY GRIP
'84 THIS IS SPINAL TAP

JOHN VICTOR SMITH
EDITOR
'79 CUBA
'81 SUPERMAN II
'83 SUPERMAN III
'84 FINDERS KEEPERS

LONNIE SMITH JR.
STUNT COORDINATOR
'84 MUTANT

KENNETH SMITH
MISCELLANEOUS
'84 STAR TREK III: THE SEARCH FOR SPOCK

LEE SMITH
ASSISTANT EDITOR
'83 YEAR OF LIVING DANGEROUSLY, THE*

LEON SMITH
EDITOR
'79 DOUBLE MCGUFFIN, THE
'80 OH! HEAVENLY DOG

LEONARD SMITH
1ST ASST. DIRECTOR
'81 HIGH RISK

LINDA GARDNER SMITH
ASSISTANT EDITOR
'80 FOR THE LOVE OF BENJI*

MARTIN SMITH
SCREENPLAY
'81 UNDER THE RAINBOW*

MARTIN CRUZ SMITH
SCREENPLAY
'79 NIGHTWING*

MAURICE SMITH
PRODUCER
'83 SCREWBALLS

MELBA SMITH
MISCELLANEOUS
'82 FRANCES

MICHAEL SMITH
ASSISTANT EDITOR
'84 ICEMAN*

MIKE SMITH
ASSISTANT EDITOR
'82 FIRST BLOOD*

NICHOLAS SMITH
EDITOR
'82 FIGHTING BACK*
'83 I AM THE CHEESE
ASSISTANT EDITOR
'80 HONEYSUCKLE ROSE*
'82 AMITYVILLE II: THE POSSESSION*

NORMAN SMITH
EDITOR
'83 STREAMERS
KEY GRIP
'80 KIDNAPPING OF THE PRESIDENT, THE

PATTI SMITH
HAIR
'79 CLASS OF MISS MACMICHAEL, THE

PETE SMITH
ART DIRECTOR
'79 CHAPTER TWO
'80 SEEMS LIKE OLD TIMES
'80 LAST MARRIED COUPLE IN AMERICA, THE
'81 PATERNITY
'82 NIGHT SHIFT

RANDEE LOIS SMITH
PROD. OFFICE COORD.
'82 DEATHTRAP

RILEY SMITH
MISCELLANEOUS
'83 REUBEN, REUBEN
'84 NOT FOR PUBLICATION

ROBERTA SMITH
LOCATIONS
'84 WOMAN IN RED, THE*

ROLAND "OZZIE" SMITH
CINEMATOGRAPHER
'80 CHEAPER TO KEEP HER

RON SMITH
HAIR
'80 BLUES BROTHERS*

RONALD SMITH
ASSOCIATE PRODUCER
'81 GHOST STORY
UNIT PROD. MANAGER
'81 GHOST STORY*
'81 HEARTBEEPS*
'83 STROKER ACE*
2ND ASST. DIRECTOR
'80 SMOKEY AND THE BANDIT II*

ROY FORGE SMITH
ART DIRECTOR
'81 LAST CHASE, THE
'84 MRS. SOFFEL*
PRODUCTION DESIGNER
'79 RUNNING
'81 LAST CHASE, THE

SCOTT SMITH
SOUND
'83 RISKY BUSINESS
'83 BABY IT'S YOU

SCOTT SMITH
ASSISTANT EDITOR
'82 SOUP FOR ONE*
'83 FLASHDANCE*
'84 KARATE KID, THE*

STEVEN PHILLIP SMITH
SCREENPLAY
'80 LONG RIDERS, THE*

SUSANNA SMITH
ART DIRECTOR
'83 STRANGE BREW*

TERRY SMITH
MISCELLANEOUS
'84 LAST STARFIGHTER, THE

TOM SMITH
MAKEUP
'79 CIRCLE OF IRON*
'80 SHINING, THE
'80 FIENDISH PLOT OF DR. FU MANCHU, THE
'81 RAIDERS OF THE LOST ARK*
'82 GANDHI
'84 INDIANA JONES AND THE TEMPLE OF DOOM
MISCELLANEOUS
'79 FEDORA

TOM SMITH
LOCATIONS
'84 CHOOSE ME*

VAN SMITH
COSTUMES
'81 POLYESTER
MAKEUP
'81 POLYESTER

VIC SMITH
2ND ASST. DIRECTOR
'83 KRULL*
'83 KEEP, THE*
'84 ELECTRIC DREAMS*
LOCATIONS
'84 TOP SECRET!*

WAYNE SMITH
MISCELLANEOUS
'79 BUCK ROGERS

WILLIAM CRAIG SMITH
ART DIRECTOR
'81 S.O.B.
'82 VICTOR/VICTORIA*
PRODUCTION DESIGNER
'79 PROPHECY

JENNIFER SMITH-ASHLEY
COSTUMES
'84 LOVE STREAMS

HALLIE SMITH-SIMMONS
MAKEUP
'79 CONCORDE-AIRPORT '79, THE*
'81 HONKY TONK FREEWAY*
'82 MEGAFORCE*
'82 PARTNERS*

ALAN SMITHEE
2ND ASST. DIRECTOR
'83 TWILIGHT ZONE, THE MOVIE*

ALLEN SMITHEE

PRODUCER
'81 STUDENT BODIES

BRIAN SMITHIES

SPECIAL EFFECTS
'81 GREAT MUPPET CAPER, THE
MISCELLANEOUS
'79 DRACULA
'82 DARK CRYSTAL, THE
'82 DARK CRYSTAL, THE
'83 OCTOPUSSY
'84 DUNE

PETER SMOKLER

CINEMATOGRAPHER
'84 THIS IS SPINAL TAP
MISCELLANEOUS
'80 ALLIGATOR

REED SMOOT

MISCELLANEOUS
'83 REVENGE OF THE NINJA

MICHAEL SMUIN

CHOREOGRAPHER
'84 COTTON CLUB, THE*
MISCELLANEOUS
'83 RUMBLEFISH

TERRY SMULEN

PROD. COORDINATOR
'82 SWORD AND THE SORCERER, THE*

PETER SNELL

EXECUTIVE PRODUCER
'82 MOTHER LODE

MARK SNOW

MUSIC
'79 SOMETHING SHORT OF PARADISE
'81 HIGH RISK

NORMA SNOW

PROD. SECRETARY
'82 LIAR'S MOON

ALLAN SNYDER

MAKEUP
'84 RACING WITH THE MOON

DAVID SNYDER

ART DIRECTOR
'80 IDOLMAKER, THE
'82 BLADERUNNER
'83 BRAINSTORM
PRODUCTION DESIGNER
'83 STRANGE BREW
'84 RACING WITH THE MOON
'84 WOMAN IN RED, THE

RON SNYDER

MAKEUP
'79 PROPHECY
'80 LAST MARRIED COUPLE
IN AMERICA, THE*
'80 LITTLE MISS MARKER*
'81 S.O.B.*
'81 BUDDY, BUDDY*
'81 BUSTIN' LOOSE*
'81 FIRST MONDAY IN OCTOBER*
'81 HARD COUNTRY
'82 I OUGHT TO BE IN PICTURES*

SHIRLEY SNYDER

PROD. COORDINATOR
'79 MUPPET MOVIE, THE*
'80 BORDERLINE

TOM SNYDER

SOUND
'83 AMERICANA*

WILLIAM SNYDER

MAKEUP
'84 NIGHT OF THE COMET

DOREEN SOAN

SCRIPT SUPERVISOR
'81 CLASH OF THE TITANS

TOM SOBECK

HAIR
'81 HARDLY WORKING*
'81 NOBODY'S PERFEKT*
'82 LOVE CHILD
'83 BLUE SKIES AGAIN
'83 PORKY'S II THE NEXT DAY

GUY SOBELL

MUSIC
'83 ANGEL OF H.E.A.T.

CAROL SOBIESKI

SCREENPLAY
'80 HONEYSUCKLE ROSE*
'82 ANNIE
'82 TOY, THE
ASSOCIATE PRODUCER
'82 ANNIE

JERRY SOBUL

1ST ASST. DIRECTOR
'79 BUCK ROGERS*
'79 FORCE OF ONE, A
'80 SERIAL
'80 PRIVATE BENJAMIN*
'82 CANNERY ROW
'82 JEKYLL AND HYDE
TOGETHER AGAIN
'83 INDEPENDENCE DAY
'84 BEST DEFENSE*
'84 UNFAITHFULLY YOURS
'84 BACHELOR PARTY
2ND ASST. DIRECTOR
'79 CHAMP, THE*

CRISTOBAL CRIADO SOLA

MAKEUP
'79 FIFTH MUSKETEER, THE

JOHN SOLDATIS

2ND ASST. DIRECTOR
'81 BEYOND THE REEF

CHRIS SOLDO

1ST ASST. DIRECTOR
'84 BIRDY
'84 NATURAL, THE*
2ND ASST. DIRECTOR
'79 ROSE, THE
'79 1941*
'80 HOLLYWOOD KNIGHTS, THE
'80 NINE TO FIVE
'81 FIRST MONDAY IN OCTOBER
'82 ANNIE*
'83 SCARFACE
'83 BLUE THUNDER*
'83 BUDDY SYSTEM, THE*

FRANCO SOLINAS

SCREENPLAY
'83 HANNA K*

RODOLFO SOLIS

SOUND
'80 GUYANA: CULT OF THE DAMNED

VICTOR SOLNICKI

EXECUTIVE PRODUCER
'79 BROOD, THE*
'80 HOG WILD*
'81 SCANNERS*
'81 GAS*
'83 VIDEODROME*

ROBERT SOLO

PRODUCER
'80 AWAKENING, THE
'82 I, THE JURY
'83 BAD BOYS

DAVID SOLOMON

ASSISTANT EDITOR
'82 MY FAVORITE YEAR*

GERALD SOLOMON

HAIR
'81 BUSTIN' LOOSE*
'82 ZOOT SUIT

JACK SOLOMON

SOUND
'79 DREAMER
'79 FRISCO KID, THE
'79 METEOR
'80 SERIAL
'80 SMOKEY AND THE BANDIT II
'81 SHARKEY'S MACHINE*
'81 CANNONBALL RUN, THE
'81 PATERNITY*
'82 MEGAFORCE
'83 STROKER ACE
'84 LAST STARFIGHTER, THE

MARIBETH SOLOMON
MUSIC
'81 TICKET TO HEAVEN*

MICHELLE SOLOTAR
UNIT MANAGER
'82 Q: QUETZALCOATL

BRUCE SOLOW
2ND ASST. DIRECTOR
'79 1941*
'80 ROADIE

HERBERT SOLOW
EXECUTIVE PRODUCER
'83 GET CRAZY

ARNOLD SOMKIN
SCREENPLAY
'84 OVER THE BROOKLYN BRIDGE

SAL SOMMATINO
PROPS
'79 LOVE AT FIRST BITE
'80 BORDERLINE
'82 CANNERY ROW
'82 MY FAVORITE YEAR
'83 STAR 80*
'83 MR. MOM

BASIL SOMNER
LOCATIONS
'83 KEEP, THE*

JUDIT SOMOGYI
MISCELLANEOUS
'80 NIJINSKY
'81 SPHINX

STEPHEN SONDHEIM
MUSIC
'81 REDS

SONYA SONES
EDITOR
'83 LET'S SPEND THE NIGHT TOGETHER*
ASSISTANT EDITOR
'79 PLAYERS*
'80 URBAN COWBOY
'82 HAMMETT*

CHARLES SONG
MISCELLANEOUS
'83 ANGEL OF H.E.A.T.

PAT SONSINI
PROD. COORDINATOR
'82 BARBAROSA*

JERI SOPANEN
CINEMATOGRAPHER
'81 MY DINNER WITH ANDRE
MISCELLANEOUS
'82 MIDSUMMER NIGHT'S SEX COMEDY, A

ANNE SOPEL
ASSISTANT EDITOR
'84 KILLING FIELDS, THE*
'84 PASSAGE TO INDIA, A*
'84 SCANDALOUS*

ROBERT SORDAL
KEY GRIP
'79 STAR TREK-THE MOTION PICTURE
'80 COMPETITION, THE
'80 TOUCHED BY LOVE
'81 BODY HEAT
'82 ANNIE
'83 BREATHLESS
'83 MAN WOMAN AND CHILD
'84 ALL OF ME
'84 HARD TO HOLD

ELVIO SORDONI
ASSISTANT EDITOR
'84 UNDER THE VOLCANO

PERRI SOREL
MAKEUP
'84 SILENT NIGHT, DEADLY NIGHT
HAIR
'84 SILENT NIGHT, DEADLY NIGHT

PETER SOREL
STILLS
'79 ROSE, THE
'79 CHINA SYNDROME, THE
'79 1941*
'79 TIME AFTER TIME
'80 SMALL CIRCLE OF FRIENDS, A
'80 BLUES BROTHERS*
'80 CLOSE ENCOUNTERS OF THE THIRD KIND SPECIAL EDITION*
'80 HOLLYWOOD KNIGHTS, THE
'80 HOW TO BEAT THE HIGH COST OF LIVING
'81 CONTINENTAL DIVIDE
'81 HONKY TONK FREEWAY
'82 MEGAFORCE
'82 MISSING
'82 NATIONAL LAMPOON'S CLASS REUNION
'82 ESCAPE ARTIST, THE*
'83 BUDDY SYSTEM, THE
'83 MAN WHO LOVED WOMEN, THE
'84 MIKE'S MURDER
'84 NO SMALL AFFAIR
'84 CANNONBALL RUN II

SWEDE SORENSON
SOUND
'80 ISLAND, THE*

DAVID SOSNA
ASSOCIATE PRODUCER
'80 BLUES BROTHERS*
1ST ASST. DIRECTOR
'79 WARRIORS, THE
'80 BLUES BROTHERS*
'82 48 HOURS
'83 JAWS 3-D*
'83 TRADING PLACES
'84 STREETS OF FIRE

RICHARD SOTO
ASSOCIATE PRODUCER
'83 BALLAD OF GREGORIO CORTEZ, THE*

JIM SOTOS
PRODUCER
'83 SWEET SIXTEEN
DIRECTOR
'83 SWEET SIXTEEN

TITO SOTTO
MUSIC
'83 BLIND RAGE

HEINZ SOTTUNG
KEY GRIP
'79 BLOODLINE

HASSINE SOUFFI
PRODUCTION MANAGER
'81 RAIDERS OF THE LOST ARK*

JOHN PHILLIP SOUSA
MUSIC
'80 FIRST FAMILY

LEONARD SOUTH
CINEMATOGRAPHER
'79 NORTH AVENUE IRREGULARS, THE
'81 AMY
MISCELLANEOUS
'79 BUCK ROGERS

KATHERINE SOUTHERN
MAKEUP
'80 HAPPY BIRTHDAY, GEMINI

JOHN SOUTHWOOD
LOCATIONS
'80 AWAKENING, THE*

PETER SOVA
CINEMATOGRAPHER
'82 DINER

JACK SOWARDS
SCREENPLAY
'82 STAR TREK II THE WRATH OF KHAN

ADRIANA SPADARO
COSTUMES
'83 HERCULES

LUCIANO SPADONI
ART DIRECTOR
'81 COMIN' AT YA!
'83 LONELY LADY, THE*
COSTUMES
'81 COMIN' AT YA!

ALBERTO SPAGNOLI
CINEMATOGRAPHER
'79 KILLER FISH
'83 HERCULES

JIM SPAHN
MISCELLANEOUS
'82 ENDANGERED SPECIES

HARRY SPALDING
SCREENPLAY
'80 WATCHER IN THE WOODS, THE*

RON SPANG
EDITOR
'79 JERK, THE*
'80 ANY WHICH WAY YOU CAN*
'80 UP THE ACADEMY*
'82 FIREFOX*

LARRY SPANGLER
PRODUCER
'84 BEAR, THE

RANDY SPANGLER
LOCATIONS
'79 10*
'81 BUDDY, BUDDY*

TONY SPANO
ASSISTANT EDITOR
'80 ROUGH CUT*
'82 JINXED

RICK SPARR
ASSOCIATE EDITOR
'84 RIVER, THE
ASSISTANT EDITOR
'81 BACK ROADS*
'81 BEAST WITHIN, THE*
'82 I OUGHT TO BE IN PICTURES*
'83 CROSS CREEK*

JOHN SPEAK
SOUND
'79 VILLAIN, THE
'80 COMPETITION, THE
'80 LITTLE DARLINGS
'80 WHOLLY MOSES!
'83 MAUSOLEUM

DAVID SPEAR
MUSIC
'81 FEAR NO EVIL*
'84 EXTERMINATOR II

JAN SPEARS
SCREENPLAY
'79 GAME OF DEATH

KAREN SPECHT
HAIR
'82 YES, GIORGIO*

KATHERINE SPECTOR
SCREENPLAY
'82 LOVE CHILD*

MAUDE SPECTOR
CASTING
'79 UNIDENTIFIED FLYING ODDBALL
'80 WATCHER IN THE WOODS, THE
'81 SPHINX*
'81 FINAL CONFLICT, THE
'81 FOR YOUR EYES ONLY*
'82 VENOM
'83 TRENCHCOAT*
'84 RAZOR'S EDGE, THE*

MYLES SPECTOR
ASSOCIATE PRODUCER
'83 ECHOES

AARON SPELLING
EXECUTIVE PRODUCER
'83 MR. MOM

DAVID SPENCE
ASSOCIATE EDITOR
'84 CLOAK AND DAGGER
ASSISTANT EDITOR
'80 WHERE THE BUFFALO ROAM
'83 PSYCHO II

MICHAEL SPENCE
EDITOR
'80 HANGAR 18
'82 BOOGENS, THE
'84 SILENT NIGHT, DEADLY NIGHT
2ND UNIT DIRECTOR
'84 SILENT NIGHT, DEADLY NIGHT

STEVE SPENCE
ART DIRECTOR
'82 SENDER, THE*
'84 KILLING FIELDS, THE*

CARMELA SPENCER
PROD. COORDINATOR
'79 CIRCLE OF IRON

DOROTHY SPENCER
EDITOR
'79 AVALANCHE EXPRESS
'79 CONCORDE-AIRPORT '79, THE

JAMES SPENCER
ART DIRECTOR
'82 SENDER, THE*
'83 TWILIGHT ZONE, THE MOVIE*
PRODUCTION DESIGNER
'80 DIE LAUGHING
'81 STRIPES
'81 KING OF THE MOUNTAIN
'82 POLTERGEIST
'84 GREMLINS

JOHN SPENCER
MISCELLANEOUS
'82 SWORD AND THE SORCERER, THE

MILTON SPENCER
ASSOCIATE PRODUCER
'80 WITHOUT WARNING*

SCOTT SPENCER
SCREENPLAY
'82 SPLIT IMAGE*

STEVEN SPENCER
ASSISTANT EDITOR
'84 ELECTRIC DREAMS*

SUE SPENCER
ASSISTANT EDITOR
'84 WINDY CITY*

HUGH SPENCER-PHILLIPS
PRODUCTION MANAGER
'82 BY DESIGN

NORRIS SPENCES
PRODUCTION DESIGNER
'83 BRITANNIA HOSPITAL

PIERRE SPENGLER
PRODUCER
'81 SUPERMAN II
'83 SUPERMAN III

R.J. SPETTER
MISCELLANEOUS
'82 TRON

LINDA SPHEERIS
ART DIRECTOR
'79 REAL LIFE*

PENELOPE SPHEERIS
PRODUCER
'79 REAL LIFE
DIRECTOR
'83 SUBURBIA
SCREENPLAY
'83 SUBURBIA

ROBERT SPIEGEL
SOUND
'81 BEYOND THE REEF

SAM SPIEGEL
PRODUCER
'83 BETRAYAL

STEVEN SPIELBERG
PRODUCER
'82 E.T. THE EXTRA-TERRESTRIAL*
'82 POLTERGEIST*
'83 TWILIGHT ZONE, THE MOVIE*
DIRECTOR
'79 1941
'80 CLOSE ENCOUNTERS OF THE THIRD KIND SPECIAL EDITION
'81 RAIDERS OF THE LOST ARK
'82 E.T. THE EXTRA-TERRESTRIAL
'83 TWILIGHT ZONE, THE MOVIE*
'84 INDIANA JONES AND THE TEMPLE OF DOOM
SCREENPLAY
'80 CLOSE ENCOUNTERS OF THE THIRD KIND SPECIAL EDITION
'82 POLTERGEIST*
EXECUTIVE PRODUCER
'80 USED CARS*
'81 CONTINENTAL DIVIDE*
'84 GREMLINS*
MISCELLANEOUS
'80 CLOSE ENCOUNTERS OF THE THIRD KIND SPECIAL EDITION

ZVI SPIELMANN
ASSOCIATE PRODUCER
'79 CIRCLE OF IRON
MISCELLANEOUS
'84 BEST DEFENSE

CAROL SPIER
ART DIRECTOR
'79 BROOD, THE
'79 FAST COMPANY
'80 HOG WILD
'81 SCANNERS
'83 VIDEODROME
PRODUCTION DESIGNER
'81 GAS
'83 RUNNING BRAVE
'83 DEAD ZONE, THE

DAVID SPIERS
ASSISTANT EDITOR
'81 DRAGONSLAYER

DAVID SPIGLE
MISCELLANEOUS
'83 CUJO

BARRY SPIKINGS
PRODUCER
'78 DEER HUNTER, THE*

JOE SPINELL
SCREENPLAY
'80 MANIAC*
EXECUTIVE PRODUCER
'80 MANIAC*

FREDDY SPINKS
MAKEUP
'83 HERCULES

HELENE SPINNER
PROD. OFFICE COORD.
'80 RAGING BULL*

DON SPINNEY
MISCELLANEOUS
'80 LAST FLIGHT OF NOAH'S ARK,THE

JEANPIERRE SPIRI-MERCANTO
PRODUCTION MANAGER
'79 MOONRAKER*

RICHARD SPITALNY
CO-PRODUCER
'84 RHINESTONE*

BARBARA SPITZ
PROD. OFFICE COORD.
'83 BRAINSTORM

JEFF SPITZ
LOCATIONS
'80 GONG SHOW MOVIE, THE

JILL SPITZ
PUBLICIST
'83 VIDEODROME

ALAN SPLET
SOUND
'83 NEVER CRY WOLF

MICHAEL SPOLAN
EDITOR
'82 CREEPSHOW*

ROGER SPOTTISWOODE
DIRECTOR
'80 TERROR TRAIN
'81 PURSUIT OF D.B. COOPER, THE
'83 UNDER FIRE
SCREENPLAY
'82 48 HOURS*

JAMES SPRACHER
STILLS
'83 SMITHEREENS

CHAIM SPREI
ASSOCIATE PRODUCER
'81 NIGHT THE LIGHTS WENT OUT IN GEORGIA, THE*

JOHN SPRINGER
PUBLICIST
'80 DRESSED TO KILL

RICK SPRINGFIELD
MUSIC
'84 HARD TO HOLD*

WAYNE SPRINGFIELD
ART DIRECTOR
'82 ANDROID*

MATT SPRINGMAN
PROPS
'79 FISH THAT SAVED PITTSBURGH, THE

EOIN SPROTT
MISCELLANEOUS
'80 SIMON
'81 ARTHUR
'82 DEATHTRAP
'82 MIDSUMMER NIGHT'S SEX COMEDY, A

CAPTAIN BARRY SPROUSE
MISCELLANEOUS
'81 STRIPES

BOB SPURLOCK
MISCELLANEOUS
'82 BLADERUNNER

ROBERT SPURLOCK
SPECIAL EFFECTS
'83 BRAINSTORM*
MISCELLANEOUS
'83 RUMBLEFISH
'83 OUTSIDERS, THE

ANTHONY SQUIRE
2ND UNIT DIRECTOR
'81 CONDORMAN
'81 EYE OF THE NEEDLE

TOM ST. AMAND
MISCELLANEOUS
'82 E.T. THE EXTRA-TERRESTRIAL
'84 INDIANA JONES AND THE TEMPLE OF DOOM

CAROLINE ST. CLAIR
PROD. COORDINATOR
'84 MAKING THE GRADE*

STEPHEN ST. JOHN
MISCELLANEOUS
'84 CITY HEAT

ANNE ST. JOHNS
CASTING
'80 TERROR TRAIN*

HURSEY ST. JOHNS
CASTING
'83 DEADLY FORCE

RICHARD ST. JOHNS
EXECUTIVE PRODUCER
'79 NIGHTWING
'79 CIRCLE OF IRON
'79 WANDERERS, THE
'80 CHANGE OF SEASONS, A
'80 FINAL COUNTDOWN, THE
'80 MOUNTAIN MEN, THE
'81 DEAD AND BURIED
'82 VENOM*

LOUIS ST. LOUIS
MUSIC
'82 GREASE 2

JOHN STABILE
KEY GRIP
'83 LOSIN' IT

JENNIFER STACE
CHOREOGRAPHER
'83 MORTUARY

EDDIE STACEY
STUNT COORDINATOR
'79 YANKS
'80 FFOLKES
'81 INCHON*
'81 DOGS OF WAR, THE*
'82 SAFARI 3000

JEFF STACEY
LOCATIONS
'84 WHERE THE BOYS ARE

JEFFREY STACEY
2ND ASST. DIRECTOR
'83 BLUE SKIES AGAIN*

MIMI STACEY
PROD. COORDINATOR
'81 NOBODY'S PERFEKT
'82 LOVE CHILD
'83 BLUE SKIES AGAIN
'84 WHERE THE BOYS ARE

GUNTHER STADELMANN
SOUND
'84 LITTLE DRUMMER GIRL, THE

PAUL STADER
2ND UNIT DIRECTOR
'80 ALLIGATOR*
STUNT COORDINATOR
'79 BEYOND THE POSEIDON ADVENTURE

ZACH STAENBERG
EDITOR
'84 POLICE ACADEMY*
ASSISTANT EDITOR
'83 TWILIGHT ZONE, THE MOVIE*

CHARLES STAFFELL
MISCELLANEOUS
'81 RAGTIME

FRED STAFFORD
EDITOR
'84 NIGHT OF THE COMET
ASSISTANT EDITOR
'79 PLAYERS*
MISCELLANEOUS
'82 CONAN THE BARBARIAN

JEFF STAGGS
ART DIRECTOR
'84 DREAMSCAPE

JOHN STAGNITTA
ASSISTANT EDITOR
'81 THIEF*

JUDY STAHELI
COSTUMES
'80 HANGAR 18
'82 BOOGENS, THE

PAUL STAHELI
ART DIRECTOR
'83 REVENGE OF THE NINJA
PRODUCTION DESIGNER
'80 HANGAR 18
'82 BOOGENS, THE

GORDON STAINFORTH
ASSISTANT EDITOR
'80 SHINING, THE*
'83 DRESSER, THE
'83 KRULL*
'84 SHEENA*

GENE STALLINGS
MISCELLANEOUS
'84 BEAR, THE

PATRICIA STALLONE
LOCATIONS
'83 SWEET SIXTEEN

SYLVESTER STALLONE
PRODUCER
'83 STAYING ALIVE*
DIRECTOR
'79 ROCKY II
'82 ROCKY III
'83 STAYING ALIVE
SCREENPLAY
'79 ROCKY II
'82 ROCKY III
'82 FIRST BLOOD*
'83 STAYING ALIVE*
'84 RHINESTONE*
MISCELLANEOUS
'79 ROCKY II

PILAR STALLWORTH
PROD. OFFICE COORD.
'84 AMERICAN DREAMER

LYNN STALMASTER
CASTING
'79 NIGHTWING
'79 ROSE, THE
'79 BEING THERE
'79 FAST BREAK
'79 GOLDENGIRL
'79 JUST YOU AND ME KID
'79 NORTH DALLAS FORTY
'79 ONION FIELD, THE
'79 PROMISES IN THE DARK
'79 PROPHECY
'79 10
'79 METEOR
'80 STIR CRAZY
'80 BLACK MARBLE, THE
'80 CHANGE OF SEASONS, A
'80 FOOLIN AROUND
'80 LOVING COUPLES
'80 MOUNTAIN MEN, THE
'80 WHOLLY MOSES!
'81 SUPERMAN II*
'81 BLOW OUT
'81 CAVEMAN
'81 CHARLIE CHAN AND THE CURSE OF THE DRAGON QUEEN
'81 LOOKER
'81 MODERN PROBLEMS*
'81 MOMMIE DEAREST*
'81 ON THE RIGHT TRACK
'81 TRUE CONFESSIONS
'82 SPLIT IMAGE*
'82 SOME KIND OF HERO
'82 AIRPLANE II: THE SEQUEL*
'82 FIRST BLOOD*
'82 HANKY PANKY*
'82 LOOKIN' TO GET OUT
'82 MAKING LOVE*
'82 OFFICER AND A GENTLEMAN, AN*
'82 TOOTSIE*
'82 YOUNG DOCTORS IN LOVE
'83 RIGHT STUFF, THE*
'83 BRAINSTORM*
'83 CLASS*
'83 MR. MOM*
'83 UNCOMMON VALOR*
'84 LONELY GUY, THE*
'84 HARRY & SON*
'84 RIVER, THE
'84 SONGWRITER
'84 SUPERGIRL*
'84 UNFAITHFULLY YOURS*

GARY STANEK
LOCATIONS
'84 NATURAL, THE*

THOMAS STANFORD
EDITOR
'81 LEGEND OF THE LONE RANGER, THE

PAUL STANHOPE
MAKEUP
'80 HOW TO BEAT THE HIGH COST OF LIVING*

PAUL STANHOPE JR.
MAKEUP
'79 SCAVENGER HUNT

JOHN STANIER
CINEMATOGRAPHER
'84 OXFORD BLUES

FRANK STANLEY
CINEMATOGRAPHER
'79 FISH THAT SAVED PITTSBURGH, THE
'79 10
'80 WHOLLY MOSES!
'81 UNDER THE RAINBOW
'82 GREASE 2
MISCELLANEOUS
'79 1941
'80 CLOSE ENCOUNTERS OF THE THIRD KIND SPECIAL EDITION

JAMES STANLEY
ASSISTANT EDITOR
'83 MR. MOM

JOE STANLEY
LOCATIONS
'79 OVER THE EDGE
'80 HEAVEN'S GATE*

MICHAEL STANLEY-EVANS
EXECUTIVE PRODUCER
'82 GANDHI

ROY STANNARD
ART DIRECTOR
'84 CHAMPIONS

LYNETTE STANSELL
ASSOCIATE PRODUCER
'79 PENITENTIARY*

PATRICK STANSFIELD
MISCELLANEOUS
'80 JAZZ SINGER, THE

ROBERT STAPLES
SPECIAL EFFECTS
'79 METEOR*

MEL STAR
KEY GRIP
'81 BEYOND THE REEF

MARTIN STARGER
EXECUTIVE PRODUCER
'79 MUPPET MOVIE, THE
'80 RAISE THE TITANIC
'80 SATURN 3
'81 GREAT MUPPET CAPER, THE
'81 HARD COUNTRY
'81 LEGEND OF THE LONE RANGER,THE
'82 SOPHIE'S CHOICE
'82 BARBAROSA

RAY STARK
PRODUCER
'79 CHAPTER TWO
'79 ELECTRIC HORSEMAN, THE
'80 SEEMS LIKE OLD TIMES
'82 ANNIE

WILBUR STARK
EXECUTIVE PRODUCER
'82 THING, THE

DAVID STARKE
LOCATIONS
'79 HEARTLAND
'80 ONE-TRICK PONY
'82 WORLD ACCORDING TO GARP, THE
'83 SURVIVORS, THE
'84 POPE OF GREENWICH VILLAGE,THE

JOHN STARKE
ASSOCIATE PRODUCER
'79 WINTER KILLS
PRODUCTION MANAGER
'80 ONE-TRICK PONY
UNIT PROD. MANAGER
'79 WARRIORS, THE
'82 WORLD ACCORDING TO GARP, THE
'83 SURVIVORS, THE*

JAISON STARKES
SCREENPLAY
'79 FISH THAT SAVED PITTSBURGH, THE*

BRUCE STARR
1ST ASST. DIRECTOR
'82 BRAINWAVES

BOB STARRETT
MISCELLANEOUS
'84 COMFORT AND JOY

TASO STAVRAKIS
SPECIAL EFFECTS
'80 HE KNOWS YOU'RE ALONE

GEORGE STAVRINOS
ART DIRECTOR
'80 UNION CITY

BOB STEADMAN
MISCELLANEOUS
'83 NEVER SAY NEVER AGAIN

CRAIG STEARNS
ART DIRECTOR
'80 FOG, THE
'84 CHILDREN OF THE CORN
'84 BODY ROCK

SPEED STEARNS
STUNT COORDINATOR
'83 METALSTORM: THE DESTRUCTION OF JARED-SYN*

ANDREW STEARS
ASSISTANT EDITOR
'84 SUPERGIRL*

JOHN STEARS
SPECIAL EFFECTS
'80 AWAKENING, THE
'80 HOPSCOTCH*
'81 OUTLAND
'84 BOUNTY, THE

MICHAEL STEELE
UNIT MANAGER
'83 SUPERMAN III*
2ND ASST. DIRECTOR
'83 RETURN OF THE JEDI*
'84 FINDERS KEEPERS
LOCATIONS
'82 GREY FOX, THE

BENITO STEFANELLI
STUNT COORDINATOR
'84 ONCE UPON A TIME IN AMERICA

BOBBIE STEIN
UNIT PUBLICIST
'84 FIRSTBORN

CHRIS STEIN
MUSIC
'80 UNION CITY
'81 POLYESTER*

EARL STEIN
SOUND
'81 ENTER THE NINJA

JEFF STEIN
DIRECTOR
'80 KIDS ARE ALL RIGHT, THE
SCREENPLAY
'80 KIDS ARE ALL RIGHT, THE
ASSOCIATE PRODUCER
'80 KIDS ARE ALL RIGHT, THE*

JENNY STEIN
ASSISTANT EDITOR
'83 NEVER CRY WOLF*

JON STEIN
SOUND
'83 MORTUARY*
'83 MY TUTOR
'84 CHILDREN OF THE CORN

MAURICE STEIN
MAKEUP
'80 HOW TO BEAT THE HIGH COST OF LIVING*
'83 MAUSOLEUM*
'84 ICE PIRATES, THE
'84 GRANDVIEW, U.S.A.*
MISCELLANEOUS
'83 MAUSOLEUM

MICHAEL STEIN
MAKEUP
'84 LOVE STREAMS

PETER STEIN
CINEMATOGRAPHER
'81 FRIDAY THE 13TH PART TWO
'83 REUBEN, REUBEN
'84 C.H.U.D.

RON STEIN
STUNT COORDINATOR
'81 CAVEMAN*
'81 TRUE CONFESSIONS
'82 ROCKY III
'83 STING II, THE
'84 STAR TREK III: THE SEARCH FOR SPOCK*
MISCELLANEOUS
'83 STING II, THE

DAVID STEINBERG
DIRECTOR
'81 PATERNITY

NORMAN STEINBERG
SCREENPLAY
'82 MY FAVORITE YEAR*
'82 YES, GIORGIO
'84 JOHNNY DANGEROUSLY*

ROBERT STEINBRECHER
PRODUCTION MANAGER
'83 NEVER CRY WOLF*

SID STEINBRIDGE
MISCELLANEOUS
'81 ESCAPE FROM NEW YORK

PETE STEINFELD
MISCELLANEOUS
'83 NIGHT IN HEAVEN, A

BRUCE STEINHEMMER
SPECIAL EFFECTS
'84 ALL OF ME

FREDRIC STEINKAMP
EDITOR
'79 FEDORA
'80 HIDE IN PLAIN SIGHT*
'82 TOOTSIE*
'84 AGAINST ALL ODDS*

WILLIAM STEINKAMP
EDITOR
'80 HIDE IN PLAIN SIGHT*
'81 KING OF THE MOUNTAIN
'82 TOOTSIE*
'84 AGAINST ALL ODDS*
ASSISTANT EDITOR
'79 FEDORA*

TESS STEINKOK
STILLS
'83 CAN SHE BAKE A CHERRY PIE?

JIM STEINMAN
MUSIC
'80 SMALL CIRCLE OF FRIENDS, A

BILL STEINMETZ
PUBLICIST
'82 FORCED VENGEANCE*

RICHARD STEIR
CASTING
'83 HOUSE ON SORORITY ROW*

MARIO STELLA
KEY GRIP
'79 HURRICANE

RAYMOND STELLA
MISCELLANEOUS
'81 HALLOWEEN II

MARY STELLAR
PROD. SECRETARY
'83 OCTOPUSSY*

KATHRYN STELLMACK
ASSOCIATE PRODUCER
'81 NIGHTHAWKS

SKIP STELOFF
EXECUTIVE PRODUCER
'80 WITHOUT WARNING*

SYD STEMBRIDGE
MISCELLANEOUS
'82 FIRST BLOOD

RICHARD STENTA
UNIT PROD. MANAGER
'82 HANKY PANKY*

LORNE STEPAK
MISCELLANEOUS
'79 MEATBALLS

JACK STEPHENS
ART DIRECTOR
'80 TESS

JOHN STEPHENS
MISCELLANEOUS
'83 HEART LIKE A WHEEL

ROD STEPHENS
EDITOR
'83 NIGHTMARES*

DAVID STEPHENSON
SOUND
'82 MOONLIGHTING

GEORGE STEPHENSON
SOUND
'79 AVALANCHE EXPRESS
'79 JAGUAR LIVES
'83 HIGH ROAD TO CHINA
'84 LASSITER

ROBERTO STERBINI
EDITOR
'79 KILLER FISH

ROBERT STERLING
EXECUTIVE PRODUCER
'79 WINTER KILLS*

JANNA STERN
SCRIPT SUPERVISOR
'82 BARBAROSA

JEFFREY STERN
ASSISTANT EDITOR
'84 BROADWAY DANNY ROSE*

JOHN STERN
MISCELLANEOUS
'79 HEARTLAND

KAREN STERN
ASSISTANT EDITOR
'80 MELVIN AND HOWARD

LEONARD STERN
DIRECTOR
'79 JUST YOU AND ME KID
SCREENPLAY
'79 JUST YOU AND ME KID*
'80 NUDE BOMB, THE*

PHIL STERN
STILLS
'79 BOULEVARD NIGHTS*
'79 1941*
'80 CHEAPER TO KEEP HER*
'81 RICHARD PRYOR: LIVE ON THE SUNSET STRIP
'83 DOCTOR DETROIT

RITA STERN
ASSISTANT EDITOR
'83 HOUSE ON SORORITY ROW

SANDOR STERN
SCREENPLAY
'79 AMITYVILLE HORROR, THE
'79 FAST BREAK

STEVEN HILLIARD STERN
DIRECTOR
'79 RUNNING
'81 DEVIL AND MAX DEVLIN, THE
SCREENPLAY
'79 RUNNING

MARTIN STERNBERG
MISCELLANEOUS
'79 VOICES

TOM STERNBERG
PRODUCER
'79 BLACK STALLION, THE*
'83 BLACK STALLION RETURNS, THE*
CO-PRODUCER
'79 APOCALYPSE NOW*

CAL STERRY
KEY GRIP
'80 USED CARS
'83 CHRISTINE
'83 FLASHDANCE
'84 STARMAN

AL STETSON
KEY GRIP
'83 NIGHT IN HEAVEN, A

MARK STETSON
MISCELLANEOUS
'82 BLADERUNNER
'83 BRAINSTORM
'84 2010

FRANKLIN STETTNER
SOUND
'82 COME BACK TO THE 5 & 10, JIMMY DEAN, JIMMY DEAN*
'82 FIGHTING BACK

ALEX STEVENS
STUNT COORDINATOR
'80 TIMES SQUARE*
'81 SCANNERS
'84 POPE OF GREENWICH VILLAGE,THE

EDMOND STEVENS
SCREENPLAY
'79 FISH THAT SAVED PITTSBURGH, THE*

JUDITH STEVENS
PRODUCTION MANAGER
'80 TIMES SQUARE

LARRY STEVENS
MISCELLANEOUS
'83 GET CRAZY

LESLIE STEVENS
SCREENPLAY
'79 BUCK ROGERS*
MISCELLANEOUS
'79 BUCK ROGERS

MORTON STEVENS
MUSIC
'81 HARDLY WORKING

ROBERT STEVENS
MISCELLANEOUS
'79 CUBA
'80 INSIDE MOVES

ROY STEVENS
2ND ASST. DIRECTOR
'81 DRAGONSLAYER*

TONY STEVENS
CHOREOGRAPHER
'82 BEST LITTLE WHOREHOUSE IN TEXAS, THE
'84 JOHNNY DANGEROUSLY
'84 WHERE THE BOYS ARE

HOUSELEY STEVENSON
EDITOR
'79 GREAT SANTINI, THE*

MICHAEL STEVENSON
2ND ASST. DIRECTOR
'80 SHINING, THE*
'80 FFOLKES*
'80 FLASH GORDON*
'80 HEAVEN'S GATE*
'81 RAGTIME*
'83 HUNGER, THE*
'84 BOUNTY, THE

MICHAEL STEVENSON
EDITOR
'79 CHAPTER TWO*
'80 SEEMS LIKE OLD TIMES
'82 ANNIE*
'82 TOY, THE*

ROBERT STEVENSON
HAIR
'82 SOME KIND OF HERO
'82 TOY, THE*
'83 FLASHDANCE

VENETIA STEVENSON
EXEC IN CHARGE PROD
'81 SOUTHERN COMFORT

ARNIE STEWART
ASSISTANT EDITOR
'79 FAST COMPANY

CHARLES STEWART
PRODUCTION DESIGNER
'83 SAVANNAH SMILES

CHUCK STEWART
SPECIAL EFFECTS
'83 BALLAD OF GREGORIO CORTEZ, THE
83 TESTAMENT
'83 FRIGHTMARE

DAVE STEWART
MISCELLANEOUS
'82 BLADERUNNER
'83 OUTSIDERS, THE

DENIS STEWART
UNIT MANAGER
'84 SILENT NIGHT, DEADLY NIGHT
1ST ASST. DIRECTOR
'84 SILENT NIGHT, DEADLY NIGHT

DONALD STEWART
SCREENPLAY
'82 MISSING*

DOUGLAS DAY STEWART
DIRECTOR
'84 THIEF OF HEARTS
SCREENPLAY
'80 BLUE LAGOON
'82 OFFICER AND A GENTLEMAN, AN
ASSOCIATE PRODUCER
'82 OFFICER AND A GENTLEMAN, AN
EDITOR
'80 ROUGH CUT
'82 JINXED
'83 RIGHT STUFF, THE*

HELEN STEWART
MAKEUP
'79 BLACK STALLION, THE

JAMES STEWART
EXECUTIVE PRODUCER
'80 WHY WOULD I LIE?*
'83 EDDIE AND THE CRUISERS*
'83 HEART LIKE A WHEEL*

JIM STEWART
ASSISTANT EDITOR
'83 MAUSOLEUM*

KAREN STEWART
PROD. COORDINATOR
'84 RUNAWAY

LIZA STEWART
COSTUME SUPERVISOR
'84 OH GOD, YOU DEVIL

MARLENE STEWART
COSTUMES
'84 BODY ROCK

PAUL STEWART
SPECIAL EFFECTS
'80 COAST TO COAST
'80 HEAVEN'S GATE*
'81 TAPS*
'83 GORKY PARK*
'83 TWILIGHT ZONE, THE MOVIE
'84 MUTANT

PETER STEWART
SPECIAL EFFECTS
'82 NATIONAL LAMPOON'S CLASS REUNION*

PENNY STEYNE
MAKEUP
'80 HOPSCOTCH*

JULIETTE STEYNING-BROWN
PROD. OFFICE COORD.
'82 SOPHIE'S CHOICE

ROBERT STIGWOOD
PRODUCER
'80 TIMES SQUARE*
'81 FAN, THE
'81 GALLIPOLI*
'82 GREASE 2*
'83 STAYING ALIVE*

RON STIGWOOD
LOCATIONS
'80 TIMES SQUARE

CLIFF STINE
MISCELLANEOUS
'79 CONCORDE-AIRPORT '79, THE

MARIA STINNETT
ASSISTANT EDITOR
'83 KISS ME GOODBYE*
'84 UNFAITHFULLY YOURS*

JOSEPH STINSON
SCREENPLAY
'83 SUDDEN IMPACT
'84 CITY HEAT*

JOHN STIRBER
SP. EFFECTS SUPERV.
'84 CONAN THE DESTROYER
MISCELLANEOUS
'81 HEARTBEEPS
'84 DUNE

MARC STIRDIVANT
SCREENPLAY
'81 CONDORMAN
ASSOCIATE PRODUCER
'82 NIGHT CROSSING

LEE STITCH
PROD. COORDINATOR
'80 PRIVATE BENJAMIN*
PROD. SECRETARY
'79 IN-LAWS, THE
'80 ALTERED STATES

KEVIN STITT
ASSISTANT EDITOR
'84 ROMANCING THE STONE*

MILAN STITT
SCREENPLAY
'79 RUNNER STUMBLES, THE

ROBERT STITZEL
SCREENPLAY
'83 BRAINSTORM*

DAVID STIVEN
EDITOR
'79 TIM
'82 ROAD WARRIOR, THE*

TOM STOCKFISCH
CASTING
'83 MY TUTOR
'84 WEEKEND PASS

JILL STOCKLAND
MAKEUP
'83 ECHOES*

WALLY STOCKLIN
PROPS
'79 STARTING OVER
'80 SIMON
'80 FIRST DEADLY SIN
'80 GLORIA
'80 NIGHT OF THE JUGGLER
'81 ROLLOVER
'82 SOPHIE'S CHOICE
'82 TEMPEST*
'84 MOSCOW ON THE HUDSON*

MICHAEL STOCKTON
PROPS
'80 KIDNAPPING OF THE PRESIDENT, THE

JOHN STODEL
MISCELLANEOUS
'82 SAFARI 3000

BARBARA STOIA
SCRIPT SUPERVISOR
'80 NIGHT OF THE JUGGLER*
'81 NIGHTHAWKS

CHRIS STOIA
2ND ASST. DIRECTOR
'83 ANGELO, MY LOVE
LOCATIONS
'82 VERDICT, THE*
'83 DANIEL
'84 GARBO TALKS*

RENATA STOIA
SCRIPT SUPERVISOR
'79 KRAMER VS. KRAMER
'80 NIGHT OF THE JUGGLER*
'81 TATTOO
'82 STILL OF THE NIGHT
'82 TEMPEST
'84 FIRSTBORN
'84 MISUNDERSTOOD

DERMOT STOKER
KEY GRIP
'84 LOVE STREAMS

J.W. STOKER
MISCELLANEOUS
'80 BRONCO BILLY

IRENE STOKES
MISCELLANEOUS
'82 PENITENTIARY II

STANZI STOKES
CASTING
'80 MOTEL HELL
'84 SILENT NIGHT, DEADLY NIGHT*
'84 TERMINATOR, THE
MISCELLANEOUS
'81 THIEF

TERESA STOKOVIC
PROD. OFFICE COORD.
'79 BEING THERE
'81 POSTMAN ALWAYS RINGS TWICE, THE
'82 FRANCES
PROD. COORDINATOR
'79 MUPPET MOVIE, THE*

DOUGLAS STOLL
LOCATIONS
'79 CHINA SYNDROME, THE
'80 SMALL CIRCLE OF FRIENDS, A*
'80 HEARTBEAT*
'81 POSTMAN ALWAYS RINGS TWICE, THE
'84 MIKE'S MURDER
'84 THIS IS SPINAL TAP

JOHN STOLL
PRODUCTION DESIGNER
'79 FIREPOWER*

NELSON STOLL
SOUND
'84 DUNE

JEFF STOLOW
LOCATIONS
'84 GHOSTBUSTERS*

DANIEL STOLTENBERG
PROPS
'81 HALLOWEEN II
'81 NIGHT THE LIGHTS WENT OUT IN GEORGIA, THE
'82 HALLOWEEN III: SEASON OF THE WITCH*

JACK STONE
MAKEUP
'79 BUCK ROGERS*

JEANNIE STONE
UNIT MANAGER
'84 SUPERGIRL
PROD. COORDINATOR
'83 PIRATES OF PENZANCE, THE

KERRY STONE
LOCATIONS
'83 KISS ME GOODBYE

L. ANDREW STONE
1ST ASST. DIRECTOR
'79 PROPHECY
'80 WHOLLY MOSES!
'80 WHEN TIME RAN OUT
'81 S.O.B.
'81 PENNIES FROM HEAVEN
'82 THAT CHAMPIONSHIP SEASON
'83 STING II, THE
'83 CLASS*
'83 FOOTLOOSE
'84 PROTOCOL*
'84 TEACHERS

MALCOLM STONE
ART DIRECTOR
'82 DARK CRYSTAL, THE*

MIKE STONE
STUNT COORDINATOR
'81 ENTER THE NINJA
MISCELLANEOUS
'81 ENTER THE NINJA

NANCY RAE STONE
2ND ASST. DIRECTOR
'83 BIG SCORE, THE
PROD. COORDINATOR
'83 RISKY BUSINESS

NOREEN STONE
SCREENPLAY
'81 AMY

OLIVER STONE
DIRECTOR
'81 HAND, THE
SCREENPLAY
'81 HAND, THE
'82 CONAN THE BARBARIAN*
'83 SCARFACE

PADDY STONE
CHOREOGRAPHER
'81 S.O.B.
'82 VICTOR/VICTORIA

PETER STONE
SCREENPLAY
'80 WHY WOULD I LIE?

RANDY STONE
CASTING
'83 JAWS 3-D

ROGER STONE
SCREENPLAY
'83 GOIN' ALL THE WAY*

RON STONE
PROPS
'84 NOT FOR PUBLICATION*

MARILYN STONEHOUSE
PRODUCTION MANAGER
'79 SILENT PARTNER, THE*
'79 LOST AND FOUND
'82 AMATEUR, THE*
'83 STRANGE INVADERS*
'83 CHRISTMAS STORY, A

JOHN STONEMAN
MISCELLANEOUS
'83 DEAD ZONE, THE

TOM STOPPARD
SCREENPLAY
'80 HUMAN FACTOR, THE

CLAUDINE STORA
ASSISTANT EDITOR
'79 LITTLE ROMANCE, A*

VITTORIO STORARO
CINEMATOGRAPHER
'79 AGATHA
'79 APOCALYPSE NOW
'81 REDS
'82 ONE FROM THE HEART

BUZZ STORCH
LOCATIONS
'83 AMERICANA

RAY STOREY
ART DIRECTOR
'79 MORE AMERICAN GRAFFITTI

KAROLA STORR
ASSISTANT EDITOR
'79 BLOODLINE*
'80 AMERICAN SUCCESS COMPANY, THE*

L. LEWIS STOUT
2ND ASST. DIRECTOR
'81 RICHARD PRYOR: LIVE ON THE SUNSET STRIP*

TOM STOVALL
ASSOCIATE PRODUCER
'83 SILKWOOD*

JAY STOVER
UNIT MANAGER
'79 DAWN OF THE DEAD

WILLIAM STOVER
ASSOCIATE PRODUCER
'79 FIVE DAYS FROM HOME

HERBERT STRABEL
ART DIRECTOR
'82 NIGHT CROSSING
'84 NEVERENDING STORY, THE*

ALAN STRACHAN
EDITOR
'80 FFOLKES
'81 FINAL CONFLICT, THE
'82 SENDER, THE

JEREMY STRACHAN
ASSISTANT EDITOR
'84 BIRDY*

HARRY STRADLING
CINEMATOGRAPHER
'80 UP THE ACADEMY
'81 S.O.B.
'81 PURSUIT OF D.B. COOPER, THE
'84 MICKI AND MAUDE

HARRY STRADLING JR.
CINEMATOGRAPHER
'79 PROPHECY
'80 CARNY
'81 BUDDY, BUDDY

ERIC STRAND
ASSISTANT EDITOR
'84 FIRESTARTER*

DR. STRANGE
SPECIAL EFFECTS
'82 BUTTERFLY

ARALEE STRANGE-MASON
2ND ASST. DIRECTOR
'79 GREAT BANK HOAX, THE

RENE STRASSER
KEY GRIP
'80 FIENDISH PLOT OF DR. FU MANCHU, THE

GARAFALIA STRATAK
HAIR
'82 SUMMER LOVERS

RICK STRATTON
MISCELLANEOUS
'80 BATTLE BEYOND THE STARS
'81 SATURDAY THE 14TH

BOB STRAUSS
STILLS
'83 LOCAL HERO*

CHRIS STRAUSS
PROD. COORDINATOR
'83 CUJO
'84 JOHNNY DANGEROUSLY
'84 RHINESTONE

JOHN STRAUSS
MUSIC SUPERVISOR
'84 AMADEUS

PETER STRAUSS
EXECUTIVE PRODUCER
'80 TOUCHED BY LOVE

ROY STREET
MISCELLANEOUS
'80 BIG RED ONE, THE

BARBRA STREISAND
PRODUCER
'79 MAIN EVENT, THE*
'83 YENTL
DIRECTOR
'83 YENTL
SCREENPLAY
'83 YENTL*

CYNTHIA STREIT
PROD. OFFICE COORD.
'83 SPRING BREAK
'83 NIGHT IN HEAVEN, A
PROD. SECRETARY
'81 FUNHOUSE, THE*

DAVID STREIT
ASSOCIATE PRODUCER
'79 ALAMBRISTA!*
LOCATIONS
'79 WANDERERS, THE
'79 WARRIORS, THE*

ANNE STRICK
PUBLICIST
'82 BORDER, THE
'82 CONAN THE BARBARIAN
'83 BAD BOYS
UNIT PUBLICIST
'84 DUNE
'84 CONAN THE DESTROYER

JOSEPH STRICK
PRODUCER
'83 NEVER CRY WOLF*

DAN STRIEPEKE
MAKEUP
'79 AMERICAN GIGOLO
'80 CAN'T STOP THE MUSIC*
'80 JAZZ SINGER, THE*
'81 CONTINENTAL DIVIDE
'82 ANNIE*
'82 MY FAVORITE YEAR
'83 DOCTOR DETROIT*
'83 FOOTLOOSE
'83 MAX DUGAN RETURNS
'84 CITY HEAT*
'84 CLOAK AND DAGGER
'84 CRACKERS*
MISCELLANEOUS
'78 DEER HUNTER, THE

KEN STRINGER
2ND ASST. DIRECTOR
'84 STAR TREK III: THE SEARCH FOR SPOCK

MICHAEL STRINGER
PRODUCTION DESIGNER
'79 ESCAPE TO ATHENA
'80 AWAKENING, THE
'80 MIRROR CRACK'D, THE

MICHAEL STRINGER
CINEMATOGRAPHER
'83 AMERICANA

SERGIO STRIZZI
STILLS
'79 BLOODLINE
'81 INCHON*

KALAI STRODE
2ND ASST. DIRECTOR
'79 NORTH DALLAS FORTY
'80 UP THE ACADEMY
'81 HONKY TONK FREEWAY*

HEIDI STROH
SCRIPT SUPERVISOR
'84 FALLING IN LOVE
'84 LITTLE DRUMMER GIRL, THE

DAVID STROHMAIER
ASSISTANT EDITOR
'79 GREAT SANTINI, THE

LOUIS STROLLER
PRODUCER
'83 EDDIE MACON'S RUN
EXECUTIVE PRODUCER
'79 SEDUCTION OF JOE TYNAN, THE
'80 SIMON
'81 FOUR SEASONS, THE
'82 VENOM*
'83 SCARFACE
UNIT PROD. MANAGER
'79 SEDUCTION OF JOE TYNAN, THE

HEIDI STROM
PROD. SECRETARY
'80 FOR THE LOVE OF BENJI*

GARY STROMBERG
PRODUCER
'79 FISH THAT SAVED PITTSBURGH, THE*

JOHN STRONG
PRODUCER
'81 EARTHLING, THE*

LEE STROSNEIDER
SOUND
'81 RICHARD PRYOR: LIVE ON THE SUNSET STRIP*

CHARLES STROUSE
MUSIC
'82 ANNIE

BARRY STRUGATZ
LOCATIONS
'81 THEY ALL LAUGHED*

DALE STRUMPELL
MISCELLANEOUS
'81 DRAGONSLAYER
'84 2010

ALAN STUART
STUNT COORDINATOR
'79 HANOVER STREET
'80 AWAKENING, THE
MISCELLANEOUS
'84 COMFORT AND JOY

WALKER STUART
ASSOCIATE PRODUCER
'83 NEVER CRY WOLF

JOHN STUCKMEYER
SCREENPLAY
'82 SWORD AND THE SORCERER, THE*
CO-PRODUCER
'82 SWORD AND THE SORCERER, THE*
PRODUCTION MANAGER
'82 SWORD AND THE SORCERER, THE*

JAMES STUEBE
SOUND
'84 NATURAL, THE*

DAVE STUMPH
COSTUME SUPERVISOR
'84 PURPLE HEARTS

ELAINE STUNDELL
PROD. OFFICE COORD.
'80 TIMES SQUARE*

BOB STURGIS
MISCELLANEOUS
'81 HEARTBEEPS

BERNIE STYLES
CASTING
'79 BELL JAR, THE
'84 LONELY GUY, THE*
MISCELLANEOUS
'80 IDOLMAKER, THE
'81 ROLLOVER
'81 HONKY TONK FREEWAY
'82 AUTHOR, AUTHOR

SUSAN STYRMOE
ASSISTANT EDITOR
'79 SAINT JACK*

KEN STYTZER
MISCELLANEOUS
'80 XANADU

JEFFREY SUDZIN
2ND ASST. DIRECTOR
'80 WITHOUT WARNING
'84 HOT DOG...THE MOVIE
KEY GRIP
'80 HOME MOVIES
2ND UNIT DIRECTOR
'84 HOT DOG...THE MOVIE

CANDACE SUERSTEDT-REHMET
1ST ASST. DIRECTOR
'81 DOGS OF WAR, THE*
2ND ASST. DIRECTOR
'80 NIGHT OF THE JUGGLER

MAURIE SUESS
ASSOCIATE PRODUCER
'81 PRIVATE LESSONS
UNIT PROD. MANAGER
'81 PRIVATE LESSONS*

SHIN SUGINO
STILLS
'79 RUNNING*
'80 MIDDLE AGE CRAZY*
'80 NOTHING PERSONAL
'82 AMATEUR, THE
'83 STRANGE BREW
'83 STRANGE INVADERS
'83 CHRISTMAS STORY, A
'84 POLICE ACADEMY

DAN SUHARD
MISCELLANEOUS
'83 OUTSIDERS, THE
'84 COTTON CLUB, THE

TIM SUHRSTEDT
CINEMATOGRAPHER
'82 ANDROID
'83 HOUSE ON SORORITY ROW
'83 SUBURBIA
MISCELLANEOUS
'80 HOME MOVIES
'80 PRIVATE EYES, THE
'84 BACHELOR PARTY

M.R. BOONYALA SUKAWASDI
LOCATIONS
'78 DEER HUNTER, THE*

JACKIE SULLIVAN
SCRIPT SUPERVISOR
'81 STRANGE BEHAVIOR
'83 NATE & HAYES

LENCOLA SULLIVAN
PROD. SECRETARY
'84 SOLDIER'S STORY, A

MICHAEL SULLIVAN
SPECIAL EFFECTS
'80 CAN'T STOP THE MUSIC

PETER SULLIVAN
MISCELLANEOUS
'82 PIRATE MOVIE, THE

TOM SULLIVAN
MISCELLANEOUS
'82 IF YOU COULD SEE WHAT I HEAR
'83 EVIL DEAD, THE

ARNE SULTAN
SCREENPLAY
'80 NUDE BOMB, THE*

EDWARD SUMMER
ASSOCIATE PRODUCER
'82 CONAN THE BARBARIAN

BOB SUMMERS
MUSIC
'80 GUYANA: CULT OF THE DAMNED*
'82 BOOGENS, THE

CATHLEEN SUMMERS
EXECUTIVE PRODUCER
'83 CLASS
ASSOCIATE PRODUCER
'80 CHANGE OF SEASONS, A
'80 MOUNTAIN MEN, THE

PAT SUMMERS
ASSISTANT EDITOR
'80 ALLIGATOR*

RAY SUMMERS
COSTUMES
'79 PROPHECY
'80 CHANGE OF SEASONS, A*
'80 FINAL COUNTDOWN, THE
'83 MAN WOMAN AND CHILD*
'83 WRONG IS RIGHT
COSTUME SUPERVISOR
'82 SIX WEEKS
'84 ALL OF ME

GRAHAM SUMNER
PROPS
'79 CIRCLE OF IRON
'81 INCHON
'82 CONAN THE BARBARIAN
'83 LORDS OF DISCIPLINE, THE*
'84 DUNE
'84 CONAN THE DESTROYER

ROBERT SUMNER
EXECUTIVE PRODUCER
'81 NESTING, THE*

EMILY SUNDBY
COSTUMES
'79 NORTH AVENUE IRREGULARS, THE*

RAY SUNDLIN
MISCELLANEOUS
'80 MOTHER'S DAY

TRACY SUNDLUN
MISCELLANEOUS
'79 GOLDENGIRL

CEDRIC SUNDSTROM
1ST ASST. DIRECTOR
'82 SAFARI 3000

MICHEL SUNE
PROPS
'79 LITTLE ROMANCE, A

SOMPOL SUNGKAWESS
2ND ASST. DIRECTOR
'84 KILLING FIELDS, THE*

MARGARET SUNSHINE
MAKEUP
'79 SEDUCTION OF JOE TYNAN, THE
'81 SO FINE*
'81 FAN, THE*

PAOLO SURDI

LOCATIONS
'83 BLACK STALLION RETURNS, THE*

TOM SURGAL

ART DIRECTOR
'80 HOME MOVIES
'82 FIRST TIME, THE
CASTING
'82 FIRST TIME, THE*

GLENN "SKIP" SURGUINE

1ST ASST. DIRECTOR
'80 OCTAGON, THE*
2ND ASST. DIRECTOR
'79 NORMA RAE

BRUCE SURTEES

CINEMATOGRAPHER
'79 DREAMER
'79 ESCAPE FROM ALCATRAZ
'81 INCHON
'82 FIREFOX
'82 HONKYTONK MAN
'83 RISKY BUSINESS*
'83 SUDDEN IMPACT
'83 BAD BOYS*
'84 BEVERLY HILLS COP
'84 TIGHTROPE

PETER SUSCHITZKY

CINEMATOGRAPHER
'80 EMPIRE STRIKES BACK, THE
'83 KRULL
'84 FALLING IN LOVE

MITCH SUSKIN

MISCELLANEOUS
'84 SPLASH

MIKHAIL SUSLOV

CINEMATOGRAPHER
'84 STRANGERS KISS

ANDREW SUSSKIND

ASSOCIATE PRODUCER
'80 LOVING COUPLES

DAVID SUSSKIND

EXECUTIVE PRODUCER
'80 LOVING COUPLES
'81 FORT APACHE, THE BRONX

KEN SUTHERLAND

MUSIC
'83 SAVANNAH SMILES

BARBARA SUTTON

HAIR
'83 LOCAL HERO

CHRISTOPHER SUTTON

LOCATIONS
'83 WICKED LADY, THE*
MISCELLANEOUS
'79 CLASS OF MISS MACMICHAEL, THE

DAVID SUTTON

STILLS
'79 FORCE OF ONE, A

KEVIN SUTTON

SOUND
'79 CLASS OF MISS MACMICHAEL, THE

LARRY SUTTON

SOUND
'82 BY DESIGN
'82 OUT OF THE BLUE
'83 GOLDEN SEAL, THE

PETER SUTTON

SOUND
'80 EMPIRE STRIKES BACK, THE
'82 DARK CRYSTAL, THE

ROD SUTTON

SOUND
'80 HANGAR 18
'84 SILENT NIGHT, DEADLY NIGHT

TOSHIRO SUZUKI

LOCATIONS
'82 CHALLENGE, THE

RAY SVEDIN

SPECIAL EFFECTS
'79 SCAVENGER HUNT*

JOSEF SVOBODA

MISCELLANEOUS
'84 AMADEUS

ELIZABETH SWADOS

MUSIC
'81 FOUR FRIENDS

KIM SWADOS

ART DIRECTOR
'78 DEER HUNTER, THE*
'79 AMITYVILLE HORROR, THE

GRANT SWAIN

PROPS
'82 GREY FOX, THE
'82 MOTHER LODE
'83 NEVER CRY WOLF*
'84 ICEMAN*

STEVE SWAN

UNIT PUBLICIST
'79 MOONRAKER*

DON SWANAGAN

ART DIRECTOR
'79 WARRIORS, THE*

BOB SWANDER

KEY GRIP
'83 CLASS

KATHE SWANSON

HAIR
'80 ORDINARY PEOPLE*
'81 ON THE RIGHT TRACK
'81 THIEF*
'83 BAD BOYS
'83 CLASS*
'84 SIXTEEN CANDLES*

TED SWANSON

EXECUTIVE PRODUCER
'81 NOBODY'S PERFEKT
ASSOCIATE PRODUCER
'79 HOT STUFF
'84 MASS APPEAL*
PRODUCTION MANAGER
'80 CADDYSHACK
'82 LOVE CHILD
UNIT PROD. MANAGER
'79 HOT STUFF
'81 NOBODY'S PERFEKT
'84 AMERICAN DREAMER
'84 MASS APPEAL

KANWAL SWAROOP

1ST ASST. DIRECTOR
'84 RAZOR'S EDGE, THE*

ROBERT SWARTHE

MISCELLANEOUS
'79 STAR TREK-THE MOTION PICTURE
'82 ONE FROM THE HEART
'83 OUTSIDERS, THE

JERRAM SWARTZ

1ST ASST. DIRECTOR
'80 ALLIGATOR
'80 BLUES BROTHERS*
'81 DEADLY BLESSING
'83 LONE WOLF MCQUADE
2ND ASST. DIRECTOR
'80 RESURRECTION

PAULA SWAUGER

2ND ASST. DIRECTOR
'84 NEVERENDING STORY, THE*

ROGER SWAYBILL

SCREENPLAY
'83 PORKY'S II THE NEXT DAY*

PATSY SWAYZE

CHOREOGRAPHER
'80 URBAN COWBOY
'82 LIAR'S MOON
'84 GRANDVIEW, U.S.A.*

TONG YEOW PARK SWEE
UNIT MANAGER
'79 SAINT JACK

ALFRED SWEENEY
PRODUCTION DESIGNER
'79 NORTH DALLAS FORTY
'80 STIR CRAZY
'80 BLACK MARBLE, THE
'81 TAPS*
'83 ROMANTIC COMEDY
'83 MR. MOM

ALFRED SWEENEY JR.
PRODUCTION DESIGNER
'79 RUNNER STUMBLES, THE

DR. JAY SWEENEY
MISCELLANEOUS
'84 2010

MATT SWEENEY
SPECIAL EFFECTS
'80 NINE TO FIVE*
'81 ON GOLDEN POND
SP. EFFECTS SUPERV.
'84 IRRECONCILABLE DIFFERENCES

MAUREEN SWEENEY
MAKEUP
'79 RUNNING*
'80 MIDDLE AGE CRAZY*

MIKE SWEETEN
MISCELLANEOUS
'80 HERBIE GOES BANANAS
'80 MIDNIGHT MADNESS

NICK SWEETMAN
PROD. OFFICE COORD.
'79 MEATBALLS*

CHUCK SWENSON
MISCELLANEOUS
'84 JOHNNY DANGEROUSLY

EZRA SWERDLOW
UNIT PROD. MANAGER
'84 BROADWAY DANNY ROSE
UNIT MANAGER
'80 STARDUST MEMORIES*
'83 KING OF COMEDY, THE
'83 ZELIG
LOCATIONS
'82 TOOTSIE*

CYRIL SWERN
SOUND
'80 NIJINSKY
'81 SPHINX

BLISS SWIFT
STILLS
'82 STARSTRUCK

BRENT SWIFT
ART DIRECTOR
'83 SPACEHUNTER: ADVENTURES IN THE FORBIDDEN ZONE*

DAVID SWIFT
SCREENPLAY
'80 FOOLIN AROUND*

GEORGE SWINK
ASSOCIATE PRODUCER
'80 WHEN TIME RAN OUT*

ROBERT SWINK
EDITOR
'79 GOING IN STYLE*
'79 IN-LAWS, THE
'81 SPHINX*

KATHY SWOR
SCRIPT SUPERVISOR
'79 TIME AFTER TIME
'80 SMALL CIRCLE OF FRIENDS, A

KEN SWOR
ASSOCIATE PRODUCER
'80 FORMULA, THE
'82 ENDANGERED SPECIES
UNIT PROD. MANAGER
'79 GREAT SANTINI, THE*
'80 FORMULA, THE
'82 DINER
'82 ENDANGERED SPECIES
1ST ASST. DIRECTOR
'79 GREAT SANTINI, THE*

STEPHANIE SWOR
PROD. COORDINATOR
'84 FLASHPOINT

SUDESH SYAL
PRODUCTION MANAGER
'84 RAZOR'S EDGE, THE*
LOCATIONS
'82 GANDHI*

ANTHEA SYLBERT
PRODUCER
'84 PROTOCOL

PAUL SYLBERT
PRODUCTION DESIGNER
'79 HARDCORE
'79 KRAMER VS. KRAMER
'80 RESURRECTION
'81 BLOW OUT
'81 WOLFEN
'83 GORKY PARK
'83 WITHOUT A TRACE
'84 POPE OF GREENWICH VILLAGE,THE

RICHARD SYLBERT
PRODUCTION DESIGNER
'79 PLAYERS
'81 REDS
'82 FRANCES
'82 PARTNERS
'83 BREATHLESS
'84 COTTON CLUB, THE
'84 FIRSTBORN

JULIAN RICHARD SYLVESTER
MISCELLANEOUS
'83 NATIONAL LAMPOON'S VACATION

KEN SYLVIA
UNIT PUBLICIST
'81 NIGHT THE LIGHTS WENT OUT IN GEORGIA, THE

DUSTY SYMONDS
ASSOCIATE PRODUCER
'84 FINDERS KEEPERS
1ST ASST. DIRECTOR
'81 SUPERMAN II
'81 FINAL CONFLICT, THE
'81 GREAT MUPPET CAPER, THE
'82 DARK CRYSTAL, THE
'83 SUPERMAN III
LOCATIONS
'80 LADY VANISHES, THE*

JAMES SYMONS
EDITOR
'79 ROCKY II*
MISCELLANEOUS
'84 OXFORD BLUES

JOHN SYRJAMAKI
2ND ASST. DIRECTOR
'81 BUSTIN' LOOSE*
'84 WHERE THE BOYS ARE*

GEORGE SZEPTYCKI
ART DIRECTOR
'80 CADDYSHACK

LASZLO SZILVASSEY
STILLS
'79 SILENT PARTNER, THE

JEANNOT SZWARC
DIRECTOR
'80 SOMEWHERE IN TIME
'83 ENIGMA
'84 SUPERGIRL

T

SONIA MARIA TABACOW
MISCELLANEOUS
'84 BLAME IT ON RIO

SYLVIO TABET
PRODUCER
'82 BEASTMASTER, THE*
EXECUTIVE PRODUCER
'80 FADE TO BLACK*
'82 BEASTMASTER, THE*
CO-PRODUCER
'84 COTTON CLUB, THE*

ALESANDRA TABOR
PROD. OFFICE COORD.
'80 TRIBUTE
'84 FLAMINGO KID, THE

DOMINIQUE TABUTEAU
2ND ASST. DIRECTOR
'84 AMERICAN DREAMER*

TED TADLOCK
CHOREOGRAPHER
'81 BODY HEAT
'84 IRRECONCILABLE DIFFERENCES

SHERRI TAFFEL-BROWN
UNIT MANAGER
'83 I AM THE CHEESE
PROD. COORDINATOR
'82 AMITYVILLE II:THE POSSESSION*

ALFONSO TAFOYA
ASSOCIATE PRODUCER
'84 C.H.U.D.

BARRY TAFT
MISCELLANEOUS
'81 ENTITY, THE

GENE TAFT
PRODUCER
'80 HONEYSUCKLE ROSE

BRIAN TAGG
EDITOR
'84 CRIMES OF PASSION

BRIAN TAGGERT
SCREENPLAY
'83 OF UNKNOWN ORIGIN

PATRICK TAGLIAFERRO
ART DIRECTOR
'84 BREAKIN 2 ELECTRIC BOOGALOO

ATTEF EL TAIEB
1ST ASST. DIRECTOR
'80 AWAKENING, THE*

DON TAIT
SCREENPLAY
'79 APPLE DUMPLING GANG RIDES AGAIN, THE
'79 UNIDENTIFIED FLYING ODDBALL
'79 NORTH AVENUE IRREGULARS, THE
'80 HERBIE GOES BANANAS
CO-PRODUCER
'80 HERBIE GOES BANANAS*

TIBOR TAKACS
PRODUCTION MANAGER
'83 SCREWBALLS

YOSIO TAKAHASHI
1ST ASST. DIRECTOR
'81 TATTOO*

GLENN TAKAKJIAN
MISCELLANEOUS
'83 RETURN OF THE ALIENS: THE DEADLY SPAWN

KAORI TERRY TAKAKUWA
PROD. SECRETARY
'84 WEEKEND PASS

KENICHI TAKASHIMA
ASSISTANT EDITOR
'83 MERRY CHRISTMAS, MR. LAWRENCE

RACHEL TALALAY
SCRIPT SUPERVISOR
'83 HOUSE ON SORORITY ROW

BRUCE TALAMON
STILLS
'83 BLUE THUNDER
'83 D.C. CAB
'83 MAN WITH TWO BRAINS, THE
'83 UNCOMMON VALOR
'84 RHINESTONE

KATHY TALBERT
CASTING
'81 NEIGHBORS
'81 REDS*
'82 SOUP FOR ONE*

BRUD TALBOT
EXECUTIVE PRODUCER
'81 COMIN' AT YA!*

RON TALSKY
COSTUMES
'79 RAVAGERS
'79 JAGUAR LIVES
'80 INSIDE MOVES
'81 CHU CHU AND THE PHILLY FLASH*
'82 THAT CHAMPIONSHIP SEASON
'84 BEAR, THE

LEE TAMAHORI
1ST ASST. DIRECTOR
'83 MERRY CHRISTMAS, MR. LAWRENCE

GIULIO TAMASSY
MISCELLANEOUS
'79 FEDORA

FLAVIO TAMBELLINI
CASTING
'84 BLAME IT ON RIO*

WINDY TAMKIN
MAKEUP
'83 MY TUTOR
'84 WEEKEND PASS

LAWRENCE TAN
MISCELLANEOUS
'79 WANDERERS, THE

MIUMI TAN
ASSISTANT EDITOR
'82 IF YOU COULD SEE WHAT I HEAR

SONNY TAN
2ND ASST. DIRECTOR
'79 SAINT JACK*

MASAO TANAKA
LOCATIONS
'81 TATTOO

GARETH TANDY
2ND ASST. DIRECTOR
'81 SUPERMAN II
'81 FOR YOUR EYES ONLY*

NED TANEN
EXECUTIVE PRODUCER
'84 SIXTEEN CANDLES

TANGERINE DREAM
MUSIC
'81 STRANGE BEHAVIOR
'81 THIEF
'83 RISKY BUSINESS
'83 KEEP, THE
'84 FIRESTARTER
'84 FLASHPOINT

WILLIAM TANNEN
DIRECTOR
'84 FLASHPOINT

JIM TANNENBAUM
SOUND
'80 STUNT MAN, THE
'81 BLOW OUT
'81 TAKE THIS JOB AND SHOVE IT
'82 ENDANGERED SPECIES
'84 BODY DOUBLE

MALCOLM TANNER
HAIR
'80 MIDDLE AGE CRAZY
'83 STRANGE BREW

PETER TANNER
EDITOR
'79 STEVIE

MICHAEL TANNERN
PRODUCER
'80 ONE-TRICK PONY

ROLAND TANTIN
SP. EFFECTS SUPERV.
'84 COUNTRY
'84 SPLASH
MISCELLANEOUS
'83 SOMETHING WICKED THIS WAY COMES

MARK TANZ
PRODUCER
'80 INSIDE MOVES*

ROBERT TAPERT
PRODUCER
'83 EVIL DEAD, THE
EXECUTIVE PRODUCER
'83 EVIL DEAD, THE*

JONATHAN TAPLIN
PRODUCER
'83 UNDER FIRE
EXECUTIVE PRODUCER
'80 CARNY
'84 GRANDVIEW, U.S.A.*

KENNETH TARAN
MISCELLANEOUS
'81 ROLLOVER

MARK TARLOV
EXECUTIVE PRODUCER
'83 CHRISTINE*

MARK TARNAWSKY
UNIT PROD. MANAGER
'83 CHAINED HEAT
LOCATIONS
'82 SWORD AND THE SORCERER, THE

BRIDGETT TARRY
PUBLICIST
'82 OFFICER AND A GENTLEMAN, AN

JAY TARSES
SCREENPLAY
'80 UP THE ACADEMY*
'81 GREAT MUPPET CAPER, THE*

MARGARET TARY
SCRIPT SUPERVISOR
'81 GOING APE!
'82 PARTNERS
'82 YOUNG DOCTORS IN LOVE

WILLIAM TASGAL
PRODUCTION MANAGER
'83 BIG SCORE, THE

TANDA TASHJIAN
STILLS
'82 BRAINWAVES*

ANN TASKER
PUBLICIST
'80 FIENDISH PLOT OF DR. FU MANCHU, THE
'81 SHOCK TREATMENT
'81 CHARIOTS OF FIRE
'81 CLASH OF THE TITANS
'82 DARK CRYSTAL, THE
'82 MONSIGNOR
'83 HUNGER, THE
'84 LASSITER
UNIT PUBLICIST
'84 JUST THE WAY YOU ARE

ALAIN TASMA
1ST ASST. DIRECTOR
'83 EXPOSED*

JULIE TASNER
ASSISTANT EDITOR
'84 MOSCOW ON THE HUDSON

MARILYN TASSO
PROD. COORDINATOR
'79 NORMA RAE

KATHY TATLOCK
STILLS
'79 HEARTLAND

WALTER TATRO
SPECIAL EFFECTS
'81 NIGHTHAWKS*

JOE TAURASO
MISCELLANEOUS
'84 LOVELESS, THE

RICHARD TAUTKUS
MISCELLANEOUS
'84 HOTEL NEW HAMPSHIRE, THE

DEAN TAVOULARIS
PRODUCTION DESIGNER
'79 APOCALYPSE NOW
'82 HAMMETT
'82 ONE FROM THE HEART
'82 ESCAPE ARTIST, THE
'83 RUMBLEFISH
'83 OUTSIDERS, THE

ANDRE TAYIR
CHOREOGRAPHER
'84 STAR TREK III: THE SEARCH FOR SPOCK

WENDY TAYLER
PUBLICIST
'82 MISSIONARY, THE
'83 PRIVATES ON PARADE

CHRIS TAYLO
HAIR
'81 SHOCK TREATMENT*

ADELE TAYLOR
HAIR
'80 COAST TO COAST
'80 HOW TO BEAT THE HIGH COST OF LIVING*
'81 BODY HEAT
'83 EDDIE MACON'S RUN
'83 NATIONAL LAMPOON'S VACATION

AL TAYLOR
CINEMATOGRAPHER
'84 MUTANT

ALBERT TAYLOR
MISCELLANEOUS
'80 BORDERLINE

ANNA TAYLOR
COSTUMES
'84 ALPHABET CITY

BARBI TAYLOR
CO-PRODUCER
'81 ROAD GAMES
MISCELLANEOUS
'80 BLUE LAGOON

BARRETT TAYLOR
ASSISTANT EDITOR
'82 DEATH VALLEY

BARRETT TAYLOR
MISCELLANEOUS
'80 WHEN TIME RAN OUT

BARRY TAYLOR
ASSISTANT EDITOR
'79 BEYOND THE POSEIDON ADVENTURE*

BILL TAYLOR
MISCELLANEOUS
'79 PRISONER OF ZENDA, THE
'80 BLUES BROTHERS
'80 CHEECH AND CHONG'S NEXT MOVIE
'80 IN GOD WE TRUST
'80 ISLAND, THE
'81 GHOST STORY
'81 HEARTBEEPS
'82 BEST LITTLE WHOREHOUSE IN TEXAS, THE
'83 PSYCHO II
'84 LONELY GUY, THE

CAMI TAYLOR
CASTING
'80 BORDERLINE*
'82 CREEPSHOW*

CAMI DEMPSEY TAYLOR
PROD. COORDINATOR
'83 LOSIN' IT
MISCELLANEOUS
'84 DREAMSCAPE

CHARLOTTE TAYLOR
MAKEUP
'84 ALPHABET CITY
HAIR
'84 ALPHABET CITY

CHRISTOPHER TAYLOR
HAIR
'81 PRIEST OF LOVE
'83 OCTOPUSSY

DAVID TAYLOR
SCREENPLAY
'82 HANKY PANKY*
'83 GET CRAZY*
'84 LASSITER
ASSOCIATE PRODUCER
'82 HANKY PANKY*

DIONE TAYLOR
HAIR
'79 NIGHTWING
'79 IN-LAWS, THE*
'79 TIME AFTER TIME
'80 ALTERED STATES
'81 RICH AND FAMOUS*
'82 STAR TREK II THE WRATH OF KHAN
'83 D.C. CAB
'83 DOCTOR DETROIT*
'84 GHOSTBUSTERS

DON TAYLOR
DIRECTOR
'80 FINAL COUNTDOWN, THE

DUNCAN TAYLOR
ASSISTANT EDITOR
'82 STARSTRUCK*

EDWARD TAYLOR
MISCELLANEOUS
'82 PERSONAL BEST

ERIC TAYLOR
SOUND
'84 BROTHER FROM ANOTHER PLANET, THE

GEOFFREY TAYLOR
ASSOCIATE PRODUCER
'84 MOSCOW ON THE HUDSON

GIL TAYLOR
CINEMATOGRAPHER
'79 DRACULA
'79 ESCAPE TO ATHENA
'80 FLASH GORDON
'82 VENOM*
'83 LOSIN' IT
'84 LASSITER

HAROLD TAYLOR
MISCELLANEOUS
'81 DRAGONSLAYER

HERB TAYLOR
MISCELLANEOUS
'79 APPLE DUMPLING GANG RIDES AGAIN, THE
'81 AMY
'81 DEVIL AND MAX DEVLIN, THE

JACK TAYLOR
ART DIRECTOR
'83 STAR 80*
'83 NIGHTMARES
'83 UNCOMMON VALOR

JACK TAYLOR JR.
ART DIRECTOR
'80 NINE TO FIVE
'81 LOOKER

JAMES TAYLOR
ART DIRECTOR
'79 LAST EMBRACE

JIM TAYLOR
STILLS
'83 RISKY BUSINESS
'83 BIG SCORE, THE

JOHN TAYLOR
ASSISTANT EDITOR
'83 DRAUGHTSMAN CONTRACT, THE

JUDY TAYLOR
CASTING
'79 AMITYVILLE HORROR, THE*
'84 RUNAWAY*

JULIET TAYLOR
CASTING
'79 MANHATTAN
'79 GREAT BANK HOAX, THE
'80 STARDUST MEMORIES
'80 CLOSE ENCOUNTERS OF THE THIRD KIND SPECIAL EDITION*
'80 WILLIE & PHIL
'81 ROLLOVER
'81 ARTHUR*
'81 FORT APACHE, THE BRONX
'81 HONKY TONK FREEWAY*
'82 SHOOT THE MOON
'82 STILL OF THE NIGHT
'82 MIDSUMMER NIGHT'S SEX COMEDY, A
'82 TEMPEST
'83 LOVESICK
'83 TERMS OF ENDEARMENT*
'83 ZELIG
'84 BIRDY
'84 BROADWAY DANNY ROSE
'84 CRACKERS
'84 FALLING IN LOVE*
'84 KILLING FIELDS, THE*
'84 MISUNDERSTOOD

LINDA TAYLOR
PROD. COORDINATOR
'84 ELECTRIC DREAMS*

MARIAN TAYLOR
SCREENPLAY
'81 DOZENS, THE*

MICHAEL TAYLOR
PRODUCER
'79 LAST EMBRACE*
'81 PURSUIT OF D.B. COOPER, THE*

NOEL TAYLOR
COSTUMES
'81 LEGEND OF THE LONE RANGER,THE

RICHARD TAYLOR
MISCELLANEOUS
'79 TIME AFTER TIME
'82 TRON
'82 TRON

RODERICK TAYLOR
SCREENPLAY
'83 STAR CHAMBER*

RON TAYLOR
MISCELLANEOUS
'80 BLUE LAGOON
'81 GALLIPOLI

RONNIE TAYLOR
CINEMATOGRAPHER
'79 CIRCLE OF IRON
'82 GANDHI*
'83 HIGH ROAD TO CHINA
'84 CHAMPIONS

VALERIE TAYLOR
MISCELLANEOUS
'80 BLUE LAGOON

LYNNE TAYLOR-CORBETT
CHOREOGRAPHER
'83 FOOTLOOSE

MOHAMED TAZI
LOCATIONS
'83 BLACK STALLION RETURNS, THE*

BILL TEAGUE
SOUND
'81 PURSUIT OF D.B. COOPER, THE*
'84 TANK

LEWIS TEAGUE
DIRECTOR
'80 ALLIGATOR
'82 FIGHTING BACK
'83 CUJO
2ND UNIT DIRECTOR
'80 BIG RED ONE, THE

TJACN TAN LENG TECK
2ND ASST. DIRECTOR
'79 SAINT JACK*

EDWARD TEETS
EXECUTIVE PRODUCER
'83 UNDER FIRE
ASSOCIATE PRODUCER
'80 THOSE LIPS, THOSE EYES
'81 SHARKEY'S MACHINE
'82 LOOKIN' TO GET OUT
UNIT PROD. MANAGER
'79 FRISCO KID, THE
'80 THOSE LIPS, THOSE EYES
'81 SHARKEY'S MACHINE
'82 LOOKIN' TO GET OUT
'83 UNDER FIRE

TONY TEIGER
PROPS
'80 HUMAN FACTOR, THE
'83 HIGH ROAD TO CHINA

JACK TEMCHIN
PRODUCER
'80 HOME MOVIES*

JERALD TEMPLE
ASSISTANT EDITOR
'83 LONE WOLF MCQUADE

TIM TENNANT
ASSOCIATE PRODUCER
'84 HOT DOG...THE MOVIE

WILLIAM TENNANT
EXECUTIVE PRODUCER
'80 HOLLYWOOD KNIGHTS, THE
'81 KING OF THE MOUNTAIN
'81 PURSUIT OF D.B. COOPER, THE*

MARILYN TENSER
PRODUCER
'80 GALAXINA
'83 MY TUTOR
'84 WEEKEND PASS

MARK TENSER
EXECUTIVE PRODUCER
'83 MY TUTOR

RANDY TEPPER
STILLS
'80 HEARTBEAT*

WILLIAM TEPPER
EXECUTIVE PRODUCER
'80 HEARTBEAT*

A. NUI BEN TERIITEHAU
PRODUCTION DESIGNER
'81 BEYOND THE REEF

EDWARD TERNES
MAKEUP
'80 LOVING COUPLES*
'81 RICH AND FAMOUS*
'83 BRAINSTORM*
'83 NIGHT IN HEAVEN, A*
'84 CHOOSE ME
'84 SONGWRITER*
'84 GRANDVIEW, U.S.A.*

ANITA TERRAIN
PROD. COORDINATOR
'81 HAND, THE
'82 SIX PACK

LINDA TERRELL
LOCATIONS
'80 SCHIZOID

DR. RICHARD TERRILE
MISCELLANEOUS
'84 2010

HOWARD TERRILL
EDITOR
'82 PARADISE

TERRY TERRILL
SCRIPT SUPERVISOR
'80 STUNT MAN, THE
'80 DEFIANCE
'81 INCREDIBLE SHRINKING WOMAN, THE
'84 SPLASH*

DENEY TERRIO
CHOREOGRAPHER
'80 IDOLMAKER, THE
'83 NIGHT IN HEAVEN, A

ALLEN TERRY
ART DIRECTOR
'83 SAVANNAH SMILES

BRIDGET TERRY
PUBLICIST
'79 RICH KIDS
'80 POPEYE
'82 DEAD MEN DON'T WEAR PLAID

JACK TERRY
PRODUCTION MANAGER
'81 REDS*
UNIT PROD. MANAGER
'79 ESCAPE FROM ALCATRAZ
'79 NORMA RAE
'80 MOUNTAIN MEN, THE

STEVE TERRY
PRODUCTION MANAGER
'82 MONTY PYTHON LIVE AT THE HOLLYWOOD BOWL

UGUR TERZIOGLU
ASSOCIATE PRODUCER
'83 YOR*

STEVE TESICH
SCREENPLAY
'79 BREAKING AWAY
'81 EYEWITNESS
'81 FOUR FRIENDS
'82 WORLD ACCORDING TO GARP, THE

PETE TESSETORE
MISCELLANEOUS
'81 FORT APACHE, THE BRONX

GAETANO TESTA
SOUND
'83 1990: THE BRONX WARRIORS

TED TESTER
ART DIRECTOR
'79 LOST AND FOUND
PRODUCTION DESIGNER
'79 SUNBURN
'81 PRIEST OF LOVE*

LAWRENCE TETENBAUM
2ND UNIT DIRECTOR
'84 POPE OF GREENWICH VILLAGE,THE

JOAN TEWKESBURY
DIRECTOR
'79 OLD BOYFRIENDS
SCREENPLAY
'83 NIGHT IN HEAVEN, A

REGINA HELENA TEXEIRA
UNIT MANAGER
'79 KILLER FISH*

GILDA TEXTER
COSTUME SUPERVISOR
'80 WHERE THE BUFFALO ROAM*

RUSSELL THACHER
ASSOCIATE PRODUCER
'83 GOLDEN SEAL, THE

RON THAL
STILLS
'83 AMERICANA*

SCOTT IRA THALER
2ND ASST. DIRECTOR
'81 DEAD AND BURIED*
'82 HALLOWEEN III: SEASON OF THE WITCH
'82 LOVE AND MONEY

SHELLEY THARAUD
PROD. SECRETARY
'79 MORE AMERICAN GRAFFITTI

TWYLA THARP
CHOREOGRAPHER
'79 HAIR
'81 RAGTIME
'84 AMADEUS

TONY THATCHER
PRODUCTION MANAGER
'80 KIDNAPPING OF THE PRESIDENT, THE

HERBERT THEISS
MISCELLANEOUS
'79 KILLER FISH

WILLIAM WARE THEISS
COSTUMES
'79 BUTCH AND SUNDANCE: THE EARLY YEARS
'83 HEART LIKE A WHEEL

BILL THEOBALD
ASSISTANT EDITOR
'79 PRISONER OF ZENDA, THE
'80 NUDE BOMB, THE

PAUL THEROUX
SCREENPLAY
'79 SAINT JACK*

GARY THIELTGES
CINEMATOGRAPHER
'82 EATING RAOUL

INGRID THIER
MAKEUP
'84 MOSCOW ON THE HUDSON*
HAIR
'84 MOSCOW ON THE HUDSON

ANDRE THIERRY
KEY GRIP
'80 QUARTET
'80 TESS

RANDY THOM
SOUND
'83 RETURN OF THE JEDI*

ANNA THOMAS
PRODUCER
'84 EL NORTE
SCREENPLAY
'84 EL NORTE*

ARMAND THOMAS
MISCELLANEOUS
'81 SCANNERS

BARRY THOMAS
SOUND
'79 AMERICAN GIGOLO
'80 CAN'T STOP THE MUSIC
'81 BACK ROADS
'81 FORCE FIVE
'83 BUDDY SYSTEM, THE
'84 MASS APPEAL

BEATRICE THOMAS
MISCELLANEOUS
'79 STARCRASH

BILL THOMAS
COSTUMES
'79 BLACK HOLE, THE
'80 FORMULA, THE
'81 DEVIL AND MAX DEVLIN, THE

BRAD THOMAS
LOCATIONS
'80 HOLLYWOOD KNIGHTS, THE

DAVE THOMAS
DIRECTOR
'83 STRANGE BREW*
SCREENPLAY
'83 STRANGE BREW*

DAVID THOMAS
LOCATIONS
'83 GET CRAZY
'84 IRRECONCILABLE DIFFERENCES*
'84 RIVER, THE*

DAVID THOMAS
PRODUCTION MANAGER
'81 HOWLING, THE

DAXSON THOMAS
PRODUCTION MANAGER
'80 HANGAR 18
'82 BOOGENS, THE

DIANE THOMAS
SCREENPLAY
'84 ROMANCING THE STONE

GARTH THOMAS
ASSOCIATE PRODUCER
'82 PINK FLOYD: THE WALL
'82 QUEST FOR FIRE*
'84 GREYSTOKE: THE LEGEND OF TARZAN, LORD OF THE APES
PRODUCTION MANAGER
'79 ALIEN

GUY THOMAS
SCREENPLAY
'80 WHOLLY MOSES!

IAN THOMAS
ART DIRECTOR
'82 GREY FOX, THE

JACKIE THOMAS
KEY GRIP
'83 HERCULES

JEREMY THOMAS
PRODUCER
'79 SHOUT, THE
'83 MERRY CHRISTMAS, MR. LAWRENCE

JOHN THOMAS
SPECIAL EFFECTS
'81 DEATH HUNT*
'82 GREY FOX, THE*
'82 MOTHER LODE*
'83 STAR 80*
'83 NEVER CRY WOLF
'84 ICEMAN
SP. EFFECTS SUPERV.
'83 GOLDEN SEAL, THE
'84 RUNAWAY

MARK THOMAS
SCRIPT SUPERVISOR
'81 GRADUATION DAY
'81 GALAXY OF TERROR

MICHAEL THOMAS
MAKEUP
'80 JUST TELL ME WHAT YOU WANT
'81 NEIGHBORS
'84 GHOSTBUSTERS*

MICHAEL THOMAS
SCREENPLAY
'83 HUNGER, THE*

R.L. THOMAS
DIRECTOR
'81 TICKET TO HEAVEN
SCREENPLAY
'81 TICKET TO HEAVEN*

ROSS THOMAS
SCREENPLAY
'82 HAMMETT*

SHEILA THOMAS
MAKEUP
'82 MOONLIGHTING

TERESA THOMAS
PROD. SECRETARY
'84 PHILADELPHIA EXPERIMENT, THE

TONY THOMAS
PRODUCER
'84 FIRSTBORN*

VICTORIA THOMAS
CASTING
'84 REPO MAN

WYNN THOMAS
ART DIRECTOR
'84 BEAT STREET

ALEX THOMPSON
CINEMATOGRAPHER
'79 CLASS OF MISS MACMICHAEL,THE
'81 EXCALIBUR
'83 KEEP, THE
'84 ELECTRIC DREAMS

ANNE THOMPSON
PUBLICIST
'81 FAN, THE
'81 KNIGHTRIDERS*
'82 HALLOWEEN III:
SEASON OF THE WITCH
'83 OSTERMAN WEEKEND, THE
'83 TERMS OF ENDEARMENT
UNIT PUBLICIST
'84 ADVENTURES OF BUCKAROO BANZAI
ACROSS THE 8TH DIMENSION, THE

CAROLINE THOMPSON
PUBLICIST
'83 JAWS 3-D

CHRIS THOMPSON
ASSISTANT EDITOR
'81 CLASH OF THE TITANS
'84 BOUNTY, THE*

CLAUDIA THOMPSON
MAKEUP
'84 MARVIN AND TIGE*
'84 MUTANT*
HAIR
'84 MARVIN AND TIGE*

DR. HUNTER THOMPSON
MISCELLANEOUS
'80 WHERE THE BUFFALO ROAM

ERNEST THOMPSON
SCREENPLAY
'81 ON GOLDEN POND

FRANKLIN THOMPSON
SCREENPLAY
'82 FORCED VENGEANCE

J. LEE THOMPSON
DIRECTOR
'81 HAPPY BIRTHDAY TO ME
'83 10 TO MIDNIGHT
'84 EVIL THAT MEN DO, THE

JIM THOMPSON
LOCATIONS
'83 OSTERMAN WEEKEND, THE*
'84 PARIS, TEXAS*

JOHN THOMPSON
EXECUTIVE PRODUCER
'83 HERCULES
2ND ASST. DIRECTOR
'82 HOME WORK
PROD. COORDINATOR
'81 ENTER THE NINJA

LARRY THOMPSON
EXECUTIVE PRODUCER
'84 CRIMES OF PASSION

MARGARET THOMPSON
ASSISTANT EDITOR
'84 SUPERGIRL*

NEVILLE THOMPSON
PRODUCER
'82 MISSIONARY, THE*
ASSOCIATE PRODUCER
'81 TIME BANDITS
LOCATIONS
'79 HANOVER STREET
'80 AWAKENING, THE*
'81 SEA WOLVES, THE

PETER THOMPSON
PUBLICIST
'79 MONTY PYTHON'S LIFE OF BRIAN

PETER LEE THOMPSON
EDITOR
'80 TWINKLE TWINKLE "KILLER" KANE*
'83 10 TO MIDNIGHT
'84 EVIL THAT MEN DO, THE
ASSISTANT EDITOR
'81 HAPPY BIRTHDAY TO ME*

ROCKY THOMPSON
MISCELLANEOUS
'84 POLICE ACADEMY

ROGER THOMPSON
HAIR
'84 CRIMES OF PASSION

SIMON THOMPSON
HAIR
'81 FRENCH LIEUTENANT'S WOMAN,THE
'84 GIVE MY REGARDS
TO BROAD STREET

TOMMY THOMPSON
EXECUTIVE PRODUCER
'79 QUINTET
'79 PERFECT COUPLE, A
'80 HEALTH
EXEC IN CHARGE PROD
'79 REMEMBER MY NAME
PRODUCTION MANAGER
'79 RICH KIDS
1ST ASST. DIRECTOR
'79 QUINTET
'79 PERFECT COUPLE, A
'79 REMEMBER MY NAME
'80 HEALTH
'81 ENTITY, THE
'82 BARBAROSA
'83 MAN WOMAN AND CHILD*

ARLY THOMSEN
KEY GRIP
'84 SILENT NIGHT, DEADLY NIGHT

BRIAN THOMSON
PRODUCTION DESIGNER
'81 SHOCK TREATMENT
'82 STARSTRUCK

PATIENCE THORESON

SCRIPT SUPERVISOR
'84 CHILDREN OF THE CORN*
'84 HOT DOG...THE MOVIE
'84 BEAR, THE*

DONALD THORIN

CINEMATOGRAPHER
'81 THIEF
'82 OFFICER AND A GENTLEMAN, AN
'83 BAD BOYS*
'84 AGAINST ALL ODDS
'84 PURPLE RAIN

ALISON THORNE

SCRIPT SUPERVISOR
'81 SHOCK TREATMENT
'82 MISSIONARY, THE
'83 FINAL OPTION, THE
'84 ANOTHER COUNTRY

KEN THORNE

MUSIC
'79 ARABIAN ADVENTURE
'81 SUPERMAN II
'83 SUPERMAN III
'84 LASSITER
'84 FINDERS KEEPERS
'84 EVIL THAT MEN DO, THE

STEVEN THORNLEY

SCREENPLAY
'80 HANGAR 18

JAMES THORNTON

SOUND
'82 PARASITE
'83 METALSTORM: THE DESTRUCTION OF JARED-SYN

JOE THORNTON

2ND ASST. DIRECTOR
'80 TOUCHED BY LOVE

RANDY THORNTON

ASSISTANT EDITOR
'79 STAR TREK-THE MOTION PICTURE*
'81 ESCAPE FROM NEW YORK
'83 OSTERMAN WEEKEND, THE

RALPH THORSON

MISCELLANEOUS
'80 HUNTER, THE

BILL THUM

PROPS
'82 FIRST BLOOD
'83 STAR 80*

JOEL THURM

CASTING
'80 AIRPLANE

DAN THURMAN

LOCATIONS
'79 MOUNTAIN FAMILY ROBINSON

JEROME TIBERGHIEN

STUNT COORDINATOR
'84 HOTEL NEW HAMPSHIRE, THE

ROSEMARY TICHLER

CASTING
'83 PIRATES OF PENZANCE, THE*

DAVID TICOTIN

2ND ASST. DIRECTOR
'82 AMITYVILLE II:THE POSSESSION*

FRANK TIDY

CINEMATOGRAPHER
'82 GREY FOX, THE
'83 SPACEHUNTER: ADVENTURES IN THE FORBIDDEN ZONE

ERNEST TIDYMAN

SCREENPLAY
'79 FORCE OF ONE, A

TONY TIERNEY

MISCELLANEOUS
'82 SWORD AND THE SORCERER, THE

C.D. TIGER

SCRIPT SUPERVISOR
'83 TESTAMENT

ERIC TILL

PRODUCER
'82 IF YOU COULD SEE WHAT I HEAR
DIRECTOR
'82 IF YOU COULD SEE WHAT I HEAR

JACK TILLAR

MUSIC
'81 MAN WHO SAW TOMORROW, THE*

JODIE TILLEN

COSTUMES
'81 THIEF
COSTUME SUPERVISOR
'82 NIGHT SHIFT

PATRICK TILLEY

SCREENPLAY
'79 LEGACY, THE*

BONNIE TIMMERMAN

CASTING
'82 FAST TIMES AT RIDGEMONT HIGH*
'83 BLACK STALLION RETURNS, THE*
'83 EASY MONEY
'83 EDDIE MACON'S RUN
'83 GORKY PARK*
'83 NIGHT IN HEAVEN, A
'83 TRADING PLACES
'83 KEEP, THE*
'84 KARATE KID, THE*
'84 POPE OF GREENWICH VILLAGE,THE
'84 C.H.U.D.

TARA TIMPONE

ASSISTANT EDITOR
'84 C.H.U.D.*

SIG TINGLOF

ART DIRECTOR
'79 JUST YOU AND ME KID

PAUL TINSLEY

SCRIPT SUPERVISOR
'80 MELVIN AND HOWARD
'84 JOY OF SEX, THE

TOMAS TINTERA

2ND ASST. DIRECTOR
'84 AMADEUS*

JOHN TINTORI

ASSOCIATE EDITOR
'84 BROTHER FROM ANOTHER PLANET, THE
KEY GRIP
'83 LIANNA
'83 LIQUID SKY

PHIL TIPPETT

MISCELLANEOUS
'80 EMPIRE STRIKES BACK, THE
'81 DRAGONSLAYER
'83 RETURN OF THE JEDI

JERRY TIRAZONA

SCREENPLAY
'83 BLIND RAGE*

GEORGE TIRL

CINEMATOGRAPHER
'84 NOT FOR PUBLICATION

STEVE TISCH

PRODUCER
'80 COAST TO COAST*
'83 RISKY BUSINESS*
EXECUTIVE PRODUCER
'83 DEAL OF THE CENTURY*

BOB TISCHLER

SOUND
'79 MR. MIKE'S MONDO VIDEO*
EDITOR
'79 MR. MIKE'S MONDO VIDEO*
MISCELLANEOUS
'79 MR. MIKE'S MONDO VIDEO

SUSAN TITLE

PROD. OFFICE COORD.
'80 STUNT MAN, THE

DR. YVES DE VESTEL TIVA

MISCELLANEOUS
'82 CONAN THE BARBARIAN

PAUL TIVERS

2ND ASST. DIRECTOR
'82 VICTOR/VICTORIA*
'84 GREYSTOKE: THE LEGEND OF TARZAN, LORD OF THE APES*

DAN TOBACK

KEY GRIP
'81 HELL NIGHT

JAMES TOBACK

PRODUCER
'82 LOVE AND MONEY
'83 EXPOSED
DIRECTOR
'82 LOVE AND MONEY
'83 EXPOSED
SCREENPLAY
'82 LOVE AND MONEY
'83 EXPOSED

JACQUE TOBEREN

ASSISTANT EDITOR
'83 EDDIE AND THE CRUISERS*

JAY TOBIAS

LOCATIONS
'83 PORKY'S II THE NEXT DAY

TIMOTHY TOBIN

ASSISTANT EDITOR
'81 POSTMAN ALWAYS RINGS TWICE, THE
'84 HOTEL NEW HAMPSHIRE, THE*

FRANCO TOCCI

KEY GRIP
'82 MONSIGNOR

JUSHO TODA

PRODUCTION DESIGNER
'83 MERRY CHRISTMAS, MR. LAWRENCE

BRENDA TODD

MAKEUP
'79 BUCK ROGERS*
'83 WAR GAMES*
'84 RIVER, THE

DELREE TODD

HAIR
'80 HOW TO BEAT THE HIGH COST OF LIVING*
'84 OH GOD, YOU DEVIL

JOY TODD

CASTING
'79 ROCKY II
'79 RUNNING*
'80 JUST TELL ME WHAT YOU WANT
'80 EXTERMINATOR, THE
'81 BUSTIN' LOOSE*
'81 BURNING, THE
'81 PRINCE OF THE CITY
'82 CHOSEN, THE
'82 FIGHTING BACK
'82 VERDICT, THE
'83 BEYOND THE LIMIT*
'83 DANIEL
'84 GHOSTBUSTERS*
'84 GARBO TALKS
'84 MOSCOW ON THE HUDSON*
'84 OVER THE BROOKLYN BRIDGE
'84 BOSTONIANS, THE
'84 ONCE UPON A TIME IN AMERICA*
MISCELLANEOUS
'80 NIGHT OF THE JUGGLER
'81 ATLANTIC CITY

MICHAEL TODD JR.

PRODUCER
'79 BELL JAR, THE*

THOMAS TODOROFF

MISCELLANEOUS
'83 BEYOND THE LIMIT

DAVID TOGURI

CHOREOGRAPHER
'84 GIVE MY REGARDS TO BROAD STREET

JERRY TOKOFSKY

EXECUTIVE PRODUCER
'81 PATERNITY
CO-PRODUCER
'84 DREAMSCAPE

MARILYN TOKUDA

MISCELLANEOUS
'83 MY TUTOR

SUSUMU TOKUNOW

SOUND
'83 PRIVATE SCHOOL
'84 BACHELOR PARTY
'84 DREAMSCAPE*

MICHAEL TOLAN

EXECUTIVE PRODUCER
'81 FOUR FRIENDS*

KEN TOM

ASSISTANT EDITOR
'80 COAST TO COAST*

GIACOMO TOMASELLI

KEY GRIP
'82 TEMPEST*
'83 1990: THE BRONX WARRIORS

PIETRO TOMASS

ASSISTANT EDITOR
'83 YOR*

DAVID TOMBLIN

1ST ASST. DIRECTOR
'80 EMPIRE STRIKES BACK, THE
'81 RAIDERS OF THE LOST ARK
'82 GANDHI
'83 RETURN OF THE JEDI
'83 NEVER SAY NEVER AGAIN
'84 INDIANA JONES AND THE TEMPLE OF DOOM*
2ND UNIT DIRECTOR
'79 PRISONER OF ZENDA, THE
'81 SUPERMAN II*
'83 RETURN OF THE JEDI

JOHN TOMICZEK

MISCELLANEOUS
'83 YELLOWBEARD

ALAN TOMKINS

ART DIRECTOR
'80 EMPIRE STRIKES BACK, THE*
'83 KEEP, THE*
'84 LASSITER*

LESLIE TOMKINS

ART DIRECTOR
'83 YENTL
'84 PASSAGE TO INDIA, A*

TOM TOMLINSON

PROPS
'84 BEVERLY HILLS COP
'84 SONGWRITER

MICHAEL TOMPANE

ASSISTANT EDITOR
'82 PERSONAL BEST*

ALICE TOMPKINS

SCRIPT SUPERVISOR
'79 MORE AMERICAN GRAFFITTI
'80 DIE LAUGHING
'82 SHOOT THE MOON
'83 RIGHT STUFF, THE
'84 BIRDY

JOE TOMPKINS
COSTUMES
'79 WHEN YOU COMIN' BACK, RED RYDER?
'80 CHEECH AND CHONG'S NEXT MOVIE
'80 COAL MINER'S DAUGHTER
'80 FOOLIN AROUND
'81 RAGGEDY MAN
'81 TRUE CONFESSIONS
'82 MISSING
'83 ROMANTIC COMEDY
'83 CROSS CREEK
'84 IRRECONCILABLE DIFFERENCES
'84 RIVER, THE
'84 SWING SHIFT

LES TOMPKINS
ART DIRECTOR
'80 SHINING, THE

PAUL TOMPKINS
LOCATIONS
'83 RUMBLEFISH

DONALD TOMS
PRODUCTION MANAGER
'84 TOP SECRET!
UNIT PROD. MANAGER
'81 DRAGONSLAYER
MISCELLANEOUS
'81 GREAT MUPPET CAPER, THE

JERRY TOMSON
KEY GRIP
'83 JOYSTICKS

NANCY TONERY
SCRIPT SUPERVISOR
'79 APOCALYPSE NOW*
'79 HAIR

TOM TONERY
PROPS
'80 TIMES SQUARE

VIVI TONINI
ASSISTANT EDITOR
'84 ONCE UPON A TIME IN AMERICA

CAMILLA TONIOLLO
ASSISTANT EDITOR
'83 LOVESICK*

PAT TONNEMA
COSTUMES
'81 MAN WHO SAW TOMORROW, THE*

ROSALBA DE BARTOLO TONTI
PROD. SECRETARY
'83 LONELY LADY, THE

ALAN TOOMAYAN
EDITOR
'82 EATING RAOUL
'84 NOT FOR PUBLICATION
ASSISTANT EDITOR
'81 SATURDAY THE 14TH*
'81 ENTER THE NINJA*

GERRY TOOMEY
2ND ASST. DIRECTOR
'84 KILLING FIELDS, THE*

MANUEL TOPETE
SOUND
'79 SUNBURN
'81 CATTLE ANNIE AND LITTLE BRITCHES
'83 AMITYVILLE 3D
'83 YELLOWBEARD*
'84 CONAN THE DESTROYER

FRANK TOPHAM
MISCELLANEOUS
'80 RAGING BULL

DANIEL TOPOLSKI
MISCELLANEOUS
'84 OXFORD BLUES

BURT TOPPER
CO-PRODUCER
'79 C.H.O.M.P.S.
2ND UNIT DIRECTOR
'79 C.H.O.M.P.S.

CHARLES TORBETT
PROPS
'79 FIFTH MUSKETEER, THE
'82 GANDHI
'84 GREYSTOKE: THE LEGEND OF TARZAN, LORD OF THE APES

STAN TORCHIA
CO-PRODUCER
'81 COMIN' AT YA!

FABIEN DAHLEN TORDJMANN
EDITOR
'79 PRIZE FIGHTER, THE
'84 MARVIN AND TIGE

LAURI TORHONEN
2ND ASST. DIRECTOR
'83 GORKY PARK*

FRANK TORO
SPECIAL EFFECTS
'83 STRANGE BREW*
'84 KARATE KID, THE

JORGE LUIS TORO
ART DIRECTOR
'84 C.H.U.D.

JOE TORRENUEVA
HAIR
'83 BREATHLESS*

GABRIEL TORRES
MISCELLANEOUS
'80 OCTAGON, THE

JOSE TORRES
1ST ASST. DIRECTOR
'83 BLIND RAGE

JOSE TORRES
MISCELLANEOUS
'79 MAIN EVENT, THE

JOSE ANTONIO TORRES
ASSISTANT EDITOR
'79 WINTER KILLS*
'81 HALLOWEEN II*

TONY TORRES
ASSISTANT EDITOR
'83 TIMERIDER*

MARIO TOSI
CINEMATOGRAPHER
'79 MAIN EVENT, THE
'80 RESURRECTION
'80 STUNT MAN, THE
'80 COAST TO COAST
'81 WHOSE LIFE IS IT ANYWAY?
'82 SIX PACK

ALBERTO TOSTZ
COSTUME SUPERVISOR
'82 YES, GIORGIO

GEORGE TOTH
MISCELLANEOUS
'81 WOLFEN

HELENA TOTH
UNIT MANAGER
'81 SPHINX*

LILLIAN TOTH
MAKEUP
'83 RISKY BUSINESS

NICHOLAS TOTH
MISCELLANEOUS
'81 WOLFEN

PETER TOTHPAL
HAIR
'80 HANGAR 18
'81 GALAXY OF TERROR
'82 ANDROID
'82 BEASTMASTER, THE
'82 BOOGENS, THE
'82 ZAPPED!
'82 PARASITE
'83 RUMBLEFISH*
'83 PRIVATE SCHOOL
'84 TERMINATOR, THE

TOTO
MUSIC
'84 DUNE

ETSU TOTOKO
2ND ASST. DIRECTOR
'82 CHALLENGE, THE*

SERGE TOUBOL
PRODUCTION MANAGER
'81 NIGHTHAWKS*
'84 RAZOR'S EDGE, THE*

VICTOR TOURJANSKY
1ST ASST. DIRECTOR
'79 PRISONER OF ZENDA, THE*
'80 POPEYE*

JEAN TOURNIER
CINEMATOGRAPHER
'79 MOONRAKER
'80 FIENDISH PLOT
OF DR. FU MANCHU, THE
MISCELLANEOUS
'83 MAN WOMAN AND CHILD

OLIVIER TOUSSAINT
MUSIC
'84 IRRECONCILABLE DIFFERENCES*

YOLANDA TOUSSEING
HAIR
'82 TOY, THE*
'84 REVENGE OF THE NERDS
'84 SIXTEEN CANDLES*
'84 GRANDVIEW, U.S.A.*

ROBERT TOWNE
PRODUCER
'82 PERSONAL BEST
DIRECTOR
'82 PERSONAL BEST
SCREENPLAY
'82 PERSONAL BEST

ROGER TOWNE
SCREENPLAY
'84 NATURAL, THE*
EXECUTIVE PRODUCER
'84 NATURAL, THE*

JIM TOWNLEY
STILLS
'81 GALLIPOLI
'81 ROAD GAMES*
'81 EARTHLING, THE
'83 YEAR OF
LIVING DANGEROUSLY, THE

JACK TOWNS
PROPS
'79 PRISONER OF ZENDA, THE*

MARVIN TOWNS JR.
1ST ASST. DIRECTOR
'83 BIG SCORE, THE

CLAYTON TOWNSEND
LOCATIONS
'84 LOVELESS, THE
'84 BEAT STREET

JEFFREY TOWNSEND
PRODUCTION DESIGNER
'83 BABY IT'S YOU
'84 RECKLESS

JENNY TOWNSEND
SCRIPT SUPERVISOR
'81 HELL NIGHT
'83 TIMERIDER

KEVIN TOWNSEND
ASSISTANT EDITOR
'80 MIDDLE AGE CRAZY*

SHERI TOWNSEND
PROD. SECRETARY
'84 HOT DOG...THE MOVIE

STEVE TOWNSEND
MISCELLANEOUS
'82 E.T. THE EXTRA-TERRESTRIAL

PETER TOWNSHEND
MUSIC
'80 KIDS ARE ALL RIGHT, THE

PHYLLIS TOWNSHEND
SCRIPT SUPERVISOR
'84 INDIANA JONES
AND THE TEMPLE OF DOOM*

GEOFFREY TOZER
ART DIRECTOR
'84 LITTLE DRUMMER GIRL, THE*

LINDA TRAINOFF
HAIR
'80 BALTIMORE BULLET, THE

JEAN-CLAUDE TRAMONT
DIRECTOR
'81 ALL NIGHT LONG

STEVEN TRAMZ
1ST ASST. DIRECTOR
'84 STONE BOY, THE
2ND ASST. DIRECTOR
'81 FOUR FRIENDS

GABRIELLA TRANI
MAKEUP
'83 LONELY LADY, THE*

MAURIZIO TRANI
MAKEUP
'83 PIRANHA II: THE SPAWNING
'83 1990: THE BRONX WARRIORS*

KAYE TRAPP
PROPS
'81 EYE FOR AN EYE, AN

ALEX TRAUNER
PRODUCTION DESIGNER
'79 FEDORA
'80 FIENDISH PLOT
OF DR. FU MANCHU, THE

GUY TRAVERS
2ND ASST. DIRECTOR
'81 TIME BANDITS

MARK TRAVIS
EXECUTIVE PRODUCER
'82 FIGHTING BACK*

NEIL TRAVIS
EDITOR
'79 HOT STUFF
'80 DIE LAUGHING
'80 IDOLMAKER, THE
'81 NOBODY'S PERFEKT
'82 SECOND THOUGHTS
'83 CUJO
'84 PHILADELPHIA EXPERIMENT, THE

MEL TRAXEL
STILLS
'79 STAR TREK-THE MOTION PICTURE
'80 SEEMS LIKE OLD TIMES
'80 IT'S MY TURN
'80 LONG RIDERS, THE*
'80 OCTAGON, THE
'81 PENNIES FROM HEAVEN
'82 I OUGHT TO BE IN PICTURES
'82 DEATH VALLEY
'83 MAX DUGAN RETURNS

RAY TRAYNOR
PROPS
'80 KIDS ARE ALL RIGHT, THE

REV. WILLIAM TREACY
MISCELLANEOUS
'79 RUNNER STUMBLES, THE

ALAN TREADWELL
UNIT PROD. MANAGER
'83 HOUSE ON SORORITY ROW

PAUL TREJO
EDITOR
'83 HOUSE ON SORORITY ROW*
ASSISTANT EDITOR
'80 EYES OF A STRANGER*

LEN TREMBLE
ASSISTANT EDITOR
'83 LONELY LADY, THE*

TONY TREMBLY
MISCELLANEOUS
'83 METALSTORM: THE DESTRUCTION OF JARED-SYN

ROSALIE WINKLER TRENCHER
PROD. OFFICE COORD.
'80 BLUE LAGOON

BRIAN TRENERRY
ASSISTANT EDITOR
'82 HOUSE OF THE LONG SHADOWS*

JERRY TRENT
CHOREOGRAPHER
'80 XANADU*

JOHN TRENT
DIRECTOR
'80 MIDDLE AGE CRAZY

LUCIO TRENTINI
UNIT PROD. MANAGER
'82 MONSIGNOR

WOLFGANG TREU
CINEMATOGRAPHER
'84 LITTLE DRUMMER GIRL, THE

RICHARD TREVOR
EDITOR
'80 HUMAN FACTOR, THE

ANDREW TRIBE
ASSOCIATE PRODUCER
'83 PIRATES OF PENZANCE, THE*

NEIL TRIFUNOVICH
SPECIAL EFFECTS
'84 POLICE ACADEMY*
'84 MRS. SOFFEL*

DEREK TRIGG
ASSISTANT EDITOR
'80 FFOLKES*
'80 FLASH GORDON*
'82 SENDER, THE*

MICHAEL TRIKILIS
PRODUCER
'82 SIX PACK

GUS TRIKONIS
DIRECTOR
'80 TOUCHED BY LOVE
'81 TAKE THIS JOB AND SHOVE IT

ROSE TRIMARCO
COSTUMES
'81 SO FINE*

TONI TRIMBLE
MAKEUP
'84 PREPPIES

EVELYN TRIMMER
HAIR
'80 NINE TO FIVE*
'81 INCREDIBLE SHRINKING WOMAN, THE*
'83 TWO OF A KIND*

DAVID TRINGHAM
1ST ASST. DIRECTOR
'79 CUBA
'79 HANOVER STREET
'80 ROUGH CUT
'81 AMERICAN WEREWOLF IN LONDON, AN
'81 OUTLAND
'83 HUNGER, THE*
'84 BOUNTY, THE

GUY TRINQUE
LOCATIONS
'81 GAS

GEORGE TRIROGOFF
ASSISTANT EDITOR
'79 WARRIORS, THE*
'82 MEGAFORCE*

JAN TROELL
DIRECTOR
'79 HURRICANE

BOB TROJAN
SPECIAL EFFECTS
'80 IDOLMAKER, THE*

EDNA TROMANS
PUBLICIST
'80 BLACK MARBLE, THE
'80 IN GOD WE TRUST
'81 ON GOLDEN POND
'82 MAKING LOVE
UNIT PUBLICIST
'79 YANKS

SONIA TROOP
PROD. SECRETARY
'84 EVIL THAT MEN DO, THE*

LINDA TROST
ASSISTANT EDITOR
'82 STARSTRUCK*

ERICH TROSTL
MISCELLANEOUS
'79 ALL THAT JAZZ

CYNNIE TROUP
SCRIPT SUPERVISOR
'79 AMERICAN GIGOLO
'80 CAN'T STOP THE MUSIC
'81 SHARKEY'S MACHINE
'82 BEST FRIENDS
'82 LOOKIN' TO GET OUT
'83 STING II, THE
'83 TO BE OR NOT TO BE

KATHY TROUT
STUNT COORDINATOR
'80 BLUE LAGOON

OSCAR GOMEZ TRUJILLO
LOCATIONS
'84 EL NORTE

DOUGLAS TRUMBULL
PRODUCER
'83 BRAINSTORM
DIRECTOR
'83 BRAINSTORM
MISCELLANEOUS
'79 STAR TREK-THE MOTION PICTURE
'80 CLOSE ENCOUNTERS OF THE THIRD KIND SPECIAL EDITION
'82 BLADERUNNER

HAL TRUSSELL
CINEMATOGRAPHER
'84 BACHELOR PARTY

BOB TSCHANZ
MISCELLANEOUS
'83 OF UNKNOWN ORIGIN

SLAVA TSUCKERMAN
PRODUCER
'83 LIQUID SKY
DIRECTOR
'83 LIQUID SKY
SCREENPLAY
'83 LIQUID SKY*
MUSIC
'83 LIQUID SKY*

SHINTARO TSUJI
EXECUTIVE PRODUCER
'82 DON'T CRY, IT'S ONLY THUNDER*

JOE TUBENS
HAIR
'79 HAIR
'79 LAST EMBRACE
'80 SMALL CIRCLE OF FRIENDS, A*
'80 ONE-TRICK PONY

JOEL TUBER
ASSOCIATE PRODUCER
'83 SILKWOOD*
1ST ASST. DIRECTOR
'84 PLACES IN THE HEART
2ND ASST. DIRECTOR
'79 RICH KIDS
'79 HAIR*
'80 ONE-TRICK PONY
'81 RAGTIME*
'83 LOCAL HERO*
'83 SILKWOOD

NANCY WOOD TUBER
PROD. OFFICE COORD.
'81 NEIGHBORS

MORTON TUBOR
EDITOR
'80 BIG RED ONE, THE

FRED TUCH
ART DIRECTOR
'81 PENNIES FROM HEAVEN*
PRODUCTION DESIGNER
'79 AVALANCHE EXPRESS

MICHAEL TUCHNER
DIRECTOR
'83 TRENCHCOAT

CHRISTOPHER TUCKER
MISCELLANEOUS
'80 ELEPHANT MAN, THE
'82 FIVE DAYS ONE SUMMER
'82 QUEST FOR FIRE

JULIA TUCKER
SCRIPT SUPERVISOR
'79 ROSE, THE
'79 CHAPTER TWO
'80 SEEMS LIKE OLD TIMES
'80 DIVINE MADNESS
'80 LAST MARRIED COUPLE

MELVILLE TUCKER
EXECUTIVE PRODUCER
'80 STIR CRAZY
'82 HANKY PANKY

PAUL TUCKER
PRODUCTION MANAGER
'82 FIRST BLOOD
'82 GREY FOX, THE
'83 GOLDEN SEAL, THE
UNIT PROD. MANAGER
'83 STAR 80*
2ND ASST. DIRECTOR
'79 PROPHECY*

PHIL TUCKER
EDITOR
'80 NUDE BOMB, THE*
'81 CHARLIE CHAN AND THE CURSE OF THE DRAGON QUEEN*

STEPHEN TUCKER
ASSISTANT EDITOR
'80 HEALTH*

FRANK TUDISCO
SCRIPT SUPERVISOR
'84 FLASHPOINT
'84 TANK

BRIAN TUFANO
CINEMATOGRAPHER
'83 LORDS OF DISCIPLINE, THE
'84 DREAMSCAPE
MISCELLANEOUS
'82 BLADERUNNER

RICHARD TUGGLE
DIRECTOR
'84 TIGHTROPE
SCREENPLAY
'79 ESCAPE FROM ALCATRAZ
'84 TIGHTROPE

VLADIMIR TUKAN
MISCELLANEOUS
'84 MOSCOW ON THE HUDSON

BARBARA TULLIVER
ASSISTANT EDITOR
'84 PLACES IN THE HEART*

MARION TUMEN
SCRIPT SUPERVISOR
'79 DREAMER
'80 NUDE BOMB, THE
'81 BACK ROADS
'82 FAST TIMES AT RIDGEMONT HIGH
'82 POLTERGEIST
'82 LOVE AND MONEY
'82 DEATH VALLEY*
'83 RISKY BUSINESS

JONATHAN TUNICK
MUSIC
'81 ENDLESS LOVE
'81 FORT APACHE, THE BRONX
'83 I AM THE CHEESE

SALLY TUNNICLIFFE
CASTING
'79 SAINT JACK*

WILLIAM TUNTKE
PRODUCTION DESIGNER
'80 NUDE BOMB, THE
'84 CLOAK AND DAGGER

KEN TUOHY
2ND ASST. DIRECTOR
'81 RAGTIME*
'83 KRULL*
LOCATIONS
'84 AMADEUS*

MICHAEL TURK
MISCELLANEOUS
'83 OCTOPUSSY

JAMES TURLEY
1ST ASST. DIRECTOR
'80 JAZZ SINGER, THE*
2ND ASST. DIRECTOR
'81 AMY*

THOMAS TURLLEY
ART DIRECTOR
'80 GALAXINA
PRODUCTION DESIGNER
'80 GALAXINA

LAWRENCE TURMAN
PRODUCER
'81 CAVEMAN*
'82 THING, THE*
'82 SECOND THOUGHTS
'84 MASS APPEAL*
SCREENPLAY
'82 SECOND THOUGHTS

JERRY TURNAGE
HAIR
'79 PERFECT COUPLE, A
'79 REMEMBER MY NAME
'80 ROADIE
'80 HEALTH

MARK TURNBULL
1ST ASST. DIRECTOR
'82 STARSTRUCK
2ND ASST. DIRECTOR
'79 MY BRILLIANT CAREER

BILL TURNER
MAKEUP
'79 DREAMER*
'79 FRISCO KID, THE*
'79 NORMA RAE*
'79 VILLAIN, THE*
'81 ...ALL THE MARBLES
'81 LEGEND OF THE LONE RANGER,THE
'81 REDS*

COBY TURNER
SCRIPT SUPERVISOR
'81 PRIVATE LESSONS

DONNA TURNER
HAIR
'79 FORCE OF ONE, A
'80 FOOLIN AROUND

DOUG TURNER
SOUND
'79 MAGICIAN OF LUBLIN, THE
'81 EXCALIBUR

ERIC TURNER
HAIR
'83 SMITHEREENS

KAORI TURNER
MISCELLANEOUS
'83 MAN WHO LOVED WOMEN, THE

MARTIN TURNER
STILLS
'84 REPO MAN

PAUL TURNER
MISCELLANEOUS
'80 BATTLE BEYOND THE STARS

PETE TURNER
STILLS
'80 CLOSE ENCOUNTERS OF THE THIRD KIND SPECIAL EDITION*

SUSAN TURNER
MISCELLANEOUS
'81 FEAR NO EVIL
'84 DREAMSCAPE

ED TURNES
MAKEUP
'83 CLASS*

CANDY CAREY TUTTLE
STUNT COORDINATOR
'83 BALLAD OF GREGORIO CORTEZ, THE
MISCELLANEOUS
'83 BALLAD OF GREGORIO CORTEZ, THE

TOM TUTTLE
MAKEUP
'79 PERFECT COUPLE, A
'80 BRONCO BILLY
'81 ON GOLDEN POND
'82 HAMMETT*
'82 LOVE AND MONEY

WILLIAM TUTTLE
MAKEUP
'79 LOVE AT FIRST BITE
'80 RESURRECTION
'80 CHANGE OF SEASONS, A*
'81 ZORRO, THE GAY BLADE

NORMAN TWAIN
ASSOCIATE PRODUCER
'84 HOTEL NEW HAMPSHIRE, THE*

TONY TWEEDALE
PUBLICIST
'79 CLASS OF MISS MACMICHAEL, THE

LYNN TWENTYMAN
SCRIPT SUPERVISOR
'79 ALL THAT JAZZ*
'81 EYEWITNESS
'82 SOUP FOR ONE
'83 AMITYVILLE 3D

ROGER TWETEN
ASSISTANT EDITOR
'82 NIGHT SHIFT*
'84 SPLASH*

DOUGLAS TWIDDY
PRODUCTION MANAGER
'80 SHINING, THE
UNIT PROD. MANAGER
'80 ROUGH CUT
MISCELLANEOUS
'81 RAIDERS OF THE LOST ARK
'84 BOUNTY, THE

S. TYER
PRODUCTION DESIGNER
'79 PHANTASM

ADRIAN TYLER
PROPS
'83 HERCULES

SUSAN TYLER
CASTING
'84 FLASHPOINT*

KATHLEEN TYNAN
SCREENPLAY
'79 AGATHA*

TRACY TYNAN
COSTUMES
'84 CHOOSE ME
'84 STRANGERS KISS

JACK TYREE
STUNT COORDINATOR
'80 HUMANOIDS FROM THE DEEP

JAN TYRELL
SCRIPT SUPERVISOR
'83 MAN FROM SNOWY RIVER, THE

JIM TYSON
COSTUME SUPERVISOR
'83 RIGHT STUFF, THE

U

DANY UBAUD
ASSOCIATE PRODUCER
'81 BURNING, THE

JEAN UBAUD
EXECUTIVE PRODUCER
'81 BURNING, THE*
MISCELLANEOUS
'81 BURNING, THE

UDANNE UDITIS
2ND ASST. DIRECTOR
'83 PORKY'S II THE NEXT DAY*

LES UDY
SOUND
'83 REVENGE OF THE NINJA

YUKIO UEDA
MAKEUP
'82 CHALLENGE, THE*

ERICA UELAND
MAKEUP
'84 CHILDREN OF THE CORN

TAKASHI UENO
CASTING
'83 MERRY CHRISTMAS, MR. LAWRENCE*
STILLS
'83 MERRY CHRISTMAS, MR. LAWRENCE*

KIYOTAKA UGAWA
PROD. COORDINATOR
'81 INCHON

RUDY UGLAND
MISCELLANEOUS
'79 BUTCH AND SUNDANCE: THE EARLY YEARS
'79 FRISCO KID, THE
'80 HEAVEN'S GATE
'80 TOM HORN
'81 EYEWITNESS
'81 ZORRO, THE GAY BLADE

PETRO UIAHOS
MISCELLANEOUS
'80 BATTLE BEYOND THE STARS

MARK ULANO
SOUND
'82 ANDROID
'82 LAST AMERICAN VIRGIN, THE
'83 ANGEL OF H.E.A.T.*
'83 CUJO
'84 BREAKIN 2 ELECTRIC BOOGALOO
'84 WEEKEND PASS

JEFFREY ULLMAN
COSTUMES
'81 MY DINNER WITH ANDRE

GOFFREDO UNDER
STUNT COORDINATOR
'83 YOR*

RON UNDERWOOD
1ST ASST. DIRECTOR
'79 TOURIST TRAP

EMMANUEL UNGARO
COSTUMES
'80 GLORIA*

ANTHONY UNGER
PRODUCER
'82 SILENT RAGE

FREDY UNGER
SPECIAL EFFECTS
'81 COMIN' AT YA!

MARIA UNGOR
UNIT MANAGER
'81 SPHINX*

JOE UNSINN
SPECIAL EFFECTS
'80 WHEN TIME RAN OUT*
'83 ALL THE RIGHT MOVES
'84 CITY HEAT
'84 JOHNNY DANGEROUSLY
'84 TIGHTROPE
SP. EFFECTS SUPERV.
'81 STRIPES
'84 REVENGE OF THE NERDS

GEOFFREY UNSWORTH
CINEMATOGRAPHER
'79 GREAT TRAIN ROBBERY, THE
'80 TESS*
'81 SUPERMAN II*

MAGGIE UNSWORTH
SCRIPT SUPERVISOR
'83 PIRATES OF PENZANCE, THE
'84 GREYSTOKE: THE LEGEND OF TARZAN, LORD OF THE APES
'84 PASSAGE TO INDIA, A

KENNETH UNTOTT
MAKEUP
'80 QUARTET*

LT. ED URBAN
MISCELLANEOUS
'84 MRS. SOFFEL

EDUARDO URBANO SR.
PROPS
'84 PURPLE HEARTS

ARNOLD URDANG
PROD. COORDINATOR
'83 MAUSOLEUM*

FRANK URIOSTE
EDITOR
'79 FAST BREAK
'80 LOVING COUPLES*
'81 ENTITY, THE
'83 AMITYVILLE 3D
'83 TRENCHCOAT
'84 CONAN THE DESTROYER
MISCELLANEOUS
'80 JAZZ SINGER, THE

MICHAEL USLAN
PRODUCER
'82 SWAMP THING*

RICHARD USSHER
UNIT MANAGER
'82 STARSTRUCK

KENNETH UTT

PRODUCER
'83 STAR 80*
ASSOCIATE PRODUCER
'79 ALL THAT JAZZ*
'81 EYEWITNESS
'82 STILL OF THE NIGHT*
PRODUCTION MANAGER
'79 ALL THAT JAZZ
'81 EYEWITNESS
'82 STILL OF THE NIGHT
'83 STAR 80

JAMES UTTERBACK

SOUND
'81 SOUTHERN COMFORT*

CARLITO UY

MISCELLANEOUS
'83 BLIND RAGE

LEONARDO VELASCO UY

EXECUTIVE PRODUCER
'83 BLIND RAGE*

MARIO UY

PROD. COORDINATOR
'83 BLIND RAGE*

V

JOST VACANO
CINEMATOGRAPHER
'84 NEVERENDING STORY, THE

MAURICE VACCARINO
PRODUCTION MANAGER
'81 ZORRO, THE GAY BLADE*
UNIT PROD. MANAGER
'79 CHAMP, THE
'80 AIRPLANE

WARREN VACHE JR.
MISCELLANEOUS
'84 COTTON CLUB, THE

PIERRE VADE
HAIR
'79 MOONRAKER*

MARIJAN VADJA
2ND ASST. DIRECTOR
'80 AMERICAN SUCCESS COMPANY,THE

STEVEN VAIL
PRODUCER
'79 SCAVENGER HUNT
SCREENPLAY
'79 SCAVENGER HUNT*

RIMAS VAINORIUS
2ND UNIT DIRECTOR
'79 PLAYERS

ANDREW VAJNA
EXECUTIVE PRODUCER
'82 AMATEUR, THE*
'82 FIRST BLOOD*

ARMANDO VALCAUDA
SPECIAL EFFECTS
'79 STARCRASH*
MISCELLANEOUS
'83 HERCULES

CARLOS VALDEMAR
SCREENPLAY
'80 GUYANA: CULT OF THE DAMNED*

DANIEL VALDES
MUSIC
'82 ZOOT SUIT

DAVID VALDES
1ST ASST. DIRECTOR
'83 RUMBLEFISH
'83 SUDDEN IMPACT
'83 OUTSIDERS, THE
'84 CITY HEAT
'84 TIGHTROPE
2ND ASST. DIRECTOR
'80 ANY WHICH WAY YOU CAN*
'80 IN GOD WE TRUST*
'80 OH GOD! BOOK II
'82 FIREFOX
'82 HAMMETT*
'82 PARTNERS

BILL VALDEZ
LOCATIONS
'80 SEEMS LIKE OLD TIMES

LUIS VALDEZ
DIRECTOR
'82 ZOOT SUIT
SCREENPLAY
'82 ZOOT SUIT

RENEE VALENTE
PRODUCER
'80 LOVING COUPLES

JOE VALENTINE
MISCELLANEOUS
'80 GONG SHOW MOVIE, THE
'82 YOUNG DOCTORS IN LOVE
'83 CHRISTINE
'84 STARMAN

VALENTINO
MISCELLANEOUS
'81 BODY AND SOUL

RICHARD GRANT VALESKO
PROPS
'79 CHAMP, THE
'79 PROMISES IN THE DARK
'80 HONEYSUCKLE ROSE

VALLI
MAKEUP
'82 PORKY'S
'83 PORKY'S II THE NEXT DAY

JOHN VALLONE
ART DIRECTOR
'79 STAR TREK-THE MOTION PICTURE*
PRODUCTION DESIGNER
'81 SOUTHERN COMFORT
'82 48 HOURS
'83 BRAINSTORM
'84 STREETS OF FIRE

HUGO VAN BAREN
KEY GRIP
'79 SAINT JACK

SEMMES VAN BROCKLIN
CASTING
'84 MAKING THE GRADE*

MARK VAN BUREN
ASSISTANT EDITOR
'80 ROUGH CUT*

MARGARETE VAN DAM
CASTING
'83 CHEECH AND CHONG'S STILL SMOKIN'

ERNST VAN DEBOVENKAMP
ART DIRECTOR
'82 HOME WORK

WILLIAM VAN DER BYL
SPECIAL EFFECTS
'79 NORMA RAE
'80 BALTIMORE BULLET, THE

EDDY VAN DER ENDEN
CINEMATOGRAPHER
'82 BUTTERFLY

PAUL VAN DER LINDEN
CINEMATOGRAPHER
'81 LAST CHASE, THE

VIOLET VAN DER STRAATEN
PROPS
'83 CHEECH AND CHONG'S STILL SMOKIN'

FRANK VAN DER VEER
MISCELLANEOUS
'79 1941
'80 FLASH GORDON
'81 CLASH OF THE TITANS
'82 CONAN THE BARBARIAN

RUUD VAN DIJK
ART DIRECTOR
'83 CHEECH AND CHONG'S STILL SMOKIN'

RICHARD VAN DYKE
SOUND
'82 I'M DANCING AS FAST AS I CAN

JOHN VAN EYSSEN
ASSOCIATE PRODUCER
'83 DANIEL

GARY VAN FLEET
PROPS
'79 PRIZE FIGHTER, THE
'80 PRIVATE EYES, THE
'84 MARVIN AND TIGE

AMY VAN GILDER
MISCELLANEOUS
'79 MUPPET MOVIE, THE

BUDDY VAN HORN
DIRECTOR
'80 ANY WHICH WAY YOU CAN
STUNT COORDINATOR
'78 DEER HUNTER, THE*
'80 HEAVEN'S GATE
'83 YELLOWBEARD

WAYNE VAN HORN
STUNT COORDINATOR
'83 SUDDEN IMPACT
'84 CITY HEAT
'84 TIGHTROPE

ANTHONY VAN LAAST
CHOREOGRAPHER
'81 EXCALIBUR
'81 OUTLAND
'83 FINAL OPTION, THE

CHAKO VAN LEUWEN
PRODUCER
'83 PIRANHA II: THE SPAWNING*

RICK VAN NESS
PRODUCTION DESIGNER
'83 AMERICANA
PRODUCTION MANAGER
'83 AMERICANA

RON VAN NOSTRAND
MISCELLANEOUS
'83 D.C. CAB

GEORGE VAN NOY
UNIT PROD. MANAGER
'79 LOVE AND BULLETS

ANITA VAN REEDE
PROD. SECRETARY
'83 CHEECH AND CHONG'S
STILL SMOKIN'

TIM VAN RELLIM
MISCELLANEOUS
'80 KIDS ARE ALL RIGHT, THE

THEADORA VAN RUNKLE
COSTUMES
'79 JERK, THE
'81 S.O.B.
'81 HEARTBEEPS*
'82 BEST LITTLE WHOREHOUSE
IN TEXAS, THE
'84 RHINESTONE*

FLOYD VAN WEY
SPECIAL EFFECTS
'80 COAL MINER'S DAUGHTER*

JUDY VAN WORMER
CHOREOGRAPHER
'79 1941*

JIM VAN WYCK
1ST ASST. DIRECTOR
'84 ICEMAN
2ND ASST. DIRECTOR
'80 FOG, THE
'81 SHARKEY'S MACHINE*
'81 ONLY WHEN I LAUGH
'82 BEST FRIENDS*
'82 BEST LITTLE WHOREHOUSE
IN TEXAS, THE*
'83 STROKER ACE*

HAROLD VANARNUM
ASSOCIATE PRODUCER
'79 LOVE AT FIRST BITE

JAMES VANCE
PRODUCTION DESIGNER
'79 NIGHTWING
'82 MAKING LOVE
'84 LONELY GUY, THE

MARILYN VANCE
COSTUMES
'82 FAST TIMES AT RIDGEMONT HIGH
'82 48 HOURS
'82 JEKYLL AND HYDE TOGETHER AGAIN
'84 STREETS OF FIRE
'84 ROMANCING THE STONE

FRANZ VANDENBURG
ASSISTANT EDITOR
'79 MY BRILLIANT CAREER

JILL VANDERMEER
PROD. OFFICE COORD.
'84 AGAINST ALL ODDS
PROD. COORDINATOR
'80 SMALL CIRCLE OF FRIENDS, A*
'84 ELECTRIC DREAMS*

LESLEY VANDERWALT
MAKEUP
'82 ROAD WARRIOR, THE

NORMAN THADDEUS VANE
DIRECTOR
'83 FRIGHTMARE
SCREENPLAY
'83 FRIGHTMARE

RICHARD VANE
LOCATIONS
'81 ZORRO, THE GAY BLADE
'82 E.T. THE EXTRA-TERRESTRIAL
'83 ROMANTIC COMEDY*
'83 TWILIGHT ZONE, THE MOVIE
'84 INDIANA JONES
AND THE TEMPLE OF DOOM*

DEREK VANLINT
CINEMATOGRAPHER
'79 ALIEN
'81 DRAGONSLAYER

PASQUALE VANNINI
PRODUCTION MANAGER
'83 1990: THE BRONX WARRIORS

GERALD VANSIER
EDITOR
'81 MY BLOODY VALENTINE*

ED VANSTON
ASSOCIATE PRODUCER
'80 FOR THE LOVE OF BENJI*

DON VARGAS
COSTUME SUPERVISOR
'82 MEGAFORCE

MARK VARGO
MISCELLANEOUS
'84 2010

FRANCO VASCOTTO
PROPS
'83 1990: THE BRONX WARRIORS*

TURI VASILE
EXECUTIVE PRODUCER
'79 KILLER FISH*

SALVADOR VASQUEZ
KEY GRIP
'83 YELLOWBEARD

JEAN-MARC VASSEUR
EDITOR
'83 HOUSE ON SORORITY ROW*

ED VAUGHAN
1ST ASST. DIRECTOR
'79 AMITYVILLE HORROR, THE

STEPHEN VAUGHAN
STILLS
'79 JERK, THE
'80 COAST TO COAST
'80 WHERE THE BUFFALO ROAM
'82 BLADERUNNER
'82 DEAD MEN DON'T WEAR PLAID
'82 PERSONAL BEST
'83 STAR 80
'83 STING II, THE
'83 TO BE OR NOT TO BE
'84 STREETS OF FIRE
'84 NATURAL, THE*

BEN VAUGHN
PRODUCER
'80 FOR THE LOVE OF BENJI

P.H. VAZAK
SCREENPLAY
'84 GREYSTOKE: THE LEGEND OF TARZAN, LORD OF THE APES*

CINDY VEAZEY
1ST ASST. DIRECTOR
'80 FRIDAY THE 13TH

FRANCIS VEBER
SCREENPLAY
'81 SUNDAY LOVERS*
'82 PARTNERS
EXECUTIVE PRODUCER
'82 PARTNERS

SAL VECCHIO
PROPS
'80 FOXES
'80 WHY WOULD I LIE?

VINNIE VECCHIO
PROPS
'80 LITTLE MISS MARKER
'82 DINER*

LADY VEELHEIM
PROPS
'82 PARADISE

WALLY VEEVERS
SPECIAL EFFECTS
'83 LOCAL HERO
MISCELLANEOUS
'80 RAISE THE TITANIC
'80 SATURN 3
'83 KEEP, THE

BAYARD VEILLER
PROD. COORDINATOR
'83 SOMETHING WICKED THIS WAY COMES*

JIM VEILLEUX
MISCELLANEOUS
'82 STAR TREK II THE WRATH OF KHAN

WILLIAM VENEGAS
PRODUCTION MANAGER
'79 WINTER KILLS*
UNIT PROD. MANAGER
'79 MAIN EVENT, THE*
'80 LAST FLIGHT OF NOAH'S ARK,THE
2ND ASST. DIRECTOR
'79 ICE CASTLES*

KATHI VENT
PROD. COORDINATOR
'83 RETURN OF THE ALIENS: THE DEADLY SPAWN

CLAUDIO VENTURA
EDITOR
'84 JUST THE WAY YOU ARE*

JAN VENTURA
SCREENPLAY
'84 BREAKIN 2 ELECTRIC BOOGALOO*

MICHAEL VENTURA
SCREENPLAY
'80 ROADIE*

PAUL VENTURA
CASTING
'84 ALPHABET CITY*

GIORGIO VENTUROLI
ASSISTANT EDITOR
'83 LONELY LADY, THE*

CECELIA VERARDI
MAKEUP
'81 FRIDAY THE 13TH PART TWO
HAIR
'81 FRIDAY THE 13TH PART TWO

CINDIE VERARDI
MAKEUP
'80 HE KNOWS YOU'RE ALONE
PROD. OFFICE COORD.
'80 MANIAC*

MARCEL VERCOUTERE
SPECIAL EFFECTS
'82 BARBAROSA

TIMEA VERESS
1ST ASST. DIRECTOR
'80 NIJINSKY*

JERRY VERHEUL
MISCELLANEOUS
'79 FAST COMPANY

GUY VERHILLE
COSTUMES
'79 DREAMER
'80 WHOLLY MOSES!
COSTUME SUPERVISOR
'84 JOY OF SEX, THE

CHRIS VERNER
SP. EFFECTS SUPERV.
'84 SCANDALOUS

STEPHEN VERONA
DIRECTOR
'79 BOARDWALK
SCREENPLAY
'79 BOARDWALK*

ED VERREAUX
MISCELLANEOUS
'83 TWILIGHT ZONE, THE MOVIE

DEBBIE VERTUE
2ND ASST. DIRECTOR
'84 OXFORD BLUES

RENE VERZIER
CINEMATOGRAPHER
'80 HOG WILD
'80 DEATH SHIP
'81 GAS
'83 OF UNKNOWN ORIGIN
MISCELLANEOUS
'80 TERROR TRAIN

EDITH VESPERINI
COSTUMES
'83 HANNA K

PIERRE VESPIER
KEY GRIP
'84 JUST THE WAY YOU ARE*

CECILIA VETTRAINO
STILLS
'84 C.H.U.D.

RENEE VIAL
ASSISTANT EDITOR
'79 FEDORA*
'84 LITTLE DRUMMER GIRL, THE*

FREDDY VIANELLIS
2ND ASST. DIRECTOR
'79 HURRICANE*
'80 FOR THE LOVE OF BENJI*
'82 TEMPEST*

MATTHEW VIBERT
PRODUCTION MANAGER
'82 QUEST FOR FIRE*
1ST ASST. DIRECTOR
'82 QUEST FOR FIRE*

CLEM VICARI
MUSIC
'80 MOTHER'S DAY*

KATHARINE VICKERS
MAKEUP
'80 FRIDAY THE 13TH

LARRY VICKERS
CHOREOGRAPHER
'80 LOVING COUPLES

SARAH VICKERS
ASSISTANT EDITOR
'82 HOUSE OF THE LONG SHADOWS*

JOSEPH VICKOCIL
MISCELLANEOUS
'83 SPACEHUNTER: ADVENTURES IN THE FORBIDDEN ZONE

SCOTT VICKREY
EDITOR
'81 THEY ALL LAUGHED*
ASSISTANT EDITOR
'79 STARTING OVER*
'80 GILDA LIVE

MARK VICTOR
SCREENPLAY
'81 DEATH HUNT*
'82 POLTERGEIST*

GABE VIDELLA
SPECIAL EFFECTS
'84 ONCE UPON A TIME IN AMERICA

TONALD VIDOR
MISCELLANEOUS
'81 STRANGE BEHAVIOR

TOMMY VIG
MUSIC
'83 SWEET SIXTEEN

BRUCK VILANCH
SCREENPLAY
'80 DIVINE MADNESS*

ED VILLA
PROPS
'80 ROADIE*

KURT VILLADSEN
EXECUTIVE PRODUCER
'84 RUNAWAY

REYNALDO VILLALOBOS
CINEMATOGRAPHER
'80 NINE TO FIVE
'80 URBAN COWBOY
'83 RISKY BUSINESS*
'83 BALLAD OF GREGORIO CORTEZ, THE
'84 BLAME IT ON RIO
'84 MIKE'S MURDER
'84 GRANDVIEW, U.S.A.
'84 WINDY CITY

CLAUDE VILLAND
SOUND
'83 HANNA K*

ROBERT VILLAR
2ND ASST. DIRECTOR
'79 BUCK ROGERS*

GEORGE VILLASENOR
EDITOR
'80 GLORIA
'84 LOVE STREAMS
ASSISTANT EDITOR
'81 FIRST MONDAY IN OCTOBER
'82 ANNIE
'82 TOY, THE*

LEOPOLDO VILLASENOR
CINEMATOGRAPHER
'80 GUYANA: CULT OF THE DAMNED

VICTOR VILLASENOR
SCREENPLAY
'83 BALLAD OF GREGORIO CORTEZ, THE

JOSE VILLAVERDE
CASTING
'83 TOUGH ENOUGH*

CLAUDIO VINALE
LOCATIONS
'79 LITTLE ROMANCE, A*

EDGARDO "BOY" VINARAO
EDITOR
'83 BLIND RAGE

BARRY VINCE
EDITOR
'79 SHOUT, THE
'82 MOONLIGHTING

CHUCK VINCENT
PRODUCER
'84 PREPPIES
DIRECTOR
'84 PREPPIES
SCREENPLAY
'84 PREPPIES*

RAFFAELE VINCENTI
PROPS
'83 BLACK STALLION RETURNS, THE

NEILL VINE-MILLER
1ST ASST. DIRECTOR
'80 AWAKENING, THE*
'84 RIDDLE OF THE SANDS

MICHAEL VINER
PRODUCER
'80 TOUCHED BY LOVE

GAIL VIOLA
COSTUMES
'84 STONE BOY, THE

DENNIS VIRKLER
EDITOR
'80 XANADU
'81 CONTINENTAL DIVIDE
'82 AIRPLANE II: THE SEQUEL
'83 GORKY PARK
'83 INDEPENDENCE DAY

KATHY VIRKLER
ASSISTANT EDITOR
'81 ONLY WHEN I LAUGH
'82 FRANCES*
'84 MASS APPEAL

MARCUS VISCIDI
LOCATIONS
'82 STILL OF THE NIGHT*

ROBERT VISCIGLIA
PROPS
'80 HEAVEN'S GATE
'84 RIVER, THE

ROBERT VISCIGLIA SR.
PROPS
'81 BODY HEAT
'83 NATIONAL LAMPOON'S VACATION

JOSEPH VISKOCIL
MISCELLANEOUS
'84 TERMINATOR, THE

JOE VITAGLIANO
CINEMATOGRAPHER
'81 DOZENS, THE

FRANCO VITALE
STILLS
'83 LONELY LADY, THE*

SAM VITALE
EDITOR
'79 WHEN A STRANGER CALLS

ATTILIO VITI
LOCATIONS
'84 ONCE UPON A TIME IN AMERICA*

ANTONIO VIVALDI
MUSIC
'81 FOUR SEASONS, THE

ESTHER VIVANTE
SCRIPT SUPERVISOR
'80 IN GOD WE TRUST*
'82 E.T. THE EXTRA-TERRESTRIAL
'83 FOOTLOOSE
'84 PROTOCOL

ALESSANDRO VIVARELLI
2ND ASST. DIRECTOR
'83 PIRANHA II: THE SPAWNING

VERA VLACILOVA
SCRIPT SUPERVISOR
'84 AMADEUS*

SANDRA VLOSEVICH-MARLEY
SCRIPT SUPERVISOR
'80 TRIBUTE

BILL VOELKER
MISCELLANEOUS
'81 CONTINENTAL DIVIDE

EDDIE LEE VOELKER
MISCELLANEOUS
'83 CHRISTINE

DAVID VOGEL
ASSOCIATE PRODUCER
'81 KNIGHTRIDERS
'82 CREEPSHOW

MATT VOGEL
SPECIAL EFFECTS
'81 MS. 45*
'81 NESTING, THE
MISCELLANEOUS
'84 C.H.U.D.

STANLEY VOGEL
EDITOR
'82 FIRST TIME, THE

SUSAN VOGELFANG
PRODUCTION MANAGER
'82 LIAR'S MOON
UNIT PROD. MANAGER
'81 STUDENT BODIES
1ST ASST. DIRECTOR
'81 STUDENT BODIES
LOCATIONS
'83 TERMS OF ENDEARMENT*

KARL HEINZ VOGELMANN
STILLS
'80 AMERICAN SUCCESS COMPANY, THE
'84 NEVERENDING STORY, THE

JUDITH VOGELSANG
2ND ASST. DIRECTOR
'79 BUCK ROGERS*
'80 LITTLE MISS MARKER
'80 WHERE THE BUFFALO ROAM
'81 HARD COUNTRY

JON VOIGHT
SCREENPLAY
'82 LOOKIN' TO GET OUT*

TED VOIGTLANDER
MISCELLANEOUS
'80 CHANGELING, THE

BETH VOIKU
CASTING
'82 DEATHWISH II*

PATRICIA VOLLMAR
ASSOCIATE PRODUCER
'79 SCALPEL*

JURGEN VOLLMER
STILLS
'84 JUST THE WAY YOU ARE*
'84 NATURAL, THE*

ROBERT VOLPE
PROPS
'81 ON THE RIGHT TRACK
'83 CLASS
'84 SIXTEEN CANDLES

RON VOLZ
MISCELLANEOUS
'80 ROADIE

PAUL VOM BRACH
MISCELLANEOUS
'82 CAT PEOPLE
'83 NATIONAL LAMPOON'S VACATION

PATRIZIA VON BRANDENSTEIN
ART DIRECTOR
'79 BREAKING AWAY
'81 RAGTIME*
PRODUCTION DESIGNER
'79 HEARTLAND
'80 TELL ME A RIDDLE
'83 SILKWOOD
'84 AMADEUS
'84 BEAT STREET
COSTUMES
'82 LITTLE SEX, A

HASSO VON HUGO
MAKEUP
'79 BLOODLINE*
'80 AMERICAN SUCCESS COMPANY,THE*
HAIR
'79 BLOODLINE*
'80 AMERICAN SUCCESS COMPANY,THE*

CHRISTA VON HUMBOLDT
COSTUMES
'80 GUYANA: CULT OF THE DAMNED
COSTUME SUPERVISOR
'83 YELLOWBEARD

GEORGE VON KIESERITZKY
ART DIRECTOR
'80 LADY VANISHES, THE*

ALLESANDRO VON NORMANN
PRODUCTION MANAGER
'79 BLACK STALLION, THE*
'83 BLACK STALLION RETURNS, THE

JESCO VON PUTTKAMER
MISCELLANEOUS
'79 STAR TREK-THE MOTION PICTURE

IRMI VON RUXLEBEN
PROD. SECRETARY
'79 FIFTH MUSKETEER, THE

AGO VON SPERL
MAKEUP
'79 FEDORA*
HAIR
'79 FEDORA*

RUDIGAN VON SPERL
MAKEUP
'79 FEDORA*
HAIR
'79 FEDORA*

NICHOLAS VON STERNBERG
CINEMATOGRAPHER
'79 TOURIST TRAP
'83 JOYSTICKS

ERNEST VON THEUMER
EXECUTIVE PRODUCER
'83 CHAINED HEAT*

TRUDY VON TROTHA
SCRIPT SUPERVISOR
'79 AVALANCHE EXPRESS*
'79 FEDORA
'80 AMERICAN SUCCESS COMPANY, THE

TORIS VON WOLFE
STILLS
'84 MAKING THE GRADE

STELLA VOTSOU
MAKEUP
'82 TEMPEST*

ANNA VOXEMBAUM
COSTUMES
'83 CAN SHE BAKE A CHERRY PIE?

RICHARD VRAA
MISCELLANEOUS
'79 ICE CASTLES

RUSSELL VREELAND
1ST ASST. DIRECTOR
'81 PRIVATE LESSONS*
'82 DEATHWISH II

LENNY VULLO
LOCATIONS
'84 GHOSTBUSTERS*
'84 FIRSTBORN

W

NAT WACHSBERGER

PRODUCER
'79 STARCRASH*
SCREENPLAY
'79 STARCRASH*

PATRICK WACHSBERGER

PRODUCER
'79 STARCRASH*

JONATHAN WACKS

PRODUCER
'84 REPO MAN*

RICK WADDELL

SOUND
'80 HOME MOVIES

GERRY WADE

PROPS
'81 BUSTIN' LOOSE*
'84 CHAMPIONS*

MARK WADE

PROPS
'79 BREAKING AWAY
'80 DEFIANCE
'80 DIE LAUGHING
'82 THAT CHAMPIONSHIP SEASON
'82 YOUNG DOCTORS IN LOVE
'83 FLASHDANCE

MARK WADE

MISCELLANEOUS
'81 PRIVATE LESSONS

TONY WADE

ASSOCIATE PRODUCER
'81 CHU CHU AND THE PHILLY FLASH
PRODUCTION MANAGER
'80 DIE LAUGHING
'80 TELL ME A RIDDLE
'81 CHU CHU AND THE PHILLY FLASH
'82 DEATHWISH II
'82 THAT CHAMPIONSHIP SEASON*
UNIT PROD. MANAGER
'80 FOOLIN AROUND
'81 PRIVATE LESSONS*
2ND UNIT DIRECTOR
'81 PRIVATE LESSONS
MISCELLANEOUS
'80 TELL ME A RIDDLE

WAYNE WADHAMS

SOUND
'80 RETURN OF THE SECAUCUS SEVEN, THE
'83 LIANNA*

MICHAEL WADLEIGH

DIRECTOR
'81 WOLFEN
SCREENPLAY
'81 WOLFEN*

JOHN WADLEY

MISCELLANEOUS
'80 SHINING, THE

ANN WADLINGTON

HAIR
'79 PROPHECY
'80 FOXES
'81 BEAST WITHIN, THE
'81 BUSTIN' LOOSE*

BILL WAGNER

MISCELLANEOUS
'79 DAWN OF THE DEAD

COL. DAVID WAGNER

MISCELLANEOUS
'82 MEGAFORCE

GARY WAGNER

MISCELLANEOUS
'81 SATURDAY THE 14TH
'81 GALAXY OF TERROR

JANE WAGNER

SCREENPLAY
'81 INCREDIBLE SHRINKING WOMAN, THE
EXECUTIVE PRODUCER
'81 INCREDIBLE SHRINKING WOMAN, THE

PETER WAGNER

KEY GRIP
'82 SUMMER LOVERS
'84 BEVERLY HILLS COP

HERB WAGREITCH

MISCELLANEOUS
'84 GHOSTBUSTERS

KEITH WAGSTAFF

CINEMATOGRAPHER
'83 MAN FROM SNOWY RIVER, THE

PAMELA WAINER

ART DIRECTOR
'83 METALSTORM: THE DESTRUCTION OF JARED-SYN

BILL WAINESS

PROPS
'79 TIME AFTER TIME

RALPH WAITE

PRODUCER
'80 ON THE NICKEL
DIRECTOR
'80 ON THE NICKEL
SCREENPLAY
'80 ON THE NICKEL

RIC WAITE

CINEMATOGRAPHER
'80 DEFIANCE
'80 LONG RIDERS, THE
'80 ON THE NICKEL
'82 BORDER, THE
'82 48 HOURS
'82 TEX
'83 CLASS
'83 FOOTLOOSE
'84 RED DAWN
MISCELLANEOUS
'83 UNCOMMON VALOR

TOM WAITS

MUSIC
'82 ONE FROM THE HEART

HANNY WAJSHONIG

ASSISTANT EDITOR
'79 ROSE, THE

PAULA WAKEFIELD

LOCATIONS
'80 OH GOD! BOOK II
'81 MODERN ROMANCE*

YANNOULLA WAKEFIELD

ASSOCIATE PRODUCER
'80 FIENDISH PLOT OF DR. FU MANCHU, THE
MISCELLANEOUS
'79 LITTLE ROMANCE, A
'83 MAN WOMAN AND CHILD

RICK WAKEMAN
MUSIC
'81 BURNING, THE
'84 CRIMES OF PASSION

NATHAN WAKS
MUSIC SUPERVISOR
'79 MY BRILLIANT CAREER

CHRIS WALAS
MISCELLANEOUS
'80 GALAXINA
'81 SCANNERS
'81 CAVEMAN

DANAE WALCZAK
LOCATIONS
'80 BLUES BROTHERS*

BOB WALD
SOUND
'80 BIG BRAWL, THE
'81 DEADLY BLESSING
'82 SILENT RAGE
'82 SPLIT IMAGE
'83 LONE WOLF MCQUADE

TOM WALDEN
ART DIRECTOR
'84 BOSTONIANS, THE*
PROPS
'81 FRIDAY THE 13TH PART TWO*

FRANK WALDMAN
SCREENPLAY
'83 TRAIL OF THE PINK PANTHER*

HARVEY WALDMAN
2ND ASST. DIRECTOR
'84 BACHELOR PARTY

TOM WALDMAN
SCREENPLAY
'83 TRAIL OF THE PINK PANTHER*

RICHARD WALDROP
PROPS
'83 REUBEN, REUBEN

KEN WALES
LOCATIONS
'82 YES, GIORGIO*

WILLIAM WALES
SCREENPLAY
'83 AMITYVILLE 3D

BEVERLY WALKER
PUBLICIST
'79 BEING THERE
'81 ABSENCE OF MALICE
'82 HAMMETT
'83 RUMBLEFISH
'83 OUTSIDERS, THE

CARDON WALKER
PROD. COORDINATOR
'83 SOMETHING WICKED
THIS WAY COMES*

CLAIRE WALKER
CASTING
'79 BLACK STALLION, THE*
'79 LOST AND FOUND*
'80 KIDNAPPING
OF THE PRESIDENT, THE
'80 TRIBUTE
'81 TICKET TO HEAVEN
'82 BY DESIGN*

DORIAN WALKER
DIRECTOR
'84 MAKING THE GRADE

GRAHAM WALKER
ART DIRECTOR
'82 ROAD WARRIOR, THE

GREG WALKER
STUNT COORDINATOR
'83 AMERICANA*

JULIA WALKER
HAIR
'80 BLUES BROTHERS*

KEN WALKER
MISCELLANEOUS
'83 RETURN OF THE ALIENS:
THE DEADLY SPAWN

LESLEY WALKER
EDITOR
'79 LOVE AND BULLETS*

LINDSAY WALKER
CASTING
'82 OUT OF THE BLUE

LOUISE WALKER
COSTUME SUPERVISOR
'79 SAINT JACK*

NANCY WALKER
DIRECTOR
'80 CAN'T STOP THE MUSIC

NANCY WALKER
PROD. SECRETARY
'82 FORCED VENGEANCE

PETE WALKER
DIRECTOR
'82 HOUSE OF THE LONG SHADOWS

RICHARD WALKER
PROPS
'84 BACHELOR PARTY

ROY WALKER
PRODUCTION DESIGNER
'80 SHINING, THE
'83 YENTL
'84 KILLING FIELDS, THE

TONI WALKER
HAIR
'80 MELVIN AND HOWARD
'80 WHERE THE BUFFALO ROAM
'81 POSTMAN ALWAYS RINGS TWICE,THE
'82 BORDER, THE
'82 FRANCES
'82 POLTERGEIST
'82 TOOTSIE*
'83 SCARFACE*
'84 COUNTRY

VIVIENNE WALKER
HAIR
'79 ...AND JUSTICE FOR ALL
'79 BEING THERE*
'80 FIRST FAMILY
'81 MOMMIE DEAREST*
'81 GOING APE!
'82 DEATHWISH II
'82 GREASE 2

LEE WALKING
SCRIPT SUPERVISOR
'82 GREY FOX, THE

BILL WALLACE
STUNT COORDINATOR
'81 NEIGHBORS

RICHARD WALLACE
2ND ASST. DIRECTOR
'79 ROLLER BOOGIE

RICK WALLACE
1ST ASST. DIRECTOR
'82 LIAR'S MOON

RIT WALLACE
ASSISTANT EDITOR
'82 PARADISE*

SCOTT WALLACE
ASSISTANT EDITOR
'80 AIRPLANE
'80 COAST TO COAST*
'83 BRAINSTORM
'84 SIXTEEN CANDLES

TOMMY LEE WALLACE
DIRECTOR
'82 HALLOWEEN III: SEASON OF THE WITCH
SCREENPLAY
'82 AMITYVILLE II: THE POSSESSION
'82 HALLOWEEN III: SEASON OF THE WITCH
PRODUCTION DESIGNER
'80 FOG, THE
EDITOR
'80 FOG, THE*

WALLY WALLACE
2ND ASST. DIRECTOR
'80 MELVIN AND HOWARD*

DEBORAH WALLACH
ASSISTANT EDITOR
'83 LOVESICK*

STUART WALLACH
ASSOCIATE PRODUCER
'80 WHY WOULD I LIE?*

ELIZABETH WALLER
COSTUMES
'81 FOR YOUR EYES ONLY

PETER WALLER
2ND ASST. DIRECTOR
'80 ISLAND, THE*
'81 REDS*
'83 GORKY PARK*
'83 YENTL
'84 LITTLE DRUMMER GIRL, THE

ROWE WALLERSTEIN
UNIT PROD. MANAGER
'81 INCREDIBLE SHRINKING WOMAN, THE

EMILY WALLIN
ASSISTANT EDITOR
'84 NO SMALL AFFAIR*

RIT WALLIS
EDITOR
'81 MY BLOODY VALENTINE*
ASSISTANT EDITOR
'81 GAS*

MARVIN WALLOWITZ
EDITOR
'79 BELL JAR, THE

IRENE WALLS
MAKEUP
'80 BLUE LAGOON

TOM WALLS
EDITOR
'79 REMEMBER MY NAME*
'80 ROADIE*
'81 HIGH RISK
'82 ENDANGERED SPECIES
'84 ICE PIRATES, THE
'84 BACHELOR PARTY

MARVIN WALOWITZ
SOUND
'80 TWINKLE TWINKLE "KILLER" KANE*

DAVID WALSH
CINEMATOGRAPHER
'79 CHAPTER TWO
'79 IN-LAWS, THE
'79 JUST YOU AND ME KID
'80 SEEMS LIKE OLD TIMES
'80 HERO AT LARGE
'80 PRIVATE BENJAMIN
'81 ONLY WHEN I LAUGH
'82 I OUGHT TO BE IN PICTURES
'82 MAKING LOVE
'83 ROMANTIC COMEDY
'83 MAX DUGAN RETURNS
'84 COUNTRY
'84 JOHNNY DANGEROUSLY
'84 UNFAITHFULLY YOURS
'84 TEACHERS

DON WALSH
MISCELLANEOUS
'80 RAISE THE TITANIC

FRANK WALSH
ART DIRECTOR
'83 LOCAL HERO*

HELENA WALSH
MISCELLANEOUS
'81 WOLFEN

JOHN WALSH
PROPS
'81 MY BLOODY VALENTINE

JOHN WALSH
MISCELLANEOUS
'84 2010

RON WALSH
1ST ASST. DIRECTOR
'80 NIGHT OF THE JUGGLER*

TERRY WALSH
STUNT COORDINATOR
'81 DRAGONSLAYER

ERNEST WALTER
EDITOR
'79 CIRCLE OF IRON

DON WALTERS
ASSOCIATE PRODUCER
'81 NESTING, THE
PRODUCTION MANAGER
'81 NESTING, THE

JIMMY WALTERS
KEY GRIP
'79 ALIEN

MARTIN WALTERS
1ST ASST. DIRECTOR
'80 NOTHING PERSONAL
'83 RUNNING BRAVE

MARVIN WALTERS
STUNT COORDINATOR
'81 DOGS OF WAR, THE*

RON WALTERS
MAKEUP
'79 FORCE OF ONE, A*
'82 HALLOWEEN III: SEASON OF THE WITCH

STEPHEN WALTERS
MISCELLANEOUS
'84 BOUNTY, THE

FRED WALTON
DIRECTOR
'79 WHEN A STRANGER CALLS
SCREENPLAY
'79 WHEN A STRANGER CALLS*

TONY WALTON
PRODUCTION DESIGNER
'80 JUST TELL ME WHAT YOU WANT
'81 PRINCE OF THE CITY
'82 DEATHTRAP
COSTUMES
'80 JUST TELL ME WHAT YOU WANT
'82 DEATHTRAP
MISCELLANEOUS
'79 ALL THAT JAZZ
'83 STAR 80

KENT WALWIN
EXECUTIVE PRODUCER
'84 HOTEL NEW HAMPSHIRE, THE*

IRENE WALZER
ASSOCIATE PRODUCER
'83 TO BE OR NOT TO BE
PUBLICIST
'81 HISTORY OF THE WORLD PART I

JOSEPH WAMBAUGH
SCREENPLAY
'79 ONION FIELD, THE
'80 BLACK MARBLE, THE

CATHERINE WANEK
2ND ASST. DIRECTOR
'84 BEST DEFENSE*

PAY LING WANG
PRODUCTION MANAGER
'84 INDIANA JONES AND THE TEMPLE OF DOOM*

CHRISTIAN WANGLER
SOUND
'79 AGATHA

WENDY WANK
ASSISTANT EDITOR
'81 THEY ALL LAUGHED*

KENN WANNBERG
MUSIC
'80 TRIBUTE
'82 AMATEUR, THE
'82 MOTHER LODE
'83 LOSIN' IT
'83 OF UNKNOWN ORIGIN
'84 PHILADELPHIA EXPERIMENT, THE

ROSE STEINBERG WAPNER
SCRIPT SUPERVISOR
'79 GOLDENGIRL

BOB WARD
KEY GRIP
'79 CHAPTER TWO*
'79 MANHATTAN
'80 STARDUST MEMORIES
'80 WINDOWS
'81 EYEWITNESS
'82 DEATHTRAP
'82 MIDSUMMER NIGHT'S SEX COMEDY, A
'82 VERDICT, THE
'83 ZELIG
'84 BROADWAY DANNY ROSE

DAVID WARD
DIRECTOR
'82 CANNERY ROW
SCREENPLAY
'82 CANNERY ROW
'83 STING II, THE

DOUG WARD
MISCELLANEOUS
'79 METEOR

JON PARKER WARD
STUNT COORDINATOR
'79 SCAVENGER HUNT

MARY WARD
HAIR
'81 SATURDAY THE 14TH

NICK WARD
PROPS
'80 MANIAC*

ROBERT WARD
SCREENPLAY
'81 CATTLE ANNIE AND LITTLE BRITCHES*

THOMAS WARD
SPECIAL EFFECTS
'82 THINGS ARE TOUGH ALL OVER*

FRED WARDELL
2ND ASST. DIRECTOR
'79 CHAMP, THE*

MARIE-CLAUDE WARDELL
SCRIPT SUPERVISOR
'82 HOME WORK

JOHN WARDLOW
STUNT COORDINATOR
'83 NEVER CRY WOLF

DICK WARLOCK
STUNT COORDINATOR
'81 ESCAPE FROM NEW YORK
'81 HALLOWEEN II
'82 HALLOWEEN III: SEASON OF THE WITCH
'82 THING, THE
'83 DEAD ZONE, THE*
'84 ANGEL

WARNER WARNASIRI
2ND ASST. DIRECTOR
'81 TARZAN, THE APE MAN

BRIAN WARNER
SPECIAL EFFECTS
'83 SUPERMAN III*
SP. EFFECTS SUPERV.
'84 FINDERS KEEPERS

MARK WARNER
EDITOR
'82 ROCKY III*
'82 48 HOURS*
'83 STAYING ALIVE*
'84 SOLDIER'S STORY, A*
ASSISTANT EDITOR
'79 BEING THERE

PAMELA WARNER
ART DIRECTOR
'82 PARASITE

SHEILA WARNER
PROD. COORDINATOR
'82 PERSONAL BEST*
'84 COUNTRY

STANLEY WARNOW
EDITOR
'79 HAIR*
'81 RAGTIME*

ANDREW WARREN
2ND ASST. DIRECTOR
'83 OCTOPUSSY*

ED WARREN
MISCELLANEOUS
'82 AMITYVILLE II: THE POSSESSION

HOWARD WARREN
SOUND
'81 NOBODY'S PERFEKT
'82 LOVE CHILD
'83 SMOKEY AND THE BANDIT III
'83 BLUE SKIES AGAIN
'84 HARRY & SON

JOHN WARREN
LOCATIONS
'81 EARTHLING, THE

GENE WARREN JR.
MISCELLANEOUS
'83 SPACEHUNTER: ADVENTURES IN THE FORBIDDEN ZONE
'84 TERMINATOR, THE

LORRAINE WARREN
MISCELLANEOUS
'82 AMITYVILLE II: THE POSSESSION

ROBERT WARREN
2ND ASST. DIRECTOR
'80 CRUISING
'80 TIMES SQUARE
'81 PRINCE OF THE CITY
'82 VERDICT, THE
'82 WORLD ACCORDING TO GARP, THE*
'83 DANIEL
'83 NIGHT IN HEAVEN, A
'83 WITHOUT A TRACE
'83 WRONG IS RIGHT*
'84 GARBO TALKS
'84 POPE OF GREENWICH VILLAGE,THE
'84 BEAT STREET

EDWARD WARSCHILKA
ASSOCIATE PRODUCER
'84 SIXTEEN CANDLES*
EDITOR
'79 MAIN EVENT, THE
'80 CHEAPER TO KEEP HER
'81 RAGGEDY MAN
'83 BRAINSTORM*
'84 SIXTEEN CANDLES

EDWARD WARSCHILKA JR.
ASSISTANT EDITOR
'81 TARZAN, THE APE MAN
'82 48 HOURS*
'83 STAYING ALIVE*
'84 SOLDIER'S STORY, A

DIONNE WARWICK
MISCELLANEOUS
'84 WOMAN IN RED, THE

NORMAN WARWICK
CINEMATOGRAPHER
'80 KIDS ARE ALL RIGHT, THE*

RICHARD WARWICK
HAIR
'82 DON'T CRY, IT'S ONLY THUNDER

PUDJI WASESO
MISCELLANEOUS
'83 YEAR OF LIVING DANGEROUSLY, THE

CHARLES WASHBURN
UNIT PROD. MANAGER
'81 BUSTIN' LOOSE*

DERIC WASHBURN
SCREENPLAY
'78 DEER HUNTER, THE
'82 BORDER, THE*

J. DENNIS WASHINGTON
ART DIRECTOR
'79 ELECTRIC HORSEMAN, THE
'83 TO BE OR NOT TO BE
'84 FINDERS KEEPERS
PRODUCTION DESIGNER
'80 TWINKLE TWINKLE "KILLER" KANE*
'81 VICTORY

JOAN WASHINGTON
MISCELLANEOUS
'83 YENTL
'84 GREYSTOKE: THE LEGEND OF TARZAN, LORD OF THE APES

RICHARD WASHINGTON
2ND UNIT DIRECTOR
'82 SWORD AND THE SORCERER, THE*
STUNT COORDINATOR
'80 NUDE BOMB, THE
'81 CHARLIE CHAN AND THE CURSE OF THE DRAGON QUEEN
'82 SOME KIND OF HERO
'82 SWORD AND THE SORCERER, THE

JUDY WASSERMIL
PROD. SECRETARY
'82 PARADISE

GORDY WATERMAN
MISCELLANEOUS
'84 NOT FOR PUBLICATION

CANDIS WATERS
SCRIPT SUPERVISOR
'80 BIG BRAWL, THE

CHUCK WATERS
STUNT COORDINATOR
'83 BAD BOYS

JIMMY WATERS
KEY GRIP
'81 VICTORY
'84 FINDERS KEEPERS

JOHN WATERS
PRODUCER
'81 POLYESTER
DIRECTOR
'81 POLYESTER
SCREENPLAY
'81 POLYESTER

ROGER WATERS
SCREENPLAY
'82 PINK FLOYD: THE WALL
MISCELLANEOUS
'82 PINK FLOYD: THE WALL
'82 PINK FLOYD: THE WALL

SHERRY WATERS
PROD. COORDINATOR
'83 SUBURBIA

TONY WATHEN
MISCELLANEOUS
'84 TOP SECRET!

DAVID WATKIN
CINEMATOGRAPHER
'79 CUBA
'79 HANOVER STREET
'81 CHARIOTS OF FIRE
'81 ENDLESS LOVE
'83 YENTL
'84 HOTEL NEW HAMPSHIRE, THE

DAVID WATKINS
SPECIAL EFFECTS
'82 GANDHI

TED WATKINS
PRODUCTION DESIGNER
'80 HAPPY BIRTHDAY, GEMINI

WILLIAM WATKINS
PRODUCTION MANAGER
'83 LORDS OF DISCIPLINE, THE
'84 AMERICAN DREAMER*
UNIT PROD. MANAGER
'81 FIRST MONDAY IN OCTOBER

BILL WATSON
MISCELLANEOUS
'83 WAR GAMES

CAROL WATSON
SCREENPLAY
'82 FRIDAY THE 13TH PART THREE IN 3D*

EARL WATSON
EDITOR
'80 GUYANA: CULT OF THE DAMNED
ASSOCIATE EDITOR
'80 SCHIZOID

IAN WATSON
ART DIRECTOR
'83 LOCAL HERO*

IRENE WATSON
SCRIPT SUPERVISOR
'83 GOIN' ALL THE WAY

BRENDA WATT
MISCELLANEOUS
'79 HOT STUFF

REUBEN WATT
2ND ASST. DIRECTOR
'84 STONE BOY, THE

ERIC WATTS
MISCELLANEOUS
'81 DRAGONSLAYER

FRANK WATTS
CINEMATOGRAPHER
'83 EDUCATING RITA

HELEN WATTS
PROD. SECRETARY
'81 ROAD GAMES*
LOCATIONS
'82 PIRATE MOVIE, THE*

ROBERT WATTS
PRODUCER
'84 INDIANA JONES AND THE TEMPLE OF DOOM
ASSOCIATE PRODUCER
'80 EMPIRE STRIKES BACK, THE*
'81 RAIDERS OF THE LOST ARK
CO-PRODUCER
'83 RETURN OF THE JEDI*

ROY WATTS
EDITOR
'82 BEASTMASTER, THE
'82 VICE SQUAD
'83 DEADLY FORCE

ROY WATTS
PRODUCER
'84 ANGEL*

FRED WAUGH
STUNT COORDINATOR
'79 BUCK ROGERS*
'81 LOOKER
'84 SPLASH*

STEVE WAX
MUSIC
'83 TOUGH ENOUGH*

JERI WAXENBERG
2ND ASST. DIRECTOR
'83 MORTUARY
PROD. COORDINATOR
'80 GALAXINA
'83 MORTUARY

ANTHONY WAYE
1ST ASST. DIRECTOR
'79 DRACULA
'79 GREAT TRAIN ROBBERY, THE
'80 ELEPHANT MAN, THE
'81 CLASH OF THE TITANS
'81 FOR YOUR EYES ONLY
'81 DOGS OF WAR, THE*
'82 FIVE DAYS ONE SUMMER
'83 OCTOPUSSY

DENNIS WAYNE
CHOREOGRAPHER
'83 ECHOES

JAMES WAYNE
SPECIAL EFFECTS
'80 FADE TO BLACK

JESSE WAYNE
STUNT COORDINATOR
'80 HOPSCOTCH
'83 TESTAMENT

JAMES WEATHERILL
1ST ASST. DIRECTOR
'80 CHANGE OF SEASONS, A*

PETER WEATHERLEY
EDITOR
'83 ENIGMA

CASSIUS WEATHERSBY
CO-PRODUCER
'83 D.C. CAB
ASSISTANT EDITOR
'82 PENITENTIARY II*
PRODUCTION MANAGER
'82 PENITENTIARY II*

ROBERT WEATHERWAX
MISCELLANEOUS
'82 THING, THE
'82 SECOND THOUGHTS
'83 OSTERMAN WEEKEND, THE

RICK WEAVER
ASSISTANT EDITOR
'79 CONCORDE-AIRPORT '79, THE

WILLIAM WEAVER
SCRIPT SUPERVISOR
'83 HANNA K*

BEVERLY WEBB
PROD. OFFICE COORD.
'82 POLTERGEIST

CHARLENE WEBB
SCRIPT SUPERVISOR
'79 SCALPEL
'82 SWAMP THING
'84 BEAR, THE*
'84 MUTANT

CHRIS WEBB
2ND ASST. DIRECTOR
'83 YEAR OF LIVING DANGEROUSLY, THE

DICK WEBB
MISCELLANEOUS
'80 AIRPLANE

DONNA WEBB
PROD. SECRETARY
'84 HARDBODIES

GORDON WEBB
ASSOCIATE PRODUCER
'80 BRUBAKER
PRODUCTION MANAGER
'82 MAKING LOVE
UNIT PROD. MANAGER
'80 BRUBAKER
'83 BUDDY SYSTEM, THE
'84 EVIL THAT MEN DO, THE
1ST ASST. DIRECTOR
'84 EVIL THAT MEN DO, THE*

JAMES WEBB JR.
SOUND
'81 TRUE CONFESSIONS*
'82 HAMMETT*

JIM WEBB
SOUND
'79 ROSE, THE*
'79 ONION FIELD, THE
'80 SMALL CIRCLE OF FRIENDS, A*
'80 LONG RIDERS, THE*
'82 ESCAPE ARTIST, THE*
'82 DEATH VALLEY
'83 FLASHDANCE
'83 OUTSIDERS, THE
'84 STREETS OF FIRE*
'84 COUNTRY*

JIMMY WEBB
MUSIC
'79 VOICES

JOYCE WEBB
SCRIPT SUPERVISOR
'82 DEATH VALLEY*

PETER WEBB
DIRECTOR
'84 GIVE MY REGARDS TO BROAD STREET

ROBERT WEBB
UNIT PROD. MANAGER
'81 AMY
1ST ASST. DIRECTOR
'79 APPLE DUMPLING GANG RIDES AGAIN, THE
'80 JAZZ SINGER, THE*

WILLIAM WEBB
ASSISTANT EDITOR
'81 BEYOND THE REEF*

BILLY WEBER
EDITOR
'82 48 HOURS*
'82 JEKYLL AND HYDE TOGETHER AGAIN
'84 BEVERLY HILLS COP*
'84 ICEMAN

CHARLES WEBER
EXECUTIVE PRODUCER
'84 CHILDREN OF THE CORN*
'84 BODY ROCK*

RICHARD WEBER JR.
MISCELLANEOUS
'79 DREAMER

JULIET WEBER
ASSISTANT EDITOR
'83 STREAMERS

PAUL WEBER
KEY GRIP
'80 AMERICAN SUCCESS COMPANY, THE

ROBERT WEBERMAN

DIRECTOR
'83 TABLE FOR FIVE

FERRIS WEBSTER

EDITOR
'79 ESCAPE FROM ALCATRAZ
'80 ANY WHICH WAY YOU CAN*
'80 BRONCO BILLY*
'82 FIREFOX*
'82 HONKYTONK MAN*

ION WEBSTER

ASSISTANT EDITOR
'81 TICKET TO HEAVEN

KEITH WEBSTER

SOUND
'79 C.H.O.M.P.S.
'81 FIRST MONDAY IN OCTOBER
'81 CARBON COPY
'82 YOUNG DOCTORS IN LOVE
'84 THIEF OF HEARTS

SONJA WEBSTER

PRODUCTION MANAGER
'82 COME BACK TO THE 5 & 10, JIMMY DEAN, JIMMY DEAN
1ST ASST. DIRECTOR
'82 COME BACK TO THE 5 & 10, JIMMY DEAN, JIMMY DEAN
LOCATIONS
'81 FOUR SEASONS, THE*

DAVID WECHTER

DIRECTOR
'80 MIDNIGHT MADNESS*
SCREENPLAY
'80 MIDNIGHT MADNESS*
CO-PRODUCER
'80 MIDNIGHT MADNESS*

JULIUS WECHTER

MUSIC
'80 MIDNIGHT MADNESS

LES WEDMAN

PUBLICIST
'82 BY DESIGN*

JO WEEKS

SCRIPT SUPERVISOR
'84 PHAR LAP

MIRIAM WEEKS

ASSISTANT EDITOR
'81 THEY ALL LAUGHED*
'83 TWILIGHT ZONE, THE MOVIE*

CHERYL WEGNER

MISCELLANEOUS
'83 METALSTORM: THE DESTRUCTION OF JARED-SYN

DEEDEE WEHLE

CASTING
'81 AMERICAN WEREWOLF IN LONDON, AN*
'83 D.C. CAB*

ROBERTA WEHLE

COSTUMES
'83 D.C. CAB

ROSEMARY WEIBELHAUS

HAIR
'84 CHILDREN OF THE CORN

KEN WEIDERHORN

DIRECTOR
'80 EYES OF A STRANGER
'84 MEATBALLS PART II

GOTZ WEIDNER

ART DIRECTOR
'84 NEVERENDING STORY, THE*

HERMAN WEIGEL

SCREENPLAY
'84 NEVERENDING STORY, THE*

JOHN WEILEY

MISCELLANEOUS
'81 EARTHLING, THE

CLAUDIA WEILL

DIRECTOR
'80 IT'S MY TURN

BRENDA WEIMAN

SCRIPT SUPERVISOR
'84 REPO MAN*

ROBERT WEIMANN

ASSISTANT EDITOR
'81 HARDLY WORKING*

JANET WEINBERG

ASSISTANT EDITOR
'79 SAINT JACK*

KEN WEINBERG

PROPS
'79 VOICES

ED. WEINBERGER

SCREENPLAY
'84 LONELY GUY, THE*

GRAHAME WEINBREN

EDITOR
'84 ALPHABET CITY

JACK WEINER

PRODUCER
'79 ESCAPE TO ATHENA*

JOSH WEINER

STILLS
'79 ALL THAT JAZZ
'79 APOCALYPSE NOW*
'80 CRUISING
'80 TIMES SQUARE
'81 ENDLESS LOVE
'81 NIGHTHAWKS
'81 TAPS
'82 SOPHIE'S CHOICE
'82 TEMPEST*
'83 BRAINSTORM*
'83 TRADING PLACES
'84 FLAMINGO KID, THE

JUDITH WEINER

CASTING
'81 HOWLING, THE*
'82 JEKYLL AND HYDE TOGETHER AGAIN*
'83 BALLAD OF GREGORIO CORTEZ, THE
'83 GET CRAZY

ROBERTA WEINER

COSTUMES
'80 CHANGELING, THE
'81 INCREDIBLE SHRINKING WOMAN, THE

ZANE WEINER

MISCELLANEOUS
'84 COTTON CLUB, THE

MERI WEINGARTEN

ASSISTANT EDITOR
'81 ARTHUR*

HERSCHEL WEINGROD

SCREENPLAY
'80 CHEAPER TO KEEP HER*
'83 TRADING PLACES*

BOB WEINSTEIN

SCREENPLAY
'81 BURNING, THE*
MISCELLANEOUS
'81 BURNING, THE

HANNAH WEINSTEIN

PRODUCER
'80 STIR CRAZY

HARVEY WEINSTEIN

PRODUCER
'81 BURNING, THE

BRUCE WEINTRAUB

ART DIRECTOR
'82 SUMMER LOVERS
PRODUCTION DESIGNER
'80 CRUISING

FRED WEINTRAUB
PRODUCER
'79 PROMISE, THE*
'80 BIG BRAWL, THE*
'80 TOM HORN
'81 FORCE FIVE
'83 HIGH ROAD TO CHINA

JERRY WEINTRAUB
PRODUCER
'80 CRUISING
'81 ALL NIGHT LONG*
'82 DINER
'84 KARATE KID, THE

JOSEPH WEINTRAUB
PRODUCER
'79 SCALPEL*
EDITOR
'79 SCALPEL

BARRY WEINTRAUB M.D.
MISCELLANEOUS
'80 RESURRECTION

SANDRA WEINTRAUB
ASSOCIATE PRODUCER
'80 TOM HORN*

GARY WEIR
SOUND
'80 KIDS ARE ALL RIGHT, THE*

PETER WEIR
DIRECTOR
'79 PICNIC AT HANGING ROCK
'81 GALLIPOLI
'83 YEAR OF LIVING DANGEROUSLY, THE
SCREENPLAY
'83 YEAR OF LIVING DANGEROUSLY, THE*

WENDY WEIR
MISCELLANEOUS
'81 GALLIPOLI
'83 YEAR OF LIVING DANGEROUSLY, THE

GARY WEIS
DIRECTOR
'80 WHOLLY MOSES!

ROCHELLE WEISBERG
EXECUTIVE PRODUCER
'81 MS. 45

SUZANNE WEISENFELD
PRODUCTION MANAGER
'79 CONCORDE-AIRPORT '79, THE*
'83 ENIGMA

STANLEY WEISER
SCREENPLAY
'80 COAST TO COAST

SUSAN WEISER-FINLEY
SCREENPLAY
'82 FIRST TIME, THE*

ALLEN WEISINGER
MAKEUP
'79 KRAMER VS. KRAMER
'80 CRUISING
'81 ENDLESS LOVE
'81 FORT APACHE, THE BRONX*
'81 WOLFEN
'82 CHOSEN, THE*
'82 HANKY PANKY*
'82 TOOTSIE*
'83 EASY MONEY
'83 NIGHT IN HEAVEN, A*
'83 TOUGH ENOUGH
'83 WITHOUT A TRACE*
'84 POPE OF GREENWICH VILLAGE,THE
HAIR
'82 CHOSEN, THE*

BOB WEISINGER
MISCELLANEOUS
'84 SHEENA

ALAN WEISMAN
MISCELLANEOUS
'80 BIG RED ONE, THE

BRENDA WEISMAN
SCRIPT SUPERVISOR
'80 WITHOUT WARNING
'82 SWORD AND THE SORCERER, THE
'82 BUTTERFLY
'83 JOYSTICKS
'84 TERMINATOR, THE

BOB WEISS
MISCELLANEOUS
'84 HARDBODIES

JULIE WEISS
COSTUMES
'82 I'M DANCING AS FAST AS I CAN
'82 SECOND THOUGHTS
'83 SPACEHUNTER: ADVENTURES IN THE FORBIDDEN ZONE
'83 INDEPENDENCE DAY
'83 TESTAMENT

HARVEY WEISS M.D.
MISCELLANEOUS
'79 SCALPEL

PEGGY WEISS
ASSISTANT EDITOR
'81 PRINCE OF THE CITY

ROBERT WEISS
PRODUCER
'80 BLUES BROTHERS
'83 DOCTOR DETROIT

GERRY WEISSBLUM
LOCATIONS
'84 MAKING THE GRADE*

BURT WEISSBOURD
PRODUCER
'81 RAGGEDY MAN*
'81 GHOST STORY

BENJAMIN WEISSMAN
EDITOR
'84 LASSITER*

MURRAY WEISSMAN
PUBLICIST
'80 CLOSE ENCOUNTERS OF THE THIRD KIND SPECIAL EDITION*

GARY WEIST
ART DIRECTOR
'79 GOING IN STYLE*
'80 DRESSED TO KILL
'83 EDDIE AND THE CRUISERS
PRODUCTION DESIGNER
'79 GREAT BANK HOAX, THE

NANCY WEIZER
ASSISTANT EDITOR
'80 COMPETITION, THE*
'80 MOUNTAIN MEN, THE*
'81 STRIPES*
'82 TOOTSIE*

ANNE WELCH
ART DIRECTOR
'83 FRIGHTMARE

BO WELCH
ART DIRECTOR
'84 SWING SHIFT

ROBERT WELCH III
ART DIRECTOR
'84 BEST DEFENSE*

BUCK WELCHER
MISCELLANEOUS
'82 OFFICER AND A GENTLEMAN, AN

ALEX WELDON
SPECIAL EFFECTS
'80 RAISE THE TITANIC

MARVIN WELDON
SCRIPT SUPERVISOR
'80 IN GOD WE TRUST*
'82 DEAD MEN DON'T WEAR PLAID

FRANK WELKER
MISCELLANEOUS
'84 CANNONBALL RUN II

COLIN WELLAND
SCREENPLAY
'79 YANKS*
'81 CHARIOTS OF FIRE

TIM WELLBURN
EDITOR
'82 ROAD WARRIOR, THE*

MICHAEL WELLER
SCREENPLAY
'79 HAIR
'81 RAGTIME

HAROLD WELLMAN
MISCELLANEOUS
'79 BEYOND THE POSEIDON ADVENTURE
'80 WHEN TIME RAN OUT

JOAN WELLMAN
PROD. SECRETARY
'84 WOMAN IN RED, THE

WENDELL WELLMAN
SCREENPLAY
'82 FIREFOX*

AMY WELLS
2ND ASST. DIRECTOR
'84 ONCE UPON A TIME IN AMERICA*

HUBERT WELLS
MISCELLANEOUS
'81 HONKY TONK FREEWAY
'84 SHEENA

LARRY WELLS
COSTUMES
'82 PORKY'S*
'83 STRANGE BREW

TERRY WELLS
PROPS
'80 AWAKENING, THE*
'80 ELEPHANT MAN, THE
'82 VENOM
'83 YENTL
'84 KILLING FIELDS, THE

TOM WELSH
COSTUME SUPERVISOR
'81 PURSUIT OF D.B. COOPER, THE*

PHILLIPPE WELT
CINEMATOGRAPHER
'84 UNTIL SEPTEMBER

WARD WELTON
MISCELLANEOUS
'83 JAWS 3-D

WIM WENDERS
DIRECTOR
'82 HAMMETT
'84 PARIS, TEXAS

CAROL WENGER
ART DIRECTOR
'81 CANNONBALL RUN, THE
'82 MEGAFORCE

CAROL LYNN WENGER
SPECIAL EFFECTS
'79 VILLAIN, THE*

CLIFF WENGER
SPECIAL EFFECTS
'80 ISLAND, THE
'82 GREY FOX, THE*
'84 BIRDY

CLIFF WENGER JR.
SPECIAL EFFECTS
'79 VILLAIN, THE*

CLIFF WENGER SR.
SPECIAL EFFECTS
'79 VILLAIN, THE*
'80 SMOKEY AND THE BANDIT II
'81 CANNONBALL RUN, THE
'82 MEGAFORCE

KATHERINE WENNINGS
EDITOR
'84 BOSTONIANS, THE*

KEN WENSEVIC
MAKEUP
'80 FOXES

STEFAN WENTA
CHOREOGRAPHER
'81 REDS*

SUSAN WENZEL
MAKEUP
'84 PURPLE RAIN*

GAIL WERBIN
EDITOR
'79 ROCK 'N ROLL HIGH SCHOOL*

ROBERT WERDEN
PUBLICIST
'78 DEER HUNTER, THE
'79 METEOR
'80 LONG RIDERS, THE
'81 PENNIES FROM HEAVEN
'81 PURSUIT OF D.B. COOPER, THE
'82 I OUGHT TO BE IN PICTURES
UNIT PUBLICIST
'81 THIEF
'83 MAX DUGAN RETURNS
'84 COUNTRY
'84 RUNAWAY

JEFF WERNER
DIRECTOR
'80 DIE LAUGHING
ASSOCIATE PRODUCER
'79 MAIN EVENT, THE

PETER WERNER
DIRECTOR
'82 DON'T CRY, IT'S ONLY THUNDER

RICHARD WERNIG
STILLS
'81 BURNING, THE*

ALBERT WERRY
MISCELLANEOUS
'81 GREAT MUPPET CAPER, THE

ALLAN WERTHEIM
1ST ASST. DIRECTOR
'80 RAGING BULL*

ROBERT WERTHEIMER
LOCATIONS
'81 ATLANTIC CITY

STEVE WERTIMER
2ND ASST. DIRECTOR
'83 STAYING ALIVE*
'83 EDDIE AND THE CRUISERS
'84 C.H.U.D.

ELIZABETH WERTZ
ASSISTANT EDITOR
'83 ECHOES*

SHELBY WERWA
LOCATIONS
'81 FOUR SEASONS, THE*

STEVE WESLAK
EDITOR
'81 LAST CHASE, THE

JAN WESLEY
ASSISTANT EDITOR
'79 ROCKY II*
'79 VOICES
'80 HOLLYWOOD KNIGHTS, THE
'82 THING, THE*

KARL WESSON

MISCELLANEOUS
'84 SILENT NIGHT, DEADLY NIGHT

ALICE WEST

2ND ASST. DIRECTOR
'79 AMERICATHON*
'81 CHEECH AND CHONG'S NICE DREAMS
'81 HARDLY WORKING*
'82 SILENT RAGE
'83 HEART LIKE A WHEEL
'83 MAN WHO WASN'T THERE, THE
'84 MEATBALLS PART II

PROD. COORDINATOR
'80 MY BODYGUARD

BRIAN WEST

CINEMATOGRAPHER
'83 LONELY LADY, THE
'84 MARVIN AND TIGE
'84 FINDERS KEEPERS

CHRISTINE WEST

COSTUME SUPERVISOR
'83 MERRY CHRISTMAS, MR. LAWRENCE

CRAIG WEST

2ND ASST. DIRECTOR
'84 TANK*

HOWARD WEST

PRODUCER
'80 IN GOD WE TRUST*

KIT WEST

SPECIAL EFFECTS
'80 BIG RED ONE, THE*
'81 SEA WOLVES, THE*

MISCELLANEOUS
'81 RAIDERS OF THE LOST ARK
'83 RETURN OF THE JEDI
'84 DUNE

ROBERT WEST

KEY GRIP
'79 AMERICATHON
'80 WHY WOULD I LIE?
'82 MY FAVORITE YEAR

ROBERT WEST SR.

KEY GRIP
'83 TO BE OR NOT TO BE

WALLY WEST

MISCELLANEOUS
'84 MOSCOW ON THE HUDSON

HERBERT WESTBROOK

ART DIRECTOR
'83 KEEP, THE*
'84 PASSAGE TO INDIA, A*

PRODUCTION DESIGNER
'81 FINAL CONFLICT, THE

FRED WESTCOTT

PROPS
'80 ON THE NICKEL

KENNETH WESTCOTT

PROPS
'82 THINGS ARE TOUGH ALL OVER
'83 WRONG IS RIGHT

THEO WESTENBERGER

STILLS
'83 NATE & HAYES

MIKE WESTGATE

SOUND
'83 MERRY CHRISTMAS, MR. LAWRENCE

DONALD WESTLAKE

SCREENPLAY
'79 HOT STUFF*

BILL WESTLEY

1ST ASST. DIRECTOR
'83 FINAL OPTION, THE
'84 KILLING FIELDS, THE

STEVE WESTLUND

PROPS
'80 BRONCO BILLY
'80 OH GOD! BOOK II
'82 PERSONAL BEST
'84 BEST DEFENSE*
'84 IRRECONCILABLE DIFFERENCES

JIM WESTMAN

1ST ASST. DIRECTOR
'80 RAISE THE TITANIC

TONY WESTMAN

MISCELLANEOUS
'82 MOTHER LODE

BOB WESTMORE

MAKEUP
'79 RAVAGERS*
'79 1941

FRANK WESTMORE

MAKEUP
'79 ...AND JUSTICE FOR ALL
'79 BEING THERE*

MARVIN WESTMORE

MAKEUP
'79 BREAKING AWAY
'79 BUDDY HOLLY STORY, THE*
'79 PROMISE, THE
'80 IDOLMAKER, THE
'82 BEST LITTLE WHOREHOUSE IN TEXAS, THE*
'82 BLADERUNNER
'84 ALL OF ME*

MICHAEL WESTMORE

MAKEUP
'79 ROCKY II
'79 CIRCLE OF IRON*
'81 TRUE CONFESSIONS
'81 VICTORY*
'82 ROCKY III
'83 STAR CHAMBER
'83 UNCOMMON VALOR*
'84 ICEMAN
'84 2010

MISCELLANEOUS
'80 RAGING BULL
'82 FIRST BLOOD

MONTY WESTMORE

COSTUMES
'82 AIRPLANE II: THE SEQUEL

MAKEUP
'79 PROMISES IN THE DARK*
'79 QUINTET
'79 REMEMBER MY NAME
'80 HEALTH
'81 BLOOD BEACH
'81 FORT APACHE, THE BRONX*
'81 PATERNITY*
'81 SUNDAY LOVERS*
'82 SOME KIND OF HERO
'82 ENDANGERED SPECIES
'82 VERDICT, THE*
'83 UNCOMMON VALOR*
'84 HARRY & SON*
'84 WOMAN IN RED, THE*

BOB WESTMORELAND

MAKEUP
'79 JUST YOU AND ME KID
'80 CLOSE ENCOUNTERS OF THE THIRD KIND SPECIAL EDITION
'80 INSIDE MOVES
'80 ISLAND, THE*
'83 TWILIGHT ZONE, THE MOVIE*

ARMAND WESTON

PRODUCER
'81 NESTING, THE

DIRECTOR
'81 NESTING, THE

SCREENPLAY
'81 NESTING, THE*

ERIC WESTON

DIRECTOR
'84 MARVIN AND TIGE

CASTING
'84 MARVIN AND TIGE*

JAY WESTON

PRODUCER
'80 NIGHT OF THE JUGGLER
'81 BUDDY, BUDDY
'81 CHU CHU AND THE PHILLY FLASH

KEN WESTON

SOUND
'84 ANOTHER COUNTRY

LINDA WESTON
MISCELLANEOUS
'81 ROLLOVER
'82 AUTHOR, AUTHOR

MAGGIE WESTON
MAKEUP
'81 TIME BANDITS*
'82 MONTY PYTHON LIVE AT THE HOLLYWOOD BOWL*
'83 MONTY PYTHON'S THE MEANING OF LIFE
HAIR
'81 TIME BANDITS*
'83 MONTY PYTHON'S THE MEANING OF LIFE

PAUL WESTON
STUNT COORDINATOR
'81 SUPERMAN II*
'83 SUPERMAN III

ROBERT WESTON
PRODUCER
'83 LONELY LADY, THE

CAROLE WESTPHALL
SCRIPT SUPERVISOR
'80 TOUCHED BY LOVE
'81 MODERN ROMANCE
'83 YELLOWBEARD*

JAMES WESTWELL
ASSOCIATE PRODUCER
'82 BY DESIGN*

BARRY WETCHER
STILLS
'83 BABY IT'S YOU
'84 RECKLESS

DAN WETHERBEE
EDITOR
'84 MAKING THE GRADE

RICHARD WETZEL
HAIR
'82 VICE SQUAD

STEVE WEVER
STILLS
'79 CHAMP, THE*
'79 HOT STUFF
'80 BRUBAKER
'80 CADDYSHACK*
'80 CARNY*
'80 HOPSCOTCH*
'81 NOBODY'S PERFEKT

HASKELL WEXLER
CINEMATOGRAPHER
'81 RICHARD PRYOR: LIVE ON THE SUNSET STRIP
'82 LOOKIN' TO GET OUT
'83 MAN WHO LOVED WOMEN, THE

JEFF WEXLER
SOUND
'79 BEING THERE
'80 BLACK MARBLE, THE
'80 NINE TO FIVE
'82 LOOKIN' TO GET OUT
'82 OFFICER AND A GENTLEMAN, AN
'83 LET'S SPEND THE NIGHT TOGETHER
'83 TABLE FOR FIVE
'84 AGAINST ALL ODDS
'84 NATURAL, THE*

MILTON WEXLER
SCREENPLAY
'83 MAN WHO LOVED WOMEN, THE*

NORMAN WEXLER
SCREENPLAY
'83 STAYING ALIVE*

TONYA WEXLER
MAKEUP
'83 TESTAMENT

KATHRYN WEYGAND
SCRIPT SUPERVISOR
'84 HARDBODIES

HAP WEYMAN
UNIT PROD. MANAGER
'81 ALL NIGHT LONG*

JOHN WHALEY
LOCATIONS
'83 TABLE FOR FIVE*

DAVID WHAN
PROPS
'79 MY BRILLIANT CAREER

JACK WHEATON
MUSIC
'82 PENITENTIARY II

CHARLES WHEELER
CINEMATOGRAPHER
'79 C.H.O.M.P.S.
'80 LAST FLIGHT OF NOAH'S ARK,THE
'81 CONDORMAN
MISCELLANEOUS
'81 PURSUIT OF D.B. COOPER, THE

HUGH WHEELER
SCREENPLAY
'80 NIJINSKY

JOHN WHEELER
EDITOR
'79 ONION FIELD, THE
'80 SERIAL
'81 GOING APE!
'82 CHALLENGE, THE
'83 STRANGE INVADERS
'84 RHINESTONE*

MR. JACK WHEELER
MISCELLANEOUS
'82 FIREFOX

PAUL WHEELER
SCREENPLAY
'79 LEGACY, THE*

ALAN WHIBLEY
SPECIAL EFFECTS
'81 EXCALIBUR*
'82 VENOM*
'83 GORKY PARK*
'83 YENTL

BOB WHITAKER
STILLS
'80 FORMULA, THE*
'84 CHAMPIONS

ALAN WHITE
KEY GRIP
'80 CHANGELING, THE

BRUCE WHITE
SOUND
'81 SHOCK TREATMENT
'83 BRITANNIA HOSPITAL
'83 LORDS OF DISCIPLINE, THE
'84 GIVE MY REGARDS TO BROAD STREET

DAVID WHITE
PUBLICIST
'79 MY BRILLIANT CAREER
'82 PIRATE MOVIE, THE

DAVID WHITE
MISCELLANEOUS
'81 NIGHTHAWKS

DELPHINE WHITE
COSTUMES
'79 FAST COMPANY
'80 HOG WILD
'81 SCANNERS
'83 VIDEODROME

DENNIS WHITE
1ST ASST. DIRECTOR
'83 REVENGE OF THE NINJA*
'83 SAVANNAH SMILES
2ND ASST. DIRECTOR
'80 HANGAR 18

DOUG WHITE
SPECIAL EFFECTS
'82 PARASITE
'83 CHAINED HEAT

DOUGLAS WHITE
MISCELLANEOUS
'83 METALSTORM: THE DESTRUCTION OF JARED-SYN

ED WHITE
SOUND
'79 PENITENTIARY

FRANK WHITE
PRODUCTION DESIGNER
'81 CLASH OF THE TITANS

GARRY MICHAEL WHITE
SCREENPLAY
'79 PROMISE, THE

GARY WHITE
1ST ASST. DIRECTOR
'82 MISSIONARY, THE

GIBONEY WHITE
SCRIPT SUPERVISOR
'79 WARRIORS, THE

IRVING WHITE
SCREENPLAY
'79 MAGICIAN OF LUBLIN, THE*

JIMI WHITE
MAKEUP
'79 DOUBLE MCGUFFIN, THE
'80 BIG BRAWL, THE
'80 FOR THE LOVE OF BENJI
'80 OH! HEAVENLY DOG
'81 DEADLY BLESSING
'82 SPLIT IMAGE
'83 TENDER MERCIES

JOAN WHITE
HAIR
'81 SUPERMAN II*
'83 SUPERMAN III*

LES WHITE
PRODUCTION MANAGER
'81 EARTHLING, THE*

MICHAEL WHITE
EXECUTIVE PRODUCER
'81 SHOCK TREATMENT*
'84 STRANGERS KISS

MICHAEL WHITE
ART DIRECTOR
'83 PRIVATES ON PARADE*

WILLIAM WHITE
1ST ASST. DIRECTOR
'80 GONG SHOW MOVIE, THE

DAVID WHITEAR
MUSIC
'82 SWORD AND THE SORCERER, THE

GEORGE WHITEAR
STILLS
'79 LEGACY, THE
'79 YANKS
'80 EMPIRE STRIKES BACK, THE
'80 FORMULA, THE*
'81 SHOCK TREATMENT
'81 FINAL CONFLICT, THE
'81 OUTLAND
'82 CONAN THE BARBARIAN*
'82 MONSIGNOR
'83 HUNGER, THE*
'83 LORDS OF DISCIPLINE, THE
'83 OCTOPUSSY*
'84 DUNE
'84 CONAN THE DESTROYER

DENNIS WHITEHEAD
EXEC IN CHARGE PROD
'84 SILENT NIGHT, DEADLY NIGHT

LOU WHITEHILL
CASTING
'79 APOCALYPSE NOW*

DENIS WHITEHOUSE
ASSISTANT EDITOR
'79 SUNBURN

ROB WHITEHOUSE
PRODUCER
'83 NATE & HAYES*

HUGH WHITEMORE
SCREENPLAY
'79 STEVIE

ERIC WHITFIELD
ASSISTANT EDITOR
'79 PERFECT COUPLE, A*
'80 HEALTH*

RICHARD WHITLEY
SCREENPLAY
'79 ROCK 'N ROLL HIGH SCHOOL*

ALBERT WHITLOCK
SPECIAL EFFECTS
'79 DRACULA
MISCELLANEOUS
'79 PRISONER OF ZENDA, THE
'80 BLUES BROTHERS
'80 CHEECH AND CHONG'S NEXT MOVIE
'80 IN GOD WE TRUST
'80 ISLAND, THE
'81 GHOST STORY
'81 HEARTBEEPS
'81 HISTORY OF THE WORLD PART I
'82 BEST LITTLE WHOREHOUSE IN TEXAS, THE
'82 CAT PEOPLE
'82 MISSING
'82 THING, THE
'83 STING II, THE
'83 PSYCHO II
'84 DUNE
'84 LONELY GUY, THE
'84 GREYSTOKE: THE LEGEND OF TARZAN, LORD OF THE APES

DALE WHITMAN
SOUND
'84 PREPPIES

PATTI WHITMAN
PROD. COORDINATOR
'80 TELL ME A RIDDLE
'81 CHU CHU AND THE PHILLY FLASH
'81 EYE FOR AN EYE, AN

TONY WHITMAN
KEY GRIP
'84 ALPHABET CITY
'84 C.H.U.D.

JOHN WHITNEY JR.
ASSOCIATE PRODUCER
'84 LAST STARFIGHTER, THE

JAMES WHITTAKER
SCREENPLAY
'82 MEGAFORCE*

BILL WHITTEN
COSTUMES
'80 FOG, THE*
'80 JAZZ SINGER, THE*
'81 BUSTIN' LOOSE*

LINDA WHITTINGSLEY
ASSISTANT EDITOR
'80 SCHIZOID*
'83 REVENGE OF THE NINJA*

JOHN WHITTLE
2ND ASST. DIRECTOR
'84 BEAR, THE

DAVID WHORF
UNIT PROD. MANAGER
'83 RIGHT STUFF, THE
'83 SMOKEY AND THE BANDIT III
1ST ASST. DIRECTOR
'79 HOT STUFF
'79 WHEN YOU COMIN' BACK, RED RYDER?
'80 CADDYSHACK
'80 DIE LAUGHING
'81 NOBODY'S PERFEKT
'82 LOVE CHILD
'84 FIRESTARTER

ROY WHYBROW
SPECIAL EFFECTS
'79 LOST AND FOUND
'81 SPHINX
SP. EFFECTS SUPERV.
'82 MOONLIGHTING

WILLIAM WIARD
DIRECTOR
'80 TOM HORN

DOUGLAS WICK
ASSOCIATE PRODUCER
'79 STARTING OVER*

RICHARD WICKERT
MISCELLANEOUS
'84 FLASHPOINT

LINNEA EBBA WICKLUND
PROD. COORDINATOR
'83 CLASS

MELINDA WICKMAN
STILLS
'80 SOMEWHERE IN TIME
'80 BLUES BROTHERS*
'80 COAL MINER'S DAUGHTER*
'80 HEALTH
'81 RAGGEDY MAN

ARTHUR WICKS
PROPS
'83 FINAL OPTION, THE
'83 YELLOWBEARD*
'83 LOCAL HERO*
'84 CHAMPIONS*
'84 SHEENA

MARK WIENER
MISCELLANEOUS
'81 CONTINENTAL DIVIDE

JAN WIERINGA
2ND ASST. DIRECTOR
'80 HUMANOIDS FROM THE DEEP

JOE WIESENFELD
SCREENPLAY
'82 BY DESIGN*

BOB WIGHTMAN
ART DIRECTOR
'79 WARRIORS, THE*

DANIEL WIGUTOW
PRODUCER
'79 LAST EMBRACE*
'81 PURSUIT OF D.B. COOPER, THE*

RALPH WIKKE
ASSISTANT EDITOR
'83 SURVIVORS, THE*

CHARLES WILBORN
SOUND
'79 ROCKY II
'79 JERK, THE
'80 BRUBAKER
'80 IT'S MY TURN*
'80 ORDINARY PEOPLE
'81 LOOKER
'81 GOING APE!
'82 ROCKY III
'82 BEST FRIENDS
'82 YES, GIORGIO
'84 BEVERLY HILLS COP
'84 ICEMAN
'84 SOLDIER'S STORY, A

BOB WILBUR
MISCELLANEOUS
'84 COTTON CLUB, THE

RONALD WILCHEWSKI
HAIR
'79 PRIZE FIGHTER, THE*

CAROLY WILCOX
MISCELLANEOUS
'81 GREAT MUPPET CAPER, THE

JOHN WILCOX
PRODUCTION MANAGER
'79 STEVIE

RICHARD WILCOX
ART DIRECTOR
'82 AMATEUR, THE

ARTHUR WILDE
LOCATIONS
'80 RAISE THE TITANIC
PUBLICIST
'79 JUST YOU AND ME KID
'80 COAL MINER'S DAUGHTER
'82 SIX PACK
'83 STAR CHAMBER
UNIT PUBLICIST
'79 ...AND JUSTICE FOR ALL
'80 MOUNTAIN MEN, THE
'81 POSTMAN ALWAYS RINGS TWICE, THE

DOROTHY WILDE
ASSOCIATE PRODUCER
'79 IN-LAWS, THE
'82 AUTHOR, AUTHOR
'82 MAKING LOVE*
MISCELLANEOUS
'84 LONELY GUY, THE

META WILDE
SCRIPT SUPERVISOR
'83 TERMS OF ENDEARMENT*

BILLY WILDER
PRODUCER
'79 FEDORA
DIRECTOR
'79 FEDORA
'81 BUDDY, BUDDY
SCREENPLAY
'79 FEDORA*
'81 BUDDY, BUDDY*

BRAD WILDER
MAKEUP
'81 CHEECH AND CHONG'S NICE DREAMS
'81 HONKY TONK FREEWAY*
'82 BEST LITTLE WHOREHOUSE IN TEXAS, THE*
'83 STAYING ALIVE
'83 GET CRAZY*
'83 TWO OF A KIND*

DON WILDER
CINEMATOGRAPHER
'79 MEATBALLS

GENE WILDER
DIRECTOR
'81 SUNDAY LOVERS*
'84 WOMAN IN RED, THE
SCREENPLAY
'81 SUNDAY LOVERS*
'84 WOMAN IN RED, THE

GENE WILDER
2ND UNIT DIRECTOR
'79 FISH THAT SAVED PITTSBURGH, THE

GLEN WILDER
STUNT COORDINATOR
'82 CANNERY ROW
'83 STAR CHAMBER
'84 FIRSTBORN*
'84 HARD TO HOLD
'84 LAST STARFIGHTER, THE

LISA WILDER
SCRIPT SUPERVISOR
'80 HAPPY BIRTHDAY, GEMINI

BURT WILEY
PROPS
'79 MORE AMERICAN GRAFFITTI
'82 SHOOT THE MOON

THOMAS WILHITE
EXEC IN CHARGE PROD
'82 TRON

TOM WILHITE
PUBLICIST
'79 APPLE DUMPLING GANG RIDES AGAIN, THE*

DON WILKERSON
2ND ASST. DIRECTOR
'80 STIR CRAZY*
'81 SHARKEY'S MACHINE*
'84 PURPLE RAIN

GARY WILKINS
SOUND
'83 MAN FROM SNOWY RIVER, THE
'83 YEAR OF LIVING DANGEROUSLY, THE
'84 PHAR LAP

RICK WILKINS
MUSIC
'80 CHANGELING, THE

BARRY WILKINSON
PROPS
'81 DRAGONSLAYER
'82 SENDER, THE
'82 VICTOR/VICTORIA
'83 PIRATES OF PENZANCE, THE
'84 GIVE MY REGARDS TO BROAD STREET*
'84 INDIANA JONES AND THE TEMPLE OF DOOM*

CHRIS WILKINSON
2ND UNIT DIRECTOR
'84 RIVER, THE

FROST WILKINSON
STILLS
'84 OVER THE BROOKLYN BRIDGE*

GARTH WILKINSON
LOCATIONS
'84 SILENT NIGHT, DEADLY NIGHT

MARC WILKINSON
MUSIC
'80 FIENDISH PLOT OF DR. FU MANCHU, THE
'83 ENIGMA*
MISCELLANEOUS
'83 ENIGMA

MARY WILKINSON
SCRIPT SUPERVISOR
'79 ALAMBRISTA!

ROBERT WILLARD
SPECIAL EFFECTS
'82 YOUNG DOCTORS IN LOVE*
'84 CLOAK AND DAGGER
'84 LONELY GUY, THE

BOYD WILLAT
ART DIRECTOR
'82 ZAPPED!

NANCY WILLEN
PUBLICIST
'83 RISKY BUSINESS
'83 SURVIVORS, THE
'83 KISS ME GOODBYE
'84 GHOSTBUSTERS
'84 MOSCOW ON THE HUDSON
UNIT PUBLICIST
'82 TEMPEST

CHRISTINE WILLEY
PROD. SECRETARY
'81 MAN WHO SAW TOMORROW, THE

BEN WILLIAMS
ASSISTANT EDITOR
'81 EARTHLING, THE*

BERNARD WILLIAMS
PRODUCER
'84 BOUNTY, THE
EXECUTIVE PRODUCER
'80 FLASH GORDON
'81 RAGTIME*
'82 AMITYVILLE II: THE POSSESSION

BILL WILLIAMS
ASSISTANT EDITOR
'80 ALLIGATOR*

BILLY WILLIAMS
CINEMATOGRAPHER
'79 SILENT PARTNER, THE
'79 BOARDWALK
'79 GOING IN STYLE
'80 SATURN 3
'81 ON GOLDEN POND
'82 GANDHI*
'82 MONSIGNOR
'83 SURVIVORS, THE

BOB WILLIAMS
MISCELLANEOUS
'82 OFFICER AND A GENTLEMAN, AN

C.S.M. MARION WILLIAMS
MISCELLANEOUS
'81 STRIPES

CHERYL WILLIAMS
HAIR
'79 MY BRILLIANT CAREER
'82 STARSTRUCK
'83 YEAR OF LIVING DANGEROUSLY, THE
'84 PHAR LAP

CHRISTINE WILLIAMS
MISCELLANEOUS
'83 ZELIG

DEAN WILLIAMS
STILLS
'80 CADDYSHACK*
'81 BEAST WITHIN, THE
'82 SIX PACK
'82 BARBAROSA
'83 EDDIE MACON'S RUN
'84 CLOAK AND DAGGER*
'84 COUNTRY*
'84 STARMAN*
'84 TANK

DENNIS WILLIAMS
MISCELLANEOUS
'82 ROAD WARRIOR, THE

DOROTHY WILLIAMS
PROD. SECRETARY
'79 ON THE YARD

DWIGHT WILLIAMS
1ST ASST. DIRECTOR
'80 FORMULA, THE*
'84 SOLDIER'S STORY, A
'84 BEAT STREET*

ELMO WILLIAMS
PRODUCER
'83 MAN WOMAN AND CHILD*

FRED WILLIAMS
MAKEUP
'81 CHARLIE CHAN AND THE CURSE OF THE DRAGON QUEEN*
'81 HARDLY WORKING*

GEORGINA WILLIAMS
HAIR
'81 S.O.B.*
'81 FORCE FIVE
'82 BARBAROSA
'82 LOVE AND MONEY

GIGI WILLIAMS
MAKEUP
'79 ROCK 'N ROLL HIGH SCHOOL
'79 ROLLER BOOGIE
'80 HOME MOVIES
'81 HOWLING, THE
'81 PRIVATE LESSONS*
'83 CHAINED HEAT*
HAIR
'79 ROCK 'N ROLL HIGH SCHOOL
'79 ROLLER BOOGIE
'80 HOME MOVIES
'81 HOWLING, THE
'83 CHAINED HEAT*

H. DELTON WILLIAMS
COSTUME SUPERVISOR
'83 BIG SCORE, THE

HOPE WILLIAMS
SCRIPT SUPERVISOR
'79 VILLAIN, THE
'80 SMOKEY AND THE BANDIT II
'80 WHOLLY MOSES!
'81 CANNONBALL RUN, THE
'82 MEGAFORCE
'83 STROKER ACE
'84 CANNONBALL RUN II

RUSSELL WILLIAMS II
SOUND
'84 MAKING THE GRADE

J. TERRY WILLIAMS
EDITOR
'80 RAISE THE TITANIC*

JAN WILLIAMS
SCREENPLAY
'80 LAST FLIGHT OF NOAH'S ARK, THE*
CO-PRODUCER
'80 LAST FLIGHT OF NOAH'S ARK, THE

JAN WILLIAMS
PRODUCER
'81 CONDORMAN

JERRY WILLIAMS
SPECIAL EFFECTS
'81 POSTMAN ALWAYS RINGS TWICE, THE
'82 BORDER, THE
'83 BREATHLESS

JOHN WILLIAMS
MUSIC
'79 DRACULA
'79 1941
'80 CLOSE ENCOUNTERS OF THE THIRD KIND SPECIAL EDITION
'80 EMPIRE STRIKES BACK, THE
'81 RAIDERS OF THE LOST ARK
'81 HEARTBEEPS
'82 E.T. THE EXTRA-TERRESTRIAL
'82 MONSIGNOR
'83 RETURN OF THE JEDI
'84 RIVER, THE
'84 INDIANA JONES AND THE TEMPLE OF DOOM

JOHN WILLIAMS
ASSISTANT EDITOR
'80 LOVING COUPLES*

JOHN WILLIAMS
MISCELLANEOUS
'78 DEER HUNTER, THE

LLANDYS WILLIAMS
COSTUME SUPERVISOR
'79 BOULEVARD NIGHTS

ADRIAN WILLIAMS M.B. MRCP
MISCELLANEOUS
'82 FRANCES

MAE WILLIAMS
CASTING
'80 FOXES*

MARLENE WILLIAMS
HAIR
'79 GOLDENGIRL
'80 ANY WHICH WAY YOU CAN
'82 HONKYTONK MAN
'83 SUDDEN IMPACT
'84 BODY DOUBLE
'84 TIGHTROPE

MIKE WILLIAMS
2ND ASST. DIRECTOR
'80 HOG WILD
'81 SCANNERS

PATRICK WILLIAMS
MUSIC
'79 BUTCH AND SUNDANCE: THE EARLY YEARS
'79 CUBA
'79 HOT STUFF
'80 HERO AT LARGE
'80 HOW TO BEAT THE HIGH COST OF LIVING
'80 IT'S MY TURN
'80 USED CARS
'80 WHOLLY MOSES!
'81 CHARLIE CHAN AND THE CURSE OF THE DRAGON QUEEN
'82 SOME KIND OF HERO
'82 BEST LITTLE WHOREHOUSE IN TEXAS, THE
'82 TOY, THE
'83 BUDDY SYSTEM, THE
'83 TWO OF A KIND
'84 ALL OF ME
'84 BEST DEFENSE
'84 SWING SHIFT
MISCELLANEOUS
'79 BREAKING AWAY

PAUL WILLIAMS
MUSIC
'79 MUPPET MOVIE, THE*

PETER WILLIAMS
ART DIRECTOR
'82 SAFARI 3000

RODNEY WILLIAMS
MISCELLANEOUS
'80 OUTSIDER, THE

ROGER NEVILLE WILLIAMS
LOCATIONS
'79 BUTCH AND SUNDANCE: THE EARLY YEARS*

RUSSELL WILLIAMS
SOUND
'82 PENITENTIARY II

SAM WILLIAMS
ASSOCIATE PRODUCER
'83 TRADING PLACES*

STACY WILLIAMS
ASSOCIATE PRODUCER
'83 MAN WOMAN AND CHILD

TOM WILLIAMS
STUNT COORDINATOR
'80 EYES OF A STRANGER

TREVOR WILLIAMS
PRODUCTION DESIGNER
'79 SILENT PARTNER, THE
'79 LOST AND FOUND
'80 CHANGELING, THE
'80 TRIBUTE
'82 AMATEUR, THE
'82 ENDANGERED SPECIES
'84 POLICE ACADEMY

DAVID WILLIAMSON
SCREENPLAY
'81 GALLIPOLI
'83 YEAR OF LIVING DANGEROUSLY, THE*
'84 PHAR LAP

FLORENCE WILLIAMSON
ASSISTANT EDITOR
'78 DEER HUNTER, THE
'79 ONION FIELD, THE
'81 LEGEND OF THE LONE RANGER,THE*
'83 STRANGE INVADERS
'84 FLAMINGO KID, THE

FRED WILLIAMSON
DIRECTOR
'83 BIG SCORE, THE

FREDDIE WILLIAMSON
MAKEUP
'81 FINAL CONFLICT, THE
'83 EDUCATING RITA
'84 KIPPERBANG

JOHN WILLIAMSON
STILLS
'84 JUST THE WAY YOU ARE*

LOYD WILLIAMSON
MISCELLANEOUS
'84 ALPHABET CITY

SAM WILLIAMSON
MISCELLANEOUS
'80 RESURRECTION

CONNIE WILLIS
SCRIPT SUPERVISOR
'79 PLAYERS

DOUG WILLIS
KEY GRIP
'79 PROMISE, THE
'80 RAISE THE TITANIC*
'80 BRUBAKER

GORDON WILLIS
DIRECTOR
'80 WINDOWS
CINEMATOGRAPHER
'79 MANHATTAN
'80 STARDUST MEMORIES
'80 WINDOWS
'81 PENNIES FROM HEAVEN
'82 MIDSUMMER NIGHT'S SEX COMEDY, A
'83 ZELIG
'84 BROADWAY DANNY ROSE

HERB WILLIS
UNIT PROD. MANAGER
'79 1941*

JIM WILLIS
SOUND
'79 FIREPOWER*
'82 CONAN THE BARBARIAN
'84 BLAME IT ON RIO

BOB WILLOUGHBY
MISCELLANEOUS
'81 NIGHTHAWKS

GEORGE WILLOUGHBY
PRODUCER
'79 BOARDWALK

GEMMA LA MANA WILLS
STILLS
'79 BUDDY HOLLY STORY, THE
'80 DIE LAUGHING
'80 FIRST FAMILY
'81 GOING APE!
'82 FRANCES
'84 GHOSTBUSTERS*

HENRY WILLS
STUNT COORDINATOR
'81 UNDER THE RAINBOW

JERRY WILLS
STUNT COORDINATOR
'81 GOING APE!
'82 FRANCES

LOU WILLS
CHOREOGRAPHER
'82 CANNERY ROW
MISCELLANEOUS
'80 POPEYE

DUNCAN WILMORE
MISCELLANEOUS
'83 RIGHT STUFF, THE
'83 WAR GAMES

HAROLD WILNER
ASSISTANT EDITOR
'79 WHEN A STRANGER CALLS

BILL WILSON
ASSOCIATE PRODUCER
'83 MR. MOM*

CAROLE WILSON
MISCELLANEOUS
'81 BLOOD BEACH

CASSANDRA WILSON
PROD. OFFICE COORD.
'83 TESTAMENT
PROD. COORDINATOR
'80 MOTEL HELL
PROD. SECRETARY
'80 FIRST FAMILY

CHRISTINE WILSON
SCRIPT SUPERVISOR
'82 OUT OF THE BLUE
'83 RUNNING BRAVE
'83 STAR 80*
'84 ICEMAN
'84 RUNAWAY

CLAY WILSON
KEY GRIP
'83 KISS ME GOODBYE

COLIN WILSON
ASSISTANT EDITOR
'81 RAIDERS OF THE LOST ARK*
'84 INDIANA JONES AND THE TEMPLE OF DOOM*
'84 FINDERS KEEPERS

GERALD WILSON
SCREENPLAY
'79 FIREPOWER

GRACE WILSON
SCRIPT SUPERVISOR
'81 ...ALL THE MARBLES

HUGH WILSON
DIRECTOR
'84 POLICE ACADEMY
SCREENPLAY
'83 STROKER ACE*
'84 POLICE ACADEMY*

IAN WILSON
CINEMATOGRAPHER
'83 PRIVATES ON PARADE

JACK WILSON
MAKEUP
'80 SOMEWHERE IN TIME*
'80 COAST TO COAST*
'80 OCTAGON, THE
'81 MODERN PROBLEMS
'83 D.C. CAB

JOE WILSON
MISCELLANEOUS
'83 TIMERIDER

JOHN WILSON
EXEC IN CHARGE PROD
'79 1941
ASSOCIATE PRODUCER
'80 USED CARS
PRODUCTION MANAGER
'84 GHOSTBUSTERS
UNIT PROD. MANAGER
'79 HARDCORE
'80 USED CARS
'83 RISKY BUSINESS
'83 BLUE THUNDER*
'83 BRAINSTORM*

JOHN WILSON
EDITOR
'83 DRAUGHTSMAN CONTRACT, THE

JOY WILSON
ASSISTANT EDITOR
'80 IT'S MY TURN*

JUDY WILSON
SCRIPT SUPERVISOR
'81 ENTER THE NINJA

LARRY WILSON
MISCELLANEOUS
'80 AIRPLANE

LESTER WILSON
CHOREOGRAPHER
'84 BEAT STREET

LINDA WILSON
ASSISTANT EDITOR
'80 FOOLIN AROUND*

MICHAEL WILSON
SCREENPLAY
'81 FOR YOUR EYES ONLY*
'83 OCTOPUSSY*
EXECUTIVE PRODUCER
'79 MOONRAKER
'81 FOR YOUR EYES ONLY
'83 OCTOPUSSY

PAUL WILSON
MISCELLANEOUS
'79 BUTCH AND SUNDANCE: THE EARLY YEARS
'81 SUPERMAN II
'81 FOR YOUR EYES ONLY
'81 HISTORY OF THE WORLD PART I
'83 KRULL

PHYLLIS WILSON
LOCATIONS
'81 TICKET TO HEAVEN

RENATE WILSON
PROD. COORDINATOR
'82 PIRATE MOVIE, THE

BOB WILSON SR.
PROPS
'84 SPLASH*

VIC WILSON
STUNT COORDINATOR
'81 GALLIPOLI*

WILLIAM WILSON
2ND ASST. DIRECTOR
'84 NEVERENDING STORY, THE*

KELLY WIMBERT
2ND ASST. DIRECTOR
'83 TENDER MERCIES

DAVID WIMBURY
ASSOCIATE PRODUCER
'84 OXFORD BLUES*
PRODUCTION MANAGER
'82 PINK FLOYD: THE WALL
'83 MONTY PYTHON'S THE MEANING OF LIFE
2ND ASST. DIRECTOR
'79 PRISONER OF ZENDA, THE*

JIM WINBURN
STUNT COORDINATOR
'80 GONG SHOW MOVIE, THE
'81 GRADUATION DAY
'81 MODERN PROBLEMS
'83 MORTUARY

SIMON WINCER
DIRECTOR
'84 PHAR LAP
EXECUTIVE PRODUCER
'83 MAN FROM SNOWY RIVER, THE*

GERI WINDSOR
CASTING
'80 CHANGELING, THE*

MAURY WINETROBE
EDITOR
'79 RAVAGERS
'79 FRISCO KID, THE*
'79 ICE CASTLES*
'80 BLACK MARBLE, THE
'80 JAZZ SINGER, THE
'81 TAPS

EARL WINGARD
PUBLICIST
'80 THOSE LIPS, THOSE EYES
'82 LOOKIN' TO GET OUT*
'83 BLUE THUNDER
'83 YELLOWBEARD
UNIT PUBLICIST
'79 NIGHTWING
'80 MOTEL HELL

LAUREN WINGATE
ASSOCIATE PRODUCER
'83 LIANNA*
LOCATIONS
'83 LIANNA*

WILLIAM WINGATE
CO-PRODUCER
'82 ZOOT SUIT*

IAN WINGROVE
SPECIAL EFFECTS
'79 LEGACY, THE
'79 GREAT TRAIN ROBBERY, THE
'81 FINAL CONFLICT, THE
'81 REDS*
'83 NEVER SAY NEVER AGAIN
'84 GIVE MY REGARDS TO BROAD STREET

ALEX WINITSKY
PRODUCER
'79 CUBA*
'83 BLUE SKIES AGAIN*
'84 IRRECONCILABLE DIFFERENCES*
'84 SCANDALOUS*
EXECUTIVE PRODUCER
'80 LADY VANISHES, THE*
'84 SWING SHIFT*

MARK WINITSKY
ASSISTANT EDITOR
'81 CUTTER'S WAY*
'84 IRRECONCILABLE DIFFERENCES

IRWIN WINKLER
PRODUCER
'79 ROCKY II*
'80 RAGING BULL*
'81 TRUE CONFESSIONS*
'82 ROCKY III*
'82 AUTHOR, AUTHOR
'83 RIGHT STUFF, THE*

TERENCE WINKLESS
SCREENPLAY
'81 HOWLING, THE*

TONY WINLEY
2ND ASST. DIRECTOR
'82 STARSTRUCK*

DEE DEE WINNER
PROD. SECRETARY
'81 FUNHOUSE, THE*

JOHN WINNER
MISCELLANEOUS
'83 SMOKEY AND THE BANDIT III

MICHAEL WINNER
PRODUCER
'79 FIREPOWER
DIRECTOR
'79 FIREPOWER
'82 DEATHWISH II
'83 WICKED LADY, THE
SCREENPLAY
'83 WICKED LADY, THE*

JOE WINOGRADOFF
2ND ASST. DIRECTOR
'84 OVER THE BROOKLYN BRIDGE

RAY WINSLADE
MISCELLANEOUS
'81 EARTHLING, THE

MARY ELLEN WINSTON
COSTUMES
'79 WARRIORS, THE*

STAN WINSTON
2ND UNIT DIRECTOR
'84 TERMINATOR, THE*
MISCELLANEOUS
'81 DEAD AND BURIED
'81 ENTITY, THE
'81 HAND, THE
'81 HEARTBEEPS
'82 PARASITE
'84 STARMAN
'84 TERMINATOR, THE

CLIVE WINTER
SOUND
'81 CHARIOTS OF FIRE
'82 PINK FLOYD: THE WALL
'83 HUNGER, THE*
'84 KILLING FIELDS, THE

RALPH WINTER
ASSOCIATE PRODUCER
'84 STAR TREK III: THE SEARCH FOR SPOCK

VINCENT WINTER
PRODUCTION MANAGER
'81 SUPERMAN II
'83 SUPERMAN III*
'84 INDIANA JONES AND THE TEMPLE OF DOOM*
UNIT MANAGER
'81 FOR YOUR EYES ONLY*
1ST ASST. DIRECTOR
'79 UNIDENTIFIED FLYING ODDBALL
LOCATIONS
'80 NIJINSKY*
'81 FOR YOUR EYES ONLY*

MILDRED JEAN WINTERS
MAKEUP
'84 FLASHPOINT

NANCY WINTERS
MISCELLANEOUS
'84 C.H.U.D.

RALPH WINTERS
EDITOR
'79 10
'80 AMERICAN SUCCESS COMPANY, THE
'81 S.O.B.
'82 VICTOR/VICTORIA
'83 CURSE OF THE PINK PANTHER*
'83 MAN WHO LOVED WOMEN, THE
'84 MICKI AND MAUDE

PETER WINTONICK
EDITOR
'79 IN PRAISE OF OLDER WOMEN*

DOUG WISE
1ST ASST. DIRECTOR
'80 PRIVATE EYES, THE
'82 STAR TREK II THE WRATH OF KHAN
2ND ASST. DIRECTOR
'79 STAR TREK-THE MOTION PICTURE
'80 FINAL COUNTDOWN, THE*

MICHAEL WISE
EXECUTIVE PRODUCER
'81 NIGHTHAWKS*

ROBERT WISE
DIRECTOR
'79 STAR TREK-THE MOTION PICTURE

PAUL WISENTHAL
MISCELLANEOUS
'80 TERROR TRAIN

HARLEY WISHNER M.D.
MISCELLANEOUS
'81 WHOSE LIFE IS IT ANYWAY?

RON WISMAN
EDITOR
'81 TICKET TO HEAVEN

DAVID WISNIEVITZ
ASSOCIATE PRODUCER
'83 BALLAD OF GREGORIO CORTEZ, THE*
PRODUCTION MANAGER
'83 BALLAD OF GREGORIO CORTEZ, THE

ELEANOR WITCOMBE
SCREENPLAY
'79 MY BRILLIANT CAREER

ALBERT WITHERICK
ART DIRECTOR
'79 UNIDENTIFIED FLYING ODDBALL
PRODUCTION DESIGNER
'81 CONDORMAN

STEPHEN WITHROW
ASSISTANT EDITOR
'82 BY DESIGN

DAN WITT
ASSOCIATE PRODUCER
'80 OH! HEAVENLY DOG
MISCELLANEOUS
'79 DOUBLE MCGUFFIN, THE

PAUL JUNGER WITT
PRODUCER
'84 FIRSTBORN*

VICKY WITT
ASSISTANT EDITOR
'82 STAR TREK II THE WRATH OF KHAN*

GLADYS WITTEN
HAIR
'79 NORTH DALLAS FORTY

DIRK WITTENBORN
SCREENPLAY
'79 MR. MIKE'S MONDO VIDEO*

WILLIAM WITTLIFF
PRODUCER
'81 RAGGEDY MAN*
'84 COUNTRY*
SCREENPLAY
'79 BLACK STALLION, THE*
'80 HONEYSUCKLE ROSE*
'81 RAGGEDY MAN
'82 BARBAROSA
'84 COUNTRY
CO-PRODUCER
'82 BARBAROSA
2ND UNIT DIRECTOR
'81 RAGGEDY MAN

ED WITTSTEIN
ART DIRECTOR
'80 FAME
PRODUCTION DESIGNER
'81 ENDLESS LOVE

ROCKLYN WITZ
HAIR
'83 METALSTORM: THE DESTRUCTION OF JARED-SYN*

JIM WITZEL
MUSIC
'82 HOME WORK*

TED WITZER
EXECUTIVE PRODUCER
'82 SIX PACK*

JOE WIZAN
PRODUCER
'79 VOICES
'83 TWO OF A KIND*
'84 UNFAITHFULLY YOURS*
EXECUTIVE PRODUCER
'79 ...AND JUSTICE FOR ALL

SCOTT WODEHOUSE
PRODUCTION MANAGER
'80 NIJINSKY*
LOCATIONS
'81 SPHINX*

ANDREW WOIK
MISCELLANEOUS
'81 NIGHT THE LIGHTS WENT OUT IN GEORGIA, THE

CHARLES WOLF
ASSISTANT EDITOR
'81 SHARKEY'S MACHINE*

GORDON WOLF
PRODUCTION MANAGER
'83 SUBURBIA

HARRY WOLF
CINEMATOGRAPHER
'80 NUDE BOMB, THE
MISCELLANEOUS
'79 PRISONER OF ZENDA, THE

HERMAN WOLF
UNIT MANAGER
'79 FIFTH MUSKETEER, THE

JEFFREY WOLF
ASSISTANT EDITOR
'80 WINDOWS

JOSEPH WOLF
EXECUTIVE PRODUCER
'81 HALLOWEEN II*
'81 HELL NIGHT*
'82 SEDUCTION, THE*
'82 HALLOWEEN III: SEASON OF THE WITCH*
'84 NIGHTMARE ON ELM STREET, A*
EXEC IN CHARGE PROD
'82 PARASITE
ASSOCIATE PRODUCER
'79 ROLLER BOOGIE
'80 FADE TO BLACK

MICHAEL WOLF
EXECUTIVE PRODUCER
'81 S.O.B.
ASSOCIATE PRODUCER
'82 PARASITE*

MICHAEL WOLF
MISCELLANEOUS
'83 SOMETHING WICKED THIS WAY COMES

RICHARD WOLF
SCREENPLAY
'81 GAS

MAURICE WOLFE
ASSOCIATE PRODUCER
'83 RUNNING BRAVE

NICK WOLFE
SOUND
'80 PRIVATE EYES, THE

ROBERT WOLFE
EDITOR
'79 ROSE, THE*
'80 HUNTER, THE
'81 ON GOLDEN POND

STEVEN WOLFE
2ND ASST. DIRECTOR
'84 WEEKEND PASS

JONATHAN WOLFF
KEY GRIP
'83 DEADLY FORCE

MARSHALL WOLINS
SCRIPT SUPERVISOR
'79 ROCKY II
'79 JERK, THE
'81 BUDDY, BUDDY

SIDNEY WOLINSKY
EDITOR
'83 MY TUTOR
'84 BEST DEFENSE
ASSISTANT EDITOR
'81 HAND, THE
'81 PENNIES FROM HEAVEN
MISCELLANEOUS
'82 YOUNG DOCTORS IN LOVE

WALTER WOLOSZCZUK
PROPS
'83 STRANGE BREW

DAVID WOLPER
EXECUTIVE PRODUCER
'81 MAN WHO SAW TOMORROW, THE

JOAN WOLPERT
PROD. COORDINATOR
'83 GET CRAZY
'84 RIVER, THE

ALBERT WOLSKY
COSTUMES
'79 ALL THAT JAZZ
'79 MANHATTAN
'79 METEOR
'80 JAZZ SINGER, THE*
'80 WILLIE & PHIL
'81 ALL NIGHT LONG
'81 PATERNITY
'82 SOPHIE'S CHOICE
'82 STILL OF THE NIGHT
'82 TEMPEST
'83 STAR 80
'83 TO BE OR NOT TO BE
'84 MOSCOW ON THE HUDSON

LYNN WOLVERTON
MAKEUP
'81 STUDENT BODIES
'82 LIAR'S MOON
HAIR
'81 STUDENT BODIES
'82 LIAR'S MOON

ROGER WOMACK
STUNT COORDINATOR
'83 PORKY'S II THE NEXT DAY*
MISCELLANEOUS
'83 PORKY'S II THE NEXT DAY

DAVID WOMARK
ASSOCIATE PRODUCER
'82 LAST AMERICAN VIRGIN, THE
1ST ASST. DIRECTOR
'84 BREAKIN 2 ELECTRIC BOOGALOO
'84 OVER THE BROOKLYN BRIDGE

ARNIE WONG
MISCELLANEOUS
'82 TRON

CLARINDA WONG
ASSISTANT EDITOR
'83 METALSTORM: THE DESTRUCTION OF JARED-SYN

SAM WONG
UNIT MANAGER
'79 GAME OF DEATH

JOE WOO JR.
ASSISTANT EDITOR
'82 BEASTMASTER, THE

CHARLES WOOD
SCREENPLAY
'79 CUBA

CHRISTOPHER WOOD
SCREENPLAY
'79 MOONRAKER

DEE DEE WOOD
CHOREOGRAPHER
'80 IN GOD WE TRUST

DOUG WOOD
KEY GRIP
'83 MORTUARY

DURINDA RICE WOOD
COSTUMES
'80 BATTLE BEYOND THE STARS

MAX WOOD
SPECIAL EFFECTS
'80 RAGING BULL*

MIKE WOOD
SPECIAL EFFECTS
'81 CHARLIE CHAN AND THE CURSE OF THE DRAGON QUEEN*
'83 AMITYVILLE 3D*
'84 FIRESTARTER*
SP. EFFECTS SUPERV.
'83 TWILIGHT ZONE, THE MOVIE

OLIVER WOOD
CINEMATOGRAPHER
'84 ALPHABET CITY

PETER WOOD
ASSOCIATE PRODUCER
'81 MAN WHO SAW TOMORROW, THE*
EDITOR
'81 MAN WHO SAW TOMORROW, THE*

SUZY WOOD
STILLS
'81 ROAD GAMES*

YVONNE WOOD
COSTUMES
'82 ZOOT SUIT

CATHIE WOODARD
PROD. COORDINATOR
'84 STONE BOY, THE

JEFFREY WOODBRIDGE
ART DIRECTOR
'84 KIPPERBANG

RAY WOODBURY
ASSISTANT EDITOR
'79 GAME OF DEATH*

JOAN WOODGATE
MISCELLANEOUS
'81 FINAL CONFLICT, THE

JOHN WOODRUFF
LOCATIONS
'80 EYES OF A STRANGER*

BILL WOODS
SPECIAL EFFECTS
'79 SILENT PARTNER, THE

JACK WOODS
EDITOR
'82 DON'T CRY, IT'S ONLY THUNDER*

MAE WOODS
ASSOCIATE PRODUCER
'84 STREETS OF FIRE

MARY ELLEN WOODS
2ND ASST. DIRECTOR
'83 SWEET SIXTEEN

ELISABETH WOODTHORPE
PROD. SECRETARY
'80 MIRROR CRACK'D, THE

BRONTE WOODWARD
SCREENPLAY
'80 CAN'T STOP THE MUSIC*

JOHN WOODWARD
UNIT MANAGER
'83 MORTUARY
LOCATIONS
'83 FLASHDANCE

RONALD WOODWARD
KEY GRIP
'81 HALLOWEEN II
'82 HALLOWEEN III: SEASON OF THE WITCH
'82 THING, THE
'83 D.C. CAB
'83 PSYCHO II
'84 ROMANCING THE STONE

JOHN WOODWORD
LOCATIONS
'83 TWO OF A KIND*

KAREN WOOKEY
SCRIPT SUPERVISOR
'79 MAIN EVENT, THE
'80 URBAN COWBOY
'81 REDS*
'83 TABLE FOR FIVE*
'84 CRACKERS
'84 ROMANCING THE STONE

DENNIS WOOLEY
ASSISTANT EDITOR
'79 IN-LAWS, THE
'81 SPHINX

PETER WOOLEY
PRODUCTION DESIGNER
'80 FATSO
'80 UP THE ACADEMY
'81 UNDER THE RAINBOW
'82 JEKYLL AND HYDE TOGETHER AGAIN
'84 HARD TO HOLD
'84 OH GOD, YOU DEVIL

STEPHANIE WOOLEY
LOCATIONS
'81 UNDER THE RAINBOW*

STEPHANIE WOOLEY
ART DIRECTOR
'84 STONE BOY, THE

CHARLES WOOLF
ASSISTANT EDITOR
'82 FRANCES*

JONATHAN WOOLF
KEY GRIP
'84 CHAMPIONS

NIGEL WOOLL
ASSOCIATE PRODUCER
'83 DRESSER, THE
PRODUCTION MANAGER
'79 YANKS
'81 REDS*
'83 KRULL*

TONY WOOLLARD
PRODUCTION DESIGNER
'82 MOONLIGHTING
'82 PIRATE MOVIE, THE

HARRY WOOLMAN
SPECIAL EFFECTS
'80 HANGAR 18

TERRY WOOLMAN
SPECIAL EFFECTS
'84 HARDBODIES

RUSS WOOLNOUGH
ASSISTANT EDITOR
'81 OUTLAND
'83 BEYOND THE LIMIT*

RALPH WOOLSEY
CINEMATOGRAPHER
'79 GREAT SANTINI, THE
'79 PROMISE, THE
'80 LAST MARRIED COUPLE IN AMERICA, THE
'80 OH GOD! BOOK II

ARTHUR WOOSTER
2ND UNIT DIRECTOR
'81 FOR YOUR EYES ONLY
'83 OCTOPUSSY
'84 CHAMPIONS
MISCELLANEOUS
'80 RAISE THE TITANIC
'81 FOR YOUR EYES ONLY
'84 RIDDLE OF THE SANDS

KATHERINE WOOTEN
SCRIPT SUPERVISOR
'80 BLUES BROTHERS
'81 HEARTBEEPS
'83 TWILIGHT ZONE, THE MOVIE

CHUCK WORKMAN
MISCELLANEOUS
'84 PROTOCOL

WALLACE WORSLEY
PRODUCTION MANAGER
'80 COAL MINER'S DAUGHTER
'82 E.T. THE EXTRA-TERRESTRIAL
UNIT PROD. MANAGER
'81 WHOSE LIFE IS IT ANYWAY?

DAVID WORTH
CINEMATOGRAPHER
'80 ANY WHICH WAY YOU CAN
'80 BRONCO BILLY

JODY TAYLOR WORTH
MUSIC SUPERVISOR
'80 UP THE ACADEMY

MARVIN WORTH
PRODUCER
'79 ROSE, THE*
'80 UP THE ACADEMY*
'82 SOUP FOR ONE
'84 FALLING IN LOVE
'84 RHINESTONE*
'84 UNFAITHFULLY YOURS*

PHIL WORTH
LOCATIONS
'80 BLUE LAGOON

HARRY WOWCHUCK
STUNT COORDINATOR
'82 PARASITE
MISCELLANEOUS
'83 TIMERIDER

EGIL WOXHOL
MISCELLANEOUS
'80 FFOLKES
'81 CLASH OF THE TITANS

ERIC WRATE
EDITOR
'82 IF YOU COULD SEE WHAT I HEAR

BOB WRIGHT
2ND ASST. DIRECTOR
'79 HANOVER STREET*
'81 CATTLE ANNIE AND LITTLE BRITCHES*
'81 OUTLAND
'82 MISSIONARY, THE

GARY WRIGHT
MUSIC
'82 ENDANGERED SPECIES

GLENN WRIGHT
COSTUMES
'80 ANY WHICH WAY YOU CAN
'80 BRONCO BILLY
'82 FIREFOX
COSTUME SUPERVISOR
'79 ESCAPE FROM ALCATRAZ
'82 HONKYTONK MAN
'84 TIGHTROPE

HARLAND WRIGHT
PRODUCTION DESIGNER
'79 DOUBLE MCGUFFIN, THE
'80 FOR THE LOVE OF BENJI

HILARY WRIGHT
COSTUMES
'84 EL NORTE
'84 TERMINATOR, THE
PROPS
'84 EL NORTE

JAKE WRIGHT
1ST ASST. DIRECTOR
'79 CLASS OF MISS MACMICHAEL, THE
'83 PRIVATES ON PARADE

JOHN WRIGHT
EDITOR
'81 ONLY WHEN I LAUGH
'82 FRANCES
'84 MASS APPEAL

AL WRIGHT JR.
SPECIAL EFFECTS
'80 BRUBAKER

LEE WRIGHT
KEY GRIP
'81 LAST CHASE, THE

PATRICK WRIGHT
PRODUCER
'83 FRIGHTMARE*

PATTI WRIGHT
PUBLICIST
'82 MONTY PYTHON LIVE AT THE HOLLYWOOD BOWL

ROBERT WRIGHT
1ST ASST. DIRECTOR
'79 FIFTH MUSKETEER, THE*

RON WRIGHT
1ST ASST. DIRECTOR
'79 MUPPET MOVIE, THE
'81 BACK ROADS
'82 HALLOWEEN III: SEASON OF THE WITCH

STEVE WRIGHT
1ST ASST. DIRECTOR
'80 PROM NIGHT
2ND UNIT DIRECTOR
'80 PROM NIGHT*

STEVE WRIGHT
MISCELLANEOUS
'84 HARDBODIES

STEWART WRIGHT
2ND ASST. DIRECTOR
'83 MAN FROM SNOWY RIVER, THE

TALLIE WRIGHT
PRODUCER
'83 FRIGHTMARE*

TOM WRIGHT
2ND UNIT DIRECTOR
'82 I OUGHT TO BE IN PICTURES
'83 STAYING ALIVE
'84 BEVERLY HILLS COP
MISCELLANEOUS
'83 MAX DUGAN RETURNS

TOM WRIGHT
STUNT COORDINATOR
'84 BROTHER FROM ANOTHER PLANET, THE*

TOM WRIGHT
MISCELLANEOUS
'79 ROCKY II

PETER WRONA JR.
MAKEUP
'80 TIMES SQUARE

DONALD WRYE
DIRECTOR
'79 ICE CASTLES
SCREENPLAY
'79 ICE CASTLES*

MARTY WUNDERLICH
PROPS
'80 TOM HORN
'81 FORCE FIVE
'81 HIGH RISK
'82 DEATH VALLEY
'83 STAR CHAMBER
'84 GREMLINS
'84 2010

ROBERT WUNSCH
EXECUTIVE PRODUCER
'80 DEFIANCE

RIKI WUOLLE
CASTING
'84 PURPLE RAIN*

STUART WURTZEL
PRODUCTION DESIGNER
'79 HAIR
'80 SIMON
'80 NIGHT OF THE JUGGLER
'81 TATTOO
'82 CHOSEN, THE
'83 BALLAD OF GREGORIO CORTEZ, THE

MICHAEL WUSCHICK
PROPS
'79 MAGICIAN OF LUBLIN, THE

AL WYATT SR.
STUNT COORDINATOR
'82 ZAPPED!*

JENNIFER WYCKOFF
PROD. SECRETARY
'84 ONCE UPON A TIME IN AMERICA

MELISSA WYE
ASSISTANT EDITOR
'82 LOOKIN' TO GET OUT*

MICHAEL WYKA
CASTING
'82 SWAMP THING*

DAVID WYLER
2ND ASST. DIRECTOR
'79 TOURIST TRAP

DONALD WYLIE
LOCATIONS
'79 ALAMBRISTA!

BOB WYMAN
EDITOR
'79 PROMISES IN THE DARK
'82 LOVE CHILD
'84 HARD TO HOLD

DAN WYMAN
MUSIC
'80 WITHOUT WARNING
'81 HELL NIGHT

GERALD WYNKOOP
MISCELLANEOUS
'79 PROMISE, THE

LISBETH WYNN-OWEN
PROD. COORDINATOR
'80 LONG RIDERS, THE
'81 SOUTHERN COMFORT
'81 THIEF
'84 STREETS OF FIRE

JIM WYNORSKI
SCREENPLAY
'83 SCREWBALLS*
EXECUTIVE PRODUCER
'83 SCREWBALLS*

Y

FRANK YABLANS
PRODUCER
'79 NORTH DALLAS FORTY
'81 MOMMIE DEAREST
'82 MONSIGNOR*
'83 STAR CHAMBER
SCREENPLAY
'79 NORTH DALLAS FORTY*
'81 MOMMIE DEAREST*

IRWIN YABLANS
PRODUCER
'81 HELL NIGHT*
'82 SEDUCTION, THE*
'84 TANK
EXECUTIVE PRODUCER
'79 ROLLER BOOGIE
'80 FADE TO BLACK*
'81 HALLOWEEN II*
'82 HALLOWEEN III: SEASON OF THE WITCH*
'82 PARASITE

YABO YABLONSKY
SCREENPLAY
'79 JAGUAR LIVES
'81 VICTORY*

SHEILA YACIMOV
HAIR
'79 RUNNING

RONY YACOV
ASSOCIATE PRODUCER
'84 BOLERO
PRODUCTION MANAGER
'80 BIG RED ONE, THE

RACHEL YAGIL
ASSISTANT EDITOR
'79 MAGICIAN OF LUBLIN, THE

ETSUKO YAGYU
COSTUMES
'82 CHALLENGE, THE

BILL YAHRAUS
EDITOR
'79 HEARTLAND
'84 COUNTRY
ASSISTANT EDITOR
'81 TRUE CONFESSIONS

LEONARD YAKIR
PRODUCER
'82 OUT OF THE BLUE*
SCREENPLAY
'82 OUT OF THE BLUE*

KIYOSHI YAMASAKI
MISCELLANEOUS
'82 CONAN THE BARBARIAN
'84 DUNE
'84 CONAN THE DESTROYER

STOMU YAMASHTA
MUSIC
'82 TEMPEST

GEORGE YANEFF
EXECUTIVE PRODUCER
'84 HOTEL NEW HAMPSHIRE, THE*

TAKIS YANNAPOULOS
ASSISTANT EDITOR
'82 SUMMER LOVERS*

DONALD YANNESSA
MISCELLANEOUS
'83 ALL THE RIGHT MOVES

ROBERT YANNETTI
2ND ASST. DIRECTOR
'84 BODY DOUBLE
'84 RIVER, THE*

LOPE YAP
LOCATIONS
'79 MORE AMERICAN GRAFFITTI

JONATHAN YARBROUGH
STUNT COORDINATOR
'81 CONTINENTAL DIVIDE

WILL YARBROUGH
SOUND
'83 D.C. CAB

GABRIEL YARED
MUSIC
'83 HANNA K

ELAINE YARISH
LOCATIONS
'81 LAST CHASE, THE*

ELI YARKONI
SOUND
'82 PARADISE

DANIEL YARUSSI
CINEMATOGRAPHER
'81 GRADUATION DAY

ALBERT YASSEUR
KEY GRIP
'84 CHEECH AND CHONG'S THE CORSICAN BROTHERS

SHOICHI YASUDA
PROPS
'83 MERRY CHRISTMAS, MR. LAWRENCE

BROCK YATES
SCREENPLAY
'80 SMOKEY AND THE BANDIT II*
'81 CANNONBALL RUN, THE

KENNETH YATES
ASSOCIATE PRODUCER
'82 SWORD AND THE SORCERER, THE*

MARIE YATES
CO-PRODUCER
'82 FRANCES

MARTHA YATES
PROD. COORDINATOR
'81 LEGEND OF THE LONE RANGER, THE

PETER YATES
PRODUCER
'79 BREAKING AWAY
'81 EYEWITNESS
'83 DRESSER, THE
DIRECTOR
'79 BREAKING AWAY
'81 EYEWITNESS
'83 DRESSER, THE
'83 KRULL

WILLIAM ROBERT YATES
EXECUTIVE PRODUCER
'81 AMY

TENA YATROUSSIS
2ND ASST. DIRECTOR
'84 RIVER, THE*

BRIG. GEN. C YEAGER, USAF
MISCELLANEOUS
'83 RIGHT STUFF, THE

JOANN YEARSLEY
SCRIPT SUPERVISOR
'83 MAUSOLEUM

LARRY YEATES
MISCELLANEOUS
'81 GALLIPOLI

RAM YEDEKAR
ART DIRECTOR
'82 GANDHI*
'83 HEAT AND DUST*
'84 PASSAGE TO INDIA, A*

SUSAN YELLAND
COSTUMES
'79 PRISONER OF ZENDA, THE
'81 SUPERMAN II*
'84 KIPPERBANG

ROBERT YERINGTON
SOUND
'84 EL NORTE

BOB YERKES
MISCELLANEOUS
'82 ONE FROM THE HEART

LUKE YERSIN
SOUND
'80 UNION CITY

ALISON YERXA
MISCELLANEOUS
'83 BRAINSTORM

SAM YIP
2ND ASST. DIRECTOR
'79 GAME OF DEATH*

JO YNOCENCIO
COSTUMES
'79 SEDUCTION OF JOE TYNAN, THE
'80 HONEYSUCKLE ROSE
'84 MISUNDERSTOOD
'84 NO SMALL AFFAIR

BOB YORBERG
MISCELLANEOUS
'84 FLAMINGO KID, THE

KRISTIN YORK
MISCELLANEOUS
'84 THIS IS SPINAL TAP

MICHAEL YORK
MISCELLANEOUS
'84 RIDDLE OF THE SANDS

TERRY YORKE
STUNT COORDINATOR
'81 TIME BANDITS*

BUD YORKIN
PRODUCER
'83 DEAL OF THE CENTURY

DONALD YORKSHIRE
1ST ASST. DIRECTOR
'81 RICHARD PRYOR: LIVE ON THE SUNSET STRIP

WENDY YORKSHIRE
2ND ASST. DIRECTOR
'81 RICHARD PRYOR: LIVE ON THE SUNSET STRIP*

RON YOSHIDA
SOUND
'84 NOT FOR PUBLICATION*

AKIRA YOSHIMURA
PRODUCTION DESIGNER
'80 GILDA LIVE*

LEO YOSHIMURA
ART DIRECTOR
'79 MR. MIKE'S MONDO VIDEO

ANDREW YOUNG
STILLS
'79 ALAMBRISTA!

CHARLES YOUNG
MISCELLANEOUS
'79 PENITENTIARY

CHRISTOPHER YOUNG
ASSISTANT EDITOR
'84 COMFORT AND JOY*

DALENE YOUNG
SCREENPLAY
'80 LITTLE DARLINGS*
'83 CROSS CREEK

DIANE YOUNG
CASTING
'83 MAN WITH TWO BRAINS, THE*

EDWARD YOUNG
PROPS
'79 SAINT JACK

ERIC YOUNG
LOCATIONS
'82 BEST FRIENDS*
MISCELLANEOUS
'83 D.C. CAB

FREDDIE YOUNG
CINEMATOGRAPHER
'79 BLOODLINE
'79 STEVIE
'80 ROUGH CUT

GABRIELLA YOUNG
MISCELLANEOUS
'81 HAND, THE

GERRY YOUNG
MISCELLANEOUS
'82 PORKY'S

HAROLD YOUNG
ASSOCIATE PRODUCER
'83 FRIGHTMARE*

IRWIN YOUNG
PRODUCER
'79 ALAMBRISTA!*

JACK YOUNG
LOCATIONS
'81 PURSUIT OF D.B. COOPER, THE
'84 FLASHPOINT
'84 CANNONBALL RUN II

JACK YOUNG
MAKEUP
'79 APOCALYPSE NOW*
'80 USED CARS*

JACK YOUNG
MISCELLANEOUS
'79 BROOD, THE

JEFF YOUNG
EXECUTIVE PRODUCER
'82 SPLIT IMAGE

JERRY YOUNG
MISCELLANEOUS
'79 FRISCO KID, THE
'81 ZORRO, THE GAY BLADE

JIM YOUNG
SCRIPT SUPERVISOR
'84 LOVELESS, THE

JOHN SACRET YOUNG
SCREENPLAY
'83 TESTAMENT

KEITH YOUNG
2ND ASST. DIRECTOR
'83 SUPERMAN III*

KURT YOUNG
KEY GRIP
'81 HOWLING, THE

NEIL YOUNG
MUSIC
'80 WHERE THE BUFFALO ROAM

RHONDA YOUNG
CASTING
'82 ROCKY III
'83 STAYING ALIVE
'84 BEVERLY HILLS COP*
'84 RHINESTONE

RICK YOUNG
PROPS
'82 BORDER, THE*
'83 BIG CHILL, THE
'84 IMPULSE

ROB YOUNG
SOUND
'82 FIRST BLOOD
'82 GREY FOX, THE
'83 RUNNING BRAVE
'84 RUNAWAY

ROBERT YOUNG
DIRECTOR
'79 RICH KIDS
'79 ALAMBRISTA!
'80 ONE-TRICK PONY
'83 BALLAD OF GREGORIO CORTEZ, THE
SCREENPLAY
'79 ALAMBRISTA!
CINEMATOGRAPHER
'79 ALAMBRISTA!

ROGER YOUNG
DIRECTOR
'84 LASSITER

STEPHEN YOUNG
PRODUCER
'79 SILENT PARTNER, THE*

TERENCE YOUNG
DIRECTOR
'79 BLOODLINE
'81 INCHON

WILLIAM YOUNG
UNIT PROD. MANAGER
'82 PERSONAL BEST*
'84 OH GOD, YOU DEVIL

GAIL YOUNGS
ASSOCIATE PRODUCER
'83 ANGELO, MY LOVE
2ND UNIT DIRECTOR
'83 ANGELO, MY LOVE

AGUSTIN YTUARTE
ART DIRECTOR
'80 HERBIE GOES BANANAS*
'82 MISSING*
'83 UNDER FIRE*

KAM YUEN
MISCELLANEOUS
'79 CIRCLE OF IRON

PAMELA YUEN
ASSISTANT EDITOR
'82 FIRST BLOOD*

MATTHEW YURICICH
MISCELLANEOUS
'79 CHINA SYNDROME, THE
'79 1941
'80 CLOSE ENCOUNTERS OF THE THIRD KIND SPECIAL EDITION
'80 WHOLLY MOSES!
'82 BLADERUNNER
'82 YES, GIORGIO
'83 BRAINSTORM

RICHARD YURICICH
ASSOCIATE PRODUCER
'83 BRAINSTORM
CINEMATOGRAPHER
'83 BRAINSTORM
MISCELLANEOUS
'79 STAR TREK-THE MOTION PICTURE
'80 CLOSE ENCOUNTERS OF THE THIRD KIND SPECIAL EDITION
'82 BLADERUNNER

STACY YURTCHUK
HAIR
'83 METALSTORM: THE DESTRUCTION OF JARED-SYN*

VERA YURTCHUK
MAKEUP
'83 METALSTORM: THE DESTRUCTION OF JARED-SYN*

Z

WILLIAM ZABALA
ASSOCIATE EDITOR
'79 SCAVENGER HUNT
ASSISTANT EDITOR
'82 BLADERUNNER

STAN ZABKA
1ST ASST. DIRECTOR
'82 FORCED VENGEANCE
2ND ASST. DIRECTOR
'80 ANY WHICH WAY YOU CAN*
'80 BRONCO BILLY*
'80 CHANGE OF SEASONS, A*

STEVE ZACHARIAS
SCREENPLAY
'84 REVENGE OF THE NERDS*

NIKE ZACHMANOGLOU
SCRIPT SUPERVISOR
'83 MORTUARY

CRAIG ZADAN
PRODUCER
'83 FOOTLOOSE*

SAUL ZAENTZ
PRODUCER
'84 AMADEUS

JOE ZAIDMAN
ASSISTANT EDITOR
'80 FORMULA, THE*

JERRY ZAKS
MISCELLANEOUS
'83 PRIVATE SCHOOL

CHARLES ZALBEN
UNIT MANAGER
'80 STARDUST MEMORIES*

ANDY ZALL
EDITOR
'84 OH GOD, YOU DEVIL

JACQUI ZAMBRANO
PROD. COORDINATOR
'84 MAKING THE GRADE*
LOCATIONS
'80 ALLIGATOR

GHEORGHE ZAMFIR
MISCELLANEOUS
'83 ANGELO, MY LOVE

ELZEMARIE ZAMPARELLI
PROPS
'82 HOME WORK

EMILIO ZAMPRIOLI
PROPS
'83 PIRANHA II: THE SPAWNING

GINO ZAMPRIOLI
MAKEUP
'84 ONCE UPON A TIME IN AMERICA*

JOHN ZANE
PRODUCTION MANAGER
'82 THAT CHAMPIONSHIP SEASON*
UNIT PROD. MANAGER
'81 CHARLIE CHAN AND THE CURSE OF THE DRAGON QUEEN
'83 10 TO MIDNIGHT

LILLI ZANGERLE
HAIR
'79 FIFTH MUSKETEER, THE*

RICHARD ZANUCK
PRODUCER
'80 ISLAND, THE*
'81 NEIGHBORS*
'82 VERDICT, THE*

JOY ZAPATA
HAIR
'79 WHEN YOU COMIN' BACK, RED RYDER?
'80 UP THE ACADEMY
'81 CHARLIE CHAN AND THE CURSE OF THE DRAGON QUEEN*
'81 UNDER THE RAINBOW
'82 TRON

ANNA ZAPPIA
PROD. COORDINATOR
'79 METEOR
'80 CHANGE OF SEASONS, A
'80 DIE LAUGHING
'80 FOOLIN AROUND
'81 LOOKER
'82 DINER
'83 TO BE OR NOT TO BE
'84 STARMAN

KARL ZASKE
ASSISTANT EDITOR
'81 ENTER THE NINJA*

PAUL ZASTUPNEVICH
COSTUMES
'79 BEYOND THE POSEIDON ADVENTURE
'80 WHEN TIME RAN OUT

KATHY ZATARGA
SCRIPT SUPERVISOR
'80 FADE TO BLACK
'81 BODY AND SOUL
'81 TAKE THIS JOB AND SHOVE IT
'83 MY TUTOR
'84 CHOOSE ME
'84 DREAMSCAPE

CAROLYN ZATZ
SCRIPT SUPERVISOR
'82 Q: QUETZALCOATL

STEVEN ZATZ
ASSISTANT EDITOR
'80 RETURN OF THE SECAUCUS SEVEN, THE*
LOCATIONS
'80 RETURN OF THE SECAUCUS SEVEN, THE

MARC ZAVAT
EXECUTIVE PRODUCER
'83 OSTERMAN WEEKEND, THE*

JEAN ZAY
COSTUMES
'81 CONDORMAN*
'84 JUST THE WAY YOU ARE

PAUL ZAZA
MUSIC
'80 PROM NIGHT*
'81 GAS
'81 MY BLOODY VALENTINE
'82 PORKY'S*
'83 CHRISTMAS STORY, A*

EROICA ZBOROWSKY
2ND ASST. DIRECTOR
'83 SPACEHUNTER: ADVENTURES IN THE FORBIDDEN ZONE*
PROD. OFFICE COORD.
'79 BLACK STALLION, THE*

WILLIAM ZBOROWSKY
PRODUCTION MANAGER
'80 TERROR TRAIN
'83 SPACEHUNTER: ADVENTURES IN THE FORBIDDEN ZONE

KRISTI ZEA

COSTUMES
'80 FAME
'81 ENDLESS LOVE
'81 TATTOO*
'82 SHOOT THE MOON
'83 EXPOSED
'83 LOVESICK
'83 TERMS OF ENDEARMENT
'84 BEST DEFENSE
'84 BIRDY
'84 UNFAITHFULLY YOURS
'84 BEAT STREET
'84 LITTLE DRUMMER GIRL, THE

NANCY ZEARFOSS

LOCATIONS
'80 IT'S MY TURN*
'83 TESTAMENT

GEORGE ZECEVIC

ASSOCIATE PRODUCER
'81 MONTENEGRO*

DAN ZECHOVAL

2ND ASST. DIRECTOR
'83 HANNA K*

FRANCO ZEFFIRELLI

DIRECTOR
'79 CHAMP, THE
'81 ENDLESS LOVE

ROLF ZEHETBAUER

PRODUCTION DESIGNER
'80 AMERICAN SUCCESS COMPANY,THE
'82 NIGHT CROSSING
'84 NEVERENDING STORY, THE

CAROLYN ZEIFMAN

ASSISTANT EDITOR
'79 BROOD, THE

BARRY ZEITLIN

EDITOR
'83 ANGEL OF H.E.A.T.

JEROME ZEITMAN

PRODUCER
'79 JUST YOU AND ME KID*
'80 HOW TO BEAT
THE HIGH COST OF LIVING*
EXECUTIVE PRODUCER
'84 JUST THE WAY YOU ARE

GARY ZELLER

SPECIAL EFFECTS
'81 SCANNERS
'81 GAS
'81 NEIGHBORS*
MISCELLANEOUS
'79 DAWN OF THE DEAD

STEVEN ZELLER

PUBLICIST
'83 SPRING BREAK
'83 SMOKEY AND THE BANDIT III

JOHN ZEMANSKY

PROPS
'79 ...AND JUSTICE FOR ALL
'79 BUTCH AND SUNDANCE:
THE EARLY YEARS
'79 PROMISE, THE
'80 BRUBAKER
'81 CUTTER'S WAY
'81 GHOST STORY
'82 BEST FRIENDS
'82 THING, THE
'82 ESCAPE ARTIST, THE
'83 SCARFACE
'83 PSYCHO II
'84 STREETS OF FIRE*

ROBERT ZEMECKIS

DIRECTOR
'80 USED CARS
'84 ROMANCING THE STONE
SCREENPLAY
'79 1941*
'80 USED CARS*

KENNETH ZEMKE

EDITOR
'82 PIRATE MOVIE, THE

MANFRED ZENDAR

MISCELLANEOUS
'80 ISLAND, THE

JIM ZENK

STILLS
'80 LONG RIDERS, THE*
'81 SOUTHERN COMFORT
'81 FOUR FRIENDS
'81 THIEF
'83 RUMBLEFISH
'83 CLASS
'83 OUTSIDERS, THE
'84 RIVER, THE
'84 SIXTEEN CANDLES
'84 TEACHERS

MICHAEL ZENON

1ST ASST. DIRECTOR
'84 POLICE ACADEMY

ALAN ZENUK

STILLS
'79 MAN, A WOMAN AND A BANK, A
'82 BY DESIGN

DON ZEPFEL

UNIT PROD. MANAGER
'83 STING II, THE
UNIT MANAGER
'82 ZOOT SUIT
1ST ASST. DIRECTOR
'79 LOVE AT FIRST BITE
'80 NUDE BOMB, THE
'81 HEARTBEEPS
'83 PSYCHO II

RONALD ZERRA

PRODUCER
'80 EYES OF A STRANGER

BARRY ZETLIN

EDITOR
'81 GALAXY OF TERROR*
ASSISTANT EDITOR
'81 SMOKEY BITES THE DUST

HARRY ZETTEL

PROPS
'81 ROAD GAMES

ADAM ZETTER

STILLS
'84 MUTANT*

HOWARD ZIEFF

DIRECTOR
'79 MAIN EVENT, THE
'80 PRIVATE BENJAMIN
'84 UNFAITHFULLY YOURS

RAFAL ZIELINSKI

DIRECTOR
'83 SCREWBALLS

BOB ZIEMBICKI

ART DIRECTOR
'81 BODY AND SOUL
'83 CHAINED HEAT
PROPS
'83 TIMERIDER

JERRY ZIESMER

1ST ASST. DIRECTOR
'79 ROCKY II
'79 APOCALYPSE NOW
'79 1941*
'81 HISTORY OF THE WORLD PART I
'82 ANNIE
'83 SCARFACE*
'83 BLUE THUNDER*
'84 RIVER, THE

SUSAN ZIETLOW-MAUST

HAIR
'80 URBAN COWBOY*
'81 ...ALL THE MARBLES
'84 FLASHPOINT

STUART ZIFF
MISCELLANEOUS
'79 CHINA SYNDROME, THE

JACK ZIGA
PRODUCTION MANAGER
'81 TAKE THIS JOB AND SHOVE IT

DICK ZIKER
STUNT COORDINATOR
'80 SMOKEY AND THE BANDIT II
'83 TO BE OR NOT TO BE
'84 RUNAWAY

ALICE ZILLER
SCRIPT SUPERVISOR
'80 FIENDISH PLOT OF DR. FU MANCHU, THE
'84 UNTIL SEPTEMBER

JONATHAN ZIMBERT
ASSOCIATE PRODUCER
'83 STAR CHAMBER*
'84 2010*

MICHAEL ZIMBRICH
2ND ASST. DIRECTOR
'81 FOR YOUR EYES ONLY*
'83 OCTOPUSSY*
'83 PRIVATES ON PARADE
'84 ANOTHER COUNTRY*
'84 GREYSTOKE: THE LEGEND OF TARZAN, LORD OF THE APES*

GEORGE ZIMINSKY
PROPS
'84 BIRDY

DAVID ZIMMERMAN
KEY GRIP
'84 JUST THE WAY YOU ARE*

DEBRA ZIMMERMAN
PROD. OFFICE COORD.
'80 MANIAC*

DON ZIMMERMAN
EDITOR
'79 BEING THERE
'80 CHANGE OF SEASONS, A
'82 ROCKY III*
'82 BARBAROSA*
'82 BEST FRIENDS
'83 STAYING ALIVE*
'84 TEACHERS

JERRY ZIMMERMAN
EXECUTIVE PRODUCER
'83 MAUSOLEUM*

JONATHAN ZIMMERMAN
2ND ASST. DIRECTOR
'79 GREAT SANTINI, THE
'79 ICE CASTLES*
'80 COMPETITION, THE*
'80 GONG SHOW MOVIE, THE

JULIE ZIMMERMAN
MAKEUP
'84 LAST NIGHT AT THE ALAMO

KEN ZIMMERMAN
PROPS
'80 RAISE THE TITANIC*

PAUL ZIMMERMAN
SCREENPLAY
'83 KING OF COMEDY, THE

VERNON ZIMMERMAN
DIRECTOR
'80 FADE TO BLACK
SCREENPLAY
'80 FADE TO BLACK

FRED ZINNEMAN
PRODUCER
'82 FIVE DAYS ONE SUMMER
DIRECTOR
'82 FIVE DAYS ONE SUMMER

TIM ZINNEMAN
PRODUCER
'80 SMALL CIRCLE OF FRIENDS, A
'80 LONG RIDERS, THE
'82 TEX
'84 IMPULSE

PETER ZINNER
EDITOR
'78 DEER HUNTER, THE
'79 FISH THAT SAVED PITTSBURGH, THE*
'80 FOOLIN AROUND
'82 OFFICER AND A GENTLEMAN, AN
MISCELLANEOUS
'83 RUNNING BRAVE

BOBBI LEIGH ZITO
STILLS
'80 MANIAC*

JOSEPH ZITO
DIRECTOR
'84 FRIDAY THE 13TH PART IV THE FINAL CHAPTER

STEPHEN ZITO
SCREENPLAY
'82 ESCAPE ARTIST, THE*

CARL ZITTRER
MUSIC
'80 PROM NIGHT*
'82 PORKY'S*
'83 CHRISTMAS STORY, A*
'83 PORKY'S II THE NEXT DAY

HADAS ZIV
2ND ASST. DIRECTOR
'84 BEST DEFENSE*

MICHAEL ZOLF
ASSOCIATE PRODUCER
'82 BY DESIGN*

CARL ZOLLO
ART DIRECTOR
'81 FEAR NO EVIL

YOSSI ZOMER
PROPS
'84 BEST DEFENSE*

VILMOS ZSIGMOND
CINEMATOGRAPHER
'78 DEER HUNTER, THE
'79 ROSE, THE
'79 WINTER KILLS
'80 CLOSE ENCOUNTERS OF THE THIRD KIND SPECIAL EDITION
'80 HEAVEN'S GATE
'81 BLOW OUT
'82 JINXED
'83 TABLE FOR FIVE
'84 NO SMALL AFFAIR
'84 RIVER, THE
MISCELLANEOUS
'82 BORDER, THE

ORLANDO ZUCCARI
KEY GRIP
'83 YOR

BERNARD ZUCH
SOUND
'79 NATURAL ENEMIES

CARL ZUCKER
UNIT MANAGER
'81 ATLANTIC CITY*
LOCATIONS
'80 WILLIE & PHIL
'83 WITHOUT A TRACE
'84 MOSCOW ON THE HUDSON*

DAVID ZUCKER
DIRECTOR
'80 AIRPLANE*
'84 TOP SECRET!*
SCREENPLAY
'80 AIRPLANE*
'84 TOP SECRET!*
EXECUTIVE PRODUCER
'80 AIRPLANE*
'84 TOP SECRET!*

JERRY ZUCKER

DIRECTOR
'80 AIRPLANE*
'84 TOP SECRET!*
SCREENPLAY
'80 AIRPLANE*
'84 TOP SECRET!*
EXECUTIVE PRODUCER
'80 AIRPLANE*
'84 TOP SECRET!*
2ND UNIT DIRECTOR
'79 ROCK 'N ROLL HIGH SCHOOL*

FRANK ZUNIGA

DIRECTOR
'83 GOLDEN SEAL, THE

STANLEY ZUPNIK

EXECUTIVE PRODUCER
'84 DREAMSCAPE*

STEFAN ZURCHER

PRODUCTION MANAGER
'84 LITTLE DRUMMER GIRL, THE*
LOCATIONS
'80 FORMULA, THE*

ALAN ZWEIBEL

SCREENPLAY
'80 GILDA LIVE*

SUSAN ZWERMAN

LOCATIONS
'79 ALL THAT JAZZ
'82 HANKY PANKY
'82 NIGHT SHIFT*
'83 SCARFACE*
'84 FLAMINGO KID, THE
'84 C.H.U.D.*

DEBORAH ZWICKER

PROD. OFFICE COORD.
'82 IF YOU COULD SEE WHAT I HEAR

To Order Additional Copies of Credits
send $75 (check or money order)
plus $3.50 postage & handling, $5 foreign
each 3 volume set to:
Magpie Press
16 Main Avenue
Wallington, New Jersey 07057

New Jersey residents add 6% sales tax